July 16–18, 2012,
Madeira, Portugal

Association for Computing Machinery

Advancing Computing as a Science & Profession

PODC'12

Proceedings of the 2012 ACM Symposium on
Principles of Distributed Computing

Sponsored by:
ACM SIGACT, ACM SIGOPS, & INESC iD Lisboa

Supported by:
Yahoo! Labs, Oracle Labs, IBM Research, & Microsoft Research

Association for Computing Machinery

Advancing Computing as a Science & Profession

The Association for Computing Machinery
2 Penn Plaza, Suite 701
New York, New York 10121-0701

Notice to Past Authors of ACM-Published Articles

ACM intends to create a complete electronic archive of all articles and/or other material previously published by ACM. If you have written a work that has been previously published by ACM in any journal or conference proceedings prior to 1978, or any SIG Newsletter at any time, and you do NOT want this work to appear in the ACM Digital Library, please inform permissions@acm.org, stating the title of the work, the author(s), and where and when published.

ISBN: 978-1-4503-1450-3

Additional copies may be ordered prepaid from:

ACM Order Department
PO Box 30777
New York, NY 10087-0777, USA

Phone: 1-800-342-6626 (USA and Canada)
+1-212-626-0500 (Global)
Fax: +1-212-944-1318
E-mail: acmhelp@acm.org
Hours of Operation: 8:30 am – 4:30 pm ET

ACM Order Number: 536120

Printed in the USA

Foreword, PODC'12 Chair's Welcome

It is our great pleasure to welcome you to the *2012 ACM Symposium on Principles of Distributed Computing – PODC'12*. This year's symposium continues its tradition of being the premier forum for presentation of research results in the area of theoretical distributed computing. During the years PODC has been the stage where many landmark results that have increased our understanding of this exciting and, in the Internet era, fundamental research endeavor have been presented. In the best tradition of theoretical discovery, the insights that have been provided have not only elucidated fundamental conceptual issues but also found their way in the real world of systems and applications. The mission of the symposium remains that of providing a high quality international forum for the timely dissemination and discussion of ideas at the frontier of current knowledge in the area of theoretical distributed computing.

The call for papers attracted 142 submissions from the Americas, Asia, and Europe. The program committee met in Rome and accepted 35 papers and 26 brief announcements that cover a wide variety of topics. In addition, this year the program includes an industrial panel where colleagues from leading technological companies will share with us their experience with the challenges presented by real, large-scale distributed systems. The keynote speech will be by David Peleg, whose outstanding research record sets a gold standard for the field. Finally, this year PODC hosts the ceremony for the 2012 Edsger W. Dijkstra Prize.

Special thanks go to Adrienne Griscti from ACM. Adrienne is used to organizing the paperwork at ACM to initiate the ACM-Sheridan Proceedings Service. Assisted by Lisa Tolles, she has taken care of processing the papers in a timely manner.

Putting together *PODC'12* was a team effort. We first thank the authors for providing the content of the program. We are grateful to the program committee and the sub-reviewers, who worked very hard in reviewing papers and providing feedback for authors. The help of the Steering Committee and of the Conference Committee was timely and invaluable. Finally, we thank the hosting organization and local organizers, our sponsors, ACM SIGOPS, ACM SIGACT, and INESC ID Lisbon and our generous corporate supporters, IBM, Microsoft Research, Oracle, and Yahoo! Labs.

We hope that you will find this program interesting and thought-provoking and that the symposium will provide you with a valuable opportunity to share ideas with other researchers and practitioners from institutions around the world.

Alessandro Panconesi
PODC'12 Chair

Table of Contents

Session 1: Shared Memory I
Session Chair: Valerie King *(University of Victoria)*

Session 2: Information Spreading, Random Walks
Session Chair: Lucia Draque Penso *(University of Ulm)*

Session 3: Communication Complexity
Session Chair: Alessandro Panconesi *(Sapienza, University of Rome)*

Session 4: Brief Announcements
Session Chair: Christian Scheideler *(University of Paderborn)*

Session 8: Ad-hoc Networks

Session Chair: Valerie King *(University of Victoria)*

Session 9: Brief Announcements

Session Chair: Lucia Draque Penso *(University of Ulm)*

Session 14: Distributed Graph Algorithms

Session 15: Shared Memory II

Author Index

PODC 2012 Symposium Organization

General Chair: Darek Kowalski *(U. of Liverpool, UK and IMDEA Networks, Spain)*

Program Chair: Alessandro Panconesi *(Sapienza, University of Rome, Italy)*

Local Arrangements Chair: Luis Rodrigues *(IST / INESC-ID Lisbon, Portugal)*

Local Arrangements Committee: Luis Rodrigues *(IST / INESC-ID Lisbon, Portugal)*
Oksana Denysyuk *(IST / INESC-ID Lisbon, Portugal)*

Publicity Chairs: Seth Gilbert *(NUS, Singapore)*
Christoph Lenzen *(Hebrew University of Jerusalem, Israel)*

Treasurer & Registration Chairs: Panagiota Fatourou *(University of Crete, Greece)*
Oksana Denysyuk *(IST / INESC-ID Lisbon, Portugal)*

Steering Committee Chair: Andrzej Pelc *(Universite du Quebec, Canada)*

Steering Committee: Panagiota Fatourou *(University of Crete, Greece)*
Pierre Fraigniaud *(CNRS and University Paris Diderot, France)*
Rachid Guerraoui *(EPFL, Switzerland)*
Darek Kowalski *(University of Liverpool, UK
and IMDEA Networks, Spain)*
Alessandro Panconesi *(Sapienza University of Rome, Italy)*
Jennifer Welch *(Texas A&M University, USA)*

Program Committee: John Byers *(Boston University, USA)*
Keren Censor-Hillel *(MIT, USA)*
Flavio Chierichetti *(Cornell University, USA)*
Edith Cohen *(AT&T Research, USA)*
Carole Delporte *(Université Paris Diderot, Paris, France)*
Michael Elkin *(Ben-Gurion University, Israel)*
Wojciech Golab *(Hewlett Packard, USA)*
Vassos Hadzilacos *(University of Toronto, Canada)*
Prasad Jayanti *(Dartmouth, USA)*
Idit Keidar *(Technion, Israel)*
Rohit Khandekar *(IBM, USA)*
Valerie King *(University of Victoria, Canada)*
Victor Luchangco *(Oracle, USA)*
Calvin Newport *(Georgetown University, USA)*
Alessandro Panconesi (chair) *(Sapienza, Rome, Italy)*
Lucia Draque Penso *(Universität Ulm, Germany)*

Additional reviewers (continued):

Kondapally Ranganath	Rabkin Ariel
Kontorovich Aryeh	Racke Harald
Koutsopoulos Andreas	Richa Andrea
Kowalski Dariusz	Riegel Torvald
Kuhn Fabian	Saia Jared
Kumaresan Ranjit	Sastry Srikanth
Kundu Ashish	Sauerwald Thomas
Kutten Shay	Schindelhauer Christian
Kuznetsov Petr	Schiper Nicolas
Langner Tobias	Schmid Stefan
Lau Francis	Schneider Scott
Lenzen Christoph	Seidel Jochen
Lev Yossi	Seshadri Arvind
Levin Dave	Shepherd Bruce
Li Xiaozhou	Shvartsman Alexander
Locher Thomas	Silberstein Mark
Lotker Zvi	Smula Jasmin
Lushman Brad	Solomon Shay
Martin Jean-Philippe	Sovran Yair
Martin Russell	Theyssier Guillaume
Milani Alessia	Tirthapura Srikanta
Milosavljevic Nikola	Travers Corentin
Mirrokni Vahab	Tredan Gilles
Mitra Sayan	Tronel Frederic
Mohassel Payman	Tuttle Mark
Moir Mark	Uitto Jara
Naden Karl	Urso Pascal
Neiman Ofer	Vaidya Nitin
Neumann Florentin	Vattani Andrea
Ogierman Adrian	Vukolic Marko
Oshman Rotem	Weiss Gera
Owens Scott	Welch Jennifer
Panagiotou Konstantinos	Welten Samuel
Pandurangan Gopal	Werneck Renato
Pareek Abhijeet	Widder Josef
Parter Merav	Xiao Zhen
Pasquale Francesco	Young Maxwell
Patterson Stacy	Zanarini Alessandro
Pelc Andrzej	Zanetti Luca
Perelman Dmitri	

PODC 2012 Sponsors & Supporters

Sponsors:

Supporters:

Oracle Labs

IBM Research

Microsoft **Research**

The 2012 Edsger W. Dijkstra Prize in Distributed Computing

The ACM-EATCS Edsger W. Dijkstra Prize in Distributed Computing is awarded to outstanding papers on the principles of distributed computing, whose significance and impact on the theory or practice of distributed computing have been evident for at least ten years. The prize is sponsored jointly by the ACM Symposium on Principles of Distributed Computing (PODC) and the EATCS Symposium on Distributed Computing (DISC).

The 2012 Prize Committee, composed of Marcos K. Aguilera (chair), Dahlia Malkhi, Keith Marzullo, Alessandro Panconesi, Andrzej Pelc, and Roger Wattenhofer, has selected

Maurice Herlihy, J. Eliot B. Moss, Nir Shavit, and Dan Touitou

to receive the 2012 Edsger W. Dijkstra Prize in Distributed Computing for the following two outstanding papers:

Maurice Herlihy and J. Eliot B. Moss.
Transactional Memory: Architectural Support for Lock-Free Data Structures.
20th Annual International Symposium on Computer Architecture, pages 289–300, May 1993.

Nir Shavit and Dan Touitou.
Software Transactional Memory.
Distributed Computing 10(2):99–116, February 1997.
(An earlier version appearing in the *14th ACM Symposium on Principles of Distributed Computing*, pages 204–213, August 1995.)

These papers established the abstraction of Transactional Memory, which has fundamentally changed parallel computing both in its theoretical foundations and in its practice.

As with many influential papers, the work by Herlihy and Moss presents a beguilingly simple idea: extend load-linked and store-conditional to allow a processor to update a collection of locations atomically. This idea arose from deep insights:

- By allowing the creator of a concurrent data structure to focus on what should be atomic rather than how it should be made atomic, transactional memory significantly raises the level of abstraction for parallel programs, thereby eliminating much of the complexity of lock-free programming.

- Because actual dynamic conflicts among operations are rare in well-written programs, a speculative implementation of atomicity can enjoy a significant performance advantage over more conservative approaches.

- Given that cache coherence protocols already track conflicts among processors, multi-location atomic update can be realized in hardware by introducing a small "transactional cache" and by making simple modifications to standard cache coherence protocols.

This last insight notwithstanding, Herlihy and Moss's proposal proved too ambitious for the hardware of the day, and their work was largely ignored within the architecture community for most of the following decade. Within the theory community, however, it inspired multiple explorations of the limits of software emulation, most notably the Software Transactional Memory work of Shavit and Touitou.

Building on earlier universal non-blocking constructions, Shavit and Touitou showed how to achieve lock freedom without the need for costly recursive helping, and thus provide effective non-blocking multi-word operations purely in software. It was the first work to demonstrate that software transactions could, under the right circumstances, outperform conservative locking.

In terms of fostering research, transactional memory has become a truly transformative idea. For example, two years ago, the second edition of the monograph by Harris, Larus, and Rajwar on Transactional Memory listed over 350 papers in the field. Google Scholar reports almost 1400 citations to Herlihy and Moss, and almost 1000 to Shavit and Touitou. The annual TRANSACT workshop, sponsored by ACM SIGPLAN, is now planning its eighth incarnation. In terms of practice, software architects have developed dozens of runtime implementations, both blocking and non-blocking, of dazzling algorithmic variety. At least four major compilers, including gcc, now support transactional memory in C++. Hardware implementations have been developed by Azul, Sun (Oracle), AMD (on paper), IBM, and Intel. The IBM and Intel implementations, in particular, ensure that hardware support is here to stay.

These two papers started the distributed computing research community along the path towards the design of general multi-word transactions; ones that in the future will most likely be based on a combination of hardware, software, and language techniques. Transactional memory serves as an outstanding example of how the distributed computing community has influenced the world.

Faster Randomized Consensus With an Oblivious Adversary

James Aspnes [*]
Yale University
aspnes@cs.yale.edu

ABSTRACT

Two new algorithms are given for randomized consensus in a shared-memory model with an oblivious adversary. Each is based on a new construction of a conciliator, an object that guarantees termination and validity, but that only guarantees agreement with constant probability. The first conciliator assumes unit-cost snapshots and achieves agreement among n processes with probability $1 - \epsilon$ in $O(\log^* n + \log(1/\epsilon))$ steps for each process. The second uses ordinary multi-writer registers, and achieves agreement with probability $1 - \epsilon$ in $O(\log \log n + \log(1/\epsilon))$ steps. Combining these constructions with known results gives randomized consensus for arbitrarily many possible input values using unit-cost snapshots in $O(\log^* n)$ expected steps and randomized consensus for up to $O(\log n \log \log n)$ possible input values using ordinary registers in $O(\log \log n)$ expected steps.

Categories and Subject Descriptors

D.1.3 [**Programming Techniques**]: Concurrent Programming—*Distributed programming*; F.2.2 [**Analysis of Algorithms and Problem Complexity**]: Nonnumerical Algorithms and Problems

General Terms

Theory, Algorithms

Keywords

Consensus, randomization, shared-memory, oblivious adversary

1. INTRODUCTION

In the **consensus** problem, a group of n processes wish to agree on a value, which must be equal to the input of some process. Consensus is known to be impossible to solve deterministically in an asynchronous message-passing [13] or

---

[*]Supported in part by NSF grant CCF-0916389.

shared-memory [17] model if even one process can fail. However, randomized algorithms can achieve wait-free consensus in bounded expected time.

The cost of consensus is strongly affected by the power of the **adversary scheduler** that chooses at each step which process should carry out the next operation. With an **adaptive adversary**, which can base its decision on the complete state of the system—including internal states of processes—the cost of consensus is well understood. A lower bound of Attiya and Censor [8] shows that $\Omega(n^2)$ expected total steps are needed even for binary consensus, where all inputs are 0 or 1, in a model that provides multi-writer multi-reader registers. Conversely, a matching upper bound was shown in the same paper, and subsequent work has demonstrated that adaptive-adversary consensus can be solved with optimal $O(n)$ expected individual step complexity [6], even if only single-writer registers are available and the inputs are arbitrary [3].

Less well understood is the complexity of randomized shared-memory consensus with an **oblivious adversary** that schedules the sequence of operations in advance without being able to observe the random choices made by the processes. Aumann [10] showed how to achieve $O(\log n)$ expected individual step complexity under a plausible weak-adversary assumption that holds for an oblivious adversary; and a more recent algorithm of Aspnes [4], based on a classic protocol of Chor, Israeli, and Li [12], simultaneously achieves $O(\log n)$ expected individual step complexity and $O(n)$ expected total step complexity under a different weak-adversary assumption.

It is clear that $O(n)$ expected total step complexity is optimal, as each process must take at least one step. A lower bound of Attiya and Censor [9] for oblivious-adversary consensus shows that the probability of failing to terminate in $O(kn)$ total steps is at least $\frac{1}{c^k}$ for some constant k, even with global coins and unit-cost snapshots. This gives a lower bound of $\Omega(n \log(1/\epsilon))$ total steps to reach agreement with probability at least $1 - \epsilon$. However, there is still the possibility that the *expected* individual step complexity even without these assumptions could be as low as $O(1)$.

We do not show such a surprising result here, although our results do show that the cost of oblivious-adversary consensus is much lower than might have been expected given the lack of improvement over the previous fifteen years. We give two algorithms for **conciliators** [4], weak consensus objects that guarantee termination and validity in all executions but guarantee agreement only with constant probability (a more formal definition is given in Section 1.2). These can be alternated with adopt-commit objects [2, 14, 18] to obtain consensus objects that guarantee agreement always, at an expected cost equal to the sum of the costs of the conciliator and the adopt-commit [4].

Our first conciliator, described in Section 2, works in the unit-cost snapshot model, and reaches agreement with constant probability after $O(\log^* n)$ operations per process. The main idea is to use the nesting property of snapshots and the properties of left-to-right maxima of random permutations to reduce an initial set of m values to $O(\log m)$ values on average in each round by assigning a random priority to each value and having each process take the value with highest priority among those it observes in a snapshot. After $O(\log^* m)$ iterations of this process, with constant probability only one value survives.

Because adopt-commit objects can be implemented using $O(1)$ snapshot operations [14], this immediately gives a randomized consensus protocol with $O(\log^* n)$ expected individual step complexity in the unit-cost snapshot model.

Our second conciliator, described in Section 3, works in the ordinary multi-writer register model, and uses a sequence of **sifting** rounds similar to those recently used by Alistarh and Aspnes [1] to implement test-and-set in $O(\log \log n)$ expected steps with an oblivious adversary. Here in each round a multi-writer register is used to eliminate values quickly. Each process chooses randomly whether to write its value to the register (and retain it for the next round), or to read the register and replace its value with the register value if it is not null. By choosing the probability of a write carefully, each round reduces the number of surviving values from m to $O(\sqrt{m})$ on average, giving a unique survivor after $O(\log \log n)$ rounds if all goes well. We give a new analysis of the sifting mechanism that shows that this indeed occurs with constant probability provided the write probabilities are chosen with the needs of the conciliator in mind.

Using this second conciliator gives $O(\log \log n)$ expected individual step complexity for randomized consensus in a multi-writer register model with an oblivious adversary, provided the range of input values is small. When the range of input values is large, the best currently known construction of an adopt-commit object [7] dominates the cost.

For both conciliators, because the oblivious adversary can't see processes' coin-flips or states, we can have each process generate a sequence of random bits associated with its input value, which then propagate along with the input value as it is adopted by other processes; we call this combination of an input value and random bits a **persona**. This allows all copies of a persona to be treated the same way in each round regardless of which processes hold them, making the number of surviving distinct personae—instead of the number of surviving processes—the relevant measure of progress.

A straightforward implementation of either conciliator leads to greater total expected step complexity than the optimal $O(n)$ bound achieved in [4]. We show (in Section 4) how to embed the $O(\log \log n)$ conciliator in a conciliator based on the consensus protocol of Chor, Israeli, and Li [12] to get a conciliator with both expected $O(\log \log n)$ individual step complexity and expected $O(n)$ total step complexity. The same technique also works for the $O(\log^* n)$ snapshot-based conciliator.

1.1 Model

We consider a standard asynchronous shared-memory model, in which n processes communicate by executing operations on shared-memory objects. These objects are either **snapshot objects**, which support an update operation and a read operation that returns a vector of the values of the most recent update operations for every process; or **atomic multi-writer multi-reader registers**, which support a write operation and a read operation that returns the value of the most recent write. In either case we treat all operations as taking one step. We do not assume any limitation on the size of registers.

Timing is controlled by an **oblivious adversary**, which specifies a **schedule** consisting of a sequence of process ids. At each step, the next process in the schedule executes one operation of its choosing. We assume that once a process has finished its protocol, any steps allocated to it become no-ops; these no-ops are not included when computing the complexity of the algorithm. Any coin-flips done by the processes are independent of the schedule chosen by the adversary.

1.2 Consensus, conciliators, and adopt-commit objects

In a **consensus** protocol, each process starts with an input and eventually decides on an output, subject to the requirements:

- **Termination.** With probably 1, each nonfaulty process decides after finitely many steps.

- **Validity.** The output value of each process is equal to the input value of some process.

- **Agreement.** All processes choose the same output value.

A conciliator [4] keeps the termination and validity conditions, but replaces agreement with:

- **Probabilistic agreement.** There is a fixed **agreement probability** $\delta > 0$ such that, for any adversary strategy, the probability that all return values are equal is at least δ.

The idea is that a conciliator attempts to produce agreement, but cannot guarantee or detect that it occurs.

An **adopt-commit protocol** [14] or **adopt-commit object** [2, 18] detects agreement, but does not create it. Our definition of an adopt-commit object uses the terminology of [4, 7]: an adopt-commit object provides a single operation $\texttt{AdoptCommit}(v)$ that returns (commit, v') or (adopt, v') for some v', subject to termination, validity (v' must equal some operation's input) and two new conditions that replace agreement:

- **Convergence.** If all operations have the same input value v, all operations return (commit, v).

- **Coherence.** If any operation returns (commit, v), then all operations return either (commit, v) or (adopt, v).

It is shown in [4] that an alternating sequence of conciliators and adopt-commit objects implements consensus, assuming each process decides immediately on v when it sees (commit, v). The idea is that some conciliator eventually produces agreement on some common value v, and the acceptance condition on the following adopt-commit means that all processes decide on that value. The additional conditions on conciliators and adopt-commit objects are used to show that validity and agreement hold. The cost of consensus using this technique is, on average, asymptotically equal to the sum of the cost of a conciliator and an adopt-commit object, because, on average, only a constant number of these objects are accessed by each process.

1.3 Notation

We use log for base-2 logarithm and ln for base-e logarithm. The **iterated logarithm function** $\log^* n$ is defined by the recurrence $\log^* n = 0$ for $n \leq 1$ and $\log^* n = 1 + \log^* \log n$ for larger n.

2. CHEAP CONSENSUS WITH CHEAP SNAPSHOTS

Here we show how to solve consensus for an unbounded range of input values in $O(\log^* n)$ expected steps using unit-cost atomic snapshot operations. We assume that an oblivious adversary schedules the order of these snapshot operations independently of the random choices made by the algorithm. Whether this is a reasonable assumption in practice is a tricky question [16], but our algorithm does demonstrate that any potential oblivious-adversary consensus lower bound greater than $\Omega(\log^* n)$ will hold only in a less benevolent model.

The basic idea of the protocol is to have a sequence of rounds, where in each round each process writes its current preference, takes a snapshot, and adopts the value out of those it sees with the highest random priority for this round. We will show that on average, if m values enter a round, $O(\log m)$ leave; thus after $O(\log^* n)$ rounds, the expected number of survivors is $O(1)$, and becomes 1 with probability at least $1 - \epsilon$ after $O(\log(1/\epsilon))$ additional rounds. To make this work, it is necessary for all copies of a given input value to share the same priority in each round. This is done by generating a vector of priorities for each process at the start of the protocol, which is then carried along with the process's input value as other processes adopt it. We refer to the combined input value and priority vector as a **persona**; the goal of the algorithm is to leave all processes with the same persona (and thus the same input value).

Pseudocode is given in Algorithm 1.

```
1  procedure conciliator(input)
2      Let priority be a vector of log* n + ⌈log(1/ε)⌉
        independent uniform random variables in [0, 1]
3      persona ← ⟨input, priority⟩
4      for i ← 1 ... log* n + ⌈log(1/ε)⌉ do
5          A_i[myId] ← persona
6          S ← snapshot(A_i)
7          Let j maximize S[j].priority[i] over all
            non-null S[j]
8          persona ← S[j]
9      return persona.input
```

Algorithm 1: Priority-based conciliator

To simplify the analysis, we assume that the priority values are uniformly chosen from the real interval $[0, 1]$. This allows us to assume that ties occur only with probability 0.

More realistically, a smaller range of priorities could be used, at the cost of a small probability that the analysis fails.

Let Y_i be the number of distinct personae remaining after i rounds of the algorithm. Let $X_i = Y_i - 1$ be the number of **excess personae** remaining after i rounds. We will show that $E[X_i]$ converges rapidly to 0. Markov's inequality can then be used to bound the probability that more than one value survives.

LEMMA 1. *Let X_i be the number of excess personae remaining after i rounds of Algorithm 1. Then*

$$E[X_{i+1}|X_i] \leq \min(\ln(X_i + 1), X_i/2). \qquad (1)$$

PROOF. For a persona to survive round $i + 1$, it must be the highest-priority persona in some view obtained by taking a snapshot of A_{i+1}. Recall that $Y_i = X_i + 1$ gives the number of distinct personae remaining after previous rounds, and that all copies of a particular persona share the same priority.

Define a view as the set of personae that appear in the result of some `snapshot` operation. Order the personae $a_1, a_2, \ldots, a_{Y_i}$ written to A_{i+1} by increasing size of the smallest view V_j that contains each a_j, breaking ties arbitrarily. Because each write to A can only add new personae, each view is a subset of any larger views. Furthermore, adding more personae to a view can only decrease the probability that any particular persona has the highest priority. It follows that a_j has the highest priority in any view (and thus survives) if and only if it has the highest priority in the smallest view that contains it, V_j.

We now wish to argue that each member of V_j is equally likely to have the highest priority, so that the probability that a_j in particular has the highest priority is exactly $1/|V_j|$. We must be a little bit careful here: while the adversary's schedule determine the order in which *processes* write and read the snapshot object, it does not determine the order in which *personae* appear, because this depends on the assignment of personae to processes, which in turn depends on the outcome of previous rounds. But the order of personae *is* fully determined by the combination of the adversary's schedule and the priorities in all rounds $i' < i + 1$. Since the priorities in round $i + 1$ are independent of these variables, the chance that a_j has the highest priority in its view is in fact $1/|V_j| \leq 1/j$.

Summing $1/j$ over all j gives a harmonic series, showing $E[Y_{i+1}|Y_i] \leq H_{Y_i} \leq \ln Y_i + 1$. So $E[X_{i+1}|X_i] \leq \ln Y_i = \ln(X_i+1)$.[1] However, because each term after the first in the harmonic series is less than or equal to $1/2$, we also have the cruder, but more accurate for small X_i, bound $E[Y_{i+1}|Y_i] \leq 1 + (Y_i - 1)/2 = 1 + X_i/2$, or $E[X_{i+1}|X_i] \leq X_i/2$. Combining these bounds gives the claimed bound (1). □

Iterating Lemma 1, plus an application of Jensen's inequality, shows that the algorithm works as advertised.

THEOREM 2. *Algorithm 1 implements a conciliator with agreement probability $1 - \epsilon$ and $O(\log^* n + \log(1/\epsilon))$ individual step complexity.*

---
[1]What we are doing here is very similar to counting **left-to-right maxima** or **outstanding values** of a random permutation. There is an extensive literature on the distribution of the number left-to-right maxima, going back to a classic paper of Rényi [19], but for our purposes a simple linearity-of-expectation bound is enough.

PROOF. Termination and validity are immediate from inspection of the code. So we concentrate on showing probabilistic agreement, specifically that the set of surviving personae converges to a singleton with probability at least $1 - \epsilon$.

Let X_i be the number of excess personae after i rounds as in Lemma 1.

Let $f(x) = \min(\ln(x + 1), x/2)$. Then (1) says that $E[X_{i+1}|X_i] \le f(X_i)$. Note that f is the minimum of increasing concave functions over $[0, \infty)$ and is thus increasing and concave itself. Because f is concave over $[0, \infty)$, we have that, for any random variable $X \ge 0$, $E[f(X)] \le f(E[X])$ by Jensen's inequality.

It follows that $E[X_{i+1}] = E[E[X_{i+1}|X_i]] \le E[f(X_i)] \le f(E[X_i])$, and in general we have $E[X_i] \le f^{(i)}(X_0) < f^{(i)}(n)$, where $f^{(i)}$ is the i-fold composition of f defined recursively by $f^{(0)}(x) = x$ and $f^{(i+1)} = f \circ f^{(i)}$.

It is not hard to show that $f(x) \le \log x$ for $x \ge 2$. Since $\log^{(i)} n \ge 2$ for $i \le \log^* n - 1$, we have $f^{(i)}(n) \le \log^{(i)} n$ for $i \le \log^* n$, and in particular have $f^{(\log^* n)}(n) \le 1$. Since $f(x) \le x/2$ always, applying f an additional $\lceil \log(1/\epsilon) \rceil$ times gives $f^{(\log^* n + \lceil \log(1/\epsilon) \rceil)}(n) \le \epsilon$ for any $\epsilon > 0$.

This gives $E[X_{\log^* n + \lceil \log(1/\epsilon) \rceil}] \le \epsilon$. But $X_{\log^* n + \lceil \log(1/\epsilon) \rceil}$ is a non-negative integer-valued random variable, so applying Markov's inequality we have $\Pr[X_{\log^* n + \lceil \log(1/\epsilon) \rceil} > 0] = \Pr[X_{\log^* n + \lceil \log(1/\epsilon) \rceil} \ge 1] \le \epsilon$. □

As noted in the introduction, alternating copies of Algorithm 1 with adopt-commit objects immediately gives an oblivious-adversary consensus protocol with $O(\log^* n)$ expected individual step complexity in the unit-cost snapshot model.

3. CHEAP CONSENSUS WITH MULTI-WRITER REGISTERS

Algorithm 2 gives an implementation of a conciliator with agreement probability $1 - \epsilon$ in which each process takes $O(\log \log n + \log(1/\epsilon))$ steps.

```
1  procedure conciliator(input)
2      Let chooseWrite be a vector of
       ⌈log log n⌉ + ⌈log_{4/3}(8/ϵ)⌉ independent random
       Boolean variables with
       Pr[chooseWrite[i] = 1] = p_i
3      persona ← ⟨input, chooseWrite⟩
4      for i ← 1 ... ⌈log log n⌉ + ⌈log_{4/3}(8/ϵ)⌉ do
5          if persona.chooseWrite[i] = 1 then
6              r_i ← persona
7          else
8              v ← r_i
9              if v ≠ ⊥ then
10                 persona ← v
11     return persona.input
```

Algorithm 2: Sifting conciliator

The basic mechanism is similar to the **sift** protocol used to reduce the number of participants in test-and-set in [1], where processes drop out when they see other processes that are not dropping out. The main difference is that in the new protocol, a process that sees another process adopts that process's persona (preferred value and random bits) and continues with the algorithm instead of dropping out.

In each round i, a process carries out exactly one operation, choosing randomly whether to write or read the register r_i. If the process writes, its persona is retained in the next round. If it reads, its persona is retained only if it sees an empty register; otherwise, it adopts whatever persona it sees. As in Algorithm 1, these random choices are controlled by vectors of random bits generated at the start of the protocol that propagate along with the input values, so that all processes with the same persona in round i take the same action.

The probabilities of each event vary from round to round and are carefully tuned to reduce the expected number of excess personae as quickly as possible. The specific probabilities used will be given after proving the following lemma.

LEMMA 3. *Let Y_i be the number of distinct personae that survive the first i rounds of Algorithm 2 and let $X_i = Y_i - 1$ be the number of excess personae. Then*

$$E[X_{i+1}|X_i] < \min \begin{cases} p_{i+1} X_i + \frac{1}{p_{i+1}}, \\ (1 - p_{i+1} + p_{i+1}^2) X_i. \end{cases}$$

PROOF. The first case of the min is more useful when X_i is large. To obtain it, we will first compute a bound on $E[Y_{i+1}|Y_i]$ and then manipulate it to obtain the stated bound on $E[X_{i+1}|X_i]$.

Order the personae $a_1, \dots, a_{Y_i}$ that appear as the persona of at least one process leaving round i by the order in which a process carrying each persona is first scheduled to write or read r_{i+1}. Observe that the assignment of personae to processes in round $i + 1$ is determined by the chooseWrite bits for rounds 1 through i and the schedule chosen by the adversary; both are independent of the round-$(i + 1)$ chooseWrite bits.

For each persona a_j, it survives round $i + 1$ if (a) some process sees a 1 in the corresponding chooseWrite[$i + 1$] bit and writes a_j; (b) some process reads a_j and adopts it; or (c) some process sees a 0 in the corresponding chooseWrite[$i + 1$] bit but sees $\perp$ when it reads. If case (b) occurs, so does case (a), since some process had to first write a_j to r_{i+1}. Case (c) occurs if persona.chooseWrite[$i + 1$] is 0 for the first process to write a_j and for all process with persona $a_{j'}$ for $j' < j$.

The probabilities of these events are p for case (a) and $(1 - p)^j$ for case (c). Summing these probabilities over all j gives $E[Y_{i+1}|Y_i] \le p_{i+1} Y_i + 1/p_{i+1} - 1$, where $1/p_{i+1} - 1 = \sum_{j=1}^{\infty} (1-p)^j$ is an upper bound on the terms from case (c).

Substituting in $X_{i+1} = Y_{i+1} - 1$ and $Y_i = X_i + 1$ gives

$$\begin{aligned} E[X_{i+1}|X_i] &\le p_{i+1}(X_i + 1) + 1/p_{i+1} - 2 \\ &= p_{i+1} X_i + 1/p_{i+1} + p_{i+1} - 2 \\ &< p_{i+1} X_i + 1/p_{i+1}. \end{aligned}$$

The second case of the min becomes useful when X_i is small, where the cavalier unbounding of bounded sums and dropping of small terms in the previous analysis causes trouble. For this bound, we consider separately the cases where the first process q reads or writes, and assume, for the sake of obtaining a simple upper bound, that all personae survive if q reads. Somewhat more formally, we have:

$$\begin{aligned}
\mathrm{E}[X_{i+1}|X_i] &= (1 - p_{i+1})\,\mathrm{E}[X_{i+1}|X_i, q \text{ reads}] \\
&\quad + p_{i+1}\,\mathrm{E}[X_{i+1}|X_i, q \text{ writes}] \\
&\leq (1 - p_{i+1})X_i + p_{i+1}^2 X_i \\
&= (1 - p_{i+1} + p_{i+1}^2)X_i.
\end{aligned}$$

□

Now let use choose the probabilities p_i.

The first bound in Lemma 3 is minimized by letting $p_1 = 1/\sqrt{X_0}$; this gives $\mathrm{E}[X_1] \leq 2\sqrt{X_0} \leq \sqrt{n-1}$.

Iterating this procedure in subsequent rounds gives a recurrence $x_0 = n - 1$, $p_{i+1} = 1/\sqrt{x_i}$, $x_{i+1} = p_i x_i + 1/p_i = 2\sqrt{x_i}$, whose solution gives

$$x_i = 2^{2 - 2^{-i+1}}(n - 1)^{2^{-i}} \tag{2}$$

and

$$p_i = 2^{1 - 2^{-i+1}}(n - 1)^{-2^{-i}}. \tag{3}$$

We will use these values of p_i for the first $\lceil \log \log n \rceil$ iterations, obtaining:

LEMMA 4. *Let X_i be the number of distinct personae that survive the first i rounds of Algorithm 2 using p_i as defined above for $i = 1 \ldots \log \log n$. Let x_i also be defined as above. Then $\mathrm{E}[X_i] < x_i$ for all i in $1 \ldots \lceil \log \log n \rceil$.*

PROOF. The proof is by induction on i, using Lemma 3 and the x_i recurrence at each step:

$$\begin{aligned}
\mathrm{E}[X_{i+1}] &= \mathrm{E}[\mathrm{E}[X_{i+1}|X_i]] \\
&\leq \mathrm{E}[p_{i+1}X_i + 1/p_{i+1}] \\
&= p_{i+1}\,\mathrm{E}[X_i] + 1/p_{i+1} \\
&\leq p_{i+1}x_i + 1/p_{i+1} \\
&= 2\sqrt{x_i} \\
&= x_{i+1}.
\end{aligned}$$

□

For $i = \lceil \log \log n \rceil$, this gives

$$\begin{aligned}
x_{\lceil \log \log n \rceil} &= 2^{2 - 2^{-\lceil \log \log n \rceil + 1}}(n - 1)^{2^{-\lceil \log \log n \rceil}} \\
&< 4n^{1/\log n} \\
&= 8.
\end{aligned}$$

For $i > \lceil \log \log n \rceil$, we switch to $p_i = 1/2$, which minimizes the coefficient $1 - p_i + p_i^2$ in the second case of the Lemma 3 bound. Now we have:

LEMMA 5. *Let X_i be the number of distinct personae that survive the first i rounds of Algorithm 2. Let $p_i = 2^{1 - 2^{-i+1}}(n - 1)^{-2^{-i}}$ for $i = 1 \ldots \lceil \log \log n \rceil$ and $1/2$ for larger i. Let $j > 0$. Then $\mathrm{E}[X_{\lceil \log \log n \rceil + j}] \leq 8 \cdot (3/4)^j$.*

PROOF. We have just shown that $\mathrm{E}[X_{\lceil \log \log n \rceil}] \leq 8$, and each subsequent round multiplies the bound by $(1 - 1/2 + (1/2)^2) = 3/4$. □

Plugging in the number of iterations from the algorithm gives:

THEOREM 6. *Algorithm 2 implements a conciliator with agreement probability $1 - \epsilon$ and $O(\log \log n + \log(1/\epsilon))$ individual step complexity.*

PROOF. Again termination and validity are easy, so we concentrate on probabilistic agreement.

From Lemma 5, after $\lceil \log \log n \rceil + \lceil \log_{4/3}(8/\epsilon) \rceil$ rounds, the expected number of excess personae X is at most

$$8 \cdot (3/4)^{\log_{4/3}(8/\epsilon)} = 8 \cdot (\epsilon/8) = \epsilon.$$

So the probability that X is nonzero is bounded by ϵ using Markov's inequality. □

The dependence on ϵ in the running time is necessary, due to the oblivious-adversary lower bound of Attiya and Censor [9]. Whether the $\log \log n$ part can be further improved is open.

To extend Algorithm 2 to an algorithm for consensus, we can alternate it with adopt-commit objects as described in [4]. For constant ϵ, this gives an expected individual step complexity equal to $O(\log \log n)$ plus the cost of the adopt-commit. Unfortunately, the best currently-known implementation of adopt-commit [7] is relatively expensive, requiring $\Theta(\log m/\log \log m)$ steps from each process if run with m possible input values. This means that we can only get $O(\log \log n)$-step consensus if the number of values m is $O(\log n \log \log n)$. It is possible that further improvements in randomized adopt-commit implementations (for an oblivious adversary) might increase this limit.

4. LINEAR EXPECTED TOTAL WORK

Algorithm 2 requires $\Theta(n \log \log n)$ additional total steps to achieve a constant probability of agreement in the worst case. With some tinkering, we can reduce this to $O(n)$ while keeping the $O(\log \log n)$ individual step complexity.

The essential idea is to embed Algorithm 2 in an outer conciliator algorithm extracted from the consensus procotocol of Chor, Israeli, and Li [12]. In the outer algorithm, there is a single register **proposal** that is initially $\bot$. At each step, a process reads **proposal** and returns its value if it is not $\bot$; otherwise, it writes its input to **proposal** with probability $\frac{1}{4n}$ and executes a step of Algorithm 2 otherwise.

In isolation, the Chor-Israeli-Li conciliator (CIL) works because some process writes **proposal** after $4n$ attempts on average, and once some process writes **proposal**, each of the remaining $n - 1$ processes has at most a $\frac{1}{4n}$ chance of overwriting the register before reading a non-null value and leaving. If no process overwrites the first value (which occurs, by the union bound, with probability at least $1 - \frac{n-1}{4n} > 3/4$), all processes will agree on it.

Embedding Algorithm 2 into CIL means that some processes may return a value obtained from Algorithm 2 while others return a value obtained from **proposal**. To reconcile these two values, we use a final combining stage that in effect implements a simple two-valued conciliator. First, an adopt-commit object forces each process to decide on the unique value if only one is present; in not, a shared coin chooses between the competing values otherwise. Using the persona technique again, we implement this shared coin by associating a random bit with each input, and having the combining stage use this bit. We show that, with constant probability, bit associated with the combining-stage inputs are equal to each other and the outcome of the adopt-commit, giving agreement on the final output value.[2]

---

[2] A similar technique was used in [5] to combine interleaved shared-coin algorithms into a single shared coin, but this re-

5

Pseudocode for the entire procedure is given in Algorithm 3.

```
1  procedure conciliator(input)
2  |   Choose coin uniformly from {0, 1}
3  |   Initialize an instance of Algorithm 2 with input
   |   ⟨input, coin⟩ and ε = 1/4.
4  |   while proposal = ⊥ do
5  |   |   with probability 1/4n do
6  |   |   |   proposal ← ⟨input, coin⟩
7  |   |   else
8  |   |   |   Run one step of the Algorithm 2 instance
9  |   |   |   if Algorithm 2 returns v then
10 |   |   |   |   r[0] ← v.input
11 |   |   |   |   return combine(0, v.coin)

12 |   v ← proposal
13 |   r[1] ← v.input
14 |   return combine(1, v.coin)
15 procedure combine(i, coin)
16 |   ⟨decide, b⟩ ← AdoptCommit(i)
17 |   if decide ≠ commit then
18 |   |   b ← coin
19 |   return r[b]
```

Algorithm 3: CIL conciliator with embedded sifter

THEOREM 7. *Algorithm 3 implements a conciliator with $O(\log \log n)$ worst-case individual step complexity, $O(n)$ expected total step complexity, and agreement probability 1/8.*

PROOF. Termination and the individual step complexity bound hold because no process can execute Line 8 more than $O(\log \log n)$ times without leaving the main loop. This implies that the main loop is also executed $O(\log \log n)$ times, because at most one iteration can skip Line 8 without writing **proposal** and causing the loop to finish anyway. The binary adopt-commit object and additional work in **combine** cost at most $O(1)$ additional steps.

For expected total steps, observe that the total expected number of iterations of the main loop is bounded by $4n$ across all processes, because each such iteration has an independent $\frac{1}{4n}$ probability of shutting the protocol down. Additional operations outside the main loop cost at most $O(n)$ more total steps.

For validity, observe that if the adopt-commit value returns ⟨commit, b⟩, then b is the index of a register to which some process's input (as returned from Algorithm 2 or written directly to **proposal**) has been written. If it returns ⟨adopt, −⟩, then both indices have appeared in inputs to the adopt-commit (by acceptance), so both registers have been initialized. In either case validity holds.

Probabilistic agreement is messier. We begin by arguing that the probability that Algorithm 2 returns a unique pair v is not affected by the embedding.

Fix a schedule S for the execution of Algorithm 3. Let $\sigma_1, \sigma_2, \ldots, \sigma_n$ be the sequence of coin-flips used in Line 5 by processes $1, 2, \ldots, n$. Observe that S and $\sigma_1 \ldots \sigma_n$ between

them determine the schedule for Algorithm 2: an easy way to see this is that if we replace Line 8 with an operation that emits the current process id, we compute the induced schedule based only on S and $\sigma_1 \ldots \sigma_n$. Because S and $\sigma_1 \ldots \sigma_n$ are independent of the input to Algorithm 2 and any coin-flips used inside it, the induced schedule is also independent of these quantities.

Conditioning on some fixed induced schedule, we have from Theorem 6 that Algorithm 2 violates probabilistic agreement with probability at most $1/4$. This continues to hold when we remove the conditioning by averaging over all values of $\sigma_1 \ldots \sigma_n$.

A second contribution to our error budget is the probability that the outer CIL mechanism produces more than one output. From the earlier discussion, this occurs with probability at most $\frac{n-1}{4n} < 1/4$.

It follows that the probability that either Algorithm 2 or the **proposal** register yield more than one output is less than $1/4 + 1/4 = 1/2$. If both conciliators produce a unique output, then **combine** produces agreement with independent probability at least $1/4$. To see this, let b_{AC} be the unique bit tagged with **commit** by the adopt-commit object (if any), and b_0 and b_1 the **coin** bits for $i = 0$ and $i = 1$. The probability that $b_0 = b_1$ is at least $1/2$ (it may be 1 if both correspond to a random bit supplied by the same process); if b_{AC} exists, the probability this common bit equals it is also $1/2$, because b_{AC} does not depend on any of the **coin** values. Multiplying these probabilities gives at least a $1/4$ chance that all processes choose the same b, which gives the at least $1/8$ probability of agreement for the algorithm as a whole. □

Essentially the same argument shows that replacing Algorithm 2 in Algorithm 3 with Algorithm 1 similarly gives an oblivious-adversary conciliator for the unit-cost snapshot model with $O(\log^* n)$ worst-case individual step complexity and $O(n)$ expected total step complexity. A similar argument is likely to work on any conciliator that is "oblivious" in the sense that it only copies its input values without examining them.

As with the algorithms in previous sections, we can use Algorithm 3 to obtain consensus by alternating it with adopt-commit objects. The resulting protocol takes an expected $O(\log \log n)$ individual steps and expected $O(n)$ total steps, for consensus on $O(1)$ possible inputs, with the input space limit as before reflecting the limitations of currently-known adopt-commit objects.

5. CONCLUSIONS

Under the assumption of an oblivious adversary, we have shown how to reduce the expected individual step complexity of consensus from $O(\log n)$ to $O(\log \log n)$ in the standard multi-writer register model and $O(\log^* n)$ in the practically irrelevant but theoretically significant unit-cost snapshot model. Many open problems remain.

Strength of the adversary.

Our results exploit the limitations of the oblivious adversary in several ways. As in previous protocols of Chandra [11] and Aumann [10], we pre-flip coins that are later shared between many processes; this requires assuming at minimum a **content-oblivious** adversary that cannot see the contents of registers or the internal states of processes.

sult depends on the output of a shared coin not always being under the control of the adversary. Unlike the shared-coin case, it is not clear that interleaving arbitrary conciliators will always give a conciliator.

We also choose between different operations probabilistically as in the protocol of Chor, Israeli, and Li [12], requiring a **weak adversary** that cannot prevent this. As the oblivious adversary is weaker than both these adversaries, our algorithms work for an oblivious adversary, but it would be interesting to examine more closely exactly what properties of the adversary are needed for either these algorithms or sublogarithmic consensus in general.

Gap between upper and lower bounds.

There is still a gap between our upper bounds of $O(\log \log n + \log(1/\epsilon))$ and $O(\log^* n + \log(1/\epsilon))$ for conciliators with agreement probability $1 - \epsilon$ and the $\Omega(1/\epsilon)$ lower bound of Attiya and Censor [9], leaving open the possibility that the dependence on n could be further reduced. It may also be the case that this dependence is necessary, and that a lower bound could be shown that mirrors the structure of the upper bound: showing that $\Omega(n^c)$ or $\Omega(\log n)$ values remain after one layer of computation in the multi-writer register or unit-cost snapshot models, respectively, in some class of executions.

Gap between consensus and test-and-set.

Many of our techniques are similar to techniques recently used for oblivious-adversary test-and-set [1, 15]. Our protocol for consensus using cheap snapshots has the same $O(\log^* n)$ expected individual step complexity as the best currently known protocol for test-and-set *without* using snapshots, due to Giakkoupis and Woelfel [15], which was developed concurrently with and independently of the present work. In the standard multi-writer register model, our protocol follows both the structure and the $O(\log \log n)$ complexity the *previous* best known test-and-set protocol of Alistarh and Aspnes [1], but this is significantly slower than the newer $O(\log^* n)$ protocol. Unfortunately, the specific technique used by Giakkoupis and Woelfel for test-and-set does not generalize immediately to consensus, because it exploits the fact that a loser in a test-and-set protocol can leave immediately without determining the identity of any specific survivor, so long as it can determine that at least one other process survives. But it may be that some similar technique could yield further improvements for oblivious-adversary consensus in the multi-writer register model.

6. REFERENCES

[1] Dan Alistarh and James Aspnes. Sub-logarithmic test-and-set against a weak adversary. In *Distributed Computing: 25th International Symposium, DISC 2011*, volume 6950 of *Lecture Notes in Computer Science*, pages 97–109. Springer-Verlag, September 2011.

[2] Dan Alistarh, Seth Gilbert, Rachid Guerraoui, and Corentin Travers. Of choices, failures and asynchrony: The many faces of set agreement. In Yingfei Dong, Ding-Zhu Du, and Oscar H. Ibarra, editors, *ISAAC*, volume 5878 of *Lecture Notes in Computer Science*, pages 943–953. Springer, 2009.

[3] James Aspnes. Randomized consensus in expected $O(n^2)$ total work using single-writer registers. In *Distributed Computing: 25th International Symposium, DISC 2011*, volume 6950 of *Lecture Notes in Computer Science*, pages 363–373. Springer-Verlag, September 2011.

[4] James Aspnes. A modular approach to shared-memory consensus, with applications to the probabilistic-write model. *Distributed Computing*, 25(2):179–188, May 2012.

[5] James Aspnes, Hagit Attiya, and Keren Censor. Combining shared coin algorithms. *Journal of Parallel and Distributed Computing*, 70(3):317–322, March 2010.

[6] James Aspnes and Keren Censor. Approximate shared-memory counting despite a strong adversary. In *SODA '09: Proceedings of the Nineteenth Annual ACM-SIAM Symposium on Discrete Algorithms*, pages 441–450, Philadelphia, PA, USA, 2009. Society for Industrial and Applied Mathematics.

[7] James Aspnes and Faith Ellen. Tight bounds for anonymous adopt-commit objects. In *23rd Annual ACM Symposium on Parallelism in Algorithms and Architectures*, pages 317–324, June 2011.

[8] Hagit Attiya and Keren Censor. Tight bounds for asynchronous randomized consensus. *Journal of the ACM*, 55(5):20, October 2008.

[9] Hagit Attiya and Keren Censor-Hillel. Lower bounds for randomized consensus under a weak adversary. *SIAM J. Comput.*, 39(8):3885–3904, 2010.

[10] Yonatan Aumann. Efficient asynchronous consensus with the weak adversary scheduler. In *PODC '97: Proceedings of the Sixteenth Annual ACM Symposium on Principles of Distributed Computing*, pages 209–218, New York, NY, USA, 1997. ACM.

[11] Tushar Deepak Chandra. Polylog randomized wait-free consensus. In *Proceedings of the Fifteenth Annual ACM Symposium on Principles of Distributed Computing*, pages 166–175, Philadelphia, Pennsylvania, USA, 23–26 May 1996.

[12] Benny Chor, Amos Israeli, and Ming Li. Wait-free consensus using asynchronous hardware. *SIAM J. Comput.*, 23(4):701–712, 1994.

[13] Michael J. Fischer, Nancy A. Lynch, and Michael S. Paterson. Impossibility of distributed consensus with one faulty process. *Journal of the ACM*, 32(2):374–382, April 1985.

[14] Eli Gafni. Round-by-round fault detectors: Unifying synchrony and asynchrony (extended abstract). In *Proceedings of the Seventeenth Annual ACM Symposium on Principles of Distributed Computing*, pages 143–152, 1998.

[15] George Giakkoupis and Philipp Woelfel. On the time and space complexity of randomized test-and-set. To appear, PODC 2012.

[16] Wojciech M. Golab, Lisa Higham, and Philipp Woelfel. Linearizable implementations do not suffice for randomized distributed computation. In Lance Fortnow and Salil P. Vadhan, editors, *STOC*, pages 373–382. ACM, 2011.

[17] Michael C. Loui and Hosame H. Abu-Amara. Memory requirements for agreement among unreliable asynchronous processes. *Advances in Computing Research*, pages 163–183, 1987.

[18] Achour Mostefaoui, Sergio Rajsbaum, Michel Raynal, and Corentin Travers. The combined power of conditions and information on failures to solve asynchronous set agreement. *SIAM Journal on Computing*, 38(4):1574–1601, 2008.

[19] Alfred Rényi. Théorie des éléments saillants d'une suite d'observations. *Annales scientifiques de l'Université de Clermont-Ferrand 2, série Mathématiques*, 8(2):7–13, 1962.

On the Liveness of Transactional Memory

Victor Bushkov
EPFL, IC, LPD
victor.bushkov@epfl.ch

Rachid Guerraoui
EPFL, IC, LPD
rachid.guerraoui@epfl.ch

Michał Kapałka
EPFL, IC, LPD
michal.kapalka@epfl.ch

ABSTRACT

Despite the large amount of work on Transactional Memory (TM), little is known about how much liveness it could provide. This paper presents the first formal treatment of the question. We prove that no TM implementation can ensure local progress, the analogous of wait-freedom in the TM context, and we highlight different ways to circumvent the impossibility.

Categories and Subject Descriptors

D.1.3 [**Programming Techniques**]: Concurrent Programming; D.2.1 [**Software Engineering**]: Requirements / Specifications

General Terms

Theory

Keywords

Concurrent programming, Liveness, Transactional memory

1. INTRODUCTION

Transactional memory (TM) [10, 13, 20] is a concurrency control paradigm that aims at simplifying concurrent programming. Each sequential process (or thread[1]) of an application performs operations on shared data within a *transaction* and then either commits or aborts the transaction. If the transaction is committed, then the effects of its operations become visible to subsequent transactions; if it is aborted, then the effects are discarded. Transactions are viewed as a simple way to write concurrent programs and hence leverage multicore architectures. Not surprisingly, a large body of work has been dedicated to implementing the paradigm and reducing its overheads.

---

[1]The technical difference between threads and processes is not important for the theoretical results of the paper.

To a large extent, however, setting the theoretical foundations of the TM concept has been neglected. Indeed, correctness conditions for TMs have been proposed in [9, 15, 4] and programming language level semantics of specific classes of TM implementations have been determined, e.g., in [1, 16, 17, 18]. All those efforts, however, focused solely on *safety*, i.e., on what TMs *should not do*. Clearly, a TM that ensures only a safety property can trivially be implemented by aborting all operations. To be meaningful, a TM has to ensure a *liveness* property [2], i.e., a guarantee about what *should be done*.

1.1 Liveness of a TM

In classical shared-memory systems, a liveness property describes when a process that invokes an operation on a shared object is guaranteed to return from this operation [14]. A widely studied such property is *wait-freedom* [11]. It ensures, intuitively, that *every* process invoking an operation eventually returns from this operation, even if other processes crash. It is the ultimate liveness property in concurrent computing as it ensures that every process makes progress.

In a transactional context, requiring such a property alone would however not be enough to ensure any meaningful progress: processes of which all transactions are *aborted* might be satisfying wait-freedom but would not be making real progress. To be meaningful, a TM liveness property should ensure transaction *commitment*, beyond operation *termination*.

One would expect from a TM that every process that keeps executing a transaction (say keeps retrying it in case it aborts) eventually commits it—a property that we call *local progress* and that is similar in spirit to wait-freedom. Not satisfying this property means that some transaction, even when retried forever, might never commit.

In fact, a TM implementation that protects transactions using a single fair global lock could ensure local progress: such a TM would execute all transactions sequentially, thus avoiding transaction conflicts. Yet, such a TM would force processes to wait for each other, preventing them from progressing independently. A process that acquires a global lock and gets suspended for a long time, or that enters an infinite loop and keeps running forever without releasing the lock, would prevent all other processes from making any progress. This would go against the very essence of wait-freedom. Hence, to be really meaningful a TM liveness property should enforce some "independent" progress.

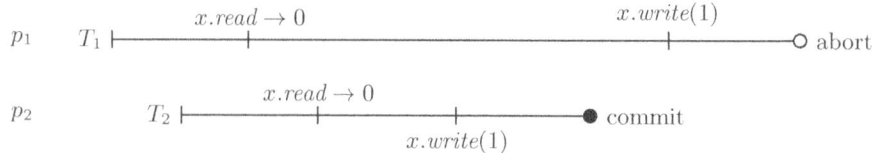

Figure 1: An illustration of the difficulty of ensuring local progress. The scenario can repeat infinitely many times preventing transaction T_1 from ever committing.

1.2 Transaction Failures

The classical way of modeling shared-memory systems in which processes can make progress independently, i.e., without waiting for each other, is to consider *asynchronous* systems in which processes can be arbitrarily slow, including failing by *crashing*. A TM implementation that is resilient to crashes enables the progress of a process even if other processes are suspended for a long time. In the same vein, one should also ensure progress in the face of *parasitic* processes—those that keep executing transactional operations without ever attempting to commit. These model long-running processes whose duration cannot be anticipated by the system, e.g., because of an infinite loop.

To illustrate the underlying challenges, consider the following example, depicted in Figure 1. Two processes, p_1 and p_2, execute transactions T_1 and T_2, respectively. Process p_1 reads value 0 from a shared variable x and then gets suspended for a long time. Then, process p_2 also reads value 0 from x, writes value 1 to x, and attempts to commit. Because of asynchrony, the processes can be arbitrarily delayed. Hence, the TM does not know whether p_1 has crashed or is just very slow, and so, in order to ensure the progress of process p_2, the TM might eventually allow process p_2 to commit T_2. But then, if process p_1 writes value 1 to x and attempts to commit T_1, the TM cannot allow process p_1 to commit, as this would violate safety. A similar situation can occur in the case of parasitic processes, say if p_1 keeps repeatedly reading from variable x. If the maximum length of a transaction is not known, the TM cannot say whether p_1 is parasitic or not, and thus may eventually allow process p_2 to commit T_2, forcing process p_1 to abort T_1 later.

1.3 Contributions

This paper first introduces the notion of a *TM-liveness* property which specifies, for each infinite execution, which processes should make progress, i.e. which processes commit transactions infinitely often. We formalize this notion by modeling TM implementations as I/O automata and focusing on infinite histories of such automata.

Since safety properties state that some events should not occur and liveness properties state that some events should eventually occur, safety and liveness requirements depend on each other. A safety requirement may make it impossible to guarantee a liveness requirement and vice versa. The question is, under what conditions which safety and liveness properties are impossible to guarantee? We address this question in the TM context by proving an impossibility result which states that no TM implementation can ensure both *local progress* and *opacity* in a fault-prone system, i.e. in a system in which any number of processes can crash or be parasitic. Opacity is the safety property ensured by most TM implementations. It states that every transaction

observes a consistent state of the system. Local progress is a TM-liveness property, highlighted above, which states that every correct process, i.e. a process which is not parasitic and does not crash, makes progress. In fact, we prove a more general result stating that no TM implementation can ensure any safety property that is at least as strong as strict serializability together with the progress of at least two correct processes and any correct process that runs alone.

2. PRELIMINARIES

2.1 Processes and Shared Memory

We assume a classical (see, e.g., [11]) asynchronous, shared memory system of n *processes* $p_1, \ldots, p_n$ that communicate by executing operations on *shared objects* (which represent the shared memory, e.g., provided in hardware). A *shared object* is a higher-level abstraction provided to processes, and implemented typically in software using a set of *base objects*.

For instance, if base objects are memory locations with basic operations such as read, write, and compare-and-swap, then shared objects could be shared data structures such as linked lists or hash tables. If a process p_i invokes an operation op on a shared object O, then p_i follows the implementation of O, possibly accessing any number of base objects and executing local computations, until p_i is returned a result of op. We assume that processes are sequential; that is, whenever a process p_i invokes an operation op on any shared object, p_i does not invoke another operation on any shared object until p_i returns from op. Invocations and responses of shared objects operations are called (invocation and response) *events*.

2.2 Transactional Memory

Let K be the set of *process identifiers*, $P = \{p_k | k \in K\}$ be a set of processes, and X be a set of shared objects called *t-variables* ("t-variable" stands for "transactional variable"). The theoretical results of the paper hold for any shared objects which can implement read and write operations. Thus, for presentation simplicity, we focus on t-variables that support *read* and *write* operations. Each t-variable can have values from set V. Let $Inv_k = \{x.write^k(v) | x \in X$ and $v \in V\} \cup \{x.read^k | x \in X\} \cup \{tryC^k\}$ be the set of invocation events of process p_k and $Res_k = \{v^k | v \in V\} \cup \{ok^k, A^k, C^k\}$ be the set of response events of process p_k, where $tryC^k$ is a commit request, C^k is a *commit event*, and A^k is an *abort event*. Also, let $Inv = \cup_{k \in K} Inv_k$ and $Res = \cup_{k \in K} Res_k$.

Since a TM is a discrete event system that receives inputs from processes and returns corresponding responses we model behavior of TM implementations using I/O automata [8]. Formally, an I/O automaton F is a quintuple (St, I, Int, O, St_0, R), where St is a (possibly infinite) set of states, I is a set of input events, Int is a set of internal events, O is a set of output events, $St_0 \subseteq St$ is the set of initial states, $R \subseteq St \times (I \cup O) \times St$ is a transition relation. The sets I, Int, and O are disjoint. An *execution* of automaton F is a (finite or infinite) sequence $s_0 \cdot e_1 \cdot s_1 \cdot e_2 \cdot s_2 \cdots$ of alternating states and events such that (I) the sequence starts from an initial state $s_0 \in St_0$, (II) for any $i \in \{1, 2, \ldots\}$ we have $(s_{i-1}, e_i, s_i) \in R$, (III) the sequence ends with a state in case the sequence is finite. The longest subsequence of an execution of automaton F such that the subsequence consists of the events from $(I \cup O)$ is called a *history H* of automaton F.

Let F be an I/O automaton such that $I = Inv$ and $O = Res$. Denote by Σ_k a set such that $\Sigma_k = \{x.write^k(v) \cdot ok^k | x.write^k(v) \in Inv_k\} \cup \{x.read^k() \cdot v^k | x.read^k() \in Inv_k$ and $v^k \in Res_k\} \cup \{tryC^k \cdot C^k\} \cup \{e \cdot A^k | e \in Inv_k\}$. Also, let $\Sigma_k^\infty = \Sigma_k^* \cup \Sigma_k^\omega$, where Σ_k^* is the set of all finite sequences over Σ_k and Σ_k^ω is the set of all infinite sequences over Σ_k. Let H be a history over $Inv \cup Res$, we define a *projection $H|p_k$* of H on process p_k as the longest subsequence of H consisting of events from $Inv_k \cup Res_k$. A history H is *well-formed* iff for every $p_k \in P$ either $H|p_k \in \Sigma_k^\infty$ or $H|p_k \in \Sigma_k^* \cdot Inv_k$ holds, i.e. $H|p_k$ is a sequence of alternating invocation and response events.

We model a *TM implementation* as an I/O automaton $F = (St, I, Int, O, St_0, R)$ such that:

- $I = Inv$ and $O = Res$.

- Every history H of F is well-formed.

- For every $k \in K$, every $e \in Inv_k$, and every history H of F such that $H|p_k \in \Sigma_k^*$, history $H \cdot e$ is a history of F. In other words, every process which is not waiting for a response must be allowed by F to send an invocation event.

Given projection $H|p_k$ of history H of some TM implementation, a *transaction* of p_k in H is a subsequence $T = e_1 \cdot \ldots \cdot e_n$ of $H|p_k$ such that e_1 is the first event in $H|p_k$ or the previous event e_0 in $H|p_k$ is either A^k or C^k, and e_n is either A^k or C^k or the last event in $H|p_k$, and no event in T, except e_n, is A^k or C^k. Transaction T is *committed* (*aborted*) if the last event in T is a commit (abort) event. Given transactions T_1 and T_2 in history H, we say that T_1 *precedes* T_2 in H, denoted by $T_1 <_H T_2$, if T_1 is committing or aborting and the last event of T_1 occurs in H before the first event of T_2. Transactions T_1 and T_2 are *concurrent* if T_1 does not precede T_2 and T_2 does not precede T_1. History H is *sequential* if no two transactions in H are concurrent to each other.

Processes communicate with each other only through a TM implementation by invoking concurrently requests (read, write, and commit requests) and receiving corresponding responses from the implementation. Processes send commit requests to the TM implementation that decides which transactions should be committed or aborted. To reduce contention between transactions, a TM implementation may use a logically separate module called a contention manager. A contention manager can force the TM implementation to abort or delay some transactions. In this work we consider a contention manager as an integral part of a TM imple-

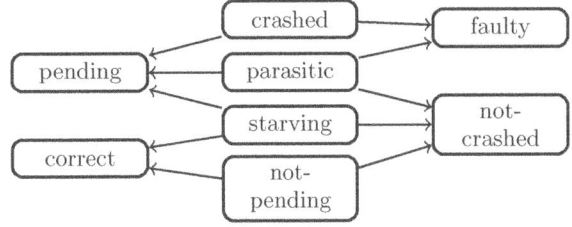

Figure 2: Classes of processes. An arrow from class c_1 to class c_2 means that every process which belongs to c_1 also belongs to c_2.

mentation. That is, all the results of the paper apply to the entire TM, including the contention manager.

The order in which processes invoke events is determined by a *scheduler*. Processes and TM implementations have no control over a scheduler. The scheduler decides which process is allowed to send an invocation to the TM implementation at given point in time. These decisions form a *schedule* which is a finite or an infinite sequence of process identifiers.

2.3 Process Failures

We say that process p_k is *pending* in infinite history H if H has only a finite number of commit events C^k. Process p_k *crashes* in infinite history H if $H|p_k \in \Sigma_k^*$. That is, from some point in time p_k stops sending invocation events.

Intuitively, a *parasitic* process is a process that keeps executing operations but, from some point in time, never attempts to commit (by invoking operation $tryC$) when given a chance to do so. Note that if starting from some moment in time every transaction of a process is prematurely aborted, i.e. aborted before the process invokes a commit request, we cannot tell whether the process will invoke a commit request, if it given a chance to do so. Therefore, we consider such processes as correct. Consider any infinite history H, and process p_k in H. If process p_k from some point in time executes infinitely many operations without being aborted and without attempting to commit, then p_k is parasitic. On the contrary, if p_k invokes operation $tryC^k$ or is aborted infinitely many times, then p_k is not parasitic. Formally, we say that process p_k is parasitic in infinite history H if $H|p_k$ is infinite and in history $H|p_k$ there are only a finite number of invocations $tryC^k$ and abort events A^k. If a process does not crash, is not parasitic, and is pending in infinite history H, then it is *starving* in H.

We say that process p_k is *correct* in infinite history H if p_k is not parasitic in H and does not crash in H. If a process is not correct in H, then it is *faulty* in H. Figure 2 depicts the relations between different classes of processes.

We define a *crash-prone system* (*parasitic-prone system*) *Sys* to be a system in which at least one process can crash (be parasitic). A *fault-prone system Sys* is a system which is crash-prone or parasitic-prone.

2.4 Safety properties of TM

A safety property S states that some events should never happen. Intuitively a safety property of TM implementations should capture the fact that all events within a transaction appear to other transactions as if they occur instanta-

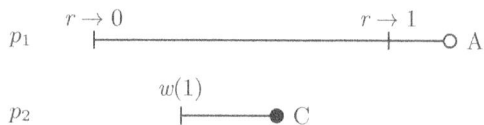

p_1 $\quad r \to 0 \qquad\qquad\qquad r \to 1$

p_2 $\qquad w(1)$

Figure 3: A history which is not opaque but strictly serializable. Hereafter, for simplicity, process and t-variable identifiers in operations are omitted, $r \to v$ means that a process invokes a read operation and receives value v, $w(v)$ means that a process invokes a write operation to write value v and receives ok, C means that a process invokes a commit request and receives a commit event, A means that a process invokes a commit request and receives an abort event.

neously. If a transaction is committed, then all the changes made by write operations within the transaction are made visible to other transactions; otherwise all the changes are rolled back. We consider two safety properties of TM implementations: strict serializability S_s and opacity S_o. Intuitively, strict serializability requires every committed transaction to observe a consistent state of the system [19], while opacity requires every transaction (even aborted or unfinished) to observe a consistent state of the system [9].

We say that history H is *equivalent* to history H' if for every process $p_k \in P$ we have $H|p_k = H'|p_k$. We obtain the *completion comp(H)* of finite history H by aborting every transaction which is neither committed nor aborted, i.e. by adding to the end of the history corresponding abort events. If $comp(H) = H$, then H is a *complete* history. We say that finite history H' *preserves the real time order* of finite history H if for any two transactions T_1 and T_2 in H if $T_1 <_H T_2$, then $T_1 <_{H'} T_2$. Let H_s be a complete sequential history and T_j be a transaction in H. Denote by $visible(T_j)$ the longest subsequence of H_s such that for every transaction T_i in the subsequence, either $j = i$ or $T_i <_{H_s} T_j$. Transaction T_j is *legal* in H_s if for every t-variable $x \in X$ history $visible(T_j)$ respects the sequential specification of x, i.e. for every transaction T_i in $visible(T_j)$ and every response event v^k in T_i, v is the value of the previous write to x invocation event in $visible(T_j)$ or v is the initial value of x if there are no write to x invocation events in $visible(T_j)$ before v^k.

A finite history H is *opaque* if there exists a sequential history H_s equivalent to $comp(H)$, such that H_s preserves the real-time order of $comp(H)$, and every transaction in H_s is legal. A finite history H is *strictly serializable* if there exists a sequential history H_s equivalent to H', where H' is obtained from H by removing every aborted or unfinished transaction, such that H_s preserves the real-time order of H, and every transaction in H_s is legal. Let M be a TM implementation represented by I/O automaton F. We say that M ensures opacity (strict serializability) iff every finite history H of F is opaque (strictly serializable).

For example, the history in Figure 1 is opaque, while the history in Figure 3 is not opaque but strictly serializable.

3. LIVENESS OF A TM

We introduce in this section the concept of a *TM-liveness* property and we give examples of such properties.

3.1 TM-liveness Properties

Basically, a TM-liveness property states whether some process p_k should make progress in some infinite history H. Clearly, progress cannot be required for crashed or parasitic processes: these processes have executions with a finite number of $tryC$ operation invocations. We define a TM-liveness property as a weakening of the strongest TM-liveness property. The strongest TM-liveness property guarantees that in every infinite history of a TM implementation every correct process makes progress.

Formally, a correct process p_k in infinite history H *makes progress* in H iff p_k is not pending H. Let H_{TM} be the set of all infinite well-formed histories.

We define *local progress*, which is analogous to wait-freedom in shared memory, as a set L_{local} of histories from H_{TM} such that infinite history $H \in H_{TM}$ belongs to L_{local} iff every correct process in H makes progress in H, or H does not have any correct process. A *TM-liveness* property L is a set of infinite histories such that $L_{local} \subseteq L \subseteq H_{TM}$. Given two TM-liveness properties L_1 and L_2, we say that L_1 is weaker (stronger) than L_2 iff $L_2 \subseteq L_1$ ($L_1 \subseteq L_2$). An infinite history H ensures TM-liveness property L iff $H \in L$.

Intuitively a TM implementation ensures a TM-liveness property iff every infinite history of the implementation ensures the property. However, we have to exclude the case when the implementation cannot produce an infinite history, i.e. when the implementation does not send response events to any invocation event of any process. We say that I/O automaton F that models some TM implementation is *live* iff every finite history H of F can be extended to some infinite history $H \cdot H'$ of F.

Let M be a TM implementation modeled by I/O automaton F. TM implementation M ensures TM-liveness property L iff F is live and every infinite history H of F ensures L.

3.2 Examples of TM-liveness Properties

3.2.1 Local Progress

A TM implementation M ensures local progress if M guarantees that every correct process makes progress.

For example, Figure 4 shows an infinite history which ensures local progress in a system with two processes and one t-variable. Both processes make progress (are not pending) in the history.

As we prove in this paper, implementing a TM that ensures opacity and local progress in any fault-prone system is impossible. That is, local progress inherently requires some form of indefinite blocking of transactions. Ensuring local progress in a system that is both crash-free and parasitic-free is possible. It suffices to use a simple TM that synchronizes all transactions using a single global starvation-free lock, and thus never aborts any transaction.

3.2.2 Global Progress

A TM implementation M ensures *global progress* if M guarantees that some correct process makes progress. We define global progress, as a TM-liveness property L_{global} such that infinite history $H \in H_{TM}$ belongs to L_{global} iff at least one correct process in H makes progress in H, or H does not have correct processes.

Figure 5 depicts an infinite history which ensures global progress in a system two processes and one t-variable. Both

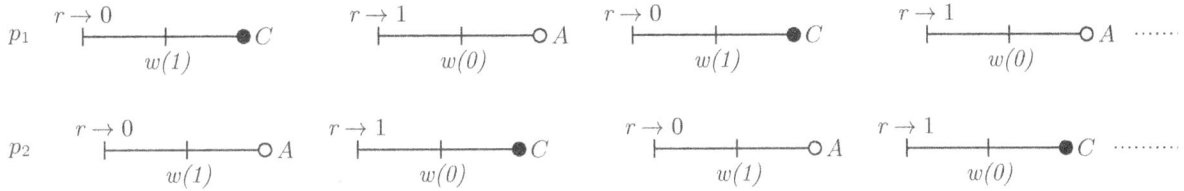

Figure 4: An infinite history with two processes and one t-variable. Each process executes an infinite number of transactions which read value 0 (read value 1) and write value 1 (write value 0).

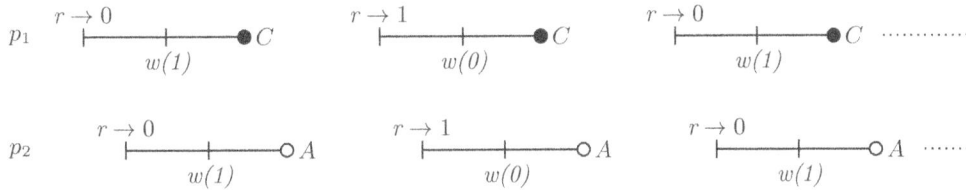

Figure 5: An infinite history with two processes and one t-variable. Processes execute an infinite number of transactions which read value 0 (read value 1) and write value 1 (write value 0).

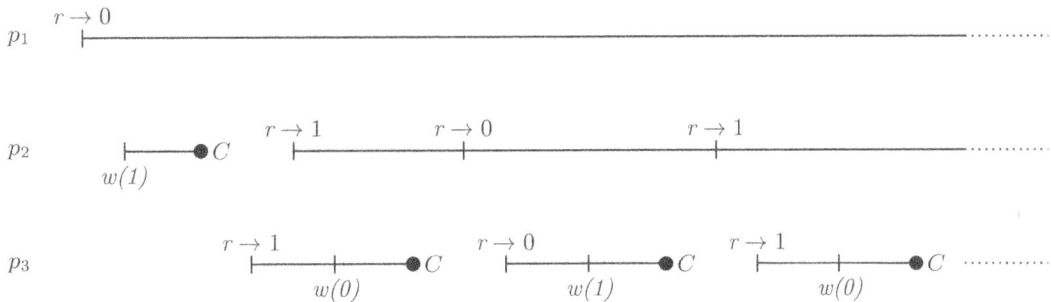

Figure 6: An infinite history with three processes and one t-variable. Process p_1 starts a transaction by invoking a read operations, but then it crashes. Process p_2 executes two transactions, but it becomes parasitic in the second transaction. Process p_3 executes an infinite number of transactions which read value 0 (read value 1) and write value 1 (write value 0).

of the processes are correct in the history. However, only process p_1 makes progress in the history.

3.2.3 Solo Progress

A TM implementation M ensures *solo progress* if M guarantees that every correct process which eventually runs alone makes progress. A correct process *runs alone* if starting from some point in time it is concurrent only to processes which are faulty. Note that in the TM context the definition of a process running alone is different from the definition in classical shared-memory systems: in the TM context a process p_k runs alone even when other process concurrently invoke operations, but p_k is the only one which invokes infinitely many commit requests.

Formally, a process p_k runs alone in infinite history H iff p_k is correct in H and no other process is correct in H. We define solo progress, as a TM-liveness property L_{solo} such that infinite history $H \in H_{TM}$ belongs to L_{solo} iff a process that runs alone in H makes progress in H, or H does not have a process that runs alone in H.

Figure 6 depicts an infinite history H_{solo} which ensures solo progress in a system with three processes and one t-variable. Process p_1 crashes, p_2 is parasitic, and p_3 runs alone and makes progress (is not pending).

Obstruction-free TM implementations [9, 12] ensure solo progress in parasitic-free systems. Lock-based TM implementations, such as TinySTM [6] and SwissTM [5], ensure solo progress in systems that are both parasitic-free and crash-free. lock-based TMs that use lazy acquire, however, such as TL2 [3], ensure solo progress in crash-free systems.

4. IMPOSSIBILITY OF LOCAL PROGRESS

Like in any distributed problem, each history of a TM implementation can be thought of as a game between the environment and the implementation. The *environment* consisting of processes and a scheduler decides on inputs (operation invocations) given to the implementation and the implementation decides on outputs (responses) returned to the environment. To prove that there is no TM implementation that ensures both opacity and local progress in a fault prone system we use the environment as an adversary that acts against the implementation. The environment wins if the resulting infinite history violates local progress. To prove the impossibility result, we show a wining strategy for the environment.

THEOREM 1. *For every fault-prone system, there does not exist a TM implementation that ensures both local progress and opacity in that system.*

PROOF. Assume otherwise, i.e. that there exists a fault-prone system **Sys** for which there exists a TM implementation M modeled by I/O automaton F that ensures local progress and opacity in **Sys**. To find a contradiction, we exhibit a winning strategy (Strategies 1 and 2 below) for the environment resulting in an infinite history of F which does not ensure local progress.

For simplicity we prove the result for TM implementations that support obstruction-free read and write operations. However, the result holds when the individual operations are not obstruction-free: obstruction freedom ensures that the implementation can produce an infinite history which corresponds to an execution of Strategy 1. If it cannot produce an infinite history, then the implementation

is not live and thus does not ensure local progress. Moreover, the result holds for more powerful shared objects that can implement objects supporting read and write operations.

By definition, fault-prone system **Sys** is a system in which at least one process can crash or be parasitic. We thus consider two different cases:

Sys is crash-prone.

Consider two processes p_1 and p_2 and the environment that interacts with M using the following strategy:

Strategy 1.

1. **Step 1.** Process p_1 invokes a read operation on t-variable x and receives as a response v'^1 or A^1. The strategy goes to Step 2.

2. **Step 2.** Process p_2 invokes a read operation on t-variable x and receives as a response v''^2 or A^2. If the response is A^2, then the strategy repeats Step 2. Otherwise p_2 invokes an operation on x, which writes to x (I) value $v' + 1$, if p_1 received v'^1 in Step1, or (II) value $v'' + 1$, if p_1 received A^1 in Step1, and receives as a response ok^2 or A^2. If the response is A^2, then the strategy repeats Step 2. Otherwise p_2 invokes $tryC^2$ operation and receives a response C^2 or A^2. If the response is A^2, the strategy repeats Step 2. Otherwise the strategy goes to Step 3.

3. **Step 3.** If p_1 received A^1 in Step 1, then the strategy goes to Step 1. Otherwise process p_1 invokes a write operation on t-variable x which writes value $v'' + 1$ to x, and then receives a response. If the response is A^1, then the strategy goes to Step 1. Otherwise p_1 invokes $tryC^1$ operation and receives a response. If the response is A^1, the strategy goes to Step 1. Otherwise the strategy stops.

We first show that there exists an infinite history of F corresponding to an execution of Strategy 1. To do so, we prove that Strategy 1 never terminates. Since individual operations of the implementation are obstruction-free, then the strategy terminates iff at Step 3 process p_1 is returned C^1 by F.

Assume some finite history H_f of F corresponding to an execution of Strategy 1 such that the last event in H_f is C^1. Since M ensures opacity, there exists a sequential finite history H_s which is equivalent to $comp(H_f)$, preserves the real-time order of $comp(H_f)$, and every transaction in H_s is legal. Since history H_f has no transactions which are neither committed nor aborted, then $comp(H_f) = H_f$. Hence H_s is equivalent to H_f and preserves the real-time order of H_f. Since H_s is a sequential history and preserves the real-time order of H_f, then H_s could only have one of the following forms, where H'_s is a prefix of H_s:

1. $H_s = H'_s \cdot x.read^1() \cdot v'^1 \cdot x.write^1(v'' + 1) \cdot ok^1 \cdot tryC^1 \cdot C^1 \cdot x.read^2() \cdot v''^2 \cdot x.write^2(v' + 1) \cdot ok^2 \cdot tryC^2 \cdot C^2$

2. $H_s = H'_s \cdot x.read^2() \cdot v''^2 \cdot x.write^2(v' + 1) \cdot ok^2 \cdot tryC^2 \cdot C^2 \cdot x.read^1() \cdot v'^1 \cdot x.write^1(v'' + 1) \cdot ok^1 \cdot tryC^1 \cdot C^1.$

In the first case, the last transaction executed by process p_2 is not legal in H_s, because p_2 reads value v'' from t-variable x the value of which is $v'' + 1$ and this violates the semantics of x. In the second case, the last transaction executed by process p_1 is not legal in H_s, because p_1 reads value v' from t-variable x the value of which is $v' + 1$, this leads to violation of the specification of x. Thus, H_f is not opaque. Since every history H_f of F that ends with commit event C^1 is not opaque and M ensures opacity, then H_f is not a history of F corresponding to the execution of the strategy. In other words, every history of F corresponding to the execution of Strategy 1 is infinite.

Consider some infinite history H of F corresponding to the execution of the above strategy. Since process p_1 never receives commit event C^1 from M, then p_1 is pending in H. Since *Sys* is crash-prone, then process p_1 can crash in history H. Therefore, we focus on the following two cases:

- **Process p_1 crashes in history H.** According to the strategy, process p_1 crashes in infinite history H iff process p_2 is pending and invokes infinitely many operations. Process p_2 invokes infinitely many operations iff the strategy executes infinitely many iterations of Step 2. At each iteration of Step 2 process p_2 either receives abort event A^2 or invokes operation $tryC^2$, thus p_2 is correct in H. Since M ensures local progress and p_2 is correct in H, then process p_2 is not pending: a contradiction. Thus, H does not ensure local progress.

- **Process p_1 does not crash in history H.** Since H is infinite and p_1 does not crash in H, then according to the strategy p_1 invokes infinitely many operations and receives infinitely many abort events. Thus, p_1 is a correct process in H. Since M ensures local progress, then p_1 makes progress in H, which means that eventually p_1 is returned commit event C^1 and history H is not infinite: a contradiction. Thus, H does not ensure local progress.

Sys is parasitic-prone. Consider two processes p_1 and p_2 and the environment that interacts with M using the following strategy:

Strategy 2.

1. **Step 1.** Process p_1 invokes a read operation on t-variable x and receives as a response v'^1 or A^1. Otherwise process p_2 invokes a read operation on x and receives as a response v''^2 or A^2. If the response is A^2, then the strategy repeats Step 1. Otherwise p_2 invokes a write operation which writes to x (I) value $v' + 1$, if p_1 received v'^1, or (II) value $v'' + 1$, if p_1 received A^1, and then p_2 receives a response. If the response is A^2, then the strategy repeats Step 1. Otherwise p_2 invokes $tryC^2$ operation and receives a response. If the response is A^2, then the strategy repeats Step 1. Otherwise the strategy goes to Step 2.

2. **Step 2.** If p_1 received A^1 in Step 1, then the strategy goes to Step 1. Process p_1 invokes a write operation on x which writes value $v'' + 1$ to x, and then p_1 receives a response. If the response is A^1, then the strategy goes to Step 1. Otherwise p_1 invokes $tryC^1$ operation and receives a response. If the response is A^1, then the strategy goes to Step 1. Otherwise the strategy stops.

First, we prove that Strategy 2 never terminates, i.e. that at Step 2 process p_1 is never returned C^1 by M in any history of M corresponding to an execution of the strategy. Assume some finite history H_f of F corresponding to an execution of Strategy 2 such that the last event in H_f is C^1. Since M

ensures opacity, there exists a sequential finite history H_s which is equivalent to $comp(H_f)$, preserves the real-time order of $comp(H_f)$, and every transaction in H_s is legal. Since history H_f has no transaction which are neither committed nor aborted, then $comp(H_f) = H_f$. Hence H_s is equivalent to H_f and preserves the real-time order of H_f. Since H_s is a sequential history and preserves the real-time order of H_f, then H_s could only have one of the following forms, where H'_s is a prefix of H_s:

1. $H_s = H'_s \cdot x.read^1() \cdot v'^1 \cdot x.write^1(v'' + 1) \cdot ok^1 \cdot tryC^1 \cdot C^1 \cdot x.read^2() \cdot v''^2 \cdot x.write^2(v' + 1) \cdot ok^2 \cdot tryC^2 \cdot C^2$

2. $H_s = H'_s \cdot x.read^2() \cdot v''^2 \cdot x.write^2(v' + 1) \cdot ok^2 \cdot tryC^2 \cdot C^2 \cdot x.read^1() \cdot v'^1 \cdot x.write^1(v'' + 1) \cdot ok^1 \cdot tryC^1 \cdot C^1$.

In the first case, the last transaction executed by process p_2 is not legal in H_s, because p_2 reads value v'' from t-variable x the value of which is $v'' + 1$ and this violates the semantics of x. In the second case, the last transaction executed by process p_1 is not legal in H_s, because p_1 reads value v' from t-variable x the value of which is $v' + 1$, this leads to violation of the specification of x. Thus, H_f is not opaque. Since every history H_f of F that ends with commit event C^1 is not opaque and M ensures opacity, then H_f is not a history of F corresponding to the execution of the strategy. In other words, every history of F corresponding to the execution of Strategy 2 is infinite.

Consider now some infinite history H of F corresponding to the execution of the above strategy. Since process p_1 never receives commit event C^1 from M, then p_1 is pending in H. Since *S* is parasitic-prone, then process p_1 can be parasitic in history H. Therefore, we focus on the following two cases:

- **Process p_1 is parasitic in history H.** According to the strategy, process p_1 is parasitic in infinite history H iff process p_2 is pending and invokes infinitely many operations at Step 1 without receiving a commit event C^2. Process p_2 invokes infinitely many operations iff the strategy executes infinitely many iterations of Step 1. At each iteration of Step 1 process p_2 either receives abort event A^2 or invokes operation $tryC^2$, thus p_2 is correct in H. Since M ensures local progress, then p_2 makes progress in H, i.e. process p_2 is not pending: a contradiction. Thus, H does not ensure local progress.

- **Process p_1 is not parasitic in history H.** According to Strategy 2 H is infinite iff process p_1 invokes infinitely many operations. Since p_1 invokes infinitely many operations and p_1 is pending in H, then p_1 receives infinitely many abort events in H. Thus, p_1 is correct in H. Since M ensures local progress, then p_1 makes progress in H, which means that eventually p_1 is returned commit event C^k and H is finite: a contradiction. Thus, H does not ensure local progress.

$\square$

5. GENERALIZING THE IMPOSSIBILITY

We generalize here the result of the previous section; namely, we determine a larger class of TM-liveness properties that are impossible to implement together with strict serializability, which is weaker than opacity, in a fault-prone system.

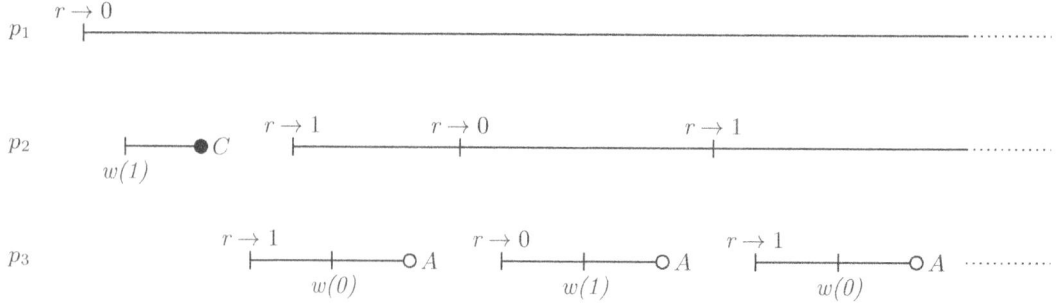

Figure 7: An infinite history with three processes and one t-variable. Process p_1 starts a transaction by invoking a read operations, but then it crashes. Process p_2 executes two transactions, but it becomes parasitic in the second transaction. Process p_3 executes an infinite number of aborting transactions which read value 0 (read value 1) and write value 1 (write value 0).

5.1 Classes of TM-liveness properties

Nonblocking TM-liveness properties.

Intuitively, we say that a TM-liveness property is *nonblocking* if it guarantees progress for every correct process that eventually runs alone. More precisely, a TM-liveness property L is nonblocking iff for every $H \in L$ if some process runs alone in H, then the process makes progress in H.

For example, Figure 4, Figure 5, and Figure 6 show infinite histories which ensure nonblocking TM-liveness properties while Figure 7 shows an infinite history which does not ensure any nonblocking TM-liveness property. TM-liveness properties that are not nonblocking are called *blocking*. Local progress, global progress, and solo progress are nonblocking. Note that solo progress is the weakest among nonblocking properties while local progress is the strongest among nonblocking properties.

Biprogressing TM-liveness properties.

Intuitively, we say that a TM-liveness property L is a *biprogressing* property if for every infinite history it guarantees that at least two correct processes make progress. More precisely, a TM-liveness property $L = \{L^1, \ldots, L^n\}$ is *biprogressing* iff for every $H \in L$ if at least two processes are correct in H, then at least two processes make progress in H.

For example, Figure 4 and Figure 6 show infinite histories which ensure a biprogressing property while Figure 5 shows an infinite history which does not ensure any biprogressing property. Local progress is a biprogressing property while global progress and solo progress are not biprogressing.

5.2 Generalized Result

We show that TM-liveness properties that are nonblocking and biprogressing are impossible to implement together with strict serializability in any fault-prone system. We start by stating the following lemma, which says, intuitively, that there exists a history in which a process executing infinitely many transactions can block the progress of all other processes if the TM ensures any nonblocking TM-liveness property. The proof of the lemma follows the same line of reasoning as in Theorem 1.

LEMMA 1. *For every TM implementation that ensures strict serializability and a nonblocking TM-liveness property in any fault-prone system, there exists an infinite history H of the implementation such that at least two processes are correct in H and at most one process makes progress in H.*

PROOF. Let M be a TM implementation ensuring strict serializability and a nonblocking TM-liveness property in a fault-prone system *Sys* and F be its I/O automaton representation. To exhibit a history in which at least two processes are correct and at most one process makes progress we consider a game between the environment and the implementation. The environment acts against the implementation and wins the game if the resulting history satisfies the requirements of the lemma.

By definition, fault-prone system *Sys* is a system in which at least one process can crash or be parasitic. We thus consider two different cases:

Sys is crash-prone. Consider two processes p_1 and p_2 that interact with M. The environment uses Strategy 1 to win the game. We can show that Strategy 1 never terminates using the same line of reasoning as in Theorem 1.

Consider some infinite history H corresponding to an execution of the strategy. Since *Sys* is crash-prone, process p_1 either crashes in history H or does not crash in H.

Assume that process p_1 crashes in history H. According to the strategy, process p_1 can crash in infinite history H only if process p_2 is pending and invokes infinitely many operations, i.e. only if p_2 is returned an infinite number of abort events at Step 2. Since p_2 is returned an infinite number of abort events, p_2 is correct in H. Because after some time only process p_2 executes operations in H (i.e. p_2 runs alone in H) and M ensures a TM-liveness property which is nonblocking, then p_2 makes progress in H, i.e. process p_2 is not pending: a contradiction. Thus, p_1 cannot crash in H.

According to the strategy, p_2 cannot crash in H since Step 2 is repeated infinitely often. Since Step 2 and Step 1 are repeated infinitely often (because p_1 does not crash in H), then p_2 receives infinitely many commit events C^2, i.e. p_2 is correct. Since process p_1 is returned infinitely many abort events A^1 at Step 1 or Step 3, process p_1 is correct. Thus, in history H both of the processes are correct and at most one process makes progress (since p_1 is never returned C^1).

Sys is parasitic-prone. Consider two processes p_1 and p_2 that interact with M. The environment uses Strategy 2 to

16

win the game. We can show that Strategy 2 never terminates using the same line of reasoning as in Theorem 1.

Consider some infinite history H corresponding to an execution of the strategy. Since Sys is parasitic-prone, process p_1 is either parasitic or not in H.

Assume that p_1 is parasitic in H. According to the strategy, p_1 can be parasitic only if p_2 is pending in H and returned A^2 infinitely often (i.e. correct). Since a correct process p_2 runs alone in H and M ensures a nonblocking TM-liveness property, then p_2 makes progress in H: a contradiction. Thus, p_1 cannot be parasitic in H.

According to the strategy, processes p_1 and p_2 do not crash because both of the processes invoke infinitely many read requests. Process p_2 cannot be parasitic in H since p_2 either invokes $tryC^2$ or is returned A^2 infinitely often at Step 1. Thus, in history H both of the processes are correct and at most one process makes progress (since p_1 is never returned C^1).

Sys is not crash-free or parasitic free. Since in Sys any number of processes can crash or be parasitic there are no restrictions on a strategy used by the environment. Thus, we can use Strategy 1 (or Strategy 2) to exhibit an infinite history that does not ensure local progress. □

By definition, a biprogressing TM-liveness property should ensure progress for at least two correct processes in every infinite history. While, by the above lemma, if the property is also nonblocking, then we can find an infinite history of any TM implementation in a fault prone system in which at least two processes are correct and at most one process makes progress: a contradiction. Thus, we have the following theorem.

THEOREM 2. *For every fault-prone system and every TM-liveness property L which is nonblocking and biprogressing there is no TM implementation that ensures strict serializability and L in that system.*

6. CONCLUDING REMARKS

We propose a framework to formally reason about liveness properties of TMs and introduce the very notion of a TM-liveness property. We prove in particular that in a system with faulty processes (crashes or parasitic), local progress cannot be ensured together with opacity, the safety property typically ensured by most TMs. We presented this impossibility result in its direct and then general form.

Local progress of transactional memory implementations is analogous to wait-freedom in concurrent computing which is the ultimate classical liveness property (for non-transactional objects) in concurrent computing. Just like wait-freedom makes sure processes do not wait for each other, local progress ensures that transactions of different processes do not wait for each other. The fact that wait-freedom was shown to be possible to implement led researchers to focus on how to achieve it efficiently. The fact that local progress is impossible to implement means that researchers have to find alternatives.

There are several ways to circumvent our impossibility result. One way is to weaken safety or TM-liveness property requirements, for example, to require only global progress. There are implementations that ensure opacity and global progress, e.g., OSTM [7]. A second way is to assume that all

transactions are static and predefined. That is a TM knows exactly which operations, on which shared variables, will be invoked in a transaction. In that case transactions can be viewed as simple operations and one can apply classical universal construction to ensure local progress [11]. However, assuming static transactions may be too limiting for certain applications. A third way is to assume a different system model instead of the multi-threaded programming model. For example, [21] shows a TM implementation that ensures local progress in an asynchronous multicore system model which assumes that a transaction can be executed by different processes and that some process crashes are detectable by the runtime system.

As we pointed out, this paper is a first step towards understanding the liveness of TMs and many problems are open. It would be interesting to determine precisely the strongest liveness property that can be ensured by a TM as well as study the impact on the impossibility of reducing the number of possible faults that a TM can face. Another possible direction for future work would be to generalize the impossibility result even further by considering classes of TM-liveness properties that guarantee progress for processes with higher priority.

7. REFERENCES

[1] M. Abadi, A. Birrell, T. Harris, and M. Isard. Semantics of transactional memory and automatic mutual exclusion. *ACM Trans. Program. Lang. Syst.*, 33(1):2:1–2:50, jan 2011.

[2] B. Alpern and F. B. Schneider. Defining liveness. *Inf. Process. Lett.*, 21(4):181–185, 1985.

[3] D. Dice, O. Shalev, and N. Shavit. Transactional locking ii. In *Proceedings of DISC'06*, pages 194–208. Springer-Verlag, 2006.

[4] S. Doherty, L. Groves, V. Luchangco, and M. Moir. Towards formally specifying and verifying transactional memory. *Electron. Notes Theor. Comput. Sci.*, 259:245–261, dec 2009.

[5] A. Dragojević, R. Guerraoui, and M. Kapalka. Stretching transactional memory. In *Proceedings of ACM PLDI'09*, pages 155–165. ACM, 2009.

[6] P. Felber, C. Fetzer, and T. Riegel. Dynamic performance tuning of word-based software transactional memory. In *Proceedings of ACM PPoPP'08*, pages 237–246. ACM, 2008.

[7] K. Fraser. *Practical Lock-Freedom*. PhD thesis, University of Cambridge, 2003.

[8] R. Gawlick, R. Segala, J. F. Søgaard-Andersen, and N. A. Lynch. Liveness in timed and untimed systems. *Information and Computation*, 141(2):119–171, mar 1998.

[9] R. Guerraoui and M. Kapalka. *Principles of Transactional Memory*. Morgan and Claypool, 2010.

[10] T. Harris, J. R. Larus, and R. Rajwar. *Transactional Memory, 2nd edition*. Morgan and Claypool, 2010.

[11] M. Herlihy. Wait-free synchronization. *ACM Trans. Program. Lang. Syst.*, 13(1):124–149, jan 1991.

[12] M. Herlihy, V. Luchangco, M. Moir, and W. N. Scherer, III. Software transactional memory for dynamic-sized data structures. In *Proceedings of ACM PODC'03*, pages 92–101. ACM, 2003.

[13] M. Herlihy and J. E. B. Moss. Transactional memory: Architectural support for lock-free data structures. *SIGARCH Comput. Archit. News*, 21(2):289–300, may 1993.

[14] M. Herlihy and N. Shavit. On the nature of progress. In *Proceedings of the 15th international conference on Principles of Distributed Systems*, pages 313–328. Springer-Verlag, 2011.

[15] D. Imbs, J. R. de Mendivil, and M. Raynal. Brief announcement: virtual world consistency: a new condition for STM systems. In *Proceedings of ACM PODC'09*, pages 280–281. ACM, 2009.

[16] S. Jagannathan, J. Vitek, A. Welc, and A. Hosking. A transactional object calculus. *Sci. Comput. Program.*, 57(2):164–186, aug 2005.

[17] V. Menon, S. Balensiefer, T. Shpeisman, A.-R. Adl-Tabatabai, R. L. Hudson, B. Saha, and A. Welc. Practical weak-atomicity semantics for java stm. In *Proceedings of ACM SPAA'08*, pages 314–325. ACM, 2008.

[18] K. F. Moore and D. Grossman. High-level small-step operational semantics for transactions. In *Proceedings of ACM POPL'08*, pages 51–62. ACM, 2008.

[19] C. H. Papadimitriou. The serializability of concurrent database updates. *J. ACM*, 26(4):631–653, oct 1979.

[20] N. Shavit and D. Touitou. Software transactional memory. In *Proceedings of ACM PODC'95*, pages 204–213, New York, NY, USA, 1995. ACM.

[21] J.-T. Wamhoff and C. Fetzer. The universal transactional memory construction. In *Proceedings of TRANSACT'11*, 2011.

On the Time and Space Complexity of Randomized Test-And-Set

(Extended Abstract)

George Giakkoupis[*][†]
INRIA Rennes-Bretagne Atlantique
Campus Universitaire de Beaulieu
35042 Rennes Cedex, France
george.giakkoupis@inria.fr

Philipp Woelfel[†]
Dept. of Computer Science
University of Calgary
Calgary, AB T2N 1N4, Canada
woelfel@ucalgary.ca

ABSTRACT

We study the time and space complexity of randomized Test-And-Set (TAS) implementations from atomic read/write registers in asynchronous shared memory models with n processes. We present an adaptive TAS algorithm with an expected (individual) step complexity of $O(\log^* k)$, for contention k, against the oblivious adversary, improving a previous (non-adaptive) upper bound of $O(\log \log n)$ (Alistarh and Aspnes, 2011). We also present a modified version of the adaptive RatRace TAS algorithm (Alistarh et al., 2010), which improves the space complexity from $O(n^3)$ to $O(n)$, while maintaining logarithmic expected step complexity against the adaptive adversary. We complement this upper bound with an $\Omega(\log n)$ lower bound on the space complexity of any TAS algorithm that has the nondeterministic solo-termination property (which is a weaker progress condition than wait-freedom). No non-trivial lower bounds on the space requirements of TAS were known prior to this work.

Categories and Subject Descriptors

D.1.3 [**Programming Techniques**]: Concurrent Programming—*Distributed programming*; F.2.2 [**Analysis of Algorithms and Problem Complexity**]: Nonnumerical Algorithms and Problems

Keywords

Test-And-Set, Leader Election, shared memory, randomization, strong/weak adversary, time/space complexity

[*]Supported by the Pacific Institute for the Mathematical Sciences (PIMS)

[†]Supported by a Discovery Grant from the Natural Sciences and Research Council of Canada (NSERC)

1. INTRODUCTION

In this paper we study the (randomized) time and space complexity of *Test-And-Set (TAS)* implementations from atomic registers in asynchronous shared memory systems with n processes. The TAS object is a fundamental synchronization primitive. It has been used in algorithms for classical problems such as mutual exclusion and renaming [3, 9].

A TAS object stores a bit, whose value is initially 0. It allows a single operation, TAS(), which sets the bit and returns its previous value. TAS objects are among the simplest natural primitives which have no deterministic wait-free linearizable implementations from atomic registers, even in systems with only two processes. In fact, in systems with two processes, a consensus protocol can be implemented deterministically from a TAS object and vice versa.

For randomized shared-memory algorithms, *adversary models* are used to describe how the scheduling is influenced by the random decisions made by processes. The strongest reasonable adversary is the *adaptive adversary*, which bases scheduling decisions on the entire past history of events including coin flips made by processes. An efficient randomized implementation of a TAS object from $O(n)$ registers dates back to 1992: Afek, Gafni, Tromp, and Vitányi [1] gave an algorithm with an expected (individual) step complexity of $O(\log n)$, which means that the maximum number of steps taken by any process has expectation $O(\log n)$. Recently, Alistarh, Attiya, Gilbert, Giurgiu, and Guerraoui [3] presented an *adaptive* algorithm called *RatRace*, in which the expected step complexity is logarithmic in k, the total number of processes accessing the TAS object. The space requirements of RatRace are higher, though, as $\Theta(n^3)$ registers are needed.

Even though non-trivial lower bounds are not known, no TAS algorithm with a sub-logarithmic expected step complexity (against the adaptive adversary) has been found, yet. The adaptive adversary, however, seems to be too strong in many cases to model realistic system behavior. Motivated by the fact that consensus algorithms benefit from weaker adversary models, Alistarh and Aspnes [2] devised a very simple but elegant TAS algorithm with an expected step complexity of $O(\log \log n)$ for the *oblivious adversary model*, where the adversary has to make all scheduling decisions at the beginning of the execution. In the following we denote this algorithm by *AA-algorithm*. Although not explicitly mentioned in the paper, the AA-algorithm even works for a slightly stronger adversary, the so-called *R/W-oblivious ad-*

versary. An R/W-oblivious adversary can take all past operations, including coin-flips, of processes into account when making scheduling decisions, but it cannot see whether a process will read or write in its next step, if that decision is made by the process at random. Since the AA-algorithm uses RatRace, its space complexity is also dominated by the $\Theta(n^3)$ registers from the RatRace implementation.

Motivated by their result, Alistarh and Aspnes asked whether any better TAS algorithm exists for the oblivious or even stronger adversary models. We answer this question in the affirmative: We present an adaptive algorithm that has expected step complexity of $O(\log^* k)$ against the oblivious adversary, where k is the maximum contention. In fact, our result holds for the slightly stronger *location-oblivious adversary*. This adversary makes scheduling decisions based on all past events (including coin-flips), but it does not know which registers processes will access in their next step, if those decisions are made at random. Further, our algorithm is the first one with sub-logarithmic expected step complexity that needs only $O(n)$ registers.

However, our algorithm is not efficient against the R/W-oblivious adversary. Instead, we present a modification of the AA-algorithm that needs only $O(n)$ registers and is adaptive, i.e., its expected step complexity is $O(\log \log k)$ if the contention is bounded by k.

The AA-algorithm has the nice property that its performance degrades gracefully when the adversary is not R/W-oblivious, and against the adaptive adversary it still achieves an expected step complexity of $O(\log n)$. This is a desirable property, as one does not need to rely on the system not to behave like an adaptive adversary. In its simple form, our adaptive algorithm with expected step complexity $O(\log^* k)$ does not exhibit this behavior—an adaptive adversary can find a schedule where processes need $\Omega(k)$ steps to complete their TAS operation (where k is the maximum contention). However, we present a general method to combine any TAS algorithm A with RatRace, so that the combined algorithm inherits the "best" complexity from both models. I.e., if A has expected step complexity $C(k)$ against an R/W-oblivious or location-oblivious adversary, then the combined algorithm has expected step complexity $O(C(k))$ against the same adversary, while at the same time it achieves $O(\log k)$ expected step complexity if the adversary is adaptive.

We complement our algorithms with lower bounds. First, we show that at least $\Omega(\log n)$ registers are needed for any randomized TAS implementation (from atomic registers) that satisfies the progress condition *nondeterministic solo-termination* [10], which is strictly weaker than wait-freedom. This is the first non-trivial lower bound on the space complexity of randomized TAS implementations.

Finally, we show for any randomized TAS implementation for two processes, that the oblivious adversary can schedule processes in such a way that for any $t > 0$ with probability at least $1/4^t$ one of the processes does not finish its TAS() method call within fewer than t steps. This result immediately implies the same lower bound on 2-process consensus, complementing a lower bound by Attiya and Censor-Hillel [6]. The authors showed for some constant c that with probability at least $1/c^t$ any randomized f-resilient n-process consensus algorithm does not terminate within $t(n-f)$ steps. However, their lower bound proof only works for $n \geq 3$ processes. Our lower bound thus fills in the missing 2-process case.

Preliminaries

We consider an asynchronous shared memory model where up to n processes communicate by reading and writing to shared atomic multi-reader multi-writer registers. Processes may fail by crashing at any time. Algorithms are randomized and can use local coin-flips to make random decisions. The scheduling and process crashes are controlled by an adversary, who at any point of an execution decides which process will take the next step. An adversary is *adaptive* if a scheduling decision is based on the entire past execution, including the results of local coin-flips. An adversary is *location-oblivious* [4] if a scheduling decision is based on any shared memory steps processes have taken in the past, and the type and argument of pending write operations (but not the register on which the operation will occur). An adversary is *R/W-oblivious* if a scheduling decision is based on any shared memory steps processes have taken in the past, and the locations of pending shared memory operations. While the R/W-oblivious adversary "knows" which register R a process is going to access in its next step, it cannot take into account whether the process reads or writes R.

We say that a randomized algorithm A has *expected step complexity* t, if for the random execution obtained by a scheduling of the "worst" adversary from a given set of adversaries, the maximum number of steps taken by any process has expectation t. The contention of an execution, usually denoted k, is the maximum number of processes taking at least one step in that execution. If the expected step complexity t is a function of k (instead of n) then we say that the algorithm is adaptive.

A Leader Election object, LeaderElect, provides a method elect(), which every process can call at most once and which returns a binary value. If some processes call elect() then at most one such call can return the value True, and if no process crashes then exactly one elect() call returns True. If a process' elect() call returns True or False, then we say the process *wins* resp. *loses* the Leader Election. It is not hard to see that any (randomized or deterministic) implementation of a LeaderElect object can be used together with one shared atomic register to implement a linearizable TAS object [11]. In this implementation, a TAS() method call consists of at most one call of elect() and in addition one read- and possibly one write-operation. Therefore, in this paper we will implement LeaderElect objects, and we don't have to worry about linearizability.

In order to implement Leader Election, we use several other objects as building blocks. One building block is a randomized 2-process LeaderElect object which uses only a constant number of registers, and where the elect() method has constant expected step complexity. Such an implementation was proposed by Tromp and Vitányi [13]. Another building block is a (deterministic) splitter object [12], Splitter, which provides the method split(). The method takes no parameters and returns a value in $\{L, R, S\}$. If a process' split() call returns S, we say that the process *wins* the splitter. If k processes call split(), at most $k-1$ receive the return value L, at most $k-1$ receive the value R, and at most one receives the value S. Thus, if only one process calls split(), the method returns S. A *randomized* splitter object [7], RSplitter, has the last two properties above, i.e., at most one split() call returns S, and if split() is called only once then it returns S. But now, if a split() call does not return S, it returns L or R independently with probability 1/2—thus it is possible that all calls return the same value in $\{L, R\}$. Deterministic and randomized splitters can both be implemented from $O(1)$ atomic registers such that any call to split() takes only a constant number of steps.

2. FAST LEADER ELECTION

In Section 2.1, we introduce the Group Election primitive, and present an implementation of a Leader Election object from Group Election objects. Then, in Sections 2.2 and 2.3, we describe randomized implementations of Group Election from registers, for the location-oblivious and the R/W-oblivious adversary models.

2.1 Leader Election from Group Election

A Group Election object, GroupElect, provides the method elect(), which takes no parameters and returns either True or False. We say that the processes whose elect() call return True get *elected*. If some processes call elect(), then at least one process must get elected. The performance of a GroupElect object is measured by the total number of processes that get elected. We define the *performance parameter* of a GroupElect object to be the smallest function $f : \{1, \ldots, n\} \to [1, n]$ such that the *expected* number of processes that get elected is at most $f(k)$, when $k \in \{1, \ldots, n\}$ processes call elect().

We now describe an implementation of a LeaderElect object from n GroupElect objects $GE_1, \ldots, GE_n$. The implementation uses also n Splitter objects $SP_1, \ldots, SP_n$, and n 2-process LeaderElect objects $LE_1, \ldots, LE_n$. Each process participates in a series of Group Elections on $GE_1, GE_2, \ldots$ If a process does not get elected in one of the Group Elections it participates in, then it immediately loses the implemented Leader Election. If a process gets elected in the Group Election on GE_i, then it tries to win splitter SP_i. If its SP_i.split() call returns L, then the process loses the Leader Election. If it returns R, then the process continues with the next Group Election, on GE_{i+1}. Finally, if the process wins SP_i, then it does not participate in other Group Elections, instead it participates in a series of 2-process Leader Elections, on objects $LE_i, LE_{i-1}, \ldots, LE_1$, until it either loses one of these elections or wins all of them. In the latter case, it wins the implemented LeaderElect object, and otherwise it loses it.

The proof of correctness of the implementation is straightforward, so we just present a sketch. First observe that at most $n - i + 1$ processes call GE_i.elect(), and thus no more than n LeaderElect objects are needed: If $j > 0$ processes call GE_i.elect(), then at most j processes call SP_i.split(), at most $j - 1$ of them receive the value R, and thus at most $j - 1$ call GE_{i+1}.elect(). Next we observe that each 2-process LeaderElect object LE_i is indeed accessed by at most two processes: the winner of SP_i and the winner of LE_{i+1} (if $i < n$). The winner of the implemented Leader-Elect object is the winner of LE_1, thus at most one process wins LeaderElect. Finally, if no process crashes then some process wins: To show this we use that at least one of the processes that call GE_i.elect() gets elected, and at least one of the processes that call SP_i.split() receives a return value other than L.

To bound the step complexity of the implementation we will use the following terminology. Let $M = (M_0, M_1, \ldots)$ be a Markov chain with state space $\{0, \ldots, n\}$ that is non-increasing. The *rate* of M is the function $r : \{1, \ldots, n\} \to$

Class GroupElect

/* Let $\ell = \lceil \log n \rceil$ */
 shared:
      int $R[1 \ldots (\ell + 1)] = [0 \ldots 0]$
      int $flag = 0$

Method elect()
1   **if** $flag$.Read() $= 1$ **return False**   2 $flag$.Write(1)   3   Choose an integer $x \in \{1, \ldots, \ell\}$ independently at random s.t. $\Pr(x = i) = 1/2^i$, for $1 \le i < \ell$, and $\Pr(x = \ell) = 1/2^{\ell-1}$ 4 $R[x]$.Write(1)   5   **if** $R[x + 1]$.Read() $= 0$ **return True**   6   **return False**

Figure 1: Group Election implementation for the location-oblivious adversary.

$[0, n]$ such that $r(j) = \mathbf{E}[M_{i+1} \mid M_i = j]$, for $1 \le j \le n$. For any non-decreasing $r : \{1, \ldots, n\} \to [0, n]$, we denote by $\Delta_r(n)$ the maximum (expected) hitting time $h_{n,0}$ over all non-increasing Markov chains on $\{0, \ldots, n\}$ with rate at most r.

Suppose now that the performance parameter of GroupElect objects GE_i is bounded by a non-decreasing function f. Let N_i be the number of processes that call GE_i.elect(), and let $i^* = \max\{i \colon N_i > 0\}$ be the total number of Group Elections executed. (Clearly, i^* is also a bound on the number of 2-process Leader Elections). If $N_i > 0$ then N_{i+1} is the number of processes that get elected on GE_i minus the number of processes whose call SP_i.split() returns a value in $\{L, S\}$. The latter number is at least one, so $\mathbf{E}[N_{i+1} \mid N_i = j] \le f(j) - 1$, for $j > 0$. It follows that $\mathbf{E}[i^*] \le \Delta_{f-1}(k)$, and thus, the expected step complexity of the implementation is $O(\Delta_{f-1}(k))$.

Thus, the following statement holds.

LEMMA 2.1. *There is a randomized implementation of a LeaderElect object with expected step complexity $O(\Delta_{f-1}(k))$, from n GroupElect objects with performance parameter at most f, and $O(n)$ registers.*

2.2 Location-Oblivious Adversary

We now present a randomized implementation of a Group Election object for the location-oblivious adversary.

LEMMA 2.2. *The construction in Figure 1 implements a GroupElect object with step complexity $O(1)$, space complexity $O(\log n)$, and performance parameter $f(k) \le 2 \log k + 6$ against the location-oblivious adversary.*

PROOF. Let A be a location-oblivious adversary and consider a random execution E obtained by A. Let i^* be the largest index such that some process p writes to $R[i^*]$ in line 4. Then p reads values 0 from $R[i^* + 1]$ in the next line, and thus returns True. Hence, at least one process gets elected.

In the rest of the proof we show the upper bound on f. Let $k' \le k$ be the number of processes that read register $flag$ in line 1 before some process writes $flag$ in the next line. The number of processes elected depends only on k'

21

(and not on k), and k' is fixed as soon as the first process writes $flag$ (that is, before any random choices are made). Thus, we can assume w.l.o.g. that k is fixed in advanced and $k' = k$.

Let $p_1, \ldots, p_k$ be the k processes participating in E in the order in which they perform their write operation in line 4, and let $\ell_1, \ldots, \ell_k$ be the respective locations in array R that they write to, i.e., process p_j writes to register $R[\ell_j]$. Since A is location-oblivious, it does not know ℓ_j before p_j writes to $R[\ell_j]$. Thus, by the principle of deferred decisions, we can assume that only after the adversary has decided the order $p_1, \ldots, p_j$ does p_j choose ℓ_j. Let X_j be the 0/1 random variable with $X_j = 1$ if and only if p_j reads a '0' in line 5, and thus gets elected. Let Y_j be the 0/1 random variable with $Y_j = 1$ if and only if none of the processes $p_1, \ldots, p_{j-1}$ writes to register $R[\ell_j + 1]$ (i.e., $\ell_{j'} \neq \ell_j + 1$, for all $j' < j$). Clearly, $X_j \leq Y_j$. Then,

$$f(k) = \mathbf{E}\left[\sum_{1 \leq j \leq k} X_j \right] = \sum_{1 \leq j \leq k} \mathbf{E}[X_j] \leq \sum_{1 \leq j \leq k} \mathbf{E}[Y_j].$$

We have

$$\mathbf{E}[Y_j] = \Pr\left(\bigwedge_{1 \leq j' < j} \ell_{j'} \neq \ell_j + 1 \right)$$
$$= \sum_{1 \leq i \leq \ell} \Pr(\ell_j = i \wedge \ell_1 \neq i+1 \wedge \cdots \wedge \ell_{j-1} \neq i+1)$$
$$= \sum_{1 \leq i \leq \ell} \Pr(\ell_j = i) \prod_{j'=1}^{j-1} \Pr(\ell_j \neq i+1)$$
$$= \sum_{1 \leq i < \ell} \frac{1}{2^i} \left(1 - \frac{1}{2^{i+1}} \right)^{j-1} + \frac{1}{2^{\ell-1}}.$$

Thus,

$$f(k) \leq \sum_{1 \leq j \leq k} \left(\sum_{1 \leq i < \ell} \frac{1}{2^i} \left(1 - \frac{1}{2^{i+1}} \right)^{j-1} + \frac{1}{2^{\ell-1}} \right)$$
$$= \sum_{1 \leq i < \ell} \frac{1}{2^i} \sum_{1 \leq j \leq k} \left(1 - \frac{1}{2^{i+1}} \right)^{j-1} + \sum_{1 \leq j \leq k} \frac{1}{2^{\ell-1}}$$
$$= \sum_{1 \leq i < \ell} \frac{1}{2^i} \cdot \frac{1 - \left(1 - \frac{1}{2^{i+1}} \right)^k}{1/2^{i+1}} + \frac{k}{2^{\ell-1}}$$
$$= 2 \sum_{1 \leq i < \ell} \left(1 - \left(1 - \frac{1}{2^{i+1}} \right)^k \right) + \frac{k}{2^{\ell-1}}.$$

We upper-bound the sum in the last line by observing that each term is at most 1, and also the i-th term is at most $1 - \left(1 - \frac{k}{2^{i+1}} \right) = \frac{k}{2^{i+1}}$, by the known inequality $(1 - \epsilon)^k \geq 1 - k\epsilon$. Thus,

$$f(k) \leq 2 \sum_{1 \leq i < \log k} 1 + 2 \sum_{\log k \leq i < \ell} \frac{k}{2^{i+1}} + \frac{k}{2^{\ell-1}}$$
$$\leq 2(\log k + 1) + 2 \frac{k}{2^{\log k}} + \frac{k}{2^{\ell-1}} \leq 2 \log k + 6,$$

since $\ell = \lceil \log n \rceil \leq \log k$. $\square$

For $f(k) \leq 2 \log k + 6$, we have $\Delta_{f-1}(k) = O(\log^* k)$. Thus, by Lemmas 2.1 and 2.2, we can combine the Leader

Election implementation in Section 2.1 with the Group Election implementation in Figure 1, to obtain a Leader Election implementation that has expected step complexity $O(\log^* k)$, from $O(n \log n)$ registers. We can improve the space complexity to $O(n)$ by observing that with probability $1 - 1/n$ only the first $O(\log n)$ GroupElect objects are used, and thus we can replace the remaining ones by dummy GroupElect objects in which all participating processes get elected.

THEOREM 2.3. *There is an adaptive randomized implementation of a* LeaderElect *object from $O(n)$ registers that has expected step complexity $O(\log^* k)$ against the location-oblivious adversary.*

2.3 R/W-Oblivious Adversary

Alistarh and Aspnes [2] presented a randomized implementation of Leader Election with $O(\log \log n)$ expected step complexity against an R/W-oblivious adversary. At the heart of their implementation is a simple Group Election algorithm, which they referred to as *sifting*. Each process participating in this Group Election either writes or reads a shared register. It writes with probability π (which is a parameter) and reads with probability $1 - \pi$, independently of other processes. A process gets elected if and only if it writes, or it reads before any process writes. The first part of the Leader Election implementation in [2] consists of $O(\log \log n)$ rounds of sifting, in which only processes that get elected in a round continue to the next one. The authors show that if the probability parameter π for each round is carefully chosen, then the number of processes that continue after round i, is at most $n^{(1-\epsilon)^i}$, with high probability.

We can use the above Group Election implementation together with the implementation in Section 2.1, to obtain a Leader Election implementation that has expected step complexity $O(\log \log n)$ and uses $O(n)$ registers. This implementation is not adaptive. However we can use a collection of non-adaptive LeaderElect objects implemented in that way, to obtain an adaptive implementation, as we sketch now. The main idea is to use $\lceil \log \log \log n \rceil$ such objects $LE_0, LE_1, \ldots$ of increasing size, such that LE_i is for $n_i = 2^{2^{2^i}}$ processes (except for $LE_{\lceil \log \log \log n \rceil}$, which is for n processes). In each LE_i, processes participate only in the first $\Theta(\log \log n_i) = \Theta(2^i)$ Group Elections, and after that, all processes that have not lost and have not won any Splitter object yet proceed to the next object LE_{i+1}. The winner of each LE_i participates in a chain of 2-process LeaderElect objects which determines the final winner. The expected step complexity of this implementation is $O(\log \log k)$. The intuition is that after $\Theta(\log \log k)$ steps a process ends up in an object LE_i of the 'right' size, such that $\log \log n_i = \Theta(\log \log k)$.

THEOREM 2.4. *There is a randomized implementation of an adaptive* LeaderElect *object from $O(n)$ registers that has expected step complexity $O(\log \log k)$ against the R/W-oblivious adversary.*

3. SPACE-EFFICIENT ADAPTIVE ADVERSARY LEADER ELECTION

We describe a Leader Election implementation for the adaptive adversary model, that has step complexity $O(\log k)$ both in expectation and w.h.p. (i.e., with probability

$1 - 1/k^{\Omega(1)}$), and uses $\Theta(n)$ registers. It is a modification of the `RatRace` algorithm proposed by Alistarh et al. [3], which has the same asymptotic step complexity, but uses $\Theta(n^3)$ registers.

3.1 Overview of RatRace

`RatRace` [3] uses two shared memory structures, a *primary tree* and a *backup grid*.

The primary tree is a complete binary tree of height $3 \log n$, where each node v is associated with an `RSplitter` (randomized splitter) object SP_v, and with a randomized 3-process `LeaderElect` object LE_v (implemented from two 2-process `LeaderElect` objects.)

Each process p starts at the root of the primary tree and moves downwards, towards the leaves, until it wins an `RSplitter` object, or it falls off the tree (which happens with low probability). Precisely, when at node v, process p calls SP_v.split(). If the call returns L or R then p moves to the left or the right child of v, respectively, provided that v is not a leaf; if v is a leaf, then the process proceeds to the backup grid as we will explain later. If p wins SP_v then it stops moving downwards, and begins to move upwards towards the root, along the same path. At each node v that p visits on its path to the root (including the node at which p won the `RSplitter` object), the process tries to win the `LeaderElect` object LE_v. If p loses LE_v then it immediately loses the implemented `LeaderElect` object; if it wins LE_v then it moves to the parent of v in the tree. The process that wins the `LeaderElect` object at the root competes against the winner of the backup grid.

The backup grid is an $n \times n$ square grid, where each node $v = (i, j) \in \{1, \ldots, n\}^2$ is associated with a (deterministic) `Splitter` object, and a randomized 3-process `LeaderElect` object. By convention, the left and right children of node (i, j) are nodes $(i + 1, j)$ and $(i, j + 1)$, respectively. Each process that falls off the primary tree, starts at node $(1, 1)$ of the grid, and proceeds in the same way as in the primary tree: first it tries to win a `Splitter` object, moving from a node to one of its children when it fails, and then tries to move back to node $(1, 1)$ along the same path, by winning all the `LeaderElect` objects along the way. The properties of deterministic splitters guarantee that the process wins a splitter before it falls off the grid.

Finally, the winners of the `LeaderElect` objects at node $(1, 1)$ of the backup grid and at the root of the primary tree participate in a randomized 2-process `LeaderElect` object, which determines the winner of `RatRace`.

3.2 Improving the Space Complexity

`RatRace` needs $\Theta(2^{3 \log n}) = \Theta(n^3)$ registers for the primary tree of height $3 \log n$, and $\Theta(n^2)$ registers for the backup $n \times n$ grid. To reduce the space complexity we will use the following structure, which we call *elimination path*. It is similar to the backup grid, but uses fewer registers.

An *elimination path of length* ℓ is an ℓ-node path where each node $i \in \{1, \ldots, \ell\}$ is associated with a deterministic `Splitter` object SP_i, and a randomized 2-process `Leader-Elect` object LE_i. A process p starts at node $i = 1$, and tries to win SP_i. If p's SP_i.split() call returns L then p loses and takes no more steps; if it returns R then p moves to the right, i.e., it moves to node $i + 1$ if $i < \ell$, or it falls off the path if $i = \ell$. Finally, if p wins SP_i then it stops moving to the right, and starts moving to the left towards node 1. From node $i > 1$, it moves to $i - 1$ only if it wins LE_i, otherwise, it loses and stops taking steps. The winner of the elimination path is the process that wins LE_1. The next claim follows from properties of deterministic splitters.

CLAIM 3.1. *If at most ℓ processes enter an elimination path of length ℓ, then no process falls off the right end of the path.*

We replace the backup grid of `RatRace` by an elimination path of length n, which has the same asymptotic step complexity as the backup grid, but uses only $\Theta(n)$ registers.

Further, we replace `RatRace`'s primary tree of height $3 \log n$, by a structure consisting of a smaller primary tree, of height $\log n$, and $n/\log n$ elimination paths EP_i, for $1 \leq i \leq n/\log n$, where each path EP_i has length $4 \log n$. The total number of registers used is $\Theta(2^{\log n} + (4 \log n) \cdot n/\log n) = \Theta(n)$. The smaller primary tree is used in the same way as before, but now any node that falls off enters one of the elimination paths EP_i instead of the backup grid. Precisely, a process that falls off the j-th leaf from the left (of the n leaves in total) moves to the beginning of path $EP_{\lceil j/\log n \rceil}$. The winner of each path EP_i moves back to the primary tree, at leaf i, and from that leaf it tries to reach the root as in the original `RatRace` algorithm. Any process that falls off a path EP_i proceeds to the elimination path of length n that replaced the backup grid. Finally, similarly to `RatRace`, the winner of that path and the winner of the primary tree compete against each other to determine the winner of the implemented `LeaderElect` object.

The step complexity of the implementation for the case of $\log k \leq (\log n)/3$ follows from the analysis of `RatRace`. For the analysis of the complementary case, $\log k > (\log n)/3$, we need the simple claim below, which guarantees w.h.p. that the number of processes that access any given path EP_i is no greater than the length of the path. Thus, by Claim 3.1, we have w.h.p. that no process enters the backup elimination path of length n, which yields an $O(\log n) = O(\log k)$ bound on the step complexity.

CLAIM 3.2. *For any fixed set of $\log n$ leaves, with probability $1 - 1/n^2$ at most $4 \log n$ processes reach those leaves.*

PROOF. The number of processes that reach the $\log n$ leaves is dominated by the number of balls that fall in a fixed set of $\log n$ bins in the classic bins-and-balls model with n balls and n bins, in which every ball is placed in a bin chosen independently and uniformly at random: We can assume that each process p comes with a uniformly random bit-string of length $\log n$. If p tries to win an `RSplitter` object of a node at distance $i - 1$ from the root but fails, then the i-th bit in the bit-string determines whether p's split() call returns L or R. Hence, the random bit-string uniquely determines the leaf that p will reach, if it does not win any `RSplitter` object along the way.

The claim then follows by applying standard Chernoff bounds. □

4. ADVERSARY INDEPENDENCE

The Leader Election implementation for the adaptive adversary presented in Section 3 has the same step complexity, $\Theta(\log k)$, even if the adversary is an oblivious one. On the other hand, the implementations in Section 2, which assume a weaker adversary, may need up to $\Theta(k)$ steps in expectation when scheduled by an adaptive adversary. In this section we describe how we can combine these implementations to obtain one that has the step complexity of RatRace against an adaptive adversary, and the step complexity of the algorithms in Section 2 against a weak adversary.

THEOREM 4.1. *For any Leader Election implementation A for the location-oblivious (resp. R/W-oblivious) adversary, there is a Leader Election implementation that has the same asymptotic step complexity as A against the location-oblivious (resp. R/W-oblivious) adversary, and it has step complexity $O(\log k)$ (both in expectation and w.p. $1 - 1/k$) against the adaptive adversary. The space complexity of this implementation is $\Theta(n)$ plus the space complexity of A.*

Combining Theorem 4.1 with Theorems 2.3 and 2.4, yields the following.

COROLLARY 4.2. *There is a Leader Election implementation that has an expected step complexity of $O(\log^* k)$ (resp. $O(\log \log k)$) against the location-oblivious (resp. R/W-oblivious) adversary, and a step complexity of $O(\log k)$ (both in expectation and w.p. $1 - 1/k$) against the adaptive adversary. The space complexity is $\Theta(n)$.*

We now present an implementation that achieves the step and space complexity prescribed in Theorem 4.1. The implementation runs both RatRace and A in parallel, in a round robin fashion. Precisely, each process executes a step of RatRace in every odd step, and a step of A in every even step. A natural way to combine the two interleaved executions would be that each process takes steps until it either wins or loses in one of the two executions; if it loses it also loses in the combined implementation, and if it wins it competes against the winner of the other execution. This approach, however, could yield a combined execution where *no* process wins. For instance, suppose that A is also RatRace. Then it is possible that a process p loses against some process q on one of the LeaderElect objects in the one execution, and at the same time q loses against p on a LeaderElect object in the other execution; thus both processes lose in the combined execution.

To solve this problem we impose the rule that if a process loses in A when it has already won a (deterministic or randomized) splitter object in RatRace, then the process continues to execute RatRace. Precisely, we use the following rules to combine the two executions with the help of an auxiliary LeaderElect object LE_{top}.

1. If a process wins in either RatRace or A then it stops taking steps in the other execution, and it tries to win LE_{top}; if it wins LE_{top} then it wins the implemented LeaderElect object, otherwise it loses.

2. If a process loses in RatRace then it stops taking steps in A, and it loses the implemented LeaderElect object.

3. If a process loses in A *and it has not yet won any of the* Splitter *or* RSplitter *objects in* RatRace, then it stops taking steps in RatRace, and it loses the implemented LeaderElect object.

We sketch the proof of the claim that it is not possible to have a failure-free execution of this combined implementation in which *no* process wins. First we consider the case when no process wins a splitter object in RatRace. Then no

processes wins or loses in RatRace, and thus RatRace has no effect on A's execution. Since A is executed without any interference, exactly one process wins A. This process will also win LE_{top}, since no process wins RatRace, and thus no other process participates in LE_{top}.

Now suppose that at least one process p wins a splitter object in RatRace but no process wins the implemented leader election. In particular, p does not win the implemented leader election, so it loses a LeaderElect object in RatRace. If this happens then some other process q wins that LeaderElect object, which implies that q won some splitter object before. Similarly to p, q can lose only if it loses a LeaderElect object in RatRace. Further, if the LeaderElect object that p lost is in a node at distance ℓ from the root, then q can only lose a LeaderElect object at distance at most $\ell - 1$ from the root. By iterating this argument, we obtain that some process w wins RatRace. By Rule 1, process w stops A and tries to win LE_{top}. Thus, there will be some process that wins LE_{top} (either w or the winner of A) and thus some process wins the implemented leader election.

Next we sketch the proof of the step complexity of the implementation. First we consider an adaptive adversary. We can view the processes that stop in RatRace because they win or lose in A, as crashed by a (randomized) adaptive adversary. (This adversary runs A in order to decide which processes to stop and when.) Since each process that wins or loses in RatRace stops taking steps in A, it follows that the step complexity of the implementation is bounded asymptotically by the step complexity of RatRace (plus the step complexity of LE_{top}).

We now consider the location-oblivious (resp. R/W-oblivious) adversary. We treat the processes that stop in A because of winning or losing RatRace, as crashed by a (randomized) location-oblivious adversary (resp. R/W oblivious adversary).[1] Unlike in the previous case, now we cannot immediately claim that the step complexity of the implementation is bounded by the step complexity of A, because a process that loses in A may continue to take steps in RatRace. Let t be the maximum number of steps of A that any process takes. Then, t is bounded by the step complexity of A. Moreover, by Rule 3, any process that loses in A but continues to take steps in RatRace must have won a splitter object at some node at distance at most t from the root. Then, from the analysis of RatRace it follows that the extra steps that those processes take are $O(t)$ in expectation and also w.p. $1 - 1/2^{\Omega(t)}$. It follows that the step complexity of the implementation is asymptotically bounded by that of A.

5. A SPACE LOWER BOUND

We prove a space lower bound of $\Omega(\log n)$ registers for any Leader Election algorithm, and thus for the implementation of TAS objects.

An algorithm satisfies *nondeterministic solo-termination*, if for any configuration and any process p, there is an execu-

---

[1]For this argument it is important that A works against a location- or R/W-oblivious adversary, rather than just against the adaptive adversary. We cannot view stopped processes as crashed by a randomized oblivious adversary, because the processes stopped and the time at which they stop may depend on random choices of A: these choices affect which processes lose in A and thus which processes stop in RatRace, and this in turn affects which processes lose in RatRace and thus stop in A.

tion in which no process other than p takes any steps, and p finishes its method call within a finite number of steps [10]. Hence, a process is guaranteed to finish its method call with positive probability, whenever there is no interference from other processes. For deterministic algorithms, nondeterministic solo-termination is the same as obstruction-freedom and weaker than wait-freedom.

THEOREM 5.1. *Any nondeterministic solo-terminating Leader Election algorithm requires $\Omega(\log n)$ registers.*

5.1 Proof Overview

We consider a Leader Election algorithm that satisfies nondeterministic solo-termination. Since we prove a space (and not a time) lower bound, we can fix the random decisions made by processes.

The idea is to use a covering argument (as introduced by Burns and Lynch [8]). Suppose n processes run a Leader Election algorithm, where n is a power of two. We let each process take steps until it is poised to write to a register (we say it *covers* that register). Now we schedule processes in rounds. Our goal is to ensure that after the k-th round every register is covered by at most $n - k$ processes. In particular, after $n - 4$ rounds every register will be covered by at most 4 processes. When we schedule processes, some processes may see others, and then they can decide to lose their Leader Election. We try to maintain as many "undecided" processes as possible. We will manage to have $\Omega(\log n)$ undecided processes at the end of the $n - 4$ rounds, and all of them are covering registers. Since every register is covered by at most 4 processes, the space lower bound follows.

In order to make this work, we have to be careful how to schedule processes in each round. We maintain the invariant that after the k-th round no process has ever written to a register that is covered by fewer than $n - k$ processes. Now consider some set $R = \{r_1, \dots, r_\ell\}$ of registers, such that each register r_j, $1 \leq j \leq \ell$, is covered by exactly $n - k$ processes. For each register r_j we choose one process q_j that covers r_j, and let it write to r_j. This way, all registers that stored any useful information will get overwritten by processes $q_1, \dots, q_\ell$. Since registers in $\overline{R}$ have not yet been written at all in the entire past execution, processes $q_1, \dots, q_\ell$ will not gain any additional information (except about themselves) when only *they* take additional steps. It follows that if we let these processes run solo, one after the other, then one of them, say q_1, must win. Since all registers in R are covered by other processes, q_1 must write to a register not in R before it can win. We stop q_1 when it is poised to write for the first time to a register that is not in R. This way, we now have increased the number of processes covering registers outside of R by one and at the same time every register in R is only covered by $n - k - 1$ processes. We may have reduced the number of "undecided" processes, because $q_2, \dots, q_\ell$ may have lost their Leader Election already.

Note that if not all of them have lost their Leader Election, then the assumption that no process knows about any other process that has not yet lost might not strictly be true anymore. We deal with this problem by grouping all processes that know about each other together, and we count always only one representative from each group when we determine the number of processes that cover a register. Whenever the representative overwrites a register at the beginning of the round, and then proceeds to take steps, we let its entire group also take steps. This way, we can maintain the invariant that one of the processes in such a group writes outside of R.

5.2 Proof of the Space Lower Bound

This section is devoted to the proof of Theorem 5.1.

We let $\mathcal{P}$ denote a set of n processes in the system, and $\mathcal{R}$ the set of registers of the system. We assume w.l.o.g. that n is a power of two. A *configuration* C is a tuple $(s_1, \dots, s_n, v_1, v_2, \dots, v_{|\mathcal{R}|})$, denoting that the i-th process is in state s_i, and the j-th register has value v_j. Configurations will be denoted by capital letters, and the initial configuration is denoted C_{init}. Two configurations $C = (s_1, \dots, s_n, v_1, \dots, v_m)$ and $C' = (s'_1, \dots, s'_n, v'_1, \dots, v'_m)$ are *indistinguishable* to the i-th process in $\mathcal{P}$, if $s_i = s'_i$ and $v_j = v'_j$ for all $j \in \{1, \dots, m\}$. Configurations C and C' are indistinguishable to a set Q of processes, if they are indistinguishable to every process $q \in Q$.

A *schedule* σ is a (possibly infinite) sequence of processes. An *execution* $E(C, \sigma)$ is a sequence of steps beginning in configuration C and moving through successive configurations one at a time. At each step, the next process p_i indicated in the schedule σ, takes the next step in its program. Since our computation model is nondeterministic, we fix the nondeterministic decisions made by processes in our lower bound proof. We use an arbitrary (but fixed) one that guarantees that each process p_i terminates within a bounded number of steps if it runs solo. If σ is a finite schedule, the final configuration of the execution $E(C, \sigma)$ is denoted $\sigma(C)$ or $C(E(C, \sigma))$. If σ and π are finite schedules then $\sigma\pi$ denotes the concatenation of σ and π; similarly, we can concatenate execution by letting $E(C, \sigma) \cdot E(\sigma(C), \pi) = E(C, \sigma\pi)$. Let Q be a set of processes, and σ a schedule. If only processes in Q appear in σ, then σ is a *Q-only* schedule and $E(C, \sigma)$ is a *Q-only* execution.

We say that in configuration C a process p *covers* a register r, if the state of p as determined by C is such that in its next step p will write register r. We assume w.l.o.g. that whenever a process writes a value to a register, that value is a pair (x, ID), where ID is the process' identifier. Initially, the second component of every pair stored in a register is $\bot$. We say process q is *visible* on register r in some configuration, if r's value is (x, q) for some x. (Thus, initially no process is visible on any register.) We say process p *sees* process q in some step of an execution, if in that step p reads a register on which q is visible. Every execution E defines a relation "$\leftrightarrow_E$" over the set $\mathcal{P}$ of processes, where $p \leftrightarrow_E q$, if $p = q$ or during E either p sees q or q sees p. Then $\leftrightarrow_E$ is reflexive and symmetric. Let $\equiv_E$ be the transitive closure of $\leftrightarrow_E$, thus $\equiv_E$ is an equivalence relation over $\mathcal{P}$.

CLAIM 5.2. *Let E be some execution starting in the initial configuration C_{init}, and $Q \subseteq \mathcal{P}$ the set of processes that finish their Leader Election algorithm during E. If $Q \neq \emptyset$ is closed w.r.t. $\equiv_E$, then exactly one process in Q wins during E.*

PROOF. Remove from E all steps by processes in $\overline{Q}$ and denote D the resulting execution. Then configurations $C(E)$ and $C(D)$ are indistinguishable to all processes in Q. It follows that during D all processes in Q finish their Leader Election with the same result as in E. Since only processes from Q take steps during D, exactly one of them wins. $\square$

CLAIM 5.3. *Let $R = \{r_1, \dots, r_\ell\} \subseteq \mathcal{R}$, $R' = \{r_{\ell+1}, \dots, r_v\} \subseteq \mathcal{R} - R$, and let E be an execution starting* in C_{init}, such that in $C(E)$ no process is visible on any register in $\overline{R}$. Further, let $Q \subseteq \mathcal{P}$ be a set that is closed w.r.t. $\equiv_E$. Suppose in $C = C(E)$, every register $r_j \in R \cup R'$, $1 \leq j \leq v$, is covered by some process $p_j \in \overline{Q}$, and every register $r_i \in R$, $1 \leq i \leq \ell$, by some process $q_i \in Q$. Then there exists a Q-only schedule β such that during $E(C, \beta)$ at least one process writes to a register in $\overline{R \cup R'}$, and no process in Q sees a process in $\overline{Q}$.

PROOF. Let σ be the Q-only schedule where each process q_j, $1 \leq j \leq \ell$, takes exactly one step, and σ' the Q-only schedule such that during the execution $E(C, \sigma\sigma')$ every process in Q finishes its algorithm. Nondeterministic solo-termination guarantees that such a schedule σ' exists. Let $\beta = \sigma\sigma'$ and $E' = E(C, \beta)$. For the purpose of a contradiction, suppose that during E' no process writes to a register in $\overline{R \cup R'}$.

During E', all register contents of registers in R are overwritten by processes in Q. Thus, throughout E', no process in $\overline{Q}$ is ever visible on any register, and thus no process in Q sees a process in $\overline{Q}$. Since in addition processes in $\overline{Q}$ take no steps during E', set Q is closed w.r.t. $\equiv_{E'}$. By assumption, it is also closed w.r.t. $\equiv_E$, and thus w.r.t. $\equiv_{E \cdot E'}$.

By the assumption that no process writes to a register in $\overline{R \cup R'}$ during execution E', in configuration $C' = C(E')$, no process is visible on a register in $\overline{R \cup R'}$. Consider a $\overline{Q}$-only execution E'' that starts in configuration C', and where first all processes $p_1, \ldots, p_v$ take exactly one step, and then we let all processes that haven't finished their algorithm, yet, run to completion. Since the algorithm satisfies nondeterministic solo-termination, such an execution E'' exists. Since in E'' processes $p_1, \ldots, p_v$ first overwrite all registers in $R \cup R'$, no process in $\overline{Q}$ sees any process in Q during E''. Trivially, no process in Q sees any process in $\overline{Q}$. Thus, Q is closed w.r.t. $\equiv_{E''}$. Since Q is closed w.r.t. $\equiv_{E \cdot E'}$, it is also closed w.r.t. $\equiv_{E \cdot E' \cdot E''}$. This implies that $\overline{Q}$ is also closed w.r.t. $\equiv_{E \cdot E' \cdot E''}$. Since all processes in Q and in $\overline{Q}$ finish their algorithm during $E \cdot E' \cdot E''$, we conclude from Claim 5.2 that some process in Q and some process in $\overline{Q}$ wins—a contradiction. $\square$

Recall that we assumed that n is a power of two.

LEMMA 5.4. For every $k \in \{0, \ldots, n-1\}$, there exists

- a schedule α_k, defining execution $E_k = E(C_{init}, \alpha_k)$ and configuration $C_k = C(E_k)$;

- a partition $(Q_1, \ldots, Q_{m_k})$ of $\mathcal{P}$; and

- m_k processes $q_j \in Q_j$, $1 \leq j \leq m_k$;

such that in configuration C_k

(a) every process q_j, $1 \leq j \leq m_k$, covers some register;

(b) no register is covered by more than $n - k$ processes in $\{q_1, \ldots, q_{m_k}\}$;

(c) if a process is visible on a register r, then r is covered by $n - k$ processes in $\{q_1, \ldots, q_{m_k}\}$;

(d) each set Q_j, $1 \leq j \leq m_k$, is closed w.r.t. $\equiv_{E_k}$; and

(e) $m_0 = n$ and $m_k \geq m_{k-1} - \lfloor m_{k-1}/(n-k+1) \rfloor + 1$ for $k > 0$.

PROOF. We prove the lemma by induction on k.

First consider the base case, $k = 0$. If we let a process p run solo when no process is visible on any register, p must win the Leader Election (by Claim 5.2). This requires that p writes to at least one register, or else some other process will win the Leader Election in a solo-run that follows p's. Hence, we can let each process run solo as long as it doesn't write to a register and stop the process when it is poised to write to a register for the first time. Thus, eventually all processes are poised to write, while at the same time no process is visible on any register. Let α_0 be the schedule that results in such an execution $E_0 = E(C_{init}, \alpha_0)$, where no process writes and where in $C_0 = C(E_0)$ every process is poised to write to a register. Further, let $m_0 = n$ and q_i the i-th process in $\mathcal{P}$ and $Q_j = \{q_j\}$ for $1 \leq j \leq n$. In C_0 all processes cover some register, no register is covered by more than $n - 0$ processes, no process is visible on any register, the sets $Q_1, \ldots, Q_n$ are equivalence classes of $\equiv_{E_0}$, and $m_0 = n$. Hence, the induction hypothesis is true for $k = 0$.

Now assume the hypothesis is true for some integer $k \in \{0, \ldots, n-2\}$. Let $\alpha_k, m_k, Q_1, \ldots, Q_{m_k}$ and $q_1, \ldots, q_{m_k}$ be given such that (a)-(e) are satisfied. Let $R = \{r_1, \ldots, r_\ell\}$ be the set of registers that are covered by exactly $n - k$ processes in $\{q_1, \ldots, q_{m_k}\}$ in configuration C_k. If $R = \emptyset$, we let $\alpha_{k+1} = \alpha_k$, and the claim for $k' = k + 1$ follows immediately from the induction hypothesis for k.

Now suppose that $R \neq \emptyset$. Choose some indices $i_1, \ldots, i_\ell \in \{1, \ldots, m_k\}$ such that process q_{i_j}, $1 \leq j \leq \ell$, covers register r_j and let $Q = Q_{i_1} \cup \cdots \cup Q_{i_\ell}$. Assume w.l.o.g. that $(i_1, \ldots, i_\ell) = (m_k - \ell + 1, \ldots, m_k)$. The set Q is closed w.r.t. $\equiv_{E_k}$ because all sets Q_j, $m_k - \ell + 1 \leq j \leq m_k$, are closed w.r.t. $\equiv_{E_k}$.

Now let R' be the set of registers covered by exactly $n - k - 1$ processes in $\{q_1, \ldots, q_{m_k}\}$. By definition, no process in Q covers a register in R', and since $n - k - 1 \geq 1$, every register in R' is covered by at least one process in $\overline{Q}$. Moreover, since $n - k \geq 2$, every register in R is covered by exactly two processes in $\{q_1, \ldots, q_{m_k}\}$ out of which exactly one is in Q. Hence, every register in R is covered by one process in Q and by at least one process in $\overline{Q}$. Finally, by induction hypothesis (c), in C_k no process is visible on any register in $\overline{R}$.

Thus, we can apply Claim 5.3. It follows that there exists a Q-only schedule β_k such during $E(C_k, \beta_k)$ at least one process writes to a register in $\overline{R \cup R'}$, and no process in Q sees a process in $\overline{Q}$. We let β'_k be the longest prefix of β_k such that in $E(C_k, \beta'_k)$ no process writes to a register in $\overline{R \cup R'}$. Thus, at the end of $E(C_k, \beta'_k)$ some process $q \in Q$ is poised to write to a register in $\overline{R \cup R'}$. We let $\alpha_{k+1} = \alpha_k \beta_k$, $E_{k+1} = E_k \cdot E(C_k, \beta'_k) = E(C_{init}, \alpha_{k+1})$, and $C_{k+1} = C(E_{k+1})$. Moreover, let $m_{k+1} = m_k - \ell + 1$, $Q_{m_{k+1}} = Q$, $q'_{m_{k+1}} = q$, and for $1 \leq j < m_{k+1}$ let $Q'_j = Q_j$ and $q'_j = q_j$.

Then processes in $Q'_1 \cup \cdots \cup Q'_{m_{k+1}-1}$ take no steps during $E(C_k, \beta'_k)$, so in C_{k+1} every process q'_j, $1 \leq j < m_{k+1}$, covers some register. By construction, at the end of execution $E(C_k, \beta'_k)$ process $q'_{m_{k+1}}$ is poised to write, so it also covers some register. This proves (a).

A process in $\{q'_1, \ldots, q'_{m_{k+1}-1}\}$ takes no step during $E(C_k, \beta'_k)$, so in configuration C_{k+1} it covers exactly the same register as in configuration C_k. Now consider some register r. If $r \in R$, then in configuration C_k register r is covered by exactly $n - k$ processes in $\{q_1, \ldots, q_{m_k}\}$. Exactly one of these $n - k$ processes is in $\{q_{m_k - \ell + 1}, \ldots, q_{m_k}\}$, and thus not in $\{q'_1, \ldots, q'_{m_{k+1}-1}\}$. Thus, exactly $n - k - 1$ processes in $\{q'_1, \ldots, q'_{m_{k+1}-1}\}$ cover register r in configuration C_{k+1}. If $r \in R'$, then in configuration C_k register r is covered by exactly $n - k - 1$ processes in $\{q_1, \ldots, q_{m_k}\}$, none of whom takes a step in $E(C_k, \beta'_k)$. Hence, in C_{k+1} every register $r \in R \cup R'$ is covered by exactly $n - k - 1$ processes in $\{q'_1, \ldots, q'_{m_{k+1}-1}\}$. Moreover, in C_{k+1} process $q'_{m_{k+1}}$ covers a register from $\overline{R \cup R'}$, so $r \in R \cup R'$ is covered by exactly $n - k - 1$ processes in $\{q'_1, \ldots, q'_{m_{k+1}}\}$. Now suppose $r \in \overline{R \cup R'}$, so in C_k register r is covered by at most $n - k - 2$ processes in $\{q_1, \ldots, q_{m_k}\}$. By construction of β'_k, during $E(C_k, \beta'_k)$ exactly one processes, namely $q'_{m_{k+1}}$, becomes poised to write to a register in $\overline{R \cup R'}$. Hence, in C_{k+1} register $r \in \overline{R \cup R'}$ is covered by at most $n - k - 1$ processes in $\{q_1, \ldots, q_{m_k}\}$, and thus also by at most $n - k - 1$ processes in $\{q'_1, \ldots, q'_{m_{k+1}}\}$. This proves (b).

Now consider a register r on which some process is visible in configuration C_{k+1}. In configuration C_k, no process is visible on a register in $\overline{R}$, and in execution $E(C_k, \beta'_k)$ no process writes to a register in $\overline{R \cup R'}$. Hence, $r \in R \cup R'$. As argued above in the proof of part (b), in C_{k+1}, every register in $R \cup R'$ is covered by exactly $n - k - 1$ processes in $\{q'_1, \ldots, q'_{m_{k+1}-1}\}$. This proves (c).

By construction and Claim 5.3, no process in Q sees any process in $\overline{Q}$ during execution $E(C_k, \beta'_k)$. Since that execution is Q-only, no process in $\overline{Q}$ sees any process during that execution. It follows that each of the sets $Q'_1 = Q_1, \ldots, Q'_{m_{k+1}-1} = Q_{m_{k+1}-1}$ (which is are subsets of $\overline{Q}$) is closed w.r.t. $\equiv_{E(C_k, \beta'_k)}$. By the induction hypothesis each of those sets is closed w.r.t. $\equiv_{E_k}$, so they are also closed w.r.t. $\equiv_{E_{k+1}}$. Similarly, $Q = Q'_{m_{k+1}}$ is closed w.r.t. $\equiv_{E(C_k, \beta'_k)}$, and since Q is the union of sets which are closed w.r.t. $\equiv_{E_k}$, Q is closed w.r.t. $\equiv_{E_{k+1}}$. This proves (d).

By construction, in configuration C_k every register in R is covered by at least $n - k$ processes from $\{q_1, \ldots, q_{m_k}\}$, so $|R| \leq \lfloor m_k/(n-k) \rfloor$. Moreover,

$$m_{k+1} = m_k - |R| + 1 \geq m_k - \left\lfloor \frac{m_k}{n-k} \right\rfloor + 1.$$

This proves (e). $\square$

Define

$$f(0) = n \quad \text{and}$$
$$f(k+1) = f(k) - \left\lfloor \frac{f(k)}{n-k} \right\rfloor + 1 \quad \text{for } k \geq 0.$$

Further, let for $k \geq 1$

$$\delta(k+1) = f(k) - f(k+1) = \left\lfloor \frac{f(k)}{n-k} \right\rfloor - 1.$$

CLAIM 5.5. *For an integer $s \geq 0$ and $k \in I(s) :=$* $\left\{ n - \dfrac{n}{2^s}, \ldots, n - \dfrac{n}{2^{s+1}} - 1 \right\}$,

(a) $f(k) = n \cdot \dfrac{s+1}{2^s} - s \cdot \left(k - n + \dfrac{n}{2^s} \right)$, *and*

(b) $\delta(k+1) = s$.

PROOF. We first argue that statement (a) implies statement (b). Let $d = k - n + n/2^s$ and suppose (a) is true.

Then

$$\delta(k+1) + 1 = \left\lfloor \frac{f(k)}{n-k} \right\rfloor = \left\lfloor \frac{n\frac{s+1}{2^s} - s \cdot (k - n + \frac{n}{2^s})}{n-k} \right\rfloor$$
$$= \left\lfloor \frac{n\frac{s+1}{2^s} - s \cdot d}{n - (d + n - n/2^s)} \right\rfloor = \left\lfloor \frac{n\frac{s+1}{2^s} - s \cdot d}{n/2^s - d} \right\rfloor$$
$$= \left\lfloor \frac{s+1 - s \cdot d \cdot 2^s/n}{1 - d \cdot 2^s/n} \right\rfloor = \left\lfloor \frac{s(1 - d \cdot 2^s/n) + 1}{1 - d \cdot 2^s/n} \right\rfloor$$
$$= \left\lfloor s + \frac{1}{1 - d \cdot 2^s/n} \right\rfloor = s + \lfloor \zeta \rfloor, \quad (1)$$

where

$$\zeta = \frac{1}{1 - d \cdot 2^s/n} = \frac{n}{n - d \cdot 2^s}.$$

Since $n - n/2^s \leq k \leq n - n/2^{s+1} - 1$, we have

$$0 \leq d \leq n/2^{s+1} - 1 - n + n/2^s = n/2^{s+1} - 1, \quad (2)$$

and thus

$$1 \leq \zeta \leq \frac{n}{n - (n/2^{s+1} - 1) \cdot 2^s} = \frac{n}{n/2 + 2^s} < 2.$$

Thus, $\lfloor \zeta \rfloor = 1$, so from (1) we obtain $\delta(k+1) + 1 = s + 1$, which proves (b).

We now prove statement (a) by induction on k. If $k = 0$, then $k \in I(0)$ and (a) is true. Thus, suppose that (a) and thus also (b) hold for some value of k. Then

$$f(k+1) = f(k) - \delta(k+1) = n\frac{s+1}{2^s} - s\left(k - n + \frac{n}{2^s}\right) - s$$
$$= n\frac{s+1}{2^s} - s\left(k + 1 - n + \frac{n}{2^s}\right). \quad (3)$$

If $k < n - n/2^{s+1} - 1$, then $k + 1 \in I(s)$ and the claim is proven. Now suppose $k = n - n/2^{s+1} - 1$, i.e., $k + 1 \in I(s+1)$. Then from (3) we get

$$f(k+1) = n \cdot \frac{s+1}{2^s} - s\left(n - \frac{n}{2^{s+1}} - n + \frac{n}{2^s}\right)$$
$$= n \cdot \frac{2s+2}{2^{s+1}} - s \cdot \frac{n}{2^{s+1}} = n \cdot \frac{s+2}{2^{s+1}}.$$

This proves (a). $\square$

PROOF OF THEOREM 5.1. We can assume w.l.o.g. that n is a power of two. Also, since we want to prove a space lower bound, we can fix arbitrary random choices by the algorithm, and thus the algorithm becomes deterministic and obstruction free.

Let $k = n - 4$. By Lemma 5.4, there exists an execution E_k that starts in configuration C_{init} and ends in configuration C_k, such that in C_k at least m_k processes cover registers, but no register is covered by more than $n - k = 4$ processes. This implies that there must be at least $\lceil m_k/4 \rceil$ registers.

Note that from part (e) of Lemma 5.4 and the definition of f, we immediately get $m_k \geq f(k)$. Since $k = n - 4$, we have $k = n - n/2^{\log n - 2}$. By the definition of $I(s)$ from Claim 5.5, $k \in I(\log n - 2)$. Thus, by that same claim,

$$m_{n-4} \geq f(n-4)$$
$$= n \cdot \frac{\log n - 1}{n/4} - (\log n - 2)\left(n - 4 - n + \frac{n}{n/4}\right)$$
$$= 4(\log n - 1).$$

Hence, at least $\log n - 1$ registers are covered in configuration C_{n-4}. $\square$

6. A 2-PROCESS TIME LOWER BOUND

THEOREM 6.1. *For any randomized TAS implementation that can be accessed by two processes, and any integer $t > 0$, there is a schedule (determined by an oblivious adversary) such that with probability at least $1/4^t$ some process does not finish its* TAS() *method within fewer than t steps.*

PROOF. The proof is by Yao's Min-Max Lemma [14]. Let $\mathcal{A}_t$ denote the set of all *deterministic* TAS algorithms for two processes in which no process takes more than t steps. Under the (standard) assumption that the domain of values for each register is countable, we have that the set $\mathcal{A}_t$ is also countable.[2] Let $\mathcal{S}_t$ denote the set of all possible schedules (i.e., sequences of process IDs) for two processes, in which each process appears exactly t times. Then,

$$|\mathcal{S}_t| = \binom{2t}{t} \leq 2^{2t}. \tag{4}$$

For any $A \in \mathcal{A}_t$ and $S \in \mathcal{S}_t$, we denote by $c(A, S)$ the indicator function that is 1 if and only if at least one of the two process in algorithm A takes t steps under schedule S. Let R be any randomized TAS implementation for two processes, and let R_t be the same algorithm except that processes are stopped after they execute their t-th step (if they have not finished before that step). We can view R_t as a probability distribution over the countable set $\mathcal{A}_t$. The probability that at least one process takes t or more steps in R under schedule S is then equal to $\mathbf{E}[c(R_t, S)]$, where $c(R_t, S)$ is now a 0/1 random variable depending on the random choices of the randomized algorithm R_t. Therefore, the probability that at least one process takes t or more steps in R for *some* schedule is

$$\max_{S \in \mathcal{S}_t} \mathbf{E}[c(R_t, S)].$$

By Yao's Min-Max Lemma, for any probability distribution D_t over the (finite) set of schedules $\mathcal{S}_t$,

$$\max_{S \in \mathcal{S}_t} \mathbf{E}[c(R_t, S)] \geq \min_{A \in \mathcal{A}_t} \mathbf{E}[c(A, D_t)].$$

We observe that for any $A \in \mathcal{A}_t$ we have $c(A, S) = 1$ for at least one $S \in \mathcal{S}_t$ because of the impossibility of deterministic wait-free implementations for TAS. Thus, by choosing D_t to be the *uniform* distribution over $\mathcal{S}_t$, we obtain that for any $A \in \mathcal{A}_t$, $\mathbf{E}[c(A, D_t)] \geq 1/|\mathcal{S}_t|$. Therefore, by (4) $\max_{S \in \mathcal{S}_t} \mathbf{E}[c(R_t, S)] \geq 1/|\mathcal{S}_t| \geq 1/2^{2t}$. And since this is true for an arbitrary randomized TAS implementation R for two processes the theorem follows. □

Conclusion

In this paper we devised several improved randomized TAS algorithms. Most importantly, we have shown that the randomized expected step complexity of TAS is $O(\log^* k)$ (where k is the contention) against the oblivious and some slightly stronger adversary models. The progress in improving randomized TAS algorithms is mirrored by recent progress on randomized consensus algorithms. Just this year, Aspnes [5] devised a randomized binary consensus

algorithm that has $O(\log \log n)$ expected step complexity against an oblivious adversary. This algorithm is based on the sifting technique from [2]. It would be interesting to know whether techniques similar to those presented here can be used to find further improvements on the randomized complexity of consensus.

Several other important problems remain open. For example even for the oblivious adversary it is still not known, whether a TAS implementation with constant expected step complexity exist. No non-trivial lower bounds on the expected step complexity of Leader Election are known, not even in the adaptive adversary model. Finally, there is still an exponential gap between the lower bound of $\Omega(\log n)$ and the upper bound of $O(n)$ for the number of registers that are required for randomized or obstruction-free TAS algorithms.

7. REFERENCES

[1] Y. Afek, E. Gafni, J. Tromp, and P. M. B. Vitányi. Wait-free test-and-set. In *Proc. of 6th WDAG*, pages 85–94, 1992.

[2] D. Alistarh and J. Aspnes. Sub-logarithmic test-and-set against a weak adversary. In *Proc. of 25th DISC*, pages 97–109, 2011.

[3] D. Alistarh, H. Attiya, S. Gilbert, A. Giurgiu, and R. Guerraoui. Fast randomized test-and-set and renaming. In *Proc. of 24th DISC*, pages 94–108, 2010.

[4] J. Aspnes. A modular approach to shared-memory consensus, with applications to the probabilistic-write model. In *Proc. of 20th PODC*, pages 460–467, 2010.

[5] J. Aspnes. Faster randomized consensus with an oblivious adversary. In *Proc. of 31st PODC*, 2012. To appear.

[6] H. Attiya and K. Censor-Hillel. Lower bounds for randomized consensus under a weak adversary. *SIAM J. on Comp.*, 39(8):3885–3904, 2010.

[7] H. Attiya, F. Kuhn, C. G. Plaxton, M. Wattenhofer, and R. Wattenhofer. Efficient adaptive collect using randomization. *Distr. Comp.*, 18(3):179–188, 2006.

[8] J. E. Burns and N. A. Lynch. Bounds on shared memory for mutual exclusion. *Inf. Comput.*, 107(2):171–184, 1993.

[9] W. Eberly, L. Higham, and J. Warpechowska-Gruca. Long-lived, fast, waitfree renaming with optimal name space and high throughput. In *Proc. of 12th DISC*, pages 149–160, 1998.

[10] F. E. Fich, M. Herlihy, and N. Shavit. On the space complexity of randomized synchronization. *J. of the ACM*, 45(5):843–862, 1998.

[11] W. Golab, D. Hendler, and P. Woelfel. An $o(1)$ RMRs leader election algorithm. *SIAM J. on Comp.*, 39:2726–2760, 2010.

[12] M. Moir and J. H. Anderson. Fast, long-lived renaming. In *Proc. of 8th WDAG*, pages 141–155, 1994.

[13] J. Tromp and P. M. B. Vitányi. Randomized two-process wait-free test-and-set. *Distr. Comp.*, 15(3):127–135, 2002.

[14] A. C.-C. Yao. Probabilistic computations: Towards a unified measure of complexity. In *Proc. of 17th FOCS*, pages 222–227, 1977.

---

[2]This assumption allows us to apply Yao's Min-Max Lemma in a straight-forward way. However, with a slightly more technical argument, a variant of the Min-Max Lemma can be used even if $\mathcal{A}_t$ is not countable.

Random Walks which Prefer Unvisited Edges. Exploring High Girth Even Degree Expanders in Linear Time

Petra Berenbrink
School of Computing Science
Simon Fraser University
Burnaby, V5A 1S6, Canada
petra@cs.sfu.ca

Colin Cooper
Dept. of Informatics
King's College London
London WC2R 2LS, UK
colin.cooper@kcl.ac.uk

Tom Friedetzky
School of Engineering and
Computing Sciences
Durham University
Durham, DH1 3LE, UK
tom.friedetzky@durham.ac.uk

ABSTRACT

In this paper, we consider a modified random walk which uses unvisited edges whenever possible, and makes a simple random walk otherwise. We call such a walk an *edge-process* (or E-process). We assume there is a rule $\mathcal{A}$, which tells the walk which unvisited edge to use whenever there are several unvisited edges. In the simplest case, $\mathcal{A}$ is a uniform random choice over unvisited edges incident with the current walk position. However we do not exclude arbitrary choices of rule $\mathcal{A}$. For example, the rule could be determined on-line by an adversary, or could vary from vertex to vertex.

For the class of connected, even degree graphs G of constant maximum degree, we characterize the vertex cover time of the E-process in terms of the edge expansion rate of G, as measured by eigenvalue gap $1 - \lambda_{\max}$ of the transition matrix of a simple random walk on G. Denote by ℓ-good, the property that every vertex is in at least one vertex induced cycle of length ℓ.

In particular, for even degree expander graphs, of bounded maximum degree, we have the following result. Let G be an n vertex ℓ-good expander graph. Any E-process on G has cover time

$$C_G(E - \text{process}) = O\left(n + \frac{n \log n}{\ell}\right).$$

This result is independent of the rule $\mathcal{A}$ used to select the order of the unvisited edges, which can be chosen on-line by an adversary.

With high probability random r-regular graphs, $r \geq 4$ even, are expanders for which $\ell = \Omega(\log n)$. Thus, for almost all such graphs, the vertex cover time of the E-process is $\Theta(n)$. This improves the vertex cover time of such graphs by a factor of $\log n$, compared to the $\Omega(n \log n)$ cover time of *any* weighted random walk.

Categories and Subject Descriptors

C.2.1 [**Network Architecture and Design**]: Distributed networks, Network topology; F.2 [**Analysis of Algorithms and Problem Complexity**]:

General Terms

Graph algorithms, network search, random walk, network design

1. INTRODUCTION

In a simple random walk on a graph, at each step a particle moves from its current vertex position to a neighbouring vertex chosen uniformly at random. Formally, a *simple* random walk $\mathcal{W}_v = (\mathcal{W}_v(t), t = 0, 1, \ldots)$ is defined as follows: $\mathcal{W}_v(0) = v$ and given $x = \mathcal{W}_v(t)$, $y = \mathcal{W}_v(t+1)$ is a randomly chosen neighbour of x.

In this paper, we consider a modified walk which uses unvisited edges whenever possible, and makes a simple random walk otherwise. We call such a walk an *edge-process* (or E-process). At each step the edge-process makes a transition to a neighbour of the currently occupied vertex as follows:

> If there are *unvisited edges* incident with the current vertex pick one and make a transition along this edge.

> If there are no unvisited edges incident with the current vertex, move to a random neighbour using a simple random walk.

If we wish, can we assume there is a rule $\mathcal{A}$, which tells the walk which unvisited edge to use whenever there is a choice. In the simplest case, this is a uniform random choice over unvisited edges incident with the current walk position. However we do not exclude arbitrary choices of rule $\mathcal{A}$. For example, the rule could be deterministic or decided on-line by an adversary, or could vary from vertex to vertex.

The E-process seems particularly adapted to searching in a physical environment, where edges can easily be marked as visited. Imagine walking in a labyrinth, and marking the entries and exits of the edges taken with a piece of chalk. Whenever all exits are marked, walk randomly.

For any process which explores a graph G by walking from vertex to vertex, the *vertex cover time*, C_G, is defined as follows. For $v \in V$, let C_v be the expected time taken for a walk W on G starting at v, to visit every vertex of G. The vertex cover time is defined as $C_G = \max_{v \in V} C_v$. It was shown by Feige [9], that for any connected n-vertex graph G, the cover time of a simple random walk satisfies $C_G \geq (1 - o(1))n \log n$. In fact, any weighted reversible random walk has a lower bound on the cover time of $C_G = \Omega(n \log n)$. Thus no reversible random walk can have an $o(n \log n)$ cover time A proof of the $\Omega(n \log n)$ lower bound on the cover time of weighted random walks, due to T. Radzik [15], is given in Section 3.1.

One random process similar to the E-process, is the *Random Walk with Choice*, (RWC(d)), of Avin and Krishnamachari [2]. The process RWC(d) selects d neighbours uniformly at random at each step, and moves to the least visited vertex among them. The paper [2] makes an experimental study of the process RWC(d) on geometric random graphs, and the toroidal grid, and finds reductions in cover time, and improved concentration of experimental results. Recently a special case of the E-process has been studied by Orenshtein and Shinkar [14] in the context of edge cover times. In [14], the next unvisited edge is chosen u.a.r. For a further discussion on edge cover time see below.

In the context of deterministic walks, the E-process has similarities with the rotor-router, or Propp machine model; see [7] for an introduction to this topic. The analysis of both processes depends on the underlying Eulerian properties of the graph. In the case of the rotor-router process, the graph is turned into an Eulerian digraph by replacing each edge with a pair of oppositely directed edges. The vertex cover time of the rotor-router model is $O(mD)$, where m is the number of edges of G, and D is the diameter, see [17].

The class of graphs we consider are connected, even degree graphs G of constant maximum degree $\Delta(G)$. That class can be further partitioned on the additional property that every vertex is in at least one vertex induced cycle of length ℓ, a property we denote by ℓ-good. We characterize the cover time of the E-process in terms of the edge expansion rate of G, as measured by eigenvalue gap $1 - \lambda_{\max}$ of the transition matrix of a simple random walk on G. A general statement of our result is the following theorem.

THEOREM 1. *Let G be a connected n vertex even degree graph, with finite maximum degree, and the additional property that every vertex is in at least one vertex induced cycle of length at least ℓ. Then,* **any** *E-process on G has cover time*

$$C_G(E - process) = O\left(n + \frac{n \log n}{\ell(1 - \lambda_{\max})}\right).$$

We briefly list a series of remarks and corollaries which arise from Theorem 1

i) The upper bound on the cover time given in Theorem 1 is independent of the rule $\mathcal{A}$ used to select unvisited edges, even if this choice is decided on-line by an adversary.

ii) For expander graphs, which have positive constant eigenvalue gap, Theorem 1 becomes

$$C_G(E - process) = O\left(n + \frac{n \log n}{\ell}\right). \quad (1)$$

In particular, for even degree expanders where each vertex is in at least one chord free cycle of length $\ell = \Omega(\log n)$, the E-process covers the graph in $\Theta(n)$ steps.

As any walk-based process must take n steps to visit every vertex, the order of our result is best possible.

iii) Examples of graphs where every vertex is in at least one chord free cycle of length $\ell = \Omega(\log n)$ include random r-regular graphs, for which we have the following corollary.

COROLLARY 2. *Let $r \geq 4$ even. Let $\mathcal{G}_r$ denote the class of random r-regular graphs. Let G be sampled uniformly at random from $\mathcal{G}_r$, then with high probability $C_G(E - process) = O(n)$.*

See Section 3 for the proof of this. Other examples which satisfy Corollary 2 are (i) connected random graphs with fixed degree sequence d, such that all degrees are even and finite, (ii) algebraically constructed even degree expanders of logarithmic girth, see [12].

iv) The lower bound on the cover time of G by *any* weighted reversible random walk is $\Omega(n \log n)$. (See Section 3.1 for a proof of this result). For expanders, the comparable cover time is given by (1). Up to $\ell = \log n$, this gives a speed up of $\Omega(\log n / \ell)$ compared to *any* random walk.

v) In Section 3.3 we give some experimental results on the performance of the E-process. Simulations suggest that for even degree random regular graphs, the cover time of the E-process is bounded (asymptotically) by the number of edges m in the graph (see Figure 1).

Could we expect an $O(n)$ cover time for the E-process on odd degree expanders? Experimentally, we find that this is not the case (see Figure 1).

vi) A practical consequence of Theorem 1, is that, in order to build 'easy to search' networks, we should ensure all vertices have even degree and few short cycles. Examples of such constructions, based on even degree random r-regular graphs, are the SWAN P2P network of [4] based on switches, and the flip based P2P network of [13]. Properties of these networks such as connectivity, diameter and mixing-rate were studied in (e.g.) [5],[6], [8].

We also make some observations on edge cover time of the E-process (see i,ii below), and on the relationship between the E-process and Propp machines (items iii-v).

i) In general upper bounds on the edge cover time of the E-process depend on the number of short cycles. The girth g of a graph G is the minimum length cycle in G. It can be shown that the E-process will cover all edges of a connected even degree graph in $O(|E| + n \log n / (1 - \lambda_2)g)$. This bound can be improved if the number of short cycles can be estimated. As an example, for even degree random regular graphs, the (**whp**) upper bound on the edge cover time is $O(n\omega)$, where $\omega \to \infty$ arbitrarily slowly.

ii) The result of [14] gives a bound for edge cover time of r-regular graphs of $O(|E| + n \log n / (1 - \lambda_{\max}))$. This is at best $O(n \log n)$ for sparse graphs, but is tight for expanders provided the number of edges $|E| = \Omega(n \log n)$. This result differs qualitatively from Theorem 1 which treats vertex cover time of constant degree expanders ($|E| = cn$, c constant).

iii) Suppose it is the case that the edges of a graph G can be distinguished as unvisited in each direction by the E-process; i.e. a first visit (x, y) and a first visit (y, x) are regarded as distinct. This converts G into an Eulerian digraph, so that the even degree restriction is no longer necessary, and Theorem 1 now holds for all connected graphs of bounded degree.

iv) Suppose the edges of the graph can be marked as unvisited in each direction. Then the ordering of the (directed) unvisited edges at each vertex made by the rule $\mathcal{A}$ is a rotor order for a rotor-router (Propp machine). The E-process acts as a hybrid of a Propp machine and a random walk, the algorithm being: *Use the rotor once at each vertex and then walk randomly. Any rotor order will do.* The power of the adversary is to set the rotor order.

v) In some rotor-router models an adversary can force a cover time of $\Omega(m \log m)$ on connected m edge graphs (see [3] for details). This phenomena partially arises because the adversary can make the walk retrace visited edges, even when unvisited edges are present at a vertex. In the E-process the adversary is less strong, and only has power to select the next unvisited edge used by the process. All transitions over visited edges are chosen randomly. Thus when $m = \Theta(n)$, and $\ell = \Omega(\log n)$, the E-process has cover time $\Theta(n)$, as compared to $\Theta(n \log n)$ cover time in the aforementioned adversarial rotor-router model.

1.1 Random walk properties

Let $G = (V, E)$ denote a connected graph, $|V| = n$, $|E| = m$, and let $d(v)$ be the degree of a vertex v. A *simple random walk* $\mathcal{W}_u$, $u \in V$, on graph G is a Markov chain modeled by a particle moving from vertex to vertex according to the following rule. The probability of transition from vertex v to vertex w is equal to $1/d(v)$, if w is a neighbour of v, and 0 otherwise. The walk $\mathcal{W}_u$ starts from vertex u at $t = 0$. Denote by $\mathcal{W}(t)$ the vertex reached at step t; $\mathcal{W}(0) = u$.

Let P be the transition matrix of a simple random walk on a graph G. Thus $P_{i,j} = 1/d(i)$ if and only if there is an edge between i and j in G. Let $P_u^{(t)}(v) = \mathbf{Pr}(\mathcal{W}_u(t) = v)$ be the t-step transition probability. We assume the random walk $\mathcal{W}_u$ on G is ergodic with stationary distribution π, where $\pi_v = d(v)/(2m)$. If this is not the case, e.g. G is bipartite, then the walk can be made ergodic, by making it lazy. A random walk is *lazy*, if it moves from v to one of its neighbours w with probability $1/(2d(v))$, and stays where it is (at vertex v) with probability $1/2$.

Let $1, \lambda_2, ..., \lambda_n$, be the eigenvalues of P, and let $\lambda_{\max} = \min(|\lambda_2|, |\lambda_n|)$. We henceforth assume that $\lambda_2 = \lambda_{\max}$ which can be achieved by making the chain lazy. This has no significant effect on our analysis.

The convergence to stationarity of a simple random walk is bounded by

$$|P_u^{(t)}(x) - \pi_x| \leq (\pi_x/\pi_u)^{1/2} \lambda_{\max}^t. \tag{2}$$

Visits to a Single Vertex.

For a random walk starting from vertex u, let H_v be the number of steps taken to reach vertex v, and let $\mathbf{E}_u(H_v)$ be the expected value of H_v; the expected hitting time of

v starting from u. If the distribution of the random walk at some step is $\rho = (\rho(u), u \in V)$, we can similarly define the hitting time from starting distribution ρ as $\mathbf{E}_\rho(H_v) = \sum_{u \in V} \rho(u) E_u(H_v)$.

For a random walk starting at a vertex chosen from the stationary distribution π, let $\mathbf{E}_\pi(H_v)$ denote the expected hitting time of vertex v from stationarity. The quantity $\mathbf{E}_\pi(H_v)$ can be expressed in the following way, (see e.g. [1], Chapter 2)

$$\mathbf{E}_\pi(H_v) = Z_{vv}/\pi_v, \tag{3}$$

where

$$Z_{vv} = \sum_{t=0}^{\infty} (P_v^{(t)}(v) - \pi_v). \tag{4}$$

Using (2), we can bound the value of $\mathbf{E}_\pi(H_v)$ as follows.

LEMMA 3.

$$\mathbf{E}_\pi(H_v) \leq \frac{1}{(1 - \lambda_{\max})\pi_v}. \tag{5}$$

Proof   Using (2) with $x = u = v$, then

$$|P_v^t(v) - \pi_v| \leq (\lambda_{\max})^t,$$

and

$$Z_{vv} = \sum_{t \geq 0} (P_v^t(v) - \pi_v) \leq \sum_{t \geq 0} (\lambda_{\max})^t = \frac{1}{1 - \lambda_{\max}}.$$

$\square$

Let T_G be the mixing time of a graph G, such that, for $t \geq T_G$,

$$\max_{u, x \in V} |P_u^{(t)}(x) - \pi_x| = O\left(\frac{1}{n^3}\right). \tag{6}$$

Let $\mathcal{A}_t(v) = \mathcal{A}_{t,u}(v)$ denote the event that $\mathcal{W}_u$ does not visit vertex v in steps $0, ..., t$. Lemma 4 gives a bound for $\mathbf{Pr}(\mathcal{A}_t(v))$ in terms of $\mathbf{E}_\pi(H_v)$ and the mixing time T.

LEMMA 4. *Let T_G be the mixing time of a random walk $\mathcal{W}_u$ on G satisfying (6). Then*

$$\mathbf{Pr}(\mathcal{A}_t(v)) \leq e^{-\lfloor t/(T_G + 3\mathbf{E}_\pi(H_v)) \rfloor}.$$

Proof   Let $\rho = (\rho_w)$ be the distribution of $\mathcal{W}_u$ on G after $T = T_G$ steps, where $\rho_w = P_u^{(T)}(w)$. Let $\mathbf{E}_\rho(H_v)$ be the expected time to hit v starting from ρ. As T satisfies (6), and $\pi_x = \Omega(1/n^2)$ for any connected graph, then $\rho_w = (1 + o(1))\pi_w$. It follows that

$$\mathbf{E}_\rho(H_v) = (1 + o(1))\mathbf{E}_\pi(H_v). \tag{7}$$

Let $H_v(\rho)$ be the time to hit v starting from ρ, then

$$\mathbf{Pr}[H_v(\rho) \geq 3\mathbf{E}_\pi(H_v)] \leq \frac{1}{e}.$$

Let $\tau = T + 3\mathbf{E}_\pi(H_v)$. By considering the process $\mathcal{W}_u$ at $\mathcal{W}(0) = u, \mathcal{W}(\tau), \mathcal{W}(2\tau), ..., \mathcal{W}(\lfloor t/\tau \rfloor \tau)$ we obtain

$$\mathbf{Pr}(\mathcal{A}_t(v)) \leq e^{-\lfloor t/\tau \rfloor}.$$

$\square$

Visits to Vertex Sets.

We can extend the results presented above to any nonempty subset S of vertices in the following way. From G we obtain a (multi)-graph $\Gamma = \Gamma_S$ by contracting S to a single vertex γ. Note that we retain multiple edges and loops in Γ_S, so that $d(S) = d(\gamma)$, and $|E(\Gamma)| = |E(G)| = m$. Let $\hat{\pi}$ be the stationary distribution of a random walk on Γ. If $v \notin S$ then $\hat{\pi}_v = \pi_v$, and $\hat{\pi}_\gamma = \pi_S \equiv \sum_{x \in S} \pi_x$.

For $u \notin S$ let $\mathcal{W}_u$ be a walk starting from u in G, and let $\widehat{\mathcal{W}}_u$ be the equivalent walk starting in Γ. Provided $\mathcal{W}_u$ does not visit S in t steps, (the event $\boldsymbol{A}_t(S, G)$), then $\widehat{\mathcal{W}}_u$ does not visit γ (the event $A_t(\gamma, \Gamma)$), and the walks have the same transition probabilities. Thus,

$$\mathbf{Pr}(\boldsymbol{A}_t(S, G)) = \mathbf{Pr}(\boldsymbol{A}_t(\gamma, \Gamma)),$$

and

$$\mathbf{E}_\pi(H_S) = \mathbf{E}_{\hat{\pi}}(H_\gamma). \tag{8}$$

It is a known result that contracting vertex sets increases the eigenvalue gap. (For a proof see e.g. [1] Chapter 3, Corollary 27.) Thus

$$1 - \lambda_{\max}(G) \leq 1 - \lambda_{\max}(\Gamma).$$

In our proofs, we will always choose a mixing time T in (6) satisfying both $T \geq T_G$, and $T \geq T_\Gamma$. It follows that, using this mixing time T, the results of Lemma 3, and Lemma 4 apply equally to Γ, and to G. Thus e.g.

COROLLARY 5. *Let $G = (V, E)$, let $|E| = m$. Let $S \subseteq V$, and let $d(S)$ be the degree of S. Then $\mathbf{E}_\pi H_S$, the expected hitting time of S from stationarity satisfies*

$$\mathbf{E}_\pi H_S \leq \frac{2m}{d(S)(1 - \lambda_{\max}(G))}.$$

2. PROOF OF MAIN RESULT

2.1 Properties of the edge-process

It is helpful to think of the progress of the E-process as a re-colouring of the edges of the graph G. We consider unvisited edges as coloured blue, and explored edges as coloured red. Let $X(t)$ be the position at step t of a particle moving according to an E-process.

Initially, the particle is at $X(0) = u$, the start vertex, and all edges of the graph G are coloured blue (unvisited). Given $X(t) = v$, $X(t + 1)$ is chosen as follows. If all edges incident with v are red (previously visited) the walk chooses $X(t + 1)$ u.a.r. from $N(v)$. If however, there are any blue (unvisited) edges incident with v, then we pick a blue edge (v, w) according to the rule $\mathcal{A}$. The walk then moves to $X(t + 1) = w$, and re-colours the edge (v, w) red (visited). We assume that the edge (v, w) is re-coloured red at the start of step $t + 1$, the instant at which the walk arrives at w. Thus we regard the transition (v, w) as being along a blue edge.

At each t the next transition is either along a blue or a red edge. We speak of the sequence of these edge transitions as the blue (sub)-walk and the red (sub)-walk. The walk thus defines red and blue phases which are maximal sequences of edge transitions when the walk is the given colour. For any vertex v, and step t, the blue (resp. red) degree of v is the number of blue (resp. red) edges incident with v at the start of step t.

OBSERVATION 6. *Assume all vertices of G are of even degree. Then a blue phase of the E-process which starts at a vertex v (at some step t), must end at v (at some step $t + \tau$).*

Proof This follows from a simple parity argument. The first blue phase starts at $t = 0$, at the start vertex u. At $t = 0$ every vertex has even blue degree. Suppose that at step t we have $X(t) = w$, where $w \neq u$. Inductively every vertex, apart from the start vertex u and the current position w have even blue degree, whereas the blue degree of u and w is odd, and hence greater than zero. The particle can thus exit w along a blue edge. When the particle leaves $w = X(t)$ making the transition $(X(t), X(t + 1))$, then the blue degree of $w = X(t)$ becomes even. If $X(t + 1) = u$, then the degree of u is even and the particle has returned to the start. If $X(t + 1) \neq u$, then the blue degree of $X(t + 1)$ and u is odd.

If the particle returns to u at step t, and the blue degree of u is zero, then the blue phase at u is completed at (the start of) step t. The particle now leaves u along a red edge $(u, v) = (X(t), X(t + 1))$, and this is the beginning of a red phase. Inductively, the blue degree of v is even when the particle arrives at v. If v has blue edges incident with it, then a blue phase begins. Otherwise the red phase continues. □

Note that it is possible for all edges incident with a vertex v to be coloured red by transitions made during the blue sub-walk, and that v has not been visited by a red walk.

Let $G[S]$ denote the subgraph of G induced by the set of vertices $S \subseteq V$. The following summarizes the consequences of Observation 6.

OBSERVATION 7. *Assume vertex v is unvisited at step t, and that the E-process is in a red phase.*

1. *All edges incident with v are blue at step t.*

2. *The blue degree of all vertices at step t is even.*

3. *Let S_v^* be the maximal blue (unvisited), edge induced subgraph obtained by fanning out in a breadth first manner from v using only blue edges. Let U^* be the vertex set of S_v^*. Then*

   (a) *The degree of v in S_v^* is $d(v)$, the degree of vertex v in G. All vertices of S_v^* have positive even degree.*

   (b) *All edges between S_v^* and $G \setminus U^*$ are red.*

   (c) *$G[U^*]$ may induce red edges, but these are not part of S_v^*.*

In the simplest case S_v^* consists of $d(v)/2$ blue cycles with common root vertex v, but otherwise vertex disjoint.

It follows from Observation 6, that if we ignore the blue phases of the E-process, then the resulting red phases describe a continuous simple random walk $W_u(t_R)$ on the graph G. Each step t_R of the walk W_u corresponds to some step $s > t_R$ in the E-process. From Observation 6 it also follows that, if X starts at u, then W_u also starts at vertex u.

At step t of the E-process, we have $t = t_R + t_B$, where t_R, t_B are the (unknown) number of red and blue edge transitions. One thing is certain however; the length of the blue walk can be at most the number of edges m of G. This is formalized in the next observation.

OBSERVATION 8. *Let $W_u(t_R)$ be a simple random walk on the graph G defined by the red phase of the E-process, and let $X_u(t)$ be the walk defined by the E-process. Then $t_R < t < t_R + m$.*

2.2 Cover time of the E-process

LEMMA 9. *Let $\mathcal{W}_u$ be a random walk starting from u in G. Let S be a set of vertices of G of size s. Let*

$$d(S) = o(m/\log n),$$

where $d(S)$ be the sum of the degrees of the vertices in S. Let

$$t = \Omega(m/s(1 - \lambda_{\max}),$$

then

$$\mathbf{Pr}(S \text{ is unvisited by } \mathcal{W}_u \text{ at step } t)$$
$$= O\left(e^{-td(S)(1-\lambda_{\max})/14m}\right).$$

Proof Contract S to a single vertex $\gamma = \gamma(S)$, retaining all resulting loops and parallel edges. Denote the resulting graph by Γ. Let $|S| = s$.

For $\lambda \leq 1$, $\lambda \leq e^{-(1-\lambda)}$. It follows from (2), for given u, x that

$$|P_u^t(x) - \pi_x| \leq \Delta^{1/2} e^{-(1-\lambda_{\max})t}, \qquad (9)$$

where Δ is the maximum degree in G or Γ as appropriate. In either case, $\Delta \leq 2m = O(n^2)$. Let

$$T = K \log n/(1 - \lambda_{\max}),$$

where $K \geq 6$. As there are at most n^2 pairs u, x, then using (9)

$$\sum_{u,x} |P_u^t(x) - \pi_x| \leq n^2 \Delta^{1/2} e^{-T(1-\lambda_{\max})} = O(1/n^3).$$

Thus T is a mixing time satisfying (6) in both G and Γ. Also, from Corollary 5 we have

$$\mathbf{E}_\pi(H_S) \leq \frac{2m}{d(S)(1 - \lambda_{\max})}.$$

For $u \notin S$ let $\mathcal{W}_u$ be a walk starting from u in G, and let $\widehat{\mathcal{W}}_u$ be the equivalent walk starting in Γ. Provided $\mathcal{W}_u$ does not visit S in t steps, (the event $\boldsymbol{A}_t(S, G)$), then $\widehat{\mathcal{W}}_u$ does not visit γ (the event $A_t(\gamma, \Gamma)$), and the walks have the same probabilities. Thus

$$\mathbf{Pr}(\boldsymbol{A}_t(S, G)) = \mathbf{Pr}(\boldsymbol{A}_t(\gamma, \Gamma)).$$

From Lemma 4 we have

$$\mathbf{Pr}(\boldsymbol{A}_t(\gamma)) \leq \exp\left(-\lfloor t/(T + 3\mathbf{E}_{\widehat{\pi}}(H_\gamma))\rfloor\right).$$

Let T_Γ be a mixing time of the random walk on Γ satisfying (6). From (9), and the conditions on $t, d(S)$ given in the lemma, we have that $T_\Gamma = o(m/d(S)(1 - \lambda))$, and thus

$$T + 3\mathbf{E}_{\widehat{\pi}}(H_\gamma) \leq \frac{7m}{d(S)(1 - \lambda_{\max})}.$$

We have the result that

$$\mathbf{Pr}(\boldsymbol{A}_t(S, G)) \leq \exp\left(-t\frac{d(S)(1 - \lambda_{\max})}{14m}\right).$$

$\square$

LEMMA 10. *Let G be a graph of maximum degree Δ. Let $\beta(s, v)$ be the number of connected edge induced subgraphs of size s rooted at vertex v in G. Then*

$$\beta(s, v) \leq 2^{s\Delta}.$$

Proof We make a crude estimate for $\beta(s, v)$ by building a digraph H_v in a breadth first manner as follows. Initially $H_v = \emptyset$ and all adjacent edges of v are in G are labeled unvisited. Mark v as processed and add it to H_v. For each edge incident with v, we label it as retained or excluded. Starting from v there are $d(v)$ unvisited edges, and so at most $2^{d(v)}$ choices for the subset of edges incident with v to retain. We process each retained edge (v, u) in increasing endpoint label order. Mark u as processed and add the retained edge (v, u) to H_v. There are at most $2^{d(u)-1}$ choices for labels (retained, excluded) of any unvisited edges incident with u.

Thus we fan out from v in a breadth-first manner using only retained edges, (u, w). We add w to H_v, and also any retained edges (x, w), where x was processed earlier than w. In general there are some number of retained and excluded edges incident with w in G, resulting from processing earlier vertices; and the remaining at most $(d(w) - 1)$ edges are unvisited. We continue until H_v has s processed vertices, and the choices at these vertices have been evaluated. The s processed vertices of H_v and any retained edges between them defines a connected subgraph of size s rooted at v, and every subgraph of size s rooted at v is found by this construction. $\square$

LEMMA 11. *Let G be an ℓ-typical graph of minimum degree δ and maximum degree Δ. With probability $1 - O(n^{-3})$, after*

$$\tau^* = O\left(m\left(1 + \frac{\Delta \log n}{\delta \min(\ell, \log n)(1 - \lambda_{\max})}\right)\right)$$

steps of the E-process, no vertex of G remains unvisited. The value of τ^* is independent of the choice of rule $\mathcal{A}$ used by the process.

In particular, if G has constant maximum degree, there exists a constant $B > 0$ such that

$$\tau^* = Bn[1 + (\log n)/\min(\ell, \log n)(1 - \lambda_{\max})].$$

Proof Let S_v^* be the maximal connected even degree blue subgraph rooted at v, as described in Observation 7. Let S_v be any connected subgraph of S_v^* of size

$$s = \min(\ell, \log n),$$

rooted at v. By Lemma 10, there are at most $2^{\Delta s}$ such possible subgraphs.

For a random walk $\mathcal{W}_u$ starting from vertex u, let $P(s, t)$ be the probability that at step t there exists an unvisited connected subgraph of size s rooted at some vertex v. Thus using Lemmas 9 and 10

$$P(s, t) \leq n 2^{\Delta s} e^{-t\frac{d(S)(1-\lambda_{\max})}{14m}}.$$

As $s = \min(\ell, \log n)$, on choosing

$$t^* = (\Delta + 7) \log n \frac{14m}{\delta s(1 - \lambda_{\max})},$$

where $\delta \geq 2$ is minimum degree, we find that

$$P(s, t^*) = O(1/n^3). \qquad (10)$$

From Observation 8, the length of the E-process walk on unvisited edges is at most m, the number of edges of G, and the step $\tau^* = \tau(t^*)$ in the E-process corresponding to the step t^* in the red phase random walk $\mathcal{W}_u$ is bounded by $\tau^* \leq m + t^*$. In particular, if Δ is constant then $m = cn$, and

$$\tau^* \leq m + t^* = B(n + (n \log n)/(\min(\ell, \log n)(1 - \lambda_{\max}))).$$

Suppose some vertex v is unvisited at τ^*. Then a blue (unvisited) edge induced subgraph S_v^* rooted at v exists at τ^*. However, from (10), **whp** any $S_v \subseteq S_v^*$ of size s, contains a vertex z already visited by $\mathcal{W}(t^*)$. Suppose this visit occurs at $t \leq t^*$, but that, at step t^*, some edges incident with z are unvisited, a necessary condition for $z \in S_v^*$. On arriving at z, the E-process completes the exploration of all edges incident with z, after which the random walk $\mathcal{W}(t)$ continues up to step t^*. Thus at τ^* all edges adjacent to z are red, which is a contradiction. $\square$

3. DISCUSSION AND EXAMPLES

3.1 Lower bound cover time for weighted random walks

For an introduction to properties of weighted random walks see [1]. The following proof that the cover time of any weighted random walk is $\Omega(n \log n)$, is due to T. Radzik [15].

For any vertex u, the expected first return time $\mathbf{E}T_u^+$ to u is $\mathbf{E}T_u^+ = 1/\pi(u)$.

The commute time $K(u, v)$ between vertices u and v, is the expected time taken to go from vertex u to vertex v and then back to vertex u. Formally, $K(u, v) = \mathbf{E}_u T_v + \mathbf{E}_v T_u$. Any walk starting from u either visits v on the way back to u or it does not. Thus $\mathbf{E}T_u^+$ is at most the commute time $K(u, v)$ between u and v.

Let S be the subset of vertices with $\pi(u) \leq 2/n$. Thus $|S| \geq n/2$. This follows because $\sum_{u \in V} \pi(u) = 1$. As $\mathbf{E}T_u^+ = 1/\pi(u)$, it follows that for $u \in S$, $\mathbf{E}T_u^+ \geq n/2$.

Let $K_S = \min_{i,j \in S} K(i, j)$ then, $K_S \geq \mathbf{E}T_u^+ \geq n/2$. From [11], we have the lower bound that

$$C_G \geq (\max_{S \subseteq V} K_S \log |S|)/2 \geq (n/4) \log(n/2).$$

3.2 Proof of Corollary 2

Random r-regular graphs, $\mathcal{G}_r$, with $r \geq 4$ even, are an example of a class of graphs for which (**whp**) $C_G(E-\text{process}) = O(n)$. To establish this let $\mathcal{G}_r'$ be the subset of $\mathcal{G}_r$ with the following properties.

(P1) G is connected, and the second eigenvalue of the adjacency matrix of G is at most $2\sqrt{r-1} + \varepsilon$, where $\varepsilon > 0$ is an arbitrarily small positive constant.

(P2) Let $s = O(\log n)$, and let $a = \lceil 2s(\log re)/\log n \rceil$. No set of vertices S of size s induces more than $s + a$ edges. In particular, for $s \leq (\log n)/(2 \log re)$ no set of vertices S of size s induces more than s edges.

LEMMA 12. *Let $\mathcal{G}_r' \subseteq \mathcal{G}_r$ be the r-regular graphs satisfying (P1), (P2). Then $|\mathcal{G}_r'| \sim |\mathcal{G}_r|$.*

Proof Friedman [10], shows the deep result that (P1) holds **whp** for random regular graphs. That (P2) holds **whp** is straightforward to establish. $\square$

Proof of Corollary 2. Let $\ell = \epsilon \log n$ for some $\epsilon > 0$. Property (P2) implies the graph is ℓ-good as follows. For any vertex v of the graph G, let U^* be the smallest non-trivial connected, even degree, vertex induced subgraph rooted at v. As $r \geq 4$, this subgraph contains at least two cycles. Let $|U^*| = k$, then U^* induces at least $k + 1$ edges. By property (P2), no subgraph on $s = \epsilon \log n$ vertices with $\epsilon = 1/(2 \log re)$ induces more than s edges, and we conclude that $|U^*| > s$.

3.3 Removing the even degree constraint?

The only place in the proofs where the even degree condition matters is the proof of Observation 6, that the walk on unvisited edges terminates at its start vertex. How important is the even degree constraint?

We consider the experimental evidence for the performance of the E-process on both even degree, and odd degree graphs. In our experiments unvisited edges are chosen uniformly at random. We generated graphs of size up to half a million vertices, using the random regular graph generator from the *NetworkX* package (http://networkx.lanl.gov/) for the programming language Python. This package implements the Steger/Wormald approach, see [16]. We used Python's built-in random number generator which is based upon the Mersenne Twister. Each data point is the average of five actual experiments.

In Figure 1 we plot the normalised cover time of the E-process, in the case where the choice of unvisited edges is random. The *normalised* cover time is the actual cover time divided by n, as a function of n. Thus, linear functions of n appear flat etc. The labeling on the graphs is as follows: The first letter indicates an E-process, and this is followed by the degree $d = r$ of the graph. In the case where the plot appears to be non-linear, a curve of the form $c \log n$, is drawn behind the normalised experimental data, and labeled $[cn \ln(n)]$. The constant c used to draw the curve was determined by inspection.

It would appear the plots for even degrees 4 and 6 are constant, i.e. the cover time is $O(n)$. On the basis of experimental evidence, the normalised cover time of 3-regular graphs is $\omega(n)$; see Figure 1. This $\omega(n)$ growth appears to be $0.93n \log n$. For degrees 5 and 7 the plot also appears to grow logarithmically. We note, however, that it is notoriously difficult to quantify such growth on the basis of finite n, and we make no claims other than to present our experiments.

4. REFERENCES

[1] D. Aldous, J. Fill. *Reversible Markov Chains and Random Walks on Graphs*, 2001. http://stat-www.berkeley.edu/users/aldous/RWG/book.html

[2] C. Avin and B. Krishnamachari. *The power of choice in random walks: An empirical study.* Proceedings of 9th ACM/IEEE International Symposium on Modeling, Analysis and Simulation of Wireless and Mobile Systems, (MSWiM-06), 219Ü-228, (2006).

[3] E. Bampas, L. Gąsieniec, N. Hanusse, D. Ilcinkas, R. Klasing, A. Kosowski. *Euler Tour Lock-in Problem in the Rotor-Router Model. I choose pointers and you choose port numbers.* Proceedings of DISC 2009, 423-435.

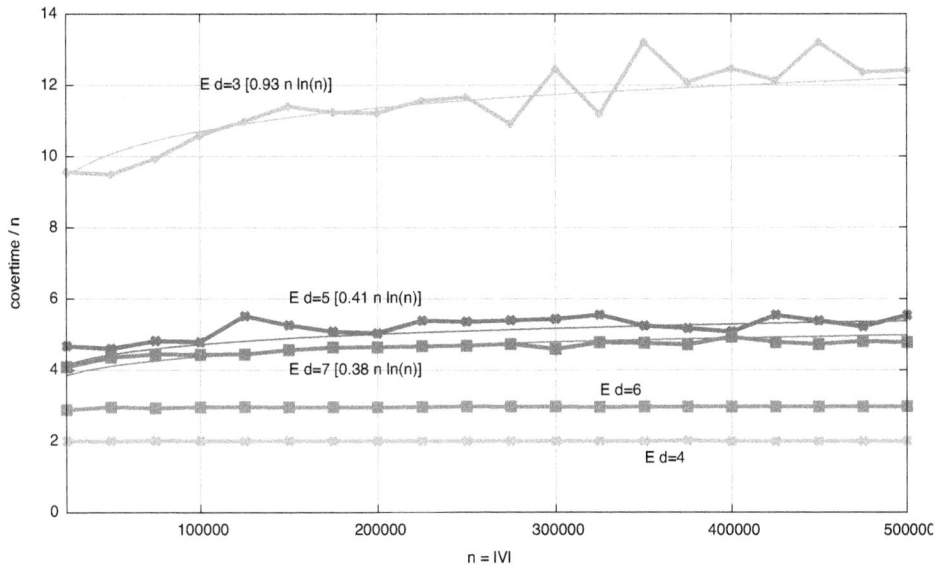

Figure 1: Normalised cover time of E-process as function of size and degree d

[4] V. Bourassa and F. Holt, *SWAN: Small-world wide area networks*. Proceedings of International Conference on Advances in Infrastructure (SSGRR 2003w), L'Aquila, Italy, 2003, paper 64.

[5] C. Cooper, M. Dyer, C. Greenhill. *Sampling regular graphs and a peer to peer network*. Combinatorics Probability and Computing 16(4) 557-593 (2007).

[6] C. Cooper, M. Dyer, A. Handley. *The Flip Markov Chain and a Randomising P2P Protocol*. Proc. of PODC 2009. 141-150, (2009).

[7] J. Cooper, B. Doerr, T. Friedrich, and J. Spencer. *Deterministic random walks on regular trees*. Proceedings of 19th ACM-SIAM Symposium on Discrete Algorithms (SODA'08), 766–772, (2008).

[8] T. Feder, A. Guetz, M. Mihail, and A. Saberi. *A local switch Markov chain on given degree graphs with application in connectivity of peer-to-peer networks*. Proc. of FOCS, 2006.

[9] U. Feige, *A tight lower bound for the cover time of random walks on graphs*. Random Structures and Algorithms 6 433–438 (1995).

[10] J. Friedman. *A proof of Alon's second eigenvalue conjecture*. Proceedings of 35th ACM Symposium on Theory of Computing, 720–724 (2003).

[11] J. Kahn, J. H. Kim, L. Lovasz, and V. H. Vu. *The cover time, the blanket time, and the Matthews bound* Proc. of FOCS'00, 467-475, (2000).

[12] A. Lubotzky, R. Phillips, and P. Sarnak, *Ramanujan graphs*, Combinatorica, 8, 261–277, (1988).

[13] P. Mahlmann and C. Schindelhauer. *Peer-to-peer networks based on random transformations of connected regular undirected graphs*. Proc. of SPAA '05, 155-164 (2005).

[14] T. Orenshtein and I. Shinkar. *Greedy random walk*. arXiv:1101.5711v3 [math.PR]

[15] T. Radzik. Private communication. (2010).

[16] A. Steger and N.C. Wormald. *Generating random regular graphs quickly*. Combinatorics, Probability & Computing 8(4): 377-396 (1999).

[17] V. Yanovski, I. A. Wagner, and A. M. Bruckstein. *A distributed ant algorithm for efficiently patrolling a network*. Algorithmica, 37:165–186, 2003.

Information Spreading in Dynamic Graphs[*]

Andrea Clementi
Dipartimento di Ingegneria
dell'Impresa
Università degli Studi di Roma
Tor Vergata
clementi@mat.uniroma2.it

Riccardo Silvestri
Dipartimento di Informatica
Sapienza Università di Roma
silvestri@di.uniroma1.it

Luca Trevisan
Department of Computer
Science
Stanford University
trevisan@stanford.edu

ABSTRACT

We present a general approach to study the flooding time (a measure of how fast information spreads) in dynamic graphs (graphs whose topology changes with time according to a random process). We consider arbitrary ergodic Markovian dynamic graph process, that is, processes in which the topology of the graph at time t depends only on its topology at time $t-1$ and which have a unique stationary distribution. The most well studied models of dynamic graphs are all Markovian and ergodic.

Under general conditions, we bound the flooding time in terms of the mixing time of the dynamic graph process. We recover, as special cases of our result, bounds on the flooding time for the *random trip* model and the *random path* models; previous analysis techniques provided bounds only in restricted settings for such models. Our result also provides the first bound for the *random waypoint* model (which is tight for the most realistic ranges of network parameters) whose analysis had been an important open question.

Categories and Subject Descriptors

G.3 [**Probability and Statistics**]: Markov processes; C.2.1 [**Computer-Communication Networks**]: Network Architecture and Design—*wireless communication*

General Terms

Theory

Keywords

Dynamic Graphs, Flooding Protocols, Markov Chains, Mobility Models.

---

[*]This work was partially supported by the PRIN 2008 research project COGENT (COmputational and GamE-theoretic aspects of uncoordinated NeTworks), funded by the Italian Ministry of University and Research.

1. INTRODUCTION

A *dynamic graph* is a probabilistic process that describes a graph whose topology changes with time. Dynamic graphs are appropriate models of wireless networks, peer-to-peer networks, social networks, and so on. There are several interesting problems on dynamic graph processes, for example load balancing, studied in [17, 29]. Here, we are interested in the speed of *information spreading*, a question that can model the spread of disease, the broadcast of files on peer-to-peer networks, of memes in social networks, etc.

The simplest model of information spreading is the process of *flooding* [4, 10, 13, 16, 18, 19, 23, 27, 28], which begins with one node in the network being given a certain piece of information, and then the application of a protocol in which, at each time step, every node that has the information spreads it to its neighbors. Recall that the neighborhood of a node changes with time, and so even though the flooding algorithm is deterministic, the process of information spread is probabilistic.

The setting of wireless networks has motivated the study of this problem in geometric models of dynamic graphs in which, at every time step, every node is mapped to a point in a metric space, and two vertices are connected if their distance is smaller than a given communication radius. The underlying metric space is usually a bounded portion of the plane, for example a square or unit disk, and the dynamics come from independent random walks performed by the individual nodes via local moves [21, 16, 11, 12, 27, 28, 24]. For example, a representative model of this type is the random walk model: n nodes are placed on a $m \times m$ grid; at each time step, every node v independently moves to a point in the grid randomly chosen among the points adjacent to the one that v occupied at the previous time step; at each time step, the edge (u, v) is present in the dynamic graph if u and v are located within distance r in the grid. In such a model, the flooding time will depend on the initial locations, on r, m and n. Usually, one is interested in a worst-case analysis with respect to the initial locations, and in a bound dependent only on r, m and n. Known analyses of such models rely rather strongly on the fact that, if we consider a fixed node v, the stationary distribution of its location (i.e. the positional distribution) on the grid under the random walk is essentially uniform.

The *random waypoint* model [7, 6, 8, 25] is another classic model of networks of mobile agents, and it is probably the most well studied one. In this model, every node chooses a random destination point in the mobility space, then he travels over the shortest path till he reaches the destination, and so on. Some analytical properties of this model have been derived such as the mixing time, the stationary node distribution, etc. [6, 8, 25]. However, bounding its flooding time (or any basic communication tasks such as routing, data collection, etc.) is still a fundamental open problem. The techniques adopted for the random walk model do not work in the random waypoint model, mainly because of the presence of long periods the node spends in deterministic trajectories and because of the strong difference between their respective stationary positional distributions. For instance, the stationary positional distribution of the random waypoint over a square is in fact far from the uniform one: it is highly biased towards the center of the square.

The above two families of models define a probabilistic process over the nodes, which then implies which pairs of nodes are connected by an edge. There are also models of probabilistic processes that are directly defined over the edges. A very general model is provided by Markovian Evolving Graphs (MEGs) introduced in [2] (see later for a formal definition). However, available techniques to analyze information spreading only concern very restricted subclasses of MEGs, such as that studied in [10], where the state (i.e. on/off) of the edges is ruled by independent copies of a simple two-state Markov chain.

Our Work

- *General Dynamic Networks.* We provide an upper bound to the flooding time of any stationary Markovian Evolving Graph (MEG) [2]. If we call $G_t = (V, E_t)$ the random variable describing the dynamic graph at time t, the process is a MEG if the sequence of random variables $\mathcal{G}([n], \{E_t\}_{t \geqslant 0}) = G_0, \ldots, G_t, \ldots$ is Markovian, that is, if the distribution G_t is completely determined by the distribution G_{t-1}, via a transformation independent of t. The class MEG is extremely general and, in particular, it includes all above-mentioned network models such as random walk and random waypoint: indeed, it is easy to verify that any of such models yields a sequence of random graphs $\mathcal{G}([n], \{E_t\}_{t \geqslant 0})$ which is Markovian. We require the Markovian sequence to converge to a unique stationary distribution, for every initial choice G_0. This stationary distribution is a probability distribution over n-vertex graphs and it will be called the stationary graph $\mathcal{G}_n$.

Our upper bound to the flooding time is a function of:
i) the edge-probability in $\mathcal{G}_n$ (that determines the expected density of the stationary graph) ii) the degree of independence among edges in $\mathcal{G}_n$ and, iii) the mixing time of the Markov chain $\mathcal{G}([n], \{E_t\}_{t \geqslant 0})$. More precisely, given edge e, node i, and node subset A, let $p(e)$ be the probability that e exists in $\mathcal{G}_n$ and let $e(i, A)$ be the binary random variable returning 1 iff an edge exists connecting i to some node in A in $\mathcal{G}_n$. Let M be an upper bound on the mixing time of $\mathcal{G}([n], \{E_t\}_{t \geqslant 0})$. Our result states that if, for some arbitrary positive reals α and β,
(i) $p(e) \geqslant \alpha$ for any link e and[1]
(ii) $\mathbf{P}(e(i, A) \cdot e(j, A)) \leqslant \beta \mathbf{P}(e(i, A)) \cdot \mathbf{P}(e(j, A))$ for arbitrary nodes i, j and arbitrary node subset A (not containing i or j),
then the flooding time is w.h.p.[2]

$$O\left(M\left(\frac{1}{n\alpha} + \beta\right)^2 \log^2 n\right) \qquad (1)$$

Our method can be applied to non-Markovian processes as well, although the results are more complex to state (see Sections 2, 3). Bounding the mixing time of dynamic networks has been the subject of several studies in the last years [1, 25, 10]: our result allows to efficiently exploit any (previous or future) bound on the mixing time for the flooding time of such MEGs. In order to get an intuition of the real meaning of Conditions (i) and (ii) (i.e. how mild they can be), we observe that mild bounds on the density and independence parameters, say $\alpha = \Omega(1/n)$ and $\beta = O(\text{polylog}(n))$, do not imply any good node/edge expansion of the single snapshot graphs G_t of the process: In every G_t there could be a large subset of all nodes (say half of them) that are isolated. In such sparse and disconnected topologies, thanks to our bound, the flooding time can be just a polylogarithmic factor away from the mixing time of the MEG. This crucial fact has strong consequences on concrete network scenarios in which the node dynamics is homogeneous as described below.

- *Node-MEGs.* Our general approach finds a natural application in a subclass of MEGs that we call node-Markovian Evolving Graphs, denoted as node-MEGs, where every node changes its state independently according to a Markov Chain $\mathcal{M}$. The state of a node can implement several dynamic features of the node (such as geometric position and destination, trajectory phase, social role, etc). Then the existence of a link between two nodes (only) depends on the current states of the two nodes according to a fixed deterministic function. Observe that node-MEGs are a relevant class of MEGs that includes every mobility model where nodes act independently over any discrete space (such as an arbitrary graph or any geometric region discretized, for instance, by using a grid of suitable resolution[3]). Random walk, random waypoint, and random trip models [7, 25, 14] have a natural realization as node-MEGs: for instance, a realization of the random waypoint as a node-MEGs is described in Subsection 4.1. Notice that in node-MEGs, nodes are indistinguishable so Condition (i) is easy-to-check: if it is satisfied (in the stationary graph) for a specific edge then it is satisfied for all edges. We then prove that if incident edges are almost pairwise independent in the stationary graph yielded by a node-MEG then Condition (ii) is satisfied for some constant β: so, checking Condition (ii) can here be reduced to check pairwise independence of incident edges in a generic node.

- *Geometric Mobility Models.* As for node-MEGs defined over geometric spaces (such as the random waypoint), we state an easy-to-check condition implying Condition (ii): we transform the pairwise-independence condition on incident edges into some mild uniformity conditions on the *single-node* positional stationary distribution (see Corollary 12). We show the former properties are satisfied by a wide class of random mobility models such as the random waypoint over a square: we thus get the first known upper bound for its flooding time. Furthermore, when the stationary graph is sparse, the obtained bound is tight up to a polylogarithmic factor, i.e., $O((L/v)\text{polylog}(n))$ where L is the diameter of the square and v is the node speed. In particular, our bound

---

[1]With an abuse of notation, event probabilities such as $\mathbf{P}(e(i, A) = 1)$ will be shortly denoted as $\mathbf{P}(e(i, A))$.

[2]We say that an event holds with high probability if it holds with probability at least $1 - 1/n$.

[3]The level of resolution does not affect the obtained bound on the flooding time, provided the resolution is high enough.

is almost tight whenever $L \sim \sqrt{n}$ and both the transmission radius and the node speed are absolute constants: this is surely the model setting that best fits opportunistic delay-tolerant Mobile Ad-hoc Networks [19, 20, 28].

- Graph Mobility Models. Our upper bound holds even when the mobility space is an arbitrary graph (the vertices of such graph are called points): in this case nodes choose randomly their trajectories from some fixed families of simple paths of the mobility graph and the mixing time is proportional to its hop-diameter. This mobility model is called *random paths* (on graphs). The parameter β in Eq. 1 is here determined by the point congestion yielded by the feasible paths of the mobility graph: informally speaking, β is small whenever the random paths do not yield high-congestion points (again, we get a somewhat mild uniformity condition on the positional stationary distribution). If this is the case, the obtained bound on the flooding time becomes tight up to some polylogarithmic factor. The random walk model on graphs can be seen as a special case of the random paths on graphs: then the obtained bound on the flooding time improves over the previous one [16] for the class of graphs where the mixing time of a random walk is shorter than the meeting time of two random walks.

By concluding about mobile networks, we want to emphasize the impact of our general method over classic models: the general conditions (i) and (ii) of our bound are transformed into mild uniformity conditions over the positional stationary distribution which can be verified by standard techniques [1, 25].

- Link-based Dynamic Networks. We show that our method can also be applied to a subclass of MEGs in which each edge evolves independently according to an arbitrary (hidden) Markov chain. Previously [10, 5], such *link-based* dynamic models had been studied only in the case in which the edge Markov chain is very simple.

Previous Works. As mentioned before, information spreading in dynamic networks has been extensively studied in the literature under a variety of scenarios and objectives (for a recent good survey see [23]). For brevity's sake, we restrict our attention to the results more directly related to our work. Previous models and results can be roughly classified in two main classes: link-based dynamic graphs and mobility models.

As for the first class, in [9], radio broadcasting is analyzed on a dynamic graph managed by a worst-case dynamic adversary and on a sequence of independent Erdös-Rény graphs. In [10], an upper bound on the flooding time for the restricted model edge-MEG has been derived. The flooding time of another simple version of edge-MEGs has been studied in [5]. The general MEG model has been introduced in [2] where some results are obtained for the cover time and hitting time of random walks. Flooding time in stationary MEGs is studied in [11]; unlike our method, the method in [11] only holds for stationary graphs which are connected and good expanders. A worst-case model of dynamic graphs has been introduced in [22]. The analysis of some communication tasks is presented under the strong stability condition called T-interval connectivity (for $T \geqslant 1$) which stipulates that for every T consecutive steps a stable connected spanning subgraph must exist.

As for mobility models, almost tight bounds on the flooding time for the random walk model have been obtained in

[21, 11, 12, 27, 28, 24]. As above discussed, their techniques strongly rely on specific properties of the adopted version of the random walk. The case of general mobility graphs has been considered in [16]: the obtained results are discussed and compared to our results in Subsection 4.1. An upper bound on a variant of the random waypoint model has been derived in [13]. In this version, nodes follows *Manhattan* paths. Similarly to the works on the random walk models, the ad-hoc analysis in [13] strongly relies on the particular node trajectories and on the specific positional distribution yielded by this model. So, its contribution strongly departs from our general approach that obtains bounds for any version of the random waypoint model.

Paper Organization. Section 2 formalizes the general model of dynamic graph and the flooding process. Section 3 provides the main theorem for the flooding time in the general model. The node-MEG model is described in Section 4 where an upper bound on the flooding time is given for this specific model. The representation of the random trip and the random paths models as specific instances of the node-MEG model is given in Subsection 4.1. Here, the flooding-time bound for node-MEGs is transformed into two useful bounds on the flooding time: the first one for the random trip and the second one for the random paths. The model edge-MEG is studied in Section 5. Finally, conclusions with open questions are discussed in Section 6. Due to lack of space some proofs are omitted (readers may find them in the full version [15]).

2. PRELIMINARIES

In this section, we introduce the general model of dynamic graphs. For any positive n, $[n]$ will denote the set $\{1, 2, \ldots, n\}$. A *dynamic graph* $\mathcal{G}([n], \{E_t\}_{t \geqslant 0})$, with node set $[n]$, is a stochastic process represented by a sequence of random variables $E_0, E_1, \ldots, E_t, \ldots$ such that, for every t, E_t is the set of edges of the dynamic graph at time t. The speed of information spreading can be studied in terms of the flooding time. Given a dynamic graph $\mathcal{G}([n], \{E_t\}_{t \geqslant 0})$ and a node $s \in [n]$, the flooding process with source s is defined as follows. At time $t = 0$, s is the only informed node; then a node v gets informed at time $t + 1$ iff an edge $e \in E_t$ exists connecting some informed node to v. Flooding over a dynamic graph is represented by the stochastic process $\{I_t\}_{t \geqslant 0}$ where $I_0 = \{s\}$ and

$$\forall t \geqslant 1 \; I_t = I_{t-1} \cup \{j \in [n] \mid \exists i \in I_{t-1} : \{i, j\} \in E_t\}$$

The random variable I_t is the set of informed nodes at time t. Clearly, it holds that $I_0 \subseteq I_1 \subseteq \cdots I_t \subseteq \cdots$. The *flooding time with source* s is the random variable $F(\mathcal{G}, s) = \min_t\{I_t = [n]\}$ and the *flooding time* is the random variable $F(\mathcal{G}) = \max_s F(\mathcal{G}, s)$.

Given a dynamic graph $\mathcal{G}([n], \{E_t\}_{t \geqslant 0})$, we define the following random variables. For every time t, for every pair of nodes $i, j \in [n]$ and for every subset of nodes $A \subseteq [n]$, let

$$e_{i,j}^t = \begin{cases} 1 & \text{if } \{i, j\} \in E_t \\ 0 & \text{otherwise} \end{cases} \quad \text{and}$$

$$e_{i,A}^t = \begin{cases} 1 & \text{if } \exists j \in A : \{i, j\} \in E_t \\ 0 & \text{otherwise} \end{cases}$$

Moreover, for any binary random variable X, the notation $\mathbf{P}(X \mid E_{t \leqslant T}) \leqslant (\text{or} \geqslant) \alpha$ stands for

$\forall$ subsets $A_0, \ldots, A_T$, with $\mathbf{P}\left(\bigwedge_{t=0}^{T}(E_t = A_t)\right) > 0$),

it holds

$$\mathbf{P}\left(X = 1 \;\middle|\; \bigwedge_{t=0}^{T}(E_t = A_t)\right) \leqslant (\text{or} \geqslant) \; \alpha$$

3. FLOODING IN DYNAMIC GRAPHS

Our goal is to evaluate the flooding time of a dynamic graph as a function of some properties of its edges. These properties are not required to show up at every snapshot, rather it suffices that they hold at the beginning of every time "epoch", where an epoch is a sequence of consecutive time steps of suitable length. When the dynamic graph is a Markovian process admitting a stationary graph, the properties above refer to the expansion properties of the stationary graph and the epoch length refers to the mixing time. However, aiming at the maximal generality, we introduce such concepts for general (non-Markovian) process.

Let M be a positive integer and let α and β be two positive reals. A dynamic graph $\mathcal{G}([n], \{E_t\}_{t \geqslant 0})$ is (M, α, β)-stationary if $\forall \tau \geqslant 1$, $\forall i, j \in [n]$ with $i \neq j$, $\forall A \subseteq [n] - \{i, j\}$, the following two conditions hold

1. Density Condition.

$$\mathbf{P}\left(e_{i,j}^{\tau M} \;\middle|\; E_{t \leqslant (\tau-1)M}\right) \geqslant \alpha$$

2. β-Independence Condition.

$$\mathbf{P}\left(e_{i,A}^{\tau M} \cdot e_{j,A}^{\tau M} \;\middle|\; E_{t \leqslant (\tau-1)M}\right) \leqslant$$

$$\beta \mathbf{P}\left(e_{i,A}^{\tau M} \;\middle|\; E_{t \leqslant (\tau-1)M}\right) \mathbf{P}\left(e_{j,A}^{\tau M} \;\middle|\; E_{t \leqslant (\tau-1)M}\right)$$

We can now state the main result of the paper.

THEOREM 1 (FLOODING TIME). *If* $\mathcal{G}([n], \{E_t\}_{t \geqslant 0})$ *is* (M, α, β)-*stationary then, with high probability, the flooding time in* $\mathcal{G}$ *is*

$$O\left(M\left(\frac{1}{n\alpha} + \beta\right)^2 \log^2 n\right)$$

3.1 Proof of Theorem 1

We will make use of the following standard inequalities in probability theory.

The Paley-Zigmund inequality. If $X \geqslant 0$ is a random variable with finite variance, and if $0 < \theta < 1$, then

$$\mathbf{P}\left(X \geqslant \theta \mathbf{E}[X]\right) \geqslant (1 - \theta^2)\frac{\mathbf{E}[X]^2}{\mathbf{E}[X^2]} \qquad (2)$$

LEMMA 2 (LEMMA 3.1 IN [3]). *Let* $X_1, \ldots, X_n$ *be a sequence of random variables with values in an arbitrary domain, and let* $Y_1, \ldots, Y_n$ *be a sequence of binary random variables, with the property that* $Y_i = Y_i(X_1, \ldots, X_n)$. *If* $\mathbf{P}(Y_i = 1 \mid X_1, \ldots, X_{i-1}) \geqslant p$ *then*

$$\mathbf{P}\left(\sum Y_i \leqslant k\right) \leqslant \mathbf{P}(B(n, p) \leqslant k)$$

where $B(n, p)$ *is binomially distributed random variable with parameters* n *and* p.

LEMMA 3 (CHERNOFF BOUND). *Let* $X_1, \ldots X_n$ *be independent binary random variables and let* $X = \sum_{i=1}^{n} X_i$ *and* $\mu = \mathbf{E}[X]$. *Then, for any* $\delta > 0$,

$$\mathbf{P}\left(X < (1 - \delta)\mu\right) < \exp\left(-\frac{\delta^2 \mu}{2}\right)$$

Expansion Properties. In what follows, we derive some expansion properties of (M, α, β)-stationary dynamic graphs. Such properties will be then exploited in the analysis of flooding.

The times τM will be called *epochs* and they will be abbreviated by τ (i.e. τ will stand for τM, with respect to a fixed (M, α, β)-stationary dynamic graph $\mathcal{G}([n], \{E_t\}_{t \geqslant 0})$). Thus, we write E_τ, $e_{i,j}^{\tau}$ and $e_{i,A}^{\tau}$ to denote $E_{\tau M}$, $e_{i,j}^{\tau M}$ and $e_{i,A}^{\tau M}$, respectively. These abbreviations will be also used for other random variables.

Let $\deg_{i,A}^{\tau}$ be the random variable counting the number of nodes in A connected to i at epoch τ, i.e., $\deg_{i,A}^{\tau} = |\{j \in A \mid \{i, j\} \in E_\tau\}|$. Observe that, thanks to Condition (1), the expected value of $\deg_{i,A}^{\tau}$ is at least $|A|\alpha$; the following lemma provides a concentration result as function of the "independence" parameter β.

LEMMA 4. *If* $\mathcal{G}([n], \{E_t\}_{t \geqslant 0})$ *is* (M, α, β)-*stationary then,* $\forall \tau \geqslant 1$, $\forall i \in [n]$, *and* $\forall A \in [n] - \{i\}$,

$$\mathbf{P}\left(\deg_{i,A}^{\tau} \geqslant \frac{|A|\alpha}{2} \;\middle|\; E_{\leqslant \tau-1}\right) \geqslant \frac{|A|\alpha}{2 + 2|A|\alpha\beta}$$

PROOF. Firstly we bound the expected square of the degree. For the sake of brevity, we omit the conditioning by $E_{\leqslant \tau-1}$. Let $\Delta = \mathbf{E}\left[\left(\deg_{i,A}^{\tau}\right)^2\right]$, then t holds that

$$
\begin{aligned}
\Delta &= \mathbf{E}\left[\left(\sum_{j \in A} e_{i,j}^{\tau}\right)^2\right] \\
&= \sum_{j,k \in A} \mathbf{E}\left[e_{i,j}^{\tau} \cdot e_{i,k}^{\tau}\right] \\
&= \sum_{j,k \in A, j \neq k} \mathbf{E}\left[e_{i,j}^{\tau} \cdot e_{i,k}^{\tau}\right] + \mathbf{E}\left[\deg_{i,A}^{\tau}\right] \quad (\text{by } (e_{i,j}^{\tau})^2 = e_{i,j}^{\tau}) \\
&\leqslant \sum_{j,k \in A, j \neq k} \beta \mathbf{E}\left[e_{i,j}^{\tau}\right] \mathbf{E}\left[e_{i,k}^{\tau}\right] + \mathbf{E}\left[\deg_{i,A}^{\tau}\right] \quad (\text{by Cond. (2)}) \\
&\leqslant \beta \mathbf{E}\left[\deg_{i,A}^{\tau}\right]^2 + \mathbf{E}\left[\deg_{i,A}^{\tau}\right]
\end{aligned}
$$

Moreover, from Condition (1), it derives that

$$\mathbf{E}\left[\deg_{i,A}^{\tau}\right] \geqslant |A|\alpha$$

Thus, from the Paley-Zigmund inequality (with $\theta = 1/2$) and the above bounds, we obtain

$$
\begin{aligned}
\mathbf{P}\left(\deg_{i,A}^{\tau} \geqslant \frac{|A|\alpha}{2}\right) &\geqslant \frac{1}{2}\frac{\mathbf{E}\left[\deg_{i,A}^{\tau}\right]^2}{\mathbf{E}\left[(\deg_{i,A}^{\tau})^2\right]} \\
&\geqslant \frac{1}{2}\frac{\mathbf{E}\left[\deg_{i,A}^{\tau}\right]^2}{\beta \mathbf{E}\left[\deg_{i,A}^{\tau}\right]^2 + \mathbf{E}\left[\deg_{i,A}^{\tau}\right]} \\
&= \frac{\mathbf{E}\left[\deg_{i,A}^{\tau}\right]}{2 + 2\beta \mathbf{E}\left[\deg_{i,A}^{\tau}\right]} \\
&\geqslant \frac{\mathbf{E}\left[\deg_{i,A}^{\tau}\right]}{2 + 2\beta \mathbf{E}\left[\deg_{i,A}^{\tau}\right]}
\end{aligned}
$$

Since function $\frac{x}{2+2\beta x}$ is decreasing, we have that

$$\mathbf{P}\left(\deg_{i,A}^\tau \geq \frac{|A|\alpha}{2}\right) \geq \frac{\mathbf{E}\left[\deg_{i,A}^\tau\right]}{2+2\beta\mathbf{E}\left[\deg_{i,A}^\tau\right]} \geq \frac{|A|\alpha}{2+2\beta|A|\alpha}$$

□

The next lemma extends Lemma 4 to the expansion of an arbitrary node subset. For every epoch τ and for every $A, B \subseteq [n]$, define the random variable counting the expansion from A to B

$$\deg_{A,B}^\tau = |\{j \in B \mid \exists i \in A : \{i,j\} \in E_\tau\}|$$

LEMMA 5. If $\mathcal{G}([n], \{E_t\}_{t \geq 0})$ is (M, α, β)-stationary then, $\forall \tau \geq 1$, $\forall A \in [n]$, and $\forall B \in [n] - A$,

$$\mathbf{P}\left(\deg_{A,B}^\tau \geq \frac{|A||B|\alpha}{4+4|A|\alpha\beta} \;\middle|\; E_{\leq\tau-1}\right) \geq \frac{|A||B|\alpha}{4+6|A||B|\alpha\beta}$$

The proof is similar to that of Lemma 4.
When the dynamic graph is sparse, the expansion rate obtained by considering a single snapshot of the process (i.e. the expansion of a node subset at time τ) does not suffice to get a good number of new informed nodes. In this case, a "dynamic" version of the expansion properties is required. For every epoch τ, for every $T \geq 1$, and for every $A \subseteq [n]$, define

$$\text{spread}_A^{\tau,T} = |\{j \in [n] - A \mid \exists \tau' \exists i \in A : \tau < \tau' \leq \tau+T \wedge \{i,j\} \in E_{\tau'}\}|$$

LEMMA 6. If $\mathcal{G}([n], \{E_t\}_{t \geq 0})$ is (M, α, β)-stationary then, $\forall \tau \geq 1$, $\forall A \subseteq [n]$ with $|A| \leq n/4$, and $\forall t \geq 0$,
$\mathbf{P}\left(\text{spread}_A^{\tau,T} < |A| \;\middle|\; E_{\leq\tau}\right) < \exp(-t)$ where

$$T = 256\left(\frac{1}{|A|n^2\alpha^2} + \frac{\beta}{n\alpha} + \frac{|A|\beta^2}{n}\right) + \left(\frac{4}{|A|n\alpha} + 3\beta\right)t$$

PROOF. For brevity's sake, we omit the conditioning by $E_{\leq\tau}$. Let S_t be the set of nodes outside A that get connected to nodes in A during the epochs in $(\tau, \tau+t]$. Formally,

$$S_0 = \emptyset \quad \text{and} \quad S_t = S_{t-1} \cup \{j \in [n] - A \mid \exists i \in A : \{i,j\} \in E_{\tau+t}\}$$

Clearly, $|S_T| = \text{spread}_A^{\tau,T}$. Let

$$\gamma = \frac{|A|n\alpha}{8+8|A|\alpha\beta}$$

Define

$$Y_t = \begin{cases} 1 & \text{if } |S_{t-1}| \geq |A| \text{ or } |S_t| \geq |S_{t-1}| + \lceil\gamma\rceil \\ 0 & \text{otherwise} \end{cases}$$

Observe that $Y_t = f_t(E_{\tau+1}, \ldots, E_{\tau+t})$ for a suitable function f_t. From the inequality $\mathbf{P}(A \vee B \mid H) \geq \mathbf{P}(B \mid H \wedge \overline{A})$, by letting $\Lambda = \mathbf{P}(Y_t = 1 \mid E_{\tau,t-1})$, it holds that

$$\begin{aligned}\Lambda &= \mathbf{P}(|S_{t-1}| \geq |A| \vee |S_t| > |S_{t-1}| + \lceil\gamma\rceil \mid E_{\tau,t-1}) \\ &\geq \mathbf{P}(|S_t| > |S_{t-1}| + \lceil\gamma\rceil \mid E_{\tau,t-1} \wedge |S_{t-1}| < |A|) \quad (3)\end{aligned}$$

where $E_{\tau,t-1}$ stands for $E_{\tau+1}, \ldots, E_{\tau+t-1}$. Assume that $|S_{t-1}| < |A|$ and let $W = [n] - A - S_{t-1}$. Since $|A| \leq n/4$, it holds that $|W| \geq \frac{n}{2}$ and

$$|S_t| > |S_{t-1}| + \lceil\gamma\rceil \quad \Leftrightarrow \quad \deg_{A,W}^{\tau+t} \geq \gamma \quad (4)$$

From Lemma 5, by letting

$$\Gamma = \mathbf{P}\left(\deg_{A,W}^{\tau+t} \geq \gamma \;\middle|\; E_{\leq\tau+t-1} \wedge |S_{t-1}| < |A|\right)$$

it holds that

$$\begin{aligned}\Gamma &\geq \mathbf{P}\left(\deg_{A,W}^{\tau+t} \geq \frac{|A||W|\alpha}{4+4|A|\alpha\beta} \;\middle|\; E_{\leq\tau+t-1} \wedge |S_{t-1}| < |A|\right) \\ &\geq \frac{|A||W|\alpha}{4+6|A||W|\alpha\beta} \\ &\geq p = \frac{|A|n\alpha}{8+6|A|n\alpha\beta} \quad (5)\end{aligned}$$

Thus, from Ineq.s 3, 4, and 5 we get

$$\mathbf{P}(Y_t = 1 \mid E_{\tau,t-1}) \geq p$$

We can now apply Lemma 2 to the r.v. $E_{\tau+1}, \ldots, E_{\tau+T}$ and r.v. $Y_1, \ldots, Y_T$

$$\mathbf{P}\left(\sum_{t=1}^T Y_t < \frac{|A|}{\gamma}\right) \leq \mathbf{P}\left(B(T,p) < \frac{|A|}{\gamma}\right)$$

Since $\text{spread}_A^{\tau,T} < |A| \Rightarrow \sum_{t=1}^T Y_t < \frac{|A|}{\gamma}$, from the above inequality we obtain

$$\mathbf{P}\left(\text{spread}_A^{\tau,T} < |A|\right) \leq \mathbf{P}\left(B(T,p) < \frac{|A|}{\gamma}\right)$$

By applying Chernoff's Bound (Lemma 3), after some calculations, we get

$$\mathbf{P}\left(B(T,p) < \frac{|A|}{\gamma}\right) \leq \exp(-t)$$

for $T = 256\left(\frac{1}{|A|n^2\alpha^2} + \frac{\beta}{n\alpha} + \frac{|A|\beta^2}{n}\right) + \left(\frac{4}{|A|n\alpha} + 3\beta\right)t$

□

The next result still concerns the "dynamic" expansion of any subset of nodes. It will be applied when the subset of informed node is large (say at least $n/2$) in order to get a good bound on the completion time of the last phase of the flooding process. Let us define the following r.v.

$$e_{i,A}^{\tau,T} = \begin{cases} 1 & \text{if } \exists\tau' \; \exists j \in A \; : \tau < \tau' \leq \tau+T \text{ and } \{i,j\} \in E_{\tau'} \\ 0 & \text{otherwise} \end{cases} \quad (6)$$

LEMMA 7. If $\mathcal{G}([n], \{E_t\}_{t \geq 0})$ is (M, α, β)-stationary then, $\forall \tau, t \geq 1$ it holds that, for every $A \subseteq [n]$ and for every $i \in [n] \setminus A$, it holds that

$$\mathbf{P}\left(e_{i,A}^{\tau,T} = 0 \;\middle|\; E_{\leq\tau}\right) \leq \exp(-t), \quad \text{where} \quad T = 2\left(\frac{1}{|A|\alpha} + \beta\right)t$$

Sketch of Proof. For brevity's sake, we omit the conditioning by $E_{\leq\tau}$. For every $s = 1, \ldots, T$, define r.v. $Y_s = e_{i,A}^{\tau+s}$. Observe that $Y_s = f_s(E_{\leq\tau+s})$ for a suitable function f_s. Lemma 4 implies

$$\mathbf{P}(Y_s = 1 \mid E_{\tau+s-1}) \geq p = \frac{|A|\alpha}{2+2|A|\alpha\beta}$$

By applying Lemma 2 to $E_{\tau+1}, \ldots, E_{\tau+T}$ and $Y_1, \ldots, Y_T$, we get

$$\mathbf{P}\left(\sum_{s=1}^{T} Y_s = 0\right) \leqslant \mathbf{P}\left(B(T, p) = 0\right) = (1 - p)^T \leqslant \exp(-t)$$

$\square$

Flooding Time. In what follows, we bound the time required to obtain at least $n/2$ informed nodes. This is the *spreading phase*.

LEMMA 8 (SPREADING PHASE). *If* $\mathcal{G}([n], \{E_t\}_{t \geqslant 0})$ *is* (M, α, β)-*stationary then,* $\forall \tau \geqslant \hat{T}$ *with*

$$\hat{T} = O\left(\left(\frac{1}{n\alpha} + \beta\right)^2 \log^2 n\right) \ then \ \mathbf{P}\left(|I_\tau| < \frac{n}{2}\right) \leqslant \frac{1}{n^2}$$

Sketch of Proof. Observe that, for any $|A|$, the bound on T for $t = \Theta(\log n)$ in Lemma 6 satisfies $T = O\left(\left(\frac{1}{n\alpha} + \beta\right)^2 \log n\right)$. From Lemma 6, after every time interval of T epochs, the size of the set of informed nodes at least doubles as far it is smaller than $n/2$, with high probability (say $1 - 1/n^2$). By a simple application of the Union Bound, we get that, after a $O(\log n)$ number of such time intervals, with high probability the number of informed nodes is at least $n/2$. $\square$
From Lemma 7, we can prove the following

LEMMA 9 (SATURATION PHASE). *Let* $\mathcal{G}([n], \{E_t\}_{t \geqslant 0})$ *be* (M, α, β)-*stationary and assume the flooding process is in some epoch* τ *such that* $|I_\tau| \geqslant n/2$. *Then, w.h.p. all nodes get informed within* $O\left(\left(\frac{1}{n\alpha} + \beta\right) \log n\right)$ *epochs.*

Finally, Theorem 1 is an easy consequence of Lemmas 8 and 9.

4. NODE MEGs

We introduce the general class of Node Markovian Evolving Graphs (in short, node-MEGs) where the behavior of the nodes is ruled by independent Markov chains. To every node is associated a Markov chain whose states contain enough information to determine whether two nodes are connected or not. Of course, this is an approach based upon hidden Markov chains to model dynamic graphs.

Let $\mathcal{M} = (S, P)$ be the Markov chain associated to every node, where S is the set of states and $P : S \times S \to \mathbb{R}$ are the transition probabilities. The connections are determined by a symmetric map $C : S \times S \to \{0, 1\}$: any two nodes i, j are connected at a given time t if $C(u, v) = 1$, where u, v are the states of i and j at time t. The symmetric map $C(\cdot, \cdot)$ is also called the connection graph of $\mathcal{M}$. A node-MEG is denoted by $NM(n, \mathcal{M}, C)$. Notice that the Markov chain $\mathcal{M}$ may depend on the number of nodes. The initial state of each node i is random with a probability distribution ι_i over the set of states S. We denote by ι the global initial probability distribution determined by the product of the probability distributions ι_i. The state of a node i at time t is a random variable s_i^t fully determined by the initial distribution ι_i and the Markov chain $\mathcal{M}$. A node-MEG $NM(n, \mathcal{M}, C)$ together with an initial probability distribution ι determines a dynamic graph $\mathcal{G}([n], \{E_t\}_{t \geqslant 0})$ where, for any $t \geqslant 0$, $E_t = \{\{i, j\} \mid C(s_i^t, s_j^t) = 1\}$. It is easy to verify that node-MEGs enjoy the following property.

FACT 10. *Given any node-MEG* NM $= NM(n, \mathcal{M}, C)$ *in its stationary state, define* P_{NM} *as the probability that any fixed pair of nodes are connected and* P_{NM2} *as the probability that two fixed nodes are both connected to another fixed one. Then, both* P_{NM} *and* P_{NM2} *do not depend on the choice of the fixed nodes: they are functions only of the stationary distribution of* $\mathcal{M}$ *and of the symmetric map* $C(\cdot, \cdot)$.

In Subsection 4.1, we will show that a wide class of mobility models turns out to be a special instance of Node-MEGs.

Flooding in Node-MEGs. We now derive some simple properties ensuring that a node-MEG $NM(n, \mathcal{M}, C)$ is a (M, α, β)-stationary dynamic graph. Since in a node-MEG, edges are not independent, the crucial condition is the β-independence. The models at hand are Markovian so the idea is to consider the model during its stationary state, that is, the time M between two consecutive epochs is proportional to the mixing time of the Markov chain $\mathcal{M}$. Moreover, the β-independence involves sets of incident edges of arbitrary size (i.e. the size of subset A): instead, thanks to the independence of node evolutions and Fact 10, in node-MEGs this condition can be relaxed to a parameterized *pairwise* independence among incident edges.

THEOREM 11. *Let* NM $= NM(n, \mathcal{M}, C)$ *be a node-MEG such that* $P_{\mathrm{NM}} \geqslant 1/n^{O(1)}$ *and* $P_{\mathrm{NM2}} \leqslant \eta(P_{\mathrm{NM}})^2$, *for some* $\eta \geqslant 1$. *Then, with high probability, the flooding time is*

$$O\left(T_{\mathrm{mix}}\left(\frac{1}{nP_{\mathrm{NM}}} + \eta\right)^2 \log^3 n\right)$$

where T_{mix} *is the mixing time of the Markov chain* $\mathcal{M}$.

4.1 Flooding in Classic Mobility Models

Geometric Mobility Models. Several mobility models can be represented as special cases of node-MEGs. Many of these are continuous-space models [7, 25] in which nodes move over a subset of $\mathbb{R}^d$. Since node-MEGs are discrete, we approximate continuous space by discretization. In the simplest and most common case, nodes move over a square of $\mathbb{R}^2$ of side length L. The square can be discretized by taking a square grid $\mathcal{Q}$ formed by $m \times m$ points regularly spaced in the square region, where m can be arbitrarily chosen.

In the standard random waypoint [7], n nodes independently move over the square: every node randomly chooses a speed in $[v_{min}, v_{max}]$ where $v_{max} = \Theta(v_{min})$ and a destination point ('waypoint') in the square and moves with the chosen speed on a straight path to this point. Then, it repeats the same process again and again. The destination points are uniformly distributed on the square. At any time two nodes are connected if they are at distance not larger than the transmission radius r.

The formal discretization of the random waypoint as a node-MEG can be done by simple and standard arguments [14], so we here provide an informal description only. The generic state of the Markov chain $\mathcal{M}$ must encode the destination point, the current point in the straight point-path the node lies, and the node speed (the latter can be defined as the number of points per time step). Then the transition matrix can be easily defined: when a node is in some internal point of a path the choice of his next state is deterministic while when he arrives at the end of a path, his next state is randomly chosen by selecting the next destination point (and thus the next path to be followed) and the speed. As usual, the connection map C is defined as follows: there is an edge between nodes u and v at time t iff their relative distance at time t is not larger than r. The *positional* probability distribution in the stationary phase is defined as the probability that a node is in point x (for any choice of x over the square) when the state of the node is random with the stationary distribution of $\mathcal{M}$. The density function of this distribution (in short, *positional function*) yielded by the random waypoint over the square will be denoted by $F_{wp}(\cdot)$. The random waypoint belongs to a general class of geometric mobility models called the *random trip model* [25] where the mobility space $\mathcal{R}$ can be any bounded connected region of $\mathbb{R}^d$ and the feasible node-trajectories can be any family of continuous curves. Any random trip model can be discretized with any level of "approximation" (in terms of grid resolution and time unit) by following the same procedure described above for the random waypoint. For this geometric class of node-MEGs, Theorem 11 can be rewritten in a very useful way.

For any $r \geqslant 0$, $D(u, r)$ denotes the set of all the points that are at Euclidean distance at most r from u. For any connected region $\mathcal{B} \subseteq \mathbb{R}^d$, define $\mathcal{B}_r = \{u \in \mathcal{B} \mid D(u, r) \subseteq \mathcal{B}\}$ and $\mathrm{vol}(\mathcal{B})$ as the volume of region $\mathcal{B}$.

COROLLARY 12. *Let* $\mathrm{NM} = NM(n, \mathcal{M}, C)$ *be a node-MEG yielded by a suitable discretization of a random trip model $\mathcal{T}$ over a bounded connected region $\mathcal{R} \subseteq \mathbb{R}^d$ with positional function $F_\mathcal{T}$. If $P_{\mathrm{NM}} \geqslant 1/n^{O(1)}$ and for some $\delta \geqslant 1$ and $\lambda > 0$ it holds that*

(a) $\forall u \in \mathcal{R}$, $F_\mathcal{T}(u) \leqslant \frac{\delta}{\mathrm{vol}(\mathcal{R})}$

(b) $\exists \mathcal{B} \subseteq \mathcal{R}$ such that $\mathrm{vol}(\mathcal{B}_r) \geqslant \lambda \mathrm{vol}(\mathcal{R})$ and $\forall u \in \mathcal{B}$, $F_\mathcal{T}(u) \geqslant \frac{1}{\delta \mathrm{vol}(\mathcal{R})}$

then, with high probability, the flooding time is

$$O\left(T_{\mathrm{mix}}\left(\frac{\delta^2 \mathrm{vol}(\mathcal{R})}{\lambda n r^d} + \frac{\delta^6}{\lambda^2}\right)^2 \log^3 n\right)$$

where T_{mix} is the mixing time of the Markov chain $\mathcal{M}$.

Sketch of Proof. Let π be the stationary distribution of the Markov chain $\mathcal{M}$ of NM. For any $x \in S$, let $u(x)$ be the point in $\mathcal{R}$ where a node is when its state is x. By assuming that the states of the nodes are random with π, let $q(x)$ be the probability that a fixed node is connected to another fixed node being in state x. Clearly,

$$q(x) = \sum_{y \in S \,:\, u(y) \in D(u(x), r)} \pi(y)$$

Since NM is a sufficiently refined discrete version of the random trip model $\mathcal{T}$, it holds that

$$q(x) \approx \int_{D(u(x), r)} F_\mathcal{T}(u) du \qquad (7)$$

From Hypothesis (b), for every $v \in \mathcal{B}_r$,

$$\forall u \in D(v, r) \qquad F_\mathcal{T}(u) \geqslant \frac{1}{\delta \mathrm{vol}(\mathcal{R})}$$

This implies that

$$\int_{D(v, r)} F_\mathcal{T}(u) du \geqslant \frac{\mathrm{vol}(D(v, r))}{\delta \mathrm{vol}(\mathcal{R})} = \frac{c_d r^d}{\delta \mathrm{vol}(\mathcal{R})} \qquad (8)$$

where c_d is a constant depending only on d. By combining (7) and (8), we have that, for every $x \in S$ with $u(x) \in \mathcal{B}_r$,

$$q(x) \gtrsim \frac{c_d r^d}{\delta \mathrm{vol}(\mathcal{R})} \qquad (9)$$

It holds that

$$\begin{aligned}
P_{\mathrm{NM}} &= \sum_{x \in S} \pi(x) q(x) \\
&\gtrsim \frac{c_d r^d}{\delta \mathrm{vol}(\mathcal{R})} \sum_{x \in S \,:\, u(x) \in \mathcal{B}_r} \pi(x) \qquad \text{(from Inequality (9))} \\
&\gtrsim \frac{c_d r^d}{\delta \mathrm{vol}(\mathcal{R})} \int_{\mathcal{B}_r} F_\mathcal{T}(u) du \\
&\gtrsim \frac{c_d r^d}{\delta \mathrm{vol}(\mathcal{R})} \frac{\mathrm{vol}(\mathcal{B}_r)}{\delta \mathrm{vol}(\mathcal{R})} \qquad \text{(from Hypothesis (b))} \\
&\gtrsim \frac{\lambda c_d r^d}{\delta^2 \mathrm{vol}(\mathcal{R})} \qquad \text{(from Hypothesis (b))} \qquad (10)
\end{aligned}$$

From (7) and Hypothesis (a), it derives that, for every $x \in S$,

$$q(x) \approx \int_{D(u(x), r)} F_\mathcal{T}(u) du \lesssim \frac{\delta \mathrm{vol}(D(u(x), r))}{\mathrm{vol}(\mathcal{R})} = \frac{\delta c_d r^d}{\mathrm{vol}(\mathcal{R})} \quad (11)$$

It holds that

$$\begin{aligned}
P_{\mathrm{NM2}} &= \sum_{x \in S} \pi(x) q(x)^2 \\
&\lesssim \left(\frac{\delta c_d r^d}{\mathrm{vol}(\mathcal{R})}\right)^2 \sum_{x \in S} \pi(x) \qquad \text{(from Inequality (11))} \\
&= \frac{\delta^2 c_d^2 r^{2d}}{\mathrm{vol}(\mathcal{R})^2}
\end{aligned}$$

From this and Inequality (10), we get

$$P_{\mathrm{NM2}} \lesssim \frac{\delta^2 c_d^2 r^{2d}}{\mathrm{vol}(\mathcal{R})^2} = \frac{\delta^6}{\lambda^2}\left(\frac{\lambda c_d r^d}{\delta^2 \mathrm{vol}(\mathcal{R})}\right)^2 \lesssim \frac{\delta^6}{\lambda^2}\left(P_{\mathrm{NM}}\right)^2$$

It follows that the node-MEG NM satisfies the hypotheses of Theorem 11 with $\eta = \delta^6/\lambda^2$ and thus, with high probability, the flooding time is

$$O\left(T_{\mathrm{mix}}\left(\frac{1}{n P_{\mathrm{NM}}} + \frac{\delta^6}{\lambda^2}\right)^2 \log^3 n\right) \leqslant$$

$$O\left(T_{\mathrm{mix}}\left(\frac{\delta^2 \mathrm{vol}(R)}{\lambda n r^d} + \frac{\delta^6}{\lambda^2}\right)^2 \log^3 n\right)$$

where we have used Inequality (10). $\square$

The useful novelty of the above corollary lies in the following fact: the pairwise-independence condition in Theorem 11 is transformed into two mild "uniformity" conditions on the positional function yielded by the mobility model. The latter only refer to the stationary positional distribution of the single node and it is often much easier to verify with respect to the pairwise condition. Indeed, a general method (the Palm Calculus) to derive explicit formulas of such function for random trip models has been introduced in [25]. As for the random waypoint on the square, the explicit positional function $F_{wp}(\cdot)$ has been derived in [26] and it is easy to verify that the two conditions of the above corollary are satisfied for some absolute constants δ and λ. Furthermore, the mixing time of the random waypoint over a square of side length L is $\Theta(L/v_{max})$ (remind we are assuming $v_{max} = O(v_{min})$)

[1, 30]. We thus obtain the following bound on the flooding time $O\left(\frac{L}{v_{max}}\left(\frac{L^2}{nr^2}+1\right)^2\log^3 n\right)$. Let us consider the case $L\sim\sqrt{n}$, $r=\Omega(1)$, and $r=O(v_{max})$; notice that this standard setting yields a stationary mobile network which is w.h.p. sparse and highly disconnected. Then the bound on the flooding time becomes $O\left(\frac{\sqrt{n}}{v_{max}}\log^3 n\right)$ which almost matches the trivial lower bound $\Omega\left(\frac{\sqrt{n}}{v_{max}}\right)$.

Graph Mobility Models. A natural generalization of random walks over a graph can be defined by considering random paths over a graph. This clearly includes the random waypoint over a graph. At every time step, a node moves along a path instead of on a single edge. More precisely, the model is specified by a graph $H(V,A)$ and a family $\mathcal{P}$ of feasible paths in H satisfying the property: for every path $h\in\mathcal{P}$, there is a path $h'\in\mathcal{P}$ such that h' starts where h ends. For any $u\in V$, let $\mathcal{P}(u)$ be the set of paths in $\mathcal{P}$ that starts at point u. The mobility model is as follows, a node at point $u\in V$ chooses uniformly at random a path in $\mathcal{P}(u)$, then it travels along the path (an edge at the time), when it reaches the end point v, it chooses uniformly at random a path in $\mathcal{P}(v)$ and travels along that path, and so on. We assume that two nodes are connected, at any given time t, if they are in the same point at time t. For any path h, let $\ell(h)$ denote the number of points of h. The representation of a random path model $RP=(H,\mathcal{P})$ as a node-MEG is straightforward. The Markov chain $\mathcal{M}_{RP}=(S,P)$ is such that:

$$S=\{(h,h_i)\mid h\in\mathcal{P},\ 2\leqslant i\leqslant\ell(h)\text{ and }h_i\text{ is the }i\text{th point of }h\};$$

the transition probabilities are as follows

$$\forall h\in\mathcal{P}\ \forall i:2\leqslant i<\ell(h)\qquad P((h,h_i),(h,h_{i+1}))=1$$

$$\forall h,h'\in\mathcal{P}:h_{\ell(h)}=h_1'\qquad P((h,h_{\ell(h)}),(h',h_2'))=\frac{1}{|\mathcal{P}(h_{\ell(h)})|}$$

all other transition probabilities are equal to zero; and the connection map is such that

$$C_{RP}((h,h_i),(h',h_j'))=1\text{ iff }h_i=h_j'$$

Observe that if $\mathcal{P}$ is the set of edges of H then the mobility model is equivalent to the random walk over H (with $\rho=1$).

We say that a path $h\in\mathcal{P}$ *passes through* a point u if $h_i=u$ for some $2\leqslant i\leqslant\ell(h)$ For any point $u\in V$, let $\#_{\mathcal{P}}(u)$ be the number of paths in $\mathcal{P}$ that passes through point u. Notice that if $\mathcal{P}$ is the set of edges of H, then $\#_{\mathcal{P}}(u)=\deg_H(u)$. A random-path model $RP=(H,\mathcal{P})$ is said to be *simple* if every path in $\mathcal{P}$ does not pass through the same point more than once, but the start and end points that may be equals. Moreover, RP is *reversible* if, for every path $h\in\mathcal{P}$, the reverse path of h also belongs to $\mathcal{P}$. We say that a random path model $(H,\mathcal{P})$ is δ-regular if

$$\forall u\in V\qquad \#_{\mathcal{P}}(u)\leqslant\delta\frac{\sum_{v\in V}\#_{\mathcal{P}}(v)}{|V|}$$

Roughly speaking δ-regularity ensures that no point is a much busier crossroad than the average. Theorem 11 then implies the following useful result.

COROLLARY 13. *Let* $NM=NM(n,\mathcal{M},C)$ *be a node-MEG yielded by a random path model* $RP=(H,\mathcal{P})$ *that is simple, reversible, δ-regular, and* $|V|\leqslant n^{O(1)}$. *Then, w.h.p the flooding time is*

$$O\left(T_{\text{mix}}\left(\frac{|V|}{n}+\delta^3\right)^2\log^3 n\right)$$

where T_{mix} *is the mixing time of the Markov chain* $\mathcal{M}$.

Sketch of Proof. It is easy to see that, any node-MEG yielded by a random-path model is a Markov Trace Model (MTM), a general class of models introduced in [14]. Since RP is simple and reversible, Theorem 11 in [14] implies that the stationary distribution π of $\mathcal{M}$ is uniform. For any state $x\in S$, let $u(x)\in V$ be the point where a node is when its state is x. By assuming that the states of the nodes are random with π, let $q(x)$ be the probability that a fixed node is connected to another fixed node being in state x. Since π is uniform and RP is simple, it holds that

$$q(x)=\sum_{y\in S\,:\,C(y,x)=1}\pi(x)=\frac{\#_{\mathcal{P}}(u(x))}{|S|}\qquad(12)$$

It follows that

$$P_{\text{NM}}=\sum_{x\in S}\pi(x)q(x)=\frac{1}{|S|^2}\sum_{x\in S}\#_{\mathcal{P}}(u(x))=\frac{1}{|S|^2}\sum_{u\in V}\#_{\mathcal{P}}(u)^2\qquad(13)$$

where the last equality derives from

$$|\{y\in S\mid u(y)=u\}|=\#_{\mathcal{P}}(u)$$

Thanks to Jensen's inequality it holds that

$$\frac{\sum_{u\in V}\#_{\mathcal{P}}(u)^2}{|V|}\geqslant\left(\frac{\sum_{u\in V}\#_{\mathcal{P}}(u)}{|V|}\right)^2=\frac{|S|^2}{|V|^2}$$

Thus, from (13), we have

$$P_{\text{NM}}\geqslant\frac{1}{|V|}\qquad(14)$$

From (12), it holds that

$$P_{\text{NM2}}=\sum_{x\in S}\pi(x)q(x)^2=\frac{1}{|S|^3}\sum_{x\in S}\#_{\mathcal{P}}(u(x))^2=\frac{1}{|S|^3}\sum_{u\in V}\#_{\mathcal{P}}(u)^3$$

Since RP is δ-regular and Ineq. (14) holds, it follows that

$$P_{\text{NM2}}=\frac{1}{|S|^3}\sum_{u\in V}\#_{\mathcal{P}}(u)^3\leqslant\frac{1}{|S|^3}\sum_{u\in V}\left(\delta\frac{\sum_{v\in V}\#_{\mathcal{P}}(v)}{|V|}\right)^3=$$

$$\frac{\delta^3}{|V|^2}\leqslant\delta^3\left(P_{\text{NM}}\right)^2$$

From this and taking into account the hypothesis $|V|\leqslant n^{O(1)}$ and Ineq. (14), Theorem 11 can be applied with $\eta=\delta^3$ obtaining that, with high probability, the flooding time is $O\left(T_{\text{mix}}\frac{|V|}{n}+\delta^3\right)^2\log^3 n\right)$. $\square$

If for every pair of points there is only one feasible simple path, then the mixing time of the relative Markov chain is $O(D)$, where D is the diameter of H. Moreover, if the model is δ-regular for $\delta=\text{polylog}(n)$ and $|V|=O(n\text{polylog}(n))$, then the above corollary implies that the flooding time is $O(D\,\text{polylog}(n))$. This is within a polylogarithmic factor from the optimum, since a trivial lower bound is $\Omega(D)$. A basic instance of this case is when H is a grid and the feasible paths are the shortest ones.

As mentioned in the Introduction, almost tight bounds for the flooding time on the random walk model over grids have been recently obtained in [11, 12, 28]. In a general graph $H(V, A)$, every node randomly chooses his next position among all points in V that are within ρ hops from his current position. The transmission radius r determines the maximal distance (again in terms of number of hops in $H(V, A)$) within which a message can be successfully transmitted. The most studied setting is $\rho = 1$ and $r = 0$: a node makes at most one hop per time step and it can infect only nodes that lies in the same point. This natural setting in general graphs has been studied in [16]: the flooding time is proved to be $O(T^* \log n)$ where T^* is the *meeting* time between two independent random walks on H.

In what follows we apply our analysis for the random path model to the special case of random walks. The δ-regularity condition over paths is transformed into a simple condition on the degree of the points. Given any $\delta \geqslant 1$, a graph $H(V, A)$ is said to be δ-regular if $(\max\{\deg(v) \mid v \in V\})/(\min\{\deg(v) \mid v \in V\}) \leqslant \delta$. Then, we can derive a simple adaptation of Corollary 13.

COROLLARY 14. *Let* $\mathrm{NM} = NM(n, \mathcal{M}, C)$ *be a node-MEG yielded by the random walk over any δ-regular mobility graph $H(V, A)$. Then, w.h.p the flooding time is*

$$O\left(T_{\mathrm{mix}}\left(\frac{\delta^2 |V|}{n} + \delta^7\right)^2 \log^3 n\right)$$

where T_{mix} is the mixing time of a random walk over H.

The above bound improves the result in [16] over a relevant and wide class of mobility graphs. Indeed, given a symmetric graph, the meeting time of two random walks is asymptotically equivalent to the first hitting time and can be much larger than the mixing time of a single random walk [1]. A natural example is that of k-augmented grids: take a grid of s points and add an edge between any pair of points whose hop-distance is not larger than k. While the meeting time is not smaller than that of a standard grid $\Theta(s \log s)$ [1, 28], the mixing time decreases in k. For instance, if $s \sim n\mathrm{polylog}(n)$ then the bound in [16] becomes $O(n\mathrm{polylog}(n))$ while our bound is $O((n\mathrm{polylog}(n))/k^2)$.

5. GENERALIZED EDGE-MEGS

The link-based dynamic model Edge-MEG has been introduced in [10] and successively studied in [4, 11, 18]. In this restricted instance of MEGs, edges evolves independently. Every edge of the n-node graph can be in two states only: *on* or *off*. At any time step, every edge changes its state according to a two-state Markovian process with probabilities p (edge birth-rate) and q (edge death-rate): if at time t an edge e exists then it will die with probability q while if e does not exists then it will come up with probability p. In [10], the authors prove an almost tight upper bound on the flooding time.

$$O\left(\frac{\log n}{\log(1 + np)}\right) \tag{15}$$

A more refined model with four states has been recently introduced and studied in [5]. Edge-MEGs do not explicitly model node's mobility, rather they are more suitable to model the link evolution in peer-to-peer networks or faulty networks.

Our main contribution here lies in the fact that Theorem 1 can be applied to the much more general version of edge-MEGs where an arbitrary (hidden) Markov chain $\mathcal{M} = (S, P)$ rules the behavior of every edge and by an arbitrary map $\chi : S \to \{0, 1\}$ that determines, in function of the state, whether the edge exists or not. This wide generalization of edge-MEG will be denoted as $EM(n, \mathcal{M}, \chi)$.

The initial state of each edge $\{i, j\}$ is random with a probability distribution $\iota_{\{i,j\}}$ over the set of states S. We denote by ι the global initial probability distribution determined by the product of the probability distributions $\iota_{\{i,j\}}$. The state of an edge $\{i, j\}$ at any time t is a random variable $s^t_{\{i,j\}}$ completely determined by the initial distribution $\iota_{\{i,j\}}$ and the Markov chain $\mathcal{M}$.

Any model $EM(n, \mathcal{M}, \chi)$ together with an initial probability distribution ι determines a dynamic graph $\mathcal{G}([n], \{E_t\}_{t \geqslant 0})$ where, for any $t \geqslant 0$, $E_t = \{\{i, j\} \mid \chi(s^t_{\{i,j\}}) = 1\}$. A crucial property of such generalized edge-MEGs is that edges are independent random variables, so it always holds that the β-independence is satisfied with $\beta = 1$. Then, when the Markov chain $\mathcal{M}$ admits a unique stationary distribution π, Theorem 1 implies that flooding time is

$$O\left(T_{\mathrm{mix}}\left(\frac{1}{n\alpha} + 1\right)^2 \log^2 n\right)$$

where T_{mix} is the mixing time of the Markov chain $\mathcal{M}$ and α is the probability an edge exists in the stationary regime (i.e. according to π). For instance, in the basic edge-MEG model with parameters p and q the mixing time is $\Theta(1/(p+q))$ and $\alpha = p/(p+q)$ [10]. We thus get an upper bound $O\left(\frac{1}{p+q}\left(\frac{p+q}{np} + 1\right)^2 \log^2 n\right)$. By comparing our bound to the (almost-tight) one in Eq. 15, we get that the former is almost tight whenever $q \geqslant np$.

6. CONCLUSIONS

We believe that significant improvements are possible to the bound in Theorem 1 along some interesting directions. We suspect that, under mild assumptions on the dynamic graph process, the factor $(\frac{1}{n\alpha} + \beta)^2$ can be improved. A more challenging task is to avoid the dependency of the bound on the mixing time of the graph process. The density and β-independence conditions can be met even at a state in which the graph process is far from the stationary distribution, and so a more refined analysis might be able to bound the flooding time without having to "wait" for the process to achieve stationarity.

Our method may prove useful in the analysis of more refined communication protocols than flooding. A simple example is a randomized protocol in which, at every step, a node that possesses the information transmits it to a randomly chosen subset of neighbors. The analysis of such a process can be reduced to the analysis of flooding in a "virtual" dynamic graph in which a subset of the edges are removed. More general communication protocols might also be reduced to flooding by folding the actions of the protocol into the dynamic graph process.

Acknowledgments. We thank Francesco Pasquale and Alessandro Pettarin for carefully reading a previous version of our paper and for providing helpful comments.

45

7. REFERENCES

[1] D. Aldous and J.A. Fill. *Reversible Markov Chains and Random Walks on Graphs.* (Chp. 14) Available at http://www.stat.berkeley.edu/ aldous/RWG/book.html, 1999.

[2] C. Avin and M. Koucky and Z. Lotker. How to explore a fast-changing world. In *Proc. of 35th ICALP'08*, LNCS, 5125, 121–132, 2008.

[3] Y. Azar, A.Z. Broder, A.R. Karlin, and E. Upfal Balanced allocation. *SIAM J. on Computing*, vol. 29(1) pp. 180-200, 1999.

[4] H. Baumann, P. Crescenzi, and P. Fraigniaud. Parsimonious flooding in dynamic graphs. In *Proc. of the 28th ACM PODC '09*, 2009.

[5] L. Becchetti, A.E.F. Clementi, F. Pasquale, G. Resta, P. Santi, and R. Silvestri. Information Spreading in Opportunistic Networks is Fast. arXiv:1107.5241v1, 2011.

[6] C. Bettstetter, G. Resta, and P. Santi. The Node Distribution of the Random Waypoint Mobility Model for Wireless Ad Hoc Networks. *IEEE Transactions on Mobile Computing*, 2, 257–269, 2003.

[7] T. Camp, J. Boleng, and V. Davies A survey of mobility models for ad hoc network research. *Wireless Communication and Mobile Computing*, 2(5):483-502, 2002.

[8] T. Camp, W. Navidi, and N. Bauer. Improving the accuracy of random waypoint simulations through steady-state initialization. In *Proc. of 15th Int. Conf. on Modelling and Simulation*, pages 319–326, 2004.

[9] A. Clementi, A. Monti, F. Pasquale, and R. Silvestri. Broadcasting in dynamic radio networks. *J. Comput. Syst. Sci.*, 75(4), 2009 (preliminary version in ACM PODC 2007).

[10] A. Clementi, C. Macci, A. Monti, F. Pasquale, R. Silvestri Flooding Time of Edge-Markovian Evolving Graphs. *SIAM J. Discrete Math.* 24(4): 1694-1712 (2010) (Ext. Abs. in *ACM PODC* 2008).

[11] A. Clementi, A. Monti, F. Pasquale, and R. Silvestri Information spreading in stationary markovian evolving graph. *IEEE Trans. Parallel Distrib. Syst.*, 22(9): 1425–1432, 2011 (Ext. Abs. in *IEEE IPDPS* 2009).

[12] A. Clementi, F. Pasquale, and R. Silvestri. Manets: High mobility can make up for low transmission power. In *Proc. of the 36th ICALP'09*, LNCS 5556, 387–398, Springer, 2009.

[13] A. Clementi, A. Monti, and R. Silvestri. Flooding over Manhattan. In Proc. of *29th ACM PODC'10*. Full version in http://arxiv.org/abs/1002.3757.

[14] A. Clementi, A. Monti, and R. Silvestri. Modelling Mobility: a Discrete Revolution. *Ad Hoc Networks*, 9(6), 998–1014, 2011 (Ext. Abs. in *ICALP'10*).

[15] A. Clementi, R. Silvestri, and L.Trevisan. Information Spreading in Dynamic Graphs. arXiv:1111.0583v2.

[16] T. Dimitriou, S. Nikoletseas, and P. Spirakis. The infection time of graphs. In *Discrete Applied Mathematics*, 154 (8), 2577–2589, 2006.

[17] B. Ghosh, F. T. Leighton, B. M. Maggs, S. Muthukrishnan, C. G. Plaxton, R. Rajaraman, A.W. Richa, R. E. Tarjan, and D. I. Zuckerman. Tight analyses of two local load balancing algorithms. *SIAM Journal on Computing*, 29(1):29-64, 1999.

[18] P. Grindrod and D.J. Higham. Evolving graphs: dynamical models, inverse problems and propagation. *Proc. R. Soc. A*, 466(2115), 753–770, 2010

[19] P. Jacquet, B. Mans, and G. Rodolakis. Information Propagation Speed in Mobile and Delay Tolerant Networks. *IEEE Transaction on Information Theory*, 56, 5001–5015, 2010.

[20] T. Karagiannis, J.-Y. Le Boudec, and M. Vojnovic. Power Law and Exponential Decay of Inter Contact Times Between Mobile Devices. In *Proc. 13th ACM MOBICOM*, 183–194, 2007.

[21] H. Kesten and V. Sidoravicius. The spread of a rumor or infection in a moving population. In *Annals of Probability*, 33 (6), 2402–2462, 2005.

[22] F. Kuhn, N. Linch, and R. Oshman. Distributed Computation in Dynamic Networks. In *Proc. 42nd ACM STOC*, 513–522. ACM, 2010.

[23] F. Kuhn, and R. Oshman. Dynamic networks: models and algorithms. *ACM SIGACT News*, 42(1), 82–96, 2011.

[24] H. Lam, Z. Liu, M. Mitzenmacher, X. Sun, Y. Wang Information Dissemination via Random Walks in d-Dimensional Space. In *Proc. 23rd ACM-SIAM SODA*, to appear 2012 (Full version in ArXive arXiv:1104.5268v2).

[25] J.-Y. Le Boudec and M. Vojnovic. The Random Trip Model: Stability, Stationary Regime, and Perfect Simulation. *IEEE/ACM Transactions on Networking*, 14(6), 1153–1166, 2006.

[26] J.-Y. Le Boudec. Understanding the simulation of mobility models with Palm calculus. *Performance Evaluation*, 64(2), 126–147, 2007.

[27] Y. Peres, A. Sinclair, P. Sousi, and A. Stauffer. Mobile Geometric Graphs: Detection, Coverage and Percolation. In *Proc. 22nd ACM-SIAM SODA*, pages 412–428. 2011.

[28] A. Pettarin, A. Pietracaprina, G. Pucci, and E. Upfal. Tight Bounds on Information Dissemination in Sparse Mobile Networks. In *Proc. 30th ACM PODC*, 355–362, 2011.

[29] Y. Rabani, A. Sinclair and R. Wanka. Local Divergence of Markov chains and the analysis of iterative load-balancing schemes *Proc. of 39th IEEE FOCS*, 694-703, 1998.

[30] T. Spyropoulos, A. Jindal, and K. Psounis. An analytical study of fundamental mobility properties for encounter based protocols. *Int. J. Auton. Adapt. Commun. Syst.*, 1(1), 4–40, 2008.

Coalescing Random Walks and Voting on Graphs[*]

Colin Cooper
Department of Informatics
King's College London
London WC2R 2LS, UK
colin.cooper@kcl.ac.uk

Robert Elsässer
Institute of Informatics
University of Paderborn
Paderborn, Germany D-33102
elsa@upb.de

Hirotaka Ono
Dept. Economic Engineering
University of Kyushu
Fukuoka 812-8581, Japan
ono@csce.kyushu-u.ac.jp

Tomasz Radzik
Department of Informatics
King's College London
London WC2R 2LS, UK
tomasz.radzik@kcl.ac.uk

ABSTRACT

In a *coalescing random walk*, a set of particles make independent discrete-time random walks on a graph. Whenever one or more particles meet at a vertex, they unite to form a single particle, which then continues the random walk through the graph. Coalescing random walks can be used to achieve consensus in distributed networks, and is the basis of the self-stabilizing mutual exclusion algorithm of Israeli and Jalfon [14].

Let $G = (V, E)$, be an undirected, connected n vertex graph. Let $C(n)$ be the expected time for all particles to coalesce, when initially one particle is located at each vertex. We study the problem of bounding the coalescence time $C(n)$ for general classes of graphs. Our general result is, that $C(n) = O(n/(\nu(1 - \lambda_2)))$, where $\nu = \sum_{v \in V} d^2(v)/(d^2 n)$, $d(v)$ is the degree of vertex v, d is the average vertex degree, and λ_2 is the second eigenvalue of the transition matrix of the random walk. The parameter ν is an indicator of the variability of vertex degrees: $1 \leq \nu = O(n)$, with $\nu = 1$ for regular graphs. Our general bound on $C(n)$ holds provided the maximum vertex degree is $O(m^{1-\epsilon})$, where m is the number of edges in the graph. This result implies, for example, that $C(n) = O(n/(1 - \lambda_2))$ for d-regular graphs with expansion parameterized by the eigenvalue gap $1 - \lambda_2$. The $O(n/(\nu(1 - \lambda_2)))$ bound is sublinear for some classes of graphs with skewed degree distributions.

A system of coalescing particles where initially one particle is located at each vertex, corresponds to the following *voter model*. Initially each vertex has a distinct opinion, and at each step each vertex changes its opinion to that of a random neighbour. The voting process can be used for leader election in a distributed context. Let $\mathbf{E}(C_v)$ be the

expected time for voting to complete, that is, for a unique opinion to emerge. It is known that $\mathbf{E}(C_v) = C(n)$, so our results imply that $\mathbf{E}(C_v) = O(n/(\nu(1 - \lambda_2)))$.

We also investigate how the voting time improves when a vertex elicits more than one opinion at each step. In a model which we call *min-voting*, each vertex initially holds a distinct opinion drawn from a linearly ordered domain. At each step each vertex takes the opinions of two random neighbours and keeps the smaller. We show that for regular graphs with very good expansion properties, voting is completed in $O(\log n)$ time with high probability. This result can be viewed as an example of the "power of two choices" in distributed voting.

Categories and Subject Descriptors

F.2.2 [**Analysis of Algorithms and Problem Complexity**]: Nonnumerical Algorithms and Problems—*Computations on discrete structures*

General Terms

Theory, Algorithms

Keywords

Random walks, Distributed voting

1. INTRODUCTION

In a *coalescing random walk*, a set of particles make independent random walks in an undirected connected graph $G = (V, E)$ with n vertices and m edges. Whenever two or more particles meet at a vertex, then they unite to form a single particle which then continues to make a random walk through the graph. The expected time for the particles to coalesce to a single particle depends on their initial positions. Let $C_k(i_1, ..., i_k)$, $2 \leq k \leq n$, be the coalescence time when there are initially k particles starting from distinct vertices $i_1, ..., i_k$. The quantity we study is

$$C(k) = \max_{i_1, ..., i_k} \mathbf{E}(C_k(i_1, ..., i_k)),$$

the worst case expected coalescence time. For the special case of two particles, $C(2)$ is more naturally referred to as the (worst case expected) *meeting time* of two random walks.

[*]Work supported by Royal Society IJP grant "Random walks, interacting particles and faster network exploration."

A system of n coalescing particles where initially one particle is located at each vertex, corresponds to another classical problem, the *voter model*, defined as follows. Initially each vertex has a distinct opinion, and at each step each vertex changes its opinion to that of a random neighbour. We will also use the term *random voting* to refer to this process.

Let C_v be the number of steps for voting to be completed, i.e., for a unique opinion to emerge. The random variable C_v has the same distribution, and hence the same expected value, as the coalescence time C_n of n coalescing particles, where one particle is initially located at each vertex, (see [2]). Thus $C(n) \equiv E(C_n) = E(C_v)$. The expected completion time $\mathbf{E}(C_v)$ of voting is also called the *voting time*, the *trapping time* or the *consensus time*.

The coalescing random walk is the key ingredient in the self-stabilizing mutual exclusion algorithm of Israeli and Jalfon [14]. Initially each vertex emits a token which makes a random walk on G. On meeting at a vertex, tokens coalesce. Provided the graph is connected, and not bipartite, eventually only one token will remain, and the vertex with the token has exclusive access to some resource. The token makes a random walk on G, so in the long run it will visit all vertices of G in proportion to their stationary distribution.

The results given in this paper. We study the problem of bounding the coalescence time $C(n)$ for general classes of graphs. Our general result is the bound

$$C(n) = O\left(\frac{n}{\nu(1-\lambda_2)}\right), \qquad (1)$$

where λ_2 is the second eigenvalue of the transition matrix of the random walk, the parameter ν is equal to

$$\nu \overset{\text{dfn}}{=} \frac{\sum_{v \in V} d^2(v)}{d^2 n}, \qquad (2)$$

$d(v)$ is the degree of vertex v, and d is the average degree. This parameter $\nu \geq 1$ measures the variability of the degree sequence, and ranges from 1 for regular graphs to $\Theta(n)$ for a star graph. Our general bound (1) on $C(n)$ holds provided the maximum degree Δ satisfies the (weak) condition that $\Delta = O(m^{1-\epsilon})$, where ϵ is an arbitrarily small positive constant. For d-regular graphs with expansion parameterized by the *eigenvalue gap* $1 - \lambda_2$, the bound (1) implies $C(n) = O(n/(1-\lambda_2))$.

The bound (1) and the correspondence between the coalescence model and the voting model mentioned earlier implies a simple voting protocol, which reaches consensus in $O(n)$ steps whenever $\nu(1 - \lambda_2)$ is greater than a positive constant. In applications of voting in distributed computing, however, one may need a faster completion time, ideally of the order of $O(\log n)$, if a graph is well connected. Continuing with the idea of voting based on adopting the opinion of a random neighbour, but aiming to speed-up the completion time, we investigate also a voting protocol when each vertex elicits more than one opinion at each step. Our specific model, which we call the *min-voting*, is defined as follows. Initially each vertex holds a distinct opinion drawn from a linearly ordered domain, and at each step each vertex takes the opinions of two random neighbours and keeps the smaller of the two (disregarding its own opinion). The two neighbours are not necessarily distinct. We establish that for regular graphs with very good expansion properties (in the sense of [7]), the min-voting is completed in $O(\log n)$ steps with high probability. Throughout this paper, "with

high probability," or **whp**, means with probability tending to 1 as $n \to \infty$. Formal statements of our results are given later in Sections 1.1 and 1.2.

Previous work on coalescing walks and voting systems. We next summarize some of what is known about these topics. In a variant of the voter model, the *two-party model*, initially there are only two opinions A and B, and the voting is completed when all vertices have the same opinion. Donnelly and Welsh [9] considered the continuous-time two-party voter model and its relation to the continuous-time coalescing random walks. In the *continuous-time* models each vertex v, independently of other vertices, waits for a random time t_v and then performs an instantaneous "action" (changing its opinion or sending the walk to a neighbouring vertex), where t_v has the exponential distribution with mean 1. Hassin and Peleg [12] and Nakata *et al.* [19] considered the *discrete-time* two-party voter model, and discussed its application to agreement problems in distributed systems. Both papers [12] and [19] focus on analysing the probability that all vertices will eventually adopt the opinion which is initially held by a given group of vertices. The central result is that the probability that opinion A wins is $d(A)/(2m)$, where $d(A)$ is the sum of the degrees of the vertices initially holding opinion A, and m is the number of edges in G.

Let $H_{u,v}$ denote the *hitting time* of vertex v starting from vertex u, that is, the random variable which gives the time taken by a random walk starting from vertex u to reach vertex v; and let $H_{\max} = \max_{u,v} \mathbf{E}(H_{u,v})$. Aldous [1] considered the continuous-time model and showed an upper bound $O(H_{\max})$ and a lower bound $\Omega(m/\Delta)$ on $C(2)$ – the meeting time of two random walks – where Δ is the maximum degree of a vertex in G. These upper and lower bounds can be far apart. For example, for a star graph (with loops), $C(2) = \Theta(1)$ whereas the bounds give $\Omega(1) \leq C(2) = O(n)$.

The $O(H_{\max})$ bound on $C(2)$ implies immediately that $C(n) = O(H_{\max} \log n)$, since the number of particles halves in $O(H_{\max})$ time, but Aldous [1] conjectured that $C(n)$ is actually $O(H_{\max})$. Earlier results by Cox [6] implied that in the continuous-time model, $C(n) = O(H_{\max})$ for constant dimension tori and grids. Aldous and Fill [2] give further bounds for the coalescence time in the continuous-time model, showing that $C(n) \leq e(\log n + 2)H_{\max}$ for regular graphs, $C(n) \leq dn^2/(4s)$ for d-regular s-edge connected graphs, $C(n) \sim n$ for complete graphs (where $f(n) \sim g(n)$ means that $f(n) = (1 \pm o(1))g(n)$). Cooper *et al.* [5] showed that Aldous' conjecture $C(n) = O(H_{\max})$ holds for discrete-time random walks on random regular graphs. They proved that for r-regular random graphs $C(n) \sim 2((r-1)/(r-2))n$, with high probability.

In parallel with our work, Oliveira [20] has recently proved that the conjecture $C(n) = O(H_{\max})$ is true for the continuous-time random walks. We do not know, however, whether this result implies the same bound for discrete-time random walks which we consider in this paper. We note that our bound (1) can be better than $O(H_{\max})$, if $\nu = \omega(1)$. Moreover, our bound can be better than $O(H_{\max})$ also when $\nu = \Theta(1)$, since there are graphs with $H_{\max} = \omega(n/(1-\lambda_2))$.

Our voting models can be viewed as selection or aggregation processes. There is a large amount of research focusing on distributed selection and aggregation in different scenarios and various settings (see e.g. [15, 16] or [3] for a survey). Here, we only mention the result of Doerr *et al.* [8], in which the following process related to min-voting is analysed. At the beginning each vertex of a complete graph has its own opinion. In each step every vertex contacts two other vertices uniformly at random, and changes its opinion to the median of the opinions of these two vertices and its own opinion. It is shown in [8] that this rule converges in $O(\log n)$ steps to a single opinion, **whp**. While there are simpler schemes which achieve consensus in $O(\log n)$ time, the protocol of [8] has the important property of being robust against an adversary which manipulates the opinions of some vertices. Our interest in the min-voting has been partially motivated by the fact that the analysis of the median voting given in [8] cannot be directly extended to sparse graphs with good expansion properties.

1.1 Our Results: Coalescence and Voting

We assume that the graphs G we consider are not bipartite, or that if G is bipartite, then each coalescing random walk is lazy and pauses with probability $1/2$ at each step. Equivalently, for the voting process, we assume that vertices may choose their own opinion with this probability. We prove the following very general theorem.

THEOREM 1. *Let G be a connected graph with n vertices, m edges, average vertex degree d, and maximum degree $\Delta = O(m^{1-\epsilon})$, for an arbitrary constant $\epsilon > 0$. Let $C(n)$ be the expected coalescence time for a system on n particles making a lazy random walk on G, where originally one particle starts at each vertex. Then, for the parameter ν defined in (2),*

$$C(n) = O\left(\frac{n}{\nu(1-\lambda_2)}\right). \qquad (3)$$

Thus by the equivalence between coalescence and voting, the expected time $\mathbf{E}(C_v)$ to complete voting on G has the same upper bound.

The parameter ν is related to the second moment of the degree distribution and measures the variability of the degree sequence. It is easy to see that $1 \leq \nu \leq \Delta/d \leq n$. The result (3) holds provided the bound $\Delta = O(m^{1-\epsilon})$, which is satisfied by many classes of graphs.

For *near regular* graphs, when the ratio of the largest to the smallest vertex degree is bounded by a constant, we have $\nu \leq \Delta/d = O(1)$, so the bound (3) becomes

$$C(n) = O\left(\frac{n}{1-\lambda_2}\right).$$

In particular, if G is an expander in the classic sense that it is regular and its eigenvalue gap $(1 - \lambda_2)$ is constant, then $C(n) = O(n)$. Oliveira's recent results [20] imply an analogous linear bound for continuous-time random walks on expanders.

As $1 - \lambda_2 \geq 1/2n^2$ for any connected graph (see e.g. Sinclair [22]) our bound shows that coalescence is completed in $O(n^3)$ expected time on any connected n vertex graph, provided the required bound on Δ. Hassin and Peleg [12] showed that the voting (hence also coalescence) is completed in expected $O(n^3 \log n)$ time on any connected graph. Our bound parameterized by the eigenvalue gap can be viewed as refinement of such absolute bounds.

For graphs with skewed degree distributions, Theorem 1 can give sublinear bounds on the coalescence and voting times as the following example shows. Mihail *et al.* [11]

results imply that for $2 < \alpha < 3$, the random $\Theta(n)$-vertex graph with $\lceil n/d^\alpha \rceil$ vertices of degree d, for $d = 3, 4, \ldots, n^{1/2}$, has an $\Omega(\log^{-2} n)$ eigenvalue gap. For this class of power law graphs, $\nu = \Theta\left(n^{(3-\alpha)/2}\right)$, so Theorem 1 implies a sublinear $O(n^{(\alpha-1)/2} \log^2 n)$ voting time. Observe that for any graph, $H_{\max} = \Omega(n)$.

There are also examples of graphs with $\nu = \Theta(1)$ for which our bound is asymptotically better than $O(H_{\max})$. Consider the graph consisting of $(\log n)$-degree expander $(1 - \lambda_2 \leq c < 1)$ with an additional vertex attached to one of the vertices of the expander. For this graph $\nu = \Theta(1)$ and $1 - \lambda_2$ is a positive constant, so $C(n) = O(n)$, but $H_{\max} = \Theta(n \log n)$.

The proof of Theorem 1 is based on the following theorem bounding the time to first meeting between any of k particles.

THEOREM 2. *For $2 \leq k \leq k^* = \log^3 n$ particles starting from arbitrary vertices in G, let M_k be the time to first meeting. If the maximum degree $\Delta = o(m/\log^6 n)$ and ν is given by (2), then*

$$\mathbf{E}(M_k) = O\left(\frac{1}{1-\lambda_2}\left(k \log n + \frac{n}{\nu k^2}\right)\right). \qquad (4)$$

Theorem 2 is proven in Sections 2–4 and Theorem 1 is proven in Section 5.

1.2 Our Results: Min-Voting on Expanders

We analyse the min-voting on d-regular graphs $G = (V, E)$ with good global expansion properties. Let $\lambda_1 \geq \lambda_2 \geq \cdots \geq \lambda_n$ be the eigenvalues of the transition matrix of the random walk on G, and let $\lambda = \max\{\lambda_2, |\lambda_n|\}$. We assume that $\lambda \leq c/\sqrt{d}$ for some constant c, where $c \ll \sqrt{d}$ if $d = O(1)$. In terms of the previous theorems, this corresponds to a second eigenvalue gap $1 - \lambda_2(P)$ of the transition matrix of size $1 - c/\sqrt{d} > 0$. We call such a connected graph an *almost Ramanujan* or *expanding* (cf. [7]).

As shown in [4, 7], these graphs satisfy the following expansion properties. For a subset of vertices $A \subseteq V$, we denote $\overline{A} = V \setminus A$. If d is large enough, then there exists a constant β such that for any constant ϕ, sufficiently small $\alpha > 0$, and any $A \subset V$ with $|A| \leq n/2$:

1. $\alpha d|A| \leq |E(A, \overline{A})| \leq \frac{d \cdot |A| \cdot |\overline{A}|}{n} + \lambda d\sqrt{|A| \cdot |\overline{A}|}$;

2. if $|A| \leq \min\{\phi n/d, n/2\}$, then $|N(A)| \geq \alpha d|A|$;

3. the number of vertices in $\overline{A}$ with at least $\alpha d|A|/n$ neighbours in A is at least $|\overline{A}| - \frac{\beta n^2}{d|A|}$.

Here $E(A, \overline{A})$ represents the set of edges between A and $V \setminus A$ and $N(A)$ is the set of neighbours of A in $V \setminus A$. In the following, we assume that d is large enough, and α, ϕ, and β do not depend on d. It is easy to see that if the definition holds for some α (where ϕ is fixed), then it also holds for values smaller than α. Hence, we assume that α is arbitrarily small and ϕ is arbitrarily large.

We obtain the following result for the min-voting on this class of graphs.

THEOREM 3. *Let $G = (V, E)$ be a d-regular almost Ramanujan graph, where d is greater than some large constant value. Applying the min-voting, after a certain number of $O(\log n)$ steps all vertices will have the same opinion, **whp**.*

The proof of this theorem consists of three parts, which correspond to three main phases of the voting. In the first part, we show that at the end of the first $(\log \log n)^2$ steps, each small opinion either is removed from the graph or resides at $\Omega(\log^2 n)$ vertices. In the second part, we show that after the subsequent $O(\log n)$ steps, at least $n/2$ vertices have the same (currently smallest) opinion in the graph (which at this time is not necessarily the initial smallest opinion). Finally, we show that after additional $O(\log n)$ steps, all vertices will adopt this opinion. The full proof of Theorem 3 is given in Section 6.

2. RANDOM WALK PROPERTIES

Let $G = (V, E)$ denote a connected undirected graph, $|V| = n$, $|E| = m$, and let $d(v)$ be the degree of a vertex v. A *simple random walk* $\mathcal{W}_u$, $u \in V$, on graph G is a Markov chain modeled by a particle moving from vertex to vertex according to the following rule. The probability of transition from vertex v to vertex w is equal to $1/d(v)$, if w is a neighbour of v, and 0 otherwise. The walk $\mathcal{W}_u$ starts from vertex u at $t = 0$. Denote by $\mathcal{W}_u(t)$ the vertex reached at step t; $\mathcal{W}_u(0) = u$.

We assume the random walk $\mathcal{W}_u$ on G is ergodic with stationary distribution π, where $\pi_v = d(v)/(2m)$. If this is not the case, e.g. G is bipartite, then the walk can be made ergodic, by making it lazy. A random walk is *lazy*, if it moves from v to one of its neighbours w with probability $1/(2d(v))$, and stays where it is (at vertex v) with probability $1/2$.

Let $P = P(G)$ be the matrix of transition probabilities of the walk and let $P_u^t(v) = \mathbf{Pr}(\mathcal{W}_u(t) = v)$. Let the eigenvalues of $P(G)$ be $\lambda_1 = 1 \geq \lambda_2 \geq \cdots \geq \lambda_n > -1$, as we assume G is not bipartite, or the random walk is lazy. Let $\lambda = \max(\lambda_2, |\lambda_n|)$. The rate of convergence of the walk is given by

$$|P_u^t(x) - \pi_x| \leq (\pi_x/\pi_u)^{1/2} \lambda^t, \qquad (5)$$

see for example, Lovász [18]. We assume henceforth that $\lambda = \lambda_2$. If not, the standard way to ensure that $\lambda = \lambda_2 = \lambda_2(G)$, is to make the chain lazy.

We use the following definition of mixing time T_G, for a graph G. For all vertices u and x in G and any $t \geq T_G$,

$$|P_u^{(t)}(x) - \pi_x| \leq o\left(\frac{1}{n^2}\right). \qquad (6)$$

For convenience we assume that $T_G = \Omega(\log n)$, even if this is not necessary.

Let $\mathbf{E}_\pi(H_w)$ denote the expected hitting time of a vertex w from the stationary distribution π. The quantity $\mathbf{E}_\pi(H_w)$ can be expressed as (see e.g. [2], Chapter 2)

$$\mathbf{E}_\pi(H_v) = Z_{vv}/\pi_v, \qquad (7)$$

where

$$Z_{vv} = \sum_{t=0}^{\infty} (P_v^{(t)}(v) - \pi_v). \qquad (8)$$

Let $A_v(t; u)$ denote the event that $\mathcal{W}_u$ does not visit vertex v in steps $0, ..., t$. The following lemma gives a bound on the probability of this event in terms of $\mathbf{E}_\pi(H_v)$ and the mixing time of the walk.

LEMMA 1. *Let $T = T_G$ be a mixing time of a random walk $\mathcal{W}_u$ on G satisfying (6). Then*

$$\mathbf{Pr}(A_v(t; u)) \leq e^{-\lfloor t/(T + 3\mathbf{E}_\pi(H_v)) \rfloor}.$$

PROOF. Let $\rho \equiv P_u^{(T)}$ be the distribution of $\mathcal{W}_u$ on G after T steps. Then (6) and the fact that $\pi_x = \Omega(1/n^2)$ for any connected graph imply

$$\mathbf{E}_\rho(H_v) = (1 + o(1))\mathbf{E}_\pi(H_v). \qquad (9)$$

Let $H_v(\rho)$ be the time to hit v starting from ρ, and let $\tau = T + 3\mathbf{E}_\pi(H_v)$. Then, noting that $\mathbf{E}_\rho(H_v) \equiv \mathbf{E}(H_v(\rho))$,

$$
\begin{aligned}
\mathbf{Pr}(A_v(\tau; u)) &= \mathbf{Pr}(A_v(T; u) \text{ and } H_v(\rho) \geq 3\mathbf{E}_\pi(H_v)) \\
&\leq \mathbf{Pr}(H_v(\rho) \geq 3\mathbf{E}_\pi(H_v)) \\
&\leq \mathbf{Pr}(H_v(\rho) \geq e \cdot \mathbf{E}(H_v(\rho))) \\
&\leq \frac{1}{e}.
\end{aligned}
$$

By restarting the process $\mathcal{W}_u$ at $\mathcal{W}_u(0) = u$, $\mathcal{W}_u(\tau)$, $\mathcal{W}_u(2\tau)$, $..., \mathcal{W}_u(\lfloor t/\tau \rfloor \tau)$, we obtain

$$\mathbf{Pr}(A_v(t; u)) \leq e^{-\lfloor t/\tau \rfloor}.$$

□

3. MULTIPLE RANDOM WALKS

We consider the coalescence of $k \geq 2$ independent random walks on a graph $G = (V_G, E_G)$. To do this we replace the k walks by a single walk as follows.

Let graph $Q = Q_k = (V_Q, E_Q)$ have vertex set $V_Q = V^k$. Thus a vertex $\boldsymbol{v}$ of Q_k is a k-tuple $\boldsymbol{v} = (v_1, v_2, ..., v_k)$ of vertices $v_i \in V_G$, $i = 1, ..., k$, with repeats allowed. Two vertices $\boldsymbol{v}, \boldsymbol{w} \in V_Q$ are adjacent if $\{v_1, w_1\}, ..., \{v_k, w_k\}$ are edges of G. There is a direct equivalence between k random walks $\mathcal{W}_{u_i}(t)$ on G with starting positions u_i and a single random walk $\mathcal{W}_{\boldsymbol{u}}(t)$ on Q_k with starting position $\boldsymbol{u} = (u_1, u_2, ..., u_k)$.

For any starting positions $\boldsymbol{u} = (u_1, ..., u_k)$ of the walks, let $M_k(\boldsymbol{u})$ be the time until the first meeting in G. Let $S_k \subseteq V(Q_k)$, the *diagonal set of vertices*, be defined by

$$S = S_k = \{(v_1, ..., v_k) : v_i = v_j \text{ some } 1 \leq i < j \leq k\}.$$

If the random walk on Q_k visits this set, two particles occupy the same vertex in the underlying graph G and a (coalescing) meeting occurs.

Since visits to a set by a random walk is not a readily manipulated quantity, an easier approach is to contract S_k to a single vertex $\gamma = \gamma_k = \gamma(S_k)$, thus replacing Q_k by a graph $\Gamma = \Gamma_k$. On contraction, all edges, including loops, are retained. Thus $d_\Gamma(\gamma) = d_Q(S)$, where d_F denotes vertex degree in graph F, and the degree $d_F(X)$ of a set X is the sum of the degrees of the vertices in X. Moreover Γ and Q have the same total degree, and the degree of any vertex of Γ other than γ is the same as in graph Q. Let π and $\hat{\pi}$ be the stationary distributions of a random walk on Q and Γ, respectively. If $\boldsymbol{v} \notin S$ then $\hat{\pi}_{\boldsymbol{v}} = \pi_{\boldsymbol{v}}$, and $\hat{\pi}_\gamma = \pi_S \equiv \sum_{\boldsymbol{x} \in S} \pi_{\boldsymbol{x}}$.

It follows that, if T_Γ is a mixing time satisfying (6) in Γ, then

$$\mathbf{E}(M_k(\boldsymbol{u})) \leq T_\Gamma + (1 + o(1))\mathbf{E}_{\hat{\pi}}(H_{\gamma_k}), \qquad (10)$$

where $\mathbf{E}_{\hat{\pi}}(H_{\gamma_k})$ is the hitting time of γ_k in Γ from stationarity.

Since we have replaced k individual walks on G by a single walk on Q_k, and then on Γ, we need to relate mixing times on T_Q and T_Γ directly to a given mixing time T_G of a single random walk on the underlying graph G. (We will need T_Γ to apply Lemma 1 to graph Γ.)

LEMMA 2. *For random walks in graphs G, Q and Γ, there are mixing times*

$$T_G = O\left(\frac{\log n}{1 - \lambda_2(G)}\right), \; T_Q = O(kT_G), \; T_\Gamma = O(kT_G), \quad (11)$$

such that

$$\max_{u,x \in V_F} |P_u^t(x) - \pi_x| = o(1/n_F^2), \quad \text{for any } t \geq T_F,$$

where F is any of the graphs G, Q or Γ, and $n_F = |V_F|$.

PROOF. The bound on T_G is well known (see for example, Sinclair [22]): use (5), observing that $\pi_x/\pi_u = O(n)$ and $\lambda_2^{1/(1-\lambda_2)}$ has a constant $c < 1$ upper bound. To use (5) also to derive bounds on T_Q and T_Γ, we need to know the eigenvalues of Q_k and Γ in terms of the eigenvalues of G. We have $\lambda_2(\Gamma) \leq \lambda_2(Q_k)$ and $\lambda_2(Q_k) = \lambda_2(G)$. This follows from established results, as we next explain.

In the jargon of Markov processes, the random walk on Q_k is known as the *tensor product chain*, and its eigenvalues are the k-wise products of the eigenvalues of G. Thus, assuming $\lambda_2(G) \geq \lambda_n(G)$, it follows that $\lambda_2(Q_k) = \lambda_2(G)$. See [17] page 168 for more details.

In the notation of [2, Ch. 3], the random walk on Γ is the random walk on Q_k with S collapsed to $\gamma(S)$. It is proved in [2, Ch. 3], Corollary 27, that if a subset A of vertices is collapsed to a single vertex, then the second eigenvalue of the transition matrix cannot increase (in that corollary the variable $\tau_2 = 1/(1 - \lambda_2)$). Thus $\lambda_2(Q) \geq \lambda_2(\Gamma)$.

We get the factor k in the bounds (11) on the mixing times T_Q and T_Γ, because $\pi_x/\pi_u = O(n^{2k})$ and we need $|P_u^T(x) - \pi_x| = o(1/n^{2k})$, as the number of vertices in graphs Q and Γ is $O(n^k)$. □

For reference, we record the salient facts for the graphs G, Q, Γ in Table 1. The bound on π_γ will be established in Lemma 4.

4. HITTING TIME FROM STATIONARITY – PROOF OF THEOREM 2

Our proof of Theorem 2 is based on Inequality (10) and on a good upper bound on the expected hitting time of vertex γ by a random walk in Γ which starts from the stationary distribution. We obtain such a bound using (7) and deriving an upper bound on $Z_{\gamma\gamma}$ (Lemma 3) and a lower bound on the stationary probability $\pi_\gamma = \widehat{\pi}_\gamma$ (Lemma 4).

LEMMA 3. *Let F be a graph with the eigenvalue gap $1 - \lambda_2$, then*

$$Z_{vv} \leq \frac{1}{1 - \lambda_2}. \quad (12)$$

In particular, for any vertex v of Q or Γ, $Z_{vv} \leq 1/(1 - \lambda_2(G))$.

PROOF. Let $\lambda_2 = \lambda_2(F)$. Using (5) with $x = u = v$, then

$$|P_v^t(v) - \pi_v| \leq \lambda_2^t,$$

and

$$Z_{vv} = \sum_{t \geq 0}(P_v^t(v) - \pi_v) \leq \sum_{t \geq 0} \lambda_2^t = \frac{1}{1 - \lambda_2}.$$

From the proof of Lemma 2, both $F = Q, \Gamma$ satisfy $(1 - \lambda_2(\Gamma)) \geq 1 - \lambda_2(Q) = 1 - \lambda_2(G)$. □

LEMMA 4. *Let $k \leq \log^3 n$. Let G be a connected n vertex, m edge graph satisfying $\Delta(G) = o(m/\log^6 n)$. Let $\gamma = \gamma_k$ in Γ be the contraction of $S = S_k$ in Q. Then there exists $c_k > 0$ constant such that*

$$\pi_\gamma = \frac{d(\gamma)}{(2m)^k} \geq \frac{c_k k^2 \nu}{n}. \quad (13)$$

PROOF. By definition, $d(\gamma) = d(S)$. For $1 \leq x < y \leq k$, define the following subsets of S:

$$S_{(x,y)} = \{(v_1, \ldots, v_k) : v_x = v_y\}.$$

We have

$$S = \bigcup_{1 \leq x < y \leq k} S_{(x,y)},$$

and

$$d\left(S_{(x,y)}\right) = (2m)^{k-2} \sum_{v \in V} d^2(v).$$

For $\{x,y\} \neq \{p,q\}$, $d\left(S_{(x,y)} \cap S_{(p,q)}\right)$ equals to

$$(2m)^{k-4} \sum_{v,u \in V} d^2(v)d^2(u), \quad \text{if } \{x,y\} \cap \{p,q\} = \emptyset, \text{ or}$$
$$(2m)^{k-3} \sum_{v \in V} d^3(v), \quad \text{if } |\{x,y\} \cap \{p,q\}| = 1.$$

Therefore, from the inclusion-exclusion principle and recalling $\sum_{v \in V} d^2(v) = \nu d^2 n$,

$$\begin{aligned}
d(S) &\geq \sum_{\{x,y\}} d\left(S_{(x,y)}\right) - \sum_{\{x,y\} \neq \{p,q\}} d\left(S_{(x,y)} \cap S_{(p,q)}\right) \\
&\geq \binom{k}{2}(2m)^k \frac{\nu}{n} - 3\binom{k}{4}(2m)^k \frac{\nu^2}{n^2} \\
&\quad - 3\binom{k}{3}(2m)^k \frac{\Delta\nu}{2mn} \\
&\geq \binom{k}{2}(2m)^k \frac{\nu}{n}\left(1 - \frac{k^2\nu}{n} - \frac{k\Delta}{2m}\right) \\
&= \binom{k}{2}(2m)^k \frac{\nu}{n}(1 - o(1)).
\end{aligned} \quad (14)$$

The last line above follows from the assumptions that $\Delta = o(m/\log^6 n)$ and $k \leq \log^3 n$, and the fact that $\nu \leq \Delta n/(2m) = o(n/\log^6 n)$. The bound (13) follows from (14). □

PROOF OF THEOREM 2. Let M_k be the time of the first meeting among $k \leq k^*$ particles in G, and let $\gamma = \gamma_k$ be the contraction of the diagonal set $S = S_k$. Using (7) for graph Γ and with $v = \gamma$, and Lemmas 3 and 4 we have, that the hitting time H_γ of γ from stationarity has expected value

$$\begin{aligned}
\mathbf{E}_\pi(H_\gamma) &\leq \frac{1}{\pi(\gamma)} \frac{1}{1 - \lambda_2} \\
&\leq \frac{1}{c_k k^2} \frac{n}{\nu} \frac{1}{1 - \lambda_2}.
\end{aligned} \quad (15)$$

Since $T_\Gamma = O(kT_G)$, and referring to (10) and Table 1,

$$\begin{aligned}
\mathbf{E}(M_k) &\leq O(kT_G) + (1 + o(1))\mathbf{E}_\pi(H_\gamma) \\
&= O\left(\frac{1}{1 - \lambda_2}\left(k\log n + \frac{n}{\nu k^2}\right)\right). \quad (16)
\end{aligned}$$

□

Graph F	n_F	π_v – stationary distribution	T_F – mixing time
G	$n_G = n$	$\pi_v = d(v)/2m$	$T_G = O(\log n/(1-\lambda_2))$
Q_k	$n_Q = n^k$	$\pi_v \leq (\Delta/2m)^k$	$T_Q = O(kT_G)$
Γ_k	$n_\Gamma \leq n^k$	$\pi_\gamma \leq (k^2(2m)^{k-2}n\Delta^2)/(2m)^k$	$T_\Gamma = O(T_Q)$

Table 1: **The main parameters of the random walks on graphs** G, Q_k **and** Γ_k.

5. COALESCENCE TIME OF RANDOM WALKS – PROOF OF THEOREM 1

Let C_k be the time for $k \leq k^* = \log^3 n$ particles to coalesce. Then, using (4), we get

$$\mathbf{E}(C_k) \leq \sum_{s=2}^{k} \mathbf{E}(M_s) = O\left(\frac{1}{1-\lambda_2}\left(k^2 \log n + \frac{n}{\nu}\right)\right), \quad (17)$$

since $\sum_s (1/s^2) \leq \pi^2/6$ is constant.

Now we consider n particles. We prove that **whp** there cannot be a subset of $k = \log^3 n$ particles which has not had a meeting by time t^*, where

$$
\begin{aligned}
t^* &= k^2 \left(T_\Gamma + 3\mathbf{E}_\pi(H_{\gamma_k})\right) \\
&= O\left(\frac{1}{1-\lambda_2}\left(k^3 \log n + \frac{n}{\nu}\right)\right).
\end{aligned}
$$

Let $\mathcal{P}(k) = \mathcal{P}(k, \boldsymbol{v})$ be the set of particles starting from vertices $\boldsymbol{v} = (v_1, ..., v_k)$. Either there has been a meeting during the mixing time T_Γ, or if not, we apply Lemma 1 to graph Γ_k, vertex γ_k, and $t = t^*$. The probability that the particles do not meet by time t is the same as the probability that the random walk in Γ_k starting from $\boldsymbol{v}$ does not visit γ_k by time t. Therefore, Lemma 1 implies that

$$
\begin{aligned}
\bar{\rho}_k &= \mathbf{Pr}(\text{no meeting among } \mathcal{P}(k) \text{ particles before } t^*) \\
&\leq e^{-k^2} = e^{-\log^6 n}.
\end{aligned}
$$

Hence

$$
\begin{aligned}
&\mathbf{Pr}(\exists \text{ a set } \mathcal{P}(k) \text{ having no meeting by } t^*) \\
&\leq \binom{n}{k}\bar{\rho}_k = O\left(e^{-\log^5 n + \log^4 n}\right).
\end{aligned}
$$

Thus by step t^* fewer than k particles remain, and an upper bound on the expected time for all particles to coalesce is

$$
\begin{aligned}
&t^* + \mathbf{E}(C_k) + O\left(n^{-(\log^4 n)/2} t^*\right) \\
&= O\left(\frac{1}{1-\lambda_2}\left(k^3 \log n + \frac{n}{\nu}\right)\right). \quad (18)
\end{aligned}
$$

The second term, $\mathbf{E}(C_k)$, (see (17)) is a bound on the expected coalescence time of the particles remaining after t^* (at most k particles remains). The last term is the expected time to coalesce, restarting the process at t^*, as many times as needed, under the assumption that some set of $k = \log^3 n$ particles had not met at that time. If $\Delta = O(m^{1-\epsilon})$, then $n/\nu = \Omega(m^\epsilon) = \Omega(k^3 \log n)$, so the bound in (18) implies the bound (3).

6. MIN-VOTING: PROOF OF THEOREM 3

Let O_p be the set of the smallest p initial opinions. If we assume, without loss of generality, that the set of the initial opinions is $\{1, 2, \ldots, n\}$, then $O_p = \{1, 2, \ldots, p\}$.

LEMMA 5. *Let V_q be the set of vertices with a certain opinion $q \in O_{\log^2 n}$ at a given time step t. Furthermore, let $W_q = \cup_{i=1}^{q} V_q$. If $\rho \leq |W_q| \leq \phi n/d$ for a certain constant ρ and opinion q, then with probability $1 - \exp(-\Theta(|W_q|))$ the size of the set W_q increases by a constant factor $c' > 1$ in a step.*

PROOF. First, we show that with probability at least $1 - \exp(-\Theta(|W_q|))$, the vertices of W_q are contacted by at least $(2 - \alpha^3)|W_q|$ edges. We consider a vertex exposure Martingale sequence $(X_i)_{1 \leq i \leq |W_q|}$, representing the number of edges contacting the vertices $v_1, \ldots, v_{|W_q|} \in V_q$. We assume that if more than $1/\alpha^2$ edges contact a vertex, then $1/\alpha^2$ of them are selected uniformly at random, which are allowed to keep their contacts. The rest is released, and the corresponding vertices may contact other vertices in the remaining steps of the exposure process. Since the released edges may choose their contacts outside W_q in the subsequent steps of the process, we only make the number of edges contacting W_q smaller. This implies that the Martingale satisfies the $1/\alpha^2$-Lipschitz condition, and the Azuma-Hoeffding bound implies that

$$
\begin{aligned}
\mathbf{Pr}(|X_{|W_q|} - X_1| &\geq \alpha^3 |W_q|) \\
&\leq 2\exp\left(-\frac{\alpha^6 |W_q|^2}{2|W_q|/\alpha^4}\right) \\
&\leq \exp(-\Theta(|W_q|)). \quad (19)
\end{aligned}
$$

Now we show that with probability $1 - \exp(-\Theta(|W_q|))$ there are at least $\alpha^2 |W_q|$ vertices, which contact exactly one vertex in W_q. Since $|W_q| \leq \phi n/d$, we have $|N(W_q)| \geq \alpha d|W_q|$. Then, the pigeonhole principle implies that at least $\alpha d|W_q|/2$ vertices in $N(W_q)$ have at most $2/\alpha$ neighbours in W_q. An arbitrary such vertex u contacts exactly one neighbour in W_q with probability at least

$$2\frac{|E(u, W_q)|}{d}\left(1 - \frac{|E(u, W_q)|}{d}\right) \geq \frac{2}{d} - \frac{2}{d^2}.$$

Since there are at least $\alpha d|W_q|/2$ such vertices, and each of these acts independently, we use Chernoff bounds to conclude that at least $\alpha^2 |W_q|$ vertices will contact exactly one vertex in W_q, with probability at least $1 - \exp(-\Theta(|W_q|))$, whenever ρ is large enough. Then, with probability $1 - \exp(-\Theta(|W_q|))$ the vertices of W_q are contacted in total by at least

$$\left(\frac{2-\alpha^3-\alpha^2}{2} + \alpha^2\right)|W_q| \geq \frac{2+\alpha^2-\alpha^3}{2}|W_q|$$

vertices, which is larger than $|W_q|$ by at least a constant factor $c' > 1$. $\square$

LEMMA 6. *After step $(\log\log n)^2$, for an arbitrary q we have $|W_q| = 0$ or $|W_q| \geq \log^2 n$, with probability at least $1 - 1/\log^{\omega(1)} n$. Furthermore, **whp** there will be at least one opinion $q \in O_{\log^2 n}$, which is contained in at least $\log^2 n$ vertices.*

PROOF. For simplicity, we assume that $d = o(n/|W_q|)$, i.e., $|N(W_q)| \geq \alpha d|W_q|$. If $|W_q| \geq \rho$, then it follows from Lemma 5 that with probability $1 - \exp(-\Theta(|W_q|))$ the number of vertices in set W_q increases by some factor $c' > 1$ in a step. Now, we consider the case when $|W_q| < \rho$. We show that with constant probability the number of vertices having some opinion at most q increases by at least 1 in a step. Since we assumed that d is large enough, and due to the fact that ρ does not depend on d, we may assume $\rho \ll d$. We know that each vertex has d neighbours, and a vertex in set W_q can have at most $|W_q| - 1$ neighbours in W_q. Then, a vertex of $N(W_q)$ contacts a neighbour in W_q with probability at least

$$1 - (1 - 1/d)^2 = 2/d - 1/d^2.$$

Since $N(W_q) \geq d - \rho$, simple Chernoff bounds imply that whenever $d > 2\rho + 1$, there will be $\rho + 1$ vertices in $N(W_q)$ contacting a vertex with some opinion $1 \ldots q$, with constant probability.

Now we describe the process by a simple random walk. Let $P' = (V', E')$ with $V' = \{u_\rho, u_{\rho+1}, \ldots, u_{\log^2 n}\}$ be a path of length $O(\log^2 n)$, in which vertex u_i represents the case when $|W_q| = i$. Furthermore, vertex $u_{\log^2 n}$ represents the case when $at\ least\ \log^2 n$ vertices have some opinion $1 \ldots q$. We also define path $P'' = (V'', E'')$ with $V'' = \{w_0, \ldots, w_\rho\}$ of length $\rho + 1$, whose vertex w_i corresponds to the case $|W_q| = i$. Note that state ρ is contained in both paths. On path P' there is a transition from each vertex u_i to the set of vertices $u_{c'i+\Omega(1)}$ with probability $1 - \exp(-\Theta(i))$. On path P'', there is a constant transition from each vertex w_i with $i > 0$ to the set of vertices $w_{i+\Omega(1)}$. Furthermore, the random walk is stopped as soon as vertex $u_{\log^2 n}$ is reached. Therefore, a random walk on the combined path $P' \cup P''$ satisfies the conditions of Lemma A.4 from [8], and we may conclude that the number of vertices with some opinion $1 \ldots q$ will exceed $\log^2 n$ within $(\log \log n)^2$ steps, with probability $1 - \log^{-\omega(1)} n$. According to Lemma 5, once some W_q reaches $\log^2 n$, it will always increase within the next $(\log \log n)^2$ steps, with probability $1 - n^{-\omega(1)}$.

Concerning the second statement of the lemma, we observe that $|W_{\log^2 n}| = \log^2 n$ at step $(\log \log n)^2$, with probability $1 - \log^{-\omega(1)} n$. Thus, there is a q with $|W_q| = |V_q| \geq \log^2 n$ at step $(\log \log n)^2$, **whp**. □

In the following, we assume that q is chosen such that $W_q = V_q$ at step $(\log \log n)^2$. That is, q is the smallest opinion, which is contained in the graph after $(\log \log n)^2$ steps. Then, it follows from the previous lemma that $|V_q| \geq \log^2 n$ at that time step, **whp**. Now we show the following lemma.

LEMMA 7. *Assume that at some time step the number of vertices with the (currently) smallest opinion q in the graph is at least $\log^2 n$. Then, after additional $O(\log n)$ steps the number of vertices with this opinion is at least $n/2$, with probability $1 - n^{-\omega(1)}$.*

PROOF. As long as $|V_q| \leq \phi n/d$, the statement of the lemma follows from Lemma 5. Therefore, we only consider the case $\phi n/d \leq |V_q| \leq n/2$. First, we assume that there are $n/40$ vertices in $V \setminus V_q$, which have more than $\alpha d|V_q|/n$, but less than $d - \alpha d|V_q|/n$ neighbours in V_q. Then, using similar Martingale arguments as in Lemma 5, Equation (19) implies that there are at least $(2-\alpha/42)|V_q|$ edges contacting

vertices in V_q. Furthermore, one of the $n/40$ vertices above contacts V_q with exactly one edge with probability

$$2\frac{\alpha d|V_q|}{nd}\left(1 - \frac{\alpha d|V_q|}{nd}\right).$$

Since there are at least $n/40$ such vertices, there will be in expectation

$$2\frac{\alpha|V_q|}{40}\left(1 - \frac{\alpha|V_q|}{40}\right)$$

vertices contacting V_q with exactly one edge. Applying simple Chernoff bounds, at least $2\alpha|V_q|/41$ vertices will contact V_q with exactly one edge, with probability $1 - n^{-\Omega(1)}$. Putting everything together, we obtain that within one step, the number of vertices with opinion q increases by a constant factor larger than 1, with probability $1 - n^{-\Omega(1)}$.

Now we show that there must exist $n/40$ vertices in $V \setminus V_q$ which have more than $\alpha d|V_q|/n$, but less than $d - \alpha d|V_q|/n$ neighbours in V_q. We know that

$$|E(V_q, V \setminus V_q)| \leq \frac{d \cdot |V_q| \cdot |V \setminus V_q|}{n} + \lambda d\sqrt{|V_q| \cdot |V \setminus V_q|}.$$

In the rest of the proof, we assume for simplicity that $\lambda = o(1)$ (a more sophisticated analysis leads to the same result if $\lambda \ll 1/\sqrt{d}$ and $d = O(1)$). Assume that there are less than $n/20$ vertices in $V \setminus V_q$ with less than $d - \alpha d|V_q|/n$ neighbours in V_q. Then, the number of edges between V_q and $V \setminus V_q$ is at least

$$\left(|V \setminus V_q| - \frac{n}{20}\right)\left(d - \alpha d\frac{|V_q|}{n}\right)$$
$$\geq \left(|V \setminus V_q| - \frac{n}{20}\right)d\left(1 - \frac{\alpha}{2}\right)$$
$$\geq \frac{9|V \setminus V_q|}{10}d\left(1 - \frac{\alpha}{2}\right), \qquad (20)$$

where $\alpha/2$ can be arbitrarily small. On the other side

$$|E(V_q, V \setminus V_q)| \leq \frac{d \cdot |V_q| \cdot |V \setminus V_q|}{n}(1 + o(1))$$
$$\leq \frac{|V \setminus V_q|}{2}d(1 + o(1)),$$

which is much smaller than the value in Equation (20) leading to contradiction.

On the other hand, the number of vertices in $V \setminus V_q$ which have less than $\alpha d|V_q|/n$ neighbours in V_q is at most

$$\frac{\beta n^2}{d|V_q|} \leq \frac{\beta n}{\phi} < \frac{n}{40},$$

if $\beta/\phi < 1/40$. This implies that at least $n/40$ vertices in $V \setminus V_q$ have more than $\alpha d|V_q|/n$, but less than $d - \alpha d|V_q|/n$ neighbours in V_q. □

Now we consider the case $|V_q| > n/2$.

LEMMA 8. *Assume that at some time step the number of vertices with the (currently) smallest opinion q in the graph is at least $n/2$. Then, after additional $O(\log n)$ steps all vertices will have opinion q, **whp**.*

PROOF. The proof basically follows the arguments given in the previous lemmas. Let $\overline{V}_q$ represent the set of vertices which do not have opinion q. We show that within one step, $\overline{V}_q$ decreases by a constant factor, with probability

$1 - n^{-\Omega(1)}$. Again, we consider two cases. First, we assume that $|\overline{V}_q| \geq \phi n/d$. Then, using the same arguments as in Lemmas 7 and 5, there are at most $(2 + \alpha/42)|\overline{V}_q|$ *edges* contacting vertices in $\overline{V}_q$. On the other hand, Lemma 7 also implies that at least $n/40$ vertices in $V \setminus \overline{V}_q$ have more than $\alpha d|\overline{V}_q|/n$, but less than $d - \alpha d|\overline{V}_q|/n$ neighbours in $\overline{V}_q$. These statements combined with the arguments of Lemma 5 imply that at least $2\alpha|\overline{V}_q|/41$ vertices will contact $\overline{V}_q$ with exactly one edge, with probability $1 - n^{-\Omega(1)}$. Then, the total number of vertices contacting $\overline{V}_q$ with both edges is at most

$$\left(2 + \frac{\alpha}{42} - \frac{2\alpha}{41}\right)\frac{|\overline{V}_q|}{2},$$

with probability $1 - n^{-\Omega(1)}$. Thus, with probability $1 - n^{-\Omega(1)}$ the number of vertices, which do not have opinion q, decreases by a constant fraction.

Now we consider the case $|\overline{V}_q| < \phi n/d$. Using the same Martingale approach as in Lemma 5, Equation (19) implies that with probability $1 - \exp(-\Theta(\overline{V}_q))$ there are at most $(2 + \alpha^3)|\overline{V}_q|$ *edges* contacting vertices in $\overline{V}_q$. On the other hand, with probability $1 - \exp(-\Theta(|\overline{V}_q|))$ there are at least $\alpha^2|\overline{V}_q|$ vertices in V_q, which contact $\overline{V}_q$ with exactly one edge. Thus, the total number of vertices which contact $\overline{V}_q$ with both edges is at most $(2 + \alpha^3 - \alpha^2)|\overline{V}_q|/2$, with probability $1 - \exp(-\Theta(|\overline{V}_q|))$. This implies that after $\log n$ steps, all but at most $\log^2 n$ vertices will have the same opinion q, with probability $1 - n^{-\Omega(1)}$.

For the case $|\overline{V}_q| \leq \log^2 n$, we use the random walk approach described in Lemma 5. However, in this case, the vertices u_i and w_i in the paths P' and P'', respectively, represent the cases when i vertices do not have opinion q. Then, a vertex u_i makes a transition to some vertex $u_{i/c' - \Omega(1)}$ with probability $1 - \exp(-\Theta(i))$, where $c' > 1$. Furthermore, a vertex w_i makes a transition to a vertex $w_{i-\Omega(1)}$ with constant probability. According to the arguments above and to Lemma 5, the random walk will reach vertex u_0 within $(\log \log n)^2$ steps, with probability $1 - \log^{-\omega(1)} n$. Thus, the lemma follows. $\square$

7. CONCLUSIONS

We have analysed two distributed voting protocols on graphs: the random voting and the min-voting. Both protocols start with the vertices of the graph having distinct opinions, and consist of a sequence of synchronized discrete steps. In each step, each vertex adopts the opinion of one of its neighbours. In the random voting, the vertex adopts the opinion of a random neighbour, while in the min-voting the vertex adopts the smaller opinion of two random neighbours. We have shown a $O(n/(\nu(1 - \lambda_2)))$ bound on the expected completion time of the random voting on general graphs, and a **whp** $O(\log n)$ bound on the completion time of the min-voting on "strong" expanders. In the bound for the random voting, the parameter ν is such that $\nu - 1$ is equal to the normalized variance of the degree sequence (hence $\nu \geq 1$, and $\nu = 1$ for regular graphs). This bound is linear for expanders, but can be sublinear for graphs with a skewed degree sequence, for example, for power law graphs. The assumption that the initial opinions are distinct was introduced only for the convenience of presentation. If the same opinions are initially hold by multiple vertices, then the voting time can only decrease.

We have obtained the bound for the random voting by analysing the dual process of coalescing random walks. We wonder if there is any random walk process related to the min-voting or to a similar voting scheme based on selecting more than one random neighbour.

One of the immediate questions regarding our analysis of the random voting is to eliminate the assumption that $\Delta = O(m^{1-\epsilon})$. To achieve this, we would need a more detailed estimation of the degree of the diagonal set S than the one derived in the proof of Lemma 4.

Regarding the min-voting, we would like to extend our $O(\log n)$ bound to the broader class of expanders which have constant eigenvalue gap. The further aim could be to develop a bound parameterized by the eigenvalue gap. In particular, is the $O(\log n/(1 - \lambda_2))$ bound on the mixing time also a bound on completing the min-voting? We note, however, that on some graphs the min-voting can be completed in time asymptotically strictly less than the mixing time.

From the point of view of possible applications of the random voting and the min-voting in distributed computing, an obvious question is how robust these processes are against an adversary which tries to win voting by corrupting opinions of one or more vertices. If the adversary substitutes the initial opinions of the vertices of some set A with its own opinion, then the adversary wins the voting with probability $d(A)/m$. Thus the random voting can be considered robust: to have a (positive) constant probability of winning, the adversary would have to corrupt a constant fraction of vertices (assuming that the graph is regular).

Comparing the random voting with the min-voting, one may say that the latter buys the speed paying for it with robustness. We argue, however, that the min-voting retains some level of robustness. If the speed of voting was the only issue, then one might consider the following simple protocol, which is mentioned in [8]. In each step every vertex v chooses a neighbour u, uniformly at random, and updates its opinion to $\min\{m_v, m_u\}$, where m_v and m_u are the current opinions of vertices v and u, respectively. This protocol, similarly to our min-voting, achieves consensus in $O(\log n)$ steps **whp** (this follows from e.g. [21] together with [10]). However, since in this voting the minimum opinion always wins, all the adversary has to do to ensure winning is to corrupt the vertex which initially has that minimum opinion, or to change the initial opinion of one vertex to an opinion which is smaller than any opinion at any other vertex. If the adversary attempts the same in our min-voting protocol, it will win only with some probability $p < 1$, since the minimum opinion is eliminated from the system with (positive) constant probability.

The above scenario motivates further analysis of the min-voting to calculate, or estimate, the probability that the minimum opinion, or more generally the i-th smallest opinion, is the winner. It also raises the question of developing a fast voting protocol with improved robustness. More specifically, we would like to develop a voting protocol, which works on expanders in $O(\log n)$ steps, but for each initial opinion, the probability that that opinion wins is only $o(1)$. We believe that our min-voting process can be used as a basis for such a scheme. Maybe some combination of the min-voting and the random voting would do? The median protocol of [8] works on complete graphs in $O(\log n)$ steps and has strong robustness properties. It is likely that the same protocol works in $O(\log n)$ steps also on expanders, but we do not see how one might try to prove this.

8. REFERENCES

[1] D. Aldous. Meeting times for independent Markov chains. *Stochastic Processes and their Applications* 38(2):185-193, August 1991.

[2] D. Aldous and J. Fill. *Reversible Markov Chains and Random Walks on Graphs*, http://stat-www.berkeley.edu/pub/users/aldous/RWG/book.html.

[3] J. Aspnes. Randomized protocols for asynchronous consensus. *Distributed Computing* 16(2-3):165-176, 2003.

[4] F.R.K. Chung: *Spectral Graph Theory.* American Mathematical Society, 1997.

[5] C. Cooper, A. M. Frieze, and T. Radzik. Multiple Random Walks in Random Regular Graphs. *SIAM J. Discrete Math.* 23(4):1738-1761, 2009.

[6] J. T. Cox. Coalescing random walks and voter model consensus times on the torus in $\mathbb{Z}^d$. *The Annals of Probability* 17(4):1333-1366, October 1989.

[7] B. Doerr, T. Friedrich, and T. Sauerwald: Quasirandom rumor spreading: expanders, push vs. pull, and robustness. In *ICALP 2009: Proceedings of the 36th International Colloquium on Automata, Languages and Programming, Part I*, Rhodes, Greece, pages 366-377, July 2009.

[8] B. Doerr, L.A. Goldberg, L. Minder, T. Sauerwald, and C. Scheideler: Stabilizing Consensus with the Power of Two Choices. In *SPAA 2011: Proceedings of the 23rd Annual ACM Symposium on Parallelism in Algorithms and Architectures*, San Jose, CA, USA, pages 149-158, June 2011, full version available at www.upb.de/cs/scheideler.

[9] P. Donnelly and D. Welsh. Finite particle systems and infection models. *Math. Proc. Camb. Phil. Soc.* 94(1):167-182, July 1983.

[10] R. Elsässer and T. Sauerwald. On the runtime and robustness of randomized broadcasting. In *ISAAC 2006: Proceedings of the 17th International Symposium on Algorithms and Computation*, Kalkota, India, pages 349-358, December 2006.

[11] C. Gkantsidis, M. Mihail, and A. Saberi. Conductance and congestion in power law graphs. In *SIGMETRICS 2003: Proceedings of 2003 ACM SIGMETRICS Intl. Conf. on Measurement and Modeling of Computer Systems*, New York, NY, USA, pages 148-159, 2003.

[12] Y. Hassin and D. Peleg. Distributed probabilistic polling and applications to proportionate agreement. *Information & Computation* 171(2):248-268, December 2001.

[13] S. Hoory, N. Linial, and A. Wigderson. Expander Graphs and their Applications. *Bulletin of the American Mathematical Society* 43(4):439-561, October 2006.

[14] A. Israeli and M. Jalfon. Token management schemes and random walks yeild self stabilizing mutual exclusion. In *PODC 1990: Proceedings of the 9th Annual ACM Symposium on Principles of Distributed Computing*, Quebec City, Quebec, Canada, pages 119-131, August 1990.

[15] D. Kempe, A. Dobra, J. Gehrke. Gossip-based computation of aggregate information. In *FOCS 2003: Proceedings of the 44th Symposium on Foundations of Computer Science*, Cambridge, MA, USA, pages 482-491, October 2003.

[16] F. Kuhn, T. Locher, R. Wattenhofer. Tight bounds for distributed selection. In *SPAA 2007: Proceedings of the 19th Annual ACM Symposium on Parallelism in Algorithms and Architectures*, San Diego, CA, USA, pages 145-153, June 2007.

[17] D. Levin, Y. Peres, and E. Wilmer. *Markov Chains and Mixing Times.* American Mathematical Society, 2009.

[18] L. Lovász. Random walks on graphs: a survey. *Bolyai Society Mathematical Studies.* Combinatorics, Paul Erdős is Eighty 2:1-46, Keszthely, Hungary, 1993.

[19] T. Nakata, H. Imahayashi, M. Yamashita. Probabilistic local majority voting for the agreement problem on finite graphs. In *COCOON 1999: Proceedings of the 5th Annual International Conference on Computing and Combinatorics*, Tokyo, Japan, pages 330-338, July 1999.

[20] R. Oliveira. On the coalescence time of reversible random walks. *Trans. Amer. Math. Soc.* 364(4): 2109-2128, 2012.

[21] T. Sauerwald. On mixing and edge expansion properties in randomized broadcasting. *Algorithmica* 56(1):349-358, January 2010.

[22] A. Sinclair. Improved bounds for mixing rates of Markov chains and multicommodity flow. *Combinatorics, Probability and Computing* 1(4):351-370, December 1992.

The Cost of Fault Tolerance in Multi-Party Communication Complexity[*]

Binbin Chen
Advanced Digital Sciences Center
Republic of Singapore
binbin.chen@adsc.com.sg

Yuda Zhao
National University of Singapore
Republic of Singapore
zhaoyuda@comp.nus.edu.sg

Haifeng Yu
National University of Singapore
Republic of Singapore
haifeng@comp.nus.edu.sg

Phillip B. Gibbons
Intel Labs
Pittsburgh, PA, USA
phillip.b.gibbons@intel.com

ABSTRACT

Multi-party communication complexity involves distributed computation of a function over inputs held by multiple distributed players. A key focus of distributed computing research, since the very beginning, has been to tolerate crash failures. It is thus natural to ask *"If we want to compute a certain function in a fault-tolerant way, what will the communication complexity be?"* This natural question, interestingly, has not been formally posed and thoroughly studied prior to this work.

Whether fault-tolerant communication complexity is interesting to study largely depends on how big a difference failures make. This paper proves that the impact of failures is significant, at least for the SUM aggregation function in general networks: As our central contribution, we prove that there exists (at least) an *exponential gap* between the non-fault-tolerant and fault-tolerant communication complexity of SUM. Our results also imply the optimality (within polylog factors) of some recent fault-tolerant protocols for computing SUM via duplicate-insensitive techniques, thereby answering an open question as well.

Part of our results are obtained via a novel reduction from a new two-party problem UNIONSIZECP that we introduce. UNIONSIZECP comes with a novel *cycle promise*, which is the key enabler of our reduction. We further prove that this cycle promise and UNIONSIZECP likely play a fundamental role in reasoning about fault-tolerant communication complexity.

Categories and Subject Descriptors

F.1 [**Computation by Abstract Devices**]: Complexity Measures and Classes; F.2 [**Analysis of Algorithms and Problem Complexity**]: Nonnumerical Algorithms and Problems

General Terms

Theory, Algorithms

---

[*]The first three authors of this paper are alphabetically ordered.

Keywords

Communication complexity, fault tolerance, aggregation functions, promise problems, wireless networks

1. INTRODUCTION

Fault tolerance in communication complexity and our exponential gap. Multi-party communication complexity [10] involves distributed computation of a function over inputs held by multiple distributed players. A key focus of distributed computing research, since the very beginning, has been to tolerate failures. (Throughout this paper, failures refer to node crash failures unless otherwise mentioned.) It is thus natural to ask *"If we want to compute a certain function in a fault-tolerant way, what will the communication complexity be?"* For the question to be meaningful, we impose two restrictions before moving forward. First, we allow the computation to ignore/omit the inputs held by those players that have failed (i.e., crashed) or been disconnected. This means that the function needs to be well-defined over any subset of the inputs. Second, we will assume that there is one special *root* player that never fails and only this player needs to learn the final result. This allows us to focus on the communication complexity of the function instead of the difficulty of, for example, achieving fault-tolerant distributed consensus. This also nicely maps to our target scenarios later in wireless sensor networks and wireless ad-hoc networks, where the root corresponds to the base station.

While the above question is natural, interestingly, it has not been formally posed and thoroughly studied — see later for our speculations on the possible reasons. Whether such fault-tolerant communication complexity is interesting to study, given the extensive research on "non-fault-tolerant" communication complexity, largely depends on how big a difference failures can make. This paper proves that the impact of failures is significant, at least for the SUM function[1] in networks with general topologies: As the central contribution of this work, we prove that there exists (at least) an *exponential gap* between the non-fault-tolerant (NFT) and fault-tolerant (FT) communication complexity of SUM. Here FT communication complexity is the smallest communication complexity among all fault-tolerant protocols that can tolerate an arbitrary number of failures, while NFT communication complexity corresponds to all pro-

---

[1]As an example where the impact of failures is *not* significant, consider the MAX function. Our technical report [11] gives a simple folklore fault-tolerant MAX protocol based on binary search, where each node sends only a logarithmic number of bits.

Communication
Complexity

$\Omega\left(\dfrac{N}{\log^2 N}\right)$ $\Omega\left(\dfrac{\sqrt{N}}{b^2 \log N}\right)$

$O(\log N)$ $O\left(\dfrac{\log N}{\log\left(\dfrac{b}{\log N}+2\right)}\right)$ $\Omega(\log N)$

$O(1)$

b

1 $2-c$ $N^{0.25-c}$ ∞

for zero-error result

Communication
Complexity

$\Omega\left(\dfrac{1}{\epsilon^2 \log N}\right)$ $\Omega\left(\dfrac{1}{\epsilon\, b^2 \log N}\right)$

$O\left(\log\dfrac{1}{\epsilon}+\log\log N\right)$ $O\left(\dfrac{a}{\log\left(\dfrac{b}{a}+2\right)}\right),$
$a=\log\dfrac{1}{\epsilon}+\log\log N$ $\Omega\left(\log\dfrac{1}{\epsilon}\right)$

$O(1)$

b

1 $2-c$ $\dfrac{1}{\epsilon^{0.5-c}}$ ∞

for (ϵ,δ)-approximate result

b: time complexity of the protocol, in terms of the number of aggregation rounds
c: any positive constant below 0.25
N: number of nodes in the network

$\Omega(...)$: FT lower bound
$O(...)$: NFT upper bound

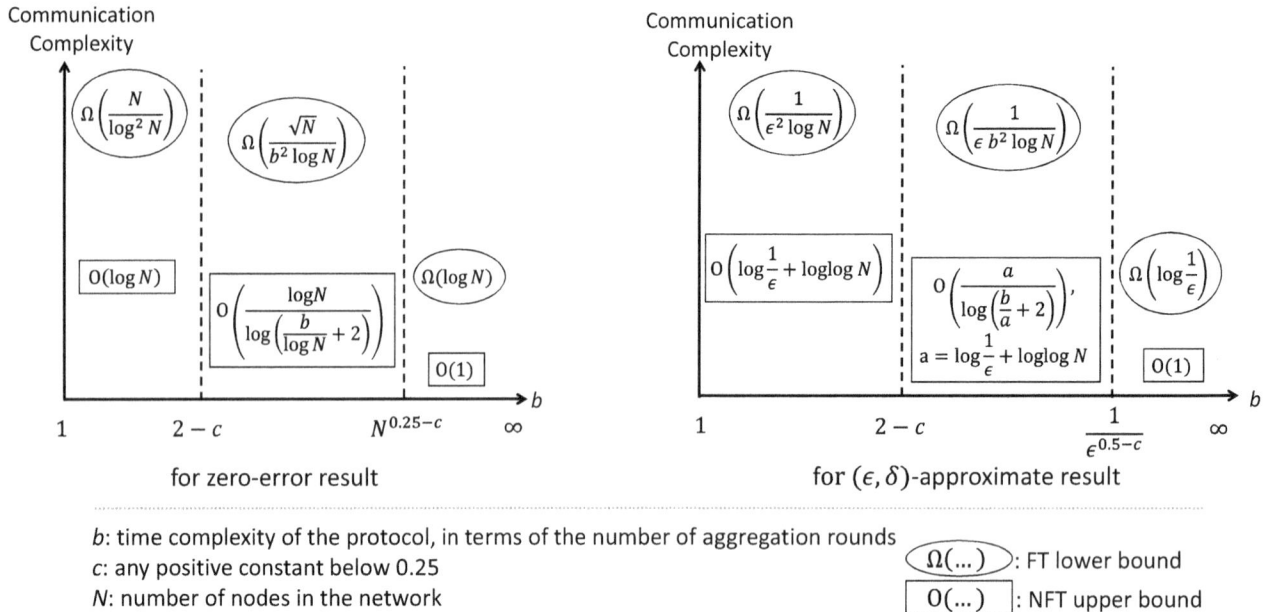

**Figure 1: Summary of our exponential gaps. All NFT upper bounds are either well-known or are obtained via standard tricks —
they are described in Section 3. All FT lower bounds are novel and are our main contributions. They are obtained in Section 4 (for
$1 \le b \le 2-c$), Section 5 (for $2-c < b \le N^{0.25-c}$ or $\frac{1}{\epsilon^{0.5-c}}$), and Section 7 (for $b > N^{0.25-c}$ or $\frac{1}{\epsilon^{0.5-c}}$).**

tocols. To our knowledge, ours is the first such result on FT communication complexity. This exponential gap attests that FT communication complexity needs to be studied separately from NFT
communication complexity.

The SUM function. Consider a synchronous wireless network (e.g.,
a wireless sensor network or a wireless ad-hoc network) with N
nodes and some arbitrary topology. Each node has a binary value,
and the SUM function asks for the sum of all the values. Note
that SUM can be easily reduced to and from some other interesting aggregation functions such as SELECTION. Communication
complexity has significant practical relevance here since i) wireless
communication usually consumes far more energy than local computation, and needs to be minimized for nodes operating on battery
power or nodes relying on energy harvesting, and ii) the capacity
of wireless networks does not scale well [18].

Existing results on SUM. In failure-free settings, by leveraging in-
network processing, a trivial tree-aggregation protocol can compute
SUM with zero-error while requiring each node to send $O(\log N)$
bits. For (ϵ,δ)-approximate results, it is possible to further reduce
to $O(\log\frac{1}{\epsilon} + \log\log N)$ bits per node for constant δ. In comparison, to tolerate arbitrary failures, we are not aware of any zero-error
protocol for computing SUM that is better than trivially having every node flood its id together with its value and thus requiring each
node to send $O(N \log N)$ bits. For (ϵ,δ)-approximate results, researchers have proposed some protocols [5, 14, 25, 26, 30] where
each node needs to send roughly $O(\frac{1}{\epsilon^2})$ bits for constant δ (after
omitting logarithmic terms of $\frac{1}{\epsilon}$ and N). All these protocols conceptually map the value of each node to exponentially weighted
positions in some bit vectors, and then estimate the sum from the
bit vectors. Same as in one-pass distinct element counting algorithms in streaming databases [1, 16], doing so makes the whole
process duplicate-insensitive. In turn, this allows each node to push
its value along multiple directions to guard against failures. Note
however, that duplicate-insensitive techniques do not need to be
one-pass, and furthermore tolerating failures does not have to use
duplicate-insensitive techniques. For example, one could repeat-

edly invoke the tree-aggregation protocol until one happens to have
a failure-free run. There is also a large body of work [3,7,12,13,20,
22,23] on computing SUM via gossip-based averaging (also called
average consensus protocols). They all rely on the mass conserva-
tion property [23], and thus are vulnerable to node failures. There
have been a few efforts [15, 21] on making these protocols fault-
tolerant. But they largely focus on correctness, without formal results on the protocol's communication complexity in the presence
of failures. Despite all these efforts, no lower bounds on the FT
communication complexity of SUM have ever been obtained, and
thus it has been unknown whether the existing protocols can be
improved.

Our results. Our main results in this paper are the first lower
bounds on the FT communication complexity (or *FT lower bounds*
in short) of SUM, for public-coin randomized protocols with zero-
error and with (ϵ,δ)-error. These FT lower bounds are (at least)
exponentially larger than the corresponding upper bounds on the
NFT communication complexity (or *NFT upper bounds* in short) of
SUM, thus establishing an exponential gap. Private-coin protocols
and deterministic protocols are also fully but implicitly covered,
and our exponential gap still applies.

Specifically, since there is a tradeoff between communication
complexity and time complexity, Figure 1 summarizes our FT lower
bounds when the time complexity of the SUM protocol is within b
aggregation rounds (defined in Section 2), for b from 1 to ∞. For
$b \le N^{0.25-c}$ or $\frac{1}{\epsilon^{0.5-c}}$ where c is any positive constant below 0.25,
the NFT upper bounds are always at most logarithmic with respect
to N or $\frac{1}{\epsilon}$, while the FT lower bounds are always polynomial.[2] For
$b > N^{0.25-c}$ or $\frac{1}{\epsilon^{0.5-c}}$, the NFT upper bounds drop to $O(1)$, while
the FT lower bounds are still at least logarithmic. Our results also
imply that under small b values, the existing fault-tolerant SUM
protocols (incurring $O(N \log N)$ or $O(\frac{1}{\epsilon^2})$ bits [5, 14, 25, 26, 30]
per node) are actually optimal within polylog factors.

---

[2]Here for (ϵ,δ)-approximate results, we only considered terms containing ϵ. Even if we take the extra terms with N into account, our
exponential gaps continue to exist as long as $\frac{1}{\epsilon^c} = \Omega(\log N)$.

Our approach. Our FT lower bounds for $b \leq 2 - c$ are obtained via a simple but interesting reduction from a two-party communication complexity problem UNIONSIZE, where Alice and Bob intend to determine the size of the union of two sets. In the reduction, without knowing Bob's input, Alice can only simulate the SUM oracle protocol's execution in part of the network. Furthermore this part is continuously shrinking due to the spreading of such unknown information. Failures play a fundamental role in the reduction — they hinder the spreading of unknown information. The FT lower bounds under $b \leq N^{0.25-c}$ or $\frac{1}{\epsilon^{0.5-c}}$ are much harder to obtain. There we introduce a new two-party problem called UNION-SIZECP, which is roughly UNIONSIZE extended with a novel *cycle promise*. Identifying this promise is a key contribution of this work, which enables the continuous injection of failures to further hinder the spreading of unknown information. We then prove a lower bound on UNIONSIZECP's communication complexity via information theoretic arguments [4]. This lower bound, coupled with our reduction, leads to FT lower bounds for SUM. We further prove a strong completeness result showing that UNIONSIZECP is *complete* among the set of *all* two-party problems that can be reduced to SUM in the FT setting via *oblivious reductions* (defined in Section 6). Namely, we prove that every problem in that set can be reduced to UNIONSIZECP. Our proof also implicitly derives the cycle promise, thus showing that it likely plays a fundamental role in reasoning about the FT communication complexity of many functions beyond SUM. Finally, our FT lower bounds under $b > N^{0.25-c}$ or $\frac{1}{\epsilon^{0.5-c}}$ are obtained by drawing a strong connection to an interesting probing game, and then by proving a lower bound on the probing game.

Other related work. Despite the developments (e.g., [8, 10, 19, 27, 28]) on different models for communication complexity, to the best of our knowledge, fault tolerance has never been considered. Among them, the closest setting to fault tolerance is perhaps unreliable channels [8, 27, 28] that either flip the bits adversarially or flip each bit iid. The specific techniques and insights there have limited applicability to our fault-tolerant setting. Under the iid unreliable channel model, there have also been some information-theoretic lower bounds [2, 17] on the rates of distributed computations. We suspect that such a lack of prior work on fault tolerance is due to two reasons. First, one needs to define correctness in a meaningful way when failures are possible, since some of the inputs can be missing. For this work, recent applications in wireless sensor networks have shown us how to do so [5]. Second, communication complexity problems tend to be challenging to study, and taking failures into account only makes things harder. For this work, we rely on several quite recent results [9, 19].

2. MODEL AND DEFINITIONS

This section describes the system model and formal definitions used throughout this paper, except in Section 8. For clarity, we defer to Section 8 various relaxed/extended versions of the system model and definitions, under which our exponential gap results continue to hold. All "log" in this paper means $\log_2$.

System model. We consider a wireless network with N *nodes* and an arbitrary undirected and connected graph G as the network topology. Each node has a unique id, and one of the N nodes is the *root*. We assume that the topology G (including the ids of each node in G) is known to all nodes. The system is synchronous and a protocol proceeds in synchronous rounds. In each round, a node (which has not failed) first performs some local computation, and then does either a *send* or *receive* operation (but not both). We also say that the node is in a *sending state* or a *receiving state* in that

round, respectively. Our results are insensitive to whether collisions are possible, but to make everything concrete, we still adopt and stick to the following commonly-used collision model. By doing a send, a node (locally) broadcasts one message to all its neighbors in G. By doing a receive, the node receives the message sent by one of its neighbors j iff node j is the only sending node among all node i's neighbors. If multiple neighbors of i send in the same round, a collision occurs and node i does not receive anything. All our results hold regardless of whether node i can distinguish silence from collision.

Failure model. The root never fails. Any other node in G may experience crash failures (but not byzantine failure), and the total number of failures can be up to $N - 1$. See Section 8 for more discussion on the number of failures. To model worst-case behavior, we have an adversary determine which nodes fail at what time. The adversary can be adaptive to the behavior of the protocol (including the coin flips) so far, but it cannot predict future coin flip results.

The SUM problem. Here each node i in G has a binary value w_i, which is initially unknown to any other node. Let $s_2 = \sum_{i=1}^{N} w_i$, and let s_1 be the sum of w_j's where by the end of the protocol's execution, node j has not failed or been disconnected from the root due to other nodes' failures. Following the same definitions from [5], a *zero-error result* of SUM is any s where $s_1 \leq s \leq s_2$, and an (ϵ, δ)-*approximate result* of SUM is any $\hat{s}$ such that for some zero-error result s, $\Pr[|\hat{s} - s| \geq \epsilon s] \leq \delta$.

Time complexity of SUM protocols. We will consider only public-coin randomized protocols. By default, a "randomized protocol" in this paper is a public-coin randomized protocol. For a randomized SUM protocol and with respect to a topology G, we define the protocol's *time complexity under G* to be the number of rounds needed for the protocol to terminate, under the worst-case values of the nodes in G, the worst-case failures (for fault-tolerant cases), and the worst-case random coin flips in the protocol. The topology G has a large impact on time complexity, and we use the notion of *aggregation rounds* to isolate such impact. We will describe the time complexity in terms of aggregation rounds. This is analogous to describing it as a multiple of, for example, the diameter of G.

In failure-free settings, an *aggregation round* in G consists of $\Lambda(G)$ rounds, where $\Lambda(G)$ is a function of the connected graph G. We will define $\Lambda(G)$ precisely later in Section 3, which describes a simple deterministic tree-aggregation protocol and then defines $\Lambda(G)$ as the number of rounds needed for that protocol to finish on G. When failures are possible, the network topology may change during execution. Let $\mathcal{G}$ be the set of all topologies that have ever appeared during the given execution. Note that a $G' \in \mathcal{G}$ may or may not be connected. For any such G' that is not connected, we define $\Lambda(G')$ to be $\Lambda(G'')$ where G'' is the connected component of G' that contains the root. To allow a fair comparison between NFT and FT communication complexity, we define an *aggregation round* in an execution with failures to be $\max_{G' \in \mathcal{G}} \Lambda(G')$ rounds. This implies that an aggregation round for an FT protocol is either the same or longer than that for an NFT protocol, which makes our gap results stronger.

NFT and FT communication complexity of SUM protocols. Classic multi-party communication complexity problems [24] usually consider the total number of bits sent by all players, since they usually use the whiteboard model where the whiteboard is the bottleneck. In our distributed computing setting with a topology G, as in other problems in such a setting, it is more natural to consider the number of bits sent by the bottleneck player. Given a randomized SUM protocol, a topology G, a value assignment to the nodes in G, and a failure adversary (if failures are considered), define a_i

to be the *expected* (with the expectation taken over coin flips in the protocol) number of bits that node i sends. The protocol's *average-case communication complexity under G* is defined as the largest a_i, across all value assignments of the nodes in G, all failure adversaries (if failures are considered), and all i's ($1 \leq i \leq N$). The protocol's *worst-case communication complexity under G* is similarly defined by considering worst-case coin flips instead of taking the expectation over the coin flips.

We define $\mathcal{R}_0^{\text{syn}}(\text{SUM}, G, b)$ ($\mathcal{R}_{\epsilon,\delta}^{\text{syn}}(\text{SUM}, G, b)$, respectively) to be the smallest average-case (worst-case, respectively) communication complexity under G across all randomized SUM protocols that can generate, in a failure-free setting, a zero-error result ((ϵ, δ)-approximate result, respectively) on G within a time complexity of at most b aggregation rounds. Here note that i) the length of an aggregation round depends on G, and ii) using the worst-case communication complexity for defining $\mathcal{R}_{\epsilon,\delta}^{\text{syn}}$ is standard practice [4, 24]. With respect to any topology G, we similarly define $\mathcal{R}_0^{\text{syn,ft}}(\text{SUM}, G, b)$ and $\mathcal{R}_{\epsilon,\delta}^{\text{syn,ft}}(\text{SUM}, G, b)$ across all fault-tolerant randomized SUM protocols.

For any given integer N, we define SUM's *NFT communication complexity* $\mathcal{R}_0^{\text{syn}}(\text{SUM}_N, b)$ and $\mathcal{R}_{\epsilon,\delta}^{\text{syn}}(\text{SUM}_N, b)$ to be the maximum $\mathcal{R}_0^{\text{syn}}(\text{SUM}, G, b)$ and $\mathcal{R}_{\epsilon,\delta}^{\text{syn}}(\text{SUM}, G, b)$, respectively, across all topology G's where G has exactly N nodes. Similarly define SUM's *FT communication complexity* $\mathcal{R}_0^{\text{syn,ft}}(\text{SUM}_N, b)$ and $\mathcal{R}_{\epsilon,\delta}^{\text{syn,ft}}(\text{SUM}_N, b)$.

Communication complexity of two-party problems. Our proofs will also need to reason about the NFT communication complexity of some two-party problems. In such a problem Π, Alice and Bob each have an input X and Y respectively, and the goal is to compute the function $\Pi(X, Y)$. For all two-party problems in this paper, we only require Alice to learn the final result. We will often use n to denote the size of Π, as compared to N which describes the number of nodes in G. The *communication complexity* of a randomized protocol for computing Π is defined to be either the average-case or worst-case (over random coin flips) number of bits sent by Alice and Bob combined. Different from the classic setting [24] for two-party problems, we will need to consider a setting with synchronous rounds[3], adapted from [19]. Here Alice and Bob proceed in synchronous rounds, where in each round Alice and Bob may simultaneously send a message to the other party. Alice, or Bob, or both may also choose not to send a message in a round. The *time complexity* of a randomized protocol for computing Π is defined to be the number of rounds needed for the protocol to terminate, over the worst-case input and the worst-case coin flips. We define $\mathcal{R}_0^{\text{syn}}(\Pi, t)$ ($\mathcal{R}_{\epsilon,\delta}^{\text{syn}}(\Pi, t)$, respectively) to be the smallest average-case (worst-case, respectively) communication complexity across all randomized protocols for Π that can generate a zero-error result ((ϵ, δ)-approximate result, respectively) within a time complexity of at most t rounds.

3. UPPER BOUNDS ON NFT COMMUNICATION COMPLEXITY OF SUM

This section describes the NFT upper bounds on SUM, which are from well-known tree-aggregation protocols coupled with some standard tricks. These are not our main contribution — instead, they serve to show the exponential gap from our FT lower bounds.

---

[3]These synchronous rounds are different from *interaction rounds*, which correspond to message exchanges. A protocol using x synchronous rounds incurs x or fewer interaction rounds since a synchronous round may or may not have any message.

Tree-aggregation protocol and defining $\Lambda(G)$. Since the topology G is known, every node can locally and deterministically construct a breadth-first spanning tree (with the root of G being the tree root) as the aggregation tree. With this tree in place, a node becomes *ready* when it receives one *aggregation message* from each of its children. Each *aggregation message* encodes the *partial sum* of all the values in the corresponding subtree. Leaf nodes are *ready* from the beginning. A ready node will combine all these aggregation messages, together with its own value, and then send a single aggregation message to its parent. With the known topology, the protocol easily avoids collision via the following simple deterministic scheduling: Out of all ready nodes, the protocol greedily and deterministically chooses a maximal set of nodes to send messages without incurring collision. A message does not need to include the sender's id — since everything is deterministic, the receiver can locally determine the sender. The function $\Lambda(G)$ is formally defined to be the number of rounds needed for the above deterministic protocol to finish on G. Thus by definition, the above protocol has a time complexity of one aggregation round.

NFT upper bounds. If each aggregation message uses $O(\log N)$ bits to encode the exact partial sum, then the above protocol is a deterministic protocol for SUM with $O(\log N)$ communication complexity and one aggregation round time complexity. For (ϵ, δ)-approximate results, it is possible to reduce the size of the aggregation message to $O(\log \frac{1}{\epsilon} + \log \log N)$ bits, using a simple private-coin protocol with similar tricks as in AMS synopsis [1] (see our technical report [11]). One can further reduce the communication complexity if the time complexity is b aggregation rounds with $b > 1$, since we can now spend b rounds in sending all the bits previously sent in one round. It is known [19] that an a-bit message sent in one round can be encoded using $a/\log \frac{b}{a}$ bits sent over b rounds, for $b \geq 2a$. To do so, one bit is sent every $\frac{b}{a} \cdot \log \frac{b}{a}$ rounds. Leveraging the round number during which the bit is sent, each such bit can encode $\log(\frac{b}{a} \cdot \log \frac{b}{a}) \geq \log \frac{b}{a}$ bits of information. Combining all the above leads to:

THEOREM 1. *For any $b \geq 1$, we have $\mathcal{R}_0^{\text{syn}}(\text{SUM}_N, b) = O(a/\log(\frac{b}{a} + 2))$ where $a = \log N$, and $\mathcal{R}_{\epsilon,\frac{1}{3}}^{\text{syn}}(\text{SUM}_N, b) = O(a/\log(\frac{b}{a} + 2))$ where $a = \log \frac{1}{\epsilon} + \log \log N$.*

4. LOWER BOUNDS ON FT COMMUNICATION COMPLEXITY OF SUM FOR $b \leq 2 - c$

The UNIONSIZE problem. In the two-party problem UNIONSIZE$_n$, Alice and Bob have length-n binary strings X and Y, respectively. Let X_i (Y_i) denote the ith bit of X (Y). Alice aims to determine $|\{i \mid X_i \neq 0 \text{ or } Y_i \neq 0\}|$. If X and Y are the characteristic vectors of two sets, then this is the size of the union of the two sets. Trivially combining a few recent results [9, 19, 29] tells us that $\mathcal{R}_0^{\text{syn}}(\text{UNIONSIZE}_n, O(\text{poly}(n))) = \Omega(\frac{n}{\log n})$ and $\mathcal{R}_{\epsilon,\frac{1}{3}}^{\text{syn}}(\text{UNIONSIZE}_n, O(\text{poly}(n))) = \Omega(\frac{1}{\epsilon^2 \log n})$ for $\epsilon \geq \frac{1}{\sqrt{n}}$ [11].

Overview of our reduction and its novelty. While the well-known reduction [29] from UNIONSIZE to the (centralized) one-pass distinct element counting problem is almost trivial, we seek a reduction from UNIONSIZE to SUM, which is less obvious. In particular, it is not immediately clear what a role failures can play. Our simple yet interesting reduction here will answer this question, which prepares for our trickier reduction in Section 5. Our reduction is based on a certain topology G. Given inputs X and Y to UNIONSIZE, each node in G has some value so that their sum is exactly

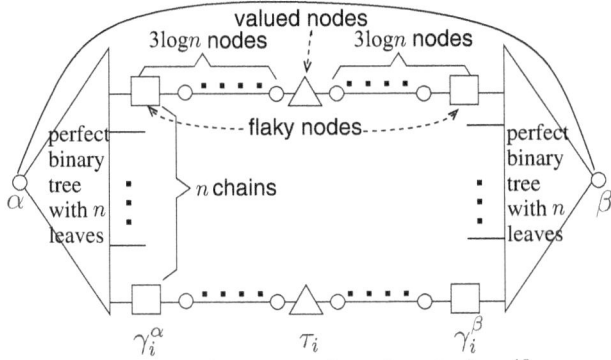

Figure 2: FT lower bound topology for $b \leq \frac{10}{9}$.

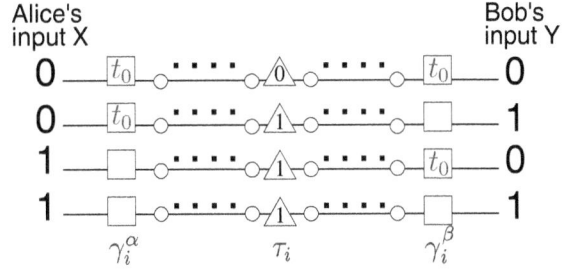

Figure 3: Values of valued nodes and failure times of flaky nodes, for $X = 0011$ and $Y = 0101$.

UNIONSIZE(X, Y). The values of some of the nodes are uniquely determined by X, and thus are known by Alice from her local knowledge of X. If the value of a node τ cannot be uniquely determined by X, then τ is *spoiled* for Alice, in the sense that Alice cannot simulate τ. (See the formal framework established in our technical report [11] for the rigorous definition of a spoiled node.) As the simulation proceeds, a spoiled node τ may causally affect its neighbor node τ', rendering Alice unable to simulate τ' and thus making τ' spoiled as well. Since the SUM protocol may have internal state, if Alice cannot simulate a node for some round, then Alice cannot simulate the node for later rounds either. In this sense, a spoiled node can never get "unspoiled" later. For each round, Alice will simply simulate the (shrinking) group of all those nodes that have not been spoiled for Alice. Bob similarly simulates all unspoiled nodes for Bob. Alice's group and Bob's may intersect.

We want the root of G to remain unspoiled for Alice when the SUM protocol ends, so that it provides the SUM result to Alice for her to determine UNIONSIZE(X, Y). To achieve this, in the reduction, Alice and Bob will need to strategically simulate the failures of certain nodes, to block the spreading of spoiled nodes. This showcases the fundamental role of failures in our reduction. At the same time, we need to avoid failing/disconnecting nodes with a value of 1 — failing/disconnecting them would enable the SUM protocol to ignore their values and potentially return a result that cannot be used to determine UNIONSIZE(X, Y). (Recall from Section 2 that a zero-error result for SUM can be any value between s_1 and s_2.) In fact, if we were not concerned with this, then simply failing all nodes except the root would keep the root unspoiled forever. Finally, it is also necessary to enlist help from Bob, who can simulate certain nodes that are spoiled for Alice. By forwarding to Alice messages sent by those nodes, Bob can further hinder the shrinking of Alice's group. The communication (between Alice and Bob) spent in doing so will be the communication complexity incurred for solving UNIONSIZE. Simulating a shrinking group of nodes and properly using failures to hinder such shrinking is the main novelty in our simple reduction.

Reducing from UNIONSIZE to SUM. For better understanding, the topology (Figure 2) we describe here works for $b \leq \frac{10}{9}$. See our technical report [11] for the topology for $b \leq 2 - c$, with the c there being any positive constant. Given UNIONSIZE$_n$ with n being a power of 2, the topology here has n parallel chains of nodes. Each chain has $6 \log n + 1$ nodes. We use γ_i^α, τ_i, and γ_i^β to denote the first, middle, and last node on the ith chain, respectively. Next we construct a perfect binary tree with all the γ_i^α's being the leaves, and let node α denote the tree root. Similarly construct a second perfect binary tree whose leaves are all the γ_i^β's, and let β be the tree root. Finally, we connect α and β with a single edge, and

let α be the root of the topology. This topology has total $N = \Theta(n \log n)$ nodes.

The inputs X and Y to UNIONSIZE$_n$ will determine the values of the τ_i's, which are called *valued nodes*. Specifically, τ_i has a binary value of 1 iff $X_i \neq 0$ or $Y_i \neq 0$ (Figure 3). All other nodes (i.e. non-valued nodes) have values of 0. X and Y also determine the failure times of the γ_i^α's and γ_i^β's, which are called *flaky nodes*. If $X_i = 0$, then γ_i^α fails at the beginning of round $t_0 = 3 \log n + 1$. Otherwise it never fails. Intuitively, t_0 is the very first round where τ_i may causally affect γ_i^α. Similarly, γ_i^β fails at the beginning of round t_0 iff $Y_i = 0$ (Figure 3). Non-flaky nodes never fail. It is worth noting that this failure adversary i) is oblivious to the SUM protocol, and ii) fails only a vanishingly small fraction (i.e., $o(N)$) of all the nodes in G.

As a key property in the above construction (and later constructions), a τ_i whose value is 1 is never disconnected from the root. This is because if τ_i's value is 1, then it must be unspoiled (by our construction) for either Alice or Bob, and thus can remain connected to α or β (and thus to the root). This in turn ensures that a zero-error result of SUM is always exactly UNIONSIZE(X, Y).

Alice will simulate the shrinking group of all the unspoiled nodes for Alice, which always contains node α. Bob similarly simulates the unspoiled nodes for Bob, including node β. (These two groups are made precise in our technical report [11].) Whenever α in the SUM protocol sends a message (whose intended recipient may or may not be β) Alice always forwards that message to Bob. Bob does the same whenever β sends a message. Alice and Bob do not exchange any additional messages. Thus the number of bits sent by Alice and Bob for solving UNIONSIZE is exactly the same as the number of the bits sent by α and β in the SUM protocol.

To obtain some intuition, let us consider some i where $X_i = 0$ and $Y_i = 1$. This makes τ_i spoiled for Alice, since Alice cannot determine τ_i's value based on X_i. To prevent τ_i from causally affecting α and thus spoiling α, Alice simulates the failure of γ_i^α before this can happen. Interestingly, since based on Y_i Bob cannot determine whether γ_i^α fails, γ_i^α becomes spoiled for Bob when it fails. Once the failure of γ_i^α can causally affect β (at round $10 \log n + 1$), Bob can no longer simulate β. The simulation must end before this happens, which is guaranteed under $b \leq \frac{10}{9}$ since an aggregation round here has no more than $8 \log n + 1$ rounds.

We obtain the following theorem by formalizing the above arguments, using an improved topology as in our technical report [11], and then trivially extending to those N values that currently do not map to any integer n for UNIONSIZE$_n$. The proof is in [11].

THEOREM 2. *For any $b \in [1, 2 - c]$ where c is any positive constant, we have* $\mathcal{R}_0^{\text{syn,ft}}(\text{SUM}_N, b) = \Omega\left(\frac{N}{\log^2 N}\right)$ *and* $\mathcal{R}_{\epsilon, \frac{1}{3}}^{\text{syn,ft}}(\text{SUM}_N, b) = \Omega\left(\frac{1}{\epsilon^2 \log N}\right)$ *for* $\epsilon \geq \frac{\sqrt{9 \log N}}{\sqrt{cN}}$.

61

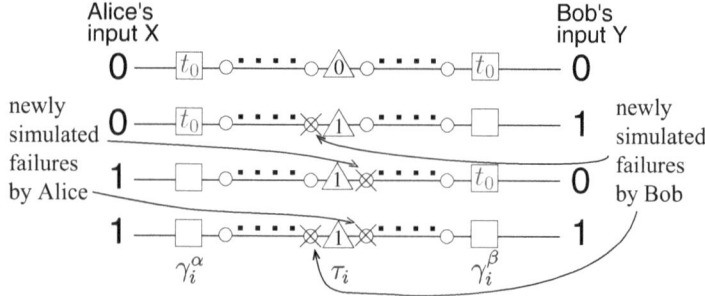

Figure 4: Why the construction from Section 4 cannot be extended to larger b.

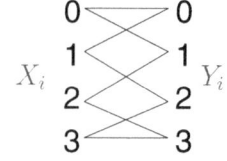

Figure 5: The cycle promise for $q = 4$.

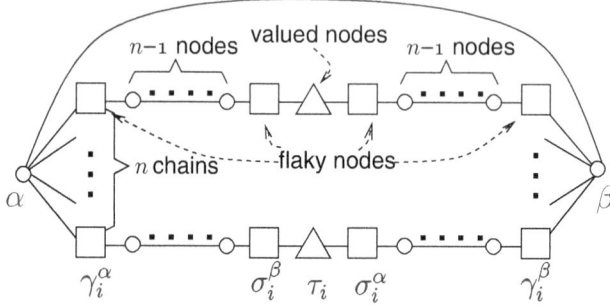

Figure 6: FT lower bound topology for $b \leq N^{0.25-c}$ or $b \leq \frac{1}{\epsilon^{0.5-c}}$.

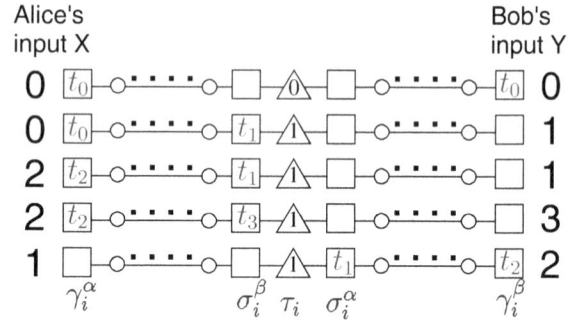

Figure 7: Values of valued nodes and failure times of flaky nodes, for $q = 4$, $X = 00221$, and $Y = 01132$.

5. LOWER BOUNDS ON FT COMMUNICATION COMPLEXITY OF SUM FOR $b \leq N^{0.25-c}$ OR $1/\epsilon^{0.5-c}$

Why the previous construction cannot be extended. The FT lower bounds in the previous section no longer hold for larger b since the failure of γ_i^α (as simulated by Alice) makes γ_i^α spoiled for Bob, which will in turn spoil β under larger b. A natural attempt to fix this is to inject new failures to prevent such propagation of spoiled nodes, as in Figure 4. Here when $Y_i = 1$, Bob simulates a new failure to the left of τ_i, to prevent the propagation of spoiled nodes due to γ_i^α. This new failure cannot be to the right of τ_i because otherwise when $X_i = 0$ (implying the failure of γ_i^α) and $Y_i = 1$, τ_i has a value of 1 and is disconnected from the root. As explained in Section 4, this prevents us from using the SUM result to determine UNIONSIZE. Similarly, Alice needs to simulate a new failure on the right side of τ_i, when $X_i = 1$. This eventually implies that when $X_i = Y_i = 1$, both of these two new failures will be introduced, again disconnecting τ_i. One could avoid this problem by adding a promise and disallowing X_i and Y_i to simultaneously be 1. Unfortunately, such a naive promise decreases the communication complexity of UNIONSIZE$_n$ to $O(\log n)$, making the final results trivial.

The UNIONSIZECP problem. To overcome the above problem, we will introduce and reduce from a new two-party communication complexity problem called UNIONSIZECP. UNIONSIZECP is intuitively UNIONSIZE extended with a novel promise which we call the *cycle promise*. This promise is not constructed ad hoc — rather, we will later see that it can be *derived*. In UNIONSIZECP$_{n,q}$ where $q \geq 2$, Alice and Bob respectively have length-n strings X and Y. The characters in the strings are integers in $[0, q-1]$. Let X_i and Y_i denote the ith character of X and Y, respectively. X and Y satisfy the following *cycle promise* where for all i: If $X_i = 0$,

then Y_i must be 0 or 1; if $X_i = q-1$, then Y_i must be $q-2$ or $q-1$; if $0 < X_i < q-1$, then Y_i must be $X_i - 1$ or $X_i + 1$. This promise is illustrated in Figure 5 as a bipartite *promise graph*, where values for X_i and Y_i are vertices and two values are connected by an edge if they satisfy the promise. Note that this promise graph is actually a cycle. Same as in UNIONSIZE, the goal in UNIONSIZECP is for Alice to determine $|\{i \mid X_i \neq 0 \text{ or } Y_i \neq 0\}|$. When $q = 2$, UNIONSIZECP degrades to UNIONSIZE. Later we will show that different from the earlier naive promise, the cycle promise does not make the communication complexity of UNIONSIZECP trivial. In our reduction to SUM, the cycle promise will enable us to continuously introduce new failures to block the spreading of spoiled nodes caused by old failures, without disconnecting any node in G with a value of 1. Those newly failed nodes then become spoiled themselves, requiring further failures to be injected, until the end of the simulation.

Reducing from UNIONSIZECP to SUM. Figure 6 illustrates the topology used in our reduction from UNIONSIZECP$_{n,q}$, which has n parallel *chains* of nodes, with each chain having $2n + 3$ nodes. We connect the first node of each chain directly to a node α, and the last node of each chain directly to a node β.[4] Finally, we connect α and β with a single edge, and let α be the root of the topology. This topology has total $N = \Theta(n^2)$ nodes. As before, Alice (Bob) will simulate a continuously shrinking group of nodes including α (β). As illustrated in Figure 7, the middle node τ_i of the ith chain is a valued node whose value is 1 iff $X_i \neq 0$ or $Y_i \neq 0$. There are 4 flaky nodes on the chain from left to right: the first node of the chain, the two neighbors of τ_i, and the last node of the chain. We use γ_i^α, σ_i^β, σ_i^α, and γ_i^β to denote these 4 nodes, respectively. Let $t_j = (j+1)n + 1$ for all $0 \leq j \leq q-1$. The flaky node γ_i^α fails

---

[4]Using binary trees will not work here. Consequently, here an aggregation round will contain more rounds than in Section 4, and in turn each chain needs to have more nodes.

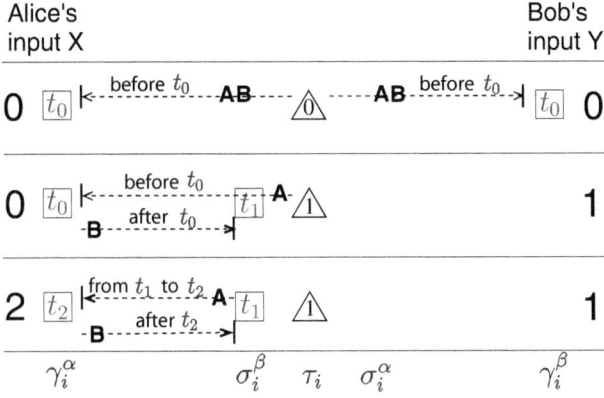

Alice's input X | Bob's input Y

Figure 8: Failures prevent the spreading of spoiled nodes. Dashed arrows labeled A (B) indicate the spreading of spoiled nodes for Alice (Bob).

at the beginning of round t_{X_i} iff X_i is even, while σ_i^α fails at the beginning of round t_{X_i} iff X_i is odd (Figure 7). Similarly, γ_i^β (σ_i^β) fails at the beginning of round t_{Y_i} iff Y_i is even (odd). Again, the failure adversary here is oblivious to the SUM protocol, and fails only a vanishingly small fraction (i.e., $o(N)$) of all the nodes in G.

To gain some intuition, consider the example in Figure 8. We say that a node is an *epicenter* for Alice's input X if it is a valued node (or a flaky node) whose value (or failure time) is not uniquely determined by X. Similarly define epicenters for Bob's input Y. Essentially, an epicenter is the source of the spreading of spoiled nodes. When $X_i = 0$, τ_i is an epicenter for Alice and thus Alice simulates the failure of γ_i^α at t_0 to block the influence of such τ_i (i.e., the top/middle scenario in Figure 8). Next since the failure of γ_i^α depends on X_i and is not uniquely determined by Y, the node γ_i^α itself now becomes an epicenter for Bob. With the cycle promise and since $X_i = 0$, Y_i must be 0 or 1. If $Y_i = 0$, then Bob does not need to be concerned, since Bob has already simulated the failure of γ_i^β at t_0 and thus blocked the potential influence of γ_i^α (i.e., the top scenario). If $Y_i = 1$ however, Bob needs to simulate the failure of σ_i^β at t_1 (i.e., the middle scenario) to block the influence of γ_i^α. Now σ_i^β again, becomes an epicenter for Alice (i.e., the middle/bottom scenario). Given the cycle promise and since $Y_i = 1$, we must have $X_i = 0$ or $X_i = 2$. If $X_i = 0$, then Alice has already simulated the failure of γ_i^α at t_0 and has already blocked the potential influence of σ_i^β (i.e., the middle scenario). If $X_i = 2$ however, Alice needs to simulate a new failure of γ_i^α at t_2 (i.e., the bottom scenario). Extending such reasoning can show that by continuously injecting new failures, we can always manage to block the spreading of spoiled nodes.

Finally, note that the simulation still cannot continue forever. Under the cycle promise, it is possible for $X_i = Y_i = q - 1$. Thus we need the SUM protocol to stop by round $t_{q-1} - 1$, since otherwise at the beginning of round t_{q-1}, Alice and Bob would simulate failures such that τ_i (with a value of 1) would be disconnected. This means that q needs to be chosen based on the SUM protocol's time complexity b: A larger q is needed when b is larger. Since the communication complexity of UNIONSIZECP depends on q (as shown next), as expected, our lower bounds here will be a function of b. We obtain the following theorem via formalizing the above reduction, using our lower bound later (Theorem 4) from UNIONSIZECP, and then trivially extending to all N values. See our technical report [11] for the proof.

THEOREM 3. *For any $b \geq 1$, we have $\mathcal{R}_0^{\text{syn,ft}}(\text{SUM}_N, b) = \Omega(\frac{\sqrt{N}}{b^2 \log N})$ and $\mathcal{R}_{\epsilon,\frac{1}{5}}^{\text{syn,ft}}(\text{SUM}_N, b) = \Omega(\frac{1}{\epsilon b^2 \log N})$ for $\epsilon \geq \frac{1}{\sqrt[4]{N}}$.*

Communication complexity of UNIONSIZECP. Since UNIONSIZECP has never been studied, there are no existing results on its communication complexity. Proving these results is thus also a contribution of our work, which may be of independent interest. On the surface, it may appear that the complexity of UNIONSIZECP should not be very different from that of UNIONSIZE. This first thought turns out to be incorrect. For $q \leq n$, our technical report [11] presents an $O(\frac{n}{q})$ upper bound protocol for $\mathcal{R}_0^{\text{syn}}(\text{UNIONSIZECP}_{n,q}, \text{poly}(n))$, implying that its communication complexity drops at least linearly with $\frac{1}{q}$. In this protocol, Alice finds the integer j with the smallest occurrence count in X, and sends Bob j and the set $\{i \mid X_i = j\}$. This takes $O(\frac{n}{q} \log n)$ bits in one round, or $O(\frac{n}{q})$ bits in poly(n) rounds [19]. Now we only need to worry about indices not in the set. For those indices, the promise graph (Figure 5) degrades to a chain, since two edges are removed from the cycle. This makes the UNIONSIZECP problem easy to solve after we apply a mapping trick [11]. To lower bound UNIONSIZECP's communication complexity, we find that the cycle promise makes it challenging to apply classic arguments based on rectangles [24].[5] But we also find that UNIONSIZECP is rather amenable to information theoretical arguments [4], which lead to the following theorem whose proof is in [11]:

THEOREM 4. $\mathcal{R}_0^{\text{syn}}(\text{UNIONSIZECP}_{n,q}, O(\text{poly}(n))) = \Omega(\frac{n}{q^2 \log n})$ *and* $\mathcal{R}_{\epsilon,\frac{1}{5}}^{\text{syn}}(\text{UNIONSIZECP}_{n,q}, O(\text{poly}(n))) = \Omega(\frac{1}{\epsilon q^2 \log n})$ *for* $\epsilon \geq \frac{1}{\sqrt{2n}}$.

6. THE FUNDAMENTAL ROLES OF CYCLE PROMISE AND UNIONSIZECP

Our reduction from UNIONSIZECP so far has led to the exponential gap result for SUM, when $b \leq N^{0.25-c}$ or $\frac{1}{\epsilon^{0.5-c}}$ for any positive constant $c < 0.25$. This restriction on b comes from the $\frac{1}{q^2}$ term in the lower bound of the communication complexity of UNIONSIZECP. Our upper bound on UNIONSIZECP indicates that such a polynomial dependency on $\frac{1}{q}$ is unavoidable because of the cycle promise. It is thus natural to ask: Can we reduce from problems without promises? Or can we reduce from problems with a different promise, to weaken the polynomial dependency on $\frac{1}{q}$ to $\log \frac{1}{q}$? For *any* possible *oblivious reduction* (defined next) from *any* two-party communication complexity problem Π to SUM, this section answers these questions in the negative. Specifically, we prove the *completeness* of UNIONSIZECP in the sense that such a Π can always be reduced to UNIONSIZECP and must have a communication complexity no larger than that of UNIONSIZECP$_{N,\lfloor \sqrt{b/3} \rfloor}$. Thus any FT lower bound on SUM, obtained in such a way via Π, must contain some polynomial term of $\frac{1}{b}$. Overcoming this polynomial term in the lower bound might still be possible, but one would have to resort to methods other than oblivious reductions from two-party problems. Our proof also (implicitly) shows that the cycle promise can be derived and that the promise likely plays a fundamental role in reasoning about many functions beyond SUM.

Reductions and oblivious reductions. Consider any two-party communication complexity problem Π, where Alice aims to learn $\Pi(X, Y)$. In a (general) reduction from Π to SUM, Alice and Bob are given some black-box *oracle* fault-tolerant protocol for SUM, and they are supposed to use this oracle to solve Π with any given input pair (X, Y). Since the (global) oracle protocol is distributed,

---

[5]Leveraging some strong results on the sperner capacity of the cyclic q-gon [6], we managed to obtain some results on $\mathcal{R}_0(\text{UNIONSIZECP})$, but not on $\mathcal{R}_{\epsilon,\delta}(\text{UNIONSIZECP})$.

it will be convenient to imagine that each node in the topology has its own oracle protocol, and invoking these protocols in a "consistent" fashion will enable the root to produce a meaningful result.

In an *oblivious reduction* to SUM, there is some fixed topology G and for each (X, Y) pair, there exists some *reference setting* specifying the value and failure time of each node in G. The reference settings are oblivious to the oracle. As explained in Section 4, a reference setting here should not fail or disconnect nodes with a value of 1. The zero-error SUM result in the reference setting should be the same as $\Pi(X, Y)$, so we can directly use it for solving Π. The reduction protocol is required to be oblivious as well. Specifically, Alice and Bob first pick a (public) random string. Next before invoking the oracle and purely based on X (Y), Alice (Bob) decides for each node in G, exactly up to which round she (he) will invoke the oracle. Note that to invoke the oracle for a certain round, Alice/Bob needs to invoke the oracle for all previous rounds as well. Alice (Bob) also decides the (initial) value of each node for which she (he) will invoke the oracle for at least one round. Requiring Alice and Bob to make these decisions beforehand is the most important aspect of oblivious reductions. We define the *reference execution* for (X, Y) to be the (global) oracle's execution under the reference setting for (X, Y) and under the chosen random string. To enable the root to generate a meaningful result, we require that the initial value, incoming messages, and coin flips fed by Alice/Bob into the oracle protocol on a node be the same as those fed into that node's oracle in the reference execution for (X, Y). Furthermore, after a node has failed in the reference execution, Alice/Bob must not invoke that node's oracle any more (since that node can no longer help out). Finally, there are two special nodes α and β in G, such that Alice and Bob will always invoke the oracle on α and β (respectively) until the root generates a result. Here α must be the root of G,[6] while β can be any other node. During the reduction, Alice (Bob) may only send to the other party all those messages sent by the oracle invocation on node α (β). This allows the establishment of a simple factor-2 relation between the communication complexity of Π and SUM.

Our previous reductions from UNIONSIZE and UNIONSIZECP to SUM are both oblivious reductions. Besides those two specific instances, the broad class of oblivious reductions further captures reductions from *any* two-party problem Π with *any* promise, using *any* topology G with *any* proper reference settings. We now present a strong result on the completeness of UNIONSIZECP:

THEOREM 5. *Consider any two-party communication complexity problem Π that can be obliviously reduced to SUM for some topology G with N nodes, with the SUM oracle protocol having a time complexity of up to b aggregation rounds where $b \geq 12$. For all $t \geq 1$, $\mathcal{R}_0^{\text{syn}}(\Pi, t) \leq \mathcal{R}_0^{\text{syn}}(\text{UNIONSIZECP}_{N, \lfloor \sqrt{b/3} \rfloor}, t)$ and $\mathcal{R}_{\epsilon, \delta}^{\text{syn}}(\Pi, t) \leq \mathcal{R}_{\epsilon, \delta}^{\text{syn}}(\text{UNIONSIZECP}_{N, \lfloor \sqrt{b/3} \rfloor}, t)$.*

The full proof is in our technical report [11], and we provide some intuition here. Let $\mathcal{X}$ be Alice's input domain in Π, and $\mathcal{Y}$ be Bob's. Let $\mathcal{L} \subseteq \mathcal{X} \times \mathcal{Y}$ be the set of all valid input pairs, given the promise in Π. If Π has no promise, then $\mathcal{L} = \mathcal{X} \times \mathcal{Y}$. Given $(X, Y) \in \mathcal{L}$, an oblivious reduction has a reference setting specifying the value of each node in G. For any node τ where $\tau \neq \alpha$ and $\tau \neq \beta$, we define τ's *(value) assignment graph* to be the bipartite graph where $\mathcal{X} \cup \mathcal{Y}$ are vertices and an edge (X, Y) exists iff $(X, Y) \in \mathcal{L}$. In addition, each edge (X, Y) has a binary label which is the value of τ in the reference setting for (X, Y). We prove that it is always possible to partition the vertices in τ's assignment graph into $2b'$

---

[6]This is largely for clarity, and can be relaxed if desired.

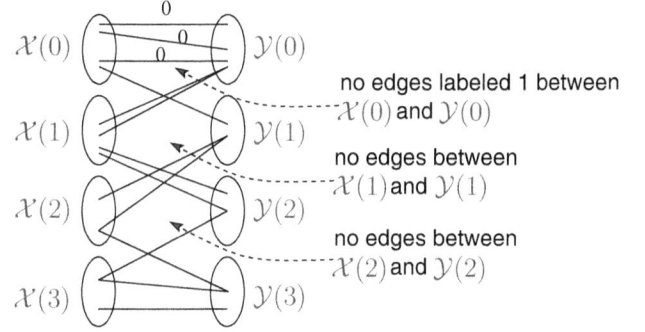

Figure 9: Example assignment graph for a given node τ and for $b' = 4$. $\mathcal{X}(0), \mathcal{Y}(0), \ldots, \mathcal{X}(3)$, and $\mathcal{Y}(3)$ are the 8 subsets, which may have different sizes and different numbers of incidental edges. All edges without labels indicated have a label of 1.

(where $b' = \lfloor \sqrt{b/3} \rfloor \geq 2$) disjoint subsets with strong properties as illustrated in Figure 9. Intuitively, this is because otherwise the reference setting for some input pair would need to have so many failures in G such that τ (with a value of 1) would be disconnected from the root. Those failures are needed to ensure that Alice (Bob) can invoke the oracle on α (β) throughout the execution.

At this point, we already have something close to the cycle promise — if we view each subset as a super vertex, then all the $2b'$ super vertices form a subgraph of a length-$2b'$ cycle. It is now possible to reduce Π to UNIONSIZECP$_{N, b'}$, by mapping an input X for Π to an input X' for UNIONSIZECP as following: Each τ in G corresponds to a unique i ($1 \leq i \leq N - 2$), and X_i' is set to be the index of the subset in τ's assignment graph to which X belongs. Finally, X_{N-1}' is set to be the (initial) value of α in the given oblivious reduction, which can be obtained purely based on X. X_N' is set to be 0. The conversion from Y to Y' is similar, with $Y_{N-1}' = 0$ and Y_N' being the value of β.

7. LOWER BOUNDS ON FT COMMUNICATION COMPLEXITY OF SUM FOR ALL b

Our previous FT lower bounds become trivial when $b > N^{0.25}$ or $\frac{1}{\epsilon^{0.5}}$. This section uses a different approach to obtain logarithmic FT lower bounds for such b, which is more than exponentially far away from the corresponding $O(1)$ NFT upper bounds for such b. We first provide some intuition under a strong *gossip assumption*. Later we will remove this key assumption, which is the key technical challenge addressed by our proof.

Under the *gossip assumption*, the root computes the sum by explicitly collecting from each node a gossip containing its value. We will show that to do so, some node will need to send $\Omega(\log N)$ messages, and hence $\Omega(\log N)$ bits even if the gossips can be fully aggregated/compressed. Here the lower bound topology will be an N-node clique with one of nodes being the root (Figure 10). Imagine for now that the adversary can fail edges in this topology, and further there is never more than one node sending messages in a round. These assumptions can be easily removed [11] once we insert some dummy nodes into each edge. Our adaptive adversary waits until exactly $\frac{N-1}{2}$ non-root nodes have sent a message (e.g., nodes 1 and 2 in Figure 10). Call these $\frac{N-1}{2}$ nodes as *marked* nodes. The adversary then fails enough edges so that each unmarked non-root node (e.g., node 3) is paired up with a marked node (e.g., node 1) and the marked node is the only gateway for the unmarked node to reach the root. Now each marked nodes has already sent a message, and yet it has one new gossip (from the

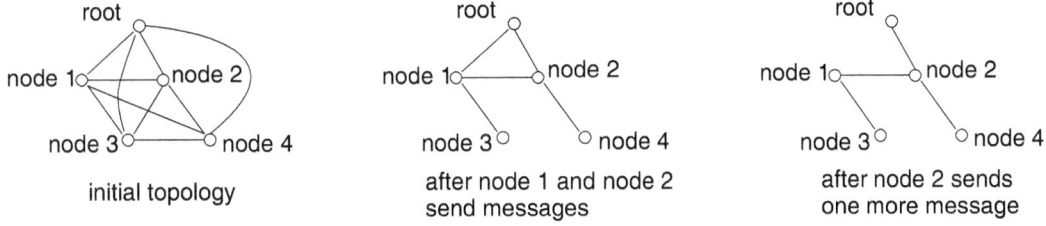

Figure 10: Example FT lower bound topology for $n = 4$ and unrestricted b.

corresponding unmarked node) to forward to the root. Next apply this procedure recursively on these $\frac{N-1}{2}$ marked nodes, and inject a second batch of edge failures when exactly $\frac{N-1}{4}$ of them (e.g., node 2) have sent a second message. Continuing this argument can easily show that for all the gossips to reach the root, some node needs to send at least $\log(N-1) + 1$ messages.

The gossip assumption is rather strong. For example, a protocol may be such that if a node's value is 0, then the root does not need to collect a gossip from that node and simply uses 0 as the default value. It is also possible that node i sends a message to node j iff node i's value is 1, and then node j conceptually relays i's value to the root, by sending a message to the root iff this value is 0. Here the root *never* collects a gossip from node i. A key challenge in our proof is to properly capture all such possibilities. To do so, we explore a single-player *probing game*, and prove a strong connection between SUM protocols and strategies in this game. We then prove a lower bound on the probing game, which eventually leads to the following FT lower bounds on SUM. See our technical report [11] for the proof of the following theorem:

THEOREM 6. *For any $b \geq 1$, we have* $\mathcal{R}_0^{\mathrm{syn,ft}}(\mathrm{SUM}_N, b) = \Omega(\log N)$ *and* $\mathcal{R}_{\epsilon, \frac{1}{3}}^{\mathrm{syn,ft}}(\mathrm{SUM}_N, b) = \Omega(\log \frac{1}{\epsilon})$ *for* $\epsilon \geq \frac{1}{N}$.

8. DISCUSSIONS AND EXTENSIONS

Putting together the NFT upper bounds (Theorem 1) and FT lower bounds (Theorem 2, 3, and 6) will directly give us the exponential gaps, as summarized in Figure 1 from Section 1. Specifically, one only needs to apply Theorem 2 for $1 \leq b \leq 2 - c$, Theorem 3 for $2 - c < b \leq N^{0.25-c}$ or $\frac{1}{\epsilon^{0.5-c}}$, and Theorem 6 for $b > N^{0.25-c}$ or $\frac{1}{\epsilon^{0.5-c}}$, with c being any positive constant below 0.25. It is worth noting that such exponential gap results apply as well to the following extensions of the model defined in Section 2.

Total number of failures. Section 2 allowed the total number of failures to be up to $N - 1$. In all the executions (of the SUM protocol) considered in our FT lower bound proofs, the failure adversary actually injects only $o(N)$ failures in G. Thus our lower bounds apply, without any modification, as long as the total number of failures is allowed to be up to any constant fraction of N. Our proofs carry over to even smaller number of failures, without disrupting the exponential gap, if we lower the degree of our polynomial lower bounds.

Private-coin and deterministic protocols. Section 2 only considered public-coin protocols. Private-coin protocols and deterministic protocols are also fully but implicitly covered by all our theorems. This is simply because the NFT upper bound protocol with zero-error in Theorem 1 is actually deterministic, while the one with (ϵ, δ)-error uses only private coins.

Allowing integer values for each node. In practice, each node in the network may have some integer value instead of a binary value. Our FT lower bounds obviously carry over to integer values. Our NFT upper bounds continue to apply as long as the integer value has a domain no larger than some polynomial of N.

Other network models. Because of the paramount practical importance of communication complexity in wireless networks, Section 2 chose to define a system model capturing wireless networks. All our theorems continue to apply regardless of whether collision is considered (i.e., whether a node can receive messages simultaneously from multiple neighbors in a round) and regardless of whether the communication is point-to-point or (local) broadcast. Note that in settings without collisions, $\Lambda(G)$ is simply the eccentricity of the root in G.

Letting all nodes know the result. We required only the root to learn the final result. To let all nodes know the result, the root in our upper bound protocol in Theorem 1 can simply broadcast the result to all nodes along some spanning tree.

Unknown topology. Assuming a known topology, as in Section 2, strengthens our FT lower bounds. For the upper bounds obtained via tree-aggregation, with unknown topologies, it suffices to simply add a distributed pre-processing phase for building a spanning tree.

Defining time complexity over average coin flips. Section 2 defined the time complexity of a protocol to be the number of rounds needed under the worst-case coin flips. Considering worst-case coin flips there was largely for clarity, as in the standard practice [4, 24] of using worst-case coin flips for defining randomized non-zero-error communication complexity. Our technical report [11] shows that defining time complexity using average-case coin flips only affects our results slightly, and our exponential gap continues to hold.

Excluding the communication complexity of the root. Section 2 defined the communication complexity of a SUM protocol to be the number of bits sent by the bottleneck node. Here it is possible for the bottleneck node to be the root. In some scenarios, one may want to exclude the root in this definition. For example, we may be concerned with communication complexity due to the power consumption of the nodes, while the root node (e.g., a base station) may not be operating on battery power. Doing so will not affect any of our theorems, once we extend the lower bound topology by attaching a new degree-1 node to the old root and letting this new node be the root [11].

9. CONCLUSIONS AND FUTURE WORK

Tolerating crash failures has been a key focus of distributed computing research from the very beginning. Adding this fault tolerance requirement to multi-party communication complexity leads to the following natural question: "If we want to compute a function in a fault-tolerant way, what will the communication complexity be?" This paper reveals that the impact of failures on communication complexity can be large, at least for the SUM aggregation function in networks with general topologies. Specifically, we show that there exists (at least) an *exponential gap* between the NFT and FT communication complexity of SUM.

This result attests that FT communication complexity needs to be studied separately from traditional NFT communication complexity. Since this paper is only the first step along this new direction of FT communication complexity, as one would imagine, the topic is rife with interesting open questions such as:

- Our lower bound topologies for SUM are carefully constructed. We are currently investigating to what extent our lower bounds can generalize to other topologies.

- We have mainly focused on the exponential gap for SUM, and have been less concerned about specific degrees of the polynomials in the FT lower bounds. Can we further strengthen these lower bounds? Note that even our lower bound on the communication complexity of UNIONSIZECP is not tight (i.e., roughly $\frac{1}{q}$ factor from the upper bound), and thus improvement might be possible even there. Similarly, our completeness result for UNIONSIZECP is for $q = \Theta(\sqrt{b})$, while our reduction actually uses a weaker $q = \Theta(b)$.

- Our lower bounds show that the bottleneck node in G will incur a large communication complexity. How many nodes in G will incur asymptotically similar communication complexity as that node? Putting it another way, how many hot spots are there?

- We have defined the FT communication complexity of SUM across all protocols that can tolerate a certain number of failures. Similar to the idea of early stopping distributed consensus protocols, among this class of protocols, it would be interesting to investigate to what extent a protocol can incur a smaller communication complexity when the number of failures *that actually happen* (denoted as f) is small. Repeatedly invoking tree-aggregation incurs a communication complexity of $O(f \log N)$ — can we do better? We are currently investigating both upper bounds and lower bounds on this.

- Our results extend to some other functions such as SELECTION, via trivial reductions to and from SUM. But clearly there are also many interesting functions whose FT communication complexity is still unknown. In particular, can we characterize the set of functions having exponential gaps?

For answering these questions, we believe that some of the insights developed in this paper (e.g., on the role of failures in the reduction and on the cycle promise) can be valuable.

10. ACKNOWLEDGMENTS

We thank Cheng Yeaw Ku and Y. C. Tay for their valuable help and pointers, and the PODC anonymous reviewers for helpful feedbacks. This work is partly supported by the research grant for the Human Sixth Sense Programme at the Advanced Digital Sciences Center from Singapore's Agency for Science, Technology and Research (A*STAR), partly supported by the research grant MOE2011-T2-2-042 "Fault-tolerant Communication Complexity in Wireless Networks" from Singapore Ministry of Education Academic Research Fund Tier-2, and partly supported by the Intel Science and Technology Center for Cloud Computing (ISTC-CC).

11. REFERENCES

[1] N. Alon, Y. Matias, and M. Szegedy. The space complexity of approximating the frequency moments. In *STOC*, May 1996.

[2] O. Ayaso, D. Shah, and M. Dahleh. Information theoretic bounds for distributed computation over networks of point-to-point channels. *IEEE Transactions on Information Theory*, 56(12):6020–6039, 2010.

[3] T. Aysal, M. Yildiz, A. Sarwate, and A. Scaglione. Broadcast gossip algorithms for consensus. *IEEE Transactions on Signal Processing*, 57(7):2748–2761, July 2009.

[4] Z. Bar-Yossef, T. S. Jayram, R. Kumar, and D. Sivakumar. An information statistics approach to data stream and communication complexity. *Journal of Computer and System Sciences*, 68(4):702–732, June 2004.

[5] M. Bawa, A. Gionis, H. Garcia-Molina, and R. Motwani. The price of validity in dynamic networks. *Journal of Computer and System Sciences*, 73(3):245–264, May 2007.

[6] A. Blokhuis. On the sperner capacity of the cyclic triangle. *Journal of Algebraic Combinatorics*, 2(2):123–124, June 1993.

[7] S. Boyd, A. Ghosh, B. Prabhakar, and D. Shah. Randomized gossip algorithms. *IEEE Transactions on Information Theory*, 52(6):2508–2530, June 2006.

[8] M. Braverman and A. Rao. Towards coding for maximum errors in interactive communication. In *STOC*, June 2011.

[9] A. Chakrabarti and O. Regev. An optimal lower bound on the communication complexity of gap-hamming-distance. In *STOC*, June 2011.

[10] A. Chandra, M. Furst, and R. Lipton. Multi-party protocols. In *STOC*, April 1983.

[11] B. Chen, H. Yu, Y. Zhao, and P. B. Gibbons. The Cost of Fault Tolerance in Multi-Party Communication Complexity. Technical Report TRA5/12, School of Computing, National University of Singapore, May 2012. Also available at http://www.comp.nus.edu.sg/~yuhf/TRA5-12.pdf.

[12] J. Chen and G. Pandurangan. Optimal gossip-based aggregate computation. In *SPAA*, June 2010.

[13] J. Chen, G. Pandurangan, and D. Xu. Robust computation of aggregates in wireless sensor networks: Distributed randomized algorithms and analysis. In *IPSN*, April 2005.

[14] J. Considine, F. Li, G. Kollios, and J. Byers. Approximate aggregation techniques for sensor databases. In *ICDE*, March 2004.

[15] I. Eyal, I. Keidar, and R. Rom. LiMoSense — Live Monitoring in Dynamic Sensor Networks. In *ALGOSENSORS*, September 2011.

[16] P. Flajolet and G. N. Martin. Probabilistic counting algorithms for data base applications. *Journal of Computer and System Sciences*, 31(2):182–209, September 1985.

[17] A. Giridhar and P. R. Kumar. Towards a theory of in-network computation in wireless sensor networks. *IEEE Communications Magazine*, 44(4):98–107, April 2006.

[18] P. Gupta and P. R. Kumar. The capacity of wireless networks. *IEEE Transactions on Information Theory*, 46(2):388–404, March 2000.

[19] R. Impagliazzo and R. Williams. Communication complexity with synchronized clocks. In *CCC*, June 2010.

[20] M. Jelasity, A. Montresor, and O. Babaoglu. Gossip-based aggregation in large dynamic networks. *ACM Transactions on Computer Systems*, 23(3):219–252, August 2005.

[21] P. Jesus, C. Baquero, and P. Almeida. Fault-tolerant aggregation by flow updating. In *DAIS*, June 2009.

[22] S. Kashyap, S. Deb, K. Naidu, R. Rastogi, and A. Srinivasan. Efficient gossip-based aggregate computation. In *PODS*, June 2006.

[23] D. Kempe, A. Dobra, and J. Gehrke. Gossip-based computation of aggregate information. In *FOCS*, October 2003.

[24] E. Kushilevitz and N. Nisan. *Communication Complexity*. Cambridge University Press, 1996.

[25] D. Mosk-Aoyama and D. Shah. Computing separable functions via gossip. In *PODC*, July 2006.

[26] S. Nath, P. Gibbons, S. Seshany, and Z. Anderson. Synopsis diffusion for robust aggregation in sensor networks. *ACM Transactions on Sensor Networks*, 4(2), March 2008.

[27] S. Rajagopalan and L. Schulman. A coding theorem for distributed computation. In *STOC*, May 1994.

[28] L. Schulman. Coding for interactive communication. *IEEE Transactions on Information Theory*, 42(6):1745–1756, 1996.

[29] D. Woodruff. Optimal space lower bounds for all frequency moments. In *SODA*, January 2004.

[30] H. Yu. Secure and highly-available aggregation queries in large-scale sensor networks via set sampling. *Distributed Computing*, 23(5):373–394, April 2011.

The Communication Complexity of Distributed Task Allocation

Andrew Drucker
Computer Science and AI
Laboratory, MIT
Cambridge, MA 02139
adrucker@mit.edu

Fabian Kuhn
Dept. of Computer Science
University of Freiburg
79110 Freiburg, Germany
kuhn@informatik.uni-freiburg.de

Rotem Oshman*
Computer Science and AI
Laboratory, MIT
Cambridge, MA 02139
rotem@csail.mit.edu

ABSTRACT

We consider a distributed task allocation problem in which m players must divide a set of n tasks between them. Each player i receives as input a set X_i of tasks such that the union of all input sets covers the task set. The goal is for each player to output a subset $Y_i \subseteq X_i$, such that the outputs $(Y_1, ..., Y_m)$ form a partition of the set of tasks. The problem can be viewed as a distributed one-shot variant of the well-known k-server problem, and we also show that it is closely related to the problem of finding a rooted spanning tree in directed broadcast networks.

We study the communication complexity and round complexity of the task allocation problem. We begin with the classical two-player communication model, and show that the randomized communication complexity of task allocation is $\Omega(n)$, even when the set of tasks is known to the players in advance. For the multi-player setting with $m = O(n)$ we give two upper bounds in the shared-blackboard model of communication. We show that the problem can be solved in $O(\log n)$ rounds and $O(n \log n)$ total bits for arbitrary inputs; moreover, if for any set X of tasks, there are at least $\alpha|X|$ players that have at least one task from X in their inputs, then $O((1/\alpha + \log m) \log n)$ rounds suffice even if each player can only write $O(\log n)$ bits on the blackboard in each round. Finally, we extend our results to the case where the players communicate over an arbitrary directed communication graph instead of a shared blackboard. As an application of these results, we also consider the related problem of constructing a directed spanning tree in strongly-connected directed networks and we show lower and upper bounds for that problem.

Categories and Subject Descriptors

F.2.2 [**Analysis of Alg. and Problem Complexity**]: Non-numerical Alg. and Problems—*comp. on discrete structures*; G.2.2 [**Discrete Mathematics**]: Graph Theory—*network problems*

General Terms

Algorithms, Theory

Keywords

task allocation, directed spanning trees, multiparty communication complexity, unidirectional links

1. INTRODUCTION

In many distributed systems, a large amount of work is performed quickly and efficiently by partitioning the work across the participants in the network. The "work" to be performed can range from computational work, such as simulating a complex physical environment or solving a complex optimization problem, to physical work, such as having robots travel to various locations to carry out assorted tasks. In all cases, effectively parceling out parts of the global goal to be performed by individual participants is key to the overall efficiency of the system. This problem has been studied in many forms and guises, from fault-tolerant task allocation (see [21]) to centralized and distributed scheduling (e.g., [8, 6, 18] and many others), from theoretical (e.g., the k-server problem [7]) to practical approaches [1].

In the current paper we study the *communication complexity* of task allocation, that is, the total number of bits that the participants need to exchange to allocate the tasks between themselves. We consider an abstract version of the problem, TASKALLOCATION$_{m,n}$, where m players must jointly perform a set of n tasks (we often assume that the set of tasks is $\{1, ..., n\}$). Each player i receives as input a set $X_i \subseteq \{1, ..., n\}$ of tasks that it is capable of performing. For example, in the case of robots performing tasks at different geographical locations, the player's input might consist of the set of locations requiring servicing that the robot can "see" with its sensors. The goal is for the players to partition the tasks between them: each player i must output a subset of tasks $Y_i \subseteq X_i$, such that $\bigcup_i Y_i = \{1, ..., n\}$ and $Y_i \cap Y_j = \emptyset$ for all $i \neq j$. To make the problem feasible, we consider only inputs $X_1, ..., X_m$ such that $\bigcup_i X_i = \{1, ..., n\}$, that is, there *exists* some partition that covers all the tasks. The players are charged for

*Rotem Oshman was supported by the Center for Science of Information (CSoI), an NSF Science and Technology Center, under grant agreement CCF-0939370.

communicating among themselves, but not for writing their output sets $Y_1, \ldots, Y_m$. We consider various models of communication between the players, from shared-blackboard to arbitrary strongly-connected communication networks.

The task allocation problem can be viewed as a restricted one-shot instance of the well-known k-server problem [7], where a centralized online algorithm assigns tasks to k servers, minimizing the total cost of servicing all tasks. In the k-server problem each (server, task) pair is associated with a *cost* for having the server perform the task, and moreover, tasks arrive continually and must be assigned in an online manner. In TASKALLOCATION, all tasks are initially known, and all have a cost of either 1 (if the task can be performed by the player) or ∞ (if it cannot). Partitioning the tasks between the players corresponds to finding a minimum-weight assignment of tasks to servers. To the best of our knowledge, the k-server problem has not been studied from the perspective of communication complexity, although distributed variants have been studied (e.g., [2, 3]). In the current paper we are not interested in competitive analysis, as the variant we consider is single-shot; extensions to weighted inputs and the online setting remain interesting directions for future work.

Our work raises several open problems, which we discuss in Section 9. In general, two-player communication complexity lower bounds have proven very useful in proving lower bounds on various distributed problems (e.g., [19, 4, 9, 16]). However, distributed computation is more accurately captured by *multi-player* communication games in the number-in-hand model, where each player knows its own input (contrast with the number-on-forehead model, where each player knows all the *other* players' input). The number-in-hand model was neglected by the communication complexity community for a time, but recently several new techniques have led to exciting advances (see [10, 11, 12]). We believe that the complexity of distributed computing in the *CONGEST* model, where bandwidth is restricted, can be analyzed in terms of a multi-player communication game. Importing problems from the distributed computing world into the communication complexity model raises issues which are not often considered in existing communication complexity lower bounds: *search problems*, where players are allowed to choose one of many possible outputs (e.g., electing a leader or reaching consensus);[1] *partial knowledge*, where each player needs to output only part of the answer (as exemplified in the TASKALLOCATION problem); and *unicast communication cost*, where we wish to charge players for the number of other players they communicate with, not just the total communication complexity as in the shared blackboard model. We believe that these issues yield new and interesting questions in multi-player communication complexity.

Contributions. Despite the apparent simplicity of the problem, TASKALLOCATION is rich enough to admit a strong lower bound: in Section 4 we show that even for two players (using public random coins), TASKALLOCATION$_{2,n}$ has a randomized communication complexity of $\Omega(n)$. We apply this bound in Section 5 to show that computing a rooted spanning tree in directed broadcast networks with diameter 2, where each message is restricted to B bits, requires $\Omega(n/B)$ rounds — even when the size of the network is fixed

---

[1]Many well-known lower bounds in communication complexity concern decision problems, but there are some cases where search problems play an important role, e.g., [13].

in advance and nodes have unique identifiers in the range $1, \ldots, n$. In Section 6 we study the communication complexity of TASKALLOCATION$_{m,n}$ in the classical multi-player setting where players communicate over a shared blackboard. We give two randomized algorithms: the first requires players to write large messages on the blackboard, but has an overall communication complexity of $O(n \log(n + m))$ and terminates in $O(\log m)$ rounds with high probability on any input. The second algorithm we give works well when no small number of players has to take care of a large set of tasks, a property that is formally captured by our definition of *task-player expansion* in Section 3. For inputs with task-player expansion α, our second randomized algorithm terminates in $O((1/\alpha + \log m) \log n)$ rounds (or better, see Theorem 6.6 in Section 6) and uses messages of size $O(\log(n + m))$. This can be shown to be optimal to within a polylog(m, n) factor. In Section 7 we extend our results to an arbitrary strongly-connected communication network between the players, with the size of individual messages bounded by B. We show that in networks of diameter D, TASKALLOCATION$_{m,n}$ can be solved in $O(D + \sqrt{m/B} \log m + n \log(n + m)/B)$ rounds, using a total of $O((m + n) \text{polylog}(m, n))$ bits of communication.

2. RELATED WORK

Scheduling and task allocation. There is a vast body of literature concerning scheduling, allocation, and related problems. Offline and online scheduling problems are a mainstay of combinatorial optimization; see [5] for a survey on multiprocessor scheduling, and [14] for a survey on the k-server problem. Distributed k-server is studied in [3], which gives a generic technique for translating centralized k-server algorithms into decentralized ones while maintaining good competitive ratio. The number of messages sent by the decentralized algorithm is counted in its cost, but messages can be unboundedly large, and indeed their size in [3] grows with the space requirements of the original centralized algorithm. To our knowledge, the communication complexity (in number of bits) of k-server has not been studied.

Distributed spanning tree in directed networks. Our motivation for studying the TASKALLOCATION problem arose from a result in [16], where two of the authors proved that counting (i.e., determining the number of nodes in the network) requires $\Omega(n/B)$ rounds in directed strongly-connected broadcast networks of diameter 2, where message size is limited to B bits. The specific network used in the lower bound of [16] only admits rooted spanning trees of constant depth, and hence the counting lower bound translates to a lower bound on finding a rooted spanning tree: if a rooted spanning tree can be found quickly, then counting could be solved in $O(1)$ additional rounds by summing up the tree, contradicting the $\Omega(n/B)$ lower bound. However, this lower bound crucially relies on the assumption that the size of the network is initially unknown to the nodes, and this did not seem to be the "reason" for the hardness of finding a spanning tree. In the current paper we use a lower bound on the TASKALLOCATION problem to obtain an $\Omega(n/B)$ lower bound on finding a rooted spanning tree even when the size n is known in advance.

Communication complexity. Strong communication complexity lower bounds are known for many interesting two-player problems; for example, for SETDISJOINTNESS, where the players must determine whether their input sets are disjoint, a tight bound of $\Omega(n)$ is shown in [20]. For a comprehensive treatment of the subject we refer to [17]. The TASKALLOCATION problem differs from classical problems such as SETDISJOINTNESS in that it is not a decision problem; on a given input there may be many permissible outputs. In addition, we do not require any of the players to know the *global* answer, only which tasks they have claimed for themselves. The problem is therefore less constrained than traditional problems. In particular, the two-player $\Omega(n)$ lower bound we give in Section 4 does not follow directly from the $\Omega(n)$ lower bound on SETDISJOINTNESS: in the TASKALLOCATION$_{2,n}$ problem we promise the players that the inputs X_1, X_2 cover all the tasks, that is, $X_1 \cup X_2 = \{1, \ldots, n\}$. With this promise, SETDISJOINTNESS becomes trivial, as X_1, X_2 are disjoint iff their sizes add up to exactly n. Moreover, when the sets are not disjoint, an element in the intersection can be found using only $O(\log^2 n)$ bits of communication (by binary search). A similar phenomenon occurs with other problems, such as INNERPRODUCT and GAPHAMMINGDISTANCE. Therefore the lower bound we give in Section 4 is proven from first principles using an information-theoretic argument, rather than appealing to existing communication complexity lower bounds.

3. PROBLEM STATEMENT

Task allocation. The *distributed task allocation* problem, denoted TASKALLOCATION$_{m,n}$, is defined over a set T of $|T| = n$ tasks and a set V of $|V| = m$ players. We often assume that $T = \{1, \ldots, n\}$. Each player $v \in V$ receives an input set $X_v \subseteq T$, with the promise that $\bigcup_{v \in V} X_v = T$. The goal is for each player to output a set $Y_v \subseteq X_v$, such that for all $u, v \in V$ we have $Y_u \cap Y_v = \emptyset$, and moreover, $\bigcup_{v \in V} Y_v = T$ (that is, $\{Y_v \mid v \in V\}$ is a partition of T).

The input assignment $\{X_v \mid v \in V\}$ induces a bipartite graph $H = (V \dot\cup T, F)$, where the edges F are given by $F := \{(v, x) \in V \times T \mid x \in X_v\}$. We call H the *task-player graph*. For convenience, for each task $i \in T$, we let $V_i := \{v \in V \mid i \in X_v\}$ denote the set of players that have task i in their input.

Communication model. In order to solve a given task allocation instance the players in V must communicate. In the current paper we assume synchronous communication, i.e., the players proceed in synchronous rounds. We consider two models of communication:

- In the classical *shared blackboard* model, the players communicate by writing messages on a shared blackboard which is visible to all other players.

- In addition, we are interested in the following *general network* model: players communicate over an arbitrary (possibly directed) graph $G = (V, E)$. In each round, every player (represented by a node of G) can send one message of B bits to all its out-neighbors in G (that is, communication is by *local broadcast*). We assume that initially the players do not know anything about the graph G except possibly its size, i.e., the number of players.

The shared blackboard model is a special case of the general network model, obtained by choosing $G := K_m$ (the complete graph on m nodes).

We are interested in the following performance measures:

- *Total communication complexity*: the total number of bits ever sent or written on the blackboard during the protocol.

- *Round complexity*: how many rounds of communication are required (where in each round each player can send/write one message).

- *Message size*: how many bits the players send or write on the blackboard in each round. This parameter is usually specified as an external constraint, and we denote it by B.

Task-player expansion. The hardness of an instance of TASKALLOCATION depends on the properties of the input assignment, represented by the task-player graph H. In particular, we will show that the complexity depends on how well tasks can be distributed among the players, as formally captured by the following definition.

DEFINITION 1 (TASK-PLAYER EXPANSION). *The task-player expansion of a task-player graph $H = (V \dot\cup T, F)$ is defined as*

$$\alpha(H) := \min_{T' \subseteq T} \frac{\left| \bigcup_{x \in T'} V_x \right|}{|T'|}.$$

Informally, when the task-player expansion is large, each set of tasks can be assigned to many different players; the problem is in some sense less constrained, which makes it easier to solve. The smallest value $\alpha(H)$ can take is $1/n$, which occurs when one player receives all the tasks in his input and the others receive nothing. The largest value, obtained when H is the complete bipartite graph, is m/n.

General definitions and notation. We conclude this section with a few general definitions and notation that will be used throughout the paper. For an integer $k \geq 1$, we denote by $[k]$ the set $[k] := \{1, \ldots, k\}$. Some of our results concern directed graphs. The graphs are always assumed strongly-connected; for a strongly-connected directed graph G, the diameter $D(G)$ is the length of the longest directed shortest path between any two nodes in G.

4. TWO-PLAYER LOWER BOUND FOR TASK ALLOCATION

We begin by analyzing the complexity of task allocation in the classic two-party model, where two players, Alice and Bob, wish to allocate n tasks between them. In this section we let TASKALLOCATION$_n$ stand for TASKALLOCATION$_{2,n}$, and we use U, V to denote the inputs to Alice and Bob respectively and A, B to denote Alice and Bob's outputs. It is assumed that $T = [n]$ and both players know n.

The tasks over which Alice and Bob "contend" are the ones in the intersection of their inputs, $U \cap V$; these tasks must be output by one player but not by both. If Alice does *not* output some task that she received in her input, then she must know that this task is in the intersection of the inputs, and that Bob will output it. The connection between task allocation and finding the intersection of the players' inputs is formalized in the following easy lemma:

LEMMA 4.1. *Let (A, B) be a valid output on instance (U, V) of TASKALLOCATION$_n$; that is, $A \cup B = [n]$, $A \cap B = \emptyset$, $A \subseteq U$, and $B \subseteq V$. Then (1) $U \setminus A \subseteq U \cap V$ and $V \setminus B \subseteq U \cap V$; and (2) $U \cap V \subseteq (U \setminus A) \cup (V \setminus B)$.*

PROOF. For (1), let $x \in U \setminus A$ (the other inclusion is similar). In particular, then, $x \notin A$, and since $A \cup B = [n]$, we must have $x \in B$. But $B \subseteq V$, and therefore $x \in U \cap V$.

For (2), let $x \in U \cap V$. Since $A \cup B = [n]$ we have $x \in A \cup B$; assume w.l.o.g. that $x \in A$. Because $A \cap B = \emptyset$ we have $x \notin B$, but on the other hand we have $x \in V$ (as $x \in U \cap V$). Together we have $x \in V \setminus B$. $\qquad\square$

THEOREM 4.2. *The randomized (public-coin) communication complexity of two-player task allocation is* $\Omega(n)$.

PROOF. Suppose the input (U, V) is generated according to the following distribution $\mathcal{D}$. Choose a random subset $X \subseteq [n]$ of size pn. Next, choose a random subset $Y \subseteq [n] \setminus X$ of size $(1-p)n/2$. Let $U := X \cup Y$ and let $V := X \cup \bar{Y} = \bar{Y}$. Let $\mathcal{C}$ be the support of the distribution (i.e., each set is of size $(1+p)n/2$, and the intersection is of size pn).

We are interested in the probability over $(U, V) \sim \mathcal{D}$ that given only U, Alice can guess $U \cap V = X$. Given U, the set X is a uniformly-chosen subset of pn elements of U. Therefore, given U, Alice's chance of guessing X is at best

$$\binom{(1+p)n/2}{pn}^{-1} \leq \left(\frac{(1+p)n/2}{pn}\right)^{-pn} = \left(\frac{1+p}{2p}\right)^{-pn} .$$

Informally, we will show that if there exists a protocol P for task allocation with communication complexity $o(n)$, then Alice can guess $X = U \cap V$ with statistically impossible accuracy (i.e., she can succeed with probability better than the bound above). For an execution of P, let A and B be the outputs of Alice and Bob, respectively. By Lemma 4.1, $U \setminus A \subseteq U \cap V$; in other words, after executing P, Alice knows that each element in her input that she did not output is in $U \cap V$. If $U \setminus A$ is large, this provides Alice with enough information to guess the remaining elements of $U \cap V$ "too accurately".

More formally, let P be a public-coin protocol for task allocation with t rounds, which succeeds with probability at least $1/2$ on each input. For each input $(U, V) \in \mathcal{C}$ we have $|U \cap V| = pn$ (by definition of $\mathcal{C}$), and by Lemma 4.1, $|(U \setminus A) \cup (V \setminus B)| \geq pn$ (in fact the lemma shows equality, but we do not require it here). Thus, if P succeeds then either $|U \setminus A| \geq pn/2$ or $|V \setminus B| \geq pn/2$; assume w.l.o.g. that with probability at least $1/4$ over both the choice of (U, V) and the coin tosses of P, the players eventually output a correct output (A, B) with $|U \setminus A| \geq pn/2$.

Now Alice can guess $X = U \cap V$ given U as follows: she simulates protocol P by guessing a t-bit transcript (in addition to P's own randomness), obtaining some output A. With probability at least $1/4 \cdot 2^{-t}$, Alice guesses a transcript for P that matches the input and P's randomness, and in addition, with this transcript and public randomness, P succeeds (so $U \setminus A \subseteq X$), and we have $|U \setminus A| \geq pn/2$. Now there are only at most

$$\binom{((1+p)n/2 - |U \setminus A|}{pn - |U \setminus A|} \leq \binom{(1+p)n/2}{pn/2}$$

$$\leq \left(\frac{(1+p)en/2}{pn/2}\right)^{pn/2} = \left(\frac{(1+p)e}{p}\right)^{pn/2}$$

possibilities for X. By choosing the most likely possibility given the transcript and the public randomness, Alice can

guess the correct value of X with probability at least

$$\left(\frac{(1+p)e}{p}\right)^{-pn/2} = \left(\frac{1+p}{2p} \cdot 2e\right)^{-pn/2} .$$

Therefore we must have

$$\frac{1}{4} \cdot 2^{-t} \cdot \left(\frac{1+p}{2p} \cdot 2e\right)^{-pn/2} \leq \left(\frac{1+p}{2p}\right)^{-pn} .$$

Simplifying yields

$$t \geq \frac{pn}{2}\left(\log\frac{1+p}{2p} - (1 + \log e)\right) - 2.$$

To obtain a non-trivial lower bound we must select p such that $\log\frac{1+p}{2p} > (1 + \log e) \approx 2.4$. For example, $p := 1/16$ satisfies this constraint.

To conclude, if P is a protocol for 2-player task allocation, then there must exist at least one input on which with probability at least $1/2$, at least $\frac{n}{32}\left(\log\frac{17}{2} - (1 + \log e)\right) - 2 = \Omega(n)$ bits are exchanged. Therefore the worst-case expected communication complexity of P is $\Omega(n)$. $\qquad\square$

Remark 1. The lower bound can be extended to a relaxed variant of TASKALLOCATION, where we allow an ε-fraction of tasks to be assigned to *both* players for a sufficiently small constant $\varepsilon \geq 0$.

Remark 2. The two-player communication complexity of TASKALLOCATION$_n$ is $O(n)$, since Alice can always just send her complete input (represented as the n-bit characteristic vector) to Bob, claim all the tasks in her input, and have Bob claim the remaining tasks. Theorem 4.2 shows that this strategy is optimal. Moreover, if we wish to find all the elements in the intersection, when the intersection is of size $\Omega(n)$, repeatedly sampling a random element is the optimal strategy up to a $\log(n)$ factor.

5. LOWER BOUND ON FINDING ROOTED SPANNING TREES

Next we show how to apply the lower bound from the previous section to obtain a lower bound on computing a rooted spanning tree. Formally, the *distributed rooted spanning tree* problem in a network $G = (V, E)$ requires each node v in the network to output a value $p_v \in V \cup \{\perp\}$, such that the edges $\{(v, p_v) \mid v \in V\}$ form a rooted spanning tree (oriented upwards toward the root) of G. (Exactly one node v may output $p_v = \perp$, and this node is the root of the tree.) In each round of the algorithm, each node $v \in V$ broadcasts B bits, which are delivered to all of v's out-neighbors in G. Each node of G initially knows the size n of the graph and has a unique identifier (UID) drawn from the set $[n]$. [2]

Our lower bound shows that finding a rooted spanning tree is hard even in a restricted class $\mathcal{G}_n$ of networks, where each $G \in \mathcal{G}_n$ is strongly-connected, has a diameter of 2, and has no simple directed path of length more than 4. (In particular, all spanning trees have depth at most 4, so the algorithm cannot be "confused" by long paths or by tall potential spanning trees.)

---

[2]In [16], two of the authors proved a weaker version of this lower bound, which relied entirely on the assumption that the size of the network is not known a-priori. We now show that this assumption did not capture "the core hardness" of finding a rooted spanning tree; the problem remains hard without it.

THEOREM 5.1. *Any algorithm for finding a rooted spanning tree in networks of $\mathcal{G}_n$ requires at least $\Omega(n/B)$ rounds to succeed with probability $1/2$.*

PROOF. We prove the theorem by reduction to the two-party task allocation problem $\text{TASKALLOCATION}_{n-2}$. Specifically, we show that if there is an algorithm for finding a rooted spanning tree in all networks of $\mathcal{G}_n$ which requires t rounds to succeed with probability $1/2$, then there is a public-coin protocol for solving $\text{TASKALLOCATION}_{n-2}$ with communication complexity $O(B \cdot t)$. The theorem then follows from Theorem 4.2.

Fix an algorithm $\mathcal{A}$ for finding a rooted spanning tree. Given inputs U, V (respectively), Alice and Bob can solve $\text{TASKALLOCATION}_{n-2}$ by simulating the execution of $\mathcal{A}$ in a network $G_{U,V} = ([n], E_{U,V})$, where

$$E_{U,V} = (\{n-1, n\} \times [n-2]) \cup \{(n-1, n), (n, n-1)\}$$
$$\cup (U \times \{n-1\}) \cup (V \times \{n\}).$$

Informally, in $G_{U,V}$ nodes $n-1$ and n represent Alice and Bob respectively, and nodes $1, \ldots, n-2$ represent the task set of the $\text{TASKALLOCATION}_{n-2}$ problem. Nodes $n-1$ and n always have edges to all nodes of the network, regardless of the input. In addition, the nodes of U have edges to node $n-1$ (that is, to "Alice") and the nodes of V have edges to node n ("Bob"). It is easy to verify that $G_{U,V} \in \mathcal{G}_n$.

Alice and Bob cooperate to simulate the execution of $\mathcal{A}$, using the public randomness to assign outcomes to the coin tosses of nodes $1, \ldots, n$; bit $n \cdot k + i - 1$ of the public random string is interpreted as bit k of node i's randomness (for $i \in [n]$ and $k = 0, 1, 2, \ldots$). Alice is responsible for locally simulating nodes $U \cup \{n-1\}$; she keeps track of these nodes' states throughout the execution. Similarly, Bob is responsible for simulating nodes $V \cup \{n\}$. (The nodes in $U \cap V$ are simulated by both players independently.)

To simulate one round of $\mathcal{A}$, the players update the states of their locally-simulated nodes as follows: Alice computes the messages output by nodes $U \cup \{n-1\}$, and Bob computes the messages output by nodes $V \cup \{n-1\}$ in the current round; then Alice and Bob send each other the messages output by nodes $n-1$ and n (resp.). Now Alice computes the new state of each node in U after receiving the messages sent by nodes $n-1$ and n, and Bob does the same for the nodes in V. Finally, Alice computes the new state of node $n-1$ after receiving the messages sent by nodes $U \cup \{n\}$, and Bob updates the state of node n after receiving the messages of nodes $V \cup \{n-1\}$. Note that in the final step, Alice and Bob know *which* nodes' messages to deliver, because Alice knows U and Bob knows V. It is not hard to see that for nodes $i \in U \cap V$, Alice and Bob agree on the local state of i at every step of the simulation.

Suppose that $\mathcal{A}$ succeeds with probability at least $1/2$ after t rounds. Then after simulating round t of the execution, with probability at least $1/2$ each node $i \in [n-2]$ outputs a parent $p_i \in [n] \cup \{\bot\}$, with exactly one node $r \in [n]$ outputting $\bot$. The edges $\{(i, p_i)\}$ form a directed spanning tree with root r. To handle the root r, the protocol concludes with one final exchange: Alice sends Bob one bit b indicating whether some node $i \in U$ (that Alice was simulating) output $p_i = \bot$. Finally the players output the following sets:

$$A = \{i \in U \mid p_i = n-1\} \cup \{r, \text{ if } r \in U \text{ and } p_r = \bot\};$$
$$B = \{i \in V \mid p_i = n\} \cup \{r, \text{ if } r \in V \text{ and } p_r = \bot \text{ and } b = 0\}.$$

It is easy to verify that A, B form a valid output on instance (U, V), as each node in $[n-2]$ except possibly r must choose either $n-1$ or n as its parent (but not both), and if $r \in [n-2]$ then it is assigned to exactly one player.

The total amount of communication used by the protocol is $2Bt + 1 = O(Bt)$, and a correct output is produced with probability at least $1/2$. ☐

The lower bound above can be shown to be nearly-tight for networks of constant diameter (and in particular, the class $\mathcal{G}_n$). More generally, in networks of diameter D it is possible to construct a rooted spanning tree in $O(D^2 + n \log n / B)$ rounds, as we will see in Section 8. It is also easy to show that $O(D + |E|/B)$ rounds suffice for networks of any diameter. The time complexity of finding a spanning tree in networks with diameter $D = \omega(\sqrt{n})$ and $|E| = \omega(n)$ remains open to the best of our knowledge.

6. MULTIPARTY COMPLEXITY IN THE SHARED BLACKBOARD MODEL

In this section we study the complexity of distributed task allocation in the shared blackboard communication model. First note that the two-player lower bound (Thm. 4.2) can be embedded into the multi-player setting, yielding the following lower bound:

THEOREM 6.1. *The shared-blackboard communication complexity of multi-player task allocation is $\Omega(n)$. Further, for any $\alpha > 0$, $n \geq 2$, and $m \geq 2/\alpha$, there is a class of inputs with task-player expansion α for which some player needs to communicate $\Omega(1/\alpha)$ bits.*

PROOF. The 2-player scenario is a special case of the multi-player shared blackboard model. Therefore, it follows from Theorem 4.2 that the communication complexity of the multi-player task allocation problem is $\Omega(n)$.

For the bound involving the expansion α, choose two players $u, v \in V$, and partition the tasks into two sets $T', T \setminus T$, where $|T'| = 2/\alpha$. All the tasks in $T' \setminus T$ are assigned to each of the players in $V \setminus \{u, v\}$. As for the tasks in T', we use them to construct a random 2-player input for the player u and v as in Theorem 4.2. Because the sub-problem defined by $\{u, v\}$ and T' is statistically independent of the problem defined by the remaining players and tasks, u and v have to solve their sub-problem by themselves. Hence, by Theorem 4.2 either u or v has to communicate at least $\Omega(1/\alpha)$ bits. ☐

In the remainder of this section we give two algorithms for task assignment in the shared blackboard model. Our algorithms show that up to logarithmic factors, the bounds of the theorem above are tight.

In both of our algorithms, each round causes some player-task assignments to become fixed for the remainder of the algorithm (i.e., some tasks become *permanently assigned*). We let $T(i)$ denote the set of tasks that have not been permanently assigned by the beginning of round i, and $V(i)$ denote the set of players that still have some unassigned tasks at the beginning of round i. Further, let $H(i)$ be the subgraph of H (the task-player graph) induced by $V(i) \cup T(i)$. In a similar manner, we use $n(i) := |T(i)|$, $m(i) := |V(i)|$ and $X_v(i)$ to denote the number of remaining tasks, the number of remaining players, and player v's remaining (unassigned) tasks at the beginning of round i.

6.1 Large Messages, Small Total Complexity

We first give a randomized algorithm that tries to minimize the overall number of bits while keeping the number of rounds small at the same time. We do not restrict B, that is, individual players can potentially send large messages, as long as the total number of bits sent in by all players in all messages is not too large.

The algorithm proceeds as follows. In round $i \geq 1$, each player $v \in V(i)$ selects a subset of its remaining tasks $X_v(i)$: each task $x \in X_v(i)$ is selected independently with probability $\min\left\{1, 2^i/m\right\}$. Then, v proposes the assignments (v, x) for all selected tasks $x \in X_v(i)$, by writing these proposals on the shared blackboard. Each task that some player proposed to claim is assigned to the smallest player that attempted to claim it (note that this requires no further communication, as all players can see all proposals). This process continues until all tasks have been assigned.

In round $\lceil \log m \rceil$, each remaining player selects each of its remaining tasks with probability 1. Therefore the algorithm terminates in at most $\lceil \log m \rceil$ rounds. In the following, we show that with high probability, the total number of announced proposals is $O(n)$.

For a task $x \in T$, let A_x be the number of proposals of the form (v, x) that are announced throughout an execution of the algorithm. The following lemma analyzes the distribution of A_x for a task x.

LEMMA 6.2. *The random variable A_x is dominated by a constant multiple of a geometric random variable, that is, for $k \geq 1$, $\mathbb{P}(A_x \geq k) \leq c\rho^k$ for constants $c > 0$ and $\rho \in (0, 1)$.*

PROOF. Let $d = |V_x|$ be the degree of task x in H, i.e., the number of players that received task x in their input. The number of proposals made for each task depends on the round in which it is assigned: if task x is not assigned before round i, the number of proposals (v, x) in round i is binomially distributed with parameters d and $2^i/m$.

Let I be the round in which task x is assigned. Note that, since each task is permanently assigned in the first round where someone attempts to claim it, proposals (v, x) for task x are only made in round I. For $k \in \{0, \ldots, d\}$ and $i \in [\lceil \log m \rceil]$, we define

$$p(k, i) := \mathbb{P}(A_x = k | I = i) = \binom{d}{k} \frac{2^{ik}}{m^k} \left(1 - \frac{2^i}{m}\right)^{d-k}.$$

We can express the probability distribution of A_x in terms of these probabilities as follows. For $k \in \{0, \ldots, d\}$, we have

$$
\begin{aligned}
\mathbb{P}(A_x = k) &= \sum_{i=1}^{\lceil \log m \rceil} p(k, i) \cdot \mathbb{P}(I = i) \\
&= \sum_{i=1}^{\lceil \log m \rceil} p(k, i) \cdot \prod_{j=1}^{i-1} p(0, j) \\
&= \sum_{i=1}^{\lceil \log m \rceil} p(k, i) \cdot \prod_{j=1}^{i-1} \left(1 - \frac{2^j}{m}\right)^d \\
&\leq \sum_{i=1}^{\lceil \log m \rceil} \underbrace{\frac{1}{k!} \cdot \left(\frac{d2^i}{m}\right)^k \cdot \prod_{j=1}^{i-1} \left(1 - \frac{2^j}{m}\right)^d}_{q(k,i)}. \quad (1)
\end{aligned}
$$

In the last inequality we used the fact that $\binom{d}{k} \leq \frac{d^k}{k!}$. Let us consider the values of the expression $q(k, i)$ from Inequality (1) for a fixed k and different i. Let i_0 be the maximal value for i such that $2^i \leq m/d$. We have $q(k, i_0) \leq 1/k!$ and $q(k, i) \leq 2^{-(i_0-i)k} q(k, i_0)$ for $i < i_0$. Because $k \geq 1$, we therefore get

$$\sum_{i=1}^{i_0} q(k, i) \leq \sum_{i=1}^{i_0} \frac{1}{k!} \cdot 2^{-(i_0-i)} \leq \frac{2}{k!}. \quad (2)$$

Further, we obtain $q(k, i_0 + 1) \leq 2^k/k!$, and for $i > i_0 + 1$ we have

$$
\begin{aligned}
q(k, i) &\leq q(k, i_0 + 1) \cdot 2^k \cdot \left(1 - \frac{2^{i-1}}{m}\right)^d \\
&\leq q(k, i_0 + 1) \cdot 2^k \cdot e^{-\frac{2^{i-1}d}{m}} \leq q(k, i_0 + 1) \cdot \left(\frac{2}{e^{2^{i-i_0-1}}}\right)^k.
\end{aligned}
$$

In the first inequality, we used the fact that $1 - x \leq e^{-x}$ for all $x \in \mathbb{R}$, and in the second inequality the fact that $i > i_0 + 1$ and $k \leq d$. Combining with (2) and applying (1), we get that

$$\mathbb{P}(A_x = k) \leq \sum_{i=1}^{\lceil \log m \rceil} q(k, i) = O\left(\frac{2^k}{k!}\right).$$

The claim of the lemma now follows because $\mathbb{P}(A_x \geq k) = \sum_{k'=k}^d \mathbb{P}(A_x = k')$. $\square$

The total number of assignment proposals throughout the execution is $A = \sum_{x \in T} A_x$. The random variables A_x are independent, and by Lemma 6.2, the sum A can be bounded from above (up to a constant factor) by the sum of n independent geometric variables. Thus we obtain the following:

LEMMA 6.3. *In an execution of the above algorithm, the total number of announced potential assignment (v, x) for $v \in V$ and $x \in T$ is at most $O(n) = O(|T|)$ with probability at least $1 - e^{-cn}$ for any constant $c > 0$.*

PROOF. Let A be the total number of announced potential assignments (v, x). By the definition of the random variables A_x, we have $A = \sum_{x \in T} A_x$. Note further that the random variables A_x are independent because they depend on disjoint set of edges of the player-task graph H and edges are picked independently.

By Lemma 6.2, each A_x is dominated by a $c \cdot Y_x$ for a constant $c > 0$ and a geometric random variable $Y_x \sim \text{Geom}(p)$ for a constant parameter $p \in (0, 1)$. Consequently, A is dominated by $c \cdot Y$, where Y is the sum of n independent geometric random variables with parameter p. Let $k > 0$ be a positive integer and let $Z \sim \text{Bin}(k, p)$ be a binomial random variable with parameter k and p. We have $Y > k$ iff in a sequence of k Bernoulli trials with success probability p, less than n succeed. We therefore have $\mathbb{P}(Y > k) = \mathbb{P}(Z < n)$. If we choose $k = \gamma n/p$ for a constant $\gamma > 1$, we have $\mathbb{E}[Z] = \gamma n$ and therefore $Z \geq n$ with probability at least $1 - e^{-\Omega(n)}$, where the hidden constant in the exponent can be made arbitrarily large if the constant γ is chosen sufficiently large. $\square$

The performance of the algorithm follows directly from the lemma above:

THEOREM 6.4. *The above algorithm solves the task assignment problem in the shared blackboard model in $O(\log m)$ rounds and with an overall communication complexity of $O(n \log(n + m))$ bits.*

6.2 Task Allocation with Small Messages

The first algorithm we presented is efficient in terms of total bit complexity and number of rounds. However, it might require individual players to send a large number of bits in a single round. We now consider the case where in each round, each player can only send a message of at most $B = O(\log(n + m))$ bits. We give an algorithm that has a good round complexity when the expansion $\alpha(H)$ of the task-player graph is large (cf. Definition 1). In the following, we assume that $\alpha(H) \leq 1$, i.e., the number of players does not exceed the number of tasks. (If $\alpha(H) > 1$, all appearances of $\alpha(H)$ in our bounds can be replaced by 1.)

Description of the algorithm. As before, the algorithm runs in rounds, and we let $H(i) = (V(i) \cup T(i), F(i))$ be the remaining task-player graph at the beginning of round i. In each round, every player v picks a random task $x \in X_v(i)$ uniformly, and proposes the assignment (v, x) by writing it on the blackboard. Task x is then permanently assigned to the smallest player u that attempted to claim it (i.e., that wrote (u, x) on the blackboard). Unassigned tasks $y \in T(i)$ for which that no assignment (v, y) was proposed in round i remain unassigned. We continue until all tasks in T have been assigned to some player.

Analysis of the running time. The algorithm above makes progress in one of two ways. Let $\lambda \in (0, \alpha(H))$ be a parameter whose value will be fixed later.

DEFINITION 2 (TASK-REDUCING ROUNDS). *We say that round i is a* task-reducing round *if given the random choices up to the beginning of round i, the expected number of tasks assigned in round i is at least $\lambda|V(i)|$.*

DEFINITION 3 (EDGE-REDUCING ROUNDS). *Round i is called* edge-reducing for player $v \in V(i)$ *if given the random choices up to the beginning of round i, in expectation at least $\left(1 - \sqrt{\lambda/\alpha(H)}\right) \cdot |X_v(i)|$ tasks from $X_v(i)$ are permanently assigned in round i.*

Informally, if a round is task-reducing, we make progress because many tasks become assigned. On the other hand, if the round is not task-reducing, this means that many players picked the same task to propose (because each player proposes one task, but not many tasks were proposed in total). Each task x proposed in round i becomes assigned to some player, and the other players v then remove this task from their remaining input $X_v(i)$, causing edge (v, i) to be removed from $H(i)$. If H has good expansion, many players are incident to (i.e., have in their input) some task among the tasks proposed in round i, and all such players now shed all edges corresponding to proposed tasks. Therefore the round is edge-reducing for a good fraction of players.

More formally, we prove the following lemma.

LEMMA 6.5. *For each round i of the algorithm, either round i is a task-reducing round, or round i is an edge-reducing task for at least a $\left(1 - \sqrt{\lambda/\alpha(H)}\right)$-fraction of the remaining players $v \in V(i)$.*

PROOF. Let $S \subseteq T(i)$ be a random variable representing the number of tasks that are assigned in round i, given the random choices up to the beginning of the round. If round i is not task-reducing, then $\mathbb{E}[S] < \lambda|T(i)|$. We will show that in this case round i is edge-reducing for a large fraction of remaining players. In the sequel all probabilities and

expectations are implicitly conditioned on events up to the beginning of round i.

Let C_u be the event that player $u \in V(i)$ picks a task $x \in X_v(i)$ that is also picked by another player $v \in V(i)$. From the assumption that the round is not task-reducing,

$$\sum_{u \in V(i)} \mathbb{P}(C_u) > |V(i)| - \mathbb{E}[S] > |V(i)| - \lambda|T(i)|$$
$$\geq |V(i)| \cdot \left(1 - \frac{\lambda}{\alpha(H)}\right). \qquad (3)$$

The last inequality follows because $|V(i)| \geq \alpha(H)|T(i)|$, by the assumption that H has task-player expansion $\alpha(H)$.

For $u \in V(i)$, let Z_u be the number of tasks in $X_u(i)$ that are assigned in round i, and let Z'_u be the number of tasks in $X_u(i)$ that are proposed by other players $v \in V(i) \setminus \{u\}$. Clearly, $Z'_u \leq Z_u$, and therefore also $\mathbb{E}[Z'_u] \leq \mathbb{E}[Z_u]$. We have

$$\mathbb{P}(C_u) = \sum_x \mathbb{P}(Z'_u = x) \cdot \mathbb{P}(C_u | Z'_u = x)$$
$$= \sum_x \mathbb{P}(Z'_u = x) \cdot x = \mathbb{E}[Z'_u] < \mathbb{E}[Z_u].$$

We need to show that for at least $\left(1 - \sqrt{\lambda/\alpha(H)}\right)|V(i)|$ players $u \in V(i)$ we have $\mathbb{E}[Z_u] \geq \left(1 - \sqrt{\lambda/\alpha(H)}\right) \cdot |V(i)|$ (i.e., round i is edge-reducing for these players). Suppose not. Then

$$\sum_{u \in V(i)} \mathbb{P}(C_u) < \sum_{u \in V(i)} \mathbb{E}[Z_u]$$
$$< \left(1 - \sqrt{\frac{\lambda}{\alpha(H)}}\right) |V(i)| \cdot 1$$
$$\quad + \sqrt{\frac{\lambda}{\alpha(H)}} \cdot |V(i)| \cdot \left(1 - \sqrt{\frac{\lambda}{\alpha(H)}}\right)$$
$$= \left(1 - \frac{\lambda}{\alpha(H)}\right) \cdot |V(i)|,$$

a contradiction to Inequality (3). $\qquad \square$

To see the intuition behind the algorithm's progress, consider the simple case where λ and $\alpha(H)$ are both constant. Then each task-reducing round causes a constant fraction of tasks to be eliminated, and each edge-reducing round causes a constant fraction of players to shed a constant fraction of their edges in the task-player graphs. After roughly $\log(n)$ edge-reducing rounds, a constant fraction of players have no tasks remaining, and they are removed from $V(i)$. To eliminate all players (and hence all tasks) we require logarithmically-many such "phases", so the overall time complexity is $O(\log n \cdot \log m)$.

In the following theorem we obtain a slightly better bound by carefully setting the parameter λ:

THEOREM 6.6. *With high probability, the algorithm runs in at most T rounds, where*

$$T = O\left(\frac{\log m \log n}{\log^2(\alpha(H) \log m)}\right) \quad \text{if } \alpha(H) = \Omega\left(\frac{1}{\log m}\right), \text{ and}$$

$$T = O\left(\frac{\log n}{\alpha(H)}\right) \quad \text{if } \alpha(H) = O\left(\frac{1}{\log m}\right).$$

PROOF. Let $\lambda \le \alpha(H)/5$ be a positive parameter. The value of λ will be fixed later. Consider some round i. We call i a task-reducing round if the expected number of tasks assigned in round i is at least $\lambda|V(i)|$. For a player $v \in V(i)$, we call round i an edge-reducing round for v if in expectation at least $\left(1-\sqrt{\lambda/\alpha(H)}\right)\cdot|X_v(i)|$ tasks from $X_v(i)$ are assigned to some player in round i. By Lemma 6.5, each round i is either a task-reducing round or an edge-reducing round for at least a $\left(1-\sqrt{\lambda/\alpha(H)}\right)$-fraction of the players in $V(i)$.

Let us first look at a task-reducing round i. For a task $x \in T(i)$, let S_x be an indicator random variable that is 1 iff task x is assigned in round i. The sum $S = \sum_{x \in T(i)} S_x$ then counts the number of tasks that are assigned to some player in round i. The picking of tasks by players can be seen as a balls-into-bins process in which each ball (player) independently chooses a random bin according to some distribution.

Consider two tasks $x \ne y \in T(i)$ and a player $v \in V(i)$ and let A_{vx} be the event that player v picks task x. We have $\mathbb{P}(A_{vx}) = 1/|X_v(i)|$. If we condition on $S_y = 0$, we have $\mathbb{P}(A_{vx}|S_y = 0) = 1/(|X_v(i)|-1) > \mathbb{P}(A_{vx})$ if $y \in X_v(i)$ and $\mathbb{P}(A_{vx}|S_y = 0) = \mathbb{P}(A_{vx})$ otherwise. We therefore have $\mathbb{P}(S_x = 1|S_y = 0) \ge \mathbb{P}(S_x = 0)$ and thus $\mathbb{P}(S_x = 1|S_y = 1) \le \mathbb{P}(S_x = 1)$. Consequently it holds that $\mathbb{E}[S_x S_y] \le \mathbb{E}[S_x] \cdot \mathbb{E}[S_y]$, i.e., S_x and S_y are negatively correlated. We therefore get $\mathrm{Var}(S) \le \sum_{x \in T(i)} \mathrm{Var}(S_x) = \sum_{x \in T(i)} \mathbb{P}(S_x = 1)\left(1 - \mathbb{P}(S_x = 1)\right) < \sum_{x \in T(i)} \mathbb{E}[S_x] = \mathbb{E}[S]$. Note that It therefore follows from Chebyshev's inequality (and because $S \ge 1$ in any case) that $S \ge \lambda|T(i)|/2$ with at least constant probability.

Let us now consider a round i that is edge-reducing for player $v \in V(i)$. Let Z_v be the number of edges of player v after round i. By assuming the round i is edge-reducing for v, we have $\mathbb{E}[Z_v] \le \sqrt{\lambda/\alpha(H)} \cdot |X_v(i)|$. Hence, by applying the Markov inequality to Z_v, we get that

$$\mathbb{P}\left(Z_v > \left(\frac{\lambda}{\alpha(H)}\right)^{1/4} \cdot |X_v(i)|\right) < \left(\frac{\lambda}{\alpha(H)}\right)^{1/4}. \quad (4)$$

Assume that there are $k = c\log_{\alpha(H)/\lambda}(n)$ edge-reducing rounds for player v for a sufficiently large constant c. Let Y be the number of these k rounds in which more than a $\sqrt[4]{\lambda/\alpha(H)}$-fraction of v's tasks remain. By (4), Y is dominated by a binomial random variable with parameters k and $\sqrt[4]{\lambda/\alpha(H)}$. As long as $Y < k - 4\log_{\alpha(H)/\lambda}(n)$, all tasks of player v get assigned to some player during these k rounds. Using a standard Chernoff bound, we get that for c sufficiently large, $Y < k - 4\log_{\alpha(H)/\lambda}(n)$ with high probability. Therefore, as soon as there are $c\log_{\alpha(H)/\lambda}(n)$ edge-reducing rounds for each player $v \in V$, all tasks have been assigned. We next show that this has to be the case after $O(\log_{\alpha(H)/\lambda}(n) \cdot \log_{\alpha(H)/\lambda}(m))$ rounds i such that round i is edge-reducing round for at least a $\left(1-\sqrt{\lambda/\alpha(H)}\right)$-fraction of the players in $V(i)$.

As before, let $k = c\log_{\alpha(H)/\lambda}(n)$ be the number of edge-reducing rounds for a player v needed to assign all tasks of v w.h.p. Consider the state at the beginning of some round i_0 and assume that there are $2k$ rounds that are edge-reducing for at least a $\left(1-\sqrt{\lambda/\alpha(H)}\right)$-fraction of the players in that round. In each round i of these ℓ rounds, there are at most $\sqrt{\lambda/\alpha(H)} \cdot |V(i_0)|$ players in $V(i)$ for which round i is not edge-reducing. For a player $v \in V(i_0)$ to still have tasks at the end of the $2k$ rounds, at least k of these

rounds are not edge-reducing for v (conditioned on the event that all the high probability events occur). The number of players for which this is the case can be at most $2k\sqrt{\lambda/\alpha(H)} \cdot |V(i_0)|/k$. Therefore, w.h.p., in these $2k$ rounds at least a $\left(1-2\sqrt{\lambda/\alpha(H)}\right)$-fraction of the players in $V(i_0)$ are removed because all their tasks get assigned. Note that we assumed that $\lambda \le \alpha(H)/5$ and therefore $2\sqrt{\lambda/\alpha(H)} \le 2/\sqrt{5} < 1$. Consequently, after at most $2k\log(m)/\log(\sqrt{\alpha(H)/4\lambda}) = O(\log_{\alpha(H)/\lambda}(n) \cdot \log_{\alpha(H)/\lambda}(m))$ rounds that are edge-reducing for at least a $\left(1 - \sqrt{\lambda/\alpha(H)}\right)$-fraction of the players, there are no players remaining and we are done. The number of rounds of the algorithm can therefore by upper bounded by

$$O\left(\frac{\log n}{\lambda} + \frac{\log m \log n}{\log^2(\alpha(H)/\lambda)}\right),$$

for any $\lambda \le \alpha(H)/5$. For $\alpha(H) = O(1/\log m)$, choosing $\lambda = \alpha(H)/5$, the first term of the above expression dominates the second one, and we get a round complexity of $O\left(\log(n)/\alpha(H)\right)$. For large $\alpha(H)$ (i.e., if $\alpha(H) = \Omega(1/\log m)$), we set $\lambda = \log(\alpha \log m)/(\alpha \log m)$, and both terms evaluate to $O\left((\log m \log n)/\log^2(\alpha \log m)\right)$. □

Since each player writes a B-bit message on the blackboard in each round, the total bit complexity of the algorithm is $mB \cdot T$, where T is the running time from Theorem 6.6. In typical scenario where $m = O(n)$, this is optimal to within polylogarithmic factors (by Theorem 6.1). However, if the number of players greatly exceeds the number of tasks, it becomes wasteful to have all the players propose task assignments in each round.

7. ARBITRARY NETWORKS

Our results for the shared-blackboard model can be translated to the more decentralized setting, where players are connected by an arbitrary communication network, using the pipelining technique from [22]. Pipelining allows k pieces of information (henceforth called *tokens*) to be disseminated to all players in $D + k$ rounds, where D is the diameter of the communication network. The strategy is quite simple: each node keeps a pool of tokens it has received but not yet sent on, and in each round selects an arbitrary token from the pool and sends it. If the message size is large enough to allow $\beta > 1$ tokens per message, we can achieve better throughput by packing multiple tokens per message. Using an inductive argument that appears in [22] (also cf. [15]), the following statement can be shown:

LEMMA 7.1. *After $d + t$ rounds, every node v has either received all the tokens that originated at nodes at distance at most d from v, or node v has received at least $\beta \cdot t$ different tokens.*

In particular, at time $D + \lceil k/\beta \rceil$, each node has either received all tokens originating anywhere in the network, or it has received at least $\beta \cdot \lceil k/\beta \rceil \ge k$ different tokens; these amount to the same thing, since there are only k tokens in total. Consequently disseminating k tokens requires $O(D + k/\beta)$ rounds.

If the diameter D and the number of tokens k are known in advance, the strategy above allows all nodes to halt in $O(D + k/\beta)$ rounds; however, if D and k are not known, the nodes may not know when they have collected all tokens. It is easier to deal with an unknown number of tokens than with an unknown diameter: if D is known but k is not, Lemma 7.1 shows that nodes may halt as soon as they reach a time $D+t$ in which fewer than $\beta \cdot t$ tokens have been received. Therefore we can still disseminate k tokens in $O(D + k/\beta)$ rounds. For the case where D is unknown, it is shown in [16] that w.h.p., an upper bound $\hat{D} \leq D + O(\sqrt{m/B} \cdot \log m)$ on D can be computed in time $\hat{D}$ (recall that m is the number of nodes in the network G). Thus we obtain:

LEMMA 7.2. *[16, 22] Even if D and k are not known to the nodes, with high probability, k tokens are disseminated (and all nodes can terminate) after $O(D + \sqrt{m/B} \log m + k/\beta)$ rounds.*

Distributed task allocation. We can now solve a given task allocation instance as follows. First, the players compute an upper bound of $\hat{D}$ on the diameter D, as described above. Then the players elect a unique leader among them (e.g., the player with the smallest ID). This can be done in $\hat{D}$ rounds. Afterwards, we start the token dissemination protocol from Lemma 7.2, using all the pairs $\{(v,x) \mid x \in X_v\}$ as our tokens. To avoid redundancy (and too many tokens), each player only forwards the first pair (v,x) that it receives for each task x; subsequent pairs (u,x) for $u \neq v$ are eliminated and not forwarded. It is not hard to show that this can be viewed as running the pipelining protocol from Lemma 7.2, except using tasks x as tokens, instead of pairs (v,x). At the end of the protocol, the leader node has received some pair (v,x) for each task x (or possibly more than one pair for some tasks); the leader now selects a permanent assignment for each task, and disseminates these assignments using the pipelining protocol.

THEOREM 7.3. $\text{TASKALLOCATION}_{m,n}$ *can be solved w.h.p. in time $O(D + \sqrt{m/B} \log m + n \log(n+m)/B)$.*

Remark. In the typical case, when $m = O(n)$, the time bound in the Theorem 7.3 simplifies to $O(D + n \log(n)/B)$. The algorithm described above is randomized, because the diameter-estimation algorithm from [16] is randomized. However, when $m = O(n)$ we can replace this part by a deterministic coarse upper bound on the diameter D: simply use pipelining to count the number of players in the network (see [15]), and use this number m as an upper bound on the diameter. This yields a deterministic $O(D + n \log(n)/B)$-round algorithm for task dissemination.

8. AN ALGORITHM FOR CONSTRUCTING ROOTED SPANNING TREES

We conclude our technical results with a simple algorithm for computing rooted spanning trees in directed broadcast networks. Our strategy is similar to the solution for task allocation in Section 7: we treat each network node as both a task and a player, where the input to player v is its set of in-children. Since we need to make sure that we do not create any cycles, we have to make task assignments in a more coordinated fashion than in Section 7. Therefore we assign children to parents in a top-down fashion, from the root towards the leaves.

We first assume that the nodes know the diameter D, or a linear upper bound on D. The first step, as in Section 7, is to select a leader r, which will serve as the root of the tree. Subsequently the algorithm runs in D phases. In the first phase, the root node r assigns all its in-neighbors as its children, and communicates this decision by applying the token dissemination protocol described in Lemma 7.2. In each subsequent phase we solve an instance of task allocation: the players are the nodes that are already assigned to some parent node and that still have unassigned in-neighbors; the tasks are all the unassigned in-neighbors of the players. Hence, the players of phase i are a subset of the nodes at in-distance $i - 1$ from the root (the ones that have in-neighbors at in-distance i from the root), and the tasks are all the nodes at in-distance i from the root. The algorithm terminates as soon as all nodes are assigned to some parent node.

THEOREM 8.1. *The above algorithm solves the spanning tree problem in $O(D^2 + n \log(n)/B)$ rounds.*

PROOF. It follows from the construction of the algorithm that in phase i all nodes at in-distance i from the root are assigned to a parent node. Therefore, the time complexity of the algorithm is determined through D sequential executions of the task assignment protocol from Section 7. Let k_i be the number of nodes at in-distance i from the root. The number of tasks in tokens in phase i is k_i. Therefore the running time of the task assignment protocol of round i is $O(D + k_i)$ (recall that we assumed that the nodes know D). Hence, the overall time complexity is

$$O\left(D^2 + \sum_{i=1}^{D} k_i \cdot \frac{\log(n)}{B}\right) = O\left(D^2 + \frac{n \log n}{B}\right).$$

$\square$

Dealing with an unknown diameter. If the diameter is initially unknown and we plug in the time complexity from Theorem 7.3, we obtain an overall time complexity of $O\big(D(D + \sqrt{n/B} \log n) + n \log(n)/B\big)$. This can be slightly improved by observing that phases do not necessarily need to be synchronized. As soon as a node receives a notification that it has been assigned to some parent node, it can start broadcasting its in-neighbors so that they can be assigned. With this modification, the additive $\sqrt{n/B} \log n$ penalty term for an unknown diameter is paid only once, instead of D times (once per phase); the penalty is dominated by the $n \log n/B$ in Theorem 8.1, so the overall time complexity from Theorem 8.1 is preserved. Note, however, that spanning tree constructed in this way is no longer a BFS tree.

9. DISCUSSION AND OPEN PROBLEMS

Our results in this paper leave several problems open. First, our lower bound from Section 5 shows that computing a spanning tree requires $\Omega(n/B)$ rounds, but the best upper bound of which we are aware, even assuming the diameter D is known in advance, is $O(\min\{D + |E|/B, D^2 + n \log n/B\})$. For dense networks with a large diameter, the bounds do not match. However, $\text{TASKALLOCATION}_{n,n}$ can be solved in $O(D + n \log n/B)$ rounds (see Section 7). The existence of a fast spanning tree algorithm implies a fast algorithm for task allocation, where we view each node as both a task and a player; the input of each player is its set of in-neighbors (viewed as "tasks"), and its output is the set of in-neighbors that chose it as their parent in the tree. The other direction is not necessarily true, since in general a task allocation may contain cycles (when we view nodes as both tasks and players). If the network is sufficiently dense, and perhaps enjoys good expansion as well, is it nevertheless possible to use a fast task allocation algorithm to find a rooted spanning tree? Can we prove that cycles are unlikely to occur, and if so, can we resolve the few cycles that do occur quickly?

Another open problem concerns task-allocation with good task-player expansion and the hardness of finding a spanning tree in directed constant-degree expanders. In a constant-degree network with bounded bandwidth B, each node only receives $O(B)$ bits of information per round. This bottleneck bounds the number of nodes with which a given node can "exchange meaningful information", even though the diameter is small. To tackle this issue in a communication-complexity setting, we could charge the protocol not just for the total bits exchanged, but also for activating the (directed) channel between two players. We could then ask what is the smallest number of channels that must be activated to solve TASKALLOCATION or other problems. All the algorithms we have given for TASKALLOCATION require either all players to exchange information with all other players (as in the shared blackboard model), or one player to exchange $\Omega(n)$ information with all other players (as in the algorithm from Section 7). A strong lower bound on the number of player-to-player channels that must be activated would yield insight into the problem and perhaps lead to a lower bound on finding spanning trees in directed constant-degree expanders.

10. REFERENCES

[1] J. Aas. Understanding the Linux 2.6.8.1 CPU scheduler. Unpublished manuscript, 2005.

[2] B. Awerbuch, S. Kutten, and D. Peleg. Competitive distributed job scheduling. In *Proc. 24th Symp. on Theory of Computing (STOC)*, pages 571–580, 1992.

[3] Y. Bartal and A. Rosen. The distributed k-server problem–a competitive distributed translator for k-server algorithms. In *Proc. 33rd Symp. on Foundations of Computer Science (FOCS)*, pages 344–353, Oct 1992.

[4] A. Das Sarma, S. Holzer, L. Kor, A. Korman, D. Nanongkai, G. Pandurangan, D. Peleg, and R. Wattenhofer. Distributed verification and hardness of distributed approximation. In *Proc. 43rd Symp. on Theory of Computing (STOC)*, pages 363–372, 2011.

[5] R. I. Davis and A. Burns. A survey of hard real-time scheduling for multiprocessor systems. *ACM Comput. Surv.*, 43:35:1–35:44, Oct. 2011.

[6] M. L. Dertouzos and A. K. Mok. Multiprocessor on-line scheduling of hard-real-time tasks. *IEEE Trans. Software Eng.*, 15(12):1497–1506, 1989.

[7] A. Fiat, Y. Rabani, and Y. Ravid. Competitive k-server algorithms. In *Journal of Computer and System Sciences*, pages 454–463, 1990.

[8] M. Frigo, C. E. Leiserson, and K. H. Randall. The implementation of the cilk-5 multithreaded language. In *Proc. 19th Conf. on Programming Language Design and Implementation (PLDI)*, pages 212–223, 1998.

[9] S. Frischknecht, S. Holzer, and R. Wattenhofer. Networks cannot compute their diameter in sublinear time. In *Proc. 22nd Symp. on Discrete Algorithms (SODA)*, pages 1150–1162, 2012.

[10] A. Gronemeier. Asymptotically optimal lower bounds on the NIH-multi-party information complexity of the AND-function and disjointness. In *Proc. 26th Symp. on Theoretical Aspects of Computer Science (STACS)*, pages 505–516, 2009.

[11] T. S. Jayram. Hellinger strikes back: A note on the multi-party information complexity of AND. In *Proc. 13th Workshop on Randomization and Computation (RANDOM)*, pages 562–573, 2009.

[12] T. S. Jayram. Information complexity: a tutorial. In *Proc. 29th Symp. on Principles of Database Systems (PODS)*, pages 159–168, 2010.

[13] M. Karchmer and A. Wigderson. Monotone circuits for connectivity require super-logarithmic depth. *SIAM J. Discrete Math.*, 3(2):255–265, 1990.

[14] E. Koutsoupias. The k-server problem. *Computer Science Review*, 3(2):105–118, 2009.

[15] F. Kuhn, N. A. Lynch, and R. Oshman. Distributed computation in dynamic networks. In *Prof. 42nd Symp. on Theory of Computing (STOC)*, pages 513–522, 2010.

[16] F. Kuhn and R. Oshman. The complexity of data aggregation in directed networks. In *Proc. of 25th Symp. on Distributed Computing (DISC)*, pages 416–431, 2011.

[17] E. Kushilevitz and N. Nisan. *Communication complexity*. Cambridge University Press, 1997.

[18] C. L. Liu and J. W. Layland. Scheduling algorithms for multiprogramming in a hard-real-time environment. *J. ACM*, 20(1):46–61, 1973.

[19] B. Patt-Shamir. A note on efficient aggregate queries in sensor networks. *Theor. Comput. Sci.*, 370(1-3):254–264, 2007.

[20] A. A. Razborov. On the distributional complexity of disjointness. *Theor. Comput. Sci.*, 106:385–390, December 1992.

[21] A. A. Shvartsman and C. Georgiou. *Cooperative Task-Oriented Computing: Algorithms and Complexity*. Morgan&Claypool Publishers, 2011.

[22] D. M. Topkis. Concurrent broadcast for information dissemination. *IEEE Trans. Softw. Eng.*, 11:1107–1112, October 1985.

Collaborative Search on the Plane without Communication

[Extended Abstract]

Ofer Feinerman[*]
The Louis and Ida Rich Career
Development Chair, The
Weizmann Institute of Science
Rehovot, Israel
feinermanofer@gmail.com

Amos Korman[†]
CNRS LIAFA, University
Diderot
Paris, France
amos.korman@liafa.jussieu.fr

Zvi Lotker
Ben-Gurion University of the
Negev
Beer-Sheva, Israel
zvilo@bgu.ac.il

Jean-Sébastien Sereni[‡]
CNRS (LIAFA, University
Diderot)
Paris, France
sereni@kam.mff.cuni.cz

ABSTRACT

We use distributed computing tools to provide a new perspective on the behavior of cooperative biological ensembles. We introduce the *Ants Nearby Treasure Search (ANTS)* problem, a generalization of the classical cow-path problem [10, 20, 41, 42], which is relevant for collective foraging in animal groups. In the ANTS problem, k identical (probabilistic) agents, initially placed at some central location, collectively search for a treasure in the two-dimensional plane. The treasure is placed at a target location by an adversary and the goal is to find it as fast as possible as a function of both k and D, where D is the distance between the central location and the target. This is biologically motivated by cooperative, central place foraging, such as performed by ants around their nest. In this type of search there is a strong preference to locate nearby food sources before those that are further away. We focus on trying to find what can be achieved if communication is limited or altogether absent. Indeed, to avoid overlaps agents must be highly dispersed making communication difficult. Furthermore, if the agents do not commence the search in synchrony, then even initial communication is problematic. This holds, in particular, with respect to the question of whether the agents can communicate and conclude their total number, k. It turns out that the knowledge of k by

the individual agents is crucial for performance. Indeed, it is a straightforward observation that the time required for finding the treasure is $\Omega(D + D^2/k)$, and we show in this paper that this bound can be matched if the agents have knowledge of k up to some constant approximation.

We present a tight bound for the competitive penalty that must be paid, in the running time, if the agents have no information about k. Specifically, this bound is slightly more than logarithmic in the number of agents. In addition, we give a lower bound for the setting in which the agents are given some estimation of k. Informally, our results imply that the agents can potentially perform well without any knowledge of their total number k, however, to further improve, they must use some information regarding k. Finally, we propose a uniform algorithm that is both efficient and extremely simple, suggesting its relevance for actual biological scenarios.

Categories and Subject Descriptors

F.2.m [**Theory of Computation**]: Analysis of Algorithms and Problem Complexity—*Miscellaneous*; G.2.1 [**Discrete Mathematics**]: Combinatorics—*Combinatorial algorithms*; G.2.2 [**Discrete Mathematics**]: Graph Theory—*Graph algorithms*

General Terms

Algorithms, Theory

Keywords

search algorithms, mobile robots, speed-up, cow-path problem, online algorithms, uniform algorithms, social insects, collective foraging, ants

[*]Supported by the Israel Science Foundation (grant 1694/10).

[†]Supported by the ANR projects DISPLEXITY and PROSE, and by the INRIA project GANG.

[‡]This author's work was partially supported by the French *Agence Nationale de la Recherche* under reference ANR 10 JCJC 0204 01.

1. INTRODUCTION

1.1 Background and Motivation

The universality of search behaviors is reflected in multitudes of studies in different fields including control systems, distributed computing and biology. We use tools from distributed computing to study a biologically inspired scenario in which a group of agents, initially located at one central location, cooperatively search for treasures in the plane. The goal of the search is to locate nearby treasures as fast as possible and at a rate that scales well with the number of participating agents.

A variety of animal species search for food around a central location that serves the search's initial point, final destination or both [47]. This central location could be a food storage area, a nest where offspring are reared or simply a sheltered or familiar environment. Central place foraging holds a strong preference to locating nearby food sources before those that are further away. Possible reasons for that are, for example: (1) decreasing predation risk [44], (2) increasing the rate of food collection once a large quantity of food is found [47], (3) holding a territory without the need to reclaim it [35, 44, 46], and (4) the ease of navigating back after collecting the food using familiar landmarks [16].

Searching in groups can increase foraging efficiency [38, p. 732]. In some extreme cases, food is so scarce that group searching is believed to be required for survival [18, 39]. Proximity of the food source to the central location is again important in this case. For example, in the case of recruitment, a nearby food source would be beneficial not only to the individual that located the source but also increase the subsequent retrieval rate for many other collaborators [60]. Foraging in groups can also facilitate the defense of larger territories [55]. Eusocial insects (e.g., bees and ants) engage in highly cooperative foraging, which can be expected as these insects reduce competition between individuals to a minimum and share any food that is found. Social insects often live in a single nest or hive, which naturally makes their foraging patterns central.

Little is known about the communication between foragers, but it is believed that in some scenarios communication may become impractical [36]. This holds, for example, if the foragers start the search at different times and remain far apart (which may be necessary to avoid unnecessary overlaps). Hence, the question of how efficient the search can be if the communication is limited, or altogether absent, is of great importance.

In this paper, we theoretically address general questions of collective searches in the particular natural setting described above. More precisely, we introduce the *Ants Nearby Treasure Search (ANTS)* problem, in which k identical (probabilistic) agents, initially placed at some central location, collectively search for a treasure in the two-dimensional plane. The treasure is placed by an adversary at some target location at distance D from the central location, where D is unknown to the agents. The goal of the agents is to find the treasure as fast as possible, where the time complexity is evaluated as a function of both k and D.

In the context of search algorithms, evaluating the time as a function of D was first introduced in a classical paper by Baeza-Yates *et al.* [10], who studied the *cow-path* problem (studied also in [20, 41, 42]). The ANTS problem generalizes the cow-path problem, as it considers multiple identical

agents instead of a single agent (a cow in their terminology). Indeed, in this distributed setting, we are concerned with the *speed-up* measure (see also, [8, 9, 27, 29]), which aims to capture the impact of using k searchers in comparison to using a single one. Note that the objectives of quickly finding nearby treasures and having significant speed-up may be at conflict. That is, in order to ensure that nearby treasures are quickly found, a large enough fraction of the search force must be deployed near the central location. In turn, this crowding can potentially lead to overlapping searches that decrease individual efficiency.

It is a rather straightforward observation that the time required for finding the treasure is $\Omega(D + D^2/k)$. Our focus is on the question of how agents can approach this bound if their communication is limited or even completely absent. In particular, as information of the size of the foraging group may not be available to the individual searchers, we concentrate our attention on the question of how important it is for agents to know (or estimate) their total number. As we later show, the lack of such knowledge may have a non-negligible impact on the performance.

1.2 Our Results

We introduce and investigate the ANTS problem, a generalization of the cow-path problem. First, we show that if the agents have a constant approximation of their total number k, then there exists a rather simple search algorithm whose expected running time is $O(D + D^2/k)$, making it $O(1)$-competitive. We then turn our attention to *uniform* searching algorithms, in which the agents are not assumed to have any information regarding k. We completely characterize the speed-up penalty that must be paid when using uniform algorithms. Specifically, we show that for a function f such that $\sum_{j=1}^{\infty} 1/f(j)$ converges, there exists a uniform search algorithm that is $O(f(\log k))$-competitive. On the other hand, we show that if $\sum_{j=1}^{\infty} 1/f(j)$ diverges, then there is no uniform search algorithm that is $O(f(\log k))$-competitive. In particular, this implies that, for every constant $\varepsilon > 0$, there exists a uniform search algorithm that is $O(\log^{1+\varepsilon} k)$-competitive, but there is no uniform search algorithm that is $O(\log k)$-competitive. Hence, the penalty for using uniform algorithms is slightly more than logarithmic in the number of agents.

In addition, we give a lower bound for the intermediate setting in which the agents are given some estimation of k. As a special case, this lower bound implies that for any constant $\varepsilon > 0$, if each agent is given a (one-sided) k^{ε}-approximation of k, then the competitiveness is $\Omega(\log k)$. Informally, our results imply that the agents can potentially perform well without any knowledge of their total number k, however, to further improve they must use some information regarding k. Finally, we propose a uniform search algorithm that is concurrently efficient and extremely simple and, as such, it may imply some relevance for actual biological scenarios.

1.3 Related Work

Our work falls within the scope of natural algorithms, a recent attempt to investigate biological phenomena from an algorithmic perspective [1, 13, 15].

Collective search is a classical problem that has been extensively studied in different fields of science. Group living and food sources that have to be actively sought after make collective foraging a widespread biological phenomenon. Social foraging theory [33] makes use of economic and game theory to optimize food exploitation as a function of the group size and the degree of cooperativity between agents in different environmental settings. Social foraging theory has been extensively compared to experimental data (see, e.g., [6, 34]) but does not typically account for the spatial characteristics of resource abundance. Central place foraging theory [47] assumes a situation in which food is collected from a patchy resource and is returned to a particular location, such as a nest. This theory is used to calculate optimal durations for exploiting food patches at different distances from the central location and has also been tested against experimental observations [35, 37]. Collective foraging around a central location is particularly interesting in the case of social insects where large groups forage cooperatively with, practically, no competition between individuals. Harkness and Mardouras [36] have conducted a joint experimental and modeling research into the collective search behavior of non-communicating desert ants. Modeling the ants' trajectories using biased random walks, they reproduce some of the experimental findings and demonstrate significant speed-up with group size. In bold contrast to these random walks, Reynolds [54] argues that Lévy flights with a power law that approaches unity is the optimal search strategy for cooperative foragers as traveling in straight lines tends to decrease overlaps between searchers.

From an engineering perspective, the distributed cooperation of a team of autonomous agents (often referred to as robots or UAVs: Unmanned Aerial Vehicles) is a problem that has been extensively studied. These models extend single agent searches in which an agent with limited sensing abilities attempts to locate one or several mobile or immobile targets [49]. The memory and computational capacities of the agent are typically large and many algorithms rely on the construction of cognitive maps of the search area that includes current estimates that the target resides in each point [64]. The agent then plans an optimal path within this map with the intent, for example, of optimizing the rate of uncertainty decrease [40]. Cooperative searches typically include communication between the agents that can be transmitted up to a given distance, or even without any restriction. Models have been suggested where agents can communicate by altering the environment to which other agent then react [61]. Cooperation without communication has also been explored to some extent [7] but the analysis puts no emphasis on the speed-up of the search process. In addition, to the best of our knowledge, no works exist in this context that put emphasis on finding nearby targets faster than faraway one. Similar problems studied in this context are pattern formation [19, 58, 59], rendezvous [2, 28], and flocking [32]. It is important to stress that in all those engineering works, the issue of whether the robots know their total number is typically not addressed, as obtaining such information does not seem to be problematic. Furthermore, in many works, robots are not identical and have unique identities.

In the theory of computer science, the exploration of graphs using mobile agents is a central question. Most of the research for graph exploration is concerned with the case of a single deterministic agent exploring a finite graph (typically, with some restrictions on the resources of the agent and/or on the graph structure). For example, in [3, 12, 21, 26] the agent explores strongly connected directed finite graphs, and

in [5, 22, 23, 24, 31, 48, 50] the agent explores undirected finite graphs. When it comes to probabilistic searching, the random walk is a natural candidate, as it is extremely simple, uses no memory, and trivially self-stabilizes. Unfortunately, however, the random walk turns out to be inefficient in a two-dimensional infinite grid. Specifically, in this case, the expected hitting time is infinite, even if the treasure is nearby.

Evaluating the time to find the treasure as a function of D, the initial distance to the treasure, was studied in the context of the cow-path problem. One of the first papers that studied the cow-path problem is a paper by Baeza-Yates et al. [10], in which the competitive ratio for deterministically finding a point on the real line is shown to be nine. Considering the two-dimensional case, Baeza-Yates et al. proved that the spiral search algorithm is optimal up to lower order terms. Randomized algorithms for the problem were studied by Kao et al. [41], for the infinite star topology. Karp et al. [42] studied an early variant of the cow-path problem on a binary tree. Recently, Demaine et al. [20] considered the cow-path problem with a double component price: the first is distance and the second is turn cost. López-Ortiz and Sweet [45] extended the cow-path problem by considering k agents. However, in contrast to the ANTS problem, the agents they consider are not identical, and the goal is achieved by (centrally) designing a different specific path for each of the k agents.

In general, the more complex setting of using multiple identical agents has received much less attention. Exploration by deterministic multiple agents was studied in, e.g., [8, 9, 27, 29]. To obtain better results when using several identical deterministic agents, one must assume that the agents are either centrally coordinated or that they have some means of communication (either explicitly, or implicitly, by being able to detect the presence of nearby agents). When it comes to probabilistic agents, analyzing the speed-up measure for k-random walkers has recently gained attention. In a series of papers, initiated by Alon et al. [4], a speed-up of $\Omega(k)$ is established for various finite graph families, including, in particular, expanders and random graphs [4, 17, 25]. While some graph families enjoy linear speed-up, for many graph classes, to obtain linear speed-up, k has to be quite small. In particular, this is true for the two-dimensional n-node grid, where a linear speed up is obtained when $k < O(\log^{1-\varepsilon} n)$. On the other hand, the cover time of 2-dimensional n-node grid is always $\Omega(n/\log k)$, regardless of k. Hence, when k is polynomial in n, the speed up is only logarithmic in k. The situation with infinite grids is even worse. Specifically, though the k-random walkers would find the treasure with probability one, the expected time to find the treasure becomes infinite.

The question of how important it is for individual processors to know their total number has recently been addressed in the context of locality. Generally speaking, it has been observed that for several classical local computation tasks, knowing the number of processors is not essential [43]. On the other hand, in the context of local decision, some evidence exist that such knowledge may be crucial for non-deterministic distributed decision [30].

2. PRELIMINARIES

We consider the ANTS problem, where k mobile *agents* (robots) are searching for a *treasure* on the two-dimensional plane. Each agent has a field of view bounded by a small positive constant, hence, for simplicity, we can assume that the agents are actually walking on the integer two-dimensional infinite grid $G := \mathbf{Z}^2$. All k agents starts the search from a central node s of G, called the *source*. An adversary locates the treasure at some node τ of G, referred to as the *target* node; the agents have no a priori information about the location of τ. The goal of the agents it to *find* the treasure: this task is accomplished once at least one of the agents visits the node τ.

The agents are probabilistic machines that can move on the grid, but cannot communicate between themselves. All k agents are identical (execute the same protocol). An agent can traverse an edge of the grid in both directions. We do not restrict the internal storage and computational power of agents, nevertheless, we note that all our upper bounds use simple procedures that can be implemented using relatively short memory. For example, with respect to navigation, our constructions only assume the ability to perform four basic procedures, namely: (1) choose a direction uniformly at random, (2) walk in a "straight" line to a prescribed distance, (3) perform a *spiral search* around a node[1], and (4) return to the source node. On the other hand, for our lower bounds to hold, we do not require any restriction on the navigation capabilities.

Regarding the time complexity, we assume that traversing an edge takes one unit of time. Furthermore, for the ease of presentation, we assume that the agents are synchronous, that is, each edge traversal costs precisely one unit of time (and all internal computations are performed in zero time). Indeed, this assumption can easily be removed if we measure the time according to the slowest edge-traversal. We also assume that all agents start the search simultaneously at the same time, denoted by t_0. This assumption can also be easily removed by starting to count the time after the last agent initiates the search. We measure the cost of an algorithm by its *expected running time*, that is, the expected time (from time t_0) until at least one of the agents finds the treasure. We denote the expected running time of algorithm $\mathcal{A}$ by $\mathcal{T}_{\mathcal{A}}(D, k)$.

The *distance* $d(u, v)$ between two nodes u and v of G is simply the hop distance between them, i.e., the number of edges on a shortest path connecting u and v in G. The distance between a node u and the source node s is simply written $d(u)$, i.e. $d(u) := d(s, u)$. Let D be the distance between the source node s and the target node τ, i.e., $D := d(\tau)$. For a node u of G and an integer r, let $B(u, r)$ be the ball of radius r centered at the node u, formally, $B(u, r) := \{v \in G : d(u, v) \leq r\}$. For short, we denote the ball of radius r around the source node s by $B(r)$, that is, $B(r) := B(s, r)$.

Note that if an agent knows D, then it can potentially find the treasure in time $O(D)$, by going to any node at distance D, and then performing a circle around the source of radius D (assuming, of course, that its navigation abilities enable it to perform such a circle). On the other hand,

without knowledge about D, an agent can find the treasure in time $O(D^2)$ by performing a spiral search around the source. When considering k agents, it is easy to see[2] that the expected running time is $\Omega(D + D^2/k)$, even if the total number of agents k is known to all agents, and even if we relax the model and allow agents to freely communicate between each other. It follows from Theorem 3.1 that if k is known to agents then there exists a search algorithm whose expected running time is asymptotically optimal, namely, $O(D + D^2/k)$. We evaluate the performance of an algorithm that does not assume the precise knowledge of k with respect to this aforementioned optimal time. Formally, let $\phi(k)$ be a function of k. An algorithm $\mathcal{A}$ is $\phi(k)$-*competitive* if

$$\mathcal{T}_{\mathcal{A}}(D, k) \leq \phi(k) \cdot (D + D^2/k),$$

for every integers k and D. We shall be particularly interested in the performances of *uniform* algorithms: these are algorithms in which no information regarding k is available to agents. (The term "uniform" is chosen to stress that agents execute the same algorithm regardless of their number, see, e.g., [43].)

3. UPPER BOUNDS

3.1 Optimal Running Time with Knowledge on k

Our first theorem asserts that agents can achieve an asymptotically optimal running time if they know the precise value of k. As a corollary, it follows that, in fact, to obtain such a bound, it is sufficient to assume that agents only know a constant approximation of k.

THEOREM 3.1. *Assume that the agents know their total number, k. Then, there exists a (non-uniform) search algorithm running in expected time $O(D + D^2/k)$.*

PROOF. For $i \in \mathbf{N}$, set $B_i := \{u : d(u) \leq 2^i\}$. Consider the following algorithm (see also Figure 1 for an illustration).

Fix a positive integer ℓ and consider the time T_ℓ until each agent completed ℓ phases i with $i \geq \log D$. Each time an agent performs phase i, the agent finds the treasure if the chosen node u belongs to the ball $B(\tau, \sqrt{t_i}/2)$ around τ, the node holding the treasure. Note that at least some constant fraction of the ball $B(\tau, \sqrt{t_i}/2)$ is contained in B_i, since $i \geq \log D$. The probability of choosing a node u in that fraction is thus $\Omega(|B(\tau, \sqrt{t_i}/2)|/|B_i|)$, which is at least β/k for some positive constant β. Thus, the probability that by time T_ℓ none of the k agents finds the treasure (while executing their respective ℓ phases i) is at most $(1 - \beta/k)^{k\ell}$, which is at most $\gamma^{-\ell}$ for some constant γ greater than 1.

---

[1] The spiral search around a node v is a particular deterministic local search algorithm (see, e.g., [10]) that starts at v and enables the agent to visit all nodes at distance $\Omega(\sqrt{x})$ from v by traversing x edges, for every integer x. For our purposes, since we are concerned only with asymptotic results, we can replace this atomic navigation procedure with any procedure that guarantees such a property. For simplicity, in the remainder of the paper, we assume that for every integer x, the spiral search of length x starting at a node v visits all nodes at distance at most $\sqrt{x}/2$ from v

[2] To see why, consider a search algorithm $\mathcal{A}$ whose expected running time is T. Clearly, $T \geq D$, because it takes time D to merely reach the treasure. Assume, towards a contradiction, that $T < D^2/4k$. In any execution of $\mathcal{A}$, by time $2T$, the k agents can visit a total of at most $2Tk < D^2/2$ nodes. Hence, by time $2T$, more than half of the nodes in $B_D := \{u : 1 \leq d(u) \leq D\}$ were not visited. Therefore, there must exist a node $u \in B_D$ such that the probability that u is visited by time $2T$ (by at least one of the agents) is less than $1/2$. If the adversary locates the treasure at u, then the expected time to find the treasure is strictly greater than T, which contradicts the assumption.

begin

Each agent performs the following double loop;

for j *from* 1 *to* ∞ **do** the *stage* j defined as follows

    for i *from* 1 *to* j **do** the *phase* i defined as follows

- Go to a node u chosen uniformly at random among the nodes in B_i;
- Perform a spiral search for time $t_i := 2^{2i+2}/k$;
- Return to the source s;

    end

end

end

Algorithm 1: The non-uniform algorithm $\mathcal{A}_k$.

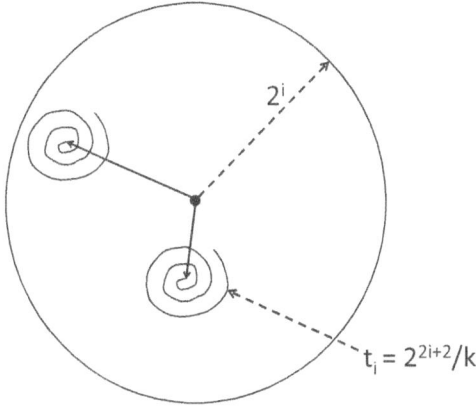

Figure 1: Illustration of two agents performing phase i.

For $i \in \mathbf{N}$, let $\psi(i)$ be the time required to execute a phase i. Note that $\psi(i) = O(2^i + 2^{2i}/k)$. Hence, the time until all agents complete stage j for the first time is

$$\sum_{i=1}^{j} \psi(i) = O(2^j + \sum_{i=1}^{j} 2^{2i}/k) = O(2^j + 2^{2j}/k).$$

Now fix $s := \lceil \log D \rceil$. It follows that for any integer ℓ, all agents complete their respective stages $s + \ell$ by time $\hat{T}(\ell) := O(2^{s+\ell} + 2^{2(s+\ell)}/k)$. Observe that by this time, all agents have completed at least $\ell^2/2$ phases i with $i \geq s$. Consequently, the probability that none of the k agents finds the treasure by time $\hat{T}(\ell)$ is at most $\gamma^{-\ell^2/2}$. Hence, the expected running time is at most

$$\mathcal{T}_{\mathcal{A}_k}(D,k) = O\left(\sum_{\ell=1}^{\infty} \frac{2^{s+\ell}}{\gamma^{\ell^2/2}} + \frac{2^{2(s+\ell)}}{k\gamma^{\ell^2/2}}\right)$$
$$= O\left(2^s + 2^{2s}/k\right) = O(D + D^2/k).$$

This establishes the theorem. $\square$

Fix a constant $\rho \geq 1$. We say that the agents have a

ρ-approximation of k, if, initially, each agent a receives as input a value k_a satisfying $k/\rho \leq k_a \leq k\rho$.

COROLLARY 3.2. *Fix a constant* $\rho \geq 1$. *Assume that the agents have a* ρ-*approximation of their total number. Then, there exists a (non-uniform) search algorithm that is* $O(1)$-*competitive.*

PROOF. Each agent a executes Algorithm $\mathcal{A}_k$ (see the proof of Theorem 3.1) with the parameter k equal to k_a/ρ. By the definition of a ρ-approximation, the only difference between this case and the case where the agents know their total number, is that for each agent, the time required to perform each spiral search is multiplied by a constant factor of at most ρ^2. Therefore, the analysis in the proof of Theorem 3.1 remains essentially the same and the running time is increased by a multiplicative factor of at most ρ^2. $\square$

3.2 Unknown Number of Agents

We now turn our attention to the case of uniform algorithms.

THEOREM 3.3. *Consider a non-decreasing function* $f: \mathbf{N} \to \mathbf{N}$ *such that* $\sum_{j=1}^{\infty} 1/f(j) < \infty$. *There exists a uniform search algorithm that is* $O(f(\log k))$-*competitive.*

PROOF. Consider the uniform search algorithm $\mathcal{A}_{\text{uniform}}$ described below. Let us analyze the performances of the algorithm and show that its expected running time is $T(D,k) := \phi(k) \cdot (D + D^2/k)$, where $\phi(k) := O(f(\log k))$. We first note that it suffices to prove the statement when $k \leq D$. Indeed, if $k > D$, then we may consider only D agents among the k agents and obtain an upper bound on the running time of $T(D,D)$, which is less than $T(D,k)$.

begin

Each agent performs the following;

for ℓ *from* 0 *to* ∞ **do** the big-stage ℓ

    for i *from* 0 *to* ℓ **do** the stage i

        for j *from* 0 *to* i **do** the phase j

- $k_j \leftarrow 2^j$;
- $D_{i,j} \leftarrow \sqrt{2^{(i+j)}/f(j)}$
- Go to the node u chosen uniformly at random among the nodes in $B(D_{i,j})$;
- Perform a spiral search starting at u for time $t_{i,j} := 2^{i+2}/f(j)$;
- Return to the source;

        end

    end

end

end

Algorithm 2: The uniform algorithm $\mathcal{A}_{\text{uniform}}$.

ASSERTION 1. *For every integer* ℓ, *the time until all agents complete big-stage* ℓ *is* $O(2^\ell)$.

For the assertion to hold, it is sufficient to prove that stage i in big-stage ℓ takes time $O(2^i)$. To this end, notice that phase j takes time $O(D_{i,j} + 2^i/f(j))$ which is at most $O(2^{(i+j)/2} +$

$2^i/f(j))$. Therefore, stage i takes time

$$O\left(\sum_{j=0}^{i}(2^{(i+j)/2}+2^i/f(j))\right)=O(2^i).$$

This establishes Assertion 1.

Set $s:=\lceil\log((D^2\cdot f(\log k))/k)\rceil+1$ and fix an integer $i\geq s$. Then, there exists $j\in\{0,\dots,i\}$ such that $2^j\leq k<2^{j+1}$.

ASSERTION 2. *There exists a constant $c\in(0,1)$ such that the probability that none of the agents finds the treasure while executing phase j of stage i is at most c.*

To see this, first note that the treasure is inside the ball $B(D_{i,j})$. Indeed, since $i\geq s$, we have

$$D_{i,j}=\sqrt{\frac{2^{i+j}}{f(j)}}\geq\sqrt{\frac{2^{s+j}}{f(j)}}>D.$$

The total number of nodes in the ball $B(D_{i,j})$ is $O(D_{i,j}^2)=O(2^{i+j}/f(j))$, and at least a third of the ball of radius $\sqrt{t_{i,j}}$ around the treasure is contained in $B(D_{i,j})$. Consequently, the probability for an agent a to choose a node u in a ball of radius $\sqrt{t_{i,j}}$ around the treasure in phase j of stage i is

$$\Omega\left(t_{i,j}/|B(D_{i,j})|\right)=\Omega\left(\frac{2^i/f(j)}{2^{i+j}/f(j)}\right)=\Omega\left(2^{-j}\right).$$

If this event happens, then the treasure is found during the corresponding spiral search of agent a. As a result, there exists a positive constant c' such that the probability that none of the k agents finds the treasure during phase j of stage i is at most $(1-c'\cdot2^{-j})^k\leq(1-c'\cdot2^{-j})^{2^j}\leq e^{-c'}$. This establishes Assertion 2.

By the time that all agents have completed their respective big-stage $s+\ell$, all agents have performed $\Omega(\ell^2)$ stages i with $i\geq s$. By Assertion 2, for each such i, the probability that the treasure is not found during stage i is at most c for some constant $c<1$. Hence, the probability that the treasure is not found during any of those $\Omega(\ell^2)$ stages is at most $1/d^{\ell^2}$ for some constant $d>1$. Assertion 1 ensures that all agents complete big-stage $s+\ell$ by time $O(2^{s+\ell})$, so the expected running time is $O(\sum_{\ell=0}^{\infty}2^{s+\ell}/d^{\ell^2})=O(2^s)=O(D^2\cdot f(\log k)/k)$, as desired. $\square$

Setting $f(x):=\lceil x^{1+\varepsilon}\rceil$ yields the following corollary.

COROLLARY 3.4. *For every positive constant ε, there exists a uniform search algorithm that is $O(\log^{1+\varepsilon}k)$-competitive.*

4. LOWER BOUNDS

4.1 A Tight Lower Bound for Uniform Algorithms

We say that a function $f:\mathbf{N}\to\mathbf{N}$ is *sub-exponential* if f is non-decreasing, and there exists a constant $c<2$ such that $f(x+1)<c\cdot f(x)$, for every $x\in\mathbf{N}$.

THEOREM 4.1. *Consider a sub-exponential function f such that $\sum_{j=1}^{\infty}1/f(j)=\infty$. There is no uniform search algorithm that is $O(f(\log k))$-competitive.*

PROOF. Suppose that there exists a uniform search algorithm with running time less than $\tau(D,k):=(D+D^2/k)\phi'(k)$. Hence, if $k\leq D$, then $\tau(D,k)\leq\frac{D^2\phi(k)}{k}$, where $\phi(k)=2\phi'(k)$. Suppose, towards a contradiction, that $\phi(k)=O(f(\log k))$.

For an integer i, set

$$k_i=2^i.$$

Let i_0 be the first integer such that for every integer $i\geq i_0$, we have $k_i>\phi(k_i)$. (The existence of i_0 is guaranteed by the fact that f is sub-exponential). Let $T\geq2^{2i_0}$ be a (sufficiently large) integer and set $D:=2T+1$. That is, for the purpose of the proof, we assume that the treasure is actually placed at some faraway distance D greater than $2T$. This means, in particular, that by time $2T$ the treasure has not been found yet. For every integer $i_0\leq i\leq\log T/2$, set

$$D_i:=\sqrt{T\cdot k_i/\phi(k_i)}.$$

Fix an integer $i\in[i_0,\log T/2]$, and consider $B(D_i)$, the ball of radius D_i around the source node. We now deal with the case where the algorithm is executed by k_i agents. For every subset S of nodes in $B(D_i)$, let $\chi(S)$ be the random variable indicating the number of nodes in S that were visited by at least one of the k_i agents by time $2T$. (We write $\chi(u)$ for $\chi(\{u\})$.)

Note that $k_i\leq D_i$ and, therefore, for each node $u\in B(D_i)$ the expected time to visit u is at most $\tau(D_i,k_i)\leq D_i^2\phi(k_i)/k_i=T$. Thus, by Markov's inequality, the probability that u is visited by time $2T$ is at least $1/2$, i.e., $\mathbf{Pr}(\chi(u)=1)\geq1/2$. Hence, $\mathbf{E}(\chi(u))\geq1/2$.

Now consider an integer i in $[i_0,\log T/2]$ and set $S_i:=B(D_i)\setminus B(D_{i-1})$. By linearity of expectation, $\mathbf{E}(\chi(S_i))=\sum_{u\in S_i}\mathbf{E}(\chi(u))\geq|S_i|/2$. Consequently, by time $2T$, the expected number of nodes in S_i that an agent visits is

$$\Omega(|S_i|/k_i)=\Omega\left(\frac{D_{i-1}(D_i-D_{i-1})}{k_i}\right)$$
$$=\Omega\left(\frac{T}{\phi(k_{i-1})}\cdot\left(\frac{\sqrt{2\phi(k_{i-1})}}{\sqrt{\phi(k_i)}}-1\right)\right)$$
$$=\Omega\left(\frac{T}{\phi(k_i)}\right),$$

where the second equality follows from the fact that $D_i=D_{i-1}\cdot\sqrt{\frac{2\phi(k_{i-1})}{\phi(k_i)}}$, and the third equality follows from the facts that $\phi(k_i)=O(f(i))$ and f is sub-exponential.

In other words, for every integer i in $[i_0,\log T/2]$, the expected number of nodes in S_i that each agent visits by time $2T$ is $\Omega\left(\frac{T}{\phi(k_i)}\right)$. Since the sets S_i are pairwise disjoint, the linearity of expectation implies that the expected number of nodes that an agent visits by time $2T$ is

$$\Omega\left(\sum_{i=i_0}^{\log T/2}\frac{T}{\phi(k_i)}\right)=T\cdot\Omega\left(\sum_{i=i_0}^{\log T/2}\frac{1}{\phi(2^i)}\right).$$

Consequently, $\sum_{i=i_0}^{\log T/2}\frac{1}{\phi(2^i)}$ must converge as T goes to infinity, and hence so does $\sum_{i=i_0}^{\log T/2}\frac{1}{f(i)}$. This contradicts the assumption on f. $\square$

Setting $f(x):=x$ yields the following statement.

COROLLARY 4.2. *There is no uniform search algorithm that is $O(\log k)$-competitive.*

4.2 A Lower Bound for Algorithms using an Approximate Knowledge of k

We now present a lower bound for the competitiveness of search algorithms assuming that agents are given approximations of their total number k. As a special case, our lower bound implies that for any constant $\varepsilon > 0$, if agents are given an estimation $\tilde{k}$ such that $\tilde{k}^{1-\varepsilon} \leq k \leq \tilde{k}$, then the competitiveness is $\Omega(\log k)$. That is, the competitiveness remains logarithmic even for relatively good approximations of k.

Formally, let $\varepsilon \colon \mathbf{N} \to (0, 1]$. We say that the agents have a k^{ε}-*approximation of* k if each agent a receives as input an estimation $\tilde{k}_a$ for k that satisfies:

$$\tilde{k}_a^{1-\varepsilon(\tilde{k}_a)} \leq k \leq \tilde{k}_a.$$

(For example, if the agents have a k^{ε}-approximation of k, where ε is the constant function equal to $1/2$, then, in particular, this means that if all agents are given the same value $\tilde{k}$, then the real number k of agents satisfies $\sqrt{\tilde{k}} \leq k \leq \tilde{k}$.)

THEOREM 4.3. *Let $\varepsilon \colon \mathbf{N} \to (0, 1]$ and assume that the agents have a k^{ε}-approximation of k. If there exists a $\phi(k)$-competitive algorithm, where ϕ is a non-decreasing function, then $\phi(k) = \Omega(\varepsilon(k)\log k)$.*

PROOF. Assume that there is a search algorithm for this case running in time $(D + D^2/k)\phi(k)$, where ϕ is non-decreasing. Suppose that all agents receive the same value $\tilde{k}$, which should serve as an estimate for k. Consider an integer W greater than $4\tilde{k}$. Set

$$T := 2W \cdot \phi(\tilde{k}) \quad \text{and} \quad j_0 := \frac{\log W}{2}.$$

For the purposes of the proof, we assume that the treasure is located at distance $D = 2T + 1$, so that by time $2T$ it is guaranteed that no agent finds the treasure.

For $i \in \mathbf{N}$, define

$$S_i := \left\{ u \,:\, 2^{j_0+i-1} < \mathrm{d}(u, s) \leq 2^{j_0+i} \right\}.$$

Fix an integer i in $\{\lceil \frac{1-\varepsilon(\tilde{k})}{2} \log \tilde{k} \rceil, \cdots, \lfloor \frac{1}{2} \log \tilde{k} \rfloor\}$. Assume for the time being, that the number of agents is $k_i := 2^{2i}$. Note that

$$\tilde{k}^{1-\varepsilon(\tilde{k})} \leq k_i \leq \tilde{k},$$

hence, k_i is a possible candidate for being the real number of agents. Observe that all nodes in S_i are at distance at most 2^{j_0+i} from the source, and that $|S_i| = \Theta(2^{2j_0+2i}) = \Theta(W \cdot k_i)$. By the definition, $j_0 \geq i + 1$. Hence, $k_i \leq 2^{j_0+i-1} < \mathrm{d}(u, s)$, and therefore using the expected running time of the algorithm, it follows that for each node $u \in S_i$, the expected time until at least one of the k_i agents covers u is at most

$$\frac{2\,\mathrm{d}(u,s)^2}{k_i} \cdot \phi(k_i) \leq 2W \cdot \phi(\tilde{k}) = T.$$

Recall that we now consider the case where the algorithm is executed with k_i agents. For every subset S of nodes of G, let $\chi(S)$ be the random variable indicating the number of nodes in S that were visited by at least one of the k_i agents by time $2T$. (As before, we write $\chi(u)$ for $\chi(\{u\})$.) By Markov's

inequality, the probability that u is visited by at least one of the k_i agents by time $2T$ is at least $1/2$, i.e., $\mathbf{Pr}(\chi(u) = 1) \geq 1/2$. Hence, $\mathbf{E}(\chi(u)) \geq 1/2$. By linearity of expectation, $\mathbf{E}(\chi(S_i)) = \sum_{u \in S_i} \mathbf{E}(\chi(u)) \geq |S_i|/2$. Consequently, by time $2T$, the expected number of nodes in S_i that a single agent visits is $\Omega(|S_i|/k_i) = \Omega(W)$.

Since this holds for any i in $\{\lceil \frac{1-\varepsilon(\tilde{k})}{2} \log \tilde{k} \rceil, \cdots, \lfloor \frac{1}{2} \log \tilde{k} \rfloor\}$, and since the sets S_i are pairwise disjoint, the linearity of expectation implies that the expected number of nodes that a single agent visits by time $2T$ is $\Omega(W \cdot \varepsilon(\tilde{k}) \log \tilde{k})$. Since $T = 2W \cdot \phi(\tilde{k})$, this implies that $\phi(\tilde{k}) = \Omega(\varepsilon(\tilde{k}) \log \tilde{k})$, as desired. This concludes the proof of the theorem. $\square$

5. HARMONIC SEARCH

The algorithms described in the Section 3 are relatively simple but still require the use of non trivial iterations, which may be complex for simple and tiny agents, such as ants. If we relax the requirement of bounding the expected running time and demand only that the treasure be found with some low constant probability, then it is possible to avoid one of the loops of the algorithms. However, a sequence of iterations still needs to be performed.

In this section, we propose an extremely simple algorithm, coined the *harmonic search algorithm*[3], which does not perform in iterations and is essentially composed of three components: (1) choose a random direction and walk in this direction for a distance of d, chosen randomly according to a distribution in which the probability of choosing d is roughly inverse proportional to d, (2) perform a local search (e.g., a spiral search) for time roughly d^2, and (3) return to the source. It turns out that this extremely simple algorithm has a good probability of quickly finding the treasure, if the number of agents is sufficiently large.

More specifically, the algorithm depends on a positive constant parameter δ that is fixed in advance and governs the performance of the algorithm. For a node u, let $p(u) := \frac{c}{\mathrm{d}(u)^{2+\delta}}$, where c is the normalizing factor, defined so that $\sum_{u \in V(G)} p(u) = 1$. (Note that c depends on δ.)

begin

    Each agent performs the following three actions;

    1. Go to a node $u \in V(G)$ with probability $p(u)$;

    2. Perform a spiral search for time $t(u) := \mathrm{d}(u)^{2+\delta}$;

    3. Return to the source;

end

    Algorithm 3: The harmonic search algorithm.

Using arguments similar to those introduced earlier, e.g., in the proofs of Theorems 3.1 and 3.3, one can prove the following result.

THEOREM 5.1. *Let $\delta \in (0, 0.8]$. For every $\varepsilon > 0$, there exists a positive real number α such that if the number k of agents is greater than αD^{δ}, then with probability at least $1 - \varepsilon$, the expected running time of the harmonic algorithm is $O(D + \frac{D^{2+\delta}}{k})$.*

---

[3]The name harmonic was chosen because of structure resemblances to the celebrated harmonic algorithm for the k-server problem — see, e.g., [11].

6. CONCLUSION AND DISCUSSION

We first presented an algorithm that assumes that agents have a constant approximation of k and runs in optimal expected time, that is, in time $O(D + D^2/k)$. We then showed that there exists a uniform search algorithm whose competitiveness is slightly more than logarithmic. We also presented a relatively efficient uniform algorithm, namely, the harmonic algorithm, that has and extremely simple structure. Our constructions imply that, in the absence of any communication, multiple searchers can still potentially perform rather well. On the other hand, our lower bounds imply that to achieve a better running time, the searchers must either communicate or utilize some information regarding k. In particular, even providing each agent with a k^ε-approximation to k (for constant $\varepsilon > 0$) does not suffice to bring the competitiveness strictly below $O(\log k)$.

Although the issue of memory is beyond the scope of this paper, our constructions are simple and can be implemented using relatively low memory. For example, going in a straight line for a distance of $d = 2^\ell$ can be implemented using $O(\log \log d)$ memory bits, by employing a randomized counting technique. In addition, our lower bounds provide evidence that in order to achieve a near-optimal running time, agents must use non-trivial memory size, required merely to store the necessary approximation of k. This may be useful to obtain a tradeoff between the running time and the memory size of agents.

From another perspective, it is of course interesting to experimentally verify whether social insects engage in search patterns in the plane which resemble the simple uniform algorithms specified above, and, in particular, the harmonic algorithm. Two natural candidates are desert ants *Cataglyphys* and honeybees *Apis mellifera*. First, these species seem to face settings that are similar to the one we use. Indeed, they cannot rely on communication during the search due to the dispersedness of individuals [36] and their inability to leave chemical trails (this is due to increased pheromone evaporation in the case of the desert ant). Additionally, the task of finding the treasure is relevant, as food sources in many cases are indeed relatively rare or patchy. Moreover, due to the reasons mentioned in Section 1, finding nearby sources of food is of great importance. Second, insects of these species have the behavioral and computational capacity to maintain a compass-directed vector flight [14, 36], measure distance using an internal odometer [56, 57], travel to distances taken from a random power law distribution [53], and engage in spiral or quasi-spiral movement patterns [51, 52, 63]. These are the main ingredients that are needed to perform the algorithms described in this paper. Finally, the search trajectories of desert ants have been shown to include two distinguishable sections: a long straight path in a given direction emanating from the nest and a second more tortuous path within a small confined area [36, 62].

7. ACKNOWLEDGMENTS.

The authors are grateful to the anonymous referees for their useful suggestions.

8. REFERENCES

[1] Y. Afek, N. Alon, O. Barad, E. Hornstein, N. Barkai, and Z. Bar-Joseph. A biological solution to a fundamental distributed computing problem. *Science*, 331(6014):183–185, 2011.

[2] N. Agmon and D. Peleg. Fault-tolerant gathering algorithms for autonomous mobile robots. *SIAM J. Comput.*, 36(1):56–82 (electronic), 2006.

[3] S. Albers and M. R. Henzinger. Exploring unknown environments. *SIAM J. Comput.*, 29(4):1164–1188, 2000.

[4] N. Alon, C. Avin, M. Koucký, G. Kozma, Z. Lotker, and M. R. Tuttle. Many random walks are faster than one. *Combin. Probab. Comput.*, 20(4):481–502, 2011.

[5] C. Ambühl, L. Gąsieniec, A. Pelc, T. Radzik, and X. Zhang. Tree exploration with logarithmic memory. *ACM Trans. Algorithms*, 7(2):Art. 17, 21, 2011.

[6] M. Arbilly, U. Motro, M. W. Feldman, and A. Lotem. Co-evolution of learning complexity and social foraging strategies. *J. Theor. Biol.*, 267(4):573–581, 2010.

[7] R. C. Arkin. Cooperation without communication: Multiagent schema-based robot navigation. *J. Rob. Syst.*, 9(3):351–364, 1992.

[8] I. Averbakh and O. Berman. A heuristic with worst-case analysis for minimax routing of two travelling salesmen on a tree. *Discrete Appl. Math.*, 68(1-2):17–32, 1996.

[9] I. Averbakh and O. Berman. $(p-1)/(p+1)$-approximate algorithms for p-traveling salesmen problems on a tree with minmax objective. *Discrete Appl. Math.*, 75(3):201–216, 1997.

[10] R. A. Baeza-Yates, J. C. Culberson, and G. J. E. Rawlins. Searching in the plane. *Inform. and Comput.*, 106(2):234–252, 1993.

[11] Y. Bartal and E. Grove. The harmonic k-server algorithm is competitive. *J. ACM*, 47(1):1–15, 2000.

[12] M. A. Bender, A. Fernández, D. Ron, A. Sahai, and S. Vadhan. The power of a pebble: exploring and mapping directed graphs. *Inform. and Comput.*, 176(1):1–21, 2002.

[13] V. Bonifaci, K. Mehlhorn, and G. Varma. Physarum can compute shortest paths. In *Proc. Symp. Discrete Algorithms*, (SODA'12), pages 233–240. SIAM, 2012.

[14] E. A. Capaldi, A. D. Smith, J. L. Osborne, S. E. Fahrbach, S. M. Farris, D. R. Reynolds, A. S. Edwards, A. Martin, G. E. Robinson, G. M. Poppy, and J. R. Riley. Ontogeny of orientation flight in the honeybee revealed by harmonic radar. *Nature*, 403:537–540, 2000.

[15] B. Chazelle. Natural algorithms. In *Proc. Symp. Discrete Algorithms*, (SODA'09), pages 422–431. SIAM, 2009.

[16] T. S. Collett, E. Dillmann, A. Giger, and R. Wehner. Visual landmarks and route following in desert ants. *J. Comp. Physiol. A: Mol. Integr. Physiol.*, 170(4):435–442, 1992.

[17] C. Cooper, A. Frieze, and T. Radzik. Multiple random walks in random regular graphs. *SIAM J. Discrete Math.*, 23(4):1738–1761, 2009/10.

[18] F. Courchamp, T. Clutton-Brock, and B. Grenfell. Inverse density dependence and the allee effect. *Trends Ecol. Evol.*, 14(10):405–410, 1999.

[19] S. Das, P. Flocchini, N. Santoro, and M. Yamashita. On the computational power of oblivious robots: forming a

series of geometric patterns. In *Proc. Symp. Principles Dist. Comput.*, (PODC'10), pages 267–276. ACM, 2010.

[20] E. D. Demaine, S. P. Fekete, and S. Gal. Online searching with turn cost. *Theoret. Comput. Sci.*, 361(2-3):342–355, 2006.

[21] X. Deng and C. H. Papadimitriou. Exploring an unknown graph. *J. Graph Theory*, 32(3):265–297, 1999.

[22] A. Dessmark and A. Pelc. Optimal graph exploration without good maps. *Theoret. Comput. Sci.*, 326(1-3):343–362, 2004.

[23] K. Diks, P. Fraigniaud, E. Kranakis, and A. Pelc. Tree exploration with little memory. *J. Algorithms*, 51:38–63, 2004.

[24] C. A. Duncan, S. G. Kobourov, and V. S. A. Kumar. Optimal constrained graph exploration. *ACM Trans. Algorithms*, 2(3):380–402, 2006.

[25] R. Elsässer and T. Sauerwald. Tight bounds for the cover time of multiple random walks. *Theoret. Comput. Sci.*, 412(24):2623–2641, 2011.

[26] R. Fleischer and G. Trippen. Exploring an unknown graph efficiently. In *Proc. Eur. Conf. Algorithms*, (ESA'05), pages 11–22. Springer-Verlag, 2005.

[27] P. Flocchini, D. Ilcinkas, A. Pelc, and N. Santoro. How many oblivious robots can explore a line. *Inform. Process. Lett.*, 111(20):1027–1031, 2011.

[28] P. Flocchini, G. Prencipe, N. Santoro, and P. Widmayer. Gathering of asynchronous robots with limited visibility. *Theor. Comput. Sci.*, 337:147–168, June 2005.

[29] P. Fraigniaud, L. Gąsieniec, D. R. Kowalski, and A. Pelc. Collective tree exploration. *Networks*, 48(3):166–177, 2006.

[30] P. Fraigniaud, A. Korman, and D. Peleg. Local distributed decision. In *Found. Comput. Sci.*, (FOCS'11), pages 708–717. IEEE, 2011.

[31] L. Gąsieniec, A. Pelc, T. Radzik, and X. Zhang. Tree exploration with logarithmic memory. In *Proc. Symp. Discrete Algorithms*, (SODA'07), pages 585–594. ACM, 2007.

[32] V. Gervasi and G. Prencipe. Coordination without communication: the case of the flocking problem. *Discrete Appl. Math.*, 144(3):324–344, 2004.

[33] L.-A. Giraldeau and T. Caraco. *Social Foraging Theory*. Princeton University Press, 2000.

[34] L.-A. Giraldeau and D. Gillis. Do lions hunt in group sizes that maximize hunters' daily food returns? *Anim. Behav.*, 36(2):611–613, 1988.

[35] L.-A. Giraldeau, D. L. Kramer, I. Deslandes, and H. Lair. The effect of competitors and distance on central place foraging eastern chipmunks, tamias striatus. *Anim. Behav.*, 47(3):621–632, 1994.

[36] R.D. Harkness and N.G. Maroudas. Central place foraging by an ant (*Cataglyphis bicolor* fab.): a model of searching. *Anim. Behav.*, 33(3):916–928, 1985.

[37] K. Holder and G. A. Polis. Optimal and central-place foraging theory applied to a desert harvester ant, *Pogonomyrmex californicus*. *Oecologia*, 72(3):440–448, 1987.

[38] B. Holldobler and E. O. Wilson. *The Ants*. Harvard University Press, 1990.

[39] J. U. M. Jarvis, N. C. Bennett, and A. C. Spinks. Food availability and foraging by wild colonies of damaraland mole-rats (*Cryptomys damarensis*): implications for sociality. *Oecologia*, 113(2):290–298, 1998.

[40] E. Kagan and I. Ben-Gal. An informational search for a moving target. In *Conv. Electr. Electron. Eng. Isr.*, pages 153–155, 2006.

[41] M.-Y. Kao, J. H. Reif, and S. R. Tate. Searching in an unknown environment: an optimal randomized algorithm for the cow-path problem. *Inform. and Comput.*, 131(1):63–79, 1996.

[42] R. M. Karp, M. Saks, and A. Wigderson. On a search problem related to branch-and-bound procedures. In *Proc. Symp. Found. Comput. Sci.*, (FOCS'86), pages 19–28. IEEE, 1986.

[43] A. Korman, J.-S. Sereni, and L. Viennot. Toward more localized local algorithms: removing assumptions concerning global knowledge. In *Proc. Symp. Principles Dist. Comput.*, (PODC'11), pages 49–58. ACM, 2011.

[44] J. R. Krebs. Optimal foraging, predation risk and territory defense. *Ardea*, 68:83–90, 1980.

[45] A. López-Ortiz and G. Sweet. Parallel searching on a lattice. In *Proc. Can. Conf. Comput. Geom.*, (CCCG'01), pages 125–128, 2001.

[46] J. C. Mitani and P. S. Rodman. Territoriality: The relation of ranging pattern and home range size to defendability, with an analysis of territoriality among primate species. *Behav. Ecol. Sociobiol.*, 5(3):241–251, 1979.

[47] G. F. Orians and N. E. Pearson. On the theory of central place foraging. *Anal. Ecol. Syst.*, pages 155–177, 1979.

[48] P. Panaite and A. Pelc. Exploring unknown undirected graphs. *J. Algorithms*, 33(2):281–295, 1999.

[49] M. M. Polycarpou, Y. Yang, and K.M. Passino. A cooperative search framework for distributed agents. In *Proc. Int. Symp. Intell. Control*, (ISIC'01), pages 1–6. IEEE, 2001.

[50] O. Reingold. Undirected connectivity in log-space. *J. ACM*, 55(4):17:1–17:24, 2008.

[51] A. M. Reynolds. Optimal random Lévy-loop searching: New insights into the searching behaviours of central-place foragers. *Europhys. Lett.*, 82(2):20001, 2008.

[52] A. M. Reynolds, A. D. Smith, R. Menzel, U. Greggers, Donald R. Reynolds, and J. R. Riley. Displaced honey bees perform optimal scale-free search flights. *Ecology*, 88(8):1955–1961, 2012/04/29 2007.

[53] A. M. Reynolds, A. D. Smith, D. R. Reynolds, N. L. Carreck, and J. L. Osborne. Honeybees perform optimal scale-free searching flights when attempting to locate a food source. *J. Exp. Biol.*, 210:3763–3770, 2007.

[54] A.M. Reynolds. Cooperative random Lévy flight searches and the flight patterns of honeybees. *Phys. Lett. A*, 354(5-6):384–388, 2006.

[55] T. W. Schoener. Theory of feeding strategies. *Annu. Rev. Ecol. Syst.*, 2:369–404, 1971.

[56] S. Sommer and R. Wehner. The ant's estimation of distance travelled: experiments with desert ants, cataglyphis fortis. *J. Comp. Physiol. A: Mol. Integr. Physiol.*, 190(1):1–6, 2004.

[57] M. V. Srinivasan, S. Zhang, M. Altwein, and J. Tautz. Honeybee navigation: Nature and calibration of the "odometer". *Science*, 287(851–853), 2000.

[58] I. Suzuki and M. Yamashita. Distributed anonymous mobile robots: formation of geometric patterns. *SIAM J. Comput.*, 28(4):1347–1363 (electronic), 1999.

[59] I. Suzuki and M. Yamashita. Erratum: "Distributed anonymous mobile robots: formation of geometric patterns" [SIAM J. Comput. **28** (1999), no. 4, 1347–1363 (electronic); mr1681010]. *SIAM J. Comput.*, 36(1):279–280 (electronic), 2006.

[60] J. F. A. Traniello. Recruitment behavior, orientation, and the organization of foraging in the carpenter ant *Camponotus pennsylvanicus* DeGeer (Hymenoptera: Formicidae). *Behav. Ecol. Sociobiol.*, 2(1):61–79, 1977.

[61] I. A. Wagner, Y. Altshuler, V. Yanovski, and A. M. Bruckstein. Cooperative cleaners: A study in ant robotics. *Int. J. Rob. Res.*, 27(1):127–151, 2008.

[62] R. Wehner, C. Meier, and C. Zollikofer. The ontogeny of foragwehaviour in desert ants, cataglyphis bicolor. *Ecol. Entomol.*, 29(2):240–250, 2004.

[63] R. Wehner and M. V. Srinivasan. Searching behaviour of desert ants, genus *Cataglyphis (Formicidae, Hymenoptera)*. *J. Comp. Physiol. A*, 142(3):315–338, 1981.

[64] Y. Yang, A.A. Minai, and M.M. Polycarpou. Decentralized cooperative search by networked uavs in an uncertain environment. In *Proc. Am. Control Conf., (ACC'04)*, volume 6, pages 5558–5563. IEEE, 2004.

Brief Announcement:
What Can be Computed without Communications? *

Heger Arfaoui
University Paris Diderot
France

Pierre Fraigniaud
CNRS and University Paris Diderot
France

ABSTRACT

When playing the boolean game (δ, f), two players, upon reception of respective inputs x and y, must respectively output a and b satisfying $\delta(a,b) = f(x,y)$, in *absence of any communication*. It is known that, for $\delta(a,b) = a \oplus b$, the ability for the players to use entangled quantum bits (qbits) helps. In this paper, we show that, for δ different from the exclusive-or operator, quantum correlations do not help. This result is an invitation to revisit the theory of distributed *checking*, a.k.a. distributed *verification*, currently sticked to the usage of decision functions δ based on the AND-operator, hence potentially preventing us from using the potential benefit of quantum effects.

Categories and Subject Descriptors

F.2.2 [**Theory of Computation**]: Analysis of Algorithms and Problem Complexity—*Nonnumerical Algorithms and Problems*

General Terms

Algorithms, Theory

Keywords

Distributed checking, Non-locality

1. TWO-PLAYER GAMES AND BOXES

This paper addresses the following 2-player problem. Alice (resp., Bob) receives a boolean x (resp., y) as input, and must return a boolean a (resp., b) as output. A *game* between Alice and Bob is defined by a pair (δ, f) of boolean functions. The objective of Alice and Bob playing game (δ, f) is, for every inputs x and y, to output values a and b satisfying

$$\delta(a,b) = f(x,y)$$

in *absence of any communication* between the two players. A game (δ, f) is said to be solvable with probability p if there exists a randomized distributed protocol satisfying, for every input pair $(x,y) \in \{0,1\}^2$, that Alice outputs a, and Bob outputs b, such that

$$\Pr[\delta(a,b) = f(x,y)] \geq p.$$

*Complete version appeared in 19th Int. Colloquium on Structural Information and Communication Complexity [1].

The literature dealing with 2-player games (see, e.g., [2, 3, 8, 14]) focuses its attention to the computational power of objects called *boxes*. A box B is characterized by the probability $\Pr[a,b|x,y]$ of outputting pair (a,b) given the input pair (x,y). A box B is thus described by a set of four probability distributions, one for each $(x,y) \in \{0,1\}^2$. There are thus infinitely many boxes, with different computational powers, in terms of their ability of solving 2-player games (δ, f)..

The absence of communication between the two players along with the assumption of causality are captured by the class of *non-signaling* boxes. A box B is non-signaling if and only if it satisfies that the marginal output distributions for Alice and Bob depend only on their respective inputs. Formally, a non-signaling box satisfies:

$$\forall a, x, \ \sum_b \Pr(a,b|x,0) = \sum_b \Pr(a,b|x,1),$$
$$\text{and} \quad \forall b, y, \ \sum_a \Pr(a,b|0,y) = \sum_a \Pr(a,b|1,y)$$

Non-signaling boxes that correspond to *classical* (i.e., non quantum) strategies are called *local* boxes. A box B is said to be local if and only if its output distributions satisfy, for every input pair (x,y) and every output pair (a,b),

$$\Pr[a,b|x,y] = \sum_{\lambda \in \Omega} \Pr[a|x,\lambda] \cdot \Pr[b|y,\lambda] \cdot \Pr(\lambda)$$

where the random variable λ is drawn from some probability space Ω. Such a probability distribution defines a box using shared randomness. The terminology "local" is referring here to the physical science concept of *local hidden variables* [9, 4].

The set of all boxes has a geometric interpretation [2], for it forms a 12-dimensional convex polytope in $[0,1]^{16}$, including the 8-dimensional convex polytope of non-signaling boxes, which includes in turn the 8-dimensional convex polytope of local boxes. The figure below provides an abstract representation of the non-signaling polytope.

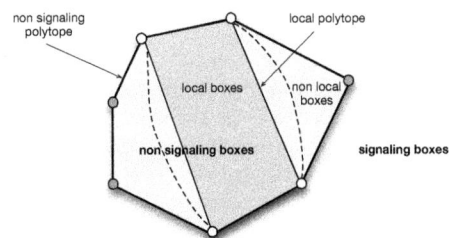

Each of the extremal vertices of the local polytope is equivalent (up to individual transformations of the inputs and outputs) to the identity box ID satisfying:

$$\Pr[a, b | x, y] = \begin{cases} 1 & \text{if } a = x \text{ and } y = b \\ 0 & \text{otherwise.} \end{cases}$$

Each of the non-local extremal vertices of the non-signaling polytope is equivalent to the PR box [5, 14] that is described by the distributions:

$$\Pr[a, b | x, y] = \begin{cases} \frac{1}{2} & \text{if } a \oplus b = x \wedge y \\ 0 & \text{otherwise.} \end{cases}$$

Non-extremal boxes are linear combinations of extremal boxes. The faces of the local polytope separating local boxes to non-local boxes are described by Bell's inequalities [4]. The doted line displayed on the figure represents the limit of the class of boxes implementable by a *quantum protocol*, that is, a protocol using correlations on quantum entangled states. This latter class strictly contains the local boxes, and is strictly included in the class of non-signaling boxes, as witnessed by the CHSH game [6]:

$$a \oplus b = x \wedge y$$

which is solved with probability 1 by the PR box, with probability $\cos^2(\pi/8)$ by a quantum box [5], and with probability $\frac{3}{4}$ by a local box, all these results being tight.

We have completed an exhaustive study of 2-player games in order to identify for which games quantum correlations help. The results of this study are reported in this BA.

2. OUR RESULTS

Essentially, we show that, for every 2-player game (δ, f) with δ different from the exclusive-or operator, every box solving (δ, f) with probabilistic guarantee p greater that the probabilistic guarantee of any local box, is signaling. Formally, we show that there are essentially two different types of non-trivial games: XOR-games and AND-games, for which the function δ respectively satisfies $\delta(a, b) = a \oplus b$, and $\delta(a, b) = a \wedge b$. An example of the former is the CHSH game $a \oplus b = x \wedge y$, while an example of the latter is the amos game: $a \wedge b = \overline{x \wedge y}$ (see [10]).

THEOREM 1. *Let (δ, f) be a 2-player game that is not equivalent to any XOR-game. Let p be the largest success probability for (δ, f) of any local boxes. Then every box solving (δ, f) with probabilistic guarantee $> p$ is signaling.*

Since quantum boxes are non-signaling, we derive that quantum effect do not help for AND-games:

COROLLARY 1. *Let (δ, f) be a 2-player game that is not equivalent to any XOR-game. Then quantum boxes solve (δ, f) with probability at most the one that can be achieved by a local box.*

These results open new perspectives in term of distributed *checking*, a.k.a. distributed *verification*, which consists in having a set of, say, n processes deciding whether their global state (obtained by the union of the local state of every individual process) satisfies some prescribed property, or not. The literature on this latter topic (see, e.g., [7, 10, 11, 13]) assumes a *decision* function δ which is applied to the set of individual decisions produced by the processes. Typically, each process should output a boolean b_i, and the global interpretation of the outputs is computed by

$$\delta(b_1, \ldots, b_n) = \bigwedge_{i=1}^{n} b_i \in \{\text{"yes","no"}\} \ .$$

The use of the AND operator is motivated by the requirement that the global state is valid if and only if all processes agree on some (local) validity condition. If this condition is violated somewhere in the system, then at least one process "rises an alarm" by outputting 0. However, recent advances in the theory of distributed checking [12] demonstrate that using other decision functions δ significantly increases the power of the "checker", or "verifier". Our results show that some functions δ, in particular the classical AND operator, do not enable to use the power of quantum computing efficiently, compared to shared randomness, at least for 2-player games. In contrast, the exclusive-or operator is known to offer high potential, as far as non-classical distributed computing is concerned. In particular, [3] proved that every boolean function f on n independent players can be implemented by a circuit of PR boxes that output booleans b_i, $i = 1, \ldots, n$, satisfying $\bigoplus_{i=1}^{n} b_i = f(x_1, \ldots, x_n)$. Our results give one more evidence of the impact of the decision function δ on the ability of "deciding" boolean predicates f.

3. REFERENCES

[1] H. Arfaoui and P. Fraigniaud. What can be computed without communication? *SIROCCO'12*, LNCS 7355, pp 135–146.

[2] J. Barrett, N. Linden, S. Massar, S. Pironio, S. Popescu, and D. Roberts. Nonlocal correlations as an information-theoretic resource. *Physical Review A* 71(2):1-11, 2005.

[3] J. Barrett and S. Pironio. Popescu-Rohrlich correlations as a unit of nonlocality. *Phys. Rev. Lett.* 95(14), 2005.

[4] J. S. Bell. On the Einstein-Podolsky-rosen paradox. *Physics*, 1(3):195–200, 1964.

[5] B. S. Cirel'son. Quantum generalizations of bell's inequality. *Letters in Math. Phys.*, 4(2):93–100, 1980.

[6] J. F. Clauser, M. A. Horne, A. Shimony, and R. A. Holt. Proposed experiment to test local hidden-variable theories. *Physical Review Letters*, 23(15):880–884, 1969.

[7] A. Das Sarma, S. Holzer, L. Kor, A. Korman, D. Nanongkai, G. Pandurangan, D. Peleg, and R. Wattenhofer. Distributed verification and hardness of distributed approximation *STOC*, 2011.

[8] F. Dupuis, N. Gisin, A. Hasidim, A. Allan Méthot, and H. Pilpel. No nonlocal box is universal. *J. Math. Phys.* 48(082107), 2007.

[9] A. Einstein, B. Podolsky, and N. Rosen. Can quantum-mechanical description of physical reality be considered complete? *Physical Review*, 47(10):777–780, 1935.

[10] P. Fraigniaud, A. Korman, and D. Peleg. Local distributed decision. *FOCS*, pp 708-717, 2011.

[11] P. Fraigniaud, S. Rajsbaum, and C. Travers. Locality and checkability in wait-free computing. *DISC*, pp 333-347, 2011.

[12] P. Fraigniaud, S. Rajsbaum, and C. Travers. Universal distributed checkers and orientation-detection tasks. Submitted, 2012.

[13] M. Naor and L. Stockmeyer. What can be computed locally? *SIAM J. Comput.* 24(6): 1259–1277 (1995).

[14] S. Popescu and D. Rohrlich. Quantum nonlocality as an axiom. *Foundations of Physics*, 24(3):379–385, 1994.

Brief Announcement: Distributed Algorithms for Throughput Performance in Wireless Networks

Eyjólfur I. Ásgeirsson
ICE-TCS, School of Science
and Engineering
Reykjavik University
eyjo@ru.is

Magnús M. Halldórsson
ICE-TCS
School of Computer Science
Reykjavik University
mmh@ru.is

Pradipta Mitra
ICE-TCS
School of Computer Science
Reykjavik University
ppmitra@gmail.com

Categories and Subject Descriptors

F.2.2 [**Nonnumerical Algorithms and Problems**]: Computations on discrete structures; C.2.4 [**Distributed Systems**]

General Terms

Algorithms, Theory

Keywords

SINR model, Network Stability

1. INTRODUCTION

Consider a continuously running wireless network where packets arrive at nodes in the network according to some stochastic process. These packets need to be be sent over the wireless channel to their intended receivers at a rate fast enough to ensure that the packet queues at nodes do not blow up. This question of ensuring the *stability* of a wireless network is a classical problem in network information theory. Our goal is to design fast, distributed algorithms that achieve this goal under significant load in the SINR model of interference.

The SINR or *physical* model of interference captures many of the realistic properties of wireless interference — such as physical aspects of wireless signal propagation and the additive nature of wireless interference [6]. This is in contrast with graph-based models, explaining the recent surge of interest in the SINR model in wireless network research.

Recent progress in the algorithmic understanding of the SINR model in particularly relevant to our work. This line of study considers problems of a classical algorithmic flavor – given a worst case instance of a wireless network, one seeks to solve certain optimization problems. Since the seminal work of Moscibroda and Wattenhofer [7] that studied scheduling in wireless networks, numerous papers have appeared solving various optimization problems [2, 4, 1]. We employ various technical insights gained from this line of work, thus importing ideas from algorithms research into the study of stability of stochastic systems.

The study of wireless network stability has an extensive history. The seminal work of Tassiulas and Ephremides [8] shows that stability can be achieved if the algorithm chooses the largest set of simultaneously schedulable transmissions

weighted by the respective queue length. This *weighted capacity* problem is NP-hard in most situations of reasonable generality, and certainly in SINR scenarios. As a result, researchers seek algorithms that stabilize the system, if arrival rates are slowed down by a factor of γ, in which case the algorithms are γ-*efficient*. In spite of numerous works in this vein, results in the SINR model have only started appearing very recently [5, 9, 3].

2. THE MODEL

The wireless network is modeled as a set L of n links, where each link $l \in L$ represents a potential transmission from a sender to a receiver. A link set may be associated with a *power assignment*, which is an assignment of a transmission power P_l to be used by each link $l \in L$.

The SINR model can be recast (see [2], for example) in the following way: the receiver of a link l successfully receives a message from the sender if $\sum_{l' \in S} a_{l'}(l) \leq 1$, where S is the set of concurrently scheduled links in the same *slot* (we assume that time is slotted.) The "affectance" $a_{l'}(l)$, a function of distances and transmission powers, captures the relative interference l' causes on l. We say that S is *feasible* if this bound is satisfied for each link in S.

Packets arrive at the sender of each link l according to a stochastic process with average arrival rate λ_l. An algorithm *stabilizes* a network for a particular arrival process if, under that arrival process the average queue size is bounded. The *throughput region* is then the set of all possible arrival rate vectors such that there exists some scheduling policy that can stabilize the network. As proved in [8], the *throughput region*, is characterized by $\Lambda = \{\lambda : \lambda \preceq \phi, \text{for some } \phi \in Co(\Omega)\}$, where Ω is the set of all maximal feasible schedules and $Co(\Omega)$ is the convex hull of Ω. The efficiency ratio γ of a scheduling algorithm is $\gamma = \sup\{\gamma : \text{all networks are stabilized for all } \lambda \in \gamma\Lambda\}$. The algorithm is then γ-efficient.

3. RESULTS AND TECHNICAL IDEAS

It is a basic result in queuing theory that in a single queue system, if the arrival rate is smaller than the departure rate, the system will be stable. Our results are achieved by mapping the wireless system to this basic single queue system. We do this in two separate ways, achieving results of different flavors and advantages.

First Approach.

In our first approach, we look at each link individually. Each link ℓ estimates its arrival rate λ_ℓ (which it can do simply by counting). In each slot, it transmits a packet from its queue with probability $4\lambda_\ell$. By carefully computing the expected interference this algorithm produces on ℓ, we manage to show that such a transmission succeeds with probability $\frac{1}{2}$. The departure rate is thus $\geq \frac{1}{2}4\lambda_\ell > \lambda_\ell$, proving the stability of the link, and finally achieving:

THEOREM 1. *There exists a distributed algorithm achieving* $\Omega(\frac{1}{\Delta^\alpha})$*-efficiency. Assuming a global synchronized clock, with some simple preprocessing* $\Omega(\frac{1}{\log \Delta})$*-efficiency can be achieved.*

The main technical idea is to reduce the system wide effects as interference measured at a single link. We do this by proving that $\sum_{l' \in S} a_{l'}(l) = O(\Delta^\alpha)$, for any feasible set S and any link l. Since the arrival process is defined on feasible sets, the above lemma can be used to compute the expected interference on the link ℓ. For linear power (where $P_\ell = \ell^\alpha$), a better version of this Lemma leads us to achieve $\Omega(1)$-efficiency.

Second Approach.

Instead of looking at a single link, we will now try to map the behavior of the whole system onto the single basic queuing system, at once. We divide time into periods, each period containing a fixed number of slots. We now take, essentially "off-the-shelf", a distributed approximation algorithm [4, 1] for solving the *scheduling* problem on a set of links. The scheduling problem is this: Given a set of links, schedule them in as few slots as possible (respecting the SINR interference model).

We then show that the approximation algorithm takes, in expectation, less than one period to schedule packets that arrive during a period. Once we show, that, we can imagine the whole system as a giant single queuing system, where the period is a slot in the new system, and the departure rate (related to the time taken by the algorithm to schedule the links) is larger than the arrival rate (expected number of packets arriving in a period), implying stability.

Intuitively, if we had a κ-factor approximation algorithm, we can expect to achieve $O(\frac{1}{\kappa})$-efficiency. In practice the situation is more complex, and the analysis requires looking into more fundamental properties of the algorithm. Nevertheless, the moral is very close to the above insight — namely, given a scheduling algorithm, we can expect to convert it into a stability achieving algorithm with efficiency corresponding to its approximation factor for the scheduling problem.

Our tool is once again bounds on $\sum_{l' \in S} a_{l'}(l)$ and $\sum_{l' \in S} a_l(l')$, and the results we achieve are:

THEOREM 2. *There exists a distributed algorithm achieving* $\Omega(\frac{1}{\log^2 n})$*-efficiency for all length-monotone, sub-linear power assignments. For the arbitrary power case,* $\Omega(\frac{1}{\log n(\log n + \log \log \Delta)})$*-efficiency can be achieved.*

4. COMPARISON AND RELATED WORK

Our first approach is extremely distributed, indeed, a more simple algorithm can hardly be imagined. The second one requires a carrier-sense primitive to be implemented in a distributed fashion. In terms of efficiency, dependence on n and Δ are incomparable.

In [5] and [9], efficiency similar to our first approach has been achieved, but using much more complicated algorithms

that require links to have free communication with neighboring links.

In concurrent and independent work [3], results very similar to our second approach has been proposed. The results are more general, applicable to multihop routes and more general interference models, but the underlying insight is close to ours. The algorithm in [3] does not need a carrier-sense primitive, but instead depends on knowing a system-wide property named "injection rate", which is a function of the interferences among links and the stochastic processes on all links. The purpose is similar, to determine or estimate period lengths.

In [3], it also shown that without a global (i.e., synchronized) clock, a rate of more than $\frac{\log n}{n}$ cannot be achieved. This analysis can be extended to prove a $\frac{\log \Delta}{\Delta^2}$ lower bound in the Euclidean plane. Our first approach does not require a global clock, and it can be specialized to a achieve a $\frac{1}{\Delta^2}$-efficiency in the plane (with $\alpha > 2$), thus obtaining essentially tight bounds for the asynchronous case.

There remain many open questions. Is constant efficiency (independent of n and Δ) possible for power assignments other than linear power? Can we achieve the current $O(\frac{1}{\log^2 n})$-efficiency results without using either carrier-sense or injection rates?

Acknowledgement

This work was supported by Iceland Research Foundation grant-of-excellence 90032021.

5. REFERENCES

[1] M. M. Halldórsson and P. Mitra. Nearly optimal bounds for distributed wireless scheduling in the SINR model. In *ICALP*, 2011.

[2] M. M. Halldórsson and P. Mitra. Wireless Capacity with Oblivious Power in General Metrics. In *SODA*, 2011.

[3] T. Kesselheim. Dynamic packet scheduling in wireless networks. In *PODC12*, 2012.

[4] T. Kesselheim and B. Vöcking. Distributed contention resolution in wireless networks. In *DISC*, 2010.

[5] L. B. Le, E. Modiano, C. Joo, and N. B. Shroff. Longest-queue-first scheduling under SINR interference model. In *MobiHoc*, 2010.

[6] R. Maheshwari, S. Jain, and S. R. Das. A measurement study of interference modeling and scheduling in low-power wireless networks. In *SenSys*, pages 141–154, 2008.

[7] T. Moscibroda and R. Wattenhofer. The Complexity of Connectivity in Wireless Networks. In *INFOCOM*, 2006.

[8] L. Tassiulas and A. Ephremides. Stability properties of constrained queueing systems and scheduling policies for maximum throughput in multihop radio networks. *IEEE Trans. Automat. Contr.*, 37(12):1936–1948, 1992.

[9] Y. Zhou, X.-Y. Li, M. Liu, Z. Li, S. Tang, X. Mao, and Q. Huang. Distributed link scheduling for throughput maximization under physical interference model. In *INFOCOM*, 2012.

Brief Announcement:
Distributed Cryptography using TrInc

Michael Backes
Saarland University and MPI-SWS
backes@mpi-sws.org

Fabian Bendun
Saarland University
bendun@cs.uni-saarland.de

Aniket Kate
MPI-SWS
aniket@mpi-sws.org

Categories and Subject Descriptors

B.8.1 [**Performance and Reliability**]: Reliability, Testing, and Fault-Tolerance; C.2.4 [**Computer-Communication Networks**]: Distributed Systems—*Distributed applications*; D.4.6 [**Software**]: Security and Protection—*Cryptographic controls*

Keywords

Trusted Counter, Commitments, Verifiable Secret Sharing

1. INTRODUCTION

Tamper-proof hardwares are prevalent in today's commodity devices, and their efficacy towards reducing the assumptions required in a variety of distributed systems is well-known. This calls for design of software modules, which can easily be implemented on the *available* tamper-proof hardwares. Although there are many proposals available in the literature in that direction, majority of those proposals asks for unsubstantiated guarantees from their hardware modules. This raises a serious question about their usability.

Recently, Levin et al. [6] implemented a small secure hardware module (TrInc), and demonstrated its utility towards Byzantine tolerant distributed systems. TrInc constitutes of a trusted non-decreasing counter and a key that provides unique, once-in-a-lifetime attestations. It prevents a malicious party from equivocating (i.e., providing conflicting values to different parties). Levin et al. observed that these rather simplistic assumptions can significantly improve performance and resilience in state machine replication and peer-to-peer systems. In this work, we extend utility of TrInc to distributed cryptography. In particular, we propose an efficient universally composable (UC) commitment scheme using TrInc(§3), and use it to improve resilience for asynchronous verifiable secret sharing (§4). The scheme can also be used to efficiently realize UC multiparty computation.

2. TrInc BASICS

In TrInc based systems, users attach a trusted piece of hardware, a *trinket*, to their devices. The TrInc API only needs an untrusted channel over which it can receive input and produce output. Although TrInc offers a possibility to create several counters having different IDs and managed by

PODC'12, July 16–18, 2012, Madeira, Portugal.
ACM 978-1-4503-1450-3/12/07.

a meta-counter, we only consider a fixed counter and a fixed key for the counter here for simplicity.

The state of the TrInc functionality reduces to a key pair, an attestation of its validity, the identity of the counter, and its value. The parts of the relevant TrInc API consists of methods $getCert()$ and $Attest(id, c', h)$. $getCert()$ returns the attestation with the public key. The method $Attest(id, c', h)$ verifies that $c \leq c'$. It then increases the counter to c' if the current value $c < c'$, and returns a signature on (id, c, c', h). We summarize state and API for TrInc in Figure 1 and refer the readers to [6] for details. Finally, TrInc has been implemented on widely available Gemalto .NET smartcards, while an implementation with the TPM standard[7] also appears to be straightforward.

3. UNIVERSALLY COMPOSABLE MPC

In 2001, Canetti and Fischlin [2] observed that Universally Composable (UC) secure implementations of MPC are impossible in the *plain* model, which only assumes authenticated channels. This followed by a series of results defining different setup assumptions to achieve UC-secure MPC. Recently, Katz [5] presented an interesting proposal to use of tamper-proof hardware tokens towards UC-secure MPC. In this framework, each party has the ability to produce and securely exchange hardware tokens. However, this requires separate hardware tokens for every communicating pair of parties. Further, these tokens has to be transferred physically in an authenticated and secure manner.

TrInc [6], on the other hand, requires a single trinket hardware per party and not for each pair. Further, as long as the authenticated links exists, trinket need not to be ex-

Notation	Meaning
K_{priv}	Unique private key of trinket
K_{pub}	Public key corresponding to K_{priv}
A	Attestation of this trinket's validity
id	Identity of this counter
c	Current value of the counter

(a) State

Function	Operation
$Attest(id, c', h)$	Verifies that id is a valid counter with some value c and key K_{pub}. Verifies that $c \leq c'$. Creates an attestation $a = (id, c, c', h)_{K_{priv}}$. Sets $c = c'$. Returns a.
$getCert()$	Returns a certificate of this trinket's validity: (K_{pub}, A).

(b) API

Figure 1: State and API of the TrInc functionality

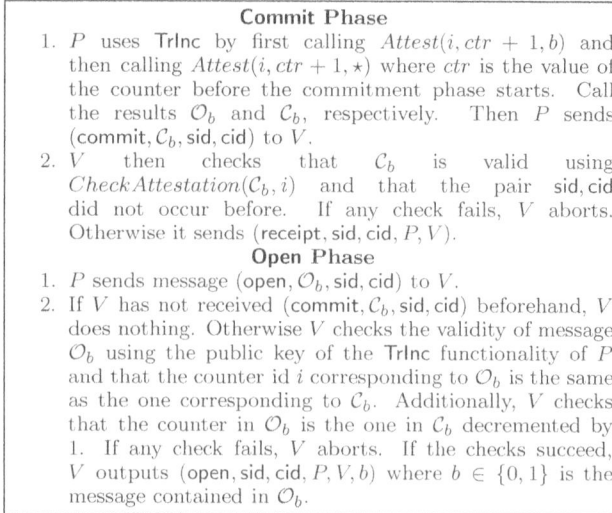

changed among the parties. Therefore, we propose use of TrInc towards UC MPC.

Canetti et al. [3] show that the problem of UC-secure MPC can be reduced to UC-secure two party commitments, TrInc can be used to design such a commitment scheme as follows: To commit to a bit $b \in \{0, 1\}$, a party uses TrInc to sign b together with the current counter value (increasing the counter by one). Then it uses TrInc to sign some constant, e.g. 2 together with the counter that is 1 bigger than the preceding one. The latter signature is sent to the other party, which now knows that the value for the counter decreased by one can not be changed any more. Figure 2 presents a pseudocode for the protocol UCC$_{\mathsf{TrInc}}$ to commit to $b \in \{0, 1\}$. The UCC$_{\mathsf{TrInc}}$ commitment scheme is perfectly hiding and computationally binding such that forging a signature for the signature scheme may allow to open to some different message. Instead of $b \in \{0, 1\}$ any other value from $\{0, 1\}^\kappa$ could be used, where κ depends on the security level of the TrInc functionality. Using collision resistant hash functions, this can be extended to values of arbitrary size $\{0, 1\}^*$.

The protocol UCC$_{\mathsf{TrInc}}$ need some setup, in which a prover P sends its public key and corresponding TrInc certificate to a verifier V using $getCert()$. On receiving a certificate V checks its validity and stores the contained public key. If the check fails, V aborts.

CLAIM 1. *If prover P has access to the TrInc functionality, then protocol UCC$_{\mathsf{TrInc}}$ realizes the ideal commitment functionality for multiple commitments $\mathcal{F}_{MCOM}$ from [2].*

4. VERIFIABLE SECRET SHARING—VSS

VSS allows an untrusted dealer (P_d) to verifiably share a secret s among n parties $\{P_1, P_2, \ldots, P_n\}$ in the presence of an adversary controlling at most t of them. In the synchronous communication setting, VSS requires $n \geq 2t + 1$ parties; however, the required number of parties increases to $n \geq 3t + 1$, when we shift to the asynchronous setting having no bounds on message transfer delays or processor speeds.

We observe that using the non-equivocation property of TrInc and signatures across parties it is possible to reduce the number of parties required for asynchronous VSS to $n \geq$

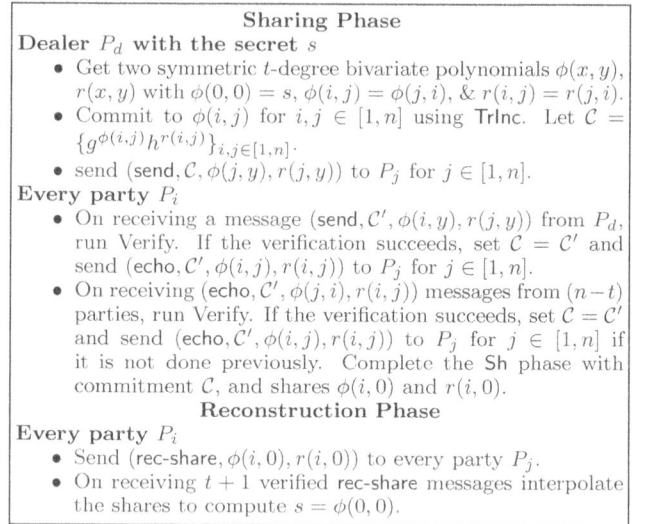

$2t + 1$. Assuming asynchronous, authenticated and private point-to-point links with eventual delivery guarantee [1], in Figure 3, we present a simple asynchronous VSS protocol $n \geq 2t + 1$ using our commitment protocol (UCC$_{\mathsf{TrInc}}$) defined in Section 3. The protocol is inspired by an omission-tolerant reliable broadcast protocol by Gopal and Toueg [4].

Note that we replace $\star$ in the UCC$_{\mathsf{TrInc}}$ protocol with Pedersen commitments of the form $g^{\phi(i,j)} h^{r_{ij}}$ to utilize their homomorphic properties. With the unconditional hiding and computational binding property of Pedersen commitments, this does not affect security of UCC$_{\mathsf{TrInc}}$.

CLAIM 2. *If dealer P_d has access to the TrInc functionality, asynchronous VSS is possible for $n \geq 2t + 1$.*

Our protocol in Figure 3 is directly applicable to asynchronous threshold cryptography and asynchronous MPC, where it reduces the resiliency bound to $n \geq 2t + 1$.

Acknowledgments. We thank our anonymous referees for their helpful advices about the commitment scheme.

5. REFERENCES

[1] C. Cachin, K. Kursawe, A.Lysyanskaya, and R. Strobl. Asynchronous Verifiable Secret Sharing and Proactive Cryptosystems. In *ACM CCS'02*, pages 88–97, 2002.

[2] R. Canetti and M. Fischlin. Universally composable commitments. In *CRYPTO*, pages 19–40, 2001.

[3] R. Canetti, Y. Lindell, R. Ostrovsky, and A. Sahai. Universally composable two-party and multi-party secure computation. In *STOC*, pages 494–503, 2002.

[4] A. S. Gopal and S. Toueg. Reliable Broadcast in Synchronous and Asynchronous Environments (Preliminary Version). In *WDAG*, pages 110–123, 1989.

[5] J. Katz. Universally composable multi-party computation using tamper-proof hardware. In *EUROCRYPT*, pages 115–128, 2007.

[6] D. Levin, J. R. Douceur, J. R. Lorch, and T. Moscibroda. Trinc: Small trusted hardware for large distributed systems. In *NSDI*, pages 1–14, 2009.

[7] http://www.trustedcomputinggroup.org/ developers/trusted_platform_module.

Brief Announcement: Reconfigurable State Machine Replication from Non-Reconfigurable Building Blocks

Vita Bortnikov
IBM Research
vita@il.ibm.com

Gregory Chockler
IBM Research
chockler@il.ibm.com

Dmitri Perelman
Technion, Israel Institute of
Technology
dima39@tx.technion.ac.il

Alexey Roytman
IBM Research
roytman@il.ibm.com

Shlomit Shachor
IBM Research
shlomiti@il.ibm.com

Ilya Shnayderman
IBM Research
ilyashn@il.ibm.com

ABSTRACT

Reconfigurable state machine replication is an important enabler of elasticity for replicated cloud services, which must be able to dynamically adjust their size as a function of changing load and resource availability. We introduce a new *generic framework* to allow the reconfigurable state machine implementation to be derived from a collection of arbitrary non-reconfigurable state machines. Our reduction framework follows the *black box* approach, and does not make any assumptions with respect to its execution environment apart from reliable channels. It allows higher-level services to leverage *speculative command execution* to ensure uninterrupted progress during the reconfiguration periods as well as in situations where failures prevent the reconfiguration agreement from being reached in a timely fashion. We apply our framework to obtain a reconfigurable speculative state machine from the non-reconfigurable Paxos implementation, and analyze its performance on a realistic distributed testbed. Our results show that our framework incurs negligible overheads in the absence of reconfiguration, and allows steady throughput to be maintained throughout the reconfiguration periods.

Categories and Subject Descriptors

C.2.4 [**Computer-Communication Networks**]: Distributed Systems; C.4 [**Performance of Systems**]: Fault Tolerance; D.1.3 [**Programming Techniques**]: Concurrent Programming—*distributed programming*

General Terms

Algorithms, Reliability, Performance

Keywords

Fault Tolerance, Replication, State Machines

1. INTRODUCTION

Replicated state machine, or RSM [2], is an important tool for maintaining integrity of distributed applications and services in failure-prone data center and cloud computing environments. In these settings, the infrastructure needs to adapt to changing resource availability, load fluctuations, variable power consumption, and data locality constraints. In order to meet these requirements, RSM must support *reconfiguration*, i.e., dynamic changes to replica set, or quorum system. It is essential to ensure that reconfiguration incurs minimum disruption to availability and performance, in order to enable building truly elastic services. The ability to perform reconfigurations in a non-disruptive fashion provides system designers with a powerful paradigm that can enable many optimizations. This includes proactive replacement of suspected or slow nodes at low cost, adapting to the changing environment characteristics (e.g. network delay, or diurnal load fluctuations, and many others).

Reconfigurable RSM has been proposed in multiple contexts (e.g., [1, 4, 5]). Each solution implemented a slightly different set of requirements, and all proved nontrivial. Designing this functionality for a realistic environment with minimal impact on performance is even more challenging. Naïve constructions follow the "brick-wall approach" in which the flow of user commands is stalled until the new configuration is installed and the state is transferred to it. Ideally, systems should strive to avoid this, and favor implementations with near-seamless hand-on, that maintain steady throughput and latency during the transition periods.

This paper introduces a framework for constructing reconfigurable state machines from collections of non-reconfigurable ones. We follow the *black box* approach that assumes nothing about the execution environment except the existence of reliable communication channels. Our reduction is both simple and generic, i.e., the underlying RSM implementation is completely opaque to the framework. Furthermore, it does not compromise efficiency, incurring negligible overhead in the absence of reconfigurations and avoiding system stalls upon reconfiguration.

The main ideas underlying our framework are as follows. Each newly proposed configuration is associated with its own instance of RSM, and all active RSM are executed concurrently to each other. The globally consistent *trunk* of commands is created by gluing together the totally ordered command sequences produced by each RSM. When switching from one RSM to another, the latter is chosen based on the outcome of the configuration agreement in the former. Our framework also relieves RSMs of state transfer responsibilities by ensuring that the latest trunk is transferred to the new configuration concurrently with the RSM execution. This way, each newly created RSM is completely independent from its predecessor, and in particular, can start executing from its initial state. We leverage this capability in our Paxos-based reconfigurable RSM implementation to supply each newly created Paxos instance with the identifier of a deterministically chosen leader thus eschewing the first phase of Paxos if the configured leader does not fail.

Another important optimization made possible by the RSM independence is the ability to *speculatively* overlap their execution with the reconfiguration protocol, thus considerably reducing the command latency during reconfiguration periods. Specifically, each RSM is made available for accepting commands for the new configuration as soon as it is proposed, and without waiting for it to be agreed upon by the parent RSM. The proposals associated with the new configuration proceed to be ordered concurrently with the reconfiguration agreement, and are added to the trunk as soon as the configuration is agreed upon. This way, our framework allows unbounded degree of parallelism in the command execution during the transition periods avoiding the performance problems of the "brick-wall" solutions. In addition, the benefits of speculation become more substantial as the network delay grows thus making speculative solutions attractive in wide-area network settings.

The modularity of our framework enables a range of additional features useful in practical settings. One such feature is supporting rolling software upgrades: i.e., the implementation of the deployed RSMs can be replaced with the newer one without stopping the system. Likewise, misbehaving or buggy RSMs can be restarted or replaced on-the-fly with the minimum impact on the system operation as per the recovery-oriented computing (ROC) [6] guidelines.

2. PRELIMINARIES

We consider an asynchronous message-passing system consisting of the (possibly infinite) set of processes P. Processes can fail by *crashing*, and communicate with each other by means of reliable FIFO channels.

The *Non-Reconfigurable Replicated State Machine* (NR-RSM) is parametrized by a configuration $C \in Config$ drawn from a fixed set of configuration identifiers *Config*. NR-RSM(C) accepts the commands submitted by the C's members and outputs a totally ordered sequence of commands. The *Reconfigurable RSM* (R-RSM) exposes additional primitives to allow the configuration to be changed dynamically at runtime, and produces a totally ordered sequence of commands and configurations.

3. REDUCTION ALGORITHM

The algorithm to obtain R-RSM given a collection of NR-RSM(C) for each configuration $C \in Config$ proceeds as follows: For each configuration C, the commands and configurations proposed in C are ordered by the C's non-reconfigurable state machine NR-RSM(C). Whenever reconfiguration from C to another configuration C' is requested, the members of C' are notified of the new configuration, and activate their local copies of the NR-RSM(C') implementation. Once a sufficient number of the copies is activated, NR-RSM(C') becomes available for ordering the incoming requests.

The sequences of commands and configurations produced by the concurrently running NR-RSM instances form a *branching* log with the branch corresponding to each NR-RSM(C) being stored at the members of C. The branching log is transformed into the single linear log, called the *trunk*, by choosing a single successor for each branch, and pruning all the other branches originating from that branch. To ensure that the branch associated with a configuration C has a unique successor in the trunk, each configuration C' proposed in C is ordered through NR-RSM(C), and the branch corresponding to the configuration that comes first in the resulting order is chosen as the C's branch successor. The commands submitted through C' are ordered *speculatively* while the agreement on C' is still in progress thus masking the reconfiguration delays, and ensuring uninterrupted transition to the new configuration.

The trunk is reconstructed locally at each process p by concatenating the log branches produced by the individual NR-RSMs so that for any two configurations C_1 and C_2, C_2 is the immediate successor of C_1 in the trunk iff C_2 was chosen as the successor of C_1 by NR-RSM(C_1). The trunk branches corresponding to the configurations C such that $p \notin members(C)$ are obtained through a separate *state transfer* mechanism, which is executed concurrently with the trunk constructions. The processes then deliver the commands and configurations in the order they appear on their trunks, which are guaranteed to be mutually consistent.

Further details of the implementation as well as the formal correctness proofs can be found in the full version of the paper.

4. IMPLEMENTATION AND EVALUATION

We used our framework to implement a full-fledged reconfigurable replication platform using non-reconfigurable Paxos [3] as its underlying non-reconfigurable RSM, and experimentally studied its performance. The results demonstrate that our system achieves high throughput and low latency in the absence of reconfigurations, which stay almost unchanged under highly dynamic reconfiguration scenarios. Specifically, the throughput is unaffected in the runs with reconfiguration rate of 5 per second, and degrades only by 20% when reconfiguration rate achieves that of 20 per second. In addition, our study indicates that the command latency in the vicinity of reconfiguration stays the same as that in the absence thereof.

5. REFERENCES

[1] L. Lamport, D. Malkhi, and L. Zhou. Stoppable paxos. [Online]. Available: http://research.microsoft.com/apps/pubs/default.aspx?id=101826, 2008.

[2] L. Lamport. Time, clocks, and the ordering of events in a distributed system. *Commun. ACM*, 21:558–565, July 1978.

[3] L. Lamport. The part-time parliament. *ACM Trans. Comput. Syst.*, 16(2):133–169, 1998.

[4] L. Lamport, D. Malkhi, and L. Zhou. Reconfiguring a state machine. Technical report, Microsoft Research, 2008.

[5] L. Lamport, D. Malkhi, and L. Zhou. Vertical paxos and primary-backup replication. In *PODC '09: Proceedings of the 28th ACM symposium on Principles of distributed computing*, pages 312–313, New York, NY, USA, 2009. ACM.

[6] D. A. Patterson et al. Recovery-oriented computing (ROC): Motivation, definition, techniques, and case studies. Technical report, UC Berkeley Computer Science Technical Report UCB//CSD-02-1175, 2002.

Brief Announcement: All-to-All Gradecast using Coding with Byzantine Failures

John F. Bridgman, III[*]
Parallel and Distributed Systems Lab
Electrical and Computer Engineering
The University of Texas at Austin
Austin, TX USA
johnfbiii@utexas.edu

Vijay K. Garg[†]
Parallel and Distributed Systems Lab
Electrical and Computer Engineering
The University of Texas at Austin
Austin, TX USA
garg@ece.utexas.edu

Categories and Subject Descriptors

C.4 [**Computer Systems Organization**]: Performance of Systems—*fault tolerance*; D.1.3 [**Programming Techniques**]: Concurrent Programming—*distributed programming*; E.4 [**Data**]: Coding and Information Theory

Keywords

Fault Tolerance, Broadcast, Distributed Algorithms

1. INTRODUCTION

Many distributed algorithms require consistent global information in the presence of faulty processes. Forward error correction codes can be used to reduce the message bit complexity when acquiring consistent global information in the presence of faulty processes. The usual method of acquiring consistent global information in the presence of faults is for every process to broadcast its information; then, every process rebroadcasts the broadcasts. The first broadcast is sometimes called first-order information and the second is sometimes referred to as second-order information. Many algorithms that tolerate Byzantine faults require this second-order information. For example, Byzantine consensus, interactive consistency, consistent broadcast, and multiconsensus all require second-order information. In order to perform a fault-tolerant broadcast, second-order knowledge is required. Because there is a bound on the number of faulty processes in most systems, rebroadcasting all the information is more than what is needed. The technique described here uses a forward error correction (FEC) code to minimize the size of the messages that are rebroadcast. If the processes collects the first broadcasts, it can encode the information using a systematic error correction code and send only the additional generated part of the code word. This will reduce the order of message size on the second broadcast from $O(n^3)$ to $O(n^2 t)$, were n is the number of processes and t is the maximum number of faulty processes. This is a significant reduc-

tion in message bit complexity in real systems where $t << n$. We show a modification to the gradecast algorithm that implements our method. Gradecast, first proposed by Feldman and Micali[1], is a broadcast algorithm for distributed systems that can handle Byzantine failures. It can be used as a basic building block to solve many important problems in distributed computing in the presence of Byzantine failures, such as agreement, clock synchronization, and approximate agreement. The full version of this paper is available as a tech report[2].

Error correction codes can be viewed as a projection from a smaller space to a larger space with good separation. Because the points in the larger space are separated, small perturbations in the point in the larger space are still close to the original mapped point and the point in the original smaller space can be recovered. Generally, the spaces are high dimensional vector spaces over finite fields and the measure of distance between two elements of the space is the number of coordinates that have a different value. *Systematic* codes can be constructed that encode a vector as the original vector concatenated with an error correction vector. Our method relies on the observation that every process is sending a value to every other process and only the faulty processes will send conflicting data. So, the vector built at each process will differ in at most t locations. This can be viewed as transmitting the vector and each process receiving a corrupted version. Then, only the error correction part of the encoded vector can be sent between processes to correct these "errors". The original vector is not actually transmitted. In a traditional application of error correction codes, an input block is encoded and then the whole output codeword is transmitted. We are not transmitting the whole codeword. Only a portion of the codeword is transmitted. A proper selection of the code allows an error correction vector that can correct t errors to be no longer than $2t + 1$.

The gradecast algorithm, first proposed by Feldman and Micali in [1], is a broadcast algorithm that gives the receivers a confidence level in the value received. Let $value_j[k]$ be the value that process P_j outputs for process P_k, $conf_j[k]$ be the confidence level process P_j outputs for process P_k, and v_k be the initial input value to the algorithm for process P_k. The confidence level returned is from the set $\{0, 1, 2\}$. The confidence level gives information about the state of other processes. The gradecast algorithm provides three properties on the confidence level allowing a process to reason about the knowledge of other processes. Property one is for all non-faulty processes P_i and P_j; and any process P_k, if

[*]This research was supported in part by the Virginia and Ernest Cockrel, Jr. Fellowship in Engineering.

[†]This research was supported in part by the NSF Grants CNS-0718990, CNS-1115808, Cullen Trust for Higher Education Endowed Professorship.

$conf_j[k] > 0$ and $conf_i[k] > 0$; then, $value_j[k] = value_i[k]$. Property two is for any non-faulty processes P_i, P_j, and any process P_k, $|conf_i[k] - conf_j[k]| \leq 1$. Property three is if P_k is non-faulty; then, for all non-faulty processes P_i, $conf_i[k] = 2$ and $value_i[k] = v_k$. The original one-to-all gradecast algorithm broadcasts a value from one process to all the other processes. We define message bit complexity as the total number of bits sent by all non-faulty processes in one invocation of the algorithm. The one-to-all gradecast algorithm has a message bit complexity of $O(mn^2)$, where m is the length of the message. Consider the case where all processes wish to broadcast a value to all other processes using gradecast. We call this all-to-all gradecast and it is used in many applications such as Byzantine agreement, approximate agreement and multiconsensus[3]. The standard implementation of all-to-all gradecast is where n instances of the one-to-all gradecast algorithm is used. This has $O(mn^3)$ message bit complexity.

We show a method, using coding, that gives an all-to-all gradecast algorithm with only $O(mtn^2)$ message bit complexity, where t is the specified maximum number of faulty processes. This is a significant reduction in message bit complexity when t is much smaller than n, which is usually the case. The execution model used by the gradecast algorithm is the standard reliable synchronous message passing model. The properties of gradecast make it a useful primitive in distributed systems. The algorithm assumes that only t out of the n processes in the system may fail; but, they may be Byzantine, that is to say, faulty in arbitrary ways. For algorithm correctness, we require that $n - 2t > t$ which simplifies to $t < n/3$. This bound is optimal because a Byzantine agreement algorithm can be build on top of gradecast that has the same requirements on t as the underlying gradecast algorithm. It has been proven that no Byzantine agreement algorithm exists for $t \geq n/3$. The algorithm assumes that the set of all messages can be encoded as members of a finite field, with one field member reserved to represent "no message" which we will denote as $\perp$. To deal with larger messages than the size of one field element the interested reader should look up code interleaving. An example of code interleaving in practical usage is the tool Parity Archive Volume Set[4].

2. ALGORITHM

This section gives our all-to-all gradecast algorithm that has $O(mtn^2)$ message bit complexity. This algorithm is based on vectorizing the gradecast algorithm presented by Feldman and Micali in [1]. Each process P_i has an input value v_i and the algorithm produces two vectors $value_i$ and $conf_i$ which are the received values and the confidence level respectively. Pseudo-code for the algorithm is provided in Figure 1. The algorithm is given from the perspective of P_i as the algorithm is symmetric. A more detailed description of the algorithm and examples are in a tech report[2].

3. REFERENCES

[1] P. Feldman and S. Micali, "Optimal algorithms for byzantine agreement," in *Proceedings of the twentieth annual ACM symposium on Theory of computing*, ser. STOC '88. New York, NY, USA: ACM, 1988, pp. 148–161. [Online]. Available: http://doi.acm.org/10.1145/62212.62225

```
P_i::
  Inputs:
    v_i : Input value for P_i
  Common knowledge:
    n : The number of processes
    t : Maximum number of faulty processes
  Variables:
    V_i[1..n] : Vector received in Step 2, initially ⊥
    Vecc_i[1..2t+1] : error correction vector for V_i
    X_i[1..n][1..n] : Matrix of decoded values in Step 3
    Y_i[1..n] : Vector of values computed in Step 3
    Yecc_i[1..2t+1] : Error correction vector for Y_i
    Z_i[1..n][1..n] : Matrix of decoded values in Step 4
    value_i[1..n] : Vector of output values
    conf_i[1..n] : Vector of confidence levels

// Step 1
for j : 1 to n do P_i.send(P_j, v_i); end
// Step 2
for j : 1 to n do V_i[j] = P_i.receive(P_j); end
Vecc_i = encode(V_i);
for j : 1 to n do P_i.send(P_j, Vecc_i); end
// Step 3
for j : 1 to n do
    X_i[j] = decode(V_i, P_i.receive(P_j));
end
∀j let Y_i[j] = x if ∃x s.t. |{k : X_i[k][j] = x}| ≥ n − t
    otherwise Y_i[j] = ⊥
Yecc_i = encode(Y_i);
for j : 1 to n do P_i.send(P_j, Yecc_i); end
// Step 4
for j : 1 to n do
    Z_i[j] = decode(Y_i, P_i.receive(P_j));
end
for j : 1 to n do
    if max_x |{k : Z_i[k][j] = x}| ≥ 2t + 1 then
        value_i[j] = arg max_x |{k : Z_i[k][j] = x}|;
        conf_i[j] = 2;
    elseif max_x |{k : Z_i[k][j] = x}| > t then
        value_i[j] = arg max_x |{k : Z_i[k][j] = x}|;
        conf_i[j] = 1;
    else value_i[j] = ⊥; conf_i[j] = 0;
    end
end
Output value_i and conf_i.
```

Figure 1: All-to-all gradecast algorithm

[2] J. F. Bridgman and V. K. Garg, "All-to-all gradecast using coding with byzantine failures," Parallel and Distributed Systems Laboratory, The University of Texas at Austin, Tech. Rep. TR-PDS-2012-001, 2012. [Online]. Available: http://maple.ece.utexas.edu/TechReports/2012/TR-PDS-2012-001.pdf

[3] M. Ben-Or, D. Dolev, and E. N. Hoch, "Simple gradecast based algorithms," Sep. 2010. [Online]. Available: http://arxiv.org/abs/1007.1049

[4] "Parchive: Parity archive tool," http://parchive.sourceforge.net/.

Brief Announcement:
There are Plenty of Tasks Weaker than Perfect Renaming and Stronger than Set Agreement*

Armando Castañeda
INRIA
Campus de Beaulieu
35042 Rennes Cedex, France

Sergio Rajsbaum
Instituto de Matemáticas
UNAM
Mexico City, Mexico

Michel Raynal
Institut Universtaire de France
& IRISA, Campus de Beaulieu,
35042 Rennes Cedex, France

ABSTRACT

In the asynchronous *wait-free* shared memory model, two families of tasks play a central role because of their implications in theory and in practice: *k-set agreement* and *M-renaming*. Let n denote the number of processes in the system. Previous research shows that $(n-1)$-set agreement can solve $(2n-2)$-renaming, for any value of n, while $(2n-2)$-renaming cannot solve $(n-1)$-set agreement, when n is odd. It is also known that, for every $n \geq 3$, n-renaming, also called *perfect renaming*, is strictly stronger than $(n-1)$-set agreement. This paper shows that when $n \geq 4$, there is a family of tasks that are strictly stronger than $(n-1)$-set agreement and strictly weaker than perfect renaming. This enlarges our view of both the nature and the structure of what are distributed computing tasks.

Categories and Subject Descriptors

D.1.3 [**Programming Techniques**]: Concurrent Programming; F.1.1 [**Computation by Abstract Devices**]: Models of Computation—*Computability Theory*; F.1.2 [**Modes of Computation**]: [Parallelism and Concurrency]

Keywords

Asynchronous wait-free read/write model, Decision task, Distributed computability, Renaming problem, k-Set agreement, Symmetry Breaking, Task solvability.

1. INTRODUCTION

A central concern in the theory of distributed computing consists in understanding the relative computability power of tasks in presence of asynchrony and failures. That is, given two tasks T and T', can T be used to *implement* T'? Here we investigate the computability power of tasks in the usual wait-free, read/write shared memory model with n asynchronous processes that can fail by crashing.

Previous works have shown that two families of tasks play a central role because of their strong implications in theory and in practice: k-set agreement and M-renaming.

*Complete version in [3]. Supported by the French ANR project DISPLEXITY devoted to the study of computability and complexity in distributed computing.

In the k-*set agreement* task [4] each process starts with a private proposal and the non-faulty processes have to agree on at mots k distinct proposals.

In the M-*renaming* task [1] the processes start with distinct initial names taken from a large input name space, and the non-faulty processes have to decide distinct names from a name space whose size is M.

Set agreement and renaming appear to be quite dissimilar tasks, one being about agreement while the other is about breaking symmetry. Thus it was surprising to know [5, 6] that, for any value of n, $(n-1)$-set agreement can be used to implement $(2n-2)$-renaming, while the opposite is impossible when n is odd. This result is extended in [2] where it is shown that *perfect renaming* (i.e., n-renaming) is strictly stronger than $(n-1)$-set agreement, namely, perfect renaming implements $(n-1)$-set agreement but not vice-versa. It is also proved in [2] that perfect renaming cannot implement $(n-2)$-set agreement, and *quasi-perfect renaming* (i.e., $(n+1)$-renaming) cannot implement $(n-1)$-set agreement. In other words, when comparing the relative power of set agreement and renaming, the strongest renaming is the only one that can solve the weakest set agreement, and this is the best it can do. Is perfect renaming the only task that has to do with breaking symmetry and is powerful enough to solve $(n-1)$-set agreement?

In an effort to expand the knowledge on the relative power of tasks, a conceptual framework has been introduced [7] to investigate the family of *generalized symmetry breaking* (GSB) tasks, which includes known tasks such as the renaming family and many other tasks which are interesting on their own.

The notation $\langle n, m, [\ell_1, \ldots, \ell_m], [u_1, \ldots, u_m] \rangle$-GSB denotes an *asymmetric* GSB task on n processes for m decision values, $[1..m]$, where each $1 \leq x \leq m$ has to be decided by at least ℓ_x and at most u_x processes. When for every $1 \leq x \leq m$, $\ell_x = \ell$ and $u_x = u$, for some ℓ and u, the task is called *symmetric* and is denoted $\langle n, m, \ell, u \rangle$-GSB. Thus, for $M \geq n+1$, M-renaming is the $\langle n, M, 0, 1 \rangle$-GSB task, and perfect renaming is the $\langle n, n, 1, 1 \rangle$-GSB task. The weak symmetry breaking task [6] is the $\langle n, 2, 1, n-1 \rangle$-GSB task. It is shown in [7] that perfect renaming is universal for the whole family of GSB tasks, in the sense that any of these tasks can be implemented from $\langle n, n, 1, 1 \rangle$-GSB.

2. A SUBFAMILY τ OF GSB TASKS

This paper investigates if the GSB family contains tasks (other than perfect renaming) that are powerful enough to solve $(n-1)$-set agreement. It shows that GSB contains a large subfamily of tasks, that we denote $\mathcal{T}$, which are strictly stronger than $(n-1)$-set agreement. Since perfect renaming is universal in the GSB family [7] and perfect renaming cannot implement $(n-2)$-set agreement [2], it follows that no GSB task can implement $(n-2)$-set agreement. Thus, the best a task of $\mathcal{T}$ can do is $(n-1)$-set agreement.

DEFINITION 1. *A GSB task belongs to $\mathcal{T}$ if and only if there are two distinct decision values λ_1 and λ_2 such that in every execution in which all processes decide, exactly one processes decides λ_1 and exactly one process decides λ_2.*

THEOREM 1. *For $n \geq 3$, every task in $\mathcal{T}$ is strictly stronger than $(n-1)$-set agreement and cannot implement $(n-2)$-set agreement.*

An example of a task in $\mathcal{T}$ is a stronger version of M-renaming in which in every execution in which all processes decide, a process decides 1 and a process decides 2, namely, the asymmetric $\langle n, M, [1,1,0,\ldots,0], [1,1,1,\ldots,1]\rangle$-GSB.

The internal structure of $\mathcal{T}$ is also investigated:

THEOREM 2. *For $n \geq 2$, $\mathcal{T}$ contains infinitely many tasks.*

THEOREM 3. *For $n = 2,3$, every task in $\mathcal{T}$ is equivalent to $\langle n,n,1,1\rangle$-GSB.*

THEOREM 4. *For $n \geq 4$, there exists a subfamily $\mathcal{T}'$ of $\mathcal{T}$ such that every task in $\mathcal{T}'$ is strictly weaker than $\langle n,n,1,1\rangle$-GSB. There exists a subfamily $\mathcal{T}''$ of $\mathcal{T}'$ such that every task in $\mathcal{T}''$ is strictly stronger than $\langle n,n+1,0,1\rangle$-GSB.*

Therefore, when $n \geq 4$, there are tasks that are "between" perfect renaming and quasi-perfect renaming, and are still powerful enough to implement $(n-1)$-set agreement (recall that quasi-perfect renaming cannot solve $(n-1)$-set agreement [2]). Figure 1 depicts the relation between $\mathcal{T}$, renaming and set agreement for $n \geq 4$. An arrow from T to T' means that the task T' can be wait-free implemented from the task T, while a crossed arrow from T to T' means that T' cannot be wait-free implemented from T.

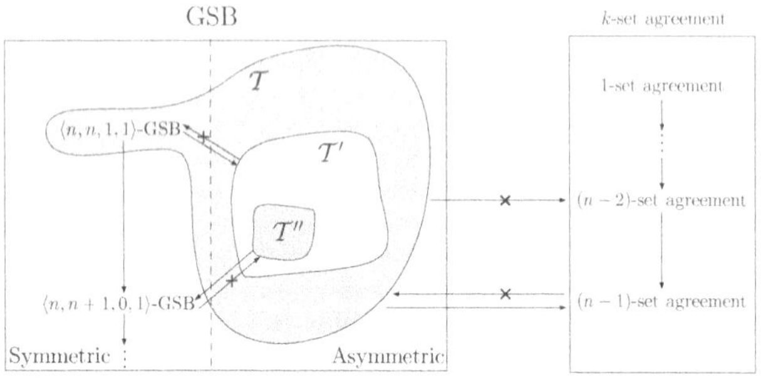

Figure 1: $\mathcal{T}$ and set agreement systems with $n \geq 4$.

It turns out that every member of $\mathcal{T}$ (except perfect renaming) is asymmetric. Hence, the question: Does it exist a symmetric GSB task distinct from perfect renaming that can solve $(n-1)$-set agreement? Almost all symmetric GSB tasks cannot implement $(n-1)$-set agreement:

THEOREM 5. *Let n, m, ℓ, u be integers such that one of the following cases holds:*

1. $m = 1$,

2. $m \geq n+1$,

3. $n = m \wedge \ell = 0 \wedge u \geq 2$,

4. $2 \leq m \leq n-1 \wedge 1 \leq \ell \leq \lfloor \frac{n}{m}\rfloor - 1 \wedge u = n - \ell(m-1)$.

Then, $\langle n, m, \ell, u\rangle$-GSB cannot implement $(n-1)$-set agreement.

The paper leaves open the question for only a (small) subfamily of symmetric GSB tasks. Hence, we conjecture that perfect renaming is the only symmetric GSB task that can solve $(n-1)$-set agreement, which would imply that the only way a GSB task, which is strictly weaker than perfect renaming, can implement $(n-1)$-set agreement is by requiring asymmetry on the decision values.

3. FUTURE RESEARCH

The are many open problems. The following is just a partial list.

1. Does it exist a GSB task that can solve $(n-1)$-set agreement and does not belong to $\mathcal{T}$? We believe $\mathcal{T}$ contains all GSB tasks that are capable to solve $(n-1)$-set agreement.

2. Does $\mathcal{T}$ contain tasks that are incomparable? We conjecture that if $n \geq 5$, $\mathcal{T}$ contains a non-small subfamily of tasks such that every two distinct members are incomparable.

3. Prove that perfect renaming is the only symmetric GSB task that can solve $(n-1)$-set agreement.

Acknowledgments

We would like to thank Damien Imbs for helpful discussions that clarified our ideas.

4. REFERENCES

[1] Attiya H., Bar-Noy A., Dolev D., Peleg D. and Reischuck R., Renaming in an Asynchronous Environment. *Journal of the ACM*, 37(3):524-548, 1990.

[2] Castañeda A., Imbs D., Rajsbaum S. and Raynal M., Renaming is Weaker than Set Agreement but for Perfect Renaming: A Map of Sub-Consensus Tasks. *10th Latin American Theoretical INformatics Symposium (LATIN 2012)*, Springer Verlag LNCS #7256, pp. 145-156, 2012.

[3] Castañeda A., Rajsbaum S. and Raynal M., There are Plenty of Tasks Weaker than Perfect Renaming and Stronger than $(n-1)$-Set Agreement. *Tech Report 1990, HAL INRIA*, 29 pages, February 2012.

[4] Chaudhuri S., More Choices Allow More Faults: Set Consensus Problems in Totally Asynchronous Systems. *Information and Computation*, 105(1):132-158, 1993.

[5] Gafni E. and Rajsbaum S., Distributed Programming with Tasks. *Proc. 10th In'l Conference on Principles of Distributed Systems (OPODIS'10)*, Springer Verlag LNCS #6490, pp. 205-218, 2010.

[6] Gafni E., Rajsbaum S. and Herlihy M., Subconsensus Tasks: Renaming is Weaker Than Set Agreement. *Proc. 20th Int'l Symposium on Distributed Computing (DISC'06)*, Springer Verlag LNCS #4167, pp.329-338, 2006.

[7] Imbs D., Rajsbaum S. and Raynal M., The Universe of Symmetry Breaking Tasks. *Proc. 18th International Colloquium on Structural Information and Communication Complexity (SIROCCO'11)*, Springer Verlag LNCS #6796, pp. 66-77, 2011.

Brief Announcement: Waiting in Dynamic Networks[*]

Arnaud Casteigts
University of Ottawa
casteig@eecs.uottawa.ca

Paola Flocchini
University ot Ottawa
flocchin@eecs.uottawa.ca

Emmanuel Godard
Université Aix-Marseille
egodard@cmi.univ-mrs.fr

Nicola Santoro
Carleton University
santoro@scs.carleton.ca

Masafumi Yamashita
Kyushu University
mak@csce.kyushu-u.ac.jp

We consider infrastructure-less highly dynamic networks, where connectivity does not necessarily hold, and the network may actually be disconnected at every time instant. These networks are naturally modeled as *time-varying* graphs. Clearly the task of designing protocols for these networks is less difficult if the environment allows *waiting* (i.e., it provides the nodes with store-carry-forward-like mechanisms such as local buffering) than if waiting is not feasible. We provide a quantitative corroboration of this fact in terms of the *expressivity* of the corresponding time-varying graph; that is in terms of the language generated by the feasible journeys in the graph. We prove that the set of languages $\mathcal{L}_{nowait}$ when no waiting is allowed contains all computable languages. On the other end, we prove that $\mathcal{L}_{wait}$ is just the family of *regular* languages. This gap is a measure of the computational power of waiting. We also study *bounded waiting*; that is when waiting is allowed at a node only for at most d time units. We prove the negative result that $\mathcal{L}_{wait[d]} = \mathcal{L}_{nowait}$.

Keywords

Time-varying graphs, dynamic networks, buffering, expressivity of TVGs

Categories and Subject Descriptors

F.1.1 [**Models of Computation**]: Networks of machines; F.4.3 [**Formal Languages**]: Classes defined by automata; D.4.4 [**Communications Management**]: Buffering

1. INTRODUCTION

In infrastructure-less highly dynamic networks, computing and performing even basic tasks (such as routing and broadcasting) is a very challenging activity due to the fact that connectivity does not necessarily hold, and the network may actually be disconnected at every time instant. Such highly dynamic systems do exist, are actually widespread, and becoming more ubiquitous; the most obvious class is that of wireless ad hoc mobile networks.

From a formal point of view, the highly dynamic features of these networks and their temporal nature are captured by the model of *time-varying* (or *evolving*) graphs, where edges between nodes

exist only at some times, a priori unknown to the algorithm designer. Formally [1], a *time-varying graph* $\mathcal{G}$ is a quintuple $\mathcal{G} = (V, E, \mathcal{T}, \rho, \zeta)$, where V is a finite set of entities or *nodes*; $E \subseteq V \times V \times \Sigma$ is a finite set of relations between these entities (*edges*), possibly labeled by symbols in an alphabet Σ. The system is studied over a given time span $\mathcal{T} \subseteq \mathbb{T}$ called *lifetime*, where $\mathbb{T}$ is the temporal domain (typically, $\mathbb{N}$ or $\mathbb{R}^+$ for discrete and continuous-time systems, respectively); $\rho : E \times \mathcal{T} \to \{0, 1\}$ is the *presence* function, which indicates whether a given edge is available at a given time; $\zeta : E \times \mathcal{T} \to \mathbb{T}$, is the *latency* function, which indicates the time it takes to cross a given edge if starting at a given date (the latency of an edge could vary in time).

A crucial aspect of dynamic networks is that a path from a node to another might still exist over time, even though at no time the path exists in its entirety. It is this fact that renders routing, broadcasting, and thus computing possible in spite of the otherwise unsurmountable difficulties imposed by the nature of those networks. Hence, the notion of "path over time", called *journey*, is a fundamental concepts and plays a central role in the definition of almost all concepts related to connectivity in time-varying graphs. Informally a journey is a walk $<e_1, e_2, ..., e_k>$ and a sequence of time instants $<t_1, t_2, ..., t_k>$ where edge e_i exists at time t_i and the latency $\zeta(e_i, t_i)$ of this edge at that time is such that $t_{i+1} \geq t_i + \zeta(e_i, t_i)$.

While the concept of journey captures the notion of "path over time" so crucial in dynamical systems, it does not yet capture additional limitations that the environment can impose during a computation. More specifically, there are systems that provide the entities with store-carry-forward-like mechanisms (e.g., local buffering); thus an entity wanting to communicate with a specific other entity at time t_0, can *wait* until the opportunity of communication presents itself. There are however environments where such a provision is not available and thus waiting is not allowed. In time-varying graphs, this distinction is the one between a *direct* journey (where $\forall i, t_{i+1} = t_i + \zeta(e_i, t_i)$), and an *indirect* journey (where $\exists i, t_{i+1} > t_i + \zeta(e_i, t_i)$).

Clearly the task of designing protocols for these networks is less difficult if the environment allows waiting than if waiting is not feasible. No quantitative corroborations of this fact exist; in fact, up to now, there are no answers to these questions: *"if waiting is allowed, how much easier is to solve problems?"*, *"what is the computational power of waiting?"*

A first difficulty in addressing these important questions is that most of the terms are qualitative, and currently there are no measures that allow to quantify even the main concepts.

We consider these qualitative questions, and examine the complexity of the environment in terms of the *expressivity* of the corresponding time-varying graph; that is in terms of the language gen-

---

[*]The results announced in this paper can be found in: A. Casteigts, P. Flocchini, E. Godard, N. Santoro, and M. Yamashita. "Expressivity of time-varying graphs and the power of waiting in dynamic networks", *CoRR*, abs/1205.1975, 2012.

erated by the feasible journeys in the graph. We establish results showing the (surprisingly dramatic) difference that the possibility of waiting creates.

We find that the set of languages $\mathcal{L}_{nowait}$ when no waiting is allowed contains all computable languages. On the other end, using algebraic properties of quasi-orders, we prove that $\mathcal{L}_{wait}$ is just the family of *regular* languages. In other words, when waiting is no longer forbidden, the power of the accepting automaton (difficulty of the environment) drops drastically from being as powerful as a Turing machine, to becoming that of a Finite-State machine. This (perhaps surprisingly large) gap is a measure of the computational power of waiting. We also study *bounded waiting*; that is when waiting is allowed at a node only for at most d time units. We prove the negative result that $\mathcal{L}_{wait[d]} = \mathcal{L}_{nowait}$; that is, the expressivity decreases only if the waiting is finite but unpredictable (i.e., under the control of the protocol designer and not of the environment).

2. OVERVIEW OF THE RESULTS

Given a dynamic network modeled as a time-varying graph $\mathcal{G}$, a journey in $\mathcal{G}$ can be viewed as a word on the alphabet of the edge labels; in this light, the class of feasible journeys defines the language $L_f(\mathcal{G})$ expressed by $\mathcal{G}$, where $f \in \{wait, nowait\}$ indicates whether or not indirect journeys are considered feasible by the environment. Hence, a time-varying graph $\mathcal{G}$ whose edges are labeled over Σ, can be viewed as a TVG-automaton $\mathcal{A}(\mathcal{G}) = (\Sigma, S, I, \mathcal{E}, F)$ where Σ is the input *alphabet*; $S = V$ is the set of *states*; $I \subseteq S$ is the set of *initial states*; $F \subseteq S$ is the set of *accepting states*; and $\mathcal{E} \subseteq S \times \mathcal{T} \times \Sigma \times S \times \mathcal{T}$ is the set of *transitions* such that $(s, t, a, s', t') \in \mathcal{E}$ iff $\exists e = (s, s', a) \in E : \rho(e, t) = 1, \zeta(e, t) = t' - t$.

Figure 1 shows an example of a deterministic TVG-automaton $\mathcal{A}(\mathcal{G})$ that recognizes the context-free language $a^n b^n$ for $n \geq 1$ (using only direct journeys). The presence and latency of the edges of $\mathcal{G}$ are specified in Table 1, where p and q are two distinct prime numbers greater than 1, v_0 is the initial state, v_2 is the accepting state, and reading starts at time $t = 1$.

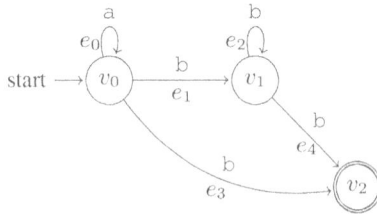

Figure 1: A TVG-automaton $\mathcal{A}(\mathcal{G})$ such that $L_{nowait}(\mathcal{G}) = \{a^n b^n : n \geq 1\}$.

e	Presence $\rho(e, t) = 1$ iff	Latency $\zeta(e, t) =$
e_0	always true	$(p-1)t$
e_1	$t > p$	$(q-1)t$
e_2	$t \neq p^i q^{i-1}, i > 1$	$(q-1)t$
e_3	$t = p$	any
e_4	$t = p^i q^{i-1}, i > 1$	any

Table 1: Presence and latency functions for the edges of $\mathcal{G}$.

We focus on the sets of languages $\mathcal{L}_{nowait} = \{L_{nowait}(\mathcal{G}) : \mathcal{G} \in \mathcal{U}\}$ and $\mathcal{L}_{wait} = \{L_{wait}(\mathcal{G}) : \mathcal{G} \in \mathcal{U}\}$, where $\mathcal{U}$ is the set of all time-varying graphs; that is, we look at the languages expressed

when waiting is, or is not allowed. For each of these two sets, the complexity of recognizing any language in the set (that is, the computational power needed by the accepting automaton) defines the level of difficulty of the environment.

We first study the expressivity of time-varying graphs when waiting is not allowed, that is the only feasible journeys are direct ones. We prove that the set $\mathcal{L}_{nowait}$ contains all computable languages.

THEOREM 2.1. *For any computable language L, there exists a time-varying graph $\mathcal{G}$ such that $L = L_{nowait}(\mathcal{G})$*

The proof is constructive.

We next examine the expressivity of time-varying graphs if indirect journeys are allowed, that is entities have the choice to wait for future opportunities of interaction rather than seizing only those that are directly available. In striking contrast with the non-waiting case, we show that the languages $\mathcal{L}_{wait}$ recognized by TVG-automata is precisely the set of *regular* languages.

THEOREM 2.2. *$\mathcal{L}_{wait}$ is the set of regular languages.*

We introduce a quasi-order on words based upon the possibility of inclusion for corresponding journeys. The fact that it is a well quasi-order cannot be derived by a simple application of classical results of the domain (eg. from [3]) but can be proved using a specific technique. The proof is algebraic and relies on a theorem by Harju and Ilie (Theorem 4.16 in [2]) that enables to characterize regularity from the closure of the sets for a well quasi-order.

In other words, we prove that, when waiting is no longer forbidden, the power of the accepting automaton (i.e., the difficulty of the environment, the power of the adversary), drops drastically from being at least as powerful as a Turing machine, to becoming that of a Finite-State Machine. This (perhaps surprisingly large) gap is a measure of the computational power of waiting.

To better understand the power of waiting, we then turn our attention to *bounded waiting*; that is when indirect journeys are considered feasible if the pause between consecutive edges in the journeys have a bounded duration $d > 0$. In other words, at each step of the journey, waiting is allowed only for at most d time units. We examine the set $\mathcal{L}_{wait[d]}$ of the languages expressed by time-varying graphs in this case and prove the negative result that the complexity of the environment is not affected by allowing waiting for a limited amount of time.

THEOREM 2.3. *For any fixed $d \geq 0$, $\mathcal{L}_{wait[d]} = \mathcal{L}_{nowait}$.*

The basic idea of the proof is to reuse the same technique as for the nowait case, but with a dilatation of time, i.e., given the bound d, the edge schedule is time-expanded by a factor d (and thus no new choice of transition is created compared to the no-waiting case). As a result, the power of the adversary is decreased only if it has no control over the length of waiting, i.e., if the waiting is unpredictable.

3. REFERENCES

[1] A. Casteigts, P. Flocchini, W. Quattrociocchi, and N. Santoro. Time-varying graphs and dynamic networks. In *Proc. 10th Int. Conf. on Ad Hoc Networks and Wireless (ADHOC-NOW)*, pages 346–359, 2011.

[2] T. Harju and L. Ilie. On quasi orders of words and the confluence property. *Theoretical Computer Science*, 200(1-2):205–224, 1998.

[3] G. Higman. Ordering by divisibility in abstract algebras. *Proceedings of the London Mathematical Society*, s3-2:326–336, 1952.

Brief Announcement: Optimal Amortized Secret Sharing with Cheater Identification

Ashish Choudhury *
Department of Computer Science
University of Bristol, United Kingdom
Ashish.Choudhary@bristol.ac.uk

ABSTRACT

We consider the problem of k-out-of-n secret sharing, capable of identifying up to t cheaters, with probability at least $(1-\epsilon)$, for a given error parameter ϵ. In any such secret sharing scheme, $t < k/2$ and the lower bound of $|\mathcal{V}_i| \geq \frac{|\mathcal{S}|-1}{\epsilon} + 1$ holds. Here $\mathcal{V}_i$ denotes the set of all possible i^{th} share, that can be assigned to the ith party and $\mathcal{S}$ denotes the set of all possible secrets. To the best of our knowledge, there does not exist any computationally efficient secret sharing scheme with $k = 2t + 1$ (the minimum value of k), where $|\mathcal{V}_i|$ exactly matches the lower bound. We show that it is possible to match this bound in the *amortized* sense.

Categories and Subject Descriptors: D. 4. 6 [Security and Protection]: Cryptographic Controls

Keywords: Information Theoretic Security.

1. INTRODUCTION

A k-out-of-n Secret Sharing (SS) scheme [5] allows a special party called the *dealer* D to share a secret among a set of n parties, such that any set of k parties can reconstruct the secret by pooling their shares, while any set of $(k-1)$ parties cannot reconstruct the secret (in the information theoretic sense) by pooling their shares. Traditional SS schemes assume that the parties will submit correct shares while reconstructing the secret. However, in a real life scenario, some of the parties may submit incorrect shares, in order to make the honest parties reconstruct an incorrect secret.

McElice and Sarwate [3] were the first to point out cheater identification in secret sharing schemes. They observed that the list of shares of a k-out-of-n Shamir secret sharing scheme [5] is nothing, but the components of the Reed-Solomon (RS) code with dimension k. So if $k + 2t + 1$ shares are revealed to reconstruct the secret, out of which at most t are corrupted, then by applying the standard RS decoding algorithm, we can identify the exact identity of the t cheaters, who produced invalid shares. But this process requires the availability of more than k shares to reconstruct the secret.

The question is whether we can do the cheater identification with the minimum number of shares (namely k), which are required to reconstruct the secret. Secret sharing with cheater identification (SSCI) is the answer to this question.

SSCI: In the model of SSCI, there exists a set $\mathcal{P} = \{P_1, \ldots, P_n\}$ of n parties and a special party called the dealer D. There exists two different static, computationally unbounded, centralized adversaries $\mathcal{A}_{Lis}$ and $\mathcal{A}_{Cheat}$. The listening adversary $\mathcal{A}_{Lis}$ can passively control any $k-1$ parties in $\mathcal{P}$. On the other hand, the cheating adversary $\mathcal{A}_{Cheat}$ can control any t parties in $\mathcal{P}$ in the Byzantine fashion. Moreover, $\mathcal{A}_{Lis}$ does not co-operate with $\mathcal{A}_{Cheat}$. This implies that $\mathcal{A}_{Cheat}$ will not get any information about the computation and communication of the parties, which may be under the control of $\mathcal{A}_{Lis}$, but not under the control of $\mathcal{A}_{Cheat}$ and vice-versa. Furthermore it is assumed that D will be honest. Any SSCI scheme consists of the following two phases:

- *Sharing Phase:* Here D takes the secret S to be shared and generates n shares $Sh_1, \ldots, Sh_n$ of S and assign Sh_i to the party P_i.

- *Reconstruction Phase:* Here a set of m parties in $\mathcal{P}$, where $m \geq k$, produce their shares to reconstruct the secret. Then the following is done:

  1. A publicly known cheater identification algorithm is applied on the m shares to identify the invalid shares. Let L be the set of parties, whose shares are identified to be invalid.
  2. If $(m - |L|) \geq k$, then a publicly known reconstruction function Rec is applied to the shares of the parties not in L, to reconstruct $\hat{S}$. Finally, $\hat{S}$ and L is the output of the reconstruction phase.
  3. If $(m - |L|) < k$, then $\perp$ and L is the output of the reconstruction phase.

Any SSCI scheme should satisfy the following properties:

- *Perfect Secrecy:* At the end of the sharing phase, $\mathcal{A}_{Lis}$ should not get any information about S in the information theoretic sense.

- *Correctness:* If any party P_i under the control of $\mathcal{A}_{Cheat}$ produces $Sh'_i \neq Sh_i$, then except with error probability ϵ, the party P_i will be included in the set L. Here $0 < \epsilon < 1/2$ is the error parameter.

For simplicity, we do not consider a *rushing* adversary, who first wait to listen the messages of the honest parties, before sending his own message for any round. However, our proposed scheme can be easily modified (by spanning the reconstruction phase over two rounds, instead of one round) to deal with a rushing $\mathcal{A}_{Cheat}$.

*The work in this paper was partially supported by EPSRC via grant EP/I03126X/1, and by the European Commission through the ICT Programme under Contract ICT−2007−216676 ECRYPT II. Part of this work was done when the author was working at the Center of Excellence in Cryptology, Indian Statistical Institute Kolkata, India.

1.1 Existing Results

Any SSCI scheme has four important parameters: (1) *Secret Space* $\mathcal{S}$: It is the set of all possible secrets. Without loss of generality, we assume that D can randomly select any element from $\mathcal{S}$ as the secret; (2) i^{th} *Share Space* $\mathcal{V}_i$: It is the set of all possible i^{th} share, which can be assigned to P_i; (3) *Eavesdropping Threshold*: It is the maximum number of parties $k-1$ which can be under the control of $\mathcal{A}_{Lis}$; (4) *Cheating Threshold*: It is the maximum number of parties t which can be under the control of $\mathcal{A}_{Cheat}$. Extensive research has been done in the past to establish bounds on $|\mathcal{V}_i|$ and to study the relationship between t and k. It is well known that in any SSCI scheme $t < k/2$ [2, 4]. So any SSCI scheme where $k = 2t + 1$ is said to have optimal cheating threshold. In [2], it is shown that in any SSCI scheme, the following lower bound holds:

$$|\mathcal{V}_i| \geq \frac{|\mathcal{S}| - 1}{\epsilon} + 1. \quad (1)$$

So any SSCI scheme, where $|\mathcal{V}_i|$ exactly matches the above bound is said to be *optimal*. The properties of the best known SSCI schemes are summarized in the following table.

	t	$|\mathcal{V}_i|$	Computational Complexity
[2]	$t < k/3$	$|\mathcal{V}_i| = |\mathcal{S}|/\epsilon^{t+2}$	Poly(k)
[4]	$t < k/3$	$|\mathcal{V}_i| = |\mathcal{S}|/\epsilon$	Poly(k)
[4]	$t < k/2$	$|\mathcal{V}_i| \approx (n \cdot (t+1) \cdot 2^{3t-1} \cdot |\mathcal{S}|)/\epsilon$	Exp(k)
[4]	$t < k/2$	$|\mathcal{V}_i| \approx ((n \cdot t \cdot 2^{3t})^2 \cdot |\mathcal{S}|)/\epsilon^2$	Exp(k) [a]

[a] In [4], two different (inefficient) schemes were presented with $t < k/2$. Here Poly$(\cdot)$ and Exp$(\cdot)$ denotes polynomial and exponential respectively.

Our Results: From the above table, we find that there exists no computationally efficient SSCI scheme with $k = 2t+1$ which satisfies the bound in Eqn. (1). We present an efficient SSCI scheme with $k = 2t + 1$ which satisfies this bound in the amortized sense, if there are large number of secrets to be shared. More specifically, our scheme allows D to share ℓ secrets from $GF(p)$, where $p = (t + 1)\ell/\epsilon$, such that $|\mathcal{V}_i| = \mathcal{O}(|\mathcal{S}|/\epsilon)$, provided $\ell = \Omega(n)$. So in applications where D has to share large number of secrets, for example secure message transmission (SMT), secure multiparty computation (MPC) and Byzantine agreement (BA), our scheme fits the bill appropriately.

1.2 Our SSCI Scheme

Let $\mathbb{F} = GF(p)$ denote a finite Galois field, where $|\mathbb{F}| = p > n$ and $p = (t + 1)\ell/\epsilon$ and let $k = 2t + 1$. Our scheme allows D to share a secret $S = (s_1, \ldots, s_\ell) \in \mathbb{F}^\ell$, where $\ell > 1$; thus $|\mathcal{S}| = p^\ell$. In our scheme, every party will get $(\ell + 3n)$ elements from $\mathbb{F}$ as his share. Thus, $|\mathcal{V}_i| = p^{\ell + 3n}$. Now if ℓ is significantly large, say $\ell = \Omega(n)$, then $|\mathcal{V}_i| = \mathcal{O}(|\mathcal{S}|/\epsilon)$. The high level idea of the protocol is as follows: for every $s_l \in S$, D generates n Shamir shares $Sh_{l,1}, \ldots, Sh_{l,n}$. Let $\sigma_i = (Sh_{1,i}, \ldots, Sh_{\ell,i})$ denote the ith share, corresponding to the ℓ secrets, which will be given to P_i. In addition to this, D authenticates each σ_i using unconditionally secure MACs. Specifically, for every pair of parties (P_i, P_j), D will select a random MAC key $key_{j,i} = (\alpha_{j,i}, \beta_{j,i})$ and compute the MAC $MAC_{i,j} = Sh_{1,i} \cdot \alpha_{j,i} + \ldots + Sh_{\ell,i} \cdot \alpha_{j,i}^\ell + \beta_{j,i}$. Then the MAC $MAC_{i,j}$ is handed over to P_i, while the MAC key $key_{j,i}$ is handed over to P_j. The interpretation is that $MAC_{i,j}$ denotes the MAC of the share σ_i of P_i under the MAC key $key_{j,i}$ of P_j. The intuition is that without

knowing the MAC key $key_{j,i}$ of an honest P_j, a corrupted P_i cannot generate a valid MAC on an incorrect σ_i', except with probability at most $\ell/|\mathbb{F}|$. This follows from the property of the above MAC [1]. Later in the reconstruction phase, if a corrupted party produces an incorrect share, then he will be caught by an honest party. The scheme is as follows:

Sharing Phase

COMPUTATION BY D: the secret is $S = (s_1, \ldots, s_\ell)$

1. For $l = 1, \ldots, \ell$, select a random polynomial $f_l(x)$ over $\mathbb{F}$ of degree at most $(k-1)$, such that $f_l(0) = s_l$. For $i = 1, \ldots, n$, compute $Sh_{l,i} = f_l(i)$. Let $\sigma_i = (Sh_{1,i}, \ldots, Sh_{\ell,i})$.

2. For every pair $i, j \in [1, \ldots, n]$, select a random MAC key $key_{j,i} = (\alpha_{j,i}, \beta_{j,i})$ and compute the $MAC_{i,j} = MAC(\sigma_i, key_{j,i}) = \sum_{l=1}^{l} \alpha_{j,i}^l \cdot Sh_{l,i} + \beta_{j,i}$.

3. For $i = 1, \ldots, n$, assign $Sh_i = (\sigma_i, MAC_{i,1}, \ldots, MAC_{i,n}, key_{i,1}, \ldots, key_{i,n})$ as the ith share of S and send Sh_i to P_i.

Reconstruction Phase

Input: A list of m shares, where $m \geq k$. Let CORE be the set of m parties who have produced their shares and let Sh_i' denote the share produced by $P_i \in$ CORE. Moreover, let $Sh_i' = \{\sigma_i', MAC_{i,1}', \ldots, MAC_{i,n}', key_{i,1}', \ldots, key_{i,n}'\}$ for each $P_i \in$ CORE. Now every party in the $\mathcal{P}$ does the following:

1. For each $P_i \in$ CORE, compute $Support_i = \{P_j \in$ CORE $: MAC_{i,j}' = MAC(\sigma_i', key_{j,i}')\}$. If $Support_i \geq t + 1$, then consider σ_i' to be valid. Otherwise, P_i is identified to be a cheater and added to a list of cheaters L, which is initially $\emptyset$. If $|L| > m - k$, then output $(\perp, L)$.

2. If $|L| \leq m - k$, then consider all valid σ_i''s (corresponding to $P_i \notin L$). Let each such $\sigma_i' = (Sha_{1,i}', \ldots, Sha_{\ell,i}')$.

3. For $l = 1, \ldots, \ell$, check using the Lagrange interpolation, whether the points $\{(i, Sh_{l,i}') : P_i \notin L\}$ lie on a unique polynomial, say $f_l'(x)$ of degree at most $(k-1)$. If not, then output $(\perp, L)$. Else output $(\hat{S}, L)$, where $\hat{S} = (f_1'(0), \ldots, f_\ell'(0))$.

THEOREM 1. *The above scheme is an SSCI scheme where* $|\mathcal{V}_i| = \mathcal{O}(|\mathcal{S}|/\epsilon)$*, provided* $\ell = \Omega(n)$.

PROOF(SKETCH): Perfect privacy follows from the fact that for every s_l, the listening adversary $\mathcal{A}_{Lis}$ gets at most $(k-1)$ points on the polynomial $f_l(x)$, where as the degree of $f_l(x)$ is $(k-1)$. So $\mathcal{A}_{Lis}$ will lack one more point to uniquely reconstruct $f_l(0)$. From the property of the MAC [1], if a corrupted $P_i \in$ CORE produces an incorrect $\sigma_i' \neq \sigma_i$, then except with probability at most $\ell/|\mathbb{F}|$, no honest party $P_j \in$ CORE will be present in $Support_i$. There will be at least $(t+1)$ honest parties in CORE and at most t corrupted parties in CORE. So from the union bound, the probability that a cheating $P_i \in$ CORE is not present in L is at most $(t+1)\ell/|\mathbb{F}| = \epsilon$. The share Sh_i contains $(\ell+3n)$ elements from $\mathbb{F}$. So $|\mathcal{V}_i| = p^{\ell+3n}$. On the other hand, $|\mathcal{S}| = p^\ell$ and $|\mathcal{S}|/\epsilon = p^\ell \cdot p/\ell(t+1)$. Now if $\ell = \Omega(n)$, then $|\mathcal{V}_i| = \mathcal{O}(p^\ell)$ and $|\mathcal{S}|/\epsilon = \mathcal{O}(p^\ell)$. Thus $|\mathcal{V}_i| = \mathcal{O}(|\mathcal{S}|/\epsilon)$. $\square$

2. REFERENCES

[1] T. Johansson, G. Kabatianskii, and B. J. M. Smeets. On the relation between A-codes and codes correcting independent errors. In *EUROCRYPT*, pages 1–11, 1993.

[2] K. Kurosawa, S. Obana, and W. Ogata. t-cheater identifiable (k, n) threshold secret sharing schemes. In *CRYPTO*, pages 410–423, 1995.

[3] R. J. McEliece and D. V. Sarwate. On sharing secrets and Reed Solomon codes. *Communications of the ACM*, 24(9):583–584, 1981.

[4] S. Obana. Almost optimum t-cheater identifiable secret sharing schemes. In *EUROCRYPT*, pages 284–302, 2011.

[5] A. Shamir. How to share a secret. *Communications of the ACM*, 22(11):612–613, 1979.

Brief Announcement: Efficient Optimally Resilient Statistical AVSS and Its Applications

Ashish Choudhury *
Department of Computer Science
University of Bristol, United Kingdom
Ashish.Choudhary@bristol.ac.uk

Arpita Patra
Department of Computer Science
ETH Zurich, Switzerland
arpita.patra@inf.ethz.ch

ABSTRACT

Asynchronous Verifiable Secret Sharing (AVSS) is a fundamental primitive in secure distributed computing. It finds significant application in problems like Asynchronous Byzantine Agreement (ABA) and Asynchronous Multiparty Computation (AMPC). In [4], we presented a new asynchronous primitive called Asynchronous Weak Commitment (AWC) and used it to construct an AVSS scheme, which is thus far the most communication efficient AVSS scheme. Through this brief announcement, we wish to make our result visible to the Distributed Computing community.

Categories and Subject Descriptors: D. 4. 6 [Security and Protection]: Cryptographic Controls

Keywords: Information Theoretic Security.

1. INTRODUCTION

VSS is a two phase (share, reconstruct) protocol, carried out among a set of n parties $\mathcal{P} = \{P_1, \ldots, P_n\}$ connected by pair-wise secure and authentic channels. In a VSS protocol, a special party in $\mathcal{P}$ called the *dealer* D wishes to share a secret s, selected from a finite field $\mathbb{F}$, among the n parties. There is a computationally unbounded adversary $\mathcal{A}_t$, who can corrupt at most t parties (possibly including D) in the Byzantine fashion. The goal is to allow D to share s during the sharing phase, such that the secrecy of s is maintained during the sharing phase if D is honest. Moreover, even if D is corrupted, it is guaranteed that D is committed to a unique value $s^\star$ during the sharing phase, which will be correctly reconstructed in the reconstruction phase, irrespective of the behavior of the corrupted parties. This property, also called the *strong commitment*, is a form of distributed commitment and it makes the VSS an important tool for many fault tolerant distributed computing problems.

AVSS extends the notion of VSS in the asynchronous networks [3], where we do not have any timing assumptions and the messages are arbitrarily delayed (however messages sent by the honest parties will be eventually delivered). The inherent difficulty in designing asynchronous protocols is that we cannot distinguish a *slow*, but honest sender from a *cor-*

rupted sender. As a result, at any step, a party has to start the computation after getting the messages from $(n-t)$ parties, ignoring the remaining t (potentially honest) parties.

Existing Results: There are two types of AVSS: *perfect* AVSS [1], which satisfies the properties of AVSS with probability 1 and *statistical* AVSS [3, 6, 5], which achieves the properties, except with probability $2^{-\Omega(\kappa)}$, for a given error parameter κ. Our focus is on the *communication complexity* (CC) of statistical AVSS, which is the total number of bits, communicated by the honest parties in the protocol. To bound the error probability by $2^{-\Omega(\kappa)}$, the computation in statistical AVSS schemes is done over $\mathbb{F} = GF(2^\kappa)$, implying that every element of $\mathbb{F}$ is represented by $\mathcal{O}(\kappa)$ bits. Statistical AVSS tolerating $\mathcal{A}_t$ is possible if and only if $n \geq 3t+1$ [3] (for perfect AVSS, $n \geq 4t+1$ is required [1]). So a statistical AVSS protocol designed with $n = 3t + 1$ parties is said to be *optimally resilient*. Such AVSS protocols are reported in [3, 6, 5], which are summarized in Table. 1.

Our Result and Its Significance: We try to further reduce the communication complexity of the best known optimally resilient statistical AVSS schemes [6, 5]. Since the Asynchronous Information Checking Protocol (AICP) [3, 6, 5] is the starting point in all the existing AVSS schemes including ours, we compare the complexity of our AVSS with the existing ones in terms of the number of invocations to the AICP. Very briefly, AICP [3, 6] provides a mechanism to authenticate data, even in the presence of a computationally unbounded $\mathcal{A}_t$. We bring efficiency in our AVSS scheme by two steps: **(1)**. By introducing a new asynchronous primitive called AWC that has weaker requirements and can be designed with better efficiency than AWSS, which is the commonly used building block in all the existing AVSS schemes. Specifically, AWC can be designed using n instances of the underlying AICP, in contrast to $\mathcal{O}(n^2)$ instances required for the AWSS of [6, 5]; **(2)**. By designing an AVSS scheme that invokes our AWC n times and thus invokes AICP $\mathcal{O}(n^2)$ times (in contrast to $\mathcal{O}(n^3)$ times required in [6, 5]).

Our AVSS has direct implications in the efficiency improvement by a factor of $\Theta(n)$ in all the primitives that use AVSS as a building block. For example **(a)** By incorporating our AVSS, the best known unconditionally secure ABA scheme of [6] with $n = 3t+1$ will now require a private communication as well as broadcast communication of $\mathcal{O}(n^5\kappa)$ bits to reach agreement on a single bit. **(b)** With our new AVSS, the best known statistical AMPC protocol of [5] with $n = 3t + 1$ will now have a communication complexity of $\mathcal{O}(n^4\kappa)$ bits per multiplication gate.

*The work in this paper was partially supported by EPSRC via grant EP/I03126X/1, and by the European Commission through the ICT Programme under Contract ICT−2007−216676 ECRYPT II.

Table 1: Existing optimally resilient statistical AVSS schemes. Here $X \xrightarrow{d} Y$ implies that primitive Y is designed using d instances of the primitive X. As AICP is the starting point in all the schemes, we count the number of AICP instances invoked in the AVSS. The fourth column denotes the number of secrets shared by the scheme. The communication complexity has two parts: the private communication done over the private channels and the public communication done through broadcasting using the Bracha's A-cast protocol [2].

Ref.	Path Followed	No. of AICP Instances	No. of Secrets	Communication Complexity (CC)
[3]	$AICP \xrightarrow{n} ARS \xrightarrow{n^2} AWSS \xrightarrow{1}$ $Two\&SumAWSS \xrightarrow{n^2} AVSS$	$\Omega(n^5)$	1	Private: $\Omega(n^9 \kappa^4)$ bits; broadcast $\Omega(n^9 \kappa^2 \log n)$ bits.
[6]	$AICP \xrightarrow{n^2} AWSS \xrightarrow{n} AVSS$	$\Theta(n^3)$	$\ell, \ell \geq 1$	Private: $\mathcal{O}(\ell n^3 \kappa + n^4 \kappa)$ bits; broadcast: $\mathcal{O}(\ell n^3 \kappa + n^4 \kappa)$ bits.
[5]	$AICP \xrightarrow{n^2} AWSS \xrightarrow{n} AVSS$	$\Theta(n^3)$	$\ell, \ell \geq 1$	Private: $\mathcal{O}(\ell n^3 \kappa + n^4 \kappa^2)$ bits; broadcast: $\mathcal{O}(n^3 \log n)$ bits.
This work	$AICP \xrightarrow{n} AWC \xrightarrow{n} AVSS$	$\Theta(n^2)$	$\ell, \ell \geq 1$	Private: $\mathcal{O}(\ell n^2 \kappa + n^3 \kappa^2)$ bits; broadcast $\mathcal{O}(n^3 \log n)$ bits.

1.1 AICP, AWSS and AWC

In an AICP, there are two special parties from $\mathcal{P}$, a Signer and an intermediary INT, along with the set of n parties from $\mathcal{P}$ acting as verifiers. An AICP consists of two phases: (1) *Signature generation phase*, where Signer generates his IC (information checking) signature on a secret $s \in \mathbb{F}$, denoted by $ICSig(\text{Signer}, \text{INT}, s)$ and hands it to INT. Signer also generates some verification information and distributes it among the n verifiers; (2) *Signature revelation phase*, where INT reveals the signature $ICSig(\text{Signer}, \text{INT}, s)$ and claims that he has received it from Signer. The verifiers then verify the signature, using the verification information and either accept or reject the claim of INT. IC signature may be considered as the information theoretically secure substitute of traditional digital signatures. It provides properties like unforgeability and non-repudiation; it also provides information theoretic security. That is, if Signer and INT are honest, then at the end of the signature generation phase, s remains secure in the information theoretic sense.

Typically AWSS [3, 6] is used to construct AVSS schemes. The properties of AWSS are similar to the AVSS, except that instead of the strong commitment, it satisfies the *weak commitment* property, which states that if D is corrupted, then depending upon the behavior of the corrupted parties, *either* $s^\star$ (the value committed by D) or $\perp$ will be reconstructed.

Our new primitive called AWC, consists of a commit phase and a decommit phase. Property wise, the sharing phase of AWSS and the commit phase of AWC demands the same; namely a distributed commitment to a unique value $s^\star$, which should be secure if D is honest. However, the difference is in the decommit phase. The decommit phase is invoked by D, where D reveals $s^\star$ and the parties verify whether $s^\star$ is the committed value. An honest D always decommits the committed secret. However, a corrupted D can decommit an incorrect $s^{\star\star} \neq s^\star$ with a negligible probability of $2^{-\Omega(\kappa)}$. The subtle difference between the reconstruction phase of AWSS and the decommit phase of AWC is about the role of D for the termination of the respective phases: the reconstruction phase of AWSS does not demand a special role by D to enforce the termination. So this phase will terminate even if a corrupted D does not participate. On contrary, the decommit phase demands a special role from D to enforce the termination. Here D actually initiates the phase; so for a corrupted D, this phase may never terminate.

The above difference intuitively suggests that D have to work/communicate "more" during the sharing phase of AWSS than the commit phase of AWC. The veracity of the intuition is confirmed by our ability to design AWC more efficiently than AWSS. The AWSS schemes of [6, 5] are based on the idea of sharing the secret using a bi-variate polynomial $F(x, y)$ of degree at most t in x and y and requires $\Theta(n^2)$ invocations of the underlying AICP to generate IC signatures on n^2 distinct points on $F(x, y)$. In contrast, we design AWC based on the Shamir secret sharing, where a univariate polynomial $f(x)$ of degree at most t is used to share the secret and only n instances of AICP are invoked to generate IC signatures on n distinct points on $f(x)$. Thus we gain $\Theta(n)$ in the communication complexity. Our scheme for a single secret is sketched below; in [4], we show how to extend it for ℓ secrets and how to design AVSS using it.

Commit Phase

GENERATING THE COMMITMENT INFORMATION : CODE FOR D

• On having a secret s, select a random polynomial $f(x)$ over $\mathbb{F}$ of degree at most t, such that $f(0) = s$ and for $i = 1, \ldots, n$, compute the ith share $Sh_i = f(i)$. Privately send Sh_i to the party P_i and ask P_i to give his IC signature on Sh_i to D.

• If $ICSig(P_i, D, Sh'_i)$ is received from P_i and if $Sh'_i = Sh_i$ then add P_i to a set WCORE, which is initially $\emptyset$. Wait till $|\text{WCORE}| = 2t + 1$ and then broadcast the set WCORE.

SIGNING THE SHARES AND VERIFYING D'S CLAIM : CODE FOR P_i

• On receiving Sh_i from D, give $ICSig(P_i, D, Sh_i)$ to D. Wait to receive a WCORE of size $2t + 1$ from the broadcast of D and once received, terminate the commit phase.

Decommit Phase

D reveals $ICSig(P_j, D, Sh_j)$ for each $P_j \in$ WCORE.

VERIFYING THE COMMITMENT : CODE FOR P_i

• Verify $ICSig(P_j, D, Sh_j)$, for every $P_j \in$ WCORE. If any of these signatures is invalid, then discard D and terminate. If $ICSig(P_j, D, Sh_j)$ is a valid signature for every $P_j \in$ WCORE, then check whether the points $\{(j, Sh_j) : P_j \in \text{WCORE}\}$ lie on a unique polynomial $f(x)$ of degree at most t. If yes, then accept $s = f(0)$ and terminate. Else discard D and terminate.

---

2. REFERENCES

[1] M. Ben-Or and R. Canetti and O. Goldreich. Asynchronous secure computation. In *STOC*, pages 52–61, 1993.

[2] G. Bracha. An asynchronous [(n-1)/3]-resilient consensus protocol. In *PODC*, pages 154–162, 1984.

[3] R. Canetti and T. Rabin. Fast asynchronous Byzantine agreement with optimal resilience. In *STOC*, pages 42–51, 1993.

[4] A. Choudhury and A. Patra. Statistical asynchronous weak commitment scheme: A new primitive to design statistical asynchronous verifiable secret sharing scheme. In *WCC* 2011. Cryptology ePrint Archive 2011/031.

[5] A. Patra, A. Choudhary, and C. P. Rangan. Efficient statistical asynchronous verifiable secret sharing with optimal resilience. In *ICITS*, pages 74–92, 2009. Cryptology ePrint Archive 2009/492.

[6] A. Patra, A. Choudhary, and C. P. Rangan. Simple and efficient asynchronous Byzantine agreement with optimal resilience. In *PODC*, pages 92–101, 2009.

Wait-Freedom with Advice

Carole Delporte-Gallet
University Paris Diderot
cd@liafa.univ-paris-diderot.fr

Hugues Fauconnier
University Paris Diderot
hf@liafa.univ-paris-diderot.fr

Eli Gafni
UCLA
eli@ucla.edu

Petr Kuznetsov
TU Berlin/Telekom Innovation Laboratories
petr.kuznetsov@tu-berlin.de

ABSTRACT

We motivate and propose a new way of thinking about failure detectors which allows us to define, quite surprisingly, what it means to solve a distributed task *wait-free using a failure detector*. In our model, the system is composed of *computation* processes that obtain inputs and are supposed to produce outputs and *synchronization* processes that are subject to failures and can query a failure detector. Under the condition that *correct* synchronization processes take sufficiently many steps, they provide the computation processes with enough *advice* to solve the given task wait-free: every computation process outputs in a finite number of its own steps, regardless of the behavior of other computation processes. Every task can thus be characterized by the *weakest* failure detector that allows for solving it, and we show that every such failure detector captures a form of set agreement. We then obtain a complete classification of tasks, including ones that evaded comprehensible characterization so far, such as renaming or weak symmetry breaking.

Categories and Subject Descriptors

C.2.4 [**Computer-Communication Networks**]: Distributed Systems; F.1.1 [**Computation by Abstract Devices**]: Models of Computation—*relations between models*

Keywords

wait-freedom, failure detectors, computation and synchronization

1. INTRODUCTION

What does it mean to solve a task? A distributed task for a set of processes can be seen as a function that maps an input vector to an output vector, one value per process. It is easy to reason correctness of a task solution by matching the outputs to the inputs with respect to the task specification. When it comes to verifying progress, however, it is getting less trivial.

On the surface, it is desirable to expect that the input vector is exactly matched by the output vector, i.e., every participating process obtains an output.[1] Unfortunately, in asynchronous or partially synchronous systems where relative processes' speeds are unbounded or very large, ensuring this property would require very long waiting. A more natural *wait-freedom* property requires that any participating process that takes sufficiently many steps obtains an output, "regardless of execution speeds of other processes" [21]. A wait-free task solution thus allows us to treat the requirement "a given participant outputs" as a *liveness* property [2, 27]: every finite execution has an extension in which the requirement is met. Naturally, wait-freedom assumes no notion of process *failures*: a process that does not take steps for a while in a given execution, always has a chance to wake up and take enough steps to output.

Failure detectors. Unfortunately, very few tasks can be solved wait-free in the basic read-write shared-memory model [15, 26, 22, 29, 5, 7]. The *failure detector* abstraction [9, 10] was proposed to circumvent these impossibilities. Intuitively, a failure detector provides each process with some (possibly incomplete and inaccurate) information about the current *failure pattern*, e.g., a list of processes predicted to take only finitely many steps in the current execution. The failure detector abstraction gives a language for capturing the weakest support from the system one may require in order to solve a given task. This gave many interesting insights on the nature of "wait-free unsolvable" tasks, starting from the celebrated result by Chandra et al. on the weakest failure detector for consensus [9].[2]

A solution of a task using a failure detector guarantees that every *correct* (a process that is predicted to take infinitely many steps by the failure pattern) eventually obtains an output. The progress of each process may thus depend on the behavior of other correct processes, and therefore failure detector-based algorithm cannot be wait-free. Con-

---

[1] A process is considered participating if it takes at least one step in the computation.

[2] Informally, $\mathcal{D}$ is the weakest failure detector to solve a task T if it (1) solves T and (2) can be deduced from any failure detector that solves T.

sequently, since the failure pattern is introduced as a part of a run, we cannot treat individual progress as a liveness property anymore: a process is not allowed to take steps after it crashes.

Wait-freedom with advice. But can we think of a system where a "hard" task can be solved so that progress of a process does not depend on the execution speeds of other processes? A straightforward way to achieve this is to assume that the processes receive *advice* from an external oracle, and an immediate question is what is the weakest oracle that allows for solving a given task so that every participating process taking enough steps outputs.

In this paper, we use the language of failure detectors to determine the relative power of such external oracles. The oracle is represented as a set of *synchronization* processes equipped with a failure detector: each synchronization process can query its failure detector module to get hints about the failures of other synchronization processes. Thus, our system only considers failures of synchronization processes. As in the classical failure-detector literature [9], the assumptions about when and where failures of synchronization processes can occur are encapsulated in an *environment*, i.e., a set of allowed failure patterns. The processes participating in a task solution by obtaining inputs and providing outputs are then called *computation* processes. The two types of processes communicate (within each type and across types) by reading and writing in the shared memory.

Now what do we mean by solving a task with a failure detector? We require that, under the condition that the synchronization processes using their failure detector behave as predicted by the environment, every computation process taking enough steps must output.

It is easy to see that the classical failure-detector model [9] is a special case of our model where there is a bijective map between computation and synchronization processes, and a computation process stops taking steps after its synchronization counterpart does. Strictly speaking, when it comes to solving tasks, our framework demands from a failure detector more than the conventional failure detector model does. Indeed, in our framework, the failure of a synchronization process does not affect computation processes, and a failure detector is supposed to help computation processes output, as long as they take enough steps. In particular, we observe that the *weakest* failure detector to solve a task T in our framework is at least as strong as the weakest failure detector for T in the conventional model [9].

Ramifications. The idea of separating computation from synchronization is not new, e.g., it is used in the celebrated Paxos protocol [25] separating *proposers* from *acceptors* and *learners*. But applying it to distributed computing with failure detectors results in a surprisingly simple model, which we call *external failure detection (EFD)*, which resolves a number of long-standing puzzles.

The use of EFD enables a complete characterization of distributed tasks, based on the "amount of concurrency" they can stand. In the classical framework, we say that a task T can be solved k-concurrently if it guarantees that in every k-concurrent run every process taking sufficiently many steps eventually outputs [17]. Informally, a run is k-concurrent if at each moment of time, there are at most k participating processes without outputs. Now, in a system of n processes,

each task T is associated with the largest k ($1 \leq k \leq n$) such that T can be solved k-concurrently.

We show that in EFD, a failure detector $\mathcal{D}$ can be used to solve a task T with "concurrency level" at most k *if and only if* $\mathcal{D}$ can be used to solve k-set agreement. More precisely, we show that, in every environment, i.e., for all assumptions on where and when failures of *synchronization* processes may occur, any failure detector that solves T is at least as strong as the anti-Ω-k failure detector [28, 30], denoted $\neg\Omega_k$. Then we describe an algorithm that uses $\neg\Omega_k$ to solve T (or any task that can be solved k-concurrently), in every environment.

Thus, any task is completely characterized through the "level of concurrency" its solution can tolerate. All tasks that can be solved k-concurrently but not $(k + 1)$-concurrently (e.g., k-set agreement) are equivalent in the sense that they require exactly the same amount of information about failures (captured by $\neg\Omega_k$) to be solved in EFD. Note that this characterization covers *all* tasks, including "colored" ones that evaded any characterization so far [14, 19, 1].

Consider, for example, the task of (j, ℓ)-renaming in which j processes come from a large set of potential participants and choose new names in a smaller name space $1, \ldots, \ell$, so that no two processes choose the same name. Surprisingly, in the conventional model, the renaming task itself can be formulated as a failure detector, so the question of the weakest failure detector for solving it results in a triviality. To avoid trivialities, additional assumptions on the scope of failure detectors are made [1].

In EFD, however, we immediately see that (j, j)-renaming (also called *strong* renaming) cannot be solved 2-concurrently and is thus equivalent to consensus.[3] More generally, determining the weakest failure detector for (j, ℓ)-renaming boils down to determining the maximal k ($1 \leq k \leq j$) such that the task can be solved k-concurrently. We show finally that $(j, j + k - 1)$-renaming can be solved k-concurrently, and, thus, using $\neg\Omega_k$.[4]

Another interesting corollary of our characterization is that if a failure detector solves k-set agreement among an arbitrary given subset of $k + 1$ processes, then it is strong enough to solve k-set agreement among *all* processes. This is a generalization of the recent result of Delporte et al. [13] that any failure detector allowing for solving consensus (1-set agreement) among each two processes, also allows for solving consensus among all processes. Years of trying to show that the phenomenon demonstrated in [13] generalizes to all $k \geq 1$ in the conventional failure-detector model [9] bore no fruits.

One important feature inherited by our EFD framework from wait-free protocols is that it leverages *simula-tion-based* computing: processes can cooperate trying bring *all* participating processes to their outputs. Simulations were instrumental in establishing tight relations between seemingly different phenomena in *asynchronous* systems [5, 7, 16, 20, 14, 18, 17], and we extend this line of research below to failure-detector models.

Roadmap. The paper is organized as follows. First, we formally define our model and our new notion of task solvability

---

[3]Note that all tasks can be solved 1-concurrently.

[4]For some values of j and k, however, the question of the maximal tolerated concurrency of $(j, j + k - 1)$-renaming is still open [8].

with a failure detector. We then present a simple inductive proof of a generalization of [13] to any $k > 1$. Then we extend the generalization even further by presenting a complete characterization of decision tasks, based on the level of concurrency they can tolerate. Then we derive the weakest failure detector for strong renaming and wrap up with obligatory concluding remarks. Proofs are partially delegated to the appendix and the full version of the paper [12].

2. THE MODEL OF EXTERNAL FAILURE DETECTION

In this section, we propose a new definition of what it means to solve a task using a failure detector and relate it to the conventional definition of [9]. Parts of our model reuse elements of [9, 10, 19, 22].

2.1 Computation and synchronization

Our system is split in two parts. The *computation* part is made up of processes that get input values for the task they intend to solve and return output values. The *synchronization* part is made up of processes that use failure detectors to help processes of the computation part.

Processes. Formally, we consider a read-write shared-memory system which consists of m *C-processes*, $\Pi^C = \{p_1, \ldots, p_m\}$, and n *S-processes*, $\Pi^S = \{q_1, \ldots, q_n\}$. We allow n and m to be arbitrary natural numbers, but, as we shall see shortly, the only "interesting" case is when $n = m$.

Intuitively, the C-processes are responsible for computation. The S-processes are responsible for synchronization and may be equipped with a failure detector module [10] that gives hints about failures of other S-processes. The processes in $\Pi^C] \cup \Pi^S$ communicate with each other via reading and writing in the shared memory.

Failure patterns and failure detectors. Since C-processes are assumed to be wait-free, we are only interested here in failures of S-processes. Hence a *failure pattern* F is a function from the time range $\mathbb{T} = \mathbb{N}$ to 2^{Π^S}, where $F(\tau)$ denotes the set of S-processes that have crashed by time τ. Once a process crashes, it does not recover, i.e., $\forall \tau : F(\tau) \subseteq F(\tau + 1)$. $faulty(F) = \cup_{\tau \in \mathbb{T}} F(\tau)$ is the set of faulty processes in F and $correct(F) = \Pi^S - faulty(F)$ is the set of correct processes in F.

A *failure detector history* H *with range* $\mathcal{R}$ is a function from $\Pi^S \times \mathbb{T}$ to $\mathcal{R}$. $H(q_i, \tau)$ is interpreted as the value output by the failure detector module of S-process q_i at time τ. A *failure detector* $\mathcal{D}$ with range $\mathcal{R}_\mathcal{D}$ is a function that maps each failure pattern to a (non-empty) set of failure detector histories with range $\mathcal{R}_\mathcal{D}$. $\mathcal{D}(F)$ denotes the set of possible failure detector histories permitted by $\mathcal{D}$ for failure pattern F.

An *environment* $\mathcal{E}$ is a set of failure patterns that describes a set of conditions on when and where failures might occur. For example $\mathcal{E}_t$ is the environment that consists of all failure patterns F such that $correct(F) \geq n - t$. We assume that for every failure pattern in the environments we consider, at least one S-process is correct.

Algorithms and runs. A distributed algorithm $\mathcal{A}$ using a failure detector $\mathcal{D}$ consists of two collections of deterministic automata, $\mathcal{A}_1^C, \ldots, \mathcal{A}_m^C$, one automaton for each C-process, and $\mathcal{A}_1^S, \ldots, \mathcal{A}_n^S$, one automaton for each S-process. In a *step*

of the algorithm, a process may read or write to a shared register, or (if it is a S-process) consult its failure-detector module.

A *state* of $\mathcal{A}$ is defined as the state of each process (state of each process being identified with the state of its corresponding automaton) and each shared object in the system. An *initial state* I of $\mathcal{A}$ specifies an initial state for every process and every shared object.

A *run of $\mathcal{A}$ using a failure detector $\mathcal{D}$ in an environment $\mathcal{E}$* is a tuple $R = \langle F, H, I, Sch, T \rangle$ where $F \in \mathcal{E}$ is a failure pattern, $H \in \mathcal{D}(F)$ is a failure detector history, I is an initial state of $\mathcal{A}$, Sch is an infinite *schedule*, i.e., a sequence of processes in $\Pi^C \cup \Pi^S$, T is a sequence of non-decreasing elements of $\mathbb{T}$. The k-th step of run R is a step of process $Sch[k]$ determined by the current state, the failure history H, $T[k]$ and the algorithm $\mathcal{A}$. If it is a step of a S-process, this process is alive ($Sch[k] \notin F(T[k])$) and the value of the failure detector for this step is given by $H(Sch[k], T[k])$.

Let $inf^S(R)$ denote the set of processes in Π^S that appear infinitely often in Sch. Respectively, $inf^C(R)$ denote the set of processes in Π^C that appear infinitely often in Sch. We say that a run $R = \langle F, H, I, Sch, T \rangle$ is *fair* if $correct(F)$ is equal to $inf^S(R)$, and $inf^C(R)$ is not empty. A *finite run* of $\mathcal{A}$ is a "prefix" of a run $\langle F, H, I, Sch, T \rangle$ of $\mathcal{A}$, i.e., a tuple $\langle F, H, I, Sch', T' \rangle$ such that $|Sch'| = |T'|$, Sch is a proper prefix of Sch, and T' is a proper prefix of T.

Tasks. We focus on a class of problems called *tasks* that are defined uniquely through inputs and outputs.

A *task* [22] is defined through a set $\mathcal{I}$ of input vectors (one input value for each C-process), a set $\mathcal{O}$ of output vectors (one output value for each C-process), and a total relation $\Delta : \mathcal{I} \mapsto 2^\mathcal{O}$ that associates each input vector with a set of possible output vectors. An input value equal to $\perp$ denotes a *not participating* process and $\perp$ output value denotes an *undecided* process.

A m-vector L' is a *prefix* of a m-vector L if L' contains at least one non-$\perp$ item and for all i, $1 \leq i \leq m$, either $L'[i] = \perp$ or $L'[i] = L[i]$. A set $\mathcal{L}$ of vectors is *prefix-closed* if for all L in $\mathcal{L}$ every prefix of L is in $\mathcal{L}$.

We assume that each element of $\mathcal{I}$ and $\mathcal{O}$ contains at least one non-$\perp$ item and also that the sets $\mathcal{I}$ and $\mathcal{O}$ are prefix-closed. Moreover, we only consider tasks that have finite sets of input vectors $\mathcal{I}$ (this assumption is used in Section 4 when we categorize tasks based on the failure detectors needed to solve them).

We stipulate that if $(I, O) \in \Delta$, then (1) if, for some i, $I[i] = \perp$, then $O[i] = \perp$, (2) for each O', prefix of O, $(I, O') \in \Delta$ and, (3) for each I' such that I is a prefix of I', there exists some O' such that O is a prefix of O' and (I', O') in Δ.

For example, in the task of (U, k)-*agreement*, where $U \subseteq \Pi^C$, input and output vectors are m-vectors, such that $I[i] = \perp$ for all $p_i \notin U$, input values are in $\{\perp, 0, \ldots, k\}$, output values are in $\{\perp, 0, \ldots, k\}$, and for each input vector I and output vector O, $(I, O) \in \Delta$ if the set of non-$\perp$ values in O is a subset of values in I of size at most k. (Π^C, k)-agreement is the conventional k-*set agreement* task [11] and $(\Pi^C, 1)$-agreement is *consensus* [15].

2.2 Solving a task in the EFD framework

Now we are ready to define what does it mean to solve a task in the external failure detection framework.

Input vector and output vector of a run. First, we assume that each automaton $\mathcal{A}_i^C$ (1) gets an input value $input_i$ as part of its initial state, and (2) contains *decide* steps such that all the next steps of $\mathcal{A}_i$ are null steps that do not affect the current state when they are executed and for each *decide* step is associated a decision value v_i.

The first step of each C-process is to write its input value to shared memory. A process that wrote its input value is called *participating*. If a C-process executes a *decide* step with decision value v, we say that the process decides v or returns v.

Given a run R, the *input vector* for the run is the m-vector I such that $I(i) = input_i$ if p_i is a participating process and $I(i) = \bot$ if p_i is a not participating process. In the same way, the *output vector* of the run is the m-vector O such that $O(i) = v$ if p_i decides v in the run and $O(i) = \bot$ if p_i does not decide in the run.

Solving a task. We say that a run R with input vector I and output vector O *satisfies* a task $T = (\mathcal{I}, \mathcal{O}, \Delta)$ if (1) $(I, O) \in \Delta$ and (2) $O(i) = \bot$ only if p_i makes a finite number of steps ($p_i \notin inf^C(R)$).

An algorithm $\mathcal{A}$ *EFD-solves* a task $T = (\mathcal{I}, \mathcal{O}, \Delta)$ *using a failure detector $\mathcal{D}$ in an environment $\mathcal{E}$* (in the rest we simply say "solves") if every fair run of $\mathcal{A}$ satisfies T. If such an algorithm exists for task T, T is *solvable with failure detector $\mathcal{D}$ in environment $\mathcal{E}$*. By extension, a failure detector $\mathcal{D}$ *solves a task T in $\mathcal{E}$* if there is an algorithm $\mathcal{A}$ that solves T using $\mathcal{D}$ in $\mathcal{E}$.

Note that we expect the algorithm to guarantee output to every C-process that takes sufficiently many steps, regardless of where and when S-processes fail. The algorithm only expects that every correct S-process in the current failure pattern takes infinitely many steps.

Comparing failure detectors. Failure detector reduction is defined as usual: failure detector $\mathcal{D}'$ is *weaker than failure detector $\mathcal{D}$ in an environment $\mathcal{E}$* if S-processes can use $\mathcal{D}$ to emulate $\mathcal{D}'$ in $\mathcal{E}$. More precisely, the automata of the C-processes of the distributed *reduction algorithm* $\mathcal{A}$ are automata with only null steps and the emulation of $\mathcal{D}'$ using $\mathcal{D}$ is made by maintaining, at each S-process q_i $\mathcal{D}'$-$output_i$ so that in any fair run with failure pattern F, the evolution of variables $\{\mathcal{D}'\text{-}output_i\}_{q_i \in \Pi^S}$ results in a history $H' \in \mathcal{D}'(F)$. We say that two failure detectors are *equivalent* in $\mathcal{E}$ if each is weaker than the other in $\mathcal{E}$.

As in the original definiton [9], if failure detector $\mathcal{D}'$ is weaker than failure detector $\mathcal{D}$ in environment $\mathcal{E}$, then every task solvable with $\mathcal{D}'$ in $\mathcal{E}$ can also be solved with $\mathcal{D}$ in $\mathcal{E}$. Now $\mathcal{D}$ is the *weakest failure detector* to solve a task T in $\mathcal{E}$ if (i) $\mathcal{D}$ solves T in $\mathcal{E}$ and (ii) $\mathcal{D}$ is weaker than any failure detector that solves T in $\mathcal{E}$. It is straightforward to extend the arguments of [23] to show that every task has a weakest failure detector.

k-concurrency. Consider the solvability of a task without the help of a failure detector. In this case the deterministic automata of the S-processes of the distributed algorithm $\mathcal{A}$ are automata with only null steps. Such an algorithm will be called *restricted*.

It is clear that tasks that are solvable with a restricted algorithm are exactly tasks that are said *wait-free* solvable in the literature (e.g. in [21, 22]).

The notion of *k-concurrent* solvability, introduced in [17], is a weaker form of solvability: a task is *k-concurrently solvable* if it is solvable only when at most k C-processes concurrently invoke the task. More precisely, a run of a distributed algorithm is *k-concurrent* if it is fair and at each time there is at most k undecided participating C-processes. A task $T = (\mathcal{I}, \mathcal{O}, \Delta)$ is *k-concurrently* solvable if there is a restricted algorithm $\mathcal{A}$ such that all k-concurrent runs R of $\mathcal{A}$ satisfy T. Note that runs of $\mathcal{A}$ in which the number of participating but not decided C-processes exceeds k at some point may not satisfy T.

A wait-free solvable task is m-concurrently solvable. Also, it is easy to show that (Appendix A):

PROPOSITION 1. *[12] Every task is 1-concurrently solvable.*

Restriction on the number of C-processes. Trivially, if a task T is solvable with a restricted algorithm then T is also solvable with any number of S-processes and any failure detector. Reciprocally, consider an algorithm $\mathcal{A}$ solving a task T with a trivial failure detector[5] in environment $\mathcal{E}_{n-1}$. If $n \geq m$ consider the following algorithm: each C-process p_i executes alternatively steps of $\mathcal{A}_{p_i}^C$ and steps of $\mathcal{A}_{q_i}^S$ and each S-process executes only null steps. It is easy to verify that in this way we emulate runs of $\mathcal{A}$ in the failure pattern in which at least all S-processes q_i with $i > m$ are crashed, and such runs satisfy task T. Hence we get:

PROPOSITION 2. *If $n \geq m$, T is solvable in $\mathcal{E}_{n-1}$ with a trivial failure detector if and only if T is solvable with a restricted algorithm.*

But if $n < m$, the S-processes may help solving the task even if they do not use their failure detection capacities. For example, with n S-processes we can implement a (Π^C, n)-set agreement in every environment. For this, each S-process waits until at least one C-process writes its input in shared memory, and then it writes this value to a shared variable V. Each C-process waits until V has been written and outputs the read value. As at least one S-process is correct, eventually V will be written and as there are n S-processes at most n values may be output. In this way the (Π^C, n)-set agreement is always solvable even without the help of any failure detector.

As we focus here on solvability where additional power of processes is only due to the failure detection, the only "interesting" scenario to consider is when the number of C-processes does not exceed the number of S-processes and more specifically the case where they are equal. *Therefore, in the following we assume that the number of C-processes is equal to the number of S-processes, we denote this number by n.*

2.3 Conventional solvability

More conventional models of computation in which there is no separation between the computation and the synchronization part may be considered as a special case of the generalized model presented here. In conventional models, each process $i \in \{1, \dots, n\}$ can be seen as running two parallel threads: p_i corresponding to the computational part and q_i corresponding to the synchronization part. Moreover failure patterns correspond: i is correct in conventional systems if

---

[5]A trivial failure detector always outputs $\bot$.

and only if q_i is correct in our setting. But, since in our model, computation and synchronization are separate, it is possible that p_i makes only a finite number of steps even if q_i is correct or vice-versa. Then we define *personified runs* of a distributed algorithm as being runs R that are fair and such that p_i crashes if and only if q_i crashes at the same time (as a result, $inf^C(R)$ is equal to $inf^S(R)$). We say that algorithm $\mathcal{A}$ solves *classically* task T with failure detector $\mathcal{D}$ in environment $\mathcal{E}$ if every personified run R of $\mathcal{A}$ satisfied T.

This definition corresponds exactly to the notion of solvability in a conventional setting as can be found in the literature [9].

As the set of personified runs of a distributed algorithm is a subset of the fair runs, we have:

PROPOSITION 3. *If a failure detector $\mathcal{D}$ solves a task T in an environment $\mathcal{E}$ then $\mathcal{D}$ classically solves T in $\mathcal{E}$.*

COROLLARY 4. *If $\mathcal{D}$ is the weakest failure detector to classically solve a task T in an environment $\mathcal{E}$, then $\mathcal{D}$ is weaker than the weakest failure detector to solve T in $\mathcal{E}$.*

Note that the converse of Proposition 3 is not true. For example, consider the $(\{p_1, p_2\}, 1)$-agreement task (consensus among p_1 and p_2). It is classically solvable in $\mathcal{E}_2$ (assuming at most 2 failures) with the failure detector $\mathcal{D}$ that, for each S-process, outputs q_1 if q_1 is correct and outputs q_2 if q_1 is faulty. But this task is not solvable in $\mathcal{E}_2$ with this failure detector (intuitively, otherwise, if q_1 is crashed we would be able to solve consensus between p_1 and p_2 without a failure detector).

It is easy to see, however, that for *colorless tasks*[6] the two notions of solvability coincide.

PROPOSITION 5. *Let T be a colorless task, T is solvable with failure detector $\mathcal{D}$ in environment $\mathcal{E}$ if and only if T is classically solvable with $\mathcal{D}$ in $\mathcal{E}$. The weakest failure detector to solve T in $\mathcal{E}$ is the weakest failure detector to classically solve T in $\mathcal{E}$.*

Failure detectors for k-set agreement. The failure detector $\neg\Omega_k$ [30] outputs, at every S-process and each time, a set of $(n-k)$ S-processes. $\neg\Omega_k$ guarantees that there is a time after which some correct S-process is never output:

$$\forall F \in \mathcal{E}, \ \forall H \in \neg\Omega_k(F), \ \exists q_i \in correct(F), \ \tau \in \mathbb{T},$$
$$\forall \tau' > \tau, \forall q_j \in correct(F) : q_i \notin H(q_j, \tau').$$

$\neg\Omega_1$ is equivalent to Ω [9] that outputs a S-process such that eventually the same correct S-process is permanently output at all correct processes.

From [19], we know that in every environment $\mathcal{E}$, $\neg\Omega_k$ is the weakest failure detector to classically solve (Π^C, k)-set agreement in $\mathcal{E}$. As (Π^C, k)-set agreement is a colorless task, from Proposition 5 we obtain:

PROPOSITION 6. *In every environment $\mathcal{E}$, $\neg\Omega_k$ is the weakest failure detector to solve (Π^C, k)-set agreement in $\mathcal{E}$.*

3. SOLVING A PUZZLE

Let U be a set of $k + 1$ C-processes. Consider a failure detector $\mathcal{D}$ that *solves k-set agreement* among the processes in U. We show that $\mathcal{D}$ actually solves k-set agreement among *all* n C-processes.

THEOREM 7. *Let U be a set of $(k + 1)$ C-processes, for some $1 \leq k < n$. For every environment $\mathcal{E}$, if a failure detector $\mathcal{D}$ solves (U, k)-set agreement in $\mathcal{E}$ then $\mathcal{D}$ solves (Π^C, k)-set agreement in $\mathcal{E}$.*

PROOF SKETCH. Without loss of generality, assume that $U = \{p_1, \ldots, p_{k+1}\}$. Let $\mathcal{A}$ be a distributed algorithm that solves the (U, k)-set agreement in $\mathcal{E}$ with $\mathcal{D}$.

Let U_x denote $\{p_1, \ldots, p_x\}$, $x = k + 1, \ldots, n$. We observe first that $\mathcal{D}$ can be used to solve $(U_x, x - 1)$-set agreement as follows. C-processes in $\{p_1, \ldots, p_{k+1}\}$ and S-processes $\{q_1, \ldots, q_n\}$ run $\mathcal{A}$ to solve k-set agreement and return the value returned by the algorithm, and processes $p_{k+2}, \ldots, p_x$ simply return their own input values. In total, at most $x - 1$ distinct input values are returned. Let $\mathcal{A}_x$ denote the resulting algorithm.

We proceed now by downward induction to show that for all $x = n$ down to k, $\mathcal{D}$ solves (Π^C, x)-set agreement.

The base case is immediate: $\{p_1, \ldots, p_n\}$ trivially solve (Π^C, n)-set agreement without any failure detector. Now suppose that $\mathcal{D}$ solves (Π^C, x)-set agreement for $x \geq k + 1$. By Proposition 6, $\mathcal{D}$ can be used to implement $\neg\Omega_x$.

Using the generic simulation technique presented in [17, 12] the C-processes, $p_1, \ldots, p_n$, can use $\neg\Omega_x$ to simulate a run of the C-part of $\mathcal{A}_x$ on $p_1, \ldots, p_x$, so that at least one simulated process takes infinitely many steps.[7] The S-part of $\mathcal{A}_x$ is executed by S-processes. In the simulation, each simulating process proposes its input value as an input value in the first step for each simulated process in $\{p_1, \ldots, p_x\}$ (this can be done, since (Π^C, x)-set agreement is a colorless task).

Suppose that the current run is fair, i.e., every correct S-process takes infinitely many steps. Therefore, we simulate a fair run of $\mathcal{A}_x$ and thus eventually some simulated C-process in $\{p_1, \ldots, p_x\}$ decides on one of the input values of the C-processes. Once a simulator finds out that a simulated process decided, it returns the decided value. Thus, eventually, every correct simulator returns. Since all decided values come from a run of $\mathcal{A}_x$, at most $x - 1$ distinct input values can be decided. Hence, $\mathcal{D}$ solves $(\Pi^C, x-1)$-set agreement. $\square$

Therefore, in our framework, we obtain a direct generalization of the fact that for a failure detector, it is as hard to solve consensus in a system of n processes as to solve consensus among each pair of processes [13]. In fact, the separation between C-processes and S-processes, implies a stronger result: solving k-set agreement among one given set of $(k + 1)$ processes is as hard (in the failure detector sense) as solving it among all n processes.

4. GENERALIZING THE PUZZLE

We showed in the previous section that solving k-set agreement among any given set of $k + 1$ C-processes requires an

---

[6]Informally, in a solution of a colorless task [7], a process is free to adopt the input or the output value of any other participating process.

[7]A "black-box" simulation of $\mathcal{A}_x$ using (Π^C, x)-set agreement objects is presented in [17]. In the full version of this paper [12], we give a direct construction using $\neg\Omega_x$.

amount of information about failures that is sufficient to solve k-set agreement among all n C-processes. We show below that this statement can be extended to any task T that cannot be solved $(k + 1)$-concurrently. We present an explicit reduction algorithm that extracts $\neg \Omega_k$ from any failure detector that solves T. Conversely, we show that a task that is k-concurrently solvable can be solved with $\neg \Omega_k$ in any environment.

Finally, we derive a complete characterization of tasks. All tasks that can be solved k-concurrently but not $(k + 1)$-concurrently are equivalent in the sense that they require the same information about failures to be solved ($\neg \Omega_k$).

4.1 Reduction to $\neg \Omega_k$

Let T be any task that cannot be solved $(k+1)$-concurrently. Let $\mathcal{E}$ by any environment. We show that every failure detector $\mathcal{D}$ that solves T in $\mathcal{E}$ can be used to implement $\neg \Omega_k$ in $\mathcal{E}$ as follows.

Let $\mathcal{A}$ be the algorithm that solves T using $\mathcal{D}$ in $\mathcal{E}$. Recall that $\mathcal{A}$ consists of two parts: $\mathcal{A}^C$ is run by the C-processes $p_1, \ldots, p_n$ and $\mathcal{A}^S$ is run by the S-processes $q_1, \ldots, q_n$.

First, we construct a restricted algorithm $\mathcal{A}_{sim}$. In $\mathcal{A}_{sim}$, C-processes $p_1, \ldots, p_n$ perform two parallel tasks. In the first task, C-processes take steps on behalf of $\mathcal{A}^C$. In the second task, they simulate a run of $\mathcal{A}^S$ on S-processes using, instead of $\mathcal{D}$, a *directed acyclic graph* (DAG) G. The DAG G contains a sample of values output by $\mathcal{D}$ in some run R of $\mathcal{A}$ [9, 30]. In $\mathcal{A}_{sim}$, S-processes take null steps.

Informally, each run of $\mathcal{A}_{sim}$ gives "turns" to the S-processes and if G provides enough information about failures to simulate the next step of a S-process q_j, the step of q_j appears in the simulated run of $\mathcal{A}$. To simulate steps of $\mathcal{A}^S$, C-processes employ BG-simulation [5, 7]. This simulation technique enables $k + 1$ processes called *simulators*, to simulate a run of any asynchronous n-processes protocol in which at least $(n - k)$ processes take infinitely many steps. Thus, if k or less participating C-processes take a finite number of steps, the resulting run of $\mathcal{A}_{sim}$ gives infinitely many turns to at least $n - k$ S-processes.

Let F be the failure pattern of the run in which G was constructed. $\mathcal{A}_{sim}$ guarantees that (1) every finite run of $\mathcal{A}_{sim}$ simulates a finite run of $\mathcal{A}$, and (2) if every S-process that is correct in F receives infinitely many turns to take steps, then the simulated run of $\mathcal{A}$ is fair, and (3) if k or less participating C-processes take only finitely many number of steps, then there are at most k S-processes that receive only finitely many turns to take steps in the simulation.

Second we construct a reduction algorithm. In such an algorithm C-processes take null steps. Our reduction algorithm consists of two components (both are run exclusively by the S-processes). In the first component, every S-process q_i queries $\mathcal{D}$, exchanges the returned values with other S-processes and maintains a DAG G_i. In the second component, each q_i locally simulates multiple $(k + 1)$-concurrent runs of $\mathcal{A}_{sim}$ using G_i, going over all combinations of inputs, exploring the runs in the depth-first manner. The simulation continues as long as some simulated C-process does not decide in the produced run of $\mathcal{A}_{sim}$. Since T cannot be solved $(k+1)$-concurrently, there must be a $(k + 1)$-concurrent run of $\mathcal{A}_{sim}$ in which some participating C-process that takes infinitely many steps never decides. The only reason for a C-process not to decide in a run of $\mathcal{A}_{sim}$ is that some correct S-process receives only finitely many turns in the simulation.

But in the simulation, at least $(n - k)$ S-processes receive infinitely many turns. Thus, by outputting the identities of the $(n - k)$ S-processes that were last to receive turns in the current run we emulate the output of $\neg \Omega_k$: we output sets of $n - k$ S-processes that eventually never contain some correct process. A detailed proof is given in Appendix B.

THEOREM 8. *Let T be a task that cannot be solved $(k+1)$-concurrently. For every environment $\mathcal{E}$, for every failure detector $\mathcal{D}$ that solves T in $\mathcal{E}$, $\neg \Omega_k$ is weaker than $\mathcal{D}$ in $\mathcal{E}$.*

4.2 Solving a k-concurrent task with $\neg \Omega_k$

In this section, instead of $\neg \Omega_k$, we use an equivalent failure detector $\overrightarrow{\Omega}_k$ [30]. Basically, $\overrightarrow{\Omega}_k$ gives a k-vector of processes such that, eventually, at least one position of the vector stabilizes on the same correct process at all correct processes.

By definition, if T is k-concurrently solvable, then there exists a restricted algorithm $\mathcal{A}$ that k-concurrently solves T.

First, we define an abstract simulation technique that, with help of $\overrightarrow{\Omega}_k$, allows us to simulate, in a system of n C-processes, runs of any restricted input-less algorithm on k C-processes (the set of non-$\perp$ input values is a singleton). Moreover, in this simulation, if ℓ simulators participate then at most $min(k, \ell)$ processes take infinitely many steps in the simulated execution. Basically, to perform a step for a simulated C-process p_i, the C-processes and the S-processes execute an instance of a leader-based consensus algorithm [10], using the item i of $\overrightarrow{\Omega}_k$ as a leader. The property of $\overrightarrow{\Omega}_k$ ensures that for some i, infinitely many consensus instances terminate.

Second, we define a restricted algorithm $\mathcal{B}$ for k C-processes that simulates a k-concurrent run of $\mathcal{A}$, using BG-simulation [6, 7] . Applying the abstract simulation technique to $\mathcal{B}$, we obtain an algorithm in which every run R simulates a run R_{sim} of $\mathcal{A}$ such that: (1) R_{sim} contains only steps of participating processes of R, (2) the inputs of the participating processes are the same in R and R_{sim}, (2) R_{sim} is k-concurrent, and (3) every C-process that takes infinitely many steps in R takes also infinitely many steps in R_{sim}. So if T is k-concurrent solvable with $\mathcal{A}$, R_{sim} satisfies T, and, consequently, R satisfies T.

To sum up, we have constructed an algorithm that solves T with $\neg \Omega_k$: with the help of S-processes and $\neg \Omega_k$, $p_1, \ldots, p_n$ simulate C-processes $p'_1, .., p'_k$ that, in turn, simulate C-processes $p''_1, .., p''_n$ taking steps in a k-concurrent execution of algorithm $\mathcal{A}$. (A detailed proof is presented in [12].)

THEOREM 9. *Let T be any k-concurrently solvable task. For every environment $\mathcal{E}$, $\neg \Omega_k$ solves T in $\mathcal{E}$.*

4.3 Task hierarchy

From Theorems 8 and 9, we deduce:

THEOREM 10. *Let T be a task that can be solved k-concurrently but not $(k + 1)$-concurrently. In every environment $\mathcal{E}$, $\neg \Omega_k$ is the weakest failure detector to solve T in $\mathcal{E}$.*

As a corollary, all tasks that can be solved k-concurrently but not $(k+1)$-concurrently (e.g., k-set agreement) are equivalent in the sense that they require exactly the same amount of information about failures (captured by $\neg \Omega_k$).

5. CHARACTERIZING THE TASK OF STRONG RENAMING

To illustrate the utility of our framework, we consider the task of (j, ℓ)-*renaming* [3]. The task is defined on n $(n > j)$ processes and assumes that in every run at most j processes participate (at least $n - j$ elements of each vector $I \in \mathcal{I}$ are $\perp$). As an output, every participant obtains a unique *name* in the range $\{1, \ldots, \ell\}$ (every non-$\perp$ element in each $O \in \mathcal{O}$ is a distinct value in $\{1, \ldots, \ell\}$).

In this section, we first focus on (j, j)-renaming (also called *strong* j-renaming). Using Theorem 10, we show that the weakest failure detector for strong j-renaming is Ω (for each $1 < j < n$). In other words, strong renaming is equivalent to consensus.

Note that in strong 2-renaming at most 2 C-processes concurrently execute steps of the algorithm. So the impossibility to achieve strong 2-renaming is equivalent to the impossibility of solving strong 2-renaming 2-concurrently. By a simple reduction to the impossibility of wait-free 2-processes consensus, we show (proofs in Appendix C):

LEMMA 11. *Strong 2-renaming cannot be solved 2-concurrently.*

By reducing to the impossibility of Lemma 11, we get a more general result:

THEOREM 12. *For all $1 < j < n$, strong j-renaming cannot be solved 2-concurrently.*

Proposition 1, Theorem 10, and Theorem 12 imply:

COROLLARY 13. *For all j $(1 < j < n)$, in every environment $\mathcal{E}$, Ω is the weakest failure detector for solving strong j-renaming in $\mathcal{E}$.*

In fact, there exists a generic algorithm (Appendix C.2) that, for all $k = 1, \ldots, j$, solves $(j, j + k - 1)$-renaming in all k-concurrent runs, and thus $(j, j + k - 1)$-renaming can be solved using $\neg\Omega_k$. For some values of k and j, $(j, j + k - 1)$-renaming can be shown to be impossible to solve $(k + 1)$-concurrently, for others determining the maximal level of concurrency of $(j, j + k - 1)$-renaming is still an open question [8].

6. CONCLUSION

This paper introduces a new model of distributed computing with failure detectors that allows processes to cooperate. A process in this model is able to advance the computation of other participating processes in the way used previously only in asynchronous simulations [5, 7, 16, 17], while using failure detectors to overcome asynchronous impossibilities. In our new framework, we derive a complete characterization of distributed tasks, based on their maximal "concurrency level": class k $(1, \ldots, n)$ consists of tasks that can be solved at most k-concurrently, and all tasks in the class are equivalent to k-set agreement.

Our framework does not have to be tied to wait-freedom. We can think of its generalization to any progress condition on computation processes encapsulated, e.g., in an *adversary* [14]. Therefore, we can pose questions of the kind: what is the weakest failure detector to solve a task T in the presence of an adversary $\mathcal{A}$? This gives another dimension to the questions explored in this paper.

7. REFERENCES

[1] Y. Afek and I. Nir. Failure detectors in loosely named systems. In *PODC*, pages 65–74. ACM Press, 2008.

[2] B. Alpern and F. B. Schneider. Defining liveness. *Inf. Process. Lett.*, 21(4):181–185, Oct. 1985.

[3] H. Attiya, A. Bar-Noy, D. Dolev, D. Peleg, and R. Reischuk. Renaming in an asynchronous environment. *Journal of the ACM*, 37(3):524–548, 1990.

[4] H. Attiya and J. Welch. *Distributed Computing. Fundamentals, Simulations, and Advanced Topics.* John Wiley & Sons, 2004.

[5] E. Borowsky and E. Gafni. Generalized FLP impossibility result for t-resilient asynchronous computations. In *STOC*, pages 91–100. ACM Press, 1993.

[6] E. Borowsky and E. Gafni. Immediate atomic snapshots and fast renaming. In *PODC*, pages 41–51. ACM Press, 1993.

[7] E. Borowsky, E. Gafni, N. A. Lynch, and S. Rajsbaum. The BG distributed simulation algorithm. *Distributed Computing*, 14(3):127–146, 2001.

[8] A. Castañeda and S. Rajsbaum. New combinatorial topology bounds for renaming: the lower bound. *Distributed Computing*, 22(5-6):287–301, 2010.

[9] T. D. Chandra, V. Hadzilacos, and S. Toueg. The weakest failure detector for solving consensus. *J. ACM*, 43(4):685–722, July 1996.

[10] T. D. Chandra and S. Toueg. Unreliable failure detectors for reliable distributed systems. *J. ACM*, 43(2):225–267, Mar. 1996.

[11] S. Chaudhuri. More choices allow more faults: Set consensus problems in totally asynchronous systems. *Information and Computation*, 105(1):132–158, 1993.

[12] C. Delporte-Gallet, H. Fauconnier, E. Gafni, and P. Kuznetsov. Wait-freedom with advice. *CoRR*, abs/1109.3056, 2012.

[13] C. Delporte-Gallet, H. Fauconnier, and R. Guerraoui. Tight failure detection bounds on atomic object implementations. *J. ACM*, 57(4), 2010.

[14] C. Delporte-Gallet, H. Fauconnier, R. Guerraoui, and A. Tielmann. The disagreement power of an adversary. *Distributed Computing*, 24(3-4):137–147, 2011.

[15] M. J. Fischer, N. A. Lynch, and M. S. Paterson. Impossibility of distributed consensus with one faulty process. *J. ACM*, 32(2):374–382, Apr. 1985.

[16] E. Gafni. The extended BG-simulation and the characterization of t-resiliency. In *STOC*, pages 85–92. ACM Press, 2009.

[17] E. Gafni and R. Guerraoui. Generalized universality. In *CONCUR 2011 - Concurrency Theory - 22nd International Conference*, pages 17–27, 2011. Full version: http://infoscience.epfl.ch/record/150307.

[18] E. Gafni and P. Kuznetsov. Turning adversaries into friends: Simplified, made constructive, and extended. In *OPODIS*, pages 380–394, 2010.

[19] E. Gafni and P. Kuznetsov. On set consensus numbers. *Distributed Computing*, 24(3-4):149–163, 2011.

[20] E. Gafni and P. Kuznetsov. Relating L-Resilience and Wait-Freedom via Hitting Sets. In *ICDCN*, pages

191–202, 2011. Full version:
http://arxiv.org/abs/1004.4701.

[21] M. Herlihy. Wait-free synchronization. *ACM Trans. Prog. Lang. Syst.*, 13(1):123–149, Jan. 1991.

[22] M. Herlihy and N. Shavit. The topological structure of asynchronous computability. *J. ACM*, 46(2):858–923, 1999.

[23] P. Jayanti and S. Toueg. Every problem has a weakest failure detector. In *PODC*, pages 75–84, 2008.

[24] L. Lamport. Time, clocks, and the ordering of events in a distributed system. *Commun. ACM*, 21(7):558–565, July 1978.

[25] L. Lamport. The Part-Time parliament. *ACM Transactions on Computer Systems*, 16(2):133–169, May 1998.

[26] M. Loui and H. Abu-Amara. Memory requirements for agreement among unreliable asynchronous processes. *Advances in Computing Research*, 4:163–183, 1987.

[27] N. A. Lynch. *Distributed Algorithms*. Morgan Kaufmann, 1996.

[28] M. Raynal. *K-anti-Omega*, August 2007. Rump session at PODC 2007.

[29] M. Saks and F. Zaharoglou. Wait-free k-set agreement is impossible: The topology of public knowledge. *SIAM J. on Computing*, 29:1449–1483, 2000.

[30] P. Zieliński. Anti-*Omega*: the weakest failure detector for set agreement. *Distributed Computing*, 22(5-6):335–348, 2010.

APPENDIX

A. 1-CONCURRENTLY SOLVABLE TASKS

Proposition 1 *Every task is 1-concurrent solvable.*

PROOF. Each C-process p_i executes the following code (1) writes its input, (2) reads the other inputs already written getting a vector I such that $I[i] = \bot$, and (3) reads all the other outputs already written getting a vector O. If O is only composed with $\bot$ then p_i is the first process, it chooses an output according to its input and Δ. Otherwise let I' obtained from I by replacing the i-th item with the input value of p_i. By definition of tasks, if $(I, O) \in \Delta$, there exists a vector O' obtained from O by replacing the i item by a non $\bot$ value such that $(I', O') \in \Delta$. Then p_i decides and outputs value $O'[i]$. Let R be a 1-concurrent run, by an easy induction on the number of participating processes we prove that R satisfies T. $\square$

B. REDUCTION TO ANTI-OMEGA-K

In this section, we show how to derive $\neg\Omega_k$ from any failure detector $\mathcal{D}$ that allows for solving a task that cannot be solved $(k+1)$-concurrently (Section 4.1). The algorithm sketched in Figure 1 describes the steps to be taken by S-processes $q_1, \ldots, q_n$ to emulate $\neg\Omega_k$. First we describe the asynchronous algorithm $\mathcal{A}_{sim}$ used by the C-processes to simulate runs of $\mathcal{A}$, given a sample of the output of $\mathcal{D}$. Then we describe how the S-processes use multiple simulated runs of $\mathcal{A}_{sim}$ to emulate the output of $\neg\Omega_k$.

Asynchronous simulation of $\mathcal{A}$. Following the technique of Chandra et al. [9], we represent a sample of the failure-detector output in the form of a directed acyclic graph (DAG).

The DAG is constructed by the S-processes by periodically querying $\mathcal{D}$ and collecting the output values: every vertex of the DAG has the form $[q_i, d, k]$ which conveys that the k-th query of $\mathcal{D}$ performed by process q_i returned value d. An edge between vertexes $[q_i, d, k]$ and $[q_j, d', k']$ conveys that the k-th query of $\mathcal{D}$ performed by q_i *causally precedes* [24] the k'-th query of $\mathcal{D}$ performed by q_j.

As in [30, 19], any such DAG G can be used to construct a *restricted* algorithm $\mathcal{A}_{sim}$.

In $\mathcal{A}_{sim}$ the C-processes $p_1, \ldots, p_n$ simulates runs of $\mathcal{A}$. The C-processes obtain input values for T and perform two parallel tasks. First, the C-processes take steps on behalf of $\mathcal{A}^C$. Second, they use BG-simulation [6, 7] to simulate a run of $\mathcal{A}^S$ on $q_1, \ldots, q_n$. But to simulate a step of an S-process, instead of $\mathcal{D}$ they use the information provided by G. More precisely, in the simulation, every S-process q_i takes steps as prescribed by $\mathcal{A}^S$, except that when q_i is about to query $\mathcal{D}$, it chooses the next vertex $[q_i, d, k]$ causally succeeding the latest simulated steps of $\mathcal{A}^S$ of all S-processes seen by q_i so far. If G was constructed in a run of $\mathcal{A}$ with failure pattern F, it is guaranteed that (1) every finite run simulated by $\mathcal{A}_{sim}$ is a run of $\mathcal{A}$ with failure pattern F, and (2) if the run of $\mathcal{A}_{sim}$ contains infinitely many simulated steps of processes in $correct(F)$ then the simulated run is a fair run of $\mathcal{A}^S$ with failure pattern F [30, 19].

$\mathcal{A}^S$ does not have inputs. Therefore, the simulation tries to promote all n S-processes (but succeed to take step for an S-process q_i if there is a matching values for q_i in G).

If the simulated run of $\mathcal{A}$ generates an output value for p_i, p_i outputs this value and leaves the computation. Note that since T cannot be solved $(k+1)$-concurrently, and all runs of $\mathcal{A}$ are safe, there must be a $(k+1)$-concurrent (simulated) run of $\mathcal{A}$ in which some participating process takes infinitely many steps without outputting a value.

Extracting $\neg\Omega_k$. Now to derive $\neg\Omega_k$, each S-process in $i \in \{1, \ldots, k\}$ collects the output of $\mathcal{D}$ in G and simulates locally multiple $(k+1)$-concurrent runs of $\mathcal{A}_{sim}$. The runs are simulated in the *corridor-based* depth-first manner [19] that works as follows.

We assume a total order on the subsets $P \subseteq \Pi^C$ so that if $P \subset P'$ then P precedes P' in the order. Each initial state I and each *schedule* σ, a sequence specifying the order in which $p_1, \ldots, p_n$ take steps of $\mathcal{A}_{sim}$, determine a unique run of $\mathcal{A}^S_{sim}$ simulated at process q_i, denoted $\alpha_i(I, \sigma)$.

For a given input vector I and a given permutation π of $p_1, \ldots, p_n$, that describes the order in which the C-processes "arrive" at the computation. Initially, we select a set P of the first $k+1$ processes in π as the participating set. Subsets $P' \subseteq P$ are then explored as "corridors" (line 16), in the deterministic order, from the narrowest (solo) corridors to wider and wider ones. Recursively, we go through simulating all runs in which only C-processes in P' take steps. In the course of simulation, if a participating C-process p_j decides, we replace it with a process that has not yet taken steps in the current computation (line 13). Since we only replace a decided process with a "fresh" non-participant, the participating set keeps the size of $k+1$ or less processes. This procedure is repeated until every C-process decides. Thus, every simulated run is $(k+1)$-concurrent. Once the exploration of the current corridor is complete (the call of *explore* in line 16 returns), we proceed to the next corridor, etc.

```
1   for all I_0, input vectors of T do
        /* All possible inputs for p_1,...,p_n */
2     for all π_0, permutations of p_1,...,p_n do
          /* All possible arrival orders */
3       P_0 := the set of first k + 1 C-processes in π_0
4       explore(I_0, ⊥, P_0, π_0)

5   function explore(I, σ, P, π)
6     ¬Ω_k-output_i := n − k S-processes that
            appear the latest in α_i(I, σ)
            (any n − k S-processes if not possible)
7     if ∃q_j ∈ Π^S: ∀σ' ∈ dom(α_i), ∃σ'', a prefix of σ':
            α_j(I, σ'') is deciding then
          /* If all schedules explored so far
             were found deciding by q_j */
8       adopt q_j's simulation
9     else
10      N := the set of undecided processes in (I, σ)
11      for all p_j ∈ P − N do
            /* For each decided process in P */
12        P := P − {p_j}
13        P := P ∪ {the first process in π that
                  does not appear in σ}
          /* Replace p_j with the next
             non-participant in π */
14        for all P' ⊆ P (in some order
                  consistent with ⊆) do
                  /*For all sub-corridors */
15          for all p_j ∈ P' (in π) do
16            explore(I, σ · p_j, P', π)
```

Figure 1: Deriving $\neg\Omega_k$: code for each S-process q_i.

If, at some point, q_i finds out that another S-process q_j made more progress in the simulation (simulated more runs than q_i), then q_i "adopts" the simulation of q_j (line 8) by adopting q_j's version of the DAG and the map α_j [19].

The output of $\neg\Omega_k$ is evaluated as the set of the ids of the latest $n − k$ processes in $q_1, \ldots, q_n$ that appear in the run of $\mathcal{A}^S_{sim}$ in the currently simulated run of $\mathcal{A}_{sim}$ (line 6). Recall that T cannot be solved $(k + 1)$-concurrently and thus there must exist a $(k + 1)$-concurrent run of $\mathcal{A}_{sim}$ in which some participating live process never decides. Since the only reason for the run of $\mathcal{A}_{sim}$ not to decide is the absence of some correct process in the simulated k-resilient run of $\mathcal{A}^S_{sim}$, and the emulated output eventually never contains some correct process— $\neg\Omega_k$ is emulated. Thus:

Theorem 8 *Let T be a task that cannot be solved $(k + 1)$-concurrently. For every environment $\mathcal{E}$, for every failure detector $\mathcal{D}$ that solves T in $\mathcal{E}$, $\neg\Omega_k$ is weaker than $\mathcal{D}$ in $\mathcal{E}$.*

PROOF SKETCH. Our reduction algorithm works as follows. Every S-process q_i runs two parallel tasks. First, it periodically queries its module of $\mathcal{D}$ and maintains its directed acyclic graph G_i, as in [9, 19]. Second, it uses G_i to locally simulate multiple runs of $\mathcal{A}_{sim}$ and emulates the output of $\neg\Omega_k$. Consider any run of the reduction algorithm. Let F be the failure pattern of that run.

First we observe that every simulated run of $\mathcal{A}_{sim}$ is $(k + 1)$-concurrent. Indeed, initially, exactly $(k + 1)$ C-processes participate and a new participant joins only after some participating C-process decides and departs.

Then we show that the correct S-processes eventually perform the same infinite sequence of recursive invocations of $explore$: $explore(I, \bot, P_0, \pi)$ invokes $explore(I, \sigma_1, P_1, \pi)$, which, in turn, invokes $explore(I, \sigma_2, P_2, \pi)$, etc. (line 14).

Indeed, all S-processes perform the simulations in the same order and since, the task is not $(k + 1)$-concurrently solvable, there must be a never deciding $(k + 1)$-concurrent run of $\mathcal{A}_{sim}$. Since all these P_ℓ are non-empty, there exists ℓ^* and P^* such that $\forall \ell \geq \ell^*$, $P_\ell = P^*$. Since we proceed from narrower corridors to wider ones, P^* is the set of live C-processes that never decide in the "first" never deciding $(k + 1)$-concurrent simulated run with a schedule σ^*.

Now we observe that all simulated runs eventually always extend a prefix $\bar\sigma^*$ of σ^* in which some simulated processes not in P^* already took all their steps in σ^*. Moreover, there is a time after all explored extensions of $\bar\sigma^*$ only contain steps of processes in P^*. By the properties of BG-simulation [5, 7], every S-process that appears only finitely often in the run of $\mathcal{A}_{sim}$ simulated by σ^* (we called these processes *blocked* by σ^*) eventually never appears in all simulated run of $\mathcal{A}$. Let U be the set of S-processes blocked by σ^*. Since the run of $\mathcal{A}_{sim}$ simulated by σ^* is $(k + 1)$-concurrent, processes in U eventually never appear among the last $n − k$ processes in $\alpha(I, \sigma)$ (line 6).

Now we observe that U must contain a correct (in F) S-process. If it is not the case, i.e., U doesn't contain a correct S-process, then the simulated run of $\mathcal{A}$ is fair and thus the simulated run of $\mathcal{A}$ must be deciding.

Thus, eventually some correct S-processes never appear in $\neg\Omega_k$-$output_i$ at every correct S-process q_i—$\neg\Omega_k$ is emulated. □

C. CHARACTERIZING THE TASK OF RENAMING

We show first that (j, j)-renaming (also called *strong j-renaming*) is not 2-concurrently solvable. Then we present a generic algorithm that, for all $k = 1, \ldots, j$, solves $(j, j + k − 1)$-renaming in all k-concurrent run, and thus $(j, j + k − 1)$-renaming can be solved (in EFD) using $\neg\Omega_k$.

C.1 Impossibility of 2-concurrent strong 2-renaming

Lemma 11 *Strong 2-renaming cannot be solved 2-concurrently.*

PROOF. We start with showing that for the special case of $j = 2$, strong renaming cannot be solved 2-concurrently. Suppose, by contradiction, that there exists a (restricted) algorithm $\mathcal{A}$ that solves $(2, 2)$-renaming 2-concurrently. Since we assumed $j < n$, we have at least 3 processes in the system. By the pigeon-hole principle, there exist two processes that decide on the same name $v \in \{1, 2\}$ in their solo runs of $\mathcal{A}$. Without loss of generality, let these processes be p_1 and p_2 and let v be 1.

Now $p1$ and $p2$ can wait-free solve 2-processes consensus as follows. Each process publishes its input and then runs $\mathcal{A}$ until it obtains a name. If the name is 1, the process decides on its input, otherwise it decides on the input of the other process. Since a process in $\{p_1, p_2\}$ obtains 1 as a name in a solo run of $\mathcal{A}$, if 1 is not obtained, then the other process participates in the run of $\mathcal{A}$ and, thus, has previously written its input. Therefore, every decided value was previously proposed. Since every obtained name is distinct, the two processes cannot decide on different values. This conclude

Shared variables: R_ℓ, $\ell = 1, \ldots, n$, initially $\bot$

```
17  Rᵢ := 1
    /* register participation */
18  repeat
19      S := {pₗ | Rₗ ≠ ⊥}
        /*get the current participating set */
20      S' := {pₗ | Rₗ = 1}
    /*get the set of not yet decided participants */
21      min₁ := min(S')
22      if (|S'| = 1 ) then
23          min₂ := min₁
24      else
25          min₂ := min(S' − min(S'))
26      if (|S| = j and (pᵢ = min₁ or pᵢ = min₂)) or
27          (|S| = j − 1 and pᵢ = min₁) then
28              take one more step of A
    /*if among two not decided with smallest ids */
29  until decided
30  Rᵢ := 0
31  return the name decided in A
```

Figure 2: A 1-resilient strong j-renaming algorithm: code for each C-process p_i.

the proof that strong 2-renaming cannot be 2-concurrently solvable. $\square$

Theorem 12 *For all $1 < j < n$, strong j-renaming cannot be solved 2-concurrently.*

PROOF. By Lemma 11, we have already the result for $j = 2$. Suppose, by contradiction, that for some $2 < j < n$, there exists an (restricted) algorithm $\mathcal{A}$ solving strong j-renaming 2-concurrently. As we deal here with 2-concurrent solvability, we are only interested by the C-processes and their algorithms. We use $\mathcal{A}$ to solve strong j-renaming in all 1-*resilient* runs, i.e., runs in which at least $j-1$ C-processes participate and take infinitely many steps. Recall that at most j C-processes participate in every run, so either $j-1$ or j processes take infinitely many steps. In the algorithm (Figure 2), every process registers its participation (line 17) and then periodically checks the current set of participants (line 19). If it finds out that it is among 2 processes with the smallest identities among j participating but not yet processes (line 26), then it starts taking steps $\mathcal{A}$ until the algorithm provides p_i with a new name. Then p_i declares that it has decided (line 30) and departs.

Note that the resulting run of $\mathcal{A}$ is 2-concurrent: either the participating set is of size $j-1$ and only the not yet decided participant with the smallest identity is allowed to take steps of $\mathcal{A}$ solo, or exactly j processes participate and the two not yet decided processes with the smallest identity are allowed to take step concurrently.

Now we observe that the run of $\mathcal{A}$ continues as long as there is at least one not yet decided participant that take steps. Indeed, either the participating set is of size $j-1$ and every participant takes an infinity number of steps (including the not yet decided one with the smallest identity) or exactly j C-processes participate and at least one of the not yet decided processes with the two smallest identity takes an infinity number of steps. Thus, every C-process that keeps taking steps of $\mathcal{A}$ in the resulting 2-concurrent run eventually decides and departs. The set of undecided participants gets smaller by one, and the next C-process with the smallest identity joins the 2-concurrent run of $\mathcal{A}$.

Shared variables:
  R_ℓ, $\ell = 1, \ldots, n$, initially $\bot$

```
32  s := 1
33  repeat forever
34      Rᵢ := (i, s, true)
        /*register new name*/
35      S := {pₗ | Rₗ ≠ ⊥}
        /*collect suggested names*/
36      if ∃(ℓ, sₗ, b) ∈ S: i ≠ ℓ and s = sₗ then
37          r := the rank of i in {ℓ | (ℓ, sₗ, b) ∈ S, b = true}
        /*rank among not yet decided participants*/
38          s := the rth integer not in
            {sₗ : | (ℓ, sₗ, b) ∈ S, i ≠ ℓ}
        /*suggest a new name among not yet suggested*/
39      else
40          Rᵢ := (i, s, false)
41          return s
```

Figure 3: A k-concurrent $(j, j+k-1)$-renaming algorithm: code for each process p_i.

But it is shown in [16] that if all 1-resilient runs of a restricted algorithm $\mathcal{A}$ satisfy strong j-renaming then there is a restricted algorithm to solve strong 2-renaming 2-concurrently, contradicting Lemma 11. $\square$

C.2 Solving renaming

Our algorithm to solve $(j, j+k-1)$-renaming k-concurrently, described in Figure 3 and proved correct in [12], essentially mimics the algorithm of [3, 4] for wait-free $(j, 2j-1)$-renaming.

In the algorithm, every process periodically selects a new name according to the set of the names not yet suggested by other processes and its rank among the set of currently not yet decided participants (lines 37 and 38).

Assuming that at most j processes participate and the run is k-concurrent, the rank of p_i can be at most k and at most $j-1$ names can be suggested by other processes. Therefore, the highest name p_i can suggest in line 34 is $j+k-1$. Moreover, no two processes claim the same s in line 34 and, thus, can output the same name. A complete proof can be found in [12].

THEOREM 14. *[12] For all $1 < k \leq j < m$, $(j, j+k-1)$-renaming can be solved k-concurrently.*

From this result and Theorem 9, we can conclude:

THEOREM 15. *For all $1 < k \leq j < m$, $(j, j+k-1)$-renaming can be solved with $\neg\Omega_k$.*

Universal Constructions that Ensure Disjoint-Access Parallelism and Wait-Freedom

Faith Ellen[*]
University of Toronto
faith@cs.toronto.edu

Panagiota Fatourou[†]
University of Crete &
FORTH-ICS
faturu@csd.uoc.gr

Eleftherios Kosmas[‡]
University of Crete &
FORTH-ICS
ekosmas@csd.uoc.gr

Alessia Milani[§]
University of Bordeaux
milani@labri.fr

Corentin Travers[§]
University of Bordeaux
travers@labri.fr

ABSTRACT

Disjoint-access parallelism and wait-freedom are two desirable properties for implementations of concurrent objects. *Disjoint-access parallelism* guarantees that processes operating on different parts of an implemented object do not interfere with each other by accessing common base objects. Thus, disjoint-access parallel algorithms allow for increased parallelism. *Wait-freedom* guarantees progress for each non-faulty process, even when other processes run at arbitrary speeds or crash.

A *universal construction* provides a general mechanism for obtaining a concurrent implementation of any object from its sequential code. We identify a natural property of universal constructions and prove that there is no universal construction (with this property) that ensures both disjoint-access parallelism and wait-freedom. This impossibility result also holds for transactional memory implementations that require a process to re-execute its transaction if it has been aborted and guarantee each transaction is aborted only a finite number of times.

Our proof is obtained by considering a dynamic object that can grow arbitrarily large during an execution. In

[*]Supported in part by the Natural Science and Engineering Research Council of Canada. Some of the work was done while visiting Labri CNRS-UMR 5800, Bordeaux, France.

[†]Supported by the European Commission under the 7th Framework Program through the TransForm (FP7-MC-ITN-238639), Hi-PEAC2 (FP7-ICT-217068), and ENCORE (FP7-ICT-248647) projects.

[‡]Supported by the project "IRAKLITOS II - University of Crete" of the Operational Programme for Education and Lifelong Learning 2007 - 2013 (E.P.E.D.V.M.) of the NSRF (2007 - 2013), co-funded by the European Union (European Social Fund) and National Resources.

[§]Supported in part by the ANR project DISPLEXITY.

contrast, we present a universal construction which produces concurrent implementations that are both wait-free and disjoint-access parallel, when applied to objects that have a bound on the number of data items accessed by each operation they support.

Categories and Subject Descriptors

E.1 [**Data Structures**]: Distributed data structures; D.1.3 [**Concurrent Programming**]: Distributed programming

General Terms

Algorithms, Theory

Keywords

disjoint-access parallelism, impossibility result, universal construction, wait-freedom

1. INTRODUCTION

Due to the recent proliferation of multicore machines, simplifying concurrent programming has become a necessity, to exploit their computational power. A *universal construction* [21] is a methodology for automatically executing pieces of sequential code in a concurrent environment, while ensuring correctness. Thus, universal constructions provide functionality similar to Transactional Memory (TM) [23]. In particular, universal constructions provide concurrent implementations of any sequential data structure: Each operation supported by the data structure is a piece of code that can be executed.

Many existing universal constructions [1, 12, 16, 17, 20, 21] restrict parallelism by executing each of the desired operations one after the other. We are interested in universal constructions that allow for increased parallelism by being disjoint-access parallel. Roughly speaking, an implementation is *disjoint-access parallel* if two processes that operate on disjoint parts of the simulated state do not interfere with each other, i.e., they do not access the same base objects. Therefore, disjoint-access parallelism allows unrelated operations to progress in parallel. We are also interested in ensuring strong progress guarantees: An implementation is *wait-free* if, in every execution, each (non-faulty) process completes its operation within a finite number of steps, even if other processes may fail (by crashing) or are very slow.

In this paper, we present both positive and negative results. We first identify a natural property of universal constructions and prove that designing universal constructions (with this property) which ensure both disjoint access parallelism and wait-freedom is not possible. We prove this impossibility result by considering a dynamic data structure that can grow arbitrarily large during an execution. Specifically, we consider a singly-linked unsorted list of integers that supports the operations APPEND(L,x), which appends x to the end of the list L, and SEARCH(L,x), which searches the list L for x starting from the first element of the list. We show that, in any implementation resulting from the application of a universal construction to this data structure, there is an execution of SEARCH that never terminates.

Since the publication of the original definition of disjoint-access parallelism [25], many variants have been proposed [2, 9, 19]. These definitions are usually stated in terms of a conflict graph. A *conflict graph* is a graph whose nodes is a set of operations in an execution. An edge exists between each pair of operations that conflict. Two operations *conflict* if they access the same data item. A *data item* is a piece of the sequential data structure that is being simulated. For instance, in the linked list implementation discussed above, a data item may be a list node or a pointer to the first or last node of the list. In a variant of this definition, an edge between conflicting operations exists only if they are concurrent. Two processes *contend* on a base object, if they both access this base object and one of these accesses is a *non-trivial* operation (i.e., it may modify the state of the object). In a disjoint-access parallel implementation, two processes performing operations op and op' can contend on the same base object only if the conflict graph of the minimal execution interval that contains both op and op' satisfies a certain property. Different variants of disjoint-access parallelism use different properties to restrict access to a base object by two processes performing operations. Note that any data structure in which all operations access a common data item, for example, the root of a tree, is trivially disjoint access parallel under all these definitions.

For the proof of the impossibility result, we introduce *feeble disjoint-access parallelism*, which is weaker than all existing disjoint-access parallelism definitions. Thus, our impossibility result still holds if we replace our disjoint-access parallelism definition with any existing definition of disjoint-access parallelism.

Next, we show how this impossibility result can be circumvented, by restricting attention to data structures whose operations can each only access a bounded number of different data items. Specifically, there is a constant b such that any operation accesses at most b different data items when it is applied sequentially to the data structure, starting from any (legal) state. Stacks and queues are examples of dynamic data structures that have this property. We present a universal construction that ensures wait-freedom and disjoint-access parallelism for such data structures. The resulting concurrent implementations are linearizable [24] and satisfy a much stronger disjoint-access parallelism property than we used to prove the impossibility result.

Disjoint-access parallelism and its variants were originally formalized in the context of fixed size data structures, or when the data items that each operation accesses are known when the operation starts its execution. Dealing with these cases is much simpler than considering an arbitrary dynamic data structure where the set of data items accessed by an operation may depend on the operations that have been previously executed and on the operations that are performed concurrently.

The universal construction presented in this paper is the first that provably ensures both wait-freedom and disjoint-access parallelism for dynamic data structures in which each operation accesses a bounded number of data items. For other dynamic data structures, our universal construction still ensures linearizability and disjoint-access parallelism. Instead of wait-freedom, it ensures that progress is *non-blocking*. This guarantees that, in every execution, from every (legal) state, *some* process finishes its operation within a finite number of steps.

2. RELATED WORK

Some impossibility results, related to ours, have been provided for transactional memory algorithms. Transactional Memory (TM) [23] is a mechanism that allows a programmer of a sequential program to identify those parts of the sequential code that require synchronization as *transactions*. Thus, a transaction includes a sequence of operations on data items. When the transaction is being executed in a concurrent environment, these data items can be accessed by several processes simultaneously. If the transaction commits, all its changes become visible to other transactions and they appear as if they all take place at one point in time during the execution of the transaction. Otherwise, the transaction can abort and none of its changes are applied to the data items.

Universal constructions and transactional memory algorithms are closely related. They both have the same goal of simplifying parallel programming by providing mechanisms to efficiently execute sequential code in a concurrent environment. A transactional memory algorithm informs the external environment when a transaction is aborted, so it can choose whether or not to re-execute the transaction. A call to a universal construction returns only when the simulated code has been successfully applied to the simulated data structure. This is the main difference between these two paradigms. However, it is common behavior of an external environment to restart an aborted transaction until it eventually commits. Moreover, meaningful progress conditions [11, 31] in transactional memory require that the number of times each transaction aborts is finite. This property is similar to the *wait-freedom* property for universal constructions. In a recent paper [11], this property is called *local progress*. Our impossibility result applies to transactional memory algorithms that satisfy this progress property. Disjoint-access parallelism is defined for transactions in the same way as for universal constructions.

Strict disjoint-access parallelism [19] requires that an edge exists between two operations (or transactions) in the conflict graph of the minimal execution interval that contains both operations (transactions) if the processes performing these operations (transactions) contend on a base object. A TM algorithm is *obstruction-free* if a transaction can be aborted only when contention is encountered during the course of its execution. In [19], Guerraoui and Kapalka proved that no obstruction-free TM can be strictly disjoint access parallel. Obstruction-freedom is a weaker progress property than wait-freedom, so their impossibility result also applies to wait-free implementations (or implementations that ensure local progress). However, it only applies to this strict variant of disjoint-access parallelism, while we consider a much weaker disjoint-access parallelism definition. It is worth-pointing out that several obstruction-free TM algorithms [18, 22, 26, 29] satisfy a weaker version of disjoint-access parallelism than this strict variant. It is unclear whether helping, which is the major technique for achieving strong progress guarantees, can be (easily) achieved assuming strict disjoint-access parallelism. For instance, consider a scenario where transaction T_1 accesses data items x and y, transaction T_2 accesses x, and T_3 accesses y. Since T_2 and T_3 access disjoint data items, strict disjoint-access parallelism says that they cannot contend on any common base objects. In particular, this limits the help that each of them can provide to T_1.

Bushkov *et al.* [11] prove that no TM algorithm (whether or not it is disjoint-access parallel) can ensure local progress. However, they prove this impossibility result under the assumption that the TM algorithm does not have access to the code of each transaction (and, as mentioned in their introduction, their impossibility result does not hold without this restriction). In their model, the TM algorithm allows the external environment to invoke actions for reading a data item, writing a data item, starting a transaction, and trying to commit or abort it. The TM algorithm is only aware of the sequence of invocations that have been performed. Thus, a transaction can be helped only after the TM algorithm knows the entire set of data items that the transaction should modify. However, there are TM algorithms that do allow threads to have access to the code of transactions. For instance, RobuSTM [31] is a TM algorithm in which the code of a transaction is made available to threads so that they can help one another to ensure strong progress guarantees.

Proving impossibility results in a model in which the TM algorithm does not have access to the code of transactions is usually done by considering certain high-level histories that contain only invocations and responses of high-level operations on data items (and not on the base objects that are used to implement these data items in a concurrent environment). Our model gives the universal construction access to the code of an invoked operation. Consequently, to prove our impossibility result we had to work with low-level histories, containing steps on base objects, which is technically more difficult.

Attiya *et al.* [9] proved that there is no disjoint-access parallel TM algorithm where read-only transactions are wait-free and *invisible* (i.e., they do not apply non-trivial operations on base objects). This impossibility result is proved for the variant of disjoint-access parallelism where processes executing two operations (transactions) concurrently contend on a base object only if there is a path between the two operations (transactions) in the conflict graph. We prove our lower bound for a weaker definition of disjoint-access parallelism and it applies even for implementations with visible reads. We remark that the impossibility result in [9] does not contradict our algorithm, since our implementation employs *visible* reads.

In [27], the concept of *MV-permissiveness* was introduced. A TM algorithm satisfies this property if a transaction aborts only when it is an update transaction that conflicts with another update transaction. An *update transaction* contains updates to data items. The paper [27] proved that

no transactional memory algorithm satisfies both disjoint access parallelism (specifically, the variant of disjoint-access parallelism presented in [9]) and MV-permissiveness. However, the paper assumes that the TM algorithm does not have access to the code of transactions and is based on the requirement that the code for creating, reading, or writing data items terminates within a finite number of steps. This lower bound can be beaten if this requirement is violated. Attiya and Hillel [8] presented a strict disjoint-access parallel lock-based TM algorithm that satisfies MV-permissiveness.

More constraining versions of disjoint-access parallelism are used when designing algorithms [5, 6, 25]. Specifically, two operations are allowed to access the same base object if they are connected by a path of length at most d in the conflict graph [2, 5, 6]. This version of disjoint-access parallelism is known as the *d-local contention property* [2, 5, 6]. The first wait-free disjoint-access parallel implementations [25, 30] had $O(n)$-local contention, where n is the number of processes in the system, and assumed that each operation accesses a fixed set of data items. Afek *et al.* [2] presented a wait-free, disjoint-access parallel universal construction that has $O(k + log^* n)$-local contention, provided that each operation accesses at most k pre-determined memory locations. It relies heavily on knowledge of k. This work extends the work of Attiya and Dagan [5], who considered operations on pairs of locations, i.e. where $k = 2$. Afek *et al.* [2] leave as an open question the problem of finding highly concurrent wait-free implementations of data structures that support operations with no bounds on the number of data items they access. In this paper, we prove that, in general, there are no solutions unless we relax some of these properties.

Attiya and Hillel [7] provide a k-local non-blocking implementation of k-read-modify-write objects. The algorithm assumes that double-compare-and-swap (DCAS) primitives are available. A DCAS atomically executes CAS on two memory words. Combining the algorithm in [7] and the non-blocking implementation of DCAS by Attiya and Dagan [5] results in a $O(k + log^* n)$-local non-blocking implementation of a k-read-modify-write object that only relies on single-word CAS primitives. Their algorithm can be adapted to work for operations whose data set is defined on the fly, but it only ensures that progress is non-blocking.

A number of wait-free universal constructions [1, 16, 17, 20, 21] work by copying the entire data structure locally, applying the active operations sequentially on their local copy, and then changing a shared pointer to point to this copy. The resulting algorithms are not disjoint access parallel, unless vacuously so.

Anderson and Moir [3] show how to implement a k-word atomic CAS using LL/SC. To ensure wait-freedom, a process may help other processes after its operation has been completed, as well as during its execution. They employ their k-word CAS implementation to get a universal construction that produces wait-free implementations of multi-object operations. Both the k-word CAS implementation and the universal construction allow operations on different data items to proceed in parallel. However, they are not disjoint-access parallel, because some operations contend on the same base objects even if there are no (direct or transitive) conflicts between them. The helping technique that is employed by our algorithm combines and extends the helping techniques presented in [3] to achieve both wait-freedom and disjoint-access parallelism.

Anderson and Moir [4] presented another universal construction that uses indirection to avoid copying the entire data structure. They store the data structure in an array which is divided into a set of consecutive data blocks. Those blocks are addressed by a set of pointers, all stored in one LL/SC object. An adaptive version of this algorithm is presented in [16]. An algorithm is *adaptive* if its step complexity depends on the maximum number of active processes at each point in time, rather than on the total number n of processes in the system. Neither of these universal constructions is disjoint-access parallel.

Barnes [10] presented a disjoint-access parallel universal construction, but the algorithms that result from this universal construction are only non-blocking. In Barnes' algorithm, a process p executing an operation op first simulates the execution of op locally, using a local dictionary where it stores the data items accessed during the simulation of op and their new values. Once p completes the local simulation of op, it tries to lock the data items stored in its dictionary. The data items are locked in a specific order to avoid deadlocks. Then, p applies the modifications of op to shared memory and releases the locks. A process that requires a lock which is not free, releases the locks it holds, helps the process that owns the lock to finish the operation it executes, and then re-starts its execution. To enable this helping mechanism, a process shares its dictionary immediately prior to its locking phase. The lock-free TM algorithm presented in [18] works in a similar way.

As in Barnes' algorithm, a process executing an operation op in our algorithm, first locally simulates op using a local dictionary, and then it tries to apply the changes. However, in our algorithm, a conflict between two operations can be detected during the simulation phase, so helping may occur at an earlier stage of op's execution. More advanced helping techniques are required to ensure both wait-freedom and disjoint-access parallelism.

Chuong *et al.* [12] presented a wait-free version of Barnes' algorithm that is not disjoint-access parallel and applies operations to the data structure one at a time. Their algorithm is *transaction-friendly*, i.e., it allows operations to be aborted. Helping in this algorithm is simpler than in our algorithm. Moreover, the conflict detection and resolution mechanisms employed by our algorithm are more advanced to ensure disjoint-access parallelism. The presentation of the pseudocode of our algorithm follows [12].

The first software transactional memory algorithm [28] was disjoint-access parallel, but it is only non-blocking and is restricted to transactions that access a pre-determined set of memory locations. There are other TM algorithms [14, 18, 22, 26, 29] without this restriction that are disjoint-access parallel. However, all of them satisfy weaker progress properties than wait-freedom. TL [14] ensures strict disjoint access parallelism, but it is blocking.

A hybrid approach between transactional memory and universal constructions has been presented by Crain *et al.* [13]. Their universal construction takes, as input, sequential code that has been appropriately annotated for processing by a TM algorithm. Each transaction is repeatedly invoked until it commits. They use a linked list to store all committed transactions. A process helping a transaction to complete scans the list to determine whether the transaction has already completed. Thus, their implementation is not disjoint-access parallel. It also assumes that no failures occur.

3. PRELIMINARIES

A *data structure* is a sequential implementation of an abstract data type. In particular, it provides a representation for the objects specified by the abstract data type and the (sequential) code for each of the operations it supports. As an example, we will consider an unsorted singly-linked list of integers that supports the operations APPEND(v), which appends the element v to the end of the list (by accessing a pointer *end* that points to the last element in the list, appending a node containing v to that element, and updating the pointer to point to the newly appended node), and SEARCH(v), which searches the list for v starting from the first element of the list.

A *data item* is a piece of the representation of an object implemented by the data structure. In our example, the data items are the nodes of the singly-linked list and the pointers *first* and *last* that point to the first and the last element of the list, respectively. The *state* of a data structure consists of the collection of data items in the representation and a set of values, one for each of the data items. A *static* data item is a data item that exists in the initial state. In our example, the pointers *first* and *last* are static data items. When the data structure is dynamic, the data items accessed by an instance of an operation (in a sequential execution α) may depend on the instances of operations that have been performed before it in α. For example, the set of nodes accessed by an instance of SEARCH depends on the sequence of nodes that have been previously appended to the list.

An operation of a data structure is *value oblivious* if, in every (sequential) execution, the set of data items that each instance of this operation accesses in any sequence of consecutive instances of this operation does not depend on the values of the input parameters of these instances. In our example, APPEND is a value oblivious operation, but SEARCH is not.

We consider an *asynchronous shared-memory* system with n processes $p_1, \ldots, p_n$ that communicate by accessing shared objects, such as *registers* and LL/SC objects. A register R stores a value from some set and supports the operations read(R), which returns the value of R, and write(R, v), which writes the value v in R. An LL/SC *object* R stores a value from some set and supports the operations LL, which returns the current value of R, and SC. By executing SC(R, v), a process p_i attempts to set the value of R to v. This update occurs only if no process has changed the value of R (by executing SC) since p_i last executed LL(R). If the update occurs, true is returned and we say the SC is successful; otherwise, the value of R does not change and false is returned.

A *universal construction* provides a general mechanism to automatically execute pieces of sequential code in a concurrent environment. It supports a single operation, called PERFORM, which takes as parameters a piece of sequential code and a list of input arguments for this code. The algorithm that implements PERFORM applies a sequence of operations on shared objects provided by the system. We use the term *base objects* to refer to these objects and we call the operations on them *primitives*. A primitive is *non-trivial* if it may change the value of the base object; otherwise, the

118

primitive is called *trivial*. To avoid ambiguities and to simplify the exposition, we require that all data items in the sequential code are only accessed via the instruction CREATEDI, READDI, and WRITEDI, which create a new data item, read (any part of) the data item, and write to (any part of) the data item, respectively.

A *configuration* provides a global view of the system at some point in time. In an *initial configuration*, each process is in its initial state and each base object has its initial value. A *step* consists of a primitive applied to a base object by a process and may also contain local computation by that process. An *execution* is a (finite or infinite) sequence $C_i, \phi_i, C_{i+1}, \phi_{i+1}, \ldots, \phi_{j-1}, C_j$ of alternating configurations (C_k) and steps (ϕ_k), where the application of ϕ_k to configuration C_k results in configuration C_{k+1}, for each $i \le k < j$. An execution α is *indistinguishable* from another execution α' for some processes, if each of these processes takes the same steps in α and α', and each of these steps has the same response in α and α'. An execution is *solo* if all its steps are taken by the same process.

From this point on, for simplicity, we use the term operation to refer to an instance of an operation. The *execution interval* of an operation starts with the first step of the corresponding call to PERFORM and terminates when that call returns. Two operations *overlap* if the call to PERFORM for one of them occurs during the execution interval of the other. If a process has invoked PERFORM for an operation that has not yet returned, we say that the operation is *active*. A process can have at most one active operation in any configuration. A configuration is *quiescent* if no operation is active in the configuration.

Let α be any execution. We assume that processes may experience *crash failures*. If a process p does not fail in α, we say that p is *correct* in α. *Linearizability* [24] ensures that, for every completed operation in α and some of the uncompleted operations, there is some point within the execution interval of the operation called its *linearization point*, such that the response returned by the operation in α is the same as the response it would return if all these operations were executed serially in the order determined by their linearization points. When this holds, we say that the responses of the operations are *consistent*. An implementation is *linearizable* if all its executions are linearizable. An implementation is *wait-free* [21] if, in every execution, each correct process completes each operation it performs within a finite number of steps.

Since we consider linearizable universal constructions, every quiescent configuration of an execution of a universal construction applied to a sequential data structure defines a state. This is the state of the data structure resulting from applying each operation linearized prior to this configuration, in order, starting from the initial state of the data structure.

Two operations *contend* on a base object b if they both apply a primitive to b and at least one of these primitives is non-trivial. We are now ready to present the definition of disjoint-access parallelism that we use to prove our impossibility result. It is weaker than all the variants discussed in Section 2.

DEFINITION 1. (**Feeble Disjoint-Access Parallelism**). *An implementation resulting from a universal construction applied to a (sequential) data structure is* feebly disjoint-access parallel *if, for every solo execution α_1 of an operation op_1 and every solo execution α_2 of an operation op_2, both starting from the same quiescent configuration C, if the sequential code of op_1 and op_2 access disjoint sets of data items when each is executed starting from the state of the data structure represented by configuration C, then α_1 and α_2 contend on no base objects. A universal construction is* feebly disjoint-access parallel *if all implementations resulting from it are feebly disjoint-access parallel.*

We continue with definitions that are needed to define the version of disjoint-access parallelism ensured by our algorithm. Fix any execution $\alpha = C_0, \phi_0, C_1, \phi_1, \ldots$, produced by a linearizable universal construction U. Then there is some linearization of the completed operations in α and a subset of the uncompleted operations in α such that the responses of all these operations are consistent. Let op be any one of these operations, let I_{op} be its execution interval, let C_i denote the first configuration of I_{op}, and let C_j be the first configuration at which op has been linearized. Since each process has at most one uncompleted operation in α and each operation is linearized within its execution interval, the set of operations linearized before C_i is finite. For $i \le k < j$, let S_k denote the state of the data structure which results from applying each operation linearized in α prior to configuration C_k, in order, starting from the initial state of the data structure. Define $DS(op, \alpha)$, the data set of op in α, to be the set of all data items accessed by op when executed by itself starting from S_k, for $i \le k < j$.

The *conflict graph* of an execution interval I of α is an undirected graph, where vertices represent operations whose execution intervals overlap with I and an edge connects two operations op and op' if and only if $DS(op, \alpha) \cap DS(op', \alpha) \ne \emptyset$. The following variant of disjoint-access parallelism is ensured by our algorithm.

DEFINITION 2. (**Disjoint-Access Parallelism**). *An implementation resulting from a universal construction applied to a (sequential) data structure is* disjoint-access parallel *if, for every execution containing a process executing* PERFORM(op_1) *and a process executing* PERFORM(op_2) *that contend on some base object, there is a path between op_1 and op_2 in the conflict graph of the minimal execution interval containing op_1 and op_2.*

The original definition of disjoint-access parallelism in [25] differs from Definition 2 in that it does not allow two operations op_1 and op_2 to read the same base object even if there is no path between op_1 and op_2 in the conflict graph of the minimal execution interval that contains them. T Also, that definition imposes a bound on the step complexity of disjoint-access parallel algorithms. Our definition is a slightly stronger version of the disjoint-access parallel variant defined in [9] in the context of transactional memory. This definition allows two operations to contend, (but not *concurrently* contend) on the same base object if there is no path connecting them in the conflict graph. This definition makes the lower bound proved there stronger, whereas our definition makes the design of an algorithm (which is our goal) more difficult. Our definition is obviously weaker than strict disjoint-access parallelism [19], since our definition allows two processes to contend even if the data sets of the operations they are executing are disjoint.

4. IMPOSSIBILITY RESULT

To prove the impossibility of a wait-free universal construction with feeble disjoint-access parallelism, we consider an implementation resulting from the application of an arbitrary feebly disjoint-access parallel universal construction to the singly-linked list discussed in Section 3. We show that there is an execution in which an instance of SEARCH does not terminate. The idea is that, as the process p performing this instance proceeds through the list, another process, q, is continually appending new elements with different values. If q performs each instance of APPEND before p gets too close to the end of the list, disjoint-access parallelism prevents q from helping p. This is because q's knowledge is consistent with the possibility that p's instance of SEARCH could terminate successfully before it accesses a data item accessed by q's current instance of APPEND. Also, process p cannot determine which nodes were appended by process q after it started the SEARCH. The proof relies on the following natural assumption about universal constructions. Roughly speaking, it formalizes that the operations of the concurrent implementation resulting from applying a universal construction to a sequential data structure should simulate the behavior of the operations of the sequential data structure.

ASSUMPTION 3 (VALUE-OBLIVIOUSNESS ASSUMPTION). *If an operation of a data structure is value oblivious, then, in any implementation resulting from the application of a universal construction to this data structure, the sets of base objects read from and written to during any solo execution of a sequence of consecutive instances of this operation starting from a quiescent configuration do not depend on the values of the input parameters.*

We consider executions of the implementation of a singly-linked list L in which process p performs a single instance of SEARCH$(L, 0)$ and process q performs instances of APPEND(L, i), for $i \geq 1$, and possibly one instance of APPEND$(L, 0)$. We may assume the implementation is deterministic: If it is randomized, we fix a sequence of coin tosses for each process and only consider executions using these coin tosses.

Let C_0 be the initial configuration in which L is empty. Let α denote the infinite solo execution by q starting from C_0 in which q performs APPEND(L, i) for all positive integers i, in increasing order. For $i \geq 1$, let C_i be the configuration obtained when process q performs APPEND(L, i) starting from configuration C_{i-1}. Let α_i denote the sequence of steps performed in this execution. Let $B(i)$ denote the set of base objects written to by the steps in α_i and let $A(i)$ denote the set of base objects these steps read from but do not write to. Notice that the sets $A(i)$ and $B(i)$ partition the set of base objects accessed in α_i. In configuration C_i, the list L consists of i nodes, with values $1, \ldots, i$ in increasing order.

For $1 < j \leq i$, let C_i^j be the configuration obtained from configuration C_0 when process q performs the first i operations of execution α, except that the j'th operation, APPEND(L, j), is replaced by APPEND$(L, 0)$; namely, when q performs APPEND$(L, 1)$, ..., APPEND$(L, j-1)$, APPEND$(L, 0)$, APPEND$(L, j+1)$, ..., APPEND(L, i). Since APPEND is value oblivious, the same set of base objects are written to during the executions leading to configurations C_i and C_i^j. Only base objects in $\cup\{B(k) \mid j \leq k \leq i\}$ can have different values in C_i and C_i^j.

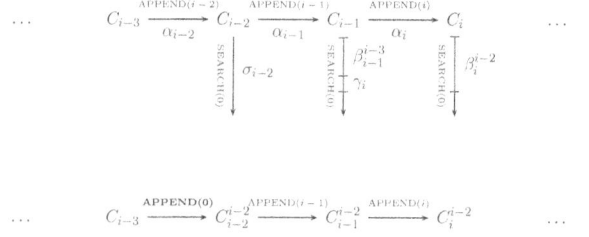

Figure 1: Configurations and Sequences of Steps used in the Proof

For $i \geq 3$, let σ_i be the steps of the solo execution of SEARCH$(L, 0)$ by p starting from configuration C_i. For $1 < j \leq i$, let β_i^j be the longest prefix of σ_i in which p does not access any base object in $\cup\{B(k) \mid k \geq j\}$ and does not write to any base object in $\cup\{A(k) \mid k \geq j\}$

LEMMA 4. *For $i \geq 3$ and $1 < j \leq i$, $\beta_i^j = \beta_{i+1}^j$ and β_{i+1}^{i-1} is a prefix of β_{i+2}^i.*

PROOF. Only base objects in $B(i+1)$ have different values in configurations C_i and C_{i+1}. Since β_i^j and β_{i+1}^j do not access any base objects in $B(i+1)$, it follows from their definitions that $\beta_i^j = \beta_{i+1}^j$. In particular, $\beta_{i+2}^i = \beta_{i+1}^i$, which, by definition contains β_{i+1}^{i-1} as a prefix. $\square$

For $i \geq 3$, let γ_{i+2} be the (possibly empty) suffix of β_{i+2}^i such that $\beta_{i+1}^{i-1}\gamma_{i+2} = \beta_{i+2}^i$. Figure 1 illustrates these definitions.

Let $\alpha' = \alpha_1\alpha_2\alpha_3\alpha_4\beta_4^2\alpha_5\gamma_5\alpha_6\gamma_6\cdots$. We show that this infinite sequence of steps gives rise to an infinite valid execution starting from C_0 in which there is an instance of SEARCH$(L, 0)$ that never terminates. The first steps of this execution are illustrated in Figure 2.

Since β_4^2 does not write to any base objects accessed in $\alpha_2\alpha_3\cdots$ and, for $i \geq 4$, $\beta_{i+1}^{i-1} = \beta_i^{i-2}\gamma_{i+1}$ does not write to any base object accessed in $\alpha_{i-1}\alpha_i\cdots$, the executions arising from α and α' starting from C_0 are indistinguishable to process q. Furthermore, since β_{i+1}^{i-1} and, hence, γ_{i+1} does not access any base object written to by $\alpha_{i-1}\alpha_i\cdots$, it follows that $\alpha_1\alpha_2\alpha_3\alpha_4\beta_4^2\alpha_5\gamma_5\cdots\alpha_j\gamma_j$ and $\alpha_1\alpha_2\alpha_3\alpha_4\cdots\alpha_j\beta_j^{j-2}$ are indistinguishable to process p for all $j \geq 4$. Thus α' is a valid execution.

Next, for each $i \geq 4$, we prove that there exists $j > i$ such that γ_j is nonempty. By the value obliviousness assumption, only base objects in $B(i-2) \cup B(i-1) \cup B(i)$ can have different values in C_i and C_i^{i-2}. Since β_i^{i-2} does not access any of these base objects, β_i^{i-2} is also a prefix of SEARCH$(L, 0)$ starting from C_i^{i-2}. Since SEARCH$(L, 0)$ starting from C_i^{i-2} is successful, but starting from C_i is unsuccessful, SEARCH$(L, 0)$ is not completed after β_i^{i-2}. Therefore β_i^{i-2} is a proper prefix of σ_i. Let b be the base object accessed in the first step following β_i^{i-2} in σ_i. For $j \geq i+1$, only base objects in $\cup\{B(k) \mid i+1 \leq k \leq j\}$ can have different values in C_i and C_j. Therefore the first step following β_i^{i-2} in σ_j is the same as the first step following β_i^{i-2} in σ_i.

To obtain a contradiction, suppose that $\beta_i^{i-2} = \beta_{i+3}^{i+1}$. Then b is the base object accessed in the first step following

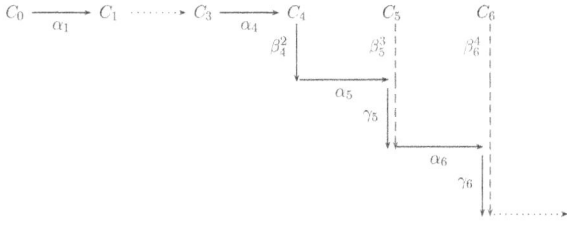

Figure 2: An Infinite Execution with a Non-terminating Search Operation

β_{i+3}^{i+1} in σ_{i+3}. By definition of β_{i+3}^{i+1}, there is some $\ell \geq i + 1$ such that the first step following β_{i+3}^{i+1} in σ_{i+3} is either an access to $b \in B(\ell)$ or a write to $b \in A(\ell)$.

Let S denote the state of the data structure in configuration $C_{\ell-1}^{\ell-3}$. In state S, the list has $\ell - 1$ nodes and the third last node has value 0. Thus, the set of data items accessed by SEARCH$(L, 0)$ starting from state S consists of $L.first$ and the first $\ell - 3$ nodes of the list. This is disjoint from the set of data items accessed by APPEND(L, ℓ) starting from state S, which consists of $L.last$, the last node of the list, and the newly appended node. Hence, by feeble disjoint access parallelism, the solo executions of APPEND(L, ℓ) and SEARCH$(L, 0)$ starting from $C_{\ell-1}^{\ell-3}$ contend on no base objects.

By the value obliviousness assumption, $B(\ell)$ is the set of base objects written to in the solo execution of APPEND(L, ℓ) starting from $C_{\ell-1}^{\ell-3}$ and $A(\ell)$ is the set of base objects read from, but not written to in that execution.

By the value obliviousness assumption, only base objects in $B(\ell-3) \cup B(\ell-2) \cup B(\ell-1)$ can have different values in $C_{\ell-1}$ and $C_{\ell-1}^{\ell-3}$. Since β_i^{i-2} does not access any of these base objects, β_i^{i-2} is also a prefix of SEARCH$(L, 0)$ starting from $C_{\ell-1}^{\ell-3}$ and the first step following β_i^{i-2} in this execution is the same as the first step following β_i^{i-2} in σ_i. Recall that this is either an access to $b \in B(\ell)$ or a write to $b \in A(\ell)$. Thus, the solo executions of APPEND(L, ℓ) and SEARCH$(L, 0)$ starting from $C_{\ell-1}^{\ell-3}$ contend on b. This is a contradiction. Hence, $\beta_i^{i-2} \neq \beta_{i+3}^{i+1}$ and it follows that at least one of γ_{i+1}, γ_{i+2}, and γ_{i+3} is nonempty.

Therefore γ_j is nonempty for infinitely many numbers j and, in the infinite execution α', process p never completes its operation SEARCH$(L, 0)$, despite taking an infinite number of steps. Hence, the implementation is not wait-free and we have proved the following result:

THEOREM 5. *No feebly disjoint-access parallel universal construction is wait-free.*

5. THE DAP-UC ALGORITHM

To execute an operation op, a process p locally simulates the execution of op's instructions without modifying the shared representation of the simulated state. This part of the execution is the simulation phase of op. Specifically, each time p accesses a data item while simulating op, it stores a copy in a local dictionary. All subsequent accesses by p to this data item (during the same simulation phase of op) are performed on this local copy. Once all instructions of op have been locally simulated, op enters its modifying phase.

```
1   type varrec
2       value val
3       ptr to oprec A[1..n]
4   type statrec
5       { ⟨simulating⟩,
6         ⟨restart, ptr to oprec restartedby⟩,
7         ⟨modifying, ptr to dictionary of dictrec changes,
8                                      value output⟩
9         ⟨done⟩
10      } status
11  type oprec
12      code program
13      process id owner
14      value input
15      value output
16      ptr to statrec status
17      ptr to oprec tohelp[1..n]
18  type dictrec
19      ptr to varrec key
20      value newval
```

Figure 3: Type definitions

At that time, one of the local dictionaries of the helpers of op becomes shared. All helpers of op then use this dictionary and apply the modifications listed in it. In this way, all helpers of op apply the same updates for op, and consistency is guaranteed.

The algorithm maintains a record for each data item x. The first time op accesses x, it makes an announcement by writing appropriate information in x's record. It also detects conflicts with other operations that are accessing x by reading this record. So, conflicts are detected without violating disjoint access parallelism. The algorithm uses a simple priority scheme, based on the process identifiers of the owners of the operations, to resolve conflicts among processes. When an operation op determines a conflict with an operation op' of higher priority, op helps op' to complete before it continues its execution. Otherwise, op causes op' to restart and the owner of op will help op' to complete once it finishes with the execution of op, before it starts the execution of a new operation. The algorithm also ensures that before op' restarts its simulation phase, it will help op to complete. These actions guarantee that processes never starve.

We continue with the details of the algorithm. The algorithm maintains a record of type oprec (lines 11-17) that stores information for each initiated operation. When a process p wants to execute an operation op, it starts by creating a new oprec for op and initializing it appropriately (line 22). In particular, this record provides a pointer to the code of op, its input parameters, its output, the status of op, and an array indicating whether op should help other operations after its completion and before it returns. We call p the owner of op. To execute op, p calls HELP (line 23). To ensure wait-freedom, before op returns, it helps all other operations listed in the tohelp array of its oprec record (lines 24-25). These are operations with which op had a conflict during the course of its execution, so disjoint-access parallelism is not violated. The algorithm also maintains a record of type varrec (lines 1-3) for each data item x, This record contains a val field, which is an LL/SC object that stores the value of x, and an array A of n LL/SC objects, indexed by process identifiers, which stores oprec records of operations that are accessing x. This array is used by operations to

```
21  value PERFORM(prog, input) by process p:
22      opptr := pointer to a new oprec record
        opptr → program := prog, opptr → input := input, opptr → output := ⊥
        opptr → owner := p, opptr → status := simulating, opptr → tophelp[1..n] := [nil, . . . , nil]
23      HELP(opptr)                                                                                        /* p helps its own operation */
24      for p' := 1 to n excluding p do                                     /* p helps operations that have been restarted by its operation op */
25          if (opptr → tohelp[p'] ≠ nil) then HELP(opptr → tohelp[p'])
26      return(opptr → output)

27  HELP(opptr) by process p:
28      opstatus := LL(opptr → status)
29      while (opstatus ≠ done)
30          if opstatus = ⟨restart, opptr'⟩ then                                                          /* op' has restarted op */
31              HELP(opptr')                                                                               /* first help op' */
32              SC(opptr → status, ⟨simulating⟩)                                           /* try to change the status of op back to simulating */
33              opstatus := LL(opptr → status)
34          if opstatus = ⟨simulating⟩ then                                                               /* start a new simulation phase */
35              dict := pointer to a new empty dictionary of dictrec records
                                                                                                           /* to store the values of the data items */
36              ins := the first instruction in opptr → program
37              while ins ≠ return(v)                                                                       /* simulate instruction ins of op */
38                  if ins is (WRITEDI(x, v) or READDI(x)) and (there is no dictrec with key x in dict)
                    then                                                                                    /* first access of x by this attempt of op */
39                      ANNOUNCE(opptr, x)                                                                  /* announce that op is accessing x */
40                      CONFLICTS(opptr, x)                                                  /* possibly, help or restart other operations accessing x */
41                      if ins = READDI(x) then val_x := x → val  else val_x := v                           /* ins is a write to x of v */
42                      add new dictrec ⟨x, val_x⟩ to dict                                                  /* create a local copy of x */
43                  else if ins is CREATEDI() then
44                      x := pointer to a new varrec record
45                      x → A[1..n] := [nil, . . . , nil]
46                      add new dictrec ⟨x, nil⟩ to dict
47                  else                                                     /* ins is WRITEDI(x, v) or READDI(x) and there is a dictrec with key x in dict */
                                                                            /* or ins is not a WRITEDI(), READDI() or CREATEDI() instruction */
48                      execute ins, using/changing the value in the appropriate entry of dict if necessary
49                  if ¬VL(opptr → status) then break                                                      /* end of the simulation of ins */
50                  ins := next instruction of opptr → program
                /* end while */
51              if ins is return(v) then                                                                   /* v may be empty */
52                  SC(opptr → status, ⟨modifying, dict, v⟩)                                               /* try to change status of op to modifying */
                                                                            /* successful iff simulation is over and status of op not changed since beginning of simulation */
53              opstatus := LL(opptr → status)
54          if opstatus = ⟨modifying, changes, out⟩ then
55              opptr → outputs := out
56              for each dictrec ⟨x, v⟩ in the dictionary pointed to by changes do
57                  LL(x → val)                                                                            /* try to make writes visible */
58                  if ¬VL(opptr → status) then return                                                     /* opptr → status = done */
59                  SC(x → val, v)
60                  LL(x → val)
61                  if ¬VL(opptr → status) then return                                                     /* opptr → status = done */
62                  SC(x → val, v)
                /* end for */
63              SC(opptr → status, done)
64              opstatus := LL(opptr → status)
        /* end while */
65  return
```

```
75  CONFLICTS(opptr, x) by process p:
76      for p' := 1 to n excluding opptr → owner do
77          opptr' := LL(x → A[p'])
78          if (opptr' ≠ nil) then                           /* possible conflict between op and op' */
79              opstatus' := LL(opptr' → status)
80          if ¬VL(opptr → status) then return
81          if (opstatus' = ⟨modifying, changes, output⟩)
82              then HELP(opptr')
83          else if (opstatus' = ⟨simulating⟩) then
84              if (opptr → owner < p') then
                                                             /* op has higher priority than op', restart op' */
85                  opptr → tohelp[p'] := opptr'
86                  if ¬VL(opptr → status) then return
87                  SC(opptr' → status, ⟨restart, opptr⟩)
88                  if (LL(opptr' → status) = ⟨modifying, changes, output⟩) then
                        HELP(opptr')
89              else HELP(opptr')                           /* opptr → owner > p' */
90      return
```

```
66  ANNOUNCE(opptr, x) by process p:
67      q := opptr → owner
68      LL(x → A[q])
69      if ¬ VL(opptr → status) then return
70      SC(x → A[q], opptr)
71      LL(x → A[q])
72      if ¬VL(opptr → status) then return
73      SC(x → A[q], opptr)
74      return
```

Figure 4: The code of Perform, Help, Announce, and Conflicts.

announce that they access x and to determine conflicts with other operations that are also accessing x.

The execution of op is done in a sequence of one or more *simulation phases* (lines 34-53) followed by a *modification phase* (lines 54-62). In a simulation phase, the instructions of op are read (lines 36, 37, and 50) and the execution of each one of them is simulated locally. The first time each process q helping op (including its owner) needs to access a data item (lines 38, 43), it creates a local copy of it in its (local) dictionary (lines 42, 46). All subsequent accesses by q to this data item (during the current simulation phase of op) are performed on this local copy (line 48). During the modification phase, q makes the updates of op visible by applying them to the shared memory (lines 56-62).

The *status* field of op determines the execution phase of op. It contains a pointer to a record of type statrec (lines 4-10) where the status of op is recorded. The status of op can be either *simulating*, indicating that op is in its simulation phase, *modifying*, if op is in its modifying phase, *done*, if the execution of op has been completed but op has not yet returned, or *restart*, if op has experienced a conflict and should re-execute its simulation phase from the beginning. Depending on which of these values *status* contains, it may additionally store another pointer or a value.

To ensure consistency, each time a data item x is accessed for the first time, q checks, before reading the value of x, whether op conflicts with other operations accessing x. This is done as follows: q announces op to x by storing a pointer opr to op's oprec in $A[opr \rightarrow owner]$. This is performed by calling ANNOUNCE (line 39). ANNOUNCE first performs an LL on $var_x \rightarrow A[p]$ (line 68), where var_x is the varrec for x and $p = opr \rightarrow owner$. Then, it checks if the status of op (line 69) remains *simulating* and, if this is so, it performs an SC to store op in $var_x \rightarrow A[p]$ (line 70). These instructions are then executed one more time. This is needed because an obsolete helper of an operation, initiated by p before op, may successfully execute an SC on $var_x \rightarrow A[p]$ that stores a pointer to this operation's oprec. However, we prove [15] that this can happen only once, so executing the instructions on lines 68-70 twice is enough to ensure consistency.

After announcing op to var_x, q calls CONFLICTS (line 40) to detect conflicts with other operations that access x. In CONFLICTS, q reads the rest of the elements of $var_x \rightarrow A$ (lines 76-77). Whenever a conflict is detected (i.e., the condition of the if statement of line 78 evaluates to true) between op and some other operation op', CONFLICTS first checks if op' is in its modifying phase (line 82) and, if so, it helps op' to complete. In this way, it is ensured that, once an operation enters its modification phase, it will complete its operation successfully. Therefore, once the status of an operation becomes *modifying*, it will next become *done*, and then, henceforth, never change. If the status of op' is *simulating*, q determines which of op or op' has the higher priority (line 84). If op' has higher priority (line 89), then op helps op' by calling HELP(op'). Otherwise, q first adds a pointer opr' to the oprec of op' into $opr \rightarrow tohelp$ (line 85), so that the owner of op will help op' to complete after op has completed. Then q attempts to notify op' to restart, using SC (line 87) to change the status of op' to *restart*. A pointer opr is also stored in the status field of op'. When op' restarts its simulation phase, it will help op to complete (lines 30-33), if op is still in its simulation phase, before it continues with the re-execution of the simulation phase of op'. This guarantees that op will not cause op' to restart again.

Recall that each helper q of op maintains a local dictionary. This dictionary contains an element of type dictrec (lines 18-20) for each data item that q accesses (while simulating op). A dictionary element corresponding to data item x consists of two fields, *key*, which is a pointer to var_x, and *newval*, which stores the value that op currently knows for x. Notice that only one helper of op will succeed in executing the SC on line 52, which changes the status of op to *modifying*. This helper records a pointer to the dictionary it maintains for op, as well as its output value, in op's *status*, to make them public. During the modification phase, each helper q of op traverses this dictionary, which is recorded in the status of op (lines 54, 56). For each element in the dictionary, it tries to write the new value into the varrec of the corresponding data item (lines 57-59). This is performed twice to avoid problems with obsolete helpers in a similar way as in ANNOUNCE.

THEOREM 6. *The* DAP-UC *universal construction (Figures 3 and 4) produces disjoint-access parallel, wait-free, concurrent implementations when applied to objects that have a bound on the number of data items accessed by each operation they support.*

6. REFERENCES

[1] Y. Afek, D. Dauber, and D. Touitou. Wait-free made fast. In *Proceedings of the 27th Annual ACM Symposium on Theory of Computing*, STOC '95, pages 538–547, New York, USA, 1995.

[2] Y. Afek, M. Merritt, G. Taubenfeld, and D. Touitou. Disentangling multi-object operations (extended abstract). In *Proceedings of the 16th Annual ACM Symposium on Principles of Distributed Computing*, PODC '97, pages 111–120, New York, USA, 1997.

[3] J. H. Anderson and M. Moir. Universal constructions for multi-object operations. In *Proceedings of the 14th Annual ACM Symposium on Principles of Distributed Computing*, PODC '95, pages 184–193, New York, USA, 1995.

[4] J. H. Anderson and M. Moir. Universal constructions for large objects. *IEEE Transactions on Parallel and Distributed Systems*, 10(12):1317–1332, 1999.

[5] H. Attiya and E. Dagan. Universal operations: unary versus binary. In *Proceedings of the 15th Annual ACM Symposium on Principles of Distributed Computing*, PODC '96, pages 223–232, New York, USA, 1996.

[6] H. Attiya and E. Hillel. Built-in coloring for highly-concurrent doubly-linked lists. In *Proceedings of the 20th International Symposium on Distributed Computing*, DISC '06, volume 4167 of *Lecture Notes in Computer Science*, pages 31–45, Springer, 2006.

[7] H. Attiya and E. Hillel. Highly-concurrent multi-word synchronization. In *Proceedings of the 9th International Conference on Distributed Computing and Networking*, ICDCN'08, pages 112–123, Springer-Verlag, Berlin, Heidelberg, 2008.

[8] H. Attiya and E. Hillel. Single-version stms can be multi-version permissive. In *Proceedings of the 12th International Conference on Distributed Computing and Networking*, ICDCN'11, pages 83–94, Springer-Verlag, Berlin, Heidelberg, 2011.

[9] H. Attiya, E. Hillel, and A. Milani. Inherent limitations on disjoint-access parallel implementations of transactional memory. In *Proceedings of the 21st Annual Symposium on Parallelism in Algorithms and Architectures*, SPAA '09, pages 69–78, New York, USA, 2009.

[10] G. Barnes. A method for implementing lock-free shared data structures. In *Proceedings of the 5th ACM Symposium on Parallel Algorithms and Architectures*, pages 261–270, 1993.

[11] V. Bushkov, R. Guerraoui, and M. Kapalka. On the liveness of transactional memory. In *Proceedings of the 31st ACM Symposium on Principles of Distributed Computing*, PODC '12, New York, USA, 2012, to appear.

[12] P. Chuong, F. Ellen, and V. Ramachandran. A universal construction for wait-free transaction friendly data structures. In *Proceedings of the 22nd ACM Symposium on Parallelism in Algorithms and Architectures*, SPAA '10, pages 335–344, New York, USA, 2010.

[13] T. Crain, D. Imbs, and M. Raynal. Towards a universal construction for transaction-based multiprocess programs. In *Proceedings of the 13th International Conference on Distributed Computing and Networking*, ICDCN '12, pages 61–75, 2012.

[14] D. Dice and N. Shavit. What Really Makes Transactions Faster? In *Proceedings of the 1st ACM SIGPLAN Workshop on Languages, Compilers, and Hardware Support for Transactional Computing*, TRANSACT '06, Ottawa, Canada, 2006.

[15] F. Ellen, P. Fatourou, E. Kosmas, A. Milani, and C. Travers. Universal Constructions that Ensure Disjoint-Access Parallelism and Wait-Freedom. Technical Report, `http://hal.inria.fr/hal-00697198/en/`, INRIA, 2012.

[16] P. Fatourou and N. D. Kallimanis. The redblue adaptive universal constructions. In *Proceedings of the 23rd international conference on Distributed computing*, DISC '09, pages 127–141, Berlin, Heidelberg, 2009.

[17] P. Fatourou and N. D. Kallimanis. A highly-efficient wait-free universal construction. In *Proceedings of the 23nd Annual ACM Symposium on Parallel Algorithms and Architectures*, pages 325 – 334, San Jose, USA, 2011.

[18] K. Fraser. *Practical lock freedom*. PhD thesis, Cambridge University Computer Laboratory, 2003. Also available as Technical Report UCAM-CL-TR-579.

[19] R. Guerraoui and M. Kapalka. On obstruction-free transactions. In *Proceedings of the 20th Annual Symposium on Parallelism in Algorithms and Architectures*, SPAA '08, pages 304–313, New York, USA, 2008.

[20] M. Herlihy. A methodology for implementing highly concurrent data structures. In *Proceedings of the 2nd ACM SIGPLAN Symposium on Principles & Practice of Parallel Programming*, PPOPP '90, pages 197–206, New York, USA, 1990.

[21] M. Herlihy. Wait-free synchronization. *ACM Transactions on Programming Languanges and Systems*, 13:124–149, January 1991.

[22] M. Herlihy, V. Luchangco, P. Martin, and M. Moir. Nonblocking memory management support for dynamic-sized data structures. *ACM Trans. Comput. Syst.*, 23:146–196, May 2005.

[23] M. Herlihy and J. E. B. Moss. Transactional memory: architectural support for lock-free data structures. In *Proceedings of the 20th Annual International Symposium on Computer Architecture*, ISCA '93, pages 289–300, New York, USA, 1993.

[24] M. Herlihy and J. M. Wing. Linearizability: A correctness condition for concurrent objects. *ACM Transactions on Programming Languages and Systems*, 12(3):463–492, July 1990.

[25] A. Israeli and L. Rappoport. Disjoint-access-parallel implementations of strong shared memory primitives. In *Proceedings of the 13th Annual ACM Symposium on Principles of Distributed Computing*, PODC '94, pages 151–160, New York, USA, 1994.

[26] V. J. Marathe, W. N. Scherer III, and M. L. Scott. Adaptive software transactional memory. In *Proceedings of the 19th International Symposium on Distributed Computing*, DISC' 05, 2005. Also available as TR 868, University of Rochester Computer Science Dept., May 2005.

[27] D. Pelerman, R. Fan, and I. Keidar. On maintaining multiple versions in stm. In *Proceedings of the 29th ACM Symposium on Principles of Distributed Computing*, PODC '10, pages 16–25, New York, USA, 2010.

[28] N. Shavit and D. Touitou. Software transactional memory. In *Proceedings of the 14th Annual ACM symposium on Principles of Distributed Computing*, PODC '95, pages 204–213, New York, USA, 1995.

[29] F. Tabba, M. Moir, J. R. Goodman, A. Hay, and C. Wang. NZTM: Nonblocking zero-indirection transactional memory. In *Proceedings of the 21st ACM Symposium on Parallelism in Algorithms and Architectures*, August 2009.

[30] J. Turek, D. Shasha, and S. Prakash. Locking without blocking: making lock based concurrent data structure algorithms nonblocking. In *Proceedings of the 11th ACM SIGACT-SIGMOD-SIGART Symposium on Principles of Database Systems*, PODS '92, pages 212–222, New York, USA, 1992.

[31] J.-T. Wamhoff, T. Riegel, C. Fetzer, and P. Felber. RobuSTM: A robust software transactional system. In *Proceedings of the 12th International Symposium on Stabilization, Safety, and Security of Distributed Systems*, SSS '10, volume 6366 of *Lecture Notes in Computer Science*, Springer-Verlag, 2010.

Generalized Lattice Agreement

[Extended Abstract]

Jose M. Falerio
Microsoft Research India
t-josfal@microsoft.com

Sriram Rajamani
Microsoft Research India
sriram@microsoft.com

Kaushik Rajan
Microsoft Research India
krajan@microsoft.com

G. Ramalingam
Microsoft Research India
grama@microsoft.com

Kapil Vaswani
Microsoft Research India
kapilv@microsoft.com

ABSTRACT

Lattice agreement is a key decision problem in distributed systems. In this problem, processes start with input values from a lattice, and must learn (non-trivial) values that form a chain. Unlike consensus, which is impossible in the presence of even a single process failure, lattice agreement has been shown to be decidable in the presence of failures. In this paper, we consider lattice agreement problems in asynchronous, message passing systems. We present an algorithm for the lattice agreement problem that guarantees liveness as long as a majority of the processes are non-faulty. The algorithm has a time complexity of $O(N)$ message delays, where N is the number of processes. We then introduce the generalized lattice agreement problem, where each process receives a (potentially unbounded) sequence of values from an infinite lattice and must learn a sequence of increasing values such that the union of all learnt sequences is a chain and every proposed value is eventually learnt. We present a wait-free algorithm for solving generalized lattice agreement. The algorithm guarantees that every value received by a correct process is learnt in $O(N)$ message delays. We show that this algorithm can be used to implement a class of replicated state machines where (a) commands can be classified as *reads* and *updates*, and (b) all update commands *commute*. This algorithm can be used to realize serializable and linearizable replicated versions of commonly used data types.

Categories and Subject Descriptors

C.2.4 [**Computer Systems Organization**]: Computer-Communication NetworksDistributed Systems; D.4.5 [**Software**]: Operating SystemsReliabilityFault Tolerance; E.1 [**Data**]: Data StructuresDistributed Data Structures

Keywords

replication, fault tolerance, lattice agreement

1. INTRODUCTION

Lattice agreement is a key decision problem in distributed systems. In this problem, each process starts with an input value belonging to a lattice, and must learn an output value belonging to the lattice. The goal is to ensure that each process learns a value that is greater than or equal to its input value, each learnt value is the join of some set of input values, and all learnt values form a chain. Unlike consensus, which is impossible in the presence of even a single failure [5], lattice agreement is decidable, and asynchronous, wait-free algorithms for shared memory distributed systems have been proposed [4, 3, 7] (see Section 7).

In this paper, we consider the lattice agreement problem in asynchronous, message passing systems. We present a wait-free algorithm for solving a single instance of lattice agreement. We also study a generalization of lattice agreement, where each process *receives* a (potentially unbounded) sequence of values from an infinite lattice, and the goal is to learn a sequence of values that form a chain. As before, we wish to ensure that every learnt value is the join of some set of received values and that every received value is eventually included in a learnt value. We present a wait-free algorithm for solving generalized lattice agreement.

One of the challenges in extending the lattice agreement algorithm to generalized lattice agreement is ensuring liveness and progress because of the potential to iterate over an unbounded chain without learning new values. Our algorithm guarantees that every received value is learnt in $O(N)$ message delays, even in the presence of failures and concurrent proposals. Our algorithm is *adaptive* [3]: its complexity depends only on the number of participants actively contending at any given point in time. If only k processes receive values, then every received value is learnt in $O(k)$ message delays. In the extreme case, if only one process receives values, our algorithm guarantees that every value is learnt in 3 message delays (including the round trip from the client to the system). Our algorithms guarantee safety properties in the presence of arbitrary non-Byzantine failures (including process failures as well as message losses). The algorithms guarantee liveness and progress as long as a majority of processes are correct and messages between correct processes are eventually delivered.

Finally, we show that generalized lattice agreement can be used to implement a special class of replicated state machines, the main motivation for our work. State machine replication [8] is used to realize data-structures that tolerate process failures by replicating state across multiple processes. The key challenge here is to execute data-structure operations on all replicas so that the replicas converge and consistency (in the form of serializability or linearizability [6]) can be guaranteed. One common approach to state machine replication is to use distributed consensus [9] among the replicas to determine the order in which operations are to be performed. Unfortunately, the impossibility of consensus means that this approach cannot guarantee liveness in the presence of failures.

Operations of a state machine can be classified as *updates* (operations that modify the state) and *reads* (operations that do not modify the state). In this paper, we consider the problem of replicating state machines when all update operations commute with each other. Recent work [12] has shown how several interesting data-structures with update operations that logically do not commute, such as sets (with adds and deletes), sequences, certain kinds of key-value tables, and graphs can be realized using a more complex data-structure with commutative update operations. Thus, commutativity of updates is a reasonable assumption in several settings.

We show that generalized lattice agreement can be used to obtain an algorithm for this class of state machines that guarantees consistency and liveness in the presence of process failures (as long as a majority of the processes are non-faulty). We are not aware of any previous algorithm that guarantees both consistency and liveness for this problem. Algorithms have been previously proposed to exploit commutativity, including generalized consensus [10]. Generalized consensus is similar to generalized lattice agreement, with some significant differences. In generalized consensus, processes propose values belonging to a partially ordered set where not all pairs of elements have a least upper bound (or join). Processes then learn a sequence of values. Generalized consensus requires values learnt by different processes to have a least upper bound, but does not require these values to be comparable (i.e., form a chain). These differences between generalized consensus and generalized lattice agreement turn out to be crucial in achieving consistency with liveness.

A straightforward approach to state machine replication using generalized consensus exploits commutativity as follows: different processes do not have to agree on the order in which commuting operations are performed. However, processes must still agree on the order of non-commuting operations. Even when all updates commute, read operations do not commute with update operations. The need to support non-commuting reads necessitates consensus in this approach and, hence, this approach cannot guarantee liveness.

The essence of our approach is to *separate* updates from reads. Note that the state of any replica corresponds to a *set-of-updates* (that have been executed to produce that state). We utilize generalized lattice agreement, on the power set lattice of the set-of-all-updates, to learn a chain of sets-of-updates. Each learnt set-of-updates represents a *consistent* state that can be used for reads. Specifically, every replica utilizes the state corresponding to its most recent learnt value to process read operations. More details on how we do this appears in the paper.

Note that generalized consensus cannot be used to separate updates from reads in this fashion. Suppose we apply generalized consensus for the state machine consisting of only update operations. Since all operations commute, generalized consensus guarantees liveness in this case. Unfortunately, the learnt values are not guaranteed to form a chain (with generalized consensus). Hence, different learnt values cannot be used to process read operations without compromising consistency.

As a simple example, consider a set data type that supports adds and reads. Assume clients issue two update commands, Add(1) and Add(2), and several reads, concurrently on an initially empty set. The adds commute with each other but the reads do not. The key to consistency is to ensure that two concurrent read operations do not return values $\{1\}$ and $\{2\}$. A conventional replicated state machine based on consensus must explicitly order reads with respect to updates, which ensures consistency but compromises liveness. In our implementation, replicas utilize our wait-free algorithm for generalized lattice agreement on the power set lattice $\mathcal{P}(\{Add(1), Add(2)\})$. Since lattice agreement guarantees that learnt values form a chain, it follows that no two reads can observe states $\{1\}$ and $\{2\}$. Furthermore, our implementation ensures that if a read returns some value of the set (say $\{1\}$), then any *subsequent* read observes a state produced by applying a larger set of commands (namely $\{1\}$, or $\{1, 2\}$).

To summarize, this paper makes the following three contributions:

- We provide a new algorithm for solving a single instance of the lattice agreement problem for asynchronous message passing system with $O(N)$ message delays. This is the first algorithm for this problem in an asynchronous message passing setting.

- We introduce the generalized lattice agreement problem and present an algorithm for this problem with an upper bound of $O(N)$ message delays for a value to be learnt.

- We use our algorithm for generalized lattice agreement to obtain an algorithm for replicated state machines with commuting updates. This is the first algorithm for this problem that guarantees both consistency and liveness.

2. SYSTEM MODEL

We are interested in lattice agreement problems in an asynchronous message passing system. We consider a system of N independent and asynchronous processes each of which have a unique identity. We assume processes are arranged as nodes in a complete graph and can communicate with each other by sending messages along edges. We make no assumptions about the order in which messages are delivered or about how long it takes for a message to be delivered. We consider non-Byzantine failures, both crash-failures of processes as well as message losses. We will refer to a process that does not fail (in a given execution) as a *correct* process.

3. LATTICE AGREEMENT

Problem Definition. Let $(\mathsf{L}, \sqsubseteq, \sqcup)$ be a semi-lattice with a partial order $\sqsubseteq$ and join (least-upper-bound) $\sqcup$. We say that two values u and v in L are *comparable* iff $u \sqsubseteq v$ or $v \sqsubseteq u$. In lattice agreement, each of the N processes starts with an initial value from the lattice and must learn values that satisfies the following conditions:

1. **Validity**. Any value learnt by a process is a join of some set of initial values that includes its own initial value.

2. **Stability**. A process can learn at most one value.

3. **Consistency**. Values learnt by any two processes are comparable.

4. **Liveness**. Every correct process eventually learns a value.

Most agreement problems are hard to solve in an asynchronous message passing system if a majority of the processes fail or if an arbitrary number of messages are lost [1]. For lattice agreement, we require that the safety properties hold even in the presence of arbitrary non-Byzantine failures (crash failures and message losses). Liveness must hold so long as a majority of processes are correct and messages between correct processes are eventually delivered.

Note that there is a subtle difference between the lattice agreement problem as stated here and the one proposed by Attiya *et al.* in [4]. Attiya *et al.* only require that any learnt value be less than or equal to the join of all initial values. The validity condition here is stricter, it restricts each learnt value to necessarily be a join of some initial values. This difference is not very significant. Any solution to the problem defined here is also a valid solution to the problem defined by Attiya *et al.*. All known algorithms for lattice agreement (for shared memory systems) as defined by Attiya *et al.* satisfy the stricter validity condition that we use here.

Algorithm. Our algorithm for lattice agreement is shown in Algorithm 1. For convenience, we consider two kinds of processes, (1) proposer processes, each of which has an initial value *initialValue*, and learns a single output value *outputValue*, and (2) acceptor processes, which help proposer processes learn output values. The algorithm permits the same process to play the roles of both a proposer and an acceptor. Let N_p denote the number of proposer processes and let N_a denote the number of acceptor processes. In this formulation, our liveness guarantees require a majority of acceptor processes to be correct.

In our formal description of the algorithm, we present every process as a collection of *guarded actions* (loosely in the style of IO-automata). A guarded action consists of a guard (precondition) predicate and an effect. We also give a name to every action to facilitate our subsequent discussion. An action is said to be *enabled* (for a process) if its corresponding precondition is true at the process. A precondition of the form $?M(x)\&\&P(x)$ is said to be true iff the process has an input message $M(x)$ satisfying the predicate $P(x)$. Here M is a message name (tag) and x is the parameter value carried by the message. A process repeatedly selects any enabled action and executes its effect *atomically*. Whenever a process executes an action whose guard includes a message predicate $?M(x)$, the matching message $M(x)$ is *consumed* and removed from the input channel.

Every proposer begins by proposing its value to all acceptors (see Propose in Algorithm 1). Each proposal is associated with a proposal number that is unique to each pro-

poser. Proposal numbers are not required to be totally ordered. The only purpose they serve is to uniquely identify proposals made by a proposer.

An acceptor may *accept* or *reject* a proposed value. Every acceptor ensures that all values that it accepts form a chain in the lattice. It does this by tracking the largest value it has accepted so far in the variable *acceptedValue*. When it gets a proposal, it accepts the proposed value iff it is greater than or equal to *acceptedValue*, and send an acknowledgment back to the proposer. If it rejects a proposed value, it sends back the *join* of the proposed value and *acceptedValue* back to the proposer along with the rejection.

This guarantees that all values accepted by a single acceptor are comparable. However, different acceptors may accept incomparable values. A value is said to be a *chosen* value iff it is accepted by a majority of acceptors. Note that any two chosen values have at least one common acceptor. Hence, any two chosen values are guaranteed to be comparable. Proposers simply count the number of acceptances every proposed value gets and whenever a proposed value gets a majority of acceptances, it knows that its proposed value is a chosen value. The proposer then executes the Decide() action, and declares the current proposed value as its output value.

This approach ensures the safety requirements of the problem. We now show how proposers deal with rejections to ensure liveness and termination. A proposer waits for a quorum of acceptors to respond to its proposal. If all these responses are acceptances, the proposer is done (since its value has been included in an output value). Otherwise, it *refines* its proposal by replacing its current value with the join of its current value and all the values it received with its rejection responses. It then goes through this process all over again, using its current value as the new proposed value. Once a proposer proposes a new value, it ignores responses it may receive for all previous proposals. This approach ensures termination since all values generated in the algorithm belong to a finite sub-lattice of L (namely, the lattice L' consisting of all values that can be expressed as the join of some set of input values).

Time complexity We now establish the complexity of the lattice agreement algorithm. In particular, we measure the time complexity [1] defined as the time it takes for a correct process to learn an output value, under the assumption that every message sent to a correct process is delivered in one unit of time. We present a simple informal argument here to show that the time complexity of the lattice agreement algorithm is $O(N)$ and defer the formal treatment to section 5. From the algorithm it can be seen that every time a proposer performs the action Refine(), it proposes a value that is strictly greater than the previously proposed value. As every proposed value is a join of some initial values, in the worst case, the Nth proposal will be the join of all initial values. Such a proposal has to be accepted. As the time between successive proposals is two units and at most N proposals are made the time complexity of the algorithm is $O(N)$. Note that if only k processes propose values, then the complexity is $O(k)$.

Algorithm 1 Lattice Agreement

1: // **Proposer process**
2: int *UID* // *Unique id for a process*
3: enum {*passive, active*} *status = passive*
4: int *ackCount, nackCount, activeProposalNumber* = 0
5: L *initialValue* // *Initial value of the process*
6: L *proposedValue, outputValue* $=\perp$
7:
8: **action** Propose()
9: **guard**: *activeProposalNumber* = 0
10: **effect**:
11:     *proposedValue = initialValue*
12:     *status = active*
13:     *activeProposalNumber++*
14:     *ackCount = nackCount* = 0
15:     Send Proposal(*proposedValue, activeProposalNumber, UID*) to all *Acceptors*
16:
17: **action** ProcessACK(*proposalNumber, value, id*)
18: **guard**: ?ACK(*proposalNumber, value, id*) && *proposalNumber = activeProposalNumber*
19: **effect**: *ackCount++*
20:
21: **action** ProcessNACK(*proposalNumber, value*)
22: **guard**: ?NACK(*proposalNumber, value*) && *proposalNumber = activeProposalNumber*
23: **effect**:
24:     *proposedValue= proposedValue* $\sqcup$ *value*
25:     *nackCount++*
26:
27: **action** Refine()
28: **guard**: *nackCount* > 0 && *nackCount + ackCount* $\geq \lceil (N_a + 1)/2 \rceil$ && *status = active*
29: **effect**:
30:     *activeProposalNumber++*
31:     *ackCount = nackCount* = 0
32:     Send Proposal(*proposedValue, activeProposalNumber, UID*) to all *Acceptors*
33:
34: **action** Decide()
35: **guard**: *ackCount* $\geq \lceil (N_a + 1)/2 \rceil$ && *status = active*
36: **effect**:
37:     *outputValue= proposedValue*
38:     *status = passive*
39:
40: // **Acceptor process**
41: L *acceptedValue* $= \perp$
42:
43: **action** Accept(*proposalNumber, proposedValue, proposerId*)
44: **guard**: ?Proposal(*proposalNumber, proposedValue, proposerId*) && *acceptedValue* $\sqsubseteq$ *proposedValue*
45: **effect**:
46:     *acceptedValue := proposedValue*
47:     Send ACK(*proposalNumber, proposedValue, proposerId*) to *proposerId*
48:
49: **action** Reject(*proposalNumber, proposedValue, proposerId*)
50: **guard**: ?Proposal(*proposalNumber, proposedValue, proposerId*) && *acceptedValue* $\not\sqsubseteq$ *proposedValue*
51: **effect**:
52:     *acceptedValue := acceptedValue* $\sqcup$ *proposedValue*
53:     Send NACK(*proposalNumber, acceptedValue*) to *proposerId*

---

4. GENERALIZED LATTICE AGREEMENT

We now generalize the lattice agreement problem, allowing processes to accept a possibly infinite sequence of input values.

Problem Definition. Let L be a join semi-lattice with a partial order $\sqsubseteq$. Consider a system with N processes. Each process p may receive an input value belonging to the lattice (from a client) at any point in time. There is no bound on the number of input values a process may receive. Let v_i^p denote the i-th input value received by a process p. The objective is for each process p to learn a sequence of output values w_j^p that satisfy the following conditions:

1. **Validity**. Any learnt value w_j^p is a join of some set of received input values.

2. **Stability**. The value learnt by any process p increases monotonically: $j < k \Rightarrow w_j^p \sqsubseteq w_k^p$.

3. **Consistency**. Any two values w_j^p and w_k^q learnt by any two processes are comparable.

4. **Liveness**. Every value v_i^p received by a correct process p is eventually included in some learnt value w_k^q of every correct process q: i.e., $v_i^p \sqsubseteq w_k^q$.

As in lattice agreement, we require that the safety properties hold even in the presence of arbitrary non-Byzantine failures (crash failures and message losses), and liveness must hold as long as a majority of processes are correct and messages between correct processes are eventually delivered.

Algorithm. The algorithm for solving one instance of lattice agreement can be extend to solve generalized lattice agreement. The extensions are described in Algorithm 2. The proposer process has two new actions Receive() and Buffer(). In generalized lattice agreement problem, input values belonging to the lattice arrive, over time, in an unbounded fashion. We model this using the action Receive(), which can be executed an unbounded number of times. In addition, the action Propose() changes to the pseudo code shown in Algorithm 2. All the other actions, ProcessACK(), ProcessNACK(), Refine() and Decide() are the same as shown in Algorithm 1. For convenience, we introduce a new type of processes called *Learners*, which learn values chosen by acceptors. We change the Accept action in acceptors to send acknowledgments to all learners.

The goal of generalized lattice agreement is to ensure that learnt values form a chain and every input value is eventually learnt. Our algorithm achieves this in two stages. First, the algorithm ensures that a received value is eventually included in the proposed value of some proposer. Second, the algorithm ensures that every value proposed by a proposer is eventually learnt, using repeated iterations of the basic lattice agreement algorithm.

The first goal above can be trivially achieved by a proposer if it replaces its current value by the join of its current value and the received value whenever any new value is received. Unfortunately, this can cause non-termination in the second stage algorithm. Recall that the informal termination argument for the basic lattice agreement algorithm exploits the fact that all computed values belong to a finite lattice. This is no longer true if every received value is immediately incorporated into proposed values.

As an example, consider a system with two proposers p_1 and p_2 and three acceptors, a_1, a_2 and a_3. Let L be a power set lattice $\mathcal{P}(\mathcal{I})$ defined over natural numbers. Consider an execution in which p_1 first proposes the value $\{1\}$, which is accepted by a_1 and a_2 (hence chosen). Subsequently p_2 proposes the value $\{2\}$. Since $\{2\} \not\sqsubseteq \{1\}$, at least one of the acceptors a_1 or a_2 will reject the proposal and update its accepted value to $\{1, 2\}$. Before p_2 refines and sends its proposal, assume p_1 receives a value $\{3\}$ and proposes $\{1, 3\}$. Since $\{1, 3\} \not\sqsubseteq \{1, 2\}$, at least one of the acceptors a_1 or a_2 will reject the proposal and update its accepted value to $\{1, 2, 3\}$. Furthermore, since L is an infinite lattice, it is easy to see that so long as proposers keep including newly received values in their proposals this process can continue without any value being chosen.

This lack of termination due to conflicting proposals is reminiscent of non-termination in Paxos. However, for the lattice agreement problem, we can guarantee termination by *controlling* when proposers can incorporate received values into new proposals. In our algorithm, a proposer *buffers* all new values it receives until it *successfully completes* its participation in a round of the basic lattice agreement problem instance. The variable *bufferedValues* contains the join of all values received since the last Propose. A proposer is said to successfully complete a round when it receives a majority of responses to its proposal that are all acceptances. When this happens, the proposer includes *bufferedValues* into its *next* proposed value during the subsequent execution of the action Propose() and moves into its next round.

With this modification, we can show that at least one of the proposers will successfully complete its round and process its buffered values. However, we cannot guarantee that all proposers will successfully complete their rounds and process their buffered values. For example, the same proposer p may successfully complete all the rounds and keep introducing new received values into the next round. As a result, none of the other proposers may ever receive a majority of acceptances to their proposals.

If a proposer does not successfully complete its round, then it will never include its buffered values into the second stage. Hence, values it receives may never be learnt. We get around this problem by making a proposer broadcast any new value it receives to all other proposers. Other proposers treat this broadcast value just like any other values they receive. Effectively all values are sent to all proposers. Since we have a liveness guarantee that at least some correct proposer will eventually successfully complete its current round and move on to its next round, and messages between correct processes are eventually delivered, we can guarantee that all received values are included in the second stage and eventually learnt.

In the next section, we formalize the notion of a round and will see that there is a distinction between a process completing a round and a process *successfully* completing a round. We will show that every process is guaranteed to complete every round, and at least one process is guaranteed to *successfully* complete a given round.

5. SAFETY AND LIVENESS

We now establish the safety and liveness properties of the generalized lattice agreement algorithm. We start with some definitions. An execution of the algorithm consists of each process executing a sequence of execution-steps. An execution-step (of a single process) consists of the execution of a single action. We identify the action executed in a step (as indicated in our algorithm description) by the name of the action and its parameters: e.g., Receive(v). If a process has one or more enabled actions, it selects one of its enabled actions (non-deterministically) and executes it atomically and repeats this process. A process may *fail* at any point in time (after which it does not execute any more execution-steps). We will use the term *correct* process (or *non-failed* process) to refer to a process that does not fail during the execution under consideration. Note that a process may fail in the middle of an execution step, and our algorithm guarantees safety properties even in this case.

Recall that N_a denotes the number of acceptor processes and N_p denotes the number of proposer processes. We will

Algorithm 2 Generalized Lattice Agreement

1: // ***Proposer Process***
2: // *All variables and actions specified in Algorithm 1 except* Propose*() are also included.*
3: L *bufferedValues* = ⊥
4:
5: **procedure** ReceiveValue(*value*)
6:    Send InternalReceive(*value*) to all *Proposers* \ {*UID*}
7:    *bufferedValues* = *value* ⊔ *bufferedValues*
8:
9: **action** Receive(*value*)
10: **guard**: ?ExternalReceive(*value*)
11: **effect**: ReceiveValue(*value*)
12:
13: **action** Buffer(*value*)
14: **guard**: ?InternalReceive(*value*)
15: **effect**: *bufferedValues* = *value* ⊔ *bufferedValues*
16:
17: **action** Propose()
18: **guard**: *status* = *passive* && *proposedValue* ⊔ *bufferedValues* ⊐ *proposedValue*
19: **effect**:
20:    *proposedValue* = *proposedValue* ⊔ *bufferedValues*
21:    *status* = *active*
22:    *activeProposalNumber*++
23:    *ackCount* = *nackCount* = 0
24:    Send Proposal(*proposedValue*, *activeProposalNumber*, *UID*) to all *Acceptors*
25:    *bufferedValues* = ⊥
26:
27: // ***Acceptor Process***
28: // *All variables and actions specified in Algorithm 1 except* Accept*() are also included.*
29: **action** Accept(*proposalNumber*, *proposedValue*, *proposerId*)
30: **guard**: ?Proposal(*proposalNumber*, *proposedValue*, *proposerId*) && *acceptedValue* ⊑ *proposedValue*
31: **effect**:
32:    *acceptedValue* := *proposedValue*
33:    Send ACK(*proposalNumber*, *proposedValue*, *proposerId*) to *proposerId* and all *Learners*
34:
35: // ***Learner process***
36: L *learntValue* = ⊥
37: int *ackCount*[int,int] // all initially 0
38:
39: **action** Learn(*proposalNumber*, *value*, *proposerId*)
40: **guard**: ?ACK(*proposalNumber*, *value*, *proposerId*)
41: **effect**:
42:    *ackCount*[*proposerId*][*proposalNumber*]++
43:    **if** (*ackCount*[*proposerId*][*proposalNumber*] ≥ ⌈(N_a + 1)/2⌉ && *learntValue* ⊏ *value*) **then**
44:      *learntValue* = *value*
45:    **endif**
46:
47: **procedure** L LearntValue()
48: **effect**:
49:    **return** *learntValue*

---

assume in the sequel that N_p is at least 2. (Otherwise, the problem and proofs are trivial.)

A set S of acceptors is said to be a *quorum* iff $|S| \geq \lceil (N_a + 1)/2 \rceil$. Note that by definition any two quorums have a non-empty intersection.

A value $v \in$ L is said to be a *received value* if and when some proposer executes the step Receive(v). A value v is said to have been *initiated* if some proposer executes an Propose step where it proposes v. A value v is said to have been *proposed* if some proposer executes either an Propose or Refine step where it proposes v. A proposal (n, v, id) is said

to have been *chosen* if some quorum of acceptors execute Accept(n, v, id). A value v is said to have been *chosen* if some proposal (n, v, id) has been chosen. A value v is said to have been *decided* if and when some proposer executes a Decide(v) step. A value v is said to have been *learnt* by a learner process p if and when p executes the step Learn(w) for some $w \sqsupseteq v$. (Note that the definition of a learnt value differs from the preceding definitions, to be consistent with the problem definition and requirements.)

5.1 Safety

Simpler proofs have been omitted in the sequel.

THEOREM 5.1. *The value of proposedValue (of any proposer), acceptedValue (of any acceptor), and learntValue (of any learner) can all be expressed as the join of some subset of previously received input values.*

PROOF. Follows by induction on the length of execution. □

COROLLARY 5.2. *Validity: Any learnt value is a join of a subset of received values.*

THEOREM 5.3. *Stability: The value of learntValue of any learner increases monotonically over time.*

LEMMA 5.4. *Values acknowledged by an acceptor increase monotonically: for any two steps* Accept(n, v, id) *and* Accept(n', v', id') *executed by the same acceptor (in that order),* $v \sqsubseteq v'$.

LEMMA 5.5. *Any two chosen values u and v are comparable.*

PROOF. Let $Quorum(u)$ be the quorum of acceptors that acknowledged a proposal with value u. Let $Quorum(v)$ be the quorum of acceptors that acknowledged a proposal with value v. Let $A = Quorum(u) \cap Quorum(v)$. By the definition of a quorum, A must be non-empty. Consider any acceptor $a \in A$. a must have acknowledged both u and v. Therefore, from Lemma 5.4, $u \sqsubseteq v$ or $v \sqsubseteq u$. □

THEOREM 5.6. *Consistency : Any two values u and v learnt by two different processes are comparable.*

PROOF. Follows from Lemma 5.5 since every learnt value is a chosen value. □

5.2 Liveness

We now show that our algorithm guarantees liveness (subject to our failure model described earlier) and derive its complexity. The key idea behind the proof is to establish that any execution can be partitioned into a sequence of *rounds* such that:

- A new value is chosen in every round, and

- Every round is guaranteed to terminate. In particular, we show that each proposer can propose at most $N_p + 1$ times within a single round.

- Every value proposed in a round is included in the value chosen in the same round.

- If a value has been received by all correct processes in a round, then it is included in a proposal in the next round.

All of the following results apply to a given execution.

LEMMA 5.7. *Values proposed by a single proposer strictly increase over time: if v_i is the value proposed by proposer p in proposal number i and v_{i+1} is the value proposed by p in proposal number $i + 1$, then $v_i \sqsubset v_{i+1}$.*

Definition Let $v_1 \sqsubset v_2 \sqsubset \cdots \sqsubset v_k$ be the set of all values chosen in a given execution. Define v_0 to be $\bot$. We partition the sequence of execution-steps of a proposer p into rounds as follows. Let v denote the value p's *proposedValue* at the end of an execution-step s. Step s is said to belong to the initial (dummy) round 0 if $v = \bot$. Step s is said to belong to the (last) round $k + 1$ if $v \not\sqsubseteq v_k$. Otherwise, step s belongs to the unique round r that satisfies $v \sqsubseteq v_r$ and $v \not\sqsubseteq v_{r-1}$. We refer to round $k + 1$ as an *incomplete* round and every other round as a *completed* round.

Note that the above definition of rounds is consistent with the ordering of events implied by message delivery: if execution-step e_1 sends a message that is processed by an execution-step e_2, then e_1 belongs to the same round as e_2 or an earlier round.

LEMMA 5.8. *Let v be a value proposed in a completed round r and let v_r be the value chosen in round r. Then, $v \sqsubseteq v_r$.*

PROOF. Follows from the definition of rounds. □

LEMMA 5.9. *A proposer executes at most one* Decide *step and at most one* Propose *in a round.*

PROOF. A proposer must alternate between Propose and Decide steps. Suppose a proposer initiates v_1, then decides v_2, then initiates v_3 and then decides v_4. We must have $v_1 \sqsubseteq v_2 \sqsubset v_3 \sqsubseteq v_4$. Note that v_2 must be a chosen value and, hence, Decide(v_2) must mark the end of a round for the proposer. The result follows. □

LEMMA 5.10. *Assume that a proposer makes at least two proposals in a round r. Let w_1 and w_2 denote the first and second value it proposes. Let v_{r-1} be the value chosen in round $r - 1$. Then, $v_{r-1} \sqsubseteq w_2$.*

PROOF. The proposer must have received responses from a quorum of acceptors for proposal w_1 before it proposes w_2. At least one of these acceptors, say a, must have acknowledged the value v_{r-1}. Furthermore, a must have acknowledged v_{r-1} before responding to proposal w_1. (Otherwise, we would have $w_1 \sqsubseteq v_{r-1}$, which contradicts the definition of rounds.) Hence, regardless of whether a ACKs or NACKs w_1, we have $v_{r-1} \sqsubseteq w_2$. □

LEMMA 5.11. *A proposer can execute at most $N_p + 1$ proposals in a single round.*

PROOF. Consider a round r in which a proposer p proposes a sequence of values $w_1 \sqsubset w_2 \sqsubset \cdots \sqsubset w_k$. Let *Prev* denote the set of all values initiated in a round $r' < r$. Let *Curr* denote the set of all values initiated in round r. Note that *Curr* can contain at most one value per proposer (from Lemma 5.9). Define *All* to be *Prev* ∪ *Curr*.

Note that each proposed value w_i can be expressed as the join of some subset of values in *All*. (This follows similar to Theorem 5.1.) Define $covered_j$ to be $\{u \in All \mid u \sqsubseteq w_j\}$. Thus, we have $w_j = \bigsqcup covered_j$.

It follows from above that $covered_1 \subset \cdots \subset covered_k$ is a strictly increasing sequence of subsets of $All = Prev \cup Curr$.

Now, we show that $covered_2 \supseteq Prev$. Let $v \in Prev$. Since v was initiated in an earlier round $r' < r$, we must have $v \sqsubseteq v_{r-1}$, where v_{r-1} is the value chosen in round $r - 1$. It follows from Lemma 5.10 that $v_{r-1} \sqsubseteq w_2$.

Putting these together, it follows that the strictly increasing sequence $covered_1 \subset \cdots \subset covered_k$ can have a length at most $N_p + 1$.

$\square$

Liveness Assumptions. Note that all the preceding results hold in the presence of arbitrary failures and message losses. The following progress guarantees, however, require the following extra assumptions: (a) A majority of acceptor processes are correct, (b) At least one proposer process is correct, (c) At least one learner process is correct, and (d) All messages between correct processes are eventually delivered. (Note that if every process simultaneously plays the roles of proposer, acceptor, and learner, then the first three assumptions simplify to the assumption that a majority of the processes are correct.)

LEMMA 5.12. *Every round eventually terminates.*

PROOF. Follows from Lemma 5.11. $\square$

LEMMA 5.13. *Every initiated value is eventually included in a chosen value.*

PROOF. Follows from Lemma 5.12 and Lemma 5.8. $\square$

LEMMA 5.14. *Every value received by a correct process is eventually proposed.*

PROOF. Consider a value u received by some correct process. By definition of Receive, u is sent to all proposers. It is eventually delivered to all correct proposers. If any correct proposer P that receives u is passive when it receives u, it will initiate u. However, if P is active, then it is in the middle of some round. It follows from Lemma 5.11 that eventually some proposer P' must execute a Decide step. Therefore, some correct process will eventually propose u. $\square$

THEOREM 5.15. *Every value received by a correct process is eventually learnt by every correct learner.*

PROOF. Implied by Lemma 5.13 and Lemma 5.14. Note that once a value is chosen, a correct learner will eventually receive the acknowledgments sent for the chosen value and learn it. $\square$

5.3 Time Complexity

We now establish the complexity of the generalized lattice agreement algorithm, in terms of the number of message delays (as described in Section 3). Recall that when a new value v is received, it is first sent to all correct proposers via the action *NewInput*. This takes one unit of time. Consider the last proposer to receive this value. By Lemma 5.11 we know that within the next N_p+1 proposals (i.e., $2 \times (N_p+1)$ units of time) some proposer will decide and will propose v in the next round. By Lemma 5.8 and Lemma 5.11, v will be chosen in the next $N_p + 1$ proposals. Every chosen value will be learnt by the learners after one message delay. Putting this all together it can be seen that every value received by a correct process is learnt in $O(N)$ units of time. Lemma 5.11 also implies that if only k processes receive values, each received value will be chosen in $O(k)$ message delays. In the extreme case, if only one process receives values, each received value can be learnt in three message delays (from the client to the proposer, from the proposer

to acceptors, and acceptors to client, assuming the client acts as a learner). This is one message delay more than the fast path of two message delays in Paxos [11]. Improving this bound while preserving wait-freedom remains an open problem.

6. STATE MACHINE REPLICATION USING LATTICE AGREEMENT

State machine replication is a general approach for implementing data-structures that can tolerate process failures by replicating state across multiple processes. In one common approach to state machine replication, replica processes receive requests or commands from clients, utilize consensus to decide on the order in which commands must be processed, and apply commands to the local replica of the state machine in that order. If the state machine is deterministic and no Byzantine faults occur, each correct process is guaranteed to generate the same responses and reach the same state. Unfortunately, the undecidability of consensus means that this approach cannot guarantee liveness in the presence of failures.

In this paper, we consider a special class of state machines. We first assume that operations of the state machine can be classified into two kinds: *updates* (operations that modify the state) and *reads* (operations that do not modify the state, but return a value). Thus, an operation that modifies the state and returns a value is not permitted. Furthermore, we assume that all update operations commute with each other and are deterministic. Several data types such as sets, sequences, certain types of key-value tables, and graphs [12] can be designed with commuting updates.

There are several approaches for implementing such state machines, each with different consistency and performance characteristics. One approach is to allow each replica process to process reads and updates in arbitrary order. This approach requires no co-ordination between processes and guarantees that as long as all commands are eventually delivered, all correct processes *eventually* reach the same state. However, this approach does not provide strong consistency guarantees, such as linearizability or serializability, for reads.

Both linearizability and serializability guarantee that the observed behavior of the replicated state machine on some set of (possibly concurrent) operations is the same as the behavior of the state machine (with no replication) for some sequential execution (the "witness") of the same set of operations. Linearizability provides the additional guarantee that any two temporally non-overlapping operations (in the execution) occur in the same order in the "witness".

One approach to guarantee linearizability, based on generalized consensus, is for processes to agree on a partial order on the commands that totally orders every read command with every update command that it does not commute with. This alternative guarantees linearizability but requires the use of consensus to compute the partial order, which is impossible in the presence of failures.

Serializability Using Lattice Agreement. Algorithm 3 describes a wait-free algorithm for state machine replication based on generalized lattice agreement that guarantees serializability. In this algorithm, the lattice L is defined to be the power set of all update commands with the partial order $\sqsubseteq$ defined to be set inclusion. (We use the term "update command" to refer to *instances* of update operations.) We

Algorithm 3 Serializable ReplicatedStateMachine
```
1: procedure ExecuteUpdate(cmd)
2:     ReceiveValue( {cmd})
3:
4: procedure State Read()
5:     return Apply(LearntValue())
```

Algorithm 4 Linearizable ReplicatedStateMachine
```
1: procedure ExecuteUpdate(cmd)
2:     ReceiveValue( {cmd})
3:     waituntil cmd ∈ LearntValue()
4:
5: procedure State Read()
6:     ExecuteUpdate(CreateNop())
7:     return Apply(LearntValue())
```

refer to a set of update commands as a *cset*. In this setting, update commands can be executed by proposers and read commands can be executed by learners. A proposer executes an update command cmd by simply executing the procedure ReceiveValue($\{cmd\}$), taking the singleton set $\{cmd\}$ to be a newly proposed value. Reads are processed by computing a state that reflects all commands in the learnt *cset* (applied in arbitrary order).

Due to the properties of generalized lattice agreement, it is easy to see that this algorithm is wait-free and serializable, with both reads and updates requiring $O(N)$ message delays. Furthermore, this algorithm guarantees *progress*: every update operation will eventually be reflected in all read operations (subject to our failure model). Note that the execution of an update command cmd completes (from a client's perspective) when the set $\{cmd\}$ has been sent to all proposers. For simplicity, assume that each process acts as a proposer, acceptor and learner. Progress is guaranteed as long as message delivery is reliable and at least a majority of the processes are correct.

Linearizability Using Lattice Agreement. We now extend the preceding algorithm to guarantee linearizability, as shown in Algorithm 4. For simplicity, we assume that each process acts as a proposer, acceptor and learner. The first challenge is to preserve the order of non-overlapping update operations: if one replica completes the execution of an update operation c_1 before another replica initiates the execution of an update operation c_2, then we must ensure that c_1 occurs before c_2 in the linearization order. This is not guaranteed by the serializable algorithm presented above.

We extend the execution of an update operation as follows. When a process executes an update command cmd, it includes the command in the next proposal (as before), and then *waits* until the command has been learnt. This preserves the order of non-overlapping update operations.

The second challenge concerns a read operation that is initiated after an update operation completes. In this case, we need to ensure that the value returned by the read operation reflects the effects of the update operation. We assume that the set of update commands includes a special *no-op* command which does not modify the state. Reads are processed by creating a new instance of the *no-op* command, executing this command, and then computing a state that reflects all commands in the learnt *cset* (applied in arbitrary order).

Optimizations. There are several simple ways of optimizing the basic algorithms presented above. Every invocation of Apply does not have to recompute state by executing all commands in LearntValue(). Instead, the implementation can exploit the monotonic nature of learnt values and the commutativity of update commands to incrementally compute state.

7. RELATED WORK

As mentioned before, the lattice agreement problem has been studied previously in an asynchronous shared memory setting [4, 3, 7]. In [7], Inoue *et al.* propose a lattice agreement algorithm which requires $O(M)$ register operations when processes are assigned identifiers in the range $[1 - M]$. The problem of assigning N processes names in a range $[0 - poly(N)]$ is referred to as the re-naming problem [2] and has been studied before. The best known algorithms for assigning identifiers in the range $[0 - O(N)]$ have a complexity of $O(N log(N))$. Hence the complexity of the Inoue *et al.* algorithm expressed in terms of number of participating processes is $O(N log(N))$, if the cost of naming is taken into account. Algorithms whose complexity depends only on the number of participant processes and not on the range of identifiers assigned to processes are called *range-independent* algorithms [3]. Further, an algorithm is *adaptive* if its complexity only depends on the number of participants actively contending at any given point in time [3]. The Inoue *et al.* algorithm is not adaptive. The algorithm proposed in [3] is both adaptive and range independent, it has a complexity of $O(N log(N))$ where N is the number of active participants. The construction of the algorithm requires a series of re-naming algorithms that are carefully put together to obtain a range independent and adaptive lattice agreement algorithm.

Some of the shared memory algorithms can be translated into message passing algorithms using emulators [1]. In particular, any shared memory algorithm that only uses single-writer multiple-reader atomic registers can be translated into a message passing algorithm with each read and write operation requiring only constant ($O(1)$) message delays. A direct emulation of the above algorithms using emulators from [1] leads to asynchronous message passing algorithms with complexity $O(N log(N))$.

In this paper we provide an asynchronous message passing algorithm for lattice agreement with complexity $O(N)$. Our algorithm is *range independent*, as it only requires the identifiers of all participating processes be unique and does not rely on any renaming steps. Our algorithm is also *adaptive* since the number of proposal refinements executed by a proposer depends only on the number of active proposers. We further show that the algorithm can be extended, without changing the complexity, to a generalization of the lattice agreement problem where processes receive a (potentially unbounded) sequence of values from a lattice and learn a sequence of values that form a chain.

8. REFERENCES

[1] Hagit Attiya, Amotz Bar-Noy, and Danny Dolev. Sharing memory robustly in message-passing systems. *J. ACM*, 42, 1995.

[2] Hagit Attiya, Amotz Bar-Noy, Danny Dolev, David Peleg, and Rüdiger Reischuk. Renaming in an

asynchronous environment. *J. ACM*, 37:524–548, July 1990.

[3] Hagit Attiya and Arie Fouren. Adaptive and efficient algorithms for lattice agreement and renaming. *SIAM J. Comput.*, 31, February 2002.

[4] Hagit Attiya, Maurice Herlihy, and Ophir Rachman. Atomic snapshots using lattice agreement. *Distrib. Comput.*, 8, March 1995.

[5] Michael J. Fischer, Nancy Lynch, and Michael S. Paterson. Impossibility of distributed consensus with one faulty process. *Journal of the ACM*, 2(32):374–382, April 1985.

[6] Maurice P. Herlihy and Jeannette M. Wing. Linearizability: a correctness condition for concurrent objects. *ACM Transactions on Programming Languages and Systems*, 12:463–492, July 1990.

[7] Michiko Inoue and Wei Chen. Linear-time snapshot using multi-writer multi-reader registers. In *Proceedings of the 8th International Workshop on Distributed Algorithms*, WDAG '94. Springer-Verlag, 1994.

[8] Leslie Lamport. The implementation of reliable distributed multiprocess systems. *Computer Networks*, 2:95–114, 1978.

[9] Leslie Lamport. The part-time parliament. *ACM Transactions on Computer Systems*, 16:133–169, May 1998.

[10] Leslie Lamport. Generalized consensus and paxos. Technical Report MSR-TR-2005-33, Microsoft Research, April 2005.

[11] Leslie Lamport. Fast paxos. *Distributed Computing*, 19:79–103, 2006.

[12] M. Shapiro, N. Preguiça, C. Baquero, and M. Zawirski. Convergent and commutative replicated data types. *Bulletin of the European Association for Theoretical Computer Science (EATCS)*, (104):67–88, 2011.

Distributed Selfish Load Balancing with Weights and Speeds

Clemens P.J. Adolphs[*]
University of British Columbia
6224 Agricultural Road
Vancouver, B.C., V6T 1Z1 Canada
cadolphs@phas.ubc.ca

Petra Berenbrink[†]
Simon Fraser University
8888 University Drive
Burnaby, B.C., V5A 1S6 Canada
petra@cs.sfu.ca

ABSTRACT

In this paper we consider neighborhood load balancing in the context of selfish clients. We assume that a network of n processors is given, with m tasks assigned to the processors. The processors may have different speeds and the tasks may have different weights. Every task is controlled by a selfish user. The objective of the user is to allocate his/her task to a processor with minimum load, where the load of a processor is defined as the weight of its tasks divided by its speed.

We investigate a concurrent probabilistic protocol which works in sequential rounds. In each round every task is allowed to query the load of one randomly chosen neighboring processor. If that load is smaller than the load of the task's current processor, the task will migrate to that processor with a suitably chosen probability. Using techniques from spectral graph theory we obtain upper bounds on the expected convergence time towards approximate and exact Nash equilibria that are significantly better than previous results for this protocol. We show results for uniform tasks on non-uniform processors and the general case where the tasks have different weights and the machines have speeds. To the best of our knowledge, these are the first results for this general setting.

Categories and Subject Descriptors

F.2.2 [**Theory of Computation**]: Nonnumerical Algorithms and Problems—*Sequencing and Scheduling*

Keywords

Load balancing, reallocation, equilibrium, convergence

[*]The research was carried out during a visit to SFU.

[†]The author was funded by an NSERC Discovery Grant "Analysis of Randomized Algorithms"

General Terms

Algorithms, Theory

1. INTRODUCTION

In this paper we consider a variant of diffusion load balancing that is motivated by game theoretic concepts. In standard diffusion load balancing a graph is given whose vertices model *processors* and whose links can be used for communication and to exchange load items (called *tasks* in the following). In the beginning the tasks are arbitrarily distributed among the processors. The load balancing process works in sequential rounds. In every round every vertex is allowed to balance its load with all its neighbors by exchanging tasks. The goal is to balance the total system load globally, meaning to minimize the load difference between the nodes with minimum and maximum load. In contrast to standard diffusion load balancing, in *selfish load balancing* it is assumed that every task belongs to a selfish user. Instead of the nodes balancing the load with their neighbors, the users are now allowed to move their tasks over to a neighboring vertex. Of course, since the users are selfish they will never move items over to nodes having larger load. The goal is for such a system to converge as soon as possible to a *Nash Equilibrium*, where no user is able to decrease the load of its task by migrating it to a neighboring processor.

We revisit the selfish load balancing protocol introduced in [6]. In each round every user is allowed to check the load of one randomly chosen neighboring processor. In more detail, let us assume that the task of a user is assigned to vertex v. Then the user randomly chooses one of the neighbors of v. If the load of the chosen neighbor is smaller, the user will migrate its task with a suitably chosen probability to that processor. Note that if the probability is too large (for example, all users move their tasks over to the random neighbor as long as its load is smaller) the system would never be able to reach a balanced state. In this paper we choose the migration probability as a function of the load difference of the two involved processors. This means that no global information is necessary.

Similarly to [6] we consider several generalizations of the model. The tasks can have different *weights* which model, for example, the runtime of the tasks. If all tasks have the same weight we call them *uniform*. The processors have different *speeds*. Again, uniform speeds means that the speeds of all processors are the same. We show results for uniform tasks on processors with speeds. We also consider the general case with weighted tasks and machines with speeds. To our best knowledge these are the first results for this general setting.

We calculate upper bounds on the expected convergence time towards approximate and exact Nash equilibria that are significantly better than the previous results in [6]. For weighted tasks we consider a protocol that is different from the one given in [6]. In our new protocol, a player will move its tasks to the neighboring node only if the player with the task with maximum weight would do the same. A justification for this is that in many realistic settings, migration will only occur if the gain from doing so exceeds some threshold. Our analysis uses techniques from spectral graph theory similar to those used in [10].

Load Balancing is an important aspect of massively parallel computations as it must be ensured that resources are used to their full efficiency. Our load balancing strategies have the advantage that the users do not need any global load information of the system, they only have to know the load of a randomly chosen neighbor. Global information is often unavailable and global coordination usually very expensive and impractical. Another advantage is that the load items are moved to neighboring nodes only, which has the effect that load items that were initially on the same node tend to stay closely together. This is important if these tasks have to exchange information.

2. MODEL AND NEW RESULTS

The parallel system is represented by an undirected graph $G = (V, E)$ with vertices representing processors and edges representing direct communication links between them. The number of processors is n. The *degree* of a vertex $v \in V$ is $\deg(v)$. The maximum degree of the network is denoted by Δ, and for two nodes v and w the maximum of $\deg(v)$ and $\deg(w)$ is d_{vw}.

We define $s_i \in \mathbb{R}$ as the speed of processor i. We assume that the smallest speed is exactly one. $s_{\max}$ is the maximum speed and $s_{\min}$ is the minimum speed of any processor. If all speeds are equal the speeds are called *uniform*. If all s_i are integer multiples of a factor ϵ, i.e. for every speed s_i there exists an integer $n_i \in \mathbb{N}$ so that $s_i = n_i \cdot \epsilon$, we call them ϵ-*speeds*. We call ϵ the *granularity* of the speed distribution. Note that ϵ does not have to be an integer itself. Let $\mathcal{S} = \sum_{i \in V} s_i$ be the total capacity of the processors. We define the *speed vector* $\mathbf{s} = (s_1, \cdots s_n)^\top$ and the *speed matrix* $S \in \mathbb{N}^{n \times n}$ with $S_{ii} = s_i$ and $S_{ij} = 0$ for $i \neq j$.

The number of tasks in the system is m. Task ℓ has weight ω_ℓ with $\omega_\ell \in (0, 1]$. In the case of uniform tasks the size of all tasks is equal and we assume the weight of all tasks is one. Define $W = \sum_{i=1}^m \omega_i(x)$ as the total load of the system and $\bar{\omega} = W/m$ as the average load.

$\mathbf{X}^t$ with $\mathbf{X}^t = X_1^t, \ldots X_n^t$ models the system state. X_i^t is the set of tasks that are assigned to processor i at the end of round t. We define $\mathbf{W}^t = W_1^t, \ldots W_n^t$ as the weight vector with W_i^t as the weight of the tasks that are assigned to processor i at the end of round t. Define $\mathbf{L}^t = S^{-1}\mathbf{W}^t$ as the *load vector* with $L_i^t = W_i^t/s_i$ as the load of the tasks assigned to processor i. Note that $\mathbf{X}^t$, $\mathbf{W}^t$ and $\mathbf{L}^t$ are vectors of random variables. We will use x^t, w_i^t and ℓ^t to denote fixed values of these variables. For a fixed state x^t, $\mathbf{e} = \mathbf{w}^t - \bar{\mathbf{w}}$ is the deviation of the actual task vector from the average load vector. It is clear that $\sum_{i \in V} e_i(x) = 0$.

A state x^t of the system is called a *Nash equilibrium* (NE) if no single task can improve its perceived load by migrating to a neighboring node while all other tasks remain where they are, i.e., $\ell_i^t - \ell_j^t \leq 1/s_j$ for all $(i, j) \in E$. A state x^t of the system is called an ε-*approximate Nash equilibrium* (ε-approximate-NE) if no single task can improve its perceived load by a factor of $(1 - \varepsilon)$, i.e. $(1 - \varepsilon) \cdot \ell_i - \ell_j \leq 1/s_j$.

The Laplacian $L = L(G)$ is a matrix widely used in graph theory. It is the $n \times n$ matrix whose diagonal elements are $L_{ii} = \deg(i)$, and the off-diagonal elements are $L_{ij} = -1$ if $(i, j) \in E(G)$ and 0 otherwise. λ_2 denotes the second smallest eigenvalue of L. The generalized Laplacian LS^{-1} [10], where S is the diagonal matrix containing the speeds s_i, is used to analyze the behavior of migration in heterogeneous networks.

2.1 Uniform Tasks

In this section we review our results for uniform tasks on machines with unequal speeds. One round of the protocol is defined as follows. Every task selects a neighboring node uniformly at random. If migrating to that node would lower the load experienced by the task, the task migrates to that node with probability proportional to the load difference and the speeds of the processors. For a detailed description of the protocol see Algorithm 1 in Section 5.

The first result concerns convergence to an approximate Nash equilibrium. We use a potential function $\Psi_0(x)$ to measure how close to such an approximate Nash equilibrium the system is. This function will be defined in Sec. 5.

Theorem 2.1 *Let* $\psi_c = 16n \cdot \Delta \cdot s_{\max}/\lambda_2$. *Algorithm 1 reaches a state* x *with* $\Psi_0(x) \leq 4 \cdot \psi_c$ *in expected time*

$$\mathcal{O}\left(\ln\left(\frac{m}{n}\right) \cdot \frac{\Delta}{\lambda_2} \cdot s_{\max}^2\right).$$

If $m \geq 8 \cdot \delta \cdot s_{\max} \cdot \mathcal{S} \cdot n^2$ *for some* $\delta > 1$, *this state is an* ε-*approximate-Nash equilibrium with* $\varepsilon = 2/(1 + \delta)$.

From the state reached in Theorem 2.1, we then go on to prove the following bound for convergence to a Nash equilibrium.

Theorem 2.2 *Let* $\psi_c = 16n \cdot \Delta \cdot s_{\max}/\lambda_2$ *and assume* $\mathbf{s}$ *consists of* ϵ-*speeds. Let* T *be the first time step in which the system is in a Nash equilibrium. Then*

$$\mathbf{E}[T] = \mathcal{O}\left(n \cdot \frac{\Delta^2}{\lambda_2} \cdot \frac{s_{\max}^4}{\epsilon^2}\right).$$

These theorems are proven in Section 5. Our bound of Theorem 2.2 is smaller by at least a factor of $\Omega(\Delta \cdot \text{diam}(G))$ than the bound found in [6] (see Observation 5.19).

We summarize the results for the most important graph classes in Table 1. The table gives an overview of asymptotic bounds on the expected runtime to reach an approximate or a exact Nash equilibrium. We omit the speeds from this table because they are independent of the graph structure and, therefore, the same for each column. We compare the results of this paper to the bounds obtained from [6]. These contain a factor $\mathcal{S} = \sum_i s_i$, which we replace with n, using $\mathcal{S} = \sum_i s_i \geq n$. The table shows that for the graph classes at hand, our new bounds are superior to those in [6].

2.2 Weighted Tasks

In Section 6, we study a slightly modified protocol (see 2) that allows tasks only to migrate to a neighboring processor

Table 1: Comparison with existing results

Graph	ε-approximate NE		Nash Equilibrium	
	This Paper	[6]	This Paper	[6]
Complete Graph	$\ln\left(\frac{m}{n}\right)$	$n^2 \cdot \ln(m)$	n^2	n^6
Ring, Path	$n^2 \cdot \ln\left(\frac{m}{n}\right)$	$n^3 \cdot \ln(m)$	n^3	n^5
Mesh, Torus	$n \cdot \ln\left(\frac{m}{n}\right)$	$n^2 \cdot \ln(m)$	n^2	n^4
Hypercube	$\ln(n) \cdot \ln\left(\frac{m}{n}\right)$	$n \cdot \ln^3(n) \cdot \ln(m)$	$n \cdot \ln^2(n)$	$n^3 \cdot \ln^5(n)$

if that would decrease their experienced load by a threshold depending on the speed of the processors. This protocol allows the tasks only to reach an approximate Nash Equilibrium.

The potential function used in the following theorem is introduced in Section 6 and is used similarly to the one in the unweighted case to measure progress towards an approximate Nash equilibrium.

Theorem 2.3 *Let* $\psi_c = 16 \cdot n \cdot \Delta/\lambda_2 \cdot s_{\max}/s_{\min}^2$. *Algorithm 2 reaches a state* x *with* $\Psi_0(x) \leq 4 \cdot \psi_c$ *in time*

$$\mathcal{O}\left(\ln\left(\frac{m}{n}\right) \cdot \frac{\Delta}{\lambda_2} \cdot \frac{s_{\max}^2}{s_{\min}}\right).$$

If $W > 8 \cdot \delta \cdot s_{\max}/s_{\min} \cdot \mathcal{S} \cdot n^2$ *for some* $\delta > 1$, *this state is an* $2/(1+\delta)$-*approximate Nash equilibrium.*

For uniform speeds the theorem gives a bound of

$$\mathcal{O}\left(\ln(m/n) \cdot \Delta/\lambda_2\right)$$

for the convergence time.

3. RELATED WORK

The work closest to ours is in [4, 5, 6]. [4] considers the case of identical machines in a complete graph. The authors introduce a protocol similar to ours that reaches a Nash Equilibria (NE) in time $\mathcal{O}(\log\log m + \text{poly}(n))$. An extension of this model to weighted tasks is studied in [5]. Their protocol converges to a NE in time polynomially in n, m, and the largest weight. In [6] the authors consider general graphs with processors with speed and weighted tasks. They use a potential function similar to ours for the analysis. The two main results of [6] for machines with speeds are presented in Table 1. [2] applies our techniques to discrete diffusive load balancing where each node sends the rounded expected flow of the randomized protocol to its neighbors.

Our paper relates to a general stream of works for selfish load balancing on a complete graph. There is a variety of issues that have been considered, starting with seminal papers on algorithms and dynamics to reach NE [12, 14]. More directly related are concurrent protocols for selfish load balancing in different contexts that allow convergence results similar to ours. Whereas some papers consider protocols that use some form of global information [13] or coordinated migration [18], others consider infinitesimal or splittable tasks [17, 3] or work without rationality assumptions [16, 1]. The machine models in these cases range from identical, uniformly related (linear with speeds) to unrelated machines. The latter also contains the case when there are

access restrictions of certain agents to certain machines. For an overview of work on selfish load balancing see, e.g., [25].

Our protocol is also related to a vast amount of literature on (non-selfish) load balancing over networks, where results usually concern the case of identical machines and unweighted tasks. In expectation, our protocols mimic continuous diffusion, which has been studied initially in [9, 7] and later, e.g., in [23]. This work established the connection between convergence, discrepancy, and eigenvalues of graph matrices. Closer to our paper are discrete diffusion processes – prominently studied in [24], where the authors introduce a general technique to bound the load deviations between an idealized and the actual processes. Recently, randomized extensions of the algorithm in [24] have been considered, e.g., [11, 19].

4. SPECTRAL GRAPH THEORY

In this section, we will briefly collect some important results of spectral graph theory that we use in our proofs. For an excellent introduction, we recommend the book by Fan Chung [8]. Many important results are collected in an overview article by Mohar [22]. We omit a discussion of the most basic properties and refer to the extensive literature.

Results in this section are, unless indicated otherwise, taken from these sources. Let us begin by defining the matrix we are interested in.

Definition 4.1 *Let* $G = (V, E)$ *be an undirected graph with vertices* $V = \{1, \ldots n\}$ *and edges* E.

The Laplacian $L(G)$ *of* G *is defined as*

$$L(G) \in \mathbb{N}^{n \times n} \qquad L(G)_{ij} = \begin{cases} \deg(i) & i = j \\ -1 & (i,j) \in E \\ 0 & \text{otherwise.} \end{cases}$$

The second-smallest eigenvalue λ_2 is closely related to the connectivity properties of G. A first, albeit weak, result is the preceding lemma. A stronger result with a corollary useful for simple estimates is given in the next lemma.

Lemma 4.2 ([21]) *Let* λ_2 *be the second-smallest eigenvalue of the unweighted Laplacian of a graph* G. *Let* $\text{diam}(G)$ *be the diameter of graph* G. *Then*

$$\text{diam}(G) \geq \frac{4}{n \cdot \lambda_2}.$$

Corollary 4.3 *Using* $\text{diam}(G) \leq n$, *we get* $\lambda_2 \geq \frac{4}{n^2}$

Lemma 4.4 *This is another useful result by Fiedler [15]. Let λ_2 be the second-smallest eigenvalue of $L(G)$. Then,*

$$\lambda_2 \leq \frac{n}{n-1} \cdot \min\{\deg(i), i \in V\}.$$

For Δ the maximum degree of graph G, it immediately follows

$$\lambda_2 \leq \frac{n}{n-1} \cdot \Delta.$$

A stronger relationship between λ_2 and the network's connectivity properties is provided via the graph's Cheeger constant.

Definition 4.5 *Let $G = (V, E)$ be a graph and $S \subset V$ a subset of the nodes. The boundary δS of S is defined as the set of edges having exactly one endpoint in S, i.e.,*

$$\delta S = \{(i, j) \in E \mid i \in S, j \in V \setminus S\}.$$

Definition 4.6 *Let $G = (V, E)$ be a graph. The isoperimetric number $i(G)$ of G is defined as*

$$i(G) = \min_{\substack{S \subset V \\ |S| \leq |V|/2}} \frac{|\delta S|}{|S|}.$$

It is also called Cheeger constant of the graph.

The isoperimetric number of a graph is a measure of how well any subset of the graph is connected to the rest of the graph. Graphs with a high Cheeger constant are also called *expanders*. The following was proven by Mohar.

Lemma 4.7 ([20]) *Let λ_2 be the second-smallest eigenvalue of $L(G)$, and let $i(G)$ be the isoperimetric number of G. Then,*

$$\frac{i^2(G)}{2\Delta} \leq \lambda_2 \leq 2i(G).$$

4.1 Generalized Laplacian Analysis

Recall the speed-matrix S from the introduction. Instead of analyzing the Laplacian L, we are interested in the *generalized Laplacian*, defined as LS^{-1}. This definition is also used by Elsässer in [10] in the analysis of continuous diffusive load balancing in heterogeneous networks. In this reference, the authors prove a variety of results for the generalized Laplacian, which we restate here in a slightly different language.

It turns out that in the discussion of the properties of this generalized Laplacian, many results carry over from the analysis of the normal Laplacian. The similarity is made manifest by the introduction of a *generalized dot-product*.

Definition 4.8 *For vectors $\mathbf{x}, \mathbf{y} \in \mathbb{R}^n$, we define the generalized dot-product with respect to S as*

$$\langle \mathbf{x}, \mathbf{y} \rangle_S := \mathbf{x}^T S^{-1} \mathbf{y} = \sum_{i \in V} \frac{x_i \cdot y_i}{s_i}$$

Lemma 4.9 *The vector space $\mathbb{R}^n$ with $\langle \cdot, \cdot \rangle_S$ forms an inner product space.*

Remark 4.10 *The fact that $\langle \cdot, \cdot \rangle_S$ is an inner product allows us to directly apply many results of linear algebra to it. For example, two vectors $\mathbf{x}$ and $\mathbf{y}$ are called orthogonal to each other, $\mathbf{x} \perp \mathbf{y}$, if $\mathbf{x} \cdot \mathbf{y} = 0$. Analogously, we call $\mathbf{x}$ and $\mathbf{y}$ orthogonal with respect to S if $\langle \mathbf{x}, \mathbf{y} \rangle_S = 0$.*

Let us now collect some of the properties of LS^{-1}. These properties have also been used in [10]. We restate them here using the notation of the generalized dot product.

Lemma 4.11 *(Compare Lemma 1 in [10]) Let L be the Laplacian of a graph, and let S be the speed-matrix, $S = \mathrm{diag}(s_1, \cdots, s_n)$. Then the following holds true for the generalized Laplacian LS^{-1}.*

(1) *The speed-vector $\mathbf{s} = (s_1, \ldots, s_n)^\top$ is (right-)eigenvector to LS^{-1} with eigenvalue 0.*

(2) *LS^{-1} is not symmetric any more. It is, however, still positive semi-definite.*

(3) *Since LS^{-1} is not symmetric, we have to distinguish left- and right-eigenvectors. Similar to the spectral theorem of linear algebra, we can find a basis of right-eigenvectors of LS^{-1} that are orthogonal with respect to S.*

For arbitrary vectors, we know that $\langle \mathbf{x}, LS^{-1}\mathbf{x} \rangle_S \geq 0$ since $S^{-1}LS^{-1}$ is positive semi-definite. The next lemma bounds the generalized dot product of certain vectors with the Laplacian with the second smallest right-eigenvector of it. A similar version can also be found in [10, Section 3].

Lemma 4.12 *Let λ_2 be the second-smallest right eigenvalue of the generalized Laplacian, LS^{-1}. Let $\mathbf{e}$ be a vector that is orthogonal to the speed vector with respect to S, i.e. $\langle \mathbf{e}, \mathbf{s} \rangle_S = 0$. Then*

$$\langle \mathbf{e}, LS^{-1}\mathbf{e} \rangle_S \geq \lambda_2 \langle \mathbf{e}, \mathbf{e} \rangle_S.$$

The next technical lemma is needed to relate the spectra of L and LS^{-1}. We require this relation because most of the useful results and bounds for λ_2 apply to the normal Laplacian only.

Lemma 4.13 *Let μ_i denote the eigenvalues of LS^{-1} in ascending order and let λ_i denote the eigenvalues of L in ascending order. Finally, let s_i denote the speeds in descending order. Then*

$$\mu_{i+j-1} \geq \frac{\lambda_i}{s_j} \qquad 0 \leq i, j \leq n, \quad 0 \leq i+j-1 \leq n \quad (1)$$

$$\mu_{i+j-n} \leq \frac{\lambda_i}{s_j} \qquad 0 \leq i, j \leq n, \quad 0 \leq i+j-n \leq n. \quad (2)$$

Corollary 4.14 *Let μ_2 denote the second smallest right eigenvalue of LS^{-1} and let λ_2 denote the second smallest eigenvalue of L. Let $s_{\max} = s_1$ be the largest speed and $s_{\min} = s_n$ the smallest speed. Then*

$$\frac{\lambda_2}{s_{\max}} \leq \mu_2 \leq \frac{\lambda_2}{s_{\min}}.$$

PROOF. Let $i = 2, j = 1$ in (1) and $i = 2, j = n$ in (2).

5. UNIFORM TASKS WITH SPEEDS

The pseudo-code of a single step of our protocol is given in Algorithm 1. Recall that d_{ij} is given by $\max\{\deg(i), \deg(j)\}$ and α is defined as $4s_{\max}$.

For the analysis we use the same (standard) *potential function* as the one used in [6]. For $r = 0, 1$, define

$$\Phi_r(x) := \sum_{i \in V} w_i(x) \cdot (w_i(x) + r)/s_i$$

The potential Φ_0 is minimized for the average task vector, $\bar{\mathbf{w}}$. We define the *normalized potential* as

$$\Psi_0(x) = \Phi_0(x) - m^2/\mathcal{S} = \sum_{i \in V}(w_i - \bar{w})^2 \,/s_i = \sum_{i \in V} e_i^2 \,/s_i.$$

We define $\Delta\Phi_r(X^t) := \Phi_r(X^{t-1}) - \Phi_r(X^t)$ as the potential drop in step t. $\Delta\Psi_0(X^t)$ is defined analogously. From the definition of Ψ_0, it becomes clear that $\Delta\Psi_0(X^t) = \Delta\Phi_0(X^t)$.

Algorithm 1: Distributed Selfish Load Balancing

---
begin
    foreach *task ℓ in parallel* **do**
        Let $i = i(l)$ be the current machine of task l
        Choose a neighboring machine j uniformly at random
        if $\ell_i - \ell_j > 1/s_j$ **then**
            Move task ℓ from node i to node j with probability

$$p_{ij} := \frac{\deg(i)}{d_{i,j}} \cdot \frac{\ell_i - \ell_j}{\alpha \cdot (1/s_i + 1/s_j) \cdot w_i}$$

        end
    end
end

The *maximum load difference* is defined as

$$L_\Delta(x) = \max_{i \in V}|w_i(x)/s_i - m/\mathcal{S}| = \max_{i \in V}|e_i/s_i|.$$

For a given state x, we define $f_{ij}(x)$ as the *expected flow* over edge (i,j), with

$$f_{ij}(x) = (\ell_i(x) - \ell_j(x))/(\alpha \cdot d_{ij} \cdot (1/s_i + 1/s_j))$$

if $\ell_i(x) - \ell_j(x) > 1/s_j$, and 0 otherwise. As an auxiliary quantity, we define

$$\Lambda_{ij}^r(x) := (2\alpha - 2) \cdot d_{ij} \cdot (1/s_i + 1/s_j) \cdot f_{ij}(x) + r/s_i - r/s_j.$$

We define the set of *non-Nash edges* as $\tilde{E}(x) := \{(i,j) \in E : f_{ij}(x) > 0\}$. This is the set of edges for which tasks have an incentive to migrate. Edges with $f_{ij}(x) = 0$ are called *Nash edges* or *balanced edges*.

Our improved bound builds upon results in [6]. In that paper, the randomized process is analyzed by lower-bounding the expected potential drop. Up to their Lemma 3.3 (restated below as Lemma 5.1) our analysis follows the steps of [6]. They then go on to link the potential drop to L_Δ. The authors show that as long as the potential Ψ_0 is large enough an edge must exist over which the load difference is at least $L_\Delta/\text{diam}(G)$. Then they show an expected multiplicative potential drop, which is used to prove convergence to an approximate Nash equilibrium. Subsequently, a constant drop in Φ_1 is used to finally converge to a Nash equilibrium.

Lemma 5.1 (Lemma 3.3 in [6]) *For any step t and any state x,*

$$\mathbf{E}[\Delta\Phi_r(X^t)|X^{t-1} = x] \geq$$
$$\sum_{(i,j)\in\tilde{E}(x)} f_{ij}(x) \cdot \left(\Lambda_{ij}^r(x) - \frac{1}{s_i} - \frac{1}{s_j}\right).$$

Here we prove a stronger bound by linking the potential drop to the Laplacian matrix. This results in a larger factor for the multiplicative drop, which then allows us to prove faster convergence to an approximate Nash equilibrium. In addition, the value of the potential Φ_1 in that approximate equilibrium is smaller than the value reached in [6]. This results in faster convergence to a Nash equilibrium using the constant drop in Φ_1. In summary, the main novelty of our analysis lies in significantly improving the bound on the expected multiplicative potential drop in Ψ_0 and the bound on Φ_1 after an approximate Nash equilibrium is reached. Other intermediate steps leading to and from these results are very similar to the steps in [6]. However, our results are also applicable to non-integer speeds. We note here that all proofs not appearing in the main text were omitted due to space limitations.

5.1 Approximate Nash Equilibrium

Lemma 5.2 *Under the condition that the system is in state x, the expected drop in the potentials Φ_0 and Ψ_0 is bounded by*

$$\mathbf{E}[\Delta\Psi_0(X^{t+1})|X^t = x] \geq$$
$$\sum_{(i,j)\in E}\left[\frac{(1 - \frac{2}{\alpha}) \cdot (\ell_i(x) - \ell_j(x))^2}{\alpha \cdot d_{i,j} \cdot \left(\frac{1}{s_i} + \frac{1}{s_j}\right)}\right] - \frac{n}{\alpha}.$$

PROOF. For brevity, we omit the argument x from all quantities. Note that we can look at the drop of either Φ_0 or Ψ_0. Substituting the particular forms of f_{ij} and Λ_{ij}^0 into the bound provided by Lemma 5.1, we arrive at

$$\mathbf{E}[\Delta\Psi_0(X^{t+1})|X^t = x]$$
$$\geq \sum_{(i,j)\in\tilde{E}}\left[\frac{(2 - \frac{2}{\alpha}) \cdot (\ell_i - \ell_j)^2}{\alpha \cdot d_{i,j} \cdot \left(\frac{1}{s_i} + \frac{1}{s_j}\right)} - \frac{(\ell_i - \ell_j)}{\alpha \cdot d_{i,j}}\right]. \quad (*)$$

We define subsets $\tilde{E}$, $\tilde{E}_1$ and $\tilde{E}_2$ of E,

$$\tilde{E} = \left\{(i,j) \in E \mid \ell_i - \ell_j \geq \frac{1}{s_j}\right\}$$
$$\tilde{E}_1 = \left\{(i,j) \in \tilde{E} \mid \ell_i - \ell_j \geq \frac{1}{s_i} + \frac{1}{s_j}\right\}$$
$$\tilde{E}_2 = \tilde{E} \setminus \tilde{E}_1.$$

Note that $\tilde{E} = \tilde{E}_1 \cup \tilde{E}_2$ and $\tilde{E}_1 \cap \tilde{E}_2 = \emptyset$. Thus, we can split the sum in $(*)$ into a sum over $\tilde{E}_1$ and a sum over $\tilde{E}_2$. We will now bound these sums individually.

Let $(i,j) \in \tilde{E}_1$ be an edge in $\tilde{E}_1$ so that $\ell_i \geq \ell_j$. Then the definition of $\tilde{E}_1$ and the non-negativity of $\ell_i - \ell_j$ allows us to deduce

$$\ell_i - \ell_j \geq \frac{1}{s_i} + \frac{1}{s_j} \Leftrightarrow \frac{1}{\frac{1}{s_i} + \frac{1}{s_j}} \cdot (\ell_i - \ell_j)^2 \geq \ell_i - \ell_j.$$

This allows us to bound

$$\sum_{(i,j)\in\tilde{E}_1}\left[\frac{(2 - \frac{2}{\alpha}) \cdot (\ell_i - \ell_j)^2}{\alpha \cdot d_{i,j} \cdot \left(\frac{1}{s_i} + \frac{1}{s_j}\right)} - \frac{(\ell_i - \ell_j)}{\alpha \cdot d_{i,j}}\right]$$
$$\geq \sum_{(i,j)\in\tilde{E}_1}\frac{(1 - \frac{2}{\alpha}) \cdot (\ell_i - \ell_j)^2}{\alpha \cdot d_{i,j} \cdot \left(\frac{1}{s_i} + \frac{1}{s_j}\right)}. \quad (*)$$

139

Next, we turn to $\tilde{E}_2$ and bound

$$\sum_{(i,j)\in\tilde{E}_2}\left[\frac{(2-\frac{2}{\alpha})\cdot(\ell_i-\ell_j)^2}{\alpha\cdot d_{i,j}\cdot\left(\frac{1}{s_i}+\frac{1}{s_j}\right)}-\frac{(\ell_i-\ell_j)}{\alpha\cdot d_{i,j}}\right].$$

The sum is over two terms, a positive and a negative one. For the first, positive term, we simply bound

$$\sum_{(i,j)\in\tilde{E}_2}\left[\frac{(2-\frac{2}{\alpha})\cdot(\ell_i-\ell_j)^2}{\alpha\cdot d_{i,j}\cdot\left(\frac{1}{s_i}+\frac{1}{s_j}\right)}\right]$$
$$\geq\sum_{(i,j)\in\tilde{E}_2}\left[\frac{(1-\frac{2}{\alpha})\cdot(\ell_i-\ell_j)^2}{\alpha\cdot d_{i,j}\cdot\left(\frac{1}{s_i}+\frac{1}{s_j}\right)}\right].\quad(**)$$

For the edges in $\tilde{E}_2$, we have $\ell_i-\ell_j<1/s_i+1/s_j$. This allows us to bound the second, negative term via

$$\sum_{(i,j)\in\tilde{E}_2}\frac{\ell_i-\ell_j}{\alpha\cdot d_{i,j}}\leq\frac{1}{\alpha}\cdot\sum_{(i,j)\in\tilde{E}_2}\frac{1}{d_{i,j}}\cdot\left(\frac{1}{s_i}+\frac{1}{s_j}\right)\quad(***)$$

Combining $(*)$, $(**)$ and $(***)$ yields

$$\mathbf{E}[\Delta\Psi_0(X^{t+1})|X^t=x]\geq$$
$$\sum_{(i,j)\in\tilde{E}}\left[\frac{(2-\frac{2}{\alpha})\cdot(\ell_i-\ell_j)^2}{\alpha\cdot d_{i,j}\cdot\left(\frac{1}{s_i}+\frac{1}{s_j}\right)}-\frac{(\ell_i-\ell_j)}{\alpha\cdot d_{i,j}}\right]\geq$$
$$\sum_{(i,j)\in\tilde{E}}\frac{(1-\frac{2}{\alpha})\cdot(\ell_i-\ell_j)^2}{\alpha\cdot d_{ij}\cdot\left(\frac{1}{s_i}+\frac{1}{s_j}\right)}-\sum_{(i,j)\in\tilde{E}_2}\frac{1}{\alpha\cdot d_{ij}}\cdot\left(\frac{1}{s_i}+\frac{1}{s_j}\right).$$
$$(\dagger)$$

In the next step, we rewrite the sum over $\tilde{E}$ in $(\dagger)$ to a sum over all edges E, using $\tilde{E}=E\setminus(E\setminus\tilde{E})$. It generally holds for any terms $X_{(i,j)}$ that

$$\sum_{(i,j)\in\tilde{E}}X_{(i,j)}=\sum_{(i,j)\in E}X_{(i,j)}-\sum_{(i,j)\in E\setminus\tilde{E}}X_{(i,j)}.$$

We will apply this to $(\dagger)$. In the following, we therefore prove an upper bound on the sum over $E\setminus\tilde{E}$. Without loss of generality, let the nodes i and j of an edge be ordered such that $\ell_i\geq\ell_j$. For edges not in $\tilde{E}$, we have, by definition, $0\leq\ell_i-\ell_j\leq\frac{1}{s_j}$, so this part can be bound by

$$\sum_{(i,j)\in E\setminus\tilde{E}}\frac{(1-\frac{2}{\alpha})}{\alpha\cdot d_{i,j}\cdot\left(\frac{1}{s_i}+\frac{1}{s_j}\right)}\cdot(\ell_i-\ell_j)^2$$
$$\leq\sum_{(i,j)\in E\setminus\tilde{E}}\frac{1}{\alpha\cdot d_{ij}}\cdot\frac{s_i}{s_i+s_j}\cdot\frac{1}{s_j}$$
$$\leq\sum_{(i,j)\in E\setminus\tilde{E}}\frac{1}{\alpha\cdot d_{ij}}\cdot\left(1-\frac{s_j}{s_i+s_j}\right)\cdot\frac{1}{s_j}$$
$$=\sum_{(i,j)\in E\setminus\tilde{E}}\frac{1}{\alpha\cdot d_{i,j}}\cdot\left(\frac{1}{s_j}-\frac{1}{s_i+s_j}\right)$$
$$\leq\sum_{(i,j)\in E\setminus\tilde{E}}\frac{1}{\alpha\cdot d_{i,j}}\cdot\left(\frac{1}{s_i}+\frac{1}{s_j}\right).$$

This bound has the same form as the bound in $(***)$, only that it goes over $E\setminus\tilde{E}$ instead of $\tilde{E}_2$. These two sets are

disjunct, since $\tilde{E}_2\subset\tilde{E}$. Therefore, we can combine the two sums into a single sum over $\tilde{E}_2\cup(E\setminus\tilde{E})=E\setminus\tilde{E}_1$. We then obtain from the following bound from $(\dagger)$.

$$\mathbf{E}[\Delta\Psi_0(X^{t+1})|X^t=x]\geq\sum_{(i,j)\in E}\left[\frac{(1-\frac{2}{\alpha})\cdot(\ell_i-\ell_j)^2}{\alpha\cdot d_{i,j}\cdot\left(\frac{1}{s_i}+\frac{1}{s_j}\right)}\right]$$
$$-\sum_{(i,j)\in E\setminus\tilde{E}_1}\frac{1}{\alpha\cdot d_{ij}}\cdot\left(\frac{1}{s_i}+\frac{1}{s_j}\right).$$
$$(\dagger\dagger)$$

The first term of this bound already has the desired form. We will now bound the second term. Since it is negative, we have to upper bound the sum itself. First, note that $E\setminus\tilde{E}_1$ is a subset of E. As the term inside the sum is non-negative, we can write

$$\sum_{(i,j)\in E\setminus\tilde{E}_1}\frac{1}{\alpha\cdot d_{ij}}\cdot\left(\frac{1}{s_i}+\frac{1}{s_j}\right)$$
$$\leq\frac{1}{\alpha}\cdot\sum_{(i,j)\in E}\left[\frac{1}{d_{ij}\cdot s_i}+\frac{1}{d_{ij}\cdot s_j}\right].$$

Recall that d_{ij} is defined as $\max\{\deg(i),\deg(j)\}$, so we can bound

$$\frac{1}{\alpha}\cdot\sum_{(i,j)\in E}\left[\frac{1}{d_{ij}\cdot s_i}+\frac{1}{d_{ij}\cdot s_j}\right]$$
$$\leq\frac{1}{\alpha}\cdot\sum_{(i,j)\in E}\left[\frac{1}{\deg(i)\cdot s_i}+\frac{1}{\deg(j)\cdot s_j}\right]$$
$$=\frac{1}{\alpha}\cdot\sum_{i\in V}\sum_{j\in\mathrm{Adj}(i)}\frac{1}{\deg(i)\cdot s_i}$$
$$=\frac{1}{\alpha}\cdot\sum_{i\in V}\frac{1}{s_i}\leq\frac{n}{\alpha}.$$

Inserting this bound into $(\dagger\dagger)$ yields the result.

We now use spectral graph theory to prove the following bound.

Lemma 5.3 *Let L be the Laplacian of the network. Let λ_2 be its second smallest eigenvalue. Then*

$$\mathbf{E}[\Delta\Psi_0(X^{t+1})|X^t=x]\geq\frac{\lambda_2}{16\Delta}\cdot\frac{1}{s_{\max}^2}\cdot\Psi_0(x)-\frac{n}{4\cdot s_{\max}}.$$

PROOF. We start from the bound obtained in Lemma 5.2. In the course of this proof, we will use Lemma 4 4.12 for the task deviation vector $\mathbf{e}$. In order to use this lemma, we have to show that $\mathbf{e}$ satisfies the lemma's condition, i.e., $\langle\mathbf{e},\mathbf{s}\rangle_S=0$. This follows via

$$\langle\mathbf{e},\mathbf{s}\rangle_S=\sum_{i\in V}\frac{e_i\cdot s_i}{s_i}=\sum_{i\in V}e_i=0.$$

We can now begin with the main proof.

$$\mathbf{E}[\Delta\Psi_0(X^{t+1})|X^t = x]$$

$$\geq \sum_{(i,j)\in E}\left[\frac{\left(1-\frac{2}{\alpha}\right)\cdot(\ell_i(x)-\ell_j(x))^2}{\alpha\cdot d_{i,j}\cdot\left(\frac{1}{s_i}+\frac{1}{s_j}\right)}\right] - \frac{n}{\alpha}$$

$$\geq \frac{\frac{1}{2}}{4\cdot s_{\max}\cdot\Delta\cdot 2}\cdot\sum_{(i,j)\in E}\left(\ell_i - \frac{m}{S} + \frac{m}{S} - \ell_j\right)^2$$
$$- \frac{n}{4\cdot s_{\max}}$$

$$\geq \frac{1}{16\Delta}\cdot\frac{1}{s_{\max}}\cdot\sum_{(i,j)\in E}\left(\frac{e_i}{s_i} - \frac{e_j}{s_j}\right)^2 - \frac{n}{4\cdot s_{\max}}$$

$$(4.11)\; = \frac{1}{16\Delta}\cdot\frac{1}{s_{\max}}\cdot(S^{-1}\mathbf{e})^\top L\left(S^{-1}\mathbf{e}\right) - \frac{n}{4\cdot s_{\max}}$$

$$= \frac{1}{16\Delta}\cdot\frac{1}{s_{\max}}\cdot\langle\mathbf{e}, LS^{-1}\mathbf{e}\rangle_S - \frac{n}{4\cdot s_{\max}}$$

$$(4.12, 4.14)\; \geq \frac{1}{16\Delta}\cdot\frac{1}{s_{\max}}\cdot\frac{\lambda_2}{s_{\max}}\langle\mathbf{e},\mathbf{e}\rangle_S - \frac{n}{4\cdot s_{\max}}$$

$$= \frac{1}{16\Delta}\cdot\frac{1}{s_{\max}}\cdot\frac{\lambda_2}{s_{\max}}\cdot\Psi_0 - \frac{n}{4\cdot s_{\max}}$$

It can be shown that as long as the expected value of the potential is sufficiently large, we can rewrite the potential drop as a multiplicative drop. Let λ_2 be the second smallest eigenvalue of the Laplacian $L(G)$ of the network. We define the *critical value* ψ_c as $\psi_c = 8\cdot n\cdot\Delta\cdot s_{\max}/\lambda_2$.

Lemma 5.4 *Let γ be defined such that $1/\gamma = \lambda_2/(32\Delta\cdot s_{\max}^2)$. Let t be a time step for which the expected value of the potential satisfies $\mathbf{E}[\Psi_0(X^t)] \geq \psi_c$. Then, the expected potential in time step $t+1$ is bounded by $\mathbf{E}[\Psi_0(X^{t+1})] \leq (1-1/\gamma)\cdot\mathbf{E}[\Psi_0(X^t)]$.*

This immediately allows us to prove the following.

Lemma 5.5 *For a given time step T, there either is a $t < T$ so that $\mathbf{E}[\Psi_0(X^t)] \leq \psi_c$, or $\mathbf{E}[\Psi_0(X^T)] \leq (1-1/\gamma)^T\cdot\mathbf{E}[\Psi_0(X^0)]$.*

As long as $\mathbf{E}[\Psi_0(X^t)] > \psi_c$ holds, the expected potential drops by a constant factor. This and several of the following results have the same form as several intermediate results in the proof of [6, Lemma 3.6], but our factor γ and the condition on $\mathbf{E}[\Psi_0(X^t)]$ are different. We can now derive a bound on the time it takes until $\mathbf{E}[\Psi_0(X^t)]$ is small.

Lemma 5.6 *Let $T = 2\gamma\cdot\ln(m/n)$. Then it holds that (1) there is a $t \leq T$ such that $\mathbf{E}[\Psi_0(X^T)] \leq \psi_c$ and (2) there is a $t \leq T$ such that the probability that $\Psi_0(X^t) \leq 4\cdot\psi_c$ is at least $\mathbf{Pr}[\Psi_0(X^t) \leq 4\cdot\psi_c] \geq 3/4$.*

Next, we show that states with $\Psi_0(x) \leq 4\cdot\psi_c$ are indeed ε-approximate Nash equilibria if the number of tasks exceeds a certain threshold. This requires one further observation.

Observation 5.7 *For any state x, we have*

$$L_\Delta(x)^2 \leq \Psi_0(x) \leq \mathcal{S}\cdot L_\Delta(x)^2.$$

Lemma 5.8 *Let $m \geq 8\cdot\delta\cdot n^2\cdot\mathcal{S}\cdot s_{\max}$ for some $\delta > 1$. Then a state x with $\Psi_0(x) \leq 4\cdot\psi_c$ is a $2/(1+\delta)$-approximate Nash equilibrium.*

Remark 5.9 If m is small, it still holds that we reach a state x with $\Psi_0(x) \leq 4\cdot\psi_c$, which is all we need to prove convergence to an exact Nash equilibrium in the next section. It is just that this intermediate state is then not an ε-approximate-Nash equilibrium.

We can now prove the main theorem.

PROOF (THEOREM 2.1). Lemma 5.8 ensures that after T steps the probability for *not* having reached a state x with $\Psi_0(x) \leq 4\cdot\psi_c$ is at most $1/4$. Hence, the expected number of times we have to repeat T steps is less than $1 + 1/4 + 1/4^2 + \cdots = 1/(1 - 1/4) < 2$. The expected time needed to reach such a state is therefore at most $2\cdot T$ with T from Lemma 5.6.

If we let the algorithm iterate until a state x with $\Psi_0(x) \leq 4\cdot\psi_c$ is obtained, Theorem 2.1 bounds the *expected* number of time steps we have to perform. However, by repeating a sufficient number of blocks with T steps, we can obtain arbitrarily high probability.

Corollary 5.10 *After $c\cdot\log_4 n$ many blocks of size T, a state with $\Psi_0(x) \leq 4\cdot\psi_c$ is reached with probability at least $1 - 1/n^c$.*

PROOF. The probability for *not* reaching a state x with $\Psi_0(x) \leq 4\cdot\psi_c$ after t steps is at most $1/4^t$. We are interested in the complementary event, so its probability is at least $1 - 1/4^t$. For $t = c\cdot\log_4 n$ the statement follows immediately.

5.2 Nash Equilibrium

We now prove the upper bound for the expected time necessary to reach an exact Nash Equilibrium (Theorem 2.2, p.). Note that we assume that the speeds are all integer multiples of ϵ. If the speeds are arbitrary non-integers, convergence can become arbitrarily slow. The convergence factor α, which was $4s_{\max}$ in the original protocol, must be changed to $4s_{\max}/\epsilon$. For non-integer speeds, we have $\epsilon < 1$, so this effectively increases α.

To show convergence towards an exact Nash Equilibrium we cannot rely solely on the potential $\Psi_0(x)$, because when the system is close to a Nash equilibrium it is possible that the potential function increases even when a task makes a move that improves its perceived load. Therefore, we use a different potential function $\Phi_1(x)$, which we define as the *shifted potential function*

$$\Psi_1(x) = \Phi_1(x) - m^2/\mathcal{S} - m\cdot n/\mathcal{S} - n^2/4\mathcal{S} + 1/4\cdot\sum_i 1/s_i.$$

Let $\bar{s}_a$ and $\bar{s}_h$ denote the arithmetic mean and the harmonic mean of the speeds, i.e., $s_a = \sum_{i\in V} s_i/n$ and $s_h = n/\sum_{i\in V} 1/s_i$. Then, we can write

$$\Psi_1(x) = \Phi_1(x) - m^2/\mathcal{S} - m\cdot n/\mathcal{S} + n/4\cdot(1/\bar{s}_h - 1/\bar{s}_a).$$

Observation 5.11 *The shifted potential $\Psi_1(x)$ has the following properties.*

1. $\Psi_1(x) = \sum_{i\in V}[(e_i + 1/2)^2/s_i] - n/4\bar{s}_a$.

2. $\Psi_1(x) \geq 0$.

3. $\Psi_1(x) = \Psi_0(x) + \sum_{i\in V} e_i/s_i + n/4\cdot(1/\bar{s}_h - 1/\bar{s}_a)$.

4. $\Delta\Psi_1(X^t) = \Delta\Phi_1(X^t)$.

141

Before we can lower-bound the expected drop in $\Psi_1(x)$, we need a technical lemma regarding a lower bound to the load difference. It is similar to [6, Lemma 3.7], which concerned integer speeds, so the result here is more general.

Lemma 5.12 *Every edge* (i, j) *with* $\ell_i - \ell_j > 1/s_j$ *also satisfies* $\ell_i - \ell_j \geq 1/s_j + \epsilon/s_i \cdot s_j$.

Potential Ψ_1 differs from potential Ψ' defined in [6] by a constant only. Therefore, potential differences are the same for both potentials and we can apply results for Ψ' to Ψ_1.

Lemma 5.13 *If the system is in a state* x *that is not a Nash equilibrium, then*

$$\mathbf{E}[\Delta \Psi_1(X^{k+1})|X^t = x] \geq \frac{\epsilon^2}{8\Delta \cdot s_{\max}^3}.$$

Since the results of the previous section apply to Ψ_0 whereas now we work with Ψ_1, we add this technical lemma relating the two.

Lemma 5.14 *For any state* x *it holds* $\Psi_1(x) \leq \Psi_0(x) + \sqrt{\Psi_0(x) \cdot n/\bar{s}_h} + n/4 \cdot (1/\bar{s}_h - 1/\bar{s}_a)$.

To obtain a bound on the expected time the system needs to reach the NE, we use a standard argument from martingale theory. Let us abbreviate $V := \epsilon^2/(8\Delta \cdot s_{\max}^3)$. We introduce a new random variable Z_t which we define as $Z_t = \Psi_1(X^t) + t \cdot V$.

Lemma 5.15 *Let* T *be the first time step for which the system is in a Nash equilibrium. Then, for all times* $t \leq T$ *we have* (1) $\mathbf{E}[Z_t|Z_{t-1} = z] \leq z$ (2) $\mathbf{E}[Z_t] \leq \mathbf{E}[Z_{t-1}]$.

Corollary 5.16 *Let* T *be the first time step for which the system is in a Nash equilibrium. Let* $t \wedge T$ *be* $\min\{t, T\}$. *Then the random variable* $Z_{t \wedge T}$ *is a super-martingale.*

Corollary 5.17 *Let* T *be the first time step for which the system is in a Nash equilibrium. Then* $\mathbf{E}[Z_T] \leq Z_0 = \Psi_1(X^0)$.

PROOF (THEOREM 2.2). First, we assume that at time $t = 0$ the system is in a state with $\mathbf{E}[\Psi_0(X^T)] \leq 4 \cdot \psi_c$. Using the non-negativity of $\Psi_1(x)$ (Observation 5.11) allows us to state

$$V \cdot \mathbf{E}[T] \leq \mathbf{E}[\Psi_1(X^T)] + V \cdot \mathbf{E}[T] = \mathbf{E}[Z_T]$$

$$(\text{Cor. } 5.17) \leq \mathbf{E}[Z_0] = \Psi_1(X^0)$$

$$(\text{Lem. } 5.14) \leq \Psi_0(X^0) + \sqrt{\Psi_0(X^0) \cdot \frac{n}{\bar{s}_h}} + \frac{n}{4} \cdot \left(\frac{1}{\bar{s}_h} - \frac{1}{\bar{s}_a}\right)$$

$$\leq 4 \cdot \psi_c + \sqrt{4 \cdot \psi_c \cdot \frac{n}{\bar{s}_h}} + \frac{n}{4}$$

Inserting the definition of ψ_c and dividing by V yields

$$\mathbf{E}[T] \leq 8\Delta \cdot \frac{s_{\max}^3}{\epsilon^2} \cdot$$

$$\left[\frac{64 \cdot n \cdot \Delta \cdot s_{\max}}{\lambda_2} + \sqrt{32 \cdot n^2 \cdot s_{\max} \cdot \frac{2\Delta}{\lambda_2}} + \frac{n}{4}\right]$$

$$\leq 607 \cdot \Delta^2 \cdot \frac{s_{\max}^4}{\epsilon^2} \cdot \frac{n}{\lambda_2}.$$

where we have used that $2\Delta/\lambda_2 \geq 1$ (Lemma 4.4) to pull that expression outside of the square root in the first line.

This bound was derived under the assumption that at $t = 0$ we had a state with $\mathbf{E}[\Psi_0(X^t)] \leq 4 \cdot \psi_c$. If this is not the case, let τ denote the number of time steps to reach such a state, and let T' denote the additional number of time steps to reach a NE from there. Combining the result from above with Theorem 2.1 allows us to write

$$\mathbf{E}[T] = \mathbf{E}[\tau + T'] = \mathcal{O}\left(\frac{n}{\lambda_2} \cdot \Delta^2 \cdot \frac{s_{\max}^4}{\epsilon^2}\right).$$

Corollary 5.18 *Similarly to Corollary 5.10, after* $c \cdot \log_4 n$ *blocks of* T *steps we have reached a Nash Equilibrium with probability at least* $1 - 1/n^c$.

Observation 5.19 *Our bound in Theorem 2.2 is asymptotically lower than the corresponding bound in [6] by at least a factor of* $\Omega(\Delta \cdot \text{diam}(G))$.

PROOF. Lemma 4.2 yields $n \cdot \text{diam}(G) \geq 4/\lambda_2$. Additionally, we have $\mathcal{S} \geq s_{\max}$, since $s_{\max}$ occurs (at least once) in the sum of all speeds. Hence, the asymptotic bound from [6] is larger than

$$\mathcal{O}\left(n \cdot \frac{\Delta^2}{\lambda_2} \cdot s_{\max}^4 \cdot [\Delta \cdot \text{diam}(G)]\right).$$

The first part of this expression is the bound of Theorem 2.2, so the expression in the square brackets is the additional factor of the bound from [6].

6. WEIGHTED TASKS

The set of tasks assigned to node i is called $x(i)$. The weight of node i becomes $w_i(x) = \sum_{\ell \in x(i)} \omega_\ell$ whereas the corresponding load is defined as $\ell_i(x) = w_i(x)/s_i$ in analogy to the unweighted case.

We present a protocol for weighted tasks that differs from the one described in [6]. A single step of that protocol is presented in Algorithm 2.

Algorithm 2: Distributed Selfish Load Balancing for weighted tasks

begin
  foreach *task* ℓ *in parallel* **do**
    Let $i = i(l)$ be the current machine of task ℓ
    Choose a neighboring machine j uniformly at random
    if $\ell_i - \ell_j > \frac{1}{s_j}$ **then**
      Move task ℓ from node i to node j with probability

$$p_{ij} := \frac{\deg(i)}{d_{i,j}} \cdot \frac{w_i - w_j}{2\alpha \cdot w_i}$$

    end
  end
end

The notable difference to the scheme in [6] is that in our case, the decision of a task ℓ to migrate or not does not depend on that task's weight. In the original protocol, a load difference of more than w_ℓ/s_j would suffice for task ℓ

to have an incentive to migrate. In the modified protocol, a task will only move if the load difference is at least $1/s_j$. The advantage of this approach is that for an edge (i, j), either all or none of the tasks on node i have an incentive to migrate. This greatly simplifies the analysis. A justification for this step is that real systems usually have a cost associated with migration, so that a task might not want to migrate if the resulting gain is only marginal. We will show that the system rapidly converges to a state where $\ell_i - \ell_j \leq 1/s_j$ for all edges (i, j). Such a system is not necessarily a Nash equilibrium as $\ell_i - \ell_j$ might still be larger than the size of a given task ω_ℓ. We will show, however, that such a state is an ε-approximate NE.

In analogy to the unweighted case, we define the expected flow f_{ij} as the expected *weight* of the tasks migrating from i to j in state x. It is given by

$$f_{ij}(x) = \frac{\ell_i(x) - \ell_j(x)}{\alpha \cdot d_{ij} \cdot \left(\frac{1}{s_i} + \frac{1}{s_j}\right) \cdot w_i(x)} \cdot \sum_{\ell \in x(i)} \omega_\ell = $$

$$\frac{\ell_i(x) - \ell_j(x)}{\alpha \cdot d_{ij} \cdot \left(\frac{1}{s_i} + \frac{1}{s_j}\right)}.$$

The potentials Φ_0 and Φ_1 are defined analogously to the unweighted case. Here, we concentrate on Φ_0 alone. The average weight per node is W/n and the task deviation e_i is defined as $w_i - W/n$. We define $\Psi_0(x)$ in analogy to the unweighted case as the normalized version of Φ_0, with $\Psi_0 = \Phi_0 - W^2/\sum_i s_i = \sum_{i \in V} e_i^2/s_i$. The auxiliary quantity $\Lambda_{ij}(x)$ is defined analogously to the unweighted case as $\Lambda_{ij}(x) = (2\alpha - 2) \cdot d_{ij} \cdot (1/s_i + 1/s_j) \cdot f_{ij}(x)$.

6.1 Approximate Nash Equilibrium

In close analogy to [6, Lemma 3.1], we first bound the drop of the potential when the flow is exactly the expected flow.

Lemma 6.1 *Let $\tilde{\Delta}\Phi_0(X^{t+1}|X^t = x)$ denote the amount by which Φ_0 would drop if the system was in state x and the flow of tasks was exactly the expected flow f_{ij}. It holds $\tilde{\Delta}\Phi_0(X^{t+1}|X^t = x) \geq \sum_{(i,j)\in\tilde{E}} f_{ij} \cdot \Lambda_{ij}$.*

This lemma and its proof are formally equivalent to Lemma 3.1 in [6] and thus we omit the proof here.

Next, we bound the variance of the process.

Lemma 6.2 *The variances of the weights on the nodes are bounded via*

$$\sum_i \frac{\mathbf{Var}[w_i(X^t)|X^{t-1} = x]}{s_i} \leq \sum_{ij} f_{ij} \cdot \left(\frac{1}{s_i} + \frac{1}{s_j}\right).$$

PROOF. As in the original reference, we introduce random variables A_i and C_i for the tasks *abandoning* and *coming to* node i, but now they count the *weight* of these tasks, not only their number. For the C_i, we again split it into Z_{ji} where Z_{ji} counts the weight migrating from j to i. Then

$$\mathbf{Var}[C_i] = \sum_{j:(j,i)\in\tilde{E}} \mathbf{Var}[Z_{ji}].$$

$$\mathbf{Var}[Z_{ji}] = \sum_{\ell \in x_j} \mathbf{Var}[\omega_\ell^{ji}].$$

Here ω_ℓ^{ji} is the random variable that is ω_ℓ if task ℓ moves from j to i and 0 otherwise. This variable follows a *Bernoulli distribution*. If p is the probability for the event to occur and if x is the value of the event, then the variance is

$$\mathbf{Var}[\mathsf{Ber}(x,p)] = x^2 \cdot p \cdot (1-p) \leq x^2 p.$$

This allows us to write

$$\mathbf{Var}[Z_{ji}] = \sum_{l \in x_j} \mathbf{Var}[\omega_\ell^{ji}]$$

$$\leq \sum_{l \in x_j} \omega_\ell^2 \cdot \frac{\ell_j - \ell_i}{\alpha \cdot d_{ij} \cdot \left(\frac{1}{s_i} + \frac{1}{s_j}\right) \cdot w_j}$$

$$\leq \sum_{l \in x_j} \omega_\ell \cdot \frac{\ell_j - \ell_i}{\alpha \cdot d_{ij} \cdot \left(\frac{1}{s_i} + \frac{1}{s_j}\right) \cdot w_j}$$

$$= \frac{\ell_j - \ell_i}{\alpha \cdot d_{ij} \cdot \left(\frac{1}{s_i} + \frac{1}{s_j}\right)} = f_{ij},$$

where we use that $\omega_\ell^2 \leq \omega_\ell$ since all tasks have weight at most 1. Hence

$$\mathbf{Var}[C_i] = \sum_{j:(j,i)\in\tilde{E}} f_{ij}.$$

Similarly, we define the random variable $A_{\ell i}$ that is ω_l if task ℓ abandons node i and 0 otherwise. It is also Bernoulli-distributed.

$$\mathbf{Var}[A_i] = \sum_{\ell \in x_i} \mathbf{Var}[A_{\ell i}]$$

$$= \sum_{\ell \in x_i} \mathbf{Var}\left[\mathsf{Ber}\left(\omega_\ell; \sum_{j:(i,j)\in\tilde{E}} \frac{\ell_i - \ell_j}{\alpha \cdot d_{ij} \cdot \left(\frac{1}{s_i} + \frac{1}{s_j}\right) \cdot w_i}\right)\right]$$

$$\leq \sum_{\ell \in x_i} \omega_\ell^2 \cdot \sum_{j:(i,j)\in\tilde{E}} \frac{\ell_i - \ell_j}{\alpha \cdot d_{ij} \cdot \left(\frac{1}{s_i} + \frac{1}{s_j}\right) \cdot w_i}$$

$$\leq \sum_{j:(i,j)\in\tilde{E}} \sum_{\ell \in x_i} \omega_\ell \cdot \frac{\ell_i - \ell_j}{\alpha \cdot d_{ij} \cdot \left(\frac{1}{s_i} + \frac{1}{s_j}\right) \cdot w_i}$$

$$= \sum_{j:(i,j)\in\tilde{E}} \frac{\ell_i - \ell_j}{\alpha \cdot d_{ij} \cdot \left(\frac{1}{s_i} + \frac{1}{s_j}\right)} = \sum_{j:(i,j)\in\tilde{E}} f_{ij}.$$

When we add the variance of C_i and A_i and sum over all nodes, we get, in formal analogy to the unweighted case,

$$\sum_i \frac{\mathbf{Var}[w_i(X^t)|X^{t-1} = x]}{s_i} = \sum_{ij} f_{ij}\left(\frac{1}{s_i} + \frac{1}{s_j}\right).$$

This allows us to formulate a bound on the expected potential drop in analogy to [6, Lemma 3.3] by combining Lemma 6.1 and Lemma 6.2.

Lemma 6.3 *The expected drop in potential Φ_0 if the system is in state x is at least*

$$E[\Delta\Phi_0(X^t)|X^{t-1} = x] \geq \sum_{(i,j)\in\tilde{E}} f_{ij}(x) \cdot (\Lambda_{ij}(x) - 2).$$

The proof is formally analogous to [6, Lemma 3.3].

PROOF OF THEOREM 2.3. The rest of the proof is the same as the proof for the unweighted case in Section 5. One may verify that, indeed, Lemma 5.2 and all subsequent results do not rely on the specific form of ℓ_i or the underlying nature of the tasks. Using the same eigenvalue techniques as in the unweighted case, this allows us to obtain a bound involving the second smallest eigenvalue of the graph's Laplacian matrix. Following the steps of the unweighted case then allows us to prove the main result of this section.

Acknowledgements

The authors thank Thomas Sauerwald for helpful discussions.

7. REFERENCES

[1] H. Ackermann, S. Fischer, M. Hoefer, and M. Schöngens. Distributed algorithms for qos load balancing. In *Proceedings of the twenty-first annual symposium on Parallelism in algorithms and architectures*, SPAA'09, pages 197–203, New York, NY, USA, 2009. ACM.

[2] C. P. J. Adolphs and P. Berenbrink. Improved Bounds for Discrete Diffusive Load Balancing. To appear at IPDPS 2012, 2012.

[3] B. Awerbuch, Y. Azar, and R. Khandekar. Fast load balancing via bounded best response. In *Proceedings of the nineteenth annual ACM-SIAM symposium on Discrete algorithms*, SODA '08, pages 314–322, Philadelphia, PA, USA, 2008. Society for Industrial and Applied Mathematics.

[4] P. Berenbrink, T. Friedetzky, L. A. Goldberg, P. W. Goldberg, Z. Hu, and R. Martin. Distributed Selfish Load Balancing. *SIAM Journal on Computing*, 37(4):1163, 2007.

[5] P. Berenbrink, T. Friedetzky, I. Hajirasouliha, and Z. Hu. Convergence to equilibria in distributed, selfish reallocation processes with weighted tasks. In L. Arge, M. Hoffmann, and E. Welzl, editors, *Proceedings of the 15th Annual European Symposium on Algorithms (ESA 2007)*, volume 4698/2007 of *Lecture Notes in Computer Science*, pages 41–52. Springer, Springer, October 2007.

[6] P. Berenbrink, M. Hoefer, and T. Sauerwald. Distributed selfish load balancing on networks. In *Proceedings of 22nd Symposium on Discrete Algorithms (SODA'11)*, pages 1487–1497, 2011.

[7] J. E. Boillat. Load balancing and Poisson equation in a graph. *Concurrency: Practice and Experience*, 2(4):289–313, Dec. 1990.

[8] F. R. K. Chung. *Spectral graph theory*. AMS Bookstore, 1997.

[9] G. Cybenko. Dynamic load balancing for distributed memory multiprocessors. *Journal of Parallel and Distributed Computing*, 7(2):279–301, Oct. 1989.

[10] R. Elsässer, B. Monien, and R. Preis. Diffusion Schemes for Load Balancing on Heterogeneous Networks. *Theory of Computing Systems*, 35(3):305–320, May 2002.

[11] R. Elsässer, B. Monien, and S. Schamberger. Distributing unit size workload packages in heterogeneous networks. *Journal of Graph Algorithms and Applications*, 10(1):51–68, 2006.

[12] E. Even-Dar, A. Kesselman, and Y. Mansour. Convergence time to Nash equilibrium in load balancing. *ACM Transactions on Algorithms*, 3(3):32–es, Aug. 2007.

[13] E. Even-Dar and Y. Mansour. Fast convergence of selfish rerouting. In *Proceedings of the sixteenth annual ACM-SIAM symposium on Discrete algorithms (SODA'05)*, pages 772–781, 2005.

[14] R. Feldmann, M. Gairing, T. Lücking, B. Monien, and M. Rode. Nashification and the coordination ratio for a selfish routing game. In J. Baeten, J. Lenstra, J. Parrow, and G. Woeginger, editors, *Automata, Languages and Programming*, volume 2719 of *Lecture Notes in Computer Science*, pages 190–190. Springer Berlin / Heidelberg, 2003.

[15] M. Fiedler. Algebraic connectivity of graphs. *Czechoslovak Mathematical Journal*, 23(2):298–305, 1973.

[16] S. Fischer, P. Mahonen, M. Schongens, and B. Vocking. Load balancing for dynamic spectrum assignment with local information for secondary users. In *New Frontiers in Dynamic Spectrum Access Networks, 2008. DySPAN 2008. 3rd IEEE Symposium on*, pages 1 –9, oct. 2008.

[17] S. Fischer and B. Vöcking. Adaptive routing with stale information. In *Proceedings of the twenty-fourth annual ACM symposium on Principles of distributed computing (PODC'05)*, pages 276–283, New York, NY, USA, 2005. ACM.

[18] D. Fotakis, A. Kaporis, and P. Spirakis. Atomic congestion games: Fast, myopic and concurrent. *Theory of Computing Systems*, 47:38–59, 2010. 10.1007/s00224-009-9198-2.

[19] T. Friedrich and T. Sauerwald. Near-perfect load balancing by randomized rounding. In *Proceedings of the 41st annual ACM symposium on Symposium on theory of computing - STOC '09*, page 121, New York, New York, USA, May 2009. ACM Press.

[20] B. Mohar. Isoperimetric numbers of graphs. *Journal of Combinatorial Theory, Series B*, 47(3):274–291, Dec. 1989.

[21] B. Mohar. Eigenvalues, diameter, and mean distance in graphs. *Graphs and Combinatorics*, 7(1):53–64, Mar. 1991.

[22] Mohar, B. The Laplacian Spectrum of Graphs. In Y. Alavi, editor, *Graph theory, combinatorics, and applications*, volume 2, pages 871–898. Wiley, 1991.

[23] S. Muthukrishnan, B. Ghosh, and M. Schultz. First- and Second-Order Diffusive Methods for Rapid, Coarse, Distributed Load Balancing. *Theory of Computing Systems*, 31(4):331–354, July 1998.

[24] Y. Rabani, A. Sinclair, and R. Wanka. Local divergence of Markov chains and the analysis of iterative load-balancing schemes. In *Proceedings 39th Annual Symposium on Foundations of Computer Science (FOCS'98)*, pages 694–703. IEEE Comput. Soc, 1998.

[25] B. Vöcking. Selfish Load Balancing. In N. Nisan, E. Tardos, T. Roughgarden, and V. Vazirani, editors, *Algorithmic Game Theory*, chapter 20. Cambridge University Press, 2007.

Making Evildoers Pay:
Resource-Competitive Broadcast in Sensor Networks

[Extended Abstract]

Seth Gilbert[*]
National University of Singapore
Department of Computer Science
Singapore, 117417
seth.gilbert@comp.nus.edu.sg

Maxwell Young
National University of Singapore
Department of Computer Science
Singapore, 117417
dcsmmry@nus.edu.sg

ABSTRACT

Consider a time-slotted, single-hop, wireless sensor network consisting of n correct devices and and $f \cdot n$ Byzantine devices where $f \geq 0$ is any constant; the Byzantine devices may or may not outnumber the correct ones. There exists a trusted sender Alice who wishes to deliver a message m over a single channel to the correct devices. There is also an evil user Carol who controls the Byzantine devices and uses them to disrupt the communication channel. For a constant $k \geq 2$, the correct and Byzantine devices each possess a meager energy budget of $O(n^{1/k})$, Alice and Carol each possess a limited budget of $\tilde{O}(n^{1/k})$, and sending or listening in a slot incurs unit cost. This setup captures the inherent challenges of guaranteeing communication despite scarce resources and attacks on the network. Given this Alice versus Carol scenario, we ask: Is communication of m feasible and, if so, at what cost?

We develop a protocol which, for an arbitrarily small constant $\epsilon > 0$, ensures that at least $(1 - \epsilon)\,n$ correct devices receive m with high probability. Furthermore, if Carol's devices expend T energy jamming the channel, then Alice and the correct devices each spend only $\tilde{O}(T^{1/(k+1)})$. In other words, delaying the transmission of m forces a jamming adversary to rapidly deplete its energy supply and, consequently, cease attacks on the network.

Categories and Subject Descriptors

C.2.1 [**Computer Communications Networks**]: Network Architecture and Design—*Wireless communication*; F.2.2 [**Analysis of Algorithms and Problem Complexity**]: Nonnumerical Algorithms and Problems—*Routing and layout*

Keywords

Byzantine fault tolerance, wireless sensor networks, energy efficiency, jamming attacks, resource competitive analysis

[*]This research was supported in part by NUS FRC grant R-252-000-443-133.

1. INTRODUCTION

Wireless sensors are continually shrinking, leading to increasingly dense networks built out of increasingly low-power devices. The concept of dense wireless sensor networks (WSNs) was popularized by the Smart Dust project [30] which provided the foundations for the well-known contemporary motes manufactured by Crossbow [11] and Dust Networks [24]. While the size of commercially available units is on the order of a few cubic centimeters, more recent endeavors such as SPECKNET [29] aim to reduce this to the cubic millimeter scale [2]. With the drive toward smaller wireless devices, it is not difficult to fathom the future deployment of highly dense WSNs and, indeed, the difficulties of communicating in such networks has been considered previously by the research community [10, 16, 32].

In this paper, we address the challenge of communicating in a dense WSN given an adversary Carol who engages in malicious interference of the wireless medium. Such *jamming attacks* have received significant attention in recent years given the ease of perpetrating such attacks and their effectiveness (see [31] and references therein). Jamming constitutes a form of denial-of-service attack that is particularly devastating given that WSN devices, including proposed future architectures [2, 8], are severely energy constrained. Therefore, the prospects for achieving communication seem dire given an attacker who controls a large number of network devices and coordinates their combined resources to jam.

In this energy-starved setting, a sensible approach is to consider the rate at which a jamming adversary is required to expend energy relative to those devices attempting to overcome the jamming. If the adversary's total cost T is substantially higher, then preventing communication for any extended duration is prohibitively expensive and forces the adversary to quickly exhaust her energy supply. Here, a useful measure of cost is the number of slots during which a device is utilizing the channel. Specifically, sending and listening operations dominate the operating costs of the Telos mote — 35mW and 38mW at 0dBm, respectively — while sleeping incurs negligible cost on the order of μW. Such a *resource-competitive* approach [20] was first explicitly studied in [22, 23] where communication between two devices is guaranteed at an expected cost of $O(T^{\varphi - 1}) = O(T^{0.62})$ per device where $\varphi = \frac{1 + \sqrt{5}}{2}$ is the golden ratio. This result places the adversary at a substantial disadvantage, but we ask: Is it possible to do better?

To address this question, we consider a general network scenario involving $(f + 1)n$ devices where f is any positive constant. A powerful adversary Carol controls $t = f \cdot n$ Byzantine devices which may deviate from the protocol arbitrarily; we emphasize that $f > 1$ is allowed. Given this attack model, a trusted sender

Alice attempts to propagate a message m to the remaining correct devices. All devices, correct and Byzantine, have a severely constrained energy budget. We exploit the following two insights: If a small *tunable* constant fraction of devices are allowed to terminate without receiving m, and we seek guarantees only with high probability, then significant improvements are possible. Given this, we derive the following main result:

THEOREM 1. *Let* $k \geq 2$. *Assume Alice has an individual budget of* $O(n^{1/k} \ln^k n)$ *and aims to deliver a message to* n *correct nodes. Assume Carol is an adaptive adversary with an individual budget of* $\tilde{O}(n^{1/k})$ *who controls* $f \cdot n$ *Byzantine nodes for any constant* $f \geq 0$. *Each node, correct and Byzantine, possesses a budget of* $O(n^{1/k})$. *Then, for* n *sufficiently large, there is a protocol that guarantees the following properties with high probability:*

- *If Carol and her Byzantine nodes jam for* T *slots, then Alice and the correct nodes each incur an individual cost of only* $\tilde{O}(T^{\frac{1}{k+1}} + 1)$ *and* $O(T^{\frac{1}{k+1}} + 1)$, *respectively.*

- *At least* $(1 - \epsilon) n$ *correct nodes receive the message for any arbitrarily small constant* $\epsilon > 0$ *and Alice and all correct nodes terminate within* $O(n^{1+(1/k)})$ *slots.*

where $\tilde{O}$ *denotes the existence of polylogarithmic terms. Additionally, if* $f < 1/24$, *then these results hold when Carol is also a reactive adversary.*

This type of "almost-everywhere" communication plays an important role in several distributed computing problems (see [12, 17, 21] and references therein). In many cases, it is sufficient to guarantee a majority of the processes receive critical information. For example, Alice and others may be attempting to implement Paxos [6], which relies on the notion of a majority quorum; therefore, m must reach a majority of the nodes. For any $t \leq (1 - \delta)n$, for a constant $\delta > 0$, our protocol guarantees this property. In general, the ability to reach a $(1 - \epsilon)$-fraction of the network is likely to be of importance in emerging WSNs.

1.1 Alice versus Carol — Our Network Model

We assume a single hop WSN with $(f + 1)n$ devices where $f \geq 0$ is a constant and where n is large; that is, the network is dense. Devices use a time division multiple access (TDMA)-like medium access control (MAC) protocol to access a single communication channel; time is divided into discrete *slots*, but no global broadcast schedule is assumed.

Nodes can detect whether a channel is in use via *clear channel assessment (CCA)* [26]. This is a common feature; for instance, it is available on the CC2420 transceiver [15] of the Telos mote, and several theoretical models feature collision detection (see [1, 4, 5, 19, 27]). Jamming is indistinguishable from the case when two or more legitimate messages collide over the channel. Furthermore, jamming or a collision can only be detected on the receiving end of the wireless channel and, when this occurs, any received data is discarded. Finally, we assume that the absence of channel activity cannot be forged; in practice, such forging would be difficult [7].

Network Participants: There are $(f + 1)n$ correct nodes in the network of which $t \leq f \cdot n$ suffer a Byzantine fault and may deviate *arbitrarily* from any prescribed protocol. Each node is limited by a sublinear *budget* of at most $C n^{1/k}$ for any constant integer $k \geq 2$ and a sufficiently large constant $C > 0$.

Messages sent by Alice can be authenticated. For example, scalable dissemination of a *small* number of public keys is possible and we may assume that her public key (and, perhaps, only hers) is known to all receivers. Other authentication schemes can be assumed [9]; this is a partially-authenticated Byzantine model since

Alice is the only participant who can be authenticated. Therefore, attempts to tamper with m or spoof Alice can be detected. However, correct nodes may be spoofed which allows Carol to repeatedly request retransmissions of m from Alice. Our protocol must be resource competitive despite such a *spoofing attack* and we address this in Section 2.2.

Finally, as a trusted sender, Alice is invested in delivering information to the network; consequently, we expect her to bear more of the communication costs; however, given the scarce energy resources of WSNs, we still enforce a fairly strict budget on Alice. Specifically, for $k = 2$, her budget is at most $C n^{1/k} \ln n$, the equivalent of only $O(\ln n)$ nodes; for general $k \geq 3$, her budget is at most $C n^{1/k} \ln^k n$ (see Section 3). Note that, for the purposes of symmetry, we concede the same to Carol (see below).

We do not assume that jamming has a uniform impact on the correct nodes. Any jamming by Carol or her Byzantine nodes can cause collisions and lost messages for some participants, while others receive the message correctly. More formally, a *ℓ-uniform adversary* (see [27]) is one who may partition the nodes into at most ℓ sets, each of which experience a different jamming schedule. We assume the worst-case, that Carol is an n-uniform adversary; therefore, she selects which nodes may detect jamming on an individual basis. Given the utility of collision detection, this capability yields a powerful advantage to Carol while abstracting many of the challenges to reliable wireless communication including hidden terminals and fading effects. Carol also possesses full information on how nodes have behaved (in terms of sending/listening) in the past and uses this knowledge to inform future attacks; that is, she *adaptive*. In this extended abstract, we assume that the actions of a node in the current slot are unknown to Carol; however, with modifications discussed in Section 4.1, our results hold when Carol possesses this information (ie. she is *reactive*) for $f < 1/24$. Finally, for the purposes of symmetry, when $k = 2$, we treat Carol as an additional Byzantine node with an individual budget of $C n^{1/k} \ln n$ to match that of Alice; for general $k \geq 3$, her budget is at most $C n^{1/k} \ln^k n$ (see Section 3).

Our Goal: Alice wishes to deliver m to as many correct nodes as possible while Carol, along with her Byzantine nodes, aims to prevent communication. Alice, Carol, correct nodes, and Byzantine nodes incur a unit cost of 1 for sending, listening, jamming, or altering messages.

We define "with high probability" (w.h.p.) to mean with probability at least $1 - n^{-c}$ for some constant $c > 0$ we can tune. Our goal is to design a protocol that guarantees w.h.p. delivery of m to as many nodes as possible while ensuring the following two properties. First, since all participants are energy starved, the protocol should be *load balanced*; that is, Alice and each correct node should incur asymptotically equal costs (up to logarithmic factors). Second, the costs incurred by Alice and each correct node should be asymptotically less than the total cost incurred by Carol and her nodes; that is, our protocol should be resource competitive.

A Note on Resource Competitiveness: We aim to show that, while Carol and her Byzantine nodes may deplete their collective budget in attacking the network, each individual correct node spends relatively little in order to achieve communication. We are focusing on an individual correct node's cost compared to the aggregate cost incurred by Carol and her Byzantine nodes; call this a *local perspective*. But why not consider a *global perspective* by using the aggregate cost of Alice and her correct nodes for comparison?

There are several points in response. First, resource competitiveness from a local perspective is not a trivial task, especially given the strict resource constraints placed on nodes. Consider the naive approach where a correct node continually sends m until the jamming stops; this yields very poor resource competitiveness since *each* node spends at least as much as the adversary. Indeed, many algorithms for communication in WSNs suffer similarly. Second, guaranteeing resource competitiveness from a local perspective bounds the relative cost incurred by any single node; that is, the adversary cannot force any particular node to spend a disproportionate amount relative the adversary. In terms of maximizing a the lifetime of a network, it might be undesirable to achieve a global advantage if some nodes end up incurring substantially more relative cost; therefore, a guarantee from a global perspective is not necessarily stronger. Furthermore, note that, from a global-perspective, we are indeed achieving a constant-factor advantage when $f > 1$. For further discussion on aspects of resource competitive analysis. we refer the reader to [20].

1.2 Related Work

There are a large number of results addressing general problems involving jamming attacks (see [31]). Closely related to our work are the results in [22] which provide the first resource-competitive communication protocol for two devices and also address a simple scenario with n devices. There are several differences between our current work and [22]. The latter provides Las Vegas protocols with expected costs and Carol's budget is completely unknown. For the 2-node and n-node scenarios in [22], the corresponding protocols are not load balanced since Alice spends roughly $D^{0.62}$ while each correct receiving node spends D. Finally, [22] can tolerate a reactive adversary only if external background communication traffic exists at no cost. In contrast, here we sacrifice a small number of nodes and focus on dense WSNs; however, our improved costs are guaranteed with w.h.p., our protocol is load-balanced, and the correct nodes themselves bear the costs for thwarting a reactive adversary. Our attack model differs in that we assume that both the correct and Byzantine nodes have roughly the same power. Specifically, Carol's collective budget is at most a constant-factor larger than the aggregate budget of the correct nodes and it is polynomially larger than any single correct node.

Work by Ashraf *et al.* [3] investigates a similar line of reasoning employing multi-block payloads, so-called "look-alike packets" (which bears some resemblance to our strategy for dealing with reactive adversaries in Section 4.1), and randomized wakeup times for receivers to force the adversary into expending more energy in order to effectively jam. Their approach is interesting but differs in many ways from our own and analytical results are not provided.

There are a number of relevant analytical results on jamming. Gilbert *et al.* [19] derive deterministic upper and lower bounds on the duration for which communication can be disrupted between two WSN devices where silence cannot be forged. Pelc and Peleg [25] examine a random jamming adversary. Koo *et al.* [5] examine the problem of multi-hop broadcast in a grid topology in the presence of jamming when the adversary's budget is exactly known. Awerbuch *et al.* [4] give a jamming-resistant MAC protocol in a single-hop network with an adaptive, rate-limited bursty jammer. Richa *et al* [27] significantly extended this work to multi-hop networks and, later, to reactive bursty adversaries [28]. In models where mutiple channels are available, Dolev *et al.* [12] address a $(1 - \epsilon)$ gossiping problem, Gilbert *et al.* [18] derive bounds on the time required for information exchange given a reactive adversary, and Dolev *et al.* [13] address secure communication while tolerating a non-reactive adversary.

In addition to pursuing a resource-competitive approach, our work differs from these related works in several ways. Our adversary is n-uniform; many previous results assume a 1-uniform adversary.

Furthermore, our adversary can be both adaptive and reactive, and she does not necessarily adhere to a particular jamming strategy (ie. bursty or random). Finally, our protocol does not rely on the availability of multiple channels; something that would likely not hold true given that Carol controls $\Theta(n)$ nodes and the number of channels is quite limited in practice.

2. OUR ALGORITHM

In this section, we focus on the case where $k = 2$. In Section 3, we present the algorithm for general k. Our communication algorithm ϵ-BROADCAST is presented in Figure 1. Recall we desire an algorithm that: (1) is load balanced and (2) is resource competitive. The constant $\epsilon > 0$ is the upper limit on the fraction of nodes that may terminate the protocol without receiving m; we assume it is set prior to deployment. For our analysis, let $\epsilon' > 0$ be an arbitrarily small constant (see Section 2.2) that we set and we will "renormalize" by ϵ' to obtain ϵ in the statement of our main result. A node u is said to be *informed* if u ever receives m; otherwise, u is said to *uninformed*. A slot that is either jammed or contains at least one transmission is called *noisy*; otherwise, it is called *silent*.

ϵ-BROADCAST proceeds in rounds indexed by i incrementing from 1 until communication is achieved. The two parameters a and b will be determined throughout the course of our analysis. Each round consists of three phases:

- *Inform Phase:* Consists of $2^{(a+b)i}$ slots. Alice send m with probability $\frac{2 \ln n}{2^{bi}}$ in each slot. Each node which has not yet received m listens to a slot with probability $\frac{2}{\epsilon' 2^{(a+\frac{b}{2})i}}$.

- *Propagation Phase:* Consists of $2^{(a+b)i}$ slots. Each node u that received m in the preceding inform phase sends m with probability $\frac{1}{n}$ and then terminates at the end of the phase. Each uninformed node listens in each slot with probability $4e(c+1)/2^{(a+(b/2))i}$ for a sufficiently large constant $c > 0$.

- *Request Phase:* Consists of $2^{(\frac{b}{2}+1)i}$ slots. In each slot, each uninformed node u sends nack with probability $1/n$ and listens with probability $\frac{c+1}{(1-e^{-64})2^i}$. If at most $5c \ln n$ noisy slots are heard (p cannot hear its own transmissions), then u terminates. Alice listens with probability $\frac{c \ln n}{(1-e^{-4\epsilon'})2^{((b/2)+1)i}}$ in each slot and she terminates if the number of noisy slots heard is at most $5c \ln n$.

Discussion: Our protocol is parameterized by the two constants a and b and these values dictate the costs to Alice and each node, respectively. In designing our protocol, we do not force values onto a and b; rather, these values are derived to achieve both load balancing and resource competitiveness. However, there are some self-evident bounds that we make explicit. Note that, in round $i = \lg n$, Alice's maximum expected cost is $\tilde{O}(n^a)$ which implies that $a \leq 1/2$ given the allowed budget. Similarly, each node's cost is $O(n^{b/2})$ which implies that $b \leq 1$.

We assume that the constant C used in the budgets for Alice, Carol, and the nodes is large enough to subsume the constants in our protocol; see the details in Section 2.3, Lemma 14. Finally, we note that there are two advantages of choosing to send/listen in each slot independently and uniformly at random. First, our analysis is primarily concerned with $i = \Omega(\log \log n)$; therefore, the expected costs for both Alice and each node are $\Omega(\log n)$ which means that these costs can be bounded to within a constant factor of their expectation via standard Chernoff bounds. Therefore, our protocol's costs are guaranteed with high probability. Second, information of how Alice and each correct node has behaved in the past conveys no information about their actions in the current slot. Therefore, our protocol does not yield any advantage to an adaptive adversary.

ϵ-BROADCAST for round i when $k = 2$

- *Inform Phase* - In each of $2^{(a+b)i}$ slots:
  - Alice sends m with probability $\frac{2\ln n}{2^{bi}}$.
  - Each uninformed node listens with probability $\frac{2}{\epsilon' 2^{(a+\frac{b}{2})i}}$.

- *Propagation Phase* - In each of $2^{(a+b)i}$ slots:
  - Each informed node sends m with probability $\frac{1}{n}$ and terminates at the end of the phase.
  - Each uninformed node listens with probability $\frac{4e(c+1)}{2^{ai+(b/2)i}}$.

- *Request Phase* - In each of $2^{(b/2+1)i}$ slots:
  - Each uninformed node sends `nack` with probability $\frac{1}{n}$, listens with probability $\frac{c+1}{(1-e^{-64e'})2^i}$, and terminates if at most $5c\ln n$ noisy slots are heard.
  - Alice listens with probability $\frac{c\ln n}{(1-e^{-4e'})2^{(b/2+1)i}}$ and terminates if at most $5c\ln n$ `nack` messages or noisy slots are heard.

Figure 1: Pseudocode for round i when $k = 2$.

2.1 Analysis of our Protocol

For the inform phase, let $X_u = 1$ if a node u receives m, otherwise let $X_u = 0$. Note that, for nodes two different nodes u and v, X_u and X_v are dependent variables. For example, if $X_u = 0$ because Alice never sent m or she was blocked, then it is more likely that $X_v = 0$. Similarly, if $X_u = 1$, then it is more likely that $X_v = 1$. The following concentration result from [14] is useful:

THEOREM 2. (*[14]*) *Let* $X_1, ..., X_\ell$ *be random variables. Let* f *be a function such that for each* $i \in \{1, ..., \ell\}$ *there is a* $c_i \geq 0$ *such that* $| E[\, f \mid X_1, ..., X_i\,] - E[\, f \mid X_1, ..., X_{i-1}\,] | \leq c_i$. *Then:*

$$Pr(f \geq E[X] + \lambda) < e^{-\frac{\lambda^2}{2\sum_{i=1}^{\ell} c_i^2}}$$

$$Pr(f \leq E[X] - \lambda) < e^{-\frac{\lambda^2}{2\sum_{i=1}^{\ell} c_i^2}}$$

Theorem 2 applies to *dependent variables*. Using this result, we show that, if Carol does not perform too much jamming, then w.h.p. there exists a set containing at least $\Theta\left(\frac{n\ln n}{2^{(b/2)i}}\right)$ informed nodes by the end of the inform phase. We define an inform phase as *blocked* if more than half of the slots in this phase are jammed; otherwise, the phase is *unblocked*. In a blocked inform phase, Carol decides which nodes, if any, receive m since she is n-uniform. We also make use of the following identity:

FACT 3. $1 - y \geq e^{-2y}$ *for any* $y \leq 1/2$.

Throughout our analysis, we are concerned with $3\lg\ln n \leq i \leq \lg n + O(1)$ as these allow us to derive concentration results; as we will see, the upper bound is a natural limit on the length of time our algorithm runs. When we speak of informed/uninformed nodes, this implicitly applies only to *correct* nodes.

LEMMA 4. *Assume at least* $\epsilon' n$ *nodes are uninformed and active at the start of an unblocked inform phase and* $3\lg\ln n \leq i \leq \lg n + O(1)$. *Then, w.h.p., the number of nodes that become newly informed by the end of this inform phase is at least* $\frac{(1-\lambda)n\ln n}{2^{(b/2)i}}$ *for some arbitrarily small constant* $\lambda > 0$ *and for* n *sufficiently large.*

PROOF. Let $s = 2^{(a+b)i}$. Define a binary random variable such that $X_u = 1$ if node u obtains m in the inform phase; otherwise, let $X_u = 0$. Let $q_j = 1$ if Carol does not jam in slot j and let $q_j = 0$ otherwise. Then $Pr(X_u = 1) = 1 - Pr(u$ fails in inform phase$) = 1 - \prod_{j=1}^{s}(1 - Pr(u$ succeeds in slot $j)) = 1 - \prod_{j=1}^{s}(1 - \frac{1}{s})$

$\frac{2\ln n}{2^{bi}}\frac{2}{\epsilon' 2^{(a+b/2)i}}\cdot q_j) \geq 1 - e^{-\frac{4\ln n}{\epsilon' 2^{(a+(3/2)b)i}}\sum_{j=1}^{s}q_j} \geq 1 - e^{-\frac{2\ln n}{\epsilon' 2^{(b/2)i}}}$ given that $\sum_{j=1}^{s}q_j \geq s/2$ since the inform phase is not blocked. Let $y = \frac{\ln n}{\epsilon' 2^{(b/2)i}}$. By Fact 3, it follows that $1 - y = 1 - \frac{\ln n}{\epsilon' 2^{(b/2)i}} \geq e^{-2\ln n/\epsilon' 2^{(b/2)i}}$ since $y \leq 1/2$ given the range of i. Therefore, we conclude that $Pr(X_u = 1) \geq 1 - e^{-\frac{2\ln n}{\epsilon' 2^{(b/2)i}}} \geq \frac{\ln n}{\epsilon' 2^{(b/2)i}}$.

Now let $f = \sum_{u=1}^{\delta n} X_u$ where $1 \geq \delta \geq \epsilon'$ and there are $\delta n \geq \epsilon' n$ uninformed nodes still active. By linearity of expectation, the expected number of nodes that receive m in the inform phase is $E[f] \geq \frac{\delta n\ln n}{\epsilon' 2^{(b/2)i}} \geq \frac{n\ln n}{2^{(b/2)i}}$. To prove a concentration result with dependent variables, we note that $| E[\, f \mid X_1, ..., X_u\,] - E[\, f \mid X_1, ..., X_{u-1}\,] | \leq c_u = 1$ and use Theorem 2. For an arbitrarily small constant $\lambda > 0$, it follows that $Pr(f < \frac{(1-\lambda)\delta n\ln n}{2^{(b/2)i}}) < e^{-\frac{\lambda^2 n^2\ln^2 n}{2^{bi} 2n}} = e^{-\Theta(\lambda^2\ln^2 n)}$ since $i \leq \lg n + O(1)$. For sufficiently large n, this implies the desired upper bound result. $\square$

Lemma 4 reveals the importance of Alice's $O(2^{ai}\ln n)$ budget as it facilitates a sufficiently large S_1. The upper bound is similar:

LEMMA 5. *Assume at least* $\epsilon' n$ *nodes are uninformed at the start of an unblocked inform phase and* $3\lg\ln n \leq i \leq \lg n + O(1)$. *Then, w.h.p., the number of nodes that become newly informed by the end of this inform phase is at most* $\frac{(1+\lambda')4n\ln n}{\epsilon' 2^{(b/2)i}}$ *for an arbitrarily small constant* $\lambda' > 0$ *and for* n *sufficiently large.*

PROOF. Let $s = 2^{(a+b)i}$ and defining X_u the same way, we have $Pr(X_u = 1) = 1 - \prod_{j=1}^{s}(1 - \frac{4\ln n}{\epsilon' 2^{(a+(3/2)b)i}}\cdot q_j)$ and note that $\frac{4\ln n}{\epsilon' 2^{(a+(3/2)b)i}} \leq 1/2$ for the range of i and sufficiently large n. Therefore, $Pr(X_u = 1) = 1 - \prod_{j=1}^{s}(1 - \frac{4\ln n}{\epsilon' 2^{(a+(3/2)b)i}}\cdot q_j) \leq 1 - e^{-\frac{4\ln n}{\epsilon' 2^{(b/2)i}}}$ using the fact that $\sum_{j=1}^{s}q_j \geq s/2$ and Fact 3. Then $Pr(X_u = 1) \leq 1 - e^{-\frac{4\ln n}{\epsilon' 2^{(b/2)i}}} \leq \frac{4\ln n}{\epsilon' 2^{(b/2)i}}$ where the inequality follows from the standard $1 - x \leq e^{-x}$. Therefore, the expected number of newly informed nodes is less than $\frac{4n\ln n}{\epsilon' 2^{(b/2)i}}$. Using Theorem 2, where $\lambda' > 0$ is an arbitrarily small constant, the probability that we have more than $\frac{(1+\lambda')4n\ln n}{\epsilon' 2^{(b/2)i}}$ newly informed nodes is superpolynomially small in n. For n sufficiently large, this yields the desired lower bound. $\square$

Therefore, so long as at least $\epsilon' n$ nodes are uninformed and active, we can generate a set S_i of at least $\Theta\left(\frac{n\ln n}{2^{(b/2)i}}\right)$ newly informed nodes for $3\lg\ln n \leq i \leq \lg n + O(1)$; note, the size of this set is always sublinear in n. Moreover, the size of this set is decreasing as i increases. This is due to the increasing length of the rounds and the limited energy afforded to each node.

In round i of the propagation phase, newly informed nodes in S_i send m to the remaining uninformed nodes. A propagation phase is *blocked* if more than half of the slots are jammed; otherwise, the phase is *unblocked*. Again, in a blocked propagation phase, Carol can decide which nodes receive m since she is n-uniform.

LEMMA 6. *Consider* $(3/b)\lg\ln n \leq i \leq \lg n + O(1)$ *and assume that the inform phase in round* i *was not blocked. Then, if the propagation phase in round* i *is not blocked, w.h.p. all nodes are informed by the end of the propagation phase.*

PROOF. Let $s = 2^{(a+b)i}$ be the number of slots and let x be the number of newly informed nodes from the inform phase. Since the inform phase was not blocked, Lemmas 4 and 5 guarantee w.h.p. that $\frac{(1-\lambda)n\ln n}{2^{(b/2)i}} \leq x \leq \frac{(1+\lambda)4n\ln n}{\epsilon' 2^{(b/2)i}}$ for some arbitrarily small constant $\lambda > 0$. In a single slot, the probability that exactly one informed node in S_i is sending is lower bounded by $x(\frac{1}{n})$

148

$(1 - \frac{1}{n})^{x-1} \geq \frac{(1-\lambda)n \ln n}{2^{(b/2)i}n} \cdot (1 - \frac{1}{n})^{((1+\lambda)4n \ln n/(\epsilon' 2^{(b/2)i})) - 1}$

$\geq \frac{(1-\lambda)\ln n}{2^{(b/2)i}} e^{-8(1+\lambda) \ln n/(\epsilon' 2^{(b/2)i})} \geq \frac{(1-\lambda)\ln n}{e \cdot 2^{(b/2)i}} \geq \frac{\ln n}{e \cdot 2^{(b/2)i+1}}$

where the second inequality follows by applying Fact 3, the third follows by noting that $2^{(b/2)i} \in \omega(\ln n)$ for $i = (3/b) \lg \ln n$ (later we show $b = 1$, thus keeping i within proper range), and the fourth follows from setting $\lambda \leq 1/2$. Note that the sublinear upper bound on the size of S_i prevents the probability of exactly one node sending from being too small. Therefore, the probability a particular uninformed node does not receive m in a single slot is at most $1 - \frac{\ln n}{2^{(b/2)i+1}} \frac{4e(c+1)}{2^{ai+(b/2)i}} q_j$ where $q_j = 0$ if Carol jams and $q_j = 1$ if she does not. The probability of a specific active and uninformed node failing to obtain m in this phase is at most

$\prod_{j=1}^{s}(1 - \frac{2(c+1)\ln n}{2^{(a+b)i}} q_j) \leq e^{-\frac{2(c+1)\ln n}{2^{(a+b)i}} \cdot \sum_1^s q_j} < n^{-(c+1)}$ since $\sum_1^s q_j \geq \frac{s}{2}$. A union bound over all nodes yields the result. $\square$

Note that any communication from S_i aimed at telling Alice the inform phase was successful could be spoofed by Carol. Therefore, S_i cannot ever replace Alice (allowing her to sleep) since it is impossible to verify that S_i was created until the protocol terminates. Furthermore, keeping S_i around for use in the propagation phase of round $i + 1$ is wasteful since S_{i+1} alone is sufficient. Increasing the sending probability of each node in S_i is also wasteful and causes nodes to exceed their budget in later rounds. Therefore, S_i terminates at the end of every propagation phase.

2.2 Request Phase: Tolerating Spoofing

A request phase in round i is said to be blocked if Carol jams more than $(1 - e^{-4\epsilon'})2^{(b/2+1)i} = \Omega(2^{(b/2+1)i})$ slots during the phase. Any constant fraction of the request phase will work; however, we choose this threshold to simplify the analysis. Again, recall that $3 \lg \ln n \leq i \leq \lg n + O(1)$. We state two important properties of Alice's termination condition:

LEMMA 7. *Assume that the request phase is unblocked. If at most $2\epsilon'n$ nodes remain active, where then w.h.p. Alice (correctly) terminates the protocol for $\epsilon' \leq 1/2$.*

PROOF. Let $s = 2^{(b/2+1)i}$. The probability that no uninformed node sends a `nack` in a particular slot is $(1 - \frac{1}{n})^{2\epsilon'n}$ for $\epsilon' \leq 1/2$. By Fact 3, we have $(1 - \frac{1}{n})^{2\epsilon'n} \geq e^{-4\epsilon'}$; therefore, the probability that a slot is noisy is $1 - (1 - \frac{1}{n})^{2\epsilon'n} \leq 1 - e^{-4\epsilon'}$. Let $Y_j = 1$ if slot j is noisy due to a `nack` message by an uninformed node; otherwise, let $Y_j = 0$. The expected number of noisy slots heard by Alice due to uninformed nodes is at most $E[\sum_1^s Y_j] \leq \sum_1^s \frac{c \ln n}{(1-e^{-4\epsilon'})2^{(b/2+1)i}} \cdot (1 - e^{-4\epsilon'}) = c \ln n$. Pessimistically, assume that each of Carol's blocked slots occurs when none of the other uninformed nodes are sending a `nack` message. Let $Z_j = 1$ if slot j is noisy due to Carol jamming; otherwise, let $Z_j = 0$. The expected number of jammed slots is at most $E[\sum_1^s Z_j] \leq \frac{c \ln n}{(1-e^{-4\epsilon'})2^{(b/2+1)i}} \cdot (1 - e^{-4\epsilon'})2^{(b/2+1)i} = c \ln n$. Therefore, the total expected number of noisy slots that Alice hears is at most $2c \ln n$. By standard Chernoff bounds, the probability of exceeding $5c \ln n$ is at most $1/n^c$. $\square$

LEMMA 8. *Assume at least $32\epsilon'n$ nodes are active at the beginning of a request phase where $\epsilon' \leq 1/32$. Then. w.h.p., Alice (correctly) does not terminate.*

PROOF. The bad event occurs if the number of noisy slots that Alice detects is less than $5c \ln n$. Since Carol cannot forge silence, we do not consider her behavior here. The probability of a noisy slot is $1 - (1 - \frac{1}{n})^{32\epsilon'n} \geq 1 - e^{-32\epsilon'}$. Therefore, as in the proof

of Lemma 7, $E[Y] \geq \sum_1^s \frac{c \ln n}{(1-e^{-2\epsilon'})} \cdot (1 - e^{-32\epsilon'}) \geq 10c \ln n$ for $s = 2^{(b/2+1)i}$ and any $\epsilon' \leq 1/32$. The result follows by standard Chernoff bounds. $\square$

We prove a similar result for uninformed nodes, although the constants differ slightly and we discuss this below.

LEMMA 9. *Assume that the request phase is unblocked. If at most $32\epsilon'n$ nodes are active, where $\epsilon' \leq 1/64$, then w.h.p. every node terminates by the end of the request phase.*

LEMMA 10. *Assume at least $1024\epsilon'n$ nodes are active at the beginning of a request phase where $\epsilon' \leq 1/1024$. The, w.h.p., none of the uninformed nodes terminate in that request phase.*

Critically, Alice should only terminate after the correct nodes terminate and, therefore, our algorithm is designed in the following way. If uninformed nodes are guaranteed w.h.p. to be active (a threshold of $1024\epsilon'n$ active nodes), then certainly Alice is guaranteed w.h.p. to be active (a threshold of $32\epsilon'n$ active nodes). Conversely, if Alice is guaranteed w.h.p. to have terminated (a threshold of $2\epsilon'n$ active nodes), then the nodes are guaranteed w.h.p. to have already terminated (a threshold of $32\epsilon'n$ active nodes).

To summarize the implications of these results, there are two bad situations: (1) if Alice or correct nodes can be tricked into perpetually executing the protocol at little cost to Carol, and (2) if Carol can cause Alice and all nodes to terminate with a large fraction of uninformed nodes. We have shown that (1) to keep Alice or nodes executing the protocol past their termination condition requires Carol to jam $\Omega(2^{(b/2+1)i})$ slots, and (2) w.h.p. Carol cannot force a large number of nodes to terminate without m.

2.3 Correctness & Resource Competitiveness

The remainder of our analysis proceeds as follows. First, we show that if no blocked phases occur, then at least $(1 - \epsilon')n$ nodes receive m. Second, when blocking phases do occur, we provide results on resource competitiveness. Finally, we prove that eventually a round is encountered where blocking must stop; consequently, at least $(1 - \epsilon')n$ nodes become informed.

LEMMA 11. *Assume that there are no blocked phases in some round $i \geq 3 \lg \ln n$ and at least $\epsilon'n$ nodes are active at the beginning of this round for any constant $\epsilon' > 0$. Then, w.h.p., all correct nodes are informed and terminate.*

PROOF. Since the inform phase of round i is not blocked, Lemmas 4 and 5 guarantee w.h.p. the creation of an S_i of appropriate size. Since the propagation phase is not blocked, Lemma 6 guarantees w.h.p. that all remaining active nodes receive m. Then, since the request phase is not blocked, Lemmas 7 and 8 guarantee w.h.p. that Alice terminates and Lemmas 9 and 10 guarantee that all nodes terminate. $\square$

Lemma 11 proves correctness in the absence of blocked phases; however, it is not yet apparent how the protocol may result in an small fraction of terminated, but uninformed, nodes. The critical observation is that we require $\epsilon'n$ active uninformed nodes at the beginning of the inform phase in order for Lemma 11 to hold.

Note that by blocking a propagation phase, an n-uniform Carol may allow $2\epsilon'n$ nodes to remain uninformed and active. By Lemma 7 and 9, Alice and all nodes then terminate. Or Carol might block a propagate phase and let all but $32\epsilon'n$ nodes become informed; in this case, all nodes terminate with $32\epsilon'n$ uninformed. Critically, when Carol blocks an inform or propagate phase, she decides how many nodes receive m since she is a n-uniform adversary; this illustrates the challenges posed by a n-uniform adversary. We now analyze resource competitiveness and begin by stating the costs when no blocked phases ever occur:

LEMMA 12. *Assume there are never any blocked phases. Then the cost to Alice is $O(\log^{3a+1} n)$ and the cost to each node is $O(\log^{(3/2)b} n)$.*

PROOF. Given no blocked phases, Lemma 11 guarantees w.h.p. that all nodes become informed and terminate by round $i = 3 \lg \ln n$ and, given that round length increases geometrically with i, the costs in this round dominates that of the earlier rounds. In the inform phase, Alice's cost is $O(\log^{3a+1} n)$ and each node's cost is $O(\log^{(3/2)b} n)$. In the propagation phase Alice is inactive while each node in S_1 incurs a cost of $\tilde{O}(1)$, and each uninformed node incurs a cost of $O(\log^{(3/2)b} n)$. In the request phase, Alice's cost is $O(\log n)$ and each node's cost is $O(\log^{(3/2)b} n)$. Summing the costs yields the claim. □

LEMMA 13. *Assume that Carol spends T over the execution of ϵ-BROADCAST and at least one phase is blocked. Then, w.h.p the cost to Alice is $\max\{\tilde{O}(T^{a/(a+b)}), \tilde{O}(T^{a/(b/2+1)})\}$ and the cost to any node is $\max\{O(T^{b/2(a+b)}), O(T^{(b/2)/(b/2+1)})\}$.*

PROOF. We analyze Alice and correct nodes separately:

Cost for Alice: There are two strategies by which Carol can prevent Alice from terminating. The first strategy is where Carol blocks during at least one of the inform or propagation phases in each round. In this case, let r be the first round where both the inform phase and propagation phase are not blocked. Then the cost to Carol is $T = \Omega(2^{(a+b)r})$. Here, the cost to Alice is dominated by the cost of the next (and last) round since cost increases geometrically; this cost is $O(2^{ar} \ln n) = O\left(T^{a/(a+b)} \ln n\right)$. The second strategy occurs when Carol blocks the request phase in order to trick Alice into believing that at least $32\epsilon' n$ nodes remain uninformed. Let $r' > r$ be the first round where Carol does not block the request phase. Note that $r' > r$ since it does Carol no good to block the request phase if the inform or propagate phases were already blocked in the round. Then, Carol's cost is $\Omega(2^{(b/2+1)r'})$ while the cost to Alice is $O(T^{\frac{a}{b/2+1}} \ln n)$ since she will proceed into the next (and, w.h.p., final) round.

Cost for a Node: There are two strategies by which Carol might prevent a node from terminating. The first strategy is where Carol blocks at least one of the inform or propagation phases in each round. Let r be the first round where this does not occur. Then, the cost to Carol is $T = \Omega(2^{(a+b)r})$ while the cost to each node is $O(T^{b/(2(a+b))})$. The second strategy occurs when Carol blocks the request phase in order to trick the informed nodes into believing that at least $1024\epsilon' n$ nodes remain uninformed. Let $r' > r$ be the first round where Carol does not block the request phase. Carol's cost is $\Omega(2^{(b/2+1)r'})$ while the cost to a node is $O(T^{(b/2)/(b/2+1)})$ since the node will proceed into the next (and final) round. □

We now state our final result for $k = 2$:

LEMMA 14. *Assume a sender Alice with a budget of at most $Cn^{1/2} \ln n$ who aims to deliver a message m to n correct nodes. Assume an adaptive adversary Carol with an individual budget of $Cn^{1/2} \ln n$ who controls an additional n Byzantine nodes. Each correct and Byzantine node possesses a budget of $Cn^{1/2}$. Then, w.h.p., ϵ-BROADCAST guarantees the following properties:*

- *If Carol and her Byzantine nodes jam for T slots, then Alice and each correct node terminates with an individual cost of $\tilde{O}(T^{\frac{1}{3}} + 1)$.*

- *At least $(1 - \epsilon)n$ correct correct nodes receive m for an arbitrarily small constant $\epsilon > 0$ within $O(n^{3/2})$ slots.*

PROOF. The worst-case resource-competitive ratios for Alice and the nodes should be equal. Lemma 13 tells us that the exponents of interest for Alice are $a/(a+b)$ and $a/(b/2+1)$. Similarly, in the case of each node, the exponents of interest are $b/(2(a+b))$ and $(b/2)(b/2+1)$. Since we can choose $a \leq 1/2$ and $b \leq 1$, we can simplify Alice's maximum cost by setting $a/(a+b) = a/(b/2+1)$ and deriving the relationship $a + b(1 - (1/2)) = 1$ (or, in general, $a + b(1 - (1/k)) = 1$). Then we can relate this to a node's cost by setting $a/(a+b) = b/(2(a+b))$ and $a/(b/2+1) = (b/2)/(b/2+1)$ yields $a = b/2$ (or, for general k, $a = b/k$). Therefore, a common solution is $b = 1$ and $a = 1/2$ (or, in general, $a = 1/k$). This yields a load-balanced solution where the cost to Alice is $O(T^{1/3} \ln n + \ln^{5/2} n)$ and the cost to each node of $O(T^{1/3} + \ln^{5/2} n)$ where the second cost term in each cost function follows from Lemma 12.

We now prove that the budgets of Alice and each node are sufficient to guarantee the claimed properties. When executing ϵ-BROADCAST, there exists some constant $d > 0$ such that the cost to each node in round i is at most $d 2^{(b/2)i} = d 2^{i/2}$; note that d depends on the parameters ϵ, c, and k in our protocol. Recall that a blocked send, propagation, and request phase are defined slightly differently in terms of the constant fraction of slots jammed. Therefore, to simplify the analysis, redefine a blocked phase in round i as one where more than $\beta \, 2^{(3/2)i}$ slots are jammed for $0 < \beta < 1$; any positive constant in the range $(0, 1)$ will yield the same resource competitive result asymptotically.

Each of the t Byzantine nodes has a budget of $C n^{1/2}$; therefore, Carol and her Byzantine nodes possess a combined budget of $C f n^{3/2} + C n^{1/2} \ln n \leq C(f + 1)n^{3/2}$. Therefore, using this budget, Carol cannot block a send, propagation, or request phase consisting of $(C/\beta)(f + 1) n^{3/2}$ slots or more. Solving for $2^{(3/2)i} = (C/\beta)(f + 1) n^{3/2}$ implies this occurs in round $i = \lg n + \frac{2}{3} \lg((C/\beta)(f+1))$.

The cost to each correct node for executing ϵ-BROADCAST in this round $i = \lg n + \frac{2}{3} \lg(2(C/\beta)(f + 1))$ is at most $d 2^{i/2} = d((C/\beta)(f + 1))^{1/3} n^{1/2}$. We must take into account previous rounds, but given the doubling of length per round, the total cost up to this round is at most $2d((C/\beta)(f + 1))^{1/3} n^{1/2}$. Therefore, so long as $C \geq (2d)^{3/2} \cdot ((f + 1)/\beta)^{1/2}$, w.h.p. a correct node does not exceed its budget. By an almost identical argument, w.h.p., Alice does not exceed her budget of $C n^{1/2} \ln n$. Therefore, for C sufficiently large, Alice and the correct nodes are guaranteed to reach a round where there are no blocked phases and, therefore, Lemma 11 guarantees that at least $(1 - \epsilon)n$ nodes are informed and terminate; the ϵ-fraction that might terminate without m follows from our observations about an n-uniform adversary. Given the doubling of the number of slots in each round, this last phase occurs within $O(n^{3/2})$ slots. □

Clearly, no algorithm can disseminate a value from sender to *any* receivers in $o(n^{3/2})$ slots given that the total budget of Carol and her Byzantine nodes allow for the channel to be jammed continuously for that length of time. The following corollary is immediate:

COROLLARY 15. *The latency for ϵ-BROADCAST is asymptotically optimal.*

Finally, we note that, in practice, each node may start with $i = 1$ (or any other agreed upon constant) and run until at least its respective estimate of $d \lg \ln n$ is reached before terminating for some constant $d \geq 3$. That is, there is no need to start at exactly round $i = 3 \lg \ln n$; indeed, nodes may not agree on such a value and we discuss this further in Section 4.2.

3. THE GENERAL CASE

For general k, it is not sufficient to simply replace $1/2$ by some function, say $(k-1)/k$, in our analysis since doing so results in a w.h.p. cost of $O(n^{(k-1)/k})$ rather than the desired $O(n^{1/k})$. Instead, the propagation of m must be extended in a non-trivial fashion by repeating the propagation phase $k - 1$ times. For a fixed round $i \in \Omega(\lg\ln n)$, we use these repeated propagation phases to prove the existence of sets of nodes $S_{i,h}$ where $h = 1, ..., k - 1$. The inform phase remains unchanged and results in the creation of the set $S_{i,1}$ consisting of $\Theta(\frac{n\ln^{k-1} n}{2^{(1-1/k)i}})$ newly informed nodes. In turn, the propagation phase utilizes $S_{i,1}$ to guarantee the creation of $S_{i,2}$ which consists of $\Theta(\frac{n\ln^{k-2} n}{2^{(1-2/k)i}})$ newly informed nodes. In general, throughout step h of the propagation phase, the existing set $S_{i,h}$ of size $\Theta(\frac{n\ln^{k-h} n}{2^{(1-h/k)i}})$ is used to create the new set $S_{i,h+1}$ of size $\Theta(\frac{n\ln^{k-h-1} n}{2^{(1-(h+1)/k)i}})$ or larger. Therefore, by at least step $h = k - 1$, the set $S_{i,k-1}$ contains $\Theta(\frac{n\ln n}{2^{i/k}})$ informed nodes which ensures that all remaining uninformed nodes can receive m if no step in creating $S_{i,h}$ is blocked. Our pseudocode for general k is given in Figure 2 with the values for $a = 1/k$ and $b = 1$ substituted.

3.1 Analysis for $k = 3$

We prove the case for $k = 3$ case which demonstrates the key features regarding how the proof must change. Notable changes are that Theorem 2 no longer suffices to prove a lower bound on the size of the sets $S_{i,h}$; although, we can still use it to obtain a useful (loose) upper bound. Our proof structure changes to handle dependencies between the variables discussed in Section 2.1. Also, Alice must now send with probability $2c\ln^k n/2^i$ and we consider $13\lg\ln n \leq i \leq \lg n + O(1)$; in general, $i = \Omega(\lg\ln n)$ for constant k. These changes are artifacts of our proof technique.

In the following, we conceptually divide the n nodes into $\frac{n\ln^2 n}{2^{2i/3}}$ groups each of size $2^{2i/3}/\ln^2 n$ nodes. We stress that these groups provide a method of counting how many nodes become informed, but such groupings play no part in the protocol. Our goal is to show that at least one member of each group becomes informed by the end of the phase. To do this, we first prove that, for every group, each slot in the inform phase has a sufficient probability of being listened to by a node in the group.

LEMMA 16. *Assume at least $\epsilon' n$ nodes are uninformed and active. Then, for any slot in the inform phase, the probability that*

at least one node in each group is listening in that slot is at least $\frac{1}{2^{i/3}\ln^2 n}$.

PROOF. In round i, consider a group of $2^{2i/3}/\ln^2 n$ nodes. Since at least $\epsilon' n$ nodes are uninformed and active, and the group membership is arbitrary, we can consider each such disjoint group to possess at least $\epsilon' 2^{2i/3}/\ln^2 n$ active nodes. Therefore, in a fixed slot, the probability that none of the nodes in a group are listening is $(1 - \frac{2}{\epsilon' 2^i})^{\epsilon' 2^{2i/3}/\ln^2 n} \leq e^{-2/(2^{i/3}\ln^2 n)}$. Therefore, the probability that at least one node in a group is listening is equal to or greater than $1 - e^{-2/(2^{i/3}\ln^2 n)} \geq \frac{1}{2^{i/3}\ln^2 n}$ by Fact 3. □

Using our analysis via groups, the next lemma states proves the existence of a set $S_{i,1}$ of at least $\frac{n\ln^2 n}{2^{2i/3}}$ nodes informed after the completion of a non-blocked inform phase.

LEMMA 17. *Assume that at least $\epsilon' n$ nodes are uninformed and active. Then, with high probability when $5\lg\ln n \leq i \leq \lg n + O(1)$, after an unblocked inform phase, there exist at least $\frac{n\ln^2 n}{2^{2i/3}}$ newly informed nodes.*

PROOF. The phase consists of $s = 2^{(4/3)i}$ slots. Since at least $\epsilon' n$ nodes are uninformed and active, Lemma 16 guarantees that the probability no nodes in a group of size $2^{2i/3}/\ln^2 n$ receive m in a fixed slot is at most $1 - (\frac{2c\ln^3 n}{2^i})(\frac{1}{2^{i/3}\ln^2 n})q_j$ where $q_j = 0$ if Carol jams and $q_j = 1$ if she does not. It follows that, over the phase, the probability of all active uninformed nodes in the group failing to obtain m is at most $\prod_{j=1}^{s}(1 - (\frac{2c\ln^3 n}{2^i})(\frac{1}{2^{i/3}\ln^2 n})q_j)$ $\leq e^{-\frac{2c\ln n}{2^{(4/3)i}}\cdot\sum_1^s q_j} \leq n^{-c}$ since $\sum_1^s q_j \geq \frac{s}{2}$. Taking a union bound over all groups, we conclude that at least one node from each of the $\frac{n\ln^2 n}{2^{2i/3}}$ groups becomes informed; this yields the result. □

While not tight, it is sufficient to use essentially the same upper bound argument as in Lemma 5:

LEMMA 18. *Assume at least $\epsilon' n$ nodes are uninformed and active at the start of an unblocked inform phase and $5\lg\ln n \leq i \leq \lg n + O(1)$. Then, w.h.p., the number of nodes that become newly informed by the end of this inform phase is at most $\frac{(1+\lambda')4n\ln^2 n}{\epsilon' 2^{i/2}}$ for an arbitrarily small constant $\lambda' > 0$ and for n sufficiently large.*

The members of the set $S_{i,1}$ are now used in the propagation phase to prove the existence of a larger set $S_{i,2}$ of size $\Theta(\frac{n\ln n}{2^{i/3}})$ informed members. Conceptually, this is proved by showing that members in $S_{i,1}$ can create at least one informed member in each of $\frac{n\ln n}{2^{i/3}}$ disjoint groups consisting of $\frac{2^{i/3}}{\ln n}$ nodes each; call each such conceptual group a *2-group*. Again, we need to lower bound the probability that a slot is covered by at least one node in such 2-group.

LEMMA 19. *Assume that at least $\epsilon' n$ nodes are uninformed and active, and assume that the inform phase was not blocked. Then, for any slot in step $h = 1$ of the propagation phase, the probability that at least one node in a 2-group is listening in that slot is at least $\frac{ec}{2^{(2/3)i}\ln n}$.*

PROOF. Let G be a 2-group consisting of $2^{i/3}/\ln n$ nodes. Since at most $(1 - \epsilon')n$ nodes have terminated, we can consider each disjoint 2-group to possess at least $\epsilon' 2^{i/3}/\ln n$ active nodes. The probability that none of the nodes in G are listening in a slot is $(1 - \frac{2ec}{\epsilon' 2^i})^{\epsilon'\cdot 2^{(i/3)}/\ln n} \leq e^{-2ec/(2^{(2/3)i}\ln n)}$. Therefore, the probability that at least one node in G is listening to a particular slot is at least $1 - e^{-2ec/(2^{(2/3)i}\ln n)} \geq ec/(2^{(2/3)i}\ln n)$ by Fact 3. □

Define a blocked step of the propagation phase to be one where more than half the slots in that step are jammed. We can now prove the existence of $S_{i,2}$:

LEMMA 20. *Assume that at least $\epsilon' n$ nodes are uninformed and active, and the inform phase was not blocked. Then, w.h.p., at least $\frac{n \ln n}{2^{i/3}}$ nodes are newly informed in an unblocked step $h = 1$ of the propagation phase for $5 \lg \ln n \leq i \leq \lg n + O(1)$.*

PROOF. The phase consists of $s = 2^{(4/3)i}$ slots. For a fixed slot, the probability that a single node from $S_{i,1}$ is sending is $p = |S_{i,1}|(\frac{1}{n})(1 - \frac{1}{n})^{|S_{i,1}|-1}$. By Lemmas 17 and 18, we know that $\frac{n \ln^2 n}{2^{2i/3}} \leq |S_{i,1}| \leq \frac{(1+\lambda')4n \ln^2 n}{\epsilon' 2^{i/2}}$, we have $p \geq \frac{\ln^2 n}{2^{2i/3}} \cdot (1 - \frac{1}{n})^{\frac{(1+\lambda')4n \ln^2 n}{\epsilon' 2^{i/2}} - 1} \geq \frac{\ln^2 n}{2^{2i/3}} e^{-2(1+\lambda')4 \ln^2 n/(\epsilon' 2^{i/2})} \geq \frac{\ln^2 n}{e 2^{2i/3}}$ in the range of i. Since at least $\epsilon' n$ nodes are uninformed and active, by Lemma 19, the probability that no nodes in a fixed 2-group receive m in a single slot is at most $1 - (\frac{\ln^2 n}{e 2^{2i/3}})(\frac{ec}{2^{(2/3)i} \ln n})q_j$ where $q_j = 0$ if Carol jams and $q_j = 1$ if she does not. It follows that the probability of all active and uninformed nodes in the 2-group failing to obtain m in this step is at most $\prod_{j=1}^{s}(1 - (\frac{c \ln n}{2^{(4/3)i}})q_j) \leq e^{-\frac{c \ln n}{2^{(4/3)i}} \cdot \sum_{1}^{s} q_j} \leq n^{-c/2}$ since $\sum_{1}^{s} q_j \geq \frac{s}{2}$. Taking a union bound over all $n \ln n/2^{i/3}$ groups yields the result. □

We need the next upper bound to ensure that members of $S_{i,2}$ will successfully send with sufficiently high probability:

LEMMA 21. *Assume at least $\epsilon' n$ nodes are active and uninformed, and both the inform phase and step $h = 1$ of the propagation phase were not blocked. Then, w.h.p. where $5 \lg \ln n \leq i \leq \lg n + O(1)$, the number of nodes that become newly informed by the end of this propagation phase is at most $\frac{(1+\lambda'')8cn \ln^2 n}{\epsilon' 2^{i/6}}$ for an arbitrary small constant $\lambda'' > 0$ and for n sufficiently large.*

Finally, we can show that all remaining nodes receive m if step $h = 2$ of the propagation phase is not blocked:

LEMMA 22. *Let $7 \lg \ln n \leq i \leq \lg n + O(1)$. Assume that in round i both the inform phase and step $h = 1$ of the propagation phase in round were not blocked. Then, if step $h = 2$ of the propagation phase in round i is unblocked, w.h.p. all nodes are informed by the end of the propagation phase.*

PROOF. Let $s = 2^{(4/3)i}$ be the number of slots. Since the inform phase and step $h = 1$ of the propagation phase were not blocked, Lemmas 20 and 21 guarantee w.h.p. that $\frac{n \ln n}{2^{i/3}} \leq |S_{i,2}| \leq \frac{(1+\lambda'')8cn \ln^2 n}{\epsilon' 2^{i/6}}$ for some arbitrarily small constant $\lambda > 0$. In a single slot, the probability that exactly one informed node in $S_{i,2}$ is sending is at least $|S_{i,2}|(\frac{1}{n})(1 - \frac{1}{n})^{|S_{i,2}|-1} \geq \frac{n \ln n}{2^{i/3} n}(1 - \frac{1}{n})^{(1+\lambda'')8cn \ln^2 n/(\epsilon' 2^{i/6})} \geq \frac{\ln n}{e 2^{i/3}}$ for $i \geq 13 \lg \ln n$ and n sufficiently large. Therefore, the probability a particular uninformed node does not receive m in a single slot is at most $1 - \frac{\ln n}{e 2^{i/3}} \frac{2ec}{2^i} q_j$ where $q_j = 0$ if Carol jams and $q_j = 0$ if she does not. The probability of a specific active and uninformed node failing to obtain m in this phase is at most $\prod_{j=1}^{s}(1 - \frac{2c \ln n}{2^{(4/3)i}} q_j) \leq e^{-\frac{2c \ln n}{2^{(4/3)i}} \cdot \sum_{1}^{s} q_j}$ which gives us the high probability guarantee since $\sum_{1}^{s} q_j \geq \frac{s}{2}$. Taking a union bound over all nodes yields the result. □

Discussion: Therefore, all nodes will receive m so long as neither the inform phase nor any steps in the propagation phase are blocked. Note that the arguments in Lemma 13 and 14 do not change so long as k is a constant (see below). Analogous to our argument when $k = 2$, when round $i = \lg n + \frac{k}{k+1} \lg(C/\beta)$ is reached, Carol and the Byzantine nodes do not have sufficient energy to block a phase (or a step of a phase) in which case, the termination conditions for Alice and the correct nodes are met. By chaining together more proofs showing the existence of $S_{i,h}$, this proof structure can be extended for any constant k.

3.2 Limits To This Approach

By increasing k, the protocol is more resource competitive; however, there is a limit. Note that, due to the steps of the propagation phase, the latency and the overall costs increases by a factor of $\Theta(k)$. Now consider if $k \geq \omega(1)$. Then, Alice and her nodes each require $\omega(n^{1/k})$ to execute the $O(k)$ propagation phase steps and this exceeds their budget.

This cannot be remedied through any $\omega(1)$-factor increase in the budget of each node. To see why, let $k = 2$ and assume that each node now has a budget of $C n^{1/2} \ln n$. Note that Carol may now block phases of length $C n^{3/2} \ln n$ which occurs for round $i = \lg n + (2/3) \lg \ln n + (2/3) \lg C$. However, in this round, each correct node must spend $2^{i/2} \ln n = \Omega(n^{1/2} \ln^{4/3} n)$; this exceeds its budget. This problem manifests for any $k = \omega(1)$.

4. EXTENSIONS TO THE PROTOCOL

In this section, we sketch how ϵ-BROADCAST can be modified to tolerate a reactive adversary when $f < 1/24$. We conclude by discussing how exact knowledge of $\ln n$ and n is not required to successfully execute ϵ-BROADCAST.

4.1 Reactive Jamming: Make Your Own Noise

Within the current time slot, a reactive adversary can detect channel activity and decide whether to jam. The ability to perform CCA makes it possible for Carol to detect such activity based on the received signal strength indicator (RSSI) which incurs negligible cost. During either the inform or propagation phases, Carol is guaranteed to interfere with the transmission of m if she jams. Such targeted jamming invalidates our analysis in Lemmas 4, 5, and 6. However, while RSSI enables Carol to detect channel activity, it provides no information about the transmitted content. Therefore, reactive jamming is only effective if the bulk of the channel activity involves the transmission of m. For example, if half of the slots contain non-critical traffic and the other half contain m, then jamming based simply on RSSI is no better than randomly jamming. While Carol might activate her transceiver in order to hear part of the transmission before deciding to jam, this is expensive.

As in [22], if there is sufficient background network traffic such that a constant fraction of the slots in each round are in use, then a reactive adversary can be tolerated. But what if such traffic is absent? Another approach is to have the correct nodes generate their own traffic. Under this strategy, we show that, for $f < 1/24$, a reactive Carol is unable to prevent communication indefinitely and our algorithm is still resource competitive. Although $f < 1/24$ implies that the aggregate energy possessed by Alice and the correct nodes exceeds that of Carol and her Byzantine nodes, we emphasize that this problem is still non-trivial. For example, it is not possible to have have Alice outspend Carol since Alice can only send the message $O(n^{1/2})$ times while Carol can jam for $\Omega(n^{3/2})$ slots. As described above, we need to have the uninformed nodes generate additional traffic in order to overcome a reactive jammer.

To do this, for the inform and propagation phases, the modified protocol specifies that each node sends a decoy message with probability $\frac{3}{4\epsilon' n}$ per slot and we assume that each correct node listens with a constant factor increase in probability (see p_u in the proof of Lemma 4). We now re-prove Lemma 4.

Lemma 4. *Assume at least $\epsilon' n$ nodes are uninformed and active at the start of an unblocked inform phase and $3 \lg \ln n \leq i \leq \lg n + O(1)$. Then, w.h.p., the number of correct nodes that become newly informed by the end of this inform phase is at least $\frac{(1-\lambda)n \ln n}{2^{i/2}}$ for an arbitrarily small constant $\lambda > 0$ and for n sufficiently large.*

PROOF. Let $s = 2^{(3/2)i}$. Let the random variable $Z_j = 1$ if a slot is occupied by one or more decoy messages; otherwise, let $Z_j = 0$. Since all correct nodes send a decoy message independently with uniform probability $\frac{3}{4\epsilon'n}$, $Pr(Z_j = 1) = 1 - (1 - \frac{3}{4\epsilon'n})^{\epsilon'n} \geq 1 - e^{-3/4} \geq 1/2$. Letting $Z = \sum_j^s Z_j$ it follows that $E[Z] \geq (1/2)s$. Conversely, using Fact 3, $Pr(Z_j = 1) \leq 1 - (1 - \frac{3}{4\epsilon'n})^n \leq 1 - e^{-3/(2\epsilon')}$; therefore, $E[Z] \leq (1 - e^{-3/(2\epsilon')})s$. By standard Chernoff bounds, for $i \geq 3\lg\ln n$, the number of slots containing one or more decoy messages, denoted by s_N, is $(1-\delta)(1/2)s \leq s_N \leq (1+\delta)(1-e^{-3/(2\epsilon')})s$ w.h.p. for $\delta > 0$ arbitrarily small depending only on sufficiently large n. By a similar argument, given $i \geq 3\lg\ln n$, the number of slots in which Alice sends m is $s_A = (1 \pm \delta')2^{i/2}\ln n$ w.h.p. for $\delta' > 0$ arbitrarily small depending only on sufficiently large n.

Redefine an inform phase as blocked if Carol jams more than $s/4$ slots *containing m or at least one decoy message*. Carol's choice to jam such a slot (or listen to it) is made without knowing whether the slot contains m or a decoy message. Therefore, for a fixed slot containing m sent by Alice, the probability that Carol fails to listen to or block this slot in a non-blocked phase is at least $1 - \frac{s/4}{s_N}$. The probability that this same slot is not used by a correct node for sending a decoy message is at least $e^{-3/(2\epsilon')}$ as determined above. Let p_u denote the probability that a node u listens to a particular slot. Assuming Alice sends m, the probability that u receives m in a fixed slot is at least $(1 - \frac{s/4}{s_N})(e^{-3/(2\epsilon')})p_u \geq (e^{-3/(2\epsilon')} - \frac{2^{(3/2)i}}{4 \cdot e^{3/(2\epsilon')} \cdot (1-\delta)(1/2)2^{(3/2)i}})p_u = (\frac{1}{e^{3/(2\epsilon')}} - \frac{(1+\delta'')}{2e^{3/(2\epsilon')}})p_u$ for small enough δ given sufficiently large n. It follows that, for sufficiently small δ''(say $\delta'' \leq 1/2$), the probability that u receives m in a slot is at least $(\frac{1}{e^{3/(2\epsilon')}} - \frac{(1+\delta'')}{2e^{3/(2\epsilon')}})p_u = \frac{p_u}{4e^{3/(2\epsilon')}}$.

As in our original proof, let $X_u = 1$ if u obtains m in the inform phase; otherwise, let $X_u = 0$. Then $Pr(X_u = 1) \geq 1 - (1 - \frac{p_u}{4e^{3/(2\epsilon')}})^{s_A} - O(1/n^{c'})$ where the last term is the probability that s_N or s_A deviate by more than δ from their respective expected values and $c' > 0$ is some constant. Redefine $p_u = \frac{16\,e^{3/(2\epsilon')}}{\epsilon'(1-\delta')2^i}$; this is a constant factor increase, so the cost to each node is asymptotically equal. Then, $Pr(X_u = 1) \geq 1 - (1 - \frac{4}{\epsilon'(1-\delta')2^i})^{(1-\delta')2^{i/2}\ln n} - O(1/n^{c'}) \geq 1 - e^{-4\ln n/(\epsilon'2^{i/2})} - O(1/n^{c''}) \geq \frac{2\ln n}{\epsilon'2^{i/2}} - O(1/n^{c'}) \geq \frac{\ln n}{\epsilon'2^{i/2}}$ for sufficiently large n. We can then apply Theorem 2 as in the original proof and obtain the desired result. □

The proofs for Lemmas 5 and 6 can be redone in a similar fashion. Now we show that communication occurs in the final round. The modifications to the sending and listening probabilities, and sending of the decoy messages, increases costs by a constant factor.

LEMMA 23. *With high probability, the modified version of ϵ-*
BROADCAST *guarantees that at least $(1-\epsilon')n$ nodes become informed when $f < 1/24$ and Carol is reactive.*

PROOF. Again, call a slot *active* if it contains either m or noise. Using the new definition of a blocked phase defined in the proof of Lemma 4 above, note that Carol and her Byzantine nodes cannot block a phase containing at least $4Cfn^{3/2}$ active slots. We can make the same argument as in Lemma 14 by using β rather than $1/4$ as the fraction of jammed slots that constitute a blocked phase; however, for simplicity we stick with $1/4$ noting that this does not affect correctness. From the proof above, w.h.p., at least $(1-\delta)(1/2)2^{(3/2)i}$ slots in a phase are active. For concreteness, set $\delta = 1/2$ which implies that, w.h.p, at least $(1/4)\,2^{(3/2)i}$ slots are active. Then, solving for i in $2^{(3/2)i}/4 = 4Cfn^{3/2}$ tells

us that, w.h.p, Carol and her Byzantine nodes cannot block round $i = \frac{2}{3}\lg(16\,Cf) + \lg n$. By our new Lemma 4, and by modifying Lemmas 5 and 6, at least $(1-\epsilon')n$ correct nodes will become informed in this round.

As shown in Lemma 14, we must ensure that Alice and the correct nodes do not exceed their respective budgets. When executing ϵ-BROADCAST, there exists some constant $d' > 0$ such that the cost to each node in round i is at most $d'\,2^{i/2}$. The cost to a correct node u is at most $d'2^{i/2} + (\frac{3}{4n} + p_u)\,2^{(3/2)i}$ where $p_u = \frac{16\,e^{3/(2\epsilon')}}{\epsilon'(1-\delta')2^i}$ and we can set $\delta' = 1/2$. Substituting for i, the cost to u for this round is at most $\mathcal{C}_u = (d'(16Cf)^{1/3} + 12\,C\,f + d''\,(C\,f)^{1/3})n^{1/2}$ where $d'' > 0$ is some constant depending only on ϵ. Because rounds double in size, the total cost to u up to and including this round is at most $2\mathcal{C}_u$. Solving for C in $C\,n^{1/2} \geq 2\mathcal{C}_u$ yields $C \geq (\frac{2d'(16f)^{1/3} + 2d''f^{1/3}}{1 - 24\,f})^{3/2}$. Therefore, for $f < 1/24$ and sufficiently large C, the correct nodes do not exceed their budget. □

We note that $f < 1/24$ is an artifact of the constants used to define a blocked phase and to provide the w.h.p. guarantees; it seems likely that this can be improved. However, the crucial point is that our modified ϵ-BROADCAST is resource competitive against a reactive Carol who controls $\Theta(n)$ Byzantine nodes, and correct nodes can bear the costs for tolerating such a reactive adversary; we do not rely on an external and free source of noise.

4.2 System-Size Parameters

As stated, the sending and listening probabilities in our protocol require knowledge of $\ln n$ and $1/n$. However, the guarantees provided by ϵ-BROADCAST still hold if each node has a constant-factor approximation to these values. Such approximations can be used instead of the true values while incurring only a constant-factor increase in cost. There are well-known "folklore" algorithms for efficiently obtaining such approximations in a distributed setting and we may hope that these are executed prior to a jamming attack.

If such approximations are not possible, our protocol still functions if all nodes share the same polynomial overestimate of n; that is, $\nu_u = n^{c'}$ for any constant $c' \geq 1$. Each node obtains the constant-factor approximation $\ell_u = \lceil c\ln n \rceil$ to use in our protocol. In the propagation phase of a fixed round i, each step (see Figure 2) is executed g times with informed nodes sending with probability $\frac{1}{2^i\,2^g}$ where $g = 1, ..., \ell_u$. At some point, $g = \ln n$ and, therefore, each informed node will complete that step of the phase with the correct sending probability to within a factor of 2. The same technique can be used in the request phase. In this case, the cost of executing ϵ-BROADCAST increases by a logarithmic factor and, consequently, the guarantees hold so long as there exists a large, but sublinear, $O(\frac{n}{\ln n})$ number of Byzantine nodes.

5. CONCLUSION AND FUTURE WORK

As the size of WSN devices decrease, communication protocols must satisfy the strict energy constraints that are unavoidable at this scale while remaining robust to malicious attacks. Our results address this challenge by demonstrating the feasibility of a critical communication primitive in the face of a powerful adversary who controls $\Theta(n)$ devices in a dense WSN. Moreover, the correct devices enjoy a significant advantage in terms of energy expenditure. A critical open question is whether these resource-competitive results have an analogue in multi-hop WSNs. It would also be of interest to examine other fundamental distributed communication problems, such as consensus or leader election, from a resource-competitive perspective.

Acknowledgements: We thank Jared Saia and Valerie King for their invaluable comments and suggestions.

6. REFERENCES

[1] D. Alistarh, S. Gilbert, R. Guerraoui, Z. Milosevic, and C. Newport. Securing Your Every Bit: Reliable Broadcast in Byzantine Wireless Networks. In *Proceedings of the Symposium on Parallelism in Algorithms and Architectures (SPAA)*, pages 50–59, 2010.

[2] D. K. Arvind, K. Elgaid, T. Krauss, A. Paterson, R. Stewart, and I. Thayne. Towards an Integrated Design Approach to Specknets. In *Proceedings of the IEEE International Conference on Communications (ICC)*, pages 3319–3324, 2007.

[3] F. Ashraf, Y.-C. Hu, and R. Kravets. Demo: Bankrupting the Jammer. In *Proceedings of the 9th International Conference on Mobile Systems, Applications, and Services (MobiSys)*, 2011.

[4] B. Awerbuch, A. Richa, and C. Scheideler. A Jamming-Resistant MAC Protocol for Single-Hop Wireless Networks. In *Proceedings of the 27th ACM Symposium on Principles of distributed computing (PODC)*, pages 45–54, 2008.

[5] V. Bhandhari, J. Katz, C.-Y. Koo, and N. Vaidya. Reliable Broadcast in Radio Networks: The Bounded Collision Case. In *Proceedings of the ACM Symposium on Principles of Distributed Computing (PODC)*, pages 258 – 264, 2006.

[6] S. Capkun, M. Cagalj, R. Rengaswamy, I. Tsigkogiannis, J.-P. Hubaux, and M. Srivastava. Paxos Made Simple. *ACM SIGACT News, Distributed Computing Column*, 32(4):51–58, 2001.

[7] S. Capkun, M. Cagalj, R. Rengaswamy, I. Tsigkogiannis, J.-P. Hubaux, and M. Srivastava. Integrity Codes: Message Integrity Protection and Authentication over Insecure Channels. *IEEE Transactions On Dependable and Secure Computing*, 5:208–223, 2008.

[8] S. Chalasani and J. M. Conrad. A Survey of Energy Harvesting Sources for Embedded Systems.

[9] H. Chan, A. Perrig, and D. Song. *Key Distribution Techniques for Sensor Networks*, pages 277–303. Kluwer Academic Publishers, 2004.

[10] Y. Chen and J. L. Welch. Location-Based Broadcasting for Dense Mobile Ad Hoc Networks. In *Proceedings of the 8th ACM International Symposium on Modeling, Analysis and Simulation of Wireless and Mobile Systems (MSWiM)*, pages 63–70, 2005.

[11] I. Crossbow Technology. http://www.xbow.com/.

[12] S. Dolev, S. Gilbert, R. Guerraoui, and C. Newport. Gossiping in a Multi-Channel Radio Network: An Oblivious Approach to Coping with Malicious Interference. In *Proceedings of the International Symposium on Distributed Computing (DISC)*, pages 208–222, 2007.

[13] S. Dolev, S. Gilbert, R. Guerraoui, and C. Newport. Secure Communication Over Radio Channels. In *Proceedings of the Symposium on Principles of Distributed Computing (PODC)*, pages 105–114, 2008.

[14] D. Dubhashi and A. Panconesi. *Concentration of Measure for the Analysis of Randomized Algorithms*. Cambridge University Press, 1st edition, 2009.

[15] C. P. from Texas Instruments. CC2420 Brochure. http://docweb.khk.be/khk/remote/technologie/PICDEM_Z/chipcon/CC2420_Brochure.pdf.

[16] V. Gau, C.-W. Huang, and J.-N. Hwang. Reliable Multimedia Broadcasting Over Dense Wireless Ad-Hoc Networks . *Journal of Communications*, 4(9):614–627, 2009.

[17] C. Georgiou, S. Gilbert, R. Guerraoui, and D. R. Kowalski. On the Complexity of Asynchronous Gossip. In *Proceedings of the 27th ACM Symposium on Principles of Distributed Computing*, pages 135–144, 2008.

[18] S. Gilbert, R. Guerraoui, D. Kowalski, and C. Newport. Interference-Resilient Information Exchange. In *INFOCOM*, pages 2249–2257, 2009.

[19] S. Gilbert, R. Guerraoui, and C. C. Newport. Of Malicious Motes and Suspicious Sensors: On the Efficiency of Malicious Interference in Wireless Networks. In *International Conference On Principles Of Distributed Systems (OPODIS)*, pages 215–229, 2006.

[20] S. Gilbert, V. King, J. Saia, and M. Young. Resource-Competitive Analysis: A New Perspective on Attack-Resistant Distributed Computing. *Submitted manuscript*, 2012.

[21] K. C. Hillel and H. Shachnai. Partial Information Spreading with Application to Distributed Maximum Coverage. In *Proceedings of the 29th Symposium on Principles of Distributed Computing*, pages 161–170, 2010.

[22] V. King, J. Saia, and M. Young. Conflict on a Communication Channel. In *Proceedings of the 30th Symposium on Principles of Distributed Computing (PODC)*, pages 277–286, 2011.

[23] V. King, J. Saia, and M. Young. Resource-Competitive Communication. http://www.maxwellyoung.net/king_saia_young_2012.pdf, 2012.

[24] D. Networks. http://www.dustnetworks.com/.

[25] A. Pelc and D. Peleg. Feasibility and Complexity of Broadcasting with Random Transmission Failures. In *Proceedings of the ACM Symposium on Principles of Distributed Computing (PODC)*, pages 334–341, 2005.

[26] I. Ramachandran and S. Roy. Clear Channel Assessment in Energy-Constrained Wideband Wireless Networks. *IEEE Wireless Communications*, 14(3):70–78, 2007.

[27] A. Richa, C. Scheideler, S. Schmid, and J. Zhang. A Jamming-Resistant MAC Protocol for Multi-Hop Wireless Networks. In *Proceedings of the International Symposium on Distributed Computing (DISC)*, pages 179–193, 2010.

[28] A. Richa, C. Scheideler, S. Schmid, and J. Zhang. Competitive and Fair Medium Access Despite Reactive Jamming. In *Proceedings of the 31st International Conference on Distributed Computing Systems (ICDCS)*, pages 507–516, 2011.

[29] SPECKNET. http://www.specknet.org/.

[30] B. Warneke, M. Last, B. Liebowitz, and K. S. J. Pister. Smart Dust: Communicating with a Cubic-Millimeter Computer. *Computer*, 34(1):44–51, 2001.

[31] M. Young and R. Boutaba. Overcoming Adversaries in Sensor Networks: A Survey of Theoretical Models and Algorithmic Approaches for Tolerating Malicious Interference. *IEEE Communications Surveys & Tutorials*, 13(4):617–641, 2011.

[32] J. Zhao and R. Govindan. Understanding Packet Delivery Performance in Dense Wireless Sensor Networks. In *Proceedings of the 1st International Conference on Embedded Networked Sensor Systems*, pages 1–13, 2003.

Distributed Public Key Schemes Secure against Continual Leakage

[Extended Abstract]

Adi Akavia
Tel-Aviv Academic College
akavia@mta.ac.il

Shafi Goldwasser
Weizmann Institute and MIT
shafi@theory.csail.mit.edu*

Carmit Hazay
Aarhus University
carmit@cs.au.dk†

ABSTRACT

In this work we study *distributed* public key schemes secure against continual memory leakage. The secret key will be shared among two computing devices communicating over a public channel, and the decryption operation will be computed by a simple 2-party protocol between the devices. Similarly, the secret key shares will be periodically refreshed by a simple 2-party protocol executed in discrete time periods throughout the lifetime of the system. The leakage adversary can choose pairs, one per device, of polynomial time computable length shrinking (or entropy shrinking) functions, and receive the value of the respective function on the internal state of the respective device (namely, on its secret share, internal randomness, and results of intermediate computations).

We present distributed public key encryption (DPKE) and distributed identity based encryption (DIBE) schemes that are secure against continual memory leakage, under the Bilinear Decisional Diffie-Hellman and 2-linear assumptions. Our schemes have the following properties:

1. Our DPKE and DIBE schemes tolerate leakage at all times, including during refresh. During refresh the tolerated leakage is a $(1/2 - o(1), 1)$-fraction of the secret memory of P_1, P_2 respectively; and at all other times (post key generation) the tolerated leakage is a $((1 - o(1)), 1)$-fraction of the secret memory of P_1, P_2 respectively.

2. Our DIBE scheme tolerates leakage from both the *master secret key* and the identity based secret keys.

3. Our DPKE scheme is CCA2-secure against continual memory leakage.

4. Our DPKE scheme also implies a secure storage system on leaky devices, where a value s can be secretely stored on devices that continually leak information about their internal state to an external attacker. The devices go through a periodic refresh protocol.

These properties improve on bounds and properties of known constructions designed to be secure against continual memory leakage in the single processor model.

Categories and Subject Descriptors

F.m [**Theory of Computation**]: Miscellaneous

Keywords

Distributed Public Key Encryption, CCA2-Security, IBE, Continual Leakage

1. INTRODUCTION

The absolute privacy of secret keys is the basic underlying assumption made in the security proof methodology of modern cryptography. Yet, as demonstrated by a large volume of works on side channel attacks [27, 7, 3, 28, 35, 21, 24, 37], when implementing cryptographic protocols in real world hardware, some information on the secret key may leak to the adversary. This turns out to completely compromise the security of well known cryptographic protocols, including for example the RSA cryptosystem and the AES [24]. To combat such threats, much recent work [36, 9, 12, 19, 26, 31, 20, 23, 1, 2, 32, 16, 34, 33, 13, 11, 15] has been done on *leakage resilient cryptography*, that is, designing cryptographic protocols that remain secure even when some information on the secret key is leaked to the adversary.

The model of leakage resilience most relevant to our work is the *Continual memory leakage* [11, 15]. In this model the memory of the computing device is viewed as consisting of two types of memory: (i) *Public memory* that stores the public key, the public randomness used by the system, and the inputs and outputs of the computation; and (ii) *Secret memory* that stores the secret key, the secret randomness used by the system, and the intermediate steps in the computations. An adversary attacking the system can see the contents of the public memory in its entirety, and on top of that the adversary is allowed to obtain a limited amount of information about the secret memory as defined next. Specifically, time is viewed as partitioned into discrete time periods, where

*ISF 700/08, BSF 2008362, DARPA Contract Number: FA8750-11-2-0225 and NSF Contract CCF-1018064

†Supported in part by The Danish National Research Foundation and The National Science Foundation of China (grant 61061130540) for the Sino-Danish Center for the Theory of Interactive Computation; The CFEM research center (supported by the Danish Strategic Research Council).

during each time period the adversary can choose an arbitrary polynomial-time computable leakage function, and obtain as a result the leakage function applied to the secret memory of the device. The only restriction on the leakage function is that it is *length shrinking* [1], namely, its output length is at most a pre-specified fraction of the number of bits of the secret memory.[1] At the end of each time-period, the secret key is *refreshed*; namely, a randomized procedure is executed that takes as input a secret key sk corresponding to a public key pk, and outputs a uniformly random secret key sk' for the same public key. We point out that leakage could happen during key refresh, can depend on the randomness used for the refreshing procedure (among other things). In summary, in this model the total leakage is *unbounded*, but leakage is bounded *within* each time period.

1.1 Our Work

In this work we study *distributed* encryption schemes resilient against continual memory leakage:[2] We propose that the secret key will be shared among two computing devices communicating over public channels, and the decryption and key refresh operations will be computed by simple 2-party protocols between the devices. The leakage adversary can now choose pairs, one per device, of polynomial time length shrinking functions, and receive the value of the respective function on the secret memory of the respective device. The secret memory contains: the secret share of the secret key as well as the device's internal randomness and results of intermediate computations. (See a detailed description of our model in Section 3.)

The advantage that this model offers is that the leakage functions chosen by the adversary are limited now to only apply to the shares of the secret memory rather than the entire secret memory at once. We remark that the choice of the leakage function can be *adaptive* based on all public information up to and including the current time period and all leakage bits from both devices obtained in *earlier* time periods, but is chosen independently of the bits leaked from the "other" device during the current time period. We believe that the limitation this model sets on leakage from the entire secret memory at once is both useful and realistic. Examples in which the distributed leakage setting is especially suitable are:

- **Symmetric Encryption:** Two processors would like to set up a symmetric encryption scheme in presence of leakage attacks. The classical solution calls for agreeing in person on a secret key based on which future decryption (and encryption) can be computed. Both processors store the common secret key in their local memory, and as such an adversary can receive leakage computed on the entire stored secret key. If instead the processors agree in person on a common secret key but each stores only a share of it, they could still decrypt and refresh the secret key via an interactive protocol, but the leakage will be restricted to be computed on

each share separately. We remark that splitting decryption keys and doing distributed decryption is *not* a new idea but was extensively pursued in the proactive world. But the motivation as well as the adversary model here are different. In the proactive setting the fear was that one of the processors could be fully compromised whereas here both processors are partially compromised in the sense that their secrets leak.

- **Auxiliary Device:** To battle leakage attacks in a public key encryption scheme, do not store the secret memory on the device in its entirety but instead add an auxiliary simpler computing gadget (say, a smart card) and store shares of the secret on the main processor and the auxiliary device respectively. To decrypt, a protocol between the main processor and the auxiliary device ensues. This will be particularly attractive, if one can make the computation on the auxiliary device much simpler than the computation on the main processor, as shall indeed be the case in the schemes proposed in this paper.

- **Secure Storage on Leaky Hardware:** Say one is merely interested in long term secret storage of data s on hardware that leaks. This problem can be solved by a distributed encryption scheme resilient to leakage as follows. Store $Enc_{pk}(s)$ on one leaky hardware device and sk on another leaky hardware device. To battle leakage the devices will periodically refresh the ciphertext (stored on the first device) and the secret key (stored on the second device) using a refresh protocol. We note that this case was addressed by an independent work of Dodis et al [17] who designed a private key encryption scheme E_{sk} and proved it is leakage resilient under the linear assumption in prime order groups. They then store $E_{sk}(s)$ on one leaky device and sk on another, and show how to refresh $E_{sk}(s)$ and sk periodically without requiring interaction between the devices.

In this work we construct a distributed public key encryption (DPKE) scheme secure against continual memory leakage, and a distributed identity based encryption (DIBE) scheme secure against continual memory leakage. The security of our schemes is under the Bilinear Decisional Diffie-Hellman (BDDH) and 2-linear (2Lin) assumptions. The schemes achieve the following properties:

Leakage Parameters: Our DPKE and DIBE schemes tolerate during key refresh periods a leakage of $((1/2 - o(1)), 1)$-fraction of the secret memory of P_1 and P_2 respectively (note that this is optimal as in these periods each device holds both the current and the next secret key share, and hence the size of the secret memory doubles); and during all other periods (post key generation) $((1 - o(1)), 1)$-fraction of the secret memory of P_1 and P_2 respectively. Assuming leakage freeness during key generation is standard. We show nevertheless that this assumption can be relaxed: Our schemes can tolerate leakage during key generation, where the leakage is up to $O(\log n)$ bits under the standard BDDH and 2Lin assumptions, and up to n^ϵ bits under the sub-exponential BDDH and standard 2Lin assumptions (for n the security parameter).

Leakage from Master Secret Key in IBE: Our DIBE

---

[1]More generally, both in [11, 15] and in our work it suffices to restrict the leakage function to be *entropy shrinking* [32], namely, requiring that the secret key has non-trivial average min-entropy conditioned on the leakage.

[2]Historical remark. An earlier version of this work (unpublished manuscript) initiated the study of distributed schemes resilient against continual memory leakage predating [29, 17].

scheme tolerates leakage from both the master secret key and the identity based secret keys.

CCA2 Security: Our DPKE scheme is CCA2-secure against continual memory leakage. Namely, it is secure even when the adversary has access to a decryption oracle (on top of access to a leakage oracle). Leakage occurs only *prior* to seeing the challenge ciphertext.

Simplicity of One of the Two Devices: In our schemes the computation performed by one of the computing devices is indeed quite simple; let's call this device P_2. All P_2 does is: (a) sample random coins $s_1, \ldots, s_\ell \in \mathbb{Z}_p$, and (b) given a list of group elements (sent from P_1), P_2 computes (and returns to P_1) the product of these elements to the power of $s_1, \ldots, s_\ell$, respectively. Thus, we may view the other device P_1 as being our main processing device (say, our computer), while P_2 can be an auxiliary device (say, a smart card) communicating with P_1.

We remarks that our DPKE scheme can also be used for securely storing data on leaky devices.

1.2 Related Works

1.2.1 Results in the Single Processor Model

There are several known constructions, which address continual memory leakage in the single processor model, of public key encryption (PKE) and identity based encryption (IBE) schemes secure against continual memory leakage. These include the PKE and IBE schemes of Brakerski et al. [11]; the PKE scheme of Lewko et al. [29] with a recent followup work by Dodis et al. [17]; and the recent IBE scheme (as well as Hierarchical IBE (HIBE) and attribute-based encryption (ABE) schemes) of Lewko et al. [30]. We also mention the work [15] that addresses identification and authenticated key agreement schemes. All these schemes consider continual memory leakage attacks, for leakage functions that are length (similarly, min-entropy) shrinking, but achieve different levels of security, leakage parameters, and efficiency.

In terms of security our DPKE scheme achieves CCA2-security, in contrast to semantic-security in [11, 29, 17]. Our DIBE achieves the same security notion as the IBE of [30].

A central ingredient in all schemes secure against continual memory leakage is designing a mechanism for periodically *refreshing* the secret key, that is, replacing the secret key by a new secret key while maintaining the same public key. The fraction of leakage bits tolerated by [11, 15, 30] differ greatly on whether or not the leakage is taking place during refreshing of the secret key. As mentioned about, during refresh our DPKE is resilient to the optimal leakage of $((1/2 - o(1)), 1)$-fraction of the secret memory of P_1 and P_2 respectively, in contrast to only $o(1)$-fraction in [11, 30], $1/258$-fraction in [29], and $1/672$-fraction in [17]. No leakage during refresh is tolerated in [15].

Another key question in the IBE case is whether leakage is allowed from the master secret key as well as the secret keys of different identities. As mentioned above, our DIBE tolerates optimal leakage of $((1 - o(1)), 1)$-fraction of the bits of the master secret key shares msk_1, msk_2 at all times other than during refresh, and optimal leakage of $((1/2 - o(1)), 1)$-fraction during refresh, in contrast to allowing no leakage from the master secret key in [11], and restricting the leakage during the refresh period to $o(1)$-fraction in [30].

Finally, our DPKE scheme is more efficient than [11, 29,

30] when considering the parameters necessary to achieve leakage fraction of $(1 - o(1))$ in [11, 29, 30]. In particular, our scheme encrypts group elements rather than single bits, encryption requires a single pairing operation (which can be provided as part of the public key) and two exponentiations (over a prime order group), and the size of our ciphertext is two group elements.[3]

1.2.2 Leakage Resilience in Distributed Setting

In our setting the two processors are cooperating rather than adversarial and are both being leaked on by an adversary. The shares of the secret key are held by two parties as means to fight the leakage adversary rather than being the initial inputs of two processors.

In several recent papers, leakage resilience in a distributed setting was considered where parties may have initial private inputs, and some of which may be faulty. This is the case in [10] where n processors want to toss a common coin in the presence of both full corruption of processors and leakage on the private state of non-corrupted processors. The works of [22, 4] consider two-party protocols with leakage for the oblivious-transfer, commitment, and zero-knowledge functionalities; identification protocols with leakage [2, 14, 15] were also considered.

1.3 Paper Organization

The rest of the paper is organized as follows. Preliminary definitions and facts appear in Section 2. We formally define our model in Section 3; state our main results and give an overview of our constructions and proof techniques in Section 4; present the construction of our DPKE semantically secure against continual memory leakage in Section 5; and give an overview of its security proof in Section 6.

2. PRELIMINARIES

We briefly review some standard definitions and facts.

A function $p(n)$ is polynomial if $\exists c > 0$ s.t. $\forall n, \, p(n) \leq n^c$. A function $\mu(n)$ is negligible if for every polynomial $p(\cdot)$, $\exists N$ s.t. $\forall n > N, \, \mu(n) < \frac{1}{p(n)}$. We denote the security parameter by n, and adopt the convention whereby a machine is said to run in polynomial-time if its number of steps is polynomial in its *security parameter* alone. We use the shorthand PPT to denote probabilistic polynomial-time. Another shorthand notation we use is $[\ell] = \{1, 2, \ldots, \ell\}$ (for natural numbers ℓ).

Let $X = \{X_n(a)\}_{n \in \mathbb{N}, a \in \{0,1\}^*}$ and $Y = \{Y_n(a)\}_{n \in \mathbb{N}, a \in \{0,1\}^*}$ be distribution ensembles. We say that X and Y are computationally indistinguishable, denoted $X \approx_c Y$, if for every family $\{C_n\}_{n \in \mathbb{N}}$ of polynomial-size circuites, there exists a negligible function $\mu(\cdot)$ such that for all $a \in \{0,1\}^*$, $|\Pr[C_n(X_n(a)) = 1] - \Pr[C_n(Y_n(a)) = 1]| < \mu(n)$.

Let $X = X_n$ and $Y = Y_n$ be random variables accepting values taken from a finite domain D. The statistical distance between X and Y is $SD(X, Y) = \frac{1}{2} \sum_{v \in D} |\Pr[X =$

---

[3]For comparison, the scheme of [11] encrypts bit-by-bit, encryption requires $\omega(n)$ exponentiations, and the ciphertext size is $\omega(n)$ group elements; the scheme of [29] encrypts bit-by-bit, the number of exponentiations for encryption (as well as the number of group elements in the ciphertexts) is constant, but these exponentiations are over composite order groups of the order of a product of four primes; and the scheme of [30] encrypts group elements, but requires $\omega(1)$ exponentiations for encryption, and the ciphertexts size is $\omega(1)$ group elements.

$v] - \Pr[Y = v]|$. We say that X and Y are ϵ-close if their statistical distance is at most $SD(X, Y) \leq \epsilon(n)$. We say that X and Y are statistically close, denoted $X \approx_s Y$, if $\epsilon(n)$ is negligible.

The min-entropy of X is $H_\infty(X) = \min_{v \in D}(-\log \Pr[X = v])$. The average min-entropy [18] defined by: $\tilde{H}_\infty(X|Y) = -\log\left(\mathbb{E}_{v \to Y}\left[2^{-H_\infty(X|Y=v)}\right]\right)$. captures the remaining uncertainty of the random variable X conditioned on the value of the random variable Y.

The leftover hash lemma says that if X is a random variable with min-entropy at least $H_\infty(X) \geq k$, and $H = \{h : D \to R\}$ is a family of pairwise independent functions (i.e., for all $x \neq y \in D$ and $a, b \in R$, $\Pr_{h \in H}[h(x) = a \ \& \ h(y) = b] = 1/|R|^2$), s.t. $\log|R| \leq k - 2\log(1/\epsilon)$, then $SD((h, h(x)), (h', r)) \leq \epsilon$ for h, x chosen independently at random from H and X respectively; and (h', r) uniformly random in $H \times R$.

2.1 Hardness Assumptions

We define bilinear mappings and the Bilinear Decisional Diffie-Hellman (BDDH) and k-Linear (kLin) assumptions.

An (admissible) bilinear map is a function $e : \mathbb{G} \times \mathbb{G} \to \mathbb{G}_T$ between two multiplicative prime order cyclic groups $\mathbb{G}, \mathbb{G}_T$ satisfying the following: (1) Bi-linearity: $\forall u, v \in \mathbb{G}$, $\forall a, b \in \mathbb{Z}_p$, $e(u^a, v^b) = e(u, v)^{ab}$. (2) Non-degeneracy: For g a generator of $\mathbb{G}$, $e(g, g)$ generates $\mathbb{G}_T$. (3) e is efficiently computable.

A parameters generating algorithm for a bilinear map e is a PPT algorithm $(p, g, e) \leftarrow \mathcal{G}(1^n)$ that, given a security parameter n (in unary), outputs an n-bits prime number p, a generator g of an order p group $\mathbb{G}$, and an admissible bilinear map $e : \mathbb{G} \times \mathbb{G} \to \mathbb{G}_T$ (for $\mathbb{G}_T$ the order p group generated by $e(g, g)$).

The Bilinear Decisional Diffie-Hellman (BDDH) assumption for $\mathcal{G}$ says that for $(p, g, e) \leftarrow \mathcal{G}(1^n)$ and a, b, c, r independent and uniformly random elements in $\mathbb{Z}_p$,

$$(p, g, e, g^a, g^b, g^c, e(g, g)^{abc}) \approx_c (p, g, e, g^a, g^b, g^c, e(g, g)^r).$$

We define the kLin and matrix kLin assumptions for $k \geq 1$ a constant. The k-Linear (kLin) assumption for $\mathcal{G}$ says that for $(p, g, e) \leftarrow \mathcal{G}(1^n)$, $g_1, \ldots, g_k \leftarrow \mathbb{G}$ and $r_0, r_1, \ldots, r_k$ independent and uniformly random elements in $\mathbb{Z}_p$,

$$(p, g, g_0, g_1, \ldots, g_k, g_1^{r_1}, \ldots, g_k^{r_k}, g_0^{\sum_{i=1}^{k} r_i})$$
$$\approx_c (p, g, g_0, g_1, \ldots, g_k, g_1^{r_1}, \ldots, g_k^{r_k}, g_0^{r_0}).$$

The matrix kLin assumption says that for every integers a and b, and every $k \leq i < j \leq \min\{a, b\}$ the ensembles $\{(p, g, g^R)\}_{R \in Rk_i(\mathbb{Z}_p^{a \times b}), n \in \mathbb{N}}$ and $\{(p, g, g^R)\}_{R \in Rk_j(\mathbb{Z}_p^{a \times b}), n \in \mathbb{N}}$ are computationally indistinguishable, where $Rk_i(\mathbb{Z}_p^{a \times b})$ is the set of all rank i matrices. The kLin assumption implies the matrix kLin assumption (see [32] Appendix A).

3. OUR MODEL

Our model extends the continual memory leakage model of [11, 15] to distributed settings. We focus here on distributed public key encryption (DPKE) schemes secure against continual memory leakage; our definitions for distributed identity based encryption (DIBE) are analogous.

3.1 Distributed Public Key Encryption

We propose that the secret key will be *shared* between two computing devices communicating over a *public chan-

nel*, and decryption will be executed by a simple 2-party protocol. Likewise, refreshing of the secret key shares will be executed by a simple 2-party protocol.

To be concrete, let us denote the two computing devices by P_1 and P_2, and their shares of the secret key by sk_1 and sk_2 respectively. Time is viewed as partitioned into discrete time periods; and *refreshing* of the secret key shares is executed at the end of each time-period.[4] Namely, at the end of each time-period a 2-party protocol is executed that takes as input secret key shares (sk_1, sk_2) corresponding to a public key pk, and outputs new secret key shares (sk_1', sk_2') for the same public key, where the new secret key shares are drawn from the same distribution as the old ones. By the termination of the refresh protocol the old secret key share sk_i has been erased from the secret memory of P_i, and the new secret key share sk_i' has been put in its place. We emphasize that the public key remains unchanged throughout the life time of the system. The definition below summarizes the above and sets some notations:

DEFINITION 3.1 (**DPKE**). *Distributed public key encryption (DPKE) schemes are defined by a tuple of algorithms and protocols $\Pi = (\mathsf{Gen}, \mathsf{Enc}, \mathsf{Dec}, \mathsf{Ref})$ where:*

- *Key generation $(pk, sk_1, sk_2) \leftarrow \mathsf{Gen}(1^n)$ is a randomized algorithm that given a security parameter n outputs the public key pk and the secret key shares sk_1, sk_2 given to devices P_1 and P_2 respectively.[5]*

- *Encryption $c \leftarrow \mathsf{Enc}_{pk}(m)$ is a randomized algorithm that given the public key pk and a message m outputs a ciphertext c. We denote $c \leftarrow \mathsf{Enc}_{pk}(m; r)$ to emphasize the randomness r used by the encryption algorithm.*

- *Decryption $m \leftarrow \mathsf{Dec}_{pk, sk_1, sk_2}(c)$ is a randomized 2-party protocol executed by P_1 and P_2. The input of P_i $(i = 1, 2)$ is (pk, sk_i, c) for pk the public key, sk_i the secret key share of P_i, and c a ciphertext. The output (outputted by either P_1 or P_2 or both) is a message m'. We require that for all m, $c \leftarrow \mathsf{Enc}_{pk}(m)$ and $m' \leftarrow \mathsf{Dec}_{pk, sk_1, sk_2}(c)$, it holds that $m' = m$.*

- *Refreshing $(sk_1', sk_2') \leftarrow \mathsf{Ref}_{pk}(sk_1, sk_2)$ is a randomized 2-party protocol executed by P_1 and P_2. The input of P_i $(i = 1, 2)$ is (pk, sk_i) for pk the public key and sk_i the current secret key share of P_i. The output is new secret key shares sk_1', sk_2' given to P_1, P_2 respectively (the old shares sk_1, sk_2 are erased). We require that for all $(pk, sk_1^0, sk_2^0) \leftarrow \mathsf{Gen}(1^n)$, $t^* \in \mathbb{N}$, and $(sk_1^t, sk_2^t) \leftarrow \mathsf{Ref}_{pk}(sk_1^{t-1}, sk_2^{t-1})$ for $t \in [t^*]$, it holds that*

$$SD((sk_1^0, sk_2^0), (sk_1^t, sk_2^t)) = 0$$

(where the probability is taken over the random coins of Gen and Ref).

We point out that our modeling assumes that the devices trust each other to follow the protocols specifications for refreshing and decryption *honestly*.

---

[4]The partition to time-periods may in fact be defined by executions of the refresh protocol, where each execution marks the end of a time-period.

[5]Without loss of generality Gen is executed by a trusted third party; otherwise, replace the trusted party by a generic 2-party protocol revealing nothing except its output; where the latter holds even if the adversary obtains during key generation the number of leakage bits considered in this work.

3.2 Continual Memory Leakage from DPKE

The memory of each computing device P_i ($i = 1, 2$) in a DPKE scheme $\Pi = (\mathsf{Gen}, \mathsf{Enc}, \mathsf{Dec}, \mathsf{Ref})$ is viewed as composed of two types of memory: (i) *Public memory* that stores the public key, the public randomness used by the system, and the public inputs and outputs of the computations executed by device P_i; and (ii) *Secret memory* that stores the share sk_i of the secret key, as well as the secret randomness of P_i, and the intermediate steps in the computations executed by P_i.

An adversary attacking the scheme can see all the following: (1) The transcript of communication to and from the devices; (2) The contents of the public memory of both devices in its entirety; and (3) A limited amount of information about the secret memory of both devices as defined next (aka, "leakage").

Essentially, during each time-period the adversary can choose a pair of polynomial time length shrinking (or entropy shrinking) functions, one per device, and receive the value of the respective function on the secret memory of the respective device. Information leakage can happen at all times, including during key refresh. The choice of the leakage function can be *adaptive* based on all public information (including the communication transcript) up to and including the current time period, and all leakage bits obtained in earlier time periods. The precise details follow.

Leakage functions. We distinguish three phases throughout the life time of the system: key generation phase, refresh phase, all other times. The content of the secret memory – and hence the input to the leakage function – varies between those phases. To address these varying inputs the adversary actually chooses two (polynomial time and length shrinking) functions per device P_i ($i = 1, 2$) at each time period t, denoted by $h_i^t, h_i^{t,\mathsf{Ref}}$, where: h_i^t is a function to be applied on the secret memory of P_i at time period t other than during refresh, and $h_i^{t,\mathsf{Ref}}$ is a function to be applied on the secret memory of P_i during refresh of time period t. In addition, the adversary chooses a (polynomial time and length shrinking) function h^{Gen} for the key generation phase.

Leakage functions can be chosen *adaptively* based on leakage and public information as said above. We point out that dependence on leakage bits in this adaptive choice is on leakage obtained in earlier time periods, not in the current one. Without loss of generality this is modeled by requiring a simultaneous choice of the leakage functions for the same time period t, namely, $(h_1^t, h_1^{t,\mathsf{Ref}}, h_2^t, h_2^{t,\mathsf{Ref}})$.

Inputs to leakage functions. For each of the aforementioned phases we specify the content of the secret memory, or equivalently, the input to the leakage function. Without loss of generality we define the latter to be solely the essential parts of the secret memory, namely, parts from which the entire secret memory is efficiently computable (given the public memory). The input to h^{Gen} is the secret randomness r^{Gen} held in memory during the key generation algorithm. The input to $h_i^{t,\mathsf{Ref}}$ and h_i^t is $(sk_i^t, r_i^{t,\mathsf{Ref}})$ and (sk_i^t, r_i^t) respectively, where: sk_i^t is the secret key share of P_i at time t; $r_i^{t,\mathsf{Ref}}$ is the secret randomness held in memory of P_i during the execution of the refresh protocol at time t; and r_i^t is the secret randomness held in memory of P_i at time t other than during the execution of the refresh protocol.

Looking ahead, to simplify the description of the security game in our security definitions we include in the input

to the leakage function also the *public information* held in memory during the current time period, denoted pub^t. This includes the communication transcript to and from both devices and the content of their public memory. This captures the adversary that first sees the public information and only then chooses its leakage functions (by encoding both the choice of leakage functions and their functionalities into the submitted functions), while simplifying the security game by allowing the leakage functions to be chosen once at the beginning of each time period.

Outputs of leakage functions. The length shrinking restriction on the leakage functions says that the sum of outputs length of the functions leaking while the share sk_i^t is in memory — that is, the functions h_i^t and $h_i^{(t-1),\mathsf{Ref}}$ — is upper bounded by a pre-specified bound b_i ($i = 1, 2$). Similarly, the output length of h^{Gen} is upper bounded by a pre-specified bound b_0. Namely, the output length is upper bounded by $\left| h^{\mathsf{Gen}}(r^{\mathsf{Gen}}) \right| \leq b_0$ and $\left| h_i^t(sk_i^t, r_i^t, pub^t) \right| + \left| h_i^{(t-1),\mathsf{Ref}}(sk_i^{(t-1)}, r_i^{(t-1),\mathsf{Ref}}, pub^{(t-1)}) \right| \leq b_i$ for $i = 1, 2$ (for $|x|$ denoting the binary representation length of x).

Leakage rate is the ratio between the number of bits being leaked (per device) per time period and the size of the secret memory of the device at that time. Namely, the leakage rate is specified by five parameters $(\rho^{\mathsf{Gen}}, \rho_1^{\mathsf{Ref}}, \rho_2^{\mathsf{Ref}}, \rho_1, \rho_2)$ for $\rho^{\mathsf{Gen}} = b_0 / \left| r^{\mathsf{Gen}} \right|$ the leakage rate during key generation; and $\rho_i^{\mathsf{Ref}} = b_i / (|sk_i| + |r_i^{\mathsf{Ref}}|)$ and $\rho_i = b_i / (|sk_i| + |r_i|)$ the rates of leakage from P_i ($i = 1, 2$) during key refresh, and during all other (post key generation) times, respectively.

3.3 Security Definitions

Our security definitions are the natural augmentation of the standard definitions by allowing the adversary to obtain continual memory leakage for as long as it chooses:

A DPKE scheme is *semantically secure against* (b_0, b_1, b_2)-*continual memory leakage* (*CPA-secure against* (b_0, b_1, b_2)-*CML*, in short) if every PPT adversary has at most a negligible advantage in winning the variant of the semantic security game, where before seeing the challenge ciphertext the adversary can receive leakage on the secret memory of both devices (as described above) for as many time periods as the adversary chooses. Here b_0, b_1, b_2 are the upper bounds for the length shrinking property as discussed above.

To model leakage on the memory state during decryption we include in the semantic security game executions of the decryption protocol. We remark that in the single processor model [11, 15] such executions are not included, because there the leakage functions is given the entire secret key and thus can simulate such executions. In contrast, in our distributed setting, the leakage function is given only one of the two secret key shares as its input and thus it cannot simulate such executions. The input ciphertexts for these executions are drawn from a (polynomial-time sampleable) distribution $\mathcal{C}$. This distribution should be thought of as modeling executions of the decryption protocol run in the background, say, by other users of the scheme (note, the adversary has no control on the choice of decryption input in a semantic security game). To simplify the presentation we assume that a single execution of the decryption protocol occurs at each time period (as achieved, say, by frequent refreshing). Extensions allowing multiple executions of the decryption protocol at each time period are simple; details omitted from this extended abstract.

DEFINITION 3.2. *A DPKE scheme* $\Pi = (\mathsf{Gen}, \mathsf{Enc}, \mathsf{Dec}, \mathsf{Ref})$ *is semantically secure against* (b_0, b_1, b_2)-*continual memory leakage (CPA-secure against* (b_0, b_1, b_2)-*CML) if for every PPT algorithm* $\mathcal{C} = \mathcal{C}(n, pk, t)$ *for sampling ciphertexts, every PPT adversary has at most a negligible advantage over 1/2 in wining the following game:*

1. **Key Generation Phase.** *The challenger generates* $(pk, sk_1^0, sk_2^0) \leftarrow \mathsf{Gen}(1^n)$, *and sends the adversary* pk.

2. **Leakage on Key Generation.** *The adversary chooses a polynomial-time computable function* h^{Gen}.

    Denote the requested leakage by $\ell^{\mathsf{Gen}} = h^{\mathsf{Gen}}(r^{\mathsf{Gen}})$ *for* r^{Gen} *the secret randomness held in memory during the execution of the key generation algorithm.*

    If $|\ell^{\mathsf{Gen}}| \leq b_0$ *then the challenger returns to the adversary* ℓ^{Gen}, *and sets* $L_i^0 \leftarrow |\ell^{\mathsf{Gen}}|$, $L_i^{0,\mathsf{Ref}} \leftarrow |\ell^{\mathsf{Gen}}|$ *(for* $i = 1, 2$) *and* $t \leftarrow 0$; *otherwise, the challenger aborts.*

3. **Leakage at Every Time Period.** *The adversary chooses a tuple* $(h_1^t, h_1^{t,\mathsf{Ref}}, h_2^t, h_2^{t,\mathsf{Ref}})$ *of polynomial-time computable functions. In response the challenger draws a random ciphertext* $c \leftarrow \mathcal{C}(n, pk, t)$, *and executes the decryption and key refresh protocols*

$$m \leftarrow \mathsf{Dec}_{pk, sk_1^t, sk_2^t}(c)$$

$$(sk_1^{t+1}, sk_2^{t+1}) \leftarrow \mathsf{Ref}_{pk}(sk_1^t, sk_2^t)$$

   Denote the requested leakage from computing device P_i *(* $i = 1, 2$*) by*

$$\ell_i^t = h_i^t(sk_i^t, r_i^t, pub^t)$$

$$\ell_i^{t,\mathsf{Ref}} = h_i^{t,\mathsf{Ref}}(sk_i^t, r_i^{t,\mathsf{Ref}}, pub^t)$$

   for sk_i^t *the secret key share of* P_i *at time* t; $(r_i^{t,\mathsf{Ref}}, r_i^t)$ *the secret randomness held in memory of* P_i *at time* t *during and not during the execution of the refresh protocol, respectively; and* $pub^t = (\mathsf{comm}^t, c, m)$ *the public information at time* t *consisting of the communication transcript* comm^t *to and from devices* P_1, P_2, *and of the input/output to the decryption protocol* c *and* m *held in their public memory.*

   If $L_i^t + |\ell_i^t| + |\ell_i^{t,\mathsf{Ref}}| \leq b_i$ *for* $i = 1, 2$, *then the challenger returns to the adversary* $(\ell_1^t, \ell_1^{t,\mathsf{Ref}}, \ell_2^t, \ell_2^{t,\mathsf{Ref}})$, *sets* $L_i^{(t+1)} \leftarrow |\ell_i^{t,\mathsf{Ref}}|$ *for* $i = 1, 2$, *and sets* $t \leftarrow t + 1$; *otherwise, the challenger aborts.*

4. **Challenge Phase.** *The adversary sends to the challenger two messages* m_0, m_1 *of equal length* $|m_0| = |m_1|$. *The challenger sends to the adversary the ciphertext* $c \leftarrow \mathsf{Enc}_{pk}(m_b)$ *for a uniformly random bit* $b \in \{0, 1\}$. *The adversary outputs* $b' \in \{0, 1\}$. *The adversary wins if* $b' = b$.

We call (b_0, b_1, b_2) *the* leakage parameter *of the game.*

Likewise, a DPKE scheme is CCA2-secure against (b_0, b_1, b_2)-continual memory leakage (CCA2-secure against (b_0, b_1, b_2)-CML, in short), if every PPT adversary has at most a negligible advantage in winning the extension of the game specified in Definition 3.2, where the adversary is given extra power in the form of access to a decryption oracle (namely, an oracle that given ciphertexts c' returns messages $m \leftarrow$ $\mathsf{Dec}(c')$); where the only restriction is that the adversary does not query the decryption oracle on the challenge ciphertext. Note that leakage occurs only *prior* to seeing the challenge ciphertext (as in the semantic-security game).

4. RESULTS & TECHNIQUES OVERVIEW

We give an overview of our constructions: Our DPKE scheme semantically secure against continual leakage (Section 4.1); our DIBE scheme semantically secure against continual leakage (Section 4.2); Our DPKE scheme CCA2-secure against continual leakage (Section 4.3). We name these schemes **DLR**, **DLR**$_{\mathrm{IBE}}$ and **DLR**$_{\mathrm{CCA2}}$, respectively (for distributed leakage resilient). The theorem below summarizes our main results.

THEOREM 4.1 (MAIN). *The following holds under BDDH and 2Lin assumptions:*

1. **DLR** *is a DPKE scheme that is CPA-secure against* (b_0, b_1, b_2)-*CML*

2. **DLR**$_{\mathrm{IBE}}$ *is a DIBE scheme that is CPA-secure against* (b_0, b_1, b_2)-*CML*

3. **DLR**$_{\mathrm{CCA2}}$ *is a DPKE scheme that is CCA2-secure against* (b_0, b_1, b_2)-*CML*

where $(b_0, b_1, b_2) = \left(\Omega(\log n), \left(1 - \frac{cn}{\lambda + cn}\right) m_1, m_2\right)$ *for* m_1, m_2 *the size of the secret key shares of* P_1, P_2 *respectively;[6]* n, λ *the security and leakage parameters of our schemes; and* $c > 0$ *a constant.*

Proof: The heart of our analysis is the proof of part 1 of the theorem; details appear in section 6. Proving parts 2 and 3 is simple given the former (cf. Sections 4.2-4.3 and the full version of this paper). ∎

The leakage rate tolerated by our schemes as derived from Theorem 4.1 is: $\rho^{\mathsf{Gen}} = o(1)$, $(\rho_1, \rho_2) = (1 - o(1), 1)$ and $(\rho_1^{\mathsf{Ref}}, \rho_2^{\mathsf{Ref}}) = (1/2 - o(1), 1/2)$. This holds because in our schemes the size of the secret memory of P_1 and P_2 (other than during refresh) is $m_1 + \log p$ and m_2 respectively; and it is $2m_1 + \log p$ and $2m_2$ respectively during refresh (when P_1, P_2 hold both the current and the next secret key shares). Our proof shows also a stronger bound on the leakage rate tolerated during refresh, showing it is $\rho_2^{\mathsf{Ref}} = 1$.

REMARK 4.1. *For our DIBE scheme* **DLR**$_{\mathrm{IBE}}$, *we note the following. First, the above leakage bounds hold both when* P_1, P_2 *are sharing the master secret key and when they are sharing an identity based secret key. Second, when generating the identity based secret key the leakage upper bound is* b_1, b_2 *bits from the secret memory of* P_1, P_2 *respectively. That is, the more restrictive leakage upper bound of* b_0 *bits applies only during generation of the* master *secret key.*

4.1 Overview of DPKE

The scheme **DLR** $= (\mathsf{Gen}, \mathsf{Enc}, \mathsf{Dec}, \mathsf{Ref})$ builds on (modifications of) the IBE scheme of Boneh-Boyen (BB) [5] and the key-dependent/leakage-resilient encryptions of Boneh-Halevy-Hamburg-Ostrovsky (BHHO) [8] / Naor-Segev (NS) [32] as described next.

---

[6] Our schemes tolerate leakage of $b_0 = n^\epsilon$ bits during key generation when assuming sub-exponential hardness of BDDH.

The *public key* of **DLR** is $pk = (p, g, e, g_1 = g^\alpha, g_2)$ for $g, e(g, g)$ generating groups $\mathbb{G}, \mathbb{G}_T$ of prime order p that are connected by a bilinear map $e: \mathbb{G} \to \mathbb{G}_T$, and for independent and uniformly random $\alpha \in \mathbb{Z}_p$ and $g_2 \in \mathbb{G}$. Note that the public key is the public parameters in BB's IBE.

The *secret key shares* are a sharing of the master secret key in BB's IBE $msk = g_2^\alpha$ using a secret sharing scheme that we construct to be refreshable, leakage resilient, and with the special property that it allows to decrypt ciphertexts of **DLR** without reconstructing its underlying secret key g_2^α. This secret sharing scheme is constructed using a secondary symmetric key encryption scheme $\Pi_{ss} = (\mathsf{Gen}_{ss}, \mathsf{Enc}_{ss}, \mathsf{Dec}_{ss})$, where the key generation algorithm Gen_{ss} chooses $sk_{ss} = (s_1, \ldots, s_\ell)$ for independent and uniformly random $s_i \in \mathbb{Z}_p$; the encryption algorithm $(a_1, \ldots, a_\ell, m \cdot \prod_{i \in [\ell]} a_i^{s_i}) \leftarrow \mathsf{Enc}_{ss}(m)$ outputs ciphertexts for independent and uniformly random $a_i \in \mathbb{G}$; and the decryption algorithm $\mathsf{Dec}_{ss}(c_1, \ldots, c_\ell, c_0)$ outputs $c_0 / \left(\prod_{i \in [\ell]} c_i^{s_i} \right)$. We use Π_{ss} to secret share g_2^α as follows. Device P_2 is given $(s_1, \ldots, s_\ell)$ the secret key of Π_{ss}, whereas P_1 is given $(a_1, \ldots, a_\ell, g_2^\alpha \cdot \prod_{i \in [\ell]} a_i^{s_i}) \leftarrow \mathsf{Enc}_{ss}(g_2^\alpha)$ a ciphertext Π_{ss} encrypting g_2^α. We note that those secret key shares are a sharing of the aforementioned master secret key $msk = g_2^\alpha$ in a leakage resilient way inspired by BHHO/NS techniques. Consequently, Π_{ss} is resilient to bounded leakage (by the leftover hash lemma); this will be crucial for our security proof for **DLR**.

Encryption is a simplified version of BB's IBE encryption. Specifically, given a message $m \in \mathbb{G}_T$, the encryption algorithm outputs a ciphertext $(g^t, m \cdot e(g_1, g_2)^t) \leftarrow \mathsf{Enc}_{pk}(m)$ for a uniformly random $t \in \mathbb{Z}_p$.

Decryption and *Refreshing* are executed via 2-party protocols. We describe the refresh protocol in details. At the outset of the refresh protocol P_1 holds a ciphertext of Π_{ss} encrypting g_2^α and P_2 holds the secret key of Π_{ss}. After each refresh stage, P_1 will hold a new random encryption of g_2^α in Π_{ss} under a new random key sk_{ss} to be held by P_2. To this end, we make use of yet another encryption scheme, denoted by $\Pi_{comm} = (\mathsf{Gen}', \mathsf{Enc}', \mathsf{Dec}')$, with useful homomorphic properties that allow us to do the following. During refresh P_1 runs Gen' and generates a secret key sk_{comm}, together with fresh new randomness a_i' (aimed to replace the a_i's), and sends ciphertexts of Π_{comm} encrypting its share and a_i''s to P_2. Upon receiving these, P_2 picks fresh new s_i''s (aimed to replace the s_i's) and sends back a ciphertext of Π_{comm} encrypting $(a_1', \ldots, a_\ell', g_2^\alpha \cdot \prod_{i \in [\ell]} a_i'^{s_i'})$. P_2 will be able to do so, although sk_{comm} is *unknown* to it, due to the homomorphic nature of Π_{comm}. Note that s_i's and a_i's are never stored unencrypted on the same device.

For our scheme to be secure we require yet one more property of Π_{comm}. Specifically, we require that ℓ independent and uniformly random plaintexts have sufficient (pseudo average min-) entropy even when conditioned on their ciphertexts in Π_{comm} together with bounded leakage from the secret key sk_{comm} and random coins used to generate these ciphertexts, as well as leakage on the plaintexts themselves. This property allows us to prove security against the adversary that chooses leakage functions based on the communication between the devices (i.e., the ciphertexts of Π_{comm}), and where the leakage is on the secret key of Π_{comm}, the random coins used for generating the ciphertexts, and on the plaintexts themselves (as all are held in the memory of

P_1). We name secret key encryption schemes Π_{comm} achieving the above two properties *homomorphic proxy secret key encryption (HPSKE)*; cf. Definition 5.1, Section 5.1.

Decryption follows in a similar manner where the parties run a protocol implementing BB's decryption algorithm.

4.2 DIBE Semantically Secure against CML

Our distribute identity based encryption semantically secure against continual leakage, named, $\mathbf{DLR}_{\text{IBE}}$, is an extension of our DPKE scheme **DLR**, where both the master secret key and the identity based secret keys are shared among two computing devices. The master secret key shares and their refreshing protocol are identical to the secret key shares and their refreshing in **DLR**. The identity based secret key shares are a sharing of the identity based secret keys in BB's IBE, while following our leakage resilient techniques for key sharing discussed above. Specifically, the BB's identity based secret key is $sk_{\mathcal{ID}} = (g^{r_1}, \ldots, g^{r_n}, M = g_2^\alpha \cdot \prod_{j \in [n]} u_{j, b_j}^{r_j})$ where $H(\mathcal{ID}) = (b_1, \ldots, b_n) \in \mathbb{Z}_p^n$ is the evaluation of an appropriate hash function H on the underlying identity $\mathcal{ID}$, and $U = (u_{i,j}) \in \mathbb{G}^{n \times 2}$ is a uniformly random matrix. Our sharing of $sk_{\mathcal{ID}}$ is with the two shares $sk_{\mathcal{ID}}^1 = (g^{r_1}, \ldots, g^{r_n}, a_1', \ldots, a_\ell', M \cdot \prod_{i \in [\ell]} a_i'^{s_i'})$ and $sk_{\mathcal{ID}}^2 = (s_1', \ldots, s_\ell')$. Refreshing these shares is a straightforward extension of the protocol for refreshing the secret key shares in **DLR**. Likewise, decryption is a straightforward extension of **DLR** decryption protocol.

4.3 DPKE CCA2-Secure against CML

Our DPKE CCA2-secure against continual memory leakage, named, $\mathbf{DLR}_{\text{CCA2}}$, is derived from our DIBE semantically secure against continual memory leakage discussed above by using a general purpose transformation from semantically secure IBE to CCA2-secure PKE. For the single processor setting where there is no leakage, such a transformation was given by Boneh et al. [6]. We use the same transformation, while extending their proof to show that CCA2-security holds even in the presence of continual leakage (as long the IBE is secure against continual leakage). Our proof (straightforwardly) extended to the distributed setting as well.

4.4 Secure Storage on Leaky Devices

Our DPKE scheme can also be used for securely storing data on continually leaky devices. We point out that storing a secret on continually leaky devices is a special case of our problem as we must implicitly maintain the secret "decryption key" of the decryption algorithm throughout its continual execution in a way that still allows to decrypt.

5. DPKE CPA-SECURE AGAINST CML

We present the details of our DPKE scheme semantically secure against continual memory leakage, named, **DLR**. For this purpose we first present the HPSKE that we use.

Throughout this section $\lambda > 0$ is a leakage parameter of the scheme; n is the security parameter; $(p, g, e) \leftarrow \mathcal{G}(1^n)$ is the output of a parameters generating algorithm (cf. Section 2) with $\mathbb{G}, \mathbb{G}_T$ denoting the order p groups generated by g and $e(g, g)$ respectively; $\mathbb{G}'$ is a group of order p (to be thought of as either $\mathbb{G}$ or $\mathbb{G}_T$); and $\ell = 7 + 3\kappa + \frac{2 \log(1/\epsilon)}{\log p}$ for $\epsilon = 2^{-n}$ and $\kappa = 1 + \frac{\lambda + 2 \log(1/\epsilon)}{\log p}$.

5.1 Building Block: HPSKE

We present the primitive we named: homomorphic proxy secret key encryption (HPSKE), and a construction for it.

DEFINITION 5.1 (HPSKE.). *A homomorphic proxy secret key encryption (HPSKE) for $\ell, \mathbb{G}'$ is a secret key encryption scheme $\Pi_{\mathsf{comm}} = (\mathsf{Gen}', \mathsf{Enc}', \mathsf{Dec}')$ with message space $\mathbb{G}'$ and ciphertexts that are tuples of elements from $\mathbb{G}'$, such that the following holds for $sk_{\mathsf{comm}} \leftarrow \mathsf{Gen}'(1^n)$:*

1. *For every two messages $m_0, m_1 \in \mathbb{G}'$ and their ciphertexts $c_i \leftarrow \mathsf{Enc}'_{sk_{\mathsf{comm}}}(m_i)$ $(i = 0, 1)$, it holds that*

$$m_0 m_1 \leftarrow \mathsf{Dec}'_{sk_{\mathsf{comm}}}(c_0 c_1)$$

   (where the product $c_0 c_1$ is computed coordinate-wise).

2. *Given ciphertexts $c_1 \leftarrow \mathsf{Enc}'_{sk_{\mathsf{comm}}}(m_1; r_1), \ldots, c_\ell \leftarrow \mathsf{Enc}'_{sk_{\mathsf{comm}}}(m_\ell; r_\ell)$ for independent and uniformly random plaintexts $m_1, \ldots, m_\ell \in \mathbb{G}'$, and given leakage $L = h(sk_{\mathsf{comm}}, m_1, \ldots, m_\ell, r_1, \ldots, r_\ell)$ for h a polynomial-time computable function of output length upper bounded by λ, there is still sufficient pseudo average min-entropy left in the plaintexts. Namely: There exists a computationally indistinguishable distribution*

$$((m_i, c_i')_{i \in [\ell]}, L') \approx_c ((m_i, c_i)_{i \in [\ell]}, L)$$

   for ciphertexts $c_i' \leftarrow \mathsf{Enc}'_{sk_{\mathsf{comm}}}(m_i; r_i')$ and leakage $L' = h(sk_{\mathsf{comm}}, m_1, \ldots, m_t, r_1', \ldots, r_t')$ such that

$$\tilde{H}_\infty(m_1, \ldots, m_t \mid c_1', \ldots, c_t', L') \geq \log p + 2\log(1/\epsilon)$$

We say that Π_{comm} is a "HPSKE for $\ell, \mathbb{G}, \mathbb{G}_T$" if it is a HPSKE for both $\ell, \mathbb{G}$ and $\ell, \mathbb{G}_T$.

REMARK 5.1. *Definition 5.1, Part 2, does not follow from existing notions of security against leakage (to the best of our knowledge). For example, the bounded leakage model [1, 32] does not allow leakage to depend on the challenge ciphertexts; and the after-the-fact leakage model [25] does not allow leakage to depend on the encryption randomness.*

LEMMA 5.2 (HPSKE EXISTS). *There exists a HPSKE scheme for $\ell, \mathbb{G}, \mathbb{G}_T$ (under 2Lin assumption).*

Proof: Fix $\mathbb{G}' \in \{\mathbb{G}, \mathbb{G}_T\}$. We show that the scheme Π_{comm} defined next is a HPSKE for $\ell, \mathbb{G}'$ (the proof is omitted from this extended abstract): The key generation algorithm $\mathsf{Gen}'(1^n)$ outputs a uniformly random secret key $sk_{\mathsf{comm}} = (\sigma_1, \ldots, \sigma_\kappa)$ in $\mathbb{Z}_p^\kappa$. The encryption algorithm $\mathsf{Enc}'_{sk_{\mathsf{comm}}}(m)$ outputs ciphertexts $(b_1, \ldots, b_\kappa, m \cdot \prod_{i \in [\kappa]} b_i^{\sigma_i})$ for independent and uniformly random $b_i \in \mathbb{G}'$. The decryption algorithm $\mathsf{Dec}'_{sk_{\mathsf{comm}}}(b_1, \ldots, b_\kappa, b_0)$ outputs $b_0 / \left(\prod_{i \in [\kappa]} b_i^{\sigma_i}\right)$. ∎

5.2 Construction of DLR

We present the scheme **DLR**. As a building block we use a HPSKE scheme $\Pi_{\mathsf{comm}} = (\mathsf{Gen}', \mathsf{Enc}', \mathsf{Dec}')$ for $\ell, \mathbb{G}, \mathbb{G}_T$ (say, as given in Section 5.1, Lemma 5.2).

CONSTRUCTION 5.3 (**DLR**). *The DPKE scheme $\mathbf{DLR} = (\mathsf{Gen}, \mathsf{Enc}, \mathsf{Dec}, \mathsf{Ref})$ is defined by the following algorithms and protocols:*

- $\mathsf{Gen}(1^n)$ *is an algorithm that, given a security parameter n, outputs the public key and secret key shares:*

$$pk = (p, g, e, e(g_1, g_2))$$
$$sk_1 = \left(a_1, \ldots, a_\ell, \Phi = g_2^\alpha \cdot \prod_{i \in [\ell]} a_i^{s_i}\right)$$
$$sk_2 = (s_1, \ldots, s_\ell)$$

  for independent and uniformly random $\alpha \in \mathbb{Z}_p$, $g_2 \in \mathbb{G}$, $s_i \in \mathbb{Z}_p$, and $a_i \in \mathbb{G}$; and for $g_1 = g^\alpha$.

- $\mathsf{Enc}_{pk}(m)$ *is an algorithm that, given a message $m \in \mathbb{G}_T$, outputs $(g^t, m \cdot e(g_1, g_2)^t)$ for a uniformly random $t \in \mathbb{Z}_p$.*

- $\mathsf{Dec}_{pk, sk_1, sk_2}(c)$ *is the following 2-party protocol executed by P_1 and P_2 on a given ciphertext $c = (A, B)$:*

  1. *P_1 samples a key $sk_{\mathsf{comm}} \leftarrow \mathsf{Gen}'(1^n)$, and sends to P_2 the ciphertexts of Π_{comm}: $\mathsf{Enc}'_{sk_{\mathsf{comm}}}(e(A, a_1))$, $\ldots, \mathsf{Enc}'_{sk_{\mathsf{comm}}}(e(A, a_\ell))$, $\mathsf{Enc}'_{sk_{\mathsf{comm}}}(e(A, \Phi))$, and $\mathsf{Enc}'_{sk_{\mathsf{comm}}}(B)$.*

  2. *Upon receiving $(d_1, \ldots, d_\ell, d_\Phi, d_B)$ from P_1, P_2 sends to P_1 the coordinate-wise product $d_B \cdot \prod_{i \in [\ell]} d_i^{s_i} / d_\Phi$.*

  3. *Upon receiving c' from P_2, P_1 outputs $\mathsf{Dec}'_{sk_{\mathsf{comm}}}(c')$.*

- $\mathsf{Ref}_{pk}(sk_1, sk_2)$ *is the following 2-party protocol executed by P_1 and P_2 on their secret key shares $sk_1 = (a_1, \ldots, a_\ell, \Phi = g_2^\alpha \prod_{i \in [\ell]} a_i^{s_i})$ and $sk_2 = (s_1, \ldots, s_\ell)$:*

  1. *P_1 chooses independent and uniformly random $a_1', \ldots, a_\ell' \in \mathbb{G}$, and sends to P_2 the ciphertext of Π_{comm}: $(\mathsf{Enc}'_{sk_{\mathsf{comm}}}(a_i), \mathsf{Enc}'_{sk_{\mathsf{comm}}}(a_i'))$ for $i \in [\ell]$ and $\mathsf{Enc}'_{sk_{\mathsf{comm}}}(\Phi)$.*

  2. *Upon receiving $((f_i, f_i')_{i \in [\ell]}, f_\Phi)$, P_2 chooses a uniformly random $(s_1', \ldots, s_\ell') \in \mathbb{Z}_p^\ell$, and sends to P_1 the coordinate-wise product: $\left(\prod_{i \in [\ell]} f_i'^{s_i'} / f_i^{s_i} \cdot f_\Phi\right)$. Next, P_2 replaces its old secret key share by*

$$sk_2 = (s_1', \ldots, s_\ell').$$

  3. *Upon receiving f, P_1 computes $\Phi' = \mathsf{Dec}'_{sk_{\mathsf{comm}}}(f)$ and replaces its old secret key share by*

$$sk_1 = (a_1', \ldots, a_\ell', \Phi').$$

Remarks

To ease the reading of our scheme in the above we overlooked some necessary implementation choices. We next specify those choices.

Optimal leakage rate. To achieve a better leakage rate we slightly change the above: In the above, we defined P_1 as holding *both* the secret key share sk_1 and the secret key sk_{comm} for encrypting the communication. To reach leakage rate $(1 - o(1))$ from P_1 we reduce the size of the secret memory of P_1 by defining it to hold only sk_{comm}; whereas instead of holding the secret key share sk_1, P_1 holds the public (coordinate-wise) encryption of sk_1 under Π_{comm}. (The latter is public as it is to be transmitted over the public channel.) We then adapt the decryption and refresh protocol so that P_1 never holds in its memory more than a single un-encrypted coordinate of sk_1. With these modifications, the secret memory of P_1 is of size $|sk_{\mathsf{comm}}| + \log p$, and our tolerated leakage is a $(1 - o(1))$-fraction of this size.

Reusing ciphertexts and hiding discrete logs of random coins.
We observe that the ciphertexts f_i's and d_i's encrypt the same set of values, only in two different groups, and reuse the ciphertexts f_i's to compute the ciphertexts d_i's. This enables us to simplify our security proof. Specifically, for every time period t, P_1 first computes the f_i's to be ciphertexts $f_i = (b_{i1}, \ldots, b_{i\kappa}, a_i \cdot \prod_{j \in [\kappa]} b_j^{\sigma_j}) \leftarrow \mathsf{Enc}'_{sk_{\mathsf{comm}}}(a_i; b_i)$ computed using fresh randomness $b_i = (b_{i1}, \ldots, b_{i\kappa})$ and the secret key $sk_{\mathsf{comm}} = (\sigma_1, \ldots, \sigma_\kappa)$; then computes $d_i = (e(A, b_{i1}), \ldots, e(A, b_{i\kappa}), e(A, a_i) \cdot \prod_{j \in [\kappa]} e(A, b_j)^{\sigma_j})$ to be the coordinate-wise pairing of f_i with A (for $c = (A, B)$ the ciphertext given as input to the decryption protocol at time period t). P_1 then sends these d_i's and f_i's during the decryption and refresh protocol (respectively) of time t.

Looking ahead, for proving **DLR** is secure we require that the discrete logarithms of the random coins b_{ij} (similarly, the a_i's) are not exposed to leakage. To achieve this we sample these elements directly as random group elements (rather than first choosing a random exponent r_{ij} and then defining $b_{ij} = g^{r_{ij}}$). This is feasible in the groups used in our scheme.

6. OUR SECURITY PROOF FOR DLR

We give an overview of our proof of Theorem 4.1, Part 1, stating that our scheme **DLR** is semantically secure against continual memory leakage.

Our proof is by a reduction to the BDDH and 2Lin assumptions. We assume for contradiction that there exists a PPT adversary $\mathcal{A}$ winning the semantic security game for **DLR** (aka, the real game) with non-negligible advantage over half; and where the leakage parameter for this semantic security game is $(b_0 = 0, b_1 = \lambda, b_2 = |sk_2|)$ for λ the leakage parameter of **DLR**, and $|sk_2|$ the size of the secret key share of P_2.[7] We then show that there exists a distinguisher $\mathcal{D}$ that breaks either the BDDH assumption or the 2Lin assumption; details below. We conclude therefore that there exists no such adversary $\mathcal{A}$. Namely, **DLR** is CPA-secure against (b_0, b_1, b_2)-CML (under BDDH and 2Lin assumptions). To conclude the proof observe that $b_1 = \left(1 - \frac{3n}{\lambda + 3n}\right) m_1$ for $m_1 = |sk_{\mathsf{comm}}|$ the size of the secret key share of P_1 (as $|sk_{\mathsf{comm}}| = \kappa \log p = \lambda + 3n$ for our parameters setting).

In the following we first define the distinguisher $\mathcal{D}$, and then outline our proof showing that $\mathcal{D}$ breaks either the BDDH or the 2Lin assumptions.

Defining the distinguisher $\mathcal{D}$. The distinguisher $\mathcal{D}$, given a BDDH tuple $(p, g, e, g^a, g^b, g^c, T)$, plays a fake semantic security game for **DLR** with $\mathcal{A}$ playing the role of the adversary, and outputs 1 iff $\mathcal{A}$ wins this fake game and 0 otherwise. When running this fake game, the distinguisher $\mathcal{D}$ simulates the role of the challenger, while deviating from the latter in how it generates the random variables used in the game:

First, the distinguisher $\mathcal{D}$ plants the BDDH tuple as part of the public key and the challenge ciphertext. Specifically, the public key is $pk = (p, g, e, e(g^a, g^b))$; and the challenge ciphertext is $C^{\mathsf{fake}} = (g^c, m_b \cdot T)$ for m_0, m_1 the messages sent to the challenger from the adversary $\mathcal{A}$, and $b \in \{0, 1\}$ uniformly random.

---

[7]Extending our proof to address leakage $b_0 > 0$ during key generation is simply by guessing those leakage bits; details omitted from this extended abstract.

Second, the distinguisher $\mathcal{D}$ samples the remaining random variables from a new distribution where, most notably, sk_1 is chosen uniformly at random, and yet, despite using this flawed share, the decryption protocol produces the correct output. To specify this distribution we fix a time period t and drop its indices (albeit the sampling itself actually takes place at once for all time periods of the game): (a) $sk_1 = (a_1, \ldots, a_\ell, \Phi) \in \mathbb{G}^{\ell+1}$ and $sk_{\mathsf{comm}} \in \mathbb{Z}_p^\kappa$ are chosen independently and uniformly random; (b) $c', d_\Phi, d_B, f_\Phi, f_i, f'_i$ are ciphertexts of Π_{comm} encrypting the plaintexts $M, e(A, \Phi)$, B, Φ, a_i, a'_i under secret key sk_{comm} (where $C = (A, B)$ and M are the input and output in the execution of the decryption protocol at time t, given to the distinguisher as advice; and a'_i is the i-th component in sk^{t+1}); (c) d_i is the coordinate-wise pairing of f_i and A (for $i = 1, \ldots, \ell$); (d) $sk_2 = (s_1, \ldots, s_\ell) \in \mathbb{Z}_p^\ell$ is chosen uniformly at random subject to the constraint that $c' = d_B \cdot \prod_{i \in [\ell]} d_i^{s_i} / d_\Phi$. Satisfying this constraint boils down to solving a system of $\kappa + 1$ linear equations (one equation per each component of c') in unknowns $s_1, \ldots, s_\ell$ and with coefficients the discrete logarithms of the corresponding ciphertexts. (e) $f = \prod_{i \in [\ell]} \left(f'^{s'_i}_i / f^{s_i}_i\right) \cdot f_\Phi$ when denoting by $sk_2^{t+1} = (s'_1, \ldots, s'_\ell)$ the next secret key share of P_2.

We elaborate on step (d). First, to ensure a solution to the said constraint exists $\mathcal{D}$ imposes a full rank requirement on the coefficients matrix (satisfied via re-sampling). Second, to ensure the solution can be found efficiently the distinguisher $\mathcal{D}$ keeps track of the discrete logarithms involved in stages (a)-(c).

$\mathcal{D}$ breaks BDDH or 2Lin. To prove that $\mathcal{D}$ breaks the BDDH or 2Lin assumptions we do the following.

First, we show that, when $T = e(g, g)^{abc}$ in the given BDDH tuple, the view of the adversary in the fake and real games is computationally indistinguishable (under 2Lin assumption). For this purpose, we define an auxiliary game that is identical to the real game except for imposing the full rank requirement as in the fake game (see above); denote by real, fake and aux the adversary's view in the real, fake, and auxiliary games, respectively. We prove that real $\approx_c$ aux with overwhelming probability (under 2Lin assumption). We then prove that aux $\approx_s$ fake by observing that the corresponding two games differ only in how they generate the random variables $(pk, C^{\mathsf{challenge}}, sk_2^t, \Phi_t)_t$ (for Φ_t the last component of sk_1^t), and proving that the following holds (even conditioned on the rest of the view): (i) The joint distribution of $(pk, C^{\mathsf{challenge}}, sk_2^t)_t$ is identical in aux and fake; (ii) The distribution of $(\Phi_t)_t$ is statistically close in aux and fake; details are omitted from this extended abstract. We conclude that real $\approx_c$ fake with overwhelming probability (under 2Lin assumption).

Now, as by our contradiction assumption $\mathcal{A}$ wins the real game with a non-negligible advantage over half, we conclude that — when $T = e(g, g)^{abc}$ — the adversary $\mathcal{A}$ wins the fake game with a non-negligible advantage over half (under 2Lin assumption). Namely, when $T = e(g, g)^{abc}$, the distinguisher $\mathcal{D}$ outputs 1 with a non-negligible advantage over half. Second, we observe that, when T is uniformly random, the distinguisher $\mathcal{D}$ outputs 1 with probability at most half, because in this case the challenge ciphertext in the fake game is uniformly random and independent of the rest of the view of the adversary, namely, the adversary $\mathcal{A}$ cannot win the game with any advantage over half. Third, we observe that when $\mathcal{A}$ is a PPT algorithm, then the distinguisher $\mathcal{D}$ is also a PPT algorithm. We conclude that (under 2Lin assumption) $\mathcal{D}$ is a PPT algorithm that distinguishes BDDH tuples with $T = e(g,g)^{abc}$ from BDDH tuples with uniform T. Namely, $\mathcal{D}$ breaks either the BDDH or the 2Lin assumptions.

7. REFERENCES

[1] A. Akavia, S. Goldwasser, and V. Vaikuntanathan. Simultaneous hardcore bits and cryptography against memory attacks. In *TCC*, pages 474–495, 2009.

[2] J. Alwen, Y. Dodis, and D. Wichs. Leakage-resilient public-key cryptography in the bounded-retrieval model. In *CRYPTO*, pages 36–54, 2009.

[3] E. Biham and A. Shamir. Differential fault analysis of secret key cryptosystems. In *CRYPTO*, pages 513–525, 1997.

[4] N. Bitansky, R. Canetti, and S. Halevi. Leakage-tolerant interactive protocols. In *TCC*, pages 266–284, 2012.

[5] D. Boneh and X. Boyen. Secure identity based encryption without random oracles. In *CRYPTO*, pages 443–459, 2004.

[6] D. Boneh, R. Canetti, S. Halevi, and J. Katz. Chosen-ciphertext security from identity-based encryption. *SIAM J. Comput.*, 36(5):1301–1328, 2007.

[7] D. Boneh, R. A. DeMillo, and R. J. Lipton. On the importance of checking cryptographic protocols for faults (extended abstract). In *EUROCRYPT*, pages 37–51, 1997.

[8] D. Boneh, S. Halevi, M. Hamburg, and R. Ostrovsky. Circular-secure encryption from decision diffie-hellman. In *CRYPTO*, pages 108–125, 2008.

[9] V. Boyko. On the security properties of oaep as an all-or-nothing transform. In *CRYPTO*, pages 503–518, 1999.

[10] E. Boyle, S. Goldwasser, and Y. T. Kalai. Leakage-resilient coin tossing. In *DISC*, pages 181–196, 2011.

[11] Z. Brakerski, Y. T. Kalai, J. Katz, and V. Vaikuntanathan. Overcoming the hole in the bucket: Public-key cryptography resilient to continual memory leakage. In *FOCS*, pages 501–510, 2010.

[12] R. Canetti, Y. Dodis, S. Halevi, E. Kushilevitz, and A. Sahai. Exposure-resilient functions and all-or-nothing transforms. In *EUROCRYPT*, pages 453–469, 2000.

[13] Y. Dodis, S. Goldwasser, Y. T. Kalai, C. Peikert, and V. Vaikuntanathan. Public-key encryption schemes with auxiliary inputs. In *TCC*, pages 361–381, 2010.

[14] Y. Dodis, K. Haralambiev, A. López-Alt, and D. Wichs. Cryptography against continuous memory attacks. In *FOCS*, pages 511–520, 2010.

[15] Y. Dodis, K. Haralambiev, A. López-Alt, and D. Wichs. Efficient public-key cryptography in the presence of key leakage. In *ASIACRYPT*, pages 613–631, 2010.

[16] Y. Dodis, Y. T. Kalai, and S. Lovett. On cryptography with auxiliary input. In *STOC*, pages 621–630, 2009.

[17] Y. Dodis, A. B. Lewko, B. Waters, and D. Wichs. Storing secrets on continually leaky devices. In *FOCS*, pages 688–697, 2011.

[18] Y. Dodis, L. Reyzin, and A. Smith. Fuzzy extractors: How to generate strong keys from biometrics and other noisy data. In *EUROCRYPT*, pages 523–540, 2004.

[19] Y. Dodis, A. Sahai, and A. Smith. On perfect and adaptive security in exposure-resilient cryptography. In *EUROCRYPT*, pages 301–324, 2001.

[20] S. Dziembowski and K. Pietrzak. Leakage-resilient cryptography. In *FOCS*, pages 293–302, 2008.

[21] K. Gandolfi, C. Mourtel, and F. Olivier. Electromagnetic analysis: Concrete results. In *CHES*, number Generators, pages 251–261, 2001.

[22] S. Garg, A. Jain, and A. Sahai. Leakage-resilient zero knowledge. In *CRYPTO*, 2011.

[23] S. Goldwasser, Y. T. Kalai, and G. N. Rothblum. One-time programs. In *CRYPTO*, pages 39–56, 2008.

[24] J. A. Halderman, S. D. Schoen, N. Heninger, W. Clarkson, W. Paul, J. A. Calandrino, A. J. Feldman, J. Appelbaum, and E. W. Felten. Lest we remember: cold-boot attacks on encryption keys. *Commun. ACM*, 52(5):91–98, 2009.

[25] S. Halevi and H. Lin. After-the-fact leakage in public-key encryption. In *TCC*, pages 107–124, 2011.

[26] Y. Ishai, A. Sahai, and D. Wagner. Private circuits: Securing hardware against probing attacks. In *CRYPTO*, pages 463–481, 2003.

[27] P. C. Kocher. Timing attacks on implementations of diffie-hellman, rsa, dss, and other systems. In *CRYPTO*, pages 104–113, 1996.

[28] P. C. Kocher, J. Jaffe, and B. Jun. Differential power analysis. In *CRYPTO*, pages 388–397, 1999.

[29] A. B. Lewko, M. Lewko, and B. Waters. How to leak on key updates. In *STOC*, pages 725–734, 2011.

[30] A. B. Lewko, Y. Rouselakis, and B. Waters. Achieving leakage resilience through dual system encryption. In *TCC*, pages 70–88, 2011.

[31] S. Micali and L. Reyzin. Physically observable cryptography (extended abstract). In *TCC*, pages 278–296, 2004.

[32] M. Naor and G. Segev. Public-key cryptosystems resilient to key leakage. In *CRYPTO*, pages 18–35, 2009.

[33] C. Petit, F.-X. Standaert, O. Pereira, T. Malkin, and M. Yung. A block cipher based pseudo random number generator secure against side-channel key recovery. In *ASIACCS*, pages 56–65, 2008.

[34] K. Pietrzak. A leakage-resilient mode of operation. In *EUROCRYPT*, pages 462–482, 2009.

[35] J.-J. Quisquater and D. Samyde. Electromagnetic analysis (ema): Measures and counter-measures for smart cards. In *E-smart*, pages 200–210, 2001.

[36] R. L. Rivest. All-or-nothing encryption and the package transform. In *FSE*, pages 210–218, 1997.

[37] B. University. Reliable computing laboratory. Side channel attacks database. http://www.sidechannelattacks.com.

Distributed Maximal Matching: Greedy is Optimal

Juho Hirvonen
juho.hirvonen@cs.helsinki.fi

Jukka Suomela
jukka.suomela@cs.helsinki.fi

Helsinki Institute for Information Technology HIIT, Department of Computer Science, University of Helsinki
P.O. Box 68, FI-00014 University of Helsinki, Finland

ABSTRACT

We study distributed algorithms that find a maximal matching in an anonymous, edge-coloured graph. If the edges are properly coloured with k colours, there is a trivial greedy algorithm that finds a maximal matching in $k - 1$ synchronous communication rounds. The present work shows that the greedy algorithm is optimal in the general case: if A is a deterministic distributed algorithm that finds a maximal matching in anonymous, k-edge-coloured graphs, then there is a worst-case input in which the running time of A is at least $k - 1$ rounds.

If we focus on graphs of maximum degree Δ, it is known that a maximal matching can be found in $O(\Delta + \log^* k)$ rounds, and prior work implies a lower bound of $\Omega(\text{polylog}(\Delta) + \log^* k)$ rounds. Our work closes the gap between upper and lower bounds: the complexity is $\Theta(\Delta + \log^* k)$ rounds. To our knowledge, this is the first linear-in-Δ lower bound for the distributed complexity of a classical graph problem.

Categories and Subject Descriptors

C.2.4 [**Computer-Communication Networks**]: Distributed Systems; F.1.3 [**Computation by Abstract Devices**]: Complexity Measures and Classes; F.2.2 [**Analysis of Algorithms and Problem Complexity**]: Nonnumerical Algorithms and Problems—*computations on discrete structures*

Keywords

distributed algorithms, lower bounds, maximal matching

1. INTRODUCTION

In the study of deterministic distributed graph algorithms, there are two parameters that are commonly used to describe the computational complexity of a graph problem: n, the number of nodes in the graph, and Δ, the maximum degree of the graph. For a wide range of problems, the complexity is well-understood as a function of n—at least if $n \gg \Delta$—but understanding the complexity as a function of Δ is one of the

major open problems in the area. For example, the maximal matching problem can be solved in $O(\Delta + \log^* n)$ rounds [15], while the best lower bound is $\Omega(\text{polylog}(\Delta) + \log^* n)$ [10–12, 14].

The present works gives the first tight lower bound that is linear in Δ for a classical graph problem. In particular, we study the problem of finding a *maximal matching in anonymous, edge-coloured graphs*. If the edges are k-coloured, the problem can be solved in $O(\Delta + \log^* k)$ rounds with an adaptation of a simple deterministic algorithm [15]. It is well-known that the complexity is $\Omega(\log^* k)$ rounds [14]; we close the case by proving a lower bound of $\Omega(\Delta)$ rounds.

1.1 Related Work

For many graph problems, the state-of-the-art algorithms are extremely fast even if the network is very large—provided that Δ is small. For example, the following problems can be solved in $O(\Delta + \log^* n)$ synchronous communication rounds (assuming $O(\log n)$-bit node identifiers):

- maximal matching [15],
- vertex colouring with $\Delta + 1$ colours [3,9],
- edge colouring with $2\Delta - 1$ colours [15].

There are also problems that can be solved in $O(\Delta)$ rounds, independently of n (even in anonymous networks without unique identifiers):

- maximal matching in 2-coloured graphs [6],
- maximal edge packing [2],
- 2-approximation of minimum vertex cover [2].

For each of these problems, the dependence on n in the running time is well-understood if $n \gg \Delta$. In particular, Linial's [14] lower bound shows that maximal matching, vertex colouring, and edge colouring require $\Omega(\log^* n)$ rounds, even if $\Delta = 2$.

However, we do not yet understand the dependence on Δ. For example, the best known lower bound for the maximal matching problem is *logarithmic* in Δ [10–12], while the above upper bounds are *linear* in Δ.

Some $\text{polylog}(\Delta)$ upper bounds are known for graph problems. For example, good approximations of fractional matchings can be found in $\text{polylog}(\Delta)$ rounds [11]; however, this does not seem to yield a deterministic $\text{polylog}(\Delta)$-time algorithm for any of the above problems. Hańćkowiak et al.'s [7] algorithm finds a maximal matching in $\text{polylog}(n)$ rounds, avoiding the linear dependence on Δ; however, it comes at the cost of a non-optimal dependence on n.

It is easy to come up with an artificial problem with the complexity of $\Theta(\Delta)$—for example, find nodes u for which

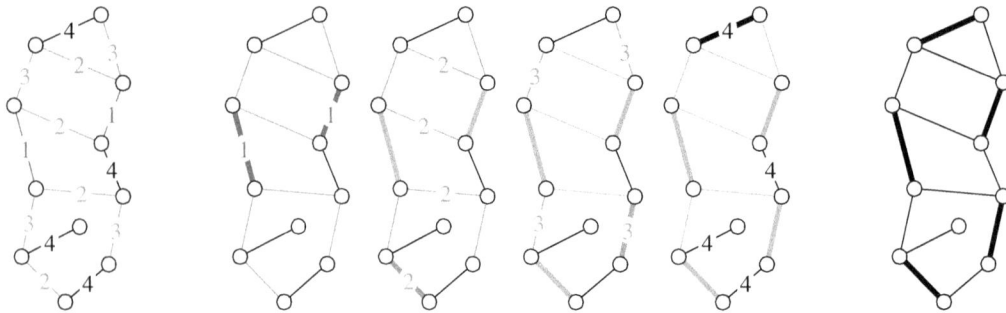

Figure 1: Greedy algorithm for $k = 4$; the thick edges indicate matching M.

there exists a node v such that the distance from u to v is smaller than the degree of v—but so far no such tight results are known for classical graph problems such as maximal matchings. The lower-bound result by Kuhn and Wattenhofer [13] comes close, but it only applies to a restricted family of algorithms.

1.2 Greedy Maximal Matching

We will focus on the task of finding a maximal matching in an edge-coloured graph, using a deterministic distributed algorithm in a network of anonymous nodes (see Section 2 for formally precise definitions and e.g. the survey [16] for more background information).

If the graph is edge-coloured with k colours, there is a very simple greedy algorithm that solves the problem in k steps: We start with an empty matching $M \leftarrow \emptyset$. Then, in step i we consider all edges of colour i in parallel. If an edge $\{u, v\}$ is of colour i, and neither u nor v is matched, we add $\{u, v\}$ to M; see Figure 1.

To analyse the exact running time of the greedy algorithm, we need to fix the model of computation. As usual, each node is a computational entity and there is an edge between two nodes if the nodes can exchange messages with each other—the same graph is both the problem instance and the network topology. Throughout this work, the running time is defined to be the number of synchronous communication rounds. Initially, each node knows the colours of its incident edges. In every round, each node in parallel (1) sends a message to each of its neighbours, (2) receives a message from each of its neighbours, and (3) updates its own state. After each round, a node can stop and announce its *local output*: whether it is matched and with which neighbour.

With these definitions, it is straightforward to verify that the running time of the greedy algorithm is at most $k - 1$ communication rounds. To see this, note that the first step of the greedy algorithm does not require any communication: if a node has an incident edge of colour 1, it is matched along this edge. Hence we have the following lemma.

LEMMA 1. *Let k be a positive integer. There exists a deterministic distributed algorithm with running time $k - 1$ that finds a maximal matching in any anonymous, k-edge-coloured graph.*

We can also easily verify that the analysis is tight, i.e., the worst-case running time of the greedy algorithm described above is exactly $k-1$ rounds. The following figure illustrates a worst-case input for $k = 4$; the construction is straightforward to generalise. In the greedy algorithm u is unmatched while

v is matched. However, radius-2 neighbourhoods of u and v are indistinguishable; in order to produce a different output, we must propagate information over distance $k - 1 = 3$: from x to u and from y to v. Hence any faithful implementation of the greedy algorithm requires at least $k - 1$ communication rounds.

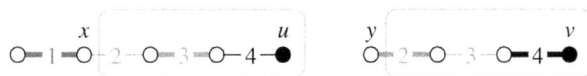

Naturally, if our goal is to find a maximal matching, there is a wide range of possible algorithms, and in many special cases we already know how to beat the greedy algorithm. However, we show that *in the general case, the greedy algorithm is optimal*. The main contribution is summarised in the following theorem.

THEOREM 2. *Let k be a positive integer. A deterministic distributed algorithm that finds a maximal matching in any anonymous, k-edge-coloured graphs requires at least $k - 1$ communication rounds.*

We prove Theorem 2 in Section 3. The lower bound holds even if we allow arbitrarily large messages and unbounded local computations, while the matching upper bound is achieved by a simple algorithm that uses only small messages, little memory, and trivial state transitions.

1.3 Special Cases

Let us now return to the case of bounded-degree graph. If $k \gg \Delta$, we can use Cole–Vishkin [4] style colour reduction techniques to considerably speed up the algorithm. For example, a straightforward adaptation of Panconesi and Rizzi's [15] algorithm finds a maximal matching in $O(\Delta + \log^* k)$ rounds.

Linial's [14] result gives us the lower bound of $\Omega(\log^* k)$; however, so far it has not been known whether $\Omega(\Delta)$ rounds is required. Our result now settles this question. The maximum degree of a k-edge-coloured graph is at most k, and we have the following corollary.

COROLLARY 1. *A deterministic distributed algorithm that finds a maximal matching in an anonymous edge-coloured graph of maximum degree Δ requires $\Omega(\Delta)$ communication rounds.*

Incidentally, our lower-bound construction is a d-regular graph with $d = k - 1$, and hence this work shows that we need d rounds even in the seemingly simple case of d-regular

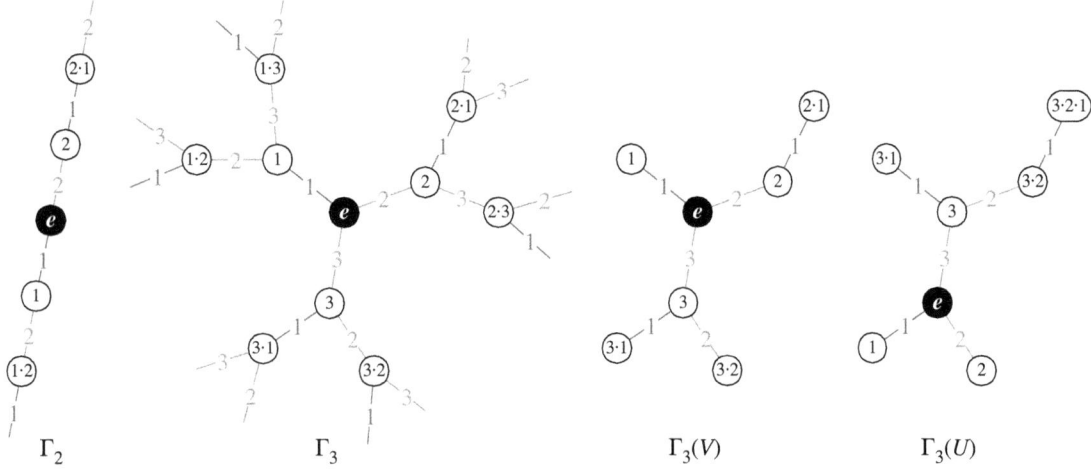

Figure 2: In this example, $V = \{e, 1, 2, 2{\cdot}1, 3, 3{\cdot}1, 3{\cdot}2\} \subseteq G_3$ **is a** 3**-colour system and** $U = \bar{3}V$. **For example,** $V[1] = U[1]$ **and** $V = V[2] \neq U[2] \neq U$.

graphs (assuming $d \geq 2$). Note that in a regular graph, an optimal fractional matching (edge packing) is trivial to find, and none of the existing lower bounds [10–12] apply—previously, we have not even had polylogarithmic-in-Δ lower bounds for such graphs.

Also note that if we study d-regular graphs with $d = k$, the problem becomes trivial: the edges of colour 1 form a perfect matching and we can solve the problem in constant time. The case of $d = k-1$ is the first non-trivial case, and it is already sufficiently rich to show that the greedy algorithm is optimal.

1.4 Future Work

Our lower-bound result covers the case of anonymous networks, including the widely-studied *port-numbering model* [1, 17] and its weaker variants [18] such as the *broadcast model* [2].

What remains open is the case of networks in which nodes have *unique identifiers*; however, the recent work [5] that bridges the gap between anonymous networks and networks with unique identifiers will likely find applications here as well.

2. PRELIMINARIES

In our lower-bound construction, we will need to manipulate edge-coloured trees, and certain group-theoretic concepts turn out to be useful.

2.1 Group G_k

Throughout this text, k is a positive integer. We use the shorthand notations $X + x = X \cup \{x\}$ and $X - x = X \setminus \{x\}$ for a set X, and $[i] = \{1, 2, \ldots, i\}$ for an integer i.

We define the group

$$G_k = \langle 1, 2, \ldots, k \mid 1^2, 2^2, \ldots, k^2 \rangle.$$

That is, the generators of group G_k are $1, 2, \ldots, k$, and we have the relations $c^2 = cc = e$ for each $c \in [k]$; we use e to denote the identity element, and we use the multiplicative notation xy or $x \cdot y$ for the group operation. Group G_k is the free product of k cyclic groups of order two, a.k.a. the group

generated by k involutions, the universal Coxeter group, or the free Coxeter group.

Let Γ_k be the Cayley graph of G_k with respect to the generators $[k]$; see Figure 2 for an illustration. In Γ_k, we have a node for each element $x \in G_k$, and there is an edge of colour $c \in [k]$ from $x \in G_k$ to $y \in G_k$ if $y = xc$. As each generator is its own inverse, there is an edge of colour c from x to y iff there is an edge of colour c from y to x; hence we can interpret Γ_k as an undirected graph. It can be verified that Γ_k is a k-regular k-edge-coloured tree; Γ_k is countably infinite if $k \geq 2$.

In the reduced form, an element $x \in G_k$ is a product $x = c_1 c_2 \cdots c_\ell$ such that $c_i \in [k]$ and $c_{i-1} \neq c_i$. The reduced form is unique; it corresponds to the sequence of edge colours along the unique path from e to x in Γ_k. We use the length of the path to define the norm $|x| = \ell$.

We use the shorthand notation $\bar{x} = x^{-1}$ for the inverse of $x \in G_k$. If $x \in G_k - e$, there is a unique $c \in [k]$ such that $|xc| = |x| - 1$; we say that c is the *tail* of x, in notation $\mathrm{tail}(x) = c$. We also define $\mathrm{head}(x) = \mathrm{tail}(\bar{x})$ and $\mathrm{pred}(x) = x\,\mathrm{tail}(x)$ for each $x \in G_k - e$.

We make the following observations: If $x, y \in G_k$, then $|\bar{x}y|$ is the length of the unique path from x to y in Γ_k; in particular, $d(x, y) = |\bar{x}y|$ defines a metric on G_k. If $|\bar{x}y| = 1$, nodes x and y are connected with an edge of colour $\bar{x}y$. We have $|\bar{x}| = |x|$ for all $x \in G_k$ and $|xy| \equiv |x| + |y| \mod 2$ for all $x, y \in G_k$. The equality $|xy| = |x| + |y|$ holds iff $x = e$, $y = e$, or $\mathrm{tail}(x) \neq \mathrm{head}(y)$.

If $V \subseteq G_k$ and $x \in G_k$, we define $xV = \{xv : v \in V\}$. If $V \subseteq G_k$, $f: V \to X$, and $x \in G_k$, we also define the function $xf: xV \to X$ as follows: $(xf)(y) = f(\bar{x}y)$ for each $y \in xV$. That is, $(xf)(xv) = f(v)$ for each $v \in V$.

2.2 Colour Systems

A non-empty set $V \subseteq G_k$ is a *k-colour system* if $v \in V - e$ implies $\mathrm{pred}(v) \in V$. That is, a colour system is a prefix-closed subset; put otherwise, we can start from any $v \in V$ and walk towards e in Γ_k without leaving V. We define the set of edges

$$E(V) = \big\{ \{\mathrm{pred}(v), v\} : v \in V - e \big\}.$$

Let $\Gamma_k(V)$ be the graph with the node set V and the edge set $E(V)$. Now $\Gamma_k(V)$ is a connected subgraph of the tree Γ_k; see Figure 2 for an example. Observe that if $\mathcal{T}$ is any k-edge-coloured tree, then we can construct a k-colour system $V \subseteq G_k$ such that $\mathcal{T}$ and $\Gamma_k(V)$ are isomorphic.

The following lemma is straightforward to verify.

LEMMA 3. *If V is a k-colour system and $u \in V$, then $\bar{u}V$ is a k-colour system. Moreover, $x \mapsto \bar{u}x$ is an isomorphism from $\Gamma_k(V)$ to $\Gamma_k(\bar{u}V)$ that preserves adjacencies and edge colours.*

For a colour system V and integer h, we define $V[h] = \{v \in V : |v| \leq h\}$. Similarly, if $f \colon V \to X$, we define that $f[h] \colon V[h] \to X$ is the restriction of f to $V[h]$. Note that $V[h]$ is a colour system. The set $u((\bar{u}V)[h]) \subseteq V$ consists of all nodes that are within distance h from $u \in V$ in $\Gamma_k(V)$.

Let $C(V, v) = \{\bar{u}v : \{u, v\} \in E(V)\}$ denote the set of colours incident to $v \in V$ in $\Gamma_k(V)$. Note that

$$C(V, v) = \{c \in [k] : vc \in V\} = (\bar{v}V)[1] - e.$$

The degree of v is $\deg(V, v) = |C(V, v)|$, and colour system V is said to be d-regular if $\deg(V, v) = d$ for all $v \in V$.

If V is a colour system and $c \in C(V, e)$, we define

$$\mathrm{prune}(V, c) = \{v \in V - e : \mathrm{head}(v) \neq c\} + e.$$

Observe that $U = \mathrm{prune}(V, c)$ is a colour system. Moreover, if V is d-regular, then $\deg(U, u) = d$ for all $u \in U - e$ and $\deg(U, e) = d - 1$.

2.3 Distributed Algorithms

For the purposes of our lower-bound result, it is sufficient to define formally what a distributed algorithm A outputs if we apply it in $\Gamma_k(V)$, where V is a colour system.

We already gave an informal definition of a distributed algorithm in Section 1.2. In particular, we assumed that the nodes are anonymous (they do not have unique identifiers), and initially each node knows the colours of the incident edges. Put otherwise, initially a node $v \in V$ knows precisely $(\bar{v}V)[1]$. Now if we let the nodes exchange all information that they have, after the first round each node $v \in V$ can reconstruct $(\bar{v}V)[2]$, and recursively, after r rounds each node knows precisely $(\bar{v}V)[r+1]$. We will use this as our definition of a distributed algorithm.

Assume that A is a function that associates a *local output* $A(V, v)$ with any colour system V and node $v \in V$. Then we say that A is a *distributed algorithm with running time r* if $(\bar{u}U)[r+1] = (\bar{v}V)[r+1]$ implies $A(U, u) = A(V, v)$.

2.4 Algorithms for Maximal Matchings

We say that a distributed algorithm A *finds a maximal matching* in colour system V if

(M1) we have $A(V, v) \in C(V, v) + \bot$ for each $v \in V$,
(M2) if $A(V, v) = c \neq \bot$ then $vc \in V$ and $A(V, vc) = c$,
(M3) if $A(V, v) = \bot$ and $c \in C(V, v)$ then $A(V, vc) \neq \bot$.

The interpretation is that $A(V, v) = \bot$ if v is unmatched and $A(V, v) = c \in C(v)$ if v is matched along the edge of colour c; see Figure 3 for an illustration. Property (M2) ensures that the output is consistent, and property (M3) ensures that the matching is maximal.

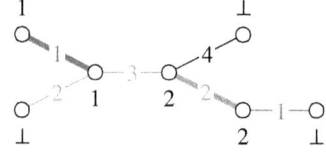

Figure 3: Encoding of a maximal matching.

3. LOWER BOUND

Let us first cover the case of $k \leq 2$.

LEMMA 4. *Let $k \in \{1, 2\}$. A deterministic distributed algorithm that finds a maximal matching in any anonymous, k-edge-coloured graphs requires at least $k - 1$ communication rounds.*

PROOF. The case of $k = 1$ is trivial. Let us then focus on the case of $k = 2$. Define the 2-colour systems $T = \{e, 1\}$, $U = \{e, 2\}$, and $V = \{e, 1, 2\}$. Now $A(T, 1) = 1$ and $A(U, 2) = 2$ for any distributed algorithm A. However, we must have either $A(V, 1) \neq 1$ or $A(V, 2) \neq 2$, even though $(\bar{1}T)[1] = (\bar{1}V)[1]$ and $(\bar{2}U)[1] = (\bar{2}V)[1]$. □

The rest of this work contains the proof of the following theorem that covers the case of $k \geq 3$.

THEOREM 5. *Let $k \geq 3$ be an integer, and let $d = k - 1$. Assume that A is a distributed algorithm that finds a maximal matching in any d-regular k-colour system. Then there are two d-regular k-colour systems U and V such that $U[d] = V[d]$, $A(U, e) \neq \bot$, and $A(V, e) = \bot$.*

In particular, the running time of A is at least $d = k - 1$. Theorem 2 follows.

3.1 Overview of the Proof

For the rest of this work, choose k, d, and A as in the statement of Theorem 5, and let r be the running time of A. All colour systems are k-colour systems.

Sections 3.2–3.7 introduce a number of concepts that we will use to present our lower-bound construction. After that, we prove Theorem 5 by induction; the base case is in Section 3.8, and the inductive step in Section 3.9.

3.2 Templates and Colour Pickers

An *h-template* is a pair (T, τ) where $T \subseteq G_k$ is an h-regular colour system and $\tau \colon T \to [k]$ associates a *forbidden colour* $\tau(t) \in [k] \setminus C(T, t)$ with each $t \in T$. The set of *free colours* is

$$F(T, \tau, t) = [k] \setminus (C(T, t) + \tau(t))$$

for each $t \in T$.

Let b be an integer with $0 \leq b \leq d - h$. A *b-colour picker* for (T, τ) is a function P that associates a subset $P(t) \subseteq F(T, \tau, t)$ of size b with each node $t \in T$. That is, a b-colour picker chooses b free colours for each node. Figure 4 gives an example with $h = 2$, $b = 1$, $d = 4$, and $k = 5$; a 2-template is an infinite path and a 1-colour picker chooses exactly one free colour for each node.

Let P and Q be colour pickers for (T, τ). We say that P and Q are *disjoint* if $P(t) \cap Q(t) = \emptyset$ for all $t \in T$. If P and Q are disjoint colour pickers for (T, τ), we can construct a colour picker R by setting $R(t) = P(t) \cup Q(t)$ for each $t \in T$.

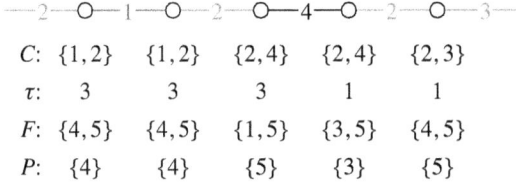

Figure 4: A 2-template and a 1-colour picker.

3.3 Extensions

Let (T, τ) be an h-template and let P be a b-colour picker for (T, τ). We will define a relation $\rightsquigarrow$ between G_k and T recursively as follows; see Figure 5 for an illustration.

(i) We have $e \rightsquigarrow e$, $c \rightsquigarrow c$ for each $c \in C(T, e)$, and $c \rightsquigarrow e$ for each $c \in P(e)$.

(ii) Assume that $x \rightsquigarrow t$ and $x \neq e$.
   We have $xc \rightsquigarrow tc$ for each $c \in C(T, t) - \mathrm{tail}(x)$, and $xc \rightsquigarrow t$ for each $c \in P(t) - \mathrm{tail}(x)$.

We make the following observations.

(a) If $x \rightsquigarrow t_1$ and $x \rightsquigarrow t_2$, we have $t_1 = t_2$.

(b) If $x \rightsquigarrow t$ and $x \neq e$, we have $\mathrm{tail}(x) \in C(T, t) \cup P(t)$.

(c) If $x \rightsquigarrow t$, $x \neq e$, and $\mathrm{tail}(x) \in C(T, t)$, we have $\mathrm{pred}(x) \rightsquigarrow t\,\mathrm{tail}(x)$.

(d) If $x \rightsquigarrow t$, $x \neq e$, and $\mathrm{tail}(x) \in P(t)$, we have $\mathrm{pred}(x) \rightsquigarrow t$.

(e) If $x \rightsquigarrow t$ and $c \in C(T, t)$, we have $xc \rightsquigarrow tc$.

(f) If $x \rightsquigarrow t$ and $c \in P(t)$, we have $xc \rightsquigarrow t$.

(g) If $x \rightsquigarrow t$ and $c \in [k] \setminus (C(T, t) \cup P(t))$, there is no $t' \in T$ with $xc \rightsquigarrow t'$.

(h) If $x \rightsquigarrow t$ then $|x| \geq |t|$.

(i) For each $t \in T$ there exists an x such that $x \rightsquigarrow t$.

Let $X = \{x \in G_k : x \rightsquigarrow t \text{ for some } t \in T\}$. Define the function $p \colon X \to T$ as follows: for each $x \in X$, let $p(x)$ be the unique element with $x \rightsquigarrow p(x)$. Let $\xi = \tau \circ p$. We say that (X, ξ, p) is the P-extension of (T, τ), in notation, $\mathrm{ext}(T, \tau, P) = (X, \xi, p)$.

Remark 1. We can interpret extensions as universal covering graphs [1] as follows. First, consider the edge-coloured tree $\mathcal{G} = \Gamma_k(T)$. Then modify $\mathcal{G}$ as follows: for each $t \in T$ and $c \in P(t)$, add a self-loop of colour c from t to itself. Now $\mathcal{G}$ is an edge-coloured multigraph; then we construct the universal covering graph $\mathcal{T}$ of $\mathcal{G}$ (i.e., we "unfold" all self-loops of $\mathcal{G}$). Graph $\mathcal{T}$ is an edge-coloured tree; it can be verified that $\mathcal{T}$ is isomorphic to $\Gamma_k(X)$.

3.4 Properties of Extensions

Let us first prove that an extension is a template.

LEMMA 6. *Assume that (T, τ) is an h-template, P is a b-colour picker for (T, τ), and $(X, \xi, p) = \mathrm{ext}(T, \tau, P)$. Then X is an $(h+b)$-regular colour system, and (X, ξ) is an $(h+b)$-template. For each $x \in X$ we have $C(X, x) = C(T, p(x)) \cup P(p(x))$.*

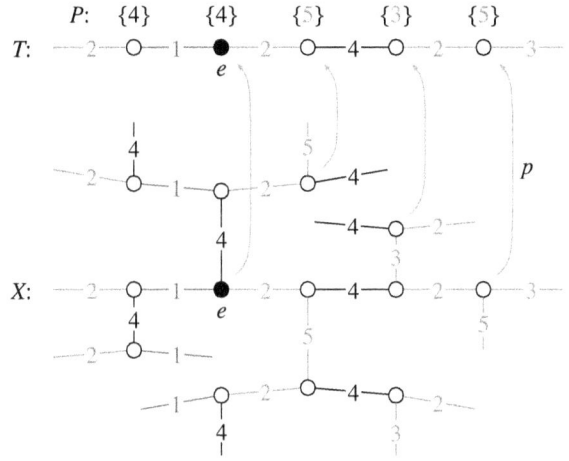

Figure 5: Here T is a 2-template and P is a 1-colour picker. The arrows illustrate the relation $\rightsquigarrow$ between X and T, and hence also function p. In this case, X is a 3-regular colour system.

PROOF. Each $x \in X - e$ has $\mathrm{pred}(x) \in X$; hence X is a colour system. If $x \in X$ and $c \in [k]$, we have $xc \in X$ iff $c \in C(T, p(x)) \cup P(p(x))$; hence $C(X, x) = C(T, p(x)) \cup P(p(x))$ and $\deg(x) = h + b$. It follows that X is $(h + b)$-regular. By assumption,

$$\xi(x) = \tau(p(x)) \notin C(T, p(x)) \cup P(p(x)) = C(X, x);$$

that is, ξ associates a valid forbidden colour with each $x \in X$, and we conclude that (X, ξ) is an $(h + b)$-template. $\square$

Next, we observe that an extension has a high degree of symmetry.

LEMMA 7. *Let $(X, \xi, p) = \mathrm{ext}(T, \tau, P)$, $x, y \in X$, and $p(x) = p(y)$. Then $\bar{x}X = \bar{y}X$, $\bar{x}\xi = \bar{y}\xi$, and $\bar{x}p = \bar{y}p$.*

PROOF. Let $w \in \bar{x}X$. Assume that $w = c_1 c_2 \cdots c_\ell$, where $c_i \in [k]$, and define $w_i = c_1 c_2 \cdots c_i$. We have $w_i \in \bar{x}X$ and $xw_i \in x\bar{x}X = X$ for all i; let $t_i = p(xw_i)$.

With these definitions, $xw_i \rightsquigarrow t_i$ for all $i = 0, 1, \ldots, \ell$. We will prove by induction that $yw_i \rightsquigarrow t_i$ for all i. The base case of $i = 0$ is trivial. Now assume that $xw_i \rightsquigarrow t_i$ and $yw_i \rightsquigarrow t_i$. As we have $xw_i c_{i+1} \rightsquigarrow t_{i+1}$, there are two possibilities. If $c_{i+1} \in C(T, t_i)$, then $t_{i+1} = t_i c_{i+1}$ and $yw_i c_{i+1} \rightsquigarrow t_i c_{i+1}$. Otherwise $c_{i+1} \in P(t_i)$, $t_{i+1} = t_i$ and $yw_i c_{i+1} \rightsquigarrow t_i$. In both cases $yw_{i+1} \rightsquigarrow t_{i+1}$.

It follows that $yw \rightsquigarrow t_\ell$, and hence $yw \in X$ with $p(yw) = t_\ell = p(xw)$. We have shown that $w \in \bar{x}X$ implies $w = \bar{y}yw \in \bar{y}X$ and

$$(\bar{y}p)(w) = (\bar{y}p)(\bar{y}yw) = p(yw) = p(xw) = (\bar{x}p)(w).$$

By symmetry, $w \in \bar{y}Y$ implies $w \in \bar{x}X$. Finally, $\bar{x}p = \bar{y}p$ implies $\bar{x}\xi = \bar{y}\xi$. $\square$

We also show that the order in which we extend does not affect the end result. If we have two disjoint colour pickers P and Q, we can first apply P and then Q, or vice versa, and we obtain the same result as if we used the colour picker $t \mapsto P(t) \cup Q(t)$ directly; in this sense, extensions commute.

LEMMA 8. *Assume that (T, τ) is a template and P and Q are disjoint colour pickers for (T, τ). Let $R(t) = P(t) \cup Q(t)$ for each $t \in T$. Let $(K, \kappa, p) = \text{ext}(T, \tau, P)$, $(L, \lambda, q) = \text{ext}(K, \kappa, Q \circ p)$, and $(X, \xi, r) = \text{ext}(T, \tau, R)$. Now $X = L$, $\lambda = \xi$, and $p \circ q = r$.*

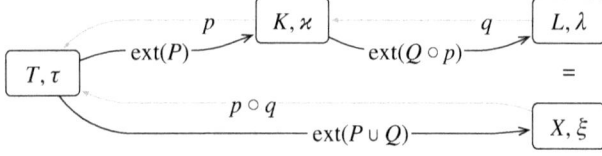

PROOF. Let $x = c_1 c_2 \cdots c_\ell$, where $c_i \in [k]$, and define $x_i = c_1 c_2 \cdots c_i$. We prove by induction that if $x_i \in X$, we also have $x_i \in L$ with $p(q(x_i)) = r(x_i)$, and if $x_i \notin X$, we also have $x_i \notin L$.

The base case $i = 0$ is trivial: $p(q(e)) = p(e) = e = r(e)$ and $e \in X \cap L$. Now assume that $x_i \in X \cap L$ and $p(q(x_i)) = r(x_i)$. There are four cases depending on c_{i+1}:

(a) Assume that $c_{i+1} \in C(T, r(x_i)) = C(T, p(q(x_i)))$. Then $c_{i+1} \in C(K, q(x_i))$, $x_{i+1} \in X \cap L$, and

$$p(q(x_{i+1})) = p(q(x_i c_{i+1}))$$
$$= p(q(x_i) c_{i+1}) = p(q(x_i)) c_{i+1} = r(x_i) c_{i+1}$$
$$= r(x_i c_{i+1}) = r(x_{i+1}).$$

(b) Assume that $c_{i+1} \in P(r(x_i)) = P(p(q(x_i))) \subseteq R(r(x_i))$. Then $c_{i+1} \in C(K, q(x_i))$, $x_{i+1} \in X \cap L$, and

$$p(q(x_{i+1})) = p(q(x_i c_{i+1}))$$
$$= p(q(x_i) c_{i+1}) = p(q(x_i)) = r(x_i)$$
$$= r(x_i c_{i+1}) = r(x_{i+1}).$$

(c) Assume that $c_{i+1} \in Q(r(x_i)) = Q(p(q(x_i))) \subseteq R(r(x_i))$. Then $c_{i+1} \in (Q \circ p)(q(x_i))$, $x_{i+1} \in X \cap L$, and

$$p(q(x_{i+1})) = p(q(x_i)) = r(x_i)$$
$$= r(x_i c_{i+1}) = r(x_{i+1}).$$

(d) Otherwise $x_{i+1} \notin X$ and $x_{i+1} \notin L$. As a consequence, $x_{i+j} \notin X$ and $x_{i+j} \notin L$ for all $j > 1$.

In conclusion, we have $X = L$, $p \circ q = r$, and $\lambda = \tau \circ p \circ q = \tau \circ r = \xi$. $\square$

3.5 Realisations

Let (T, τ) be an h-template. Define a $(d - h)$-colour picker P by setting $P(t) = F(T, \tau, t)$ for each $t \in T$. Let $(V, g, p) = \text{ext}(T, \tau, P)$. We say that (V, p) is the *realisation* of template (T, τ), in notation, $(V, p) = \text{real}(T, \tau)$.

Intuitively, V is a concrete problem instance—it is always a d-regular colour system, and hence we can apply algorithm A to V. Templates can be seen as compact, schematic representations of problem instances.

Lemma 7 has the following corollary.

COROLLARY 2. *Let $(V, p) = \text{real}(T, \tau)$. If $u, v \in V$ and $p(u) = p(v)$, then $\bar{u}V = \bar{v}V$. In particular, $A(V, u) = A(V, v)$.*

Put otherwise, if (T, τ) is a template with the realisation (V, p), each node $t \in T$ represents an *equivalence class* $p^{-1}(t) \subseteq V$ of nodes with identical outputs. For each $t \in T$,

we define $A(T, \tau, t) = A(V, v)$ where $v \in p^{-1}(t)$; by Corollary 2, this does not depend on the choice of v.

We define $M(T, \tau) = \{\{u, v\} \in E(T) : A(T, \tau, u) = A(T, \tau, v) = \bar{u}v\}$. Note that $M(T, \tau)$ is always a matching in the tree $\Gamma_k(T)$, but the matching is not necessarily maximal. If $S \subseteq T$, we also define $M(T, S, \tau) = \{\{u, v\} \in M(T, \tau) : u, v \in S\}$, the restriction of $M(T, \tau)$ to S.

Lemma 8 has the following corollary; it shows that a template and its extensions have the same realisations.

COROLLARY 3. *Let*

$$(K, \kappa, p) = \text{ext}(T, \tau, P),$$
$$(X, r) = \text{real}(T, \tau),$$
$$(L, q) = \text{real}(K, \kappa).$$

Then $X = L$, $p \circ q = r$, and $A(K, \kappa, x) = A(T, \tau, p(x))$ for all $x \in K$.

The following lemma is yet another application of the symmetry that we have in extensions: if a template has free colours (i.e., $h < d$), then an algorithm produces a perfect matching in the realisation of the template.

LEMMA 9. *Assume that (T, τ) is an h-template with $h < d$. Then $A(T, \tau, t) \neq \perp$ for all $t \in T$.*

PROOF. Let $(V, p) = \text{real}(T, \tau)$, $t \in T$, and $v \in p^{-1}(t)$. If $h < d$, there exists a $c \in F(T, \tau, t)$. Let $u = vc$; we have $p(u) = p(v) = t$, $c \in C(V, v)$, and

$$A(V, u) = A(V, v) = A(T, \tau, t).$$

Now $A(T, \tau, t) = \perp$ would contradict property (M3). $\square$

3.6 Zero-Templates

Let $Z = \{e\}$ be the colour system with only one node. For each $c \in [k]$, let $\hat{c}$ denote the function $\hat{c}: Z \to [k]$ that maps $\hat{c}(e) = c$. Now $(Z, \hat{c})$ is a 0-template for each $c \in [k]$.

If A is the greedy algorithm, we have $A(Z, \hat{1}, e) = 2$ and $A(Z, \hat{3}, e) \neq 2$. The following lemma generalises this observation.

LEMMA 10. *There are distinct colours $c_1, c_2, c_3 \in [k]$ such that $A(Z, \hat{c}_1, e) = c_2$ and $A(Z, \hat{c}_3, e) \neq c_2$.*

PROOF. For each $c \in [k]$, let $h(c) = A(Z, \hat{c}, e)$. By Lemma 9, we have $h(c) \in [k]$ for each $c \in [k]$. Moreover, $h(c) \in [k] - \hat{c}(e) = [k] - c$. Hence we have a function $h: [k] \to [k]$ that does not have any fixed points.

First, assume that $h(h(1)) \neq 1$. Then we can choose $c_1 = h(1)$, $c_2 = h(h(1))$, and $c_3 = 1$.

Second, assume that $h(h(1)) = 1$. Let $c \in [k] - \{1, h(1)\}$. If $h(c) = h(1)$, we can choose $c_1 = h(1)$, $c_2 = 1$, and $c_3 = c$. If $h(c) \neq h(1)$, we can choose $c_1 = 1$, $c_2 = h(1)$, and $c_3 = c$. $\square$

3.7 Compatible Templates and Critical Pairs

Let $h \geq 1$. We say that templates (S, σ) and (T, τ) are *h-compatible* if

(C1) $S[h] = T[h]$,
(C2) $\sigma[h - 1] = \tau[h - 1]$.

We emphasise that h-compatible templates are not necessarily h-templates.

We say that (S, σ) and (T, τ) form an *h-critical pair* if they are h-compatible h-templates and they satisfy the following additional properties:

$$
\begin{array}{llcl}
K: & \bullet\!\!-\!c_2\!-\!\circ^e & X: & \bullet\!\!-\!c_2\!-\!\circ^e \\
\kappa: & c_1 \quad c_1 & \xi: & c_1 \quad c_3 \\
A(K,\kappa): & c_2 \quad c_2 & A(X,\xi): & ? \quad ?
\end{array}
$$

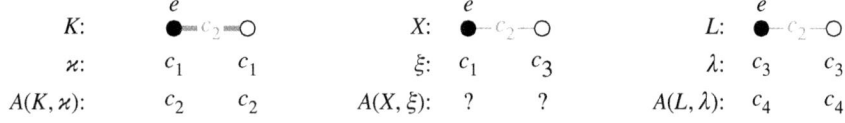

Figure 6: A 1-critical pair.

(C3) $A(T,\tau,e) \notin C(T,e)$,

(C4) $A(S,\sigma,s) \in C(S,s)$ for each $s \in S$.

If $h < d$, Lemma 9 and property (C3) imply that $A(T,\tau,e) \in F(T,\tau,e)$. Property (C4) implies that $M(S,\sigma)$ is a perfect matching in $\Gamma_k(S)$, while property (C3) implies that $M(T,\tau)$ cannot be a perfect matching in $\Gamma_k(T)$.

Remark 2. A reader familiar with Linial's neighbourhood graphs [14] may want to interpret h-compatible templates as adjacent nodes in an h-neighbourhood graph.

3.8 Base Case

In this section we show that there exists a 1-critical pair. Choose $c_1, c_2, c_3 \in [k]$ as in Lemma 10 and let $c_4 = A(Z, \hat{c}_3, e)$. Note that $c_4 \neq c_2$; however, we may have $c_4 = c_1$.

Let $K = L = X = \{e, c_2\}$. Define $\kappa(e) = \kappa(c_2) = \xi(e) = c_1$ and $\lambda(e) = \lambda(c_2) = \xi(c_2) = c_3$. Now (K,κ), (L,λ), and (X,ξ) are 1-templates; the construction is illustrated in Figure 6.

If $p(e) = p(c_2) = e$ and $P(e) = c_2$, we have

$$
(K,\kappa,p) = \text{ext}(Z, \hat{c}_1, P),
$$
$$
(L,\lambda,p) = \text{ext}(Z, \hat{c}_3, P).
$$

Therefore $A(K,\kappa,v) = c_2$ for each $v \in K$ and $A(L,\lambda,v) = c_4$ for each $v \in L$.

Now we construct 1-templates (S_1, σ_1) and (T_1, τ_1) as follows:

(i) If $A(X,\xi,e) \neq c_2$, we choose $(S_1, \sigma_1) = (K,\kappa)$ and $(T_1, \tau_1) = (X, \xi)$.

(ii) If $A(X,\xi,e) = c_2$, we choose $(S_1, \sigma_1) = (\bar{c}_2 X, \bar{c}_2 \xi)$ and $(T_1, \tau_1) = (\bar{c}_2 L, \bar{c}_2 \lambda)$.

LEMMA 11. *Templates (S_1, σ_1) and (T_1, τ_1) form a 1-critical pair.*

PROOF. We have $S_1[1] = T_1[1] = K = L = X = \{e, c_2\}$, verifying property (C1). To verify (C2), note that case (i) implies $\sigma_1(e) = \tau_1(e) = c_1$ and case (ii) implies $\sigma_1(e) = \tau_1(e) = c_3$. To verify property (C3), observe that $A(T_1, \tau_1, e) \neq c_2$ while $C(T_1, e) = \{c_2\}$. To verify property (C4), observe that $A(S_1, \sigma_1, s) = c_2$ and $C(S_1, s) = \{c_2\}$ for all $s \in S_1$. $\square$

3.9 Inductive Step

Now assume that (S_h, σ_h) and (T_h, τ_h) form an h-critical pair, where $1 \leq h < d$. In this section, we will construct an $(h+1)$-critical pair (S_{h+1}, σ_{h+1}) and (T_{h+1}, τ_{h+1}).

Recall that Lemma 9 implies that $A(S_h, \sigma_h, s) \neq \bot$ for all $s \in S_h$ and $A(T_h, \tau_h, t) \neq \bot$ for all $t \in T_h$. We define two colour pickers as follows; see Figures 7 and 8 for illustrations.

(i) Define a 1-colour picker Q for (T_h, τ_h) as follows. Let $t \in T_h$. If $A(T_h, \tau_h, t) \in F(T_h, \tau_h, t)$, we choose $Q(t) = \{A(T_h, \tau_h, t)\}$. Otherwise we choose an arbitrary free colour $c \in F(T_h, \tau_h, t)$ and set $Q(t) = \{c\}$.

(ii) Define a 1-colour picker P for (S_h, σ_h) as follows. Let $s \in S_h$. If $|s| \leq h-1$, we have $s \in T_h$ and $F(S_h, \sigma_h, s) = F(T_h, \tau_h, s)$; hence we can choose $P(s) = Q(s)$. Otherwise we choose an arbitrary free colour $c \in F(S_h, \sigma_h, s)$ and set $P(s) = \{c\}$.

Let $(K, \kappa, p) = \text{ext}(S_h, \sigma_h, P)$, $(L, \lambda, q) = \text{ext}(T_h, \tau_h, Q)$, and $\chi = A(T_h, \tau_h, e)$. We make the following observations:

(a) (K, κ) and (L, λ) are $(h+1)$-templates,

(b) (K, κ) and (L, λ) are h-compatible,

(c) $\{e, \chi\} \in E(K)$ and $\{e, \chi\} \in E(L)$,

(d) $p(e) = p(\chi) = e$ and $q(e) = q(\chi) = e$,

(e) $\bar{\chi}K = K$, $\bar{\chi}\kappa = \kappa$, $\bar{\chi}L = L$, and $\bar{\chi}\lambda = \lambda$,

(f) $A(K, \kappa, v) \in C(K, v)$ for each $v \in K$, i.e., $M(K, \kappa)$ is a perfect matching in $\Gamma_k(K)$,

(g) $A(L, \lambda, v) \in C(L, v)$ for each $v \in L$, i.e., $M(L, \lambda)$ is a perfect matching in $\Gamma_k(L)$,

(h) $\{e, \chi\} \notin M(K, \kappa)$ but $\{e, \chi\} \in M(L, \lambda)$.

Now we will use (K, κ) and (L, λ) to construct a new $(h+1)$-template (X, ξ); refer to Figure 7. Let $K_1 = \text{prune}(K, \chi)$, $L_1 = \chi \text{ prune}(\bar{\chi}L, \chi)$, and $X = K_1 \cup L_1$. Define $\xi: X \to [k]$ as follows: $\xi(v) = \kappa(v)$ for all $v \in K_1$ and $\xi(v) = \lambda(v)$ for all $v \in L_1$. We make the following observations:

(a) (X, ξ) is an $(h+1)$-template,

(b) (X, ξ), (K, κ), and (L, λ) are pairwise h-compatible,

(c) $(\bar{\chi}X, \bar{\chi}\xi)$, $(\bar{\chi}K, \bar{\chi}\kappa)$, and $(\bar{\chi}L, \bar{\chi}\lambda)$ are pairwise h-compatible.

(d) $(\bar{y}X, \bar{y}\xi)$ and $(\bar{y}K, \bar{y}\kappa)$ are $(h+1)$-compatible for any $y \in K_1$,

(e) $(\bar{y}X, \bar{y}\xi)$ and $(\bar{y}L, \bar{y}\lambda)$ are $(h+1)$-compatible for any $y \in L_1$.

Hence we have a family of $(h+1)$-compatible $(h+1)$-templates; however, we need to construct an $(h+1)$-critical pair.

LEMMA 12. *There is a node $y \in X$ such that $A(X, \xi, y) \notin C(X, y)$.*

PROOF. We say that an edge $\{u, v\}$ is *distant* if $|u| > r+1$ and $|v| > r+1$; otherwise it is *near*.

Set $M(K, \kappa)$ is a perfect matching in $\Gamma_k(K)$. Moreover, $\{e, \chi\} \notin M(K, \kappa)$; therefore we have either $\{u, v\} \subseteq K_1$ or $\{u, v\} \cap K_1 = \emptyset$ for each $\{u, v\} \in M(K, \kappa)$. It follows that $\bigcup M(K, K_1, \kappa) = K_1$. Let $K_3' \subseteq M(K, K_1, \kappa)$ consist of the edges that are distant, and let $K_2' = M(K, K_1, \kappa) \setminus K_3'$ consist of the edges that are near. Define $K_2 = \bigcup K_2'$ and $K_3 = \bigcup K_3'$; see Figure 7 for an illustration.

171

Set $M(L, \lambda)$ is a perfect matching in $\Gamma_k(L)$. Moreover, $\{e, \chi\} \in M(L, \lambda)$; this is the unique edge that joins L_1 and $L \setminus L_1$. Therefore we have $\bigcup M(L, L_1, \lambda) = L_1 - \chi$. Let $L_3' \subseteq M(L, L_1, \lambda)$ consist of the edges that are distant, and let $L_2' = M(L, L_1, \lambda) \setminus L_3'$ consist of the edges that are near. Define $L_2 = (\bigcup L_2') + \chi$ and $L_3 = \bigcup L_3'$.

It follows that

(a) K_3, K_2, L_2, and L_3 form a partition of X,

(b) $(\bar{v}K)[r+1] = (\bar{v}X)[r+1]$ and $(\bar{v}\kappa)[r+1] = (\bar{v}\xi)[r+1]$ for any $v \in K_3$,

(c) $(\bar{v}L)[r+1] = (\bar{v}X)[r+1]$ and $(\bar{v}\lambda)[r+1] = (\bar{v}\xi)[r+1]$ for any $v \in L_3$,

(d) $A(K, \kappa, v) = A(X, \xi, v)$ for any $v \in K_3$,

(e) $A(L, \lambda, v) = A(X, \xi, v)$ for any $v \in L_3$,

(f) $\{u, v\} \in K_3' \cup L_3'$ implies $\{u, v\} \in M(X, \xi)$,

(g) K_2 is a finite set with an even number of nodes,

(h) L_2 is a finite set with an odd number of nodes.

By a parity argument, there is a node $y \in K_2 \cup L_2$ such that $y \notin \bigcup M(X, \xi)$, i.e., $A(X, \xi, y) \notin C(X, y)$. $\square$

Now choose y as in Lemma 12, and define (S_{h+1}, σ_{h+1}) and (T_{h+1}, τ_{h+1}) as follows:

(a) If $y \in K_1$, define $S_{h+1} = \bar{y}K$, $\sigma_{h+1} = \bar{y}\kappa$, $T_{h+1} = \bar{y}X$, and $\tau_{h+1} = \bar{y}\xi$.

(b) If $y \in L_1$, define $S_{h+1} = \bar{y}L$, $\sigma_{h+1} = \bar{y}\lambda$, $T_{h+1} = \bar{y}X$, and $\tau_{h+1} = \bar{y}\xi$.

LEMMA 13. *Templates (S_{h+1}, σ_{h+1}) and (T_{h+1}, τ_{h+1}) form an $(h+1)$-critical pair.*

PROOF. First, assume that $y \in K_1$. We have already observed that $(S_{h+1}, \sigma_{h+1}) = (\bar{y}K, \bar{y}\kappa)$ and $(T_{h+1}, \tau_{h+1}) = (\bar{y}X, \bar{y}\xi)$ are $(h+1)$-compatible. Moreover, we have

$$A(T_{h+1}, \tau_{h+1}, e) = A(X, \xi, y) \notin C(X, y) = C(T_{h+1}, e),$$
$$A(S_{h+1}, \sigma_{h+1}, s) = A(K, \kappa, ys) \in C(K, ys) = C(S_{h+1}, s)$$

for each $s \in S_{h+1}$. Hence (S_{h+1}, σ_{h+1}) and (T_{h+1}, τ_{h+1}) form an $(h+1)$-critical pair.

The case of $y \in L_1$ is analogous. $\square$

By induction, there are d-templates (S_d, σ_d) and (T_d, τ_d) that form a d-critical pair. Theorem 5 follows by choosing $U = S_d$ and $V = T_d$.

4. ACKNOWLEDGEMENTS

We thank Mika Göös and anonymous reviewers for comments and feedback, and Petteri Kaski, Christoph Lenzen, Joel Rybicki, and Roger Wattenhofer for discussions. This work was supported in part by the Academy of Finland, Grants 132380 and 252018, the Research Funds of the University of Helsinki, and the Finnish Cultural Foundation.

A preprint of this work is available [8]. For presentation slides, see http://www.cs.helsinki.fi/jukka.suomela/mm-lb.

5. REFERENCES

[1] Dana Angluin. Local and global properties in networks of processors. In *Proc. STOC 1980*, pages 82–93. ACM Press, 1980.

[2] Matti Åstrand and Jukka Suomela. Fast distributed approximation algorithms for vertex cover and set cover in anonymous networks. In *Proc. SPAA 2010*, pages 294–302. ACM Press, 2010.

[3] Leonid Barenboim and Michael Elkin. Distributed $(\Delta + 1)$-coloring in linear (in Δ) time. In *Proc. STOC 2009*, pages 111–120. ACM Press, 2009.

[4] Richard Cole and Uzi Vishkin. Deterministic coin tossing with applications to optimal parallel list ranking. *Information and Control*, 70(1):32–53, 1986.

[5] Mika Göös, Juho Hirvonen, and Jukka Suomela. Lower bounds for local approximation. In *Proc. PODC 2012*. ACM Press, 2012.

[6] Michał Hańćkowiak, Michał Karoński, and Alessandro Panconesi. On the distributed complexity of computing maximal matchings. In *Proc. SODA 1998*, pages 219–225. SIAM, 1998.

[7] Michał Hańćkowiak, Michał Karoński, and Alessandro Panconesi. On the distributed complexity of computing maximal matchings. *SIAM J. Discrete Math.*, 15(1):41–57, 2001.

[8] Juho Hirvonen and Jukka Suomela. Distributed maximal matching: greedy is optimal, 2011. Manuscript, arXiv:1110.0367 [cs.DC].

[9] Fabian Kuhn. Weak graph colorings: Distributed algorithms and applications. In *Proc. SPAA 2009*, pages 138–144. ACM Press, 2009.

[10] Fabian Kuhn, Thomas Moscibroda, and Roger Wattenhofer. What cannot be computed locally! In *Proc. PODC 2004*, pages 300–309. ACM Press, 2004.

[11] Fabian Kuhn, Thomas Moscibroda, and Roger Wattenhofer. The price of being near-sighted. In *Proc. SODA 2006*, pages 980–989. ACM Press, 2006.

[12] Fabian Kuhn, Thomas Moscibroda, and Roger Wattenhofer. Local computation: Lower and upper bounds, 2010. Manuscript, arXiv:1011.5470 [cs.DC].

[13] Fabian Kuhn and Roger Wattenhofer. On the complexity of distributed graph coloring. In *Proc. PODC 2006*, pages 7–15. ACM Press, 2006.

[14] Nathan Linial. Locality in distributed graph algorithms. *SIAM J. Comput.*, 21(1):193–201, 1992.

[15] Alessandro Panconesi and Romeo Rizzi. Some simple distributed algorithms for sparse networks. *Distrib. Comput.*, 14(2):97–100, 2001.

[16] Jukka Suomela. Survey of local algorithms. *ACM Comput. Surveys*. To appear.

[17] Masafumi Yamashita and Tsunehiko Kameda. Computing on anonymous networks: Part I—characterizing the solvable cases. *IEEE Trans. Parallel Distrib. Systems*, 7(1):69–89, 1996.

[18] Masafumi Yamashita and Tsunehiko Kameda. Leader election problem on networks in which processor identity numbers are not distinct. *IEEE Trans. Parallel Distrib. Systems*, 10(9):878–887, 1999.

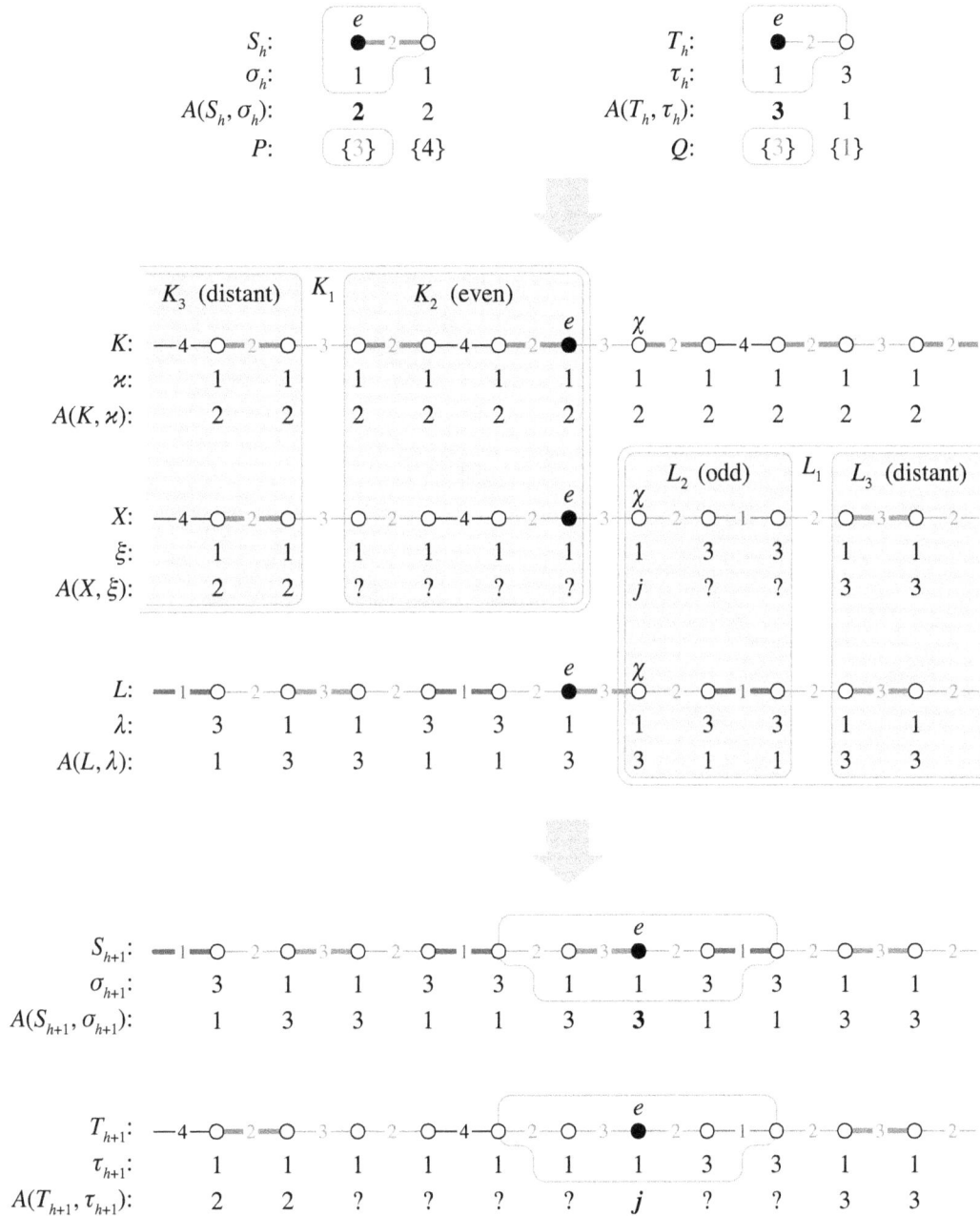

Figure 7: Inductive step. In this example, $h = 1$ and $\chi = 3$. We assume that $j \notin \{2,3\}$, and thus we can choose $y = \chi$ in Lemma 12.

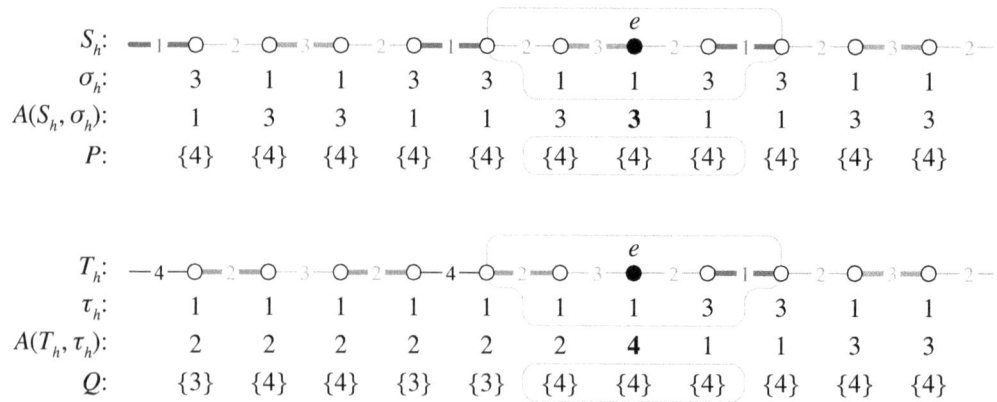

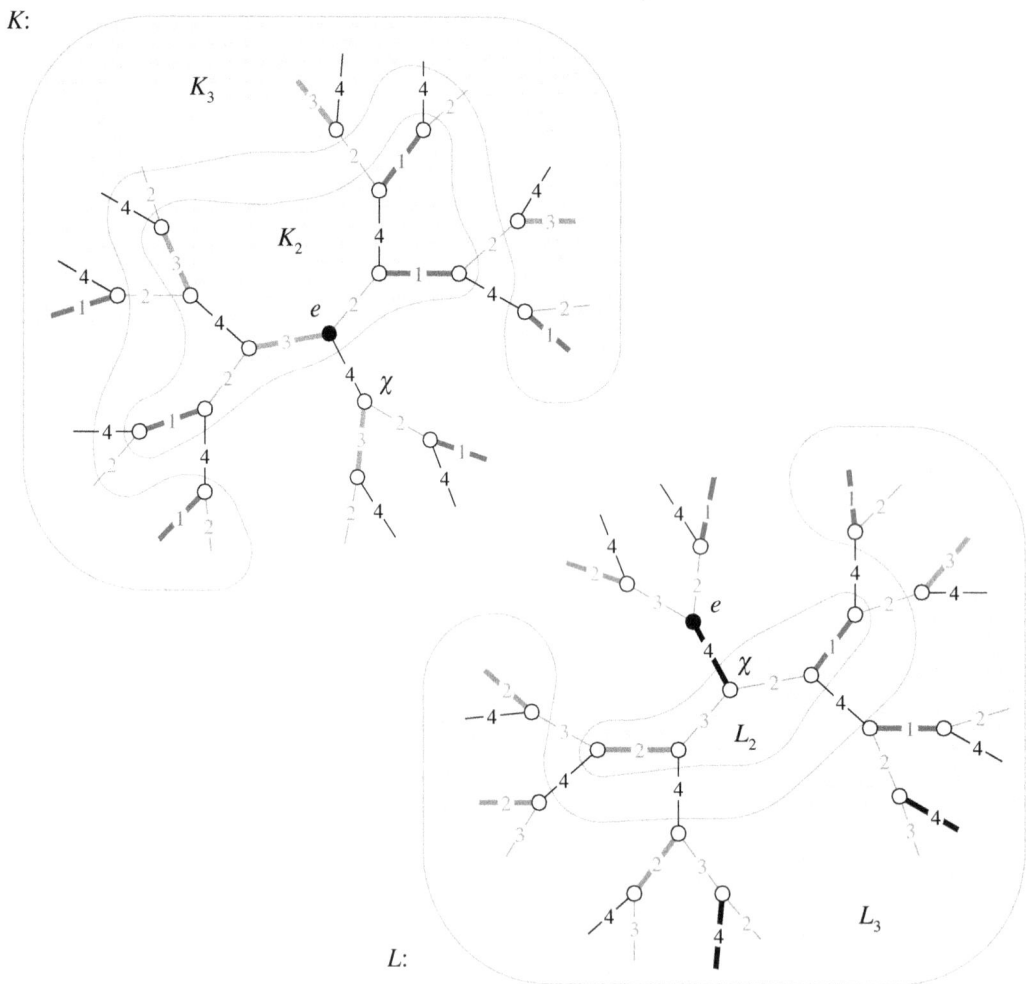

Figure 8: Inductive step. In this example, $h = 2$ and $\chi = 4$.

Lower Bounds for Local Approximation

Mika Göös
mika.goos@cs.helsinki.fi

Juho Hirvonen
juho.hirvonen@cs.helsinki.fi

Jukka Suomela
jukka.suomela@cs.helsinki.fi

Helsinki Institute for Information Technology HIIT, Department of Computer Science, University of Helsinki
P.O. Box 68, FI-00014 University of Helsinki, Finland

ABSTRACT

In the study of deterministic distributed algorithms it is commonly assumed that each node has a unique $O(\log n)$-bit identifier. We prove that for a general class of graph problems, local algorithms (constant-time distributed algorithms) do not need such identifiers: a port numbering and orientation is sufficient.

Our result holds for so-called *simple* PO-*checkable graph optimisation problems*; this includes many classical packing and covering problems such as vertex covers, edge covers, matchings, independent sets, dominating sets, and edge dominating sets. We focus on the case of bounded-degree graphs and show that if a local algorithm finds a constant-factor approximation of a simple PO-checkable graph problem with the help of unique identifiers, then the same approximation ratio can be achieved on anonymous networks.

As a corollary of our result and by prior work, we derive a tight lower bound on the local approximability of the *minimum edge dominating set problem*.

Our main technical tool is an algebraic construction of *homogeneously ordered graphs*: We say that a graph is (α, r)-homogeneous if its nodes are linearly ordered so that an α fraction of nodes have pairwise isomorphic radius-r neighbourhoods. We show that there exists a finite (α, r)-homogeneous $2k$-regular graph of girth at least g for any $\alpha < 1$ and any r, k, and g.

Categories and Subject Descriptors

C.2.4 [**Computer-Communication Networks**]: Distributed Systems; F.1.3 [**Computation by Abstract Devices**]: Complexity Measures and Classes; F.2.2 [**Analysis of Algorithms and Problem Complexity**]: Nonnumerical Algorithms and Problems—*computations on discrete structures*

Keywords

approximation algorithms, deterministic distributed algorithms, edge dominating set, local algorithms, unique identifiers

1. INTRODUCTION

In this work, we study deterministic distributed algorithms under three different assumptions; see Figure 1a for illustrations.

(ID) *Networks with unique identifiers.* Each node is given a unique $O(\log n)$-bit label.

(OI) *Order-invariant algorithms.* There is a linear order on nodes.

Equivalently, the nodes have unique labels, but the output of an algorithm is not allowed to change if we relabel the nodes while preserving the relative order of the labels.

(PO) *Anonymous networks with a port numbering and orientation.* For each node, there is a linear order on the incident edges, and for each edge, there is a linear order on the incident nodes.

Equivalently, a node of degree d can refer to its neighbours by integers $1, 2, \ldots, d$, and each edge is oriented so that the endpoints know which of them is the head and which is the tail.

While unique identifiers are often useful, we will show that they are seldom needed in local algorithms (constant-time distributed algorithms): there is a general class of graph problems such that local algorithms in PO are able to produce as good approximations as local algorithms in OI or ID.

1.1 Graph Problems

We study graph problems that are related to the structure of an unknown communication network. Each node in the network is a computer; each computer receives a *local input*, it can exchange messages with adjacent nodes, and eventually it has to produce a *local output*. The local outputs constitute a solution of a graph problem—for example, if we study the dominating set problem, each node produces one bit of local output, indicating whether it is part of the dominating set. The *running time* of an algorithm is the number of synchronous communication rounds.

From this perspective, the models ID, OI, and PO are easy to separate. Consider, for example, the problem of finding a maximal independent set in an n-cycle. In ID model the problem can be solved in $\Theta(\log^* n)$ rounds [6, 18], while in OI model we need $\Theta(n)$ rounds, and the problem is not solvable at all in PO, as we cannot break symmetry—see Figure 1b. Hence ID is strictly stronger than OI, which is strictly stronger than PO.

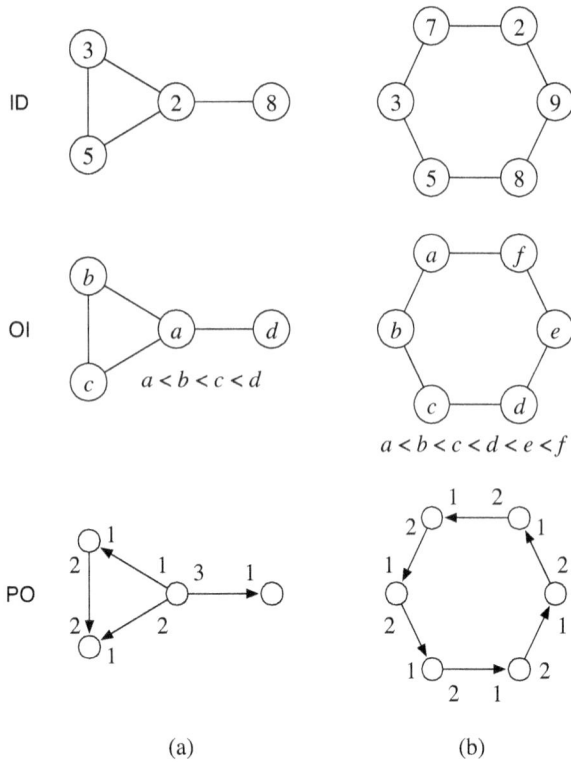

Figure 1: **(a) Three models of distributed computing. (b) In model ID, the numerical identifiers break symmetry everywhere—for example, in a cycle, a maximal independent set can be found in $O(\log^* n)$ rounds. In model OI, we can have a cycle with only one "seam", and in model PO we can have a completely symmetric cycle.**

1.2 Local Algorithms

In this work we focus on *local algorithms*, i.e., distributed algorithms that run in a constant number of synchronous communication rounds, independently of the number of nodes in the network [20,23]. The above example separating ID, OI, and PO no longer applies, and there has been a conspicuous lack of *natural* graph problems that would separate ID, OI, and PO from the perspective of local algorithms.

Indeed, there are results that show that many problems that can be solved with a local algorithm in ID also admit a local algorithm in OI or PO. For example, the seminal paper by Naor and Stockmeyer [20] studies so-called *locally checkable labellings*, or LCL problems for short—these include problems such as graph colouring and maximal matchings on bounded-degree graphs. The authors show that ID and OI are indeed equally expressive among LCL problems. The followup work by Mayer, Naor, and Stockmeyer [19] hints of a stronger property:

(i) *Weak 2-colouring* is an LCL problem that can be solved with a local algorithm in ID model [20]. It turns out that the same problem can be solved in PO model as well [19].

Granted, contrived counterexamples do exist: there are LCL problems that are solvable in OI but not in PO. However, most of the classical graph problems that are studied in the

field of distributed computing are *optimisation problems*, not LCL problems.

1.3 Local Approximation

In what follows, we will focus on graph problems in the case of *bounded-degree graphs*; that is, there is a known constant Δ such that the degree of any node in any graph that we may encounter is at most Δ. Parity often matters; hence we also define $\Delta' = 2\lfloor \Delta/2 \rfloor$.

In this setting, the best possible approximation ratios are surprisingly similar in ID, OI, and PO. The following hold for any given $\Delta \geq 2$ and $\epsilon > 0$:

(ii) *Minimum vertex cover* can be approximated to within factor 2 in each of these models [3,5]. This is tight: $(2 - \epsilon)$-approximation is not possible in any of these models [9,17,23].

(iii) *Minimum edge cover* can be approximated to within factor 2 in each of these models [23]. This is tight: $(2 - \epsilon)$-approximation is not possible in any of these models [9,17,23].

(iv) *Minimum dominating set* can be approximated to within factor $\Delta' + 1$ in each of these models [4]. This is tight: $(\Delta' + 1 - \epsilon)$-approximation is not possible in any of these models [9,17,23].

(v) *Maximum independent set* cannot be approximated to within any constant factor in any of these models [9,17].

(vi) *Maximum matching* cannot be approximated to within any constant factor in any of these models [9,17].

This phenomenon has not been fully understood: while there are many problems with identical approximability results for ID, OI, and PO, it has not been known whether these are examples of a more general principle or merely isolated coincidences. In fact, for some problems, tight approximability results have been lacking for ID and OI, even though tight results are known for PO:

(vii) *Minimum edge dominating set* can be approximated to within factor $4 - 2/\Delta'$ in each of these models [22]. This is tight for PO but only near-tight for ID and OI: $(4 - 2/\Delta' - \epsilon)$-approximation is not possible in PO [22], and $(3 - \epsilon)$-approximation is not possible in ID and OI [9,17,23].

In this work we prove a theorem unifying all of the above observations—they are indeed examples of a general principle. As a simple application of our result, we settle the local approximability of the minimum edge dominating set problem by proving a tight lower bound in ID and OI.

1.4 Main Result

A *simple graph problem* Π is an optimisation problem in which a feasible solution is a subset of nodes or a subset of edges, and the goal is to either minimise or maximise the size of a feasible solution. We say that Π is a PO-*checkable graph problem* if there is a local PO-algorithm A that recognises a feasible solution. That is, $\mathsf{A}(\mathcal{G}, X, v) = 1$ for all nodes $v \in V(\mathcal{G})$ if X is a feasible solution of problem Π in graph $\mathcal{G}$, and $\mathsf{A}(\mathcal{G}, X, v) = 0$ for some node $v \in V(\mathcal{G})$ otherwise—here

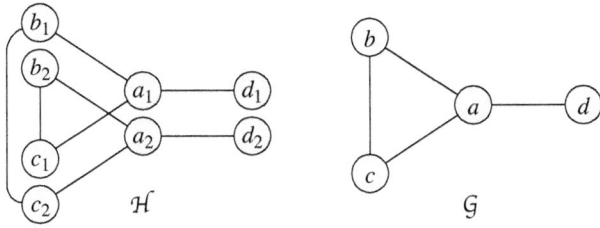

Figure 2: Graph $\mathcal{H}$ is a lift of $\mathcal{G}$. The covering map $\varphi\colon V(\mathcal{H}) \to V(\mathcal{G})$ maps $a_i \mapsto a$, $b_i \mapsto b$, $c_i \mapsto c$, and $d_i \mapsto d$ for each $i = 1, 2$. The fibre of $a \in V(\mathcal{G})$ is $\{a_1, a_2\} \subseteq V(\mathcal{H})$; all fibres have the same size.

$A(\mathcal{G}, X, v)$ is the output of a node v if we run algorithm A on graph $\mathcal{G}$ and the local inputs form an encoding of X.

Let $\varphi\colon V(\mathcal{H}) \to V(\mathcal{G})$ be a surjective graph homomorphism from graph $\mathcal{H}$ to graph $\mathcal{G}$. If φ preserves vertex degrees, i.e., $\deg_{\mathcal{H}}(u) = \deg_{\mathcal{G}}(\varphi(u))$, then φ is called a *covering map*, and $\mathcal{H}$ is said to be a *lift* of $\mathcal{G}$. The *fibre* of $u \in V(\mathcal{G})$ is the set $\varphi^{-1}(u)$ of pre-images of u. We usually consider n-lifts that have fibres of the same cardinality n. It is a basic fact that a connected lift $\mathcal{H}$ of $\mathcal{G}$ is an n-lift for some n. See Figure 2 for an illustration.

Let $\mathcal{F}$ be a family of graphs. We say that $\mathcal{F}$ is *closed under lifts* if $\mathcal{G} \in \mathcal{F}$ implies $\mathcal{H} \in \mathcal{F}$ for all lifts $\mathcal{H}$ of $\mathcal{G}$. A family is *closed under connected lifts* if $\mathcal{G} \in \mathcal{F}$ implies $\mathcal{H} \in \mathcal{F}$ whenever $\mathcal{H}$ and $\mathcal{G}$ are connected graphs and $\mathcal{H}$ is a lift of $\mathcal{G}$.

Now we are ready to state our main theorem.

THEOREM 1 (MAIN THEOREM). *Let Π be a simple PO-checkable graph problem. Assume one of the following:*

– *General version: $\mathcal{F}$ is a family of bounded degree graphs, and it is closed under lifts.*

– *Connected version: $\mathcal{F}$ is a family of connected bounded degree graphs, it does not contain any trees, and it is closed under connected lifts.*

If there is a local ID-algorithm A that finds an α-approximation of Π in $\mathcal{F}$, then there is a local PO-algorithm B that finds an α-approximation of Π in $\mathcal{F}$.

While the definitions are somewhat technical, it is easy to verify that the result is widely applicable:

(a) Vertex covers, edge covers, matchings, independent sets, dominating sets, and edge dominating sets are simple PO-checkable graph problems.

(b) Bounded-degree graphs, regular graphs, and cyclic graphs are closed under lifts.

(c) Connected bounded-degree graphs, connected regular graphs, and connected cyclic graphs are closed under connected lifts.

1.5 An Application

The above result provides us with a powerful tool for proving lower-bound results: we can easily transfer negative results from PO to OI and ID. We demonstrate this strength by deriving a new lower bound result for the minimum edge dominating set problem.

THEOREM 2. *Let $\Delta \geq 2$, and let A be a local ID-algorithm that finds an α-approximation of a minimum edge dominating set on connected graphs of maximum degree Δ. Then $\alpha \geq \alpha_0$, where $\alpha_0 = 4 - 2/\Delta'$ and $\Delta' = 2\lfloor \Delta/2 \rfloor$. This is tight: there is a local ID-algorithm that finds an α_0-approximation.*

PROOF. By prior work [22], it is known that there is a connected Δ'-regular graph $\mathcal{G}_0$ such that the approximation factor of any local PO-algorithm on $\mathcal{G}_0$ is at least α_0. Let $\mathcal{F}_0$ consist of all connected lifts of $\mathcal{G}_0$, and let $\mathcal{F}$ consist of all connected graphs of degree at most Δ. We make the following observations.

(a) We have $\mathcal{F}_0 \subseteq \mathcal{F}$; by assumption, A finds an α-approximation in $\mathcal{F}_0$.

(b) Family $\mathcal{F}_0$ consists of connected graphs of degree at most Δ. As $\mathcal{G}_0$ is not a tree, family $\mathcal{F}_0$ does not contain any trees. Moreover, $\mathcal{F}_0$ is by construction closed under connected lifts. Hence we can apply the connected version of the main theorem: there is a local PO-algorithm B that finds an α-approximation in $\mathcal{F}_0$.

(c) However, $\mathcal{G}_0 \in \mathcal{F}_0$, and hence $\alpha \geq \alpha_0$.

The matching upper bound is presented in prior work [22]. □

1.6 Overview

Informally, our proof of the main theorem is structured as follows.

(a) Fix a graph problem Π, a graph family $\mathcal{F}$, and an ID-algorithm A as in the statement of Theorem 1. Let r be the running time of ID-algorithm A.

(b) Let $\mathcal{G} \in \mathcal{F}$ be a graph with a port numbering and orientation.

(c) Section 3.2: We construct a certain lift $\mathcal{G}_\epsilon \in \mathcal{F}$ of $\mathcal{G}$. Graph $\mathcal{G}_\epsilon$ inherits the port numbering and the orientation from $\mathcal{G}$.

(d) Section 4.1: We show that there exists a linear order $<_\epsilon$ on the nodes of $\mathcal{G}_\epsilon$ that gives virtually no new information in comparison with the port numbering and orientation. If we have an OI-algorithm A' with running time r, then we can simulate A' with a PO-algorithm B' almost perfectly on $\mathcal{G}_\epsilon$: the outputs of A' and B' agree for a $(1 - \epsilon)$ fraction of nodes. We deduce that the approximation ratio of A' on $\mathcal{F}$ cannot be better than the approximation ratio of B' on $\mathcal{F}$.

(e) Section 4.2: We apply Ramsey's theorem to show that the unique identifiers do not help, either. We can construct a PO-algorithm B that simulates A in the following sense: there exists an assignment of unique identifiers on a lift $\mathcal{H} \in \mathcal{F}$ of $\mathcal{G}_\epsilon$ such that the outputs of A and B agree for a $(1 - \epsilon)$ fraction of nodes. We deduce that the approximation ratio of A on $\mathcal{F}$ cannot be better than the approximation ratio of B on $\mathcal{F}$.

Now if graph $\mathcal{G}$ was a directed cycle, the construction would be standard; see, e.g., Czygrinow et al. [9]. In particular, $\mathcal{G}_\epsilon$ and $\mathcal{H}$ would simply be long cycles, and $<_\epsilon$ would order the nodes along the cycle—there would be only one "seam" in $(\mathcal{G}_\epsilon, <_\epsilon)$ that could potentially help A' in comparison with B', and only an ϵ fraction of nodes are near the seam.

However, the case of a general $\mathcal{G}$ is more challenging. Our main technical tool is the construction of so-called homogeneous graphs; see Section 3.1. Homogeneous graphs are regular graphs with a linear order that is useless from the perspective of OI-algorithms: for a $(1 - \epsilon)$ fraction of nodes, the local neighbourhoods are isomorphic. Homogeneous graphs trivially exist; however, our proof calls for homogeneous graph of an arbitrarily high degree and an arbitrarily large girth (i.e., there are no short cycles—the graph is locally tree-like). In Section 5 we use an algebraic construction to prove that such graphs exist.

1.7 Discussion

In the field of distributed algorithms, the running time of an algorithm is typically analysed in terms of two parameters: n, the number of nodes in the graph, and Δ, the maximum degree of the graph. In our work, we assumed that Δ is a constant—put otherwise, our work applies to algorithms that have a running time independent of n but arbitrarily high as a function of Δ. The work by Kuhn et al. [13–15] studies the dependence on Δ more closely: their lower bounds on approximation ratios apply to algorithms that have, for example, a running time sublogarithmic in Δ.

While our result is very widely applicable, certain extensions have been left for future work. One example is the case of planar graphs [9], [16, §13]. The family of planar graphs is not closed under lifts, and hence Theorem 1 does not apply. Another direction that we do not discuss at all is the case of randomised algorithms; if each node has access to a stream of random bits, the distinction between ID, OI, and PO essentially vanishes, as the random bits can be used to generate unique identifiers w.h.p.

2. THREE MODELS OF DISTRIBUTED COMPUTING

In this section we make precise the notion of a *local algorithm* in each of the models ID, OI and PO. First, we discuss the properties common to all the models.

We start by fixing a graph family $\mathcal{F}$ where every $\mathcal{G} = (V(\mathcal{G}), E(\mathcal{G})) \in \mathcal{F}$ has maximum degree at most $\Delta \in \mathbb{N}$. We consider algorithms A that operate on graphs in $\mathcal{F}$; the properties of A (e.g., its running time) are allowed to depend on the family $\mathcal{F}$ (and, hence, on Δ). We denote by $\mathsf{A}(\mathcal{G}, u) \in \Omega$ the output of A on a node $u \in V(\mathcal{G})$. Here, Ω is a finite set of possible outputs of A in $\mathcal{F}$. If the solutions to Π are sets of vertices, we shall have $\Omega = \{0, 1\}$ so that the solution produced by A on $\mathcal{G}$, denoted $\mathsf{A}(\mathcal{G})$, is the set of nodes u with $\mathsf{A}(\mathcal{G}, u) = 1$. Similarly, if the solutions to Π are sets of edges, we shall have $\Omega = \{0, 1\}^{\Delta}$ so that the ith component of the vector $\mathsf{A}(\mathcal{G}, u)$ indicates whether the ith edge incident to u is included in the solution $\mathsf{A}(\mathcal{G})$—in each of the models a node will have a natural ordering of its incident edges.

Let $r \in \mathbb{N}$ denote the constant running time of A in $\mathcal{F}$. This means that a node u can only receive messages from nodes within distance r in $\mathcal{G}$, i.e., from nodes in the radius-r neighbourhood

$$B_{\mathcal{G}}(u, r) = \big\{ v \in V(\mathcal{G}) : \mathrm{dist}_{\mathcal{G}}(u, v) \le r \big\}.$$

Let $\tau(\mathcal{G}, u)$ denote the structure $(\mathcal{G}, u)$ restricted to the vertices $B_{\mathcal{G}}(u, r)$, i.e., in symbols, $\tau(\mathcal{G}, u) = (\mathcal{G}, u) \restriction B_{\mathcal{G}}(u, r)$. Then $\mathsf{A}(\mathcal{G}, u)$ is a function of the data $\tau(\mathcal{G}, u)$ in that

$$\mathsf{A}(\mathcal{G}, u) = \mathsf{A}(\tau(\mathcal{G}, u)).$$

The models ID, OI and PO impose further restrictions on this function.

2.1 Model ID

Local ID-algorithms are not restricted in any additional way. We follow the convention that the vertices have unique $O(\log n)$-bit labels, i.e., an instance $\mathcal{G} \in \mathcal{F}$ of order $n = |V(\mathcal{G})|$ has $V(\mathcal{G}) \subseteq \{1, 2, \ldots, s(n)\}$ where $s(n)$ is some fixed polynomial function of n. Our presentation assumes $s(n) = \omega(n)$, even though this assumption can often be relaxed as we discuss in Remark 1.

2.2 Model OI

A local OI-algorithm A does not directly use unique vertex identifiers but only their relative *order*. To make this notion explicit, let the vertices of $\mathcal{G} \in \mathcal{F}$ be linearly ordered by $<$, and call $(\mathcal{G}, <)$ an *ordered graph*. Denote by $\tau(\mathcal{G}, <, u)$ the restriction of the structure $(\mathcal{G}, <, u)$ to the r-neighbourhood $B_{\mathcal{G}}(u, r)$, i.e., in symbols,

$$\tau(\mathcal{G}, <, u) = (\mathcal{G}, <, u) \restriction B_{\mathcal{G}}(u, r).$$

Then, the output $\mathsf{A}(\mathcal{G}, <, u)$ depends only on the *isomorphism type* of $\tau(\mathcal{G}, <, u)$, so that if $\tau(\mathcal{G}, <, u) \simeq \tau(\mathcal{G}', <', u')$ then $\mathsf{A}(\mathcal{G}, <, u) = \mathsf{A}(\mathcal{G}', <', u')$.

2.3 Model PO

In the PO model the nodes are considered anonymous and only the following node specific structure is available: a node can communicate with its neighbours through ports numbered $1, 2, \ldots, \deg(u)$, and each communication link has an orientation.

2.3.1 Edge-Labelled Digraphs

To model the above, we consider *L-edge-labelled directed graphs* (or *L-digraphs*, for short) $\mathcal{G} = (V(\mathcal{G}), E(\mathcal{G}), \ell_{\mathcal{G}})$, where the edges $E(\mathcal{G}) \subseteq V(\mathcal{G}) \times V(\mathcal{G})$ are directed and each edge $e \in E(\mathcal{G})$ carries a label $\ell_{\mathcal{G}}(e) \in L$. We restrict our considerations to *proper* labellings $\ell_{\mathcal{G}} : E(\mathcal{G}) \to L$ that for each $u \in V(\mathcal{G})$ assign the incoming edges $(v, u) \in E(\mathcal{G})$ distinct labels and the outgoing edges $(u, w) \in E(\mathcal{G})$ distinct labels; we allow $\ell_{\mathcal{G}}(v, u) = \ell_{\mathcal{G}}(u, w)$. We refer to the outgoing edges of a node by the labels L and to the incoming edges by the formal letters $L^{-1} = \{\ell^{-1} : \ell \in L\}$. In the context of L-digraphs, covering maps $\varphi : V(\mathcal{H}) \to V(\mathcal{G})$ are required to preserve edge labels so that $\ell_{\mathcal{H}}(u, v) = \ell_{\mathcal{G}}(\varphi(u), \varphi(v))$ for all $(u, v) \in E(\mathcal{H})$.

A port numbering on $\mathcal{G}$ gives rise to a proper labelling $\ell_{\mathcal{G}}(v, u) = (i, j)$, where u is the ith neighbour of v, and v is the jth neighbour of u; see Figure 3. We now fix L to contain every possible edge label that appears when a graph $\mathcal{G} \in \mathcal{F}$ is assigned a port numbering and an orientation. Note that $|L| \le \Delta^2$.

2.3.2 Views

The information available to a PO-algorithm computing on a node $u \in V(\mathcal{G})$ in an L-digraph $\mathcal{G}$ is usually modelled as follows [1, 23, 24]. The *view* of $\mathcal{G}$ from u is an L-edge-labelled rooted (possibly infinite) directed tree $\mathcal{T} = \mathcal{T}(\mathcal{G}, u)$, where the vertices $V(\mathcal{T})$ correspond to all non-backtracking walks on $\mathcal{G}$ starting at u; see Figure 3c. Formally, a k-step walk can be identified with a word of length k in the letters $L \cup L^{-1}$. A non-backtracking walk is a *reduced* word where neither $\ell \ell^{-1}$ nor $\ell^{-1} \ell$ appear. If $w \in V(\mathcal{T})$ is a walk on $\mathcal{G}$ from u to v, we define $\varphi(w) = v$. In particular, the root of $\mathcal{T}$ is the

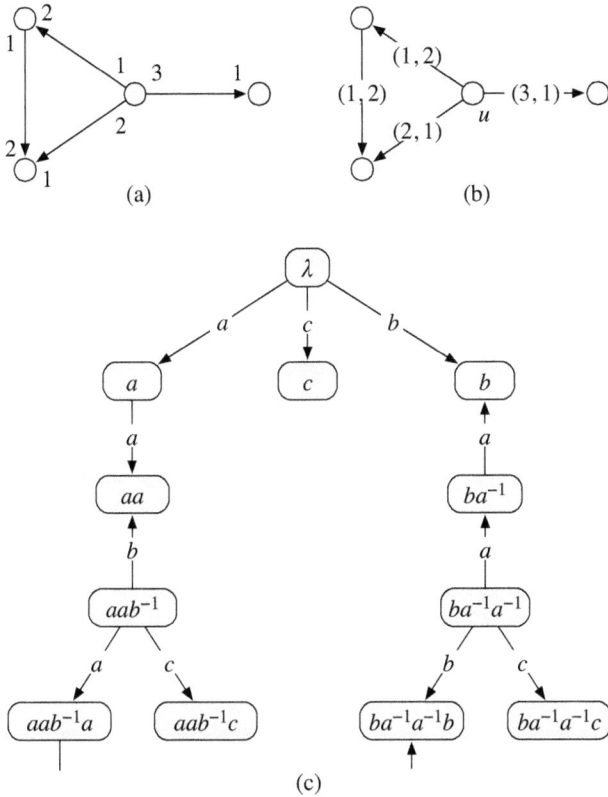

Figure 3: (a) A graph $\mathcal{G}$ with a port numbering and an orientation. (b) A proper labelling $\ell_\mathcal{G}$ that is derived from the port numbering. We have an L-digraph with $L = \{a, b, c\}$, $a = (1,2)$, $b = (2,1)$, and $c = (3,1)$. (c) The view of $\mathcal{G}$ from u is an infinite directed tree $\mathcal{T} = \mathcal{T}(\mathcal{G}, u)$; there is a covering map φ from $\mathcal{T}$ to $\mathcal{G}$ that preserves adjacencies, orientations, and edge labels. For example, $\varphi(\lambda) = \varphi(aab^{-1}) = u$.

empty word λ with $\varphi(\lambda) = u$. The directed edges of $\mathcal{T}$ (and their labels) are defined in such a way that $\varphi \colon V(\mathcal{T}) \to V(\mathcal{G})$ becomes a covering map. Namely, $w \in V(\mathcal{T})$ has an out-neighbour $w\ell$ for every $\ell \in L$ such that $\varphi(w)$ has an outgoing edge labelled ℓ.

2.3.3 *Local* PO-*Algorithms*

The inability of a PO-algorithm B to detect cycles in a graph is characterised by the fact that $\mathsf{B}(\mathcal{G}, u) = \mathsf{B}(\mathcal{T}(\mathcal{G}, u))$. In fact, we *define* a local PO-algorithm as a function B satisfying

$$\mathsf{B}(\mathcal{G}, u) = \mathsf{B}(\tau(\mathcal{T}(\mathcal{G}, u))).$$

An important consequence of this definition is that the output of a PO-algorithm is invariant under lifts, i.e., if $\varphi \colon V(\mathcal{H}) \to V(\mathcal{G})$ is a covering map of L-digraphs, then $\mathsf{B}(\mathcal{H}, u) = \mathsf{B}(\mathcal{G}, \varphi(u))$. The intuition is that nodes in a common fibre are always in the same state during computation as they see the same view.

The following formalism will become useful. Denote by $(\mathcal{T}^*, \lambda)$ the complete L-labelled rooted directed tree of radius r with $V(\mathcal{T}^*)$ consisting of reduced words in the letters $L \cup L^{-1}$, i.e., every non-leaf vertex in $\mathcal{T}^*$ has an outgoing edge and an incoming edge for each $\ell \in L$; see Figure 4. The

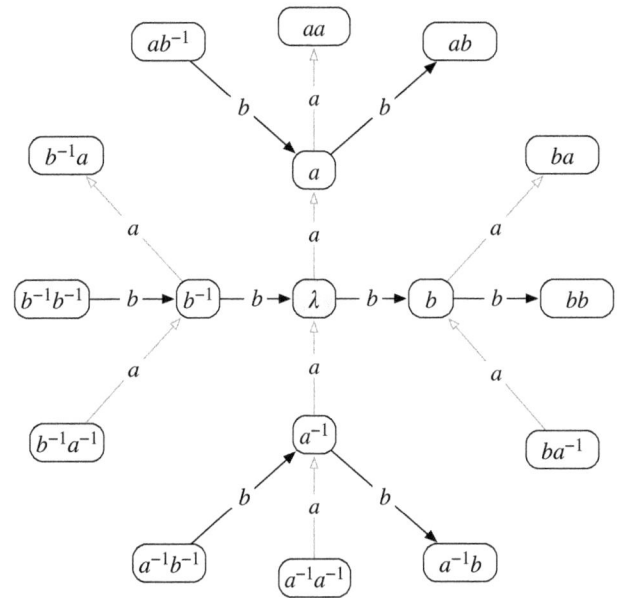

Figure 4: The complete L-labelled rooted directed tree $(\mathcal{T}^*, \lambda)$ of radius $r = 2$, for $L = \{a, b\}$.

output of B on every graph $\mathcal{G} \in \mathcal{F}$ is completely determined after specifying its output on the subtrees of $(\mathcal{T}^*, \lambda)$. More precisely, let $\mathfrak{W}$ consist of vertex sets $W \subseteq V(\mathcal{T}^*)$ such that $(\mathcal{T}^*, \lambda) \upharpoonright W = \tau(\mathcal{T}(\mathcal{G}, u))$ for some $\mathcal{G} \in \mathcal{F}$ and $u \in V(\mathcal{G})$. Then a function $\mathsf{B} \colon \mathfrak{W} \to \Omega$ defines a PO-algorithm by identifying

$$\mathsf{B}((\mathcal{T}^*, \lambda) \upharpoonright W) = \mathsf{B}(W).$$

3. ORDER HOMOGENEITY

In this section we introduce some key concepts that are used in controlling the local symmetry breaking information that is available to a local OI-algorithm.

3.1 Homogeneous Graphs

In the following, we take the *isomorphism type* of an r-neighbourhood $\tau = \tau(\mathcal{G}, <, u)$ to be some canonical representative of the isomorphism class of τ.

Definition 1. Let $(\mathcal{H}, <)$ be an ordered graph. If there is a set $U \subseteq V(\mathcal{H})$ of size $|U| \geq \alpha|\mathcal{H}|$ such that the vertices in U have a common r-neighbourhood isomorphism type τ^*, then we call $(\mathcal{H}, <)$ an (α, r)-*homogeneous graph* and τ^* the associated *homogeneity type* of $\mathcal{H}$.

Homogeneous graphs are useful in fooling OI-algorithms: an (α, r)-homogeneous graph forces any local OI-algorithm to produce the same output in at least an α fraction of the nodes in the input graph. However, there are some limitations to how large α can be: Let $(\mathcal{G}, <)$ be a connected ordered graph on at least two vertices. If u and v are the smallest and the largest vertices of $\mathcal{G}$, their r-neighbourhoods $\tau(\mathcal{G}, <, u)$ and $\tau(\mathcal{G}, <, v)$ cannot be isomorphic even for $r = 1$. Thus, non-trivial finite graphs are not $(1, 1)$-homogeneous. Moreover, an ordered $(2k-1)$-regular graph cannot be $(\alpha, 1)$-homogeneous for any $\alpha > 1/2$; this is the essence of the weak 2-colouring algorithm of Naor and Stockmeyer [20].

Our main technical tool will be a construction of graphs that satisfy the following properties:

(1) $(1 - \epsilon, r)$-homogeneous for any $\epsilon > 0$ and r,
(2) $2k$-regular for any k,
(3) large girth,
(4) finite order.

Note that it is relatively easy to satisfy any three of these properties:

(1), (2), (3) Infinite $2k$-regular trees admit a $(1, r)$-homogeneous linear order; see Figure 5 for an example.

(1), (2), (4) We can construct a sufficiently large k-dimensional toroidal grid graph (cartesian product of k directed cycles) and order the nodes lexicographically coordinate-wise; see Figure 6 for an example. However, these graphs have girth 4 when $k \geq 2$.

(1), (3), (4) A sufficiently large directed cycle is $(1 - \epsilon, r)$-homogeneous and has large girth. However, all the nodes have degree 2.

(2), (3), (4) It is well known that regular graphs of arbitrarily high girth exist.

Our construction satisfies all four properties simultaneously.

THEOREM 3. *Let* $k, r \in \mathbb{N}$. *For every* $\epsilon > 0$ *there exists a finite* $2k$-*regular* $(1 - \epsilon, r)$-*homogeneous connected graph* $(\mathcal{H}_\epsilon, <_\epsilon)$ *of girth larger than* $2r + 1$. *Furthermore, the following properties hold:*

(a) *The homogeneity type* τ^* *of* $(\mathcal{H}_\epsilon, <_\epsilon)$ *does not depend on* ϵ.

(b) *The graph* $\mathcal{H}_\epsilon$ *and the type* τ^* *are* k-*edge-labelled digraphs.*

We defer the proof of Theorem 3 to Section 5. There, it turns out that Cayley graphs of *soluble* groups suit our needs: The homogeneous toroidal graphs mentioned above are Cayley graphs of the abelian groups $\mathbb{Z}_n^k$. Analogously, we use the decomposition of a soluble group into abelian factors to guarantee the presence of a suitable ordering. However, to ensure large girth, the groups we consider must be sufficiently far from being abelian, i.e., they must have large derived length [7].

3.2 Homogeneous Lifts

We fix some notation towards a proof of Theorem 1. By Theorem 3 we let $(\mathcal{H}_\epsilon, <_\epsilon)$, $\epsilon > 0$, be a family of $2|L|$-regular $(1 - \epsilon, r)$-homogeneous connected graphs of girth $> 2r + 1$ interpreted as L-digraphs. The homogeneity type τ^* that is shared by all $\mathcal{H}_\epsilon$ is then of the form $\tau^* = (\mathcal{T}^*, <^*, \lambda)$, where $\mathcal{T}^*$ is the complete L-labelled tree of Section 2.3.

We use the graphs $\mathcal{H}_\epsilon$ to prove the following theorem.

THEOREM 4. *Let* $\mathcal{G}$ *be an* L-*digraph. For every* $\epsilon > 0$ *there exists a lift* $(\mathcal{G}_\epsilon, <_{\mathcal{G}_\epsilon})$ *of* $\mathcal{G}$ *such that a* $(1 - \epsilon)$ *fraction of the vertices in* $(\mathcal{G}_\epsilon, <_{\mathcal{G}_\epsilon})$ *have* r-*neighbourhoods isomorphic to a subtree of* $\tau^* = (\mathcal{T}^*, <^*, \lambda)$. *Moreover, if* $\mathcal{G}$ *is connected,* $\mathcal{G}_\epsilon$ *can be made connected.*

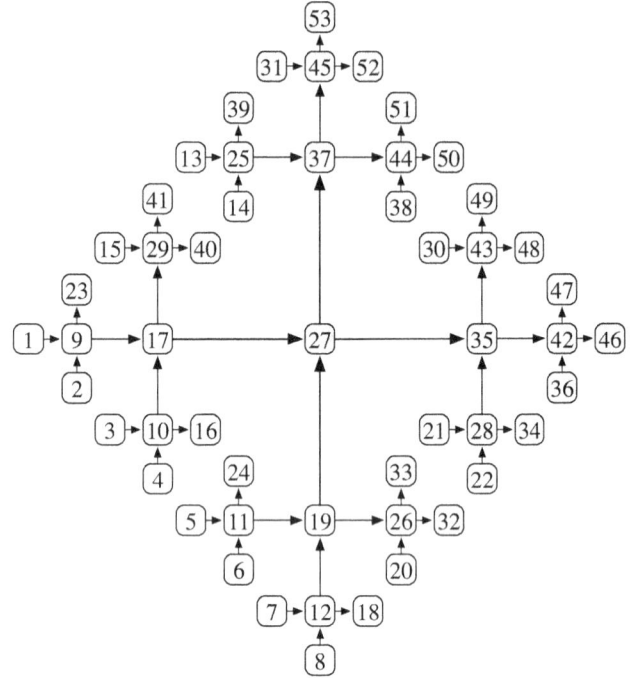

Figure 5: A fragment of a 4-regular infinite ordered tree $(\mathcal{G}, <)$. **The numbering of the nodes indicates a** $(1, r)$-**homogeneous linear order in the neighbourhood of node** 27; **grey nodes are larger than** 27 **and white nodes are smaller than** 27.

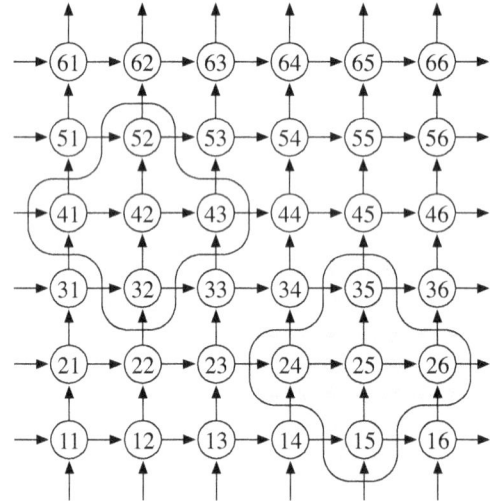

Figure 6: A 4-regular graph $\mathcal{G}$ **constructed as the cartesian product of two directed 6-cycles. We define the ordered graph** $(\mathcal{G}, <)$ **by choosing the linear order** $11 < 12 < \cdots < 16 < 21 < 22 < \cdots < 66$. **The radius-1 neighbourhood of node** 25 **is isomorphic to the radius-1 neighbourhood of node** 42. **In general, there are** 16 **nodes (fraction** 4/9 **of all nodes) that have isomorphic radius-1 neighbourhoods; hence** $(\mathcal{G}, <)$ **is** $(4/9, 1)$-**homogeneous. It is also** $(1/9, 2)$-**homogeneous.**

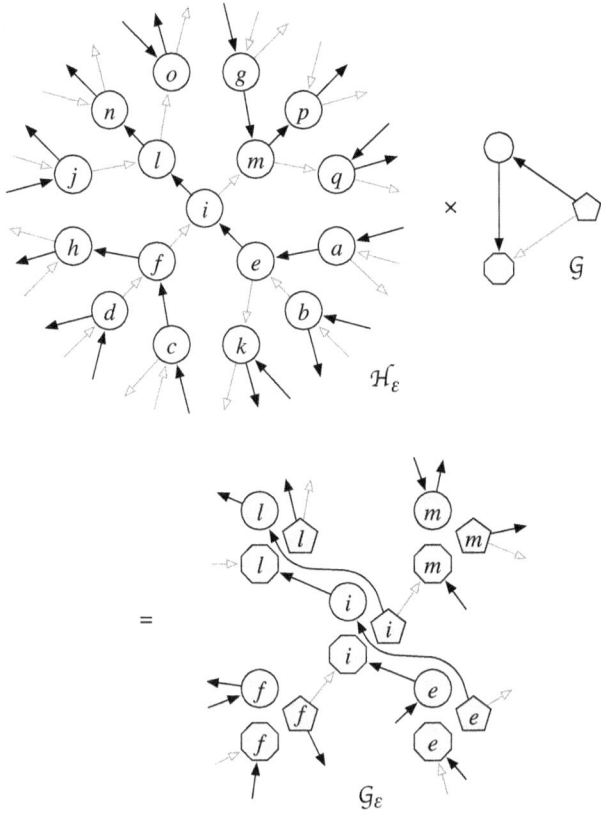

Figure 7: Homogeneous lifts. In this example $L = |2|$, and the two labels are indicated with two different kinds of arrows. Graph $\mathcal{H}_\epsilon$ is a homogeneous $2|L|$-regular ordered L-digraph with a large girth—in particular, the local neighbourhood of a node looks like a tree. Graph $\mathcal{G}$ is an arbitrary L-digraph, not necessarily ordered. Their product $\mathcal{G}_\epsilon$ is a lift of $\mathcal{G}$, but it inherits the desirable properties of $\mathcal{H}_\epsilon$: a high girth and a homogeneous linear order.

PROOF. For brevity, write

$$(\mathcal{C}, <_{\mathcal{C}}) = (\mathcal{G}_\epsilon, <_{\mathcal{G}_\epsilon}), \quad (\mathcal{H}, <_{\mathcal{H}}) = (\mathcal{H}_\epsilon, <_\epsilon).$$

Our goal is to construct $(\mathcal{C}, <_{\mathcal{C}})$ as a certain product of $(\mathcal{H}, <_{\mathcal{H}})$ and $\mathcal{G}$; see Figure 7. This product is a modification of the common lift construction of Angluin and Gardiner [2].

The lift $\mathcal{C}$ is defined on the product set

$$V(\mathcal{C}) = V(\mathcal{H}) \times V(\mathcal{G})$$

by "matching equi-labelled edges": the out-neighbours of $(h, g) \in V(\mathcal{C})$ are vertices $(h', g') \in V(\mathcal{C})$ such that $(h, h') \in E(\mathcal{H})$, $(g, g') \in E(\mathcal{G})$ and $\ell_{\mathcal{H}}(h, h') = \ell_{\mathcal{G}}(g, g')$. An edge $((h, g), (h', g')) \in E(\mathcal{C})$ inherits the common label $\ell_{\mathcal{H}}(h, h') = \ell_{\mathcal{G}}(g, g')$.

The properties of $\mathcal{C}$ are related to the properties of $\mathcal{G}$ and $\mathcal{H}$ as follows.

(a) The projection $\varphi_{\mathcal{G}} : V(\mathcal{C}) \to V(\mathcal{G})$ mapping $(h, g) \mapsto g$ is a covering map. This follows from the fact that each edge incident to $g \in V(\mathcal{G})$ is always matched against an edge of $\mathcal{H}$ in the fibre $V(\mathcal{H}) \times \{g\}$.

(b) The projection $\varphi_{\mathcal{H}} : V(\mathcal{C}) \to V(\mathcal{H})$ mapping $(h, g) \mapsto h$ is not a covering map in case $\mathcal{G}$ is not $2|L|$-regular. In any case $\varphi_{\mathcal{H}}$ is a graph homomorphism, and this implies that $\mathcal{C}$ has girth $> 2r + 1$.

Next, we define a partial order $<_p$ on $V(\mathcal{C})$ as $u <_p v \iff \varphi_{\mathcal{H}}(u) <_{\mathcal{H}} \varphi_{\mathcal{H}}(v)$, for $u, v \in V(\mathcal{C})$. Note that this definition leaves only pairs of vertices in a common $\varphi_{\mathcal{H}}$-fibre incomparable. But since $\mathcal{H}$ has large girth, none of the incomparable pairs appear in an r-neighbourhood of $\mathcal{C}$. We let $<_{\mathcal{C}}$ be any completion of $<_p$ into a linear order. The previous discussion implies that $<_{\mathcal{C}}$ satisfies $\tau(\mathcal{C}, <_{\mathcal{C}}, u) = \tau(\mathcal{C}, <_p, u)$ for all $u \in V(\mathcal{C})$.

Let $U_{\mathcal{H}} \subseteq V(\mathcal{H})$, $|U_{\mathcal{H}}| \geq (1 - \epsilon)|\mathcal{H}|$, be the set of type τ^* vertices in $(\mathcal{H}, <_{\mathcal{H}})$. Set $U_{\mathcal{C}} = \varphi_{\mathcal{H}}^{-1}(U_{\mathcal{H}})$ so that $|U_{\mathcal{C}}| \geq (1-\epsilon)|\mathcal{C}|$. Let $u \in U_{\mathcal{C}}$. By our definition of $<_p$, $\varphi_{\mathcal{H}}$ maps the r-neighbourhood $\tau_u = \tau(\mathcal{C}, <_{\mathcal{C}}, u)$ into $\tau(\mathcal{H}, <_{\mathcal{H}}, \varphi_{\mathcal{H}}(u)) \simeq \tau^*$ while preserving the order. But because τ^* is a tree, $\varphi_{\mathcal{H}}$ must be injective on the vertex set of τ_u so that τ_u is isomorphic to a subtree of τ^* as required.

Finally, suppose $\mathcal{G}$ is connected. Then, by averaging, some connected component of $\mathcal{C}$ will have vertices in $U_{\mathcal{C}}$ with density at least $(1-\epsilon)$. This component satisfies the theorem. $\square$

4. PROOF OF MAIN THEOREM

Next, we use the tools of the previous section to prove Theorem 1. For clarity of exposition we first prove Theorem 1 in the special case where A is an OI-algorithm. The subsequent proof for an ID-algorithm A uses a somewhat technical but well-known Ramsey type argument.

4.1 Proof of Main Theorem for OI-algorithms

We will prove the general and connected versions of Theorem 1 simultaneously; for the proof of the connected version it suffices to consider only connected lifts below. We do not need the assumption that $\mathcal{F}$ does not contain any trees.

Let Π be as in the statement of Theorem 1. Suppose an OI-algorithm A finds an α-approximation of Π in $\mathcal{F}$. We define a PO-algorithm B simply by setting for $W \in \mathfrak{W}$,

$$\mathsf{B}(W) = \mathsf{A}((\mathcal{T}^*, <^*, \lambda) \upharpoonright W).$$

Now, Theorem 4 translates into saying that for every $\mathcal{G} \in \mathcal{F}$ and $\epsilon > 0$ we have that $\mathsf{A}(\mathcal{G}_\epsilon, <_{\mathcal{G}_\epsilon}, u) = \mathsf{B}(\mathcal{G}_\epsilon, u)$ for at least a $(1 - \epsilon)$ fraction of nodes $u \in V(\mathcal{G}_\epsilon)$. The claim that B works as expected follows essentially from this fact as we argue next.

For simplicity, we assume the solutions to Π are sets of vertices so that $\mathsf{A}(\mathcal{G}) \subseteq V(\mathcal{G})$; solutions that are sets of edges are handled similarly.

Fix $\mathcal{G} \in \mathcal{F}$ and let $\varphi_\epsilon : V(\mathcal{G}_\epsilon) \to V(\mathcal{G})$, $\epsilon > 0$, be the associated covering maps.

4.1.1 Feasibility

Let us first show that algorithm B finds a feasible solution of Π on $\mathcal{G}$. Let V be a local PO-algorithm verifying the feasibility of a solution for Π; we may assume V also runs in time r. For $\epsilon > 0$ sufficiently small, each $v \in V(\mathcal{G})$ has a pre-image $v' \in \varphi_\epsilon^{-1}(v)$ such that A and B agree on the vertices $\bigcup_{v \in V(\mathcal{G})} B_{\mathcal{G}_\epsilon}(v', r)$. Thus, V accepts the solution $\mathsf{B}(\mathcal{G}_\epsilon)$ on the vertices v'. But because $\varphi_\epsilon(\{v' : v \in V(\mathcal{G})\}) = V(\mathcal{G})$ it follows that V accepts the solution $\mathsf{B}(\mathcal{G}) = \varphi_\epsilon(\mathsf{B}(\mathcal{G}_\epsilon))$ on every node in $\mathcal{G}$.

4.1.2 Approximation

Now we proceed to show that algorithm B finds an α-approximation of Π on $\mathcal{G}$. We assume Π is a minimisation problem; maximisation problems are handled similarly. Let $X \subseteq V(\mathcal{G})$ and $X_\epsilon \subseteq V(\mathcal{G}_\epsilon)$ be some optimal solutions of Π.

As $\epsilon \to 0$, the solutions $\mathsf{B}(\mathcal{G}_\epsilon)$ and $\mathsf{A}(\mathcal{G}_\epsilon)$ agree on almost all the vertices. Indeed, a simple calculation shows that $|\mathsf{B}(\mathcal{G}_\epsilon)| \leq f(\epsilon) \cdot |\mathsf{A}(\mathcal{G}_\epsilon)|$ for some f with $f(\epsilon) \to 1$ as $\epsilon \to 0$. Furthermore,

$$\frac{|\mathsf{B}(\mathcal{G})|}{|X|} = \frac{|\varphi_\epsilon^{-1}(\mathsf{B}(\mathcal{G}))|}{|\varphi_\epsilon^{-1}(X)|} \leq \frac{|\mathsf{B}(\mathcal{G}_\epsilon)|}{|X_\epsilon|} \leq \frac{f(\epsilon) \cdot |\mathsf{A}(\mathcal{G}_\epsilon)|}{|X_\epsilon|} \leq f(\epsilon)\alpha,$$

where the first equality follows from φ_ϵ being an n-lift, and the first inequality follows from $\varphi_\epsilon^{-1}(\mathsf{B}(\mathcal{G})) = \mathsf{B}(\mathcal{G}_\epsilon)$ and the fact that $\varphi_\epsilon^{-1}(X)$ is a feasible solution so that $|X_\epsilon| \leq |\varphi_\epsilon^{-1}(X)|$. Since the above inequality holds for every $\epsilon > 0$ we must have that $|\mathsf{B}(\mathcal{G})|/|X| \leq \alpha$, as desired.

4.2 Proof of Main Theorem for ID-algorithms

We extend the above proof to the case of local ID-algorithms A by designing "worst-case" vertex identifiers for the instances in $\mathcal{F}$ in order to make A behave similarly to a PO-algorithm on tree neighbourhoods. To do this we use the Ramsey technique of Naor and Stockmeyer [20]; see also Czygrinow et al. [9]. For a reference on Ramsey's theorem see Graham et al. [12].

We use the following notation: if $(X, <_X)$ and $(Y, <_Y)$ are linearly ordered sets with $|X| \leq |Y|$, we write $f \colon (X, <_X) \hookrightarrow (Y, <_Y)$ for the unique order-preserving injection $f \colon X \to Y$ that maps the ith element of X to the ith element of Y. A t-set is a set of size t, and the set of t-subsets of X is denoted $X^{(t)}$.

Write $\Omega^{\mathfrak{W}}$ for the family of functions $\mathfrak{W} \to \Omega$; recall that each $\mathsf{B} \in \Omega^{\mathfrak{W}}$ can be interpreted as a PO-algorithm. Set $k = |\Omega^{\mathfrak{W}}|$ and $t = |\mathcal{T}^*|$. We consider every t-subset $A \in \mathbb{N}^{(t)}$ to be ordered by the usual order $<$ on $\mathbb{N}$. For $W \in \mathfrak{W}$ we let $f_{W,A} \colon (W, <^*) \hookrightarrow (A, <)$ so that the vertex-relabelled tree $f_{W,A}((\mathcal{T}^*, \lambda) \restriction W)$ has the $|W|$ smallest numbers in A as vertices. Define a k-colouring $c \colon \mathbb{N}^{(t)} \to \Omega^{\mathfrak{W}}$ by setting

$$c(A)(W) = \mathsf{A}(f_{W,A}((\mathcal{T}^*, \lambda) \restriction W)).$$

For each $m \geq t$ we can use Ramsey's theorem to obtain a number $R(m) \geq m$, so that for every $R(m)$-set $I \subseteq \mathbb{N}$ there exists an m-subset $J \subseteq I$ such that $J^{(t)}$ is monochromatic under c, i.e., all t-subsets of J have the same colour. In particular, for every interval

$$I(m, i) = [(i - 1)R(m) + 1, iR(m)], \quad i \geq 1,$$

there exist an m-subset $J(m, i) \subseteq I(m, i)$ and a colour (i.e., an algorithm) $\mathsf{B}_{m,i} \in \Omega^{\mathfrak{W}}$ such that $c(A) = \mathsf{B}_{m,i}$ for all t-subsets $A \subseteq J(m, i)$.

This construction has the following property.

PROPOSITION 1. *Suppose $m \geq |\mathcal{G}_\epsilon| + t$. Algorithms A and $\mathsf{B}_{m,i}$ produce the same output on at least a $(1 - \epsilon)$ fraction of the vertices in the vertex-relabelled L-digraph $f_{m,i}(\mathcal{G}_\epsilon)$, where*

$$f_{m,i} \colon (V(\mathcal{G}_\epsilon), <_{\mathcal{G}_\epsilon}) \hookrightarrow (J(m, i), <).$$

PROOF. By Theorem 4, let $U \subseteq V(f_{m,i}(\mathcal{G}_\epsilon))$, $|U| \geq (1 - \epsilon)|\mathcal{G}_\epsilon|$, be the set of vertices u with $\tau(f_{m,i}(\mathcal{G}_\epsilon), <, u)$ isomorphic to a subtree of $\mathcal{T}^*$. In particular, for a fixed $u \in U$ we can choose $W \in \mathfrak{W}$ such that $\tau(f_{m,i}(\mathcal{G}_\epsilon), <, u) \simeq (\mathcal{T}^*, <^*, \lambda) \restriction W$. Now, as m is large, there exists a t-set $A \subseteq J(m, i)$ such that

$\tau(f_{m,i}(\mathcal{G}_\epsilon), u) = f_{W,A}((\mathcal{T}^*, \lambda) \restriction W)$. Thus, A and $\mathsf{B}_{m,i}$ agree on u by the definition of $\mathsf{B}_{m,i}$. $\square$

For every $n \in \mathbb{N}$ some colour appears with density at least $1/k$ (i.e., appears at least n/k times) in the sequence $\mathsf{B}_{m,1}, \mathsf{B}_{m,2}, \ldots, \mathsf{B}_{m,n}$. Hence, let B_m be a colour that appears with density at least $1/k$ among these sequences for infinitely many n. Let B be a colour appearing among the B_m for infinitely many m. We claim B satisfies Theorem 1. In fact, Theorem 1 follows from the following proposition together with the considerations of Section 4.1.

PROPOSITION 2. *For every $\mathcal{G}_\epsilon$ there exists an n-lift $\mathcal{H}$ of $\mathcal{G}_\epsilon$ such that $V(\mathcal{H}) \subseteq \{1, 2, \ldots, s(|\mathcal{H}|)\}$ and $\mathsf{A}(\mathcal{H}, u) = \mathsf{B}(\mathcal{H}, u)$ for a $(1 - \epsilon)$ fraction of nodes $u \in V(\mathcal{H})$. Moreover, if $\mathcal{G}_\epsilon$ is connected and not a tree, $\mathcal{H}$ can be made connected.*

PROOF. Let m be such that $m \geq |\mathcal{G}_\epsilon| + t$ and $\mathsf{B} = \mathsf{B}_m$. For infinitely many n there exists an n-set $I \subseteq [nk]$ of indices such that $\mathsf{B} = \mathsf{B}_{m,i}$ for $i \in I$. Consider the following n-lift of $\mathcal{G}_\epsilon$ obtained by taking disjoint unions:

$$\mathcal{H} = \bigcup_{i \in I} f_{m,i}(\mathcal{G}_\epsilon).$$

Algorithms A and B agree on a $(1 - \epsilon)$ fraction of the nodes in $\mathcal{H}$ by Proposition 1. Furthermore, we have $|\mathcal{H}| = n|\mathcal{G}_\epsilon|$ and $V(\mathcal{H}) \subseteq \{1, 2, \ldots, nkR(m)\}$. We are assuming that $s(n) = \omega(n)$ so choosing a large enough n proves the non-connected version of the claim.

Finally, suppose $\mathcal{G}_\epsilon$ is connected and not a tree. We may assume that there is an edge $e = (u, v) \in E(\mathcal{G}_\epsilon)$ so that $\mathcal{G}_\epsilon$ remains connected when e is removed and that a $(1 - \epsilon)$ fraction of vertices in $\mathcal{G}_\epsilon$ have r-neighbourhoods not containing e that are isomorphic into τ^*. Now $\mathcal{H}$ above is easily modified into a connected graph by redefining the directed matching between the fibre $\{u_i\}_{i \in I}$ of u and the fibre $\{v_i\}_{i \in I}$ of v. Namely, let π be a cyclic permutation on I and set

$$E' = \left(E(\mathcal{H}) \smallsetminus \{(u_i, v_i)\}_{i \in I} \right) \cup \{(u_i, v_{\pi(i)})\}_{i \in I}.$$

Then $\mathcal{H}' = (V(\mathcal{H}), E')$ is easily seen to be a connected n-lift of $\mathcal{G}_\epsilon$ satisfying the claim. $\square$

Remark 1. Above, we assumed that instances $\mathcal{G}$ have node identifiers $V(\mathcal{G}) \subseteq \{1, 2, \ldots, s(n)\}$, $n = |\mathcal{G}|$, for $s(n) = \omega(n)$. By choosing identifiers more economically as in the work of Czygrinow et al. [9] one can show lower bounds for the graph problems of Section 1.3 even when $s(n) = n$.

5. CONSTRUCTION OF HOMOGENEOUS GRAPHS OF LARGE GIRTH

In this section we prove Theorem 3. Our construction uses Cayley graphs of semi-direct products of groups. First, we recall the terminology in use here; for a standard reference on group theory see, e.g., Rotman [21], and for more background information, see the full version of this work [11].

5.1 Semi-Direct Products

Let G and H be groups with H acting on G as a group of automorphisms. We write $h \cdot g$ for the action of $h \in H$ on $g \in G$ so that the mapping $g \mapsto h \cdot g$ is an automorphism of G. The *semi-direct product* $G \rtimes H$ is defined to be the set $G \times H$ with the group operation given by

$$(g, h)(g', h') = (g(h \cdot g'), hh').$$

5.2 Cayley Graphs

The *Cayley graph* $\mathcal{C}(G,S)$ of a group G with respect to a finite set $S \subseteq G$ is an S-digraph on the vertex set G such that each $g \in G$ has an outgoing edge (g, gs) labelled s for each $s \in S$. We require that $1 \notin S$ so as not to have any self-loops. We do not require that S is a generating set for G, i.e., the graph $\mathcal{C}(G,S)$ need not be connected.

If $\varphi \colon H \to G$ is an onto group homomorphism and $S \subseteq H$ is a set such that the mapping φ is injective on $S \cup \{1\}$, then φ naturally induces a covering map of digraphs $\mathcal{C}(H,S)$ and $\mathcal{C}(G, \varphi(S))$.

5.3 Proof of Theorem 3

Let $n \in \mathbb{N}$ be an even number. We consider three families of groups, $\{H_i\}_{i \geq 1}$, $\{W_i\}_{i \geq 1}$, and $\{U_i\}_{i \geq 1}$, that are variations on a common theme. The families are defined iteratively as follows:

$$H_1 = \mathbb{Z}_n, \qquad W_1 = \mathbb{Z}_2, \qquad U_1 = \mathbb{Z},$$
$$H_{i+1} = H_i^2 \rtimes \mathbb{Z}_n, \quad W_{i+1} = W_i^2 \rtimes \mathbb{Z}_2, \quad U_{i+1} = U_i^2 \rtimes \mathbb{Z}.$$

Here, the cyclic group $\mathbb{Z}_n = \{0, 1, \dots, n-1\}$ acts on the direct product $H_i^2 = H_i \times H_i$ by cyclically permuting the coordinates, i.e., the subgroup $2\mathbb{Z}_n \leq \mathbb{Z}_n$ acts trivially and the elements in $1 + 2\mathbb{Z}_n$ swap the two coordinates. The groups $\mathbb{Z}_2$ and $\mathbb{Z}$ act analogously in the definitions of W_i and U_i.

The underlying sets of the groups H_i, W_i, and U_i consist of $d(i)$-tuples of elements in $\mathbb{Z}$, for $d(i) = 2^i - 1$, so that $W_i \subseteq H_i \subseteq U_i$ as sets. Interpreting these tuples as points in $\mathbb{R}^{d(i)}$ we immediately get a natural embedding of every Cayley graph of these groups in $\mathbb{R}^{d(i)}$. This geometric intuition will become useful later.

(a) The groups W_i are i-fold iterated regular wreath products of the cyclic group $\mathbb{Z}_2$. These groups have order $|W_i| = 2^{d(i)}$ and they are sometimes called *symmetric 2-groups*; they are isomorphic to the Sylow 2-subgroups of the symmetric group on 2^i letters [21, p. 176].

(b) The groups U_i are natural extensions of the groups W_i by the free abelian group of rank $d(i)$: the mapping $\varphi_i \colon U_i \to W_i$ that reduces each coordinate modulo 2 is easily seen to be an onto homomorphism with abelian kernel $(2\mathbb{Z})^{d(i)} \simeq \mathbb{Z}^{d(i)}$.

(c) The groups H_i are intermediate between U_i and W_i in that the mapping $\psi_i \colon U_i \to H_i$ that reduces each coordinate modulo n is an onto homomorphism, and the mapping $\varphi_i' \colon H_i \to W_i$ that reduces each coordinate modulo 2 is an onto homomorphism. In summary, the following diagram commutes:

$$
\begin{array}{ccc}
U_i & \xrightarrow{\psi_i} & H_i \\
& \searrow{\scriptstyle\varphi_i} & \downarrow{\scriptstyle\varphi_i'} \\
& & W_i
\end{array}
$$

Our goal will be to construct a suitable Cayley graph $\mathcal{H}$ of some H_i. We will use the groups W_i to ensure $\mathcal{H}$ has large girth, whereas the groups U_i will guarantee that $\mathcal{H}$ has an almost-everywhere homogeneous linear ordering.

5.3.1 Girth

Gamburd et al. [10] study the girth of random Cayley graphs and prove, in particular, that a random k-subset of W_i generates a Cayley graph of large girth with high probability when $i \gg k$ is large. We only need the following weaker version of their result [10, Theorem 6]; see the full version of this work [11] for an alternative, constructive proof.

THEOREM 5 (GAMBURD ET AL.). *Let $k, r \in \mathbb{N}$. There exists an $i \in \mathbb{N}$ and a set $S \subseteq W_i$, $|S| = k$, such that the girth of the Cayley graph $\mathcal{C}(W_i, S)$ is larger than $2r + 1$.*

Fix a large enough $j \in \mathbb{N}$ and a k-set $S \subseteq W_j$ so that $\mathcal{C}(W_j, S)$ has a girth larger than $2r + 1$. Henceforth, we omit the subscript j and write H, W, U, φ, ψ and d in place of H_j, W_j, U_j, φ_j, ψ_j and $d(j)$. Interpreting S as a set of elements of H and U (so that $\varphi(S) = \psi(S) = S$) we construct the Cayley graphs

$$\mathcal{H} = \mathcal{C}(H, S), \quad \mathcal{W} = \mathcal{C}(W, S), \quad \text{and} \quad \mathcal{U} = \mathcal{C}(U, S).$$

As each of these graphs is a lift of $\mathcal{W}$, none have cycles of length at most $2r + 1$ and their r-neighbourhoods are trees.

5.3.2 Linear Order

Next, we introduce a *left-invariant* linear order $<$ on U satisfying

$$u < v \implies wu < wv, \qquad \text{for all } u, v, w \in U.$$

Such a relation can be defined by specifying a *positive cone* $P \subseteq U$ of elements that are greater than the identity $1 = 1_U$ so that

$$u < v \iff 1 < u^{-1}v \iff u^{-1}v \in P.$$

A relation $<$ defined this way is automatically left-invariant; it is transitive iff $u, v \in P$ implies $uv \in P$; and every pair $u \neq v$ is comparable iff for all $w \neq 1$, either $w \in P$ or $w^{-1} \in P$. The existence of a P satisfying these conditions follows from the fact that U is a torsion-free soluble group (e.g., [8]), but it is easy enough to verify that setting

$$P = \big\{ (u_1, u_2, \dots, u_i, 0, 0, \dots, 0) \in U : \\ 1 \leq i \leq d \text{ and } u_i > 0 \big\} \tag{1}$$

satisfies the required conditions above.

Because U acts (by multiplication on the left) on $\mathcal{U}$ as a vertex-transitive group of graph automorphisms, it follows that the structures $(\mathcal{U}, <, u)$, $u \in U$, are pairwise isomorphic. A fortiori, the r-neighbourhoods $\tau(\mathcal{U}, <, u)$, $u \in U$, are all pairwise isomorphic. Let τ^* be this common r-neighbourhood isomorphism type.

5.3.3 Transferring the Linear Order on U to $\mathcal{H}$

Let $V(\mathcal{H})$ be ordered by restricting the order $<$ on U to the set $V(\mathcal{H}) = \mathbb{Z}_n^d$ underlying the group H. Note that $<$ is not a left-invariant order on H (indeed, no non-trivial finite group can be left-invariantly ordered). Nevertheless, we will argue that, as $n \to \infty$, almost all $u \in V(\mathcal{H})$ have r-neighbourhoods of type τ^*.

The neighbours of a vertex $u \in V(\mathcal{U})$ are elements us where

$$s \in S \cup S^{-1} \subseteq [-1, 1]^d.$$

The right multiplication action of $s \in S \cup S^{-1}$ on u can be described in two steps as follows: First, the coordinates of

s are permuted (as determined by u) to obtain a vector s'. Then, us is given as the standard addition of the vectors u and s' in $\mathbb{Z}^d \subseteq \mathbb{R}^d$. Hence, $us \in u + [-1, 1]^d$, and moreover,

$$B_{\mathcal{U}}(u, r) \subseteq u + [-r, r]^d. \qquad (2)$$

This means that vertices close to u in the graph $\mathcal{U}$ are also close in the associated geometric $\mathbb{R}^d$-embedding.

Consider the set of inner nodes $I = [r, (n-1) - r]^d$. Let $u \in I$. By (2), the vertex set $B_{\mathcal{U}}(u, r)$ is contained in $\mathbb{Z}_n^d$. This implies that the cover map ψ is the identity on $B_{\mathcal{U}}(u, r)$ and consequently the r-neighbourhood $\tau(\mathcal{H}, <, u)$ *contains* the ordered tree $\tau(\mathcal{U}, <, u) \simeq \tau^*$. If $\tau(\mathcal{H}, <, u)$ had any additional edges to those of $\tau(\mathcal{U}, <, u)$, this would entail a cycle of length at most $2r + 1$ in $\mathcal{H}$, which is not possible. Thus, $\tau(\mathcal{H}, <, u) \simeq \tau^*$. The density of elements in $\mathcal{H}$ having r-neighbourhood type τ^* is therefore at least

$$\frac{|I|}{|\mathcal{H}|} = \frac{(n - 2r)^d}{n^d} \geq 1 - \epsilon,$$

for large n.

Finally, to establish Theorem 3 it remains to address $\mathcal{H}$'s connectedness. But if $\mathcal{H}$ is not connected, an averaging argument shows that some connected component must have the desired density of at least $(1 - \epsilon)$ of type τ^* vertices.

6. ACKNOWLEDGEMENTS

We thank anonymous reviewers for their helpful feedback, and Christoph Lenzen and Roger Wattenhofer for discussions. This work was supported in part by the Academy of Finland, Grants 132380 and 252018, the Research Funds of the University of Helsinki, and the Finnish Cultural Foundation. The full version of this work is available online [11].

7. REFERENCES

[1] Dana Angluin. Local and global properties in networks of processors. In *Proc. 12th Symposium on Theory of Computing (STOC 1980)*, pages 82–93. ACM Press, New York, 1980.

[2] Dana Angluin and A. Gardiner. Finite common coverings of pairs of regular graphs. *Journal of Combinatorial Theory, Series B*, 30(2):184–187, 1981.

[3] Matti Åstrand, Patrik Floréen, Valentin Polishchuk, Joel Rybicki, Jukka Suomela, and Jara Uitto. A local 2-approximation algorithm for the vertex cover problem. In *Proc. 23rd Symposium on Distributed Computing (DISC 2009)*, volume 5805 of *LNCS*, pages 191–205. Springer, Berlin, 2009.

[4] Matti Åstrand, Valentin Polishchuk, Joel Rybicki, Jukka Suomela, and Jara Uitto. Local algorithms in (weakly) coloured graphs, 2010. Manuscript, arXiv:1002.0125 [cs.DC].

[5] Matti Åstrand and Jukka Suomela. Fast distributed approximation algorithms for vertex cover and set cover in anonymous networks. In *Proc. 22nd Symposium on Parallelism in Algorithms and Architectures (SPAA 2010)*, pages 294–302. ACM Press, New York, 2010.

[6] Richard Cole and Uzi Vishkin. Deterministic coin tossing with applications to optimal parallel list ranking. *Information and Control*, 70(1):32–53, 1986.

[7] Marston Conder, Geoffrey Exoo, and Robert Jajcay. On the limitations of the use of solvable groups in

[8] Paul Conrad. Right-ordered groups. *The Michigan Mathematical Journal*, 6:267–275, 1959.

[9] Andrzej Czygrinow, Michał Hańćkowiak, and Wojciech Wawrzyniak. Fast distributed approximations in planar graphs. In *Proc. 22nd Symposium on Distributed Computing (DISC 2008)*, volume 5218 of *LNCS*, pages 78–92. Springer, Berlin, 2008.

[10] Alex Gamburd, Shlomo Hoory, Mehrdad Shahshahani, Aner Shalev, and Balint Virág. On the girth of random Cayley graphs. *Random Structures & Algorithms*, 35(1):100–117, 2009.

[11] Mika Göös, Juho Hirvonen, and Jukka Suomela. Lower bounds for local approximation, 2012. Manuscript, arXiv:1201.6675 [cs.DC].

[12] Ronald L. Graham, Bruce L. Rothschild, and Joel H. Spencer. *Ramsey Theory*. John Wiley & Sons, New York, 1980.

[13] Fabian Kuhn, Thomas Moscibroda, and Roger Wattenhofer. What cannot be computed locally! In *Proc. 23rd Symposium on Principles of Distributed Computing (PODC 2004)*, pages 300–309. ACM Press, New York, 2004.

[14] Fabian Kuhn, Thomas Moscibroda, and Roger Wattenhofer. The price of being near-sighted. In *Proc. 17th Symposium on Discrete Algorithms (SODA 2006)*, pages 980–989. ACM Press, New York, 2006.

[15] Fabian Kuhn, Thomas Moscibroda, and Roger Wattenhofer. Local computation: Lower and upper bounds, 2010. Manuscript, arXiv:1011.5470 [cs.DC].

[16] Christoph Lenzen. *Synchronization and Symmetry Breaking in Distributed Systems*. PhD thesis, ETH Zurich, January 2011.

[17] Christoph Lenzen and Roger Wattenhofer. Leveraging Linial's locality limit. In *Proc. 22nd Symposium on Distributed Computing (DISC 2008)*, volume 5218 of *LNCS*, pages 394–407. Springer, Berlin, 2008.

[18] Nathan Linial. Locality in distributed graph algorithms. *SIAM Journal on Computing*, 21(1):193–201, 1992.

[19] Alain Mayer, Moni Naor, and Larry Stockmeyer. Local computations on static and dynamic graphs. In *Proc. 3rd Israel Symposium on the Theory of Computing and Systems (ISTCS 1995)*, pages 268–278. IEEE, Piscataway, 1995.

[20] Moni Naor and Larry Stockmeyer. What can be computed locally? *SIAM Journal on Computing*, 24(6):1259–1277, 1995.

[21] Joseph J. Rotman. *An Introduction to the Theory of Groups*, volume 148 of *Graduate Texts in Mathematics*. Springer, New York, 1995.

[22] Jukka Suomela. Distributed algorithms for edge dominating sets. In *Proc. 29th Symposium on Principles of Distributed Computing (PODC 2010)*, pages 365–374. ACM Press, New York, 2010.

[23] Jukka Suomela. Survey of local algorithms. *ACM Computing Surveys*. To appear.

[24] Masafumi Yamashita and Tsunehiko Kameda. Computing on anonymous networks: Part I— characterizing the solvable cases. *IEEE Transactions on Parallel and Distributed Systems*, 7(1):69–89, 1996.

Weak Models of Distributed Computing, with Connections to Modal Logic

Lauri Hella, Matti Järvisalo, Antti Kuusisto, Juhana Laurinharju,
Tuomo Lempiäinen, Kerkko Luosto, Jukka Suomela, and Jonni Virtema

LH, AK, JV: School of Information Sciences, University of Tampere
MJ, JL, TL, JS: Helsinki Institute for Information Technology HIIT,
Department of Computer Science, University of Helsinki
KL: Department of Mathematics and Statistics, University of Helsinki

ABSTRACT

This work presents a classification of weak models of distributed computing. We focus on deterministic distributed algorithms, and we study models of computing that are weaker versions of the widely-studied port-numbering model. In the port-numbering model, a node of degree d receives messages through d input ports and it sends messages through d output ports, both numbered with $1, 2, \ldots, d$. In this work, VV_c is the class of all *graph problems* that can be solved in the standard port-numbering model. We study the following subclasses of VV_c:

VV: Input port i and output port i are not necessarily connected to the same neighbour.

MV: Input ports are not numbered; algorithms receive a multiset of messages.

SV: Input ports are not numbered; algorithms receive a set of messages.

VB: Output ports are not numbered; algorithms send the same message to all output ports.

MB: Combination of MV and VB.

SB: Combination of SV and VB.

Now we have many trivial containment relations, such as $SB \subseteq MB \subseteq VB \subseteq VV \subseteq VV_c$, but it is not obvious if, e.g., either of $VB \subseteq SV$ or $SV \subseteq VB$ should hold. Nevertheless, it turns out that we can identify a *linear order* on these classes. We prove that $SB \subsetneq MB = VB \subsetneq SV = MV = VV \subsetneq VV_c$. The same holds for the constant-time versions of these classes.

We also show that the constant-time variants of these classes can be characterised by a corresponding *modal logic*. Hence the linear order identified in this work has direct implications in the study of the expressibility of modal logic. Conversely, we can use tools from modal logic to study these classes.

Categories and Subject Descriptors

C.2.4 [**Computer-Communication Networks**]: Distributed Systems

Keywords

anonymous networks, deterministic distributed algorithms, graph problems, modal logic, port-numbering model

1. INTRODUCTION

We introduce seven complexity classes, VV_c, VV, MV, SV, VB, MB, and SB, each defined as the class of *graph problems* that can be solved with a deterministic distributed algorithm in a certain variant of the widely-studied *port-numbering model*. We present a *complete characterisation* of the containment relations between these classes, as well as their constant-time counterparts, and identify connections between these classes and questions related to *modal logic*.

1.1 Distributed Algorithms

For our purposes, a distributed algorithm is best understood as a state machine $\mathcal{A}$. In a distributed system, each node is a copy of the same state machine $\mathcal{A}$. Computation proceeds in synchronous steps. In each step, each machine

(1) sends messages to its neighbours,

(2) receives messages from its neighbours, and

(3) updates its state based on the messages that it received.

If the new state is a stopping state, the machine halts.

Let us now formalise the setting studied in this work. We use the notation $[k] = \{1, 2, \ldots, k\}$. For each positive integer Δ, let $\mathcal{F}(\Delta)$ consist of all simple undirected graphs of maximum degree at most Δ. A *distributed algorithm* for $\mathcal{F}(\Delta)$ is a tuple $\mathcal{A} = (Y, Z, z_0, M, m_0, \mu, \delta)$, where

- Y is a finite set of stopping states,

- Z is a (possibly infinite) set of intermediate states,

- $z_0 \colon \{0, 1, \ldots, \Delta\} \to Z$ defines the initial state depending on the degree of the node,

- M is a (possibly infinite) set of messages,

- $m_0 \in M$ is a special symbol for "no message",

- $\mu \colon Z \times [\Delta] \to M$ is a function that constructs the outgoing messages,

- $\delta \colon Z \times M^{\Delta} \to Y \cup Z$ defines the state transitions.

To simplify the notation, we extend the domains of μ and δ to cover the stopping states: for all $y \in Y$, we define $\mu(y, i) = m_0$ for any $i \in [\Delta]$, and $\delta(y, \vec{m}) = y$ for any $\vec{m} \in M^{\Delta}$. In other words, a node that has stopped does not send any messages and does not change its state any more.

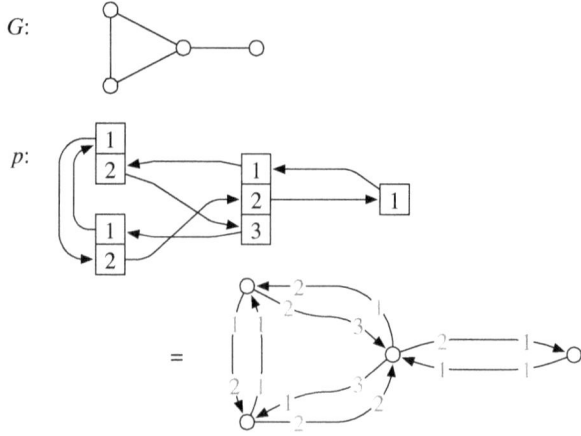

Figure 1: A port numbering p of graph G. Here we present p using two different notations.

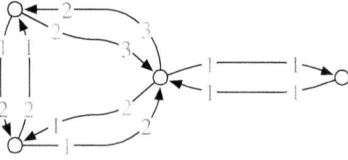

Figure 2: Consistent port numbering.

1.2 Port Numbering

Now consider a graph $G = (V, E) \in \mathcal{F}(\Delta)$. We write $\deg(v)$ for the degree of node $v \in V$. A *port* of G is a pair (v, i) where $v \in V$ and $i \in [\deg(v)]$. Let $P(G)$ be the set of all ports of G. Let $p \colon P(G) \to P(G)$ be a bijection. Define

$$A(p) = \{(u, v) : p((u, i)) = (v, j) \text{ for some } i \text{ and } j\},$$
$$A(G) = \{(u, v) : \{u, v\} \in E\}.$$

We say that p is a *port numbering* of G if $A(p) = A(G)$; see Figure 1. The intuition here is that a node $v \in V$ has $\deg(v)$ communication ports; if it sends a message to its port (v, i), and $p((v, i)) = (u, j)$, the message will be received by its neighbour u from port (u, j).

We say that a port numbering is *consistent* if p is an involution, i.e.,

$$p\big(p((v, i))\big) = (v, i) \text{ for all } (v, i) \in P(G).$$

See Figure 2 for an example.

1.3 Execution of an Algorithm

For a fixed distributed algorithm $\mathcal{A}$, graph G, and port numbering p, we can define the *execution* of $\mathcal{A}$ in (G, p) recursively as follows.

The state of the system at time $t = 0, 1, \ldots$ is represented as a state vector $x_t \colon V \to Y \cup Z$. At time 0, we have $x_0(u) = z_0(\deg(u))$ for each $u \in V$.

Now assume that we have defined the state x_t at time t. Let $(u, i) \in P(G)$ and $(v, j) = p^{-1}((u, i))$. Define

$$a_{t+1}(u, i) = \mu(x_t(v), j).$$

In words, $a_{t+1}(u, i)$ is the message received by node u from port (u, i) in round $t + 1$, or equivalently the message sent

by node v to port (v, j). For each $u \in V$ we define a vector $\vec{a}_{t+1}(u)$ of length Δ as follows:

$$\vec{a}_{t+1}(u) = \big(a_{t+1}(u, 1),\, a_{t+1}(u, 2),\, \ldots,\, a_{t+1}(u, \deg(u)),$$
$$m_0, m_0, \ldots, m_0 \big).$$

That is, we simply take all messages received by u, in the order of increasing port number; the padding with the dummy messages m_0 is just for notational convenience so that $\vec{a}_{t+1}(u) \in M^\Delta$. Finally, we define the new state of a node $u \in V$ as follows:

$$x_{t+1}(u) = \delta(x_t(u), \vec{a}_{t+1}(u)).$$

We say that $\mathcal{A}$ *stops in time* T in (G, p) if $x_T(u) \in Y$ for all $u \in V$. If $\mathcal{A}$ stops in time T in (G, p), we say that $S = x_T$ is the *output* of $\mathcal{A}$ in (G, p). Here $S(u) = x_T(u)$ is the *local output* of $u \in V$.

1.4 Graph Problems

A *graph problem* is a function Π that associates with each undirected graph $G = (V, E)$ a set $\Pi(G)$ of *solutions*. Each solution $S \in \Pi(G)$ is a mapping $S \colon V \to Y$; here Y is a finite set that does not depend on G.

We emphasise that this definition is by no means universal; however, it is convenient for our purposes and covers a wide range of classical graph problems:

- Finding a *subset of vertices*. A typical example is the task of finding a *maximal independent set*: $Y = \{0, 1\}$, and each solution S is the indicator function of a maximal independent set.

- Finding a *partition of vertices*. A typical example is the task of finding a *vertex 3-colouring*: $Y = \{1, 2, 3\}$, and each solution S is a valid 3-colouring of the graph.

- Deciding *graph properties*. A typical example is deciding if a graph is *Eulerian*: Here $Y = \{0, 1\}$. If G is Eulerian, there is only one solution S with $S(v) = 1$ for all $v \in V$. If G is not Eulerian, valid solutions are mappings S such that $S(v) = 0$ for at least one $v \in V$. Put otherwise, all nodes must accept a yes-instance, and at least one node must reject a no-instance.

The idea is that a distributed algorithm $\mathcal{A}$ *solves* a graph problem if, for any graph G and for any port numbering of G, the output of $\mathcal{A}$ is a valid solution $S \in \Pi(G)$. However, the fact that we study graphs of bounded degree requires some care; hence the following somewhat technical definition.

Let Π be a graph problem. Let $T \colon \mathbb{N} \times \mathbb{N} \to \mathbb{N}$. Let $\mathcal{A} = (\mathcal{A}_1, \mathcal{A}_2, \ldots)$ be a family of distributed algorithms. We say that $\mathcal{A}$ *solves* Π *in time* T if the following hold for any $\Delta \in \mathbb{N}$, any graph $G \in \mathcal{F}(\Delta)$, and any port numbering p of G:

(a) Algorithm $\mathcal{A}_\Delta$ stops in time $T(\Delta, |V|)$ in (G, p).
(b) The output of $\mathcal{A}_\Delta$ is in $\Pi(G)$.

We say that $\mathcal{A}$ *solves* Π *in time* T *assuming consistency* if the above holds for any consistent port numbering p of G. Note that we do not even require that $\mathcal{A}$ stops if the port numbering happens to be inconsistent.

We say that $\mathcal{A}$ *solves* Π or $\mathcal{A}$ *is an algorithm* for Π if there is any function T such that $\mathcal{A}$ solves Π in time T. We say that $\mathcal{A}$ *solves* Π *in constant time* or $\mathcal{A}$ *is a local algorithm* for Π if $T(\Delta, n) = T'(\Delta)$ for some $T' \colon \mathbb{N} \to \mathbb{N}$, independently of n.

1.5 Algorithm Classes

Now we are ready to introduce the concepts studied in this work: variants of the definition of a distributed algorithm.

For a vector $\vec{a} = (a_1, a_2, \ldots, a_\Delta) \in M^\Delta$ we define

$$\mathrm{set}(\vec{a}) = \{a_1, a_2, \ldots, a_\Delta\},$$
$$\mathrm{multiset}(\vec{a}) = \big\{(m, n) : m \in M, n = |\{i \in [\Delta] : m = a_i\}|\big\}.$$

In other words, $\mathrm{multiset}(\vec{a})$ discards the ordering of the elements of $\vec{a}$, and $\mathrm{set}(\vec{a})$ furthermore discards the multiplicities.

Let Vector be the set of all distributed algorithms, as defined in Section 1.1. We define three subclasses of distributed algorithms, Set $\subseteq$ Multiset $\subseteq$ Vector, and Broadcast $\subseteq$ Vector:

- $\mathcal{A} \in$ Multiset if $\mathrm{multiset}(\vec{a}) = \mathrm{multiset}(\vec{b})$ implies $\delta(x, \vec{a}) = \delta(x, \vec{b})$ for all $x \in Z$,

- $\mathcal{A} \in$ Set if $\mathrm{set}(\vec{a}) = \mathrm{set}(\vec{b})$ implies $\delta(x, \vec{a}) = \delta(x, \vec{b})$ for all $x \in Z$.

- $\mathcal{A} \in$ Broadcast if $\mu(x, i) = \mu(x, j)$ for all $x \in Z$ and $i, j \in [\Delta]$.

Classes Multiset and Set are related to *incoming* messages. Intuitively, an algorithm in class Vector considers a *vector* of incoming messages, while an algorithm in Multiset considers a *multiset* of incoming messages, and an algorithm in Set considers a *set* of incoming messages. Algorithms in Multiset and Set do not have any access to the numbering of incoming ports.

Class Broadcast is related to *outgoing* messages. Intuitively, an algorithm in class Vector constructs a *vector* of outgoing messages, while an algorithm in Broadcast can only *broadcast* the same message to all neighbours. Algorithms in Broadcast do not have any access to the numbering of outgoing ports.

1.6 Problem Classes

So far we have defined classes of algorithms; now we will define seven classes of problems:

$\Pi \in \mathsf{VV_c}$: there is an algorithm $\mathcal{A} \in$ Vector that solves Π assuming consistency,

$\Pi \in \mathsf{VV}$: there is an algorithm $\mathcal{A} \in$ Vector that solves Π,

$\Pi \in \mathsf{MV}$: there is an algorithm $\mathcal{A} \in$ Multiset that solves Π,

$\Pi \in \mathsf{SV}$: there is an algorithm $\mathcal{A} \in$ Set that solves Π,

$\Pi \in \mathsf{VB}$: there is an algorithm $\mathcal{A} \in$ Broadcast that solves Π,

$\Pi \in \mathsf{MB}$: there is an algorithm $\mathcal{A} \in$ Multiset $\cap$ Broadcast that solves Π,

$\Pi \in \mathsf{SB}$: there is an algorithm $\mathcal{A} \in$ Set $\cap$ Broadcast that solves Π.

We will also define the constant-time variants of the classes:

$\Pi \in \mathsf{VV_c}(1)$: there is a local algorithm $\mathcal{A} \in$ Vector that solves Π assuming consistency,

$\Pi \in \mathsf{VV}(1)$: there is a local algorithm $\mathcal{A} \in$ Vector that solves Π, etc.

Note that consistency is irrelevant for all other classes; we only define the consistent variants of VV and VV(1). The classes are summarised in Figure 3a. Figure 4 summarises what information is available to an algorithm in each class.

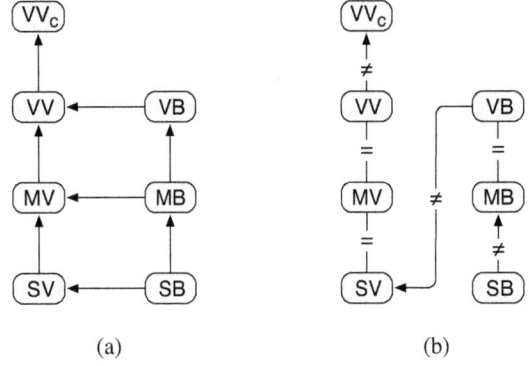

Figure 3: (a) Trivial subset relations between the classes. (b) The linear order identified in this work.

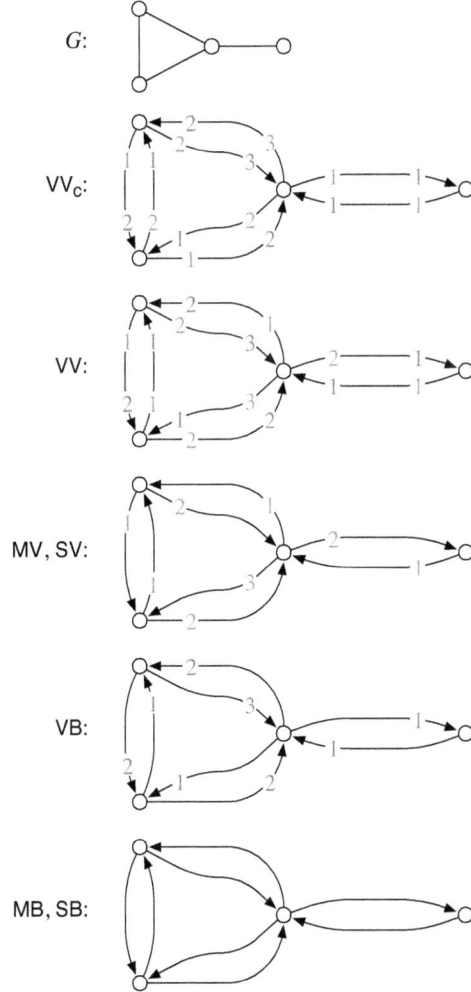

Figure 4: Auxiliary information that is available to a distributed algorithm in each class.

2. CONTRIBUTIONS

This work is a systematic study of the complexity classes VV_c, VV, MV, SV, VB, MB, and SB, as well as their constant-time counterparts. Our main contributions are two-fold.

First, we present a complete characterisation of the containment relations between these classes. The definitions of the classes imply the partial order depicted in Figure 3a. For example, classes VB and SV are seemingly orthogonal, and it would be natural to assume that neither $VB \subseteq SV$ nor $SV \subseteq VB$ holds. However, we show that this is not the case. Unexpectedly, the classes form a linear order (see Figure 3b):

$$SB \subsetneq MB = VB \subsetneq SV = MV = VV \subsetneq VV_c. \qquad (1)$$

In summary, instead of seven classes that are possibly distinct, we have precisely four distinct classes. These four distinct classes of algorithms can be concisely characterised as follows, from the strongest to the weakest:

(1) consistent port numbering (class VV_c),
(2) no incoming port numbers (class SV and equivalent),
(3) no outgoing port numbers (class VB and equivalent),
(4) neither (class SB).

We also show an analogous result for the constant-time versions:

$$\begin{aligned} SB(1) \subsetneq MB(1) = VB(1) \subsetneq SV(1) \\ = MV(1) = VV(1) \subsetneq VV_c(1). \end{aligned} \qquad (2)$$

The main technical achievement here is proving that $SV = MV$; this together with the ideas of a prior work [3] leads to the linear orders (1) and (2).

Second, we identify a novel connection between distributed computational complexity and modal logic. In particular, the classes $VV_c(1)$, VV(1), MV(1), SV(1), VB(1), MB(1), and SB(1) have natural characterisations using certain variants of modal logic. This correspondence allows one to apply tools from the field of modal logic—in particular, bisimulation—to facilitate the proofs of (1) and (2). Conversely, we can lift our results from the field of distributed algorithms to modal logic, by re-interpreting the relations identified in (2).

3. MOTIVATION AND RELATED WORK

In this work, we study *deterministic* distributed algorithms in *anonymous* networks—all state transitions are deterministic, all nodes run the same algorithm, and initially each node knows only its own degree. This is a fairly weak model of computation, and traditionally research has focused on stronger models of distributed computing.

3.1 Stronger Models

There are two obvious extensions:

(a) *Networks with unique identifiers*: initially, all nodes are labelled with $O(\log n)$-bit, globally unique identifiers. With this extension, we arrive at Linial's [17] model of computation; Peleg [21] calls it the *local* model.

(b) *Randomised distributed algorithms*: the nodes have access to a stream of random bits. The state transitions can depend on the random bits.

Both of these extensions lead to a model that is strictly stronger than any of the models studied in this work. The problem of finding a maximal independent set is a good example of a graph problem that separates the weak models from the above extensions. This problem is clearly not in VV_c—a cycle with a symmetric port numbering is a simple counterexample—while it is possible to find a maximal independent set *quickly* in both of the above models.

3.2 Port-Numbering Model

While most of the attention is on stronger models, one of the weaker models has been studied extensively since the 1980s. Unsurprisingly, it is the strongest of the family, model VV_c, and it is commonly known as the *port-numbering model* in the literature.

The study of the port-numbering model was initiated by Angluin [2] in 1980. Initially the main focus was on problems that have a *global* nature—problems in which the local output of a node necessarily depends on the global properties of the input. Examples of papers from the first two decades after Angluin's pioneering work include Attiya et al. [4], Yamashita and Kameda [25–27], and Boldi and Vigna [9], who studied global functions, leader election problems, spanning trees, and topological properties.

Based on the earlier work, the study of the port-numbering model may look like a dead end: positive results were rare. However, very recently, distributed algorithms in the port-numbering model have become an increasingly important research topic—and surprisingly, the study of the port-numbering model is now partially motivated by the desire to understand distributed computing in *stronger* models of computation.

The background is in the study of *local algorithms*, i.e., constant-time distributed algorithms. The research direction was initiated by Naor and Stockmeyer [19] in 1995, and initially it looked like another area where most of the results are negative—after all, it is difficult to imagine a non-trivial graph problem that could be solved in constant time. However, since 2005, we have seen a large number of local algorithms for a wide range of graph problems; see the survey [22] for an overview.

At first sight, constant-time algorithms in stronger models and distributed algorithms in the port-numbering model seem to be orthogonal concepts. However, in many cases a local algorithm is also an algorithm in the port-numbering model. Indeed, a formal connection between local algorithms and the port-numbering model has been recently identified [13].

3.3 Weaker Models

While the study of the port-numbering model has been recently revived, it is also time to question whether its role as the the standard model in the study of anonymous networks is justified. First, the definition is somewhat arbitrary—it is not obvious that VV_c is the "right" class, instead of VV, for example. Second, while the existence of a port numbering is easily justified in the context of wired networks, weaker models such as Broadcast and Set seem to make more sense from the perspective of wireless networks.

If we had no positive examples of problems in classes below VV_c, there would be little motivation for pursuing further. However, the recent work related to the vertex cover problem [3] calls for further investigation. It turned out that 2-approximation of vertex cover is a graph problem that is not only in $VV_c(1)$, but also in $MB(1)$—that is, we have a non-trivial graph problem that does not require any access to either outgoing or incoming port numbers. One ingredient of the vertex cover algorithm is the observation that $MB(1) = VB(1)$, which raises the question of the existence of other similar collapses in the hierarchy of weak models.

We are by no means the first to investigate the weak models. Computation in models that are strictly weaker than the standard port-numbering model has been studied since the 1990s, under various terms [1, 3, 7–9, 11, 16, 20, 23, 24, 28]—see the full version of this work [14] for an overview. Questions related to specific problems, models, and graph families have been studied previously, and indeed many of the techniques and ideas that we use are now standard—this includes the use of symmetry and isomorphisms, local views, covering graphs (lifts) and universal covering graphs, and factors and factorisations. Mayer, Naor, and Stockmeyer [18, 19] made it explicit that the parity of node degrees makes a huge difference in the port-numbering model, and Yamashita and Kameda [26] discussed factors and factorisations in this context.

However, it seems that a comprehensive classification of the weak models from the perspective of solvable graph problems has been lacking. Our main contribution is putting all pieces together in order to provide a complete characterisation of the relations between the weak models and the complexity classes associated with them. We also advocate a new perspective for studying the weak models—the connections with modal logic can be used to complement the traditional graph-theoretic approaches, and in particular bisimulation is a very convenient tool that complements the closely related graph-theoretic concept of covering graphs.

3.4 Distributed Algorithms and Modal Logic

Modal logic (see Section 4) has, of course, been applied previously in the context of distributed systems. However, our perspective is a radical departure from the traditional approach.

In the textbook approach, possible worlds are possible states of the (distributed) system and accessibility relations are possible state transitions. We turn this setting upside down.

In our approach, possible worlds correspond to machines and accessibility relations correspond to communication links. Hence a Kripke model is, in essence, an encoding of the structure of a computer network.

While such an interpretation is of course always possible, it turns out to be particularly helpful in the study of weak models of distributed computing. With this interpretation, for example, a local algorithm in Set ∩ Broadcast corresponds to a formula in modal logic, while a local algorithm in Multiset ∩ Broadcast corresponds to a formula in *graded* modal logic—local algorithms are exactly as expressive as such formulas, and the running time of an algorithm equals the modal depth of a formula. Standard techniques from the field of modal logic can be directly applied in the study of distributed algorithms, and conversely our classification of the weak models of distributed computing can be rephrased as a result that characterises the expressibility of modal logics in certain classes of Kripke models.

4. CONNECTIONS WITH MODAL LOGIC

In this section, we show how to characterise each of the classes $SB(1)$, $MB(1)$, $VB(1)$, $SV(1)$, $MV(1)$, $VV(1)$, and $VV_c(1)$ by a corresponding modal logic, in the spirit of descriptive complexity theory (see Immerman [15]). For each class there is a modal logic such that every algorithm in the class can be described by a formula in the modal logic, and conversely, each formula defines an algorithm in the class.

4.1 Logics ML, GML, MML, and GMML

Our characterisation uses *basic modal logic* ML, *graded modal logic* GML, *multimodal logic* MML, and *graded multimodal logic* GMML—see, e.g., Blackburn, de Rijke, and Venema [5] or Blackburn, van Benthem, and Wolter [6] for further details on modal logic.

Basic modal logic, ML, is obtained by extending propositional logic by a single (unary) modal operator $\Diamond$. More precisely, if Φ is a finite set of proposition symbols, then the set of ML(Φ)-formulas is given by the following grammar:

$$\varphi := q \mid (\varphi \wedge \varphi) \mid \neg\varphi \mid \Diamond\varphi, \quad \text{where } q \in \Phi.$$

The semantics of ML is defined on Kripke models. A *Kripke model* for the set Φ of proposition symbols is a tuple $K = (W, R, \tau)$, where W is a nonempty set of *states* (or *possible worlds*), $R \subseteq W^2$ is a binary relation on W (*accessibility relation*), and τ is a *valuation* function $\tau : \Phi \to \mathcal{P}(W)$.

The truth of an ML(Φ)-formula φ in a state $v \in W$ of a Kripke model $K = (W, R, \tau)$ is defined recursively in the obvious way. For the modal case it holds that

$$K, v \models \Diamond\varphi \quad \text{iff}$$
$$K, w \models \varphi \text{ for some } w \in W \text{ s.t. } (v, w) \in R.$$

The syntax of *graded modal logic* [12], GML, extends the syntax of ML with the rules $\Diamond_{\geq k}\varphi$, where $k \in \mathbb{N}$. The semantics of these graded modalities $\Diamond_{\geq k}$ is the following:

$$K, v \models \Diamond_{\geq k}\varphi \quad \text{iff}$$
$$\left|\{w \in W : (v, w) \in R \text{ and } K, w \models \varphi\}\right| \geq k.$$

Up to this point we have considered modal logics with only one modality $\Diamond$. *Multimodal logic*, MML, is the natural generalisation of ML that allows an arbitrary (finite) number of modalities. Given a set I of indices and a finite set Φ of proposition symbols, the set of MML(I, Φ)-formulas is defined by the same grammar as for ML(Φ) with $\Diamond\varphi$ replaced by $\langle\alpha\rangle\varphi$, for each $\alpha \in I$.

The Kripke models corresponding to the multimodal language MML(I, Φ) are of the form

$$K = (W, (R_\alpha)_{\alpha \in I}, \tau),$$

where $R_\alpha \subseteq W^2$ for each $\alpha \in I$. The truth of an MML(I, Φ)-formula in K is defined in the obvious way.

We can naturally extend MML by graded modalities $\langle\alpha\rangle_{\geq k}$ for each $\alpha \in I$ and $k \in \mathbb{N}$ and obtain *graded multimodal logic* GMML(I, Φ).

Let $\mathcal{L}$ be a modal logic and φ an $\mathcal{L}$-formula. The *modal depth* of φ, denoted by $\text{md}(\varphi)$, is the largest number of nested modalities in φ.

Given a modal logic $\mathcal{L}$ and a Kripke model K for $\mathcal{L}$, each $\mathcal{L}$-formula φ *defines* a subset $\{v \in W : K, v \models \varphi\}$ of the set of states in K; this set is denoted by $\|\varphi\|^K$.

4.2 Bisimulation and Definability

We will now define one of the most important concepts in modal logic, bisimulation. The objective is to characterise definability in the corresponding modal logics, so that if two states w and w' are bisimilar they cannot be separated by any formula of the corresponding logic. Bisimulation can be defined in a canonical way for each of the logics ML, GML, MML, and GMML.

Bisimulation for MML is defined as follows. Let $K = (W, (R_\alpha)_{\alpha \in I}, \tau)$ and $K' = (W', (R'_\alpha)_{\alpha \in I}, \tau')$ be Kripke models for a set Φ of proposition symbols. A nonempty relation $Z \subseteq W \times W'$ is a *bisimulation* between K and K' if the following conditions hold.

(B1) If $(v, v') \in Z$, then $v \in \tau(q)$ iff $v' \in \tau'(q)$ for all $q \in \Phi$.

(B2) If $(v, v') \in Z$ and $(v, w) \in R_\alpha$ for some $\alpha \in I$, then there is a $w' \in W'$ such that $(v', w') \in R'_\alpha$ and $(w, w') \in Z$.

(B3) If $(v, v') \in Z$ and $(v', w') \in R'_\alpha$ for some $\alpha \in I$, then there is a $w \in W$ such that $(v, w) \in R_\alpha$ and $(w, w') \in Z$.

If there is a bisimulation Z such that $(v, v') \in Z$, we say that v and v' are bisimilar w.r.t. MML.

FACT 1. *Let $\mathcal{L}$ be one of the modal logics ML, MML, GML and GMML, and let K and K' be Kripke models, $v \in W$ and $v' \in W'$. If v and v' are bisimilar w.r.t. $\mathcal{L}$, then for all $\mathcal{L}$-formulas φ we have $K, v \models \varphi$ iff $K', v' \models \varphi$.*

4.3 Characterising Constant Time Classes

There is a natural correspondence between the framework for distributed computing defined in this paper and the logics ML, GML, MML, and GMML. For any input graph G and port numbering p of G, the pair (G, p) can be transformed into a Kripke model $K(G, p) = (W, (R_\alpha)_{\alpha \in I}, \tau)$ in a canonical way. Given a local algorithm $\mathcal{A}$, its execution can then be simulated by a modal formula φ. The crucial idea is that the truth condition for a diamond formula $\langle \alpha \rangle \psi$ is interpreted as communication between the nodes:

$$K, v \models \langle \alpha \rangle \psi \quad \text{iff} \quad v \text{ receives the message "}\psi \text{ is true"}$$
$$\text{from some } u \text{ such that } (v, u) \in R_\alpha.$$

Conversely, given a modal formula φ, the evaluation of its truth in the Kripke model $K(G, p)$ can be done by a local algorithm $\mathcal{A}$.

The general idea of the correspondence between modal logic and distributed algorithms is described in Table 1.

We define four different Kripke models $K_i(G, p)$ for (G, p), reflecting the fact that algorithms in the lower classes do not use all the information encoded in the port numbering. Let $G = (V, E) \in \mathcal{F}(\Delta)$, and let p be a port numbering of G. The accessibility relations used in $K_1(G, p)$ are the following:

$$R_{(i,j)} = \left\{ (u, v) \in V \times V : p((v, j)) = (u, i) \right\}$$

for each pair $(i, j) \in [\Delta] \times [\Delta]$. For algorithms in classes below **Vector** we need alternative accessibility relations with corresponding restrictions on their information about p. For each $i \in [\Delta]$ we define that

$$R_{(i,*)} = \bigcup_{j \in [\Delta]} R_{(i,j)} \quad \text{and} \quad R_{(*,i)} = \bigcup_{j \in [\Delta]} R_{(j,i)}.$$

In addition we define that $R_{(*,*)} = \bigcup_{(i,j) \in [\Delta] \times [\Delta]} R_{(i,j)}$. Note that $R_{(*,*)} = \{(u, v) : \{u, v\} \in E\}$ is the edge set E interpreted as a symmetric relation.

In addition to the accessibility relations, we encode the local information on the degrees of vertices into a valuation $\tau : \Phi_\Delta \to \mathcal{P}(V)$, where $\Phi_\Delta = \{q_i : i \in [\Delta]\}$. The valuation τ is given by $\tau(q_i) = \{v \in V : \deg(v) = i\}$.

Table 1: Correspondence between modal logic and distributed algorithms.

Modal logic	Distributed algorithms
Kripke model K	$\begin{cases} \text{input graph } G = (V, E) \\ \text{port numbering } p \end{cases}$
states W	nodes V
relations R_α, $\alpha \in I$	edges E, port numbering p
valuation τ proposition symbols	$\Big\}$ node degrees (initial state)
formula φ	algorithm $\mathcal{A}$
formula φ is true in world v	node v outputs 1
modal depth of φ	running time of $\mathcal{A}$

The four versions of a Kripke model corresponding to graph G and port numbering p are now defined as follows:

$$K_1(G, p) = (V, (R_\alpha)_{\alpha \in I_{\Delta,1}}, \tau), \quad \text{where} \quad I_{\Delta,1} = [\Delta] \times [\Delta],$$
$$K_2(G, p) = (V, (R_\alpha)_{\alpha \in I_{\Delta,2}}, \tau), \quad \text{where} \quad I_{\Delta,2} = \{*\} \times [\Delta],$$
$$K_3(G, p) = (V, (R_\alpha)_{\alpha \in I_{\Delta,3}}, \tau), \quad \text{where} \quad I_{\Delta,3} = [\Delta] \times \{*\},$$
$$K_4(G, p) = (V, (R_\alpha)_{\alpha \in I_{\Delta,4}}, \tau), \quad \text{where} \quad I_{\Delta,4} = \{(*,*)\}.$$

For each $i \in \{1, 2, 3, 4\}$, we denote the class of all Kripke models of the form $K_i(G, p)$ by $\mathcal{K}_i$. Furthermore, we denote by $\mathcal{K}_0$ the subclass of $\mathcal{K}_1$ consisting of the models $K_1(G, p)$, where p is a consistent port numbering of G.

In order to give a precise formulation of the correspondence between modal logics and the constant time classes of graph problems, we define now the concept of modal formulas solving graph problems. W.l.o.g., we consider here only problems Π such that the solutions $S \in \Pi(G)$ are functions $V \to \{0, 1\}$, or equivalently, subsets of V.

Let $\mathcal{L}$ be a modal logic, let $i \in \{1, 2, 3, 4\}$, and let $\Psi = (\psi_1, \psi_2, \ldots)$ be a sequence of modal formulas such that $\psi_\Delta \in \mathcal{L}(I_{\Delta,i}, \Phi_\Delta)$ for each $\Delta \in \mathbb{N}$. Then Ψ *defines a solution* for a graph problem Π on the class $\mathcal{K}_i$ if for all $\Delta \in \mathbb{N}$, all $G \in \mathcal{F}(\Delta)$, and all port numberings p of G, the subset $\|\psi_\Delta\|^{K_i(G,p)}$ defined by the formula ψ_Δ in the model $K_i(G, p)$ is in set $\Pi(G)$. Furthermore, the sequence Ψ defines a solution for Π on the class $\mathcal{K}_0$, if the condition above with $i = 1$ holds for all *consistent* port numberings p.

Note that any sequence $\Psi = (\psi_1, \psi_2, \ldots)$ of modal formulas as above gives rise to a canonical graph problem Π_Ψ that it solves: for each graph G, the solution set $\Pi_\Psi(G)$ simply consists of the sets $\|\psi_\Delta\|^{K_i(G,p)}$ where $G \in \mathcal{F}(\Delta)$ and p ranges over the (consistent) port numberings of G.

Let $\mathcal{L}$ be a modal logic, let $i \leq 4$, and let C be a class of graph problems. We say that $\mathcal{L}$ *captures* C on $\mathcal{K}_i$ if the following two conditions hold:

- If $\Psi = (\psi_1, \psi_2, \ldots)$ is a sequence of formulas such that $\psi_\Delta \in \mathcal{L}(I_{\Delta,i}, \Phi_\Delta)$ for all $\Delta \in \mathbb{N}$, then $\Pi_\Psi \in C$.

- For every graph problem $\Pi \in C$ there is a sequence $\Psi = (\psi_1, \psi_2, \ldots)$ of formulas such that $\psi_\Delta \in \mathcal{L}(I_{\Delta,i}, \Phi_\Delta)$ for all $\Delta \in \mathbb{N}$, which defines a solution for Π on $\mathcal{K}_i$.

The main result of this section is that the constant time version of each of the classes VV$_c$, VV, MV, SV, VB, MB,

Table 2: The intended meaning of the subformulas.

Subformulas of ψ_Δ	Algorithm $\mathcal{A}_\Delta$
$\varphi_{\ell,t}$ is true in world v	bit ℓ of local state $x_t(v)$ is 1
$\vartheta_{m,j,t}$ is true in world v	node v sends message m to port j in round t
$\chi_{m,i,j,t}$ is true in world v	node v receives message m from port i in round t, the message was sent by a neighbour to port j

Table 3: Constructing the formula ψ_Δ, given an algorithm $\mathcal{A}_\Delta$.

Recursive definition of the formulas	Execution of $\mathcal{A}_\Delta$
$\varphi_{\ell,0}$: Boolean combination of $q_i \in \Phi_\Delta$	initialisation: $x_0(u) = z_0(\deg(u))$
$\vartheta_{m,j,t+1}$: Boolean combination of $\varphi_{\ell,t}$, $\ell \le L$	local computation: $m = \mu(x_t(v), j)$
$\chi_{m,i,j,t+1} = \langle \alpha \rangle \vartheta_{m,j,t+1}$ with $\alpha = (i,j)$	communication: construct $\vec{a}_{t+1}(v)$
$\varphi_{\ell,t+1}$: Boolean combin. of $\varphi_{k,t}$, $k \le L$, and $\chi_{m,i,j,t+1}$, $m \in M$, $i,j \in [\Delta]$	local computation: $x_{t+1}(v) = \delta(x_t(v), \vec{a}_{t+1}(v))$

and SB is captured by one of the modal logics MML, ML, GMML, and GML on an appropriate class $\mathcal{K}_i$.

THEOREM 1. *(a) MML captures* $\mathsf{VV_c}(1)$ *on* $\mathcal{K}_0$.
(b) MML captures $\mathsf{VV}(1)$ *on* $\mathcal{K}_1$.
(c) GMML captures $\mathsf{MV}(1)$ *on* $\mathcal{K}_2$.
(d) MML captures $\mathsf{SV}(1)$ *on* $\mathcal{K}_2$.
(e) MML captures $\mathsf{VB}(1)$ *on* $\mathcal{K}_3$.
(f) GML captures $\mathsf{MB}(1)$ *on* $\mathcal{K}_4$.
(g) ML captures $\mathsf{SB}(1)$ *on* $\mathcal{K}_4$.

PROOF SKETCH. We describe here the idea behind the proof of (b); other cases are similar.

Assume first that $\Psi = (\psi_1, \psi_2, \ldots)$ is a sequence of formulas with $\psi_\Delta \in \mathrm{MML}(I_{\Delta,1}, \Phi_\Delta)$ for each $\Delta \in \mathbb{N}$. We describe a local algorithm $\mathcal{A}_\Delta \in \mathsf{Vector}$ that simulates the recursive evaluation of the truth of ψ_Δ on a Kripke model $K_1(G, p)$.

The idea is that in the j:th step of computation of the algorithm $\mathcal{A}_\Delta$ each node u sends the truth values of subformulas of ψ_Δ of modal depth $j - 1$ in u to its neighbours. After receiving these truth values from its neighbours each node u computes the values of subformulas of ψ_Δ of modal depth j. Now after $\mathrm{md}(\psi_\Delta)$ computation steps of the algorithm $\mathcal{A}_\Delta$ each node u knows whether ψ_Δ holds in it or not.

For the other direction, assume that Π is a graph problem in $\mathsf{VV}(1)$. Thus, there is a sequence $\mathcal{A} = (\mathcal{A}_1, \mathcal{A}_2, \ldots)$ of local algorithms in Vector that solves Π. We will encode information on the states of computation and messages sent during the execution of $\mathcal{A}_\Delta$ on an input (G, p) by suitable formulas of MML.

Using the definitions of Section 1.1, let $\mathcal{A}_\Delta = (Y, Z, z_0, M, m_0, \mu, \delta)$, and let T be the running time of $\mathcal{A}_\Delta$. We use a binary encoding for the states $x_t(v)$ of nodes in the computation of $\mathcal{A}_\Delta$; let L be the length of this encoding. We assume w.l.o.g. that the output of the algorithm is the first bit of x_T. We will build a formula $\psi_\Delta \in \mathrm{MML}(I_{\Delta,1}, \Phi_\Delta)$ that simulates $\mathcal{A}_\Delta$ from the following subformulas:

- $\varphi_{\ell,t}$ for $\ell \le L$ and $t \le T$,
- $\vartheta_{m,j,t}$ for $m \in M$, $j \in [\Delta]$ and $t \in [T]$,
- $\chi_{m,i,j,t}$ for $m \in M$, $i,j \in [\Delta]$ and $t \in [T]$.

The intended meaning of these subformulas is given in Table 2, and their recursive definitions are given in Table 3.

Given an input (G, p) to the algorithm $\mathcal{A}_\Delta$, the output on a node v is 1 if and only if

$$v \in \|\varphi_{0,T}\|^{K_1(G,p)}.$$

Thus, defining $\psi_\Delta := \varphi_{0,T}$ we get $\|\psi_\Delta\|^{K_1(G,p)} \in \Pi(G)$ for all $G \in \mathcal{F}(\Delta)$ and all port numberings p of G. Hence we conclude that the sequence $\Psi = (\psi_1, \psi_2, \ldots)$ defines a solution to Π.

As an additional remark, we note that $\mathrm{md}(\psi_\Delta)$ is equal to the running time T of $\mathcal{A}_\Delta$. $\square$

5. RELATIONS BETWEEN THE CLASSES

Now we are ready to prove relations (1) and (2) that we gave in Section 2.

5.1 Equality MV = SV

Theorem 2 is the most important technical contribution of this work. Informally, it shows that *outgoing* port numbers necessarily break symmetry even if we do not have *incoming* port numbers—provided that we are not too short-sighted.

THEOREM 2. *Let* Π *be a graph problem and let* $T : \mathbb{N} \times \mathbb{N} \to \mathbb{N}$. *Assume that there is an algorithm* $\mathcal{A}_1 \in \mathsf{Multiset}$ *that solves* Π *in time* T. *Then there is an algorithm* $\mathcal{A}_2 \in \mathsf{Set}$ *that solves* Π *in time* $T + O(\Delta)$.

To prove Theorem 2, we define the following local algorithm $\mathcal{A}'_\Delta \in \mathsf{Set}$. Each node v constructs two sequences, $\beta_t(v)$ and $B_t(v)$ for $t = 0, 1, \ldots, 2\Delta$. Before the first round, each node v sets $\beta_0(v) = \emptyset$ and $B_0(v) = \emptyset$. Then in round $t = 1, 2, \ldots, 2\Delta$, each node v does the following:

(1) Set $\beta_t(v) = (\beta_{t-1}(v), B_{t-1}(v))$.
(2) For each port i, send $(\beta_t(v), \deg(v), i)$ to port i.
(3) Let $B_t(v)$ be the set of all messages received by v.

Let $G = (V, E) \in \mathcal{F}(\Delta)$, and let p be a port numbering of graph G. We will analyse the execution of $\mathcal{A}'_\Delta$ on (G, p). If $p((v, i)) = (u, j)$, we define that $\pi(v, u) = i$. That is, $\pi(v, u)$ is the outgoing port number in v that is connected to u. Let

$$m_t(u, v) = (\beta_t(u), \deg(u), \pi(u, v))$$

denote the message that node u sends to node v in round t; it follows that $m_t(u, v) \in B_t(v)$ for all $\{u, v\} \in E$.

We begin with the following technical lemma. We emphasise that in the statement of the lemma, the sets $\{u, w\}$, $\{v_1, v_2, \ldots, v_k\}$, and $\{v'_1, v'_2, \ldots, v'_{k+1}\}$ may intersect—for example, we may have $u = v_1 = v'_1$.

LEMMA 1. *Suppose that all of the the following hold for some $t \geq 4$:*

(a) *Nodes u and w are two distinct neighbours of v.*
(b) *Nodes $v_1, v_2, \ldots, v_k$ are k distinct neighbours of v.*
(c) *We have $\beta_t(u) = \beta_t(w) = \beta_t(v_i)$ for all $i = 1, 2, \ldots, k$.*
(d) *We have $\deg(u) = \deg(w)$ and $\pi(u, v) = \pi(w, v)$.*

In particular, node v receives the same message from u and w in round t. Then the following holds:

(e) *There are $k + 1$ distinct neighbours of v, denoted by $v'_1, v'_2, \ldots, v'_{k+1}$, such that*
$$\beta_{t-2}(u) = \beta_{t-2}(w) = \beta_{t-2}(v'_i)$$
for all $i = 1, 2, \ldots, k + 1$.

PROOF. From $\beta_t(u) = \beta_t(w)$ it follows that $\beta_{t-2}(u) = \beta_{t-2}(w)$. This implies $m_{t-2}(u, v) = m_{t-2}(w, v)$.

For all $i = 1, 2, \ldots, k$, node v_i receives the message
$$m_{t-1}(v, v_i) = (\beta_{t-1}(v), \deg(v), \pi(v, v_i))$$
from v in round $t - 1$. By assumption, we have $\beta_t(v_i) = \beta_t(v_j)$ for all i, j, which implies $B_{t-1}(v_i) = B_{t-1}(v_j)$. Now $m_{t-1}(v, v_i) \in B_{t-1}(v_i)$ implies $m_{t-1}(v, v_j) \in B_{t-1}(v_i)$ for all i, j.

In any port numbering, we have $\pi(v, v_i) \neq \pi(v, v_j)$ for $i \neq j$; hence $m_{t-1}(v, v_i) \neq m_{t-1}(v, v_j)$, and $B_{t-1}(v_1)$ contains k distinct messages. That is, node v_1 has k distinct neighbours, $u_1, u_2, \ldots, u_k$, such that
$$\begin{aligned}(\beta_{t-1}(u_i), \deg(u_i), \pi(u_i, v_1)) &= m_{t-1}(u_i, v_1) = m_{t-1}(v, v_i) \\ &= (\beta_{t-1}(v), \deg(v), \pi(v, v_i)).\end{aligned}$$

In particular, $\beta_{t-1}(u_i) = \beta_{t-1}(v)$ for all i.

Now let us investigate the messages that the nodes u_i receive in round $t - 2$. We have
$$m_{t-2}(v_1, u_i) = (\beta_{t-2}(v_1), \deg(v_1), \pi(v_1, u_i)).$$

However, $\beta_{t-1}(u_i) = \beta_{t-1}(v)$ implies $B_{t-2}(u_i) = B_{t-2}(v)$ for all i. In particular, $m_{t-2}(v_1, u_i) \in B_{t-2}(v)$ for all i. Now $\pi(v_1, u_i) \neq \pi(v_1, u_j)$ implies $m_{t-2}(v_1, u_i) \neq m_{t-2}(v_1, u_j)$ for all $i \neq j$.

To summarise, v receives the following messages in round $t - 2$: k distinct messages,
$$m_{t-2}(v_1, u_i) = (\beta_{t-2}(v_1), \deg(v_1), \pi(v_1, u_i))$$
for $i = 1, 2, \ldots, k$, and two identical messages,
$$m_{t-2}(u, v) = m_{t-2}(w, v) = (\beta_{t-2}(u), \deg(u), \pi(u, v)).$$

Moreover, $\beta_{t-2}(v_1) = \beta_{t-2}(u)$. Hence v receives at least $k + 1$ messages in round $t - 2$, each of the form $(\beta_{t-2}(u), \cdot, \cdot)$. Hence v has at least $k + 1$ distinct neighbours v'_i with $\beta_{t-2}(u) = \beta_{t-2}(v'_i)$. $\square$

LEMMA 2. *If a node v receives the same message from its neighbours u and w in round $2t$, and v has k distinct neighbours $v_1, v_2, \ldots, v_k$ such that $\beta_{2t}(v_i) = \beta_{2t}(u) = \beta_{2t}(w)$ for all $i = 1, 2, \ldots, k$, then v has at least $t + k - 1$ neighbours.*

PROOF. The proof is by induction on t. The base case $t = 1$ is trivial. For the inductive step, apply Lemma 1. $\square$

Hence if a node v has two neighbours u and w with $m_{2t}(u, v) = m_{2t}(w, v)$, node v has at least $t + 1$ neighbours. As the maximum degree of graph G is at most Δ, we know that $m_{2\Delta}(u, v) \neq m_{2\Delta}(w, v)$ whenever u and w are two distinct neighbours of v. In particular,
$$(\beta_{2\Delta}(u), \deg(u), \pi(u, v)) \neq (\beta_{2\Delta}(w), \deg(w), \pi(w, v)).$$

Once we have finished running $\mathcal{A}'_\Delta$, which takes $O(\Delta)$ time, we can *simulate* the execution of $\mathcal{A}_1 \in$ Multiset with an algorithm $\mathcal{A}_2 \in$ Set as follows: if a node u in the execution of $\mathcal{A}_1$ sends the message a to port i, algorithm $\mathcal{A}_2$ sends the message
$$(\beta_{2\Delta}(u), \deg(u), i, a)$$
to port i. Now all messages received by a node are distinct. Hence given the set of messages received by a node v in $\mathcal{A}_2$, we can reconstruct the multiset of messages received by v in $\mathcal{A}_1$. This concludes the proof of Theorem 2.

COROLLARY 1. *We have* $\mathsf{MV} = \mathsf{SV}$ *and* $\mathsf{MV}(1) = \mathsf{SV}(1)$.

PROOF. Immediate from Theorem 2. $\square$

5.2 Equalities VB = MB and VV = MV

The following theorems are implicit in prior work [3]; we give more detailed proofs in the full version of this work [14]. The basic idea is that $\mathcal{A}_2$ augments each message with the full communication history, and orders the incoming messages lexicographically by the communication histories—the end result is equal to the execution of $\mathcal{A}_1$ in the same graph G for a very specific choice of incoming port numbers.

THEOREM 3. *Let Π be a graph problem and let $T : \mathbb{N} \times \mathbb{N} \rightarrow \mathbb{N}$. Assume that there is an algorithm $\mathcal{A}_1 \in$ Vector that solves Π in time T. Then there is an algorithm $\mathcal{A}_2 \in$ Multiset that solves Π in time T.*

THEOREM 4. *Let Π be a graph problem and let $T : \mathbb{N} \times \mathbb{N} \rightarrow \mathbb{N}$. Assume that there is an algorithm $\mathcal{A}_1 \in$ Broadcast that solves Π in time T. Then there is an algorithm $\mathcal{A}_2 \in$ Multiset $\cap$ Broadcast that solves Π in time T.*

COROLLARY 2. *We have* $\mathsf{VB} = \mathsf{MB}$, $\mathsf{VB}(1) = \mathsf{MB}(1)$, $\mathsf{VV} = \mathsf{MV}$, *and* $\mathsf{VV}(1) = \mathsf{MV}(1)$.

5.3 Separating the Classes

Trivially, $\mathsf{SB} \subseteq \mathsf{MB} \subseteq \mathsf{MV}$ and $\mathsf{SB}(1) \subseteq \mathsf{MB}(1) \subseteq \mathsf{MV}(1)$. Together with Corollaries 1 and 2 these imply
$$\mathsf{SB} \subseteq \mathsf{MB} = \mathsf{VB} \subseteq \mathsf{SV} = \mathsf{MV} = \mathsf{VV},$$
$$\mathsf{SB}(1) \subseteq \mathsf{MB}(1) = \mathsf{VB}(1) \subseteq \mathsf{SV}(1) = \mathsf{MV}(1) = \mathsf{VV}(1).$$

Now we proceed to show that the subset relations are proper. We only need to come up with a graph problem that separates a pair of classes—here the connections to modal logic and bisimulation are a particularly helpful tool.

For the case of $\mathsf{VB} \neq \mathsf{SV}$, the separation is easy: we can consider the problem of breaking symmetry in a star graph.

THEOREM 5. *There is a graph problem Π such that $\Pi \in \mathsf{SV}(1)$ and $\Pi \notin \mathsf{VB}$.*

PROOF. An appropriate choice of Π is the (artificial) problem of selecting a leaf node in a star graph. More formally, we have the set of outputs $Y = \{0, 1\}$. We define $\Pi(G)$ as follows, depending on G:

(a) $G = (V, E)$ is a k-star for a $k > 1$. That is, $V = \{c, v_1, v_2, \ldots, v_k\}$ and $E = \{\{c, v_i\} : i = 1, 2, \ldots, k\}$. Then we have $S \in \Pi(G)$ if $S \colon V \to Y$, $S(c) = 0$, and there is a j such that $S(v_j) = 1$ and $S(v_i) = 0$ for all $i \neq j$.

(b) $G = (V, E)$ is not a star. Then we do not restrict the output, i.e., $S \in \Pi(G)$ for any function $S \colon V \to Y$.

It is easy to design a local algorithm $\mathcal{A}_1 \in \mathsf{Set}$ that solves Π: First, all nodes send message i to port i for each i; then a node outputs 1 if it has degree 1 and if it received the set of messages $\{1\}$.

It is equally easy to see that an algorithm $\mathcal{A}_2 \in \mathsf{Broadcast}$ cannot solve the problem. Let G be a k-star, and let p be any port numbering of G. Now in the Kripke model $K_3(G, p)$, all leaf nodes are bisimilar w.r.t. MML. Equivalently, in any execution of $\mathcal{A}_2$ on (G, p), all leafs are in the same state at each time step. $\square$

COROLLARY 3. *We have* $\mathsf{VB} \neq \mathsf{SV}$ *and* $\mathsf{VB}(1) \neq \mathsf{SV}(1)$.

PROOF. Follows from Theorem 5. $\square$

To show that $\mathsf{SB} \neq \mathsf{MB}$, we can consider, for example, the problem of identifying nodes that have an odd number of neighbours with odd degrees.

THEOREM 6. *There is a graph problem* Π *such that* $\Pi \in \mathsf{MB}(1)$ *and* $\Pi \notin \mathsf{SB}$.

PROOF. We define Π as follows. Let $G = (V, E)$ and $S \colon V \to \{0, 1\}$. We have $S \in \Pi(G)$ if the following holds: $S(v) = 1$ iff v is a node with an odd number of neighbours of an odd degree.

The problem is trivially in $\mathsf{MB}(1)$: first each node broadcasts the parity of its degree, and then a node outputs 1 if it received an odd number of messages that indicate the odd parity.

To see that the problem is not in SB, it is sufficient to argue that the white nodes in the following graphs are bisimilar, yet they are supposed to produce different outputs.

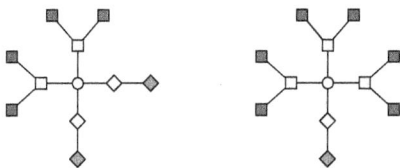

More precisely, we can partition the nodes in five equivalence classes (indicated with the shading and shapes in the above illustration), and the nodes in the same equivalence class are bisimilar in the Kripke model $K_4(G, p)$ w.r.t. ML; recall that the model is independent of the choice of the port numbering p. Equivalently, in the execution of any algorithm $\mathcal{A} \in \mathsf{Set} \cap \mathsf{Broadcast}$, all nodes in the same equivalence class have the same state and hence produce the same output. $\square$

COROLLARY 4. *We have* $\mathsf{SB} \neq \mathsf{MB}$ *and* $\mathsf{SB}(1) \neq \mathsf{MB}(1)$.

PROOF. Follows from Theorem 6. $\square$

Finally, to separate VV and $\mathsf{VV_c}$, we can use the construction of Figure 5—there a consistent port numbering necessarily breaks symmetry, while an inconsistent port numbering may be symmetric.

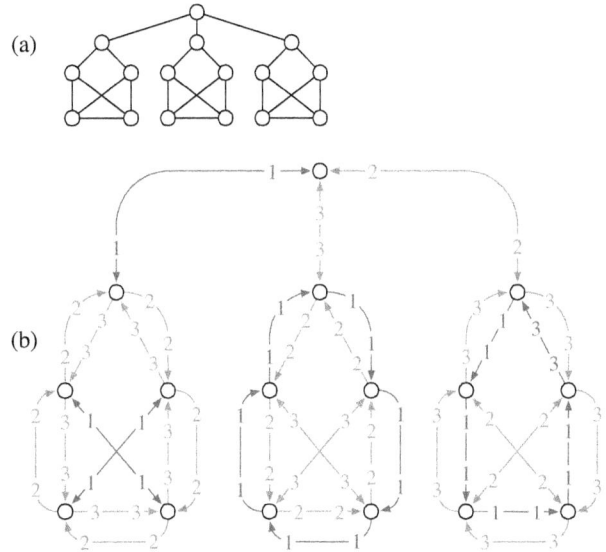

Figure 5: (a) A 3-regular graph G that does not have a 1-factor [10, Figure 5.10]. (b) A port numbering of G.

THEOREM 7. *There is a graph problem* Π *such that* $\Pi \in \mathsf{VV_c}(1)$ *and* $\Pi \notin \mathsf{VV}$.

PROOF. We define Π so that for the graph $G = (V, E)$ illustrated in Figure 5a, $\Pi(G)$ consists of all non-constant functions $S \colon V \to \{0, 1\}$, that is, we have $u, v \in V$ with $S(u) \neq S(v)$. For all other graphs $\Pi(G)$ consists of all functions $S \colon V \to \{0, 1\}$.

Let us first prove that the problem is in $\mathsf{VV_c}(1)$. Let G be the graph of Figure 5a. Graph G is 3-regular. It can be verified that G does not have any 1-factor (perfect matching); hence it does not have any 2-factor, either. Now the arguments of Yamashita and Kameda [26, Section 5.1] imply that in any consistent port numbering of G, there are two nodes with distinct local views; moreover, it suffices to focus on radius-T local views for a (small) constant T. We define that the *type* of a node is an encoding of its radius-T local view (as an integer, using some canonical encoding). Now in G we have always nodes of at least two different types. Hence we can solve the problem as follows: a node outputs 1 iff it is adjacent to a node with a strictly smaller type. This produces a non-constant output in G, for any port numbering p, and it stops in constant time in any graph; hence it is a local algorithm that solves Π.

To see that an algorithm $\mathcal{A} \in \mathsf{Vector}$ cannot solve the problem without assuming consistency, consider the port numbering p in Figure 5b. If we reverse the arrows, the same figure can be interpreted as an illustration of the Kripke model $K_1(G, p)$, and it is straightforward to verify that all nodes are bisimilar w.r.t. MML. $\square$

COROLLARY 5. *We have* $\mathsf{VV_c} \neq \mathsf{VV}$ *and* $\mathsf{VV_c}(1) \neq \mathsf{VV}(1)$.

PROOF. Follows from Theorem 7. $\square$

In summary, we have established that the classes we have studied form a linear order of length four—see (1) and (2) in Section 2. As a corollary of (2) and Theorem 1, we can make, for example, the following observations.

COROLLARY 6. *(a)* MML *captures the same class of problems on* $\mathcal{K}_1$ *and* $\mathcal{K}_2$.

(b) Both MML *and* GMML *capture the same class of problems on* $\mathcal{K}_2$.

(c) The class of problems captured by MML *becomes strictly smaller if we replace* $\mathcal{K}_2$ *with* $\mathcal{K}_3$.

(d) MML *on* $\mathcal{K}_3$ *captures the same class of problems as* GML *on* $\mathcal{K}_4$.

To keep the proofs of Theorems 5, 6, and 7 as simple as possible, we introduced graph problems that were highly contrived. An interesting challenge is to come up with *natural* graph problems that separate the classes. Another challenge is to come up with *decision problems* that separate the classes.

6. ACKNOWLEDGEMENTS

We thank anonymous reviewers for their helpful feedback, and Mika Göös and Joel Kaasinen for discussions and comments. This work was supported in part by Academy of Finland (grants 129761, 132380, 132812, and 252018), the research funds of University of Helsinki, and Finnish Cultural Foundation.

The full version of this work is available online [14].

7. REFERENCES

[1] Yehuda Afek, Noga Alon, Ziv Bar-Joseph, Alejandro Cornejo, Bernhard Haeupler, and Fabian Kuhn. Beeping a maximal independent set. In *Proc. DISC 2011*, volume 6950 of *LNCS*, pages 32–50. Springer, 2011.

[2] Dana Angluin. Local and global properties in networks of processors. In *Proc. STOC 1980*, pages 82–93. ACM Press, 1980.

[3] Matti Åstrand and Jukka Suomela. Fast distributed approximation algorithms for vertex cover and set cover in anonymous networks. In *Proc. SPAA 2010*, pages 294–302. ACM Press, 2010.

[4] Hagit Attiya, Marc Snir, and Manfred K. Warmuth. Computing on an anonymous ring. *J. ACM*, 35(4):845–875, 1988.

[5] Patrick Blackburn, Maarten de Rijke, and Yde Venema. *Modal Logic*, volume 53 of *Cambridge Tracts in Theoretical Computer Science*. Cambridge University Press, 2001.

[6] Patrick Blackburn, Johan van Benthem, and Frank Wolter, editors. *Handbook of Modal Logic*, volume 3 of *Studies in Logic and Practical Reasoning*. Elsevier, 2007.

[7] Paolo Boldi, Shella Shammah, Sebastiano Vigna, Bruno Codenotti, Peter Gemmell, and Janos Simon. Symmetry breaking in anonymous networks: characterizations. In *Proc. ISTCS 1996*, pages 16–26. IEEE, 1996.

[8] Paolo Boldi and Sebastiano Vigna. Computing vector functions on anonymous networks. In *Proc. SIROCCO 1997*, pages 201–214. Carleton Scientific, 1997.

[9] Paolo Boldi and Sebastiano Vigna. An effective characterization of computability in anonymous networks. In *Proc. DISC 2001*, volume 2180 of *LNCS*, pages 33–47. Springer, 2001.

[10] J. A. Bondy and U. S. R. Murty. *Graph Theory with Applications*. North-Holland, New York, 1976.

[11] Krzysztof Diks, Evangelos Kranakis, Adam Malinowski, and Andrzej Pelc. Anonymous wireless rings. *Theoret. Comput. Sci.*, 145(1–2):95–109, 1995.

[12] Kit Fine. In so many possible worlds. *Notre Dame J. Formal Logic*, 13(4):516–520, 1972.

[13] Mika Göös, Juho Hirvonen, and Jukka Suomela. Lower bounds for local approximation. In *Proc. PODC 2012*. ACM Press, 2012.

[14] Lauri Hella, Matti Järvisalo, Antti Kuusisto, Juhana Laurinharju, Tuomo Lempiäinen, Kerkko Luosto, Jukka Suomela, and Jonni Virtema. Weak models of distributed computing, with connections to modal logic, 2012. Manuscript, arXiv:1205.2051 [cs.DC].

[15] Neil Immerman. *Descriptive Complexity*. Graduate Texts in Computer Science. Springer, 1999.

[16] Fabian Kuhn and Roger Wattenhofer. On the complexity of distributed graph coloring. In *Proc. PODC 2006*, pages 7–15. ACM Press, 2006.

[17] Nathan Linial. Locality in distributed graph algorithms. *SIAM J. Comput.*, 21(1):193–201, 1992.

[18] Alain Mayer, Moni Naor, and Larry Stockmeyer. Local computations on static and dynamic graphs. In *Proc. ISTCS 1995*, pages 268–278. IEEE, 1995.

[19] Moni Naor and Larry Stockmeyer. What can be computed locally? *SIAM J. Comput.*, 24(6):1259–1277, 1995.

[20] Nancy Norris. Computing functions on partially wireless networks. In *Proc. SIROCCO 1995*, pages 53–64. Carleton Scientific, 1996.

[21] David Peleg. *Distributed Computing: A Locality-Sensitive Approach*. SIAM Monographs on Discrete Mathematics and Applications. SIAM, 2000.

[22] Jukka Suomela. Survey of local algorithms. *ACM Comput. Surveys*. To appear.

[23] Stephen Wolfram. Statistical mechanics of cellular automata. *Reviews of Modern Physics*, 55(3):601–644, 1983.

[24] Masafumi Yamashita and Tsunehiko Kameda. Electing a leader when processor identity numbers are not distinct (extended abstract). In *Proc. WDAG 1989*, volume 392 of *LNCS*, pages 303–314. Springer, 1989.

[25] Masafumi Yamashita and Tsunehiko Kameda. Computing functions on asynchronous anonymous networks. *Mathematical Systems Theory*, 29(4):331–356, 1996.

[26] Masafumi Yamashita and Tsunehiko Kameda. Computing on anonymous networks: Part I—characterizing the solvable cases. *IEEE Trans. Parallel Distrib. Systems*, 7(1):69–89, 1996.

[27] Masafumi Yamashita and Tsunehiko Kameda. Computing on anonymous networks: Part II—decision and membership problems. *IEEE Trans. Parallel Distrib. Systems*, 7(1):90–96, 1996.

[28] Masafumi Yamashita and Tsunehiko Kameda. Leader election problem on networks in which processor identity numbers are not distinct. *IEEE Trans. Parallel Distrib. Systems*, 10(9):878–887, 1999.

Aggregation in Dynamic Networks

Alejandro Cornejo
MIT CSAIL
Cambridge, MA
acornejo@csail.mit.edu

Seth Gilbert
NUS
Singapore
seth.gilbert@comp.nus.edu.sg

Calvin Newport
Georgetown University
Washington, DC
cnewport@cs.georgetown.edu

ABSTRACT

The aggregation problem assumes that every process starts an execution with a unique token (an abstraction for data). The goal is to collect these tokens at a minimum number of processes by the end of the execution. This problem is particularly relevant to mobile networks where peer-to-peer communication is cheap (e.g., using 802.11 or Bluetooth), but uploading data to a central server can be costly (e.g., using 3G/4G). With this in mind, we study this problem in a dynamic network model, in which the communication graph can change arbitrarily from round to round.

We start by exploring *global* bounds. First we prove a negative result that shows that in general dynamic graphs no algorithm can achieve any measure of competitiveness against the optimal offline algorithm. Guided by this impossibility result, we focus our attention to dynamic graphs where every node interacts, at some point in the execution, with at least a p-fraction of the total number of nodes in the graph. We call these graphs p-clusters. We describe a distributed algorithm that in p-clusters aggregates the tokens to $O(\log n)$ processes with high probability.

We then turn our attention to *local* bounds. Specifically we ask whether its possible to aggregate to $O(\log n)$ processes in parts of the graph that locally form a p-cluster. Here we prove a negative result: this is only possible if the local p-clusters are sufficiently isolated from the rest of the graph. We then match this result with an algorithm that achieves the desired aggregation given (close to) the minimal required p-cluster isolation. Together, these results imply a "paradox of connectivity": in some graphs, increasing connectivity can lead to inherently worse aggregation performance.

We conclude by considering what seems to be a promising performance metric to circumvent our lower bounds for local aggregation algorithms. However, perhaps surprisingly, we show that no aggregation algorithm can perform well with respect to this metric, even in very well connected and very well isolated clusters.

Categories and Subject Descriptors

F.2.2 [**Analysis of Algorithms and Problem Complexity**]: Non-numerical Algorithms and Problems—*computations on discrete structures*; G.2.2 [**Discrete Mathematics**]: Graph Theory—*network problems*

General Terms

Algorithms, Theory

Keywords

dynamic graphs, aggregation

1. INTRODUCTION

In the aggregation problem every process starts the execution with a piece of information which is abstractly represented as a unique *token*. At the end of the execution every token must be uploaded to a central server. During the execution processes use peer-to-peer communication to consolidate the tokens at a minimum number of processes. The performance of an aggregation algorithm is described by the number of processes with tokens to upload at the end of the execution (the fewer the tokens the better the performance). This problem is motivated by the following observation: in many networks, local links between processes are far cheaper (in terms of expense, required infrastructure, and energy) than the long distance links needed to communicate with a central server. By using local links to aggregate tokens at a small number of processes, we reduce the total number of expensive long distance links required at the end of the execution to upload all the tokens.

Implicit in this cost analysis is the assumption that, in practice, it consumes less bandwidth/energy to upload a collection of x tokens from a single source than to have x distinct sources each upload one token. There are many different rationales for this assumption. For example, each long distance connection induces a fixed overhead independent of the size of the packet data payload. This comes from both the handshaking required to connect with the central server, and the fixed size of the packet header. In addition, the data represented by abstract tokens in our model is often, in reality, either compressible or summarizable (e.g., the server only needs an average, max, or min over the values). This also leads to great bandwidth/energy reductions when we can collect the values at a small number of sources before uploading.

One setting in which this problem is particularly relevant is mobile networks. To give a concrete example, consider a traffic reporting system, such as CarTel [5], which uses drivers' smartphones to upload traffic observations to a central traffic server. With major cellphone carriers such as AT&T eliminating their unlimited data plans, uploading these observations might deplete users' limited minutes. In addition, cellular links drain device batteries (a 3G link, for example, can use orders of magnitude more battery power than a local 802.11 or Bluetooth link [14]). A good aggregation algorithm in this setting could leverage free, low-energy local links (i.e., 802.11 or Bluetooth) to reduce the usage of expensive, high-energy long distance links (i.e., 3G).

In the remainder of this section we outline our contributions and we describe some of the related work.

Problem Setup.

Aggregation is a problem of deep interest to practitioners. In this paper, however, we show that it also produces a set of interesting problems for theoreticians to tackle. We study both upper and lower bounds for randomized solutions to the aggregation problem in a synchronous dynamic network model. We model the communication topology as a *dynamic graph* where the edge set can change arbitrarily from round to round. We adopt this model for two reasons. First, it matches the unpredictable topology observed in real mobile networks, a setting where the aggregation problem is particularly relevant. Second, dynamic graphs generalize a diversity of different topology assumptions and results in this model, therefore, are widely applicable (c.f., the discussion in [11]).

Global Results.

We start by showing a negative result which proves that no aggregation algorithm is competitive with the optimal offline algorithm in every dynamic graph (with respect to the number of processes required to upload all the tokens). Specifically, we show there are dynamic graphs where the optimal offline algorithm can aggregate to a single process, but with high probability any randomized algorithm will aggregate to $\Omega(n)$ processes, where n is the network size. Chastened by this impossibility result, we redirect our ambition to identifying natural structures that enable aggregation algorithms to perform well and which arise in real-world dynamic graphs. This search leads us to the notion of a *p-cluster* (where $p \in (0, 1]$). We say a dynamic graph is a *p*-cluster if by the end of the execution every node has interacted with at least *p*-fraction of all nodes. We highlight that we do not restrict when these connections occur or in what order. In particular we do not assume these connections are random, which would imply a graph with expander-like properties and would simplify significantly the task of aggregation. In contrast, we model these connections as being picked by an adversary. We describe a randomized algorithm CLUSTERAGGREGATE$_p$ that with high probability aggregates all tokens to $\mathcal{O}(\log n)$ processes when executing on a *p*-cluster.

Local Results.

In the second part of this paper, we turn our attention to proving performance guarantees that depend not on the "global" structure of the dynamic graph but on its "local" structure. For example, consider a dynamic graph that is not itself a *p*-cluster, but that includes many subsets of nodes that locally form *p*-clusters. We would like our aggregation

algorithms to *discover these hidden structures* and locally aggregate well.

Consider, for example, a hypothetical aggregation algorithm which ensures that, for every subset of nodes that form a 1-cluster (i.e., clique) in the dynamic graph, there is at most one process that uploads tokens at the end of the execution (i.e., at most one "uploader"). Such an algorithm (which is, in fact, easy to obtain) would guarantee the following property: given a dynamic graph G, where η is the size of the minimum clique cover of G: for every execution of the algorithm, the number of uploaders is at most η. Such results having the interesting property that they leverage the existence of hidden structure, even while finding such structure may be NP-complete (as is finding the minimum clique cover).

Here, we focus on leveraging the existence of local *p*-clusters in the graph. We first prove that the ability to aggregate well in a local *p*-cluster depends on the isolation of this cluster with respect to the rest of the graph. In more detail, a subset of nodes is a (p, r)-cluster if: (a) the nodes form a *p*-cluster amongst themselves; and (b) a node in the cluster has at most r neighbors outside the cluster. We prove that for any aggregation algorithm that guarantees at most k uploaders in each (p, r)-cluster, r must be $O(k^2)$: in other words, more aggregation requires more isolation. Notice that this result has interesting echoes of classical complexity theory, where good polynomial-time approximations of the largest clique problem require sufficient isolation of the cliques in the graph.

On the positive side, we then extend our analysis of CLUSTERAGGREGATE$_p$ showing that it guarantees, with high probability, to aggregate all the data in every $(p, O(\log n))$-cluster to $\mathcal{O}(\log n)$ nodes in that cluster. By the previous lower bound result, this performance is within a log factor of the optimal, both in terms of the amount of isolation required and on the total number of broadcasters.

Together, these results imply a "paradox of connectivity": in some graphs, increasing connectivity can lead to inherently worse aggregation performance. Intuitively we would expect the performance of aggregation protocols to improve as the networks become more connected, allowing more sharing of information. What we show, though, is that when clusters are relatively isolated, we can achieve good performance, limiting the number of uploaders in each cluster. By contrast, as connectivity increases, the performance worsens and it is impossible to achieve the same bounds on the number of uploaders per cluster.

To conclude we turn our attention to an alternative local performance metric. The metric used up to this point counts the number of processes in a cluster that upload. The alternative metric, by contrast, counts the number of processes that upload a token *on behalf* of a process in a cluster. Though the metric seems like a promising alternative to circumvent our previous lower bounds, we prove, perhaps surprisingly, that it is impossible to satisfy. In more detail, we show no aggregation algorithm can guarantee to perform well with respect to this metric, even if we require it to only work in very isolated and very well connected clusters (i.e., $(1, 1)$-clusters).

Related Work.

Dynamic networks have received a lot of attention in recent years. Though many different dynamic network models have been proposed (see [11] for a good overview), the variant most relevant to our work was introduced in [9], where the authors studied gossip in the context of a communication topology that could change arbitrarily from round to round. In subsequent work, prioritized gossip [3], consensus [10], and random linear network coding [4] were also studied in the same model. In [9, 10, 4] the network was assumed to be connected at every round: such a constraint is similar to our global p-clusters property. Our study of local p-clusters, by contrast, has some echoes of the study of prioritized gossip in [3], which also sidestepped global constraints and proved guarantees relative to local connectivity properties.

Our model differs from the existing models in [9, 3, 10, 4], however, in one crucial respect. These previous studies assume *broadcast communication*: in each round, each process can broadcast a message which is received by its arbitrary neighbor set. In this paper, by contrast, we assume *unicast communication*: in each round, each process is arbitrarily paired with at most one of other process with which it can interact. Such unicast communication has been previously studied, among other dynamic settings, in the context of gossip–e.g., [2]—and population protocols (see, [1]). In the former, the choice of pair is typically random, not arbitrary, while in the latter, the protocols are assumed to have limited memory.

Finally, there exists a sizable corpus of work on aggregation in networks, much of it centered on the collection, combination, and uploading of data (or functions on the data, such as average value) in resource-constrained sensor networks; c.f., [12, 6, 8]. The topic has proven applicable in other settings as well, such as gathering information from components in a telecommunications system [13].

2. MODEL

We consider a synchronous network with unpredictable connectivity topology. Namely, we model communication using a *dynamic graph* $D = (V, \mathcal{E})$, where V is a static set of nodes, and $\mathcal{E} : \{1, ..., t\} \to 2^{V \times V}$ is a function mapping each round number $r \in \{1, ..., t\}$ to a set of undirected edges $\mathcal{E}(r)$ that captures the connectivity in that round. The parameter $t \geq 1$ is the *duration* of the dynamic graph. Different dynamic graphs can have different durations.[1] We constrain these graphs to behave as *interaction graphs*: in each round r, each process u is included in at most one edge in $\mathcal{E}(r)$, and there are no self-edges. Thus, for each round r, the static graph $(V, \mathcal{E}(r))$ is a matching. For each round $r \in \{1, ..., t\}$ in the execution, the edge set $\mathcal{E}(r)$ defines which pairs of processes *interact* by sending each other their state and performing some local computations.

To simplify definitions and notation, we assume V is fixed and known for all dynamic graphs. This allows us to define an *algorithm* $\mathcal{A}$ as a collection of $|V|$ randomized *processes*, one for each $u \in V$. It follows that processes have unique ids (as they can agree on a mapping from V to an id space) and know $n = |V|$.

---

[1]In this paper we study algorithms that run for a fixed duration and then terminate. This follows because in practice aggregation is something that occurs over a fixed interval, as in "take a sensor reading, aggregate for t seconds, upload the data, then start over with a new reading." By giving durations to dynamic graphs, when we later say that an algorithm must work with all dynamic graphs, it follows automatically that must work for all durations.

Aggregation Problem.

At the beginning of every execution α, each process u is passed a unique *token* $\alpha.\sigma[u]$. Similarly, at the end of any execution α each process u produces an output (potentially empty) $\alpha.\gamma[u]$. We call $\alpha.\sigma$ the *input assignment* of α, and $\alpha.\gamma$ the *output assignment* of α.

An *aggregation algorithm*, must ensure that every token in the input assignment is subsequently output exactly once in the output assignment. In other words, tokens are neither lost nor duplicated. Formally:

Definition 1 (Aggregation Algorithm). An algorithm $\mathcal{A}$ is an aggregation algorithm if and only if at the end of every execution α of $\mathcal{A}$ we have:

- *No Loss:* $\bigcup_{u \in V} \alpha.\gamma[u] = \bigcup_{u \in V} \alpha.\sigma[u]$.
- *No Duplication:* $\forall u, v \in V, u \neq v : \alpha.\gamma[u] \cap \alpha.\gamma[v] = \emptyset$.

Uploaders.

A natural metric for the performance of an aggregation algorithm is the total number of processes that end up broadcasting at least one token at the end of the execution. In the rest of the paper we call any such process an *uploader*. The smaller the number of uploaders, the better the performance of an aggregation algorithm. Formally, given an execution α, the set of uploaders is the set of nodes which upload at the end of the execution $\{u \mid u \in V \wedge \alpha.\gamma[u] \neq \emptyset\}$.

Token Ownership.

We can leverage the conditions of Definition 1 to prove that every aggregation algorithm must satisfy a property we call *token ownership*. In the paragraph below we define this property informally. This should be sufficient for understanding the lower bound proofs that follow. The informal description is followed by a formal proof.

At the end of every execution prefix of an aggregation algorithm, each process u *owns* a set of tokens T_u such that the following two properties are true: (1) if we extend this execution prefix such that process u interacts with no other processes for the remainder of the execution, then with probability 1 it will output T_u at the end of this extension; and (2) for every token $x \in T_u$, either u received x as its input, or there is some other process v that received x as its input and there is a sequence of interactions in the prefix that starts with v and ends with u.

In other words, at the end of every round, every process has to commit to a set of tokens that it will definitely output if it finishes the execution in isolation. Furthermore, these tokens have to be tokens it actually heard about. To reiterate: these are not extra conditions that we impose on aggregation algorithms, we prove below that they follow from the definition of such algorithms.

Formally, fix some execution *prefix* β of an aggregation algorithm, and a process $u \in V$. We use $i(\beta, u)$ to describe every extension of β in which process u has no further communication with other nodes (that is, u is *isolated* in the extension of β). The following lemma formalizes property (1) of token ownership:

Lemma 1. *Fix some execution prefix β of an aggregation algorithm, and a node $u \in V$. For every $\alpha, \alpha' \in i(\beta, u)$, $\alpha.\gamma[u] = \alpha'.\gamma[u]$. That is, in all isolated extensions of β, u outputs the same tokens.*

Proof. The lemma follows from the *no loss* and *no duplication* conditions of Definition 1. If there existed a pair $\alpha, \alpha' \in i(\beta, u)$ such that $\alpha.\gamma[u] \neq \alpha'.\gamma[u]$, then there would be a probability greater than 0 that one of these two properties would be violated in some execution. □

We say $(u, r) \leadsto_G (v, r')$, for $u, v \in V$, rounds $r' \geq r \geq 1$, and dynamic graph $G = (V, \mathcal{E})$, if and only if: (a) $u = v$; or (b) there is a sequence of edges, $e_r = \{u, u_r\}, e_{r+1} = \{u_r, u_{r+1}\}, ..., e_{r'} = \{u_{r'}, v\}$, such that for every $i \in \{r, ..., r'\}$: $e_i \in \mathcal{E}(i)$, (Informally, $(u, r) \leadsto_G (v, r')$ indicates that there exists a sequence of edges by which u can pass information it knows at the beginning of r to v by r' in G.) The following lemma formalizes property (2) of token ownership:

Lemma 2. *Let α be an execution of an aggregation algorithm with dynamic graph G of duration t. For every $u \in V$ and token $x \in \alpha.\gamma[u]$: there exists $v \in V$ such that $x = \alpha.\sigma[v]$ and $(v, 1) \leadsto_G (u, t)$. That is, if u outputs a token x then there is a path from the process that started with x to u in G.*

Proof. If this lemma did not hold then some process v might output a token x even though there is no path from a process that started with x to process v. We consider two cases: First, if there is a path from every process to v in this execution, then the execution violates the no loss property of Definition 1. Second, if there are instead some processes that do not have paths to v, it is possible that one of these processes started with x, in which case process v may have made a lucky guess by outputting x. However, because there is no interaction with these processes and v, this execution is indistinguishable with respect to v from one in which none of these processes started with x: and in this execution the no loss property is once again violated. □

Notice that as a result of these lemmas, there is no benefit to *copying* tokens: each must be owned by a single process at any given time.

3. GLOBAL BOUNDS

3.1 The Impossibility of a Competitive Aggregation Algorithm

The amount of achievable aggregation in a given execution is affected by the dynamic graph for which the execution is defined. For example, if the dynamic graph isolates all nodes we cannot blame the algorithm for requiring n uploaders at the end of the execution. With this in mind, it makes sense to judge an algorithm's performance relative to the best achievable performance in the graph.

We could hope to find an algorithm that guarantees (with high probability) at most $k \cdot f(n)$ uploaders in any dynamic graph where the offline optimal algorithm (which knows G in advance) guarantees at most k uploaders. Ideally we would like $f(n)$ to a reasonably small function (i.e. $f(n) \in$ polylog(n)). Our first result, however, proves that no algorithm can provide these guarantees.

Theorem 3. *For every aggregation algorithm $\mathcal{A}$ there is a dynamic graph G where the offline optimal algorithm guarantees 1 uploader but w.h.p., the system $(\mathcal{A}, G)$ produces an execution with $\Omega(n)$ uploaders.*

Proof. We define dynamic graph $G = (V, \mathcal{E})$ with a duration of $\lfloor n/2 \rfloor + 2$ rounds, but it is straightforward to extend it longer durations. Parition V into pairs of nodes (omitting one node if $|V|$ is odd). Define $\mathcal{E}(1)$ to consist of one edge $\{u, v\}$ for each pair $\{u, v\}$ from our partition. Next, for each pair, randomly select one node to be *isolated* and another to be *social*. In the next round we do not include any isolated node in an edge. Also, we choose a single *super*-social node to visit every other social node (and the node omitted in round 1 for the case where $|V|$ is odd). The fact that the offline optimal algorithm would guarantee 1 uploader follows from the possibility of aggregating all information at the super-social node.

Here we deploy the concept of *token ownership* which tells us that at the end of every round, every process must *own* a set of tokens (potentially empty) that it will output if it continues the execution in isolation. Furthermore, this set can only contain tokens it could have heard about at this point. It follows that after the first round of any execution in G, for each pair $\{u, v\}$, at least one of these two processes owns at least one token. Call this the *committed process* (breaking ties arbitrarily in the case where both would output a token). When constructing G we choose the isolated node at random. For each pair, therefore, the probability that we isolate a committed process is $\frac{1}{2}$. Notice, any isolated committed process outputs at least one token. We thus expect $\Theta(n)$ committed processes that correspond to isolated nodes, and Chernoff tells us that with high probability we are not more than a constant factor away from this expectation. It follows that, w.h.p., $\mathcal{A}$ combined with G generates an execution where the number of uploaders is $\Omega(n)$. □

3.2 Aggregating in Well-Connected Dynamic Graphs

The previous lower bound tells us that it is impossible for an aggregation algorithm to be competitive with an optimal offline algorithm in all dynamic graphs. However this result relied on dynamic graphs in which a large fraction of the nodes had only a small number of connections with the rest of the graph. We should not be surprised that it is hard to aggregate well in the presence of such minimal and fleeting connections. Here we present an aggregation algorithm that is competitive as long as the graph is well-connected, which we formalize with the natural notion of a *p-cluster*:

Definition 2 (*p*-Cluster). *A dynamic graph G is a p-cluster for some $p \in (0, 1]$ iff every $u \in V$ is included in an edge in G with at least $\lfloor p|V| \rfloor$ different nodes.*

We emphasize that we do not assume the connections of a node in a *p*-cluster to be random (which would simplify the task of aggregation). In contrast, we consider the worst possible set of connections, modeling them as picked by an adaptive online adversary.

Below we present an algorithm tailored to aggregate well in *p*-clusters.

Algorithm.

A process can be in one of two states, either *active* or *inactive*. At the end of the execution (i.e. all time t) all active processes will upload their tokens. Initially every process is active and therefore a potential uploader. When starting the algorithm each process u initializes a TAGCOUNT$_u$ variable to zero, and selects an identifier ID$_u$ of $\Theta(\log n)$

bits at random. Consider the interaction between processes u and v. If $\text{ID}_u \leq \text{ID}_v$ then process u does nothing. On the other hand, if $\text{ID}_u > \text{ID}_v$ then process u increases its TAGCOUNT_u variable. If in addition process v is active and $\text{TAGCOUNT}_u \geq c_p \log n$ then process u hands off all its tokens to process v *and* switches to the inactive state. Here $c_p \in \Theta(1/p)$ is a sufficiently large constant which depends on p which we will determine later.

Algorithm 1 CLUSTERAGGREGATION$_p$ at process u

1: ACTIVE$_u \leftarrow$ **true**
2: ID$_u \leftarrow$ random string of $\Theta(\log n)$ bits
3: TAGCOUNT$_u \leftarrow 0$
4: **for** each interaction with process v **do**
5:     **if** ID$_u >$ID$_v$ **then**
6:         **if** ACTIVE$_v$ and TAGCOUNT$_u \geq c_p \log n$ **then**
7:             hand off tokens to process v
8:             ACTIVE$_u \leftarrow$ **false**
9:         TAGCOUNT$_u \leftarrow$TAGCOUNT$_u$+1
10: **if** ACTIVE$_u$**then** upload tokens

We reiterate that all active process broadcast data at the end of the execution, and a process only hands off its tokens and becomes inactive when encountering an active process. Therefore the CLUSTERAGGREGATION algorithm satisfies the no loss and integrity conditions by construction, it remains only to show that when the algorithm is executed in p-cluster with high probability the number of active nodes is at most $\mathcal{O}(\log n)$.

Moreover, also by construction it follows that the $c_p \log n$ processes with the smallest random identifier in the graph cannot get tagged $c_p \log n$ times, and therefore they cannot become inactive.

Fact 1. The processes with the smallest $c_p \log n$ identifiers remain active throughout the execution.

The following theorem captures the main result of this section.

Theorem 4. *Fix a constant $p \in (0,1]$. For every p-cluster dynamic graph G the system (CLUSTERAGGREGATION$_p$, G) produces w.h.p., an execution with $\mathcal{O}(\log n)$ uploaders.*

Since the node identifiers are chosen uniformly at random from a space of $\Theta(\log n)$ bits, the probability that they are not unique can be made less than n^{-c} for any constant c. Hence, we can use a union bound to show that w.h.p., the random identifiers are unique. Thus for simplicity and without loss of generality, in the rest of the proof we assume that the random identifiers generated are unique.

Let S be the set of $\mathcal{O}(\log n)$ processes with the smallest random identifiers. To prove theorem 4 it suffices to show that with high probability at the end of the execution only the processes in S will remain active. Since by assumption the graph is a p-cluster, it follows that any process will have met with at least $p|V|$ different processes. Specifically, we divide the interactions of every process in $V \setminus S$ into two groups of size $p|V|/2$. We will then show that with high probability a process is tagged $c_p \log n$ times in the first group of the interactions by a subset of the processes in S, and is subsequently deactivated in the second group of the interactions by a process in S (with which it had not interacted).

To prove theorem 4 we need two technical lemmas. The first lemma shows that, given a set $Q \subseteq V$ of processes selected according to some property of their random identifier (i.e., smallest, largest, etc.), during the first half of the interactions a fixed process $u \in V \setminus Q$ interacts with no more (and no less) than a constant fraction of the processes in Q. The proof follows from a generalization of the Chernoff bound to Hypergeometric random variables.

Lemma 5. *Let X_u be a random variable that counts the number of processes in Q a process $u \in V \setminus Q$ meets in the first $p|V|/2$ interactions. $\Pr\left[X_u \leq \frac{p}{4}|Q|\right] \leq e^{-\frac{p}{16}|Q|}$ and $\Pr\left[X_u \geq \frac{3p}{4}|Q|\right] \leq e^{-\frac{p}{24}|Q|}$*

Before we can prove the above lemma, we need to state a slight generalization of the traditional Chernoff bound.

Generalized Chernoff Bounds. *Let Z be a random variable with Binomial or Hypergeometric distribution, and let $\mu = \mathbb{E}[Z]$. Then:*

$$\Pr[Z \geq (1+\delta)\mu] \leq e^{-\frac{\delta^2 \mu}{3}} \text{ and } \Pr[Z \leq (1-\delta)\mu] \leq e^{-\frac{\delta^2 \mu}{2}}.$$

The Binomial distribution describes the number of successes in a sequence of draws *with* replacement, and can be expressed as a sum of independent random variables representing each draw. On the other hand, the Hypergeometric distribution describes the number of successes in a sequence of draws *without* replacement, and hence the draws are not independent.

Typically, the Chernoff bound applies to random variables with a binomial distribution. However, as noted by [7], it seems reasonable to expect that drawing samples without replacement would produce smaller random fluctuations than sampling with replacement, so the fact that the Chernoff bound also holds for the Hypergeometric distribution is not entirely surprising. We omit the proof of this generalized bound since it can be found in Theorem 2.1 and 2.10 in [7].

Now lemma 5 follows by a straightforward application of this generalized Chernoff bound.

Proof of lemma 5. We have a total of $|V|$ processes, we are interacting with $p|V|/2$ of them (without replacement), and we want to count how many times we meet a process in $Q \subseteq V$. Observe that X_u has a Hypergeometric distribution, and hence $\mathbb{E}[X_u] = \frac{p}{2}|Q|$. The theorem follows from the generalized Chernoff bounds (with $\delta = \frac{1}{2}$). $\square$

Therefore, assuming $|Q|$ is "large", with high probability a process $u \in V \setminus Q$ will see no more and no less than a constant fraction of the process in Q during the first half of the interactions.

Our second technical lemma shows that w.h.p., a process $u \in V \setminus Q$ will encounter in the second half of the interactions a process with which it hadn't interacted before. To prove this we leverage lemma 5, and observe that at every interaction a process u has a probability of meeting a process in Q which is $\mathcal{O}(|Q|/|V|)$.

Lemma 6. *Assume $|Q| \geq 48/p$. The probability that a process $u \in V \setminus Q$ does not interact with a new process of Q in the last $p|V|/2$ interactions is less than $e^{-\frac{p}{48}|Q|}$.*

Proof. Fix $u \in V \setminus Q$ and let I_1 and I_2 correspond to the first $p|V|/2$ interactions, and the remaining interactions (at least $p|V|/2$) respectively.

Define X as the event that process u does not meet a single process of Q in the interactions of I_2. We want to show that the probability that X occurs is exponentially small (on $|Q|$). Define Y as the event that process u meets with more than $\frac{3p}{4}|Q|$ fraction of the processes in Q during the interactions I_1. By lemma 5 $\Pr[Y] \leq e^{-\frac{p}{24}|Q|}$.

Now consider $\Pr[X|\neg Y]$, that is the event that process u does not meet a single process in Q during the interactions of I_2, conditioned on the fact that there are at least $\frac{1}{4}|Q|$ processes with which it didn't interact in I_1. Observe that until process u meets one of those $\frac{1}{4}|Q|$ remaining processes in Q, then at every interaction of I_2 it will meet a process in Q with probability at least $\frac{1}{4}|Q|/|V|$. Therefore:

$$\Pr[X|\neg Y] \leq \left(1 - \frac{1}{4}\frac{|Q|}{|V|}\right)^{\frac{p}{2}|V|} \leq e^{-\frac{p}{8}|Q|}$$

Finally, by the law of total probability we have $\Pr[X] = \Pr[X|Y]\Pr[Y] + \Pr[X|\neg Y]\Pr[\neg Y] \leq \Pr[Y] + \Pr[X|\neg Y] \leq e^{-\frac{p}{8}|Q|} + e^{-\frac{p}{24}|Q|} \leq 2e^{-\frac{p}{24}|Q|} \leq e^{-\frac{p}{24}|Q|+1}$, and since $|Q| \geq 48/p$ then $\Pr[X] \leq^{-\frac{p}{48}|Q|}$ $\square$

With these technical lemmas in place we are ready to prove theorem 4.

Proof of theorem 4. Let S be the set of $5c_p \log n$ processes with smallest identifier, and let A be the set of $c_p \log n$ processes with smallest identifier, clearly $A \subset S$. Define $B = S \setminus A$ as the remaining $4c_p \log n = |B|$ processes in S. By Fact 1 the processes in A remain active throughout the execution.

To prove the theorem it suffices to show that w.h.p., all processes in $V \setminus S$ become inactive. In particular we will show that the probability that a fixed process in $V \setminus S$ remains active is at most $1/n^2$, and then union bound over all processes.

Fix a process $u \in V \setminus S$. If process u meets $|B|/4$ processes of B in the first $p|V|/2$ interactions it will get tagged at least $c_p \log n$ times, and if in the remaining interactions it meets a process of A it will become inactive.

Instantiating lemma 5 with $Q = B$, the probability that process u *does not* interact with at least $|B|/4$ processes within the first $p|V|/2$ interactions is at most $e^{-p|B|/16}$. Similarly, instantiating lemma 6 with $Q = A$, the probability that in the remaining interactions process u *does not* meet a process of A is at most $e^{-p|A|/48}$. Therefore, the probability that process u remains active is at most $e^{-p|B|/16} + e^{-p|A|/48}$. Finally, by letting $c_p \geq 3 \cdot 48/p$ we have that the probability that node u remains active is at most $1/n^2$ which concludes the theorem.

$\square$

We remark that by tweaking the constants, the same proof can be used to show the same statement holds with probability at least $1 - 1/n^c$ for any constant c. This fact will be useful later.

4. LOCAL BOUNDS

In practice, a lot of the networks where aggregation is interesting are large. For example, consider a network of thousands of taxicabs spanning a large metropolitan city. In this setting, it is unlikely that the global network of taxicabs, spanning the whole city, form a p-cluster (some cabs will inevitably be stuck in the boondocks). At the same time, however, there are likely plenty of clusters of cabs *within the network* that locally form p-clusters (e.g., at areas of high density like downtown or at the airport). The question we pursue in this section is whether we can find algorithms that successfully find and leverage these local structures that are hidden within the larger global topology.

In doing so, we discover the following interesting *paradox of connectivity*. Intuitively it might seem that aggregation protocols perform only better on better connected networks: at worst, a protocol could ignore the extraneous communication links. In fact, however, we observe the following: when the local clusters are relatively isolated, we can develop aggregation protocols that work well, minimizing the number of uploaders in each cluster; by contrast, when the clusters have more communication with the rest of the network, it becomes impossible to achieve efficient aggregation.

We must begin, however, by generalizing our definitions of a cluster to describe a well-connected sub-graph within a larger graph.

Definition 3 ((p, r)-Cluster). Fix some $p \in (0, 1]$ and $r \in \{0, ..., n\}$. We say a subset of $S \subseteq V$ forms a (p, r)-cluster in dynamic graph G, iff: 1) every $u \in S$ has a link in G to at least $\lfloor p|S| \rfloor$ different nodes in S; and 2) no node $u \in S$ has a link to more than r nodes in $V \setminus S$.

Observe that if $r = 0$ then we require clusters to be completely isolated from the rest of the graph, whereas, letting $r = n$ imposes no isolation requirements.

4.1 The Necessity of Cluster Isolation

Intuition.

In this subsection we show that if an aggregation algorithm guarantees no more than k nodes in every (p, r)-cluster then r cannot be much bigger than k^2. In other words, *more aggregation requires more isolation.*

At a high-level, our lower bound works by constructing two dynamic graphs and arguing that if r is larger than $O(k^2)$ then any aggregation algorithm will fail (with constant probability) to guarantee k uploaders in every (p, r)-cluster in one of the two dynamic graphs.

To simplify the theorem statement and the proof we introduce the following definition.

Definition 4. Fix $p \in (0, 1]$ and $r, k \in \{1, ..., n\}$. Then $\mathcal{A}$ is a (p, r, k)-**cluster-aggregation algorithm** if in every dynamic graph G w.h.p., $(G, \mathcal{A})$ generates an execution where every (p, r)-cluster in G has at most k uploaders.

Theorem 7. *Fix some $p \in (1/2, 3/4)$ and $k \leq \sqrt{n/40}$. For any $r > 30k^2$ there does not exist a (p, r, k)-cluster-aggregation algorithm.*

Proof. Assume for contradiction that $\mathcal{A}$ is a (p, r, k)-cluster-aggregation algorithm for $r > 40k^2$.

We will construct a pair of dynamic graphs and we will argue that when $\mathcal{A}$ is executed on either of these two graphs, with constant probability there will exist a (p, r)-cluster with more than k uploaders, reaching a contradiction.

We begin by defining some constants $q = 5k$, $m = 2k$, and $\ell = m\left(\frac{p}{1-p}\right)$. A few observations regarding these constants: (1) $m < \ell < 3m$; (2) $\ell/(m+\ell) \geq p$; and (3) $q\ell < r$.

We partition the first $q\ell + qm$ nodes into sets $X_1, \ldots, X_q$ and $Y_1, \ldots, Y_q$, where for $i \in \{1, \ldots, q\}$ we have $|X_i| = \ell$ and $|Y_i| = m$. Notice that since $k \leq \sqrt{n/40}$ then $q(\ell + m) \leq (5k)(8k) \leq n$, and hence this partitioning is possible. In the following we only deal with the $q\ell + qm$ nodes partitioned and assume the other nodes are isolated in both graphs we construct.

Let $X = \bigcup_{i=1}^q X_i$, and $Z_i = X_i \cup Y_i$. In both graphs, the first set of rounds consist of nodes in X interacting with each other, while the remaining nodes are isolated. That is, the nodes X form a clique in the both dynamic graphs (in fact we will argue that X is a (p, r)-clique in both graphs). After all nodes in X have interacted with each other we differentiate the graphs G_1 and G_2.

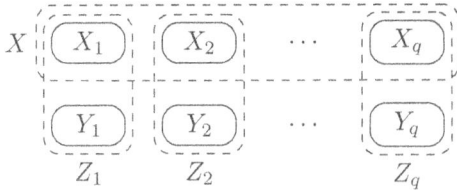

Figure 1: **For every $i \in \{1, \ldots, q\}$ we have $|X_i| = \ell$ and $|Y_i| = m$. In both G_1 and G_2 the nodes in the component $X = \bigcup_{i=1}^q X_i$ interact as a clique. For every $i \in \{1, \ldots, q\}$ the nodes in Z_i interact as a complete bipartite graph between X_i and Y_i in G_1, and a (not-complete) bipartite graph between X_i and Y_i in G_2.**

Constructing G_1.

For each $i \in \{1, \ldots, q\}$ we schedule each of the m nodes of Y_i to interact with each of the ℓ nodes of X_i. We schedules these interactions in m *passes*, each consisting of ℓ interactions. In each pass, for each i, one node from Y_i interacts with every node in X_i in some arbitrary order. During the pass, there are no other interactions.

Thus, at the end of the duration G_1, the nodes in X have interacted in a clique, and for each i the nodes in $Z_i = X_i \cup Y_i$ interact in a complete bipartite graph between X_i and Y_i. Notice that the nodes in Y_i have no direct interactions with each other.

First observe that the nodes in X form a (p, r)-cluster: (i) every node in X interacts with every other node in X, and (ii) each node in X interacts with at most $m = 2k < r$ nodes not in X.

In addition observe that for every i the nodes in Z_i form a (p, r)-cluster: (i) since $\ell/(m+\ell) \geq p$, every node in Z_i interacts with at least a p fraction of the other nodes in Z_i; and (ii) each node in Y_i only interacted with nodes in X_i while each node in X_i has interacted with at most $q\ell$ nodes outside Z_i. Since $q\ell < (4k+4)(6k) < 48k^2 < r$ (by assumption on r), it follows that the nodes in Z_i form a (p, r)-cluster.

Constructing G_2.

Graph G_2 is almost identical to G_1 with the following exception: for each $i \in \{1, \ldots, q\}$ we pick a random number n_i uniformly from the set $\{1, \ldots, m\}$. After the n_i^{th} pass in the interaction between X_i and Y_i we then isolate all nodes in X_i and Y_i for the remainder of the graph. In other words, G_2 is defined like G_1 with the exception that, for each i, the interactions between X_i and Y_i are aborted at a random point. We refer to this as the "abort point". As before, observe that X is a (p, r)-cluster, although it may no longer be true that every Z_i is a (p, r)-cluster.

Indistinguishability argument.

We now analyze the behavior of $\mathcal{A}$ when executed on these two dynamic graphs. First consider an execution in G_1. Let A_i be the nodes in Z_i whose processes upload tokens at the end of their interactions. Observe that if $\exists i$ such that $A_i \cap Y_i > k$ then the (p, r)-cluster formed by Z_i has more than k uploaders. Let p' be the probability that that an execution of $\mathcal{A}$ in G_1 leads to this case. Since, with high probability, the number of uploaders is $\leq k$, we conclude that $p' \leq 1/n$.

Consider the case where $A_i \cap Y_i \leq k$, which occurs with probability at least $(1 - 1/n)$. In this case, the tokens of at least $m - k = k$ nodes in Y_i are transferred to a node in X_i.

We now turn our attention to G_2. For the purpose of this discussion, fix some i. Notice that for processes in Y_i that interact with X_i before the "abort point," the executions G_1 and G_2 are indistinguishable. Recall that in G_1, for each Y_i, there are at least k processes that rely on some other processes to upload their token. Thus, for each of these processes, if the abort point in G_2 occurs after their interaction with X_i, they will continue to rely on other processes to upload their token, as they cannot distinguish G_1 and G_2.

For a given execution on graph G_2, let $v \in Y_i$ be the node that interacts with X_i in the last pass before the abort point. If v chooses not to upload its token (i.e., if it is one of those $\geq k$ processes in Y_i that rely on some other process to upload its token), then some process in X_i must upload the token of v since there are no further interactions after the abort point at which its token might be aggregated. (This follows from the no-loss property and the notion of token ownership defined in Section 2).

We thus conclude with the following analysis. With probability at least $(1 - 1/n) \geq 1/2$, for every Y_i there are at least k nodes that rely on a process in X_i to upload their token. Moreover, with probability at least $k/m = 1/2$ the abort point occurs immediately after one of these $\geq k$ nodes interacts with X_i. Thus, with probability $\geq 1/4$, at least one node in X_i needs to upload tokens. In total, then, the expected number of nodes in X that upload tokens is at least $q/4 > k$. We conclude that with constant probability, the number of nodes in X that upload tokens is greater than k, which contradicts our assumption that $\mathcal{A}$ is a (p, k, r)-cluster-aggregation algorithm. □

4.2 An Upper Bound for Isolated Cliques

Here we show that for any $r \in \mathcal{O}(\log n)$ the CLUSTER-AGGREGATION$_p$ algorithm aggregates the tokens to $\mathcal{O}(\log n)$ uploaders in every subset $S \subseteq V$ which forms a (p, r)-cluster. This comes within a $\mathcal{O}(\log n)$ factor of the minimal amount of isolation established by theorem 7.

Theorem 8. *Fix a constant $p \in (0, 1]$, $r \in \mathcal{O}(\log n)$. For every dynamic graph G the system (CLUSTERAGGREGATION$_p$, G) produces w.h.p., an execution where every (p, r)-cluster has $\mathcal{O}(\log n)$ uploaders.*

The proof of this theorem follows the same spirit as theorem 4. The key difference is that, in the context of a (p, r)-cluster, Fact 1 is no longer true. Specifically, consider any set $S \subset V$ which forms a (p, r)-cluster. It still holds that the $c_p \log n$ processes with the smallest random identifier in a set S cannot be tagged $c_p \log n$ times by other processes inside S. However, the nodes in S *can be* tagged $c_p \log n$ times (or more) by processes which are outside S.

Nevertheless, observe that since $r = r_0 \log n$ for some sufficiently large constant r_0, then by letting $c_p \geq 2_r 0$ we can guarantee $c_p \log n \geq 2r$, which implies that $c_p \log n - r \geq \frac{1}{2} c_p \log n$. Therefore, if we consider the $c_p \log n$ processes with the smallest identifiers in S, only half of them can get tagged by processes outside S, and therefore we have the following fact (in the same spirit as Fact 1).

Fact 2. Assume $c_p \geq 2r_0$. In every subset $S \subseteq V$ which forms a (p, r)-cluster, the processes with the smallest $\frac{1}{2} c_p \log n$ identifiers remain active throughout the execution.

With this fact in place, we can essentially reuse the proof of theorem 4 to show that if we fix a (p, r)-cluster, then with high probability we aggregate to $\mathcal{O}(\log n)$ nodes in that cluster. Since trivially there are never more than $\mathcal{O}(n)$ (p, r)-clusters, we can union bound over all clusters and show that with high probability CLUSTERAGGREGATION$_p$ aggregates to $\mathcal{O}(\log n)$ processes in all (p, r)-clusters of a dynamic graph.

4.3 The Impossibility of Cover Aggregation in Cliques

Motivated by considering clusters embedded within a larger dynamic graph, here we consider an alternative natural measure for the performance of an aggregation algorithm (rather than the number of uploaders in every local cluster).

Specifically we propose considering for every local cluster, the number of nodes that upload a token *on behalf* of a node in the cluster. We call such nodes, the *cover-uploaders* of a cluster. Observe that the number of *cover-uploaders* of a cluster is a trivial upper bound on the number of *uploaders* for the same cluster, but the reverse is not true.

It is possible, for example, that no process in a local cluster uploads a token, but that many processes outside the cluster upload tokens on their behalf (i.e., no uploaders in the cluster but plenty of cover-uploaders outside the cluster).

For a $(p, 0)$-cluster the cover-uploaders are equivalent to the uploaders, so we turn our attention to larger values of r. Our main results below shows that even for $r = 1$ (i.e., almost completely isolated clusters), there are no aggregation algorithms that can guarantee less than $n^{1/3}$ cover-uploaders in every (p, r)-cluster. This is a strong separation with the number of uploaders, where we just proved that for polylog r we can guarantee polylog uploaders in every (p, r)-cluster.

Theorem 9. *For every aggregation algorithm $\mathcal{A}$ there exists a dynamic graph G where the system $(\mathcal{A}, G)$ produces with constant probabilty an execution where one $(1, 1)$-cluster has $\Omega(n^{1/3})$ cover-uploaders.*

Proof. Fix any aggregation algorithm $\mathcal{A}$ that guarantees at most k cover-uploaders in every $(1, 1)$-cluster. To show that $k \geq n^{1/3}$, we will construct a dynamic graph G which contains a $(1, 1)$-cluster where with constant probability the number of cover-uploaders is at least $n^{1/3}$.

To simplify notation, in the following assume that $k + 1$ divides n (for the case where this does not hold, our bound on k differs only by a constant factor). To define G we first partition the nodes into $n/(k + 1)$ clusters $C_1, \ldots, C_{n/(k+1)}$ where each cluster has exactly $k + 1$ nodes. We define the random set U of size $n/(k + 1)$ which contains for each C_i a single node u_i which was selected uniformly at random. In the first half of the execution we let all nodes in each C_i interact with each other (i.e., each C_i is a complete graph), and in the remainder of the execution, the nodes in U remain isolated, while all nodes in $V \setminus U$ interact with each other (thus $V \setminus U$ is a $(1, 1)$-cluster).

With G defined, we can examine the execution of $\mathcal{A}$ in this graph. Observe that if we were to stop the execution after all the interactions in each C_i cluster, then every C_i is a $(1, 0)$-cluster. Moreover since $|C_i| > k$, we can assume that with constant probability some aggregation must have occurred in every cluster (otherwise if we extend the execution with all nodes being isolated we would have proved the theorem). It follows that every cluster C_i has at least one *responsible* process v_i that owns at least two tokens, in the sense that it will output these two tokens if isolated from this point forward (as established by the notion of token ownership from Section 2).

Since in the rest of the execution the nodes in U are isolated, each of the responsible processes in U will broadcast a token on behalf of a unique process from $V \setminus U$ (and recall that the processes in $V \setminus U$ form a $(1, 1)$-cluster). Because the nodes nodes in U are picked uniformly at random, we expect $|U|/(k + 1) = n/(k + 1)^2$ processes in U to upload at the end of the execution. Therefore with constant probability the number of cover-uploaders (nodes which upload tokens on behalf) of the $(1, 1)$-cluster defined by $V \setminus U$ is at least $n/(k + 1)^2$. Finally, this implies that with constant probability $k \geq n^{1/3}$, since if $k \leq n^{1/3} - 1$ then the number of (cover-)uploaders in U is at least $k + 1$ (which would be a contradiction). $\square$

5. CONCLUSION

In this paper, we studied the problem of aggregating values to a small number of processes in the dynamic network model. We proved that no algorithm guarantees a good competitive ratio if we make no assumptions on the topology changes. With this in mind, we presented new connectivity metrics that allow for better bounds for both global and local aggregation.

Several interesting open questions remain. It might prove productive, for example, to connect our results to existing graph metrics which have already been well-studied in the graph algorithm literature. This might highlight unexpected connections between the dynamic aggregation problem other known results. There are also related problems that might yield useful bounds in our dynamic setting; for example: aggregating data to a small number of predetermined *gateway* processes. Finally, we note it would be interesting to implement our algorithms in simulation to judge their performance when combined with real world dynamic network topology traces.

6. ACKNOWLEDGMENTS

This research was supported by Singapore MOE AcRF-2 grant MOE2011-T2-2-042, NSF Award CNS-1035199, NSF

Award CCF-0937274 NSF Award CCF-0726514, NSF Award
CCF-0939370 and AFOSR Award FA9550-08-1-0159.

7. REFERENCES

[1] J. Aspnes and E. Ruppert. An Introduction to
Population Protocols. *Bulletin of the European
Association for Theoretical Computer Science*,
93:98–117, 2007.

[2] K. Censor Hillel and H. Shachnai. Partial Information
Spreading with Application to Distributed Maximum
Coverage. In *Proceedings of the International
Symposium on Principles of Distributed Computing*,
2010.

[3] A. Cornejo and C. Newport. Prioritized Gossip in
Vehicular Networks. In *Proceedings of the
International Workshop on Discrete Algorithms and
Methods for Mobile Computing and Communications*,
2010.

[4] B. Haeupler. Analyzing Network Coding Gossip Made
Easy. *Arxiv preprint arXiv:1010.0558*, 2010.

[5] B. Hull, V. Bychkovsky, Y. Zhang, K. Chen,
M. Goraczko, A. Miu, E. Shih, H. Balakrishnan, and
S. Madden. CarTel: a Distributed Mobile Sensor
Computing System. In *Proceedings of the Conference
on Embedded Networked Sensor System*, 2006.

[6] C. Intanagonwiwat, D. Estrin, R. Govindan, and
J. Heidemann. Impact of Network Density on Data
Aggregation in Wireless Sensor Networks. In
*Proceedings of the Conference on Distributed
Computing Systems*, 2002.

[7] S. Janson, T. Luczak, and A. Rucinski. *Random
Graphs*. John Wiley & Sons Inc., 2000.

[8] L. Krishnamachari, D. Estrin, and S. Wicker. The
Impact of Data Aggregation in Wireless Sensor
Networks. In *Proceedings of the Conference of
Distributed Computing Systems*, 2002.

[9] F. Kuhn, N. Lynch, and R. Oshman. Distributed
Computation in Dynamic Networks. In *Proceedings of
the Symposium on Theory of Computing*, 2010.

[10] F. Kuhn, Y. Moses, and R. Oshman. Coordinated
Consensus in Dynamic Networks. In *Proceedings of the
International Symposium on Principles of Distributed
Computing*, 2011.

[11] F. Kuhn and R. Oshman. Dynamic networks: models
and algorithms. *ACM SIGACT News*, 42(1):82–96,
2011.

[12] S. Madden, M. Franklin, J. Hellerstein, and W. Hong.
Tag: a Tiny Aggregation Service for Ad-Hoc Sensor
Networks. *ACM SIGOPS Operating Systems Review*,
36(SI):131–146, 2002.

[13] R. Pinheiro, A. Poylisher, and H. Caldwell. Mobile
Agents for Aggregation of Network Management Data.
In *Proceedings of the International Symposium on
Mobile Agents*, 1999.

[14] A. Thiagarajan, L. Ravindranath, H. Balakrishnan,
S. Madden, and L. Girod. Accurate, Low-Energy
Trajectory Mapping for Mobile Devices. In
*Proceedings of the Symposium on Networked Systems
Design and Implementation*, 2011.

Distributed Connectivity of Wireless Networks*

Magnús M. Halldórsson   Pradipta Mitra

ICE-TCS, School of Computer Science, Reykjavik University, 101 Reykjavik, Iceland
mmh@ru.is   ppmitra@gmail.com

ABSTRACT

We consider the problem of constructing a communication infrastructure from scratch, for a collection of identical wireless nodes. Combinatorially, this means a) finding a set of links that form a strongly connected spanning graph on a set of n points in the plane, and b) scheduling it efficiently in the SINR model of interference. The nodes must converge on a solution in a distributed manner, having no means of communication beyond the sole wireless channel.

We give distributed connectivity algorithms that run in time $O(poly(\log \Delta, \log n))$, where Δ is the ratio between the longest and shortest distances among nodes. Given that algorithm without prior knowledge of the instance are essentially limited to using uniform power, this is close to best possible. Our primary aim, however, is to find efficient structures, measured in the number of slots used in the final schedule of the links. Our main result is algorithms that match the efficiency of centralized solutions. Specifically, the networks can be scheduled in $O(\log n)$ slots using (arbitrary) power control, and in $O(\log n(\log \log \Delta + \log n))$ slots using a simple oblivious power scheme. Additionally, the networks have the desirable properties that the latency of a converge-cast and of any node-to-node communication is optimal $O(\log n)$ time.

Categories and Subject Descriptors

F.2.2 [**Nonnumerical Algorithms and Problems**]: Computations on discrete structures; C.2.4 [**Distributed Systems**]

General Terms

Algorithms, Theory

Keywords

SINR model, Wireless Connectivity

*This work was supported by Iceland Research Foundation grant-of-excellence 90032021.

1. INTRODUCTION

We consider the problem of constructing a communication infrastructure from scratch, for a collection of identical wireless nodes. Combinatorially, this means finding a set of links that form a strongly connected spanning graph on a set of points in the plane, and scheduling it efficiently in the SINR model of interference. The nodes must converge on a solution in a distributed manner, having no means of communication beyond the sole wireless channel. The issue is how quickly and how well: the time it takes to form the structure and the efficiency of the final schedule produced.

The importance of creating a connected structure spanning a set of wireless nodes can hardly be overstated. This may underlie a "multi-hop" wireless network, where any two nodes can communicate through path(s) specified by such a structure. In an ad-hoc network, such a structure may provide the underlying backbone for synchronized operation of the network. In a wireless sensor network, the structure can double as an information aggregation mechanism.

The efficiency of a structure is closely intertwined with the issue of interference, the distinguishing feature of wireless communication. Interference implies that only a limited number of transmissions can be successful simultaneously; this number depending on spatial distribution of the links, power settings, etc. We adopt the SINR (or physical) model of interference, that has been shown both theoretically and experimentally to be a more faithful representation of reality than many of the traditional graph-based models [18, 22].

Achieving an efficient schedule involves deciding power levels for the links – which may either be fully instance-dependent ("arbitrary"), or be chosen in an "oblivious" manner, depending only on the length of each link. Recent centralized results show that it is possible to connect any link set using $O(\log n)$ slots [11], whereas the use of oblivious power is bound to involve a factor of $\log \log \Delta$ [8, 4, 11], where Δ is the ratio between shortest and longest distance in the network.

Achieving connectivity is a distributed problem *par excellence*. Distributed algorithms often assume "free" local communication. In contrast, since the purpose in this paper is to build a communication infrastructure from scratch, we assume that the only mode of communication allowed is transmission in the single wireless channel, which succeeds if the required signal-to-interference-and-noise ratio is achieved. We also do not assume a *carrier sensing* primitive (see, e.g., [26]) that allows nodes to estimate the amount of activity on the channel.

Given that the nodes have no information about distances

to nearby nodes, they are in effect limited to using a pre-defined fixed power initially. It is known that usage of such a simple power scheme can necessarily require a linear number of slots to connect the nodes [21]. A more refined bound is $\log \Delta$, where Δ is the ratio between maximum to the minimum distance among the nodes. We provide a distributed algorithm that forms a (initial) connected network in time $O(\log \Delta \cdot \log n)$, which is probably close to the best possible.

The quality or efficiency of the *final* structure is another story. Once the initial (and possibly inefficient) network is formed, we are interested in retooling the network, still in a distributed fashion, but using the existing network, to find improved connectivity structures. We provide two approaches to this. First, we show that the initial network has nice geometric properties that allows us to use (distributed) power control to make it much more efficient. Second, we propose a more sophisticated approach — instead of simply changing the power settings of the links of initial network, we leverage the initial tree to construct *new* set of links (and their power settings) that can be scheduled even more efficiently, while still achieving connectivity. This suggest a novel interplay between different layers — a network layer (i.e., the initial tree) that goes back and retools both itself (choosing new links) and the MAC layer (changing power settings and schedules).

The challenge raised in this paper can then be stated as follows:

> Is there a distributed algorithm, running in time $O(poly(\log \Delta, \log n))$, that results in a nearly optimal strongly connected structure in the SINR model?

We answer this question affirmatively, giving algorithms that match the best upper bounds known for centralized algorithms. This holds both for oblivious power assignments as well as when allowing arbitrary power assignments. In particular, using arbitrary power, we find and schedule a bidirectional tree in $O(\log n)$ slots that has the property that both aggregation computation and any pairwise communication can be achieved in optimal logarithmic time.

The rest of the paper is organized as follows. We introduce the model and key definitions in Sec. 3, and discuss related results in Sec. 2. Our results are described in Sec. 4. Section 5 contains technical definitions and clarifications that are essential for the analysis but not needed to understand the results. The algorithm for the initial network construction is given and analyzed in Sec. 6. Our two approaches to finding extremely efficient schedules are presented in Sec. 7 and Sec. 8, respectively. Several proofs and construction details have been deferred to appendices.

2. RELATED WORK

Connectivity was the first problem studied from a worst-case perspective in the SINR model. In a seminal paper, Moscibroda and Wattenhofer [21] formalized the problem and proposed an algorithm that connects arbitrary set of n points in $O(\log^4 n)$ slots. This was improved to $O(\log^3 n)$ [23], $O(\log^2 n)$ [20], and recently to $O(\log n)$ [11]. All these works deploy centralized algorithms. No non-trivial lower bound is known. Somewhat orthogonally, a large body of work exists on randomly deployed wireless networks, starting with the influential work by Gupta and Kumar [7]. Work in this setting for connectivity includes [1], which studied

the probability of there existing a path between two nodes in a randomly deployed network. In [25], minimum energy connectivity structures is studied for randomly deployed networks, but interference is essentially ignored.

Distributed connectivity of wireless networks has also been the subject of research. In [28], connectivity in mobile networks was studied from a graph-theoretic perspective with no explicit interference model. Indeed, connectivity maintenance problem has been well studied in control theory and robotics [28, 19, 3], but with different underlying assumptions, typically without the use of the SINR interference model. Sensor connectivity has also been studied [13] without reference to any particular interference model. In [24], a heuristic was proposed for connectivity maintenance in multi-hop wireless networks. A more rigorous study was done in [27] but with the assumption of an underlying MAC layer that resolves interference problems.

Two fundamental problems that deal with a given set of links relate to this work. *Capacity*: find the largest feasible subset of links, and *Scheduling*: partition the link set into the fewest number of feasible sets. For the former, constant-factor algorithms were given for uniform power [5, 12], mean and linear power (and most other oblivious power assignments) [10], and power control [14]. These imply a logarithmic factor for the corresponding scheduling problems. Distributed algorithm was given for *Scheduling* with oblivious power [15] and shown to achieve $O(\log n)$-approximation [9].

Distributed algorithms have also been given for local broadcasting [6] and dominating set [26] in the SINR model. Both of these problem are, however, local in nature.

The Minimum-Latency Aggregation Scheduling problem is closely related to connectivity, where the latency for transmitting messages to a sink is to be minimized. A large literature is known, but the first worst-case analysis in the SINR model was given in [16], with a $O(\log^3 n)$ bound on the schedule length by a centralized algorithm and $O(\log \Delta)$ by a distributed algorithm. The centralized bound was improved to optimal $O(\log n)$ in [11].

3. MODEL AND PRELIMINARIES

Given is a set P of n wireless nodes located at points on the plane. Without loss of generality, assume that the minimum distance between any two points is 1. The nodes have synchronized clocks, and start running the distributed algorithm simultaneously using slotted time. Each node knows its location and has a globally unique ID. A single message is large enough to contain the ID and the location of a node. A receiver of a message thus always knows its distance from the sender and can identify the sender uniquely.

A *link* is a directed edge between two nodes, indicating a transmission from the first node (the sender) to the second (the receiver). A link between u and v is denoted by (u, v); ℓ will also be used to indicate a generic link. A link set L naturally induces a set of senders $S(L)$ and a set of receivers $R(L)$. The link (y, x) is known as the *dual* of link (x, y), following [15]. A link set X is a dual of set Y if X consists of the duals of the links in Y. The degree of a node u in a linkset L is the number of links incident on u in L. The *distance* between two nodes u and v is denoted by $d(u, v)$ (this is also the *length* of the link (u, v)). Let Δ denote the maximum length of a possible link. A *length class* refers to a set of links whose lengths differ by a factor of at most 2.

In the SINR model of interference, a non-transmitting node v successfully receives a message transmitted by node u if,

$$\frac{P_u/d(u,v)^\alpha}{N + \sum_{w \in S \setminus \{u\}} P_w/d(w,v)^\alpha} \geq \beta \ , \qquad (1)$$

where N is the ambient *noise*, β is the required SINR level, $\alpha > 2$ is the so-called path loss constant, P_w is the *power* used by node w, and S is the set of senders transmitting simultaneously. A set L of links is *feasible* if the above constraint holds for all $v \in R(L)$ where $S = S(L)$. We do not impose any limit on the power a node can use.

The goal is to identify a set $\mathcal{T}$ of links that both *strongly connects* the wireless nodes and can be scheduled efficiently (i.e., can be partitioned into few feasible sets). Additionally, we seek low latency constructions.

A *converge-cast* tree is a directed rooted spanning tree where all links are oriented towards the root (i.e., for each link, the receiver is a parent of the sender). An *aggregation tree* is a converge-cast tree along with a schedule of the links that has the property that each link (x, y) in the tree is scheduled after all links involving descendants of x. A *dissemination tree* is the opposite: a broadcast tree (spanning arborescence) with links oriented away from the root, with the opposite property for the schedule. In both cases, the scheduling order follows link directions and paths in the trees.

Definition 1. A **bi-tree** is an aggregation tree with a complementary dissemination tree, using the same links in the opposite direction and same schedule in opposite order.

Note that with a bi-tree, any node-node communication can be achieved within time equal to the length of the schedule. The same holds for computing an aggregation or a broadcast.

The following power assignments are of interest. An oblivious power assignment is one where power assigned to a sender u is a (simple) function of $d(u, v)$, where v is the intended receiver. The oblivious assignment we are most interested in is the "mean power" assignment $\mathcal{M}$ where $P_u^{\mathcal{M}} = d(u, v)^{\alpha/2}$. We also use uniform power $\mathcal{U}$ that assigns the same power to all transmitting nodes, and the "linear power" assignment $\mathcal{L}$ where $P_u^{\mathcal{L}} = d(u, v)^\alpha$. Note that a sender can transmit to different receivers at different times, and may use different powers. Finally, we also consider solutions achievable with arbitrary power assignments, where the algorithm is free to use any assignment. We let $\Upsilon = O(\log \log \Delta + \log n)$ denote the best ratio known for the cost of using oblivious power; namely, it is known that for any set of links, the ratio between the maximum size of feasible subset using arbitrary power vs. using mean power is at most Υ [8, 10].

4. OUR RESULTS

We give the first distributed algorithms with performance guarantees for connectivity problems in the SINR model. We first provide a basic algorithm:

THEOREM 1. *There exists a distributed algorithm that computes a bi-tree $\mathcal{T}$ in $O(\log \Delta \cdot \log n)$ slots.*

We can improve this solution by using scheduling with non-uniform (but oblivious) power assignments. Recall $\Upsilon = O(\log \log \Delta + \log n)$.

THEOREM 2. *The bi-tree $\mathcal{T}$ can be re-scheduled in $O(\Upsilon \cdot \log^3 n)$ slots using mean power.*

We then intersperse the connectivity-building and the scheduling to get solutions matching the best centralized solutions known.

THEOREM 3. *There exists a distributed algorithm (building on the first one) that finds and schedules a bi-tree in $O(\log n)$ slots (with arbitrary power), using time $O(\Upsilon \cdot \log \Delta \cdot \log n)$. A variation finds and schedules a bi-tree in $O(\Upsilon \cdot \log n)$ slots with mean power, using time $O(\Upsilon \log \Delta \cdot \log^2 n)$.*

In particular, the bi-tree property ensures that aggregation, broadcast, and pairwise communication can all be achieved in optimal $O(\log n)$ steps.

Technically, this work combines ingredients from numerous recent works on the SINR model [8, 10, 14, 15, 9, 11]. In addition, we derive a number of properties, most of which deal with the concept of *affectance* in relation to connectivity structures; intuitively, affectance measures the interference of one transmission on the reception of another transmission, relative to the signal strength of the latter. We explicitly define a previously considered geometric property of *sparsity*, and show it to imply small average affectance. We give novel algorithms for finding large feasible subsets in such sparse link sets. And, we introduce randomized transmission strategies to estimate affectance in terms of transmission successes.

5. TECHNICAL NOTES

Our algorithms require the following knowledge about the instance: The number of nodes, n, up to a polynomial factor; the minimum distance (assumed to be 1); and the maximum distance Δ. We do not treat Δ as a constant, although it is small in many systems. Knowledge of Δ is mainly needed for stopping criteria; it can be avoided by computing the size of the tree, if precise knowledge of n is available.

In describing our algorithm, we refer to some messages as *broadcasts* and some as *acknowledgments*. In terms of if and how these messages succeed, they are identical and work as dictated by Eqn. 1. The difference lies in when these messages are transmitted and what they contain. A broadcast refers to an exploratory message sent to no node in particular, only containing the sender's ID and location. An acknowledgment is transmitted as a response to a previous message (typically a broadcast) and contains IDs of both the sender (the acknowledger) and the initial broadcaster. Thus, receivers receiving an acknowledgment can determine if it was addressed to them or not.

All our results are proved to be true "with high probability" (w.h.p., for short), where the term means that the relevant event occurs with probability $1 - \frac{1}{n^c}$, for some suitably large c[1]. We frequently prove a lemma to hold, w.h.p., for a node u, or a link (u, v). It will always be clear that such a result can be safely union bounded over all nodes, or all possible links, to derive a high probability result for the whole algorithm. The only case that needs care is when we union bound over slots in the algorithm. The number of slots in our first algorithm is a function of $\log \Delta$, which can

---

[1]This can be amplified to hold for *any* c, by scaling up the constant factors.

be arbitrarily larger than n. Union bounding is still safe for the following reason. The algorithm proceeds by considering links belonging to the same length class, and there can be at most $\log \Delta$ of such classes (thus the dependence on $\log \Delta$). However, since there are at most n^2 links in the network, only n^2 classes can actually be non-empty (in the full version, we provide a more refined $O(n)$ upper bound). During empty length classes, nothing happens with probability 1 and thus the union bounding incurs no "cost".

Affectance. We use the notion of *affectance*, introduced in [5, 12] and refined in [15] to the threshold-ed form used here. The affectance $a_w^{\mathcal{P}}(\ell)$ on link $\ell = (u, v)$ *from* a sender w, with a given power assignment $\mathcal{P}$, is the interference of w on u relative to the power received, or

$$a_w^{\mathcal{P}}(\ell) = \min \left\{ 1 + \epsilon, c(u, v) \frac{P_w}{P_u} \cdot \left(\frac{d(u, v)}{d(w, v)} \right)^\alpha \right\},$$

where ϵ is some arbitrary fixed constant (say 0.1), $c(u, v) = \beta/(1 - \beta N d(u, v)^\alpha / P_u)$ depends only on the parameters of the link ℓ. We drop $\mathcal{P}$ when clear from context. For a set S of senders and a link ℓ, $a_S(\ell) = \sum_{w \in S} a_w(\ell)$.

Using such notation, Eqn. 1 can be rewritten as $a_S(\ell) \leq 1$, which we adopt. When dealing with links $\ell = (u, v)$ and $\ell' = (u', v')$ we mean $a_\ell(\ell')$ to mean $a_u(\ell')$. Extending this to a link set L, we use the notation $a_L(\ell)$ to mean $a_S(\ell)$ where $S = S(L)$ are the senders in L. For two sets X and Y, $a_X(Y)$ thus means $\sum_{\ell \in Y} a_{S(X)}(\ell)$. From its definition, it is clear that $c(u, v) \geq \beta$. We require that $c(u, v) \leq 2\beta$, and point out how to achieve this during the description of the algorithms. This simply means that nodes always transmit with power high enough for the intended (or potentially intended, in case of a broadcast) links to comfortably succeed in the presence of noise (but no other interference).

6. INITIAL TREE CONSTRUCTION

The general template for the algorithm is as follows. At any given time, a subset of the nodes is *active*, with initially all nodes active and in the end only one node. Links are formed between pairs of active nodes, by a node u broadcasting, and another node v acknowledging that message in the next round. When such a communication succeeds, links (u, v) and (v, u) become part of the network and node u becomes inactive (and forms no further links). The still active node v is u's parent in the eventual aggregation tree. The link (u, v) is then part of the aggregation tree and the link (v, u) is part of the dissemination tree.

In what follows, $\lambda_1, \lambda_2 \ldots, \gamma_1, \gamma_2 \ldots$ are constants.

The algorithm proceeds in $\lceil \log \Delta \rceil$ rounds, each containing $\lambda_1 \log n$ slot-pairs (a slot-pair is simply two consecutive slots). Each node u maintains a link set L_u storing incoming and outgoing links along with a time stamp. The final set $\mathcal{T}$ is then simply $\cup_u L_u$. In this initial tree construction, slots in the schedule of the links correspond simply to the time stamps.

At the beginning of each slot-pair in round r, each active node decides to be a *broadcaster* with iid probability p ($p \leq \frac{1}{2}$ to be determined), and *listener* otherwise. Then,

- During the first slot, a broadcaster u transmits a message and a listener v listens for messages.

- During the second slot, a listener v that received a message from u such that $2^{r-1} \leq d(u, v) < 2^r$ in the

previous slot does the following with iid probability p: add the links (u, v) and (v, u) to L_v with appropriate slot numbers and return an acknowledgment. A broadcaster u listens for acknowledgments during this slot, and on receiving one (say, from v) adds (u, v) and (v, u) to L_u, and becomes *inactive*.

Note that a node only forms links with nodes at distance in the range $[2^{r-1}, 2^r)$ during round r. Since each node knows this range it can easily choose a power that ensures $c(u, v) \leq 2\beta$ for all $d(u, v) \in [2^{r-1}, 2^r)$. Setting the power to $2\beta N 2^{r\alpha}$ suffices. We say that a link (u, v) is *successfully formed* between nodes u and v during a slot-pair if all of the following happen: a) the transmission (u, v) is successful in the first slot, b) it is successfully acknowledged in the second slot (i.e., the link (v, u) successfully transmits), and c) both nodes store (u, v) and (v, u) in their set of links with the appropriate time stamps. Note that when this happens, u becomes inactive, by the description of the algorithm. The sole link that is outgoing from a given node is also the last one to be scheduled, thus ordering satisfies the leaf-to-root order of aggregation trees.

Remarks. Two technical clarifications. First, note that a listener v can store a failed link, since it does not necessarily know whether an acknowledgment (v, u) succeeded. However, this is not a problem, since: a) Node u remains active if the acknowledgment fails and connects itself later to some node (or eventually becomes the root), b) Transmission of the link (v, u) is not problematic for other links, since links transmitting in that slot *did* succeed in the presence of that transmission. In any case, it is easy to efficiently "clean up" such stray links after the whole network is formed. Second, as constructed, the dissemination tree has the opposite order of links in the schedule (links closer to the root are scheduled later, instead of earlier, as the definition calls for). This is also easily fixable after the network is formed by a reversal process initiated by the root. We omit these details in this version.

6.1 Analysis

We first show that short links have a high probability of succeeding.

LEMMA 1. *Assume that at the beginning of round r, the minimum distance between active nodes is at least 2^{r-1}. Consider any slot-pair in the round and active nodes u and v with $d(u, v) < 2^r$. Then, with probability at least $\frac{1}{4} p^2 (1-p)$, the link (u, v) is successfully formed in that slot-pair. Similarly, with probability at least $\frac{1}{4} p^2 (1-p)$, the link (v, u) is successfully formed.*

PROOF. Let $\rho = 2^{r-1}$. Let M_r be the set of currently active nodes and let $\ell = (u, v)$. Let B_r be the set of broadcasters during the slot-pair. First, note that by the description of the algorithm

$$\mathbb{P}(u \in B_r \text{ and } v \notin B_r) = p(1-p) .$$

For $t = 0, 1, \ldots$ define C_t to be the ball around v of radius $\rho(t+1)$ and define the annulus A_t as $A_0 = C_0$, $A_t = C_t \backslash C_{t-1}$ for $t \geq 1$. From this it is easily computed that the area of A_t is

$$\text{Area}(A_t) = \pi \rho^2 (2t + 1) \qquad (2)$$

Now, by the definition of ρ, balls of radius $\frac{\rho}{4}$ around any pair of points in M_r do not intersect (since the minimum distance between active nodes is ρ). Combining this with Eqn. 2, we see that A_t contains at most $16(2t + 1) \leq 48t$ nodes in M_r.

For $x \in M_r \cap A_0$, $a_x(\ell) \leq 1 + \epsilon$, simply by the definition of affectance. For $x \in M_r \cap A_t$ for $t \geq 1$, $d(x, v) \geq \rho \cdot t$ and thus $a_x(\ell) \leq c_\ell \frac{(2\rho)^\alpha}{(\rho \cdot t)^\alpha} \leq 2\beta \left(\frac{2}{t}\right)^\alpha$, where $c_\ell \equiv c(u, v) \leq 2\beta$. Note that for any x, $\mathbb{P}(x \in B_r) = p$.

Thus,

$$\mathbb{E}(a_{B_r}(\ell)) = \mathbb{E}(a_{B_r \cap A_0}(\ell)) + \sum_{t \geq 1} \mathbb{E}(a_{B_r \cap A_t}(\ell))$$

$$\leq 16(1 + \epsilon)p + p2\beta \sum_{t \geq 1} \left(\frac{2}{t}\right)^\alpha 48t$$

$$\leq 16(1 + \epsilon)p + 96p\beta 2^\alpha \frac{1}{\alpha - 2} ,$$

using the bound $\zeta(x) = \sum_{n \geq 1} \frac{1}{n^x} \leq \frac{1}{x-1}$ on the Riemann zeta function. Thus, for any $p \leq (64(1 + 6\beta 2^\alpha \frac{1}{\alpha-2}))^{-1}$, we get that $\mathbb{E}(a_{B_r}(\ell)) \leq 1/2$. By Markov's inequality, $a_{B_r}(\ell) \leq 1$ with probability at least $\frac{1}{2}$ (recall that this means that the link ℓ succeeds). Thus,

$$\mathbb{P}(a_{B_r}(\ell) \leq 1 \text{ and } u \in B_r \text{ and } v \notin B_r) \geq \frac{1}{2}p(1 - p) ,$$

A similar argument proves that the probability of $\ell_r = (v, u)$ succeeding is at least $\frac{1}{2}p$ and thus the link (u, v) is formed with probability at least $\frac{1}{4}p^2(1 - p)$. The argument for the potential formation of link (v, u) is identical. $\square$

Now we can claim that,

LEMMA 2. *At the beginning of each round r, the distance between active nodes is at least 2^{r-1}, w.h.p.*

PROOF. (Sketch.) The claim is clearly true for round 1 (since the minimum distance in the system is 1). Now inductively assume that it is true for round r. Consider any two nodes u, v that are active at the beginning of round $r + 1$ with $d(u, v) < 2^{r+1}$. Consider any slot-pair in which they are both active. By Lemma 1, the probability of both of them remaining active after this slot pair is at most $1 - \frac{1}{4}p^2(1 - p) \leq 1 - \frac{1}{8}p^2$. Thus, the probability of both of them remaining active over $\lambda_1 \log n$ slot-pairs is $\leq (1 - \frac{1}{8}p^2)^{\lambda_1 \log n}$. Setting $\lambda_1 = \frac{80}{p^2}$, this probability can be upper bounded by $\frac{1}{n^{10}}$. This proves the Lemma (after union bounding). $\square$

We can now prove the first main result.

PROOF. [of Thm. 1] By Lemma 2 it is clear that within $O(\log \Delta)$ rounds, and thus $O(\log \Delta \cdot \log n)$ slots, at most one active node remains (since the maximum distance among nodes is Δ). Since nodes only cease to be active by forming links with an active node, it is also clear that exactly one node remains active. When nodes cease to be active, they do so only by connecting in both directions to still-active nodes (by the description of the algorithm). By induction, the whole network is then strongly connected to the single node active at the end. This last active node is the root of both the aggregation and dissemination trees. $\square$

We can also show that the network formed has low degree, where the degree of a node is its number $|L_u|$ of incident links.

THEOREM 4. *The probability of a link having degree d is at most $e^{\frac{-p^2 d}{8}}$. As a result, the maximum degree is $O(\log n)$, w.h.p.*

PROOF. Let u be a node and consider any round r and any slot-pair in the round where u is active. Suppose there is another active node v with $d(u, v) < 2^r$. Then by Lemma 1, u ceases to be active after this slot-pair, with probability at least $\frac{1}{4}p^2(1-p) \geq \frac{1}{8}p^2$. Note that in slot-pairs where no such v exists, u does not form a link. Thus, the degree of a node is upper bounded by the number of slot pairs where such a v exists, and u remains active after wards. The probability of there being d such slot pairs is at most $(1 - \frac{1}{8}p^2)^d \leq e^{\frac{-p^2 d}{8}}$.

Setting $d = \frac{1}{p^2}80 \log n$ gives us the second part of the lemma. $\square$

7. SPARSITY AND POWER CONTROL

In this section, we show that the link set $\mathcal{T}$ produced by the algorithm of Sec. 6 can actually be scheduled in considerably fewer slots (in terms of dependence on Δ) using mean power, thus proving Thm. 2. This leads to an algorithm to reschedule the same links with this improved power assignment. The main idea is to show that the produced link set has certain geometric properties that allows such improved scheduling.

Definition 2. A set L of links is ψ-**sparse** if, for every closed ball B in the plane,

$$B \cap L(8 \cdot rad(B)) \leq \psi ,$$

where $rad(B)$ is the radius of B, $L(d)$ is the set of links in L of length at least d, and $B \cap Q$ denotes the links in a set Q with at least one endpoint in ball B.

It was shown in [11] that the sparsity property (not explicitly defined there) is connected to a property named *amenability* in [11], which via an algorithm in [14] and results in [10] imply the following:

THEOREM 5 ([11]). *Let L be a ψ-sparse link set, for some $\psi \geq 1$. Then any $L' \subseteq L$ contains a feasible subset of size $\Omega \left(\frac{|L'|}{\psi}\right)$. The set L can be scheduled in $O(\psi \log n)$ slots.*

Furthermore, any $L' \subseteq L$ contains a subset of size $\Omega \left(\frac{|L'|}{\psi \cdot \Upsilon}\right)$ that is feasible under mean power assignment. The set L can be scheduled in $O(\psi \cdot \Upsilon \cdot \log n)$ slots using mean power.

We provide a short overview of these ideas for reference in Appendix B.

We now claim a sparsity result for the network $\mathcal{T}$ formed by the algorithm.

LEMMA 3. *If D is a disc of radius ρ in the plane, then the number of links in $\mathcal{T}$ longer than 8ρ that have at least one endpoint in D is $O(\log n)$, w.h.p.*

PROOF. Let $L = L(8 \cdot \rho) \cap D$. We first claim that at most one node inside D is incident to a link in L. For contradiction, assume that there are two such nodes u and v. Now, by the description of the algorithm, links of length 8ρ or higher can only be formed in rounds $\log \rho + 4$ or higher. Thus, both u and v were active during round $\log \rho + 4$. However, $d(u, v) \leq 2\rho$ and thus by Lemma 2, at the end of round $\log \rho + 2$, at most one of them could remain active. This is a contradiction. The proof of the Lemma is now complete by Thm. 4. $\square$

By union bounding over all ρ and all balls (by careful selection, there are only polynomially many of them that are relevant), this implies:

THEOREM 6. *The set $\mathcal{T}$ of links produced by the algorithm is $O(\log n)$-sparse.*

We now propose the following extension of the algorithm to schedule the links using significantly fewer slots.

> The sender of each link ℓ in $\mathcal{T}$ sets its power to mean power, $\ell^{\alpha/2}$. The links then use the distributed algorithm from [15] to compute a schedule of the links using this power assignment.

We can now prove Thm. 2.

PROOF. Thm. 5 and Thm. 6 imply that $\mathcal{T}$ can be scheduled in $O(\Upsilon \cdot \log^2 n)$ slots using mean power. The distributed scheduling algorithm of [15] produces a $O(\log n)$-approximation [9], giving the Theorem. (See Appendix C for a technical note on the approximation factor in [9].) □

The resulting schedule, however, does not necessarily satisfy the ordering property of bi-trees.

8. MATCHING CENTRALIZED BOUNDS

In this section, we prove Thm. 3. The difference with Sec. 7 are threefold. First, we achieve more efficient final schedules. Second, unlike Sec. 7, we produce bi-trees. The third is a difference in approach. While the algorithm in Sec. 7 merely rescheduled the links in the original tree, in this section, we shall actually build a *new* tree with superior properties, but will do so by using the original tree.

We use **Init** to refer to the algorithm from Sec. 6 that constructs the initial bi-tree. For any link set L which is a subset of a directed rooted tree, we call a node u a "top level node" with respect to L if no link of form (v, w) is in L (i.e., the link between v and its parent in the rooted tree, if such a link exists, is not present in L).

In what follows, we focus on forming the aggregation tree part for simplicity (constructing the dissemination tree portion of the bi-tree is essentially identical). The algorithmic framework is as follows.

Algorithm 1 TreeViaCapacity

1: Set $i = 0$ and $P_i = P$ (the original input set).
2: **for** $i = 0, 1, 2 \ldots$ **until** $|P_i| = 1$ **do**
3:     Construct (aggregation) tree $\mathcal{T}$ on P_i using **Init**.
4:     Find a feasible subset $\mathcal{T}' \subset \mathcal{T}$
5:     Let P_{i+1} be the set of top level nodes w.r.t. $\mathcal{T}'$.
6: **end for**

If $\mathcal{T}'$ is large, then this process ends quickly.

THEOREM 7. *Assume that in each iteration, $\mathbb{E}(|\mathcal{T}'|) = \delta|\mathcal{T}|$ for some $\delta > 0$. Then, the process ends after $O(\frac{1}{\delta} \log n)$ iterations and the links produced form an aggregation tree connecting the nodes in $O(\frac{1}{\delta} \log n)$ slots, w.h.p.*

PROOF. First we show that:

CLAIM 1. $\mathbb{E}(|P_{i+1}|) \leq (1 - \frac{1}{2}\delta)|P_i|$, *for any P_i such that $|P_i| \geq 2$.*

PROOF. Suffices to pro Recall that $|\mathcal{T}'| \geq \delta|\mathcal{T}| = \delta(|P_i| - 1)$. Consider any link $(u, v) \in \mathcal{T}'$. Clearly, this link rules out u as a top level node. Also, since $\mathcal{T}$ is an aggregation tree, there can be at most one outgoing link from each node u. Thus, $\mathbb{E}(|P_{i+1}|) \leq |P_i| - \mathbb{E}(|\mathcal{T}'|) \leq |P_i| - \delta(|P_i| - 1) \leq (1 - \frac{1}{2}\delta)|P_i|$ (for $|P_i| \geq 2$). □

This can be used to show that the process ends in $O(\frac{1}{\delta} \log n)$ steps, w.h.p.

CLAIM 2. $\mathbb{P}(|P_t| > 1) \leq \frac{1}{n^4}$ *for $t = 10\frac{1}{\delta} \log n$.*

PROOF. Since P_i is non-increasing in i, for contradiction, condition on all $P_i \geq 2$ for $i \leq t$. Then we can apply the above Lemma to show that

$$\mathbb{E}(|P_t|) \leq \left(1 - \frac{1}{2}\delta\right)^{10\frac{1}{\delta} \log n} \frac{1}{n} \leq \frac{1}{n^4} ,$$

from which the claim follows by Markov's inequality. □

By the definition of top level nodes, nodes not in P_{i+1} are connected to some node in P_i by a link. Thus, the final structure is clearly a converge-cast tree. The ordering on schedules is also guaranteed by the way the algorithm proceeds (it is easy to see that nodes can be involved in at most one link in a feasible set, thus the ordering is not violated within $\mathcal{T}'$).

Finally, since each iteration uses a single slot, the bound on iterations immediately implies the bound on the number of slots in the schedule. The theorem follows.

To implement the above scheme, we need to show that $\mathcal{T}'$ can always be found for a large enough δ to claim the results in Thm. 3.

We do this in two steps: in the first step a $O(1)$-sparse subset $\mathcal{T}(M) \subseteq \mathcal{T}$ is chosen, and in the second step a subset of $\mathcal{T}(M)$ is chosen as $\mathcal{T}'$. The first step is identical for mean power and arbitrary power case. The set $\mathcal{T}(M)$ is defined in the following result, whose proof is in Appendix A.

THEOREM 8. *Let M be the set of nodes of degree at most $\rho = \frac{160}{p^2}$ in $\mathcal{T}$, and let $\mathcal{T}(M)$ be the links in $\mathcal{T}$ induced by M. Then, $\mathcal{T}(M)$ is $O(1)$-sparse and $\mathbb{E}(|\mathcal{T}(M)|) = \Omega(|\mathcal{T}|)$.*

To actually compute $\mathcal{T}(M)$ in a distributed fashion, note that nodes can easily decide if they are in M (by counting the number of links adjacent to them). One sweep through the existing network $\mathcal{T}$ is enough for each node to detect which of their links (if any) are in $\mathcal{T}(M)$.

Selecting $\mathcal{T}'$ is also reasonably easy for mean power, but more involved for arbitrary powers. The following two subsections deal with these cases separately. Note that we keep the original network around at all times, which is useful for controlling the construction of the new one. Running these networks in parallel can be achieved with simple time-division multiplexing.

8.1 Finding $\mathcal{T}'$ with mean power

Assume that $\mathcal{T}(M)$ is known. It can be shown that the *average affectance* in the linkset $\mathcal{T}(M)$ (under mean power) is small, or $O(\Upsilon)$ (proof in Appendix A).

LEMMA 4. *Affectance within $\mathcal{T}(M)$ under mean power satisfies $a^{\mathcal{M}}_{\mathcal{T}(M)}(\mathcal{T}(M)) = \gamma_1 \Upsilon |\mathcal{T}(M)|$, for some constant γ_1.*

Lemma 4 implies, after some basic manipulation, that there exists Q with $|Q| \geq \frac{1}{2}|\mathcal{T}(M)|$, such that $a^{\mathcal{M}}_{\mathcal{T}(M)}(\ell) \leq 2\gamma_1\Upsilon$ for all $\ell \in Q$.

The following *sampling* mechanism produces a large feasible set in expectation (see [4]): Each link in $\mathcal{T}(M)$ transmits with iid probability $\frac{1}{4\gamma_1\Upsilon}$, with the successful links forming the set $\mathcal{T}'$. Since each transmitting link in Q succeeds with probability $\geq \frac{1}{2}$, the expected size of $\mathcal{T}'$ is at least $\frac{1}{2\gamma_1\Upsilon}|Q| = \Omega(\frac{1}{\Upsilon}|\mathcal{T}(M)|)$. Combining this with Thm. 8, we get that

LEMMA 5. $\mathbb{E}(|\mathcal{T}'|) = \Omega(\frac{1}{\Upsilon}\mathbb{E}(|\mathcal{T}(M)|)) = \Omega(\frac{1}{\Upsilon}|\mathcal{T}|)$.

Thus, Thm. 7 can be invoked with $\delta = \Omega(\frac{1}{\Upsilon})$, to obtain the second half of Thm. 3:

THEOREM 9. *There exists a distributed algorithm that forms and schedules a bi-tree in $O(\Upsilon \cdot \log n)$ slots using mean power. This algorithm completes in time $O(\Upsilon \log \Delta \cdot \log^2 n)$.*

PROOF. The performance of the final solution follows from Thm. 7, as mentioned above. Let us the bound the total running time. The algorithm **Init** needs to be invoked $O(\Upsilon \cdot \log n)$ times, for a total cost of $O(\Upsilon \cdot \log \Delta \cdot \log^2 n)$. After forming $\mathcal{T}$ with each such invocation, identifying $\mathcal{T}(M)$ costs $O(\log \Delta \log n)$ (the cost of $\mathcal{T}$). Computing $\mathcal{T}'$ is cheap since the sampling is done in parallel. One technical aspect to note is that while the nodes choose $\mathcal{T}'$, they nodes need to know if their transmission succeeded; this can be done without substantial loss of performance using an extra acknowledgment slot, as we have seen before. The runtime bound of the theorem then follows. $\square$

This theorem completes the proof of the second half of Thm. 3.

8.2 Finding $\mathcal{T}'$ with arbitrary power

In this case, we want to find a large set $\mathcal{T}'$, given $\mathcal{T}(M)$, and then choose a power assignment making the set feasible.

We start with the link selection step. Leveraging the fact that our input instance $\mathcal{T}(M)$ is sparse, we implement a distributed version of a centralized algorithm for choosing such a set proposed in [14].

The following algorithm was shown in [14] to give constant factor approximation for finding the largest feasible subset of any given linkset: Given a linkset R, let the selected set be L, initially empty. Go through all links in ascending order of length (breaking ties arbitrarily). If the condition

$$a^{\mathcal{L}}_L(\ell) + a^{\mathcal{U}}_\ell(L) \leq \tau , \qquad (3)$$

holds, for a constant τ, then the link ℓ is added to L (Eqn. 1 of [14] can be seen to be essentially equivalent to the above equation).

For simplicity, we assume in this abstract that that receivers can measure the SINR of a successful link (i.e., can measure if the link succeeded with a desired threshold τ or not). This assumption can be removed.

Assume the formation of $\mathcal{T}$ using **Init** required R rounds. Our selection algorithm **Distr-Cap** has the following outline.

> **Distr-Cap** contains R phases. In phase i, links in $\mathcal{T}(M)$ that were formed in round i of **Init** decide whether or not to add themselves to the selected set $\mathcal{T}'$.

By the description of **Init**, links formed in the same round belong to the same length class (also, links formed in a particular round are smaller than all links formed in later rounds).

For all i, phase i of **Distr-Cap** consists of one slot-pair. Let Q be the links participating in this phase (i.e., links formed during round i of **Init**). During the first slot of the phase, the following happens:

1. All links ℓ in $\mathcal{T}'$ (the set selected so far) transmit using linear power (i.e. $P_\ell = \ell^\alpha$).

2. Links in Q transmit with iid probability p (small constant) using linear power.

3. Receivers in Q record a success if they received a message across the link with SINR $\leq \tau/4$. Let $\tilde{Q}$ be the set of links that recorded success.

During the second slot:

1. Links in $\mathcal{T}'_d$ (dual of $\mathcal{T}'$) transmit using linear power (i.e., the receivers of $\mathcal{T}'$ transmit using linear power).

2. Links in $\tilde{Q}_d$ (dual of $\tilde{Q}$) transmit with iid probability $\gamma_2^2 \cdot p$ for some $\gamma_2 < 1$, using linear power.

3. Receivers in $\tilde{Q}_d$ record a success if they received a message across the link with SINR $\leq \frac{\gamma_2 \cdot \tau}{4}$.

Thus, at the end of a second slot, a success is recorded at a sender of a (original) link in Q, if the transmission succeeded in both directions (the original link and the dual) with the required SINR threshold. Let Q^* be the set of links that succeeded. The updated solution is then $\mathcal{T}' \leftarrow \mathcal{T}' \cup Q^*$, which simply means that links add themselves to $\mathcal{T}'$ if they succeeded in both directions.

We now analyze this algorithm. The following sub-subsections show that the selected solution is feasible and large (a constant factor approximation to the largest feasible subset), respectively.

8.2.1 $\mathcal{T}'$ is feasible

We now show that $\mathcal{T}'$ satisfies Eqn. 3. It suffices to show that for all $\ell \in \mathcal{T}'$, if $L \subseteq \mathcal{T}'$ are the links no larger than ℓ then:

$$a^{\mathcal{L}}_L(\ell) + a^{\mathcal{U}}_\ell(L) \leq \tau .$$

The following two Lemmas imply the above.

LEMMA 6. $a^{\mathcal{L}}_L(\ell) \leq \frac{\tau}{4}$.

PROOF. To see this, note the selection of $\tilde{Q}$ in the first slot of each slot-pair. We claim that during this slot, all links in L are transmitting with linear power. For links in L that were selected in an earlier phase, this is obviously true. For links in Q that will be selected in L, this is true as well, since eventual admission in L is only possible (though not guaranteed) if the link decided to transmit during the first slot.

The proof of the Lemma is completed by noting the SINR threshold used in the selection of $\tilde{Q}$. $\square$

LEMMA 7. $a^{\mathcal{U}}_\ell(L) \leq \frac{\tau}{4}$.

PROOF. The selection process implemented during the second slot guarantees that $a^{\mathcal{L}}_{L_d}(\ell_d) \leq \frac{\gamma_2\tau}{4}$, where L_d is the dual set of L and ℓ_d is the dual of ℓ (this follows the proof of the previous Lemma almost verbatim).

To complete the proof, we use a result from [15, Obs. 4]. It was shown that for a constant γ_2, and links ℓ and ℓ',

CLAIM 3. $\gamma_2 a_{\ell_d'}^{\mathcal{L}}(\ell_d) \leq a_\ell^{\mathcal{U}}(\ell') \leq \frac{1}{\gamma_2} a_{\ell_d'}^{\mathcal{L}}(\ell_d)$.

Using this claim, we get that

$$a_\ell^{\mathcal{U}}(L) = \sum_{\ell' \in L} a_\ell^{\mathcal{U}}(\ell') \leq \sum_{\ell' \in L_d} \frac{1}{\gamma_2} a_{\ell_d'}^{\mathcal{L}}(\ell_d) = \frac{1}{\gamma_2} a_{L_d}^{\mathcal{L}}(\ell_d) \leq \frac{\tau}{4} \ ,$$

as required. $\square$

8.2.2 $\mathcal{T}'$ is large

Define, following [11, 14],

$$f_\ell(\ell') = \begin{cases} a_{\ell'}^{\mathcal{U}}(\ell) + a_\ell^{\mathcal{L}}(\ell') & \text{if } \ell \leq \ell', \\ 0 & \text{otherwise.} \end{cases}$$

This definition is essentially equivalent to the definition of that of $f_\ell(\ell')$ of [11] and of $w(\ell, \ell')$ of [14] (also see Appendix B). Those definitions are presented in terms of distances. The reason why we choose to define $f_\ell(\ell')$ in terms of affectances here, instead of distances, is that affectances (or their SINR equivalents) can be measured by the link receivers and thus used as a selection criteria. For a set X, define $f_\ell(X) = \sum_{\ell' \in X} f_\ell(\ell')$ and $f_X(\ell') = \sum_{\ell \in X} f_\ell(\ell')$.

Recall that the input set $\mathcal{T}$ is $O(1)$-sparse, which is of crucial importance. Consider once again the execution of the algorithm for phase i. Let $\mathcal{T}'_{i-1}$ be the selected set at the end of phase $i-1$. As before, let Q be the links considered in phase i and Q^* be the links that succeeded in that phase. Since $\mathcal{T}$ is $O(1)$-sparse, so is Q.

LEMMA 8. Let Q' be the subset of links ℓ in Q with $f_{\mathcal{T}'}(\ell) \leq \gamma_2^2 \cdot \tau/8$. Then, $\mathbb{E}(|Q^*|) = \Omega(|Q'|)$.

PROOF. Consider any link $\ell \in Q'$. We shall show below that $\mathbb{P}(\ell \in Q^*) = \Omega(1)$, which implies the Lemma.

In the first slot, ℓ transmits with probability p. We claim that:

CLAIM 4. $\mathbb{P}(a_T^{\mathcal{L}}(\ell) \leq \tau/8) \geq \frac{1}{2}$, where T are the links in Q transmitting.

PROOF. Let ρ be such that length class in phase i covers lengths in $[\rho, 2\rho]$. Since Q is $O(1)$-sparse, it follows that balls of radius ρ contain only a constant number of nodes that have links in Q. The claim now follows from arguments essentially identical to those in Lemma 1, after setting the probability p sufficiently small. $\square$

Since $\ell \in Q'$, we see that $a_{\mathcal{T}'_{i-1}}^{\mathcal{L}}(\ell) \leq \tau/8$, by the definition of Q'. Thus, if $a_T^{\mathcal{L}}(\ell) \leq \tau/8$, then $a_{T \cup \mathcal{T}'_{i-1}}^{\mathcal{L}}(\ell) \leq \tau/4$, and the transmission is recorded as a success. Thus, ℓ transmits and is recorded as a success with probability $\frac{1}{2}p$. In other words,

$$\mathbb{P}(\ell \in \tilde{Q}) \geq \frac{1}{2}p \ . \tag{4}$$

Now, condition on ℓ being in $\tilde{Q}$. Then ℓ_d transmits with probability $\gamma_2 p$. The following claim can be proven using Claim 3 and is similar to Claim 4.

CLAIM 5. $\mathbb{P}(a_{T_d}^{\mathcal{L}}(\ell_d) \leq \frac{\gamma_2 \cdot \tau}{8}) \geq \frac{1}{2}$, where $T_d \subseteq \tilde{Q}_d$ are the (dual) links transmitting in this slot.

Following a argument similar to the one used for the first slot, we see that in the second slot, such a transmission is recorded as a success as well.

Thus, $\mathbb{P}(\ell \in Q^* | \ell \in \tilde{Q}) \geq \frac{1}{2}\gamma_2 p$. Combining this with Eqn. 4, we get $\mathbb{P}(\ell \in Q^*) \geq \frac{1}{4}\gamma_2 p^2 = \Omega(1)$, completing the proof of the Lemma. $\square$

This leads to the desired bound on the size of $\mathcal{T}'$.

THEOREM 10. The set $\mathcal{T}'$ chosen by the algorithm satisfies $\mathbb{E}(|\mathcal{T}'|) = \Omega(|\mathcal{T}(M)|)$.

PROOF. By Thm. 5, there exists a set $O \subseteq \mathcal{T}$ such that O is feasible and $|O| = \Omega(|\mathcal{T}|)$. Thus, it suffices to show that $\mathbb{E}(|\mathcal{T}'|) = \Omega(|O|)$ for any feasible set O.

Thm. 1 of [14] shows that for a feasible link set R and any link ℓ,

$$f_\ell(R) = O(1) \ . \tag{5}$$

Consider the set $R = O \setminus \mathcal{T}'$. We divide R further into two subsets: $R_1 = \{\ell' \in R : f_{\mathcal{T}'}(\ell') > \gamma_2^2 \tau/8\}$ and $R_2 = R \setminus R_1$. Summing Eqn. 5 for all $\ell \in \mathcal{T}'$,

$$f_{\mathcal{T}'}(R) = O(|\mathcal{T}'|) \ . \tag{6}$$

By definition of R_1, $f_{\mathcal{T}'}(R_1) > \frac{1}{8}\gamma_2^2 \tau |R_1|$. Assume first that $|R_1| \geq |R|/2$. Then, we get, $f_{\mathcal{T}'}(R_1) > \frac{1}{16}\gamma_2^2 \tau |R|$, which combined with Eqn. 6 gives, $|\mathcal{T}'| = \Omega(f_{\mathcal{T}'}(R)) \geq f_{\mathcal{T}'}(R_1) = \Omega(|R|)$. Since $|O| \leq |\mathcal{T}'| + |R|$, this clearly implies that $|\mathcal{T}'| = \Omega(|O|)$. Otherwise assume, $|R_1| < |R|/2$ and thus $|R_2| > |R|/2$. But Lemma 8 implies that $\Omega(|R_2|)$ links were chosen by the algorithm (in expectation), from which $\mathbb{E}(|\mathcal{T}'|) = \Omega(|O|)$ follows. $\square$

8.2.3 Computing the power assignment

So far we have dealt with the *selection* of a large set of feasible links. Once the link set $\mathcal{T}'$ is identified, we must select the power assignments for this set. Given a set of links that are known to be feasible, there exists a large body of work proposing algorithms that converge to a power assignment making the assignment feasible. For example, two recent ones are [17] and [2]. Using such an algorithm as a black box, we can find the appropriate power assignment.

THEOREM 11. There exists a distributed algorithm that connects the nodes in $O(\log n)$ slots. Assuming that there exists an algorithm to find the power assignment for a feasible set in time η, this algorithm completes in time $O(\log n(\log \Delta \cdot \log n + \eta))$.

As an example, if we select the algorithm from [17], η can be bounded by $O(\log \Delta(\log n + \log \log \Delta))$. This proves the first part of Thm. 3.

9. CONCLUSIONS

Our distributed algorithms have efficiency and effectiveness that appear to be close to best possible. An interesting direction would be to treat dynamic situations, including asynchronous node wakeup, node and link failures, and mobility.

10. REFERENCES

[1] C. Bettstetter. On the connectivity of ad hoc networks. *The Computer Journal*, 47(4):432–447, 2004.

[2] J. Dams, M. Hoefer, and T. Kesselheim. Convergence time of power-control dynamics. In *ICALP (2)*, pages 637–649, 2011.

[3] D. Dimarogonas and K. Johansson. Bounded control of network connectivity in multi-agent systems. *Control Theory & Applications*, 4(8):1330 – 1338, 2010.

[4] A. Fanghänel, T. Kesselheim, H. Räcke, and B. Vöcking. Oblivious interference scheduling. In *PODC*, pages 220–229, August 2009.

[5] O. Goussevskaia, M. M. Halldórsson, R. Wattenhofer, and E. Welzl. Capacity of Arbitrary Wireless Networks. In *Infocom*, pages 1872–1880, April 2009.

[6] O. Goussevskaia, T. Moscibroda, and R. Wattenhofer. Local Broadcasting in the Physical Interference Model. In *DialM-POMC*, August 2008.

[7] P. Gupta and P. R. Kumar. The Capacity of Wireless Networks. *IEEE Trans. Information Theory*, 46(2):388–404, 2000.

[8] M. M. Halldórsson. Wireless scheduling with power control. *ACM Trans. Algorithms*, 2012. To appear. See also http://arxiv.org/abs/1010.3427.

[9] M. M. Halldórsson and P. Mitra. Nearly optimal bounds for distributed wireless scheduling in the SINR model. In *ICALP*, 2011.

[10] M. M. Halldórsson and P. Mitra. Wireless Capacity with Oblivious Power in General Metrics. In *SODA*, 2011.

[11] M. M. Halldórsson and P. Mitra. Wireless Connectivity and Capacity. In *SODA*, 2012.

[12] M. M. Halldórsson and R. Wattenhofer. Wireless Communication is in APX. In *ICALP*, pages 525–536, July 2009.

[13] C.-F. Huang, Y.-C. Tseng, and H.-L. Wu. Distributed protocols for ensuring both coverage and connectivity of a wireless sensor network. *ACM Trans. Sen. Netw.*, 3, March 2007.

[14] T. Kesselheim. A Constant-Factor Approximation for Wireless Capacity Maximization with Power Control in the SINR Model. In *SODA*, 2011.

[15] T. Kesselheim and B. Vöcking. Distributed contention resolution in wireless networks. In *DISC*, pages 163–178, August 2010.

[16] H. Li, Q.-S. Hua, C. Wu, and F. C.-M. Lau. Minimum-latency aggregation scheduling in wireless sensor networks under physical interference model. In *MSWiM*, pages 360–367, 2010.

[17] Z. Lotker, M. Parter, D. Peleg, and Y. A. Pignolet. Distributed power control in the SINR model. In *Infocom*, pages 2525–2533, 2011.

[18] R. Maheshwari, S. Jain, and S. R. Das. A measurement study of interference modeling and scheduling in low-power wireless networks. In *SenSys*, pages 141–154, 2008.

[19] J. Meng and M. Egerstedt. Connectedness preserving distributed coordination control over dynamic graphs. In *Proc. of American Control Conference*, pages 3591–3596, 2005.

[20] T. Moscibroda. The worst-case capacity of wireless sensor networks. In *IPSN*, pages 1–10, 2007.

[21] T. Moscibroda and R. Wattenhofer. The Complexity of Connectivity in Wireless Networks. In *Infocom*, 2006.

[22] T. Moscibroda, R. Wattenhofer, and Y. Weber. Protocol Design Beyond Graph-Based Models. In *Hotnets*, November 2006.

[23] T. Moscibroda, R. Wattenhofer, and A. Zollinger. Topology control meets SINR: The scheduling complexity of arbitrary topologies. In *MOBIHOC*, pages 310–321, 2006.

[24] R. Ramanathan and R. Rosales-Hain. Topology control of multihop wireless networks using transmit power adjustment. In *Infocom*, pages 404 – 413, 2000.

[25] V. Rodoplu and T. H. Meng. Minimum energy mobile wireless networks. *IEEE JSAC*, 17(8):1333–1344, 1999.

[26] C. Scheideler, A. W. Richa, and P. Santi. An $O(\log n)$ dominating set protocol for wireless ad-hoc networks under the physical interference model. In *MobiHoc*, pages 91–100, 2008.

[27] R. Wattenhofer, L. Li, P. Bahl, and Y.-M. Wang. Distributed topology control for power efficient operation in multihop wireless ad hoc networks. In *Infocom*, pages 1388–1397, 2001.

[28] M. M. Zavlanos and G. J. Pappas. Distributed connectivity control of mobile networks. In *Proc. of American Control Conference*, pages 3591–3596, 2007.

APPENDIX

A. MISSING PROOFS

Proof of Thm. 8

PROOF. Recall that M is the set of nodes of degree at most $\rho = \frac{160}{p^2}$ in $\mathcal{T}$. For sets X and Y, let $\mathcal{E}(X, Y)$ be the number of links with senders in X and receivers in Y. We claim that setting $\mathcal{T}(M) = \mathcal{E}(M, M)$ fulfills the properties claimed in the theorem.

The $O(1)$-sparsity follows by noting that the nodes in M have degree $O(1)$; the proof of Lemma 3 can be followed verbatim using the constant-degree bound instead of the $O(\log n)$-bound employed there.

Thus, what remains to be proven is that $\mathbb{E}(|\mathcal{E}(M, M)|) = \Omega(n) = \Omega(|\mathcal{T}|)$. Let $M' = P \setminus M$ (recall that P is the set of all nodes). Since $\mathcal{T}$ is a tree, $|\mathcal{T}| = n - 1$. Then, since the number of unique links adjacent to M is at least $\frac{1}{2}M\rho$, it is easily computed that $|M'| \leq \frac{2n}{\rho}$ and thus $|M| \geq n(1 - \frac{2}{\rho})$. We show in Lemma 9 below that $\mathbb{E}(|\mathcal{E}(M', P)|) \leq \frac{n}{e^9}$. Note that since $\mathcal{T}$ is a connected tree, $|\mathcal{E}(M, P)| \geq |M| - 1$. Thus,

$$\mathbb{E}(|\mathcal{E}(M, M)|) \geq \mathbb{E}(|\mathcal{E}(M, P)|) - \mathbb{E}(|\mathcal{E}(M, M')|)$$
$$\geq \mathbb{E}(|M|) - 1 - \mathbb{E}(|\mathcal{E}(M', P)|)$$
$$\geq n\left(1 - \frac{2}{\rho}\right) - \frac{n}{e^9} = \Omega(n) \,,$$

which implies the theorem. □

LEMMA 9. $\mathbb{E}(|\mathcal{E}(M', P)|) \leq \frac{n}{e^9}$.

PROOF. Recall that by Thm. 4, $\mathbb{P}(deg(u) \geq d) \leq e^{\frac{-p^2 d}{8}}$, where $deg(u)$ is the degree of u. This implies that $\mathbb{P}(deg(u) \in [d, 2d)) \leq e^{\frac{-p^2 d}{8}}$. Since $\rho = \frac{160}{p^2}$, we can verify using basic calculus that $e^{p^2 \rho 2^t / 8} \geq \rho^2 2^{2t+2}$, for all t. Using this bound, we get,

$$\mathbb{E}(|\mathcal{E}(M', P)|) \leq n \sum_{t=0}^{\infty} \mathbb{P}(deg(u) \in [\rho 2^t, \rho 2^{t+1})) \rho 2^{t+1}$$

$$\leq n \sum_{t=0}^{\infty} e^{\frac{-p^2 \rho 2^t}{8}} \rho 2^{t+1} \leq n \sum_{t=0}^{\infty} e^{\frac{-p^2 \rho 2^t}{16}} \leq n \sum_{t=0}^{\infty} e^{-10 \cdot 2^t}$$

$$= \frac{n}{e^{10}} + n \sum_{t=1}^{\infty} \frac{1}{e^{10 \cdot 2^t}} \leq \frac{n}{e^{10}} + \frac{n}{e^{10}} \sum_{t=1}^{\infty} \frac{1}{e^{2^t}} \leq \frac{2n}{e^{10}} \leq \frac{n}{e^9} .$$

$\square$

Proof of Lemma 4

PROOF. The proof of this Lemma follows ideas from [8] and [10]. We need to relate the idea of sparsity to the idea of "independence" used in [8].

We say that a set of links is q-independent if any two of them, $\ell = (x, y)$ and $\ell' = (x', y')$, satisfy the constraint $d(x, y') \cdot d(y, x') \geq q^2 d(x, y) \cdot d(x', y')$.

We claim,

CLAIM 6. *Let C be a sufficiently large constant. Let Q be a C-independent set, and for any link ℓ in $\mathcal{T}'$, let Q^ℓ be the links in Q longer than ℓ. Then, $a_\ell(Q^\ell) + a_{Q^\ell}(\ell) = O(\Upsilon)$.*

PROOF. Partition Q^ℓ into two sets: Q_l^ℓ, with links length at least $d(x, y) \cdot 2(2\beta n)^{2/\alpha}$, and Q_s^ℓ, with the remaining links. It follows from [8, Lemma 4.4] that $a_{Q_l^\ell}^{\mathcal{M}}(\ell) + a_\ell^{\mathcal{M}}(Q_l^\ell) = O(\log \log \Delta)$. On the other hand, Q_s^ℓ can be partitioned into $O(\log n)$ length classes. For such sets, it is known [8] that C-independence, for some constant C, implies feasibility. Let Z be such a set. By Lemma 7 of [15], $a_Z^{\mathcal{M}}(\ell) = O(1)$. Since Z belongs to a single length class, it is also possible to show (following arguments similar to [15]) that $a_\ell^{\mathcal{M}}(Z) = O(1)$. Thus, $a_{Q_s^\ell}^{\mathcal{M}}(\ell) + a_\ell^{\mathcal{M}}(Q_s^\ell) = O(\log n)$, summing over the $O(\log n)$ such Z's. The claim follows. $\square$

By Lemma 10 below, we know that $\mathcal{T}'$ can partitioned into a constant number of C-independent sets. Let $Q_1, Q_2, \ldots, Q_t$ be a partition of L' into t different C-independent sets. For a link ℓ, let $Q_i^\ell = \{\ell' \in Q_i : \ell' \geq \ell\}$. Then,

$$a_{\mathcal{T}'}^{\mathcal{M}}(\mathcal{T}') \leq \sum_{\ell=(x,y) \in \mathcal{T}'} \sum_{i=1}^{t} a_\ell^{\mathcal{M}}(Q_i^\ell) + a_{Q_i^\ell}^{\mathcal{M}}(\ell)$$

$$= t|\mathcal{T}'|O(\Upsilon) = O(|\mathcal{T}'|\Upsilon) ,$$

since $t = O(1)$.

LEMMA 10. *$\mathcal{T}'$ can be partitioned into a constant number of C-independent sets.*

PROOF. Consider any link ℓ. We claim that there are $O(1)$ links ℓ' at least as long as ℓ such that ℓ and ℓ' are *not* C-independent. This claim proves the lemma by the following algorithm. Sort the links in an ascending order of their length, breaking ties arbitrarily.

Now consider the graph on links where there is an edge between links if they are not C-independent.

By the claim, all links have $O(1)$ edges to links after them in the ascending order. Such a graph is $O(1)$-colorable, where each color represents an independent set in graph theoretic sense, and thus a C-independent set according to our definition.

Now we prove the claim. Recall that $\mathcal{T}'$ is γ_3-sparse for some constant γ_3. Consider the link $\ell = (u, v)$ and a ball of radius $(2C)^2 \cdot d(u, v)$ around u. By a basic geometric argument, this ball can be covered by $O(1)$ balls of radius $d(u, v)/8$. By the definition of sparsity, there can be at most γ_3 links of length $d(u, v)$ or higher that have one endpoint in each of the smaller balls. Thus, the larger ball also contains only $O(1)$ such links. We now claim that all other links, i.e., $\ell' = (u', v')$ such that $\min(d(u', u), d(v', u)) \geq (2C)^2 \cdot d(u, v)$ are such that ℓ and ℓ' are C-independent. First, assume that $d(u', v) \geq \frac{1}{4}d(u', v')$. Then $d(u', v) \cdot d(u, v') \geq \frac{1}{4}d(u', v') \cdot (2C)^2 \cdot d(u, v) = C^2 d(u', v')d(u, v)$ which implies C-independence. On the other hand, if $d(u', v) < \frac{1}{4}d(u', v')$, then $d(u, v') \geq d(u', v') - d(u', v) - d(u, v) \geq d(u', v') - \frac{5}{4}d(u', v) \geq \frac{11}{16}d(u', v')$, from which C-independence follows by similar computations. $\square$

B. A SHORT PRIMER ON SPARSITY, AMENABILITY AND FEASIBILITY

In [11], a set of links L was defined to be η-**amenable** if the following holds: for any link ℓ (ℓ not necessarily a member of L), $\sum_{\ell' \in L} f_\ell(\ell') \leq \eta$, for a function f (see Eqn. 8.2.2), for some η. Actually, in [11], η is implicitly considered to be a constant, and just the term **amenable** is used. The definition extends naturally to arbitrary η. It was shown in [14] that an η-**amenable** set L has a feasible subset of size $\Omega\left(\frac{1}{\eta}|L|\right)$.

Now the final ingredient needed is to tie sparsity to feasibility (and thus get Thm. 5). We claim that sparsity as defined in this paper implies amenability. This is implicit in [11]. Specifically, in proving the main Lemma 4 of [11], it is first shown that the structure in question (which happens to be a Minimum Spanning Tree on the set of nodes) is $O(1)$-sparse (Lemma 5) and then this is used to show that the structure is amenable (which then implies a large feasible subset).

C. A NOTE ON THE APPROXIMATION FACTOR FOR DISTRIBUTED SCHEDULING

If acknowledgments have to be explicitly implemented, the algorithm of [15, 9] produces a schedule length of $O((T+T') \cdot \log n)$, where T is the optimal schedule for the input link set, and T' is the optimal schedule for the dual set of the input set, which may be larger than $O(T \log n)$. For our instance, this problem simply is not relevant. The constructed link set $\mathcal{T}$ *is its own dual*, and thus a $O(\log n)$-approximation factor can be safely asserted.

Leader Election in Shared Spectrum Radio Networks

Sebastian Daum
University of Lugano
Lugano, Switzerland
sebastian.daum@usi.ch

Seth Gilbert
NUS
Singapore
seth.gilbert@comp.nus.edu.sg

Fabian Kuhn
University of Freiburg
Freiburg, Germany
kuhn@informatik.uni-
freiburg.de

Calvin Newport
Georgetown University
Washington D.C.
cnewport@cs.georgetown.edu

ABSTRACT

We study the *leader election problem* in the context of a congested single-hop radio network. We assume a collection of N synchronous devices with access to a shared band of the radio spectrum, divided into $\mathcal{F}$ frequencies. To model unpredictable congestion, we assume an abstract *interference adversary* that can choose up to $t < \mathcal{F}$ frequencies in each round to disrupt, preventing communication. The devices are individually activated in arbitrary rounds by an adversary. On activation, a device does not know how many other devices (if any) are also active. The goal of the leader election problem is for each active device to output the id of a leader as soon as possible after activation, while preserving the safety constraint that all devices output the *same* leader, with high probability.

We begin by establishing a lower bound of $\Omega\left(\frac{\log^2 N}{(\mathcal{F}-t)\log\log N} + \frac{\mathcal{F}t}{\mathcal{F}-t} \cdot \log N\right)$ rounds, through reduction to an existing result in this model [5]. We then set out to prove this bound tight (within $\log\log N$ factors). For the case where $t = 0$, we present a novel randomized algorithm, based on a strategy of recruiting *herald nodes*, that works in $O\left(\frac{\log^2 N}{\mathcal{F}} + \log N\right)$ time. For $1 \le t \le \mathcal{F}/6$, we present a variant of our herald algorithm in which multiple real (potentially disrupted) frequencies are used to simulate each non-disrupted frequency from the $t = 0$ case. This algorithm works in $O\left(\frac{\log^2 N}{\mathcal{F}} + t\log N\right)$ time. Finally, for $t > \mathcal{F}/6$ we show how to improve the *trapdoor protocol* of [5], used to solve a similar problem in a non-optimal manner, to solve leader election in optimal $O\left(\frac{\log N + \mathcal{F}t}{\mathcal{F}-t} \cdot \log N\right)$ time, for (only) these large values of t. We also observe that if $\mathcal{F} = \omega(1)$ and $t \le (1-\epsilon)\mathcal{F}$ for a constant $\epsilon > 0$, our protocols beat the classic $\Omega(\log^2 N)$ bound on wake-up in a single frequency radio network, underscoring the observation that more frequencies in a radio network allows for more algorithmic efficiency—even if devices can each only participate on a single frequency at a time, and a significant fraction of these frequencies are disrupted adversarially.

Categories and Subject Descriptors

C.2.1 [**Network Architecture and Design**]: Wireless Communication;
F.2.2 [**Analysis of Algorithms and Problem Complexity**]: Non-numerical Algorithms and Problems—*computations on discrete structures*

General Terms

Algorithms, Theory

Keywords

wireless network, leader election, shared spectrum, disruption

1. INTRODUCTION & RELATED WORK

Due to the growing number of wireless devices, the systems community has placed new emphasis on developing shared spectrum networks [19]. Such networks allow multiple unrelated protocols to share the same band of the radio spectrum, each dynamically adjusting its use based on the local behavior it observes. Many of the most widely-deployed wireless standards—including WiFi [12], Bluetooth [2], and Zigbee [23]—operate in shared spectrum networks, and with the recent opening of broadcast television bands for secondary use by networked devices, more such standards are sure to follow [1]. Shared spectrum networks, however, introduce new algorithmic challenges. A protocol operating in this environment encounters a communication medium that is being used concurrently in a dynamic and unpredictable fashion. Even tasks as basic as finding other nearby devices become complex in this unpredictable setting [22].

In this paper, we study the foundational problem of *leader election* in the shared spectrum setting. We argue that discovering nearby devices and then electing a leader to coordinate their behavior (e.g., by disseminating a frequency hopping pattern or spread spectrum code [20]) is a key building block in the construction of efficient protocols in these complex networks. In addition, techniques to solve leader election in single-hop radio networks have also proved useful for solving more basic problems like computing maximal independent sets for clustering or colorings to coordinate channel access in a multi-hop setting [16, 18]. Formally, we

*The research in this paper was supported by NUS FRC grant R-252-000-443-133 and by the Swiss National Science Foundation under grant n. 200021-135160

capture the dynamics of shared spectrum communication using the well-studied *t-disrupted* radio network model [4–8, 11, 17, 20, 21]. We present the first known optimal solution to leader election in this setting (within log log factors). As detailed below, this optimal solution also beats a classic lower bound on communication in a non-shared, single-frequency radio network—providing further evidence of the surprising computational power of multiple frequency network models (see also [8]).

Leader Election Results. We study leader election in the *t-disrup-ted* network model, which describes a congested single-hop synchronous radio network consisting of $\mathcal{F} > 0$ communication frequencies. In each round, each active device can choose a single frequency on which to participate. Concurrent broadcasts on the same frequency lead to message loss on that frequency, due to collision. We assume no collision detection. To capture the unpredictable interference caused by unrelated protocols using the same shared spectrum, we introduce an abstract *interference adversary* that can choose up to $t < \mathcal{F}$ frequencies in each round to *disrupt*—preventing communication. We assume t is a known upper bound. The leader election problem assumes N devices that are activated in an arbitrary pattern by an adversary. On being activated, a device has no *a priori* knowledge of which other devices (if any) are also active. Some devices might never be activated. The goal is to output the id of a leader as soon as possible, while maintaining the safety property that all active devices output the same id, with high probability. The time complexity of a leader election algorithm is measured as the maximum number of rounds from when a device is activated to when it outputs a leader id.

We start by establishing a lower bound of $\Omega\big(\frac{\log^2 N}{(\mathcal{F}-t)\log\log N} + \frac{\mathcal{F}t}{\mathcal{F}-t}\cdot\log N\big)$ rounds, through reduction to our previous bound on the *wireless synchronization problem* in this same model [5]. Notice, the *trapdoor protocol* presented in [5] can be adapted to solve leader election in $O\big(\frac{\mathcal{F}}{\mathcal{F}-t}\log^2 N + \frac{\mathcal{F}t}{\mathcal{F}-t}\log N\big)$ time, which is not tight with respect to this lower bound. In the remainder of the paper, we set out to close this gap.

To accomplish this goal, we present three different algorithms, each optimal with respect to a different subset of the range of possible t values. For the case where $t = 0$, we present a randomized algorithm that works in $O\big(\frac{\log^2 N}{\mathcal{F}} + \log N\big)$ time. This algorithm uses a novel strategy of recruiting *herald* nodes to advance a leadership case on behalf of a potential leader. To understand the intuition behind this strategy, imagine that $\mathcal{F} = \log N$. Our algorithm, in this case, assigns an exponential distribution of probabilities to the channels, and active devices choose their channels according to this distribution; they then broadcast on the selected channel with constant probability. At a high-level, we can show that with constant probability, there will be a favored channel in this round that has only a single broadcaster. The receivers on this favored channel are then responsible for *heralding* this single broadcaster by announcing it on a special announcement channel, also with constant probability. We can prove that $O(\log N)$ rounds will be sufficient to ensure that with high probability, a single such announcement is promulgated to the whole active network, and subsequently to all devices that are eventually activated.

For $1 < t \le \mathcal{F}/6$, we present a variant of our herald algorithm in which multiple real (potentially disrupted) frequencies are used to simulate each undisrupted frequency from the $t = 0$ case. This algorithm works in $O\big(\frac{\log^2 N}{\mathcal{F}} + t\log N\big)$ time. Finally, for $t > \mathcal{F}/6$ we improve the trapdoor protocol of [5] to work in $O\big(\frac{\log N + \mathcal{F}t}{\mathcal{F}-t}\cdot\log N\big)$ time for these values of t. This improvement matches the lower bound (within log log factors). It is important to note that it

requires t to be large. That is, for smaller t, this particular algorithm is no longer optimal—whereas our above herald-style algorithms are.

The most relevant existing result is the trapdoor protocol [5] mentioned above. This protocol can be adapted to solve the leader election problem in our model. As the time complexity is not tight with the lower bound, our protocols close this gap. In fact, the original problem solved by the trapdoor protocol is "wireless synchronization," and our protocols can be adapted to solve this problem as well. Thus, not only do we present the first known tight leader election bounds in this model, we also present the first known tight wireless synchronization bounds. Also relevant is the work of Meier et al. [15], which studies bounds on device discovery in the *t-disrupted* model. They focus primarily on the case where there are only 2 devices that start simultaneously, but t is unknown—showing unknown t algorithms that can come within a $\log^2 \mathcal{F}$ competitive ratio of the optimal known t algorithms, in terms of expected performance. We focus instead on a case where there are an unknown number of nodes started adversarially, but t is known.

The Computational Power of Frequency Diversity. Notice that for $t = 0$ and $\mathcal{F} = \omega(1)$ our herald protocol beats the classic $\Omega(\log^2 n)$ bound on a single device broadcasting alone in a single frequency, non-disrupted radio model [10, 14] (i.e., our model with $\mathcal{F} = 1$ and $t = 0$). Indeed, our algorithms show that this advantage can be maintained even for relatively large amounts of disruption (i.e., for $\mathcal{F} - t =: \epsilon\mathcal{F} = \omega(1)$ and $t/\epsilon = o(\log N)$). Put another way, the presence of multiple communication frequencies adds non-trivial power to a radio network model, even if devices can each only use one frequency per round *and* a significant fraction of frequencies are disrupted. (A similar result was presented in [8], which proved that global broadcast can be solved faster in the *t-disrupted* radio network model than in the classical undisrupted, single-frequency model.)

2. MODEL & DEFINITIONS

We model randomized distributed algorithms in a synchronous single hop radio networking consisting of multiple communication channels and bounded disruption. In more detail, we assume time is divided into synchronized slots, called *rounds*. We assume that N devices—which we call *nodes*—begin each execution *inactive*. At the beginning of each round, an adversary decides which devices (if any) to make *active*, at which point they start executing with a round number of 1 (that is, we assume no *a priori* knowledge of a global round number). The radio network consists of $\mathcal{F} \ge 1$ disjoint and distinguishable narrowband communication frequencies — throughout the paper we use the notion of frequency and channel interchangeably.

In each round, each active node can choose a single frequency on which to participate by either broadcasting or receiving. If a single node broadcasts on a given frequency in a given round, then all nodes receiving on that frequency receive its message. If two or more nodes broadcast on the same frequency in the same round, then the message is lost due to collision. Nodes are incapable of *collision detection*, i.e., nodes can not distinguish between a collision and no message being broadcasted. We emphasize that nodes learn nothing about the behavior on other frequencies.

The multi-frequency open spectrum networks we model here are prone to disruption generated by unrelated protocols and other source of electromagnetic emission. We capture this unpredictable disruption with an *interference adversary* that can disrupt up to $\mathcal{F}$ frequencies per round. By disrupting a frequency, the adversary prevents any node from receiving a message on that frequency. That is, a node receives a message on a frequency only if a single node broadcasts on that frequency *and* it is not disrupted. We assume the interference adversary knows the algorithm being executed by the nodes, and the entire history prior to the current round, but does not know the private randomness used by nodes to make random choices.

Each node knows the $\mathcal{F}$ frequencies, an upper bound to the number of nodes, N, and an upper bound t to the number of disrupted frequencies.

Mathematical Preliminaries. We frequently need to say that an event A happens with probability close to 1. If the probability that A does not occur is exponentially small in some parameter k, i.e., if $\mathbb{P}(A) = 1 - e^{-ck}$ for some constant $c > 0$, we say that A happens with very high probability w.r.t. k, abbreviated as w.v.h.p.(k). We say that an event happens with high probability w.r.t. a parameter k, abbreviated as w.h.p.(k), if it happens with probability $1 - k^{-c}$, where the constant $c > 0$ can be chosen arbitrarily (possibly at the cost of adapting some other involved constants). If an event happens w.h.p.(N), we just say it happens with high probability (w.h.p.).

In order to show concentration of random variables, we will make use of the notion of negative association as defined in [13]. In particular, consider an experiment in which weighted balls are thrown independently into n bins according to some given distribution. For $i \in [n]$, let X_i be the total weight of balls in bin i and for an arbitrary parameter $a \geq 0$ and $i \in [n]$, let Y_i and Z_i be indicator random variables such that $Y_i = 1$ iff $X_i \leq a$ and $Z_i = 1$ iff $X_i \geq a$. It can be shown that the following lemma holds (see e.g., [9, 13]):

LEMMA 2.1. *The random variables $X_1, \ldots, X_n$ (or any subset of these random variables) are negatively associated. The same is true for the random variables $Y_1, \ldots, Y_n$ and for the random variables $Z_1, \ldots, Z_n$.*

Specifically, negative association is useful because as, e.g., shown in [9], for the sum of negatively associated random variables, the usual Chernoff bounds hold. We will make use of the following bounds:

LEMMA 2.2. *For a parameter $a > 0$, let $X_1, \ldots, X_n$ be independent or negatively associated non-negative random variables with $X_i \leq a$. Further, let $X := X_1 + \cdots + X_n$ and $\mu := \mathbb{E}[X]$. For $\delta > 0$, it holds that*

$$\mathbb{P}\left(X \geq (1+\delta)\mu\right) \leq \left(\frac{e^\delta}{(1+\delta)^{1+\delta}}\right)^{\mu/a}.$$

For $\delta \leq 1$, the bound can by upper bounded by $\mathbb{P}(X \geq (1+\delta)\mu) \leq e^{-\delta^2\mu/3a}$, for $\delta > 1$, it holds that $\mathbb{P}(X \geq (1+\delta)\mu) \leq e^{-\delta \ln(1+\delta)\mu/2a}$. Further, for every $\delta \in (0, 1)$,

$$\mathbb{P}\left(X \leq (1-\delta)\mu\right) \leq \left(\frac{e^{-\delta}}{(1-\delta)^{1-\delta}}\right)^{\mu/a} \leq e^{-\frac{\delta^2}{2a} \cdot \mu}.$$

LEMMA 2.3. *Assume there are k bins and n balls with non-negative weights $w_1, \ldots, w_n \leq 1/4$, as well as a parameter $q \in (0, 1]$. Assume that $\sum_{i=1}^n w_i = c \cdot k/q$ for some constant $c \geq 1$. Each ball is independently selected with probability q and each selected ball is thrown into a uniformly random bin. With probability w.v.h.p.(k), there are at least $k/4$ bins in which the total weight of all balls is between $c/3$ and $2c$.*

Due to lack of space we only provide a proof sketch and refer to [3] for the full proof.

PROOF SKETCH. We introduce random variables X_i that count the weight in each bin and Bernoulli random variables Y_i (Z_i) that count the number of bins with more than $c/3$ (less than $2c$) total weight. Then we apply Chernoff bounds to the negatively associated Y_i (Z_i). Note that Y_i and Z_j are not negatively associated. Careful assembling of the dependent variables $Y = \sum Y_i$ and $Z = \sum Z_i$ allows us to conclude that the number of bins, for which both conditions hold, are in $\Theta(k)$ w.v.h.p.(k). □

In addition, we need a few simple results in our analysis, which we sum up in the following proposition:

PROPOSITION 2.4. *1. $x \in \left[0, \frac{1}{2}\right) \Rightarrow e^{-\frac{3}{2}x} \leq 1 - x \leq e^{-x}$*

2. Let $n, k \in \mathbb{N}$, $\lambda_i \in [0, \frac{1}{k}]$ for $i = 1, 2, \ldots, n$ and $\sum_{i=1}^n \lambda_i = 1$. Then $\sum_{i=1}^n \lambda^2 \leq \frac{1}{k}$.

3. PROBLEM

The goal of the leader election problem is for active nodes to agree on a single active node to play the role of the leader. Formally, we say an algorithm *solves the leader election problem within $f(\mathcal{F}, t, N)$ rounds* if it guarantees the following properties are satisfied w.h.p.(N), when executed in a network with parameters $\mathcal{F}$, t, N:

1. *Liveness:* Every node that is activated outputs the id of an active node as leader within $f(\mathcal{F}, t, N)$ rounds of being activated.

2. *Well-Formedness:* Every node that is activated performs no more than a single output.

3. *Safety:* No two nodes output different leaders.

We call an algorithm that solves the leader election problem a *leader election algorithm.*

4. LOWER BOUND

We establish a lower bound on leader election that we will subsequently prove to be tight (within log log factors) in the remainder of this paper. This bound, presented below, requires that the leader election algorithm in question is also *regular* [5]. An algorithm is regular if there exists a sequence of pairs $(F_1, b_1), (F_2, b_2), \ldots$, where each F_i is a probability distribution over frequencies and b_i is a probability, such that for each node u and local round r, as u has not received a message through its first r rounds, it chooses its frequency and whether or not to broadcast according to F_r and b_r, respectively. Once u receives a message we no longer restrict its behavior. Notice, all the algorithms described in this paper are regular.

We continue with the main bound:

THEOREM 4.1. *Let $\mathcal{A}$ be a regular algorithm that solves the leader election problem in $f(\mathcal{F}, t, N)$ rounds. It follows that $f(\mathcal{F}, t, N) = \Omega\left(\frac{\log^2(N)}{(\mathcal{F}-t)\log\log(N)} + \frac{\mathcal{F}t}{\mathcal{F}-t} \cdot \log N\right)$.*

To prove this theorem, our strategy is to first prove that any leader election algorithm must satisfy a specific communication property. We then leverage a lemma that was adapted from our study of a related problem [5], to bound such algorithms, yielding the result claimed by our theorem.

In more detail, the lemma we adapt from [5] bounds a type of algorithm that we call *vocal*. Formally, we say an algorithm is *vocal with probability* p, if for every activation pattern[1] that includes at least 2 nodes, with probability at least p some node receives a message from another. In the setting of non-disrupted single frequency radio networks (i.e., our model with $\mathcal{F} = 1$ and $t = 0$), Jurdzinski and Stachowiak [14] proved a classic bound of $\Omega\left(\frac{\log^2(N)}{\log\log(N)}\right)$ rounds for a vocal algorithm to deliver its first message (a problem they called *wake-up*). In fact, the lemma we adapt from [5], relies, in part, on a generalization of the Jurdzinski and Stachowiak argument to a setting with multiple frequencies and disruption. Notice that Farach-Colton et al. [10] later removed the $\log\log(N)$ factor, but the same techniques we used to generalize [14] did not apply.

It is tempting to claim it is obvious that any solution to leader election must be vocal, and therefore any bound on vocal algorithms applies to leader election. And in fact there are studies of other radio network problems that make this exact claim without justification. Here we emphasize that more care is needed. Though our intuition might tell us that *some* communication is required for meaningful coordination, this is not necessarily always the case. Indeed, for any number of advanced radio network problems, one can devise algorithms that, for some activation pattens, solve the problem with no messages ever being received. Silence, in other words, can convey information. Accordingly, our first task is to formally argue that to solve leader election with high probability requires that the algorithm is vocal with an almost as high probability:

LEMMA 4.2. *If algorithm $\mathcal{A}$ solves the leader election problem with probability at least $1 - \epsilon$, then with probability at least $1 - 3\epsilon$, $\mathcal{A}$ is vocal, and at least one node waits to output a leader until after the first message is received.*

PROOF. Assume for contradiction that $\mathcal{A}$ is vocal in the required manner with probability less than $1 - 3\epsilon$. It follows that there exists an activation pattern P that activates at least 2 nodes, such that with probability at least 3ϵ, $\mathcal{A}$ with pattern P generates a *silent* execution in which every node elects a leader before any node receives a message. Let u and v be two nodes activated in P. Our strategy is to argue that u and v cannot distinguish a silent execution with pattern P from executions where they are alone. This will lead to a non-trivial probability that at least one of these nodes fails to solve leader election.

To formalize this intuition we need to formalize our treatment of randomness. In more detail, assume that at the beginning of each execution, a sufficiently large collection of bits is generated for the system, where each bit is determined with independent randomness. These bits are then partitioned among all N processes, and processes that end up activated use their bits to resolve their probabilistic choices. Let B be the set of all possible bit strings that could be generated for an execution. By definition, every $s \in B$ is equally likely to be generated.

Let $B_S \subset B$ be the subset of strings that, when combined with activation pattern P, generate a silent execution. By our above assumption, $|B_S| > 3\epsilon|B|$. Let $B_S^L \subseteq B_S$ be the subset of strings from B_S that, when combined with activation pattern P, are not only silent but also solve leader election (that is, all nodes output the same node as leader, and it is an active node). Given our assumption about $\mathcal{A}$ solving leader election with probability $1 - \epsilon$, it follows

$$|B_S^L| > 2\epsilon|B|.$$

Let S_P be the set of nodes activated in P. Define $\ell : B_S^L \to S_P$, such that $\forall s \in B_S^L$, $\ell(s)$ is the single node in S_P to be the elected

leader when we run $\mathcal{A}$ with s and activation pattern P. A simple counting argument tells us:

$$\exists u \in S_P, \frac{|\{s \in B_S^L : \ell(s) = u\}|}{|B_S^L|} \leq 1/2.$$

That is, at least one node is not elected leader in more than half of these bit strings.

Moving on, let $B_S^{L,\bar{u}} \subseteq B_S^L$ be the strings in B_S^L where u is not elected leader. The key observation is that for any $s \in B_S^{L,\bar{u}}$, an execution of $\mathcal{A}$ with s with an activation pattern that only activates u is indistinguishable through u's leader output w.r.t. an execution with u in pattern P, as in both cases, u makes the same random choices and receives no messages, before outputting a leader. For these strings, when u is run alone, it elects some other node as leader, which violates the properties of leader election. To complete the proof, we note that by construction:

$$|B_S^{L,\bar{u}}| \geq (1/2)|B_S^L| > \epsilon.$$

We have, therefore, identified an activation pattern (u being activated alone) for which $\mathcal{A}$ solves leader election with probability *less* than $1 - \epsilon$. A contradiction. □

We can now present our main lemma regarding vocal algorithms. This lemma is adapted from the proof arguments presented for Theorems 1 and 4 from [5].

LEMMA 4.3 (FROM [5]). *Let $\mathcal{A}$ be a regular vocal algorithm that guarantees that a message is received within $f(\mathcal{F}, t, N)$ rounds of the first activation, with probability at least $1 - 1/N$. It follows that $f(\mathcal{F}, t, N) = \Omega\left(\frac{\log^2(N)}{(\mathcal{F}-t)\log\log(N)} + \frac{\mathcal{F}t}{\mathcal{F}-t} \cdot \log N\right).$*

Returning to Theorem 4.1, the proof follows from the combination of Lemmas 4.2 and 4.3.

5. BASIC HERALD ALGORITHM

We start our description of algorithms with the simplest case, when there are no disrupted frequencies, i.e., $t = 0$. This allows us to present the basic ideas and techniques without having to worry about many of the technical difficulties that arise in the more general setting.

The described protocol runs in $O\left(\frac{\log^2 N}{\mathcal{F}} + \log N\right)$, which is tight (up to log log factors).

Algorithm Description. Detailed pseudo-code of the algorithm of this section and of Section 6 is given in Algorithm 1. For the case $t = 0$, which we analyze in this section, lines 15 and 29 can basically be omitted and in the upcoming analysis we write $\mathcal{H}$ and $\mathcal{L}$ instead of $(\mathcal{H}, 0)$ and $(\mathcal{L}, 0)$ respectively.

For convenience, we define $F := \mathcal{F} - 2$ and assume that the $\mathcal{F}$ frequencies are $1, \ldots, F$, as well as two special frequencies $\mathcal{H}$ and $\mathcal{L}$. W.l.o.g., we assume that $F \leq \log N$, otherwise, we just only use the first $2 + \log N$ channels. We also assume for simplicity that N is a power of 2 and that F divides $\log N$. W.l.o.g., we assume the first round in which any node wakes up to be round 1.

After awaking, a node u considers itself *waiting* (state W). It stays in this state for $\Theta(\log N)$ rounds (we call that Phase 0) in which it only listens on channels $\mathcal{L}$ and $\mathcal{H}$ (with prob. $1/2$ on each of them). If u does not receive any message during Phase 0, it switches to the state *competing* (C), where it behaves as follows.

The algorithm acts in phases. Each phase lasts for $l := c \log N$ rounds, where c is an appropriately chosen constant. There are a total of $2\frac{\log N}{F} + 1$ phases. If a node finishes its last phase while

---

[1]By *activation pattern*, we mean the description of which nodes are activated in an execution and during which global round.

Algorithm 1:

$t = 0$: Basic herald algorithm for the undisrupted case
$t > 0$: Herald algorithm for disrupted channels

State description: W – waiting, C – competing, H – herald,
L – leader, E – eliminated

```
1  begin
2  |  if t = 0 then
3  |  |  phase-length := c log N + 1
4  |  |  sub-channel-set := {0}
5  |  else
6  |  |  phase-length := c(F + log N/t) + 1
7  |  |  sub-channel-set := {1, 2, . . . , 2t}
8  |  set phase := 0; count := 0; age := 0; state := W
9  |  while state ≠ E do
10 |  |  count := count + 1; age := age + 1
11 |  |  if count = phase-length then
12 |  |  |  count := 1; phase := phase + 1
13 |  |  if phase = 1 and state = W then  state := C
14 |  |  if phase = 2 log N/F + 2 and state = C then  state := L
15 |  |  Pick s uniformly at random out of sub-channel-set
16 |  |  switch state do
17 |  |  |  case W :  With prob. 1/2, listen on channel
   |  |  |     (H, s), otherwise listen on channel (L, s)
18 |  |  |  case C :
19 |  |  |  |  Randomly pick r ∈ [0, 1)
20 |  |  |  |  Let I :=
   |  |  |  |    max { i : r ≥ (2^(i−F) · 2^((F/2)(phase−1)))/(4N) }
21 |  |  |  |  if I > F or I = 0 then
22 |  |  |  |  |  With prob. 1/2, listen on channel (H, s),
   |  |  |  |  |     otherwise listen on channel (L, s)
23 |  |  |  |  else
24 |  |  |  |  |  On channel (I, s) with probability π_ℓ
   |  |  |  |  |     listen or otherwise broadcast (id, age)
25 |  |  |  case H :
26 |  |  |  |  Broadcast bc on channel (H, s)
27 |  |  |  |  if bc ≠ (id, age) then state := E else
   |  |  |  |     state := C
28 |  |  |  case L :
29 |  |  |  |  if t > 0 and age > c'(log² N/F + t log N)
   |  |  |  |     then Consider yourself a leader
30 |  |  |  |  On channel (L, s) with prob. 1/2 listen,
   |  |  |  |     otherwise broadcast (id, age)

31 Upon receiving a message msg = (msg.id, msg.age):
32 if current channel/block is H or L then
33 |  if msg.age ≥ age and msg.id ≠ id then  state := E
34 else                           // can only happen if state = C
35 |  state := H
36 |  if msg.age ≥ age then
37 |  |  bc := (msg.age + 1, msg.id)
38 |  else
39 |  |  bc := (age + 1, id)
```

→ lines 15 and 29 marked with arrows

still competing, then it declares itself a leader (state L) and starts broadcasting on channel $\mathcal{L}$ with probability $\frac{1}{2}$ in each round.

In a given round, a competing node chooses one of the available channels—each of them with a different probability. The highest probability is assigned to channels $\mathcal{H}$ and $\mathcal{L}$, which have a special role among all channels. If a competing node u chooses channels $\mathcal{L}$ or $\mathcal{H}$ then it listens in that round, if it chooses a channel $i \in [F]$, u listens with constant probability $\pi_\ell \leq \frac{1}{2}$ and transmits with probability $1 - \pi_\ell$ (the value of π_ℓ is determined at the end of the proof of Lemma 5.2). Once awake (i.e., active), each node u keeps track of its age $age(u)$ by counting the number of rounds it has been awake.

Most of the time a node spends listening; if it ever hears a message, then it follows these rules:

1. First assume that a node u hears a message on channel $\mathcal{H}$ or $\mathcal{L}$. The message contains the name and age of a node v. Note that v is not necessarily the sender of that message. If $u \neq v$ and $age(v) \geq age(u)$, then u immediately considers itself *eliminated* (state E). Eliminated nodes only listen on channel $\mathcal{L}$ to learn of a leader election. If u is older than v then u does not react to the message.

2. If a node u hears a message containing the name and age of a node v on a channel other than $\mathcal{H}$ or $\mathcal{L}$, then u considers itself a *herald* (state H) for exactly one round (i.e., for the following round). In that round, u broadcasts a message on channel $\mathcal{H}$. If the herald u is strictly older than the age of v in the message it received, then u broadcasts its own name and (current) age on channel $\mathcal{H}$. If not, then it broadcasts the name and age of v instead (adding 1 round to comprise the fact that there is a one-round-delay). A node u that heralds the name of a node $v \neq u$ also considers itself eliminated.

A competing node in the first phase chooses one of the $\mathcal{F}$ channels using the following probabilities: It selects channel $i \in [F]$ with probability $\frac{2^{i-F}}{4N}$ and with half of the remaining probability for channels $\mathcal{H}$ and $\mathcal{L}$, respectively. Each time a node progresses to a new phase all those probabilities (except of those for channels $\mathcal{H}$ and $\mathcal{L}$) are multiplied by $2^{\frac{F}{2}}$. Channels $\mathcal{H}$ and $\mathcal{L}$ always get the remaining probability. After $2\frac{\log N}{F} + 1$ phases, the chances for channels $F, F-1, F-2, \ldots$ are $\frac{1}{4}, \frac{1}{8}, \frac{1}{16}, \ldots$, respectively. Channel $\mathcal{H}$ and $\mathcal{L}$ are therefore both always chosen with probability more than $\frac{1}{4}$.

Analysis. The goal of the remainder of Section 5 is to prove the main theorem of the section.

THEOREM 5.1. *With high probability, for $t = 0$ Algorithm 1 elects exactly one leader and it does so in $O\left(\frac{\log^2 N}{F}\right)$ rounds after the first node wakes up.*

In any round, for a competing node v we denote with $p_v(m)$ the probability of v choosing channel m and we denote by P_m the sum of the probabilities of all nodes to choose channel m, i.e., $P_m := \sum_v p_v(m)$. Note that $P_F = 2^m P_{F-m}$ and therefore $P_F \approx \frac{1}{2} \sum_{m=1}^{F} P_m$. When making a statement about the probability mass, we refer to P_F. If we state that a constant fraction of the probability mass is eliminated we mean that a collection of notes, which contribute a constant fraction to the probability mass, are eliminated. Further, in any round, $\mathcal{A}$ is the age which separates younger and older nodes in such a way that both groups contribute roughly one half of the whole probability mass. In more precise mathematical terms:

$$\mathcal{A} \; := \; \min\left\{ h \in \mathbb{N}_0 : \sum_{v:age(v)\le h} p_v(F) > \frac{P_F}{2} \right\}$$

$$= \; \max\left\{ h \in \mathbb{N}_0 : \sum_{v:age(v)\ge h} p_v(F) \ge \frac{P_F}{2} \right\}.$$

A herald is called *old*, if it broadcasts on channel $\mathcal{H}$ the id of an *old* node u, where u is old if $age(u) \ge \mathcal{A}$. We call a round in which exactly one node u becomes an old herald a *successful round*. We next show that under the appropriate circumstances, each round is successful with constant probability. In the round following a successful round, all nodes listening on channel $\mathcal{H}$ receive the old herald's message. Since the herald's message contains the fingerprint of an old node and each other node listens on channel $\mathcal{H}$ at least with probability $\frac{1}{4}$, we are able to show that in expectation at least a constant fraction of the probability mass is eliminated when this happens.

LEMMA 5.2. *A round r during an execution of Algorithm 1 for which $P_F \in \left[\frac{1}{2}, 2^{F-1}\right]$ is a successful round with constant probability.*

PROOF. The conditions of the lemma imply that for one channel $\lambda \in \{1,\dots,F\}$ it holds that P_λ is in $[\frac{1}{2}, 1)$. We will prove two claims:

W.l.o.g., assume that of all nodes $V = \{v_1,\dots,v_n\}$ the nodes $v_1,\dots v_\kappa$ are those being awake and that $age(v_1) \ge \dots \ge age(v_\kappa)$. Let i_0 be the smallest value such that $age(v_{i_0}) < \mathcal{A}$, i.e., $v_1,\dots,v_{i_0-1}$ are old and $v_{i_0},\dots,v_\kappa$ are not. Further, let c_{ij} be the probability that on channel λ exactly nodes v_i and v_j are present in the current round, but no other node. We denote by $p_l(m)$ the probability that node v_l is on channel m. We have

$$c_{ij} \; = \; p_i(\lambda)p_j(\lambda)\prod_{k\neq i,j}\left(1-p_k(\lambda)\right)$$

$$\overset{\text{(Prop. 2.4.1)}}{\ge} \; p_i(\lambda)p_j(\lambda)e^{-\frac{3}{2}P_\lambda} =: c'_{ij}.$$

So the probability of having exactly two nodes on channel λ is lower bounded by the sum over all c'_{ij} with $i < j$. Since $c'_{ij} = c'_{ji}$ for all i,j, we can sum over all c'_{ij} (without restrictions in i and j), which is $P_\lambda^2 e^{-\frac{3}{2}P_\lambda}$, deduct $\sum_i c'_{ii}$ and multiply the result with $\frac{1}{2}$. However, we need also to make sure that at least one of the nodes v_i, v_j is old, so we also refrain from including any c'_{ij} for which both $i,j \ge i_0, i \neq j$. Call the event of having exactly two nodes on channel λ with at least one of them being old D_λ. Then,

$$\mathbb{P}(D_\lambda) \ge \frac{1}{2}\left(\underbrace{\sum_{i,j} c'_{ij}}_{=P_\lambda^2 e^{-\frac{3}{2}P_\lambda}} - \sum_{i<i_0} c'_{ii} - \underbrace{\left(\sum_{i\ge i_0} c'_{ii} + \sum_{i,j\ge i_0, i\neq j} c'_{ij} \right)}_{=:C'_0} \right).$$

Set $\delta_i := \frac{p_i(\lambda)}{P_\lambda}$ for $i < i_0$ (all old nodes) and $\delta_{i_0} := \frac{\sum_{j\ge i_0} p_j(\lambda)}{P_\lambda}$ (all young nodes together). Note that the δ_i's are not defined for $i \in \{i_0+1,\dots,n\}$, however, they still 'consider' the probabilities of all nodes. Now we have that $\delta_i \le \frac{1}{2}$ for all i (including i_0) and our choice of δ_{i_0} also ensures that $\sum_{i=1}^{i_0}\delta_i = 1$, which allows us to apply Proposition 2.4.2. Furthermore it holds that $c'_{ii} = \delta_i^2 P_\lambda^2 e^{-\frac{3}{2}P_\lambda}$ and $C'_0 = \delta_{i_0}^2 P_\lambda^2 e^{-\frac{3}{2}P_\lambda}$. We get

$$\mathbb{P}(D_\lambda) \ge \frac{1}{2}P_\lambda^2 e^{-\frac{3}{2}P_\lambda}\left(1 - \sum_{i<i_0}\delta_i^2 - \delta_{i_0}^2\right) \ge \frac{1}{4}P_\lambda^2 e^{-\frac{3}{2}P_\lambda} = \Omega(1)$$

We call a transmission on a channel $m \in [F]$ *successful*, if *exactly one* node transmits on that channel, *exactly one* node listens and at least one of those nodes is old—we denote that event by A_m. The probability of having a successful transmission on some channel m conditioned on having exactly two nodes on that channel is $2\pi_\ell(1-\pi_\ell) \ge \pi_\ell$. Since we also know that $\mathbb{P}(D_\lambda) = \Omega(1)$, we have

$$\mathbb{P}(A_\lambda) = \Omega(\pi_\ell).$$

That finishes the proof of our first claim. We continue with proving the second one.

To have a successful round, we have to have exactly one old herald being created in that round. This probability is lower bounded by the probability that this herald is created on channel λ while none is created on any other channel. Let B_m be the event that *exactly one* node transmits and *at least one* node listens on channel m:

$$\mathbb{P}(\text{successful round}) \;\ge\; \mathbb{P}(A_\lambda)\left(1 - \mathbb{P}\left(\bigcup_{m\in[F]\setminus\lambda} B_m \,\middle|\, A_\lambda\right)\right)$$

$$\ge\; \mathbb{P}(A_\lambda)\left(1 - \sum_{m\in[F]\setminus\lambda}\mathbb{P}(B_m|A_\lambda)\right).$$

When we condition on A_λ, there are $\kappa - 2$ nodes that are on channels different from λ. Let $u_1,\dots,u_{\kappa-2} \subset \{v_1,\dots,v_\kappa\}$ be these nodes. Let i,j,k be in $\{1,\dots\kappa-2\}$ in the following calculations. Conditioning on A_λ the probability for any node u_k being on channel m increases by $(1-p_k(\lambda))^{-1}$. That is,

$$\mathbb{P}(u_k \text{ is on channel } m|A_\lambda) = \frac{p_k(m)}{1-p_k(\lambda)},$$

and moreover we have

$$\mathbb{P}(u_k \text{ is not transmitting on channel } m|A_\lambda) = 1 - \frac{(1-\pi_\ell)p_k(m)}{1-p_k(\lambda)}.$$

Let $B_m^{i,j}$ be the event that u_i is on channel m, no other node transmits on channel m, and u_j listens on channel m. For $m \in [F] \setminus \lambda$, we have

$$\mathbb{P}\left(B_m^{i,j}|A_\lambda\right) = \frac{p_i(m)}{1-p_i(\lambda)}(1-\pi_\ell)\frac{p_j(m)}{1-p_j(\lambda)}\pi_\ell$$

$$\prod_{k\notin\{i,j,\kappa-1,\kappa\}}\left(1 - \frac{(1-\pi_\ell)p_k(m)}{1-p_k(\lambda)}\right)$$

$$= p_i(m)p_j(m)\pi_\ell\overbrace{(1-\pi_\ell)(1-p_{\kappa-1}(\lambda))(1-p_\kappa(\lambda))}^{\le 1}$$

$$\prod_{k\le\kappa}\frac{1-p_k(\lambda)-(1-\pi_\ell)p_k(m)}{1-p_k(\lambda)}$$

$$\prod_{k=i,j,\kappa-1,\kappa}\left(1 - \underbrace{p_k(\lambda)-(1-\pi_\ell)p_k(m)}_{\le\frac{1}{4}+\frac{1}{8}}\right)^{-1}$$

$$\overset{\text{(Prop. 2.4.1)}}{\le} p_i(m)p_j(m)\,\pi_\ell\, e^{\frac{3}{2}P_\lambda}\, e^{-P_\lambda-P_m(1-\pi_\ell)}(8/5)^4$$

$$\le p_i(m)p_j(m)\,\pi_\ell\, e^3 e^{-\frac{P_m}{2}}.$$

Because $B_m = \bigcup_{i,j\in[\kappa-2], i\neq j} B_m^{i,j}$, applying a union bound yields

$$\mathbb{P}(B_m|A_\lambda) \le \sum_{i,j\in[\kappa-2], i\neq j}\mathbb{P}(B_m^{i,j}|A_\lambda) \le P_m^2 e^3 \pi_\ell e^{-\frac{P_m}{2}} =: C_m.$$

For a fixed value m this value is in $O(\pi_\ell)$.

We now upper bound the sum over all C_m. We set $\lambda' := \min\{\lambda + 4, F\}$. Remember that $P_{m+1} = 2P_m \; \forall m \in \{1, \ldots, F-1\}$. Then:

$$\frac{C_{m+1}}{C_m} = 4e^{-P_m + \frac{P_m}{2}} = 4e^{-\frac{P_m}{2}} < \frac{1}{2}, \quad \forall m \geq \lambda'$$

$$\frac{C_{m-1}}{C_m} = \frac{1}{4}e^{-\frac{P_m}{4} + \frac{P_m}{2}} = \frac{1}{4}e^{\frac{P_m}{4}} < \frac{1}{2}, \quad \forall m \leq \lambda$$

That is, the further a frequency is away from λ, the smaller the probability that there is a herald created, more precisely, after some constant distance from channel λ, probabilities drop by at least $\frac{1}{2}$ with each step within the frequencies (actually way more). We thus make use of geometric series to upper bound all frequencies outside $[\lambda, \ldots, \lambda']$ simultaneously by $C_\lambda + C_{\lambda'}$. As mentioned above $C_m = O(\pi_\ell)$ for a fixed m. Thus, in total, we have

$$\sum_{m \neq \lambda} \mathbb{P}(B_m | A_\lambda) \leq \sum_m C_m \leq C_\lambda + C_{\lambda'} + \sum_{m=\lambda}^{\lambda'} C_m = O(\pi_\ell).$$

Choosing π_ℓ small enough but still constant, then this value is less than 1. On the other hand, since we choose π_ℓ to be a constant the event A_λ happens with constant probability and thus the probability of a successful round is also a constant, concluding the proof. $\square$

Because in every round with constant probability an old herald is created, we can argue that in expectation all listening nodes on channel $\mathcal{H}$ of the same or lower age as the age being heralded are eliminated. By the definition of $\mathcal{A}$ we have that every time a successful round happens, a constant fraction of the probability mass is eliminated with constant probability.

LEMMA 5.3. *With high probability, at all times, it holds that $P_F \leq 2^{F-1}$. Further, with high probability, there are no $l/2$ consecutive rounds in which $P_F \geq \frac{1}{2}$.*

PROOF. There are two ways for P_F to increase: Either a node is already actively contributing to P_F and finishes a phase or it switches from the waiting state to the competing state. The former allows an increase of that node's contribution by $2^{\frac{F}{2}}$ while the latter is an absolute increase from 0 to $\frac{1}{4N}$. However, there are at most N nodes that can switch from the waiting state to the competing state, so that contribution is at most $\frac{1}{4}$, thus comparably small.

Thus, within $l = c \log N$ rounds (i.e., within the time of one phase), P_F can not increase by more than a factor of $2^{\frac{F}{2}}$ and an additive value of $\frac{1}{4}$. This guarantees that for P_F to exceed 2^{F-1} it must hold for at least l rounds that $P_F \geq \frac{1}{2}$, so all the requirements for lemma 5.2 are fulfilled.

If the constant c in the algorithm is chosen large enough, applying Chernoff bounds guarantees that, w.h.p., there are $\Omega(\log N)$ successful rounds. Each of these rounds eliminates a constant fraction of the probability mass in expectation (by choice of $\mathcal{A}$ and since the probability of listening on channel $\mathcal{H}$ is at least $\frac{1}{4}$). But since $\log N = \Omega(F)$, w.h.p., l rounds are thus sufficient have P_F drop back to a value smaller than $\frac{1}{2}$, a contradiction.

Using an identical argument and that $P_F \leq 2^{F-1}$ at all times, it also follows that $P_F \geq 1/2$ cannot hold for $l/2$ consecutive rounds. $\square$

PROOF OF THEOREM 5.1. The running time is clear from the construction of the algorithm as well is the fact that at least one leader is elected since among the nodes that wake up in round 1, there is at least one node that finishes its last phase without being eliminated.

For the sake of contradiction, assume that more than one leader is elected with probability more than $1/N$ (or any polynomial in N). W.l.o.g., let v_1 and v_2 be elected leaders with $age(v1) \geq age(v2)$.

Assume first that $age(v_2) \geq age(v_1) + l/2$. Then they both are in the last phase for at least $l/2$ rounds. In that time interval it holds that $p_1(F) = p_i(F) = \frac{1}{4}$, i.e., $P_F \geq \frac{1}{2}$ for $l/2$ consecutive rounds, a contradiction to the second claim of Lemma 5.3. Hence, w.h.p., $age(v_2) < age(v_1) + l/2$. But then, v_1 is already a leader for $l/2$ rounds before any other node becomes a leader. W.h.p. this is sufficiently long for v_2 to hear node v_1 on channel $\mathcal{L}$ before becoming a leader. Consequently, there is only one leader w.h.p. $\square$

6. HERALD ALGORITHM TOLERATING DISRUPTION

In this section, we address the problem of up to $t \in [1, \rho\mathcal{F}]$ nonfunctional frequencies, for some constant $\rho < 1/3$. We will show that a slight adaption of the basic herald algorithm provides an asymptotically optimal algorithm under the assumption that ρ is known to all nodes. For simplicity[2], we assume that the number of disrupted channels is $t \leq \mathcal{F}/6$. Also for simplicity, we assume that $2t$ divides $\mathcal{F}$. As discussed in Section 2, the adversary can freely decide which channels to disrupt just before a round starts.

The algorithm we present works similar to the algorithm in the case $t = 0$, except that each used channel in the original algorithm is replaced by a *block* of $2t$ channels with a total of $F + 2 = \frac{\mathcal{F}}{2t}$ blocks. Similarly to Section 5, we again assume that $F \leq \log N$. If it is not, we can just only use the first $2t(\log N + 2)$ channels. Analogously to the algorithm in Section 5, we name two of the blocks $\mathcal{H}$ and $\mathcal{L}$ and the remaining blocks $1, 2, \ldots, F$. Each block consists of $2t$ *sub-channels* and in a particular block b for a particular sub-channel s the corresponding channel is denoted by *channel* (b, s). Each round nodes choose a block b in the same manner as they choose channels in in the case $t = 0$. On the selected block b, they choose a uniformly random sub-channel s. After choosing a channel (b, s), nodes continue in the same manner as in the case $t = 0$. The second change is that for a competing node each phase now only lasts for $\Theta(F + \frac{\log N}{t})$ rounds. The third change is that a node that moves to state L does not immediately consider itself a leader, but it first becomes a *candidate*. Candidates listen or broadcast their id and age on a uniformly random channel on block $\mathcal{L}$. If a candidate does not get eliminated after being in state L for $\Theta(t \log N)$ rounds, it considers itself a *leader*. Any node that receives a message on $\mathcal{L}$ can calculate itself from the age being broadcasted whether that node is already a leader or not.

Detailed pseudo-code of the algorithm is given in Algorithm 1 in Section 5.

Analysis. Analogously to section 5 we denote with P_m the sum of all nodes' probabilities to choose block m. $\mathcal{A}$ and the notion of an old herald are also analogously defined. With $l = c(F + \frac{\log N}{t})$ we denote the length of one phase. Our primary goal of this subsection is to prove the following main theorem of the section.

THEOREM 6.1. *With high probability, Algorithm 1 elects exactly one leader and it does so in $O\left(\frac{\log^2 N}{F} + t \log N\right)$ rounds after the first node wakes up.*

First we prove in Lemma 6.2 that once the total probability mass exceeds a certain threshold, w.v.h.p.(t) each round $\Omega(t)$ heralds of age $\mathcal{A}$ or higher are created. In Lemma 6.3 we show that also

---

[2]A natural generalization yields $t < \rho\mathcal{F}$ for any $\rho < 1/3$: divide channels into blocks of $t(1 + \epsilon)$ instead of blocks of size $2t$.

the total number of heralds created each round is of order $O(t)$ w.v.h.p.(t). Both together provide for the fact that each round, w.v.h.p.(t), a constant fraction of the total probability mass is eliminated. Since that happens w.v.h.p.(t), a phase does not need to last longer than $\Theta\left(F + \frac{\log N}{t}\right)$ rounds to guarantee a probability mass reduction of order $\Omega(2^F)$ w.h.p.(N). We finally show that, w.h.p., at any time the number of nodes in state L is in $O(t)$. $\Theta(t \log N)$ rounds after the first nodes move to state L, one of them can safely declare itself a leader.

LEMMA 6.2. *If $P_F \in [2t, 2^F t]$ in any round, then w.v.h.p.(t) $\Omega(t)$ heralds are created, which herald the name and age of a node of age at least $\mathcal{A}$ on one of the channels in block $\mathcal{H}$ in the following round.*

PROOF. Following the lines of the proof for Lemma 5.2 we get that there is a block λ for which $P_\lambda \in [2t, 4t]$. Let $Dis_\lambda \subset \{1, 2, \ldots, 2t\}$ be the subset of disrupted sub-channels in block λ and let $t_\lambda := |Dis_\lambda| \le t$. Then define $q := 1 - \frac{t_\lambda}{2t} \in (0, 1]$, $k := 2t - t_\lambda$, $c := \frac{qP_\lambda}{k} = \frac{P_\lambda}{2t} \ge 1$ and $w_i := p_i(\lambda)$ for $i = 1, 2, \ldots, n$, where $p_i(\lambda)$ denotes the probability of node i to choose block λ. Note that $\sum_{i=1}^{n} w_i = P_\lambda$. We now apply Lemma 2.3, where the bins are the set of $k := 2t - t_\lambda \ge t$ undisrupted sub-channels in block λ, i.e., the channels $[2t] \setminus Dis_\lambda$. W.v.h.p.$(t)$ we get that on at least $k/4 \ge t/4$ of these sub-channels the total probability mass to choose block λ is in $[1/3, 4]$.

Clearly the age of a node has no impact regarding the choice of a sub-channel. Thus, due to symmetry and with analogous reasoning as in Lemma 5.2, we get that, independently, on each of those $k/4$ channels, with constant probability a herald is created that broadcasts the age of an old node in the following round. Hence, in expectation, the number of heralds created on block λ is $\Omega(t)$. Using a standard Chernoff bound (cf. Lemma 2.2), we also get that w.v.h.p.(t) that number is $\Omega(t)$. □

In the case $t = 0$ we needed to make sure that there is a constant chance to have exactly one herald being created. Here we need to be more thorough to maintain an optimal running time: we need to make sure that $\Theta(t)$ heralds are created w.v.h.p.(t) in *each round*.

LEMMA 6.3. *If $P_F \in [2t, 2^F t]$ in any round, then w.v.h.p.(t) $O(t)$ heralds are created.*

Due to lack of space we omit the details of this lengthy and technical proof. Here we provide a proof sketch and refer to [3] for the full proof.

PROOF SKETCH. In the case $t = 0$ we could show that on channels $i \ne \lambda$ no other herald is created with at least constant probability. We can not proceed analogously here for several reasons. First, for $t = 0$ the probability mass between consecutive channels did differ by a factor exactly 2. Here this is still true for blocks, but it is certainly not true for different channels on the same block. Second, the probability to have no herald created outside block λ is not a constant anymore. Third, we do not merely need a constant probability to bound the number of additional heralds, we need a very high probability that no more than $O(t)$ heralds are created.

We define the *node-range* $R_i := [2^{i-1} + 1, 2^i]$ and say that a channel is in node-range i iff the number of nodes on it is in R_i. We also let H_i be the number of heralds created on all channels in range i and set $\gamma := \ln(1/\pi_\ell)$. The proof is now carried out as follows:

(I) For $\xi \ge 0$, the total number of nodes in all blocks b for $b \le \lambda + \xi$ is $O(2^\xi t)$ w.v.h.p.(t).

(II) W.v.h.p.(t), for every $i \ge 0$, all blocks b with $b > \lambda + i$ together have at most $O(t)$ channels with at most 2^i nodes.

(III) W.v.h.p.(t), for every $i \ge 1$, there are at most νt channels in node-range R_i for a large constant ν.

(IV) W.v.h.p.(t), channels in node-ranges larger than $\log t$ do not create any heralds at all.

(V) Next we show that $\mathbb{P}(H_i \ge 2^i e^{1 - \frac{\gamma}{2} 2^{i-1}} \nu t + x + 2^i) \le e^{-\gamma x/4}$. Essentially, x measures how much H_i exceeds a safe value which would guarantee a total of $O(t)$ heralds over all node ranges.

(VI) In the last step, we use a probabilistic argument to union bound over all 'bad cases' to show that w.v.h.p.(t) on channels in node-range between 1 and $\log t$, in total only $O(t)$ heralds are created.

The last step concludes the claim. □

Both lemmas provide that for $P_F \ge 2$ the total number of heralds created in a single round is in $\Theta(t)$.

LEMMA 6.4. *With high probability, at all times, it holds that $P_F < t2^F$. Further, for appropriately chosen constant c, with high probability, there are no $l/2$ consecutive rounds in which $P_F \ge 2t$.*

PROOF. As in the case of the analysis in Section 5, there are two ways in which P_F can increase. Either some nodes switch to a new phase or there are new nodes switching from the waiting into the competing state. Analogously to the argument in the proof of Lemma 5.3, within the time of one phase, P_F can only increase by a factor of $2^{F/2}$ and a small additive amount. In order for P_F to exceed $t2^F$, P_F therefore has to be at least $2t$ for l consecutive rounds (i.e., for the duration of one phase). We show that for c sufficiently large, w.h.p., this cannot be the case.

Consider some round in which $P_F \in [2t, t2^F]$ and assume that there are $\hat{t} \in \{t, \ldots, 2t\}$ channels on block $\mathcal{H}$ that are undisrupted. Let $X_1, X_2, \ldots, X_{\hat{t}}$ be the random variables counting the number of heralds on each of the $\hat{t}$ undisrupted channels in block $\mathcal{H}$. By Lemma 2.1 the random variables $X_1, \ldots, X_{\hat{t}}$ are negatively associated. The same is true for the indicator random variables $X_{i, \le \alpha}$ that take value 1 iff $X_i \le \alpha$, where $i \in [\hat{t}]$ and $\alpha \ge 0$. We define $X_{\le \alpha} := \sum_{i=1}^{\hat{t}} X_{i, \le \alpha}$ and we let $p_{\le \alpha}$ denote the probability that at most α heralds are on a specific single channel. Let $2\eta t$ be the number of heralds on block $\mathcal{H}$ for this round for some $\eta = \Theta(t)$. We then have

$$p_0 := p_{\le 0} = \left(1 - \frac{1}{2t}\right)^{2\eta t} \overset{\text{(Prop. 2.4.1)}}{\ge} e^{-\frac{3}{2}\eta},$$

$$p_{\le 1} = p_0 + \eta t \cdot \frac{1}{2t}\left(1 - \frac{1}{2t}\right)^{2\eta t - 1}$$

$$= p_0 \left(1 + \frac{2\eta t}{2t - 1}\right) \ge p_0 (1 + \eta).$$

Since η is a constant, the two probabilities p_0 and $p_{\le 1}$ are constant as well. Therefore

$$\mu_{\le \alpha} := \mathbb{E}[X_{\le \alpha}] = p_{\le \alpha}\hat{t}.$$

We can apply Lemma 2.2 to get that for $\delta \le 1$,

$$\mathbb{P}(|X_{\le \alpha} - \mu_{\le \alpha}| \ge \delta\mu_{\le \alpha}) \le e^{-\delta^2 \Theta(t)}.$$

In other words, for constant δ the $X_{\le \alpha}$ are close to their expected values w.v.h.p.(t). Therefore if we choose δ small enough ($\delta <$

$\eta/(2\eta + 4))$, w.v.h.p.(t), we obtain

$$
\begin{aligned}
X_{\leq 1} - X_{\leq 0} &\geq (1-\delta)\mu_{\leq 1} - (1+\delta)\mu_{\leq 0} \\
&\geq ((1-\delta)(1+\eta) - (1+\delta)) \cdot p_0 \hat{t} \\
&= (\eta - \delta(2+\eta)) \cdot p_0 \hat{t} = \Theta(t).
\end{aligned}
$$

Therefore, w.v.h.p.(t), a constant fraction of the undisrupted channels on block $\mathcal{H}$ have exactly one herald. By Lemmas 6.2 and 6.3, w.v.h.p.(t), there are $\Theta(t)$ heralds and a constant fraction of these heralds has age at least $\mathcal{A}$. By symmetry, the $\Theta(t)$ heralds that broadcast alone on some undisrupted channel of block $\mathcal{H}$ are a uniformly random subset of all heralds. Hence, w.v.h.p.(t), a constant fraction of the heralds that broadcast alone on an undisrupted channel of $\mathcal{H}$ are old. Each node that listens on $\mathcal{H}$ therefore has a constant probability of picking a sub-channel with exactly one old herald.

Because each node has a constant probability to listen on $\mathcal{H}$, w.v.h.p.(t), a constant fraction of the total probability contributing to P_F is eliminated in *each* round for which $P_F \geq 2t$. Assume that for constants $\hat{\gamma} > 0$ and $\hat{s} > 1$, with probability $p := 1 - e^{-\hat{\gamma}t}$, a $1/\hat{s}$-fraction of the total probability mass is eliminated and let us call a round successful if an $1/\hat{s}$-fraction of the total probability mass is eliminated. In order to get from some $P_F < t2^F$ to $P_F < 2t$ w.h.p., we need $\Theta(F)$ successful rounds in a time span of l rounds w.h.p.(N).

If $1-p = e^{-\hat{\gamma}t}$ is more than e^{-3}, then t is less than $3/\hat{\gamma} = O(1)$, having a phase lasting $\Omega(\log N)$ rounds, each being successful with a constant probability. A standard Chernoff argument gives us that $\Theta(l)$ of them are successful w.h.p.(N).

If $1 - p$ is less than e^{-3}, then we apply Chernoff again to show that less than a constant fraction of l rounds are *not* successful. By choosing $\delta = e^{\hat{\gamma}t-1} \geq e^2$ and letting X count the number of unsuccessful rounds we get:

$$
\begin{aligned}
\mathbb{P}(X \geq l/2) &< \mathbb{P}(X \geq e \cdot e^{-\hat{\gamma}t} l) = \mathbb{P}(X \geq (1+\delta)\mu) \\
&\leq e^{-\mu \overbrace{((\delta+1)\ln(\delta+1) - \delta)}^{>0}} \\
&\underset{\mu = e^{-\hat{\gamma}t}l}{\leq} e^{-l(e^{-1}(\hat{\gamma}t-1) - e^{-1} + e^{-\hat{\gamma}t})} \\
&\underset{l \geq c\frac{\log N}{t}}{\leq} N^{-\frac{c}{t}\frac{\hat{\gamma}t-2}{e}} \leq N^{-c\frac{\hat{\gamma}}{3e}}
\end{aligned}
$$

That is, w.h.p.(N), a constant fraction of l rounds are successful. If c is chosen large enough, it follows in the same way that, w.h.p., the maximum number of consecutive rounds in which $P_F \geq 2t$ is less than $l/2$. $\qquad\square$

LEMMA 6.5. *With high probability, at all times, the number of candidates is $O(t)$.*

PROOF. We show that at all times, the number of candidates is less than $16t$ with probability at least $1 - N^{-d}$, where the constant d can be chosen arbitrarily. For the sake of contradiction, assume that there is a first round r_0 in which the number of candidates is at least $16t$ with probability more than N^{-d}.

We first show that between round $r' = r_0 - l/2$ and r_0 at most $8t$ of all active nodes switch to state L. Assume that this is not the case. All these $8t$ nodes are therefore together in the last competing phase for at least $cF/2$ rounds. Because in these rounds, all $8t$ nodes choose channel F with probability $1/4$, this implies that there are $cF/2$ consecutive rounds in which $P_F \geq 2t$, something that does not happen w.h.p. according to Lemma 6.4.

Hence, w.h.p., more than $8t$ of the candidates have already been active in round r'. Because we also assumed that r_0 is the first time,

where the number of candidates is at least $16t$, this also implies that overall between rounds r' and r_0, there are less than $24t$ different candidates, i.e., $n \in [8t, 24t)$ different candidates.

Consider some round $r \in [r', r_0)$. Assume that in round r, $\hat{t} \in [t, 2t]$ of the $2t$ channels in block $\mathcal{L}$ are not disrupted. Each of the n candidates picks a uniformly random channel. Applying Lemma 2.3 with parameters $q = \hat{t}/(2t)$, $k = \hat{t}$, and $w_i = 1$ for $i \in [n]$—which implies $c = \frac{n}{2t} \in [4, 12)$— we get that w.v.h.p.$(t)$, on at least $\hat{t}/4$ channels, there are between $\lceil 4/3 \rceil = 2$ and 24 nodes. On all these channels, independently, there is a constant probability that exactly one candidate broadcasts. Hence, w.v.h.p.(t), there are $\Theta(t)$ channels on $\mathcal{L}$ on which exactly one candidate broadcasts. Let a be the median age of the candidates. As the set of the candidates broadcasting on these channels is a uniformly random subset of all candidates in the given round, w.v.h.p.(t), there are also $\Theta(t)$ channels on which a candidate of age at least a broadcasts. Independently, each of the $\Theta(t)$ candidates of age at most a listens with constant probability on one of these channels. Therefore, w.v.h.p.(t), a constant fraction of the candidates is eliminated in each round $r \in [r', r_0)$. For c large enough, this implies that in the $l/2$ rounds in the interval $[r', r_0)$, w.h.p., more than $8t$ candidates are eliminated, a contradiction to the assumption that the number of candidates in round r_0 is at least $16t$. $\qquad\square$

PROOF OF THEOREM 6.1. Analogously to the proof of Theorem 5.1 we have that at least one node v becomes a leader, i.e., it moves through $\Theta\left(\frac{\log N}{F}\right)$ phases of length $\Theta\left(F + \frac{\log N}{t}\right)$ each and is a candidate for $\Theta(t \log N)$ rounds. In total that gives a running time of

$$
\Theta\left(\frac{\log N}{F}\left(F + \frac{\log N}{t}\right) + t \log N\right) = \Theta\left(t \log N + \frac{\log^2 N}{\mathcal{F}}\right).
$$

Assume that besides v another node v' becomes a leader. Then v' is a candidate for $\Theta(t \log N)$ rounds in which also v is either a candidate or a leader, that broadcasts its id and age on some channel $(\mathcal{L}, s)$ with probability $1/2$ each of those rounds. Since the number of candidates is in $O(t)$ during all those rounds, w.h.p., there is a constant probability that v broadcasts alone on an undisrupted channel in block $\mathcal{L}$. On the other hand v' listens with probability $1/2$ on block $\mathcal{L}$ and thus listens on the same channel on which v broadcasts with probability $\Omega(1/t)$, i.e., in (t) rounds there is a constant chance for v' to hear v. Thus, w.h.p., v' is eliminated within $O(t \log N)$ rounds, contradicting the initial assumption. $\qquad\square$

7. IMPROVED TRAPDOOR PROTOCOL

In this section, we provide a leader election protocol that is tight (within log log factors) for $t > \mathcal{F}/6$. Our strategy is to modify the trapdoor protocol of [5] to produce a new protocol, which we call the *truncated trapdoor protocol*, that behaves in an optimal manner for t values in this range.

In the trapdoor protocol, when a node is activated, it attempts to make it through $\log N$ phases without being knocked out. For each round of each phase i a node chooses a channel with uniform randomness. If the node is *inactive* (i.e., has been knocked out already) it listens. Otherwise it is *active*, and it broadcasts its id and age (i.e., rounds it has been active) with probability $\frac{2^{i-1}}{N}$. If an active node receives a message from another active node of the same age or older, the node is knocked out and becomes inactive. If a node makes it through all $\log N$ phases without being knocked out, it declares itself the leader, and subsequently selects a channel at random in each round, broadcasting its id with probability $1/2$. If any node hears from a leader, it outputs the leader id and halts.

In the version of the protocol presented in [5], the first $\log N - 1$ phases were of length $\Theta\left(\frac{\mathcal{F}}{\mathcal{F}-t}\log N\right)$ and the final phase had length $O\left(\frac{\mathcal{F}t}{\mathcal{F}-t}\cdot\log N\right)$. Here, we consider a more efficient variant where each of the first $\log N - 1$ phases is reduced to length $l = O\left(\frac{\log(N)}{\mathcal{F}-t}\right)$. Below, we prove that the truncated trapdoor protocol still solves leader election. Our analysis requires that $t > \mathcal{F}/6$. We assume w.l.o.g. that $\mathcal{F} - t = O(\log N)$. For a given round let $p(v)$ be the probability that v broadcasts in that round (i.e., $p(v) = 2^{i-1}/N$ if node v is in phase i). For each round, we define $P := \sum_v p(v)$. We prove that P is bounded:

LEMMA 7.1. *With high probability, at all times, it holds that $P \le 4\mathcal{F} + 1$.*

PROOF SKETCH. For the sake of contradiction, assume that P exceeds $4\mathcal{F} + 1$ with probability larger than $1/N^d$, for a given constant d. In l rounds, P can only increase by a factor of 2 and by an additive amount of 1 contributed by newly activated nodes (which start in phase 1 with broadcast probability $1/N$). Hence, if P exceeds $4\mathcal{F} + 1$, it must have been between $2\mathcal{F}$ and $4\mathcal{F} + 1$ for l consecutive rounds before this point.

Consider some such round r, during which $P \in [2\mathcal{F}, 4\mathcal{F} + 1]$. Let $\hat{t} \ge \mathcal{F} - t$ be the number of non-disrupted channels in round r. We can apply Lemma 2.3 to show that, w.v.h.p.($\mathcal{F} - t$), in round r there are at least $(\mathcal{F} - t)/4$ channels on which the total broadcast probability of all nodes is between $2/3$ and 10. The parameters for the lemma are $k = \hat{t}$, $q = \hat{t}/\mathcal{F}$, $w_v = p(v)$ and consequently, $c \in [2, 5]$.

Now consider one such channel with a total broadcast probability between $2/3$ and 10. We can choose an age a such that at least half of the total broadcast probability comes from nodes of age at most a, and at least half of the total broadcast probability comes from nodes of age at least a. We also note that because the total broadcast probability is at least $2/3$, and because an individual node cannot broadcast with probability more than $1/2$, we know we are dealing with at least 2 nodes. With constant probability, therefore, there is exactly one node v of age at least a that transmits on our selected channel. Assume this event occurs. It follows: all nodes of age at most a (except v) receive the message and are knocked out. Therefore, with constant probability, a constant fraction of the probability mass on the channel is eliminated. This happens independently on all channels that match our broadcast probability bound. As proved above, there at least $(\mathcal{F} - t)/4$ such channels, w.v.h.p.($\mathcal{F} - t$).

By repeating this argument $c \log(N)/(\mathcal{F} - t)$ times, for a sufficiently large constant c, we get that with high probability, at least $2/3$ of the initial probability mass of P is eliminated and hence P becomes less than $2\mathcal{F}$. By choosing the constant c large enough, we therefore get a contradiction to the assumption that P exceeds $4\mathcal{F} + 1$ with probability more than N^{-d}. $\square$

The above lemma replaces Lemma 9 of [5], which we can then combine with the argument for Theorem 10 of that same paper to get the following:

THEOREM 7.2. *With high probability, the truncated trapdoor protocol elects exactly one leader within $O\left(\frac{\log N + \mathcal{F}t}{\mathcal{F}-t}\cdot\log N\right)$ rounds after the first node wakes up.*

8. REFERENCES

[1] P. Bahl, R. Chandra, T. Moscibroda, R. Murty, and M. Welsh. White Space Networking with Wi-Fi like Connectivity. In *Proceedings of the ACM SIGCOMM Conference*, 2009.

[2] Bluetooth Consortium. *Bluetooth Specification Version 2.1*, July 2007.

[3] S. Daum, S. Gilbert, F. Kuhn, and C. Newport. Leader election in shared spectrum radio networks. Technical Report 269, University of Freiburg, Department of Computer Science, 2012.

[4] S. Dolev, S. Gilbert, R. Guerraoui, D. R. Kowalski, C. Newport, F. Kuhn, and N. Lynch. Reliable Distributed Computing on Unreliable Radio Channels. In *the Proceedings of the 2009 MobiHoc S³ Workshop*, 2009.

[5] S. Dolev, S. Gilbert, R. Guerraoui, F. Kuhn, and C. Newport. The wireless synchronization problem. In *Proc. 28th Symp. on Principles of Distributed Computing (PODC)*, pages 190–199, 2009.

[6] S. Dolev, S. Gilbert, R. Guerraoui, and C. Newport. Gossiping in a Multi-Channel Radio Network: An Oblivious Approach to Coping with Malicious Interference. In *Proc. Int. Symp. on Distributed Comp. (DISC)*, 2007.

[7] S. Dolev, S. Gilbert, R. Guerraoui, and C. Newport. Secure Communication Over Radio Channels. In *Proc. Int. Symp. on Principles of Distributed Computing (PODC)*, 2008.

[8] S. Dolev, S. Gilbert, M. Khabbazian, and C. Newport. Leveraging Channel Diversity to Gain Efficiency and Robustness for Wireless Broadcast. In *Proc. Int. Symp. on Distributed Comp. (DISC)*, 2011.

[9] D. Dubhashi and D. Ranjan. Balls and bins: A study in negative dependence. *Random Structures & Algorithms*, 13(2):99–124, 1998.

[10] M. Farach-Colton, R. J. Fernandes, and M. A. Mosteiro. Lower Bounds for Clear Transmissions in Radio Networks. In *Proc. Latin American Symp. on Theoretical Informatics*, 2006.

[11] S. Gilbert, R. Guerraoui, D. Kowalski, and C. Newport. Interference-Resilient Information Exchange. In *Proc. Conf. on Computer Communication (INFOCOM)*, 2009.

[12] IEEE 802.11. Wireless LAN MAC and Physical Layer Specifications, June 1999.

[13] K. Joag-Dev and F. Proschan. Negative association of random variables, with applications. *Annals of Statistics*, 11(1):286–295, 1983.

[14] T. Jurdzinski and G. Stachowiak. Probabilistic Algorithms for the Wakeup Problem in Single-Hop Radio Networks. In *Proc. Int. Symp. on Algorithms and Computation*, pages 535–549, 2002.

[15] D. Meier, Y. A. Pignolet, S. Schmid, and R. Wattenhofer. Speed Dating Despite Jammers. In *Proceedings of the International Conference on Distributed Computing in Sensor Systems*, 2009.

[16] T. Moscibroda and R. Wattenhofer. Maximal independent sets in radio networks. In *Proc. 24th Symp. on Principles of Distributed Computing (PODC)*, pages 148–157, 2005.

[17] C. Newport. *Distributed Computation on Unreliable Radio Channels*. PhD thesis, MIT, 2009.

[18] J. Schneider and R. Wattenhofer. Coloring unstructured wireless multi-hop networks. In *Proc. 28th Symp. on Principles of Distributed Computing (PODC)*, pages 210–219, 2009.

[19] M. Sherman, A. Mody, R. Martinez, C. Rodriguez, and R. Reddy. IEEE Standards Supporting Cognitive Radio and Networks, Dynamic Spectrum Access, and Coexistence. *IEEE Communications Magazine*, 46(7):72–79, 2008.

[20] M. Strasser, C. Pöpper, and S. Capkun. Efficient Uncoordinated FHSS Anti-jamming Communication. In *Proc. Int. Symp. on Mobile Ad Hoc Networking and Computing (MOBIHOC)*, 2009.

[21] M. Strasser, C. Pöpper, S. Capkun, and M. Cagalj. Jamming-resistant Key Establishment using Uncoordinated Frequency Hopping. In *the Proceedings of the IEEE Symposium on Security and Privacy*, 2008.

[22] R. Zhang, Y. Zhang, and X. Huang. JR-SND: Jamming-Resilient Secure Neighbor Discovery in Mobile Ad Hoc Networks. In *Proceedings of the International Conference on Distributed Computing Systems*, 2011.

[23] ZigBee Alliance. Zigbee specification. *ZigBee Document 053474r06*, 1, 2005.

Brief Announcement: Achieving Reliability in Master-Worker Computing via Evolutionary Dynamics

Evgenia Christoforou
University of Cyprus
christoforou.evgenia
@ucy.ac.cy

Antonio Fernández Anta
Institute IMDEA Networks
& Univ. Rey Juan Carlos
antonio.fernandez@imdea.org

Chryssis Georgiou
University of Cyprus
chryssis@ucy.ac.cy

Miguel A. Mosteiro
Rutgers University
& Univ. Rey Juan Carlos
mosteiro@cs.rutgers.edu

Angel (Anxo) Sánchez
Matemáticas, Univ. Carlos III
& BIFI, Univ. Zaragoza
anxo@math.uc3m.es

ABSTRACT

This work considers Internet-based task computations in which a master process assigns tasks, over the Internet, to rational workers and collect their responses. The objective is for the master to obtain the correct task outcomes. For this purpose we formulate and study the dynamics of evolution of Internet-based master-worker computations through reinforcement learning.

Categories and Subject Descriptors

C.2.4 [**Computer-Communication Networks**]: Distributed Systems

General Terms

Algorithms, Reliability, Theory

Keywords

Internet-based task computing, Evolutionary dynamics, Reinforcement learning, Algorithmic mechanism design.

1. INTRODUCTION

Motivation and prior work: As an alternative to expensive supercomputing parallel machines, Internet is a feasible computational platform for processing complex computational jobs. Several Internet-based applications operate on top of this global computation infrastructure. Examples are the volunteer-based "@home" projects such as SETI. In SETI, for example, there is a machine, call it the *master*, that sends tasks, across the Internet, to volunteers' computers, call them *workers*. These workers execute and report back some result. However, these workers may not be trustworthy (limiting the platforms potentials) and it might be at their best interest to report incorrect results; that is, workers, or their owners, can be viewed as *rational* [2]. In SETI, the master attempts to minimize the impact of these bogus results by assigning the same task to several workers and comparing their outcomes (i.e., redundant task allocation is employed).

Prior work has shown that it is possible to design algorithmic mechanisms with reward/punish schemes so that the master can reliably obtain correct task results. We view these mechanisms as one-shot in the following sense: In a round, the master sends a task to be computed to a collection of workers, and the mechanism, using auditing and reward/punish schemes guarantees (with high probability) that the master gets the correct task result. For another task to be computed, the process is repeated (with the same or different collection of workers) but without taking advantage of the knowledge gained. *A detailed account of related work can be found in [4].*

Given a long running computation (such as SETI-like master-worker computations), it can be the case that the best interests, and hence the behavior of the workers, might change over time. So, one wonders: Would it be possible to design a mechanism for performing many tasks, over the course of a possibly infinite computation, that could positively exploit the repeated interaction between a master and the same collection of workers?

Our approach: In this work we provide a positive answer to the above question. To do so, we introduce the concept of *evolutionary dynamics* under the biological and social perspective and relate them to Internet-based master-worker task computing. More specifically, we employ *reinforcement learning* [3] to model how system entities or learners interact with the environment to decide upon a strategy, and use their experience to select or avoid actions according to the consequences observed. Positive payoffs increase the probability of the strategy just chosen, and negative payoffs reduce this probability. Payoffs are seen as parameterizations of players' responses to their experiences. Empirical evidence [1] suggests that reinforcement learning is more plausible with players that have information only on the payoffs they receive and not of the strategies involved. This fits nicely to our master-worker computation problem: the workers have no information about the master and the other workers' strategies and they don't know the set of strategies that led to the payoff they receive. The workers have only information about the strategies they choose at each round of the evolution of the system and their own received payoffs. The master also has minimal information about the workers and their intentions (to be truthful or not). Thus, we employ reinforcement learning for both the master and the workers in an attempt to build a reliable computational platform.

Our contributions: (Full details in [4].)

- We *initiate* the study of the evolutionary dynamics of Internet-based master-worker computations through reinforcement learning.

- We develop and analyze a mechanism based on reinforcement learning to be used by the master and the workers. In particular, in each round, the master allocates a task to the workers and decides whether to audit or not their responses with a certain probability $p_\mathcal{A}$. Depending on whether it audits or not, it applies a different reward/punish scheme, and adjusts the probability $p_\mathcal{A}$ for the next round (a.k.a. the next task execution). Similarly, in a round, each worker i decides whether it will truthfully compute and report the correct task result, or it will report an incorrect result, with a certain probability p_{Ci}. Depending on the success or not of its decision, measured by the increase or the decrease of the worker's *utility*, the worker adjusts probability p_{Ci} for the next round.

- We show necessary and sufficient conditions under which the mechanism ensures *eventual correctness*, that is, we show the conditions under which, after some finite number of rounds, the master obtains the correct task result in every round, with minimal auditing, while keeping the workers satisfied (w.r.t. their utility).

- Finally, we show that our mechanism, when adhering to the above-mentioned conditions, reaches eventual correctness quickly. In particular, we show analytically, probabilistic bounds on the convergence time, as well as bounds on the expected convergence time. Our analysis is complemented with simulations.

2. ALGORITHMIC MECHANISM

The mechanism is composed by an algorithm run by the Master and an algorithm run by each worker.

Master's Algorithm: At each round, the master sends a task to all workers in W ($|W| = n$) and, when all answers are received, the master audits the answers with probability $p_\mathcal{A}$; auditing means that the master computes the task by itself, and checks which workers have truthfully reported the correct task result. We assume that there is a value $p_\mathcal{A}^{min} > 0$ so that at all times $p_\mathcal{A} \geq p_\mathcal{A}^{min}$. In the case the answers are not audited, the master accepts the value contained in the majority of answers and continues to the next round with the same probability of auditing. In the case the answers are audited, the value $p_\mathcal{A}$ of the next round is reinforced; meaning that $p_\mathcal{A}$ is modified according to the outcome of the round as follows:

$$p_\mathcal{A} = \min\{1, \max\{p_\mathcal{A}^{min}, p_\mathcal{A} + \alpha_m(\tfrac{cheaters(r)}{n} - \tau)\}\}.$$

The master initially has scarce or no information about the environment (e.g., workers initial p_C). Therefore, a safe approach for the master is to initially set $p_\mathcal{A} = 0.5$. Observe that, in a round r, when the answers are not audited, the master has no information about the number of cheaters $cheaters(r)$. Thus, $p_\mathcal{A}$ remains the same as in the previous round. When the answers are audited, the master can safely extract $cheaters(r)$ and the master adapts the auditing probability $p_\mathcal{A}$ accordingly.

A discount factor, which we call *tolerance* and denote by τ, expresses the master's tolerable ratio of cheaters (typically, we will assume $\tau = 1/2$). Hence, if the proportion of cheaters is larger than τ, $p_\mathcal{A}$ will be increased, and otherwise, $p_\mathcal{A}$ will be decreased. The amount by which $p_\mathcal{A}$ changes depends on the difference between these values, modulated by

a *learning rate* α_m. This latter value determines to what extent the newly acquired information will override the old information.

After the master has received all answers, rewards/penalizes the workers appropriately. The following workers' payoff parameters are considered: (1) $WP_\mathcal{C}$: worker's punishment for being caught cheating; (2) $WC_\mathcal{T}$: worker's cost for computing the task; (3) $WB_\mathcal{Y}$: worker's benefit from master's acceptance. Furthermore, in every round, a worker i has an *aspiration* a_i, that is, the minimum benefit it expects to obtain in a round. To motivate the workers to participate in the computation, the master must ensure that $WB_\mathcal{Y} \geq a_i$. We assume that the master knows the aspirations (it may be included in a contract the master and the worker agree before the start of the computation).

Workers' Algorithm: At each round, each worker receives a task from the master and, with probability $1 - p_{Ci}$ calculates the task, and replies to the master with the correct answer. (Initially, p_{Ci} could be set to 0.5.) If the worker decides to cheat, it fabricates an answer, and sends the incorrect response to the master. Flag S_i models the decision of a worker i to cheat ($S_i = -1$) or not ($S_i = 1$). After receiving its payoff, each worker i changes its p_{Ci} according to the payoff Π_i received, the chosen strategy S_i, and its aspiration a_i as follows: $p_{Ci} = \max\{0, \min\{1, p_{Ci} - \alpha_w(\Pi_i - a_i)S_i\}\}$.

The workers have a learning rate α_w. We assume that all workers have the same learning rate, that is, they learn in the same manner (see also the discussion in [3]; the learning rate is called step-size there); note that our analysis can be adjusted to accommodate also workers with different learning rates.

Overview of results: We analyze the evolution of the master-worker system as a Markov chain and we show that:

THEOREM 1. *If $p_\mathcal{A} > 0$ then, in order to guarantee with positive probability that, after some finite number of rounds, the system achieves eventual correctness, it is* **necessary** *and* **sufficient** *to set $WB_\mathcal{Y} \geq a_i + WC_\mathcal{T}$ for all $i \in Z$ in some set $Z \subseteq W$ such that $|Z| > n/2$.*

We call the time (number of rounds) taken to achieve eventual convergence as *convergence time*. We show, both in expectation and with high probability, that when our mechanism adheres to the conditions of Theorem 1, it can reach convergence time quickly. Our analysis is complemented with simulation results that further demonstrate the practicality of our mechanism. Full details can be found in [4].

Acknowledgments: This work is supported by the Cyprus Research Promotion Foundation grant ТПЕ/ПЛНРО/0609(ВЕ)/05, NSF grants CCF-0937829, CCF-1114930, Comunidad de Madrid grant S2009TIC-1692, Spanish MOSAICO and RESINEE grants and MICINN grant TEC2011-29688-C02-01, and National Natural Science Foundation of China grant 61020106002.

3. REFERENCES

[1] C. F. Camerer. Behavioral game theory: Experiments in strategic interaction. *Roundtable Series in Behavioral Economics*, 2003.

[2] J. Shneidman and D.C. Parkes. Rationality and self-interest in P2P networks. In *IPTPS 2003*, pp. 139–148.

[3] C. Szepesvári. *Algorithms for Reinforcement Learning*. Synthesis Lectures on Artificial Intelligence and Machine Learning, Morgan & Claypool publishers, 2010.

[4] Technical report of this work: http://www.cs.ucy.ac.cy/~chryssis/EvolMW-TR.pdf

Brief Announcement: Breaking the O(nm) Bit Barrier, Secure Multiparty Computation with a Static Adversary [*]

Varsha Dani
University of New Mexico
Dept. of Computer Science
Albuquerque, NM 87131-1386
varsha@cs.unm.edu

Valerie King
University of Victoria
Dept. of Computer Science
P.O. Box 3055; Victoria, BC;
Canada V8W 3P6
val@cs.uvic.ca

Mahnush Movahedi
University of New Mexico
Dept. of Computer Science
Albuquerque, NM 87131-1386
movahedi@cs.unm.edu

Jared Saia
University of New Mexico
Dept. of Computer Science
Albuquerque, NM 87131-1386
saia@cs.unm.edu

ABSTRACT

We describe scalable algorithms for secure multiparty computation (SMPC). We assume a synchronous message passing communication model, but we do not assume the existence of a broadcast channel. Our main result holds for the case where there are n players, of which a $1/3 - \epsilon$ fraction are controlled by an adversary, for ϵ any positive constant. We describe an SMPC algorithm for this model that requires each player to send $\tilde{O}(\frac{n+m}{n} + \sqrt{n})$ messages and perform $\tilde{O}(\frac{n+m}{n} + \sqrt{n})$ computations to compute any function f, where m is the size of a circuit to compute f. We also consider a model where all players are rational. In this model, we describe a Nash equilibrium protocol that solves SMPC and requires each player to send $\tilde{O}(\frac{n+m}{n})$ messages and perform $\tilde{O}(\frac{n+m}{n})$ computations. These results significantly improve over past results for SMPC which require each player to send a number of bits and perform a number of computations that is $\theta(nm)$.

Categories and Subject Descriptors

F.2.0 [**Theory**]: Analysis of Algorithms and Problem Complexity

Keywords

Secure Multiparty Computation, Game Theory

1. INTRODUCTION

In 1982, A. Yao posed a problem that has significantly impacted the weltanschauung of computer security research [13]:

[*]A full version of this paper is available as *Breaking the O(nm) Bit Barrier: Secure Multiparty Computation with a Static Adversary* at www.cs.unm.edu/~saia/papers Varsha Dani, Mahnush Movahedi and Jared Saia are partially supported by NSF CAREER Award 0644058,NSF CCR-0313160, and an AFOSR MURI grant. Valerie King is supported by an NSERC grant.

Can we design a protocol to allow some millionaires to determine who is the wealthiest without revealing any additional information about their wealth? This problem is an example of the celebrated *secure multiparty computation (SMPC)* problem. In the SMPC problem, there are n players. Each player i has a private input x_i. Further, there is a n-ary function f that is known to all players. The goal is to ensure: 1) all players learn the value $f(x_1, x_2, \ldots, x_n)$; and 2) the inputs remain as private as possible: each player i learns nothing about the private inputs other than what is revealed by $f(x_1, x_2, \ldots, x_n)$ and x_i.

The main complication is the fact that up to a $1/3$ fraction of the players are assumed to be controlled by an adversary that is trying to prevent the computation of the function. We assume that the adversary is *static*, meaning that it must select the set of bad players at the start of the algorithm.

This problem formulation is quite powerful. If f returns the input that is in the majority, then SMPC enables voting. SMPC also can enables group digital signatures and anonymous message transmission. In short, the only limitation is determined by whether or not the function f is computable.

There have been thousands of papers addressing the SMPC problem. However, there is a striking barrier that prevents wide-spread use: current algorithms to solve SMPC are not resource efficient. In particular, if there are n players and the function f can be computed by a circuit with m gates, then most algorithms require each player to send a number of messages and perform a number of computations that is $\Omega(mn)$ (see, for example, [6, 3, 1, 9]).

Recent years have seen exciting improvements in the *amortized* cost of SMPC [5, 4]. However, the results for these algorithm hold only in the amortized case where m is much larger than n, and all of them have additional additive terms that are large polynomials in n (e.g. n^6). Thus, there is still a strong need for SMPC algorithms that are efficient in both n and m.

2. OUR RESULTS

The main result of this paper is as follows.

THEOREM 1. *Assume there are n players, no more than a $1/3$ fraction of which are bad. If the good players follow our* *algorithm, then with high probability, they can solve SMPC, while ensuring each player sends $\tilde{O}(\frac{n+m}{n} + \sqrt{n})$ messages, and performs $\tilde{O}(\frac{n+m}{n} + \sqrt{n})$ computations.*

An additional result of this paper deals with the situation where all players are rational. The rational players' utility functions are such that they prefer to learn the output of the function, but other players not learn the output [11, 7, 8, 12]. Our main result in this model is the following.

THEOREM 2. *Assume there are n rational players with utility function given as above. Then, there exists a protocol such that 1) it is a Nash equilibrium for all players to run this protocol and 2) when all players run the protocol then, with high probability, they solve SMPC, while ensuring each player sends $\tilde{O}(\frac{n+m}{n})$ messages, and performs $\tilde{O}(\frac{n+m}{n})$ computations.*

In the theorems, we assume good players strictly follow the protocol, and thus do not form coalitions for gossiping. However, we can maintain privacy even with a coalition set of size $q/3$ where $q = \Theta(\log(n))$.

3. OUR APPROACH

The main idea behind reducing the amount of communication required for the computation is that rather than having each player communicate with all the other players, we will subdivide the players into groups called *quorums* of logarithmic size.

First we create a collection of quorums, using the algorithm from [10]. Then, for every player i, we assign i a quorum Q_i. Each player i computes a value R_i selected uniformly at random from all values in the field $\mathbb{F}$. It then computes the value of its private input plus R_i and sends it to all players in Q_i. Finally, it uses the verifiable secret sharing algorithm from [2] to create shares of R_i, and to send one share to each player in Q_i.

Next, for every gate g in the circuit C that computes f, we assign g a quorum Q_g. Then from the the bottom (input gates) of the circuit to the top, we ensure the following for every gate g: the players in Q_g all learn the sum of the output of g plus a mask-value R_g selected uniformly at random from the field $\mathbb{F}$. Shares of R_g are held by the players in the quorum, but the value is unknown to any individual. This ensures that no player learns any information about the output of g. During the computation of a gate, g, we perform a HEAVYWEIGHT-SMPC [2] to compute the masked output of that gate. To do so, the quorums associated with the inputs to that gate all provide information about the gate inputs, and the players in Q_g provide information to create the value R_g. This procedure is repeated to compute the values for the gates in the next layer of the circuit.

At the top gate of the circuit, the output of f is computed and sent down to all players through all-to-all communication in the quorums.

4. CONCLUSION

We have designed SMPC algorithms that are significantly more efficient than previous works. Our first algorithm works for traditional SMPC and our second algorithms works for the case where all players are rational. Both of our algorithms work in the partially synchronous communication model. However, we are currently working on improving them to work in the fully asynchronous model.

5. REFERENCES

[1] B. Applebaum, Y. Ishai, and E. Kushilevitz. From secrecy to soundness: efficient verification via secure computation. *Automata, Languages and Programming*, pages 152–163, 2010.

[2] M. Ben-Or, S. Goldwasser, and A. Wigderson. Completeness theorems for non-cryptographic fault-tolerant distributed computing. In *Proceedings of the Twentieth ACM Symposium on the Theory of Computing (STOC)*, pages 1–10, 1988.

[3] P. Bogetoft, D. Christensen, I. Damgård, M. Geisler, T. Jakobsen, M. Krøigaard, J. Nielsen, J. Nielsen, K. Nielsen, J. Pagter, et al. Secure multiparty computation goes live. *Financial Cryptography and Data Security*, pages 325–343, 2009.

[4] I. Damgård, Y. Ishai, M. Krøigaard, J. Nielsen, and A. Smith. Scalable multiparty computation with nearly optimal work and resilience. *Advances in Cryptology–CRYPTO 2008*, pages 241–261, 2008.

[5] I. Damgård and J. Nielsen. Scalable and unconditionally secure multiparty computation. In *Proceedings of the 27th annual international cryptology conference on Advances in cryptology*, pages 572–590. Springer-Verlag, 2007.

[6] K. Frikken. Secure multiparty computation. In *Algorithms and theory of computation handbook*, pages 14–14. Chapman & Hall/CRC, 2010.

[7] S. Gordon and J. Katz. Rational secret sharing, revisited. *Security and Cryptography for Networks*, pages 229–241, 2006.

[8] J. Halpern and V. Teague. Rational secret sharing and multiparty computation: extended abstract. In *Proceedings of the thirty-sixth annual ACM symposium on Theory of computing*, page 632. ACM, 2004.

[9] W. Henecka, A. Sadeghi, T. Schneider, I. Wehrenberg, et al. Tasty: Tool for automating secure two-party computations. In *Proceedings of the 17th ACM conference on Computer and communications security*, pages 451–462. ACM, 2010.

[10] V. King, S. Lonergan, J. Saia, and A. Trehan. Load balanced scalable byzantine agreement through quorum building, with full information. In *International Conference on Distributed Computing and Networking (ICDCN)*, 2011.

[11] G. Kol and M. Naor. Games for exchanging information. In *Proceedings of the 40th annual ACM symposium on Theory of computing*, pages 423–432. ACM, 2008.

[12] A. Lysyanskaya and N. Triandopoulos. Rationality and adversarial behavior in multi-party computation. *Advances in Cryptology-CRYPTO 2006*, pages 180–197, 2006.

[13] A. Yao. Protocols for secure computations. In *Proceedings of the 23rd Annual Symposium on Foundations of Computer Science*, pages 160–164, 1982.

Brief Announcement: Maintaining Large Dense Subgraphs on Dynamic Networks

Atish Das Sarma
eBay Research Labs
eBay Inc.
San Jose, CA, USA.
atish.dassarma@gmail.com

Ashwin Lall
Department of Mathematics
and Computer Science
Denison University
Granville, OH, USA.
lalla@denison.edu

Danupon Nanongkai
Theory and Applications of
Algorithms Research Group
University of Vienna,
Vienna, Austria.
danupon@gmail.com

Amitabh Trehan
Information Systems group
Faculty of Industrial
Engineering and
Management,
Technion, Haifa, Israel
amitabh.trehaan@gmail.com

ABSTRACT

In distributed networks, some groups of nodes may have more inter-connections, perhaps due to their larger bandwidth availability or communication requirements. In many scenarios, it may be useful for the nodes to know if they form part of a dense subgraph, e.g., such a dense subgraph could form a high bandwidth backbone for the network. In this work, we address the problem of self-awareness of nodes in a dynamic network with regards to graph density, i.e., we give distributed algorithms for maintaining dense subgraphs (subgraphs that the member nodes are aware of). The only knowledge that the nodes need is that of the *dynamic diameter D*, i.e., the maximum number of rounds it takes for a message to traverse the dynamic network. For our work, we consider a model where the number of nodes are fixed, but a powerful adversary can add or remove a limited number of edges from the network at each time step. The communication is by broadcast only and follows the CONGEST model in the sense that only messages of $O(\log n)$ size are permitted, where n is the number of nodes in the network.

Our algorithms are continuously executed on the network, and at any time (after some initialization) each node will be aware if it is part (or not) of a particular dense subgraph. We give algorithms that approximate both the *densest subgraph*, i.e., the subgraph of the highest density in the network, and the *at-least-k-densest subgraph* (for a given parameter k), i.e., the densest subgraph of size at least k. We give a $(2 + \epsilon)$-approximation algorithm for the densest subgraph problem. The at-least-k-densest subgraph is known to be NP-hard for the general case in the centralized setting and the best known algorithm gives a 2-approximation. We present an algorithm that maintains a $(3 + \epsilon)$-approximation in our distributed, dynamic setting. Our algorithms run in $O(D \log_{1+\epsilon} n)$ time.

ACM Classification

C.2.1 [**Computer Systems Organization**]: Computer-Communication Networks: Network Architecture and Design-*Distributed networks, Network communications, Wireless communication*; C.2.4 [**Computer Systems Organization**]: Distributed Systems; C.4 [**Computer Systems Organization**]: Performance of Systems- *Reliability, availability, and serviceability*; H.3.4 [**Information Systems**]: Information Storage and Retrieval: Systems and Software - *Distributed systems, Information networks*

Keywords

Dynamic networks, Distributed, Graph density, Subgraph density, Approximate, Probablistic, Estimation, aggregation

1. INTRODUCTION

Density is a very well studied graph property with a wide range of applications stemming from the fact that it is an excellent measure of the strength of inter-connectivity between nodes. While several variants of graph density problems and algorithms have been explored in the classical setting, there is surprisingly little work that addresses this question in the distributed computing framework. This paper focuses on decentralized algorithms for identifying dense subgraphs in dynamic networks.

Finding dense subgraphs has received a great deal of attention in graph algorithms literature because of the robustness of the property. The density of a subgraph only gradually changes when edges come and go in a network, unlike other graph properties such as connectivity that are far more sensitive to graph perturbation. Density measures the *strength* of a set of nodes by the graph induced on them from the overall structure. The power of density lies in locally observing the strength of *any* set of nodes, large or small, independent of the entire network.

Consider, for example, a distributed network that requires a small set of nodes, say *hubs*, that are treated as central and can be used as a backbone for communication amongst them. It is conceivable and even likely that they would incur a larger communication interaction between them, and therefore demand larger connectivity structure, lower latency, and higher resilience to failures. Therefore, a peer-to-peer network would like to retain this structure, or at least identify such nodes, even as the graph evolves over time.

In this paper, we expand the static CONGEST [4] model and consider a dynamic setting where the graph edges may change continually. We present algorithms for approximating the (at least size k) densest subgraph in a dynamic graph model to within constant factors. Our algorithms are not only designed to compute size-constrained dense subgraphs, but also track or maintain them through time, thereby allowing the network to be aware of dense subgraphs even as the network changes. They are fully decentralized and adapt well to rapid network failures or modifications. This gives the densest subgraph problem a special status among global graph problems : while most graph problems are hard to approximate in $o(\sqrt{n})$ time even on static networks [5], the densest subgraph problem can be approximated quickly, even in the dynamic setting. Khuller and Saha [2] considered the problem of finding densest subgraphs with size restrictions and showed that these are NP-hard. Khuller and Saha [2] and also Andersen and Chellapilla [1] gave constant factor approximation algorithms. Some of our algorithms are based off of those presented in [2].

1.1 Model: Edge-dynamic distributed

Here, we briefly describe our model. Consider an undirected, unweighted, connected n-node graph $G = (V, E)$, with the vertices representing processors with unbounded computational power but having only local knowledge. The communication is synchronous, and occurs in discrete pulses, called *rounds*. However, the nodes are only allowed to *broadcast*, i.e., if they send a message in a round, they send the same message to every neighbor. All the nodes wake up simultaneously at the beginning of round 1 and can only broadcast an arbitrary message of size $O(\log n)$ in each round, which is successfully received in the same round. Our algorithms work in an edge dynamic network model i.e. an edge deletion/addition model. We consider a sequence of (undirected) graphs $G_0, G_1, \ldots$ on n nodes, where, for any t, G_t denotes the state of the dynamic network $G(V, E)$ at time t, where the adversary deletes and/or inserts upto r edges at each step, i.e., $E(G_{t+1}) = (E(G_t) \setminus E_U) \cup E_V$, where $E_U \subseteq E(G_t)$ and $E_V \subseteq E(\overline{G_t})$, $|E_U| + |E_V| = r$. Also, following the notion in [3], we define the *dynamic diameter* of the dynamic network $G(V, E)$, denoted by D, to be the maximum time a message needs to traverse the network at any time. To measure the efficiency of our algorithms, we will concentrate on their running times in terms of number of rounds.

1.2 Problem definition

Let G $= (V, E)$ be an undirected graph and $S \subseteq V$ be a set of nodes. Let us define the following:
Graph Density: The density of a graph $G(V, E)$ is defined as $|E|/|V|$.
SubGraph Density: The density of a subgraph defined by a subset of nodes S of $V(G)$ is defined as its induced density. We will use $\rho(S)$ to denote the density of the subgraph induced by S. The problem we address in this paper is to construct distributed algorithms to discover the following:

- **(Approximate) Densest subgraphs:** The densest

subgraph problem is to find a set $S^* \subseteq V$, s.t. $\rho(S^*) = \max \rho(S)$ over all $S \subseteq V$. A α-approximate solution S' will be a set $S' \subseteq V$, s.t. $\rho(S') \geq \frac{\rho(S^*)}{\alpha}$.

- **(Approximate) at-least-k-densest subgraphs:** The densest at-least-k-subgraph problem is the previous problem restricted to sets of size at least k, i.e., to find a set $S^{k*} \subseteq V, |S^{k*}| \geq k$, s.t. $\rho(S^{k*}) = \max \rho(S)$ over all $S \subseteq V, |S| \geq k$. A α-approximate solution S^k will be a set $S^k \subseteq V, |S^k| \geq k$, s.t. $\rho(S^k) \geq \frac{\rho(S^{k*})}{\alpha}$.

2. ALGORITHMS AND RESULTS

The nature of our algorithms is such that we *continuously* maintain an approximation to the densest subgraph in the dynamic network, *at all times*. This means that, at all times (except for a short initialization period), all nodes are aware of whether they are part of the approximated at-least-k densest subgraphs, for all k. In particular, we give approximation algorithms for the densest and at-least-k-densest subgraph problems which are efficient even on dynamic distributed networks. We develop algorithms that, for any $\epsilon > 0$, $(2 + \epsilon)$-approximate the densest subgraph, and $(3 + \epsilon)$-approximate the at-least-k-densest subgraph, in $O(D \log_{1+\epsilon} n)$ time provided the density is high enough. Formally:

Theorem 2.1. *There exists an algorithm that for any dynamic graph with dynamic diameter D and parameter r returns a subgraph at time t such that, w.h.p., the density of the returned subgraph is a $(2 + \epsilon)$-approximation to the density of the densest subgraph at time t if the densest subgraph has density at least $\Omega(Dr \log nr)$.*

Theorem 2.2. *There exists an algorithm that for any dynamic graph with dynamic diameter D and parameter r returns a subgraph of size at least k at time t such that, w.h.p., the density of the returned subgraph is a $(3+\epsilon)$-approximation to the density of the densest at least k subgraph at time t if the densest at least k subgraph has density at least $\Omega(Dr \log n/k)$.*

Further, our general theorems also imply the following for static graphs (by simply setting $r = 0$). No such results were known in the distributed setting even for static graphs.

Corollary 2.3. *In a static distributed graph, there is an algorithm that obtains, w.h.p., $(2 + \epsilon)$-approximation to the densest subgraph problem in $O(D \log n)$ rounds of the CONGEST model.*

Corollary 2.4. *In a static distributed graph, there is an algorithm that obtains, w.h.p, $(3 + \epsilon)$-approximation to the k-densest subgraph problem in $O(D \log n)$ rounds of the CONGEST model.*

3. REFERENCES

[1] Reid Andersen and Kumar Chellapilla. Finding dense subgraphs with size bounds. In *WAW '09: Proceedings of the 6th International Workshop on Algorithms and Models for the Web-Graph*, pages 25–37, 2009.

[2] Samir Khuller and Barna Saha. On finding dense subgraphs. In *ICALP (1)*, pages 597–608, 2009.

[3] Fabian Kuhn, Rotem Oshman, and Yoram Moses. Coordinated consensus in dynamic networks. In *PODC*, pages 1–10, 2011.

[4] David Peleg. *Distributed computing: a locality-sensitive approach*. Society for Industrial and Applied Mathematics, Philadelphia, PA, USA, 2000.

[5] Atish Das Sarma, Stephan Holzer, Liah Kor, Amos Korman, Danupon Nanongkai, Gopal Pandurangan, David Peleg, and Roger Wattenhofer. Distributed verification and hardness of distributed approximation. In *STOC*, pages 363–372, 2011.

Brief Announcement:
Decentralized Network Supercomputing
in the Presence of Malicious and Crash-Prone Workers*

Seda Davtyan
Computer Science & Engineering
University of Connecticut
seda@engr.uconn.edu

Kishori M. Konwar
Immunology and Microbiology
University of British Columbia
kishori@interchange.ubc.ca

Alexander A. Shvartsman
Computer Science & Engineering
University of Connecticut
aas@cse.uconn.edu

ABSTRACT

Internet supercomputing is an approach to solving parti-
tionable, computation-intensive problems by harnessing the
power of a vast number of interconnected computers. For the
problem of using network supercomputing to perform a large
collection of independent tasks, our prior work introduced
the decentralized approach, and provided a synchronous algorithm that is able to perform all tasks with high probability (*whp*), while dealing with malicious behaviors under a
rather strong assumption that the *average* probability of live
(non-crashed) processors returning bogus results remains inferior to $1/2$ during the computation. There the adversary
is severely limited in its ability to crash processors that normally return correct results. This work develops an efficient
synchronous decentralized algorithm that is able to deal with
a much stronger adversary. We consider a failure model with
crashes, where given the initial set of processors P, an adversary is able to crash any subset F of processors, where
$|F| \le f \cdot n$, for a constant f $(0 < f < 1)$, under the constraint
that there exists a subset $H \subseteq P - F$, with $|H| = \Omega(n)$,
called the *hardened* set, such that the *average* probability of
a processor in H returning a bogus result is inferior to $1/2$.
Here any processor may return bogus results, and H may be
much *smaller* than $P - F$, while the average probability of
processors in $P - F$ returning a bogus result may be *greater*
than $1/2$. We develop an efficient randomized algorithm for
n processors and t tasks $(n \le t)$, where each live processor is
able to determine locally when all tasks are performed, and
obtain the results of all tasks. We prove that in $\Theta(\frac{t}{n} \log n)$
rounds all live workers know the results of all tasks *whp*,
and that these results are correct *whp*. The work complexity of the algorithm is $\Theta(t \log n)$, the message complexity is
$\Theta(n \log n)$, and the bit complexity is $O(tn \log^3 n)$.

Categories and Subject Descriptors: F.2.0 [Theory of
Computation]: ANALYSIS OF ALGORITHMS AND PROBLEM
COMPLEXITY – *General*

General Terms: Algorithms, Reliability

Keywords: Distributed Algorithms, Fault-Tolerance, Randomized Algorithms, Communication, Internet Supercomputing

*This work is supported in part by the NSF award 1017232.

1. INTRODUCTION

Internet supercomputing comes at a cost substantially
lower than acquiring a supercomputer, or building a cluster of powerful machines [1, 2, 3]. The promise of scalable
network supercomputing depends on the availability of efficient decentralized algorithms—algorithms that do not depend on centralized control—able to deal with computers
that may return bogus results and/or crash. A phenomenon
of increasing concern is that workers may return incorrect
results due to unintended failures, or may claim to have
performed assigned work so as to obtain incentives, such as
earning a higher rank in the system. A typical Internet supercomputer consists of a *master* server and a large number
of computers called *workers* that perform computation on
behalf of the master. Earlier approaches explored ways of
improving the quality of the results obtained from untrusted
workers in the master-worker setting, e.g., [5, 6, 7] present
work-efficient algorithms where the master can determine
the correct results *whp*.

Our prior work [4] removes the assumption of an infallible
and bandwidth-unlimited master processor. However, in [4]
the adversary is severely limited in its ability to crash processors that normally return correct results. In this work we
aim to provide a decentralized solution that is able to deal
with a much stronger adversary.

2. THE PROBLEM AND SYSTEM MODEL

We consider the problem of performing t tasks in a distributed system of n workers $(n \le t)$ *without* centralized
control. The tasks are constant-time, independent, and admit at-least-once execution semantics. We assume that the
workers can obtain the tasks from some repository. The
fully-connected message-passing system is synchronous and
the workers communicate using authenticated messages. The
crash-prone workers can return incorrect results. The weakly
adaptive adversary decides on the subset of processors to
crash prior to the beginning of the computation. The computation is structured in *rounds*, where in each round a
processor sends and receives messages and performs a local polynomial computation, where the local computation
time is negligible compared to message latency.

Let P be the initial set of processors. For each $i \in P$,
we define p_i to be the probability of processor i returning
incorrect results, independently of other processors. We define H to be a *hardened set* in an execution of a specific
algorithm, if no processors in H crash, and $\frac{1}{|H|} \sum_{i \in H} p_i <
\frac{1}{2} - \varepsilon$, for some constant $\varepsilon > 0$, i.e., the average probability

of processors in H returning incorrect results is inferior to $\frac{1}{2}$: we use ε to prevent the average probability of misbehavior becoming arbitrarily close to $\frac{1}{2}$ as n grows arbitrarily large.

We consider a linearly bounded adversary that can crash any subset F of processors, such that $|F| \leq f \cdot n$, for a constant f, where $0 < f < 1$, provided that each execution has a hardened set of processors $H \subseteq P - F$, with $|H| > h \cdot n$, where $0 < h < 1 - f$. Note that, unlike in [4], the average probability of non-crashed processors returning bogus results can become *greater* than $1/2$.

3. ALGORITHMICS

We developed a randomized algorithm solving our cooperation problem for n workers and $t = n$ tasks. The algorithm naturally generalizes for $t \geq n$ tasks, where each processor deals with fixed groups of $\lceil t/n \rceil$ tasks.

One of the main challenges in our algorithm is for every processor to find a subset of processors whose calculated results will be used to compute the final result for every task. To improve efficiency we select a subset of processors S that maximizes the total average probability of computing results correctly, i.e., given the existence of the hardened set H, we want to select a subset S, where $H \subseteq S \subset P$, that maximizes $\sum_{s \in S}(1 - p_s)$, subject to $\frac{1}{|S|} \sum_{s \in S} p_s < \frac{1}{2} - \varepsilon$.

In solving the stated optimization problem, that we call SELECT, we assume that the probabilities $\{p_s\}$ are known. This assumption is made for simplicity only, as it is easily removed using our algorithms in [7], where $\{p_s\}$ are efficiently estimated with arbitrary accuracy. We developed a linear time algorithm for SELECT that uses a greedy approach. First, the processor identifiers are sorted in the decreasing order of $\{1 - p_s\}$. Then we iteratively select processors in the sorted order, keeping in mind the constraint on the average probability of returning result incorrectly for the subset $S \subset P$ of selected processors.

Now we detail the main algorithm that works in synchronous rounds. In every round a processor performs a random task and communicates its cumulative knowledge to one other randomly chosen processor. The number of rounds performed by the algorithm is an external (compile-time) parameter K. We prove that $K = \frac{1}{h} 2L$ rounds are sufficient to obtain the high probability guarantee, for a certain L that is shown to be $\Theta(\log n)$.

Each worker i maintains two arrays of size linear in n. Array $R_i(1..n)$ is used to accumulate knowledge from different processors. Each element $R_i(j)$ is a set of results (initially empty) for task j, containing triples $\langle v_j, i, r \rangle$ representing the result v_j computed for task j by processor i in round r. The second array, $Results_i(1..n)$, stores the final results.

The algorithm iterates through three stages, *Receive, Compute*, and *Send*, where a single iteration comprises one *round*.

Receive Stage: Each processor receives messages sent during the previous round. The messages consist of the sender's collection of the results. Upon receiving the messages a processor updates its own local copy of the sets by taking a union (this excludes duplicated triples).

Compute Stage: If the round count is less than $\frac{1}{h} L$, then processor i randomly selects task j, computes the result v_j, and adds the triple $\langle v_j, i, r \rangle$ to $R_i(j)$.

If the round count reached K, each processor i goes over $R_i(j)$ for each task j and extracts the set of processors that calculated the results. Among these processors, it then selects a subset of processors S using algorithm SELECT. The result is then chosen to correspond to the plurality of the results calculated by processors in S (in the analysis we prove that in fact a majority exists). The results are stored locally in array $Results_i[1..n]$. The processor halts.

Send Stage: Each processor i chooses a target processor k randomly from P and sends to k its results $R_i(1..n)$.

4. ALGORITHM ANALYSIS

For $t = n$ we prove that in $\Theta(\log n)$ rounds *whp* every task is performed $\Theta(\log n)$ times, possibly by different workers. Moreover, we prove that if a task has been performed $\Theta(\log n)$ times then *whp* in $\Theta(\log n)$ rounds of the algorithm each worker will acquire the results for every task.

We proved the following theorem that states our main result: *The algorithm computes all n tasks correctly at every processor in $\Theta(\log n)$ rounds* whp.

We further show that for $t \geq n$ the *time complexity* of the algorithm is $\Theta(\frac{t}{n} \log n)$, the *work complexity* of the algorithm is $\Theta(t \log n)$, the *message complexity* of the algorithm is $\Theta(n \log n)$ and the *bit complexity* is $O(t \, n \log^3 n)$. The *space complexity* of the algorithm is $\Theta(t \, n \log^2 n)$.

5. SIMULATIONS

We developed a simulation of the algorithm for $t = n$. We let $L = \frac{1}{h} k \log n$, for constant $k > 0$. We carried out simulations for up to $n = 1000$ processors. For each chosen (n, k) pair we ran the simulation 100 times. We assumed that initially the average probability of returning incorrect result is inferior to 0.3. We let 60% of the processors return incorrect results with probability 0.1, we denote this set of processors by P_1, and the remaining 40% return incorrect results with probability 0.6, this set is denoted by P_2; here $P = P_1 \cup P_2$. We let $\frac{2}{3}$ of the processors in P_1 crash, thus "ruining" the preset probabilistic balance between P_1 and P_2. Using procedure SELECT we then chose a subset of processors S, with $H \subseteq S$, such that the average probability of returning incorrect result stays inferior to 0.3. The empirical data shows that even for the modest values of k in $\{2, 3, 4\}$ after $\Theta(\log n)$ rounds the correct results of every task are known to all workers with very few exceptions.

6. REFERENCES

[1] Distributed.net. http://www.distributed.net/.
[2] Internet primenet server.
    http://mersenne.org/ips/stats.html.
[3] Seti@home. http://setiathome.ssl.berkeley.edu/.
[4] S. Davtyan, K. M. Konwar, and A. A. Shvartsman. Robust network supercomputing without centralized control. In *Proc. 15th Int-l Conference on Principles of Distributed Systems*, OPODIS '11, 2011.
[5] A. Fernandez, C. Georgiou, L. Lopez, and A. Santos. Reliably executing tasks in the presence of untrusted entities. In *SRDS*, pages 39–50, 2006.
[6] A. Fernández, Ch. Georgiou, and M. Mosteiro. Algorithmic mechanisms for internet-based master-worker computing with untrusted and selfish workers. In *Proc. 24th IEEE Int'l Symp. on Parallel and Distributed Processing*, pages 1–11, 2010.
[7] K. M. Konwar, S. Rajasekaran, and A. A. Shvartsman. Robust network supercomputing with malicious processes. In *Proc. 17th Int-l Symposium on Distributed Computing (DISC 2006)*, pages 474–488, 2006.

Brief Announcement: Order-preserving Renaming in Synchronous Message Passing Systems with Byzantine Faults

Oksana Denysyuk
INESC-ID, Instituto Superior Técnico
Universidade Técnica de Lisboa, Portugal
oksana.denysyuk@ist.utl.pt

Luís Rodrigues
INESC-ID, Instituto Superior Técnico
Universidade Técnica de Lisboa, Portugal
ler@ist.utl.pt

ABSTRACT

Renaming is a fundamental problem in distributed computing which consists in a set of processors picking distinct names from a given namespace. We are interested in a stronger variant of the problem in which the processors have to pick new names according to the initial order of their original *ids*.

We assume a fully connected synchronous message passing system consisting of N processors, t of which can exhibit Byzantine behavior. In a synchronous model, renaming can be solved using consensus. However, it is known that renaming is "easier" than consensus. Therefore, in this work we are mainly concerned with the efficiency of performing renaming and briefly describe two contributions in this direction. The first contribution consists in an order-preserving renaming algorithm for $N > 3t^2$ with *constant* step complexity and target namespace of size $N^2 + Nt$. As a second contribution we present an order preserving renaming algorithm with $\mathcal{O}(\log N)$ step complexity and target namespace of size $2N$, for $N > 3t$.

Full version of this paper is available in [2].

Categories and Subject Descriptors

F.2.2 [**Theory of Computation**]: Analysis of Algorithms and Problem Complexity—*Nonnumerical Algorithms and Problems*

General Terms

Theory, Algorithms, Reliability

Keywords

Renaming problem; Byzantine failures; synchronous message passing model.

1. INTRODUCTION

The renaming problem was originally introduced in [1] in the asynchronous message-passing model with crash failures, in which solving consensus is known to be impossible [3].

Renaming can be informally described as follows: a set of processors $\{p_1, \cdots, p_N\}$ with unique identifiers, or *ids*,

belonging to the range $[1 \cdots N_{max}]$ pick new names from a given namespace $\{1, \cdots, M\}$, where $M \ll N_{max}$. Below we summarize the system model used in this paper.

The processors are arranged in a synchronous network of an a priory known size N, in which each pair of nodes is connected by a direct communication link. The communication between two processors is performed by message passing. The links of each processor are labeled by $1, \cdots, N$, where the links $1, \cdots, N-1$ are to the remaining processors and link N is a self-loop. It is assumed that the processors know the label of the link through which any message is received.

Each correct processor has a unique identifier, originally only known to the processor itself. The processors include their *id* in every message they exchange with other processors. Up to t processors may be faulty and exhibit an arbitrary behavior (these processors are named Byzantine processors); faulty processors may send messages with arbitrary content. Communication channels are assumed to be reliable.

The renaming problem can be formally defined by the following conditions (e.g. [1]):

Validity: each new name is an integer in the set $\{1, \cdots, M\}$.

Termination: each correct processor outputs a new name.

Uniqueness: no two correct processors output the same new name.

A stronger version of renaming can be obtained by adding the following property:

Order Preserving: new names of the correct processors preserve the order imposed by their original identifiers.

The particular case in which the size of the target namespace is equal to N is called *strong* renaming.

Contributions

The main contributions of this paper are two new algorithms to solve order preserving Byzantine renaming. Algorithm 1 has constant step complexity and tolerates upto $N > 3t^2$ Byzantine faults using the target name-space of size $N^2 + Nt$.

We then employ the previous solution to devise Algorithm 2 with optimal fault tolerance and the target namespace of size $2N$. This algorithm works by successive approximation, with provable convergence rate. The step complexity of Algorithm 2 is $\mathcal{O}(\log N)$. Both algorithms presented in this paper are deterministic.

To our knowledge, our work is the first to address the order preserving renaming in the given model.

2. CONSTANT TIME ALGORITHM

In this section we assume that t, the number of Byzantine processors, is limited by $N > 3t^2$, and give a high level description of Algorithm 1 that implements an order preserving renaming.

For each of the links $1 \leq i \leq n$ the algorithm holds the id of the processor to which the link is connected ($lnk[i].id$). Since the Nth link is a self-loop, $lnk[N].id$, (or $myId$), is the id of the current processor. The main steps of Algorithm 1 can be summarized as follows.

In Round 1, the processors start by sending their own id through all the links.

In Round 2, the processes initialize the $lnk[i].id$ variables based on the information sent in the previous round. Subsequently, the processors broadcast all the ids they received in Round 1. We call these second messages $echoes$. Note that ids belonging to correct processors (or correct ids, for short) will be echoed at least $N - t$ times.

In Round 3, the nodes start by checking the validity of the echoed messages. Messages that are clearly faulty are discarded. Namely, an echoed message is discarded if one of the following conditions holds: i) no message has been received via the incoming link in the previous round; ii) the message has more ids than the number of processors (which is known); or iii) the intersection of the echoed set and the set collected in Round 2 differs by more than $N - t$ entries. As noted, at least $N - t$ ids must be included in the echo message from a correct processor. This sanity test limits the power of the Byzantine nodes.

After all echo messages have been processed, the distances between the known ids are set as follows. The offset for each id is simply the value of the $counter$, or N, if $counter \geq N - t$. The latter adjustment will guarantee that the offsets of the correct ids are always N. Finally, $newId$ is assigned by summing the offsets of all the ids up to, and including, the given id.

Algorithm 1 runs in constant time employing only two all-to-all communication rounds and achieves the target namespace of size $N^2 + Nt$.

3. LOG-TIME ALGORITHM

In this section, we assume that the number of Byzantine processors is bounded by $N > 3t$. The constant time algorithm from previous section serves as an initial building block for our second renaming scheme. Here, $newIds$ calculated in Algorithm 1 are used as intermediate names for the processors. Since a larger proportion of processors are allowed to exhibit arbitrary behavior, there may be larger discrepancies to the $newId$ values used by distinct correct processors for selecting their name. As a result, without any additional algorithmic steps the outputs would not satisfy the order preserving property.

The idea of Algorithm 2 is to reduce the discrepancies among $newIds$ by running a variant of approximate agreement. In the task of approximate agreement processors start with some real values and output values that are within some bounded distance from each other. In our algorithm, this is achieved by averaging the $newId$ values calculated in Algorithm 1.

In addition to the usual properties of the approximate agreement, our algorithm must guarantee that the values converge preserving the initial ordering. This is ensured by performing a series of additional verifications to the $newIds$ proposed by the processors. In this way, after a logarithmic number of steps $newIds$ calculated by each correct processor are approximately the same. Another important property of our instance of an approximate agreement is that the $newId$ values converge preserving some minimal spacing. Thus, the $newIds$ at each correct processor will be well distributed over the intermediate namespace. This, in turn, allows to compact the final namespace from $N^2 + Nt$ to $2N$.

4. CONCLUSIONS

In this paper, we presented the first renaming algorithm that runs in constant time and tolerates the number of Byzantine faults bounded by $N > 3t^2$. Our work is complemented by a second contribution that consists in the algorithm for order-preserving renaming for $N > 3t$. This bound on the number of Byzantine faults is optimal [4].

From theoretical point of view, the algorithms point out an interesting research direction of exploring the tradeoffs between the number of Byzantine faults, the size of target namespace and the running time of the renaming algorithms in the given model. Namely, the bounds on the minimum size of the target namespace, and the number of Byzantine faults, for constant time renaming, remain an intriguing open problem.

Acknowledgements

This work was partially supported by the FCT (INESC-ID multi annual funding through the PIDDAC Program fund grant and by the project PTDC/EIA- EIA/102212/2008).

5. REFERENCES

[1] Hagit Attiya, Amotz Bar-Noy, Danny Dolev, David Peleg, and Rüdiger Reischuk. Renaming in an asynchronous environment. *J. ACM*, 37:524–548, July 1990.

[2] Oksana Denysyuk and Luis Rodrigues. Order-preserving renaming in synchronous message passing systems with byzantine faults. Arxiv preprint arXiv:1205.0477v1, 2012.

[3] Michael J. Fischer, Nancy A. Lynch, and Michael S. Paterson. Impossibility of distributed consensus with one faulty process. *J. ACM*, 32:374–382, April 1985.

[4] Michael Okun, Amnon Barak, and Eli Gafni. Renaming in synchronous message passing systems with byzantine failures. *Distributed Computing*, 20:403–413, 2008.

Brief Announcement: An Obstacle to Scalability in Wireless Networks*

András Faragó
Department of Computer Science
The University of Texas at Dallas
800 W. Campbell Road
Richardson, Texas 75080
farago@utdallas.edu

ABSTRACT

We generalize the well known random geometric graph based network topology model to a higher level of abstraction, to allow the inclusion of many different models. We explore the asymptotic relationship between node degrees and connectivity in this general model.

Categories and Subject Descriptors

C.2.1 [**Computer-Communication Networks**]: Network Architecture and Design—*Network Topology, Wireless Communication*

General Terms

Theory, Performance

Keywords

Ad hoc network, connectivity, fundamental limits

I. INTRODUCTION

In the random network topologies of wireless ad hoc and sensor networks it is a well known phenomenon that the requirement of asymptotic connectivity implies that the expected degree of an average node tends to infinity, approximately at least in the order of $\log n$, where n is the number of nodes (see, e.g., [3]). This is clearly an obstacle to scalability, as a real node cannot handle an unbounded number of links within bounded processing time. We call it the *lack of degree scalability*. To explore this phenomenon, and to find out whether it can be relieved by changing some conditions, we set up a general modeling framework that contains many different relevant random graph models as special cases. In this general framework we identify an "innocent looking" sufficient condition that is responsible for the lack of degree scalability. As our simple general condition is directly checkable in most specific cases, even in complicated ones, it can serve as powerful tool to show that a possibly complex random network topology model lacks degree scalability. Often this would otherwise be rather hard to prove via direct analysis of the stochastic geometry of the model.

---
*Research is supported by NSF Grant CNS-1018760.

PODC'12, July 16–18, 2012, Madeira, Portugal.
ACM 978-1-4503-1450-3/12/07.

II. RANDOM GRAPH MODELS AND DEGREE SCALABILITY

Let us first explain what we mean by random graphs and a random graph model in the most general sense. In full generality, by a *random graph* on a fixed number n of nodes we mean a random variable, denoted by G_n, that takes its values in the set of all undirected graphs on n nodes. At this point, it is still completely general, it can be generated by any mechanism, with arbitrary dependencies among its parts. Thus, a *random graph model* is given by a sequence of graph valued random variables:

$$\mathcal{M} = (G_n; \; n \in \mathbf{N}).$$

Let us denote by $e(G_n)$ the number of edges in the graph. The *expected average degree* of G_n is denoted by $\overline{d}(n)$ and is defined by

$$\overline{d}(n) = \frac{2\mathrm{E}(e(G_n))}{n}$$

based on the fact that the actual average degree in any graph G on n nodes is $2e(G)/n$.

Definition 1 (Degree scalability) *A random graph model* $\mathcal{M} = (G_n; \; n \in \mathbf{N})$ *is called* degree scalable *if there exists a constant C with* $\overline{d}(n) \leq C$ *for every n, and*

$$\lim_{n \to \infty} \Pr(G_n \text{ is connected}) = 1.$$

One may hope that if less than full connectivity is required asymptotically, then there is a better chance to keep the node degrees bounded. To this end, let us define a weaker version of connectivity and a corresponding weaker version of degree scalability.

Definition 2 (β-connectivity) *For a real number* $0 \leq \beta \leq 1$, *a graph G on n nodes is called β-connected if G contains a connected component on at least βn nodes.*

When we consider a sequence of graphs with different values of n, then the parameter β may depend on n. When this is the case, we write β_n-connectivity. Note that even if $\beta_n \to 1$, this is still weaker than full connectivity in the limit. For example, if $\beta_n = 1 - 1/\sqrt{n}$, then we have $\beta_n \to 1$, but each graph on n nodes can still have $n - \beta_n n = \sqrt{n}$ nodes that are not part of the largest connected component.

Definition 3 (Weak degree scalability) *A random graph model* $\mathcal{M} = (G_n; \; n \in \mathbf{N})$ *is called* weakly degree scalable *if there exists a constant C with* $\overline{d}(n) \leq C$ *for every*

n, and there exists a sequence $\beta_n \to 1$ of reals, such that

$$\lim_{n \to \infty} \Pr(G_n \text{ is } \beta_n\text{-connected}) = 1.$$

III. THE ABSTRACT GEOMETRIC RANDOM GRAPH MODEL

Let us now introduce a model that reflects a typical feature of geometric random graph models. This feature is that in geometric random graphs the primary random choice is picking random nodes from some domain and then the edges are already determined by some geometric property (typically some kind of distance) of the random nodes. We elevate this approach to an abstract level, which includes many different models, as special cases. Our abstract geometric model is built using the following components:

1. Node variables. The nodes are represented by an infinite sequence $X_1, X_2, \ldots$ of random variables, called *node variables*. They take their values in an arbitrary (nonempty) set S, which is called the *domain* of the model. In most practical cases the domain is a simple subset of the Euclidean plane or of the 3-dimensional space. In general, however, S can be any abstract set from which we can choose random elements. When we want to generate a random graph on n nodes, then we use the first n entries of the sequence, that is, $X_1, \ldots, X_n$ represent the nodes in G_n. It is important to note that we do not require the node variables to be independent.

2. Edge functions. We denote by $Y_{ij}^{(n)} \in \{0, 1\}$ the indicator of the edge between nodes X_i, X_j in the random graph G_n. To express the geometric nature, we assume there are functions $f^{(n)}$ such that the edge indicators are expressible as

$$Y_{ij}^{(n)} = f^{(n)}(X_i, X_j, \xi_{ij}).$$

Here the ξ_{ij} random variables are independent of all other random variables in the model. They are only needed if we also want to include independent randomization, to cover cases when the node positions do not determine *deterministically* the existence of edges.

III.1 An Important Special Property: Name Invariance

Let us first recall a useful concept from probability theory, called exchangeability.

Definition 4 (Exchangeable random variables) *A finite sequence $\xi_1, \ldots, \xi_n$ of random variables is called exchangeable if for any permutation σ of $\{1, \ldots, n\}$, the joint distribution of $\xi_1, \ldots, \xi_n$ is the same as the joint distribution of $\xi_{\sigma(1)}, \ldots, \xi_{\sigma(n)}$. An infinite sequence of random variables is called exchangeable if every finite initial segment of the sequence is exchangeable.*

Exchangeability can be equivalently defined such that for any k of the random variables, say, $\xi_{j_1}, \ldots, \xi_{j_k}$, their joint distribution is always the same (for a given k); it does not depend on which particular set of k indices is selected. Note that independent, identically distributed (i.i.d.) random variables are always exchangeable, but the converse is not true, so this is a larger family. Now let us introduce the condition that we use to restrict the arbitrary dependence of node variables.

Definition 5 (Name invariance) *An abstract geometric random graph model is called* name invariance, *if its node variables are exchangeable.*

We call it the *name invariance* of the model because it means the names (the indices) of the nodes are irrelevant in the sense that the joint probabilistic behavior of any fixed number of nodes is invariant to renaming (reindexing) the nodes. In particular, it also implies that each single node variable X_i has the same probability distribution. Name invariance is naturally satisfied with the typically used random node choices. It allows, however, dependencies among the nodes. An example is a randomly clustered node distribution. Such a distribution can be generated, e.g., by randomly selecting clusterheads among the independent random nodes, and keeping only those nodes that are within a given distance to a clusterhead, while discarding the rest.

IV. RESULTS ON DEGREE SCALABILITY

Theorem 1. *If an abstract geometric random graph model is name invariant, then it cannot be degree scalable.*

The proof is based on another theorem, which is interesting on its own right. As a further notation, the (random) number of isolated nodes in G_n is denoted by I_n. Recall that the expected average degree of G_n is defined as $\overline{d}(n) = 2\mathrm{E}(e(G_n))/n$.

Theorem 2. *Let G_n be a random graph generated by any name invariant abstract geometric random graph model. Then the expected number of isolated nodes in G_n satisfies*

$$\mathrm{E}(I_n) \geq n \left(1 - \frac{\overline{d}(n)}{n-1}\right)^{n-1}.$$

Remark: It is worth noting that even when $\mathrm{E}(I_n) \to \infty$ is the case, this fact alone may not *a priori* preclude the possibility of asymptotically almost sure connectivity. For example, if G_n is connected with probability $1 - 1/\sqrt{n}$ and consists of n isolated nodes with probability $1/\sqrt{n}$, then $\mathrm{E}(I_n) = n/\sqrt{n} \to \infty$, but $\Pr(G_n \text{ is connected}) = 1 - 1/\sqrt{n} \to 1$.

Interestingly, we can prove that name invariance excludes even weak degree scalability. Thus, this general property implies that the bounded expected average degree excludes even that the random graph is *almost* connected in the limit, in the sense that a vanishing fraction of nodes (for example, $\sqrt{n}$ out of n) are possibly isolated.

Theorem 3. *If an abstract geometric random graph model is name invariant, then it cannot be weakly degree scalable.*

The key message of these theorems is that a flat random wireless network topology is not scalable, even if we allow an extremely liberal choice of conditions, via the abstract geometric random graph model, covering many relevant cases. The proofs, with further extensions, can be found in [1, 2].

V. REFERENCES

[1] A. Faragó, "Scalability of Node Degrees in Random Wireless Network Topologies", *IEEE JSAC* Vol. 27, Sept. 2009, pp. 1238–1244.

[2] A. Faragó, "Asymptotically Optimal Trade-off between Local and Global Connectivity in Wireless Networks", *Performance Evaluation*, vol. 68, 2011, pp. 142–156.

[3] P. Gupta and P.R. Kumar, "The Capacity of Wireless Networks" *IEEE Trans. Information Theory*, Vol. 46, 2000, pp. 388–404.

Brief Announcement:
On the Resilience of Routing Tables

Joan Feigenbaum
Yale University
joan.feigenbaum@yale.edu

Brighten Godfrey
UIUC
pbg@illinois.edu

Aurojit Panda
UC Berkeley
apanda@cs.berkeley.edu

Michael Schapira
Hebrew University
schapiram@huji.ac.il

Scott Shenker
UC Berkeley
shenker@eecs.berkeley.edu

Ankit Singla
UIUC
singla2@illinois.edu

Categories and Subject Descriptors

C.2.2 [**Network Protocols**]: Routing Protocols

Keywords

Internet routing, fault tolerance

ABSTRACT

Many modern network designs incorporate "failover" paths into routers' forwarding tables. We initiate the theoretical study of such *resilient routing tables*.

1. INTRODUCTION

The core mission of computer networks is delivering packets from one point to another. To accomplish this, the typical network architecture uses a set of forwarding tables (that dictate the outgoing link at each router for each packet) and a routing algorithm that establishes those forwarding tables, recomputing them as needed in response to link failures or other topology changes. While this approach provides the ability to *recover* from an arbitrary set of failures, it does not provide sufficient *resiliency* to failures because these routing algorithms take substantial time to reconverge after each link failure. As a result, for periods of time ranging from 10s of milliseconds to seconds (depending on the network), the network may not be able to deliver packets to certain destinations. In comparison, packet forwarding is several orders of magnitude faster: a 10 Gbps link, for example, sends a 1500 byte packet in 1.2 μsec.

In order to provide higher availability we must design networks that are more resilient to failures. To this end, many modern network designs incorporate various forms of "backup" or "failover" paths into the forwarding tables that enable a router (or switch), when it detects that one of its attached links is down, to use an alternate outgoing link. We call these *resilient routing tables* since they embed failover information into the routing table itself and do not entail changes in packet headers (and so require no change in the low-level packet forwarding hardware). Because these failover decisions are purely local — based only on the packet's destination, the packet's incoming link, and the set of active incident links — they occur much more

rapidly than the global recovery algorithms used in traditional routing protocols and thus result in many fewer packet losses.

While such resilient routing tables are widely used in practice (*e.g.,* ECMP), there has been little theoretical work on their inherent power and limitations. In this short note we initiate the theoretical study of resilient routing tables and take the first few steps in this research direction. We prove that routing tables can always provide resilience against single failures (so long as the network remains topologically connected). We show, in contrast, that perfect resilience is not achievable in general (*i.e.,* there are cases in which no set of routing tables can guarantee packet delivery even when the graph remains connected). We leave open the question of closing the large gap between our positive and negative results. Other interesting open questions include exploring resilient routing tables in the context of specific families of graphs, randomized forwarding rules, and more.

The literature is replete with discussions of how to make routing more resilient, but these approaches differ from ours in one or more important respects: (a) use bits in the packet headers to determine when to switch from primary to backup paths (this includes MPLS Fast Reroute [6]); (b) encode failure information in packet headers to allow nodes to make failure-aware forwarding decisions (see [3, 5] and work on fault-tolerant compact routing [7]); (c) use graph-specific properties to achieve resilience [2]; and (d) modify routing tables on the fly [4].

Because of space limitations, full proofs can be found in our technical report [1].

2. MODEL

The network is modeled as an undirected graph $G = (V, E)$, in which the vertex set V consists of source nodes $\{1, 2, \ldots, n\}$ and a *unique* destination node $d \notin [n]$. Each node $i \in [n]$ has a *forwarding function* $f_i^d : E_i \times 2^{E_i} \to E_i$, where E_i is the set of node i's incident edges. f_i^d maps incoming edges to outgoing edges as a function of which incident edges are up. We call an n-tuple of forwarding functions $f^d = (f_1^d, \ldots, f_n^d)$ a *forwarding pattern*.

Consider the scenario that a set of edges $F \subseteq E$ fails. A *forwarding path* in this scenario is a loop-free route in the graph $H^F = (V, E \setminus F)$ such that for every two consecutive edges e_1, e_2 on the route which share a mutual node i it holds that $f_i^d(e_1, E_i \setminus F) = e_2$.

Intuitively, our aim is to guarantee that whenever a node

PODC'12, July 16–18, 2012, Madeira, Portugal.
ACM 978-1-4503-1450-3/12/07.

is connected to the destination d, it also has a forwarding path to the destination. Formally, we say that a forwarding pattern f is *t-resilient* if for every failure scenario $F \subseteq E$ such that $|F| \leq t$, if there exists some route from a node i to d in H^F then there also exists a forwarding path from i to d in H^F.

3. POSITIVE RESULT

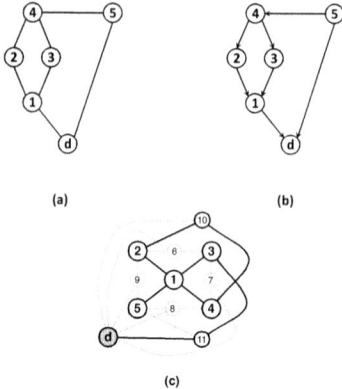

(a)   (b)

(c)

We now present our main result, which establishes that for every given network it is possible to efficiently compute a 1-resilient forwarding pattern.

THEOREM 3.1. *For every network there exists a 1-resilient forwarding pattern and, moreover, such a forwarding pattern can be computed in polynomial time.*

We prove Theorem 3.1 constructively; we present an algorithm that efficiently computes a 1-resilient forwarding pattern. We now give an intuitive exposition of our algorithm. We first orient the edges in G so as to compute a directed acyclic graph (DAG) D in which each edge in E is utilized. Our results hold regardless of how the DAG D is computed. An example network and corresponding DAG appear in figures (a) and (b), respectively. The DAG D naturally induces forwarding rules at source nodes; each node's incoming edge in D is mapped to its first active outgoing edge in D, given some arbitrary order over the node's outgoing edges (*e.g.*, node 4 in the figure forwards traffic from node 5 to node 2 if the edge to 2 is up, and to node 3 otherwise).

Intuitively, the next step is to identify a "problematic" node, that is, a node that is bi-connected to the destination in G but not in the partial forwarding pattern computed thus far, and add forwarding rules so as to "fix" this situation. Once this is achieved, another problematic node is identified and fixed, and so on. Observe that nodes 1-4 in the figure are all problematic. Observe also that adding the two following forwarding rules fixes node 4 (*i.e.*, makes node 4 bi-connected to the destination in the forwarding pattern): (a) when both of node 4's outgoing edges in D are down, traffic reaching 4 from node 5 is sent back to 5; and (b) when node 5's direct edge to the destination is up, traffic reaching node 5 from node 4 is sent along this edge. Thus, the algorithm builds the forwarding functions at nodes gradually, as more and more forwarding rules are added to better the resilience of the forwarding pattern.

Implementing the above approach, though, requires care; the order in which problematic nodes are chosen, and the exact manner in which forwarding rules are fixed, are important. Intuitively, our algorithm goes over problematic nodes

in the topological order $<_D$ induced by the DAG D (visiting problematic nodes closer to the destination in D first), and when fixing a problematic node i, forwarding rules are added until a minimal node in $<_D$ whose entire sub-DAG in D does not traverse i is reached. We prove that this scheme outputs the desired forwarding pattern in a computationally-efficient manner.

4. NEGATIVE RESULT

We say that a forwarding pattern f is *perfectly resilient* if it is ∞-resilient — so that regardless of the failure scenario $F \subseteq E$, if there exists some route from a node i to the destination d in H^F then there also exists a forwarding path from i to d in H^F. We next prove that forwarding patterns cannot always achieve perfect resilience.

THEOREM 4.1. *There exists a network for which no perfectly resilient forwarding pattern exists.*

We now present the intuition for the proof of Theorem. Consider the example network in figure (c). We show that after certain failures, no forwarding pattern on the original graph allows each surviving node in the destination's connected component to reach the destination. In figure (c), the surviving links are shown in bold; all other links fail.

We argue that in any perfectly resilient forwarding pattern f^d, node 1 has to route packets in some cyclic ordering of its neighbors. By the topology's symmetry, we can suppose w.l.o.g. that this ordering is 2, 3, 4, 5, 2, *i.e.*, f^d is defined such that 1 forwards packets from 2 to 3, packets from 3 to 4, *etc.* Note that a forwarding loop is formed when a packet repeats a directed edge in its path (rather than just a node). To show that this occurs, consider the path taken by packets sent by 5 after the failures. It can be shown that to achieve perfect resilience, packets sent $1 \rightarrow 2$ must not loop back and so must travel $2 \rightarrow 10 \rightarrow 4 \rightarrow 1$. As a result the packet travels $5 \rightarrow 1 \rightarrow 2 \rightarrow 10 \rightarrow 4 \rightarrow 1 \rightarrow 5 \rightarrow 1$ which is a loop since the edge $5 \rightarrow 1$ is repeated.

5. REFERENCES

[1] Joan Feigenbaum, P. Brighten Godfrey, Aurojit Panda, Michael Schapira, Scott Shenker, and Ankit Singla. Technical report YALEU/DCS/TR-1454. On the resilience of routing tables. 2012.

[2] Nate Kushman, Srikanth Kandula, Dina Katabi, and Bruce M. Maggs. R-BGP: Staying connected in a connected world. In *NSDI*, 2007.

[3] K. Lakshminarayanan, M. Caesar, M. Rangan, T. Anderson, S. Shenker, and I. Stoica. Achieving convergence-free routing using failure-carrying packets. In *SIGCOMM*, 2007.

[4] Junda Liu, Baohua Yan, Scott Shenker, and Michael Schapira. Data-driven network connectivity. In *HotNets*, 2011.

[5] S.S. Lor, R. Landa, and M. Rio. Packet re-cycling: eliminating packet losses due to network failures. In *HotNets*, 2010.

[6] P. Pan, G. Swallow, and A. Atlas. RFC 4090 Fast Reroute Extensions to RSVP-TE for LSP Tunnels. May 2005.

[7] Koichi Wada and Kimio Kawaguchi. Efficient fault-tolerant fixed routings on (k+1)-connected digraphs. *Discrete Applied Mathematics*, 1992.

Brief Announcement: A Tight RMR Lower Bound for Randomized Mutual Exclusion

George Giakkoupis[*][†]
INRIA Rennes-Bretagne Atlantique
Campus Universitaire de Beaulieu
35042 Rennes Cedex, France
george.giakkoupis@inria.fr

Philipp Woelfel[†]
Dept. of Computer Science
University of Calgary
Calgary, AB T2N 1N4, Canada
woelfel@ucalgary.ca

ABSTRACT

The Cache Coherent (CC) and the Distributed Shared Memory (DSM) models are standard shared memory models, and the Remote Memory Reference (RMR) complexity is considered to accurately predict the actual performance of mutual exclusion algorithms in shared memory systems. In [12] we prove a tight lower bound for the RMR complexity of deadlock-free randomized mutual exclusion algorithms in both the CC and the DSM model with an adaptive adversary. Our lower bound establishes that an adaptive adversary can schedule n processes in such a way that each enters the critical section once, and the total number of RMRs is $\Omega(n \log n / \log \log n)$ in expectation. This matches an upper bound of Hendler and Woelfel [14].

Categories and Subject Descriptors

D.1.3 [**Programming Techniques**]: Concurrent Programming—*Distributed programming*; F.2.2 [**Analysis of Algorithms and Problem Complexity**]: Nonnumerical Algorithms and Problems

Keywords

Mutual exclusion, Lower bound, Remote memory references, RMRs, Strong adversary, Randomization

1. INTRODUCTION

We consider asynchronous shared memory systems with n processes, that provide atomic registers and compare&swap objects.

The *mutual exclusion* problem, introduced by Dijkstra in 1965 [9], is a fundamental and well-studied problem in asynchronous computing. Processes coordinate their access to a shared resource by serializing the execution of a piece of code, called *critical section*. Since processes may have to wait for other processes to leave the critical section, the number of steps processes execute, can be unbounded. Therefore, the efficiency of mutual exclusion algorithms is measured in terms of the number of *remote memory references*

[*]Supported by the Pacific Institute for the Mathematical Sciences (PIMS)

[†]Supported by a Discovery Grant from the Natural Sciences and Research Council of Canada (NSERC)

(RMRs). In shared memory systems, some of the memory is placed local to each process, while the rest of the memory is remote, e.g., in other processing units or in dedicated storage. For example, in *cache-coherent* (CC) systems, each processor maintains local copies of (remote) shared variables in its cache; the consistency of copies in different caches is ensured by a coherence protocol. In *distributed shared-memory* (DSM) systems, on the other hand, each shared variable is permanently locally accessible to a single processor and remote to all other processors.

RMRs are orders of magnitude slower than accesses to the local memory. Therefore, the performance of many algorithms for shared memory multiprocessor systems depends critically on the number of RMRs they incur [4, 19]. *Local-spin* algorithms, which perform busy-waiting by repeatedly reading locally accessible shared variables, achieve bounded RMR complexity and have practical performance benefits [4]. In fact, recent mutual exclusion research has almost entirely focused on the RMR complexity (see, e.g., [3, 2, 18, 5, 8, 15, 16, 17, 6, 13, 14]).

For distributed systems with strong atomic primitives, such as fetch&increment or swap and compare&swap, there are mutual exclusion algorithms with $O(1)$ RMR complexity (e.g., [19]), meaning that every process incurs only a constant number of RMRs per passage through the critical section. If only atomic registers and compare&swap objects are supported, then the most efficient deterministic mutual exclusion-algorithms have an RMR complexity of $O(\log n)$ [20]. Anderson and Kim [1] conjectured that this is optimal. Following several lower bound proofs [7, 17, 10], Attiya, Hendler, and Woelfel [5] proved this conjecture true. More recently, randomized techniques have been employed to speed up the efficiency of mutual exclusion algorithms. Hendler and Woelfel [14] presented a randomized algorithm, where each process incurs an expected number of $O(\log n / \log \log n)$ RMRs per passage through the critical section. The algorithm works in a strong adaptive adversary model, where scheduling decisions can depend on all past events, including local coin flips.

Recently, Bender and Gilbert [6] presented a very different approach to solving mutual exclusion. Their algorithm employs approximate counting techniques to guarantee with high probability an amortized RMR complexity of $O(\log^2(\log n))$ per passage through the critical section in the CC model, albeit only for a weak, oblivious adversary model. I.e., in their model the schedule is independent of the random decisions made by processes.

Results. In reality, the speed of operations can depend on the random decisions of processes. E.g., the location of register accesses may be decided at random, but due to the memory hierarchy and architecture, the speed of such accesses is not uniform. It would therefore be desirable to achieve a similar RMR complexity as in the algorithm of Bender and Gilbert [6], for stronger adversaries. The strongest reasonable adversary is the adaptive adversary, and thus, an algorithm with low RMR complexity for this adversary would guarantee efficiency independent of the system behavior. However, in the face of the fact that the best known algorithm for the adaptive adversary [14] has an $O(\log n/\log\log n)$ expected RMR complexity per passage through the critical section, Bender and Gilbert [6] noted that their "choice of a weaker adversary seems fundamental." We show that this is indeed the case, by proving that any deadlock-free mutual exclusion algorithm for the n-process CC or DSM model has an expected RMR complexity of $\Omega(\log n/\log\log n)$ per passage through the critical section, against an adaptive adversary. This lower bound holds even for one-time mutual exclusion algorithms. Specifically, there is an adaptive adversary that schedules n processes in such a way that every process enters the critical section once, and the expectation of the total number of RMRs is $\Omega(n\log n/\log\log n)$. This is the first non-trivial lower bound for the RMR complexity of randomized mutual exclusion against an adaptive adversary; for weaker adversary models no lower bounds are known.

Proof Technique. We define a *randomized adaptive* adversary, i.e., the adversary makes random scheduling decisions but the distribution over these decisions is independent of processes' future coin flips. We prove our lower bound on the expected RMR complexity of *any deterministic* mutual exclusion algorithm scheduled by the above randomized adversary. Our result then follows from Yao's Principle [21].

Our randomized adversary schedules processes in rounds, but in every round only a small, randomly chosen fraction of the processes takes steps. This way, it is difficult for processes to "find" other processes. With every process we associate a potential such that the difference between the total potential initially and after all processes have finished is $\Omega(n\log n/\log\log n)$, and we argue that the expected decrease in potential per round is proportional to the expected number of RMRs executed in that round.

Our lower bound proof is very different from previous lower bounds for deterministic mutual exclusion [7, 17, 10, 5]. Potential functions have been used before to show lower bounds for *deterministic* shared memory algorithm for various problems (see, e.g., [11]). However, we are not aware of any lower bound proofs for *randomized* shared memory algorithms that use potential function techniques.

2. REFERENCES

[1] James H. Anderson and Yong-Jik Kim. Fast and scalable mutual exclusion. In *Proc. of 13th DISC*, pages 180–194, 1999.

[2] James H. Anderson and Yong-Jik Kim. Adaptive mutual exclusion with local spinning. In *Proc. of 14th DISC*, pages 29–43, 2000.

[3] James H. Anderson and Yong-Jik Kim. An improved lower bound for the time complexity of mutual exclusion. *Distr. Comp.*, 15:221–253, 2002.

[4] Thomas E. Anderson. The performance of spin lock alternatives for shared-memory multiprocessors. *IEEE Trans. Parallel Distrib. Syst.*, 1(1):6–16, 1990.

[5] Hagit Attiya, Danny Hendler, and Philipp Woelfel. Tight RMR lower bounds for mutual exclusion and other problems. In *Proc. of 40th ACM STOC*, pages 217–226, 2008.

[6] Michael Bender and Seth Gilbert. Mutual exclusion with $O(\log^2\log n)$ amortized work. In *Proc. of 52nd FOCS*, pages 728–737, 2011.

[7] Robert Cypher. The communication requirements of mutual exclusion. In *Proc. of 7th SPAA*, pages 147–156, 1995.

[8] Robert Danek and Wojciech M. Golab. Closing the complexity gap between FCFS mutual exclusion and mutual exclusion. *Distr. Comp.*, 23(2):87–111, 2010.

[9] Edsger W. Dijkstra. Solution of a problem in concurrent programming control. *Commun. ACM*, 8:569, 1965.

[10] Rui Fan and Nancy A. Lynch. An $\Omega(\log n)$ lower bound on the cost of mutual exclusion. In *Proc. of 25th PODC*, pages 275–284, 2006.

[11] Faith Ellen Fich, Danny Hendler, and Nir Shavit. Linear lower bounds on real-world implementations of concurrent objects. In *Proc. of 46th FOCS*, pages 165–173, 2005.

[12] George Giakkoupis and Philipp Woelfel. Tight RMR lower bounds for randomized mutual exclusion. In *Proc. of 44th ACM STOC*, 2012. To appear.

[13] Danny Hendler and Philipp Woelfel. Adaptive randomized mutual exclusion in sub-logarithmic expected time. In *Proc. of 29th PODC*, pages 141–150, 2010.

[14] Danny Hendler and Philipp Woelfel. Randomized mutual exclusion with sub-logarithmic RMR-complexity. *Distr. Comp.*, 24(1):3–19, 2011.

[15] Prasad Jayanti. Adaptive and efficient abortable mutual exclusion. In *Proc. of 22nd PODC*, pages 295–304, 2003.

[16] Prasad Jayanti, Srdjan Petrovic, and Neha Narula. Read/write based fast-path transformation for FCFS mutual exclusion. In *Proc. of 31st SOFSEM*, pages 209–218, 2005.

[17] Yong-Jik Kim and James H. Anderson. A time complexity bound for adaptive mutual exclusion. In *Proc. of 15th DISC*, pages 1–15, 2001.

[18] Yong-Jik Kim and James H. Anderson. Nonatomic mutual exclusion with local spinning. *Distr. Comp.*, 19(1):19–61, 2006.

[19] John M. Mellor-Crummey and Michael L. Scott. Algorithms for scalable synchronization on shared-memory multiprocessors. *ACM Trans. Comput. Syst.*, 9(1):21–65, 1991.

[20] Jae-Heon Yang and James H. Anderson. A fast, scalable mutual exclusion algorithm. *Distr. Comp.*, 9(1):51–60, 1995.

[21] Andrew Chi-Chih Yao. Probabilistic computations: Towards a unified measure of complexity. In *Proc. of 17th FOCS*, pages 222–227, 1977.

Brief Announcement – From Sequential to Concurrent: Correctness and Relative Efficiency

Vincent Gramoli
School of Information
Technologies
University of Sydney

Petr Kuznetsov, Srivatsan
Ravi[*]
TU Berlin/Telekom Innovation
Laboratories

Categories and Subject Descriptors

F.0 [**Theory of Computation**]: General

General Terms

Algorithms, Theory

Keywords

Concurrency, Synchronization

1. INTRODUCTION

How to turn a sequential implementation of a data structure (a hash table, a list, a tree, etc.) into a correct and, preferably, efficient concurrent one? What if we provide an environment in which a user can *locally* run the sequential code so that the resulting execution is *globally* correct.

One way to do this is to use *locks* to make sure that critical parts of a sequential program can only be accessed in an exclusive mode. An implementation that grabs a lock on the whole data structure before executing a sequential operation imposes a serial order but ignores all the benefits provided by the multiprocessing power of modern machines. Efficient fine-grained locking requires lots of intelligence, since it must be based on good understanding of which parts of the sequential code to protect at what time.

A more automated approach is to use transactional memory (TM) and treat each (sequential) operation as a transaction. If the transaction commits, the corresponding operation returns the response computed based on the values read in the course of the transaction. Otherwise, if the transaction aborts, the operation does not take effect. This approach promises to make use of the hardware concurrency at low intellectual cost. But does this simplicity bring a considerable efficiency degradation with respect to fine-grained locking?

To tackle this question, we first define the meaning of a correct transformation of a sequential program into a concurrent one. More precisely, we model an execution of a

[*]The research leading to these results has received funding from the European Union Seventh Framework Programme (FP7/2007-2013) under grant agreement N 238639, ITN project TRANSFORM, and grant agreement N 248465, the S(o)OS project.

concurrent implementation as a sequence of invocations and responses of the high-level operations on the data structure, operations on the sequential implementation of the data structure (e.g., reads and writes to the items of a linked-list), plus accesses to synchronization primitives (e.g., transaction delimiters or acquisitions and releases of locks). Now we say that an execution is *locally serializable* if the sequence of sequential events corresponding to each high-level operation is consistent with *some* sequential execution. In addition, the *high-level* history of every execution, i.e., the subsequence of high-level invocation and response, must be *linearizable* [6] with respect to the sequential object type. The combination of local serializability and linearizability gives our novel correctness criterion which we call *LS-linearizability*, where LS stands for "locally serializable." Note that we can easily think of implementations that are linearizable but not LS-linearizable (do not look sequential locally), as well as locally serializable but not linearizable (do not make sense globally). In this sense, the two properties indeed complement each other.

Once we are done with a correctness definition for a concurrent "wrapper" of a sequential data structure, what can we say about its performance? This paper proposes a metric to evaluate the performance of such an implementation via the "amount of concurrency" it allows for. We associate the implementation with the set of *schedules* (interleavings of steps of the sequential program) it *accepts*, i.e., is able to process. Now we can compare different concurrent implementations (or implementation classes) for a given sequential data structure (or a class of data structures) based on the sets of accepted schedules, similar to how TM classes were compared [2].

We then show how this metric can be used to compare implementations exploiting different synchronization techniques, in particular, various forms of fine-grained locking or transactional memory for different data structures. The full version of this paper can be found in [3].

2. PRELIMINARY DEFINITIONS

An *execution* of a concurrent implementation is a sequence of invocations and responses of high-level operations, (atomic) read and write events and *synchronization* events (e.g., lock acquisitions and releases or transaction delimiters). In this paper, we primarily focus on two synchronization techniques: locks and transactional memory (TM). A *history exported by an execution E* is a subsequence of invocation-response and read-write events related to high-level operations that *take effect*. For lock-based implementations, the history of an execution E is determined by removing all synchronization (acquire/release) events. For a TM-based implementation, the history is determined by, additionally, removing all events related to *aborted* or *incomplete* transactions. By convention, every execution of a sequential implementation I_S is already a history. Histories H and H' are *equivalent* if, for every process p_i, $H|p_i=H'|p_i$. A *high-level history* $\tilde{H}$ is a sequence of invocations and responses on high-level objects (e.g., a subsequence of a given history).

3. LS-LINEARIZABILITY

Let H be a history, and let π be a high-level operation in H. Then $H|\pi$ denotes the subsequence of H consisting of the events of π. Let I_S be a sequential implementation of an object of type τ and Σ be the set of histories of I_S.

DEFINITION 1. *A history H is* locally serializable *with respect to I_S if for all high-level operations π in H, there exists $S_\pi \in \Sigma$ such that $H|\pi = S_\pi|\pi$.*

Note that local serializability stipulates that the execution is witnessed sequential by every high-level operation in isolation. Two different operations (even when invoked by the same process) are not required to witness the same sequential execution.

DEFINITION 2. *A history H is* LS-linearizable *with respect to (I_S, τ) if (1) H is locally serializable with respect to I_S, and (2) the corresponding high-level history $\tilde{H}$ is linearizable with respect to τ.*

We show that LS-linearizability is *compositional* [6] (i.e., holds under composition).

3.1 Concurrency Relations

A *schedule* is an equivalence class of histories that agree on the order of events but possibly not on read values or high-level responses. Intuitively, a schedule describes the order in which high-level operations, reads and writes are invoked by the user. We say that an implementation I *accepts* a schedule S if there exists an execution of I which exports a history that exhibits the order of S. Given an implementation I, let $\mathcal{S}(I)$ denote the set of schedules accepted by I. Intuitively, $\mathcal{S}(I)$ reflects the "amount of concurrency" provided by I.

A *synchronization technique* is a set of concurrent implementations. Given a sequential implementation I_S of an object type τ and a synchronization technique $\mathcal{A}$, let $\mathcal{T}_\mathcal{A}(I_S, \tau)$ denote the set of LS-linearizable (with respect to (I_S, τ)) implementations in $\mathcal{A}$. Let I_S be a sequential implementation of a type τ. We say that a synchronization technique $\mathcal{A}$ provides *less concurrency* than a synchronization technique $\mathcal{B}$ with respect to (I_S, τ), and we write $\mathcal{A} \preceq_{(I_S, \tau)} \mathcal{B}$, iff $\forall I \in \mathcal{T}_\mathcal{A}(I_S, \tau), \exists I' \in \mathcal{T}_\mathcal{B}(I_S, \tau), \mathcal{S}(I) \subseteq \mathcal{S}(I')$. We say that $\mathcal{A}$ provides *strictly less concurrency* than $\mathcal{B}$ with respect to (I_S, τ), and we write $\mathcal{A} \prec_{(I_S, \tau)} \mathcal{B}$, iff $(\mathcal{A} \preceq_{(I_S, \tau)} \mathcal{B}) \wedge (\mathcal{B} \not\preceq_{(I_S, \tau)} \mathcal{A})$. If $\mathcal{A} \preceq_{(I_S, \tau)} \mathcal{B}$ for all (I_S, τ), then we say that $\mathcal{A}$ provides less concurrency than $\mathcal{B}$ and write $\mathcal{A} \preceq \mathcal{B}$.

4. LOCKING VS. TRANSACTIONAL MEMORY

We now describe how the language we have introduced can be applied to a real-world implementation of a concurrent data structure. To this end, we consider an object of type *integer set* (disallowing duplicates), implemented using a *sorted linked list* data structure (denoted I_S). We assume that the type is specified by the *Insert*, *Remove* and *Contains* operations.

We first prove that *hand-over-hand* locking technique [1] provides strictly more concurrency w.r.t (I, set) than a wide class of strictly serializable TM-based implementations that resolve *read-write conflicts* between concurrent transactions by forcefully aborting or delaying some of them [4, 5] (we denote these classes of implementations by HOH and M_0, respectively).

THEOREM 3. $M_0 \prec_{(I_S, set)} HOH$.

However, we now show how TMs with stronger progress guarantees than *conflict-resolving* can accept schedules that no lock-based implementation can accept.

Allowing TMs to maintain multiple versions of transactional objects enables implementations with stronger progress guarantees than conflict-resolving. This allows multiversion TMs to accept schedules which cannot be accepted by *any* lock-based implementation. Let M_1 denote the class of multiversion strict serializable TM implementations that guarantee *mv-permissiveness* [7].

THEOREM 4. $M_1 \not\preceq \mathcal{L}$.

However, maintaining multiple versions is known to come at a significant cost [7], therefore it is not obvious that using mv-permissive TMs results in performance improvements. In response to this, we describe a class M_2 of *single-version* strict serializable TM implementations accepting schedules that cannot be accepted by *any* lock-based implementation. This class of TMs provide a slightly stronger progress guarantee than the minimal progress provided by the *conflict-resolving* TMs, but weaker than *mv-permissiveness*. Specifically, while transactions with a non-empty read-set may abort on observing a read-write conflict, read-only transactions may abort only when at least two transactional objects in the read-set experience read-write conflicts.

THEOREM 5. $M_2 \not\preceq \mathcal{L}$.

5. REFERENCES

[1] R. Bayer and M. Schkolnick. Readings in database systems. pages 129–139, San Francisco, CA, USA, 1988. Morgan Kaufmann Publishers Inc.

[2] V. Gramoli, D. Harmanci, and P. Felber. On the input acceptance of transactional memory. *Parallel Processing Letters*, 20(1):31–50, 2010.

[3] V. Gramoli, P. Kuznetsov, and S. Ravi. From sequential to concurrent: Correctness and relative efficiency. *CoRR*, abs/1203.4751, 2012.

[4] M. Herlihy. SXM: C# software transactional memory, 2005. www.cs.brown.edu/ mph/SXM/README.doc.

[5] M. Herlihy, V. Luchangco, M. Moir, and W. N. Scherer, III. Software transactional memory for dynamic-sized data structures. In *PODC*, pages 92–101, 2003.

[6] M. Herlihy and J. M. Wing. Linearizability: A correctness condition for concurrent objects. *ACM Trans. Program. Lang. Syst.*, 12(3):463–492, 1990.

[7] D. Perelman, R. Fan, and I. Keidar. On maintaining multiple versions in STM. In *PODC*, pages 16–25, 2010.

Asynchronous Failure Detectors

Alejandro Cornejo
Computer Science and
Artificial Intelligence Lab, MIT
acornejo@csail.mit.edu

Nancy Lynch
Computer Science and
Artificial Intelligence Lab, MIT
lynch@csail.mit.edu

Srikanth Sastry
Computer Science and
Artificial Intelligence Lab, MIT
sastry@csail.mit.edu

ABSTRACT

Failure detectors — oracles that provide information about process crashes — are an important abstraction for crash tolerance in distributed systems. Although current failure-detector theory provides great generality and expressiveness, it also poses significant challenges in developing a robust hierarchy of failure detectors. We address some of these challenges by proposing a variant of failure detectors called *asynchronous failure detectors* and an associated modeling framework. Unlike the traditional failure-detector framework, our framework eschews real time completely. We show that asynchronous failure detectors are sufficiently expressive to include several popular failure detectors. Additionally, we show that asynchronous failure detectors satisfy many desirable properties: they are self-implementable, guarantee that stronger asynchronous failure detectors solve more problems, and ensure that their outputs encode no information other than process crashes. We introduce the notion of a failure detector being *representative* of a problem to capture the idea that some problems encode the same information about process crashes as their weakest failure detectors do. We show that a large class of problems, called *finite problems*, do not have representative failure detectors.

Categories and Subject Descriptors

C.2.4 [**Computer-Communication Networks**]: Distributed Systems; D.4.5 [**Operating Systems**]: Reliability—*fault-tolerance*; F.1.1 [**Computation by Abstract Devices**]: Models of Computation—*computability theory*

General Terms

Algorithms, Reliability, Theory

Keywords

Asynchronous System, Fault-Tolerance, Asynchronous Failure Detector, I/O Automata

PODC'12, July 16–18, 2012, Madeira, Portugal.
Copyright 2012 ACM 978-1-4503-1450-3/12/07 ...$10.00.

1. INTRODUCTION

Failure detectors [5] are a popular mechanism for designing asynchronous distributed algorithms for crash-prone systems. Conceptually, they provide (potentially unreliable) information about process crashes in the system. This information may be leveraged by asynchronous algorithms for crash tolerance. Technically, failure detectors are specified by constraints on their possible outputs, called *histories*, relative to the actual process crashes in the system, called the *fault pattern*. The fault pattern is the 'reality', and the history is an 'approximation' of that reality. A failure detector is a function that maps every fault pattern (the 'reality') to a set of admissible histories (the 'approximations'). The *stronger* a failure detector is, the closer its admissible 'approximations' are to the 'reality'.

We explore the modeling choices made in the traditional failure-detector framework, and we focus on a variant of failure detectors called *asynchronous failure detectors*. We also offer an alternative modeling framework to study the properties of asynchronous failure detectors. Briefly, asynchronous failure detectors are a variant of failure detectors that can be specified without the use of real time, are self-implementable, and interact with the asynchronous processes *unilaterally*; in unilateral interaction, the failure detector provides outputs to the processes continually without any queries from the processes. We show that asynchronous failure detectors retain sufficient expressiveness to include many popular and *realistic* [7] failure detectors while satisfying several desirable properties.

1.1 Background and Motivation

The canonical works [5, 4] pioneered the theory of failure detectors. Results in [5] showed how *sufficient* information about process crashes can be encoded in failure detectors to solve problems in asynchronous systems. Complementary work in [4] showed that some information about crashes is actually *necessary*; in particular, they showed that Ω is a "weakest" failure detector to solve consensus in crash-prone asynchronous systems. Their proposed proof technique has been used to demonstrate weakest failure detectors for many problems in crash-prone asynchronous systems (cf. [8, 24, 11, 14]). Recent results have shown that a large class of problems have a weakest failure detector [17] while yet another class of problems do not have a weakest failure detector [3].

From a modeling perspective, failure detectors mark a departure from conventional descriptions of distributed systems. Conventionally, the behavior of all the entities in a distributed system model — processes, channels, and other entities — are either all asynchronous or are all constrained by the passage of real time. In contrast, in the failure-detector model, only the failure-detector behavior is constrained by real time, whereas the behavior of all other entities is asynchronous. The differences between the two styles of models have been the subject of recent work [6, 17] which has brought the theory of failure detectors under additional scrutiny. We discuss five aspects of failure-detector theory that remain unresolved: self-implementability, interaction mechanism, the kind of information provided by a failure detector, comparing failure-detector strengths, and the relationship between weakest failure detectors and partial synchrony.

Self-Implementability. Failure detectors need not be *self-implementable*. That is, there exist failure detectors (say) D such that it is not possible for any asynchronous distributed algorithm to implement an admissible behavior of D despite having access to the outputs from D. Since a failure detector D' is stronger then a failure detector D iff D' can implement D, we arrive at an unexpected result that a failure detector D need not be comparable to itself.

Jayanti et. al. resolve the issue of self-implementability in [17] by separating the notion of a failure detector from an *implementation of a failure detector*. A failure detector provides outputs to each process at each time instant, but a failure-detector implementation provides outputs only upon being queried. An implementation of a failure detector D is said to be correct if, for every query, the output of the implementation is a valid output of D for some time in the interval between the query and the output. In effect, the definition of "implementing a failure detector" in [17] collapses multiple classes of distinct failure detectors into a single equivalence class.[1] The broader impact of results from [17] on the landscape of failure-detector theory remains unexplored.

Interaction Mechanism. The mechanism proposed in [17] explicitly requires that failure-detector implementations interact with processes via a query-based interface. An alternative interface is one in which failure-detector implementations provide outputs to processes unilaterally and continually, without queries. To our knowledge, the motivation for choosing either interface has not been adequately elucidated despite non-trivial consequences of the choice. For instance, recall that self-implementability of a failure detector in [17] depends critically on the query-based interface. Also, the so-called 'lazy' implementations of failure detectors [10] depend on a query-based interface to ensure communication efficiency; an analogous optimization is not known with a unilateral interface. Therefore, the significance and consequences of the interaction model merit investigation.

Information About Crashes Alone. Whether or not failure detectors can provide information about events other than process crashes has a significant impact on the weakest failure detectors for problems such as Non-Blocking Atomic Commit [14, 15] and Uniform Reliable Broadcast [1, 16]. In order to restrict failure detectors to the ones that give

information only about crashes, the authors in [1] consider failure detectors that are exclusively a function of the fault pattern. In [14], the authors further restrict the universe of failure detectors to *timeless* failure detectors, which provide information only about the set of processes that crash, and no information about *when* they crash. To our knowledge, the necessary and sufficient conditions for failure detectors to provide information about crashes alone remains unresolved.

Comparing Failure Detectors. Not all information provided by failure detectors may be useful in an asynchronous system. For instance, if a failure detector provides the current real-time in its outputs (in addition to other information), the processes cannot use this information because passage of real time is not modeled in an asynchronous system. Suppose we consider two failure detectors D and D' where D is timeless, and D' provides all the information provided by D; additionally D' provides the current real time as well. Clearly, D' is strictly stronger than D. However, since the asynchronous system cannot use the information about real time provided by D', there exist no problems that can be solved in an asynchronous system with D', but that cannot be solved with D. This leads to a curious conclusion: there exist failure detectors (say) D and D' such that D' is strictly stronger than D, and yet D' cannot solve a harder problem than D. This begs the following question: what does the relative strength of failure detectors tell us about the relative hardness of problems they solve?

Weakest Failure Detectors and Partial Synchrony. Failure detectors are often viewed as distributed objects that encode information about the temporal constraints on computation and communication necessary for their implementation; the popular perception is that several failure detectors are substitutable for partial synchrony in distributed systems [19, 21, 20]. Therefore, if a failure detector D is the weakest to solve a problem P, then a natural question follows: is the synchronism encoded in the outputs of D the minimal synchronism necessary to solve P in a crash-prone partially synchronous system? Work to date suggests that the answer is affirmative for some problems [19, 22] and negative for others [6]. To our knowledge, there is no characterization of the problems for which the aforementioned question is answered in the affirmative or in the negative.

Summary. Based on our understanding of the state of the art, we see that failure-detector theory is a very general theory of crash tolerance with important results and novel methods. These results and methods provide a qualitative understanding of the amount of information about crashes necessary and sufficient to solve various problems in asynchronous systems. However, the generality of the theory makes it difficult to develop a robust hierarchy of failure detectors and to determine the relative hardness of solving problems in crash-prone asynchronous systems.

1.2 Contribution

In this paper, we examine a new variant of failure detectors called *asynchronous failure detectors* (AFDs) and we show that they satisfy many desirable properties. We define AFDs through a set of basic properties that we expect any "reasonable" failure detector to satisfy. We demonstrate the expressiveness of AFDs by defining many traditional failure detectors as AFDs. Restricting our focus to AFDs offers several advantages.

---

[1]For example, consider the instantaneously perfect failure detector $\mathcal{P}^+$ [6] which always outputs the exactly the set of crashed processes and the perfect failure detector $\mathcal{P}$ [5] which never suspects live processes and eventually and permanently suspects crashed processes. Under the definition of "implementing a failure detector" from [17], an implementation of $\mathcal{P}^+$ is indistinguishable from an implementation of $\mathcal{P}$.

First, AFDs are self-implementable and their specification does not require real time. Therefore, unlike current failure-detector models, all the entities in the distributed system are asynchronous. In order to specify AFDs, we propose a new modeling framework that completely eschews real time, which allows us to view failure detectors as problems within the asynchronous model. This allows us to compare failure detectors as we compare problems; it also allows us to compare problems with failure detectors, and vice versa.

Second, AFDs provide outputs to the processes unilaterally, without queries. Therefore we preserve the advantages offered by the framework in [17] while ensuring failure detectors provide information only about process crashes.

Third, the hierarchy of AFDs ordered by their relative strength induces an analogous hierarchy of problems ordered by their relative hardness. In fact, if an AFD D is strictly stronger than another AFD D', then we show that the set of problems solvable with D is a strict superset of the set of problems solvable by D.

Fourth, AFDs clarify a relationship between a weakest failure detector to solve a problem and the minimal synchronism that is necessary and sufficient to solve the same problem. We introduce the concept of representative AFDs for a problem. Briefly, an AFD D is "representative" of a problem P iff D is sufficient to solve P and D can be extracted from a (blackbox) solution to P. By construction, the synchronism encoded by the outputs of a representative AFD for a problem P is also the minimal synchronism sufficient to solve P. We show that finite problems (such as consensus and set agreement) do not have a representative AFD, but they have a weakest failure detector [17].

2. I/O AUTOMATA

We use the I/O Automata framework [18] for specifying the system model and failure detectors. Briefly, in the I/O framework each component of a distributed system is modeled as a state machine, where different components interact with each other through input and output actions. This section provides an overview of I/O-Automata-related definitions used in this paper. See [18, Chapter 8] for a thorough description of the I/O Automata framework.

2.1 Definitions

An I/O automaton (or simply, an automaton) is a (possibly infinite) state machine. Formally, an I/O automaton consists of five components: a signature, a set of states, a set of initial states, a state-transition relation, and a set of tasks. We describe these components next.

Actions, Signature, and Tasks. The state transitions in an automaton are associated with named *actions*; the set of actions of an automaton A is denoted $act(A)$. Actions are classified as *input*, *output*, or *internal*, and they constitute the *signature* of the automaton. The set of input, output, and internal actions of an automaton A are denoted $input(A)$, $output(A)$, and $internal(A)$, respectively. Input and output actions are collectively called *external* actions, and output and internal actions are collectively called *locally controlled* actions. The locally controlled actions of an automaton are partitioned into *tasks*.

Internal actions of an automaton are visible only to the automaton itself whereas external actions are visible to other automata as well; automata interact with each other through external actions. Unlike locally controlled actions, input actions arrive from the outside and are assumed not to be under the automaton's control.

States. The set of states of an automaton A is denoted $states(A)$. A non-empty subset $init(A) \subseteq states(A)$ is designated to be the set of *initial states*.

State-Transition relation. The state transitions in an automaton A are restricted by a *state-transition relation*, denoted $trans(A)$, which is a set of tuples of the form (s, a, s') where $s, s' \in states(A)$ and $a \in act(A)$. Each such tuple (s, a, s') is a *transition*, or a *step*, of A.

For a given state s and an action a, if $trans(A)$ has some step of the form (s, a, s'), then a is said to be *enabled* in s. Every input action in A is enabled in all the states of A. A task C, which consists of a set of locally controlled actions, is said to be *enabled* in a state s iff some action in C is enabled in state s.

Intuitively, each step of the form (s, a, s') denotes the following behavior: the automaton A, in state s, performs action a and changes its state to s'.

2.2 Executions And Traces

Now we describe how an automaton executes. An *execution fragment* of an automaton A is a finite sequence $s_0, a_1, s_1, a_2, \ldots, s_{k-1}, a_k, s_k$, or an infinite sequence $s_0, a_1, s_1, a_2, \ldots, s_{k-1}, a_k, s_k, \ldots$, of alternating states and actions of A such that for every $k \geq 0$, action a_{k+1} is enabled in state s_k. An execution fragment that starts with an initial state is called an *execution*. Each occurrence of an action in an execution fragment is said to be an *event*.

A *trace* of an execution denotes only the externally observable behavior. Formally, the trace t of an execution α is the subsequence of α consisting of all the external actions. We say that t is a trace of an automaton A if t is the trace of some execution of A. When referring to specific events in a trace, we use the following convention: if t contains at least x events, then $t[x]$ denotes the xth event in the trace t, and otherwise, $t[x] = \bot$. Throughout this article, we assume that no action is named $\bot$.

It is useful to consider subsequences of traces that contain only certain events. We accomplish this through the notion of a *projection*. Given a sequence of actions t and a set of actions B, the projection of t over B, denoted $t|_B$, is the subsequence of t consisting of exactly the events from B.

2.3 Composing I/O Automata

A collection of I/O automata may be composed by matching output actions of some automata with the same-named input actions of others. Specifically, each output of an automaton may be matched with same-named input of any number of other automata. Upon composition, all the actions with the same name are performed together.

2.4 Fairness

When considering executions of a composition of I/O automata, we are interested in the executions in which all the automata get fair turns to perform steps; such executions are called fair executions.

Recall that in each automaton, the locally controlled actions are partitioned into tasks. An execution fragment α of an automaton A is said to be a *fair execution fragment* iff the following two conditions hold for every task C in A. (1) If α is finite, then no action in C is enabled in the final state of α. (2) If α is infinite, then either (a) α contains infinitely many events from C, or (b) α contains infinitely many occurrences of states in which C is not enabled.

A trace t of A is said to be a *fair trace* if t is the trace of a fair execution of A.

2.5 Deterministic Automata

We define an action a (of an automaton A) to be *deterministic* iff for every state s, there exists at most one transition of the form (s, a, s') in $trans(A)$. We define an automaton A to be *task deterministic* iff (1) for every task C and every state s of A, at most one action in C is enabled in s, and (2) all the actions in A are deterministic. An automaton is said to be *deterministic* iff it is task deterministic, has exactly one task, and has a unique start state.

3. CRASH PROBLEMS

This section provides definitions of problems, distributed problems, crashes, crash problems and asynchronous failure detectors.

3.1 Problems

A *problem* P is a tuple (I_P, O_P, T_P) where I_P and O_P are disjoint sets of actions and T_P is a set of (finite or infinite) sequences over these actions.

Distributed Problems. Here, we introduce a fixed finite set Π of n location IDs; we assume that Π does not contain the element $\perp$.

For a problem P, we define a mapping $loc : I_P \cup O_P \to \Pi \cup \{\perp\}$ which associates an action to a location ID or $\perp$. For an action a, if $loc(a) = i$ and $i \in \Pi$, then a is said to *occur at* i. Problem P is said to be *distributed* over Π if, for every action $a \in I_P \cup O_P$, $loc(a) \in \Pi$.

For convenience, the location of each action is included in the name of the action as a subscript; for instance, if an action a occurs at i, then the action is named a_i.

Crash Problems. We posit the existence of a set of actions $\{crash_i | i \in \Pi\}$, denoted $\hat{I}$; according to our conventions $loc(crash_i) = i$. A problem $P \equiv (I_P, O_P, T_P)$ that is distributed over Π, is said to be a *crash problem* iff, for each $i \in \Pi$, $crash_i$ is an action in I_P; that is, $\hat{I} \subseteq I_P$.

Given a sequence $t \in T_P$, $faulty(t)$ denotes the set of locations at which a *crash* event occurs in t. Similarly, $live(t)$ denotes the set of locations for which a *crash* event does not occur in t. The locations in $faulty(t)$ are said to be *faulty* in t, and the locations in $live(t)$ are said to be *live* in t.

For convenience, we assume that for any two distinct crash problems $P \equiv (I_P, O_P, T_P)$ and $P' \equiv (I_{P'}, O_{P'}, T_{P'})$, $(I_P \cup O_P) \cap (I_{P'} \cup O_{P'}) = \hat{I}$. The foregoing assumption simplifies the issues involving composition of automata; we discuss these in Section 5.

3.2 Asynchronous Failure Detectors

Recall that a failure detector is an oracle that provides information about crash failures. In our modeling framework, we view failure detectors as a special type of crash problems and are called *asynchronous failure detectors*. A necessary condition for a crash problem $P \equiv (I_P, O_P, T_P)$ to be an asynchronous failure detector is *crash exclusivity*, which states that $I_P = \hat{I}$; that is, the actions I_P are exactly the *crash* actions. Crash exclusivity guarantees that the only inputs to a failure detector are the *crash* events, and hence, failure detectors provide information only about

crashes. An asynchronous failure detector also satisfies additional properties, but before describing these properties formally we need some auxiliary definitions.

Let $D \equiv (\hat{I}, O_D, T_D)$ be a crash problem. For each $i \in \Pi$, $\mathcal{F}_i$ is the set of actions in O_D at i; thus, $O_D = \cup_{i \in \Pi} \mathcal{F}_i$. We begin by defining the following terms. Let t be an arbitrary sequence over $\hat{I} \cup O_D$.

Valid sequences. The sequence t is said to be *valid* iff (1) for every $i \in \Pi$, no event in O_D occurs at i after a $crash_i$ event in t, and (2) if no $crash_i$ event occurs in t, then t contains infinitely many events in O_D at i.

Sampling. A sequence t' is a *sampling* of t iff (1) t' is a subsequence t, (2) for every location $i \in \Pi$, (a) if i is live in t, then $t'|_{\mathcal{F}_i} = t|_{\mathcal{F}_i}$, and (b) if i is faulty in t, then i is faulty in t' and $t'|_{\mathcal{F}_i}$ is a prefix of $t|_{\mathcal{F}_i}$.

Constrained reordering. Let t' be a permutation of events in t; t' is *constrained reordering* of t iff, for every pair of events e and e', if (1) e precedes e' in t and (2) either $loc(e) = loc(e')$, or $e \in \hat{I}$, then e precedes e' in t' as well.

Now we define an asynchronous failure detector. A crash problem of the form $D \equiv (\hat{I}, O_D, T_D)$ (which satisfies crash exclusivity) is an *asynchronous failure detector* (AFD, for short) iff D satisfies the following properties.

Validity. Every sequence $t \in T_D$ is valid.

Closure Under Sampling. For every sequence $t \in T_D$, every sampling of t is in T_D.

Closure Under Constrained Reordering. For every sequence $t \in T_D$, every constrained reordering of t is in T_D.

A brief motivation for the above properties is in order. The validity property ensures that after a location crashes, no outputs occur at that location, and if a location does not crash, outputs occur infinitely often at that location. Closure under sampling permits a failure detector to 'skip' or 'miss' any suffix of outputs at a faulty location. Finally, closure under constrained reordering permits 'delaying' output events at any location.

3.3 Examples of AFDs

Here, we specify some of the failure detectors that are most widely used and cited in literature, as AFDs.

The Leader Election Oracle. Informally, Ω continually outputs a location ID at each location; eventually and permanently, Ω outputs the ID of a unique live location at all the live locations.

We specify our version of $\Omega \equiv (\hat{I}, O_\Omega, T_\Omega)$ as follows. The action set $O_\Omega = \cup_{i \in \Pi} \mathcal{F}_i$, where, for each $i \in \Pi$, $\mathcal{F}_i = \{FD\text{-}\Omega(j)_i | j \in \Pi\}$. T_Ω is the set of all valid sequences t over $\hat{I} \cup O_\Omega$ that satisfy the following property: *if $live(t) \neq \emptyset$, then there exists a location $l \in live(t)$ and a suffix t_{suff} of t such that, $t_{suff}|_{O_\Omega}$ is a sequence over the set $\{FD\text{-}\Omega(l)_i | i \in live(t)\}$.*

Perfect and Eventually Perfect Failure Detectors. Here we specify two popular failure detectors among the canonical failure detector from [5]: the perfect failure detector $\mathcal{P}$ and the eventually perfect failure detector $\Diamond\mathcal{P}$. Informally, $\mathcal{P}$ never suspects any location (say) i until event $crash_i$ occurs, and it eventually and permanently suspects crashed locations; $\Diamond\mathcal{P}$ eventually and permanently never suspects live locations and eventually and permanently suspects faulty locations.

We specify our version of $\mathcal{P} \equiv (\hat{I}, O_\mathcal{P}, T_\mathcal{P})$ as follows. The action set $O_\mathcal{P} = \cup_{i \in \Pi} \mathcal{F}_i$, where, for each $i \in \Pi$, $\mathcal{F}_i = \{FD\text{-}\mathcal{P}(S)_i | S \in 2^\Pi\}$. $T_\mathcal{P}$ is the set of all valid sequences

t over $\hat{I} \cup O_{\mathcal{P}}$ that satisfy the following two properties. (1) For every prefix t_{pre} of t, if $i \in live(t_{pre})$, then for each $j \in \Pi$ and for every event of the form $FD\text{-}\mathcal{P}(S)_j$ in t_{pre}, $i \notin S$. (2) There exists a suffix t_{sus} of t such that, for every $i \in faulty(t)$, for each $j \in \Pi$, and for every event of the form $FD\text{-}\mathcal{P}(S)_j$ in t_{sus}, $i \in S$.

We specify our version $\Diamond\mathcal{P} \equiv (\hat{I}, O_{\Diamond\mathcal{P}}, T_{\Diamond\mathcal{P}})$ as follows. The action set $O_{\Diamond\mathcal{P}} = \cup_{i \in \Pi} \mathcal{F}_i$, where, for each $i \in \Pi$, $\mathcal{F}_i = \{FD\text{-}\Diamond\mathcal{P}(S)_i | S \in 2^{\Pi}\}$. $T_{\Diamond\mathcal{P}}$ is the set of all valid sequences t over $\hat{I} \cup O_{\Diamond\mathcal{P}}$ that satisfy the following two properties. (1) There exists a suffix t_{trust} of t such that, for every pair of locations $i, j \in live(t)$, and for every event of the form $FD\text{-}\Diamond\mathcal{P}(S)_j$ in t_{trust}, $i \notin S$. (2) There exists a suffix t_{sus} of t such that, for every $i \in faulty(t)$, for each $j \in live(t)$, and for every event of the form $FD\text{-}\Diamond\mathcal{P}(S)_j$ in t_{sus}, $i \in S$.

It is easy to see that $\Omega \equiv (\hat{I}, O_{\Omega}, T_{\Omega})$, $\mathcal{P} \equiv (\hat{I}, \hat{O}, T_{\mathcal{P}})$ and $\Diamond\mathcal{P} \equiv (\hat{I}, \hat{O}, T_{\Diamond\mathcal{P}})$ satisfy all the properties of an AFD and the proof of the aforementioned assertion is left as an exercise for the reader. Similarly, it is straightforward to specify failure detectors like Ω^k and Ψ_k as AFDs.

4. SYSTEM MODEL AND DEFINITIONS

An asynchronous system is modeled as the composition of a collection of the following I/O automata: process automata, channel automata, a crash automaton, and possibly other automata (including a failure-detector automata).

Process Automata. The system contains a collection of n process automata: one process automaton at each location. Each process automaton is a deterministic automaton whose actions occur at a single location. A process automaton whose actions occur at i is denoted $proc(i)$. It has an input action $crash_i$ which is an output from the crash automaton; when $crash_i$ occurs, it permanently disables all locally controlled actions of $proc(i)$. The process automaton $proc(i)$ sends and receives messages through a set of output actions $\{send(m, j)_i | m \in \mathcal{M} \wedge j \in \Pi \setminus \{i\}\}$, and a set of input actions $\{receive(m, j)_i | m \in \mathcal{M} \wedge j \in \Pi \setminus \{i\}\}$, respectively. In addition, process automata may interact with the environment automaton and other automata through additional actions.

A *distributed algorithm* A is a collection of process automata, one at each location; for convenience, we write A_i for the process automaton $proc(i)$ at i.

Channel Automata. For every ordered pair (i, j) of distinct locations, the system contains a channel automaton $C_{i,j}$. The input actions are $\{send(m, j)_i | m \in \mathcal{M}\}$, which are outputs from the process automaton at i. The output actions are $\{receive(m, i)_j | m \in \mathcal{M}\}$, which are inputs to the process automaton at j. Each such channel automaton implements a *reliable FIFO link*.

Crash Automaton. The crash automaton contains the set $\{crash_i | i \in \Pi\} \equiv \hat{I}$ of output actions and no input actions. Every sequence over $\hat{I}$ is a fair trace of the crash automaton.

Environment Automaton. The environment automaton, denoted $\mathcal{E}$, models the external world with which the distributed system interacts. The external signature of the environment matches the input and output actions of the process automata that do not interact with other automata in the system. The set of fair traces that constitute the externally observable behavior of $\mathcal{E}$ specifies "well-formedness" restrictions, which vary from one system to another.

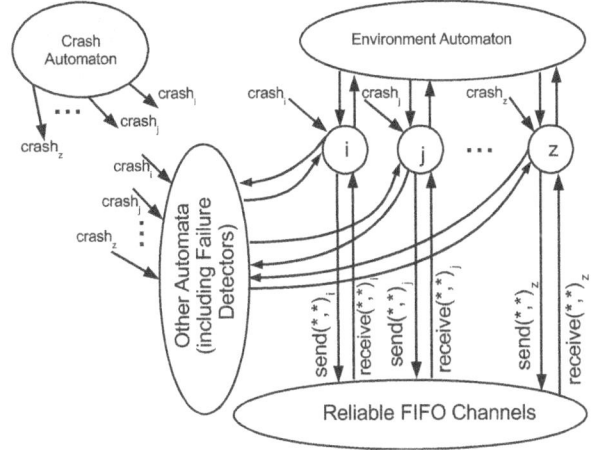

Figure 1: Interaction diagram for a message-passing asynchronous distributed system augmented with a failure detector automaton.

Other Automata. The system may contain other automata with which the process automata and the crash automaton interact. Typically, these automata *solve* a crash problem, as defined in the next section.

5. SOLVING PROBLEMS

In this section, we define what it means for an automaton to solve a crash problem and for a distributed algorithm to solve a crash problem. We also define what it means for a system to solve a crash problem P using another crash problem P'. We use the aforementioned definitions to define what it means for an AFD to be sufficient to solve a crash problem, and vice versa.

5.1 Solving a Crash Problem

An automaton U *solves* a crash problem $P \equiv (I_P, O_P, T_P)$ in an environment $\mathcal{E}$, if (1) the input actions of U are I_P, and the output actions of U are O_P, (2) the input actions of $\mathcal{E}$ are O_P, and the output actions of $\mathcal{E}$ are $I_P \setminus \hat{I}$, and (3) the set of fair traces of the composition of U, $\mathcal{E}$, and the crash automaton is a subset of T_P.

A distributed algorithm A *solves a crash problem P in an environment $\mathcal{E}$* (or, A solves P in $\mathcal{E}$), iff the automaton $\hat{A}$, which is obtained by composing A with the channel automata, solves P in $\mathcal{E}$. A crash problem P is said to be *solvable* in an environment $\mathcal{E}$, iff there exists a distributed algorithm A such that A solves P in $\mathcal{E}$. If a crash problem is not solvable in $\mathcal{E}$, then it is said to be *unsolvable* in $\mathcal{E}$.

5.2 Using One Crash Problem to Solve Another

Often, an unsolvable crash problem P may be solvable in a system that contains an automaton that solves some *other* unsolvable crash problem P'. We describe the relationship between P and P' as follows.

A distributed algorithm A *solves a crash problem P using another crash problem P' in an environment $\mathcal{E}$* (or succinctly, A solves P using P' in $\mathcal{E}$), iff the following is true. Let $\hat{A}$ be the composition of A with the channel automata, the crash automaton, and the environment $\mathcal{E}$. For every fair trace t of $\hat{A}$, if $t|_{I_{P'} \cup O_{P'}} \in T_{P'}$, then $t|_{I_P \cup O_P} \in T_P$.

We say that a crash problem $P' \equiv (I_{P'}, O_{P'}, T_{P'})$ *is sufficient to solve* a crash problem $P \equiv (I_P.O_P, T_P)$, in environment $\mathcal{E}$, denoted $P' \succeq_{\mathcal{E}} P$ iff there exists a distributed algorithm A that solves P using P' in $\mathcal{E}$. If $P' \succeq_{\mathcal{E}} P$, then also we say that P *is solvable using* P' in $\mathcal{E}$. If no such distributed algorithm exists, then we state that P is *unsolvable* using P' in $\mathcal{E}$, and we denote it as $P' \not\succeq_{\mathcal{E}} P$.

It is worth noting that in the foregoing definition, the problems P and P' must be distinct in order for automata composition to be applicable. However, it is useful to consider problems that are "sufficient to solve themselves"; that is, given a crash problem P and an environment $\mathcal{E}$, it is useful to define the following relation: $P \succeq_{\mathcal{E}} P$. We do so using the notion of renaming.

5.2.1 Renaming and Self-Implementability

A crash problem $P' \equiv (I_{P'}, O_{P'}, T_{P'})$ is said to be a *renaming* of a crash problem $P \equiv (I_P, O_P, T_P)$ iff (1) $(I_P \cup O_P) \cap (I_{P'} \cup O_{P'}) = \hat{I}$, and there exist bijections $r_{IO} : I_P \cup O_P \rightarrow I_{P'} \cup O_{P'}$ and $r_T : T_D \rightarrow T_{P'}$ such that, (1) for each $a \in \hat{I}$, $r_{IO}(a) = a$, for each $a \in I_P \setminus \hat{I}$, $r_{IO}(a) \in I_{P'} \setminus \hat{I}$, for each $a \in O_P$, $r_{IO}(a) \in O_{P'}$, (2) for each action $a \in I_P \cup O_P$, $loc(a) = loc(r_{IO}(a))$, and (3) for each $t \in T_P$ and for each $x \in \mathbb{N}^+$, if $t[x] \neq \bot$, then $r_T(t)[x] = r_{IO}(t[x])$.

Now, we can define the solvability of a crash problem P using itself as follows. We say that a crash problem P is *self-implementable* in environment $\mathcal{E}$, denoted $P \succeq_{\mathcal{E}} P$, iff there exists a renaming P' of P such that $P \succeq_{\mathcal{E}} P'$.

5.3 Using and Solving AFDs

Since an AFD is simply a kind of crash problem, we have automatic definitions for the following notions. (1) A distributed algorithm A solves an AFD D in environment $\mathcal{E}$. (2) A distributed algorithm A solves a crash problem P using an AFD D in environment $\mathcal{E}$. (3) An AFD D is sufficient to solve a crash problem P in environment $\mathcal{E}$. (4) A distributed algorithm A solves an AFD D using a crash problem P in environment $\mathcal{E}$. (5) A crash problem P is sufficient to solve an AFD D in environment $\mathcal{E}$. (6) A distributed algorithm A solves an AFD D' using another AFD D in environment $\mathcal{E}$. (7) An AFD D is sufficient to solve another AFD D' in environment $\mathcal{E}$. (8) An AFD D is self-implementable in environment $\mathcal{E}$.

We remark that when we talk about solving an AFD, the environment $\mathcal{E}$ has no output actions because the AFD has no input actions except for $\hat{I}$, which are inputs from the crash automaton. Therefore, we have the following lemma.

LEMMA 1. *For a crash-problem P, an AFD D, and an environment $\mathcal{E}$, if $P \succeq_{\mathcal{E}} D$, then for any other environment $\mathcal{E}'$ with the same external signature as $\mathcal{E}$, $P \succeq_{\mathcal{E}'} D$.*

Consequently, when we refer to an AFD D being solvable using a crash problem (or an AFD) P, we generally omit the reference to the environment automaton and simply say that P is sufficient to solve D; we denote this relationship by $P \succeq D$. Analogously, when we refer to a D being unsolvable using P, we denote this relationship by $P \not\succeq D$.

Finally, if an AFD D is sufficient to solve another AFD D', then we state that D *is stronger than* D', and we denote that $D \succeq D'$. If $D \succeq D'$, but $D' \not\succeq D$, then we say that D is *strictly stronger than* D', and we denote that $D \succ D'$.

Next, we consider reflexivity of the $\succeq$ relation between AFDs. We show that for every AFD D, $D \succeq D$ must be true; that is, every AFD is self-implementable.

6. SELF-IMPLEMENTABILITY OF AFDS

Within the traditional definitions of failure detectors, it is well known that not all failure detectors self-implementable (see [6] for a detailed discussion). In contrast we show that every AFD is self-implementable. Recall that an AFD D is self-implementable, denoted $D \succeq D$, iff there exists a renaming D' of D such that $D \succeq D'$.

Algorithm For Self-Implementability. We provide a distributed algorithm $\mathcal{A}^{self}$ that demonstrates self implementability of an arbitrary AFD D. First, we fix an arbitrary AFD $D \equiv (\hat{I}, O_D, T_D)$. Let $D' \equiv (\hat{I}, O_{D'}, T_{D'})$ be a renaming of D. Let $r_{IO} : O_D \rightarrow O_{D'}$ and $r_T : T_D \rightarrow T_{D'}$ be the bijections that define the renaming. That is, for each $t \in T_D$ and for each $x \in \mathbb{N}^+$, if $t[x] \neq \bot$, then $r_T(t)[x] = r_{IO}(t[x])$. The $\mathcal{A}^{self}$ automaton leverages the information provided by AFD D to solve D'.

The distributed algorithm $\mathcal{A}^{self}$ is a collection of automata $\mathcal{A}_i^{self}$, one for each location $i \in \Pi$. Each automaton $\mathcal{A}_i^{self}$ has the following signature. (1) An input action $crash_i$ which is the output action from the crash automaton. (2) The set of input actions $\mathcal{F}_i = \{d | d \in O_D \wedge (loc(d) = i)\}$ which are outputs of the failure-detector automaton D. (3) The set of output actions $\mathcal{F}_i' = \{r_{IO}(d) | d \in \mathcal{F}_i\}$.

At each location i, $\mathcal{A}_i^{self}$ maintains a queue fdq of elements from the range O_D; fdq is initially empty. When event $d \in \mathcal{F}_i$ occurs at location i, $\mathcal{A}_i^{self}$ adds d to the queue fdq. The precondition for action $d' \in \mathcal{F}_i'$ at i is that the head of the queue fdq at i is $r_{IO}^{-1}(d')$. When this precondition is satisfied, and event d' occurs at i, the effect of this event is to remove $r_{IO}^{-1}(d')$ from the head of fdq. Finally, when event $crash_i$ occurs, the effect of this event is to disable the output actions $\mathcal{F}_i'$ permanently. The pseudocode for $\mathcal{A}^{self}$ is available in Algorithm 1.

Algorithm 1 Algorithm for showing self-implementability of asynchronous failure-detector.

The automaton $\mathcal{A}_i^{self}$ at each location i.
Signature:
    input $d_i : O_D$ at location i, $crash_i$
    output $d_i' : O_{D'}$ at location i
Variables:
    fdq: queue of elements from O_D, initially empty
    failed: Boolean, initially *false*
Actions:
    input *crash*
    effect
        failed := *true*
    input d
    effect
        add d to fdq
    output d'
    precondition
        $(\neg failed) \wedge (fdq \text{ not empty}) \wedge (r_{IO}^{-1}(d') = head(fdq))$
    effect
        delete head of fdq

Correctness. The proof of correctness follows from closure under sampling and closure under constrained reordering, but is omitted due to space constraints.

THEOREM 2. *The distributed algorithm $\mathcal{A}^{self}$ uses AFD D to solve a renaming of D.*

From Theorem 2 we have the following as a corollary.

COROLLARY 3. *Every AFD is self-implementable: for every AFD D, $D \succeq D$.*

An immediate consequence of Corollary 3 is that we can take the union of the relation $\succeq$ between distinct AFDs and the $\succeq$ relation comparing an AFD and claim that the $\succeq$ relation is transitive. This is captured in the following lemma.

LEMMA 4. *Given AFDs D, D', and D'', if $D \succeq D'$ and $D' \succeq D''$, then $D \succeq D''$.*

7. AFDS AND OTHER CRASH PROBLEMS

In this section, we explore the relative solvability among AFDs and the consequences of such relative solvability on other crash problems that can be solved using AFDs. Section 7.1 shows that if an AFD D' is strictly stronger than another AFD D, then the set of problems that D' can solve in a given environment is a strict superset of the set of problems solvable by D in the same environment. Section 7.2 revisits the traditional notion of a *weakest failure detector* for a problem and defines what it means for an AFD to be a *weakest* to solve a crash problem in a given set of environments. We also introduce the notion of an AFD begin *representative* of a problem in a given set of environments. Section 7.3 shows that a large class of problems, which we call *finite problems*, do not have a representative AFD.

7.1 Comparing AFDs

Traditionally, as defined in [4], a failure detector $\mathcal{D}$ is stronger than a failure detector $\mathcal{D}'$ if $\mathcal{D}$ is sufficient to solve $\mathcal{D}'$. This definition immediately implies that every problem solvable in some environment using $\mathcal{D}'$ is also solvable in the same environment using $\mathcal{D}$. However, this definition does not imply the converse; if in every environment every problem solvable using $\mathcal{D}'$ is also solvable using $\mathcal{D}$, then it is not necessarily the case that $\mathcal{D}$ is stronger than $\mathcal{D}'$.

We demonstrate that in our framework, the converse must also be true; that is, given two AFDs D and D', every crash problem solvable using D' in a some environment is also solvable using D in the same environment iff D is stronger than D'. This is captured by the following theorem:

THEOREM 5. *For every pair of AFDs D and D', $D \succeq D'$ iff for every crash problem P, and every environment $\mathcal{E}$, $D' \succeq_{\mathcal{E}} P \rightarrow D \succeq_{\mathcal{E}} P$.*

PROOF. The proof is immediate for the case where $D = D'$. For the remainder of the proof we fix D and D' to be distinct AFDs.

Claim 1: Let $D \succeq D'$. Fix P to be a crash problem and $\mathcal{E}$ to be an environment. If $D' \succeq_{\mathcal{E}} P$, then $D \succeq_{\mathcal{E}} P$.

PROOF. Assume $D' \succeq_{\mathcal{E}} P$. There exists a distributed algorithm $\mathcal{A}^P$ such that for every fair trace t of the composition of $\mathcal{A}^P$, with the crash automaton, the channel automata, and $\mathcal{E}$, if $t|_{\hat{I} \cup O_{D'}} \in T_{D'}$, then $t|_{I_P \cup O_P} \in T_P$.

Since $D \succeq D'$, there exists a distributed algorithm $\mathcal{A}^{D'}$ such that for every fair trace t of the composition of $\mathcal{A}^{D'}$ with the crash automaton and the channel automata, $t|_{\hat{I} \cup O_D} \in$

$T_D \Rightarrow t|_{\hat{I} \cup O_{D'}} \in T_{D'}$. Let $\mathcal{A}$ be a distributed algorithm where each $\mathcal{A}_i$ at location i is obtained by composing $\mathcal{A}_i^P$ and $\mathcal{A}_i^{D'}$. Let T_A be the set of all fair traces t of the composition of $\mathcal{A}$ with the crash automaton and the channel automata such that $t|_{\hat{I} \cup O_D} \in T_D$. By the construction of $\mathcal{A}^{D'}$, we know that for each such trace t, $t|_{\hat{I} \cup O_{D'}} \in T_{D'}$. Then, by the construction of $\mathcal{A}^P$, we have that $t|_{I_P \cup O_P} \in T_P$, which immediately implies $D \succeq_{\mathcal{E}} P$. □

Claim 2: If, for every crash problem P and every environment $\mathcal{E}$, $D' \succeq_{\mathcal{E}} P \rightarrow D \succeq_{\mathcal{E}} P$, then $D \succeq D'$.

PROOF. Suppose $D' \succeq_{\mathcal{E}} P \rightarrow D \succeq_{\mathcal{E}} P$, for every crash problem P and environment $\mathcal{E}$. Specifically, $D' \succeq D' \rightarrow D \succeq D'$. Applying Corollary 3, we conclude $D \succeq D'$. □

The theorem follows directly from Claims 1 and 2. □

COROLLARY 6. *Given two AFDs D and D' where $D \succ D'$, there exists a crash problem P and an environment $\mathcal{E}$ such that $D \succeq_{\mathcal{E}} P$, but $D' \not\succeq_{\mathcal{E}} P$; that is, there exists some problem P and an environment $\mathcal{E}$ such that D is sufficient to solve P in $\mathcal{E}$, but D' is not sufficient to solve P in $\mathcal{E}$.*

PROOF. If $D \succ D'$, then $D' \not\succeq D$. By the contrapositive of Theorem 5, there exists a problem P and an environment $\mathcal{E}$ such that $D \succeq_{\mathcal{E}} P$ and $D' \not\succeq_{\mathcal{E}} P$. □

7.2 Weakest and Representative AFDs

The issue of weakest failure detectors for problems was originally tackled in [4] in which a failure detector D is defined as a *weakest* to solve a problem P if the following two conditions are satisfied: (1) D is sufficient to solve P, and (2) any failure detector D' that is sufficient to solve P is stronger than D. This definition can be directly translated to our framework as follows.

An AFD D is *weakest* for a crash problem P in an environment $\mathcal{E}$ iff (1) $D \succeq_{\mathcal{E}} P$ and (2) for every AFD D' such that $D' \succeq_{\mathcal{E}} P$, $D' \succeq D$. An AFD D is a *weakest* for a crash problem P in a set of environments $\widehat{\mathcal{E}}$ iff for every $\mathcal{E} \in \widehat{\mathcal{E}}$, D is weakest for P in $\mathcal{E}$.

There have been many results that demonstrate weakest failure detectors for various problems. The proof techniques used to demonstrate these results have been of two distinct styles. The first proof technique was first proposed in [4] and is as follows. To show that D_P, which is sufficient to solve P, is the weakest failure detector to solve problem P it considers an arbitrary failure detector D that is sufficient to solve the problem P using an algorithm $\mathcal{A}$. It then constructs a distributed algorithm that exchanges the failure detector D's outputs and then continually simulates runs of $\mathcal{A}$ using the set of D's outputs available so far. From these simulations, an admissible output for D_P is extracted. This proof technique has been used to determine a weakest failure detector for the so-called one-shot problems such as consensus [4] and k-set consensus[11].

The second proof technique is simpler and follows from mutual reducibility. To show that D_P, which is sufficient to solve P, is the weakest failure detector to solve problem P, it uses a solution to P as a 'black box' to design a distributed algorithm whose outputs satisfy D_P. This proof technique has been used to determine a weakest failure detector for long-lived problems such as mutual exclusion [9, 2], contention managers [12], and dining philosophers [22].

A natural question is, "does the mutual-reducibility based proof technique work for determining weakest failure detectors for one-shot problems?" We answer this question negatively by introducing the notion of a representative AFD.

Representative AFD. Informally, an AFD is representative of a crash problem if the AFD can be used to solve the crash problem and conversely, a solution to the problem can be used to solve (or implement) the AFD.

Formally, an AFD D is *representative* of a problem P in an environment $\mathcal{E}$ iff $D \succeq_{\mathcal{E}} P$ and $P \succeq D$. An AFD D is *representative* of problem P in a set of environments $\widehat{\mathcal{E}}$ iff for every environment $\mathcal{E} \in \widehat{\mathcal{E}}$, D is representative of P in $\mathcal{E}$.

Observe that if an AFD D is representative of a crash problem P in $\widehat{\mathcal{E}}$, then D is also a weakest AFD to solve P in $\widehat{\mathcal{E}}$. However, the converse need not be true. Specifically if D is a weakest AFD to solve problem P in $\widehat{\mathcal{E}}$, it is not necessary for D to be representative of P in $\widehat{\mathcal{E}}$.

In particular, we highlight that the weakest failure detector results in [23, 22, 13] establish that the eventually perfect failure detector is representative for eventually fair schedulers, dining under eventual weak exclusion, and boosting obstruction-freedom to wait-freedom, respectively.

Next, we show that a large class of problems (which we call finite problems) do not have a representative failure detector despite having a weakest failure detector.

7.3 Finite Problems and Representative AFDs

In this subsection we define the notion of a finite problem, which captures what is often referred to as one-shot problems. Informally speaking, finite problems are those that have a bounded number of interactions with the environment. Examples of finite problems include consensus, leader election, terminating reliable broadcast, and k-set agreement. Examples of problems that are not finite problems include mutual exclusion, Dining Philosophers, synchronizers, and other long-lived problems.

Before we define finite problems we need some auxiliary definitions. A problem P is *crash independent* if, for every finite prefix t_{pre} of a trace $t \in T_P$, $t_{pre}|_{I_P \cup O_P \setminus \hat{I}}$ is a finite prefix of some $t' \in T_P$ such that $t'|_{\hat{I}}$ is empty. In other words, for every prefix t_{pre} of every trace $t \in T_P$, the subsequence of t_{pre} consisting of exactly the non-crash events is a prefix of some crash-free trace in T_P. For each $t \in T_P$, let $len(t)$ denote the length of the subsequence of t that consists of all non-crash events. A problem P has *bounded length* if there exists a $b_P \in \mathbb{N}^+$ such that, for every $t \in T_P$, $len(t) \leq b_P$.

If a problem P is crash independent and has bounded length we say that P is a *finite problem*.

Before we state the main theorem of this section, recall that an *unsolvable problem* is one that cannot be solved in a purely asynchronous system (i.e. without failure detectors).

THEOREM 7. *If P is a finite problem that is unsolvable in an environment $\mathcal{E}$ then P does not have a representative AFD in $\mathcal{E}$.*

Proof sketch. Suppose by contradiction that P is a finite problem that is unsolvable in an environment $\mathcal{E}$, and some AFD D is representative of P in $\mathcal{E}$. Therefore, there exists a distributed algorithm A^P that uses P to solve D, and conversely there exists a distributed algorithm A^D which uses D to solve P in $\mathcal{E}$. First we state the following lemma.

LEMMA 8. *There exists a crash-free finite execution α_{ref} of A having a trace t_{ref} such that (1) $t_{ref}|_{I_P \cup O_P} \in T_P$, (2) there are no messages in transit in the final state of α_{ref}, and (3) for every fair execution α' that extends α_{ref}, the suffix of α' following α_{ref} has no events in $I_P \cup O_P \setminus \hat{I}$.*

Before proving Lemma 8, we show why it implies the theorem. From Lemma 8, and crash independence of P, it follows that for any fair execution α' (and its associated trace t') of A that extends α_{ref} then $t'|_{I_P \cup O_P} \in T_P$. Since A solves D using P we have that $t'|_{I_D \cup O_D} \in T_D$.

For each $i \in \Pi$, let s_i be the state of process automaton at i at the end of α_{ref} and let f_i denote the sequence of events from O_D at location i in α_{ref}. Next, we describe a distributed algorithm A' which, in every fair execution, guarantees that each process i will first output the sequence f_i and then behave as A^P would behave when starting at state s_i.

The distributed algorithm A' which is identical to A^P except in the following ways at each $i \in \Pi$. (1) A'_i has an additional variable fdq_i that is a queue of failure-detector outputs and its initial value is f_i. (2) The initial values of all other variables in A'_i corresponds to the state s_i. (3) For every output action $a_i \in O_D$ at i, A'_i has two actions $int(a_i)$ and a_i: (a) $int(a_i)$ is an internal action whose associated state transitions are the same as action a_i in A^P_i except that, additionally, $int(a_i)$ enqueues the element a_i to fdq_i. (b) a_i is enabled when element a_i is at the head of fdq_i. The effect of a_i is to delete the element a_i from the head of fdq_i. (4) A'_i does not contain any action from $I_P \cup O_P \setminus \hat{I}$.

By construction and the FIFO property of the queues in A' we have the following lemma.

LEMMA 9. *For every fair execution α (and its trace t) of A' with the channel automata and the crash automaton, there exists a fair execution α_{A^P} (and its trace t_{A^P}) of the composition of A^P with the crash automaton, and the channel automaton where $t_{A^P}|_{I_P \cup O_P} \in T_P$ such that the following is true. (1) α_{ref} is a prefix of α_{A^P}. (2) $t|_{\hat{I} \cup O_D}$ is constrained reordering of a sampling of $t_{A^P}|_{\hat{I} \cup O_D}$.*

Lemma 9 implies that any fair execution α of A' produces a trace t such that $t|_{I_D \cup O_D} \in T_D$, and therefore A' solves D. Therefore, by composing A'_i and A^P_i (and their respective channel automata) at each location i, we obtain a distributed algorithm that solves P in $\mathcal{E}$; that is, P is solvable in $\mathcal{E}$. But P is assumed to be unsolvable in $\mathcal{E}$. Thus, we have a contradiction, and that completes the proof of Theorem 7. $\square$

Proof of Lemma 8. Let σ be the set of all fair executions of A such that for any trace t produced by an execution in σ it is true that $t|_{I_P \cup O_P} \in T_P$. Let α_{max} be an execution in σ which produces the trace t_{max} that maximizes $len(t_{max}|_{I_P \cup O_P})$.

Let $\alpha_{s.pre}$ be the shortest prefix of the execution α_{max} which contains all events of $I_P \cup O_P$. Since P is bounded length it follows that such a prefix exists and is finite, and furthermore, any extension of $\alpha_{s.pre}$ does not include any events from $I_P \cup O_P \setminus \hat{I}$ because $len(t_{max}|_{I_P \cup O_P})$ is maximal. We extend $\alpha_{s.pre}$ to another finite execution α_{pre} by appending *receive* events for every message that is in transit at the end of $\alpha_{s.pre}$ such so that no message is in transit (and the channels are 'quiescent') at the end of α_{pre}

Let Π_C be the set of crashed locations in α_{pre}, and observe that by assumption after the first $crash_i$ event in α_{pre},

$proc(i)$ does not perform any outputs in α_{pre}. Let α_{ref} be identical to α_{pre} except that all crash events have been removed. For a location $i \notin \Pi_C$ the executions α_{pre} and α_{ref} are indistinguishable, and therefore $proc(i)$ must produce the same output in both executions. For a location $i \in \Pi_C$ the executions α_{pre} and α_{ref} are indistinguishable up to the point where the first event $crash_i$ occurs in α_{pre}, and after that point there is no other output at i in α_{pre}; therefore $proc(i)$ must produce the same output in both executions. Thus, α_{ref} is a finite crash-free execution that fulfills the requirements for the lemma. $\square$

8. WEAKEST AFD FOR CONSENSUS

In a seminal result [4], Chandra et. al. established that Ω is a weakest failure detector to solve crash-tolerant binary consensus. Recasting the arguments from [4] in our modeling framework yields a simpler proof. The proof is split into two parts, which we discuss separately.

In the first part, as in [4], we construct a tree of possible executions of an AFD-based solution to consensus. However, in [4], each edge of such a tree corresponds to a single event whereas in our framework, each edge corresponds to a task, which represents a collection of events. Therefore, we reduce the number of cases for which we have analyze the tree. Specifically, we look for transitions from a bivalent to a monovalent execution.[2] Furthermore, the proof in [4] considers a forest of executions, where each tree in the forest corresponds to a single configuration of the inputs to consensus. In contrast, our framework treats inputs for consensus as events that are performed by the environment automaton. Therefore, we need analyze only a single tree of executions. These, two factors simplify the analysis of AFD-based consensus significantly and yield the following (paraphrased) claim, which may be of independent interest.

Claim. In the tree of all possible executions of a system solving consensus using an AFD, the events responsible for the transition from a bivalent to a univalent execution occur at a live location.

The second part of the proof uses the above claim to show that Ω is a weakest AFD to solve consensus. The arguments are similar to the ones presented in [4], but are simplified by the above claim.

As in [4], we present a distributed algorithm A^Ω which receives the outputs from the AFD D (which is sufficient to solve consensus) and solves Ω. The process automata exchange the AFD outputs among each other. Based on their current knowledge of the AFD outputs at various locations, A_i^Ω at each location i continually determines a finite "canonical" FD sequence, denoted t_i, which is a prefix of some sequence in T_D. Furthermore, as the execution proceeds, A_i^Ω at each location i obtains increasingly longer sequences of AFD outputs from other locations. Thus, at each live location i, A_i^Ω constructs increasingly longer canonical FD sequences t_i. Eventually, at each live location i, t_i converges to some unique sequence in $t_{ref} \in T_D$. More importantly, for any finite prefix t_{pre} of t_{ref}, eventually and permanently, the canonical sequences t_i at each live location i are extensions of t_{pre}.

---

[2]Briefly, an execution of the system is v-valent (where v is either 0 or 1) if the only possible decision at each location, in the execution or any fair extension of the execution, is v. A v-valent execution is monovalent. If an execution is not monovalent, then it is bivalent.

Periodically, at each location i, A_i^Ω uses its canonical sequence t_i to construct a finite tree of executions of depth d_i, where d_i is the length of t_i. From this tree, it determines the "earliest" transition from a bivalent execution to a monovalent execution of consensus. The location of the process associated with this transition is provided as the output of Ω at i. Note that the earliest such transition in the tree of executions is determined uniquely by the nodes within some finite depth (say) d of the tree. Let $t_{pre.d}$ be the prefix of t_{ref} of length d. Eventually and permanently, the canonical sequence t_i at each live location are extensions of $t_{pre.d}$. Therefore, eventually and permanently, A_i^Ω at every live location i determines the same "earliest" transition from a bivalent execution to a monovalent execution of consensus. From the claim established in the first part, we know that the the events responsible for the "earliest" transition from a bivalent to a univalent execution occur at a some live location (say) l. Therefore, eventually and permanently, A_i^Ω at every live location i determines l to be the output of the Ω AFD, which is a unique correct location. Thus A^Ω implements the Ω AFD using D. Thus, we show that Ω is a weakest AFD for consensus.

9. DISCUSSION

Query-Based Failure Detectors. Our framework models failure detectors as crash problems that interact with process automata unilaterally. In contrast, many traditional models of failure detectors employ a query-based interaction [4, 17]. Since the inputs to AFDs are only the crash events, the information provided by AFDs can only be about process crashes. In contrast, query-based failure detectors receive inputs from the crash events and the process automata. The inputs from process automata may "leak" information about other events in the system to the failure detectors We illustrate the ability of query-based failure detectors to provide such additional information with the following example.

Applying Theorem 7 we know that consensus does not have representative failure detectors. However, if we consider the universe of query-based failure detectors, we see that consensus has a representative query-based failure detector, which we call a *participant failure detector*. A participant failure detector outputs the same location ID to all queries at all times and guarantees that the process automaton whose associated ID is output has queried the failure detector at least once (observe that this does not imply that said location does not crash, just that the location was not crashed initially).

It is easy to see how we can solve consensus using the participant failure detector. Each process automaton sends its proposal to all the process automata before querying the failure detector. The output of the failure detector must be a location whose process automaton has already sent its proposal to all the process automata. Therefore, each process automaton simply waits to receive the proposal from the process automaton whose associated location ID is output by the failure detector and then decide on that proposal.

Similarly, solving participant failure detector from a solution to consensus is also straightforward. The failure detector implementation is as follows. Upon receiving a query, the process automaton inputs its location ID as the proposal to the solution to consensus. Eventually, the consensus solution decides on some proposed location ID, and therefore, the ID of some location whose process automaton queried the failure detector implementation. In response to all queries, the implementation simply returns the location ID decided by the consensus solution.

Thus, we see that query-based failure detectors may provide information about events other than crashes. Furthermore, unlike representative failure detectors, a representative query-based failure detector for some problem P is not guaranteed to be a weakest failure detector for problem P. In conclusion, we argue that unilateral interaction for failure detectors is more reasonable than a query-based interaction.

Future Work. Our work introduces AFDs, but the larger impact of AFD-based framework on the existing results from traditional failure-detector theory needs to be assessed. The exact set of failure detectors than can be specified as AFDs remains to determined. It remains to be seen if weakest failure detectors for various problems are specifiable as AFDs, and if not, then the weakest AFDs to solve these problems are yet to be determined. We are yet to investigate if the results in [17] hold true for AFDs and if every problem (as defined in [17]) has a weakest AFD. The exact characterization of problems that have a representative AFD and the problems that do not have a representative AFD is unknown.

10. ACKNOWLEDGMENTS

This work is supported in part by NSF Award Numbers CCF-0726514, CCF-0937274, and CNS-1035199, and AFOSR Award Number FA9550-08-1-0159. This work is also partially supported by Center for Science of Information (CSoI), an NSF Science and Technology Center, under grant agreement CCF-0939370.

11. REFERENCES

[1] M. K. Aguilera, S. Toueg, and B. Deianov. Revisiting the weakest failure detector for uniform reliable broadcast. In *Proc. of 13th International Symposium on Distributed Computing*, pages 19–34, 1999.

[2] V. Bhatt, N. Christman, and P. Jayanti. Extracting quorum failure detectors. In *Proc. of 28th ACM symposium on Principles of distributed computing*, pages 73–82, 2009.

[3] V. Bhatt and P. Jayanti. On the existence of weakest failure detectors for mutual exclusion and k-exclusion. In *Proc. of the 23rd International Symposium on Distributed Computing*, pages 311–325, 2009.

[4] T. D. Chandra, V. Hadzilacos, and S. Toueg. The weakest failure detector for solving consensus. *Journal of the ACM*, pages 685–722, 1996.

[5] T. D. Chandra and S. Toueg. Unreliable failure detectors for reliable distributed systems. *J. ACM*, 43(2):225–267, 1996.

[6] B. Charron-Bost, M. Hutle, and J. Widder. In search of lost time. *Information Processing Letters*, 2010.

[7] C. Delporte-Gallet, H. Fauconnier, and R. Guerraoui. A realistic look at failure detectors. In *Proc. of International Conference on Dependable Systems and Networks*, pages 345–353, 2002.

[8] C. Delporte-Gallet, H. Fauconnier, R. Guerraoui, V. Hadzilacos, P. Kouznetsov, and S. Toueg. The weakest failure detectors to solve certain fundamental problems in distributed computing. In *Proc. of 23rd ACM Symposium on Principles of Distributed Computing*, pages 338–346, 2004.

[9] C. Delporte-Gallet, H. Fauconnier, R. Guerraoui, and P. Kouznetsov. Mutual exclusion in asynchronous systems with failure detectors. *Journal of Parallel and Distributed Computing*, pages 492–505, 2005.

[10] C. Fetzer, F. Tronel, and M. Raynal. An adaptive failure detection protocol. In *Proc. of the Pacific Rim International Symposium on Dependable Computing*, pages 146–153, 2001.

[11] E. Gafni and P. Kuznetsov. The weakest failure detector for solving k-set agreement. In *Proc. of 28th ACM symposium on Principles of distributed computing*, pages 83–91, 2009.

[12] R. Guerraoui, M. Kapalka, and P. Kouznetsov. The weakest failure detectors to boost obstruction-freedom. *Distributed Computing*, pages 415–433, 2008.

[13] R. Guerraoui, M. Kapalka, and P. Kouznetsov. The weakest failure detectors to boost obstruction-freedom. *Distributed Computing*, pages 415–433, 2008.

[14] R. Guerraoui and P. Kouznetsov. On the weakest failure detector for non-blocking atomic commit. In *Proc. of 17th IFIP World Computer Congress - TC1 Stream / 2nd IFIP International Conference on Theoretical Computer Science: Foundations of Information Technology in the Era of Networking and Mobile Computing*, pages 461–473, 2002.

[15] R. Guerraoui and P. Kouznetsov. The weakest failure detector for non-blocking atomic commit. Technical report, EPFL, 2003.

[16] J. Y. Halpern and A. Ricciardi. A knowledge-theoretic analysis of uniform distributed coordination and failure detectors. In *Proc. of 18th ACM symposium on Principles of distributed computing*, pages 73–82, 1999.

[17] P. Jayanti and S. Toueg. Every problem has a weakest failure detector. In *Proc. of 27th ACM symposium on Principles of distributed computing*, pages 75–84, 2008.

[18] N. A. Lynch. *Distributed Algorithms*. Morgan Kaufmann, 1996.

[19] S. M. Pike, S. Sastry, and J. L. Welch. Failure detectors encapsulate fairness. In *14th International Conference Principles of Distributed Systems*, pages 173–188, 2010.

[20] S. Rajsbaum, M. Raynal, and C. Travers. Failure detectors as schedulers (an algorithmically-reasoned characterization). Technical Report 1838, IRISA, Université de Rennes, France, 2007.

[21] S. Rajsbaum, M. Raynal, and C. Travers. The iterated restricted immediate snapshot model. In *Proc of 14th International Conference on Computing and Combinatorics*, pages 487–497, 2008.

[22] S. Sastry, S. M. Pike, and J. L. Welch. The weakest failure detector for wait-free dining under eventual weak exclusion. In *Proc. of 21st ACM Symposium on Parallelism in Algorithms and Architectures*, pages 111–120, 2009.

[23] Y. Song, S. M. Pike, and S. Sastry. The weakest failure detector for wait-free, eventually fair mutual exclusion. Technical Report TAMU-CS-TR-2007-2-2, Texas A&M University, 2007.

[24] N. C. Vibhor Bhatt and and P. Jayanti. Extracting quorum failure detectors. In *Proc. of 28th ACM Symposium on Principles of Distributed Computing*, pages 73–82, 2009.

Simulations and Reductions for Colorless Tasks

Maurice Herlihy[*]
Brown University
Computer Science Department
Providence, RI 02912, USA
mph@cs.brown.edu

Sergio Rajsbaum[†]
Instituto de Matemáticas
Universidad Nacional Autónoma de México
Ciudad Universitaria, D.F. 04510, México
rajsbaum@math.unam.mx

ABSTRACT

If one model of computation can simulate another, then the existence (or non-existence) of an algorithm in the simulated model reduces to a related question about the simulating model. The *BG-simulation* algorithm uses this approach to prove that k-set agreement cannot be solved when t processes can crash, $1 \leq t \leq k$, by reduction to the wait-free case, where it is known that $n + 1$ processes cannot solve n-set agreement, and similarly for any other *colorless* task. We give a definition, expressed in the language of combinatorial topology, for what it means for one model of distributed computation to simulate another with respect to the ability to solve colorless tasks. This definition is not linked to specific models or specific protocols. We show how to exploit elementary topological arguments to show when a simulation *exists*, without the need for an explicit construction. We use this approach to generalize the BG-simulation and to unify a number of simulation relations linking various models, some previously known, some not.

Categories and Subject Descriptors

D.1.3 [**Programming Techniques**]: Concurrent Programming; F.1.1 [**Computation by Abstract Devices**]: Models of Computation—*Computability Theory*; F.1.2 [**Computation by Abstract Devices**]: Modes of Computation—*Parallelism and Concurrency*

General Terms

Algorithms, Theory

1. INTRODUCTION

In complexity theory, it is common to prove results by *reduction* from one problem to another. For example, textbooks typically prove from first principles that satisfiabil-

---

[*]Supported by NSF 000830491.

[†]Supported by a UNAM PAPIIT Research Project.

ity is NP-complete, but then use reductions to show that other problems are also NP-complete. Reductions have also been applied to distributed computing. Perhaps the best-known reduction technique is the *BG-simulation* algorithm [5], which can be used to reduce impossibility results in t-resilient models to impossibility results in wait-free models.

The BG-simulation algorithm was used to prove that k-set agreement cannot be solved when t processes can crash, $1 \leq t \leq k$, by reduction to the wait-free case, where it was known that $n + 1$ processes cannot solve n-set agreement. Moreover, as shown in [5] the BG-simulation algorithm can be used to obtain similar reductions for any *colorless* task. These are tasks where all that matters are the *sets* of input or output values, not which process has which. Any legal starting configuration remains legal if any process adopts any other process's input value, and similarly for legal halting configurations and output values. Both consensus and k-set agreement are examples of such tasks.

There are several reasons reductions based on explicit simulations may be difficult to apply more broadly. First, while there are several examples of explicit simulations (see related work in Section 6) and precise formal definitions for some [5], there is no systematic definition of what it means for one arbitrary model to simulate another. Second, the construction of such explicit simulations is *ad-hoc*: a new, specialized algorithm must be crafted for each pair of models. This search is rendered more difficult by the absence of a systematic test for when a simulation exists: one can only hunt for an explicit simulation algorithm, with no assurance it exists.

This paper addresses these limitations in several ways. First, we give a general definition, expressed in the language of combinatorial topology, for what it means for one model to simulate another. This definition is not linked to specific models or specific protocols. Second, we show how to exploit elementary topological arguments to show when a simulation *exists*, without the need for an explicit construction. The existence conditions we give are in terms of a model's connectivity, and likely to be easier to determine in general than devising pair-wise simulations. Many techniques are known for computing a model's connectivity, and indeed for many models the connectivity has already been computed [12, 13, 15, 16, 18, 17, 19, 20]. Notice that the important results derived from simulations, such as the impossibility of t-resilient k-set agreement, depend only on the *existence* of a simulation, not on the specific mechanisms employed by any particular simulation.

2. COMBINATORIAL TOPOLOGY

We review here a few standard notions from topology [1, 25]. A *simplicial complex* is a higher-dimensional generalization of a graph. A simplicial complex is given by a finite set V, along with a collection of subsets $\mathcal{K}$ of V closed under containment. An element of V is called a *vertex* of $\mathcal{K}$, and each set in $\mathcal{K}$ is called a *simplex*, usually denoted by lower-case Greek letters. A subset of a simplex is called a *face* of that simplex. For brevity, we sometimes abuse notation by using σ to refer both to a simplex, and to the complex consisting of σ and its faces. The *dimension* $\dim \sigma$ of a simplex σ is $|\sigma| - 1$. We use "k-simplex" as shorthand for "k-dimensional simplex", and similarly for "k-face". The k-*skeleton* of a complex $\mathcal{K}$, $\mathrm{skel}^k \mathcal{K}$, is the complex formed by all simplices of $\mathcal{K}$ of dimension k or less. A *facet* of $\mathcal{K}$ is a maximal simplex, and $\mathcal{K}$ is *pure* if all its facets have the same dimension.

Let $\mathcal{K}$ and $\mathcal{L}$ be complexes. A *vertex map* f carries vertices of $\mathcal{K}$ to vertices of $\mathcal{L}$. If f also carries simplices of $\mathcal{K}$ to simplices of $\mathcal{L}$, it is called a *simplicial map*. A *carrier map* $\Delta : \mathcal{K} \rightarrow 2^{\mathcal{L}}$ maps each simplex of $\mathcal{K}$ to a subcomplex of $\mathcal{L}$, so that

$$\Delta(\sigma \cap \tau) \subseteq \Delta(\sigma) \cap \Delta(\tau) \tag{1}$$

for all $\sigma, \tau \in \mathcal{K}$. In other words, carrier maps preserve intersections. It follows that if σ' is a face of σ, then $\Delta(\sigma') \subseteq \Delta(\sigma)$.

It is sometimes convenient to give simplices and complexes a *geometric* interpretation. Let $\mathcal{K}$ be a complex with vertices $v_0, \ldots, v_N$. For each vertex v_i, let $|v_i| \in \mathbb{R}^{N+1}$ be the point whose i^{th} co-ordinate is 1, and the rest 0. For each n-simplex $\sigma = \{v_{i_0}, \ldots, v_{i_n}\}$, let $|\sigma|$ be the convex hull of the points $|v_{i_0}|, \ldots, |v_{i_n}|$. We call

$$|\mathcal{K}| = \cup_{\sigma \in \mathcal{K}} |\sigma|$$

the *polyhedron* of $\mathcal{K}$.

Informally, a *subdivision* of a geometric complex $\mathcal{A}$ is constructed by "dividing" the simplices of $\mathcal{A}$ into smaller simplices. More precisely, a subdivision of a geometric complex $\mathcal{A}$ is a geometric complex $\mathcal{B}$ such that (1) each simplex of $\mathcal{B}$ is contained in a simplex of $\mathcal{A}$, and (2) each simplex of $\mathcal{A}$ is the union of finitely many simplices of $\mathcal{B}$.

Definition 1. The *barycentric* subdivision of a simplex σ, written $\mathrm{Bary}\, \sigma$, is the complex whose vertices are faces of σ. A set of vertices $\sigma_0, \ldots, \sigma_k$ forms a simplex if $\sigma_0 \subset \cdots \subset \sigma_k$.

The barycentric subdivision of a complex $\mathcal{A}$, written $\mathrm{Bary}\, \mathcal{A}$, is constructed by taking the barycentric subdivision of each of its simplices. Geometrically, the vertex corresponding to $\tau \subseteq \sigma$ is usually placed at the barycenter (centroid) of τ. Sometimes it is useful to apply repeated subdivisions: $\mathrm{Bary}^N \mathcal{K}$ is the complex constructed by taking N repeated barycentric subdivisions.

A complex $\mathcal{K}$ is k-*connected* if every continuous map of the k-sphere to $|\mathcal{K}|$ can be extended to a continuous map of the $(k+1)$-disk. (Informally, it has no "holes" in dimensions k or less.) By convention, a complex is (-1)-*connected* if and only if it is nonempty. It is 0-connected if it is path-connected, and 1-connected if it is simply-connected.

FACT 1. *The $(n-1)$-skeleton of an n-simplex is homeomorphic to an $(n-1)$-sphere.*

FACT 2. *Any n-simplex is homeomorphic to an n-disk.*

3. PROTOCOLS AND TASKS

A *colorless task* is given by a triple $(\mathcal{K}, \mathcal{L}, \Delta)$, where $\mathcal{K}$, the *input complex*, defines the sets of possible input values, $\mathcal{L}$, the *output complex*, defines the sets of possible output values, and $\Delta : \mathcal{K} \rightarrow 2^{\mathcal{L}}$ is a carrier map that defines which sets of output values are valid for which sets of input values.

Each input value is a vertex of $\mathcal{K}$, and a set of input values σ is a simplex in $\mathcal{K}$ if there is an initial system state where σ is the processes' set of input values. Symmetrically, a set of output values τ is a simplex in $\mathcal{L}$ if there is a final system state where τ is the processes' set of output values. Operationally, the processes are initially assigned vertices from a simplex σ in $\mathcal{K}$, and they halt after choosing vertices from a simplex τ in $\mathcal{L}$, where $\tau \in \Delta(\sigma)$. Colorless tasks are a special case of tasks, usually denoted $(\mathcal{I}, \mathcal{O}, \Delta)$ in the literature since [20], where each vertex of the input complex $\mathcal{I}$ and $\mathcal{O}$ specifies not only a value (input or output), but to which process the value is associated. Given a colorless task, the corresponding task is easily defined, see e.g. [14].

The classic example of a colorless task is k-set agreement [7]. A general form of this task is specified by an input complex $\mathcal{K}$, which can be an arbitrary complex, and the output complex is $\mathrm{skel}^{k-1} \mathcal{K}$, the $(k-1)$-skeleton of $\mathcal{K}$. Operationally, the processes choose a subset of their inputs of size at most k, corresponding to a face of the input simplex of dimension at most $k-1$.

Informally, in a protocol for an input complex $\mathcal{K}$ processes repeatedly exchange information, where the timing and medium of the exchanges is determined by the model of computation. For example, in a synchronous message-passing model of computation, processes might repeatedly broadcast their states to one another. Each protocol defines an associated *protocol complex* $\mathcal{P}$. A vertex v of the protocol complex is a pair consisting of a process name, $\mathrm{name}(v)$, and that process's final state, $\mathrm{value}(v)$. A set of vertices with distinct process names forms a simplex if there is an execution at the end of which each process has that state. If $\mathcal{P}$ is a protocol and σ an input simplex of $\mathcal{K}$, we use $\mathcal{P}(\sigma)$ to mean the complex generated by all executions in which the processes start with input values taken from σ. For the simulations in this paper, it is important to focus on the structural properties of a protocol complex, and hence we take the following as a definition.

Definition 2. A *protocol* is a carrier map $\mathcal{P}(\cdot)$ that takes each input simplex $\kappa \in \mathcal{K}$ to a protocol complex $\mathcal{P}(\kappa)$.

Definition 3. A protocol *solves* a colorless task $(\mathcal{K}, \mathcal{L}, \Delta)$ if there is a simplicial map $\delta : \mathcal{P}(\mathcal{K}) \rightarrow \mathcal{L}$ carried by Δ: for every input simplex κ in $\mathcal{K}$, $\delta(\mathcal{P}(\kappa)) \subseteq \Delta(\kappa)$.

Operationally, each process finishes the protocol in a local state that is a vertex of $\mathcal{P}$, and then applies δ to choose an output value.

These relations are illustrated in the left-hand diagram of Figure 1. Along the horizontal arrow, Δ carries each input simplex κ of $\mathcal{K}$ to a subcomplex of $\mathcal{L}$. Along the diagonal arrow, a protocol, here denoted $\mathcal{P}'$, carries each κ to a subcomplex of its protocol complex, which is mapped to a subcomplex of $\mathcal{L}$ along the vertical arrow by the simplicial map δ'. The diagram *semi-commutes*: the subcomplex of $\mathcal{L}$ reached through the diagonal and vertical arrows is contained in the subcomplex reached through the horizontal arrow.

In a distributed system, failures may be correlated for processes running on the same node, in the same network partition, or managed by the same provider. In a multiprocessor, failures may be correlated for processes running on the same core, the same processor, or the same card. Such situations are typically modeled by *adversary* schedulers that can cause certain subsets of processes to fail, perhaps in a non-uniform way [26].

The most straightforward way to characterize adversaries is to enumerate the *faulty sets*: all sets of processes that fail in some execution. We assume that the faulty sets are closed under inclusion: if F is the complete set of processes that fail in some execution, then for any $F' \subset F$, there is an execution in which F' is the complete set of processes that fail.

We require faulty sets to be closed under inclusion because we want to respect the principle that fault-tolerant algorithms should continue to be correct if run in a system that displays *fewer failures* than anticipated. For example, here is a simple consensus protocol for a three-process system whose only faulty set is $\{P_1, P_2\}$: P_0 decides its input, and P_1 and P_2 wait until they fail. This algorithm would be incorrect, however, if P_1 unexpectedly failed to fail. We think it is absurd to consider as legitimate algorithms that are correct *only if* certain failures occur.

Enumerating failure sets can be cumbersome, so we use a more succinct and flexible way to characterize adversaries. A *core* [23, 24] is a minimal set of processes that will not all fail in any execution. For the wait-free adversary, the entire set of processes is the only core, and for the t-faulty adversary, any set of $t + 1$ processes is a core. In a three-process system, for the adversary with faulty sets $\emptyset$, $\{P_0\}$, $\{P_1\}$, $\{P_2\}$, and $\{P_1 P_2\}$, the cores are $\{P_0, P_1\}$ and $\{P_0, P_2\}$.

Informally, a model of computation is given by a set of process names, a communication medium, such as shared memory or message-passing, a timing model, such as synchronous or asynchronous, and a failure model, given by an adversary.

Definition 4. A *model of computation* M is given by a set of process names Π, an input complex $\mathcal{K}$, an adversary $\mathbb{A}$, and a (countably infinite) family of protocols.

Definition 5. A model of computation M *solves* a colorless task $(\mathcal{K}, \mathcal{L}, \Delta)$ if there is a protocol $\mathcal{P}$ in M that solves that task.

4. SIMULATION

What does it mean for one model of computation to simulate another? A simulation is defined in terms of two models of computation, a model R (called the *real* model) and a model V (called the *virtual model*). They have the same input complex $\mathcal{K}$, but their process names, protocol complexes, and adversaries may differ. For example, the real model might be the $(t + 1)$-process wait-free read-write protocols, and the virtual model the $(n + 1)$-process t-resilient read-write protocols.

Informally, the real model simulates the virtual model if, for each protocol in the virtual model, there is a protocol in the real model by which real processes choose compatible virtual executions, where each virtual process has the same input as some real process.

Definition 6. A (real) model R *simulates* a (virtual) model V if, for each protocol $\mathcal{P}'$ in V, there exists a real protocol

$\mathcal{P}$ in R and a simplicial map,

$$\phi : \mathcal{P}(\mathcal{K}) \rightarrow \mathcal{P}'(\mathcal{K}),$$

such that for each simplex κ in $\mathcal{K}$, ϕ carries each simplex of $\mathcal{P}(\kappa)$ to a simplex of $\mathcal{P}'(\kappa)$.

Informally, each processes executing the real protocol chooses a simulated execution in the virtual protocol, where each virtual process has the same input as some real process. Note that distinct real processes may choose the same simulated execution.

These relations are illustrated in the middle diagram of Figure 1. Along the diagonal arrow, $\mathcal{P}'$ carries each input simplex κ of $\mathcal{K}$ to a subcomplex of its protocol complex $\mathcal{P}'(\mathcal{K})$. Along the vertical arrow, $\mathcal{P}$ carries each input simplex κ of $\mathcal{K}$ to a subcomplex of its own protocol complex, which is carried to a subcomplex of $\mathcal{P}'(\mathcal{K})$ by the simplicial map ϕ. The diagram semi-commutes: the subcomplex of $\mathcal{P}'(\mathcal{K})$ reached through the vertical and horizontal arrows is contained in the subcomplex reached through the diagonal arrow.

The BG-simulation is usually explained in terms of a wait-free $(t + 1)$-process read-write protocol where the processes compute compatible virtual executions of an $(n + 1)$-process t-resilient read-write protocol. Here, we replace this operational view with a combinatorial approach: the real protocol (the BG-simulation) and the virtual protocol (the t-resilient computation) each defines a protocol complex generated by the set of all possible executions. The BG-simulation implicitly defines a simplicial map carrying vertices of the (real) BG-simulation complex to vertices of the (virtual) simulated protocol complex. Reformulated in the language of simplicial maps, the notion of simulation extends naturally to any pair of computational models, not just the individual cases considered in the literature.

THEOREM 1. *If model* R *simulates model* V, *then any colorless task that has a protocol in* V *has a protocol in* R.

PROOF. Recall that if V has a protocol for a colorless task $(\mathcal{K}, \mathcal{L}, \Delta)$, then there a protocol complex $\mathcal{P}'(\mathcal{K})$ and a simplicial map $\delta' : \mathcal{P}'(\mathcal{K}) \rightarrow \mathcal{L}$ carried by Δ. If model R simulates model V, then for any protocol $\mathcal{P}' \in V$, there is a protocol $\mathcal{P} \in R$ and a simplicial map $\phi : \mathcal{P}(\mathcal{K}) \rightarrow \mathcal{P}'(\mathcal{K})$, such that for each simplex κ in $\mathcal{K}$, $\phi(\mathcal{P}(\kappa)) \subseteq \mathcal{P}'(\kappa)$.

Let δ be the composition of ϕ and δ'. By construction,

$$\delta'(\phi(\mathcal{P}(\kappa))) \subseteq \delta'(\mathcal{P}'(\kappa)) \subseteq \Delta(\kappa),$$

so R also solves $(\mathcal{K}, \mathcal{L}, \Delta)$. $\square$

Figure 1 illustrates how these relations fit together.

The important point about Theorem 1 is that it depends only on the *existence* of a simplicial map: the explicit construction of any particular simulation algorithm, however clever, serves only to establish that simulation is possible. Combinatorial topology provides powerful tools for proving the existence (or non-existence) of maps. An approach that uses topological arguments to show that such maps exist is both more general and ultimately, simpler, removing the need to devise case-by-case simulation algorithms. Finally, the kinds of topological connectivity arguments needed to show the existence of such simplicial maps are well-established for a wide variety of standard models [13, 15, 16, 17, 18, 19, 20].

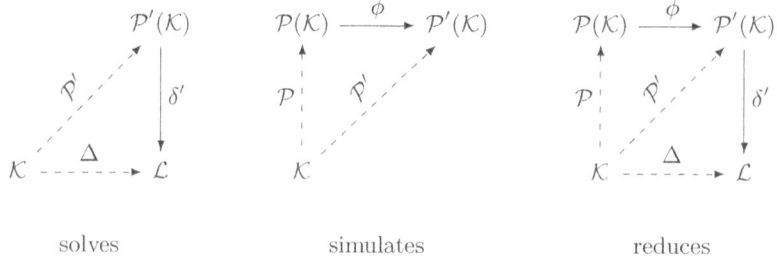

Figure 1: Carrier maps are shown as dashed arrows, simplicial maps as solid arrows. On the left, $\mathcal{P}'$ via δ' solves the colorless task $(\mathcal{K}, \mathcal{L}, \Delta)$. In the middle, $\mathcal{P}$ simulates $\mathcal{P}'$ via ϕ. On the right, $\mathcal{P}$ via the composition of ϕ and δ' solves $(\mathcal{K}, \mathcal{L}, \Delta)$.

Model	Connectivity	Source
read-write memory	$c - 1$	[18]
message-passing	$c - 1$	[17]
(m, k)-set agreement	$\lfloor \frac{c}{m} \rfloor k + \min(k, c \bmod m) - 1$	[13]
Limited-scope failure detector $S_{x,q}$	$(f - x + \min(q, k) - 1)$	[12]

Figure 2: Connectivity of various $(n + 1)$-process models

5. APPLICATIONS

We will use connectivity arguments to show the existence of the desired simplicial maps. Figure 2 summarizes the connectivity of protocol complexes for several models of computation. The first three lines describe models running against an adversary with minimal core size c. The first model uses asynchronous read-write memory, the second asynchronous message-passing, and the third asynchronous read-write memory augmented by objects that solve (m, k)-set agreement. The last model employs *limited-scope failure detectors* [12]: there are q disjoint clusters of processes that share a failure detector $S_{x,q}$ that ensures that some correct process in each cluster is never suspected by any process in that cluster. (This model is motivated by the notion that processes can detect failures more accurately within clusters than across clusters.) This last model is included to show how our technique can establish the existence of simulations between very different models of computation.

THEOREM 2. *Let $\mathcal{A}$ be a pure k-dimensional complex, $\mathcal{B}$ a complex, and $\Delta : \mathcal{A} \to 2^{\mathcal{B}}$ a carrier map such that for every simplex α in $\mathcal{A}$, $\Delta(\alpha)$ is k-connected. Then there exists a simplicial map*

$$\phi : \mathrm{Bary}^r \, \mathcal{A} \to \mathcal{B},$$

for sufficiently large $r > 0$, such that ϕ is carried by Δ: for every simplex α in $\mathcal{A}$, $\phi(\mathrm{Bary}^r \, \alpha) \subseteq \Delta(\alpha)$.

PROOF. We inductively construct a continuous map

$$f_\ell : |\operatorname{skel}^\ell \mathcal{A}| \to |\mathcal{B}|$$

such that $f_\ell(\alpha) \subseteq |\Delta(\alpha)|$. For the base case, when ℓ is zero, choose f_0 to send each vertex a of $\mathcal{A}$ to some vertex in $\Delta(a)$, which is non-empty because it is k-connected, for $k \geq -1$.

For the induction step, assume we have such a map $f_{\ell-1}$ that sends the set of $(\ell-1)$-faces of α to $|\Delta(\alpha)|$. These $(\ell-1)$ faces form an $(\ell-1)$-sphere (Fact 1), and because $\Delta(\alpha)$ is k-connected, for $k \geq \ell$, $f_{\ell-1}$ can be extended to a continuous map $f_\ell : |\alpha| \to \Delta(\alpha)$ of the ℓ-disk α (Fact 2). Because all

```
 1  // N is the number of rounds
 2  // code for P_i
 3  protocol BaryAgree[N: int]
 4      // input is vertex of σ
 5      // output is vertex of Bary^N σ
 6      // array of barycentric agreement protocol objects
 7      shared mem: array[0..N][0..n] of vertex := {⊥, ..., ⊥}
 8      method propose(v: vertex): vertex
 9          mem[0][i] := v;
10          for r := 0 to N−1 do
11              snap := snapshot(mem[r])
12              mem[r+1][i] := barycenter(u ∈ snap and u ≠ ⊥)
13          return mem[N][i]
14      end
15  end
```

Figure 3: Barycentric agreement protocol

such maps agree on the intersections of their domains, they extend to a continuous map on all of $|\operatorname{skel}^\ell \mathcal{A}|$.

The Simplicial Approximation Theorem [27, p.89] states that $f_\ell : |\mathcal{A}| \to |\mathcal{B}|$ can be approximated by a simplicial map $\phi : \mathrm{Bary}^r \, \mathcal{A} \to \mathcal{B}$, for sufficiently large $r > 0$, satisfying the conditions of the theorem. $\square$

Theorem 2 is a statement about combinatorial topology. We will apply this theorem to computing by taking $\mathcal{A}$ to be the task's input complex, and $\mathcal{B}$ the virtual protocol complex.

As a building block, we use the wait-free *barycentric agreement* protocol shown in Figure 3. The task inputs are the vertices of a simplex σ, and the outputs are the vertices of a simplex of the iterated barycentric subdivision $\mathrm{Bary}^r \, \sigma$, for some known $r > 0$. The protocol proceeds in rounds. The processes share a two-dimensional array mem[][], initially all $\perp$. In round 0, P_i writes its input vertex to mem[0][i]. In round r, takes a snapshot of row r, computes the barycenter of the vertices it reads, and writes the results to mem$[r+1][i]$. All processes finish on (not necessarily distinct) vertices of a simplex in Bary$^r \sigma$.

5.1 Read-Write Simulations

Consider a real model of computation R in which the $n+1$ real processes communicate via read-write memory, failures are controlled by an adversary $\mathbb{A}$, and C is a core for $\mathbb{A}$ of minimal size c.

THEOREM 3. *If, for every input simplex σ, each virtual protocol complex $\mathcal{P}'(\sigma)$ in V is $(c-1)$-connected, then any read-write model with minimal core size c simulates V.*

PROOF. Here is the simulation. Let σ be an input simplex. If we focus on the processes in the minimal core C, their values lie on a simplex in skel$^{c-1} \mathcal{K}$, a pure $(c-1)$-dimensional complex. Because $\mathcal{P}'(\sigma)$ is $(c-1)$-connected, Theorem 2 states that there is a simplicial map

$$\phi : \text{Bary}^r \text{skel}^{c-1} \mathcal{K} \to \mathcal{P}(\mathcal{K})$$

carrying each input simplex σ to $\mathcal{P}'(\sigma)$. Each process in C applies ϕ to its input, yielding a vertex in $\mathcal{P}'(\sigma)$, and writes that vertex to a shared-memory array.

Each process not in C simply waits for a process in C to write its vertex, and then chooses that vertex. Because C is a core, some vertex will eventually be written, and the vertices chosen all lie on a single simplex of $\mathcal{P}'(\sigma)$.

This simulation is a protocol $\mathcal{P}$ of the real model R, and the final choice of vertex in $\mathcal{P}'$ induces a simplicial map $\mathcal{P}(\mathcal{K}) \to \mathcal{P}'(\mathcal{K})$, which defines a simulation. □

COROLLARY 1. *A read-write model with minimum core size c can simulate a read-write or message-passing model with minimum core size c' if $c \leq c'$.*

COROLLARY 2. *All read-write models with minimum core size c are equivalent for colorless tasks [9, 18].*

COROLLARY 3. *A read-write model with minimum core size c can simulate an (m, k)-set agreement model with minimum core size c' if $c \leq \lfloor \frac{c'}{m} \rfloor k + \min(k, c' \bmod m)$.*

COROLLARY 4. *A read-write model with minimum core size c can simulate a limited-scope failure detector model if $c \leq f - x + \min(q, k)$.*

While the BG-simulation provides an explicit construction for special cases of the first two corollaries, we know of no explicit simulation protocol for the last.

5.2 Set-Agreement Simulations

Observe that c processes that share (m, k)-set agreement objects can solve (c, d)-set agreement, where

$$d(c, m, k) = \left\lfloor \frac{c}{m} \right\rfloor k + \min(k, c \bmod m).$$

There are $\lfloor \frac{c}{m} \rfloor$ (m, k)-set agreement objects accessed by m processes each, and each yields at most k distinct values. If m does not divide c exactly, then there are $c \bmod m$ leftover processes that share an additional set-agreement object. If $c \bmod m < k$, then at most $c \bmod m$ values are chosen, and otherwise at most k.

THEOREM 4. *If, for every input simplex σ, each virtual protocol complex $\mathcal{P}'(\sigma)$ in V is $(d(c, m, k) - 1)$-connected, then the (m, k)-set agreement model with minimum core size c simulates V.*

PROOF. Let σ be an input simplex. If we focus on the processes in the minimal core C, their values lie on a simplex in skel$^{c-1} \mathcal{K}$, a pure $(c-1)$-dimensional complex. These processes then use a set of wait-free (m, k)-set agreement objects to agree on a subset of at most $d(c, m, k)$ of their inputs. Because $\mathcal{P}'(\sigma)$ is $d(c, m, k) - 1)$-connected, Theorem 2 states that there is a simplicial map

$$\phi : \text{Bary}^r \text{skel}^{d(c,m,k)-1} \mathcal{K} \to \mathcal{P}(\mathcal{K})$$

carrying each input simplex σ to $\mathcal{P}'(\sigma)$. Each process in C applies ϕ to its input, yielding a vertex in $\mathcal{P}'(\sigma)$, and writes that vertex to a shared-memory array.

As before, each process not in C simply waits for a process in C to write its vertex, and then chooses that vertex. Because C is a core, some vertex will eventually be written, and the vertices chosen all lie on a single simplex of $\mathcal{P}'(\sigma)$. □

COROLLARY 5. *An (m, k)-set agreement model with minimum core size c can simulate a read-write or message-passing model with minimum core size c' if $d \leq c'$.*

COROLLARY 6. *An (m, k)-set agreement model with minimum core size c can simulate an (m', k')-set agreement model with minimum core size c' if $d(c, m, k) \leq d(c', m', k')$.*

COROLLARY 7. *An (m, k)-set agreement model with minimum core size c can simulate a limited-scope failure detector model if $d(c, m, k) \leq f - x + \min(q, k)$.*

These corollaries generalize results of Imbs and Raynal [22].

6. RELATED WORK

The BG-simulation was introduced in [2] with the goal of extending the wait-free set agreement impossibility result to the t-resilient case. It was formalized and studied in more detail in the journal version [5] of that paper, where the tasks for which it can be used were identified, as the colorless tasks. This class of tasks was introduced in [14] under the name *convergence* tasks, to study decidability issues. The BG-simulation was then used in [3, 8] to study the set agreement partial order [13].

Variants and extensions of the BG-simulation have also been considered [21]. This simulation of [22] considers processes that can communicate with objects that are more powerful than read/write registers, and shows that consensus numbers have a multiplicative power with respect to process failures. Considering the restriction of the applicability of the BG-simulation to colorless tasks, an extended version was described in [10].

Other simulations have been studied. The one presented in [6] is used to prove an equivalence of t-resilient and wait-free implementation of consensus using shared objects. Simulations for iterated models, where each shared object can be accessed only once, were considered in [4, 11].

Junqueira and Marzullo [24] introduced the core/survivor-set formalism for characterizing general adversaries used here, and derived the first lower bounds for synchronous consensus against such an adversary. Delporte-Gallet et al. [9]

were the first to prove several important lower bounds on k-set agreement in asynchronous read-write memory against a more general adversary. Herlihy and Rajsbaum [18] gave the first direct application of combinatorial topology to the asynchronous read-write memory model against an adversary.

7. CONCLUSIONS

To understand the possible reductions among a set of N models of computation, we would have to devise $O(N^2)$ explicit pair-wise simulations, each simulation intimately connected with the detailed structure of two models. Each simulation is likely to be a protocol of non-trivial complexity, requiring a non-trivial operational proof.

The approach proposed here by contrast, requires computing the topological connectivity of the protocol complexes for each of the N models. Each such computation is a combinatorial exercise of the kind that has already been undertaken for many different models of computation. We think that this approach is more systematic, and, arguably, reveals more about the underlying structure of the models than explicit simulation algorithms.

We note that the definitions and constructions in this paper work only for colorless tasks. For arbitrary tasks, we can also define simulation in terms of maps between protocol complexes, but these maps require additional structure (they might be *color-preserving*, mapping real to virtual processes in a one-to-one way). More general notions of simulation are a promising area for future work.

8. REFERENCES

[1] M. A. Armstrong. *Basic Topology (Undergraduate Texts in Mathematics)*. Springer, July 1983.

[2] Elizabeth Borowsky and Eli Gafni. Generalized FLP impossibility result for t-resilient asynchronous computations. In *STOC '93: Proceedings of the twenty-fifth annual ACM symposium on Theory of computing*, pages 91–100, New York, NY, USA, 1993. ACM.

[3] Elizabeth Borowsky and Eli Gafni. The implication of the borowsky-gafni simulation on the set-consensus hierarchy. Technical Report 930021, University of California, Los Angeles. Computer Science Dept, 1993.

[4] Elizabeth Borowsky and Eli Gafni. A Simple Algorithmically Reasoned Characterization of Wait-Free Computations (Extended Abstract). In *PODC '97: Proceedings of the sixteenth annual ACM symposium on Principles of distributed computing*, pages 189–198, New York, NY, USA, 1997. ACM.

[5] Elizabeth Borowsky, Eli Gafni, Nancy Lynch, and Sergio Rajsbaum. The BG distributed simulation algorithm. *Distributed Computing*, 14(3):127–146, 2001.

[6] Tushar Chandra, Vassos Hadzilacos, Prasad Jayanti, and Sam Toueg. Generalized irreducibility of consensus and the equivalence of t-resilient and wait-free implementations of consensus. *SIAM J. Comput.*, 34:333–357, February 2005.

[7] Soma Chaudhuri, Maurice Herlihy, Nancy A. Lynch, and Mark R. Tuttle. A Tight Lower Bound for k-Set Agreement. In *In Proceedings of the 34th IEEE Symposium on Foundations of Computer Science*, pages 206–215, 1993.

[8] Soma Chaudhuri and Paul Reiners. Understanding the Set Consensus Partial Order Using the Borowsky-Gafni Simulation (Extended Abstract). In *Proceedings of the 10th International Workshop on Distributed Algorithms*, pages 362–379, London, UK, 1996. Springer-Verlag.

[9] Carole Delporte-Gallet, Hugues Fauconnier, Rachid Guerraoui, and Andreas Tielmann. The Disagreement Power of an Adversary. In Idit Keidar, editor, *Distributed Computing*, volume 5805 of *Lecture Notes in Computer Science*, chapter 6, pages 8–21. Springer Berlin / Heidelberg, Berlin, Heidelberg, 2009.

[10] Eli Gafni. The extended BG-simulation and the characterization of t-resiliency. In *Proceedings of the forty-first annual ACM symposium on Theory of computing*, STOC '09, pages 85–92, New York, NY, USA, 2009. ACM.

[11] Eli Gafni and Sergio Rajsbaum. Distributed programming with tasks. In *Proc. 14th International Conference on Principles of Distributed Systems*, pages 205–218. Springer, 2010.

[12] Maurice Herlihy and Lucia Draque Penso. Tight bounds for k-set agreement with limited-scope failure detectors. *Distrib. Comput.*, 18:157–166, December 2005.

[13] Maurice Herlihy and Sergio Rajsbaum. Set consensus using arbitrary objects (preliminary version). In *PODC '94: Proceedings of the thirteenth annual ACM symposium on Principles of distributed computing*, pages 324–333, New York, NY, USA, 1994. ACM.

[14] Maurice Herlihy and Sergio Rajsbaum. The decidability of distributed decision tasks (extended abstract). In *STOC '97: Proceedings of the twenty-ninth annual ACM symposium on Theory of computing*, pages 589–598, New York, NY, USA, 1997. ACM.

[15] Maurice Herlihy and Sergio Rajsbaum. Algebraic spans. *Mathematical Structures in Computer Science*, 10(4):549–573, 2000.

[16] Maurice Herlihy and Sergio Rajsbaum. A classification of wait-free loop agreement tasks. *Theor. Comput. Sci.*, 291(1):55–77, 2003.

[17] Maurice Herlihy and Sergio Rajsbaum. Concurrent computing and shellable complexes. In Nancy Lynch and Alexander Shvartsman, editors, *Distributed Computing*, volume 6343 of *Lecture Notes in Computer Science*, pages 109–123. Springer, 2010.

[18] Maurice Herlihy and Sergio Rajsbaum. The topology of shared-memory adversaries. In *Proceeding of the 29th ACM SIGACT-SIGOPS symposium on Principles of distributed computing*, PODC '10, pages 105–113, New York, NY, USA, 2010. ACM.

[19] Maurice Herlihy, Sergio Rajsbaum, and Mark Tuttle. An Axiomatic Approach to Computing the Connectivity of Synchronous and Asynchronous Systems. *Electron. Notes Theor. Comput. Sci.*, 230:79–102, 2009.

[20] Maurice Herlihy and Nir Shavit. The topological structure of asynchronous computability. *J. ACM*, 46(6):858–923, 1999.

[21] Damien Imbs and Michel Raynal. Visiting gafni's reduction land: from the BG simulation to the extended bg simulation. In *11th International Symposium on Stabilization, Safety, and Security of Distributed Systems*, SSS '09, pages 369–383, Berlin Heildelberg, Germany, 2009. Springer.

[22] Damien Imbs and Michel Raynal. The multiplicative power of consensus numbers. In *Proceedings of the 29th ACM SIGACT-SIGOPS symposium on Principles of distributed computing*, PODC '10, pages 26–35, New York, NY, USA, 2010. ACM.

[23] Flavio Junqueira, Keith Marzullo, Maurice Herlihy, and Lucia Penso. Threshold protocols in survivor set systems. *Distributed Computing*, 23:135–149, 2010.

[24] Flavio P. Junqueira and Keith Marzullo. Designing Algorithms for Dependent Process Failures. Technical report, 2003.

[25] Dmitry Koslov. *Combinatorial Algebraic Topology*. Springer, 2007.

[26] Petr Kuznetsov. Understanding non-uniform failure models. *Bulletin of the EATCS*, 106:53–77, February 2012.

[27] James Munkres. *Elements of Algebraic Topology*. Prentice Hall, 2 edition, January 1984.

A Closer Look at Fault Tolerance

Gadi Taubenfeld
The Interdisciplinary Center, P.O.Box 167, Herzliya 46150, Israel
tgadi@idc.ac.il

ABSTRACT

The traditional notion of fault tolerance requires that *all* the correct participating processes eventually terminate, and thus, is not sensitive to the *number* of correct processes that should properly terminate as a result of failures. Intuitively, an algorithm that in the presence of any number of faults always guarantees that all the correct processes except maybe one properly terminate, is more resilient to faults than an algorithm that in the presence of a single fault does not even guarantee that a single correct process ever terminates. However, according to the standard notion of fault tolerance both algorithms are classified as algorithms that can not tolerate a single fault.

To overcome this difficulty, we generalize the traditional notion of fault tolerance in a way which enables to capture more sensitive information about the resiliency of an algorithm. Then, we present several algorithms for solving classical problems which are resilient under the new notion. It is well known that, in an asynchronous systems where processes communicate either by reading and writing atomic registers or by sending and receiving messages, important problems such as, consensus, set-consensus, election, perfect renaming, implementations of a test-and-set bit, a shared stack, a swap object and a fetch-and-add object have no deterministic solutions which can tolerate even a single fault. We show that while, some of these problems have solutions which guarantee that in the presence of *any* number of faults most of the correct processes will properly terminate; other problems do not even have solutions which guarantee that in the presence of just *one* fault at least one correct process properly terminates.

Categories and Subject Descriptors

F.0 [**Theory of Computation**]: General

General Terms

Algorithms, Reliability, Theory

Keywords

Fault tolerance, shared memory, message passing, election, test-and-set, renaming, consensus, set-consensus, stack, swap, fetch-and-add.

1. INTRODUCTION

1.1 Motivation

According to the standard notion of fault tolerance, an algorithm is *t*-resilient if in the presence of up to *t* faults, *all* the correct processes can still properly complete their operations and terminate. Thus, an algorithm is *not t*-resilient, if as a result of *t* faults there is *some* correct process that can not properly terminate. This traditional notion of fault tolerance is not sensitive to the *number* of correct processes that may or may not complete their operations as a result of the failure of other processes.

Consider for example the renaming problem, which allows processes, with distinct initial names from a large name space, to get distinct new names from a small name space. A renaming algorithm that in the presence of any number of faults always guarantees that *most* of the correct processes, but not necessarily all, get distinct new names is clearly more resilient than a renaming algorithm that in the presence of a single fault does not guarantee that even one correct process ever gets a new name. However, using the standard notion of fault tolerance, it is not possible to compare the resiliency of such algorithms – as both are simply not even 1-resilient. This motivates us to suggest and investigate a more general notion of fault tolerance.

We have generalized the traditional notion of fault tolerance by allowing a limited number participating correct processes not to terminate in the presence of faults. Every process that do terminate is required to return a correct result. Thus, our definition guarantees safety but may sacrifice liveness (termination), for a limited number of processes, in the presence of faults. The consequences of violating liveness are often less sever than those of violating safety. In fact, there are systems that can detect and abort processes that run for too long. Sacrificing liveness for few of the processes allows us to increase the resiliency of the whole system.

1.2 Model and Basic Definitions

Our model of computation consists of an asynchronous collection of *n* processes that communicate either by reading and writing atomic registers or by sending and receiving messages. The processes have unique identifiers. With an atomic register, it is assumed that operations on the register occur in some definite order. That is, reading or writing an atomic register is an indivisible action.

With required participation every process must eventually execute its code. However, a more interesting and practical situation is one in which participation is not required, as is usually assumed when solving resource allocation problems. Unless explicitly stated, when the shared memory model is considered, it is assumed that participate is *not* required. When the message passing model is considered, it is assumed that: participate is required, a process starts participating spontaneously or when receiving a first message. Once a process starts participating it may fail by *crashing*.

In the literature, it is common to assume that the identifiers of the n processes are integers taken from the range $\{1, ..., n\}$. However, there may be situations when there are many more identifiers than processes. For example, there might be a small number of processes, say 50, but their identifiers can be taken from the range $\{0, ..., 2^{32}\}$. In such a case identifiers cannot be easily used to index registers, and hence it is better to use symmetric algorithms.

> **Symmetric Algorithms:** A symmetric algorithm is an algorithm in which the only way for distinguishing processes is by comparing identifiers, which are unique. Identifiers can be written, read and compared, but there is no way of looking inside any identifier. Thus, identifiers cannot be used to index shared registers.

Designing symmetric algorithms is especially important, when the designed algorithms are intended to be used as a building blocks in an environment where the processes' name space is not known in advance. Most of the algorithms presented in this paper are symmetric.

1.3 Fault Tolerance

For the rest of the paper, n denotes the number of processes, t denotes the number of faulty processes, and $N = \{0, 1, ..., n\}$.

> **Definition:** For a given function $f : N \to N$, an algorithm is (t, f)-*resilient* if in the presence of t' faults at most $f(t')$ participating correct processes may *not* properly terminate their operations, for every $0 \le t' \le t$.

It seems that (t, f)-*resiliency* is interesting only when requiring that $f(0) = 0$. That is, in the absence of faults all the participating processes must properly terminate. The standard definition of t-resiliency is equivalent to (t, f)-resiliency where $f(t') = 0$ for every $0 \le t' \le t$. Thus, the familiar notion of *wait-freedom* is equivalent to $(n - 1, f)$-resiliency where $f(t') = 0$ for every $0 \le t' \le n - 1$. The new notion of (t, f)-resiliency is quite general, and in this paper we focus mainly on the following three levels of resiliency.

- An algorithm is *almost-t-resilient* if it is (t, f)-*resilient*, for a function f where $f(0) = 0$ and $f(t') = 1$, for every $1 \le t' \le t$. Thus, in the presence of any number of up to t faults, all the correct participating processes, except maybe one process must properly terminate.

- An algorithm is *partially-t-resilient* if it is (t, f)-*resilient*, for a function f where $f(0) = 0$ and $f(t') = t'$, for every $1 \le t' \le t$. Thus, in the presence of any number

$t' \le t$ faults, all the correct participating processes, except maybe t' of them must properly terminate.

- An algorithm is *weakly-t-resilient* if it is (t, f)-*resilient*, for a function f where $f(0) = 0$, and in the presence of any number of up to $t \ge 1$ faults, if there are *two* or more correct participating processes then one correct participating process must properly terminate. (Notice that for $n = 2$, if one process fails the other one is not required to terminate.)

For $n \ge 3$ and $t < n/2$, the notion of weakly-t-resiliency is strictly weaker than the notion of partially-t-resiliency. For $n \ge 3$, the notions of weakly-t-resiliency is strictly weaker than the notion of almost-t-resiliency. For $n \ge 3$ and $t \ge 2$, the notions of partially-t-resiliency is strictly weaker than almost-t-resiliency. For all n, partially-1-resiliency and almost-1-resiliency are equivalent. For $n = 2$ these three notions are equivalent. We say that an algorithm is *almost-wait-free* if it is *almost-$(n - 1)$-resilient*, thus, in the presence of any number of faults, all the participating correct processes, except maybe one process must terminate. We say that an algorithm is *partially-wait-free* if it is *partially-$(n - 1)$-resilient*, thus, in the presence of any number of $t \le n - 1$ faults, all the correct participating processes, except maybe t of them must properly terminate.

In an asynchronous shared memory system which supports atomic registers or in a message passing system, important problems such as consensus, set-consensus, election, perfect renaming, implementations of a test-and-set bit, a shared stack, a swap object and a fetch-and-add object, have no solutions which can tolerate even a single fault. Rather surprisingly, as we will show later, while some of these problems have solutions which satisfy almost-wait-freedom, other problems do not even have weakly-1-resilient solutions.

1.4 Contributions

New Definitions. We generalize the traditional notion of fault tolerance. Together with the technical results, the new definitions provide a deeper understanding of complexity and computability issues which are involved in the development of fault-tolerant algorithms.

Election. In this problem one or more processes independently initiate their participation in an election to decide on a leader. Each participating process should eventually output either 0 or 1 and terminate. At most one process may output 1, and in the absence of faults exactly one of the *participating* processes should output 1. The process which outputs 1 is the elected leader. It is known that there is no 1-resilient election algorithm, when processes communicate either by reading and writing atomic registers or by sending and receiving messages. We show that:

> (1) *There is an almost-wait-free symmetric election algorithm using $\lceil \log n \rceil + 2$ atomic registers.*
> (2) *There is an almost-wait-free symmetric election algorithm with $n^2 - n$ message complexity.*

Message complexity is the total number of message sent. The known space lower bound for election in the absence of faults is $\lceil \log n \rceil + 1$ atomic registers [33].

Test-and-set. A test-and-set bit is an object that supports two operations called *test-and-set* and *reset*. A test-and-set operation on a single bit takes as argument a shared bit b, assigns the value 1 to b, and returns the previous value of b (which can be either 0 or 1). A reset operation takes as argument a shared registers b and writes the value 0 into b. We show that:

> (1) There is an almost-wait-free symmetric implementation of a test-and-set bit for n processes using $n+1$ atomic registers. (2) Any implementation of a test-and-set bit for n processes using registers must use at least n registers, even in the absence of faults.

It is known that in asynchronous systems where processes communicate using atomic registers there are no 1-resilient implementations of a test-and-set bit [28].

Perfect Renaming. A *perfect* renaming algorithm allows n processes with initially distinct names from a large name space to acquire distinct new names from the set $\{1, ...n\}$. A *one-shot* renaming algorithm allows each process to acquire a distinct new name just once. A *long-lived* renaming algorithm allows processes to repeatedly acquire distinct names and release them. We show that:

> (1) There is a partially-wait-free symmetric one-shot perfect renaming algorithm using (a) $n-1$ almost-wait-free election objects, or (b) $O(n \log n)$ registers, or (c) $O(n^3)$ messages. (2) There is a partially-wait-free symmetric long-lived perfect renaming algorithm using either $n-1$ almost-wait-free test-and-set bits or $O(n^2)$ registers.

It is known that in asynchronous systems where processes communicate either by atomic registers or by sending and receiving messages, there is no 1-resilient perfect renaming algorithm [7, 30, 35].

Fetch-and-add, swap, stack. A *fetch-and-add* object supports an operation which takes as arguments a shared register r, and a value *val*. The value of r is incremented by *val*, and the old value of r is returned. A *swap* object supports an operation which takes as arguments a shared registers and a local register and atomically exchange their values. A shared stack is a linearizable object that supports push and pop operations, by several processes, with the usual stack semantics. We show that:

> There are partially-wait-free implementations of a fetch-and-add object, a swap object, and a stack object using atomic registers.

The result complements the results that in asynchronous systems where processes communicate using registers there are no 1-resilient implementations of fetch-and-add, swap, and stack objects [13, 22].

Consensus and Set-consensus. The *k-set consensus* problem is to find a solution for n processes, where each process starts with an input value from some domain, and must choose some participating process' input as its output. All n processes together may choose no more than k distinct output values. The 1-set consensus problem, is the familiar consensus problem. We show that:

> (1) For $n \geq 3$ and $1 \leq k \leq n-2$, there is no weakly-k-resilient k-set-consensus algorithm us-

ing either atomic registers or sending and receiving messages. In particular, for $n \geq 3$, there is no weakly-1-resilient consensus algorithm using either atomic registers or messages. (2) For $n \geq 3$ and $1 \leq k \leq n-2$, there is no weakly-k-resilient k-set-consensus algorithm using almost-wait-free test-and-set bits and atomic registers.

Our results strengthen the know results that, in asynchronous systems where processes communicate either by atomic registers or by sending and receiving messages, there is no 1-resilient consensus algorithm [20, 28], and there is no k-resilient k-set-consensus algorithm [12, 23, 32].

1.5 Related Work

In [33] it is proved that, in the absence of failures, $\lceil \log n \rceil + 1$ registers are necessary and sufficient for symmetric election, assuming that only the elected leader is required to ever terminate, while n registers are necessary and sufficient for deadlock-free symmetric mutual exclusion. We use some key ideas from [33], in our implementations of an almost-wait-free election object and an almost-wait-free test-and-set bit. The impossibility result that there are no election algorithm and no perfect renaming algorithm that can tolerate a single crash failure was first proved for the asynchronous message-passing model in [8, 30], and later has been extended for the shared memory model in [35].

The one-shot renaming problem was first solved for message-passing systems [8], and later for shared memory systems [11]. In [17] a long-lived wait-free renaming algorithm was presented. Several of the many papers on renaming are [1, 3, 4, 5, 9, 10, 14, 18, 21, 23, 26, 29].

The consensus problem was formally defined in [31]. The impossibility result that there is no consensus algorithm that can tolerate even a single crash failure was first proved for the asynchronous message-passing model in [20], and later has been extended for the shared memory model with atomic registers, in [28]. The impossibility result that, for $1 \leq k \leq n-1$ there is no k-resilient k-set-consensus algorithm for n processes using atomic registers, is from [12, 23, 32].

Extensions of the notion of fault tolerance, which are different from those considered in this paper, were proposed recently in[19], where a precise way is presented to characterize adversaries by introducing the notion of disagreement power: the biggest integer k for which the adversary can prevent processes from agreeing on k values when using registers only; and it is shown how to compute the disagreement power of an adversary. The ability to solve consensus under various symmetric and asymmetric progress conditions was studied in [25, 34].

A comprehensive discussion of wait-free synchronization is given in [22]. In [6], a class of objects called Common2 is defined. Each object in Common2 has a wait-free implementation from registers together with any other object in Common2. Commonly used objects such as test-and-set, fetch-and-add, swap, and stack are in Common2 [2, 6]. In [24], the related notion of a non-blocking is introduced. It guarantees that some correct process with a pending operation, will always be able to complete its operation in a finite number of its own steps regardless of the execution speed of other processes. For one-shot objects wait-freedom and non-blocking are the same.

2. ALMOST-WAIT-FREE SYMMETRIC ELECTION

In the leader election problem, processes do not have inputs. Each participating process should eventually output either 0 or 1 and terminate. At most one process may output the value 1, and in the absence of faults exactly one of the participating processes should output 1. The process which outputs 1 is elected as a leader. It is not require that the processes know the identity of the leader. The elected leader must be one of the participating processes, thus, there can not be an a priori leader.

In asynchronous systems where processes communicate either using atomic registers or by sending and receiving messages, election is impossible with one faulty process [20, 30, 35]. We show below that almost-wait-free symmetric election is possible in such asynchronous systems. This possibility result for election is later used for solving perfect renaming. We point out that, it follows from the results presented in Section 6 for the consensus problem, that for a stronger definition of election in which it is required that the processes know (i.e., output) the identity of the leader, even weakly-1-resilient strong-election is impossible.

2.1 Election using atomic registers

In [33], an election algorithm which is *not* weakly-1-resilient is presented. It is correct under the following assumptions: (1) processes never fail, and (2) only the elected leader is required to terminate. The election algorithm presented below, is based on the algorithm from [33].

THEOREM 2.1. *There is an almost-wait-free symmetric election algorithm using $\lceil \log n \rceil + 2$ atomic registers.*

The algorithm below is for n processes each with a unique identifier taken from some (possibly infinite) set which does not include 0. The algorithm uses the shared registers $turn$ and $done$ and the array of registers V. All these registers are initially 0. Also, for each process, the local variables $level$ and j are used. We denote by $e.turn$, $e.done$ and $e.V[*]$ the shared registers of the specific election algorithm (object) named e. This should simplify the construction of algorithms that use election as a basic building block.

AN ALMOST-WAIT-FREE SYMMETRIC ELECTION: process p's program.

```
function election (e: object_name) return:value in {0,1};
1    e.turn := p;
2    for level := 1 to ⌈log n⌉ do
3        repeat
4            if e.done = 1 then return(0) fi;   /*not leader*/
5            if e.turn ≠ p then
6                for j := 1 to level − 1 do
7                    if e.V[j] = p then e.V[j] := 0 fi od;
8                return(0) fi              /* not the leader */
9            until e.V[level] = 0;
10           e.V[level] := p;
11           if e.turn ≠ p then
12               for j := 1 to level do
13                   if e.V[j] = p then e.V[j] := 0 fi od;
14               return(0) fi              /* not the leader */
15   od;
16   e.done := 1; return(1).              /* leader! */
end_function
```

The process that is last to write to $e.turn$ (line 1) attempts to become the leader. It does so, by waiting for each of the registers $e.V[j]$ to be 0 (lines 3-9) and then sets the register to its id (line 10). A process becomes the leader if it manages to write its id into all the registers during the period that $e.turn$ equals its id. Any process that notices that $e.turn$ is no longer equals its id, gives up on becoming the leader, and erase any write it has made (lines 6 & 12).

There are runs of the algorithm in which every process manages to set $\lceil \log n \rceil$ registers before discovering that another process has modified $e.turn$, and as a result has to set back to 0 some of the registers before terminating. Proving the correctness of the algorithm is rather challenging, due to the existence of such runs.

In [33], it has been proven that, even in the absence of faults, any election algorithm for n processes must use at least $\lceil \log n \rceil + 1$ registers. (This lower bound holds even for non-symmetric algorithms.) Thus, our algorithm which uses $\lceil \log n \rceil + 2$ registers, provides an almost tight space upper bound.

2.2 Correctness proof

The proof of the election algorithm is an adaptation of the proof for the algorithm from [33] which guarantees that only the leader terminates, and is correct only in the absence of faults. The fact that our election algorithm uses $\lceil \log n \rceil + 2$ atomic registers is obvious from inspecting the algorithm.

THEOREM 2.2 (LIVENESS). *In the absence of faults, at least one leader is elected.*

PROOF. Assume to the contrary that no leader is elected. Let r be an infinite run with no faults where no leader is elected, and let p be the last processes to write to $turn$ in run r. Let q be the process with the highest value of $level$ when p writes to $turn$. At some point q will notice that $turn \neq q$, and set back to 0, all the entries of the array V which equal to q. Repeat this argument with the new highest process. Thus, any entry of the array V which process p may wait on, will eventually be set back to 0, enabling p to proceed until it is elected. A contradiction. □

We say that a process is at level k, when the value of its private $level$ register is k.

LEMMA 2.3. *For any $k \in \{1, ..., \lceil \log n \rceil\}$, out of all the processes that are in level k during a time interval where $V[k]$ continuously holds the value 0, at most one process can: (1) continue level $k+1$ or (2) change any register other than $V[k]$.*

PROOF. Assume that a set of processes $p_1, ..., p_\ell$ are at level k, and during the time interval where $V[k]$ continuously holds the value 0, they all notice that $V[level] = 0$ when executing the until statement in line 9. One of these processes, say p_1, must be the last to update $turn$. If $k = 1$, each process in $\{p_2, ..., p_\ell\}$ will notice that $turn$ is different from its id (line 11), possibly write 0 into $V[1]$, and return 0. Assume $k > 1$. Before p_1 has set $turn$ to its id, each of the other processes at level k, must have seen in level $k − 1$ that $turn$ is equal to its id. This means that before any of the processes $p_2, ..., p_\ell$ could execute the assignment at line 10, p_1 has already set $V[1], ..., V[k−1]$ to its id. Thus, when each process at level k, other than p_1, executes the if statement in line 11, it finds out that $turn$ is different from its id, possibly write 0 into $V[k]$, and returns 0, without a need to write 0 to any of the registers $V[1], ..., V[k-1]$. Process p_1, may continue to level $k+1$ or itself notices that $turn \neq p_1$ and sets some or all of the registers $V[1], ..., V[k-1]$ to 0, but its is the only process, among the processes $p_1, ..., p_\ell$, that may set any register other than $V[k]$. □

THEOREM 2.4   (SAFETY). *At most one leader is elected.*

For proving the theorem, an accounting system of credits is used. Initially, the number of credits is $2n-1$. New credits can not be created during the execution of the algorithm. The credit system ensures that a process acquires exactly 2^{k-1} credits before it can reach level k. Being elected is equivalent to reaching level $\log n + 1$. Thus, the credit system ensures that a process must acquire $2^{\log n + 1 - 1} = n$ credits before it can be elected. Once a process is elected, it may not release any of its credits. Thus, it is not possible for two processes to get elected.

With out loss of generality it is assumed that n, the number of processes, is a power of 2. Initially, each process holds 1 credit, and each register $V[k]$ where $1 \leq k \leq \log n$ holds 2^{k-1} credits. Thus, the total number of credits is $n + \sum_{k=1}^{\log n} 2^{k-1} = 2n - 1$. As a results of an operation taken by a process credits may be transferred from a register to a process and vice versa. We list below all possible operations by processes and their effect:

- No credits are transferred when a process (1) checks the value of a register, (2) writes into $turn$, or (3) executes a *return* statement.

- When a process writes its id into register $V[k]$, changing $V[k]$'s value from 0 to its id, 2^{k-1} credits are transferred from $V[k]$ to that process. When a process writes 0 into register $V[k]$ which does not already holding 0, 2^{k-1} credits are transferred to $V[k]$ from that process.

- Let one or more processes notice that $V[k] = 0$. By Lemma 2.3, at most one of them can continue level $k+1$. Assume one of them continues to level $k+1$. By Lemma 2.3, the processes that do not continue to the next level can only execute $V[k] := 0$, transferring to $V[k]$ the 2^{k-1} credits they have by getting this far. Then 2^{k-1} credits are take from $V[k]$, and are assigned to the process that continues to the next level, giving it the 2^k credits it needs for level $k+1$.

- Let one or more processes notice that $V[k] = 0$, and assume no one of them continues to level $k+1$. By Lemma 2.3, at most one of these processes, say process p, changes any register other than $V[k]$. As before, the remaining processes can transfer their credits by setting $V[k]$ to 0. Then, if p is the last to set $V[k]$, 2^{k-1} credits are taken from $V[k]$, and are assigned to p. Thus, p has 2^k credits available, 2^{k-1} credits from reaching level k, plus 2^{k-1} credits from $V[k]$. Setting to 0 every variable from $V[1]$ to $V[k]$ accounts for $2^k - 1$ credits, so p has enough credits and no new credits should be created by p when it sets to 0 multiple registers.

As already mentioned, initially, the number of credits is $2n-1$. No new credits are created, and a process must acquire

n credits before it can be elected. Once a process is elected, it may not release any of its credits. Thus, it is not possible for two processes to get elected. □

THEOREM 2.5   (ALMOST-WAIT-FREEDOM). *In the absence of faults, every participating process eventually terminates. In the presence of faults, every correct participating process, except maybe one, eventually terminates.*

PROOF. Once a leader is elected and returns, all correct participating processes will eventually find out that $done = 1$ and properly terminate. In particular, in the absence of faults, since by Theorem 2.2 at least leader is eventually elected, all the participating processes will terminate. Also, regardless of the number of faults, a correct process which is not the last to write into $turn$, will eventually either notices this fact and terminates or be elected and terminates. Thus, in the presence of faults, only the last process to write into $turn$ may be blocked. □

2.3   Election in a message passing system

We present a simple election algorithm in which the process with the maximum identifer is elected.

THEOREM 2.6. *There is an almost-wait-free symmetric election algorithm with $n^2 - n$ message complexity.*

PROOF. In the algorithm each process sends its identifer to every other process, and collects, through the messages seen, identifiers of other processes. As soon as a process collects an identifer which is bigger than itself it returns 0. If a process collects the identifiers of all the other $n-1$ processes, and finds out that it is the process with the maximum identifer, it returns 1. In the code below $my.id$ refers to the identifier of the process executing the algorithm, and $message.val$ refers to the value of the message received. Each process has a local $counter$ variable which is initially set to 0.

ALMOST-WAIT-FREE SYMMETRIC ELECTION ALGORITHM: program for a process with identifier $my.id$.

```
1 send my.id to all the other processes;
2 each time a message is received do
3     if my.id < message.val then
4         return(0) else counter := counter + 1 fi;
5     if counter = n − 1 then return(1) fi      /* leader! */
6 od
```

Clearly, in the absence of faults exactly one process is elected and it is always the process with the maximum identifer. In the presence of faults, only the correct participating process with the maximum identifier *among* the currently participating processes may not terminate, all the other processes will get a message from it, return 0 and terminate. The message complexity is $n^2 - n$, since each process sends one message to each other process. □

3.   ALMOST-WAIT-FREE SYMMETRIC TEST-AND-SET BIT

We show that n registers are necessary and $n+1$ registers are sufficient for implementing a single almost-wait-free test-and-set bit using registers for n processes. A test-and-set bit supports two atomic operations called *test-and-set* and *reset*. A test-and-set operation takes as argument a shared bit b, assigns the value 1 to b, and returns the previous value of b (which can be either 0 or 1). A reset operation takes as argument a shared bit b and writes the value 0 into b.

The *sequential specification* of an object specifies how the object behaves in sequential runs, that is, in runs when its operations are applied sequentially. The sequential specification of a test-and-set bit is quite simple. In sequential runs, the first test-and-set operation returns 0, a test-and-set operation that happens immediately after a reset operation also returns 0, and all other test-and-set operations return 1. We require that, although operations of processes may overlap, each operation should appear to take effect instantaneously. In particular, operations that do not overlap should take effect in their "real-time" order. This correctness requirement is called *linearizability* [24].

3.1 Upper bound

The algorithm below is for n processes each with a unique identifier taken from some (possibly infinite) set which does not include 0. It makes use of exactly n registers which are long enough to store a process identifier and one atomic bit. The algorithm is based on the symmetric mutual exclusion algorithm presented in [33].

THEOREM 3.1. *There is an almost-wait-free symmetric algorithm which implements a test-and-set bit using atomic registers. The algorithm is for n processes and uses $n + 1$ atomic registers.*

The algorithm uses a register called *turn* to indicate who has priority to return 1, $n - 1$ *lock* registers to ensure that at most one process will return 1 between resets, and a bit call *winner* to indicate whether some process already returned 1. Initially the values of all these shared registers are 0. In addition each process has a private boolean variable call *locked*. We denote by $b.turn$, $b.winner$ and $b.lock[*]$ the shared registers of the specific test-and-set *bit* named b.

AN ALMOST-WAIT-FREE SYMMETRIC TEST-AND-SET BIT: process p's program.

function *test-and-set* (b:bit) **return**:value in $\{0, 1\}$;
1   **if** $b.turn \neq 0$ **then** *return*(0) **fi**;   /* lost */
2   $b.turn := p$;
3   **repeat**
4   **for** $j := 1$ **to** $n - 1$ **do**   /* get locks */
5   **if** $b.lock[j] = 0$ **then** $b.lock[j] := p$ **fi od**
6       $locked := 1$;
7   **for** $j := 1$ **to** $n - 1$ **do**   /* have all locks? */
8   **if** $b.lock[j] \neq p$ **then** $locked := 0$ **fi od**;
9   **until** $b.turn \neq p$ **or** $locked = 1$ **or** $b.winner = 1$;
10 **if** $b.turn \neq p$ **or** $b.winner = 1$ **then**
11   **for** $j := 1$ **to** $n - 1$ **do**   /* lost, release locks */
12   **if** $b.lock[j] = p$ **then** $b.lock[j] := 0$ **fi od**
13   *return*(0) **fi**;
14 $b.winner := 1$; *return*(1).   /* wins */
end_function

function *reset* (b:bit);   /* access bit b */
1   $b.winner := 0$; $b.turn := 0$;   /* release locks */
2   **for** $j := 1$ **to** $n - 1$ **do**
3   **if** $b.lock[j] = p$ **then** $b.lock[j] := 0$ **fi od**.
end_function

In the test-and-set operation, a process, say p, initially checks whether $b.turn = 0$, and if so returns 0. Otherwise, p takes

priority by setting $b.turn$ to p, and attempts to obtain all the $n - 1$ locks by setting them to p. This prevents other processes that also saw $b.turn = 0$ and set $b.turn$ to their ids from entering. That is, if p obtains all the locks before the other processes set $b.turn$, they will not be able to get any of the locks since the values of the locks are not 0. Otherwise, if p sees $b.turn \neq p$ or $b.winner = 1$, it will release the locks it holds, allowing some other process to proceed, and will return 0. In the reset operation, p sets $b.turn$ to 0, so the other processes can proceed, and releases all the locks it currently holds.

3.2 Correctness proof

We prove that our implementation is linearizable w.r.t. the sequential specification of a test-and-set bit mentioned earlier. For that it is enough to prove the following theorems. We say that run is *well structured*, if in that run a reset operation may be initiated only by a process that its last operation (before applying the reset operation) is a test-and-set operation which has returned 0. We say that a process is a *winner* in a given finite run, if the *last* completed operation of that process in the run is a test-and-set operation which has returned 0.

THEOREM 3.2   (SAFETY). *There is at most one winner in any well structured run.*

PROOF. Assume some process p is a winner. We show that no other process can become a winner before p preforms a reset operation. When process p last accessed *turn* and the $n - 1$ locks, the value of each of these n shared registers was p. Any other process has to set all the $n - 1$ locks and see *turn* set to its value for it to become a winner. But a process always checks a lock before writing it, and can only change one lock which has been already set (and not released yet) by some other process. So if all the n shared registers have the value p, and each of the remaining $n - 1$ processes can overwrite at most one such register, at least one shared register must still hold the value p, preventing processes other than p from becoming winners.   □

We say that a pending test-and-set operations is *potentially successful* if no process has become a winner since the operation was issued.

THEOREM 3.3   (LIVENESS). *In the absence of faults, at least one process will eventually become a winner, in any given run with potentially successful pending test-and-set operations.*

PROOF. Assume to the contrary that no process will become a winner. Since no process becomes a winner, *turn* is not set back to 0, and hence *turn* must eventually have a nonzero value, say p, and this value will not change thereafter. Every participating process other than p will eventually notice *turn* = p, it will release the locks it holds, will return 0 and thereafter will not update any other registers because *turn* is not zero. At this point, since process p always finds *turn* = p, nothing is preventing process p from getting all the locks and becoming a winner. A contradiction.   □

THEOREM 3.4   (ALMOST-WAIT-FREEDOM). *In the absence of faults, every participating process (i.e, pending operation) eventually returns. In the presence of faults, every correct participating process, except maybe one, eventually returns.*

PROOF. Once some process becomes the winner and returns 1, as long as the winner does not initiate a reset operation, all correct participating processes will eventually find out that $done = 1$ and return 0. In particular, in the absence of faults, since by Theorem 3.3 at least one process will eventually become the winner, all the participating processes will return. Also, regardless of the number of faults, a correct process which is not the last to write *turn*, will eventually either notice this fact and return 0 or becomes the winner and returns 1. Thus, in the presence of faults, only the last process to write *turn* may be blocked. □

3.3 Lower bound

We show that the $n + 1$ space upper bound is almost tight.

OBSERVATION 3.5. *Even in the absence of faults, any implementation of a test-and-set bit for n processes using atomic registers must use at least n atomic registers.*

PROOF. In [15, 16], it is proven that any deadlock-free mutual exclusion algorithm for n processes must use at least n shared registers. On the other hand, it is trivial to implement a deadlock-free mutual exclusion algorithm for n processes using a single test-and-set bit, say x, as follows: A process first keeps on accessing x until, in one atomic step, it succeeds to change x from 0 to 1. Then, the process can safely enter its critical section. The exit code is to reset x to 0. It is trivial to show that the algorithm satisfies mutual exclusion and is deadlock-free. The result follows. □

4. PARTIALLY-WAIT-FREE SYMMETRIC PERFECT RENAMING

A *renaming* algorithm allows processes with initially distinct initial names from a large name space to acquire distinct new names from a small name space. A *perfect* renaming algorithm allows n processes with initially distinct names from a large name space to acquire distinct new names from the set $\{1, ... n\}$. A *one-shot* renaming algorithm allows each process to acquire a distinct new name just once. A *long-lived* renaming algorithm allows processes to repeatedly acquire distinct names and release them (however, once a process acquires a new name it must first release it before trying to acquire another one).

It is well known that, in asynchronous systems where processes communicate either by reading and writing atomic registers or by sending and receiving messages, there is no 1-resilient perfect renaming algorithm [7, 30, 35]. Contrary to this impossibility result, we show that there is a partially-wait-free perfect renaming algorithm in such systems. A *partially-wait-free* renaming algorithm, should guarantee that t failures, where $1 \leq t \leq n-1$, may prevent at most t correct participating processes from acquiring new names.

THEOREM 4.1. *There is a partially-wait-free symmetric one-shot perfect renaming algorithm using either (1) $n-1$ almost-wait-free election objects, (2) $O(n \log n)$ registers, or (3) $O(n^3)$ messages.*

PROOF. First we present an algorithm which uses $n-1$ almost-wait-free election objects. The election objects are indexed $1,2,....,n-1$. Each process scans the objects, in order, starting with object number 1. At each step, the process applies the election operation, and either: moves to

the next object if it is not elected in object $i < n-1$, stops if it is being elected, or stops if it not elected in object $n-1$. The process is assigned either the name equal to the index of the object on which its election operation has succeeded, or n if it is not elected in all $n-1$ objects. Notice that at most $n-i+1$ processes may participate in object i, for $1 \leq i \leq n-1$. Thus, by Theorem 2.1, the almost-wait-free, election object indexed i, where $1 \leq i \leq n-1$, can be implemented using $\lceil \log(n-i+1) \rceil + 2$ atomic registers. Thus, the number of registers used are at most:

$$3(n-1) + \sum_{i=2}^{n} \log i = 3(n-1) + \log n! = O(n \log n).$$

Finally, by Theorem 2.6, there is an implementation of an almost-wait-free symmetric election object for n processes which has $n^2 - n$ message complexity. The result follows. □

THEOREM 4.2. *There is a partially-wait-free symmetric long-lived perfect renaming algorithm using either $n-1$ almost-wait-free test-and-set bits or $O(n^2)$ atomic registers.*

PROOF. First we present an algorithm which uses $n-1$ almost-wait-free test-and-set bit bits. The bits have initial values 0, and are indexed $1,2,....,n-1$. Each process scans the bits, in order, starting with bit number 1. At each step, the process applies a *test-and-set* operation, and either: moves to the next bit if the returned value is 1 in bit $i < n-1$, stops when the returned value is 0, or stops if the returned value is 1 in bit $n-1$. The process is assigned the name equal to the index of the bit on which its (last) *test-and-set* operation returned 0, or n if the returned value is 1 in all $n-1$ bits. A process which is assigned the name i can later release this name by applying a *reset* operation to the i'th bit setting its value back to 0. A process which is assigned the name n doesn't have to access any shared bit to release the name n. At most $n-i+1$ processes may concurrently access the bit indexed i, for $1 \leq i \leq n-1$. Thus, by Theorem 3.1, the bit indexed i, where $1 \leq i \leq n-1$, can be implemented using $n-i+2$ registers. Thus, the number of registers used are:

$$\sum_{i=2}^{n} (i+1) = \frac{n^2 + 3n - 4}{2}.$$

The result follows. □

5. PARTIALLY-WAIT-FREE FETCH-AND-ADD, SWAP, AND STACK

A *fetch-and-add* object supports one operation, which takes as arguments a shared register r, and a value *val*. The value of r is incremented by *val*, and the old value of r is returned. A *swap* object supports one operation, which takes as arguments a shared registers and a local register and atomically exchange their values. A concurrent *stack* is a linearizable object that supports push and pop operations, by several processes, with the usual stack semantics. A *sequential* process is a process that has at most one pending operation at any given time.

LEMMA 5.1. *Assume that there is a wait-free implementation for n sequential processes of an object o using wait-free test-and-set bits and atomic registers. Then, there is a partially-wait-free implementation for n processes of o using atomic registers only.*

PROOF. Let A be a wait-free implementation for n sequential processes of an object o using wait-free test-and-set bits and registers. Let A' be the implementation A where each wait-free test-and-set bit is replaced with an almost-wait-free test-and-set bit. While executing A', a failure of a process with a pending test-and-set operation, may prevent at most one other process from completing its operation in A'. Thus, a failure of t processes may prevent at most t other process from completing their operations. This implies that A' is a partially-wait-free implementation of o using almost-wait-free test-and-set bits and registers. By Theorem 3.1, we can replace each almost-wait-free test-and-set bit in A', by an implementation using atomic registers. The result follows. □

THEOREM 5.2. *There are partially-wait-free implementations for n processes of a fetch-and-add object, a swap object, and a stack object using atomic registers only.*

PROOF. In [6], a class of shared objects called Common2 were defined. Each object in Common2 is known to have a wait-free implementation from registers together with any other object in Common2, for an arbitrary number of sequential processes. Commonly used primitives such as test-and-set, fetch-and-add, swap, and stack are in Common2 [2, 6]. Thus, any of the objects in Commom2 has a wait-free implemention using registers and wait-free test-and-set bits, for arbitrary number of sequential processes. (The implementations presented in [6] are not symmetric.) This last observation together with Lemma 5.1 implies that there are partially-wait-free implementations for n processes of a fetch-and-add object, a swap object, and a stack object using atomic registers only. □

6. IMPOSSIBILITY RESULTS FOR CONSENSUS AND SET-CONSENSUS

The *k-set consensus* problem is to find a solution for n processes, where each process starts with an input value from some domain, and must choose some participating process' input as its output. All n processes together may choose no more than k distinct output values. The 1-set consensus problem, is the familiar consensus problem for n processes.

The consensus and set-consensus problems belong to a class of problems called *colorless tasks*. Colorless tasks (also called convergence tasks [13]) allow a process to adopt an input or output value of any other participating process, so the task can be defined in terms of input and output sets instead of vectors.

For proving the following lemma we need to assume a model where participation is required. Recall that with required participation every process must eventually execute its code.

LEMMA 6.1. *Assume a model where participation is required, $n \geq 3$ and $t \leq n - 2$. When processes communicate either by reading and writing atomic registers or by sending and receiving messages, for any colorless task T: there is a weakly-t-resilient algorithm which solves T if and only if there is a t-resilient algorithm which solves T.*

PROOF. Let A be a weakly-t-resilient algorithm using atomic registers which solves T. We use A to implement a t-resilient algorithm, called A', which uses atomic registers

and solves T. An additional shared register called *output* is used, which has initial value $\perp$. Every process executes as in A, and before it terminates it writes its output into *output*. During its execution of A, a process also continuously checks whether *output* $\neq \perp$, and in case the test is positive, it adopts the value of *output* as its own output value and terminates. Since participation is required, $n \geq 3$ and $t \leq n - 2$, one correct process will eventually terminate. Once one correct process writes its output into *output*, it is guaranteed that each participating correct will eventually either terminates according its code in A, or will notice that *output* $\neq \perp$, and properly terminates. The resulting algorithm is A'. Proving the other direction is trivial. The proof for the case where communication is by sending and receiving messages is almost the same. Instead of writing to *output*, a process sends its decision to everyone before terminating. Each process that receives a message with such a decision value, decides on that value, sends it to everyone and terminates. □

The following results hold for a model where participation is required, and thus also hold for a model where participation is not required.

THEOREM 6.2. *For $n \geq 3$, there is no weakly-1-resilient consensus algorithm using either reading and writing atomic registers or sending and receiving messages.*

PROOF. The proof follows from Lemma 6.1 and the known result that there is no 1-resilient consensus algorithm using either reading and writing atomic registers or sending and receiving messages [20, 28]. This known impossibility result was proved for a model where participation is required and thus also trivially holds for a model where participation is not required. □

THEOREM 6.3. *For $n \geq 3$ and $1 \leq k \leq n - 2$, there is no weakly-k-resilient k-set-consensus algorithm using either reading and writing atomic registers or sending and receiving messages.*

PROOF. The proof follows from Lemma 6.1 and the known result the there for $1 \leq k \leq n - 1$, is no k-resilient k-set-consensus algorithm for n processes using atomic registers [12, 23, 32]. The impossibility result for the message passing model follows immediately from the one for the shared memory model. This known impossibility result was proved for a model where participation is required and thus also trivially holds for a model where participation is not required. □

COROLLARY 6.4. *For $n \geq 3$ and $1 \leq k \leq n-2$, there is no weakly-k-resilient k-set-consensus algorithm using almost-wait-free test-and-set bits and atomic registers.*

PROOF. The proof follows immediately from Theorem 3.1 and Theorem 6.3. □

7. DISCUSSION

We have refined the traditional notion of t-resiliency by defining the finer grained notion of (t, f)-resiliency. In particular, we have extended the investigation of fault-tolerance by presenting several new notions: weakly-t-resiliency, partially-t-resiliency and almost-t-resiliency.

In the traditional notion of t-resiliency it is assumed that failures are *uniform*: processes are equally probable to fail, and failure of one process does not affect the reliability of the other processes. As discussed in [27], in real systems, failures may be correlated because of software or hardware features shared by subsets of processes. Our new resiliency notions can be defined similarly also for such *non-uniform* failure models, and it would be interesting to extend our results to cover such failure models.

All our results are presented in the context of crash failures in asynchronous systems, it would be interesting to consider also other types of failures such as omission failures and Byzantine failures, and to consider synchronous systems. Another interesting direction would be to extend the results for other objects. In particular, is there an almost-wait-free (or even a weakly-wait-free) implementation of a shared *queue* object from registers? We have assumed that the number of processes is finite and known, it would be interesting to consider also the case of unbounded concurrency. Considering failure detectors in the context of the new definition is another interesting direction.

Several other questions are left open. We have presented a symmetric almost-wait-free implementation of a test-and-set bit from registers. Are there similar symmetric almost-wait-free implementations for, stack, swap and fetch-and-add objects from registers? In case that there is no almost-wait-free perfect renaming, what is the smallest m for which there is a solution for almost-wait-free renaming in which a process always gets a distinct name in the range $\{1, ..., m\}$? Finally, are there implementations which are more space, time or message efficient than the implementations presented?

8. REFERENCES

[1] Y. Afek, H. Attiya, A. Fouren, G. Stupp, and D. Touitou. Long-lived renaming made adaptive. In *Proc. 18th ACM Symp. on Principles of Distributed Computing*, pages 91–103, May 1999.

[2] Y. Afek, E. Gafni, and A. Morrison. Common2 extended to stacks and unbounded concurrency. In *Proc. 25th ACM Symp. on Principles of Distributed Computing*, pages 218–227, 2006.

[3] Y. Afek and M. Merritt. Fast, wait-free $(2k - 1)$-renaming. In *Proc. 18th ACM Symp. on Principles of Distributed Computing*, 105–112, 1999.

[4] Y. Afek, G. Stupp, and D. Touitou. Long-lived adaptive collect with applications. In *Proc. 40th IEEE Symp. on Foundations of Computer Science*, pages 262–272, Oct. 1999.

[5] Y. Afek, G. Stupp, and D. Touitou. Long lived adaptive splitter and applications. *Distributed Computing*, 30:67–86, 2002.

[6] Y. Afek, E. Weisberger, and H. Weisman. A completeness theorem for a class of synchronization objects (extended abstract). In *Proc. 12th ACM Symp. on Principles of Distributed Computing*, pages 159–170, 1993.

[7] H. Attiya, A. Bar-Noy, D. Dolev, D. Koller, D. Peleg, and R. Reischuk. Achievable cases in an asynchronous environment. In *Proc. 28th IEEE Symp. on Foundations of Computer Science*, 337–346, Oct. 1987.

[8] H. Attiya, A. Bar-Noy, D. Dolev, D. Koller, D. Peleg, and R. Reischuk. Renaming in an asynchronous environment. *Journal of the Association for Computing Machinery*, 37(3):524–548, July 1990.

[9] H. Attiya and A. Fouren. Polynomial and adaptive long-lived $(2k - 1)$-renaming. In *Proc. 14th International Symp. on Distributed Computing: Lecture Notes in Computer Science 1914*, pages 149–163, Oct. 2000.

[10] H. Attiya and A. Fouren. Algorithms adapting to point contention. *Journal of the ACM*, 50(4):144–468, 2003.

[11] A. Bar-Noy and D. Dolev. Shared memory versus message-passing in an asynchronous. In *Proc. 8th ACM Symp. on Principles of Distributed Computing*, pages 307–318, 1989.

[12] E. Borowsky and E. Gafni. Generalizecl FLP impossibility result for t-resilient asynchronous computations. In *Proc. 25th ACM Symp. on Theory of Computing*, pages 91–100, 1993.

[13] E. Borowsky, E. Gafni, N. A. Lynch, and S. Rajsbaum. The BG distributed simulation algorithm. *Distributed Computing*, 14(3):127–146, 2001.

[14] A. Brodsky, F. Ellen, and P. Woelfel. Fully-adaptive algorithms for long-lived renaming. *Distributed Computing*, 24(2):119–134, 2011.

[15] J. Burns and A. Lynch. Mutual exclusion using indivisible reads and writes. In *18th annual allerton conference on communication, control and computing*, pages 833–842, Oct. 1980.

[16] J. Burns and N. Lynch. Bounds on shared-memory for mutual exclusion. *Information and Computation*, 107(2):171–184, Dec. 1993.

[17] J. Burns and G. Peterson. The ambiguity of choosing. In *Proc. 8th ACM Symp. on Principles of Distributed Computing*, pages 145–158, Aug. 1989.

[18] A. Castaneda, S. Rajsbaum, and M. Raynal. The renaming problem in shared memory systems: An introduction. *Computer Science Review*, 5(3):229–251, 2011.

[19] C. Delporte-Gallet, H. Fauconnier, R. Guerraoui, and A. Tielmanns. The disagreement power of an adversary. In *Proc. 28th ACM Symp. on Principles of Distributed Computing*, pages 288–289, 2009.

[20] M. Fischer, N. Lynch, and M. Paterson. Impossibility of distributed consensus with one faulty process. *Journal of the ACM*, 32(2):374–382, 1985.

[21] E. Gafni, M. Merritt, and G. Taubenfeld. The concurrency hierarchy, and algorithms for unbounded concurrency. In *Proc. 20th ACM Symp. on Principles of Distributed Computing*, pages 161–169, Aug. 2001.

[22] M. P. Herlihy. Wait-free synchronization. *ACM Trans. on Programming Languages and Systems*, 13(1):124–149, Jan. 1991.

[23] M. P. Herlihy and N. Shavit. The topological structure of asynchronous computability. *Journal of the ACM*, 46(6):858–923, July 1999.

[24] M. P. Herlihy and J. M. Wing. Linearizability: a correctness condition for concurrent objects. *toplas*, 12(3):463–492, 1990.

[25] D. Imbs, M. Raynal, and G. Taubenfeld. On asymmetric progress conditions. In *Proc. 29th ACM Symp. on Principles of Distributed Computing*, pages 55–64, 2010.

[26] M. Inoue, S. Umetani, T. Masuzawa, and H. Fujiwara.

Adaptive long-lived $O(k^2)$-renaming with $O(k^2)$ steps. In *15th international symposium on distributed computing*, 2001. *LNCS 2180* Springer Verlag 2001, 123–135.

[27] P. Kuznetsov. Understanding non-uniform failure models. *Distributed computing column of the Bulletin of the European Association for Theoretical Computer Science (BEATCS)*, 106:54–77, 2012.

[28] M. Loui and H. Abu-Amara. Memory requirements for agreement among unreliable asynchronous processes. *Advances in Computing Research*, 4:163–183, 1987.

[29] M. Moir and J. H. Anderson. Wait-free algorithms for fast, long-lived renaming. *Science of Computer Programming*, 25(1):1–39, Oct. 1995.

[30] S. Moran and Y. Wolfstahl. Extended impossibility results for asynchronous complete networks. *Information Processing Letters*, 26(3):145–151, 1987.

[31] M. Pease, R. Shostak, and L. Lamport. Reaching agreement in the presence of faults. *Journal of the ACM*, 27(2):228–234, 1980.

[32] M. Saks and F. Zaharoglou. Wait-free k-set agreement is impossible: The topology of public knowledge. *SIAM Journal on Computing*, 29, 2000.

[33] E. Styer and G. L. Peterson. Tight bounds for shared memory symmetric mutual exclusion problems. In *Proc. 8th ACM Symp. on Principles of Distributed Computing*, pages 177–191, Aug. 1989.

[34] G. Taubenfeld. The computational structure of progress conditions. In *24th international symposium on distributed computing (DISC 2010)*, Sept. 2010. *LNCS 6343* Springer Verlag 2010, 221–235.

[35] G. Taubenfeld and S. Moran. Possibility and impossibility results in a shared memory environment. *Acta Informatica*, 33(1):1–20, 1996.

A Simple Approach for Adapting Continuous Load Balancing Processes to Discrete Settings

[Extended Abstract]

Hoda Akbari
Simon Fraser University
Burnaby, Canada
hodaa@sfu.ca

Petra Berenbrink[*]
Simon Fraser University
Burnaby, Canada
petra@sfu.ca

Thomas Sauerwald
Max Planck Institute for
Informatics
Saarbruecken, Germany
sauerwal@mpi-inf.mpg.de

ABSTRACT

We introduce a general method that converts a wide class of continuous neighborhood load balancing algorithms into a discrete version. Assume that initially the tasks are arbitrarily distributed among the nodes of a graph. In every round every node is allowed to communicate and exchange load with an arbitrary subset of its neighbors. The goal is to balance the load as evenly as possible. Continuous load balancing algorithms that are allowed to split tasks arbitrarily can balance the load perfectly, so that every node has exactly the same load. Discrete load balancing algorithms are not allowed to split tasks and therefore cannot balance the load perfectly.

In this paper we consider the problem in a very general setting, where the tasks can have arbitrary weights and the nodes can have different speeds. Given a neighborhood load balancing algorithm that balances the load perfectly in t rounds, we convert the algorithm into a discrete version. This new algorithm is deterministic and balances the load in t rounds so that the difference between the average and the maximum load is at most $2\,d \cdot w_{\max}$, where d is the maximum degree of the network and $w_{\max}$ is the maximum weight of any task. Compared to the previous methods that work for general graphs [12], our method achieves asymptotically lower discrepancies (e.g. $\mathcal{O}(1)$ vs. $\mathcal{O}(\log n)$ for constant-degree expanders and $\mathcal{O}(r)$ vs. $\mathcal{O}(n^{1/r})$ for r-dimensional tori) in the same number of rounds.

For the case of uniform weights we present a randomized version of our algorithm balancing the load so that the difference between the minimum and the maximum load is at most $O(\sqrt{d \log n})$ if the initial load on every node is large enough.

*This author's work was supported by an NSERC Discovery Grant "Analysis of Randomized Algorithms".

Categories and Subject Descriptors

C.2.4 [**Computer Systems Organization**]: Computer-Communication Networks—*Distributed Systems*

Keywords

load balancing, discrete diffusion, randomized

1. INTRODUCTION

In this paper we consider neighborhood load balancing in arbitrary networks. The network is modeled as a graph, the nodes model processors and the edges communication links. The balancing approach works in sequential rounds. In the beginning the tasks are arbitrarily distributed among the processors. We distinguish between the *continuous* and *discrete* case. In the former case tasks can be split into arbitrarily small pieces, whereas in the latter case tasks may not be divided. For the continuous model, it is not difficult to design a distributed algorithm that balances the load perfectly. However, for algorithms in the discrete case, the final load difference between minimally loaded and maximally loaded processors usually depends on the structural properties of the graph such as the maximum degree and/or the expansion. Two well-known continuous neighborhood load balancing algorithms are *diffusion* and *dimension exchange*. In diffusion, in every round every node balances its load with all neighbors. Dimension exchange algorithms use in each round at most one edge per node for load balancing, and each node sends half of its load to one of its neighbors through this edge.

Neighborhood load balancing schemes have the advantage that they are very simple and that the processors do not need any global information to base their balancing decisions on. Another advantage is that balancing with neighbors has the tendency to keep load items initiated by one processor in the neighborhood of the processor. This is an advantage if these load items are not independent and information has to be passed between them. Neighborhood load balancing schemes have applications in various areas such as job scheduling, routing, mesh computations, simulating molecular dynamics, electrostatic plasma, and computational fluid dynamics [11]. The area has received much attention by the researchers in past decades addressing the problem in a wide variety of settings.

In this paper we present a general framework that translates a continuous load balancing process into a discrete version. We assume that the discrete load balancing algorithm knows the load that is transferred over any edge of the network by its continuous counterpart. While this knowledge is not required for most of the previously analyzed algorithms, this knowledge is easy to gather: in every round the nodes simply have to store their "real" discrete load and also the load that they would have in the continuous setting. Together with the tasks that they send to their neighbors due to the discrete load balancing process, they also send them the information how much load they would have received in the continuous case.

Our approach works for a wide class of continuous algorithms, as will be formally specified in Section 1.2. This class is quite general, it contains both the first order diffusion and dimension exchange processes. Our discrete version of a continuous load balancing algorithm achieves a maximum load of average load plus d, which is the maximum degree of the graph. The runtime of our discrete version is *exactly* the same time that it takes for the continuous algorithm to balance the load in the network completely. We also present a randomized variant with the same runtime that results in a load difference of $\sqrt{d \log n}$, which is advantageous for networks with large degrees. A more detailed overview of our results as well as a comparison with the existing results can be found in Table 1.

Our method can also be applied to continuous algorithms in more general settings. In the heterogeneous model processors have different speeds, proportional to the amount of work they can perform in a time unit. Our approach also applies to weighted tasks, where the weight of a task is proportional to the amount of computational resources needed to process that task.

1.1 Model

We model the network by an undirected graph $G = (V, E)$, where $n = |V|$. The nodes represent the processors and the edges model the communication links. $N(i)$ is the set of direct neighbors of node i and $d_i = |N(i)|$ is the degree of node i; We will use d to refer to the maximum degree.

Initially there are in total m tasks which are assigned arbitrarily to the n nodes of the graph G. Tasks may be of different weights and the maximum task weight is denoted by $w_{\max}$. W is the total weight of the tasks, i.e., the sum of the weights of all tasks. When tasks are identical, they are called tokens. The processors can have different speeds; s_i is the speed of processor i. We assume the speeds are integral and w.l.o.g. $s_1 = 1$, and for all $2 \leqslant i \leqslant n$, we have $s_i \geqslant 1$. We define $S = s_1 + s_2 + \cdots + s_n$ as the *capacity* of the network. The *load* x_i of processor i is defined as the total weight of its tasks. The *makespan* ℓ_i of processor i is defined as the total weight of its tasks divided by its speed, i.e., x_i/s_i. The makespan of an assignment $(x_1, \ldots, x_n)$ is the maximum makespan of any processor. The *discrepancy* of an assignment is defined as the difference between the minimum and maximum makespan. The *unbalancedness* is defined as the difference between the maximum makespan and W/S, which is the makespan of the balanced allocation.

For a fixed system, let $x(t) = (x_1(t), \ldots, x_n(t))$ denote the load vector in the beginning of the round t of the process, so $x(1)$ is the load vector that describes the initial distribution of the m tasks. We use $y_{i,j}(t) \geqslant 0$ to represent the load

transferred from node i to node j at round t, so we have:

$$x_i(t+1) = x_i(t) - \sum_{j \in N(i)} (y_{i,j}(t) - y_{j,i}(t))$$

We define $f_{i,j}(t)$ as the total load transferred from i to j by the end of the round t, which is

$$f_{i,j}(t) = \sum_{\tau \leqslant t} (y_{i,j}(\tau) - y_{j,i}(\tau))$$

To distinguish between the processes we will use the names of these processes as superscript in the above definitions. We will use $\mathcal{P}$ for a continuous algorithm and $\mathfrak{D}(\mathcal{P})$ for its discrete counterpart. We define:

$$e_{i,j}(t) = f_{i,j}^{\mathcal{P}}(t) - f_{i,j}^{\mathfrak{D}(\mathcal{P})}(t),$$

as the difference in the flow forwarded over the edge (i,j) by $\mathcal{P}$ and $\mathfrak{D}(\mathcal{P})$ at the end of the round t. Note that $e_{i,j}(t) = -e_{j,i}(t)$ and $f_{i,j}(t) = -f_{j,i}(t)$.

The *balancing time* of a continuous algorithm is the time it takes for the algorithm until every node has a load that is very close to its load in the ideally balanced state; that is,

$$\tau = \tau(x(1), G) = \{\min t \colon \forall i \colon |x_i(t) - W \cdot s_i/S| \leqslant 1\}$$

With this notation, we are ready to describe our results.

1.2 Summary of the Results

In Section 2 we present and analyze an algorithm that transforms a continuous process $\mathcal{P}$ into its discrete counterpart which we call $\mathfrak{D}(\mathcal{P})$. To distinguish between the two processes we will use $\mathcal{P}$ and $\mathfrak{D}(\mathcal{P})$ as superscripts in the definitions of Section 1.1. We restrict the continuous process to the set of all *iterative matrix based load balancing processes* in which $x^{\mathcal{P}}(t+1) = x^{\mathcal{P}}(t)P(t)$, where $P(t)$ is the round matrix in round t. By the nature of its usage, it is required that for all $i, j, 0 \leqslant P_{ij}(t) \leqslant 1$ and also for all i, $\sum_j P_{ij}(t) = 1$. If j is not a neighbor of i, then $P_{ij}(t)$ must be zero. We also require that for all t, i and j, $P_{ij}(t) \cdot s_i = P_{ji}(t) \cdot s_j$. This class is quite general as it contains first order diffusion and dimension exchange processes.

THEOREM 1.1. *Let $x(1)$ be an arbitrary initial load distribution of weighted tasks on an arbitrary graph G. Let $\mathcal{P}$ be a continuous iterative matrix based load balancing process that starting from $x(1)$ on G, balances in time τ. Let $\mathfrak{D}(\mathcal{P})$ be its discrete counterpart following the transformation of Algorithm 1.*

Then for all $t \geqslant \tau$ the unbalancedness of $x^{\mathfrak{D}(\mathcal{P})}(t)$ is at most $2d \cdot w_{\max} + 2$. If additionally we have $x_i(1)/s_i \geqslant d \cdot w_{\max}$ for $1 \leqslant i \leqslant n$ then the discrepancy of $x^{\mathfrak{D}(\mathcal{P})}(t)$ is at most $2d \cdot w_{\max} + 2$.

For the special case of uniform tasks, this gives a bound of $2d + 2$ on the difference between the average and the maximum load.

In Section 3 we present Algorithm 2, a scheme that transforms the continuous balancing process into a randomized discrete process. It can be applied to uniform tasks and heterogeneous networks, and achieves $\mathcal{O}(\sqrt{d \log n})$ unbalancedness which is an improved bound for graphs whenever $d = \Omega(\log n)$.

THEOREM 1.2. *Let $x(1)$ be an arbitrary initial load distribution of uniform tasks on an arbitrary graph G. Let $\mathcal{P}$ and*

τ be as in Theorem 1.1 and assume $\tau \leqslant n^{\kappa}$ for an arbitrary constant $\kappa > 0$. Let $\mathfrak{D}(\mathcal{P})$ be the discrete counterpart of $\mathcal{P}$ following the transformation of Algorithm 2.

Then, the unbalancedness of $X^{\mathfrak{D}(\mathcal{P})}(\tau)$ is at most $d/4 + \mathcal{O}(\sqrt{d \log n})$ w.h.p[1]. If additionally, for a properly chosen constant $c > 0$ and $1 \leqslant i \leqslant n$ we have $x_i(1)/s_i \geqslant d/4 + c\sqrt{d \log n}$, then w.h.p. the discrepancy of $X^{\mathfrak{D}(\mathcal{P})}(\tau)$ is at most $\mathcal{O}(\sqrt{d \log n})$.

1.3 Related Work

In this section we discuss previous results that are most relevant to our work. In the first two sections we review results for unweighted tasks and processors with uniform speeds. In the last section we review results for the general model with weights and speeds. See Table 1 for more details and comparison with our results.

Continuous models.

The original diffusion algorithm (first-order load balancing scheme (FOS)) was introduced in [3] and [2]. Muthukrishnan et al. [11] introduce the second-order load balancing (SOS) in which the amount of load transmitted over the links depends on the current state of the network as well as the network's state in the previous round. In this approach it is possible that a node has to forward more load items to its neighbors than it actually has. Muthukrishnan et al. [11] introduce so called *I Owe You* (IOU) units to account for the difference between the actual and the ideal load transferred over each edge. The authors bound the convergence time for several network topologies including mesh, hypercube and expanders. For results about the dimension exchange model see [7, 9, 12]. As mentioned in Muthukrishnan et al. [11], Rabani et al. [12], the FOS scheme converges in time $\mathcal{O}(\log(Kn)/(1 - \lambda_{\max}))$ where $\lambda_{\max}$ denotes the second largest eigenvalue of the diffusion matrix $\mathbf{P}$ in absolute value and K is the initial discrepancy. This upper bound is usually tight up to constant factors, which means that the continuous process is rather well understood. It also shows that as long as K is not too large, the convergence time of the continuous process is always polynomial in n.

Discrete Diffusion.

Rabani et al. [12] derive a general technique that approximates a continuous process by a discrete process. The discrete process first calculates the continuous flow for every edge of the network and then it rounds this value down. To quantify the deviation of the discrete load from the idealized process, they propose a natural measure, the *local divergence* Ψ_1. The local divergence measures the sum of load differences across all edges in the network, aggregated over time. Rabani et al. [12] give a general bound on the divergence in terms of $\lambda_{\max}$.

Subramanian and Scherson [13] propose the idea of *Randomized Rounding* on the continuous flow. In [7] the authors analyze a randomized version of the dimension-exchange algorithm using randomly generated or deterministic matchings. In their algorithm, the decision to round up or down

[1] We say an event occurs *with high probability (w.h.p)* if its probability is at least $1 - \mathcal{O}(n^{-\alpha})$ for an arbitrary constant $\alpha > 0$.

is randomized. Friedrich et al. [8] analyze a deterministic modification of the standard diffusion algorithm. The idea is that each edge keeps tracks of its own rounding errors and in each step an edge's decision to round up or down is done such that the sum of its rounding errors is minimized. The authors were only able to analyze this protocol on hypercubes and constant-dimensional torus graphs. [8] also consider a randomized version of the diffusion algorithm. Their approach is edge-based. Edges decide independently at random whether to round up or down. The probabilities are chosen such that, in expectation, the behavior of the continuous diffusion algorithm is mimicked. They present a general upper bound for their approach in terms of $\lambda_{\max}$. Note that both algorithms in Friedrich et al. [8] may generate negative load due to the edge-based rounding.

Berenbrink et al. [1] propose a discrete randomized diffusion algorithm that avoids negative load. Instead of rounding up or down on any edge, every vertex distributed the excess tokens on its own by randomly sampling the neighbors (without replacement). The authors obtain general discrepancy results that are based on the so-called *refined local divergence*. Bounding the refined local divergence for specific graph clases like expanders, tori and hypercubes, they obtain corresponding bounds on the discrepancy.

Heterogenous Networks.

Elsässer, Monien, and Preis [5] extend the first and second order schemes for continuous load balancing to heterogeneous networks consisting of processors with different speeds and links with different capacities. For the case of processors with speeds, they generalize the analysis of [12] and bound the convergence time by $\mathcal{O}(\log(Kns_{\max})/(1 - \lambda_{\max}))$, where K is the initial discrepancy and $s_{\max}$ is the maximum speed [5]. [4, 6] address the problem in discrete settings. In these results [4, 6], coarse balancing is achieved in the first phase of the algorithm using first order diffusion and always round down approach [12]; the second phase is fine balancing which consists of concurrent random walks.

2. DETERMINISTIC FLOW IMITATION

For reasons of simplification we assume in this section that G is a d-regular graph. The proofs can easily be generalized to graphs with maximum degree d.

Figure 1 shows round t of our deterministic transformation scheme. The algorithm keeps track of the total flow $f_{i,j}^{\mathcal{P}}(t)$ that is sent over the edge (i, j) by the continuous algorithm. It calculates the difference in the flow forwarded over the edge by the continuous and the discrete algorithm $\widehat{y}_{i,j}^{\mathcal{P}}(t) := (f_{i,j}^{\mathcal{P}}(t) - f_{i,j}^{\mathfrak{D}(\mathcal{P})}(t-1))$. It then tries to find a set $\mathcal{S}_{ij}$ of tasks with a total weight $|\mathcal{S}_{ij}|$ of that difference. These load items will be forwarded over the edge (i, j). In the case of uniform tasks, the amount of load sent from i to its neighbor j is $\lceil f_{i,j}^{\mathcal{P}}(t) - f_{i,j}^{\mathfrak{D}(\mathcal{P})}(t-1) \rceil$. In the case of weighted flows $\mathcal{S}_{ij}$ is chosen in a way that $f_{i,j}^{\mathcal{P}}(t) - f_{i,j}^{\mathfrak{D}(\mathcal{P})}(t) \leqslant w_{\max}$.

It might happen that the node i does not contain enough load items. In that case the algorithm will create new, artificial load items and send them to the corresponding neighbors (or equivalently, we may think of an attached infinite source of tokens from which the node gets some load items). Later we will show that this will never happen if the initial load of the processors is large enough.

		RSW [12]	FS [7]	FGS [8]	BCFFS [1]	Alg. 1	Alg. 2
Unbalancedness	Graph with max. degree d	$\mathcal{O}(\frac{d\log n}{1-\lambda_{\max}})$				$2d+2$	$\mathcal{O}(\sqrt{d}\log n)$
	d-regular graph		$\mathcal{O}(\frac{d\log\log n}{1-\lambda_{\max}})$		$\mathcal{O}(\frac{d\log\log n}{1-\lambda_{\max}})$	$2d+2$	$\mathcal{O}(\sqrt{d}\log n)$
	d-regular expander	$\mathcal{O}(d\log n)$	$\mathcal{O}(d\log\log n)$		$\mathcal{O}(d\log\log n)$	$2d+2$	$\mathcal{O}(\sqrt{d}\log n)$
	Hypercube	$\mathcal{O}(\log^2 n)$	$\mathcal{O}(\log^2 n)$	$\mathcal{O}(\log n)$	$\mathcal{O}(\log n)$	$\mathcal{O}(\log n)$	$\mathcal{O}(\log n)$
	r-dimensional torus, $r=O(1)$	$\mathcal{O}(n^{1/r})$	$\mathcal{O}(n^{1/2r}\sqrt{\log n})$	$\mathcal{O}(1)$	$\mathcal{O}(\sqrt{\log n})$	$\mathcal{O}(1)$	$\mathcal{O}(1)$
Avoids Negative Load		✓	✗	✗	✓	✓	✓
Deterministic		✓	✗	✓	✗	✓	✗

Table 1: Comparison of the *flow imitation* scheme with existing results.

Algorithm 1 $\mathfrak{D}(\mathcal{P})$: Discretized $\mathcal{P}$ using *flow imitation*: the process on node i at round t

---

for each neighbor j of i
    Compute $f_{i,j}^{\mathcal{P}}(t)$
    $\widehat{y}_{i,j}^{\mathcal{P}}(t) \leftarrow f_{i,j}^{\mathcal{P}}(t) - f_{i,j}^{\mathfrak{D}(\mathcal{P})}(t-1)$

    while $\widehat{y}_{i,j}^{\mathcal{P}}(t) - |\mathcal{S}_{ij}| \geqslant w_{\max}$
        if $\mathcal{S}_i = \emptyset$ **then**
            $q \leftarrow$ a unit weight task generated by the
                     attached infinite source
        else
            $q \leftarrow$ arbitrary task removed from $\mathcal{S}_i$
        Add q to $\mathcal{S}_{ij}$

    $y_{i,j}^{\mathfrak{D}(\mathcal{P})}(t) \leftarrow |\mathcal{S}_{ij}|$

Before proceeding with the proof of this theorem, we observe some basic results.

OBSERVATION 2.1. *Suppose for all neighboring pairs i and j and for all $t \geqslant 0$, we have:*

$$P_{ij}(t) \cdot s_i = P_{ji}(t) \cdot s_j$$

Furthermore, suppose for some $\ell \geqslant 0$, for all i, $x_i^{\mathcal{P}}(1) \geqslant s_i \cdot \ell$. Then for all $1 \leqslant i \leqslant n$ and $t \geqslant 1$ we have $x_i^{\mathcal{P}}(t) \geqslant s_i \cdot \ell$.

PROOF. The proof is by induction on t. Suppose that for all i we have $x_i^{\mathcal{P}}(t) \geqslant s_i \cdot \ell$. In the following, we prove this yields $x_i^{\mathcal{P}}(t+1) \geqslant s_i \cdot \ell$:

$$x_i^{\mathfrak{D}(\mathcal{P})}(t+1) = x_i^{\mathcal{P}}(t)\left(1 - \sum_{j \in N(i)} P_{ij}(t)\right)$$
$$+ \sum_{j \in N(i)} x_j^{\mathcal{P}}(t) \cdot P_{ji}(t)$$
$$\geqslant \ell \cdot s_i \cdot \left(1 - \sum_{j \in N(i)} P_{ij}(t)\right) + \ell \cdot \sum_{j \in N(i)} s_j \cdot P_{ji}(t)$$
$$= s_i \cdot \ell \qquad \text{(since } P_{ij}(t) \cdot s_i = P_{ji}(t) \cdot s_j\text{)}$$

This completes the inductive proof. $\square$

OBSERVATION 2.2. *As long as Algorithm 1 is allowed to access the infinite source we have:*

$$|e_{i,j}(t)| < w_{\max}$$

PROOF. Recall that $e_{i,j}(t) = f_{i,j}^{\mathfrak{D}(\mathcal{P})}(t) - f_{i,j}^{\mathcal{P}}(t)$ and observe that $e_{i,j}(t) = -e_{j,i}(t)$. Thus it suffices to prove that the inequality holds for an arbitrary edge direction. In the following, we prove that $f_{i,j}^{\mathfrak{D}(\mathcal{P})}(t) - f_{i,j}^{\mathcal{P}}(t) < w_{\max}$.

Fix an edge (i,j) and observe that

$$f_{i,j}^{\mathcal{P}}(t) - f_{i,j}^{\mathfrak{D}(\mathcal{P})}(t-1) = (-1) \cdot \left(f_{j,i}^{\mathcal{P}} - f_{j,i}^{\mathfrak{D}(\mathcal{P})}(t-1)\right)$$

Assume $f_{i,j}^{\mathcal{P}}(t) - f_{i,j}^{\mathfrak{D}(\mathcal{P})}(t-1) \geqslant 0$ (otherwise we switch i and j). From the definition of Algorithm 1, since $f_{j,i}^{\mathcal{P}}(t) - f_{j,i}^{\mathfrak{D}(\mathcal{P})}(t-1) \leqslant 0$ it follows that $y_{j,i}^{\mathfrak{D}(\mathcal{P})}(t) = 0$. Therefore

$$f_{i,j}^{\mathfrak{D}(\mathcal{P})}(t) = f_{i,j}^{\mathfrak{D}(\mathcal{P})}(t-1) + y_{i,j}^{\mathfrak{D}(\mathcal{P})}(t)$$

After exiting the loop for node i, we have

$$f_{i,j}^{\mathcal{P}}(t) - f_{i,j}^{\mathfrak{D}(\mathcal{P})}(t-1) - \|\mathcal{S}_{ij}\| < w_{\max}$$

or

$$f_{i,j}^{\mathcal{P}}(t) - f_{i,j}^{\mathfrak{D}(\mathcal{P})}(t-1) - y_{i,j}^{\mathfrak{D}(\mathcal{P})}(t) < w_{\max}$$

which yields:

$$f_{i,j}^{\mathcal{P}}(t) - f_{i,j}^{\mathfrak{D}(\mathcal{P})}(t) < w_{\max} \qquad (2.1)$$

Let w be the weight of the last task added to $\mathcal{S}_{ij}$. Before adding this task, the loop condition was fulfilled. hence we have $f_{i,j}^{\mathcal{P}}(t) - f_{i,j}^{\mathfrak{D}(\mathcal{P})}(t) + w \geqslant w_{\max}$, which yields:

$$f_{i,j}^{\mathcal{P}}(t) - f_{i,j}^{\mathfrak{D}(\mathcal{P})}(t) \geqslant w_{\max} - w \geqslant 0 \qquad (2.2)$$

Combining Equations (2.1) and (2.2), we obtain $|f_{i,j}^{\mathfrak{D}(\mathcal{P})}(t) - f_{i,j}^{\mathcal{P}}(t)| < w_{\max}$ as needed. $\square$

OBSERVATION 2.3. *Let $1 \leqslant i \leqslant n$, $j \in N(i)$ and $t \geqslant 1$. Assume $y_{i,j}^{\mathfrak{D}(\mathcal{P})}(t) > 0$, then we have*

$$y_{i,j}^{\mathfrak{D}(\mathcal{P})}(t) \leqslant y_{i,j}^{\mathcal{P}}(t) - y_{j,i}^{\mathcal{P}}(t) + e_{i,j}(t-1)$$

PROOF. We observe:

$$y_{i,j}^{\mathcal{P}}(t) - y_{j,i}^{\mathcal{P}}(t) + e_{i,j}(t-1)$$
$$= y_{i,j}^{\mathcal{P}}(t) - y_{j,i}^{\mathcal{P}}(t) + f_{i,j}^{\mathcal{P}}(t-1) - f_{i,j}^{\mathfrak{D}(\mathcal{P})}(t-1)$$
$$= f_{i,j}^{\mathcal{P}}(t) - f_{i,j}^{\mathfrak{D}(\mathcal{P})}(t-1)$$
$$= \widehat{y}_{i,j}^{\mathcal{P}}(t)$$

It remains to prove $y_{i,j}^{\mathcal{D}(\mathcal{P})}(t) \leqslant \widehat{y}_{i,j}^{\mathcal{P}}(t)$. Let w be the weight of the last task added to $\mathcal{S}_{ij}$ in round t. Before adding this task, the loop condition of Algorithm 1 was fulfilled and we had $\widehat{y}_{i,j}^{\mathcal{P}}(t) - (|\mathcal{S}_{ij}| - w) \geqslant w_{\max}$. After the loop, we have $y_{i,j}^{\mathcal{D}(\mathcal{P})}(t) = |\mathcal{S}_{ij}|$. This yields

$$\widehat{y}_{i,j}^{\mathcal{P}}(t) - y_{i,j}^{\mathcal{D}(\mathcal{P})}(t) \geqslant w_{\max} - w \geqslant 0,$$

as needed. □

OBSERVATION 2.4. *For $1 \leqslant i \leqslant n$ and $t \geqslant 1$ we have:*

(1) $x_i^{\mathcal{D}(\mathcal{P})}(t) = x_i^{\mathcal{P}}(t) + \sum_{j \in N(i)} e_{i,j}(t-1)$.

(2) $\left| x_i^{\mathcal{D}(\mathcal{P})}(t) - x_i^{\mathcal{P}}(t) \right| < d \cdot w_{\max}$.

PROOF. The proof of (1) is by induction on t. For $t = 1$, we have $x_i^{\mathcal{D}(\mathcal{P})}(1) = x_i^{\mathcal{P}}(1)$ and for all i, j, $E_{i,j}(-1) = 0$. Therefore the equation holds.

As the induction hypothesis, suppose for $\tau \geqslant 1$ we have:

$$x_i^{\mathcal{D}(\mathcal{P})}(\tau) = x_i^{\mathcal{P}}(\tau) + \sum_{j \in N(i)} e_{i,j}(\tau-1)$$

It remains to prove that the statement holds for $t = \tau + 1$ as well. We have:

$$x_i^{\mathcal{D}(\mathcal{P})}(\tau+1) = x_i^{\mathcal{D}(\mathcal{P})}(\tau) + \sum_{j \in N(i)} (y_{j,i}^{\mathcal{D}(\mathcal{P})}(\tau) - y_{i,j}^{\mathcal{D}(\mathcal{P})}(\tau))$$

$$= x_i^{\mathcal{P}}(\tau) + \sum_{j \in N(i)} e_{i,j}(\tau-1) + \sum_{j \in N(i)} \left(y_{j,i}^{\mathcal{D}(\mathcal{P})}(\tau) - y_{i,j}^{\mathcal{D}(\mathcal{P})}(\tau) \right)$$

$$= x_i^{\mathcal{P}}(\tau) +$$
$$\sum_{j \in N(i)} \left(f_{i,j}^{\mathcal{P}}(\tau-1) - f_{i,j}^{\mathcal{D}(\mathcal{P})}(\tau-1) + y_{j,i}^{\mathcal{D}(\mathcal{P})}(\tau) - y_{i,j}^{\mathcal{D}(\mathcal{P})}(\tau) \right)$$

$$= \left(x_i^{\mathcal{P}}(\tau+1) - \sum_{j \in N(i)} (y_{j,i}^{\mathcal{P}}(\tau) - y_{i,j}^{\mathcal{P}}(\tau)) \right)$$
$$+ \sum_{j \in N(i)} \left(f_{i,j}^{\mathcal{P}}(\tau-1) - f_{i,j}^{\mathcal{D}(\mathcal{P})}(\tau) \right)$$

$$= x_i^{\mathcal{P}}(\tau+1)$$
$$+ \sum_{j \in N(i)} \left(f_{i,j}^{\mathcal{P}}(\tau-1) + y_{i,j}^{\mathcal{P}}(\tau) - y_{j,i}^{\mathcal{P}}(\tau) - f_{i,j}^{\mathcal{D}(\mathcal{P})}(\tau) \right)$$

$$= x_i^{\mathcal{P}}(\tau+1) + \sum_{j \in N(i)} \left(f_{i,j}^{\mathcal{P}}(\tau) - f_{i,j}^{\mathcal{D}(\mathcal{P})}(\tau) \right)$$

$$= x_i^{\mathcal{P}}(\tau+1) + \sum_{j \in N(i)} e_{i,j}(\tau)$$

This finishes the proof of (1). For (2), we apply (1) to get

$$\left| x_i^{\mathcal{D}(\mathcal{P})}(t) - x_i^{\mathcal{P}}(t) \right| = \left| \sum_{j \in N(i)} e_{i,j}(t-1) \right| \leqslant \sum_{j \in N(i)} |e_{i,j}(t-1)|$$

Now, the result can be obtained using Observation 2.2. □

The following lemma shows that if the initial load of each processor is large enough the infinite sources will never be used.

LEMMA 2.5. *Suppose for all $1 \leqslant i \leqslant n$ we have:*

$$x_i^{\mathcal{P}}(1) \geqslant d \cdot s_i \cdot w_{\max}$$

Then we never use the infinite source, i.e. for all $1 \leqslant i \leqslant n$ and $t \geqslant 1$ we have:

$$x_i^{\mathcal{D}(\mathcal{P})}(t) - \sum_{j \in N(i)} y_{i,j}^{\mathcal{D}(\mathcal{P})}(t) \geqslant 0.$$

PROOF. Since for all $i, x_i^{\mathcal{P}}(1) \geqslant d \cdot s_i \cdot w_{\max}$ we can apply Observation 2.1 and show that for all i and t,

$$x_i^{\mathcal{P}}(t) \geqslant d \cdot s_i \cdot w_{\max}$$

For the sake of contradiction, let us assume there is some round $\widehat{t}$ in which we use the infinite source for the first time. Let i be an arbitrary node with insufficient load, so that we have:

$$x_i^{\mathcal{D}(\mathcal{P})}(\widehat{t}) - \sum_{j \in N(i)} y_{i,j}^{\mathcal{D}(\mathcal{P})}(\widehat{t}) < 0$$

Let $L = \{ j \in N(i) : y_{i,j}^{\mathcal{D}(\mathcal{P})}(\widehat{t}) > 0 \}$ be the set of neighbors of node i to which i sends some load in round $\widehat{t}$. We get:

$$x_i^{\mathcal{D}(\mathcal{P})}(\widehat{t}) - \sum_{j \in L} y_{i,j}^{\mathcal{D}(\mathcal{P})}(\widehat{t}) \geqslant x_i^{\mathcal{P}}(\widehat{t}) + \sum_{j \in N(i)} e_{i,j}(\widehat{t}-1) \quad (2.3)$$
$$- \sum_{j \in L} \left(y_{i,j}^{\mathcal{P}}(\widehat{t}) - y_{j,i}^{\mathcal{P}}(\widehat{t}) + e_{i,j}(\widehat{t}-1) \right)$$

$$= x_i^{\mathcal{P}}(\widehat{t}) + \sum_{j \in N(i)} e_{i,j}(\widehat{t}-1)$$
$$- \sum_{j \in L} \left(x_i^{\mathcal{P}}(\widehat{t}) \cdot P_{ij}(\widehat{t}) - x_j^{\mathcal{P}}(\widehat{t}) \cdot P_{ji}(\widehat{t}) + e_{i,j}(\widehat{t}-1) \right)$$

$$= x_i^{\mathcal{P}}(\widehat{t}) \left(1 - \sum_{j \in L} P_{ij}(\widehat{t}) \right) + \sum_{j \in N(i) - L} e_{i,j}(\widehat{t}-1)$$
$$+ \sum_{j \in L} x_j^{\mathcal{P}}(\widehat{t}) \cdot P_{ji}(\widehat{t})$$

$$\geqslant d \cdot s_i \cdot w_{\max} \cdot \left(1 - \sum_{j \in L} P_{ij}(\widehat{t}) \right) + \sum_{j \in N(i) - L} e_{i,j}(\widehat{t}-1)$$
$$+ \sum_{j \in L} d \cdot s_j \cdot w_{\max} \cdot P_{ji}(\widehat{t})$$

$$= d \cdot s_i \cdot w_{\max} + \sum_{j \in N(i) - L} e_{i,j}(\widehat{t}-1) \quad (2.4)$$

$$\geqslant d \cdot s_i \cdot w_{\max} - |N(i) - L| \cdot w_{\max} \quad (2.5)$$

$$\geqslant d \cdot s_i \cdot w_{\max} - d \cdot w_{\max} \geqslant 0 \quad \text{(Since } s_i \geqslant 1\text{)} \quad (2.6)$$

where in Equation (2.3) we use Observations 2.4 and 2.3, Equation (2.4) follows from the assumption $P_{ij}(\widehat{t}) \cdot s_i = P_{ji}(\widehat{t}) \cdot s_j$, and Equation (2.5) results from Observation 2.2.

This contradicts our initial assumption that $x_i^{\mathcal{D}(\mathcal{P})}(\widehat{t}) - \sum_{j \in N(i)} y_{i,j}^{\mathcal{D}(\mathcal{P})}(\widehat{t}) < 0$ and the proof follows. □

PROOF OF THEOREM 1.1. First we prove the result for the case where for $1 \leqslant i \leqslant n$ we have:

$$x_i(1) \geqslant d \cdot w_{\max}$$

Under this assumption, by Lemma 2.5 no infinite source is used, and therefore the total load remains unchanged. By Part (2) of the Observation 2.4, we have:

$$\left| x_i^{\mathcal{D}(\mathcal{P})}(t) - x_i^{\mathcal{P}}(t) \right| < d \cdot w_{\max}$$

On the other hand, by the definition of convergence time, we have:

$$\left| x_i^{\mathcal{P}}(t) - W \cdot s_i/S \right| \leqslant 1$$

Hence we can conclude

$$\left| x_i^{\mathfrak{D}(\mathcal{P})}(t) - W \cdot s_i/S \right| < d \cdot w_{\max} + 1$$

Since $s_i \geqslant 1$, this yields:

$$\left| x_i^{\mathfrak{D}(\mathcal{P})}(t)/s_i - W/S \right| < d \cdot w_{\max} + 1$$

Similarly we can show:

$$\left| x_j^{\mathfrak{D}(\mathcal{P})}(t)/s_j - W/S \right| < d \cdot w_{\max} + 1$$

The result now follows by combining the last two inequalities using the triangle inequality. The general case can be reduced to the first case by simply adding $\lceil d \cdot w_{\max} \rceil \cdot s_i$ *dummy* unit weight tasks to each processor i before the process begins. Note that this does not affect the convergence time of the continuous process, because the extra load is completely balanced. Let us denote the new total load by W'. We have:

$$W' = W + \sum_i \lceil d \cdot w_{\max} \rceil \cdot s_i$$
$$\leqslant W + (d \cdot w_{\max} + 1) \cdot S$$

Hence,

$$W'/S \leqslant W/S + d \cdot w_{\max} + 1 \qquad (2.7)$$

We use $x_i^{\mathfrak{D}(\mathcal{P})}(\tau)$ as an upper bound on the final load of the node i. Following the steps of the first case we get:

$$x_i^{\mathfrak{D}(\mathcal{P})}(t)/s_i - W'/S < d \cdot w_{\max} + 1$$

Combined with Equation (2.7) this yields $x_i^{\mathfrak{D}(\mathcal{P})}(t)/s_i < W/S + 2d \cdot w_{\max} + 2$, as required. $\quad\square$

3. RANDOMIZED FLOW IMITATION

In this section we analyze a randomized version of Algorithm 1 that can be applied for balancing uniform tasks. Instead of always rounding down the flow that has to be sent over an edge, Algorithm 2 uses randomized rounding. The notation we use in this section is the same as defined in Section 2. We use uppercase letters to express random variables. As an example $f_{i,j}^{\mathcal{P}}(t)$ is the flow sent over edge (i,j) in round t by the continuous process, while $F_{i,j}^{\mathfrak{D}(\mathcal{P})}(t)$ is the corresponding random variable for the discrete process.

Algorithm 2 calculates the flow $\widehat{Y}_{i,j}(t) := f_{i,j}^{\mathcal{P}}(t) - F_{i,j}^{\mathfrak{D}(\mathcal{P})}(t-1)$ that has to be sent over edge (i,j) as before. To calculate the flow that is actually sent, $\widehat{Y}_{i,j}(t)$ is randomly rounded up or down, with a probability depending on the value of its fractional part. Suppose $\widehat{Y}_{i,j}(t) > 0$ in some round t. Then the discrete flow $Y_{i,j}^{\mathfrak{D}(\mathcal{P})}(t)$ that is sent over the edge is a random variable determined by the following randomized rounding scheme. For a real x, we use $\{x\} = x - \lfloor x \rfloor$ to denote the fractional part of x. Then

$$Y_{i,j}^{\mathfrak{D}(\mathcal{P})}(t) = \begin{cases} \lfloor \widehat{Y}_{i,j}(t) \rfloor + 1 & \text{with probability } \{\widehat{Y}_{i,j}(t)\}, \\ \lfloor \widehat{Y}_{i,j}(t) \rfloor & \text{otherwise.} \end{cases}$$
$$(3.1)$$

In Algorithm 2 we use $Z_{i,j}(t)$, which is a zero-one random variable indicating whether we should round up. Once we know all the random choices in round t, we can calculate the load of processor i by the following fomula:

$$X_i^{\mathfrak{D}(\mathcal{P})}(t+1) = X_i^{\mathfrak{D}(\mathcal{P})}(t) - \sum_{j \in N(i)} (Y_{i,j}^{\mathfrak{D}(\mathcal{P})}(t) - Y_{j,i}^{\mathfrak{D}(\mathcal{P})}(t))$$

Algorithm 2 $\mathfrak{D}(\mathcal{P})$: Discretized $\mathcal{P}$ using randomized *flow imitation*: the process on node i at round t

---

for each neighbor j of i in parallel
    Compute $f_{i,j}^{\mathcal{P}}(t)$
    $\widehat{Y}_{i,j}(t) \leftarrow f_{i,j}^{\mathcal{P}}(t) - F_{i,j}^{\mathfrak{D}(\mathcal{P})}(t-1)$
    if $\widehat{Y}_{i,j}(t) > 0$ **then**
        Toss a coin with head probability $\{\widehat{Y}_{i,j}(t)\}$
        $Z_{i,j}(t) \leftarrow \begin{cases} 1 & \text{if head comes up;} \\ 0 & \text{otherwise.} \end{cases}$
        $Y_{i,j}^{\mathfrak{D}(\mathcal{P})}(t) \leftarrow \lfloor \widehat{Y}_{i,j}(t) \rfloor + Z_{i,j}(t)$
        Send $Y_{i,j}^{\mathfrak{D}(\mathcal{P})}(t)$ tokens to j
        if there are not enough tokens **then**
            Generate the required amount using the attached infinite source

---

We will show that with high probability the roundings errors only sum up to a small value. To begin, we note the following observations:

OBSERVATION 3.1. *For an arbitrary edge (i,j) and $t \geqslant 0$ we have*

$$E_{i,j}(t) = y_{i,j}^{\mathcal{P}}(t) - y_{j,i}^{\mathcal{P}}(t) + E_{i,j}(t-1) - (Y_{i,j}^{\mathfrak{D}(\mathcal{P})}(t) - Y_{j,i}^{\mathfrak{D}(\mathcal{P})}(t))$$

PROOF. Recall that $E_{i,j}(t) = f_{i,j}^{\mathcal{P}}(t) - F_{i,j}^{\mathfrak{D}(\mathcal{P})}(t)$. The right side of the equation can be simplified as below:

$$y_{i,j}^{\mathcal{P}}(t) - y_{j,i}^{\mathcal{P}}(t) + E_{i,j}(t-1) - \left(Y_{i,j}^{\mathfrak{D}(\mathcal{P})}(t) - Y_{j,i}^{\mathfrak{D}(\mathcal{P})}(t) \right)$$
$$= \left(y_{i,j}^{\mathcal{P}}(t) - y_{j,i}^{\mathcal{P}}(t) + f_{i,j}^{\mathcal{P}}(t-1) \right)$$
$$\quad - \left(F_{i,j}^{\mathfrak{D}(\mathcal{P})}(t-1) + Y_{i,j}^{\mathfrak{D}(\mathcal{P})}(t) - Y_{j,i}^{\mathfrak{D}(\mathcal{P})}(t) \right)$$
$$= f_{i,j}^{\mathcal{P}}(t) - F_{i,j}^{\mathfrak{D}(\mathcal{P})}(t)$$
$$= E_{i,j}(t).$$

$\square$

OBSERVATION 3.2. *For an arbitrary edge (i,j) and $t \geqslant 0$, if $Y_{i,j}^{\mathfrak{D}(\mathcal{P})}(t) > 0$ then $Y_{j,i}^{\mathfrak{D}(\mathcal{P})}(t) = 0$.*

PROOF. If $Y_{i,j}^{\mathfrak{D}(\mathcal{P})}(t) > 0$ then according to Algorithm 2 we have $\widehat{Y}_{i,j}(t) > 0$; therefore:

$$f_{j,i}^{\mathcal{P}}(t) - F_{j,i}^{\mathfrak{D}(\mathcal{P})}(t-1) < 0$$

which yields $Y_{i,j}^{\mathfrak{D}(\mathcal{P})}(t) = 0$. $\quad\square$

OBSERVATION 3.3. *Recall $\widehat{Y}_{i,j}(t)$ is defined as $y_{i,j}^{\mathcal{P}}(t) - y_{j,i}^{\mathcal{P}}(t) + E_{i,j}(t-1)$ and suppose $\widehat{Y}_{i,j}(t) > 0$. Then we have:*

$$E_{i,j}(t) = \begin{cases} 1 - \{\widehat{Y}_{i,j}(t)\} & \text{if } Z_{i,j}(t) = 1 \\ -\{\widehat{Y}_{i,j}(t)\} & \text{otherwise.} \end{cases}$$

PROOF. Since $\widehat{Y}_{i,j}(t) > 0$, $\widehat{Y}_{j,i}(t) = -\widehat{Y}_{i,j}(t) < 0$ and therefore $Y_{j,i}^{\mathfrak{D}(\mathcal{P})}(t) = 0$. Hence, using Observation 3.1 we get:

$$E_{i,j}(t) = y_{i,j}^{\mathcal{P}}(t) - y_{j,i}^{\mathcal{P}}(t) + E_{i,j}(t-1) - Y_{i,j}^{\mathfrak{D}(\mathcal{P})}(t)$$
$$= \widehat{Y}_{j,i}(t) - Y_{i,j}^{\mathfrak{D}(\mathcal{P})}(t)$$

The proof follows from the definition of $Y_{i,j}^{\mathfrak{D}(\mathcal{P})}(t)$ in Algorithm 2. □

Observation 3.3 shows that $E_{i,j}(t)$ is the error in the randomized rounding of $\widehat{Y}_{j,i}(t)$. An example makes it clear how the errors are computed: Suppose we want to round 9.3; we round up with probability 0.3 getting an error of $+0.7$, or round down with probability 0.7 with error of -0.3.

Now we show that w.h.p. the discrete process does not deviate much from the continuous process. We identify some *undesirable* events and we show in the next lemma that each of these events happens only with a small probability. In our proofs, we make use of Lemma A.1 which is a simple adaptation of the Hoeffding bound [10] for sums of randomized rounding errors.

We define:

$$H_i(t) := \{j \in N(i) : y_{i,j}^{\mathcal{P}}(t) - y_{j,i}^{\mathcal{P}}(t) + E_{i,j}(t-1) > 0\},$$

to denote the set of neighbors of i to which i probably sends some tokens in round t and

$$L_i(t) := N(i) - H_i(t),$$

which contains the rest of i's neighbors.

LEMMA 3.4. *Assume $T \leq n^{\kappa}$ for an arbitrary constant $\kappa > 0$ and that $\alpha > 0$ is an arbitrary constant. For an arbitrary node i, round $t \leq T$ and suitable constant $c > 0$ we have*

(1) $\mathbf{Pr}\left[\left|X_i^{\mathfrak{D}(\mathcal{P})}(t+1) - x_i^{\mathcal{P}}(t+1)\right| \geq c \cdot \sqrt{d \lg n}\right] \leq (n^{\alpha+1} \cdot T)^{-1}.$

(2) $\mathbf{Pr}\left[\left|\sum_{j \in H_i(t)} E_{i,j}(t)\right| \geq c \cdot \sqrt{d \lg n}\right] \leq (n^{\alpha+1} \cdot T)^{-1}.$

(3) $\mathbf{Pr}\left[\sum_{j \in L_i(t+1)} E_{i,j}(t) \leq -\frac{d}{4} - c \cdot \sqrt{d \lg n}\right] \leq (n^{\alpha+1} \cdot T)^{-1}.$

PROOF. We begin with the proof of (1).

Proof of (1).

Define

$$\Delta := X_i^{\mathfrak{D}(\mathcal{P})}(t+1) - x_i^{\mathcal{P}}(t+1)$$

It is easy to see that that Observation 2.4 also holds for the randomized scheme, so we have:

$$\Delta = \sum_{j \in N(i)} E_{i,j}(t)$$

Assume $E_{i,j}(t-1)$ is fixed for all the edges (i,j). Then each of the random variables $E_{i,j}(t)$ can assume at most two different values and the probability to round up or down is independent for all edges (See Observation 3.3). Let the random variable $E_i(t)$ be a vector denoting the error values

of the edges connected to i at the end of the round t. By the law of total probability we have:

$$\mathbf{Pr}\left[\,|\Delta| \geq \delta\,\right] = \tag{3.2}$$
$$\sum_{\mathcal{E}_i} \mathbf{Pr}\left[\,|\Delta| \geq \delta \mid E_i(t-1) = \mathcal{E}_i\,\right] \cdot \mathbf{Pr}\left[\,E_i(t-1) = \mathcal{E}_i\,\right] \tag{3.3}$$

Note that each $E_{i,j}(t)$ is the random variable indicating the error in the randomized rounding of $\widehat{Y}_{i,j}(t)$ (Observation 3.3). We can apply Lemma A.1 to bound Δ, resulting in:

$$\mathbf{Pr}\left[|\Delta| \geq \delta \mid E_i(t-1) = \mathcal{E}\right] \leq 2 \exp\left(-2\delta^2/d\right)$$

Hence,

$$\mathbf{Pr}\left[\,|\Delta| \geq \delta\,\right] =$$
$$\sum_{\mathcal{E}} \mathbf{Pr}\left[\,|\Delta| \geq \delta \mid E_i(t-1) = \mathcal{E}\,\right] \cdot \mathbf{Pr}\left[\,E_i(t-1) = \mathcal{E}\,\right]$$
$$\leq \sum_{\mathcal{E}} 2 \exp\left(-2\delta^2/d\right) \cdot \mathbf{Pr}\left[\,E_i(t-1) = \mathcal{E}\,\right]$$
$$= 2 \exp\left(-2\delta^2/d\right). \tag{3.4}$$

As $T \leq n^{\kappa}$ we can choose a constant c such that setting $\delta = c \cdot \sqrt{d \lg n} \geq \sqrt{d \lg(2n^2 T)/2}$ yields the desired bound.

Proof of (2).

This proof is similar to the proof of (1). Define

$$\Delta := \sum_{j \in H_i(t)} E_{i,j}(t)$$

Recall the definition of $H_i(t) = \{j \in N(i) : y_{i,j}^{\mathcal{P}}(t) - y_{j,i}^{\mathcal{P}}(t) + E_{i,j}(t-1) > 0\}$. Observe that $|H_i(t)| \leq d$. Conditioned on $E_i(t-1) = \mathcal{E}_i$, the set $H_i(t)$ is fixed. Hence we can apply Lemma A.1 and obtain:

$$\mathbf{Pr}\left[|\Delta| \geq \delta \mid E_i(t-1) = \mathcal{E}_i\right] \leq 2 \exp\left(-2\delta^2/d\right)$$

Following the same steps as in (1) we obtain the desired result.

Proof of (3).

Recall that

$$L_i(t+1) = \{j \in N(i) : y_{i,j}^{\mathcal{P}}(t+1) - y_{j,i}^{\mathcal{P}}(t+1) + E_{i,j}(t) \leq 0\},$$

so intuitively the set is biased toward containing lower values of $E_{i,j}(t)$. However, we can change the summation and use different random variables so that we can still apply Hoeffding bounds. Define

$$E_{i,j}^{-}(t) := \min\{E_{i,j}(t), 0\}$$

We have:

$$\sum_{j \in N(i)} E_{i,j}^{-}(t) \leq \sum_{j \in L_i(t+1)} E_{i,j}(t) \tag{3.5}$$

Fix an arbitrary node i, let $\Delta = \sum_{j \in N(i)} E_{i,j}^{-}(t)$ and $p_{ij} = \{\widehat{Y}_{i,j}(t)\}$. We have:

$$\mathbf{Ex}\left[E_{i,j}^{-}(t) \mid E_i(t-1) = \mathcal{E}_i\right] = -p_{ij} \cdot (1 - p_{ij}) + 0 \cdot p_{ij}$$
$$\geq -1/4,$$

where the last step follows from a simple minimization of $f(p_{ij}) = (1 - p_{ij}) + 0 \cdot p_{ij}$. The random variables $E_{i,j}^-(t)$ are independent ranging over intervals of length no more than one. Again, we can apply Hoeffding bounds using $\delta = c \cdot \sqrt{d \lg n} \geqslant \sqrt{\lg(2n^{\alpha+1}T)/2d}$ with the same constant c as in the previous parts. Hence,

$$\mathbf{Pr}\left[\Delta < -\frac{d}{4} - c \cdot \sqrt{d \lg n} \;\middle|\; E_i(t-1) = \mathcal{E}\right] \leqslant \frac{1}{2n^{\alpha+1} \cdot T}$$
(3.6)

By Equation (3.5), we can replace Δ with $\sum_{j \in L_i(t+1)} E_{i,j}(t)$ in the Equation (3.6) to obtain the desired bound. $\square$

LEMMA 3.5. *Assume $\tau \leqslant n^\kappa$ for an arbitrary constant κ and assume that $\alpha > 0$ is a fixed constant. Suppose for all $1 \leqslant i \leqslant n$ we have*

$$x_i^{\mathcal{P}}(1) \geqslant s_i \cdot (d/4 + 2c \cdot \sqrt{d \lg n})$$

Then for a suitably chosen constant c we have

(1) $\mathbf{Pr}\Big[$ *for all $1 \leqslant t \leqslant \tau$ and $1 \leqslant i \leqslant n$,*
$$\left|X_i^{\mathfrak{D}(\mathcal{P})}(t) - x_i^{\mathcal{P}}(t)\right| > c \cdot \sqrt{d \lg n}\Big] < n^{-\alpha}$$

(2) No infinite source is used, i.e
$$\mathbf{Pr}\Big[\text{ for some } 1 \leqslant t \leqslant \tau \text{ and some } 1 \leqslant i \leqslant n,$$
$$X_i^{\mathfrak{D}(\mathcal{P})}(t) - \sum_{j \in H_i(t)} Y_{i,j}^{\mathfrak{D}(\mathcal{P})}(t) < 0\Big] < 2n^{-\alpha}$$

PROOF. We choose the value of c as computed by the Lemma 3.4 for the same value of α and $T = \tau$.

Proof of (1).

The proof follows by applying the union bound to Part (1) of the Lemma 3.4.

Proof of (2).

We have to show that the load of every node i at the beginning of every round $t \leqslant \tau$ is large enough to satisfy their outgoing demands. Recall that $H_i(t)$ is defined so that no load is transferred from i to any of its neighbors not in $H_i(t)$. It suffices to prove that for arbitrary $i, t \leqslant \tau$,

$$X_i^{\mathfrak{D}(\mathcal{P})}(t) - \sum_{j \in H_i(t)} Y_{i,j}^{\mathfrak{D}(\mathcal{P})}(t) \geqslant 0$$

We have:

$$X_i^{\mathfrak{D}(\mathcal{P})}(t) - \sum_{j \in H_i(t)} Y_{i,j}^{\mathfrak{D}(\mathcal{P})}(t) = X_i^{\mathfrak{D}(\mathcal{P})}(t)$$
$$- \sum_{j \in H_i(t)} \left(y_{i,j}^{\mathcal{P}}(t) - y_{j,i}^{\mathcal{P}}(t) + E_{i,j}(t-1) - E_{i,j}(t)\right) \quad (3.7)$$
$$= x_i^{\mathcal{P}}(t) + \sum_{j \in N(i)} E_{i,j}(t-1)$$
$$- \sum_{j \in H_i(t)} \left(y_{i,j}^{\mathcal{P}}(t) - y_{j,i}^{\mathcal{P}}(t) + E_{i,j}(t-1) - E_{i,j}(t)\right) \quad (3.8)$$
$$= x_i^{\mathcal{P}}(t) + \sum_{j \in N(i)} E_{i,j}(t-1) - \sum_{j \in H_i(t)} \Big(x_i^{\mathcal{P}}(t) \cdot P_{ij}(t)$$
$$- x_j^{\mathcal{P}}(t) \cdot P_{ji}(t) + E_{i,j}(t-1) - E_{i,j}(t)\Big)$$
$$= x_i^{\mathcal{P}}(t)\left(1 - \sum_{j \in H_i(t)} P_{ij}(t)\right) + \sum_{j \in L_i(t)} E_{i,j}(t-1)$$

$$+ \sum_{j \in H_i(t)} x_j^{\mathcal{P}}(t) \cdot P_{ji}(t) + \sum_{j \in H_i(t)} E_{i,j}(t)$$

$$\geqslant s_i \cdot (d/4 + 2c \cdot \sqrt{d \lg n})\left(1 - \sum_{j \in H_i(t)} P_{ij}(t)\right)$$
$$+ \sum_{j \in L_i(t)} E_{i,j}(t-1)$$
$$+ (d/4 + 2c \cdot \sqrt{d \lg n}) \cdot \sum_{j \in H_i(t)} s_j \cdot P_{ji}(t)$$
$$+ \sum_{j \in H_i(t)} E_{i,j}(t) \quad (3.9)$$
$$= s_i \cdot (d/4 + 2c \cdot \sqrt{d \lg n}) + \sum_{j \in L_i(t)} E_{i,j}(t-1)$$
$$+ \sum_{j \in H_i(t)} E_{i,j}(t) \quad (\text{Since } P_{ij}(t) \cdot s_i = P_{ji}(t) \cdot s_j)$$
(3.10)

where Equation (3.8) follows from Observation 2.4, Equation (3.9) is obtained using Observation 2.1, in Equation (3.7) we use Observations 3.2 and 3.1. The proof follows by considering $s_i \geqslant 1$ and applying union bound to parts (2) and (3) of Lemma 3.4. $\square$

PROOF OF THEOREM 1.2. First we prove that the result holds if for all i, $x_i(1) \geqslant d/4 + c \cdot \sqrt{d \lg n}$. For arbitrary constant $\alpha > 0$, let $c = 2c'$ where c' is the constant computed in Lemma 3.5. Applying the union bound to combine both parts of the Lemma 3.5 we obtain that with probability of at least $1 - 3n^{-\alpha}$ the infinite sources are never used and that for all i,

$$\left|X_i^{\mathfrak{D}(\mathcal{P})}(t) - x_i^{\mathcal{P}}(t)\right| < c' \cdot \sqrt{d \lg n}$$

On the other hand, using the definition of convergence time we get

$$\left|x_i^{\mathcal{P}}(t) - W \cdot s_i/S\right| \leqslant 1$$

Hence, we can conclude that

$$\left|X_i^{\mathfrak{D}(\mathcal{P})}(t) - W \cdot s_i/S\right| < c' \cdot \sqrt{d \lg n} + 1$$

Since $s_i \geqslant 1$, we have

$$\left|X_i^{\mathfrak{D}(\mathcal{P})}(t)/s_i - W/S\right| < c' \cdot \sqrt{d \lg n} + 1$$

Similarly we can show that

$$\left|X_j^{\mathfrak{D}(\mathcal{P})}(t)/s_j - W/S\right| < c' \cdot \sqrt{d \lg n} + 1$$

The result now follows by combining the last two inequalities using the triangle inequality.

The general case can be reduced to the first case by simply adding $\lceil d/4 + 2c' \cdot \sqrt{d \lg n} \rceil \cdot s_i$ *dummy* tokens to each processor i before the process begins. Note that this does not affect the convergence time of the continuous process, because the extra load is completely balanced. Let us denote the new total load by W'. We have:

$$W' = W + \sum_i \lceil d/4 + 2c' \cdot \sqrt{d \lg n} \rceil \cdot s_i$$
$$\leqslant W + S \cdot \left(d/4 + c \cdot \sqrt{d \lg n} + 1\right)$$

Hence,

$$W'/S \leqslant W/S + d/4 + c \cdot \sqrt{d \lg n} + 1 \qquad (3.11)$$

We use $X_i^{\mathfrak{D}(\mathcal{P})}(\tau)$ as an upper bound of the real final load of the node i. Following the steps of the first case we get

$$X_i^{\mathfrak{D}(\mathcal{P})}(\tau)/s_i - W'/S < c' \cdot \sqrt{d \lg n} + 1$$

Combined with Equation (3.11) this yields

$$X_i^{\mathfrak{D}(\mathcal{P})}(\tau)/s_i < W/S + d/4 + 3c' \cdot \sqrt{d \lg n} + 1,$$

as required. $\square$

References

[1] P. Berenbrink, C. Cooper, T. Friedetzky, T. Friedrich, and T. Sauerwald. Randomized diffusion for indivisible loads. In *Proceedings of the 22nd ACM-SIAM Symposium on Discrete Algorithms (SODA'11)*, pages 429–439, 2011.

[2] J. E. Boillat. Load balancing and poisson equation in a graph. *Concurrency and Computation: Practice and Experience*, 2:289–314, 1990.

[3] G. Cybenko. Dynamic load balancing for distributed memory multiprocessors. *Journal of Parallel and Distributed Computing*, 7:279–301, 1989.

[4] R. Elsässer and T. Sauerwald. Discrete load balancing is (almost) as easy as continuous load balancing. In *Proceedings of the 29th ACM Symposium on Principles of Distributed Computing (PODC'10)*, pages 346–354, 2010.

[5] R. Elsässer, B. Monien, and R. Preis. Diffusion schemes for load balancing on heterogeneous networks. *Theory Comput. Syst.*, 35(3):305–320, 2002.

[6] R. Elsässer, B. Monien, and S. Schamberger. Distributing unit size workload packages in heterogeneous networks. *J. Graph Algorithms Appl.*, 10(1):51–68, 2006.

[7] T. Friedrich and T. Sauerwald. Near-perfect load balancing by randomized rounding. In *Proceedings of the 41st Annual ACM Symposium on Theory of Computing (STOC'09)*, pages 121–130, 2009.

[8] T. Friedrich, M. Gairing, and T. Sauerwald. Quasirandom load balancing. In *Proceedings of the 21st Annual ACM-SIAM Symposium on Discrete Algorithms (SODA'10)*, pages 1620–1629, 2010.

[9] B. Ghosh and S. Muthukrishnan. Dynamic load balancing by random matchings. *J. Comput. Syst. Sci.*, 53:357–370, 1996.

[10] W. Hoeffding. Probability inequalities for sums of bounded random variables. *Journal of the American Statistical Association*, 58(301):13–30, 1963.

[11] S. Muthukrishnan, B. Ghosh, and M. H. Schultz. First- and second-order diffusive methods for rapid, coarse, distributed load balancing. *Theory Comput. Syst.*, 31(4):331–354, 1998.

[12] Y. Rabani, A. Sinclair, and R. Wanka. Local divergence of markov chains and the analysis of iterative load-balancing schemes. In *Proceedings of the 39th IEEE Symposium on Foundations of Computer Science (FOCS'98)*, pages 694–703, 1998.

[13] R. Subramanian and I. D. Scherson. An analysis of diffusive load-balancing. In *Proceedings of the 6th ACM Symposium on Parallel Algorithms and Architectures (SPAA'94)*, pages 220–225, 1994.

APPENDIX

A. HOEFFDING BOUND: ADAPTATION FOR RANDOMIZED ROUNDING

LEMMA A.1. *Let $X_1, \ldots, X_k$ be k independent random variables, and $p_1, \ldots, p_k$ be k values where for all $i, 0 < |p_i| < 1$. Suppose X_i is $1 - p_i$ with probability p_i and $-p_i$ otherwise. If we define the random variable $X = \sum_{1 \leqslant i \leqslant k} X_i$, then we have for any $\delta > 0$ that*

$$\mathbf{Pr}\left[\, |X| \geqslant \delta \,\right] \leqslant 2 \exp\left(-2\delta^2/k\right).$$

PROOF. We first note that for each i, we have $\mathbf{Ex}[X_i] = (1 - p_i) \cdot p_i + (-p_i) \cdot (1 - p_i) = 0$; hence by the linearity of expectation we get $\mathbf{Ex}[X] = \sum_{1 \leqslant i \leqslant k} \mathbf{Ex}[X_i]$. Also, for each i, $-p_i \leqslant X_i \leqslant 1 - p_i$. Therefore, we can apply the Hoeffding bound [10] to get $\mathbf{Pr}\left[\, |X| \geqslant \delta \,\right] \leqslant 2 \exp\left(-2\delta^2/k\right)$, as required. $\square$

Dynamic Packet Scheduling in Wireless Networks

Thomas Kesselheim[*]
RWTH Aachen University
Department of Computer Science
52056 Aachen, Germany
kesselheim@cs.rwth-aachen.de

ABSTRACT

We consider protocols that serve communication requests arising over time in a wireless network that is subject to interference. Unlike previous approaches, we take the geometry of the network and power control into account, both allowing to increase the network's performance significantly. We introduce a stochastic and an adversarial model to bound the packet injection. Although taken as the primary motivation, this approach is not only suitable for models based on the signal-to-interference-plus-noise ratio (SINR). It also covers virtually all other common interference models, for example the multiple-access channel, the protocol model, the radio-network model, and distance-2 matching. Packet-routing networks allowing each edge or each node to transmit or receive one packet at a time can be modeled as well.

Starting from an algorithm for the respective scheduling problem with static transmission requests, we build distributed stable protocols. This is more involved than in previous, similar approaches because the algorithms we consider do not necessarily scale linearly when scaling the input instance. We can guarantee a throughput that is as large as the one of the original static algorithm. In particular, for SINR models the competitive ratios of the protocol in comparison to optimal ones in the respective model are between constant and $O(\log^2 m)$ for a network of size m.

Categories and Subject Descriptors

C.2.1 [**Computer-Communication Networks**]: Network Architecture and Design—*Wireless Communication, Distributed Networks*; F.2.2 [**Analysis of Algorithms and Problem Complexity**]: Non Numerical Algorithms and Problems

---
[*]Supported by DFG through UMIC Research Centre at RWTH Aachen University.

Keywords

Dynamic Scheduling, Wireless Network, SINR, Adversarial Queuing Theory

1. INTRODUCTION

In order to exploit the full potential of wireless communication, it is crucial to suitably deal with the effect of interference, being one of the main limits of a wireless network's performance. Simultaneous transmissions may collide but only if they are not far enough apart. So in order to utilize the available time as efficient as possible, parallel communication has to be going on in spite of interference. In recent time, the resulting algorithmic problems have attained much interest, particularly the ones in the SINR model. Here, interference constraints are modeled much more realistically than in conventional models derived from graph theory. The SINR model takes accumulation of interference into account and allows to consider the effects of power control. That is, for each transmission an individual power can be selected. Theoretical and practical studies have shown that this way the network's performance can be drastically improved. So far, algorithmic studies in the SINR model have mainly considered problems of a static nature. In a typical problem formulation, one is given a set of n transmission requests and has to compute a schedule of minimum length such that all transmissions can be carried out successfully, possibly with the freedom of selecting the transmission powers. Although algorithmically challenging, this is a very limited view as neglects the fact that transmission requests actually arise over time.

For communication requests arriving in a network by adversarial injection or a stochastic process over time, algorithmic research has mainly considered two scenarios. In *packet-routing networks* the focus lies on multi-hop communication in a wireline network. That is, packets have to use intermediate nodes until reaching their target node. The restriction is that on each communication link only a single packet may be transmitted in a time slot. In scheduling problems on a *multiple-access channel*, a number of users have to share a channel but only one user can successfully transmit over the channel at a time. Although both approaches have also been applied in the context of wireless networks, they do not take the geometry of the network into consideration. Packet routing networks neglect all effects of interference between communication links. In contrast, the multiple-access-channel model overestimates interference as it does not take the locality of interference into consideration.

In this paper, we aim at bridging the gap between these different settings. We consider a general model for dynamic packet injection that allows to take the aspects of interference into account. For example, this includes the mentioned advantages of the SINR model such as the spatial separation of transmission but also different transmission powers and the fact if transmission powers are fixed or if they can be chosen by the protocol. In order to cover these different variants, our approach is quite general. Although the SINR model was the primary motivation, this has the interesting consequence that virtually all interference models are covered, such as the multiple-access channel, the radio-network model, the protocol model, and distance-2 matching. Furthermore packet-routing networks allowing that each edge or each node transmits or receives one packet at a time can be modeled as well.

We study *stable* scheduling protocols. That is, the expected time for each packet from injection until delivery (latency) is bounded. Our objective is to build protocols of maximal throughput that guarantee stability. In order to express this performance, we say that a protocol is γ-*competitive* if the following holds. Assuming that there is some way an optimal protocol could serve all arising transmission requests, our protocol would be able to do so as well if time was stretched by the factor γ. Technically, we consider transmission requests arising from stochastic and adversarial injection. In the stochastic model, the injection by a finite number of independent users has to be a convex combination of feasible sets, scaled by factor γ. In addition to that, we adapt the popular model of a window adversary. During each interval of length w, the adversary may only inject packets that could be served in that time, scaled by γ.

We make use of the results for scheduling static transmission requests by giving a black-box transformation to the dynamic model. For a number of algorithms, the exact throughput bound can be transferred to the dynamic case. Using comparisons to the optimal static schedule length, this yields competitive ratios that are as good as the approximation factor of the static algorithms.

1.1 Our Contribution

We introduce a model for adversarial and stochastic packet injection in a wireless network that is suitable for SINR models. Like in a packet-routing network, injected packets may have to use intermediate nodes in order to reach the final destination. For this purpose, the network nodes correspond to vertices of a graph that are connected by an edge if a transmission can take place between them. Due to the diversity in assumptions, we model the aspects of interference in a generic and abstract way. We choose a suitable matrix W quantifying the relative amount of interference of one edge on another one. Based on this matrix, we define an adversarial and a stochastic injection model, limiting the average amount of packets injected per time slot by the injection rate ρ as follows. If $F(e)$ is the average number of packets injected by time step using edge e then each entry of the vector $W \cdot F$ has to be bounded by ρ.

The definition is motivated by *linear contention measures* as they are used in the SINR model. They quantify the amount of contention that has to be resolved in a static scheduling instance. Considering a static single-hop instance in which n packets have to be transmitted from their sender to the respective receiver, the contention measure defined by the matrix W is given as $C = \max_{e \in E} \sum_{e' \in E} W_{e,e'} R(e')$. Here, $R(e)$ denotes the number of packets that have to be transmitted via the edge e. Examples of existing static scheduling algorithms generate schedules of length $O(C \cdot \log n)$ or $O(C + \log^2 n)$ with high probability for the respective contention measure C.

In related work [18, 34, 37] typically a protocol for dynamic injection is built by repeatedly running a static algorithm for a suitably long time. In our case this does not have the desired effect in general. For example, when scaling the number of communication requests per edge, an $O(C \cdot \log n)$ schedule length increases super-linearly since both C and n increase. Thus, having more packets the throughput decreases. In order to deal with this problem we show in the first step how to transform these algorithms to ones that are suitable for dense instances. We exploit the fact that there are only m possible communication links. This allows us to improve the scaling behavior of an algorithm computing schedules of length $f(n) \cdot I$ with high probability to $O(f(m \log m)) \cdot I + g(m,n)$, where $f(m)$ only depends on the network size and $g(m,n)$ grows sub-linearly in n.

The algorithms resulting from the first transformation are suitable to be used in the dynamic scenario. Here, we divide time into sufficiently long time frames. In each of them, the static algorithm is executed with the intention that each injected packet is transmitted via one hop in each time frame. However, packets may fail due to too many injected packets or collisions in the algorithm. These packets are treated by separate executions of the algorithm. This protocol is shown to be stable for injection rates corresponding to the throughput of the respective static algorithm. As a result, we obtain the static approximation factor as the competitive ratio. In particular, for the SINR model we achieve competitive ratios between constant and $O(\log^2 m)$. The expected latency of a packet is also shown to be poly-logarithmic in the size of the network.

Depending on the properties of the algorithm, we obtain a distributed protocol. In order to run the transformation, the network nodes only need the knowledge of a global clock, and the size of the network, the injection rate, and (for the case of adversarial injection) the window size. It is reasonable that this information is available to each network node as it is static, that is, it does not depend on the packet injections and can be set at the deployment time. Furthermore, we show that being aware of a global clock is inevitable. When assuming only local clocks, no protocol for the SINR model with uniform transmission powers can be $m/2 \ln m$-competitive. Achieving $O(m)$-competitiveness is trivial by falling back to the multiple-access channel model.

1.2 Related Work

The analysis of stochastically arriving transmission requests in a wireless network has first been considered in the context of ALOHA [1]. Here, a multiple-access channel is considered, that is only one transmission request can be served at a time. Over the years, this work has been continued under a large number of different assumptions, e.g. if there are finitely or infinitely many users or how much feedback the transmitters get, see e.g. [24, 35, 18, 17] or [9] for an overview.

A different approach for dynamic scheduling in wireless networks has been considered by Tassiulas and Ephremides

[38]. They consider a network with arbitrary interference constraints, where in each round transmission requests arise by an independently, identically distributed process. Tassiulas and Ephremides prove optimality of a protocol that selects in each round a maximum weight set of communication links. The protocol is optimal because it is stable for any injection for which there is some stable protocol. However, this protocol is neither distributed nor can it be computed in polynomial time in general. Viewed from this perspective, we show how to approximate this optimal protocol. Very recently and independently of our work, there has been some similar progress having the same aim by Asgeirsson et al. [5] and Pei and Kumar [33]. The fundamental difference between these protocols and ours lie in the amount of information that is assumed to be known to the network nodes. In contrast to Asgeirsson et al. [5] we assume to have access to a global clock, which allows to obtain significantly better results as we show in Section 8. Pei and Kumar [33] in turn do not only need a global clock but assume that even more information on the geometry of the network is available, which makes more coordination possible.

The probably most popular approach to bound adversarial packet injection was presented by Borodin et al. [8] and refined by Andrews et al. [3]. The general idea is that there is some window size w. The adversary is (λ, w)-bounded if during any interval of w time steps for any edge $e \in E$ at most $\lambda \cdot w$ packets are injected having the edge e on their path. Andrews et al. show that very simple local policies such as *shortest-in-system* (SIS) guarantee that for each $\lambda < 1$ the number of undelivered packets in the system is bounded at any time. The protocol by Aiello et al. [2] achieves essentially the same result but does not have to know the routing paths. It only suffices that there are paths (only known to the adversary) that make the adversary (λ, w)-bounded.

The model of a (λ, w)-bounded adversary has also been applied to the multiple-access channel [7, 11, 10]. The idea is that in each time interval of length w at most $\lambda \cdot w$ packets can arrive. Chlebus et al. [11] show that quite simple deterministic protocols are stable for all $\lambda < 1$, whereas stability for $\lambda = 1$ is impossible for distributed protocols. Further adaptations of the window adversary also consider wireless networks [4, 12]. However, in these cases interference is again completely neglected. To the best of our knowledge adversarial injection taking locality of interference into account has not yet been considered.

While commonly the only criterion is bounded delay, Rabani and Tardos [34], and Scheideler and Vöcking [37] show how to achieve small delays by transforming static packet-routing algorithms. The second part of our transformation is inspired by the one of Scheideler and Vöcking and structurally similar. However, in order to achieve stability they use SIS as a fallback solution, which is known to yield stability. This is not possible in our case since no stable protocols have been known up to now. Furthermore, their analysis and way to cope with dependencies is complex and tailored to the packet-routing case. For this reason, our analysis does not have much in common with the one by Scheideler and Vöcking.

Since a seminal work by Moscibroda and Wattenhofer [31], algorithmic research has started considering scheduling wireless transmissions in the SINR model. As already mentioned, this model takes accumulation effects of interference and the possibility of selecting transmission powers

into account. These different transmission powers offer a new degree of freedom to the problem depending on if the powers are specified as part of the input or if they can be set by the algorithm. For the first problem of dealing with fixed transmission powers, e.g. uniform powers, a number of algorithms have been proposed, centralized [19, 23] and distributed [16, 29, 21] ones. For the problem in which transmission powers can be set by the algorithm one approach is to set transmission powers obliviously, depending on the distance between the sender and the receiver [15, 20, 22]. While this approach can achieve only trivial approximation factors in terms of n, there is also a centralized algorithm achieving an $O(\log n)$ approximation guarantee [27].

When considering conflict graphs with a small inductive independence number [26, 25], a similar abstraction as in this paper is used. However, we aim at building distributed protocols in this paper whereas the approach in [26] is rather appropriate for centralized, LP-based approximations.

2. FORMAL DEFINITION OF THE NETWORK MODEL

We assume the wireless network to be modeled as a directed graph $G = (V, E)$. The vertex set V corresponds to the set of network nodes. The set E indicates the set of possible communication links between two nodes. As the graph is not necessarily complete, we assume that packets might need to be transmitted via intermediate nodes before reaching their final destination. These paths are fixed for each packet, e.g., by routing tables. They may, in principle, visit nodes multiple times. They are only restricted to have length at most D. We will use $m := \max\{|E|, D\}$ as the significant network size.

Via each communication link at most one packet may be transmitted per time step. Furthermore, transmissions on different links are also subject to interference. Generalizing multiple variants of the SINR model but also packet-routing networks, the multiple access channel and a broad class of wireless interference models (see Sections 6 and 7), we employ a *linear contention measure*. It quantifies the contention in a static single-hop scheduling instance. We will assume that there is some algorithm computing a solution for the static scheduling problem that can be bounded in terms of the measure. Furthermore, to get a bound on the competitiveness, we will need the property that the contention measure can also serve as a lower bound on the optimal schedule length.

To define the measure formally, we assume that there is some matrix W expressing the (relative) impact that a transmission on one link has to a transmission on another one. It is chosen later on based on the geometry and the interference assumptions. More precisely, for two edges e and e', the quantity $W_{e,e'} \in [0, 1]$ indicates, how much a transmission on e is interfered by a transmission on e'. We assume that $W_{e,e} = 1$ for all $e \in E$. Given a set of paths let $R(e)$ denote the number of paths including edge e somewhere. The contention measure induced by the vector R is now given by $C := \|W \cdot R\|_\infty = \max_e \sum_{e'} W_{e,e'} \cdot R(e')$.

For example, the case of packet-routing networks can be captured by setting W to the identity matrix and receive the congestion as the contention measure. For the multiple-access channel, we can set W to the matrix whose entries are all 1. In this case C is simply the total number of packets to be delivered. In both cases the contention measure is trivially a lower bound on the optimal schedule length. The respective algorithms for the static scenario are discussed in Section 7.

Note that we do not state explicitly here what makes a transmission successful. In our final protocol, all transmissions will be carried out by the algorithm our transformation is applied on. We will only assume that there is some algorithm generating schedules of length at most $f(n) \cdot C$ or $f(m) \cdot C + g(n, m)$ in case of n packets. For our considerations, it is not important if, for example, acknowledgment transmissions have to be carried out.

2.1 Injection Models

For communication requests arising over time, we adapt two famous models: time-independent, finite-user stochastic injection and injection by a window adversary. In either case, the injected packets are assumed to have a fixed path through the network. We bound the average contention measure of all communication requests injected per time slot. If $F(e)$ is the average number of packets that have to be transmitted via edge e, the injection rate λ is the largest component of the vector $W \cdot F$.

For the stochastic model, we take the following assumptions. We assume that there is a finite number of packet generators each of which injects at most one packet per time slot at random. The probability distribution is identical in each time slot and independent among different generators or different time slots. Formally, let $X_{g,P}^t$ be 1 if generator g injects in time slot t a packet that shall be routed along path P. We assume these random variables to have the following three properties. (a) The injection in each time step is identically distributed. That is for any pair t_1 and t_2 the random variables $X_{g,P}^{t_1}$ and $X_{g,P}^{t_2}$ have to be identically distributed for all g and P. (b) The injection of different generators and in different time slots is independent. Formally, we require independence of any subset of random variables $X_{g,P}^t$ in which no pair shares both the same t and the same g. (c) Each generator only injects a single packet per time slot. That is for any fixed t, and g only one of the $X_{g,P}^t$ can be 1. We require each component of $W \cdot F$ to be bounded by λ, where $F(e) = \sum_g \sum_{P:e \in P} \mathbf{E} \left[X_{g,P}^t \right]$.

Furthermore, we consider a (w, λ)-bounded adversary for an arbitrary $w \in \mathbb{N}$. That is, considering an arbitrary interval of w time slots, we require that the contention measure induced by all links of the respective paths is at most $w \cdot \lambda$. Formally, let $R(e)$ be the number of packets including edge e on the path injected during that interval. Then each component of the vector $W \cdot R$ is bounded by $w \cdot \lambda$.

3. STATIC ALGORITHMS FOR LARGE PACKET NUMBERS

All existing approaches to use static scheduling algorithms in a dynamic environment [18, 34, 37] share the idea of running the algorithm repeatedly for a suitably long time. As in these cases the schedule length grows linearly, this does not decrease the throughput and at the same time failures are less likely. In our case, however, the situation is different. Consider for example an algorithm that computes a schedule of length $O(C \cdot \log n)$ for n packets with high probability. Then doubling all packets does not only double the number of time slots used as both C and n are doubled. Our solu-

tion to this problem is to exploit that there are only m different links that can be used for transmissions. Starting e.g. from an $O(C \cdot \log n)$ algorithm, our transformation yields an $O(C \cdot \log m + \log n \cdot \log^2 m + \log^2 n \cdot \log m)$-algorithm. That is, for sufficiently many transmission requests, the schedule length becomes linear in C.

More precisely, we assume that there is some algorithm $\mathcal{A}(C, n)$ that generates a schedule of length $f(n) \cdot C$ with probability $1 - 1/n$ if the contention measure is at most C and the number of packets is at most n. Algorithm 1 runs $\mathcal{A}$ repeatedly on randomly selected subsets of the communication requests. Each edge randomly selects delay values for all waiting packets. The algorithm is then executed on all packets having received the same delay, assuming the contention measure of these packets to be at most $\chi = 6(\ln m + 9)$. Having an contention measure of at most χ, the number of packets can also be at most $m \cdot \chi$ as we have $W_{e,e} = 1$ for all $e \in E$. Thus, we know that $f(m\chi) \cdot \chi$ time slots suffice for the execution with probability at least $1 - 1/m\chi$. For each packet not being successfully transmitted, the same step is repeated with a smaller maximum delay. At some point not many packets remain. These are dealt with by running $\mathcal{A}$ without using the random-partition technique.

Algorithm 1: Transformation to get a schedule length that is independent of the number of packets

---

set $\chi = 6(\ln m + 9)$;
for $i := 1$ to $\xi = \lceil \log(C/2\phi\chi \log n) \rceil$ **do**
    assign each remaining packet a delay of at most $\lceil 2^{-i+1} \cdot C/\chi \rceil$;
    execute $\mathcal{A}(\chi, m \cdot \chi)$ for $f(m\chi) \cdot \chi$ steps on all packets that received the same delay;

for $i := 1$ to $\lceil \phi \rceil + 1$ **do**
    execute $\mathcal{A}(2\phi\chi \log n, n)$ on the remaining packets;

In the analysis, we show that with high probability the contention measure induced by the remaining transmission requests reduces by a factor of two in each iteration of the for loop. Thus, after ξ iterations, the contention measure has become as small as $O(\log n \cdot \log m)$ and for this reason the original algorithm can schedule all remaining packets with it in $O(f(n) \cdot \log n \cdot \log m)$ steps.

THEOREM 1. *If $\mathcal{A}(C, n)$ uses at most $f(n) \cdot C$ steps with probability at least $1 - 1/n$, then, for each constant ϕ, Algorithm 1 uses at most $2 \cdot f(m\chi) \cdot C + O(f(m\chi) \cdot \log n \cdot \log m + f(n) \cdot \log n \cdot \log m)$ steps with probability at least $1 - 1/n^\phi$.*

PROOF. The number of time slots Algorithm 1 uses can be obtained by summing up the numbers of time slots used by all iterations of $\mathcal{A}$. In order to bound the success probability, let $C^{(i)}$ be the contention measure induced by the remaining transmission requests after the ith iteration of the for loop, $C^{(0)} = C$. We claim that with probability at least $1 - 1/n^\phi$ all of the following events occur: For all $i \in [\xi]$, we have $C^{(i)} \leq 2^{-i} \cdot C$, and all remaining packets are successfully transmitted in one of the last $\lceil \phi \rceil + 1$ executions of $\mathcal{A}$.

In order to bound the probability of a failure, we consider the first event that does not occur. That is, let us assume that for i, we have $C^{(i-1)} \leq 2^{-(i-1)} \cdot C$. Given this event, we now bound the probability that $C^{(i)} \leq 2^{-i} \cdot C$.

CLAIM 2. *For all $i \in [\xi]$ we have*

$$\mathbf{Pr}\left[C^{(i)} > 2^{-i} \cdot C \;\middle|\; C^{(i-1)} \leq 2^{-(i-1)} \cdot C\right] \leq \frac{2^i}{2^\xi} \cdot \frac{1}{4n^\phi} \;.$$

PROOF (OUTLINE). Let $i \in [\xi]$ be fixed. In the ith iteration each of the remaining packets is assigned a delay value uniformly at random from the set $[\psi]$, where $\psi = \lceil 2^{-i+1} \cdot C/\chi \rceil$.

Let $R_j^{(i-1)}(e)$ be the number of packets for link e having been assigned delay j in the ith iteration.

A packet might not be successfully transmitted in the ith iteration for two reasons. Either we have $\|W \cdot R_j^{(i-1)}\|_\infty > \chi$ or in spite of the fact that the contention measure was small enough algorithm $\mathcal{A}$ did not transmit all packets successfully.

In the first case, we set $Y_j = \|W \cdot R_j^{(i-1)}\|_\infty/\chi$, otherwise we set $Y_j = 0$. If in contrast, we had a failure of the algorithm, we set $Z_j = 1$ and otherwise $Z_j = 0$. These definitions yield $C^{(i)} \leq \sum_{j=1}^{\psi} Y_j \cdot \chi + \sum_{j=1}^{\psi} Z_j \cdot \chi$.

Let us first consider the random variables Y_j. Using Chernoff bounds one can show that for all $j \in [\psi]$ we have $\mathbf{E}\left[e^{4 \cdot Y_j}\right] \leq 2$. The random variables Y_j are not independent. Nevertheless, we have $\mathbf{E}\left[\prod_{j=1}^{\psi} e^{4 \cdot Y_j}\right] \leq \prod_{j=1}^{\psi} \mathbf{E}\left[e^{4 \cdot Y_j}\right]$ by applying the FKG inequality (see, e.g., [14, Theorem 9]). For this reason, we get

$$\mathbf{Pr}\left[\sum_{j=1}^{\psi} Y_j \geq \frac{\psi}{4}\right] = \mathbf{Pr}\left[e^{4\sum_{j=1}^{\psi} Y_j} \geq e^\psi\right]$$

$$\leq e^{-\psi} \prod_{j=1}^{\psi} \mathbf{E}\left[e^{4 \cdot Y_j}\right]$$

$$\leq e^{-\psi} \cdot 2^\psi \leq 2^{-\frac{\psi}{4}} \;.$$

Let us now turn to the random variables Z_j. We have $Z_j = 1$ if the respective execution of $\mathcal{A}$ failed in spite of the fact that the contention measure was small enough. By assumption, the probability of this event is at most $\frac{1}{m\chi} \leq \frac{1}{8e}$. Thus, $\mathbf{E}[Z_j] \leq \frac{1}{8e}$ and $\mathbf{E}\left[\sum_{j=1}^{\psi} Z_j\right] \leq \frac{\psi}{8e}$. As these are independent 0/1 random variables, we can apply a a Chernoff bound to get

$$\mathbf{Pr}\left[\sum_{j=1}^{\psi} Z_j \geq \frac{\psi}{4}\right] \leq 2^{-\frac{\psi}{4}} \;.$$

Combining the two bounds and using the definition of ψ, we have

$$\mathbf{Pr}\left[C^{(i)} > 2^{-i} \cdot C \;\middle|\; C^{(i-1)} \leq 2^{-(i-1)} \cdot C\right]$$

$$\leq \mathbf{Pr}\left[\sum_{j=1}^{\psi} Z_j + \sum_{j=1}^{\psi} Y_j \geq \frac{\psi}{2}\right] \leq 2 \cdot 2^{-\frac{\psi}{4}} \leq \frac{2^i}{2^\xi} \cdot \frac{1}{4n^\phi} \;.$$

This completes the proof of the claim. □

Having shown this bound for each iteration, we can now take the sum over all $i \in [\xi]$ to get

$$\sum_{i=1}^{\xi} \mathbf{Pr}\left[C^{(i)} > 2^{-i} \cdot C \;\middle|\; C^{(i-1)} \leq 2^{-(i-1)} \cdot C\right]$$

$$\leq \sum_{i=1}^{\xi} \frac{2^i}{2^\xi} \cdot \frac{1}{4n^\phi} \leq 2 \cdot \frac{1}{4n^\phi} \;.$$

Now let us consider the last $\lceil \phi \rceil + 1$ executions of $\mathcal{A}$. Provided that $C^{(\xi)} \leq 2^{-\xi} \cdot C \leq 2\phi\chi \log n$, by our assumption the probability that not all packets are successfully transmitted in one execution is at most $1/n$. Having $\lceil \phi \rceil + 1$ independent repeats, this failure probability reduces to $1/2n^\phi$. Taking another union bound, this shows that the combined failure probability is at most $1/n^\phi$.

4. DYNAMIC SCHEDULING PROTOCOL FOR STOCHASTIC INJECTION

We are now prepared to transform the static algorithm into a protocol for dynamic packet injection. In this section, we consider the stochastic injection. In the next section, the results are transferred to the adversarial injection model. The assumption we make is that there is some algorithm $\mathcal{A}(C, n)$ for static scheduling instances. Given at most n communication requests of contention measure at most C, it computes a schedule of length $f(m) \cdot C + g(m, n)$ with probability at least $1 - 1/2n^4$. Here, f is a function independent of n, and g is a function growing sublinearly in n. Such an algorithm can, for example, be obtained by the transformation presented in the previous section. Given this algorithm, we build a stable protocol for each injection rate $\lambda < \frac{1}{f(m)}$.

Let $\lambda = (1 - \varepsilon)/f(m)$. Without loss of generality, we assume that $\varepsilon \leq 1/2$. We divide time into frames of length T. We require that $T \geq \frac{100 f(m)}{\varepsilon^3} + \frac{48 f(m) \ln m}{\varepsilon^2}$ and furthermore that $T \geq \frac{4 f(m)}{\varepsilon^2} \cdot g\left(m, \frac{m}{f(m)} \cdot T\right)$. The latter condition is fulfilled for sufficiently large T because $g(m, n)$ grows sublinearly in n. For example, if $f(m) = O(\log m)$ and $g(m, n) = O(\log n \cdot \log^2 m + \log^2 n \cdot \log m)$, as derived in the previous section, it suffices to have $T = O\left(\frac{\log^4 m}{\varepsilon^2}\right)$. Furthermore, we set $J = (1 + \varepsilon) \cdot \lambda \cdot T$.

Each time frame of length T itself consists of two phases. Each packet is intended to make one hop towards its final destination during the first phase of a time frame. In order to achieve this goal, after injection a packet waits for the next time frame to begin. Here, $\mathcal{A}(J, m \cdot J)$ is executed for $T' = f(m) \cdot J + g(m, m \cdot J)$ time slots on the set containing the respective next hop on the path of each packet that has not failed so far. In this execution packets can fail to reach their next hop destination. If this happens, a packet is referred to as *failed* and will from now on be only scheduled for transmission in the second phase, the *clean-up phase*. The clean-up phase consists of the remaining $T - T'$ time slots of the time frame. Here, the algorithm is executed another time but only on the following set of packets. Each edge e with a non-empty buffer of failed packets performs a random experiment. With probability $1/m$ it selects the failed packet from its buffer whose failure is longest ago. With the remaining probability no packet from the buffer of failed packets on this edge is selected in this round. On the selected packets, we execute $\mathcal{A}(1, m \cdot J)$ for $f(m) \cdot 1 + g(m, m \cdot J)$ time steps. If T fulfills the bounds mentioned before, these are at most $T - T'$ steps. So both phases fit into a time frame.

In order to prove stability, we have to consider the failed packets. Each packet that does not fail will reach its final destination after at most D time frames. The central question is therefore whether the clean-up phases are able to keep the buffers of failed packets small. In the following two sections, we show that both queue lengths and packet latency are bounded in expectation, proving the protocol to be stable.

4.1 Queue Lengths

In order to show the stability of the protocol, we show in this section that in expectation queue lengths are bounded. As previously stated, it suffices to bound the lengths of buffers for failed packets. Packets that do not fail spend at most $D + 1$ time frames in the system. Having a bounded (expected) number of packets injected per time step, they do not have to be considered anymore.

THEOREM 3. *The expected queue lengths (i.e. number of undelivered packets) are bounded at any time.*

To prove the theorem, we consider as a potential function Φ the sum of the numbers of remaining hops all failed packets have to cross. In a clean-up phase this quantity reduces if a transmission is successfully carried out. Obviously, this potential function is an upper bound on the summed buffer sizes as well.

First, we bound the increase of the potential function in a time frame. This is due to colliding packets. The increase may depend on the previous value of the potential function. For example, if all packets collided in the previous time frames, collisions are less likely. Fortunately, we can use the following pessimistic assumption. The probability of a collision is maximal (and therefore the potential increase) if no packets have collided before. Therefore we will assume for the bound on the potential increase that all injected packets have reached the current time frame without failing. This may yield that we account for failed packets multiple times: We add its contribution to the potential function in each time frame it would fail. However, this assumption allows us to treat the potential like a Markov chain.

LEMMA 4. *For each $i \in \mathbb{N}$ the probability that the potential increases by at least $i \cdot m^2 J + 1$ is at most $(mJ)^{-4-i}$.*

PROOF (OUTLINE FOR $i = 0$). Let C be the contention measure of all transmission requests that were originally meant to be served in this phase. As we have $W_{e,e} = 1$ for all $e \in E$ and path lengths are at most D, the potential increase in case of a failure can be bounded by $D \cdot |E| \cdot C \leq m^2 C$. Using a Chernoff bound, one can show that

$$\mathbf{Pr}\left[C \geq (1 + \varepsilon)\lambda T\right] \leq m \cdot \left(\frac{e^\varepsilon}{(1 + \varepsilon)^{1+\varepsilon}}\right)^{\lambda T} . \quad (1)$$

As mentioned earlier there are two possible reasons for this event to occur. On the one hand, the network is overloaded in the time frame, that is $C > J$. We use the fact that $T \geq \frac{100 f(m)}{\varepsilon^3} + \frac{48 f(m) \ln m}{\varepsilon^2}$ to get $\lambda T \geq A \cdot \ln(mJ)$, where $A = -5 / \ln\left(\frac{e^\varepsilon}{(1+\varepsilon)^{1+\varepsilon}}\right)$. Combined with Equation (1), we get

$$\mathbf{Pr}\left[C \geq J\right] = \mathbf{Pr}\left[C \geq (1 + \varepsilon)\lambda T\right]$$
$$\leq m \left(\frac{e^\varepsilon}{(1 + \varepsilon)^{1+\varepsilon}}\right)^{A \ln(mJ)}$$
$$= m \left(\frac{1}{mJ}\right)^5 = \frac{1}{2(mJ)^4} .$$

Still, in the case $C \leq J$, packets may fail. This is due to the fact that internal randomization of the algorithm can

result in failures. We required the algorithm to have a failure probability of at most $1/2(mJ)^4$ in this case. Combining the two bounds, this shows the claim for the case $i = 0$. $\square$

For the potential decrease in clean-up phases we use a very pessimistic but simple assumption. In the worst case all failed packets are in the same buffer. Even in this case, the potential decreases with probability at least $1/2em$.

LEMMA 5. *The probability that a non-zero potential decreases is at least $1/2em$.*

PROOF. Having non-zero potential, at least one buffer contains failed packets. For this reason, the probability that at least one packet is selected is at least $1/m$. With probability at least $(1 - 1/m)^{m-1} \geq 1/e$ no other packet is selected. The success probability of the algorithm is at least $1/2$. All events are independent. $\square$

Combining these two bound we get the following facts on the Markov chain's drift, that is, its expected change. The drift is finite for each state and in the case of non-zero potential it is negative. This already yields that the Markov chain is ergodic [32]. However, we can also bound the probability distribution quantitatively.

LEMMA 6. *Let Δ be an integer random variable that only values -1, 0, $i \cdot H + 1$ for some $H \in \mathbb{N}$, having the following distribution:*

- $\mathbf{Pr}\left[\Delta = -1\right] = q$,

- $\mathbf{Pr}\left[\Delta = 0\right] = (1 - a - q)$, *and*

- $\mathbf{Pr}\left[\Delta = i \cdot H + 1\right] = \frac{a}{1-b} \cdot b^i$,

where $b \leq \frac{1}{8}$, $a \leq \frac{q}{4H}$.

Let Φ be another, independent, non-negative integer random variable. If $\mathbf{Pr}\left[\Phi \geq k\right] \leq \left(1 - \frac{1}{H}\right)^k$ for all $k \in \mathbb{N}$, then this bound also holds for $\max\{\Phi + \Delta, 0\}$.

PROOF. For $k = 0$ the bound trivially holds. So let us consider $k > 0$. Considering all possible values of Δ, we have that $\mathbf{Pr}\left[\max\{\Phi + \Delta, 0\} \geq k\right]$ is

$$\mathbf{Pr}\left[\Delta = -1, \Phi \geq k + 1\right] + \mathbf{Pr}\left[\Delta = 0, \Phi \geq k\right]$$
$$+ \sum_{i=0}^{\infty} \mathbf{Pr}\left[\Delta = i \cdot H + 1, \Phi \geq k - (i \cdot H + 1)\right] .$$

Using the definitions and the independence, this is at most

$$q \cdot \left(1 - \frac{1}{H}\right)^{k+1} + (1 - q - a)\left(1 - \frac{1}{H}\right)^k$$
$$+ \sum_{i=0}^{\infty} \frac{a}{1-b} b^i \cdot \left(1 - \frac{1}{H}\right)^{k-(i \cdot H + 1)} .$$

We now apply the fact that $b \leq 1/8$ and $H \geq 2$. This yields

$$\sum_{i=0}^{\infty} b^i \cdot \left(1 - \frac{1}{H}\right)^{-i \cdot H} \leq \sum_{i=0}^{\infty} (4b)^i \leq 2$$

and

$$\frac{1}{1-b}\left(1 - \frac{1}{H}\right)^{-1} \leq \frac{5}{2} .$$

For this reason, the probability is at most

$$\left(1 - \frac{1}{H}\right)^k \left(q \cdot \left(1 - \frac{1}{H}\right) + (1 - q - a) + 5a\right)$$

$$\leq \left(1 - \frac{1}{H}\right)^k \left(1 - \frac{1}{H}q + 4a\right) \ .$$

As we have $a \leq \frac{q}{4H}$, this is at most $\left(1 - \frac{1}{H}\right)^k$. $\square$

Lemmas 4 and 5 show that the potential change is stochastically dominated by Δ in the lemma when setting $H = m^2 J$, $a = (mJ)^{-4}$, $b = (mJ)^{-1}$, and $q = (2em)^{-1}$. Thus the lemma shows that $\mathbf{Pr}[\Phi(t) \geq k] \leq \left(1 - \frac{1}{m^2 J}\right)^k$ at any time t. That is, we have $\mathbf{E}[\Phi(t)] \leq m^2 J$ at any time t. As Φ is an upper bound on the lengths of queues for failed packets, this completes our proof of Theorem 3.

4.2 Packet Latency

Keeping the insights from the previous section in mind, we can now bound the expected time that a packet spends in the network between the time of injection and reaching its final destination (*latency*). In particular, we show that for each packet with a path length d, the expected latency is $O(d \cdot T)$. That is, it takes $O(d)$ time frames. Starting from an $O(C \cdot \mathrm{polylog}\, n)$-algorithm, this means the expected latency is bounded by $O(d \cdot \mathrm{polylog}\, m)$.

THEOREM 7. *The expected latency of a packet of path length d is $O(d \cdot T)$.*

Due to space limitations, the full formal proof can only be found in the full version. Nevertheless, we strive to give an overview over the main ideas here.

For packets that do not fail, this bound is trivial since they take one hop in each time frame. Therefore, it is crucial how much time it takes from the moment a packet fails until its delivery. Fortunately, this can be related to the potential after the time frame of failure.

OBSERVATION 8. *The expected remaining number of time frames a packet spends in the network between failure and reaching its destination is at most $2em\Phi$, where Φ is the potential after the time frame of failure.*

PROOF. In order to show this claim, we consider the following simplified model that works as an upper bound for the clean-up phases. At the time of failure, all remaining hops of a packet are added to the tail of a FIFO queue. In each time frame, one hop is dequeued with probability $1/2em$. If the queue length is Φ after adding the hops of a packet, this packet will spend in expectation $2em \cdot \Phi$ time frames in the queue.

For the actual network, the potential Φ after the time frame of failure is exactly the number of successful transmission the failed packet has to wait for until it is delivered. Just as in the FIFO queue, in each time frame there is a successful transmission with probability at least $1/2em$. Therefore, the expected number of time frames the packet spends in the network is at most $2em \cdot \Phi$. $\square$

We can combine this insight with the bounds on the probability distribution of Φ obtained in the previous section. This way, we get bounds on the probability distribution of time a failed packet spends in the system. To show the theorem, we take into consideration that it is very unlikely for

a packet to fail. This step has to be done carefully because the involved random variable can be correlated. Nevertheless, we can show that in each time frame for each packet the probability of a failure in this time frame multiplied by the expected remaining time in case of this failure is bounded by a constant.

5. DYNAMIC SCHEDULING PROTOCOL FOR ADVERSARIAL INJECTION

In order to transfer the achieved results of the previous section to the adversarial injection model, we adapt an approach by Scheideler and Vöcking [37]. The idea is to assign each packet a random delay at the time of injection. Then this packet is kept at the generator node until the delay has elapsed. After this time it is treated as if it was actually injected at this time.

We consider an adversarial injection of rate $\lambda = (1 - \varepsilon)/f(m)$. For each packet a delay value δ from 0 to $\delta_{\max} - 1$ is chosen uniformly at random, where $\delta_{\max} = \lceil 2(D + w)/\varepsilon \rceil$. Like in the stochastic model, it waits until the beginning of the next time frame, but now it spends another δ time frames waiting. Afterwards it is treated like in the stochastic model with $\lambda' = (1 - \varepsilon/2)/f(m)$.

THEOREM 9. *The expected queue lengths are bounded at any time. The expected latency of a packet is $O(D \cdot w \cdot T/\varepsilon)$.*

6. APPLICATION TO SINR-BASED ALGORITHMS

In the SINR model, the network nodes are assumed to be located in a metric space. This allows to model the signal propagation as follows. If some node transmits at power level p then at distance d this signal is received at a strength of p/d^α, where α is the so-called path-loss exponent. A transmission can successfully be received if the *signal-to-interference-plus-noise ratio* (SINR) is above some threshold β. That is, a transmission via a link $\ell = (s, r)$ if for the set $S \subseteq E$ of simultaneous transmissions we have

$$\frac{p(\ell)}{d(s,r)^\alpha} \geq \beta \left(\sum_{\substack{\ell' = (s', r') \in S \\ \ell \neq \ell'}} \frac{p(\ell')}{d(s', r)^\alpha} + N \right) \ .$$

We choose the impact matrix W depending on whether the transmission powers are fixed for the respective links or they can be chosen for each transmission by the protocol.

6.1 Fixed Power Assignments

Let us first consider the case in which the network links use fixed transmission powers. That is the power value used for a transmission over link ℓ is always $p(\ell)$. We define the weight matrix W based on the the relative amount of interference of one link on another one, the so-called *affectance* [23, 29]. For two links $\ell, \ell' \in E$ it is defined as

$$a_p(\ell, \ell') = \min\left\{ 1, \beta \frac{p(\ell)}{d(s, r')^\alpha} \Big/ \left(\frac{p(\ell')}{d(s', r')^\alpha} - \beta N \right) \right\} \ .$$

We achieve the best competitive ratios when dealing with a linear power assignment. That is, $p(\ell)$ is proportional to $d(\ell)^\alpha$ for each link ℓ – and thus the received signal strength is the same for any link. In this case, we set the matrix entries to $W_{\ell,\ell'} = a_p(\ell',\ell)$. With this definition the contention measure C is apart from constant factors the measure of interference defined in [16]. For this reason, we can use the algorithm from [16] that achieves a schedule length of $O(C + \log^2 n)$ whp. Applying the transformation, we get a protocol allowing for injection rates $\Omega(1)$. The lower bound on C in [16] states that for each set of transmission requests that can be served in a single step we have $C = O(1)$. Thus the optimally achievable injection rate is $O(1)$ as well. That is, independent of the network size we are only a constant factor worse.

COROLLARY 10. *For linear power assignments there is a stable, constant-competitive distributed protocol.*

Generalizing linear power assignments, we consider power assignments that are (sub-)linear and monotone. That is for two links $\ell, \ell' \in E$ with $d(\ell) \leq d(\ell')$ we have $p(\ell) \leq p(\ell')$ and $p(\ell)/d(\ell)^\alpha \geq p(\ell')/d(\ell')^\alpha$. In this case, we set the matrix W to $W_{\ell,\ell'} = \max\{a_p(\ell,\ell'), a_p(\ell',\ell)\}$ if $d(\ell) \leq d(\ell')$ and $W_{\ell,\ell'} = 0$ otherwise. We apply the distributed algorithm in [29]. This algorithm needs for n packet $O(\bar{A} \cdot \log n)$ steps, where $\bar{A}$ denotes the *maximum average affectance* that is defined by $\bar{A} = \max_{M \subseteq \mathcal{R}} \text{avg}_{\ell' \in M} \sum_{\ell \in M} a_p(\ell,\ell') = \max_{M \subseteq \mathcal{R}} \frac{1}{|M|} \sum_{\ell' \in M} \sum_{\ell \in M} a_p(\ell,\ell')$. Here, $\mathcal{R}$ denotes the multiset of all transmission requests. We observe that for the contention measure C defined by the matrix W, we have $C \geq \bar{A}/2$. Therefore, we can apply the transformation from Section 3 to get a distributed algorithm computing schedules of length $O(C \cdot \log m + \log m \cdot \log^2 m)$ with high probability. This yields a protocol that is stable for all injection rates in $\Omega(1/\log m)$. Furthermore, the lower bounds on the optimal schedule length in [29] show that all stable protocols are limited by some injection rate $O(\log m)$.

COROLLARY 11. *For monotone (sub-)linear power assignments there is a stable, $O(\log^2 m)$-competitive distributed protocol.*

At this point, one has to remark that in [21] an improved analysis of the algorithm in [29] has been presented. It remains an open problem to fit this analysis into our framework.

6.2 Powers Chosen by the Algorithm

There are two approaches to face the setting in which each transmission may use an individual power. On the one hand, one can still define fixed transmission powers for each link in an oblivious fashion, that is, without taking into consideration which transmissions actually take place. Using linear power assignments as described in the previous section, the results in [16] yield a $O(\log \Delta \cdot \log m)$-competitive protocols. Here, Δ is the ratio between the length of the longest and the shortest link. Using square-root power assignments [15, 20], we get $O(\log \log \Delta \cdot \log^2 m)$-competitive protocols. Considering fading metrics, that is the setting where α is greater than the doubling dimension, the protocols are $O(\log \Delta)$ respectively $O(\log \log \Delta \cdot \log m)$-competitive.

We can also exploit the possibility of selecting powers for each transmission individually. For this case only centralized approximation algorithms are known [27]. In this case, we set for two links $\ell = (s,r), \ell' = (s',r') \in E$ the weight $W_{\ell,\ell'} = \min\left\{1, \frac{d(s,r)^\alpha}{d(s,r')^\alpha} + \frac{d(s,r)^\alpha}{d(s',r)^\alpha}\right\}$ if $d(\ell) \leq d(\ell')$ and 0

otherwise. The algorithm in [27] yields schedule lengths of $O(C \cdot \log n)$ with this measure. We have lower bounds of $O(1)$ in fading metrics resp. $O(\log m)$ in general metrics.

COROLLARY 12. *For arbitrary transmission powers, there is a stable centralized protocol, that is $O(\log m)$-competitive in fading metrics and $O(\log^2 m)$-competitive in general metrics.*

This protocol has the drawback of being centralized and for this reason not being applicable in practical settings. However, this results shows the problem tractable is in general. In order to construct a distributed protocol, a possible solution could be to spend some time for preprocessing. Even an $O(C \cdot \log m + \text{poly}(m))$ algorithm could be used to get the same competitive ratio.

7. FURTHER APPLICATIONS

Defining the matrix W and using the right static algorithm, we can immediately get results for old and new models. For example, for packet routing, setting W to the identity matrix and using the trivial single-hop algorithm, we get stable protocols for all $\lambda < 1$. For the multiple-access channel we set $W_{e,e'} = 1$ for all $e, e' \in E$. Using an algorithm that is acknowledgement-based and works without station ids, we can build stable protocols for all $\lambda < 1/e$. When using station ids and also the other transmissions as feedback, we achieve stability for all $\lambda < 1$. See the full version for the algorithms and [18] for details on this duality.

Going beyond these models, we can introduce a conflict graph on the network links. In this graph, the set of vertices is the set of network links E and (possibly weighted) directed edges indicate if (or to what extent) a transmission on one link is interfered by a transmission on another link. Implementing for example the *node constraint model*, that is that each node can only transmit or receive a single packet in each step, we have edges between links that share an endpoint. In this case, we can get constant-competitive since the conflict graph has bounded independence and the algorithm from [16] can be adapted.

For the more general case that the conflict graph has inductive independence number ρ, we can build $O(\rho \cdot \log m)$-competitive protocols. Conflict graphs with constant ρ for example result from the radio network model in disk graphs, the protocol model or distance-2 matching in disk graphs. For the definition of the inductive independence number and the respective algorithm see the full version.

8. ASPECTS OF DISTRIBUTED PROTOCOLS

In general, it is desirable to design distributed dynamic scheduling protocols. In order to apply our transformation we require the nodes to have access to a global clock (in order to build the time frames), and to know the network size m, the injection rate λ and (in the adversarial model) the window size w. The other properties depend on the algorithm the protocol was derived from. Particularly, the amount of feedback the protocol needs is identical to the one of the static algorithm. For example, we can start from a static *acknowledgement-based* algorithm, that is, the only feedback it gets is whether it its own transmission was received. Transforming this algorithm, the dynamic protocol

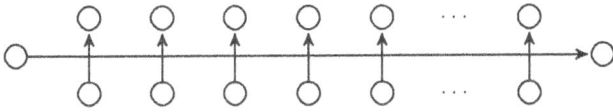

Figure 1: The instance considered in the proof of Theorem 13.

will also be acknowledgement-based. Furthermore, if the algorithm is the same for all nodes, we derive a symmetric protocol.

Fortunately, the required information for the transformation does not depend on the state of the network and is thus available at the time of deployment. So our protocol can be considered distributed if the static algorithm is. However, at this point the natural question arises whether all these assumptions are necessary, particularly the knowledge of a global clock, allowing the construction of common time frames. For the multiple-access channel it can be shown that having only local clocks does not weaken the protocols significantly. Even with an acknowledgement-based protocol local clocks can be synchronized [18]. In our case this is different.

THEOREM 13. *There is no stable acknowledgement-based protocol with local clock for the SINR model with uniform transmission powers that is $m/2 \ln m$-competitive.*

The formal proof of this theorem can be found in the full version. The main idea is to exploit the inherent asymmetry of the SINR model. In the multiple-access-channel model, we have that in case of a collision due to interference all involved transmissions fail. In the SINR model this is different. A transmission can be successful but harm another one at the same time. The instance considered in the proof of Theorem 13 consists of a number of small parallel links (Figure 1). These links are not able to coordinate each other because they do not interfere. Hence, a transmission via the large link is impossible in almost every step.

9. DISCUSSION AND OPEN PROBLEMS

In this paper we have shown a general technique to transfer results from static to dynamic packet scheduling in a wireless network. This transformation is independent of the respective interference model. All accesses to the wireless network are performed via a given algorithm for static problems. Improving, adapting or extending this static algorithm suffices to build a new dynamic protocol. This gives a strong motivation for studies of the static scheduling problems.

A possible direction for future work could be considering unreliable networks in the given models. Unreliable communication has been an emerging topic in related fields. For example, stochastic interference constraints based on Rayleigh fading have been considered [13]. As shown in [13], the static single-hop algorithms applied in Section 6 yield very similar results in the Rayleigh-fading setting. Hence, our transformation directly applies. For adversarial interference constraints, an adversarial jammer [6, 36] and unreliable transmission links [30] in the radio-network model have been considered. In principle, our transformation can also be applied to these settings by adapting the respective static algorithm.

Another possible future direction includes the study of flexible data rates. That is, wireless devices adapt to the

current interference conditions, e.g., by slowing down a file transfer. Very recently [28], centralized algorithms for static scheduling problems have been presented. Combining these results with distributed algorithms and dynamically arising communication requests remains an open problem.

Furthermore, it could be interesting which information is really necessary in which model to design the protocol. We have shown that the global clock is inevitable for our transformation. However, it remains an open question whether knowing the network size, the injection rate, and the window size is really necessary to build a protocol.

The last aspect to be mentioned here is that we sticked to the traditional notions of stability here. That is, queue lengths and packet latencies were analyzed in expectation. In a practical environment, however, packets waiting too long for their delivery will presumably be outdated and thus have to be dropped. Probably, by allowing packet losses, one could develop protocols that are closer to actual applications.

10. REFERENCES

[1] N. Abramson. The ALOHA system: another alternative for computer communications. In *Proceedings of the November 17-19, 1970, fall joint computer conference*, AFIPS '70 (Fall), pages 281–285, 1970.

[2] W. Aiello, E. Kushilevitz, R. Ostrovsky, and A. Rosén. Adaptive packet routing for bursty adversarial traffic. In *Proceedings of the 30th annual ACM symposium on Theory of computing (STOC)*, pages 359–368, 1998.

[3] M. Andrews, B. Awerbuch, A. Fernández, J. M. Kleinberg, F. T. Leighton, and Z. Liu. Universal stability results for greedy contention-resolution protocols. In *Proceedings of the 37th IEEE Annual Symposium on Foundations of Computer Science (FOCS)*, pages 380–389, 1996.

[4] M. Andrews and L. Zhang. Routing and scheduling in multihop wireless networks with time-varying channels. In *Proceedings of the 15th ACM-SIAM Symposium on Discrete Algorithms (SODA)*, pages 1031–1040, 2004.

[5] E. I. Asgeirsson, M. M. Halldórsson, and P. Mitra. A fully distributed algorithm for throughput performance in wireless networks. In *Proceedings of the 46th Annual Conference on Information Sciences and Systems (CISS)*, 2012.

[6] B. Awerbuch, A. Richa, and C. Scheideler. A jamming-resistant MAC protocol for single-hop wireless networks. In *Proceedings of the 27th ACM Symposium on Principles of Distributed Computing (PODC)*, pages 45–54, 2008.

[7] M. A. Bender, M. Farach-Colton, S. He, B. C. Kuszmaul, and C. E. Leiserson. Adversarial contention resolution for simple channels. In *Proceedings of the 17th ACM Symposium on Parallelism in Algorithms and Architectures (SPAA)*, pages 325–332, 2005.

[8] A. Borodin, J. Kleinberg, P. Raghavan, M. Sudan, and D. P. Williamson. Adversarial queuing theory. *Journal of the ACM*, 48:13–38, January 2001.

[9] B. S. Chlebus. Randomized communication in radio networks. In *Handbook on Randomized Computing*, pages 401–456. Kluwer Academic Publishers, 2001.

[10] B. S. Chlebus, D. R. Kowalski, and M. A. Rokicki. Stability of the multiple-access channel under maximum broadcast loads. In *Proceedings of the 9th International Symposium on Stabilization, Safety, and Security of Distributed Systems (SSS)*, pages 124–138, 2007.

[11] B. S. Chlebus, D. R. Kowalski, and M. A. Rokicki. Adversarial queuing on the multiple access channel. *ACM Transactions on Algorithms*, 8(1):5:1–5:31, 2012.

[12] V. Cholvi and D. R. Kowalski. Bounds on stability and latency in wireless communication. *IEEE Communications Letters*, 14(9):842–844, 2010.

[13] J. Dams, M. Hoefer, and T. Kesselheim. Scheduling in wireless networks with Rayleigh-fading interference. In *Proceedings of the 24th ACM Symposium on Parallelism in Algorithms and Architectures (SPAA)*, 2012. To appear.

[14] D. P. Dubhashi and D. Ranjan. Balls and bins: A study in negative dependence. *Random Structures and Algorithms*, 13(2):99–124, 1998.

[15] A. Fanghänel, T. Kesselheim, H. Räcke, and B. Vöcking. Oblivious interference scheduling. In *Proceedings of the 28th ACM Symposium on Principles of Distributed Computing (PODC)*, pages 220–229, 2009.

[16] A. Fanghänel, T. Kesselheim, and B. Vöcking. Improved algorithms for latency minimization in wireless networks. *Theoretical Computer Science*, 412(24):2657–2667, 2011.

[17] L. Goldberg, M. Jerrum, S. Kannan, and M. Paterson. A bound on the capacity of backoff and acknowledgement-based protocols. In *Proceedings of the 27th International EATCS Colloquium on Automata, Languages and Programming (ICALP)*, pages 705–717, 2000.

[18] L. A. Goldberg, P. D. Mackenzie, M. Paterson, and A. Srinivasan. Contention resolution with constant expected delay. *Journal of the ACM*, 47:1048–1096, 2000.

[19] O. Goussevskaia, R. Wattenhofer, M. M. Halldórsson, and E. Welzl. Capacity of arbitrary wireless networks. In *Proceedings of the 28th Conference of the IEEE Communications Society (INFOCOM)*, pages 1872–1880, 2009.

[20] M. M. Halldórsson. Wireless scheduling with power control. In *Proceedings of the 17th annual European Symposium on Algorithms (ESA)*, pages 361–372, 2009.

[21] M. M. Halldórsson and P. Mitra. Nearly optimal bounds for distributed wireless scheduling in the sinr model. In *Proceedings of the 38th International EATCS Colloquium on Automata, Languages and Programming (ICALP)*, pages 625–636, 2011.

[22] M. M. Halldórsson and P. Mitra. Wireless capacity with oblivious power in general metrics. In *Proceedings of the 22nd ACM-SIAM Symposium on Discrete Algorithms (SODA)*, pages 1538–1548, 2011.

[23] M. M. Halldórsson and R. Wattenhofer. Computing wireless capacity. unpublished manuscript, 2010.

[24] J. Håstad, F. T. Leighton, and B. Rogoff. Analysis of backoff protocols for multiple access channels. *SIAM Journal on Computing*, 25:740, 1996.

[25] M. Hoefer and T. Kesselheim. Secondary spectrum auctions for symmetric and submodular bidders. In *Proceedings of the 13th ACM Conference on Electronic Commerce (EC)*, 2012. To appear.

[26] M. Hoefer, T. Kesselheim, and B. Vöcking. Approximation algorithms for secondary spectrum auctions. In *Proceedings of the 23rd ACM Symposium on Parallelism in Algorithms and Architectures (SPAA)*, pages 177–186, 2011.

[27] T. Kesselheim. A constant-factor approximation for wireless capacity maximization with power control in the SINR model. In *Proceedings of the 22nd ACM-SIAM Symposium on Discrete Algorithms (SODA)*, pages 1549–1559, 2011.

[28] T. Kesselheim. Approximation algorithms for wireless link scheduling with flexible data rates. *CoRR*, abs/1205.1331, 2012.

[29] T. Kesselheim and B. Vöcking. Distributed contention resolution in wireless networks. In *Proceedings of the 24th International Symposium on Distributed Computing (DISC)*, pages 163–178, 2010.

[30] F. Kuhn, N. Lynch, C. Newport, R. Oshman, and A. Richa. Broadcasting in unreliable radio networks. In *Proceedings of the 29th ACM Symposium on Principles of Distributed Computing (PODC)*, pages 336–345, 2010.

[31] T. Moscibroda and R. Wattenhofer. The complexity of connectivity in wireless networks. In *Proceedings of the 25th Conference of the IEEE Communications Society (INFOCOM)*, pages 1–13, 2006.

[32] A. Pakes. Some conditions for ergodicity and recurrence of markov chains. *Operations Research*, pages 1058–1061, 1969.

[33] G. Pei and V. A. Kumar. Low-complexity scheduling for wireless networks. In *Proceedings of the 13th ACM International Symposium Mobile Ad-Hoc Networking and Computing (MOBIHOC)*, 2012.

[34] Y. Rabani and E. Tardos. Distributed packet switching in arbitrary networks. In *Proceedings of the 28th annual ACM symposium on Theory of computing (STOC)*, pages 366–375, 1996.

[35] P. Raghavan and E. Upfal. Stochastic contention resolution with short delays. *SIAM Journal on Computing*, 28(2):709–719, 1999.

[36] A. Richa, C. Scheideler, S. Schmid, and J. Zhang. A jamming-resistant MAC protocol for multi-hop wireless networks. In *Proceedings of the 24th International Symposium on Distributed Computing (DISC)*, pages 179–193, 2010.

[37] C. Scheideler and B. Vöcking. From static to dynamic routing: Efficient transformations of store-and-forward protocols. *SIAM Journal on Computing*, 30(4):1126–1155, 2000.

[38] L. Tassiulas and A. Ephremides. Stability properties of constrained queueing systems and scheduling policies for maximum throughput in multihop radio networks. *IEEE Transactions on Automatic Control*, 37(12):1936–1948, 1992.

Competitive and Fair Throughput for Co-Existing Networks Under Adversarial Interference

Andrea Richa, Jin Zhang
Computer Science and
Engineering, SCIDSE
Arizona State University
Tempe, AZ 85287, USA
{aricha,jzhang82}@asu.edu

Christian Scheideler
Department of Computer
Science
University of Paderborn
D-33102 Paderborn, Germany
scheideler@upb.de

Stefan Schmid
Deutsche Telekom
Laboratories & TU Berlin
D-10587 Berlin, Germany
stefan@net.t-labs.tu-
berlin.de

ABSTRACT

This paper initiates the formal study of a fundamental problem: How to efficiently allocate a shared communication medium among a set of K co-existing networks in the presence of arbitrary external interference? While most literature on medium access focuses on how to share a medium among *nodes*, these approaches are often either not directly applicable to co-existing networks as they would violate the independence requirement, or they yield a low throughput if applied to multiple networks. We present the randomized medium access (MAC) protocol CoMAC which guarantees that a given communication channel is shared fairly among competing and independent networks, and that the available bandwidth is used efficiently. These performance guarantees hold in the presence of arbitrary external interference or even under adversarial jamming. Concretely, we show that the co-existing networks can use a $\Omega(\varepsilon^2 \min\{\varepsilon, 1/poly(K)\})$-fraction of the non-jammed time steps for successful message transmissions, where ε is the (arbitrarily distributed) fraction of time which is not jammed.

Categories and Subject Descriptors

C.2.5 [**Computer-Communication Networks**]: Local and Wide-Area Networks—*Access schemes*; F.2.2 [**Analysis of Algorithms and Problem Complexity**]: Nonnumerical Algorithms and Problems—*Sequencing and scheduling*

General Terms

Algorithms, Reliability, Theory

Keywords

Wireless Ad-hoc Networks, MAC Protocols, Jamming

1. INTRODUCTION

The decentralized allocation of a communication medium among a set of wireless nodes does not only constitute one of the most fundamental theoretical problems in distributed computing, but is also of direct practical relevance. Today, a chunk of the wireless spectrum is often simultaneously used by many devices belonging to different, so-called *co-existing networks*. It is expected that the popularity of wireless mobile devices will further increase the resource sharing by such networks in the future.

Interestingly, not much is known today on how a given spectrum can be shared efficiently and fairly among co-existing networks, especially in environments with uncontrollable external interference. Existing distributed MAC protocols (typically based on random backoff schemes) are either not resistant to the unpredictable unavailability of the medium at all, or are optimized towards a single network only, in the sense that the nodes of a network collaboratively seek to coordinate the access among themselves [24]. However, the state-of-the-art protocols fail if multiple networks are collocated (as illustrated, for example, in our simulation study in Section 4).

This paper is the first to present (and rigorously prove the performance of) a robust MAC protocol suited for co-existing networks exposed to a harsh environment with unpredictable or even adversarial interference.

1.1 Model

We attend to a simplified scenario where a set of n wireless nodes V are located within transmission range of each other and need to communicate over a single shared channel. The wireless nodes belong to K co-existing networks N_i with node sets V_i, i.e., $V = V_1 \cup V_2 \cup \ldots \cup V_K$, for some constant K (which is of unknown to the nodes). For simplicity we will assume that these networks are node disjoint. However, by emulating multiple instances, a node may also participate in several networks simultaneously; the performance guarantees derived in this paper would still hold.

We aim to design a distributed MAC protocol for these wireless nodes. Although the protocol is used by all nodes $v \in V$, it should not depend on any knowledge of how many nodes n there are in total, on the number of co-existing networks K, or on the size of the co-existing network v belongs to. Moreover, it should ensure that the K networks are independent in the sense that no communication is required between different networks.

Co-existing wireless networks appear in many scenarios where different wireless networks share the same wireless medium. For example, consider a major conference, e.g., organized by the United Nations, where participants from different countries use their hand-held devices to communicate with the other representatives of their country. We assume that the different networks only share the same medium access protocol, but are otherwise different and inter-network communication may not be desired or possible (except, e.g., for multi-national participants). Another scenario where ensuring fairness among co-existing networks is crucial are emergency response networks, where many emergency response services, such as fire squads, police, and paramedics, all arrive simultaneously at some accident or disaster scene and have to share the wireless medium in a fair and even manner in order to establish their own separate communication networks.[1]

This paper presents a robust and fair medium access (MAC) protocol CoMAC that makes effective use of the few and arbitrarily distributed time periods where a wireless medium is available. We model interference—due to simultaneous transmissions, co-existing networks, changes in the environment that affect the wireless medium, etc., and, when applicable, intentional jamming—generally as an *adversary*, which we may sometimes simply refer to as the *jammer* (even when a malicious jammer is not present in the environment and interference may be caused by other factors). Our adversary may behave in an *adaptive* manner: we assume that the adversary has full knowledge of the protocol and its history, and that it uses this knowledge to decide on whether to jam at a certain moment in time.

Let us use the simplifying notation $N(v)$ to denote the network node $v \in V$ belongs to. We assume that a node v can distinguish among the following events at some time t: (1) idle channel (no node in V transmits and there is no outside interference, including jamming activity, at time t); (2) successful transmission of a packet in network $N(v)$ (which occurs every time a single node in $N(v)$ transmits, and no other node in V nor the adversary transmits); and (3) medium busy (due to a transmission by a node in some co-existing network different from network $N(v)$, or to simultaneous transmissions by two or more nodes in $N(v)$, or to external interference or jamming).

How to design such a distributed medium access protocol which shares the bandwidth fairly among the K networks, without sacrificing performance? At first sight this may seem impossible: as the total number of co-existing networks and the number of devices is not known, a node cannot guess its fair share of the channel time. This paper shows that this is indeed possible, even in the presence of a powerful adaptive adversarial jammer, referred to as a $(T, 1 - \varepsilon)$-*bounded* (adaptive) adversary, which can jam the medium an arbitrary $(1 - \varepsilon)$ fraction of the time for an arbitrarily small constant $\varepsilon > 0$ and which hence models a wide range of external interference scenarios or jammers. For the ease of presentation, we assume a synchronous environment where time proceeds in *rounds* (also called *steps*). Formally, the $(T, 1 - \varepsilon)$-bounded adversary is defined as follows: for some $T \in \mathbb{N}$ and a constant $0 < \varepsilon < 1$, the adversary may jam at most $(1 - \varepsilon)w$ of the time steps, for any time window of size $w \geq T$. In the following, we will use the notation $N = \max\{T, n\}$ to denote the maximum over the adversarial window size and n.

Assuming backlogged traffic at the wireless devices, we require that our MAC protocol fulfill the following properties: (1) *c-competitiveness*: Given a time interval I, we define $g(I)$ as the number of time steps in I that are non-jammed, and $s(I)$ as the total number of time steps in I in which a successful transmission happens in any network. A MAC protocol is called *c-competitive* against some $(T, 1 - \varepsilon)$-bounded adversary if, for any sufficiently large time interval I, $s(I) \geq c \cdot g(I)$. (2) *Fairness*: The probabilities of having a successful transmission in any two networks N_i and N_j, where $i, j \in [1, K]$, do not differ by much; moreover, the nodes inside a network share the bandwidth fairly as well.

Note that the nodes have no knowledge of how many nodes

are there in the same network as itself, nor do the nodes know how many other networks are co-existing and how many nodes are there in each of these co-existing networks, respectively. However, we assume that the nodes have a common parameter $\gamma \in O(1/(\log T + \log \log n))$. The assumption that nodes know γ is not critical for the scalability of our protocol, as it requires only a polynomial estimate of T and an even rougher estimate of n.

Although the presented CoMAC protocol converges fast and is therefore expected to work well under continuously entering and leaving nodes, in this paper we will just focus on a synchronous setting where nodes do not join or leave.

1.2 Related Work

The classic approach to design efficient MAC protocols is to use random backoff schemes (e.g., [5, 6, 12, 13, 18, 22]). However, these works do not take into account adversarial interference and are hence not robust against it. Generally, in a random backoff protocol, each node periodically attempts to transmit a message starting with a certain probability p. If the message transmission fails (due to interference), the node may retry sending the message in the next time steps with polynomially or exponentially decreasing probabilities (for example, $p^2, p^4, p^8, \ldots$) until the message is successfully transmitted or the minimum allowable probability is reached. Thus, in a dense network (as in our single-hop scenario), an adversary with knowledge of the MAC protocol could simply wait until the nodes have reached transmission probabilities that are inversely proportional to the number of nodes and then start jamming the medium, forcing the nodes to lower their transmission probabilities to a point where a competitive throughput is not achievable.

There also exist several interesting results on protocols that are robust to more complex or even adversarial interference (see, e.g., [7] or [29] for a nice overview). There are two basic approaches in the literature. The first assumes randomly corrupted messages (e.g., [21]), which is much easier to handle than adaptive adversarial jamming [4]. The second line of work either bounds the number of messages that the adversary can transmit or disrupt with a limited energy budget (e.g. [1, 11, 16, 17]), or bounds the number of channels the adversary can jam (e.g. [8, 9, 10, 19]). The protocols in, e.g., [17] can tackle adversarial jamming at both the MAC and network layers, where the adversary may not only jam the channel but also introduce malicious (fake) messages (possibly with address spoofing). However, these solutions depend on the fact that the adversarial jamming budget is finite, so it is not clear whether the protocols would work under heavy continuous jamming. (The result in [11] seems to imply that a jamming rate of 0.5 is the limit whereas the handshaking mechanisms in [17] seem to require an even lower jamming rate.)

Our work is motivated by the jamming-resistant single network MAC protocols studied in [3, 23, 24]. In particular, our adversarial model was introduced by Awerbuch et al. [3] who present a single-hop MAC protocol that guarantees a constant throughput against an adaptive adversary that can block the medium a constant fraction of the time. The MAC protocol and the throughput guarantees were subsequently generalized to multi-hop networks [23, 26], and also the adversary was strengthened further such that it can even jam the medium *reactively*, i.e., it has a binary feedback whether the medium will be idle or busy in the current round [24], before it has to make a decision whether to jam the current round. It has also been shown that the MAC protocol can serve as a basis to design robust applications such as leader election [25].

However, the performance achieved by the MAC protocols described in [3, 23, 24] drops sharply if multiple networks are collo-

---

[1] Whereas in some scenarios it may be desirable that messages are broadcast across all emergency unit networks, for better immediate response action to a disaster/accident, in the longer run, it is still important to be able to differentiate among the different ad-hoc networks established.

cated. This is due to the fact that in these protocols, each individual co-existing network will strive to achieve a constant competitive throughput in the non-jammed time periods, which requires a constant cumulative access probability *per co-existing network*. As we will explain in the next section in more detail, this necessarily leads to a throughput which is exponentially small in the number of co-existing networks.

It turns out that in a co-existing scenario, the nodes must strike a good balance between a less aggressive (more cooperative) medium access strategy while remaining robust against external interference. We will show that this can be achieved by monitoring the availability of the wireless medium over time and adjusting the sending probabilities or backoffs according to the fraction of observed *idle time periods*. (A similar approach is used in the *Idle-Sense* [14] Distributed Coordination Function to synchronize the nodes' contention windows.) Implicitly synchronizing access via idle time periods is also the key to enable fairness between co-existing networks. The performance analysis of such an algorithm however is involved, as the distributed and randomized decisions exhibit many non-trivial dependencies. Nevertheless, we are able to rigorously prove good competitive throughput and fairness properties, which is also confirmed by our simulation study.

Interestingly, although co-existing networks are ubiquitous and many different aspects are discussed intensively (e.g., the packet inter-arrival time and fairness in co-existing 802.11a/g and 802.11n networks [2], interference cancelation phenomena [27], transmission capacities in multi-antenna adhoc networks [15], or even explicit inter-network communication for frequency cooperation [30]) in different contexts (e.g., in the current debate on white space liberalization [20] where primary TV and microphone users announcing their reservations in a central database are given strict priority), we are not aware of any work on the design of MAC protocols for independent co-existing networks with rigorous formal competitive throughput and fairness guarantees.

1.3 Our Contributions

To the best of our knowledge, this is the first paper to present a robust medium access protocol which provably performs well in an environment with co-existing networks. The COMAC protocol features a guaranteed competitive throughput in the presence of co-existing networks as well as a wide range of external interference patterns that can be subsumed and modeled as a $(T, 1-\varepsilon)$-bounded adaptive adversary blocking the medium a $(1-\varepsilon)$ fraction of all time. Moreover, it features fairness among co-existing networks and within an individual network. Finally, the protocol is attractive for its simple design. Our main theoretical result is summarized in the following theorem.

THEOREM 1.1. *The* COMAC *medium access protocol guarantees that in a backlogged scenario, if executed for* $\Omega(\frac{1}{\varepsilon} \log N \max\{T, \frac{1}{\varepsilon\gamma^2} \log^3 N\})$ *many time steps,* COMAC *achieves a competitive throughput of* $\Omega(\varepsilon^2 \min\{\varepsilon, 1/poly(K)\})$ *w.h.p., for any* $(T, 1 - \varepsilon)$-*bounded adaptive adversary that arbitrarily jams the medium up to a* $(1 - \varepsilon)$ *fraction of the time, and which has complete knowledge of the protocol history. Moreover, the cumulative probabilities among different networks, as well as the access probabilities of individual nodes within the same network, differ only by a small factor.*

Simulations complement our theoretical asymptotic bounds.

2. MAC FOR CO-EXISTING NETWORKS

Before presenting the formal MAC algorithm, we explain its variables and provide some intuition.

2.1 Intuition

In the COMAC protocol, each node v maintains a medium access probability p_v which determines the probability that v transmits a message in a communication round. The nodes adapt and synchronize (inside a co-existing network) their p_v values over time (which as a side-effect also guarantees fairness within the network) in a multiplicative-increase multiplicative-decrease manner in order to ensure a throughput that is as good as possible. More precisely, the sending probabilities are changed by a factor of $(1 + \gamma)$. Moreover, we impose an upper bound of $\hat{p}$ on p_v, for some constant $0 < \hat{p} < 1$. As we will see, unlike in most classic backoff protocols, our adaptation rules for p_v ensure that the adversary cannot influence p_v much by adaptive jamming.

In addition, each node maintains two variables, a threshold variable T_v and a counter variable c_v. T_v is used to estimate the adversary's time window T. A good estimation of T can help the nodes recover from a situation where they experience high interference in the network. In times of high interference, T_v will be increased and the sending probability p_v will be decreased.

While these concepts have already been used in our other protocols in [3, 23, 24], they are not sufficient to ensure a jamming-resistant protocol that also works well in case of co-existing networks. The basic problem lies in the fact that all of these protocols aim at reaching a constant cumulative probability, irrespective of the adversarial jamming, so that a good throughput can be obtained in those steps that are not jammed. In co-existing networks, however, this is not a good idea: Suppose that we have K co-existing networks such that each has a constant cumulative probability. Then the overall cumulative probability would be $\Theta(K)$ and therefore, the probability of having a successful transmission in any network would be as low as $\Theta(K)e^{-\Theta(K)}$, which is *exponentially* low in K.

Hence, a less aggressive approach than the one pursued in [3, 23, 24] is needed. Ideally, this approach should also make sure that the available bandwidth is shared in a fair way among the networks. Surprisingly, a relatively simple change in the protocol in [24] can achieve jamming-resistance, a good throughput in co-existing networks, and also fairness. The basic idea behind this change is to remember the latest idle time step, and whenever there is a new idle time step, then *with a probability* q_v *that is inversely proportional to the time difference to the previous idle time step,* p_v *and* T_v *are adapted.* (The protocol in [24] would *always* adapt p_v and T_v in case of an idle channel.) Since this probabilistic rule turned out to be very hard to analyze, we transformed it into a deterministic rule that shows the same performance in the experiments.

2.2 Algorithm

Now we are ready to provide the detailed and formal description of the COMAC algorithm. Initially, each node v sets $p_v = \hat{p}$ ($\hat{p} \leq 1/24$), $c_v = T_v = 1$, and $q_v = 0$. In the following, $L_v \geq 1$ is the time that went by from v's viewpoint since the last idle time step. (If there has not yet been an idle time step, $L_v = \infty$.)

In each step, each node v does the following: v decides with probability p_v to send a message along with the tuple (c_v, T_v, p_v). If it decides not to send a message, it checks the following two conditions:

1. If v senses an idle channel, then $q_v := q_v + 1/L_v$. If $q_v \geq 1$ then

   - $p_v := \min\{(1+\gamma)p_v, \hat{p}\}$, $T_v := \max\{1, T_v - 1\}$, and

- $q_v := q_v - 1$.

2. If v successfully receives a message from node u with the tuple (c_u, T_u, p_u) then

   - $p_v := (1 + \gamma)^{-1} p_u$, $c_v = c_u$, and $T_v = T_u$.

Afterwards, v sets $c_v := c_v + 1$. If $c_v > T_v$ then it does the following: v sets $c_v := 1$, and if there was no idle step among the past T_v time steps, then $p_v := (1 + \gamma)^{-1} p_v$ and $T_v := T_v + 2$.

3. ANALYSIS

For the analysis of our protocol we will use the following notation. We are given $K \geq 2$ co-existing networks denoted by $N_1, \ldots, N_K$. Each network N_i consists of a node set V_i where $n_i = |V_i| \geq 2$ (otherwise, the network would be irrelevant). The cumulative probability due to nodes in N_i is given by $P_i = \sum_{v \in V_i} p_v$, and the cumulative probability over all co-existing networks is given by $P = \sum_{i=1}^{K} P_i$. Whenever we consider some specific time step t, $P_i(t)$ is the value of P_i at time t and $P(t)$ is the value of P at time t.

3.1 Basic Observations

Given that we have a single-hop network, any idle time period is observed by all nodes in all co-existing networks. Hence, the q_v and L_v values of all nodes are identical if all start at the same time (otherwise, two idle time steps suffice to synchronize the L_v values so that the increase of the q_v's is synchronized from that point on, which would also be sufficient for our analysis to go through). Henceforth, we will drop the subscript v from q_v and L_v. Since after the first successful transmission in N_i, the T_v and c_v values are synchronized among the nodes in N_i, we arrive at the following fact, which establishes fairness within a network.

FACT 3.1. *After the first successful transmission in network N_i, the access probabilities p_v of the nodes $v \in V_i$ differ by a factor of at most $(1 + \gamma)$.*

Throughout our analysis, we will make use of generalized Chernoff bounds that are derived from [28].

LEMMA 3.2. *Consider any set of random variables $X_1, \ldots, X_n$ with values in $[0, 1]$. If there exist values $p_1, \ldots, p_n \in [0, 1]$ with $\mathbb{E}[\prod_{i \in S} X_i] \leq \prod_{i \in S} p_i$ for every set $S \subseteq \{1, \ldots, n\}$, then it holds for $X = \sum_{i=1}^{n} X_i$ and $\mu = \sum_{i=1}^{n} p_i$ and any $\delta > 0$ that*

$$\mathbb{P}[X \geq (1 + \delta)\mu] \leq \left(\frac{e^\delta}{(1 + \delta)^{1+\delta}} \right)^\mu \leq e^{-\frac{\delta^2 \mu}{2(1+\delta/3)}}$$

If, on the other hand, it holds that $\mathbb{E}[\prod_{i \in S} X_i] \geq \prod_{i \in S} p_i$ for every set $S \subseteq \{1, \ldots, n\}$, then it holds for any $0 < \delta < 1$ that

$$\mathbb{P}[X \leq (1 - \delta)\mu] \leq \left(\frac{e^{-\delta}}{(1 - \delta)^{1-\delta}} \right)^\mu \leq e^{-\delta^2 \mu / 2}$$

The following lemma follows immediately from the Taylor series of the exponential function.

LEMMA 3.3. *For all $0 < x < 1$ it holds that $e^{-x/(1-x)} \leq 1 - x \leq e^{-x}$.*

This implies the following lemma.

LEMMA 3.4. *For any non-jammed time step,*

$$e^{-\frac{P}{1-\hat{p}}} \leq \mathbb{P}[channel\ is\ idle] \leq e^{-P} \quad and$$

$$P_i \cdot e^{-\frac{P}{1-\hat{p}}} \leq \mathbb{P}[successful\ msg\ transmission\ in\ N_i] \leq \frac{P_i}{1-\hat{p}} \cdot e^{-P}$$

3.2 Cumulative Probability

In the following, we will derive the first fundamental property of our protocol: we show that the overall cumulative probability $P = \sum_{i=1}^{K} P_i$ converges to some range of values so that the contention on the wireless medium is moderate. This is a necessary condition for a good performance. Our proof framework basically follows the framework of [3] but the proof arguments significantly differ in various places when it comes to analyzing the specifics of our new protocol. We refer to Section 2 of [3] for a comparison.

The proof works by induction over sufficiently large time frames. Let I be a time frame consisting of $\frac{\alpha}{\varepsilon} \log N$ *subframes* I' of size $f = \max\{T, \frac{\alpha \beta^2}{\varepsilon \gamma^2} \log^3 N\}$ rounds, where α and β are sufficiently large constants and $N = \max\{T, n\}$. Let $F = \frac{\alpha}{\varepsilon} \log N \cdot f$ denote the size of I.

First, we show that for any subframe I' in which initially the overall cumulative probability is at least $1/(f^2(1 + \gamma)^{2\sqrt{f}})$, also afterwards this cumulative probability is at least $1/(f^2(1+\gamma)^{2\sqrt{f}})$, w.h.p.

LEMMA 3.5. *For any subframe $I' = [t_0, t_1]$ in which $P(t_0) \geq 1/(f^2(1 + \gamma)^{2\sqrt{f}})$, also $P(t_1) \geq 1/(f^2(1 + \gamma)^{2\sqrt{f}})$ w.h.p.*

PROOF. We start with the following claim about the maximum number of times nodes decrease their probabilities in I' due to $c_v > T_v$.

CLAIM 3.6. *If in subframe I', T_v is decreased at most k times, then node v increases T_v by 2 at most $k/2 + \sqrt{f}$ many times.*

PROOF. Only an idle time step can potentially reduce T_v by 1. If there is no idle time step during the last T_v many steps, T_v is increased by 2. Suppose that $k = 0$. Then the number of times a node v increases T_v by 2 is upper bounded by the largest possible ℓ so that $\sum_{i=0}^{\ell} T_v^0 + 2i \leq f$, where T_v^0 is the initial value of T_v. For any $T_v^0 \geq 1$, $\ell \leq \sqrt{f}$, so the claim is true for $k = 0$. For each decrease of T_v, the current T_v as well as all subsequent values of T_v (until a T_v is reached with $T_v = 1$) get reduced by one. Hence, for an arbitrary value of $k \geq 0$ we are searching for the maximum ℓ so that $\sum_{i=0}^{\ell} \max\{T_v^0 + 2i - k, 1\} \leq f$. This ℓ is at most $k/2 + \sqrt{f}$, which proves our claim. $\square$

This claim allows us to prove that the overall cumulative probability P will exceed a certain threshold in a subframe w.h.p.

CLAIM 3.7. *Suppose that in $I' = [t_0, t_1)$, $P(t_0) \in [1/(f^2(1 + \gamma)^{\sqrt{2f}}), 1/f^2]$. Then there is a time step t in I' with $P(t) \geq 1/f^2$, w.h.p.*

PROOF. Suppose that there are g non-jammed time steps in I'. Let k_0 be the number of these steps with an idle channel and k_1 be the number of these steps with a successful message transmission in any of the co-existing networks. Let the binary random variable X_i be 1 if and only if the nodes increase their access probabilities in the i-th idle time step in I', and let $X = \sum_{i=1}^{k_0} X_i$. Furthermore, let k_2 be the maximum number of times a node v increases T_v by 2 in I'.

Suppose for the moment that $P(t_0) = 1/f^2$. If all time steps t in I' satisfy $P(t) \leq 1/f^2$, then it must hold that the total decrease of $P(t)$ in I' (due to successful transmissions and cases in which access probabilities are decreased when $c_v > T_v$), which is at most $(1 + \gamma)^{k_1 + k_2}$, has to be at least as large as the total increase of $P(t)$ (due to idle time steps), which is equal to $(1 + \gamma)^X$. Hence, we must have that $X \leq k_1 + k_2$. For an arbitrary initial probability $P(t_0) \leq 1/f^2$, we must therefore have

$$X - \log_{1+\gamma}((1/f^2)/P(t_0)) \leq k_1 + k_2 \quad (1)$$

to avoid a time step t in I' with $P(t) > 1/f^2$. Our goal is to show that this inequality is violated w.h.p., which implies that I' has a time step t with $P(t) > 1/f^2$ w.h.p.

Next, we focus on k_2. Consider some fixed $k_0 \geq 2$ (as we will see later, $k_0 \geq 2$ w.h.p.). Let L_i be the L-value of the nodes at the i-th idle time step (note that they are all the same) and let $q_i = 1/L_i$ denote the increase of the q-values of the nodes in the i-th idle time step. Also, let $\bar{q} = \frac{1}{k_0 - 1} \sum_{i=2}^{k_0} q_i$. Certainly, the number of times any node v decreases T_v in I' is bounded by the number of times q is at least 1, which is at most $\lceil \sum_{i=1}^{k_0} q_i \rceil \leq \lceil 1 + (k_0 - 1)\bar{q} \rceil$. Hence, it follows from Claim 3.6 that

$$k_2 \leq \lceil \bar{q}(k_0 - 1) + 1 \rceil / 2 + \sqrt{f} \quad (2)$$

On the other hand, the number of times any node v increases p_v in I' is at least $\lfloor \sum_{i=2}^{k_0} q_i \rfloor = \lfloor (k_0 - 1)\bar{q} \rfloor$ (because due to Fact 3.1 it follows from $P(t) \leq 1/f^2$ that $p_v(t) < \hat{p}$ for all v). Plugging this together with (2) into (1) and using the fact that $P(t_0) \geq 1/(f^2(1+\gamma)^{\sqrt{2f}})$, we obtain

$$\lfloor (k_0 - 1)\bar{q} \rfloor - \lceil (k_0 - 1)\bar{q} + 1 \rceil / 2 \leq \sqrt{2f} + k_1 + \sqrt{f}$$
$$\Rightarrow \quad (k_0 - 1)\bar{q}/2 \leq k_1 + 4\sqrt{f} \quad (3)$$

given that f is large enough. It remains to lower bound $\bar{q}$ and k_0 and to upper bound k_1 in order to arrive at a contradiction.

We start with $\bar{q}$. Let $\bar{L} = \frac{1}{k_0 - 1} \sum_{i=2}^{k_0} L_i$. Since $\sum_{i=2}^{k_0} L_i < f$, it holds that $\bar{L} < \frac{f}{k_0 - 1}$. Moreover, we make use of the following well-known fact.

FACT 3.8. *For any sequence of positive numbers $x_1, \ldots, x_n$ it holds for its arithmetic mean $A = (1/n) \sum_{i=1}^n x_i$ and its harmonic mean $H = ((1/n) \sum_{i=1}^n 1/x_i)^{-1}$ that $A \geq H$.*

Hence, it follows that $\bar{L} \geq 1/(\frac{1}{k_0 - 1} \sum_{i=2}^{k_0} 1/L_i)$ and therefore, $\frac{1}{k_0 - 1} \sum_{i=2}^{k_0} 1/L_i \geq 1/\bar{L}$. This in turn implies that

$$\bar{q} \geq 1/\bar{L} \geq \frac{k_0 - 1}{f}$$

Next we provide an upper bound for k_1 that holds w.h.p. Certainly, for any time step t with $P(t) \leq 1/f^2$,

$$\mathbb{P}[\geq 1 \text{ message transmitted at step } t] \leq 1/f^2.$$

Hence, $\mathbb{E}[k_1] \leq g \cdot (1/f^2) \leq 1/f$. In order to prove an upper bound on k_1 that holds w.h.p., we can use the general Chernoff bounds stated in Lemma 3.2. For any step t let the binary random variable Y_t be 1 if and only if at least one message is transmitted successfully at time t and $P(t) \leq 1/f^2$. Then

$$\mathbb{P}[Y_t = 1] = \mathbb{P}[P(t) \leq 1/f^2] \cdot$$
$$\mathbb{P}[\text{successful msg transmission} \mid P(t) \leq 1/f^2]$$
$$\leq 1/f^2.$$

Moreover, it certainly holds for any set S of time steps prior to some time step t that

$$\mathbb{P}[Y_t = 1 \mid \prod_{s \in S} Y_s = 1] \leq 1/f^2.$$

Therefore, we have

$$\mathbb{P}[\prod_{s \in S} Y_s = 1]$$
$$= \mathbb{P}[Y_1 = 1] \cdot \mathbb{P}[Y_2 = 1 | Y_1 = 1] \cdot \mathbb{P}[Y_3 = 1 | \prod_{s=1,2} Y_s = 1] \cdots$$
$$\cdot \mathbb{P}[Y_{|S|} = 1 | \prod_{s=1,2,\ldots,|S|-1} Y_s = 1]$$
$$\leq (1/f^2)^{|S|}$$

and

$$\mathbb{E}[\prod_{s \in S} Y_s = 1] = \mathbb{P}[\prod_{s \in S} Y_s = 1] \leq (1/f^2)^{|S|}.$$

Thus, the Chernoff bounds and our choice of f imply that w.h.p. either $\sum_{t \in I'} Y_t < \varepsilon^2 f/8$ and $P(t) \leq 1/f^2$ throughout I', or there must be a time step t in I' with $P(t) > 1/f^2$, which would finish the proof. Therefore, unless $P(t) > 1/f^2$ at some point in I', $k_1 < \varepsilon^2 f/8$ w.h.p.

Next we prove a lower bound on k_0 that holds w.h.p. For any time step t with $P(t) \leq 1/f^2$ it holds that

$$\mathbb{P}[\text{channel is idle}] \geq e^{-P(t)/(1-\hat{p})} \geq 1 - \frac{P(t)}{1 - \hat{p}} \geq 1 - 1/f$$

Hence, $\mathbb{E}[k_0] \geq g \cdot (1 - 1/f) \geq \varepsilon f(1 - 1/f)$. Using similar arguments as for k_1, it follows that $k_0 > (7/8)\varepsilon f$ w.h.p. unless $P(t) > 1/f^2$ at some point in I'. When combining the bounds for $\bar{q}$ and k_0, we obtain

$$(k_0 - 1)\bar{q}/2 \geq \frac{(k_0 - 1)^2}{2f} \geq (7/8)^2 \varepsilon^2 f/2$$
$$> \varepsilon^2 f/8 + 4\sqrt{f} > k_1 + 4\sqrt{f}$$

w.h.p., if f is large enough, which violates Inequality (3) and therefore completes the proof of Claim 3.7. $\square$

Similarly, we can also prove that once the cumulative probability exceeds a certain threshold, it cannot become too small again.

CLAIM 3.9. *Suppose that for the first time step t_0 in I', $P(t_0) \geq 1/f^2$. Then there is no time step t in I' with $P(t) < \frac{1}{f^2(1+\gamma)^{\sqrt{2f}}}$, w.h.p.*

PROOF. Consider some fixed subinterval $I'' = [t_1, t_2]$ in I' with the property that $P(t_1) \geq 1/f^2$ and $P(t) \leq 1/f^2$ for all other t in I'' (i.e., we will use conditional probabilities based on $P(t) \leq 1/f^2$ like in the bound for k_1 in the proof of Claim 3.7). Suppose that there are g non-jammed time steps in I''. If $g \leq \beta \log N$ for a (sufficiently large) constant β, then it follows for the probability $P(t_2)$ at the end of I'' that

$$P(t_2) \geq \frac{1}{f^2} \cdot (1 + \gamma)^{-((3/2)\beta \log N + \sqrt{f})} \geq \frac{1}{f^2(1+\gamma)^{\sqrt{2f}}}$$

given that f is large enough (i.e., $\varepsilon = \Omega(1/\log^3 N)$). This is because in the worst case for the decrease of $P(t)$ all non-jammed time steps are successful. In this case, $P(t)$ is decreased at most

$\beta \log N$ times due to these steps. Moreover, from Claim 3.6 it follows that $P(t)$ can be decreased another at most $\beta \log N/2 + \sqrt{f}$ times due to $c_v > T_v$.

So suppose that $g > \beta \log N$. Let X be the number of time steps in I'' in which $P(t)$ increases and k_1 be the maximum number of time steps in I'' (over all networks) with a successful message transmission. Furthermore, let k_2 be the maximum number of times a node v increases T_v in I''. If $P(t_2) < \frac{1}{f^2(1+\gamma)\sqrt{2f}}$ then it must hold that the total increase in $P(t)$ (which is equal to $(1+\gamma)^X$) is at most the total decrease in $P(t)$ (which is at most $(1+\gamma)^{k_1+k_2}$), or in other words,

$$X \leq k_1 + k_2.$$

From the previous claim we know that this is not true w.h.p. given that $P(t) \leq 1/f^2$ for all $t > t_1$ in I'' and the constant β is sufficiently large to achieve polynomially small probability bounds. Since there are at most f^2 possible values for t_1 and t_2, there is no time step t_2 in I' with $P(t_2) < \frac{1}{f^2(1+\gamma)\sqrt{2f}}$ w.h.p., which completes the proof. □

Combining Claims 3.7 and 3.9 completes the proof of Lemma 3.5. □

Next we show an upper bound for $P(t)$. In the following, $K' = O(K)$ is a sufficiently large constant $\geq K$.

LEMMA 3.10. *For any subframe* $I' = [t_0, t_1)$ *with* $T_v \leq (3/4)\sqrt{F}$ *for all nodes* v *at the beginning of* I', $P(t_1) \leq 12 \ln K'$ *w.m.p.*

PROOF. First, we will show that if $P(t) \geq 4 \ln K'$ throughout I', then for each N_i, there must be a step t' with $P_i(t') \leq (2 \ln K')/K'$ w.h.p., and once such a step is reached, we show that $P_i(t'') < (4 \ln K')/K'$ w.m.p. for all time steps t'' following t'. Hence, there must be a time step t'' in I' with $P_i(t'') < (4 \ln K')/K'$ for all i, w.m.p., contradicting the assumption that $P(t) \geq 4 \ln K'$ throughout I'. Once we have that, we will show that at the end of I', $P(t_1) \leq 12 \ln K'$ w.m.p.

Consider some fixed network i. Let k_0 be the number of idle steps in I' and k_1 be the number of successful time steps for network i. Moreover, let X be the total number of times $P_i(t)$ is increased by $(1+\gamma)$ due to an idle channel in I'. For N_i to avoid a time step t' in I' with $P_i(t') \leq (2 \ln K')/K'$, we must have that the total increase of $P_i(t)$ (which is equal to $(1+\gamma)^X$) is at least the total decrease of $P_i(t)$ once we have reached a point t with $P_i(t) = (2 \ln K')/K'$, which is the case after at most $\log_{1+\gamma}(n_i \cdot \hat{p})$ reductions of $P_i(t)$. Hence, we must have

$$X \geq k_1' - \log_{1+\gamma}(n_i \cdot \hat{p}) \qquad (4)$$

where k_1' is the total decrease (in the exponent) of $P_i(t)$ due to successful transmissions to avoid a time step t' in I' with $P_i(t') \leq (2 \ln K')/K'$. Notice that k_1' is not equal to k_1 because if, for example, a node successfully transmits twice in a row, $P_i(t)$ does not get decreased the second time.

In order to contradict this bound, we first need to have a closer look at what happens when there is a successful transmission in N_i.

CLAIM 3.11. *If the node* v *successfully transmitting a message in* N_i *at time* t *is different from the node that previously successfully transmitted a message in* N_i, *then* $P_i(t+1) \in [\frac{1}{1+\gamma} P_i(t), \frac{1}{\sqrt{1+\gamma}} P_i(t)]$ *for any* $n_i \geq 2$.

PROOF. The lower bound is obvious. Moreover, it follows from the protocol that

$$
\begin{aligned}
P_i(t+1) &= p_{v,t} + \sum_{w \in V_i \setminus \{v\}} \frac{1}{1+\gamma} \cdot p_{v,t} \\
&= \frac{1}{1+\gamma} \cdot P_i(t) + \frac{\gamma}{1+\gamma} \cdot p_{v,t} \\
&\leq \frac{1}{1+\gamma} \cdot P_i(t) + \frac{\gamma}{1+\gamma} \cdot \frac{P_i(t)}{n_i} \\
&= \frac{1}{1+\gamma} \left(1 + \frac{\gamma}{n_i}\right) P_i(t) \\
&\leq \frac{1}{1+\gamma} (1+\gamma)^{1/n_i} P_i(t) \leq \frac{1}{\sqrt{1+\gamma}} P_i(t)
\end{aligned}
$$

given that $n_i \geq 2$. □

If the same node v successfully transmits again at time t, then $P_i(t+1) = P_i(t)$, which only happens with probability at most $(1+\gamma)/n_i$ because in this case the transmitting node has an access probability that is by a $(1+\gamma)$ factor larger than the other access probabilities in N_i. Hence, on expectation, at least $1/3$ of the time steps with successful transmission, $P_i(t)$ is reduced by at least $(1+\gamma)^{1/2}$, which implies that $\mathbb{E}[k_1'] \geq k_1/6$.

Based on this insight, the next claim shows that under certain conditions, Inequality (4) is not true w.h.p. Let g_i be the number of *useful* time steps for N_i, which are time steps that are either idle or successful for N_i in I'.

CLAIM 3.12. *If all time steps* $t \in I'$ *satisfy* $P(t) \geq 4 \ln K'$ *and* $g_i \geq \delta \log_{1+\gamma} N$ *for a sufficiently large constant* δ, *then* $X + \log_{1+\gamma} n_i < k_1'$ *w.h.p.*

PROOF. It is easy to see that for any useful time step t,

$$\mathbb{P}[t \text{ successful for } N_i] \geq P_i(t) \cdot \mathbb{P}[t \text{ idle}] \qquad (5)$$

and therefore $\mathbb{E}[k_1] \geq \frac{2 \ln K'}{K'} \mathbb{E}[k_0]$ unless there is a time step t with $P_i(t) < (2 \ln K')/K'$. For a given number of useful time steps g_i, since $k_0 + k_1 = g_i$ and therefore also $\mathbb{E}[k_0] + \mathbb{E}[k_1] = g_i$, $\mathbb{E}[k_1] \geq \frac{2 \ln K'}{K'}(g_i - \mathbb{E}[k_1])$, which implies that $\mathbb{E}[k_1] \geq \frac{\ln K'}{K'} \cdot g_i$ if $K' = O(K)$ is a sufficiently large constant. Since $\mathbb{E}[k_1'] \geq k_1/6$, $g_i = \Omega(\log_{1+\gamma} N)$, and for each useful time step there is an independent probability whether this time step is idle or successful, it follows from the Chernoff bounds that $k_1' \geq \frac{\ln K'}{8K'} g_i$ w.h.p.

Next we bound X. Let the binary random variable X_j denote the increase of $P_i(t)$ by $(1+\gamma)^{X_j}$ in the j-th idle time step. Then $X = \sum_{j=1}^{k_0} X_j$. Moreover, let L_j be the number of time steps between the $(j-1)$-th and j-th idle time steps. It holds that

$$\mathbb{P}[t \text{ idle}] \leq e^{-P(t)} \leq 1/(K')^4$$

for every $t \in I'$ given that $P(t) \geq 4 \ln K'$. Hence,

$$
\begin{aligned}
\mathbb{E}[X_j] &= \sum_{\ell \geq 1} \mathbb{P}[L_j = \ell] \cdot 1/\ell \leq \sum_{\ell \geq 1} \frac{1}{(K')^4}\left(1 - \frac{1}{(K')^4}\right)^{\ell-1} \cdot \frac{1}{\ell} \\
&\leq \frac{1}{(K')^4 - 1} \sum_{\ell \geq 1} e^{-\ell/(K')^4}/\ell \leq \frac{1}{(K')^4 - 1} \cdot 2\ln(K')^4 \\
&= \frac{4 \ln K'}{(K')^4 - 1}
\end{aligned}
$$

and therefore, $\mathbb{E}[X] \leq \frac{4 \ln K'}{(K')^4 - 1} \cdot k_0 \leq \frac{4 \ln K'}{(K')^4 - 1} \cdot g_i$. Since the upper bound on $\mathbb{E}[X_j]$ holds independently for each j, it follows from the Chernoff bounds that $X \leq \frac{6 \ln K'}{(K')^4} \cdot g_i$ w.h.p.

Since $g_i = \Omega(\log_{1+\gamma} N)$, $X + \log_{1+\gamma} n_i < k_1'$ w.h.p. if $K' = O(K)$ is sufficiently large, which completes the proof of the claim. □

Otherwise, suppose that $g_i < \delta \log_{1+\gamma} N$. For every node v it follows from the COMAC protocol and the choice of f and F that if initially $T_v \leq (3/4)\sqrt{F}$, then T_v can be at most $\sqrt{F}$ during I'. Let us cut I' into m intervals of size $2\sqrt{F}$ each. It is easy to check that if β in the definition of f is sufficiently large compared to δ, then $m \geq 3\delta \log_{1+\gamma} N$. Since there are less than $\delta \log_{1+\gamma} N$ useful steps in N_i in I', at least $2\delta \log_{1+\gamma} N$ of these intervals do not contain any useful step, which implies that p_v is reduced by $(1+\gamma)$ by each $v \in V_i$ in each of these intervals.

Hence, altogether, every p_v gets reduced by a factor of at least $(1+\gamma)^{-2\delta \log_{1+\gamma} N}$ during I' in N_i. The useful time steps can only raise that by at most $(1+\gamma)^{\delta \log_{1+\gamma} N}$, so altogether we must have $P_i(t') \leq (2\ln K')/K'$ at some time point t' in I', w.h.p.

Next we prove the following claim, which implies that for all $t'' > t'$ in I', $P_i(t'') < (4\ln K')/K'$ w.m.p.

CLAIM 3.13. *If all time steps $t \in I'$ satisfy $P(t) \geq 4\ln K'$ and initially $P_i(t) \leq (2\ln K')/K'$, then for all steps $t \in I'$, $P_i(t) \leq (4\ln K')/K'$ w.m.p.*

PROOF. Consider some fixed subinterval $I'' = [t_1, t_2]$ in I' with the property that $P_i(t_1) \leq (2\ln K')/K'$ and $P_i(t) \geq (2\ln K')/K'$ for all other t in I''. Suppose that there are g_i useful time steps in I''. If $g_i \leq \ln_{1+\gamma} 2$, then it follows for the probability $P_i(t_2)$ at the end of I'' that $P_i(t_2) \leq \frac{2\ln K'}{K'} \cdot (1+\gamma)^{\ln_{1+\gamma} 2} \leq \frac{4\ln K'}{K'}$. Otherwise, suppose that $g_i > \ln_{1+\gamma} 2$, which is at least $1/(2\gamma) = \Omega(\ln f)$. Let X be the number of time steps in I'' in which $P_i(t)$ increases and k_1 be the number of time steps in I'' with a successful transmission in N_i. Furthermore, let k_2 be the maximum number of times a node $v \in V_i$ increases T_v in I''. If $P(t_2) > (4\ln K')/K'$ then it must hold that the total increase in $P_i(t)$ (which is equal to $(1+\gamma)^X$) is at least the total decrease in $P(t)$ (which is at most $(1+\gamma)^{k_1+k_2}$) plus $\ln_{1+\gamma} 2$, or formally,

$$X \geq k_1' + \ln_{1+\gamma} 2 \qquad (6)$$

where k_1' is the total decrease (in the exponent) of $P_i(t)$ due to successful transmissions. We know that $\mathbb{E}[k_1'] \geq k_1/6$. Also, from the proof of the previous claim it follows that $\mathbb{E}[k_1] \geq \frac{\ln K'}{K'} g_i$ if $K' = O(K)$ is a sufficiently large constant, unless there is a time step t in I' with $P_i(t) < (2\ln K')/K'$. Since $g_i = \Omega(\ln f)$, it follows from the Chernoff bounds that $k_1' \geq \frac{\ln K'}{8K'} g_i$ w.m.p. On the other hand, it follows from the proof of the previous claim that $X \leq \frac{6\ln K'}{(K')^4} \cdot g_i$ w.m.p. Hence, inequality (6) is violated w.m.p., which implies that $P_i(t_2) \leq \frac{4\ln K'}{K'}$ w.m.p. Since there are at most f^2 different values of t_1 and t_2, there is no time step t_2 in I' with $P_i(t_2) > \frac{4\ln K'}{K'}$ w.m.p., which completes the proof. □

Combining the insights above, it follows that there must be a time step t in I' with $P(t) < 4\ln K'$ w.m.p. To finish the proof, we need the following claim.

CLAIM 3.14. *If for the first time step t_0 in I', $P(t_0) \leq 4\ln K'$, then $P(t) \leq 12\ln K'$ for all time steps t in I' w.m.p.*

PROOF. Consider some subinterval $I'' = [t_1, t_2]$ in I' with the property that $P(t_1) \leq 4\ln K'$ and $P(t) \geq 4\ln K'$ for all $t > t_1$ in I''. Suppose that there are g useful time steps in I'', where a time step is useful if there was either a successful transmission in some network or the channel is idle. If

$g \leq \log_{1+\gamma} 2$, then certainly $P(t) \leq 12\ln K'$ for all t in I'. So suppose that $g > \log_{1+\gamma} 2$. Consider some fixed network N_i. Let X be the number of time steps in I'' in which $P_i(t)$ increases and k_1 be the number of time steps in I'' with a successful message transmission in N_i. Furthermore, let k_2 be the maximum number of times a node $v \in V_i$ increases T_v in I''. If $P(t_2) > 12\ln K'$ then there must be a network N_i with $P_i(t_2) > \max\{(8\ln K')/K', 2P_i(t_1)\}$. To see this, let I_1 be the set of all i with $P_i(t_1) < (4\ln K')/K'$ and I_2 be the set of all other i. As long as for all i, $P_i(t_2) \leq \max\{(8\ln K')/K', 2P_i(t_1)\}$, it must hold that $P(t_2) \leq \sum_{i\in I_1} (8\ln K')/K' + \sum_{i\in I_2} 2P_i(t_1) \leq (8\ln K')/K' \cdot K + 2P(t_1) \leq 12\ln K'$ if $K' = O(K)$ is sufficiently large.

First, consider the case that for some i with $P_i(t_1) \geq (4\ln K')/K'$, $P_i(t_2) > 2P_i(t_1)$. Then the total increase of $P_i(t)$ in I'' (which is equal to $(1+\gamma)^X$ is at least the total decrease in $P_i(t)$ plus $\log_{1+\gamma} 2$. Hence,

$$X \geq k_1' + \log_{1+\gamma} 2 \qquad (7)$$

where k_1' is the total decrease (in the exponent) of $P(t)$ due to successful transmissions in N_i. From Inequality (5) we know that $\mathbb{E}[k_1] \geq \frac{4\ln K'}{K'} \cdot \mathbb{E}[k_0]$ and therefore $\mathbb{E}[k_1] \geq \frac{2\ln K'}{K'} \cdot g$ if $K' = O(K)$ is large enough. Since $\mathbb{E}[k_1'] \geq k_1/6$ and $g = \Omega(\ln f)$ it follows from the Chernoff bounds that $k_1' \geq \frac{\ln K'}{4K'} \cdot g$ w.m.p. On the other hand, we also know that $X \leq \frac{6\ln K'}{(K')^4} \cdot g$ w.m.p., which implies that Inequality (7) is violated w.m.p. Hence, $P_i(t_2) \leq 2P_i(t_1)$ w.m.p.

For the case that $P_i(t_1) < (4\ln K')/K'$ let t_1' be the first step in I'' with $P_i(t_1') \geq (4\ln K')/K'$. If t_1' does not exist, we are done, and otherwise we prove in the same way as above that w.m.p. $P_i(t_2) \leq (12\ln K')/K'$.

Since there are at most f^2 ways of choosing t_1 and t_2, there is no time step t in I' with $P(t) \leq 12\ln K'$ w.m.p., which completes the proof. □

All claims combined imply Lemma 3.10. □

A proof similar to Lemma 3.10 also implies the following result.

COROLLARY 3.15. *For any subframe I' that satisfies $P(t) \leq 12\ln K'$ at the beginning of I', all time steps t of I' satisfy $P(t) \leq 36\ln K'$ w.m.p.*

We also need to show that for a constant fraction of the non-jammed time steps in a subframe where initially $P(t) \leq 12\ln K'$, $P(t)$ is also lower bounded by a constant for a sufficiently large fraction of time steps t.

LEMMA 3.16. *For any subframe I' in which initially $P(t_0) \geq 1/(f^2(1+\gamma)^{2\sqrt{J}})$, at least $\varepsilon/8$ of the non-jammed steps t satisfy $P(t) \geq \varepsilon\hat{p}/4$, w.h.p.*

PROOF. Let G be the set of all non-jammed time steps in I' and S be the set of all steps t in G with $P(t) < \varepsilon\hat{p}/4$. Let $g = |G|$ and $s = |S|$. If $s \leq (1-\varepsilon/8)g$, we are done. Hence, consider the case that $s \geq (1-\varepsilon/8)g$.

Suppose that $P(t)$ must be increased ℓ many times to get from its initial value up to a value of $\varepsilon\hat{p}/4$. (If $P(t_0) \geq \varepsilon\hat{p}/4$ then $\ell = 0$.) Let k_0 be the number of time steps in S with an idle channel and k_1 be the number of time steps in S with a successful message transmission in any of the co-existing networks. Let the binary random variable X_i be 1 if and only if the nodes increase their access probabilities in the i-th idle time step in S, and let

$X = \sum_{i=1}^{\ell} X_i$. Furthermore, let k_2 be the maximum number of times a node v decreases p_v due to $c_v > T_v$ in I'. For S to be feasible (i.e., probabilities can be assigned to each $t \in S$ so that $P(t) < \varepsilon \hat{p}/4$), we must have

$$X \leq \ell + k_1 + k_2 \tag{8}$$

For the special case that $\ell = k_2 = 0$ this follows from the fact that whenever there is a successful message transmission, $P(t)$ is reduced by $(1 + \gamma)^{-1}$, at most. On the other hand, whenever the nodes decide to increase $P(t)$ for some $t \in S$, $P(t)$ can indeed increase because of $P(t) < \varepsilon \hat{p}/4$ and therefore $p_v < \hat{p}$ for all v. Thus, if $X > k_1$, then one of the steps in S would have to have a probability of at least $\varepsilon \hat{p}/4$, violating the definition of S. ℓ comes into the formula due to the startup cost of getting to a value of $\varepsilon \hat{p}/4$, and k_2 comes into the formula since the reductions of the $p_v(t)$ values due to $c_v > T_v$ allow up to k_2 additional decreases of $P(t)$ for S to stay feasible.

Certainly, $\ell \leq 2\log_{1+\gamma} f + 2\sqrt{f}$. Moreover, for k_1 it holds that $\mathbb{E}[k_1] \leq \varepsilon \hat{p}/4 \cdot s$ and therefore, $k_1 \leq \varepsilon \hat{p}/2 \cdot s$ w.h.p. For k_2 it holds that $k_2 \leq (X + \varepsilon g/8)/2 + \sqrt{f}$. Hence, Inequality (8) implies that

$$
\begin{aligned}
X &\leq 2\log_{1+\gamma} f + 2\sqrt{f} + \varepsilon \hat{p} s/2 + (X + \varepsilon g/8)/2 + \sqrt{f} \\
\Rightarrow X &\leq (\hat{p} + 1/16)\varepsilon g + 8\sqrt{f}
\end{aligned}
\tag{9}
$$

if f is sufficiently large. It remains to compute a lower bound for X.

Let X' be the total number of times $P(t)$ is increased over all time steps in G, k'_0 be the number of idle time steps in G, and $\bar{q}$ be the average increase of the q_v-values in I'. From the proof of Claim 3.7 we know that $\bar{q} \geq (k'_0 - 1)/f$ and that $X' \geq \lfloor (k'_0 - 1)\bar{q} \rfloor$. Moreover, $X \geq X' - \varepsilon g/8$. Hence, $X \geq \lfloor (k_0 - 1)^2/f \rfloor - \varepsilon g/8$. We know that $\mathbb{E}[k_0] \geq (1 - \varepsilon \hat{p}/4)s$ and therefore, $k_0 \geq 3g/4$ w.h.p. Hence, $X \geq g^2/(4f) - \varepsilon g/8 \geq \varepsilon g/8$ w.h.p. Since this violates Inequality (9), the lemma follows. $\square$

In the following, let us call a subframe I' *good* if its initial step t_0 satisfies $P(t_0) \leq 12 \ln K'$. Combining the results above, we get:

LEMMA 3.17. *For any good subframe I', there are at least $\varepsilon^2 f/8$ non-jammed time steps t in I' with $P(t) \in [\varepsilon \hat{p}/4, 36 \ln K']$ w.m.p.*

Consider now the first eighth of frame I, called J. The following lemma follows directly from Lemma 2.14 in [3].

LEMMA 3.18. *If at the beginning of J, $p_v \geq 1/(f^2(1+\gamma)^{2\sqrt{f}})$ and $T_v \leq \sqrt{F}/2$ for all nodes v, then we also have $p_v \geq 1/(f^2(1+\gamma)^{2\sqrt{f}})$ at the end of J for every v and the number of non-jammed time steps t in I' with $P(t) \in [\varepsilon \hat{p}/4, 36 \ln K']$ is at least $\varepsilon^2 f/16$ w.h.p.*

We finally need the following lemma, which follows from Lemma 2.15 in [3].

LEMMA 3.19. *If at the beginning of J, $T_v \leq \sqrt{F}/2$ for all v, then it holds that also $T_v \leq \sqrt{F}/2$ at the end of J w.h.p.*

Inductively using Lemmas 3.18 and 3.19 on the eighths of frame I implies that COMAC satisfies the property of Lemmas 3.18 for the entire I and at the end of I, $p_v \geq 1/(f^2(1+\gamma)^{2\sqrt{f}})$ and $T_v \leq \sqrt{F}/2$ for all v w.h.p. Since our results hold with high probability, we can also extend them to any polynomial number of frames.

3.3 Throughput

Summarizing the results above, we obtain the following result for the throughput.

THEOREM 3.20. *For any polynomial sequence of time steps of length at least F, COMAC achieves a competitive throughput of $\Omega(\varepsilon^2 \min\{\varepsilon, 1/poly(K)\})$ for any constants ε and K.*

3.4 Fairness

Finally, we show that COMAC also ensures a limited degree of fairness. Note that by Lemma 3.4, we can directly bound the probabilities of having a successful transmission within networks N_i and N_j by their respective cumulative probabilities, which we bound on the following theorem.

THEOREM 3.21. *If all nodes v initially start with access probability $\hat{p}$, then it takes at most F time steps until a time step is reached in which the difference between minimum and maximum cumulative probability of a network is at most $O(K^2)$.*

PROOF. Consider the potential function summing up the differences of the networks' cumulative probabilities compared to the minimum probability $\Phi = \sum_i |x_i - x_{\min}|$ where $x_i = \log_{1+\gamma} P_i$ and $x_{\min} = \min_i x_i$. We focus on the events with a successful transmission, since only successful transmissions can change the difference among individual network probabilities. Assume that a successful transmission occured in N_i, if $x_i > x_{\min}$, then the change in Φ, denoted by $\Delta\Phi$, satisfies $\Delta\Phi = -1$. If $x_i = x_{\min}$, then $\Delta\Phi \leq K$. Hence, $\mathbb{E}[\Delta\Phi] \leq -\mathbb{P}[x_i > x_{\min}$ successful$] + K\mathbb{P}[x_i = x_{\min}$ successful$]$. Suppose that $x_{\max} \geq x_{\min} + \log_{1+\gamma}(2K^2)$. Then, $\mathbb{P}[x_i > x_{\min}$ successful$] \geq 2K \cdot \mathbb{P}[x_i = x_{\min}$ successful$]$ as there can be up to $K - 1$ many N_i with $x_i = x_{\min}$. Certainly, $\mathbb{P}[x_i > x_{\min}$ successful$] + \mathbb{P}[x_i = x_{\min}$ successful$] = 1$ given that there is a successful transmission. Hence in this case, $\mathbb{P}[x_i > x_{\min}$ successful$] \geq \frac{2K}{2K+1}$, which implies that $\mathbb{E}[\Delta\Phi] \leq -\frac{2K}{2K+1} + \frac{K}{2K+1} = -\frac{K}{2K+1} \leq -1/3$, whenever there is a successful transmission.

Now, let us define the random variable X_t as follows for the t-th successful transmission: $X_t = 1$ if either $x_{\max} < x_{\min} + \log_{1+\gamma}(2K^2)$ (i.e., we reached our goal) or the successful transmission is from a network N_i with $x_i > x_{\min}$; and $X_t = -K$ otherwise.

Suppose that there are s successful transmissions across all networks. Let $X = \sum_{t=1}^{s} X_t$. Then it holds that $\mathbb{E}[X] \geq s/3$. In order to apply Chernoff bounds, let us define $Y_t = (X_t + K)/(K + 1)$ and $Y = \sum_{t=1}^{s} Y_t$. Then Y_t is a binary random variable with $\mathbb{E}[Y_t] \geq (K + 1/3)/(K + 1)$ and therefore $\mathbb{E}[Y] \geq s(K + 1/3)/(K + 1)$. Since the upper bound on $\mathbb{E}[Y_t]$ holds irrespective of previous Y_j's, it follows from the Chernoff bounds that $\mathbb{P}[Y \leq (1 - \delta)s(K + 1/3)/(K + 1)] \leq e^{-\delta^2 s/3}$, for any $0 < \delta < 1$. Since $Y = (X + s \cdot K)/(K + 1)$, we get $\mathbb{P}[X \leq (1 - \delta)s/3 - \delta sK] \leq e^{-\delta^2 s/3}$. If we choose $\delta = 1/(6(K+1/3))$ then $\mathbb{P}[Y \leq (1-\delta)s(K+1/3)/(K+1)] = \mathbb{P}[X \leq s/6]$ and hence, $\mathbb{P}[X \leq s/6] \leq e^{-\delta^2 s/3}$. Now, from Theorem 3.20 we know that $s = \Omega(\varepsilon^2 \min\{\varepsilon, 1/poly(K)\}F)$ w.h.p., so $s = \omega(K \log N)$. This implies that when running the protocol for F time steps, $X > K \log N$ w.h.p. Thus, if the initial value of the potential Φ_0 is at most $K \log N$, we must have reached a point where $x_{\max} < x_{\min} + \log_{1+\gamma}(2K^2)$ as otherwise we would end up with a negative potential. It remains to bound Φ_0.

Given that all nodes start with the same access probability $\hat{p}$, the maximum initial difference between P_i and P_j for any i and j is N and therefore, $x_{\max} < x_{\min} + \log_{1+\gamma} N$. Hence, $\Phi_0 \leq K \log_{1+\gamma} N$, which implies the theorem. $\square$

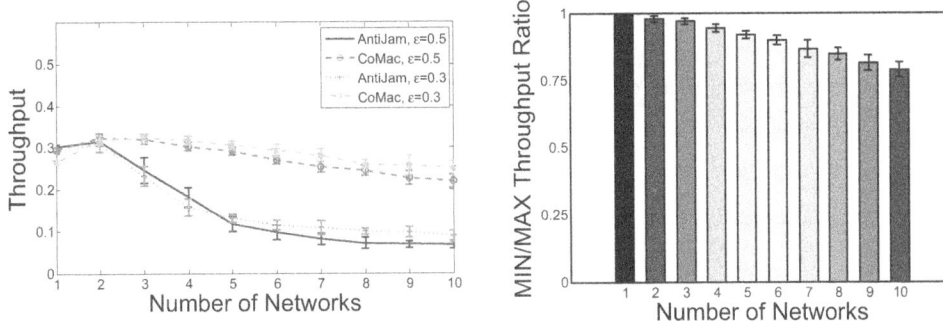

Figure 1: *Left:* Throughput of COMAC and ANTIJAM [24] as a function of the number of co-existing networks and for two different adversaries ($\varepsilon = \{0.5, 0.3\}$). The total number of nodes for each $K = 1, \ldots, 10$ is 500, and each co-existing network has the same size (up to an additive node due to rounding). The protocol is executed for 7000 rounds, and the result is averaged over 10 runs. The adversary is modeled in a simplified manner and simply jams each round with independent probability $1 - \varepsilon$. *Right:* Fairness as the min/max competitive throughput ratio for $\varepsilon = 0.3$.

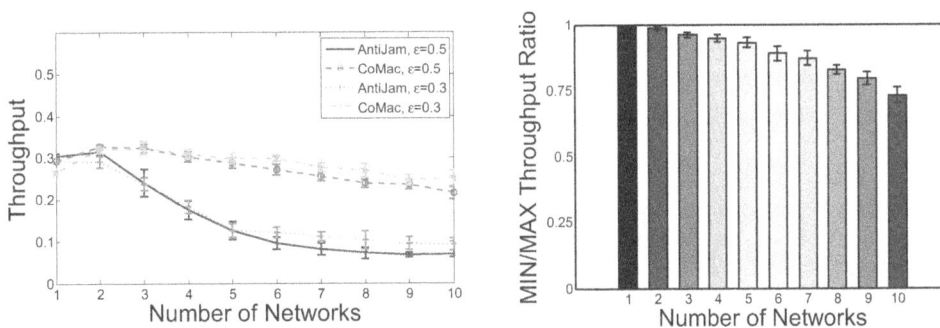

Figure 2: *Left:* Throughput and fairness of COMAC and ANTIJAM [24] for a setting like in Figure 1 but where the size of the co-existing networks is heterogenous, i.e., the i-th largest network is roughly 1.5 times the size of $(i + 1)$-largest network. *Right:* Fairness as the min/max competitive throughput ratio for $\varepsilon = 0.3$.

Fact 3.1 ensures that the access probabilities of the nodes within a network differs by at most a $(1 + \gamma)$ factor, ensuring fairness within each network N_i.

4. SIMULATION

Although the focus of this paper is on the formal, asymptotic and worst-case performance guarantees achieved by COMAC, we also briefly report on some of our quantitative insights from a simulation study. We are interested in: (i) how the competitive throughput of all the networks changes when the number of networks varies;[2] (ii) the fairness of COMAC, i.e., whether the successful transmissions are evenly distributed among all the networks. Also, we compare COMAC to the state-of-the-art jamming resistant MAC protocol ANTIJAM in [24], and find that COMAC indeed better suits co-existing networks.

There is a total of 500 nodes among all the co-existing networks, and the number of networks K ranges from 1 to 10. All the results are averaged over 10 runs, and the confidence intervals are provided as well. More specifically, we conduct competitive throughput and fairness experiments in two different scenarios.

[2]The competitive throughput of all the networks is defined as the fraction of non-jammed time steps that are used for successful transmissions among all K networks.

Scenario 1: The size of individual networks are the same, namely $|V_i| \in \{\lfloor 500/K \rfloor, \lceil 500/K \rceil\}$. In Figure 1 (*left*) we study the *competitive throughput*, i.e., the fraction of non-jammed time steps that are used for successful transmissions among all K networks. We observe that for a single network ($K = 1$) the competitive throughput of COMAC is relatively worse compared to ANTIJAM as p_v is raised more strictly when the channel is idle. However, COMAC is always better than ANTIJAM when there is more than one network ($K > 1$) as the additional interference introduced by co-existing networks is bounded. For example, when $K = 10$, the competitive throughput of COMAC is still above 20% even when adversary can jam 70% of all time steps, while the competitive throughput of ANTIJAM is below 10%. Note that there is a trend towards smaller competitiveness for larger K, as expected from our formal worst-case analysis. Figure 1 (*right*) studies the fairness of COMAC in terms of min/max competitive throughput ratio, where the minimum and maximum competitive throughput are selected from the K co-existing networks. The closer this ratio is to 1, the fairer the protocol. Obviously COMAC is fair in a sense that even when $K = 10$, the min/max competitive throughput ratio is above 0.78.

Scenario 2: The size of i-th largest network is roughly 1.5 times the size of $(i+1)$-th largest network. Figure 2 shows that even when the size of individual networks vary a lot, CoMAC still achieves a better competitive throughput (above 20% when $K = 10$) compared to AntiJam (below 10% when $K = 10$), and more importantly, CoMAC is still fair in a sense that the min/max competitive throughput ratio when $K = 10$ is still above 0.73.

5. CONCLUSION

Motivated by our observation that MAC algorithms optimized for a single network often yield a poor performance in scenarios with multiple co-existing networks due to too high sending probabilities, this paper presented the first protocol for provably robust, efficient and fair medium allocation among a set of co-existing networks (e.g., of a multi-nation conference or of an emergency network). Interestingly, with simple adaptions, our protocol could even be used in scenarios where the throughput is required to be distributed according to some specific proportions (i.e., not necessarily fairly) among the co-existing networks. For instance, a spectrum owner may require the co-existing networks to use only a share of the medium that corresponds to the negotiated or auctioned share. We believe that our work raises a series of interesting questions for future research. For example, we have assumed a rather naive interference model and it would be interesting to generalize our results for the SINR physical interference model.

Acknowledgments

We would like to thank Çiğdem Şengül and Ruben Merz from Telekom Innovation Laboratories for interesting discussions. This work was supported in part by NSF awards CCF-0830791 and CCF-0830704, and by DFG projects SCHE 1592/2-1 and SFB 901.

6. REFERENCES

[1] L. Anantharamu, B. S. Chlebus, D. R. Kowalski, and M. A. Rokicki. Medium access control for adversarial channels with jamming. In *Proc. 18th International Conference on Structural Information and Communication Complexity (SIROCCO)*, pages 89–100, 2011.

[2] H. Asai, K. Fukuda, and H. Esaki. Towards characterization of wireless traffic in coexisting 802.11a/g and 802.11n network. In *Proc. ACM CoNEXT Student Workshop*, 2010.

[3] B. Awerbuch, A. Richa, and C. Scheideler. A jamming-resistant mac protocol for single-hop wireless networks. In *Proc. PODC*, 2008.

[4] E. Bayraktaroglu, C. King, X. Liu, G. Noubir, R. Rajaraman, and B. Thapa. On the performance of IEEE 802.11 under jamming. In *Proc. INFOCOM*, 2008.

[5] M. A. Bender, M. Farach-Colton, S. He, B. C. Kuszmaul, and C. E. Leiserson. Adversarial contention resolution for simple channels. In *Proc. SPAA*, pages 325–332, 2005.

[6] B. S. Chlebus, D. R. Kowalski, and M. A. Rokicki. Adversarial queuing on the multiple-access channel. In *Proc. PODC*, pages 92–101, 2006.

[7] S. Dolev, S. Gilbert, R. Guerraoui, D. R. Kowalski, C. Newport, F. Kuhn, and N. Lynch. Reliable distributed computing on unreliable radio channels. In *Proc. 2009 MobiHoc S3 Workshop*, 2009.

[8] S. Dolev, S. Gilbert, R. Guerraoui, and C. Newport. Gossiping in a Multi-Channel Radio Network (An Oblivious Approach to Coping With Malicious Interference). In *Proc. 21st International Symposium on Distributed Computing (DISC)*, pages 208–222, 2007.

[9] S. Dolev, S. Gilbert, R. Guerraoui, and C. Newport. Secure communication over radio channels. In *Proc. 27th ACM Symposium on Principles of Distributed Computing (PODC)*, pages 105–114, 2008.

[10] S. Gilbert, R. Guerraoui, D. R. Kowalski, and C. C. Newport. Interference-resilient information exchange. In *Proc. 28th IEEE International Conference on Computer Communications (INFOCOM)*, pages 2249–2257, 2009.

[11] S. Gilbert, R. Guerraoui, and C. Newport. Of malicious motes and suspicious sensors: On the efficiency of malicious interference in wireless networks. In *Proc. OPODIS*, 2006.

[12] L. A. Goldberg, P. D. Mackenzie, M. Paterson, and A. Srinivasan. Contention resolution with constant expected delay. *Journal of the ACM*, 47(6):1048–1096, 2000.

[13] J. Hastad, T. Leighton, and B. Rogoff. Analysis of backoff protocols for mulitiple access channels. *SIAM Journal on Computing*, 25(4):740–774, 1996.

[14] M. Heusse, F. Rousseau, R. Guillier, and A. Duda. Idle sense: an optimal access method for high throughput and fairness in rate diverse wireless LANs. *SIGCOMM Comput. Commun. Rev.*, 35(4):121–132, 2005.

[15] J. Ji and W. Chen. Transmission capacity of two co-existing wireless ad hoc networks with multiple antennas. In *Proc. IEEE International Conference on Communications (ICC)*, pages 1–6, 2011.

[16] V. King, J. Saia, and M. Young. Conflict on a communication channel. In *Proc. 30th Annual ACM Symposium on Principles of Distributed Computing (PODC)*, pages 277–286, 2011.

[17] C. Koo, V. Bhandari, J. Katz, and N. Vaidya. Reliable broadcast in radio networks: The bounded collision case. In *Proc. PODC*, 2006.

[18] B.-J. Kwak, N.-O. Song, and L. E. Miller. Performance analysis of exponential backoff. *IEEE/ACM Transactions on Networking*, 13(2):343–355, 2005.

[19] D. Meier, Y. A. Pignolet, S. Schmid, and R. Wattenhofer. Speed dating despite jammers. In *Proc. DCOSS*, June 2009.

[20] G. Nychis, R. Chandra, T. Moscibroda, I. Tashev, and P. Steenkiste. Reclaiming the white spaces: spectrum efficient coexistence with primary users. In *Proc. 7th Conference on Emerging Networking Experiments and Technologies (CoNEXT)*, 2011.

[21] A. Pelc and D. Peleg. Feasibility and complexity of broadcasting with random transmission failures. In *Proc. PODC*, 2005.

[22] P. Raghavan and E. Upfal. Stochastic contention resolution with short delays. *SIAM Journal on Computing*, 28(2):709–719, 1999.

[23] A. Richa, C. Scheideler, S. Schmid, and J. Zhang. A jamming-resistant mac protocol for multi-hop wireless networks. In *Proc. DISC*, 2010.

[24] A. Richa, C. Scheideler, S. Schmid, and J. Zhang. Competitive and fair medium access despite reactive jamming. In *Proc. 31st IEEE ICDCS*, 2011.

[25] A. Richa, C. Scheideler, S. Schmid, and J. Zhang. Self-stabilizing leader election for single-hop wireless networks despite jamming. In *Proc. 12th ACM MobiHoc*, 2011.

[26] A. Richa, C. Scheideler, S. Schmid, and J. Zhang. Towards jamming-resistant and competitive medium access in the SINR model. In *Proc. 3rd Annual ACM S3 Workshop*, 2011.

[27] A. Santoso, Y. Tang, B. Vucetic, A. Jamalipour, and Y. Li. Interference cancellation in coexisting wireless local area networks. In *Proc. 10th IEEE Singapore International Conference on Communication Systems*, pages 1–7, 2006.

[28] J. Schmidt, A. Siegel, and A. Srinivasan. Chernoff-Hoeffding bounds for applications with limited independence. *SIAM Journal on Discrete Mathematics*, 8(2):223–250, 1995.

[29] M. Young and R. Boutaba. Overcoming adversaries in sensor networks: A survey of theoretical models and algorithmic approaches for tolerating malicious interference. *IEEE Communications Surveys and Tutorials*, 13(4):617–641, 2011.

[30] G. Zhou, J. A. Stankovic, and S. H. Son. Crowded spectrum in wireless sensor networks. In *Proc. 3rd Workshop on Embedded Networked Sensors (EmNets)*, 2006.

On the (Limited) Power of Non-Equivocation

Allen Clement
MPI-SWS
aclement@mpi-sws.org

Flavio Junqueira
Yahoo! Research
fpj@yahoo-inc.com

Aniket Kate
MPI-SWS
aniket@mpi-sws.org

Rodrigo Rodrigues
CITI / Universidade Nova de Lisboa
rodrigo.rodrigues@fct.unl.pt

ABSTRACT

In recent years, there have been a few proposals to add a small amount of trusted hardware at each replica in a Byzantine fault tolerant system to cut back replication factors. These trusted components eliminate the ability for a Byzantine node to perform equivocation, which intuitively means making conflicting statements to different processes.

In this paper, we define non-equivocation and study its power in the context of distributed protocols that assume a Byzantine fault model. We show that non-equivocation alone does not allow for reducing the number of processes required to reach agreement in the presence of Byzantine faults in the asynchronous communication model, by proving a lower bound of $n > 3f$ processes for agreement with non-equivocation. However, when we add the ability to guarantee the transferable authentication of network messages (e.g., using digital signatures), we show that it is possible to use non-equivocation to transform any protocol that works under the crash fault model into a protocol that tolerates Byzantine faults, without requiring an increase in the number of processes.

Categories and Subject Descriptors

B.8.1 [**PERFORMANCE AND RELIABILITY**]: Reliability, Testing, and Fault-Tolerance; C.2.4 [**Computer-Communication Networks**]: Distributed Systems—*Distributed applications*; D.4.6 [**OPERATING SYSTEMS**]: Security and Protection—*Cryptographic controls*

General Terms

Algorithms, Reliability, Security, Theory

Keywords

Non-equivocation, Transferable authentication, Trusted hardware

1. INTRODUCTION

The Byzantine fault model [15] is an important foundation for building protocols that offer strong guarantees in the presence of processes that fail in ways other than silently crashing. This model has been adopted by a series of practical replicated systems [5] that are resilient to arbitrary faults, which can originate from issues ranging from software bugs to malicious attacks.

In recent years, several proposals [7, 16] have emerged to add a trusted hardware component to each process running in a Byzantine fault tolerant replicated system in order to make the replication protocols more efficient, most notably by reducing the number of processes that are required to build a replicated state machine. The capability behind this trusted component is to prevent a Byzantine process from equivocating other nodes, which intuitively means making conflicting statements to two or more other processes. Since this can be enforced using a very simple design that can be implemented on today's hardware, the expectation is that this new capability might be widely adopted in the design of more efficient secure distributed systems.

In this paper we set to study the power of non-equivocation. To this end, we formally define non-equivocation in the context of a distributed system with Byzantine processes, and we study whether non-equivocation can aid in finding efficient solutions to the problems of agreement and reliable broadcast.

Our first finding is that non-equivocation is unable to reduce the number of processes required to solve Byzantine agreement in an asynchronous system. In particular, we prove a lower bound of $3f + 1$ processes to solve agreement in a system model that considers both Byzantine faults and non-equivocation. This proof does not contradict the benefits in terms of reducing replication factors achieved by systems like A2M [7] and TrInc [16], since the proof assumes the nonexistence of a primitive that allows for the transferable authentication of network messages (e.g., digital signatures). The second result in this paper focuses precisely on the system model where the unforgeability of network messages can be guaranteed. In this setting, we show how we can use non-equivocation to obtain a generic transformation from a protocol that works under the crash fault model into a protocol that provides the same guarantees under the Byzantine fault model, without requiring an increase in the number of processes. Such transformation can be used, for instance, to solve consensus with $2f + 1$ processes.

With this work, and namely by introducing a new system

model where Byzantine processes are constrained in their behavior by the presence of trusted hardware, we hope to initiate the formal study of the role of trusted computing in the design of secure distributed protocols, an area that is gaining increasing visibility in the security community. Furthermore, we envision that our generic transformation can be an initial step in a research avenue of building distributed protocols that are secure by design, at the cost of adding inexpensive trusted hardware at each process plus a modest increase in protocol complexity.

1.1 Related Work

Chun et al. [7] observe that one of the most disruptive behaviors of Byzantine processes is lying in different ways to different clients or servers. They coin the term *equivocation* for this adversarial behavior, and propose a small trusted computing facility, attested append-only memory (A2M), that makes protocol designs immune to equivocation and enables a lower degree of replication. In particular, using the non-equivocation mechanism from A2M, they provide a Byzantine fault-tolerant state machine replication system that requires only $2f + 1$ replicas instead of $3f + 1$ required in the general Byzantine environment [5]. Levin et. al. [16] reduce the hardware trust assumption required for non-equivocation to a trusted non-decreasing counter and a key that provides unique, once-in-a-lifetime attestations. Nevertheless, the general idea that these papers convey is that using a non-equivocation mechanism results in an improved resiliency bound, which we show not to be true, at least from using non-equivocation *per se*. We instead find that, along with non-equivocation, the use of digital signatures as transferable authentication in A2M and TrInc results in an improved resiliency bound.

The concept of transforming a protocol tolerating f crashes to a protocol tolerating f Byzantine faults with translations using more processes is not new. Bracha [4] defined such a translation for a crash-tolerant consensus protocol to tolerate the same number of Byzantine faults. Coan [8] generalizes this translation to a larger variety of consensus and related protocols. Ho, Dolev, and van Renesse [13] observe that Coan's generalized translation is suitable only for consensus and related problems, and does not work for arbitrary distributed protocols. They instead define the concept of ordered authenticated reliable broadcast (OARcast) over FIFO communication links, and use an OARcast protocol to convert a crash-tolerant system into a system tolerating the same number of Byzantine faults. In follow-up work [14], they further improve their translation to be more scalable and reconfigurable and prove the practicality of the translation by applying it to a link-based routing protocol and an overlay multicast protocol.

Our generic translation provides significant improvement over the above discussed translations: using non-equivocation and transferable authentication mechanisms, we translate a crash-tolerant protocol to a Byzantine fault tolerant protocol without asking for any additional processes or any additional messages (though substantially increasing the message size); we do not restrict our links to be FIFO; finally, our translation is simple, and easy to analyze and specialize for various distributed protocols.

Furthermore, small trusted hardware components have been considered as part of hybrid fault models [18]. Such devices enable a smaller number of replicas and reduce the communication complexity as shown for distributed cryptographic protocols in the security literature [2, 11]. Although these systems inherently use the concepts of non-equivocation and transferable authentication, they do not formally define or study the power of non-equivocation and transferable authentication.

2. SYSTEM MODEL

This section presents our system model, and precisely defines the capability of non-equivocation.

2.1 Fault and communication model

The system consists of n processes $p_1, \ldots, p_n$ connected by a network such that processes are pairwise connected by an asynchronous channel, *i.e.*, messages between two processes can be arbitrarily delayed, or reordered. However, we assume messages are eventually delivered. At most f of n processes may exhibit *faulty* behavior. The remaining processes are *correct*. We consider in this work two distinct models for faulty processes:

Crash. A faulty process does not execute further steps once it crashes;

Byzantine. A faulty process may deviate arbitrarily from the correct behavior of the protocol it implements.

2.2 Computation Model

A system S consists of a complete graph of system processes and an algorithm for each process in the graph. An algorithm for a process is a (possibly infinite state) automaton, which has an initial state Σ_0 and performs the following actions in each step it takes:

- it receives a message through the incoming channels;

- given its state and the message received, it moves to a new state and sends a (possibly empty) set of messages through the outgoing channels.

This allows us to define a *process behavior* $\mathcal{B}_{p,h}$ for process p as a sequence of the form: $\Sigma_{p,0}, (\mathcal{R}_{p,1}, \Sigma_{p,1}, \mathcal{S}_{p,1}), (\mathcal{R}_{p,2}, \Sigma_{p,2}, \mathcal{S}_{p,2}), \ldots, (\mathcal{R}_{p,h}, \Sigma_{p,h}, \mathcal{S}_{p,h})$ such that

- $\Sigma_{p,0}$ is an initial state of the process,

- $\mathcal{R}_{p,j}$ is the jth set of messages received by p^1,

- $\Sigma_{p,j}$ is the state of the process p after processing the message $\mathcal{R}_{p,j}$ while in state $\Sigma_{p,j-1}$, and

- $\mathcal{S}_{p,j}$ is the set of messages (if any) sent by p after entering in the state $\Sigma_{p,j}$.

2.3 Authentication

An authenticated message m is accompanied by an authentication token σ_{p_i} that allows a recipient p_j to verify that p_i generated the message using $verify(m, \sigma_{p_i})$. A key property of message authentication is that authentication tokens are *unforgeable*: if p_i is non-faulty then $verify(m, \sigma_{p_i})$ evaluates to true if and only if p_i generated the message m; for a faulty p_i, $verify(m, \sigma_{p_i}) \wedge verify(m', \sigma_{p_i}) \Rightarrow m = m'$. An authentication token provides *transferable authentication* if correct processes p_j and p_k always evaluate $verify(m, \sigma_{p_i})$

---

[1] In some cases $\mathcal{R}_{p,j}$ will be a singleton set.

in the same way, when p_k receives message m and authentication token σ_{p_i} from p_j. An authentication token provides *non-transferable authentication* if process p_j can evaluate $verify(m, \sigma_{p_i})$ to true while process p_k may not be able to correctly evaluate it. For example, digital signatures provide transferable authentication while arrays of MACs provide non-transferable authentication [1].

2.4 Non-equivocation

A process p equivocates if it sends different messages to different replicas in the same round while it was supposed to send the same message according to the protocol. To prevent equivocation, the system model provides the protocol designer with the capability of *non-equivocation*. This capability consists of being able to validate a pair (k, m) from a process p, where key $k \in \mathbb{N}$ and m is an arbitrary message, with the guarantee that the same key k cannot be used to validate contradicting messages from process p. Let $valid_p(k, m)$ be a predicate that evaluates to true if and only if k validates m and (k, m) has been generated by p. Non-equivocation guarantees that $valid_p(k, m) \wedge valid_p(k, m') \Rightarrow m = m'$. Note that the *valid* predicate is generally realized using the *verify* predicate of the authentication mechanism discussed in Section 2.3.

3. LOWER BOUNDS

In this section, we study the lower bounds for the reliable broadcast primitive using the non-equivocation Byzantine model considered in A2M [7] and TrInc [16]. Contrary to the belief, subjacent to these papers, that the non-equivocation restriction on a Byzantine adversary improves the degree of replication from $n \geq 3f + 1$ to $n \geq 2f + 1$, we observe that signatures (or transferable authentication) also play an instrumental role along with the non-equivocation restriction in improving the resiliency bound. In particular, we prove that assuming at most f Byzantine faults in an asynchronous system of n processes, the non-equivocation restriction and transferable-authentication tokens together, but not individually, are sufficient to improve the resiliency bound to $n \geq 2f + 1$.

Note that our resiliency results also apply to other related distributed computing primitives such as consensus, state machine replication and verifiable secret sharing, since they are stronger problems compared to the reliable broadcast problem we target [6].

3.1 Definition

We start by defining the Reliable Broadcast (r-broadcast) primitive.

r-broadcast is a fundamental primitive for synchronization among a group of processes, which can be characterized by the following *liveness* and *safety* properties.

DEFINITION 1. *In an asynchronous system of n processes having a distinguished sender s and an f-limited adversary with point-to-point authenticated links, a **reliable broadcast (r-broadcast) protocol** satisfies the following liveness and safety conditions:*

Liveness.

> **Sender Termination (L1).** *If the sender is correct and sends m, then the sender delivers m.*

> **Completeness (L2).** *If a correct process delivers a message, then all correct processes deliver a message.*

Safety.

> **Validity (S1).** *If the sender is correct and a correct process delivers a message m, then the sender must have sent m.*

> **Agreement (S2).** *If a correct node p_i delivers m_i and another correct node p_j delivers m_j, then $m_i = m_j$.*

> **Integrity (S3).** *A correct node delivers at most one message.*

Note that the r-broadcast primitive cannot guarantee termination of a protocol instance for a faulty sender. It follows from the impossibility of guaranteeing consensus in the asynchronous setting with even a single crash fault [10].

The r-broadcast primitive only needs $n \geq f+1$ in the crash fault model [12] while it requires $n \geq 3f+1$ in the Byzantine model [3]. We include the corresponding resilience-optimal r-broadcast protocols in Appendix A.

3.2 Analysis

We now show two lower bound claims for the degree of replication of r-broadcast when considering non-equivocation and transferable authentication. The first claim assumes that faulty processes cannot equivocate, but there is no transferable authentication. The second claim makes the opposite assumption: the model does not give access to non-equivocation, but does allow for transferrable authentication.

In the following proofs, we use the notion of locality. If two isomorphic subsystems consisting of correct processes are such that corresponding processes start in the same initial states and corresponding input edges to the subsystems carry the same messages, then the two subsystems exhibit identical behavior, independent of the overall systems. This property is called the *locality axiom* [9].

CLAIM 3.1. *Suppose an asynchronous system of n processes such that at most f processes fail under the Byzantine model and $n < 3f + 1$. If processes do not implement transferable authentication and faulty processes cannot equivocate, then there is no solution for r-broadcast.*

PROOF. Proof by contradiction. Suppose that there exists a protocol that solves r-broadcast with $n < 3f+1$ without using transferable authentication even when the adversary cannot equivocate. Without loss of generality, we assume that $n = 3f$.

Suppose that we partition the set of processes n into disjoint subsets A, B, and C, such that each subset contains exactly f processes. Using this partition of the set of processes, we construct several runs of the protocol, the last of which violates a safety property. In all runs there is a distinguished process $s \in A$ that broadcasts a message.

Run 1. Processes in C crash at the beginning of the run (time t_0):

- Process s broadcasts m', all processes in C crash at time t_0, and all other processes are correct;

303

- Messages between A and B are delivered in a timely fashion;

- By the Liveness and Agreement properties of r-broadcast, all processes in A and B deliver m' by time t.

Run 2. Processes in A crash after processes in B have delivered m', and messages to and from C are arbitrarily delayed:

- Process s broadcasts m', all processes in A crash at time t and all other processes are correct;

- Messages between A and B are delivered in a timely fashion and the steps of processes in A and B are the same as in Run 1 until time t;

- Processes in B deliver m' by time t, since they cannot differentiate Run 2 from Run 1;

- Messages between B and C are delayed until time t', t' arbitrarily large and $t' > t$;

- Messages between A and C are not delivered (processes in A are faulty in this run);

- By the Agreement property of r-broadcast, processes in C deliver m' by time $t'' > t'$.

Run 3. All processes are correct, but messages from and to processes in C are arbitrarily delayed:

- Process s broadcasts m', and all processes are correct;

- Messages between A and B are delivered in a timely fashion and the steps of processes in A and B are the same as in Run 1 until time t;

- Processes in B have all delivered m' by time t, since they can't differentiate Run 3 from Run 2;

- Messages between B and C are delayed until time t';

- Messages between A and C are delayed until time $t''' > t''$.

- Processes in C deliver m' by time t'', since they cannot distinguish Run 3 from Run 2.

Run 4. All processes in B are faulty:

- Process s broadcasts m, processes in B are faulty, and all other processes are correct;

- Messages between processes in B and C are delayed until time t' and the steps of processes in B and C are the same as in Run 3, in which the sender broadcasts m';

- Messages between A and C are delayed until time t''';

- Processes in C deliver m' by time t'', since they cannot distinguish Run 4 from Run 3;

- By Liveness, process s delivers m.

Run 4 constitutes a violation of the Agreement property and contradicts the assumption of a protocol that solves r-broadcast for $n \leq 3f$ processes. $\square$

Note that in the proof of Claim 3.1, Run 4 is valid even if faulty processes cannot equivocate. This is because Byzantine processes in B (in Run 4, Step 2) repeat sequences of messages of another run, while not equivocating. Correct processes in C cannot distinguish between Run 3 and Run 4, since there is no transferable authentication scheme implemented by assumption.

The next theorem considers the opposite setting, where Byzantine nodes can equivocate, but the system model allows for transferable authentication.

CLAIM 3.2. *Suppose an asynchronous system of n processes such that at most f processes fail under the Byzantine model and $n < 3f + 1$. If processes implement transferable authentication and faulty processes can equivocate, then there is no solution for r-broadcast.*

PROOF. Proof by contradiction. Suppose that there exists a protocol such that it solves r-broadcast with $n < 3f + 1$ assuming transferable authentication and that faulty processes can equivocate. Without loss of generality, we assume that $n = 3f$.

Suppose that we partition the set of processes n into disjoint subsets A, B, and C, such that each subset contains exactly f processes. Using this partition of the set of processes, we construct three runs. In all runs there is a distinguished process $s \in A$ that broadcasts a message.

Run 1. Processes in B crash:

- Process s broadcasts m and all processes in B crash at the beginning of the run (t_0);

- By the agreement and the liveness properties of r-broadcast all process in A and C eventually deliver m by time t.

Run 2. Processes in C crash:

- Process s broadcasts m' and all processes in C crash at the beginning of the run (t_0);

- By the agreement and the liveness properties of r-broadcast all process in A and B eventually deliver m' by time t'.

Run 3. Processes in A are faulty:

- Processes in A execute the same steps as in Run 1 when exchanging messages with processes in C;

- Processes in A execute the same steps as in Run 2 when exchanging messages with processes in B;

- Messages between B and C are delayed until time $\max\{t, t'\}$;

- Processes in C cannot distinguish Run 3 from Run 1, and they deliver m;

- Processes in B cannot distinguish Run 3 from Run 2, and they deliver m'.

Run 3 constitutes a violation of the Agreement property and contradicts the assumption of a protocol that solves r-broadcast for $n \leq 3f$ processes. $\square$

Note that in the proof of Claim 3.2 the faulty processes in Run 3 do not violate transferable authentication, although the first two steps of the run possibly violate non-equivocation. We also note the similarity between the argument in the proof of the theorem and the argument provided by Pease, Shostak, and Lamport for interactive consistency [17]; we adapted it to the r-broadcast problem.

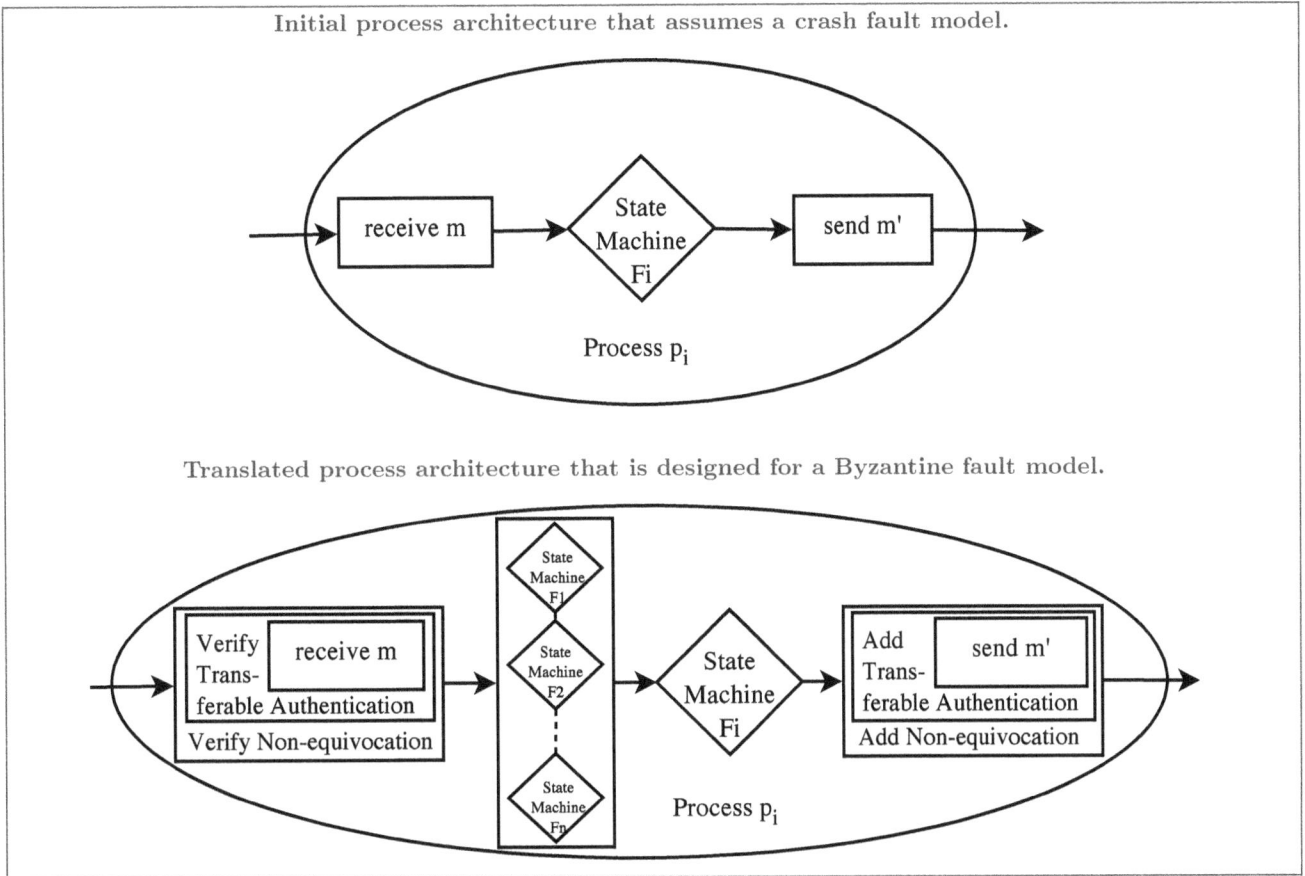

Figure 1: Overview of the translation from a crash fault tolerant system to a Byzantine fault tolerant system.

4. TRANSLATION

In this section we demonstrate the power of combining non-equivocation with transferable authentication. In particular, we show that there exists a translation of a distributed protocol that can tolerate f crash faults into one that tolerates f Byzantine faults using the same number of processes and the same number of (longer) messages. This transformation makes use of both non-equivocation and digital signatures. This result implies that we can solve Byzantine agreement with only $2f + 1$ processes, thus confirming the potential of non-equivocation evidenced by A2M [7] and TrInc [16].

4.1 Requirements

The basic idea of the translation mechanism is to replace the primitives for sending and receiving messages through the network with a more complex protocol that provides the same key guarantees about the contents of the delivered messages that are expected by the original protocol in the crash fault model.

This strategy is similar to the one used by another proposal by Ho *et al.* [13, 14] for transforming protocols that tolerate crash faults into protocols that provide the same guarantees in the Byzantine fault model. In particular, they identify the following key safety properties that are expected by a crash fault tolerant protocol regarding the messages that are delivered by the network, and that must also be provided by our translation mechanism.

Safety. If the sender p_i is correct and a correct process p_j *receives* a message m from p_i, then the sender p_i must have executed *send* with m.

Integrity. If a correct process *receives* a message m, then m is a valid state machine message.

Regarding the Integrity property, message m sent by process p_i is valid if it corresponds to the output of applying a sequence of valid messages to the state machine of the process (and considering that external inputs, like messages coming from clients of a replicated service, are valid), i.e., there is a correct process behavior $B_{p_i,h} = \Sigma_0, (\mathcal{R}_1, \Sigma_1, \mathcal{S}_1), (\mathcal{R}_2, \Sigma_2, \mathcal{S}_2), \ldots, (\mathcal{R}_h, \Sigma_h, \mathcal{S}_h)$ such that $m \in \mathcal{S}_h$ and all $\mathcal{R}_i$ are valid.

Ho *et al.* [13, 14] also include the liveness property that if a correct sender p_i *sends* a message to a correct process p_j, then process p_j will *receive* the message eventually. This property is generally satisfied by asynchronous communication models assumed by many distributed protocols, e.g., the r-broadcast primitive in Section 3.1. However, it is not considered mandatory for every crash fault tolerant protocol, and to make our list of requirements more generic, we do not include this liveness property in the list.

The previous generic transformation work [13, 14] stated another property, which we modify in our set of requirements. The original missing property stated that the transformed network implements a first in, first out (FIFO) policy [13, 14]. However, this is insufficient, since two correct

```
upon B-receiving a message $((k_p, m, \mathcal{R}_p, \mathcal{S}_p), \sigma_p)$ from $p$:
    verify$((k_p, m, \mathcal{R}_p, \mathcal{S}_p), \sigma_p)$
    Check that $k_p = |\mathcal{R}_p| = |\mathcal{S}_p|$
    For all the messages in $\mathcal{R}_p$ and $\mathcal{S}_p$ check authenticity
    Instantiate copy of state machine in initial state, feed messages inputs in $\mathcal{R}_p$, confirm outputs match those in $\mathcal{S}_p$
    For all the messages in $\mathcal{R}_p$, recursively apply same checks to ensure checks were made by sender
    if all checks pass then
        Deliver T-receive message $m$ from $p$
        add $((k_p, m, \mathcal{R}_p, \mathcal{S}_p), \sigma_p)$ to the set of received messages $\mathcal{R}$
    end if

upon receiving a T-send$(m)$ to set $P$ from the state machine:
    Increment $k$
    $\sigma_p$ = GenerateAuthentication $(k, m, \mathcal{R}, \mathcal{S})$
    B-send $((k, m, \mathcal{R}, \mathcal{S}), \sigma_p)$ to all processes in $P$
    Add $((k, m, \mathcal{R}, \mathcal{S}), \sigma_p)$ to the set of sent messages $\mathcal{S}$
```

Figure 2: Pseudocode for the generic translation

processes might receive contradictory but valid messages from a Byzantine process (i.e., the final output of two forks, both corresponding to correct executions) without violating FIFO since each correct process only receives one of the two messages. This is a situation that crash fault tolerant protocols do not expect, and may not be ready to handle. We therefore modify this final requirement as follows.

Consistency. If correct processes p_1 and p_2 receive valid messages $m_i \in \mathcal{S}_i$ and $m_j \in \mathcal{S}_j$ respectively from process p_g, then either (a) $B_{p_g,i}$ is a prefix of $B_{p_g,j}$, (b) $B_{p_g,j}$ is a prefix of $B_{p_g,i}$, or (c) $B_{p_g,i} = B_{p_g,j} \wedge \mathcal{S}_i = \mathcal{S}_j$ (where $B_{p_g,x}$ is the process behavior that supports the validity of message m_x).

4.2 Translation Implementation

Now, we show a translation, defined as a set of wrapper functions for processes to send and receive messages, that meets the above listed properties. Given that the terms send and receive will be overloaded, we will make the following distinction throughout our description:

- B-send and B-receive refer to the lower level sending and receiving of messages through the network in the Byzantine model (i.e., used by the implementation of the translation).

- T-send and T-receive are the resultant higher level primitives, i.e., the interface exported by the translation layer to the implementation of the original crash fault tolerant protocol sitting above that layer.

The goal of the translation layer is to implement T-send and T-receive primitives that satisfy the three requirements defined in Section 4.1 despite f Byzantine faults, by leveraging the non-equivocation and transferable authentication mechanisms. Note that our transformation encapsulates and runs instances of the state machine. Consequently, it is not independent of the state machine, and does not clearly separate the communication layer and the application layer.

The safety requirement can be ensured by retrying the B-send attempts and by authenticating messages in B-send and B-receive. Our assumption of transferable authentication is thus sufficient (and even too strong since non-transferable authentication would also suffice).

The integrity requirement requires the receiver to obtain a guarantee that a message from process p_i is based on a

sequence of valid messages. In this case, the transferable authentication mechanism helps by allowing p_i to prove the validity of its output message to its receivers by attaching the corresponding signatures (or authentication tokens) of p_i's inputs that led to sending the output message. Then by replaying these authentic inputs, the integrity requirement can be validated.

Finally, the consistency requirement can be enforced through non-equivocation, simply by including a sequence number in the key associated with each outgoing message, thus forcing a total order on the outputs of each process, and by forcing the sender process to also transmit all the previous sequence numbers in each message step.

We therefore reach the translation mechanism that is depicted in a block diagram in Figure 1. In Figure 2 we present the pseudocode for the translation.

The idea is that to T-send a message a node must pass it through a non-equivocation layer and a transferable authentication layer. The non-equivocation layer causes the output of the ith state transition that is sent to be associated with key k, and passes the (k, m) message to the next layer. The transferable authentication layer associates with each outgoing message the sequence of signed inputs that led to generating this message, and also signs the message before B-sending it.

On the receiver side, the transferable authentication layer checks that the message is signed by the correct sender, replays the execution of the sequence of inputs encapsulated in the message, checking if the output matches the payload that was received, and recursively applies these checks to every message in the sequence, to ensure that the messages were based on valid inputs. The non-equivocation layer merely has to check that the key k matches the number of inputs in the sequence.

We present a correctness argument for this transformation in Appendix B.

5. CONCLUSION AND FUTURE WORK

Non-equivocation is a practical capability available to the design of systems that tolerate Byzantine faults. It has received some attention from the designers of distributed systems in recent years because of the important practical features it enables: a simple implementation and a lower degree of replication.

In this paper, we formally defined non-equivocation, and showed that, contrary to the belief implied by the initial proposals for using hardware support for non-equivocation, this capability by itself does not decrease the number of replicas required to solve problems like consensus in the Byzantine fault model. However, coupled with transferable authentication, it is possible to reduce the degree of replication. To demonstrate it, we show a generic transformation from a crash-tolerant protocol into one that is Byzantine tolerant, using non-equivocation and transferable authentication, requiring the same number of processes as the crash-tolerant counterpart.

This work opens some near term follow-up research directions, namely it would be interesting to make our translation mechanism more efficient. The current translation uses an expensive mechanism of replaying the execution of almost the entire system to ensure that the message that is received is legitimate. While it shows that a translation exists without increasing the number of processes, it is also clearly not a practical strategy and can be highly optimized, *e.g.*, by reusing previous verifications, and also by using checkpointing mechanisms that allow nodes to agree on a correct view of the system.

Given the potential of non-equivocation to enable more efficient protocols that tolerate Byzantine faults, and the viability of the concept that has been shown by the existence of efficient hardware implementations and its application to existing distributed systems, we believe that the formal study of non-equivocation is an important research direction. Furthermore, the translation we provide is an important initial step towards the design and implementation of distributed systems that are secure by construction, and yet efficient in the required number of processes.

Acknowledgments

We thank our anonymous referees for their helpful comments and advice. Flavio Junqueira has been partially supported by the INNCORPORA - Torres Quevedo Program from the Spanish Ministry of Science and Innovation, co-funded by the European Social Fund.

6. REFERENCES

[1] A. S. Aiyer, L. Alvisi, R. A. Bazzi, and A. Clement. Matrix Signatures: From MACs to Digital Signatures in Distributed Systems. In *22nd International Symposium on Distributed Computing (DISC '08)*, pages 16–31, 2008.

[2] G. Avoine and S. Vaudenay. Optimal Fair Exchange with Guardian Angels. In *Proc. 4th International Workshop Information Security Applications (WISA '03)*, pages 188–202, 2003.

[3] G. Bracha. An Asynchronous [(n-1)/3]-Resilient Consensus Protocol. In *Proc. 3rd ACM Symposium on Principles of Distributed Computing (PODC '84)*, pages 154–162, 1984.

[4] G. Bracha. Asynchronous Byzantine Agreement Protocols. *Information and Computation*, 75(2):130–143, 1987.

[5] M. Castro and B. Liskov. Practical Byzantine Fault Tolerance and Proactive Recovery. *ACM Transactions on Computer Systems (TOCS)*, 20(4):398–461, 2002.

[6] T. D. Chandra and S. Toueg. Unreliable failure detectors for reliable distributed systems. *Journal of the ACM*, 43:225–267, March 1996.

[7] B.-G. Chun, P. Maniatis, S. Shenker, and J. Kubiatowicz. Attested append-only memory: making adversaries stick to their word. In *21st ACM Symposium on Operating Systems Principles (SOSP '07)*, pages 189–204, 2007.

[8] B. A. Coan. A Compiler that Increases the Fault Tolerance of Asynchronous Protocols. *IEEE Trans. Computers*, 37(12):1541–1553, 1988.

[9] M. J. Fischer, N. A. Lynch, and M. Merritt. Easy impossibility proofs for distributed consensus problems. In *Proc. 4th ACM Symposium on Principles of Distributed Computing (PODC '85)*, pages 59–70, 1985.

[10] M. J. Fischer, N. A. Lynch, and M. Paterson. Impossibility of Distributed Consensus with One Faulty Process. *Journal of ACM*, 32(2):374–382, 1985.

[11] M. Fort, F. C. Freiling, L. D. Penso, Z. Benenson, and D. Kesdogan. TrustedPals: Secure Multiparty Computation Implemented with Smart Cards. In *Proc. 11th European Symposium on Research in Computer Security (ESORICS '06)*, pages 34–48, 2006.

[12] V. Hadzilacos and S. Toueg. A Modular Approach to Fault-Tolerant Broadcasts and Related Problems. Technical report, Ithaca, NY, USA, 1994.

[13] C. Ho, D. Dolev, and R. van Renesse. Making Distributed Applications Robust. In *11th International Conference Principles of Distributed Systems (OPODIS '07)*, pages 232–246, 2007.

[14] C. Ho, R. van Renesse, M. Bickford, and D. Dolev. Nysiad: Practical Protocol Transformation to Tolerate Byzantine Failures. In *4th USENIX Symposium on Networked Systems Design and Implementation (NSDI '08)*, pages 175–188, 2008.

[15] L. Lamport, R. E. Shostak, and M. C. Pease. The Byzantine Generals Problem. *ACM Trans. Program. Lang. Syst.*, 4(3):382–401, 1982.

[16] D. Levin, J. R. Douceur, J. R. Lorch, and T. Moscibroda. TrInc: Small Trusted Hardware for Large Distributed Systems. In *6th USENIX Symposium on Networked Systems Design and Implementation (NDSI '09)*, pages 1–14, 2009.

[17] M. C. Pease, R. E. Shostak, and L. Lamport. Reaching Agreement in the Presence of Faults. *Journal of the ACM*, 27(2):228–234, 1980.

[18] P. E. Veríssimo. Travelling through wormholes: a new look at distributed systems models. *SIGACT News*, 37(1):66–81, Mar. 2006.

APPENDIX

A. RELIABLE BROADCAST PROTOCOLS

We consider two reliable broadcast protocol in the asynchronous setting from the literature. In Figure 3, we present a r-broadcast protocol [12] in the crash fault model for $n \geq f + 1$, while in Figure 4, we include a r-broadcast protocol [3] in the Byzantine model for $n \geq 3f + 1$.

```
broadcast protocol for process p_i during session (τ, s)

upon a message (τ, in, r-broadcast, m) /* for the sender s*/
    for all j ∈ [1, n] do
        send the message (τ, s, send, m) to p_j
    end for
    output (τ, s, out, m)

upon a message (τ, s, send, m) from p_m for the first time:
    for all j ∈ [1, n] do
        send the message (τ, s, send, m) to p_j
    end for
    output (τ, s, out, m)
```

Figure 3: Reliable Broadcast for $n \geq f + 1$ for the crash Model [12]

```
broadcast protocol for process p_i during session (τ, s)

upon initialization:
    for all m do
        e_m ← 0; r_m ← 0
    end for

upon a message (τ, in, r-broadcast, m) /*for the sender s*/
    for all j ∈ [1, n] do
        send the message (τ, s, send, m) to p_j
    end for

upon a message (τ, s, send, m) from s for the first time:
    for all j ∈ [1, n] do
        send the message (τ, s, echo, m) to p_j
    end for

upon a message (τ, s, echo, m) from p_ℓ for the first time:
    e_m ← e_m + 1
    if e_m = ⌈(n+f+1)/2⌉ ∧ r_m < f + 1 then
        for all j ∈ [1, n] do
            send the message (τ, s, ready, m) to p_j
        end for
    end if

upon a message (τ, s, ready, m) from p_ℓ for the first time:
    r_m ← r_m + 1
    if r_m = f + 1 ∧ e_m < ⌈(n+f+1)/2⌉ then
        for all j ∈ [1, n] do
            send the message (s, τ, ready, m) to p_j
        end for
    else if r_m = n − f then
        output (τ, s, out, m)
    end if
```

Figure 4: Bracha's Reliable Broadcast for $n \geq 3f + 1$ for the Byzantine Fault Model [3]

B. A CORRECTNESS ARGUMENT FOR THE GENERIC TRANSLATION

We present an argument that the translation satisfies the safety, integrity, and consistency properties. We note that many crash fault tolerant protocols also require liveness; i.e, if a correct sender p_i sends a message to a correct process p_j, then process p_j will receive the message eventually. As we discussed in Section 4.1, this requirement is satisfied by the asynchronous communication model itself, e.g., our communication model defined in Section 2 for the r-broadcast primitive.

Safety.

Our (transferable) authentication mechanism ensures that a faulty process cannot impersonate a correct process. Therefore, if the sender p_i is correct and a correct process p_j receives a message m from p_i, then the sender p_i must have executed send with m.

Integrity.

Integrity requires that if a correct process p_j receives a message m, then m is a valid state machine message. It is provable using the transferable authentication mechanism in a recursive manner as follows:

In our translated system, every sender p_s attaches a proof of correctness in the form of transferable authentication tokens to a message sent to a receiver p_r. The transferable authentication tokens include the corresponding messages ($\mathcal{R}_i$ for $i \in [1, h]$) p_s received. These messages also carry authentication tokens σ_i for $i \in [1, h]$, which process p_r uses to verify the authenticity of $\mathcal{R}_i$. When these verification are successful, p_r sequentially runs the received messages $\mathcal{R}_i$ for $i \in [1, h]$ through a state machine Σ_{p_s} for p_s starting from the initial state $\Sigma_{p_s,0}$. If the received message m corresponds to the state $\Sigma_{p_s,h}$, p_r is ensured that m is a valid message.

Consistency.

Consistency requires that if correct processes p_1 and p_2 receive valid messages $m_i \in \mathcal{S}_i$ and $m_j \in \mathcal{S}_j$ respectively from process p_g, then either (a) $B_{p_g,i}$ is a prefix of $B_{p_g,j}$, (b) $B_{p_g,j}$ is a prefix of $B_{p_g,i}$, or (c) $B_{p_g,i} = B_{p_g,j} \wedge \mathcal{S}_i = \mathcal{S}_j$.

We ensure this properties using the non-equivocation mechanism. As we discuss in the pseudocode, every message sent by a sender p_g is registered in its local non-equivocation mechanism. This enforces a total order on the messages sent sender p_g. Jointed with integrity, this itself can be sufficient to consistency. However, we further simplify the consistency enforcement by mandating p_g to transmit all the previous sequence numbered messages along with its current message. This ensures that a receiver does not miss any past of messages. Resultantly, when two receivers p_1 and p_2 hear from the same sender p_g their behaviors corresponding to the sender p_g will follow the exact same state transition path. However, as p_g may not send all messages, a behavior of process (say) p_1 can form a prefix of a behavior by process p_2, and vice versa.

On the Price of Equivocation in Byzantine Agreement

Alexander Jaffe
University of Washington
ajaffe@cs.washington.edu

Thomas Moscibroda
Microsoft Research Asia
moscitho@microsoft.com

Siddhartha Sen
Princeton University
sssix@cs.princeton.edu

ABSTRACT

In the Byzantine agreement problem, a set of n processors, any f of whom may be arbitrarily faulty, must reach agreement on a value proposed by one of the correct processors. It is a celebrated result that unless $n > 3f$, Byzantine agreement is impossible in a variety of computation and communication models. This is due to the fact that faulty processors can *equivocate*, that is, say different things to different processors. If this ability is mitigated, for example by assuming a global broadcast channel, then $n > 2f$ is sufficient. With very few exceptions, the literature on Byzantine agreement has been confined to the $n > 2f$ and $n > 3f$ paradigms.

We bridge the gap between these two paradigms by assuming partial broadcast channels among sets of three processors, observing that equivocation is fundamentally an act involving three parties: a faulty processor that lies (inconsistently) to two correct processors. We characterize the conditions under which Byzantine agreement is possible for all $n = 2f + h$, h an integer in $[1..f]$, by giving asymptotically tight bounds on the number of necessary and sufficient partial broadcast channels. We prove these bounds by a reduction to a problem in extremal combinatorics, which itself is a natural generalization of a well-studied hypergraph coloring problem. Algorithmically, we show that deciding whether a given set of broadcast channels enables Byzantine agreement is co-NP-complete. Although partial broadcast channels have been studied in prior work, the bounds obtained on the number of required channels were sub-optimal by up to a factor of $\Theta(n^2)$. Moreover, this work has been confined to the synchronous model. In contrast, we apply our results to several distinct models and provide stronger motivation for using partial broadcast channels in practice, drawing from recent work in the systems community.

Categories and Subject Descriptors

G.2.2 [**Discrete Mathematics**]: Graph Theory—*graph labeling, hypergraphs*; F.2.2 [**Analysis of Algorithms and Problem Complexity**]: Nonnumerical Algorithms and Problems—*computations on discrete structures*

Keywords

Byzantine agreement, partial broadcast, hypergraph coloring, expander graphs

1. INTRODUCTION

One of the most celebrated results in distributed computing theory is the bound on the redundancy required to solve the *Byzantine Agreement* problem. In this problem, a set of n processors, each with an initial value and any f of whom may be arbitrarily faulty, must reach agreement on a value proposed by one of the correct processors.[1] Lamport, Shostak, and Pease showed in 1982 that in the standard communication model of a complete synchronous network of pairwise authenticated channels, Byzantine agreement is possible if and only if $n > 3f$ [31], implying a significant amount of redundancy. Moreover, the $n > 3f$ bound is remarkably robust to changes in the underlying communication and computation model [9, 18, 28].

A closer inspection of these results reveals that the fundamental reason for requiring $n > 3f$ processors is that faulty processors can *equivocate*, *i.e.*, say different things to different processors. For instance, in a synchronous system with 3 processors, a single faulty processor can consistently send different messages to the two correct processors and make them agree to different values [31]. In asynchronous systems, the adversary's ability to delay messages (in addition to its ability to equivocate) can confound the correct processors even if cryptography is used [18]. Thus, several researchers have considered using stronger communication primitives such as broadcast channels. Broadcast channels mitigate equivocation by ensuring that a message appears identically at all recipients on the channel. In the synchronous model, Rabin and Ben-Or [37] introduced a global broadcast channel and achieved Byzantine agreement (in fact, any multiparty protocol) if and only if $n > 2f$. Fitzi and Maurer [20] added $\Theta(n^3)$ *partial broadcast* channels among every set of three processors to achieve Byzantine agreement if and only if $n > 2f$. Ravikant et al. [38] reduced the number of 3-processor channels required for $n = 2f + h$, where h is an integer in $[1..f]$, assuming sufficient connectivity in the underlying network. However, they get asymptotically tight results only for the same case $h = 1$ as Fitzi and Maurer do. Finally, Considine et al. [14] generalized partial broadcast to sets of $b > 3$ processors, achieving reliable broadcast (but not consensus) when $n > f(b+1)/(b-1)$.

The above overview of previous work illustrates that the gap between $n > 3f$ and $n > 2f$ represents a fundamental *price of equivocation*. In this paper, we give a complete and tight characterization of this price, by studying the relationship between the fraction of processor 3-tuples that are prevented from equivocating, modeled as 3-processor partial broadcast channels, and the fault resilience required to solve Byzantine agreement. Specifically, we study the use, application, and algorithmic implications of 3-processor broadcast channels to Byzantine agreement. We view these channels as

---

[1] This variant of the problem is called *consensus*. The variant where only a single processor has an initial value is called *reliable broadcast*. Consensus implies reliable broadcast, but the reverse is only true if faulty processors are in the minority, *i.e.* $n > 2f$.

3-hyperedges in the processor graph. Whereas prior work has almost exclusively focused on resilience $n > 2f$, we show that the range $n \geq 2f + h$, where $h \in [1..f]$ allows for significantly more efficient constructions by requiring asymptotically fewer than $\binom{n}{3} = \Theta(n^3)$ 3-hyperedges, assuming standard requirements on the connectivity of the underlying graph [34, 38]. We derive asymptotically tight bounds for all $h \in [1..f]$. Interestingly, this problem turns out to be a natural generalization of a well-studied *hypergraph coloring problem*. Although prior work has been limited to the synchronous model, we show how to apply our results to various other models as well.

The motivation for studying 3-hyperedges is two-fold. First, a 3-hyperedge (x, y, z) represents the fundamental unit of equivocation: a faulty processor x says different things to correct processors y and z. Second, while it is possible (and likely more efficient) to create a single or larger broadcast channel with x and the processors it has 3-hyperedges with, the expressiveness of 3-hyperedges may be useful in practice. For example, if hyperedges (x, y, z) and (x, y, w) exist but not (x, z, w), then a protocol may require x to use partial broadcast when sending a message to y and z or to y and w, but not when sending a message to z and w.

1.1 Results and outline

Let H be a 3-uniform hypergraph on n vertices (representing processors), where each 3-hyperedge represents a partial broadcast channel. Our main result is an asymptotically tight characterization of the necessary and sufficient number of 3-hyperedges required to achieve Byzantine agreement despite f faulty processors, for all $n \geq 2f + h$, h a positive integer in $[1..f]$. h is thus the parameter that interpolates between the well-studied cases $n > 2f$ and $n > 3f$. As in prior work [38], we assume the underlying graph is at least $(2f + 1)$-connected. Let $T_n(h)$ denote the minimum m such that there exists an H with m 3-hyperedges that achieves Byzantine agreement. We show:

- $T_n(h(n)) = \Theta\left(\frac{n^3}{h(n)^2}\right)$

For comparison, the only other existing work that gives results on this trade-off is by Ravikant et al. [38], who obtain an upper bound of $T_n(h(n)) = O((f - h(n) + 1)f^2) = O((n - 3h(n) + 1)n^2)$, which is up to a factor of $\Theta(n^2)$ off the correct bound, depending on $h(n)$. They also give a near-tight bound for the case $n = 2f + 1$, but this result is asymptotically identical to the trivial solution of including all 3-hyperedges. Their constructions are elementary and use a clever and simple recursive structure, though the analysis is nontrivial. We improve on their results by using the power of expander graphs, building hypergraphs out of existing expander constructions in order to exploit their high connectivity. Although we can prove our bound on $T_n(h(n))$ using a simple probabilistic method argument, in this work we are concerned with *explicit constructions*. A strong motivation for this goal is given by the following result.

Theorem 1. *Given a 3-uniform hypergraph $H = (V, E)$ with $|V| = n$, it is co-NP-complete to decide, for any $n = 2f + h$, $h \in [1..f]$, whether Byzantine agreement is possible in H despite f faulty processors.*

The proof of this theorem, a reduction from balanced bipartite independent set, can be found in Section 6. Since it is intractable to detect the possibility of Byzantine agreement in general, it is possible that explicit construction is the only reliable means of exploiting the efficiency gains of sparse fault-tolerant hypergraphs.

Our final result gives an exact bound for $U_n(h(n))$, the minimum m such that any H with m hyperedges achieves Byzantine agreement:

- $U_n(h(n)) = \binom{n}{3} - \frac{n - h(n)}{2} \cdot h(n)^2 + 1$

Section 1.2 discusses the application of our results to upper and lower bounds for Byzantine agreement in various models. Section 2 formally defines the problem and proves an equivalence to a more natural combinatorial problem, which we use in the remainder of the paper. Section 3 proves the lower bound on $T_n(h(n))$ using a graph projection and counting arguments. Section 4 describes explicit constructions of H that match the upper bound on $T_n(h(n))$; we rely on a "lifting" procedure that converts existing constructions of Ramanujan graphs into hypergraphs with expander-like properties. Section 5 proves the bound on $U_n(h(n))$ using multivariate minimization techniques. Section 7 concludes with some open problems. Due to space constraints, some proofs are omitted and deferred to the full version of this paper.

1.2 Algorithms and applications

The results of this paper naturally give rise to new upper and lower bounds for Byzantine agreement in various models (augmented with partial broadcast channels). Specifically, our results apply to any proof that relies on the following intersection property between quorums of processors (made precise in Section 2), which we call *f-tolerance*: Consider a quorum of size $n - f$; although $n - f$ is the number of correct processors, a quorum of this size may still contain up to f faulty processors. Given two such quorums, the correct processors of one quorum may disagree with those of the other because faulty processors common to both may equivocate, unless their intersection contains at least one correct processor: $2(n - f) - n > f \implies n > 3f$. The key insight is that we get the same guarantee by replacing the correct processor x with a 3-hyperedge (x, y, z) such that y and z are correct processors in distinct quorums. Even if x is faulty, hyperedge (x, y, z) prevents it from equivocating to y and z and making their quorums agree on inconsistent values.

Ravikant et al. [38] prove that Byzantine agreement is possible in the synchronous model if and only if a set of conditions which includes f-tolerance holds. The remaining conditions are the standard connectivity requirements of the underlying graph, which we also assume in our setting. Thus Theorem 1 in their paper implies lower and upper bounds for Byzantine agreement in our setting as well. However, the hypergraphs they construct are suboptimal: they provide a tight bound only for $n = 2f + 1$ [38, Sections 5.2 and 5.3] and loose upper bounds for any $n = 2f + h, h \in [1..f]$ [38, Section 5.1]. By replacing their construction with ours from Section 4, we reduce the number of 3-hyperedges and the message complexity of their protocol by up to a factor of $\Theta(n^2)$.

In the asynchronous model, we can adapt the lower bound of Bracha and Toueg [9] to show that f-tolerance is necessary for Byzantine agreement. The proof is essentially the same as Theorem 3 in their paper, except that instead of any two $(n - f)$-sized quorums, a pair of quorums that violates f-tolerance must be used. We can obtain upper bounds for any $n = 2f + h$ by modifying the protocols of Bracha and Toueg [9, Figure 2] or Bracha [8], for example. We do this by overlaying our hypergraph construction onto the processor graph and requiring x to use hyperedge (x, y, z), if it exists, when sending a message to both y and z. Although this reduces the efficiency of the protocol, the relevant correctness proofs ([9, Theorem 4] and [8, Sections 3.2 and 6]) are readily adapted because they rely on f-tolerance. Similarly, there has been tremendous recent interest in the systems community on designing efficient Byzantine agreement protocols in a partially synchronous model with cryptography (*e.g.*, [4, 12, 15, 27, 29]). This model is subject to Bracha and Toueg's lower bound [9], and essentially all upper bounds are derivatives of Castro and Liskov's protocol [11], which relies on f-tolerance for correctness [11, Invariants A.1.4 and A.1.5]. Therefore we can improve the resiliency of these protocols as above. This reduces their replication costs, which is often cited as an obstacle to practical deployment [27, 39, 43, 44].

There are several ways to implement 3-hyperedges in practice. One way is to use multicast groups; another is to use a shared cyptographic key; another is to use trusted primitives like an *append-only log* [12] or *trusted incrementer* [32]. Depending on the implementation, it may not always be possible to force a processor x to use a 3-hyperedge *a priori*, but it is always possible for y and z to generate a proof of misbehavior (POM) [2] against x *a posteriori* if x violates the protocol. Several systems [2, 26, 29] use POMs in this manner. Finally, if each 3-hyperedge is allowed to fail with some probability [20], our hypergraph construction reduces the probability of failure because there are fewer 3-hyperedges to union bound over.

1.3 Other related work

If cryptography is used, consensus is possible in the synchronous model when $n > 2f$ [18, 31]. Whereas consensus cannot be solved in the asynchronous model [19], the $n > 3f$ bound applies in this model when using randomized algorithms that terminate almost surely [9] or with probability $1 - \varepsilon$ for fixed $\varepsilon > 0$ [28], even if cryptography is used [18]. The same bound also applies in partially synchronous models [18].

Partial broadcast was first considered by Franklin, Wright, and Yung [22, 23] in the context of secure point-to-point communication over an incomplete network. Stronger primitives based on trusted subsystems and cryptography have also been used, such as *weak sequenced broadcast* [1] to solve weak Byzantine agreement in the asynchronous model, and *append-only log* [12] and *trusted incrementer* [32] to solve Byzantine agreement in a partially synchronous model. These primitives achieve resilience $n > 2f$.

We mention two other lines of work that are related to ours. The first considers hybrid fault models that combine Byzantine and crash failures (*e.g.*, [25, 30]), in which optimal bounds on resilience [25, 30] depend on the number of faults of each type. The second considers a non-threshold adversary characterized by an *adversary structure* (*e.g.*, [5, 21]), or a monotone set of subsets of processors any one of which may be faulty. It is known [21] that Byzantine agreement is possible if and only if no three sets cover all processors.

2. PROBLEM DEFINITION AND AN EQUIVALENCE

We model a system of n processors as a 3-uniform, n-vertex hypergraph $H = (V, E)$ where each edge $(x, y, z) \in E$ represents a partial broadcast channel. For a fixed integer f, we analyze the conditions under which Byzantine agreement is possible in H, when up to f processors are faulty. As in prior work [38], we assume the underlying graph is at least $(2f + 1)$-connected (*e.g.*, via a complete set of 2-hyperedges (edges) connecting the processors). As explained in Section 1.2, this problem is equivalent to ensuring that in the intersection of any two size-$(n - f)$ quorums S and T, there exists a node z that cannot equivocate between correct nodes $x \in S, y \in T$. We assume w.l.o.g. that $S \cap T$ contains only faulty nodes, because a correct node in $S \cap T$ would prevent equivocation.

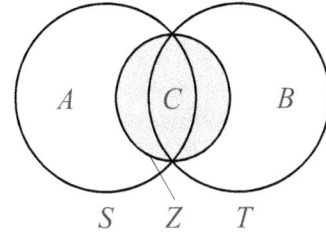

Figure 1: The relationship between sets S, T, Z of f-tolerance and sets A, B, C of h-disjointness. Shaded regions contain faulty nodes. The diagram above shows $C \subset Z$, but in general $C \subseteq Z$.

This reduces the possibility of Byzantine agreement to the following property of H.

Definition 1. *A 3-uniform hypergraph $H = (V, E)$ with $|V| = n$ vertices is f-tolerant if $\forall S, T, Z \subset V$ and $S \neq T$ satisfying the conditions below, $\exists x \in S \setminus Z, y \in T \setminus Z, z \in S \cap T$ for which $(x, y, z) \in E$:*

- $|Z| \leq f$,
- $|S|, |T| \geq n - f$,
- $S \cap T \subseteq Z \subset S \cup T$.

The property as defined is somewhat unwieldy, because the sets S, T, and Z can overlap in a variety of ways. To simplify our problem statement, we introduce a new property on disjoint sets and show its equivalence. Consider the sets $A = S \setminus Z$, $B = T \setminus Z$, and $C = S \cap T$; A, B, and C are disjoint because $S \cap T \subseteq Z$. A and B contain the correct nodes in quorums S and T, respectively, and C contains the faulty nodes in their intersection. (There may be other faulty nodes in the two quorums, limiting the size of A and B, but only in sum.) We will shortly redefine f-tolerance in terms of the following notion.

Definition 2. *A 3-uniform hypergraph $H = (V, E)$ with $|V| = n$ vertices is h-disjoint if for all disjoint $A, B, C \subset V$ satisfying the conditions below, $\exists x \in A, y \in B, z \in C$ for which $(x, y, z) \in E$:*

- $|A|, |B|, |C| \geq h$,
- $|A| + |B| + |C| \geq \frac{n+3h}{2}$.

Figure 1 illustrates the equivalence of f-tolerance and h-disjointness. Note that although A, B, and C are symmetric in the above definition, we will often distinguish them as in Figure 1 for ease of exposition. The following theorem makes this equivalence precise, with proof deferred to the full version:

Theorem 2. *Let H be a 3-uniform hypergraph on n vertices, and integer $f \geq \frac{n}{3}$. Then H is f-tolerant if and only if H is $(n - 2f)$-disjoint.*

h-disjointness is equivalent to the notion of $(3, f)$-hyper-$(3f - n + 1)$-connectedness in [38]. However, we find our definition to be simpler and more clearly related to the hypergraph coloring literature, discussed below. The remainder of this paper characterizes the hypergraphs that are h-disjoint by deriving tight bounds on the necessary and sufficient number of edges, $T_n(h)$ and $U_n(h)$ respectively. As we observed in Section 1.2, these results imply new upper and lower bounds for Byzantine agreement in different models. We start with $T_n(h)$:

Definition 3. *For positive integers n and h, $T_n(h)$ is the minimum m such that there exists an h-disjoint 3-uniform hypergraph with m edges.*

2.1 Related Combinatorial Problems

h-disjointness can be seen as a generalization of a rich body of work on *mixed hypergraph coloring* and *the upper chromatic number* (see Voloshin's book [42]). We present a single definition that essentially captures all of these concepts. A *k-heterochromatic coloring* of a hypergraph $H = (V, E)$ is a surjection $\chi : V \to [k]$ such that the restriction of χ to some $e \in E$ is injective. In other words, some edge has no repeated color. When H is k-uniform, this is equivalent to some edge being k-chromatic, as in h-disjointness.

A primary line of research in this area sought to analyze $f(n, k)$, the minimum number of edges among k-heterochromatically colorable, k-uniform, n-vertex hypergraphs [6, 7, 10, 17, 41], which was recently resolved up to lower order terms by Bujtás and Tuza [10]. The specific (earlier) result that is relevant to this paper is $f(n, 3) = \frac{n(n-2)}{3}$. h-disjointness has immediate connections to $f(n, 3)$, but introduces the additional concepts of *balance* and *partiality* in colorings, controlled by h. When $h = 1$, h-disjointness is equivalent to the condition that there is a trichromatic edge for all *small partial* colorings A, B, C, with $|A|, |B|, |C|$ non-empty, but total size only $|A| + |B| + |C| = (n+3)/2$. This condition is strictly stronger than requiring all complete colorings to have a trichromatic edge, because every complete coloring contains a small partial coloring. In contrast, when $h = f = n/3$, h-disjointness is equivalent to the condition that there is a trichromatic edge for all *balanced complete* colorings, with $|A| = |B| = |C| = n/3$. This is strictly weaker than restricting all complete colorings to have a trichromatic edge. For $1 < h < n/3$ the condition will be that all somewhat small, somewhat balanced colorings have a trichromatic edge.

Thus we may already state that $T_n(1) \geq f(n, 3) = \frac{n(n-2)}{3}$ and $T_n(n/3) \leq f(n, 3) = \frac{n(n-2)}{3}$. As we will see, we can in fact do much better and show a smooth transition $T_n(h) = \Theta\left(\frac{n^3}{h(n)^2}\right)$. In particular, this gives $T_n(1) = \Theta(n^3)$, and $T_n(n/3) = \Theta(n)$, both a factor of n from $f(n, 3)$.

3. LOWER BOUNDS

In this section, we will give asymptotically tight bounds on $T_n(h(n))$ for all non-decreasing functions $h(n)$. We will need the following notion of a hypergraph-projection.

Definition 4. *Let $H = (V, E)$ be a 3-uniform hypergraph, and $W \subseteq V$ a subset of its vertices. We define the* projection of H by W *as the* **graph** $H_W = (V_W, E_W)$. *The vertex set V_W is defined as $V \setminus W$. The edge set E_W has an edge (u, v) if and only if E has an edge (u, v, w), for some $w \in W$.*

This definition allows us to apply graph-theoretic theorems to hypergraphs, with potentially little loss. We extend the technique of [40], [7], [16], used to prove the aforementioned lower bound on k-heterochromatically colorable hypergraphs. They consider a hypergraph H for which every k-coloring contains a k-chromatic hyperedge, and proceed to lower bound the size of its edge set in two steps. First, they lower bound the number of edges in the projection of H by each $(k-2)$-vertex subset. Then, they upper bound the number of possible edge-projections of each hyperedge, giving a lower bound on the number of original hyperedges.

Our analysis is similar, with an added layer of complexity in lower bounding the number of edges in each projection. Because $h(n)$-disjointness implies that hyperedges cross somewhat balanced partitions of subsets of the vertices, we cannot assume that the projections are connected graphs. For large $h(n)$, we can only assume

very weak conditions on the projections' connectivity. For small $h(n)$, we can assume conditions even stronger than connectedness. To address this, we prove a pair of results on the number of edges in a simple graph having appropriate connectivity conditions.

3.1 Linear $h(n)$

We first consider the regime in which $h(n)$ is linear in n. In fact, the bound we derive below holds for all legitimate $h(n)$, but it is asymptotically optimal only for linear $h(n)$. In the subsequent subsection, we will give a bound that holds for a smaller range of $h(n)$, but is asymptotically optimal for sublinear $h(n)$.

Theorem 3. *For any positive $h(n)$ that is bounded above everywhere by $\frac{n}{3}$,*

$$T_n(h(n)) \geq \frac{3}{4}n(1 - o(1)).$$

PROOF. Let $H = (V, E)$ be a 3-uniform hypergraph on n vertices. Consider a coloring A, B, C of V, for which $|C| \leq n/3$. To satisfy $h(n)$-disjointness, H must contain a hyperedge that is trichromatic in A, B, C. In particular, for any bisection $(S, \bar{S})$ of $V \setminus C$, there is an edge in H_C crossing $(S, \bar{S})$. We will use the following lemma, with proof deferred to the full version.

Lemma 4. *For **graph** $G = (V, E)$, $|V| = n$, if all bisections are crossed by at least one edge, then $|E| \geq n/2$.*

To apply Lemma 4, observe that since $|V_C| \geq 2n/3$, we have $|E_C| \geq n/3$. Now we sum over all $|C| = n/3$.

$$\sum_{\substack{C \subset V \\ |C| = n/3}} |E_C| \geq \binom{n}{n/3} n/3. \tag{1}$$

In order to turn this into a bound on $|E|$, we need to upper bound the extent to which hyperedges in E are overcounted in (1). A hyperedge in E induces a (single) edge in E_C only if one of its vertices is in C, and two of them are not. For a given hyperedge in E, there are three possible vertices that could be in C. Conditioned on that vertex being in C, and the two other vertices being outside C, there are at most $\binom{n-3}{n/3-1}$ ways to choose the remaining vertices of C. Hence each edge in E contributes 1 to $|E_C|$ for at most $3 \cdot \binom{n-3}{n/3-1}$ distinct C.

Dividing out the maximum contribution of each edge gives our desired lowered bound:

$$
\begin{aligned}
|E| &\geq \frac{\binom{n}{n/3} n/3}{3 \cdot \binom{n-3}{n/3-1}} \\
&= \frac{n!(n)(n/3-1)!(2n/3-2)!}{9(n-3)!(n/3)!(2n/3)!} \\
&= \frac{(n-1)(n-2)}{4n/3-2} \\
&= \frac{3}{4}n(1 - o(1)).
\end{aligned}
$$

$\square$

3.2 Sublinear $h(n)$

Theorem 5. *For any function $h(n)$ that is bounded above everywhere by $\frac{n}{6}$,*

$$T_n(h(n)) \geq \Omega_n\left(\frac{n^3}{h(n)^2}\right).$$

PROOF. First we will need a (weakened) generalization of Lemma 4.

Definition 5. *Let $G = (V,E)$ be a graph on n vertices. For integers a,b, we say that G is (a,b)-crossing if for all disjoint $X, Y \subseteq V$ such that $|X| = a$ and $|Y| = b$, there is an edge from X to Y. (That is, $\exists x \in X, y \in Y : (x,y) \in E$.)*

Lemma 6. *For positive $i \leq n/2$, every $(i, n/2)$-crossing graph on n vertices has at least $\frac{n^2}{2(n-i)} \left(\frac{n}{2i} - 1 \right)$ edges.*

PROOF. Note that the bound is vacuous for $i = n/2$, so assume $i \leq n/2 - 1$. First observe that every subset of size i must have at least $n/2 - i + 1$ edges leaving it. This can be seen by contradiction: assume that some set X of size i has at most $n/2 - i$ edges leaving it, and hence at most $n/2 - i$ vertices in its neighborhood. Then take as Y the set of vertices in $V \setminus X$ with no edge to X. This set is of size at least $n - |X| - (n/2 - i) = n/2$. Since there is no edge from X to Y, the graph cannot be $(i, n/2)$-crossing.

We now show that the lemma in fact holds for any graph having the above boundary property. There are $\binom{n}{i}$ vertex sets of size i. We count at least $n/2 - i + 1$ edges out of each set. Each edge can only be counted for the sets that it leaves; there are $2\binom{n-2}{i-1}$ of these, because we must choose one of the two vertices, not choose the other one, and choose $i - 1$ other vertices. Hence, the total number of edges is at least

$$\frac{\binom{n}{i}}{2\binom{n-2}{i-1}} (n/2 - i + 1) = \frac{n!(i-1)!(n-i-1)!}{2i!(n-i)!(n-2)!} (n/2 - i + 1)$$

$$= \frac{n(n-1)}{2i(n-i)} (n/2 - i + 1)$$

$$= \frac{n}{2(n-i)} \left((n-1)\left(\frac{n}{2i} - 1 \right) + \frac{n-1}{i} \right)$$

$$> \frac{n}{2(n-i)} \left((n-1)\left(\frac{n}{2i} - 1 \right) + \frac{n}{2i} - 1 \right)$$

$$= \frac{n^2}{2(n-i)} \left(\frac{n}{2i} - 1 \right).$$

Now consider an $h(n)$-disjoint hypergraph $H = (V,E)$ on n vertices. For convenience, let $h = h(n)$. Since H is h-disjoint, there must exist a hyperedge for every A, B, C satisfying the conditions of Definition 2. In particular, consider a $C \subseteq V$ of size $|C| = h$. As in Section 3.1, we will show that the graph projection of H by C has many edges.

For $C \subseteq V$ having size $|C| = h$, let $G_C = (V_C, E_C)$ be the projection of H by C. We bound the size of each $|E_C|$. H is h-disjoint, so for any disjoint $A, B \subseteq V \setminus C$ such that $|A|, |B| \geq h$ and $|A| + |B| \geq \frac{n+3h}{2} - h = \frac{n+h}{2}$, there exists an edge $(x,y,z) \in E$ with $x \in A, y \in B, z \in C$. In other words, graph G_C has the following property: for $D \subseteq V_C$ with $|D| \geq \frac{n+h}{2}$, for all $A \subseteq D, B = D \setminus A$ with $|A|, |B| \geq h$, there is an edge in E_C from A to B.

When $h = 1$, the above says that each subset of V_C of size $\frac{n+1}{2}$ is connected. In generality, we would like to lower bound the number of edges in $|E_C|$, which we can do with Lemma 6. First let $n' = |V_C|$, so $n' = n - h$. Observe that G_C is $(h, n'/2)$-crossing, by choosing A as any set of size h, B as any disjoint set of size $\frac{n'}{2}$, and $D = A \cup B$, so that $|D| = |A| + |B| = h + \frac{n'}{2} = h + \frac{n-h}{2} = \frac{n+h}{2}$. Hence $|E_C| \geq \frac{n'^2}{2(n'-h)} \left(\frac{n'}{2h} - 1 \right)$.

Now we must bound the extent to which each hyperedge is overcounted. A hyperedge can only be counted towards a given E_C if

exactly one of its vertices is contained in C. There are then $\binom{n-3}{h-1}$ ways to choose the rest of the vertices. So each hyperedge contributes to $|E_C|$ for at most $3\binom{n-3}{h-1}$ values of C.

There are exactly $\binom{n}{h}$ sets C. Hence the total number of edges in H must be at least

$$|E| \geq \frac{\binom{n}{h}}{3\binom{n-3}{h-1}} \left(\frac{n'^2}{2(n'-h)} \right) \left(\frac{n'}{2h} - 1 \right).$$

We have assumed that $h \leq n/6$, so $\frac{3}{2} \leq \frac{n}{4h}$ and hence

$$\frac{n'}{2h} - 1 = \frac{n-h}{2h} - 1 = \frac{n}{2h} - \frac{3}{2} \geq \frac{n}{4h}.$$

Similarly,

$$\frac{n'^2}{2(n'-h)} = \frac{(n-h)^2}{2(n-2h)} \geq \frac{(n-(n/6))^2}{2(n-2)} = \frac{25n^2}{72(n-2)}.$$

Then

$$|E| \geq \frac{\binom{n}{h}}{3\binom{n-3}{h-1}} \left(\frac{25n^3}{288h(n-2)} \right)$$

$$= \frac{n!(h-1)!(n-2-h)!}{3h!(n-3)!(n-h)!} \left(\frac{25n^3}{288h(n-2)} \right)$$

$$\geq \frac{25n^4}{864h^2(n-2)} = \Omega\left(\frac{n^3}{h^2} \right).$$

4. UPPER BOUNDS

In this section, we give an asymptotically tight upper bound on $T_n(h(n))$ for almost all n, and all $1 \leq h(n) \leq n/3$. We do this by constructing near-Ramanujan expander graphs and converting them to "lifted" hypergraphs with expander-like properties. Our construction hence depends on the existence of sufficiently good expanders. These are probabilistically guaranteed to exist for all n; recall, however, that we are primarily interested in explicit constructions. Our result is fully constructive, with the exception that it relies on expander graphs that can be explicitly constructed for an infinite but incomplete set of values of n. As such, our result is only fully constructive for these n, which we do not consider a substantial weakness. To 'fill in the missing values' would require advances in explicit expander construction, which would immediately imply corresponding extensions of our algorithm.

Much of the difficulty of our analysis comes in explicitly bounding the degree. This is necessary to achieve an eigenvalue gap that can guarantee edges are well-distributed enough to induce a hyperedge across all "reasonable" colorings.

In what follows, an *algebraic* (n, d, λ)-*expander* will refer to an n-vertex, d-regular graph whose adjacency matrix has $\max(|\lambda_2|, |\lambda_n|) = \lambda$, where $\lambda_1 \geq \ldots \geq \lambda_n$ are the matrix eigenvalues.

Definition 6. *For graph $G = (V,E)$, we define a lifted 3-uniform hypergraph $L(G) = (V, E')$ as follows. The edge set E' contains (x,y,z) if and only if at least two of the edges (x,y), (y,z), and (x,z) are present in G.*

In other words, for a given vertex x in G, we make hyperedges out of x and every pair of its neighbors. We claim that for an (n, d, λ)-expander G with the right parameters, hypergraph $H = L(G)$ is $h(n)$-disjoint and has a number of edges given by:

Theorem 7. $T_n(h(n)) \leq O\left(\frac{n^3}{h(n)^2}\right)$.

PROOF. We construct a lifted 3-uniform hypergraph $H = L(G)$, where G is an (n,d,λ)-expander. Our goal is to determine the minimum λ such that H is $h(n)$-disjoint, as a function of d. Then using an expander G for which an upper bound on λ is known, we can derive a sufficient lower bound on d and hence the number of hyperedges in H.

To demonstrate $h(n)$-disjointness, we consider each partial 3-coloring A, B, C satisfying the conditions of Definition 2, and show that H contains a trichromatic edge for each such coloring. By the construction of H, it suffices to show that some set of vertices in C has edges in G to both A and B. Our main tool will be the Expander Mixing Lemma, which states that if $G = (V, E)$ is an (n,d,λ)-expander, then for any $S, T \subseteq V$, $\left| |E(S,T)| - \frac{d|S| \cdot |T|}{n} \right| \leq \lambda \sqrt{|S| \cdot |T|}$. Additionally, we will need the following variant of the expander mixing lemma. We have not found this precise lemma in the literature, so we give a proof of it below.

Lemma 8 (Expander Vertex-Boundary Lemma). *Let $G = (V, E)$ be an (n,d,λ)-expander. Then for any sets $S, T \subseteq V$,*

$$|S \cap N(T)| \geq |S| - \frac{2\lambda n}{d}\sqrt{\frac{|S|}{|T|}},$$

where $N(T)$ is the set of vertices having a neighbor in T.

PROOF. The intuition is that if S is large, then the subset of S with edges to T cannot be small, because by the expander mixing lemma, a small set would have a small number of edges to T, but S must have a large number of edges to T. Let $S_T = S \cap N(T)$ and $s = |S|, t = |T|, s_T = |S_T|$. Then by definition $E(S,T) = E(S_T, T)$. By the expander mixing lemma, we have:

$$|E(S,T)| \geq \frac{d}{n}st - \lambda\sqrt{st} \quad \text{and} \quad |E(S_T,T)| \leq \frac{d}{n}s_T t + \lambda\sqrt{s_T t}.$$

Combining the inequalities and solving for s_T gives:

$$
\begin{aligned}
s_T &\geq s - \lambda\frac{n}{d\sqrt{t}}(\sqrt{s} + \sqrt{s_T}) \\
&\geq s - \frac{2\lambda n}{d}\sqrt{s/t},
\end{aligned}
$$

where the last inequality follows because $s_T \leq s$. $\qquad\square$

Using these tools, we prove the following main lemma:

Lemma 9. *Let $A, B, C \subseteq V$ be colors of sizes $a \leq b \leq c$, respectively, of the vertices of $H = L(G)$. Define $\mathscr{F}(a,b,c) = \sqrt{\frac{cb}{a}}\left(\sqrt{a+b} - \sqrt{b}\right)$. If*

$$\lambda < \frac{d}{n}\mathscr{F}(a,b,c),$$

then H contains a trichromatic edge.

Before proving the lemma, we show how it implies the theorem. By picking a G with $\lambda < \frac{d}{n}\mathscr{F}(a,b,c)$, we ensure that H contains a trichromatic edge for all colorings A, B, C. But the conditions of h-disjointness do not require all colorings to have this property, and in particular we can show:

Claim 10. *For $a \leq b \leq c$ satisfying the conditions of Definition 2, $\mathscr{F}(a,b,c) \geq k\sqrt{h(n-h)}$ for a fixed constant $k > 0$.*

PROOF. We wish to show that:

$$\sqrt{\frac{cb}{a}}\left(\sqrt{a+b} - \sqrt{b}\right) \geq k\sqrt{n(n-h)}$$

for some constant $k > 0$. To do this, we will show that $\sqrt{c} \geq k_1\sqrt{n-h}$ and $\sqrt{\frac{b}{a}}\left(\sqrt{a+b} - \sqrt{b}\right) \geq k_2\sqrt{h}$ for constants $k_1, k_2 > 0$, from which the theorem follows (with $k = k_1 k_2$) because the LHS and RHS are non-negative in both inequalities. The conditions $a \leq b \leq c$ and $a+b+c = \frac{n+3h}{2}$ imply that $c \geq \frac{1}{3}\left(\frac{n+3h}{2}\right)$. Since both sides are positive, we have:

$$\sqrt{c} \geq \sqrt{\frac{1}{6}(n+3h)} > \sqrt{\frac{1}{6}(n-h)} = k_1\sqrt{n-h}$$

for $k_1 = \sqrt{\frac{1}{6}}$.

To lower bound the $\sqrt{\frac{b}{a}}\left(\sqrt{a+b} - \sqrt{b}\right)$ expression, we relax the $c \geq b$ and $a+b+c = \frac{n+3h}{2}$ constraints, and leave only the constraints $b \geq a$ and $a \geq h$. Now, since $a, b > 0$, we have for fixed a:

$$
\begin{aligned}
\frac{d}{db}\left(\sqrt{\frac{b}{a}}\left(\sqrt{a+b} - \sqrt{b}\right)\right) &= \frac{d}{db}\left(\sqrt{\frac{b^2}{a} + b} - \frac{b}{\sqrt{a}}\right) \\
&= \frac{\frac{2b}{a} + 1}{2\sqrt{\frac{b^2}{a} + b}} - \frac{1}{\sqrt{a}} \\
&= \frac{2 + \frac{a}{b}}{2\sqrt{a}\sqrt{1 + \frac{a}{b}}} - \frac{1}{\sqrt{a}} \\
&= \frac{2 + \frac{a}{b} - 2\sqrt{1 + \frac{a}{b}}}{2\sqrt{a}\sqrt{1 + \frac{a}{b}}} \\
&= \frac{\left(1 - \sqrt{1 + \frac{a}{b}}\right)^2}{2\sqrt{a}\sqrt{1 + \frac{a}{b}}}
\end{aligned}
$$

which is always positive, indicating that the function is monotonically increasing in b. Thus in order to minimize the function for fixed a, we choose b as small as possible, namely $b = a$. This gives:

$$\sqrt{\frac{b}{a}}\left(\sqrt{a+b} - \sqrt{b}\right) \geq \left(\sqrt{2} - 1\right)\sqrt{a} \geq k_2\sqrt{h(n)}$$

for $k_2 = \sqrt{2} - 1$. Thus the claim holds for $k = k_1 k_2 = \frac{\sqrt{2}-1}{\sqrt{6}}$. $\qquad\square$

Thus it suffices to construct a G with $\lambda < \frac{dk}{n}\sqrt{h(n-h)}$. A Ramanujan graph has $\lambda \leq 2\sqrt{d-1} < 2\sqrt{d}$ and hence can be used if $2\sqrt{d} < \frac{dk}{n}\sqrt{h(n-h)}$. Rearranging gives $d > \frac{4n^2}{k^2 h(n-h)}$, which is satisfied if $d > \frac{6n}{k^2 h}$, since $h \leq n/3$. That is, if G is Ramanujan with $d = \Theta\left(\frac{n}{h}\right)$, then $H = L(G)$ is h-disjoint. Since H has a hyperedge for every pair of edges from a given vertex in G, H has maximum degree $O\left(\frac{n^2}{h^2}\right)$ and thus at most $O\left(\frac{n^3}{h^2}\right)$ hyperedges.

To prove the bound, it suffices to assert the existence of Ramanujan graphs for every n and d. In fact, a much stronger theorem holds: for every $\varepsilon > 0$ and even $d \geq 4$, a random d-regular graph on n vertices satisfies $\lambda \leq 2\sqrt{d-1} + \varepsilon$ with high probability [24]. Both ε and the requirement that d be even have an insubstantial effect on the final number of edges. $\qquad\square$

We now give a proof of the main lemma. The idea is to first apply the expander vertex-boundary lemma to A and C, then the expander

314

mixing lemma to B and the subset of C with neighbors in A. In so doing, we certify that A contains a vertex with edges to both B and C, in G. By the definition of a lifted hypergraph, this ensures that H contains a hyperedge crossing all three colors. Since we show this for arbitrary A,B,C satisfying the size bounds of Definition 2, this verifies the h-disjointness of H.

PROOF OF LEMMA 9. Let $C_A = C \cap N(A)$ and $a = |A|, b = |B|$, $c = |C|, c_A = |C_A|$. By Lemma 8,

$$c_A \geq c - \frac{2\lambda n}{d}\sqrt{\frac{c}{a}}. \qquad (2)$$

To prove the existence of a trichromatic edge in H, it suffices to show that $|E_G(C_A, B)| > 0$. By the expander mixing lemma,

$$|E_G(C_A, B)| \geq \frac{dbc_A}{n} - \lambda\sqrt{bc_A}.$$

Hence there exists an edge from C_A to B when $\frac{dbc_A}{n} > \lambda\sqrt{bc_A}$, which is equivalent to $c_A > \frac{\lambda^2 n^2}{bd^2}$, because all variables are non-negative. Substituting c_A with (2) and solving gives $\frac{n^2}{bd^2}\lambda^2 + \frac{2n}{d}\sqrt{\frac{c}{a}}\lambda - c < 0$. By the quadratic equation, this is equivalent to

$$\left(\lambda - \frac{\sqrt{c}bd}{n}\left(\sqrt{\frac{1}{b} + \frac{1}{a}} - \sqrt{\frac{1}{a}}\right)\right) \cdot$$
$$\left(\lambda + \frac{\sqrt{c}bd}{n}\left(\sqrt{\frac{1}{b} + \frac{1}{a}} + \sqrt{\frac{1}{a}}\right)\right) < 0.$$

Because λ is positive, the LHS is negative when the first term is negative. Thus we need:

$$\lambda < \frac{\sqrt{c}bd}{n}\left(\sqrt{\frac{1}{b} + \frac{1}{a}} - \sqrt{\frac{1}{a}}\right)$$
$$= \frac{\sqrt{c}bd}{n}\frac{\sqrt{a+b} - \sqrt{b}}{\sqrt{ab}}$$
$$= \frac{d}{n}\sqrt{\frac{cb}{a}}\left(\sqrt{a+b} - \sqrt{b}\right).$$

This concludes the proof of the lemma, and hence of Theorem 7. □

We also give a (slightly less general) explicit construction of such hypergraphs.

Theorem 11. *There is an algorithm that, for an infinite number of integers n, and any $h(n)$ bounded above by $n/3$, efficiently constructs an $h(n)$-disjoint, n-disjoint hypergraph with $O\left(\frac{n^3}{h(n)^2}\right)$ hyperedges.*

In other words, by applying an explicit Ramanujan construction, we constructively achieve the result of Theorem 7, for an infinite number of values of n.

PROOF. Extending the classic works of Lubotzky-Phillips-Sarnak [33], Margulis [35], and Morgenstern [36] on explicit constructions of Ramanujan graphs, Cioabă and Murty [13] give a construction that comes very close to the Ramanujan bound for nearly any graph size and degree.

Theorem 12 (Cioabă and Murty [13]). *Let $d \in \mathbb{Z}^+$ be such that $d - 1$ is composite. For any positive ε, there exists an infinite sequence of graphs $\{G_i\}_{i=0}^{\infty}$ such that G_i is an $(n_i, d, (2+\varepsilon)\sqrt{d-1})$-expander, and $n_i > n_{i-1} \ \forall \ i > 0$.*

Recall that Lemma 9 and Claim 10 together imply it suffices to construct an (n, d, λ)-expander G, where $\lambda < \frac{dk}{n}\sqrt{h(n)(n-h(n))}$ for a fixed k.

Pick $d = \frac{2(2+\varepsilon)^2 n}{k^2 h(n)}$. Then [13] gives an algorithm to construct (n, d, λ)-expanders with $\lambda = \frac{(2+\varepsilon)^2}{k}\sqrt{\frac{2n}{h(n)}}$. Then observe:

$$\frac{dk}{n}\sqrt{h(n)(n-h(n))} = \frac{2(2+\varepsilon)^2 nk}{k^2 h(n)n}\sqrt{h(n)(n-h(n))}$$
$$\geq \frac{2(2+\varepsilon)^2}{k}\sqrt{\frac{n(2/3)}{h(n)}}$$
$$> \frac{(2+\varepsilon)^2}{k}\sqrt{\frac{2n}{h(n)}} = \lambda,$$

proving the theorem. □

5. A SUFFICIENCY CONDITION FOR h-DISJOINTNESS

In this section we consider a complementary question to that of the previous sections. Namely: how many hyperedges are necessary to ensure that *every* 3-uniform hypergraph of that size is $h(n)$-disjoint? Equivalently, what is the densest 3-uniform hypergraph that is *not* $h(n)$-disjoint? This question is relevant in practice, as it may be impossible in some systems to implement the set of 3-hyperedges exactly. The theorem below gives guarantees on reliability in such an oblivious setting.

Definition 7. *For integer $h \leq n/3$, the sufficiency number $U_n(h)$ is the minimum integer such that, for a 3-uniform hypergraph $H = (V, E)$ on n vertices, $|E| \geq U_n(h)$ implies that H is h-disjoint.*

Theorem 13. *For $h \leq n/3$,*

$$U_n(h) = \binom{n}{3} - \frac{n-h}{2} \cdot h^2 + 1.$$

In other words, $\frac{n-h}{2} \cdot h^2$ is the minimum number of edges one can remove from the complete 3-uniform n-vertex hypergraph, in order to ensure it is not h-disjoint.

PROOF. Let $H = (V, E)$ be an n-vertex 3-uniform hypergraph that is not h-disjoint. By definition, there must be some partial coloring A, B, C of the vertices with $a = |A|, b = |B|, c = |C|$, such that there is no edge crossing A, B, C, and moreover $a, b, c \geq h$ and $a + b + c \geq \frac{n+3h}{2}$. For any 3-coloring, the complete 3-uniform hypergraph contains exactly abc crossing hyperedges. Hence for some a, b, c having the properties above, abc is the smallest number of edges that can be removed from the complete graph to make it not h-disjoint.

Claim 14. *For integers $a, b, c \geq h$ such that $a + b + c \geq \frac{n+3h}{2}$, abc is minimized by taking $a = h, b = h, c = \frac{n-h}{2}$.*

PROOF. We will assume for the proof that $n \equiv h \pmod 2$. The second case is proved similarly.

First note that since $a + b + c \geq \frac{n+3h}{2}$, abc is minimized by taking $a + b + c = \frac{n+3h}{2}$. Decreasing the sum can always decrease the product. Hence, we may assume w.l.o.g. that $c = \frac{n+3h}{2} - a - b$, and minimize $g(a,b) = ab\left(\frac{n+3h}{2} - a - b\right)$. This gives the following optimization problem, for arbitrary n and h:

minimize $\quad g(a,b)$

subject to $\quad a \geq h, \qquad b \geq h, \qquad a + b \leq \dfrac{n+h}{2}$

The constraints are linear and hence define halfspaces in the (a,b)-plane. These halfspaces define P, a polytope (triangle) in which the solution must lie. In particular, the optimal solution must either be a global minimum of $g(a,b)$ (and hence a root of the gradient); a minimum along one of the faces of the polytope; or a vertex of the polytope. We check each case in turn.

Proposition 15. *The following three facts about the constrained optima of $g(a,b)$ hold.*

- *The gradient of g has a single root inside P, and it is a global maximum.*

- *The minimum value of g along the faces of P is $\dfrac{(n+h)^2}{16} h$.*

- *The minimum value of g at a vertex of P is $\dfrac{h^2(n-h)}{2}$.*

The proof of the proposition appears in the appendix. We now observe how it implies the theorem.

Comparison. There are only two possible minima in the polytope: $\frac{h(n+h)^2}{16}$ and $\frac{h^2(n-h)}{2}$. Observe that

$$
\begin{aligned}
\frac{(n+h)^2}{16} &= \frac{n^2 + h^2 + 2nh}{16} \\
&= \frac{(n^2 + 9h^2 - 6nh) - 8h^2 + 8nh}{16} \\
&= \frac{(n-3h)^2}{16} + \frac{h(n-h)}{2} \\
&\geq \frac{h(n-h)}{2}.
\end{aligned}
$$

Therefore $\frac{h(n+h)^2}{16} \geq \frac{h^2(n-h)}{2}$, so $\frac{h^2(n-h)}{2}$ is the minimum of the constrained $g(a,b)$. Recall that this was obtained by setting two faces to tight. In other words, set any two of a,b,c to h, and the other to $\frac{n-h}{2}$. $\qquad\square$

By the claim, removing $\frac{h^2(n-h)}{2}$ edges from the complete 3-uniform hypergraph ensures that a given valid coloring has no trichromatic edge. As a result, the hypergraph cannot be h-disjoint. Conversely, removing fewer edges cannot remove all the edges crossing any valid coloring. Hence $U_n(h) = \binom{n}{3} - \frac{n-h}{2} \cdot h^2 + 1$. This completes the proof of Theorem 13. $\qquad\square$

6. HARDNESS OF DECIDING h-DISJOINTNESS

In this section, we take a first step towards addressing algorithmic questions related to h-disjointness. In particular, given a 3-uniform hypergraph H, we would like to determine the minimum value $h_{opt}(n)$ such that H is $h_{opt}(n)$-disjoint, or barring this, an approximate value h that is as close to $h_{opt}(n)$ as possible. This question has practical value because it allows us to evaluate an existing hypergraph, or perhaps one constructed via the methods described in Section 4, for h-disjointness. Here we show that deciding whether H is h-disjoint is *co-NP*-complete.

Theorem 1 (restated). *Given a 3-uniform hypergraph $H = (V, E)$ with $|V| = n$, it is co-NP-complete to decide, for integers $h \leq n/3$, whether H is h-disjoint.*

PROOF. The complement problem to h-disjointness is that of finding a disjoint $A, B, C \subseteq V$ satisfying the conditions of Definition 2 such that $\forall x \in A, y \in B, z \in C$, it holds that $(x, y, z) \notin E$. A certificate for this problem is the sets A, B, C, and it can be verified in $O(|A||B||C|)$ time by checking that all hyperedges (x, y, z) are not in E. Since complement h-disjointness is in *NP*, it follows that h-disjointness is in *co-NP*.

We show that complement h-disjointness is *NP*-hard by a reduction from balanced bipartite independent set (BBIS), which is *NP*-complete [3]. Given a balanced bipartite graph $G(X \cup Y; E)$ with $|X| = |Y| = n/2$ and a positive integer t, the decision BBIS problem is to find sets $A \subseteq X$, $B \subseteq Y$ with $|A| = |B| = t$ with no edges between A and B. Given an instance of the BBIS problem, we construct an instance of complement h-disjointness as follows. Create an empty 3-uniform hypergraph H with $n' = n + (n-t)$ vertices, where the first n vertices represent the vertices of G. On the $n-t$ vertices, create a complete 3-uniform hypergraph Z. Add a hyperedge (u, v, w) for each pair of vertices $u, v \in Z$ and every $w \in G$. Add a hyperedge (u, v, w) for each pair of vertices $u, v \in X$ and every $w \in Z$; do the same for every pair of vertices $u, v \in Y$. Finally, add a hyperedge (u, v, w) for each *edge* $(u, v) \in G$ and every $w \in Z$. The input to the complement h-disjointness problem is the hypergraph H and the positive integer $h = t$.

Given a solution (A, B) with $|A| = |B| = t$ to BBIS, we claim that A, B, Z is a solution to complement h-disjointness. Since $t \leq |X| = |Y| = n/2$, it follows that $|Z| = n-t \geq t$, so all $|A|, |B|, |Z| \geq t$. Also, $|A| + |B| + |Z| = t + t + (n-t) = \frac{n + (n-t) + 3t}{2} = \frac{n' + 3t}{2}$. Now, for a hyperedge to cross the sets A, B, Z, there must be some $u \in A, v \in B, w \in Z$ such that $(u, v, w) \in H$. By our construction, all but one type of hyperedge in H involve vertices in at most two of the sets $A \subseteq X$, $B \subseteq Y$, and Z. The exception are hyperedges (u, v, w) where $(u, v) \in G$ and $w \in Z$. But since there are no edges crossing A, B, there is no hyperedge that crosses A, B, Z. Thus A, B, Z is a solution to complement h-disjointness.

In the reverse direction, suppose we have a solution A, B, C to complement h-disjointness. Since $|A| + |B| + |C| \geq \frac{n' + 3t}{2} = n + t$, some vertices in Z must appear in the sets A, B, C. We claim that these vertices must appear in exactly one set. This is because if Z appears in all three sets, then there would exist a hyperedge crossing all three sets, since Z is a complete 3-uniform hypergraph. Similarly, Z cannot appear in exactly two sets, because then there would exist a hyperedge connecting two vertices of Z (one in each set) and a vertex in the third set (a vertex in G), also by our construction. Thus Z participates in exactly one set; assume w.l.o.g. that this set is C. We now claim that the vertices in X appear in at most two sets, and if they appear in two sets, one of those sets must be C. If X appears in both A and B, then there would exist a hyperedge connecting two vertices of X (one in each set) to a vertex of C, because C contains at least some vertices of Z by our argument above. Therefore, X appears in either A or B, but not both. The same argument shows that this is also true of Y. Combining these arguments with the fact that A, B, C are non-empty, it follows that the vertices of X and Y are split across A, B (though they may appear together in C). Since Z appears in C, A and B consist entirely of vertices in G. Finally, the same argument used in the forward direction above shows that there cannot exist an edge $(u, v) \in G$ between A and B, since then there would exist a hyperedge (u, v, w) to a vertex $w \in Z$ in C. Thus, since $|A|, |B| \geq t$, we can remove excess vertices so that $|A| = |B| = t$ and the resulting sets are a solution to BBIS. $\qquad\square$

7. CONCLUSIONS & OPEN PROBLEMS

This paper studies the price of equivocation in distributed systems. Our tight bounds on the number of 3-processor partial broadcast channels required for Byzantine agreement describe the amount of equivocation a system can tolerate for a given level of redundancy. Our results thus capture the *equivocation vs. redundancy trade-off*, an important metric in the cost-benefit analysis of a fault-tolerant system.

Several interesting theoretical questions remain. For example, given the hardness of deciding a system's resilience (h-disjointness) based on its partial broadcast channels, we are interested in approximation algorithms for this value. We would also like to understand the combinatorial properties of h-disjointness in greater depth. Can it be shown that h-disjoint hypergraphs *must* fundamentally be built on an underlying expander? How do our definitions and results scale to k-uniform hypergraphs, for $k > 3$?

On the practical side, it would be very interesting to find a realistic network that achieves h-disjointness naturally based on its broadcast (*e.g.*, network hub) and point-to-point (*e.g.*, network switch) connections, instead of constructing partial broadcast channels explicitly.

References

[1] I. Abraham, M. K. Aguilera, and D. Malkhi. Fast asynchronous consensus with optimal resilience. In *24th International Symposium on Distributed Computing (DISC)*, pages 4–19, 2010.

[2] A. S. Aiyer, L. Alvisi, A. Clement, M. Dahlin, J.-P. Martin, and C. Porth. BAR fault tolerance for cooperative services. In *20th Symposium on Operating Systems Principles (SOSP)*, pages 45–58, 2005.

[3] Alon, Duke, Lefmann, Rodl, and Yuster. The algorithmic aspects of the regularity lemma. *J. Algorithms*, 16, 1994.

[4] L. Alvisi, A. Clement, M. Dahlin, M. Marchetti, and E. Wong. Making Byzantine fault tolerant systems tolerate Byzantine faults. In *6th Symposium on Networked Systems Design and Implementation (NSDI)*, pages 153–168, 2009.

[5] S. Amitanand, I. Sanketh, K. Srinathant, V. Vinod, and C. P. Rangan. Distributed consensus in the presence of sectional faults. In *22nd Symposium on Principles of Distributed Computing (PODC)*, pages 202–210, 2003.

[6] J. L. Arocha and J. Tey. The size of minimum 3-trees. *J. Graph Theory*, 54(2):103–114, 2007.

[7] J. L. Arocha, J. Bracho, and V. Neumann-Lara. On the minimum size of tight hypergraphs. *J. Graph Theory*, 16(4): 319–326, 1992.

[8] G. Bracha. An asynchronous $\lceil(n-1)/3\rceil$-resilient consensus protocol. In *3rd Symposium on Principles of Distributed Computing (PODC)*, pages 154–162, 1984.

[9] G. Bracha and S. Toueg. Asynchronous consensus and broadcast protocols. *J. ACM*, 32(4):824–840, 1985.

[10] C. Bujtas and Z. Tuza. Smallest set-transversals of k-partitions. *Graph. Comb.*, 25:807–816, 2009.

[11] M. Castro. *Practical Byzantine Fault-Tolerance*. PhD thesis, Massachusetts Institute of Technology, 2000.

[12] B.-G. Chun, P. Maniatis, S. Shenker, and J. Kubiatowicz. Attested append-only memory: Making adversaries stick to their word. In *21st Symposium on Operating Systems Principles (SOSP)*, pages 189–204, 2007.

[13] S. M. Cioaba. *Eigenvalues, expanders and gaps between primes*. PhD thesis, Queen's University, 2005.

[14] J. Considine, M. Fitzi, M. K. Franklin, L. A. Levin, U. M. Maurer, and D. Metcalf. Byzantine agreement given partial broadcast. *J. Cryptology*, 18(3):191–217, 2005.

[15] J. Cowling, D. Myers, B. Liskov, R. Rodrigues, and L. Shrira. HQ replication: A hybrid quorum rotocol for Byzantine fault tolerance. In *7th Symposium on Operating Systems Design and Implementation (OSDI)*, pages 177–190, 2006.

[16] K. Diao, P. Zhao, and H. Zhou. About the upper chromatic number of a co-hypergraph. *Discrete Math.*, 220:67–73, 2000.

[17] K. Diao, G. Liu, D. Rautenbach, and P. Zhao. A note on the least number of edges of 3-uniform hypergraphs with upper chromatic number 2. *Discrete Math.*, 306(7):670–672, 2006.

[18] C. Dwork, N. Lynch, and L. Stockmeyer. Consensus in the presence of partial synchrony. *J. ACM*, 35(2):288–323, 1988.

[19] M. J. Fischer, N. A. Lynch, and M. S. Paterson. Impossibility of distributed consensus with one faulty process. *J. ACM*, 32 (2):374–382, 1985.

[20] M. Fitzi and U. Maurer. From partial consistency to global broadcast. In *32nd Symposium on Theory of Computing (STOC)*, pages 494–503, 2000.

[21] M. Fitzi and U. M. Maurer. Efficient byzantine agreement secure against general adversaries. In *12th International Symposium on Distributed Computing (DISC)*, pages 134–148, 1998.

[22] M. Franklin and M. Yung. Secure hypergraphs: Privacy from partial broadcast (extended abstract). In *27th Symposium on the Theory of Computing (STOC)*, pages 36–44, 1995.

[23] M. K. Franklin and R. N. Wright. Secure communications in minimal connectivity models. In *Advances in Cryptology (EUROCRYPT)*, pages 346–360, 1998.

[24] J. Friedman. A proof of Alon's second eigenvalue conjecture. In *35th Symposium on Theory of Computing (STOC)*, pages 720–724, 2003.

[25] J. A. Garay and K. J. Perry. A continuum of failure models for distributed computing. In *6th International Workshop on Distributed Algorithms (WDAG)*, pages 153–165, 1992.

[26] A. Haeberlen, P. Kouznetsov, and P. Druschel. Peerreview: practical accountability for distributed systems. In *21st Symposium on Operating Systems Principles (SOSP)*, pages 175–188, 2007.

[27] R. Kapitza, J. Behl, C. Cachin, T. Distler, S. Kuhnle, S. V. Mohammadi, W. Schröder-Preikschat, and K. Stengel. CheapBFT: resource-efficient byzantine fault tolerance. In *European Conference on Computer Systems (EuroSys)*, pages 295–308, 2012.

[28] A. Karlin and A. C. Yao. Probabilistic lower bounds for byzantine agreement and clock synchronization. Unpublished manuscript, 1984.

[29] R. Kotla, L. Alvisi, M. Dahlin, A. Clement, and E. Wong. Zyzzyva: Speculative Byzantine fault tolerance. In *21st Symposium on Operating Systems Principles (SOSP)*, pages 45–58, 2007.

[30] L. Lamport. Lower bounds for asynchronous consensus. In *Future Directions in Distributed Computing*, pages 22–23,

2003.

[31] L. Lamport, R. Shostak, and M. Pease. The Byzantine generals problem. *ACM Trans. Program. Lang. Syst.*, 4(3):382–401, 1982.

[32] D. Levin, J. R. Douceur, J. R. Lorch, and T. Moscibroda. TrInc: Small trusted hardware for large distributed systems. In *6th Symposium on Networked Systems Design and Implementation (NSDI)*, pages 1–14, 2009.

[33] A. Lubotzky, R. Phillips, and P. Sarnak. Ramanujan graphs. *Combinatorica*, 8(3):261–277, 1988.

[34] N. A. Lynch. *Distributed Algorithms*. Morgan Kaufmann, 1996.

[35] G. A. Margulis. Explicit group-theoretical constructions of combinatorial schemes and their application to the design of expanders and concentrators. *Probl. Inf. Transm.*, 24(1):39–46, 1988.

[36] M. Morgenstern. Existence and explicit constructions of $q+1$ regular ramanujan graphs for every prime power q. *J. Comb. Theory Ser. B*, 62(1):44–62, 1994.

[37] T. Rabin and M. Ben-Or. Verifiable secret sharing and multiparty protocols with honest majority (extended abstract). In *21st Symposium on Theory of Computing (STOC)*, pages 73–85, 1989.

[38] D. V. S. Ravikant, M. Venkitasubramaniam, V. Srikanth, K. Srinathan, and C. P. Rangan. On byzantine agreement over (2, 3)-uniform hypergraphs. In *18th International Symposium on Distributed Computing (DISC)*, pages 450–464, 2004.

[39] M. Serafini, P. Bokor, D. Dobre, M. Majuntke, and N. Suri. Scrooge: Reducing the costs of fast byzantine replication in presence of unresponsive replicas. In *41st International Conference on Dependable Systems and Networks (DSN)*, pages 353–362, 2010.

[40] F. Sterboul. An extremal problem in hypergraph coloring. *J. Comb. Theory Ser. B*, 22(2):159 – 164, 1977.

[41] V. I. Voloshin. On the upper chromatic number of a hypergraph. *Australas. J. Combin.*, 11:25–45, 1995.

[42] V. I. Voloshin. *Coloring Mixed Hypergraphs: Theory, Algorithms and Applications*, volume 17 of *Fields Institute Monographs*. AMS, 2002.

[43] T. Wood, R. Singh, A. Venkataramani, P. J. Shenoy, and E. Cecchet. ZZ and the art of practical BFT execution. In *6th European Conference on Computer Systems (EuroSys)*, pages 123–138, 2011.

[44] J. Yin, J.-P. Martin, A. Venkataramani, L. Alvisi, and M. Dahlin. Separating agreement from execution for Byzantine fault tolerant services. In *19th Symposium on Operating Systems Principles (SOSP)*, pages 253–267, 2003.

APPENDIX

Proof for Sufficiency Condition

PROOF OF PROPOSITION 15. We explore the three claims below.

Global minimum. The gradient of g has only a single root in the polytope.

$$\nabla g(a,b) = \left[\frac{b(n+3h)}{2} - 2ab - b^2, \frac{a(n+3h)}{2} - 2ab - a^2 \right].$$

We may assume that $a \neq 0, b \neq 0$, since otherwise $[a,b]$ is not in the polytope. Hence $\frac{b(n+3h)}{2} - 2ab - b^2 = 0$ is equivalent to $a = \frac{n+3h}{4} - \frac{b}{2}$. Symmetrically, $b = \frac{n+3h}{4} - \frac{a}{2}$. So $a = \frac{n+3h}{4} - \left(\frac{n+3h}{8} - \frac{a}{4} \right)$, i.e. $\frac{3}{4}a = \frac{n+3h}{8}$, i.e. $a = \frac{n+3h}{6}$. Symmetrically, $b = \frac{n+3h}{6}$. Therefore the only root of the gradient that may be in the polytope is $\left[\frac{n+3h}{6}, \frac{n+3h}{6} \right]$.

We now show that $\left[\frac{n+3h}{6}, \frac{n+3h}{6} \right]$ must be a maximum by examining the second derivatives of $g(a,b)$. The second derivatives are

- $g_{aa}(a,b) = -2b = -\frac{n+3h}{3}$
- $g_{bb}(a,b) = -2a = -\frac{n+3h}{3}$
- $g_{ab}(a,b) = \frac{n+3h}{2} - 2a - 2b = -\frac{n+3h}{6}$.

The second derivative test says that if $g_{aa}(a,b)$ is negative, and $g_{aa}(a,b) \cdot g_{bb}(a,b) - g_{ab}(a,b)^2$ is positive, then $[a,b]$ is a local maximum. Indeed, $-\frac{n+3h}{3}$ is negative, and $\left(-\frac{n+3h}{3} \right)^2 - \left(-\frac{n+3h}{6} \right)^2$ is positive. Therefore the only root that may be within the polytope is a global maximum, so it cannot possibly be the minimum point of the polytope.

Faces. We consider the points along the faces of each constraint. In other words, we set the constraints to tight, then globally optimize the resulting function.

First make $a \geq h$ tight. $a = h$ means the new objective function is $hb \left(\frac{n+3h}{2} - h - b \right) = hb \left(\frac{n+h}{2} - b \right)$. We differentiate to find the optimum value of b for this function.

$$\frac{d}{db} hb \left(\frac{n+h}{2} - b \right) = \frac{h(n+h)}{2} - 2hb,$$

which is 0 only at $b = \frac{n+h}{4}$. Thus $g \left(h, \frac{n+h}{4} \right) = h \left(\frac{n+h}{4} \right) \cdot \left(\frac{n+h}{2} - \frac{n+h}{4} \right) = \frac{h(n+h)^2}{16}$ is a potential global minimum for g.

By symmetry, setting $b \geq h$ tight gives the same potential minimum.

Finally, set $a + b \leq \frac{n+h}{2}$ tight. Then the new objective function is $\left(\frac{n+h}{2} - b \right) b \left(\frac{n+3h}{2} - \left(\frac{n+h}{2} - b \right) - b \right) = \left(\frac{n+h}{2} - b \right) bh$. We differentiate to find the optimum value of b of this new function.

$$\frac{d}{db} \left(\frac{n+h}{2} - b \right) bh = \frac{h(n+h)}{2} - 2bh,$$

which is 0 only when $b = \frac{n+h}{4}$. Plugging this and $a = \frac{n+h}{4}$ (by symmetry) into g gives $g(a,b) = (\frac{n+h}{4})^2 (\frac{n+3h}{2} - \frac{n+h}{2}) = \frac{(n+h)^2}{16} h$, the same value found for the other two constraints.

Vertices. We now consider the value of g at the three intersections of the three halfspaces. (Note that the faces only intersect in at most one point because they are unique and on two variables.)

Setting $a = h$ and $a + b = \frac{n+h}{2}$ gives $b = \frac{n-h}{2}$, hence $g(a,b) = h \cdot \frac{n-h}{2} \left(\frac{n+3h}{2} - h - \frac{n-h}{2} \right) = h \cdot \frac{n-h}{2} \cdot h$.

By symmetry, setting $b = h$ and $a + b = \frac{n+h}{2}$ also gives $g(a,b) = \frac{h^2(n-h)}{2}$.

Finally, setting $a = h$ and $b = h$ gives $g(a,b) = h^2 \left(\frac{n+3h}{2} - 2h \right) = \frac{h^2(n-h)}{2}$, again. □

Byzantine Broadcast in Point-to-Point Networks using Local Linear Coding *

Guanfeng Liang
University of Illinois
Electrical and Computer Engineering
Urbana, Illinois
guanfeng.liang@gmail.com

Nitin H. Vaidya
University of Illinois
Electrical and Computer Engineering
Urbana, Illinois
nhv@illinois.edu

ABSTRACT

The goal of Byzantine Broadcast (BB) is to allow a set of fault-free nodes to agree on information that a source node wants to broadcast to them, in the presence of Byzantine faulty nodes. We consider design of efficient algorithms for BB in *synchronous* point-to-point networks, where the rate of transmission over each communication link is limited by its "link capacity". The throughput of a particular BB algorithm is defined as the average number of bits that can be reliably broadcast to all fault-free nodes per unit time using the algorithm without violating the link capacity constraints. The *capacity* of BB in a given network is then defined as the supremum of all achievable BB throughputs in the given network, over all possible BB algorithms.

We develop NAB – a Network-Aware BB algorithm – for tolerating f faults in arbitrary point-to-point networks consisting of $n \geq 3f + 1$ nodes and having $\geq 2f + 1$ directed node disjoint paths from each node i to each node j. We also prove an upper bound on the capacity of BB, and conclude that NAB can achieve throughput at least 1/3 of the capacity. When the network satisfies an additional condition, NAB can achieve throughput at least 1/2 of the capacity. To the best of our knowledge, NAB is the first algorithm that can achieve a constant fraction of capacity of Byzantine Broadcast (BB) in general point-to-point networks.

Categories and Subject Descriptors

C.2.4 [**Distributed Systems**]: Distributed applications

General Terms

Algorithms, Theory

*This research is supported in part by National Science Foundation award 1059540 and Army Research Office grant W-911-NF-0710287. Any opinions, findings, and conclusions or recommendations expressed here are those of the authors and do not necessarily reflect the views of the funding agencies or the U.S. government.

Keywords

Broadcast, Byzantine faults, capacity, directed graph

1. INTRODUCTION

The problem of Byzantine Broadcast (BB) – also known as the Byzantine Generals problem [11] – was introduced by Pease, Shostak and Lamport in their 1980 paper [19]. Since the first paper on this topic, Byzantine Broadcast has been the subject of intense research activity, due to its many potential practical applications, including replicated fault-tolerant state machines [5], and fault-tolerant distributed file storage [20]. Informally, Byzantine Broadcast (BB) can be described as follows. There is a source node that needs to broadcast a message (also called its *input*) to all the other nodes such that even if some of the nodes are *Byzantine faulty*, all the fault-free nodes will still be able to agree on an identical message; the agreed message is identical to the source's input if the source is fault-free.

We consider the problem of maximizing the *throughput* of Byzantine Broadcast (BB) in *synchronous* networks of point-to-point links, wherein each directed communication link is subject to a "capacity" constraint. Informally speaking, *throughput* of BB is the number of bits of Byzantine Broadcast that can be achieved per unit time (on average), under the worst-case behavior by the faulty nodes. Despite the large body of work on BB [7, 6, 3, 10, 2, 18], performance of BB in *arbitrary* point-to-point network has not been investigated previously. When capacities of the different links are not identical, previously proposed algorithms can perform poorly. In fact, one can easily construct example networks in which previously proposed algorithms achieve throughput that is arbitrarily worse than the optimal throughput. Our prior work [13] introduces a BB algorithm that achieves the optimal throughput in 4-node networks with arbitrary link capacity constraints. But this does not apply to networks with > 4 nodes.

Problem Formulation

We consider a *synchronous* system consisting of n nodes, named $1, 2, \cdots, n$, with one node designated as the *sender* or *source* node. In particular, we will assume that node 1 is the source node. Source node 1 is given an *input* value x containing L bits, and the goal here is for the source to broadcast its input to all the other nodes. The following conditions must be satisfied:

Termination: Every fault-free node i must eventually decide on an *output* value of L bits; let us denote the output value of fault-free node i as y_i.

Agreement: All fault-free nodes must agree on an identical output value, i.e., there exists y such that $y_i = y$ for each fault-free node i.

Validity: If the source node is fault-free, then the agreed value must be identical to the input value of the source, i.e., $y = x$.

Failure Model

The faulty nodes are controlled by an adversary that has a complete knowledge of the network topology, the algorithm, and the input value x. No secret is hidden from the adversary. The adversary can take over up to f nodes at any point during execution of the algorithm, where $f < n/3$. These nodes are said to be *faulty*. The faulty nodes can engage in any kind of deviations from the algorithm, including sending incorrect or inconsistent messages to the neighbors. We assume that the set of faulty nodes remains *fixed* across different instances of execution of the BB algorithm. When a faulty node fails to send a message to a neighbor as required by the algorithm, we assume that the recipient node interprets the missing message as being some default value. We also assume that $f > 0$, since the case when $f = 0$ is trivial.

Network Model

We assume a synchronous point-to-point network modeled as a directed simple graph $\mathcal{G}(\mathcal{V}, \mathcal{E})$, where the set of vertices $\mathcal{V} = \{1, 2, \cdots, n\}$ represents the nodes in the network, and the set of edges $\mathcal{E}$ represents the links in the network. With a slight abuse of terminology, we will use the terms *edge* and *link*, and *node* and *vertex*, interchangeably. We assume that $n \geq 3f + 1$ since it is necessary for the existence of a correct BB algorithm [7]. We also require that there exist $\geq 2f + 1$ directed node disjoint paths from each node i to each node j in the network.

In the given network, links may not exist between all node pairs. For each directed link $e = (i, j) \in \mathcal{E}$, its *capacity*, denoted as z_e, specifies the maximum amount of information that can be transmitted on that link per unit time. Specifically, we assume that up to $z_e \tau$ bits can be reliably sent from node i to node j over time duration τ (for any non-negative τ). This is a deterministic model of *capacity* that has been commonly used in other work [12, 4, 8, 9]. All link capacities are assumed to be positive integers.[1] Propagation delays on the links are assumed to be zero (relaxing this assumption does not impact the correctness of results shown for large input sizes). We also assume that each node correctly knows the identity of the nodes at the other end of its links.

Throughput and Capacity of BB

When defining the throughput of a given BB algorithm in a given network, we consider Q independent instances of BB. The source node is given an L-bit input for each of these Q instances, and the *validity* and *agreement* properties need to be satisfied for each instance *separately* (i.e., independent of the outcome for the other instances).

For any BB algorithm $\mathcal{A}$, denote $t(\mathcal{G}, L, Q, \mathcal{A})$ as the duration of time required, in the worst case, to complete Q instances of L-bit Byzantine Broadcast, without violating the capacity constraints of the links in $\mathcal{G}$. Throughput of algo-

---

rithm $\mathcal{A}$ in network $\mathcal{G}$ for L-bit inputs is then defined as

$$T(\mathcal{G}, L, \mathcal{A}) = \lim_{Q \to \infty} \frac{LQ}{t(\mathcal{G}, L, Q, \mathcal{A})}.$$

We then define capacity C_{BB} as follows.

Capacity C_{BB} of Byzantine Broadcast in network $\mathcal{G}$ is defined as the supremum over the throughput of all algorithms $\mathcal{A}$ that solve the BB problem and all values of L. That is,

$$C_{BB}(\mathcal{G}) = \sup_{\mathcal{A}, L} T(\mathcal{G}, L, \mathcal{A}).$$

2. ALGORITHM OVERVIEW

This section provides an overview of the structure of NAB – a Network-Aware Byzantine broadcast algorithm – for arbitrary point-to-point networks. Each instance of our NAB algorithm performs Byzantine broadcast of an L-bit value. We assume that the NAB algorithm is used repeatedly, and during all these repeated executions, the cumulative number of distinct faulty nodes is upper bounded by f. Due to this assumption, the algorithm can perform well by amortizing the cost of fault tolerance over a large number of executions. Larger values of L also result in better performance for the algorithm. The algorithm is intended to be used for sufficiently large L and Q, to be elaborated later in Section 5.

The k-th instance of NAB executes on a network corresponding to graph $\mathcal{G}_k(\mathcal{V}_k, \mathcal{E}_k)$, defined as follows:

- For the first instance, $k = 1$, and $\mathcal{G}_1 = \mathcal{G}$. Thus, $\mathcal{V}_1 = \mathcal{V}$ and $\mathcal{E}_1 = \mathcal{E}$.
- The k-th instance of NAB occurs on graph $\mathcal{G}_k$ in the following sense: (i) all the fault-free nodes know the node and edge sets $\mathcal{V}_k$ and $\mathcal{E}_k$, (ii) only the nodes corresponding to the vertices in $\mathcal{V}_k$ need to participate in the k-th instance of BB, and (iii) only the links corresponding to the edges in $\mathcal{E}_k$ are used for communication in the k-th instance of NAB (communication received on other links is ignored).
- During the k-th instance of NAB using graph $\mathcal{G}_k$, if misbehavior by some faulty node(s) is detected, then, as described later, additional information is gleaned about the potential identity of the faulty node(s). In this case, $\mathcal{G}_{k+1}$ is obtained by removing from $\mathcal{G}_k$ appropriately chosen edges and possibly some vertices, based on dispute control [1].
  On the other hand, if during the k-th instance, no misbehavior is detected, then $\mathcal{G}_{k+1} = \mathcal{G}_k$.

The k-th instance of NAB algorithm consists of three phases, as described next. The main contributions of this paper are (i) the algorithm used in Phase 2 below, and (ii) a performance analysis of NAB.

If graph $\mathcal{G}_k$ does *not* contain the source node 1, then (as will be clearer later) by the start of the k-th instance of NAB, all the fault-free nodes already know that the source node is surely faulty; in this case, the fault-free nodes can agree on a default value for the output, and terminate the algorithm. Hereafter, we will assume that the source node 1 is in $\mathcal{G}_k$.

Phase 1: Unreliable Broadcast

In Phase 1, source node 1 broadcasts L bits to all the other nodes in $\mathcal{G}_k$. This phase makes no effort to detect or tolerate

---

[1] Rational link capacities can be turned into integers by choosing a suitable time unit. Irrational link capacities can be approximated by integers with arbitrary accuracy by choosing a suitably long time unit.

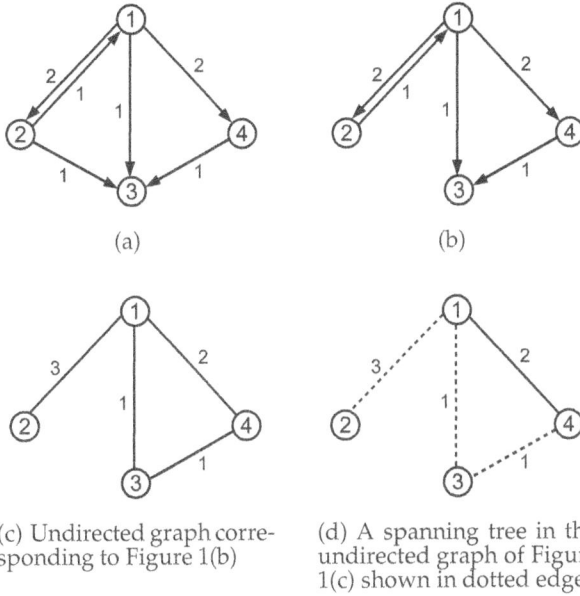

(a)

(b)

(c) Undirected graph corresponding to Figure 1(b)

(d) A spanning tree in the undirected graph of Figure 1(c) shown in dotted edges

Figure 1: Example graphs. Numbers next to the edges indicate link capacities.

misbehavior by faulty nodes. Now let us analyze the time required to perform unreliable broadcast in Phase 1.

$MINCUT(\mathcal{G}_k, 1, j)$ denotes the minimum cut in the directed graph $\mathcal{G}_k$ from source node 1 to node j. Let us define

$$\gamma_k = \min_{j \in \mathcal{V}_k} MINCUT(\mathcal{G}_k, 1, j).$$

$MINCUT(\mathcal{G}_k, 1, j)$ is equal to the maximum flow rate possible from node 1 to node $j \in \mathcal{V}_k$. It is well-known [17] that γ_k is the maximum rate achievable for broadcast from node 1 to *all* the other nodes in $\mathcal{V}_k$, under the capacity constraints on the links in $\mathcal{E}_k$ (this can be achieved using γ_k unit-capacity spanning trees embedded in $\mathcal{G}_k$ [15]). Thus, the least amount of time in which L bits can be broadcast by node 1 in graph $\mathcal{G}_k$ is given by L/γ_k. To simplify the analysis, we ignore propagation delays. Analogous results can be obtained in the presence of propagation delays as well [12].

Clearly, γ_k depends on the capacities of the links in $\mathcal{G}_k$. For example, if $\mathcal{G}_k$ were the directed graph in Figure 1(a), then $MINCUT(\mathcal{G}_k, 1, 2) = 2$, $MINCUT(\mathcal{G}_k, 1, 3) = 3$, and $MINCUT(\mathcal{G}_k, 1, 4) = 2$; hence $\gamma_k = 2$.

At the end of the broadcast operation in Phase 1 of the k-th instance of NAB, each node should have received L bits. One of the following four outcomes will occur:

(i) The source node 1 is fault-free, and all the fault-free nodes correctly receive the source node's L-bit input for the k-th instance of NAB, or

(ii) The source node 1 is fault-free, but some of the fault-free nodes receive incorrect L-bit values due to misbehavior by some faulty node(s), or

(iii) The source node 1 is faulty, but all the fault-free nodes still receive an identical L-bit value in Phase 1, or

(iv) The source node is faulty, and all the fault-free nodes do not receive an identical L-bit value in Phase 1.

The values received by the fault-free nodes in cases (i) and (iii) satisfy the *agreement* and *validity* conditions, whereas in cases (ii) and (iv) at least one of the two conditions is violated.

Phase 2: Failure Detection

Phase 2 performs the following two operations. As stipulated in the fault model, a faulty node may not follow the algorithm specification correctly.

(Step 2.1) Equality check: Using an *Equality Check* algorithm, the nodes in $\mathcal{V}_k$ perform a comparison of the L-bit value they received in Phase 1, to determine if all the nodes received an identical value. The source node 1 also participates in this comparison operation (treating its input as the value "received from" itself).

Section 3 presents the Equality Check algorithm, which is designed to *guarantee* that if the values received by the fault-free nodes in Phase 1 are *not identical*, then at least one fault-free node will detect the *mismatch*.

(Step 2.2) Agreeing on the outcome of equality check: Using a previously proposed Byzantine broadcast algorithm, such as [19], each node performs Byzantine broadcast of a 1-bit *flag* to other nodes in $\mathcal{G}_k$ indicating whether it detected a mismatch during equality check.

If any node broadcasts in step 2.2 that it has detected a mismatch, then subsequently *Phase 3 is performed*. On the other hand, if no node announces a mismatch in step 2.2 above, then *Phase 3 is not performed*; in this case, each fault-free node agrees on the value it received in Phase 1, and the k-th instance of *NAB is completed*.

We will later prove that, when Phase 3 is *not* performed, the values agreed above by the fault-free nodes satisfy the *validity* and *agreement* conditions for the k-th instance of NAB. On the other hand, when Phase 3 is performed during the k-th instance of NAB, as noted below, Phase 3 results in correct outcome for the k-th instance. When Phase 3 is performed, Phase 3 determines $\mathcal{G}_{k+1}$; otherwise, $\mathcal{G}_{k+1} = \mathcal{G}_k$.

Phase 3: Dispute Control

Phase 3 employs a *dispute control* mechanism that has also been used in prior work [1, 14]. Appendix A provides the details of the dispute control algorithm used in Phase 3. Here we summarize the outcomes of this phase – this summary should suffice for understanding the main contributions of this paper.

The dispute control in Phase 3 has very high overhead, due to the large amount of data that needs to be transmitted. From the above discussion of Phase 2, it follows that Phase 3 is performed *only if* at least one faulty node misbehaves during Phases 1 or 2. The outcomes from Phase 3 performed during the k-th instance of NAB are as follows.

Outcome 1: Phase 3 results in correct Byzantine broadcast for the k-th instance of NAB. This is obtained as a byproduct of the dispute control mechanism.

Outcome 2: By the end of Phase 3, either one of the nodes in $\mathcal{V}_k$ is correctly identified as faulty, or/and at least one pair of nodes in $\mathcal{V}_k$, say nodes a, b, is identified as being "in dispute" with each other. When a node pair a, b is found *in dispute*, it is guaranteed that (i) *at least* one of these two nodes is faulty, and (ii) at least one of the directed edges (a, b) and (b, a) is in $\mathcal{E}_k$. Note that the dispute control phase *never* finds two fault-free nodes in dispute with each other.

Outcome 3: Phase 3 in the k-th instance computes graph $\mathcal{G}_{k+1}$. In particular, any nodes that can be inferred as being faulty based on their behavior so far are excluded from $\mathcal{V}_{k+1}$; links attached to such nodes are excluded from $\mathcal{E}_{k+1}$. In Appendix A we elaborate on how the faulty nodes are identified. Then, for each node pair in $\mathcal{V}_{k+1}$, if that node pair has been found in dispute at least in one instance of NAB so far, the links between the node pair are excluded from $\mathcal{E}_{k+1}$. Phase 3 ensures that all the fault-free nodes compute an identical graph $\mathcal{G}_{k+1} = (\mathcal{V}_{k+1}, \mathcal{E}_{k+1})$ to be used during the next instance of NAB.

Consider two special cases for the k-th instance of NAB:

Case 1: If graph $\mathcal{G}_k$ does not contain the source node 1, it implies that all the fault-free nodes are aware that node 1 is faulty. In this case, they can safely agree on a default value as the outcome for the k-th instance of NAB.

Case 2: Similarly, if the source node is in $\mathcal{G}_k$ but at least f other nodes are excluded from $\mathcal{G}_k$, that implies that the remaining nodes in $\mathcal{G}_k$ are all fault-free; in this case, algorithm NAB can be reduced to just Phase 1.

Observe that during each execution of Phase 3, either a new pair of nodes *in dispute* is identified, or a new node is identified as faulty. Once a node is found to be in dispute with $f + 1$ distinct nodes, it can be identified as faulty, and excluded from the algorithm's execution. Therefore, dispute control needs to be performed at most $f(f + 1)$ times over repeated executions of NAB. Thus, even though each dispute control phase is expensive, the bounded number ensures that the amortized cost over a large number of instances of NAB is small, as reflected in the performance analysis of NAB (in Section 5 and Appendix C).

3. EQUALITY CHECK ALGORITHM WITH PARAMETER ρ_K

We now present the Equality Check algorithm (Algorithm 1 below) used in Phase 2, which has an integer parameter ρ_k for the k-th instance of NAB. Later in this section, we will elaborate on the choice of ρ_k, which is dependent on capacities of the links in $\mathcal{G}_k$.

Let us denote by x_i the L-bit value received by fault-free node $i \in \mathcal{V}_k$ in Phase 1 of the k-th instance. For simplicity, we do not include index k in the notation x_i. To simplify the presentation, let us assume that L/ρ_k is an integer. Thus we can represent the L-bit value x_i as ρ_k symbols from Galois Field $GF(2^{L/\rho_k})$. In particular, we represent x_i as a vector $\mathbf{X_i} = [\mathbf{X_i(1)}, \mathbf{X_i(2)}, \cdots, \mathbf{X_i(\rho_k)}]$, where each symbol $X_i(j) \in GF(2^{L/\rho_k})$ can be represented using L/ρ_k bits. As discussed earlier, for convenience, we assume that all the link capacities are integers.

In the Equality Check algorithm, z_e symbols of size L/ρ_k bits are transmitted on each link e of capacity z_e. Therefore, the Equality Check algorithm requires time duration L/ρ_k.

3.1 Salient Feature of the Algorithm

In the Equality Check algorithm, a single round of communication occurs between adjacent nodes. No node is required to forward packets received from other nodes during the algorithm. This implies that, while a faulty node may send incorrect packets to its neighbors, it cannot tamper information sent between fault-free nodes. This feature of Equality Check is important in being able to prove its correctness despite the presence of faulty nodes in $\mathcal{G}_k$.

3.2 Choice of Parameter ρ_k

We define a set Ω_k as follows using the disputes identified through the first $(k - 1)$ instances of NAB.

Algorithm 1 Equality Check in $\mathcal{G}_k$ with parameter ρ_k

Each node $i \in \mathcal{V}_k$ should performs these steps:

1. On each outgoing link $e = (i, j) \in \mathcal{E}_k$ whose capacity is z_e, node i transmits z_e linear combinations of the ρ_k symbols in vector $\mathbf{X_i}$, with the weights for the linear combinations being chosen from $GF(2^{L/\rho_k})$.

   More formally, for *each* outgoing edge $e = (i, j) \in \mathcal{E}_k$ of capacity z_e, a $\rho_k \times z_e$ matrix $\mathbf{C_e}$ is specified as a part of the algorithm. Entries in $\mathbf{C_e}$ are chosen from $GF(2^{L/\rho_k})$. Node i sends to node j a vector $\mathbf{Y_e}$ of z_e symbols obtained as the matrix product $\mathbf{Y_e} = \mathbf{X_i C_e}$. Each element of $\mathbf{Y_e}$ is said to be a "coded symbol". The choice of the matrix $\mathbf{C_e}$ affects the correctness of the algorithm, as elaborated later.

2. On each incoming edge $d = (j, i) \in \mathcal{E}_k$, node i receives a vector $\mathbf{Y_d}$ containing z_d symbols from $GF(2^{L/\rho_k})$. Node i then checks, for each incoming edge d, whether $\mathbf{Y_d} = \mathbf{X_i C_d}$. The check is said to fail iff $\mathbf{Y_d} \neq \mathbf{X_i C_d}$.

3. If checks of symbols received on any incoming edge fail in the previous step, then node i sets a 1-bit *flag* equal to MISMATCH; else the *flag* is set to NULL. This flag is broadcast in *Step 2.2* in Phase 2 above.

$$\Omega_k = \{ H \mid H \text{ is a subgraph of } \mathcal{G}_k \text{ containing } (n - f) \text{ nodes}$$
$$\text{such that no two nodes in } H \text{ have been found}$$
$$\textit{in dispute} \text{ through the first } (k - 1) \text{ instances } \}$$

As noted in the discussion of Phase 3 (Dispute Control), fault-free nodes are never found in dispute *with each other* (fault-free nodes may be found in dispute with faulty nodes, however). This implies that $\mathcal{G}_k$ includes all the fault-free nodes. There are at least $n - f$ fault-free nodes in the network. This implies that set Ω_k is non-empty.

Corresponding to a directed graph $H(V, E)$, let us define an *undirected* graph $\overline{H}(V, \overline{E})$ as follows: (i) both H and $\overline{H}$ contain the same set of vertices, (ii) undirected edge $(i, j) \in \overline{E}$ if either $(i, j) \in E$ or $(j, i) \in E$, and (iii) capacity of undirected edge $(i, j) \in \overline{E}$ is defined to be equal to the sum of the capacities of directed links (i, j) and (j, i) in E (if a directed link does not exist in E, here we treat its capacity as 0). For example, Figure 1(c) shows the undirected graph corresponding to the directed graph in Figure 1(b).

Define a set of undirected graphs $\overline{\Omega}_k$ as follows. $\overline{\Omega}_k$ contains undirected version of each directed graph in Ω: $\overline{\Omega}_k = \{\overline{H} | H \in \Omega_k\}$. Define

$$U_k = \min_{\overline{H} \in \overline{\Omega}_k} \min_{i, j \in \overline{H}} MINCUT(\overline{H}, i, j)$$

as the minimum value of the *undirected* MINCUTs between all pairs of nodes in all the undirected graphs in the set $\overline{\Omega}_k$. For instance, suppose that $n = 4$, $f = 1$ and the graph shown in Figure 1(a) is $\mathcal{G}$, whereas $\mathcal{G}_k$ is the graph shown in Figure 1(b). Thus, nodes 2 and 3 have been found in dispute previously. Then, Ω_k and $\overline{\Omega}_k$ each contain two subgraphs, one subgraph corresponding to the node set $\{1, 2, 4\}$, and the other subgraph corresponding to the node set $\{1, 3, 4\}$. In this example, $U_k = 2$.

Parameter ρ_k is chosen such that

$$\rho_k \leq \frac{U_k}{2}.$$

Under such constraint on ρ_k, we will prove the correctness of the Equality Check algorithm, with its execution time being L/ρ_k.

3.3 Correctness of Equality Check

The correctness of Algorithm 1 depends on the choices of the parameter ρ_k and the set of coding matrices $\{\mathbf{C_e}|e \in \mathcal{E}_k\}$. Let us say that a set of coding matrices is *correct* if the resulting Equality Check (Algorithm 1) satisfies the following requirement:

(EC) **if** there exists a pair of fault-free nodes $i, j \in \mathcal{G}_k$ such that $\mathbf{X_i} \neq \mathbf{X_j}$ (i.e., $x_i \neq x_j$),
then the 1-bit flag at *at least one* fault-free node is set to MISMATCH.

Recall that $\mathbf{X_i}$ is a vector representation of the L-bit value x_i received by node i in Phase 1 of NAB. Two consequences of the above correctness condition are:

Consequence 1: If some node (possibly the source node) misbehaves during Phase 1 leading to outcomes (ii) or (iv) for Phase 1, then at least one fault-free node will set its flag to MISMATCH. In this case, the fault-free nodes (possibly including the sender) do not share identical L-bit values $\mathbf{X_i}$'s as the outcome of Phase 1.

Consequence 2: If no misbehavior occurs in Phase 1 (thus the values received by fault-free nodes in Phase 1 are correct), but MISMATCH flag at some fault-free node is set in *Equality Check*, then misbehavior must have occurred in Phase 2.

The following theorem shows that when $\rho_k \leq U_k/2$, and when L is sufficiently large, there exists a set of coding matrices $\{\mathbf{C_e}|e \in \mathcal{E}_k\}$ that are correct.

THEOREM 1. *For $\rho_k \leq U_k/2$, if the entries of the coding matrices $\{\mathbf{C_e}|e \in \mathcal{E}_k\}$ in step 1 of Algorithm 1 are chosen independently and uniformly at random from $GF(2^{L/\rho_k})$, then $\{\mathbf{C_e}|e \in \mathcal{E}_k\}$ is correct with probability $\geq 1 - 2^{-L/\rho_k}\left[\binom{n}{n-f}(n-f-1)\rho_k\right]$. Note that when L is large enough, $1 - 2^{-L/\rho_k}\left[\binom{n}{n-f}(n-f-1)\rho_k\right] > 0$.*

Proof sketch: The complete proof of Theorem 1 is presented in Appendix B. Our goal is to prove that property (EC) above holds with a non-zero probability. That is, regardless of which (up to f) nodes in $\mathcal{G}$ are faulty and what values $\mathbf{X_i}$'s equal to, whenever $\mathbf{X_i} \neq \mathbf{X_j}$ for some pair of fault-free nodes i and j in $\mathcal{G}_k$ during the k-th instance, at least one fault-free node (which may be different from nodes i and j) will set its 1-bit flag to MISMATCH. To prove this, we consider every subgraph of $H \in \Omega_k$ (see definition of Ω_k above). By definition of Ω_k, no two nodes in H have been found in dispute through the first $(k-1)$ instances of NAB. Therefore, H represents one *potential* set of $n - f$ fault-free nodes in $\mathcal{G}_k$. For each edge $e = (i, j)$ in H, steps 1-2 of Algorithm 1 together have the effect of checking whether or not $(\mathbf{X_i} - \mathbf{X_j})\mathbf{C_e} = 0$. Without loss of generality, for the purpose of this proof, rename the nodes in H as $1, \cdots, n-f$. Denote $\mathbf{D_i} = \mathbf{X_i} - \mathbf{X_{n-f}}$ for $i = 1, \cdots, (n-f-1)$, then

$$(\mathbf{X_i} - \mathbf{X_j})\mathbf{C_e} = 0 \Leftrightarrow \begin{cases} (\mathbf{D_i} - \mathbf{D_j})\mathbf{C_e} = 0 & , \text{ if } i, j < n-f; \\ \mathbf{D_i}\mathbf{C_e} = 0 & , \text{ if } j = n-f; \\ -\mathbf{D_j}\mathbf{C_e} = 0 & , \text{ if } i = n-f. \end{cases}$$

Define $\mathbf{D_H} = [\mathbf{D_1}, \mathbf{D_2}, \cdots, \mathbf{D_{n-f-1}}]$. Let m be the sum of the capacities of all the directed edges in H. As elaborated in Appendix B, we define $\mathbf{C_H}$ to be a $(n-f-1)\rho_k \times m$ matrix whose entries are obtained using the elements of $\mathbf{C_e}$ for each edge

e in H in an appropriate manner. For the suitably defined $\mathbf{C_H}$ matrix, we can show that the comparisons in steps 1-2 of Algorithm 1 at *all* the nodes in $H \in \Omega_k$ are equivalent to checking whether or not $\mathbf{D_H}\mathbf{C_H} = 0$.

We show that for a particular subgraph $H \in \Omega_k$, when $\rho_k \leq U_k/2$, $m \geq (n-f-1)\rho_k$ and L is large enough, with non-zero probability $\mathbf{C_H}$ contains a $(n-f-1)\rho_k \times (n-f-1)\rho_k$ invertible submatrix if the set of coding matrices $\{\mathbf{C_e}|e \in \mathcal{E}_k\}$ are generated randomly as described in Theorem 1. In this case $\mathbf{D_H}\mathbf{C_H} = 0$ if and only if $\mathbf{D_H} = 0$, i.e., $\mathbf{X_1} = \mathbf{X_2} = \cdots = \mathbf{X_{n-f}}$. In other words, if all nodes in subgraph H are fault-free, and $\mathbf{X_i} \neq \mathbf{X_j}$ for two fault-free nodes i, j, then $\mathbf{D_H}\mathbf{C_H} \neq 0$ and hence the check in step 2 of Algorithm 1 fails at some fault-free node in H.

We then further show that, for large enough L, with a non-zero probability, this is also *simultaneously* true for all subgraphs $H \in \Omega_k$. This implies that, for large enough L, correct coding matrices ($\mathbf{C_e}$ for each $e \in \mathcal{E}_k$) can be found. Notice that for a given network, the correctness of a set of coding matrices is *independent* of the values of x_i's. This set of matrices are specified as a part of the algorithm specification.

4. CORRECTNESS OF NAB

For Phase 1 (Unreliable Broadcast) and Phase 3 (Dispute Control), the proof that the outcomes claimed in Section 2 indeed follows directly from the prior literature cited in Section 2 (and elaborated in Appendix A). Now consider two cases:

Case 1 – The values received by the fault-free nodes in Phase 1 are *not identical*: Then the correctness of Equality Check ensures that a fault-free node will detect the mismatch, and consequently Phase 3 will be performed. As a byproduct of Dispute Control in Phase 3, the fault-free nodes will correctly agree on a value that satisfies the *validity* and *agreement* conditions.

Case 2 – The values received by the fault-free nodes in Phase 1 are identical: If no node announces a mismatch in step 2.2, then the fault-free nodes will agree on the value received in Phase 1. It is easy to see that this is a correct outcome. On the other hand, if some node announces a mismatch in step 2, then Dispute Control will be performed, which will result in correct outcome for the broadcast of the k-th instance. Thus, in all cases, NAB will lead to correct outcome in each instance.

5. THROUGHPUT AND CAPACITY

5.1 Throughput of NAB for Large L and Q

In this section, we present a lower bound on the achievable throughput with NAB when the input size L for each instance and the number of instances Q are both "large" (in an order sense) compared to n. Complete proof can be found in Appendix C. Two consequences of L and Q being large:

L **being large** ($\omega(n^\alpha)$ for some constant $\alpha > 0$): the overhead of 1-bit broadcasts performed in step 2.2 of Phase 2 becomes negligible when amortized over the L bits being broadcast by the source in each instance of NAB.

Q **being large** ($\omega(n^{\beta+2})$ for some constant $\beta > 0$): the average overhead of dispute control per instance of NAB becomes negligible. Recall that dispute control needs to be performed at most $f(f + 1)$ times over Q executions of NAB.

It then suffices to consider only the time it takes to complete the Unreliable Broadcast in Phase 1 and Equality Check in Phase 2. For the k-th instance of NAB, as discussed previously, the unreliable broadcast in Phase 1 can be done in L/γ_k time units (see definition of γ_k in Section 2). We now define

$$\Gamma = \{ H \mid H \text{ is a subgraph of } \mathcal{G} \text{ containing source node 1} \\ \text{such that } \mathcal{G}_k \text{ may equal } H \text{ in some execution of} \\ \text{NAB for some } k \}$$

Appendix D provides a systematic construction of the set Γ. Define the minimum value of all possible γ_k:

$$\gamma^* = \min_{\mathcal{G}_k \in \Gamma} \gamma_k = \min_{\mathcal{G}_k \in \Gamma} \min_{j \in \mathcal{V}_k} MINCUT(\mathcal{G}_k, 1, j).$$

Then an upper bound of the execution time of Phase 1 in all instances of NAB is L/γ^*.

With parameter $\rho_k = U_k/2$, the execution time of the Equality Check in Phase 2 is L/ρ_k. Recall that U_k is defined as the minimum value of the MINCUTs between all pairs of nodes in all undirected graphs in the set $\overline{\Omega}_k$. As discussed in Appendix B.2, $\overline{\Omega}_k \subseteq \overline{\Omega}_1$, where $\mathcal{G}_1 = \mathcal{G}$. Hence $U_k \geq U_1$ in all possible $\mathcal{G}_k$. Define

$$\rho^* = \frac{U_1}{2} = \min_{\overline{H} \in \Omega_1} \min_{\text{nodes } i,j \text{ in } \overline{H}} MINCUT(\overline{H}, i, j).$$

Then $\rho_k \geq \rho^*$ for all possible $\mathcal{G}_k$ and the execution time of the Equality Check is upper-bounded by L/ρ^*. So the throughput of NAB for large Q and L can be lower bounded by

$$\lim_{L \to \infty} T(\mathcal{G}, L, NAB) \geq \frac{L}{L/\gamma^* + L/\rho^*} = \frac{\gamma^* \rho^*}{\gamma^* + \rho^*}. \quad (1)$$

To simplify the discussion above, we ignored propagation delays. Appendix C also describes how to approach this bound even when propagation delays are considered.

5.2 An Upper Bound on Capacity of BB

We prove (in Appendix E) the following upper bound of the capacity of BB:

THEOREM 2. *In point-to-point network $\mathcal{G}(\mathcal{V}, \mathcal{E})$, the capacity of Byzantine broadcast (C_{BB}) with node 1 as the source satisfies the following upper bound: $C_{BB}(\mathcal{G}) \leq \min(\gamma^*, 2\rho^*)$.*

Given the throughput lower bound $T_{NAB}(\mathcal{G})$ in (Eq.1) and the upper bound on $C_{BB}(\mathcal{G})$ from Theorem 2, the result below can be obtained through simple calculation. Readers are referred to Appendix G of our report [15] for the proof.

THEOREM 3. *In point-to-point network $\mathcal{G}(\mathcal{V}, \mathcal{E})$:*

$$\lim_{L \to \infty} T(\mathcal{G}, L, NAB) \geq \min(\gamma^*, 2\rho^*)/3 \geq C_{BB}(\mathcal{G})/3.$$

Moreover, when $\gamma^* \leq \rho^*$:

$$\lim_{L \to \infty} T(\mathcal{G}, L, NAB) \geq \min(\gamma^*, 2\rho^*)/2 \geq C_{BB}(\mathcal{G})/2.$$

6. CONCLUSION

This paper presents NAB, a network-aware Byzantine broadcast algorithm for point-to-point networks. We derive an upper bound on the capacity of Byzantine broadcast, and show that NAB can asymptotically achieve throughput at least 1/3 fraction of the capacity over a large number of execution instances, when L is large. The fraction can be improved to at least 1/2 when the network satisfies an additional condition.

7. REFERENCES

[1] Z. Beerliova-Trubiniova and M. Hirt. Efficient multi-party computation with dispute control. In *IACR Theory of Cryptography Conference (TCC)*, 2006.

[2] Z. Beerliova-Trubiniova and M. Hirt. Perfectly-secure mpc with linear communication complexity. In *IACR Theory of Cryptography Conference (TCC)*, 2008.

[3] P. Berman, J. A. Garay, and K. J. Perry. Bit optimal distributed consensus. In *Computer science*. Plenum Press, 1992.

[4] N. Cai and R. W. Yeung. Network error correction, part II: Lower bounds. *Communications in Information and Systems*, 2006.

[5] M. Castro and B. Liskov. Practical Byzantine fault tolerance. In *USENIX Symposium on Operating Systems Design and Implementation (OSDI)*, 1999.

[6] B. A. Coan and J. L. Welch. Modular construction of a Byzantine agreement protocol with optimal message bit complexity. *Journal of Information and Computation*, 1992.

[7] M. J. Fischer, N. A. Lynch, and M. Merritt. Easy impossibility proofs for distributed consensus problems. In *ACM symposium on Principles of Distributed Computing (PODC)*, 1985.

[8] T. Ho, B. Leong, R. Koetter, M. Medard, M. Effros, and D. Karger. Byzantine modification detection in multicast networks using randomized network coding (extended version). Technical report, (http://www.its.caltech.edu/ tho/multicast.ps), 2004.

[9] S. Jaggi, M. Langberg, S. Katti, T. Ho, D. Katabi, and M. Medard. Resilient network coding in the presence of Byzantine adversaries. In *IEEE International Conference on Computer Communications (INFOCOM)*, 2007.

[10] V. King and J. Saia. Breaking the $O(n^2)$ bit barrier: Scalable Byzantine agreement with an adaptive adversary. In *ACM symposium on Principles of Distributed Computing (PODC)*, 2010.

[11] L. Lamport, R. Shostak, and M. Pease. The Byzantine generals problem. *ACM Transaction on Programming Languages and Systems*, 1982.

[12] S.-Y. Li, R. Yeung, and N. Cai. Linear network coding. *IEEE Transactions on Information Theory*, 2003.

[13] G. Liang and N. Vaidya. Capacity of Byzantine agreement with finite link capacity. In *IEEE International Conference on Computer Communications (INFOCOM)*, 2011.

[14] G. Liang and N. Vaidya. Error-free multi-valued consensus with Byzantine failures. In *ACM Symposium on Principles of Distributed Computing (PODC)*, 2011.

[15] G. Liang and N. Vaidya. Byzantine broadcast in point-to-point networks using local linear coding. Technical report, arXiv (http://arxiv.org/abs/1106.1845), June 2011 (revised May 2012).

[16] E. M. Palmer. On the spanning tree packing number of a graph: a survey. *Journal of Discrete Mathematics*, 2001.

[17] C. H. Papadimitriou and K. Steiglitz. *Combinatorial Optimization: Algorithms and Complexity*. Courier Dover Publications, 1998.

[18] A. Patra and C. P. Rangan. Communication optimal multi-valued asynchronous Byzantine agreement with optimal resilience. Cryptology ePrint Archive, 2009.

[19] M. Pease, R. Shostak, and L. Lamport. Reaching

agreement in the presence of faults. *Journal of the ACM (JACM)*, 1980.

[20] A. Silberschatz, P. B. Galvin, and G. Gagne. *Operating System Concepts*, chapter 17 Distributed File Systems. Addison-Wesley, 1994.

APPENDIX

Some details are omitted for the sack of space. Please see [15] for the complete proofs.

A. DISPUTE CONTROL

The dispute control algorithm motivated by the work in [1] is performed in the k-th instance of NAB only if at least one node misbehaves during Phases 1 or 2. The goal of dispute control is to learn some information about the identity of at least one faulty node. In particular, the dispute control algorithm will identify a new node as being faulty, or/and identify a new node pair in dispute (at least one of the nodes in the pair is guaranteed to be faulty). The steps in dispute control in the k-th instance of NAB are as follows:

(DC1) Each node i in $\mathcal{V}_k$ uses a previously proposed Byzantine broadcast algorithm, such as [6] (extended to use $2f + 1$ node disjoint paths; see Appendix C), to broadcast to all other nodes in $\mathcal{V}_k$ all the messages that this node i claims to have received from other nodes, and sent to the other nodes, during Phases 1 and 2 of the k-th instance. Source node 1 also uses an existing Byzantine broadcast algorithm [6] to broadcast its L-bit input for the k-th instance to all the other nodes. Thus, at the end of this step, all the fault-free nodes will reach correct agreement for the output for the k-th instance.

(DC2) If for some node pair $a, b \in \mathcal{V}_k$, a message that node a claims above to have sent to node b mismatches with the claim of received messages made by node b, then node pair a, b is found in dispute. In step DC1, since a Byzantine broadcast algorithm is used to disseminate the claims, all the fault-free nodes will identify identical node pairs in dispute.

It should be clear that a pair of fault-free nodes will never be found in dispute with each other in this step.

(DC3) The NAB algorithm is deterministic in nature. Therefore, the messages that should be sent by each node in Phases 1 and 2 can be completely determined by the messages that the node receives, and, in case of node 1, its initial input. Thus, if the claims of the messages sent by some node i are inconsistent with the messages it claims to have received, and its initial input (in case of node 1), then that node i must be faulty. Again, all fault-free nodes identify these faulty nodes identically. Any nodes thus identified as faulty until now (including all previous instances of NAB) are deemed to be "in dispute" with all their neighbors (to whom the faulty nodes have incoming or outgoing links).

It should be clear that a fault-free node will never be found to be faulty in this step.

(DC4) Consider the node pairs that have been identified as being in dispute in DC2 and DC3 of at least one instances of NAB so far. We will say that a set of nodes F_i, where $|F_i| \le f$, "explains" all the disputes so far, if for each pair a, b found in dispute so far, at least one of a and b is in F_i.

It should be easy to see that for any set of disputes that may be observed, there must be at least one such set that *explains* the disputes. It is easy to argue that the nodes in the set intersection $\bigcap_{\delta=1}^{\Delta} F_\delta$ must be necessarily faulty (in fact, the

nodes in the set intersection are also guaranteed to include nodes identified as faulty in step DC3).

Then, $\mathcal{V}_{k+1}$ is obtained as $\mathcal{V}_k - \bigcap_{\delta=1}^{\Delta} F_\delta$. $\mathcal{E}_{k+1}$ is obtained by removing from $\mathcal{E}_k$ edges incident on nodes in $\bigcap_{\delta=1}^{\Delta} F_\delta$, and also excluding edges between all node pairs that have been found in dispute so far.

As noted earlier, the above dispute control phase may be executed in at most $f(f + 1)$ instances of NAB.

B. PROOF OF THEOREM 1

To prove Theorem 1, we first prove that when the coding matrices are generated at random as described, for a particular subgraph $H \in \Omega_k$, with non-zero probability, the coding matrices $\{\mathbf{C}_e | e \in \mathcal{G}_k\}$ define a matrix $\mathbf{C}_\mathbf{H}$ (as defined later) such that $\mathbf{D}_\mathbf{H} \mathbf{C}_\mathbf{H} = 0$ if and only if $\mathbf{D}_\mathbf{H} = 0$. Then we prove that this is also *simultaneously* true for all subgraphs $H \in \Omega_k$.

B.1 For a given subgraph $H \in \Omega_k$

Consider any subgraph $H \in \Omega_k$. For each edge $e = (i, j)$ in H, we "expand" the corresponding coding matrix $\mathbf{C}_e$ (of size $\rho_k \times z_e$) to a $(n - f - 1)\rho_k \times z_e$ matrix $\mathbf{B}_e$ as follows: $\mathbf{B}_e$ consists $n - f - 1$ blocks, each block is a $\rho_k \times z_e$ matrix:

- If $i \ne n - f$ and $j \ne n - f$: the i-th and j-th block equal to $\mathbf{C}_e$ and $-\mathbf{C}_e$, respectively. The other blocks are all set to 0: $\mathbf{B}_e^T = \begin{pmatrix} 0 \cdots 0 & \mathbf{C}_e^T & 0 \cdots 0 & -\mathbf{C}_e^T & 0 \cdots 0 \end{pmatrix}$. Here $()^T$ denotes the transpose of a matrix or vector.
- If $i = n - f$: the j-th block equals to $-\mathbf{C}_e$, and the other blocks are all set to 0 matrix: $\mathbf{B}_e^T = \begin{pmatrix} 0 \cdots 0 & -\mathbf{C}_e^T & 0 \cdots 0 \end{pmatrix}$.
- If $j = n - f$: the i-th block equals to $\mathbf{C}_e$, and the other blocks are all set to 0 matrix: $\mathbf{B}_e^T = \begin{pmatrix} 0 \cdots 0 & \mathbf{C}_e^T & 0 \cdots 0 \end{pmatrix}$.

Let $D_{i,\beta} = X_i(\beta) - X_{n-f}(\beta)$ for $i < n - f$ as the difference between $\mathbf{X}_i$ and $\mathbf{X}_{n-f}$ in the β-th element. Recall that $\mathbf{D}_i = \mathbf{X}_i - \mathbf{X}_{n-f} = \begin{pmatrix} D_{i,1} & \cdots & D_{i,\rho_k} \end{pmatrix}$ and $\mathbf{D}_\mathbf{H} = \begin{pmatrix} \mathbf{D}_1 & \cdots & \mathbf{D}_{n-f-1} \end{pmatrix}$. So $\mathbf{D}_\mathbf{H}$ is a row vector of $(n - f - 1)\rho_k$ elements from $GF(2^{L/\rho_k})$ that captures the differences between $\mathbf{X}_i$ and $\mathbf{X}_{n-f}$ for all $i < n - f$. It should be easy to see that $(\mathbf{X}_i - \mathbf{X}_j)\mathbf{C}_e = 0 \Leftrightarrow \mathbf{D}_\mathbf{H} \mathbf{B}_e = 0$. So for edge e, steps 1-2 of Algorithm 1 have the effect of checking whether or not $\mathbf{D}_\mathbf{H} \mathbf{B}_e = 0$.

If we label the set of edges in H as $e1, e2, \cdots$, and let m be the sum of the capacities of all edges in H, then we construct a $(n - f - 1)\rho_k \times m$ matrix $\mathbf{C}_\mathbf{H}$ by concatenating all expanded coding matrices: $\mathbf{C}_\mathbf{H} = \begin{pmatrix} \mathbf{B}_{e1} & \mathbf{B}_{e2} & \cdots \end{pmatrix}$, where each column of $\mathbf{C}_\mathbf{H}$ represents one coded symbol sent in H over the corresponding edge. Then steps 1-2 of Algorithm 1 for all edges in H have the same effect as checking whether or not $\mathbf{D}_\mathbf{H} \mathbf{C}_\mathbf{H} = 0$. So to prove Theorem 1, we need to show that there exists $\mathbf{C}_\mathbf{H}$ such that $\mathbf{D}_\mathbf{H} \mathbf{C}_\mathbf{H} = 0 \Leftrightarrow \mathbf{D}_\mathbf{H} = 0$.

It is obvious that if $\mathbf{D}_\mathbf{H} = 0$, then $\mathbf{D}_\mathbf{H} \mathbf{C}_\mathbf{H} = 0$ for any $\mathbf{C}_\mathbf{H}$. So all left to show is that there exists $\mathbf{C}_\mathbf{H}$ such that $\mathbf{D}_\mathbf{H} \mathbf{C}_\mathbf{H} = 0 \Rightarrow \mathbf{D}_\mathbf{H} = 0$. It is then sufficient to show that $\mathbf{C}_\mathbf{H}$ (probably with columns permuted) contains a $(n - f - 1)\rho_k \times (n - f - 1)\rho_k$ submatrix $\mathbf{M}_\mathbf{H}$ that is *invertible*, because when such an invertible submatrix exist, $\mathbf{D}_\mathbf{H} \mathbf{C}_\mathbf{H} = 0 \Rightarrow \mathbf{D}_\mathbf{H} \mathbf{M}_\mathbf{H} = 0 \Rightarrow \mathbf{D}_\mathbf{H} = 0$.

Now we describe how one such submatrix $\mathbf{M}_\mathbf{H}$ can be obtained. Notice that each column of $\mathbf{C}_\mathbf{H}$ represents one coded symbol sent on the corresponding edge. A $(n - f - 1)\rho_k \times (n - f - 1)$ submatrix $\mathbf{S}$ of $\mathbf{C}_\mathbf{H}$ is said to be a "spanning matrix" of H if the edges corresponding to the columns of $\mathbf{S}$ form an undirected spanning tree of $\overline{H}$, the *undirected* representation of H. In Figure 1(d), an undirected spanning tree of the undirected graph in Figure 1(c) is shown in dotted edges. It is worth pointing out that an undirected spanning tree in an undirected graph $\overline{H}$ does not necessarily correspond to a directed spanning tree in the corresponding directed graph H. For example, the directed edges in Figure 1(b) corresponding to the dotted undirected edges in Figure 1(d) do not form a spanning tree in the directed graph in Figure 1(b).

It is known that in an undirected graph whose MINCUT equals to U, at least $U/2$ undirected unit-capacity spanning trees can be embedded [16]. This implies that $\mathbf{C_H}$ contains a set of $U_k/2$ spanning matrices such that no two spanning matrices in the set covers the same column in $\mathbf{C_H}$. Let $\{\mathbf{S_1}, \cdots, \mathbf{S}_{\rho_k}\}$ be one set of $\rho_k \leq U_k/2$ such spanning matrices of H. Then union of these spanning matrices forms an $(n - f - 1)\rho_k \times (n - f - 1)\rho_k$ matrix $\mathbf{M_H} = \begin{pmatrix} \mathbf{S_1} & \cdots & \mathbf{S}_{\rho_k} \end{pmatrix}$. $\mathbf{M_H}$ is not necessarily a submatrix of $\mathbf{C_H}$, but it is always a submatrix of a column-permuted version $\mathbf{C_H}$.

Next, we will show that when the set of coding matrices are generated as described in Theorem 1, with non-zero probability we obtain an invertible square matrix $\mathbf{M_H}$. When $\mathbf{M_H}$ is invertible, $\mathbf{D_H M_H} = 0 \Leftrightarrow \mathbf{D_H} = 0 \Leftrightarrow \mathbf{X_1} = \cdots = \mathbf{X_{n-f}}$.

For the following discussion, it is convenient to reorder the elements of $\mathbf{D_H}$ into $\tilde{\mathbf{D}}_H = \begin{pmatrix} D_{1,1} \cdots D_{n-f-1,1} \cdots D_{1,\rho_k} \cdots D_{n-f-1,\rho_k} \end{pmatrix}$, so that the $(\beta-1)(n-f-1)+1$-th through the $\beta(n-f-1)$ elements of $\tilde{\mathbf{D}}_H$ represent the difference between $\mathbf{X_i}$ ($i = 1, \cdots, n-f-1$) and $\mathbf{X_{n-f}}$ in the β-th element.

We also reorder the rows of each spanning matrix $\mathbf{S_q}$ ($q = 1, \cdots, \rho_k$) accordingly. It can be showed that after reordering, $\mathbf{S_q}$ becomes $\tilde{\mathbf{S}}_q = \begin{pmatrix} \mathbf{A_q S_{q,1}} \\ \vdots \\ \mathbf{A_q S}_{q,\rho_k} \end{pmatrix}$.

Here $\mathbf{A_q}$ and $\mathbf{S_{q,p}}$ are all $(n - f - 1) \times (n - f - 1)$ square matrices. $\mathbf{A_q}$ is called the *adjacency* matrix of the spanning tree corresponding to $\mathbf{S_q}$ and is formed as follows. Suppose that the r-th column of $\mathbf{S_q}$ corresponds to a coded symbol sent over a directed edge (i, j) in H, then
1. If $i \neq n - f$ and $j \neq n - f$, then the r-th column of $\mathbf{A_q}$ has the i-th element as 1 and the j-th element as -1, the remaining entries in that column are all 0;
2. If $i = n - f$, then the j-th element of the r-th column of $\mathbf{A_q}$ is set to -1, the remaining elements of that column are all 0;
3. If $j = n - f$, then the i-th element of the r-th column of $\mathbf{A_q}$ is set to 1, the remaining elements of that column are all 0.

For example, suppose $\overline{H}$ is the graph shown in Figure 1(c), and $\mathbf{S_q}$ corresponds to a spanning tree of H consisting of the dotted edges in Figure 1(d). Suppose that we index the corresponding directed edges in the graph shown in Figure 1(b) in the following order: (1,2), (1,3), (4,3). The resulting adjacency matrix $\mathbf{A_q} = \begin{pmatrix} 1 & 1 & 0 \\ -1 & 0 & 0 \\ 0 & -1 & -1 \end{pmatrix}$.

On the other hand, each square matrix $\mathbf{S_{q,p}}$ is a diagonal matrix. The r-th diagonal element of $\mathbf{S_{q,p}}$ equals to the p-th coefficient used to compute the coded symbol corresponding to the r-th column of $\mathbf{S_q}$. In the previous example, suppose the second column of $\mathbf{S_q}$ corresponds to a coded packet $aX_1(1) + bX_1(2)$ being sent on link (1,3). Then the second diagonal elements of $\mathbf{S_{q,1}}$ and $\mathbf{S_{q,2}}$ are a and b, respectively.

After the reordering, $\mathbf{M_H}$ can be written as $\tilde{\mathbf{M}}_H$ that has the following structure: $\tilde{\mathbf{M}}_H = \begin{pmatrix} \mathbf{A_1 S_{1,1}} & \mathbf{A_2 S_{2,1}} & \cdots & \mathbf{A}_{\rho_k} \mathbf{C}_{\rho_k, \rho_k} \\ \vdots & & \ddots & \vdots \\ \mathbf{A_1 S}_{1,\rho_k} & \mathbf{A_2 S}_{2,\rho_k} & \cdots & \mathbf{A}_{\rho_k} \mathbf{S}_{\rho_k, \rho_k} \end{pmatrix}$.

Notice that $\tilde{\mathbf{M}}_H$ is obtained by permuting the rows of $\mathbf{M_H}$. So showing $\mathbf{M_H}$ is invertible is equivalent to showing $\tilde{\mathbf{M}}_H$ is invertible.

Define $\mathbf{M_q} = \begin{pmatrix} \mathbf{A_1 S_{1,1}} & \cdots & \mathbf{A_q S_{q,1}} \\ \vdots & \ddots & \vdots \\ \mathbf{A_1 S_{1,q}} & \cdots & \mathbf{A_q S_{q,q}} \end{pmatrix}$ for $1 \leq q \leq \rho_k$. Note that $\mathbf{M_{q1}}$ is a sub-matrix of $\mathbf{M_{q2}}$ when $q1 < q2$, and $\mathbf{M}_{\rho_k} = \tilde{\mathbf{M}}_H$. We prove the following lemma:

LEMMA 1. *For any $\rho_k \leq U_k/2$, with probability at least $\left(1 - \frac{n-f-1}{2^{L/\rho_k}}\right)^{\rho_k}$, matrices $\tilde{\mathbf{M}}_H$ and $\mathbf{M_H}$ are invertible.*

PROOF. We now show that each $\mathbf{M_q}$ is invertible with probability at least $\left(1 - \frac{n-f-1}{2^{L/\rho_k}}\right)^{q}$ for all $q \leq \rho_k$. The proof is by induction, with $q = 1$ being the base case.

Base Case: $q = 1$.

For $q = 1$, $\mathbf{M_1} = \mathbf{A_1 S_{1,1}}$. As showed in Appendix C.3 of [15], $\mathbf{A_q}$ is always invertible and $\det(\mathbf{A_q}) = \pm 1$. Since $\mathbf{S_{1,1}}$ is a $(n - f - 1)$-by-$(n - f - 1)$ diagonal matrix, it is invertible provided that all its $(n - f - 1)$ diagonal elements are non-zero. Remember that the diagonal elements of $\mathbf{S_{1,1}}$ are chosen uniformly and independently from $GF(2^{L/\rho_k})$. The probability that they are all non-zero is $\left(1 - \frac{1}{2^{L/\rho_k}}\right)^{n-f-1} \geq 1 - \frac{n-f-1}{2^{L/\rho_k}}$.

Induction Step: $q < \rho_k$ to $q + 1 \leq \rho_k$.

For this part, we rewrite $\mathbf{M_{q+1}} = \begin{pmatrix} \mathbf{M_q} & \mathbf{P_q} \\ \mathbf{F_q} & \mathbf{A_{q+1} S_{q+1,q+1}} \end{pmatrix}$, where $\mathbf{P_q} = \begin{pmatrix} \mathbf{A_{q+1} S_{q+1,1}} \\ \vdots \\ \mathbf{A_{q+1} S_{q+1,q}} \end{pmatrix}$ is an $(n-f-1)q$-by-$(n-f-1)$ matrix, and $\mathbf{F_q} = \begin{pmatrix} \mathbf{A_1 S_{1,q+1}} & \cdots & \mathbf{A_q S_{q,q+1}} \end{pmatrix}$ is an $(n-f-1)$-by-$(n-f-1)q$ matrix. Assuming that $\mathbf{M_q}$ is invertible, we transform $\mathbf{M_{q+1}}$ into $\mathbf{M'_{q+1}}$ as follows:

$$\mathbf{M'_{q+1}} = \begin{pmatrix} \mathbf{I_{(n-f-1)q}} & 0 \\ 0 & \mathbf{A_{q+1}^{-1}} \end{pmatrix} \begin{pmatrix} \mathbf{M_q} & \mathbf{P_q} \\ \mathbf{F_q} & \mathbf{A_{q+1} S_{q+1,q+1}} \end{pmatrix} \begin{pmatrix} \mathbf{I_{(n-f-1)q}} & -\mathbf{M_q^{-1} P_q} \\ 0 & \mathbf{I_{(n-f-1)}} \end{pmatrix}$$
$$= \begin{pmatrix} \mathbf{M_q} & 0 \\ \mathbf{A_{q+1}^{-1} F_q} & \mathbf{S_{q+1,q+1}} - \mathbf{A_{q+1}^{-1} F_q M_q^{-1} P_q} \end{pmatrix}.$$

Here $\mathbf{I_{(n-f-1)q}}$ and $\mathbf{I_{(n-f-1)}}$ each denote a $(n-f-1)q \times (n-f-1)q$ and a $(n-f-1) \times (n-f-1)$ identity matrices. Note that $|\det(\mathbf{M'_{q+1}})| = |\det(\mathbf{M_{q+1}})|$, since in the first equation above, the matrix multiplied at the left has determinant ± 1, and the matrix multiplied at the right has determinant 1.

Observe that the diagonal elements of the $(n - f - 1) \times (n - f - 1)$ diagonal matrix $\mathbf{S_{q+1,q+1}}$ are chosen independently from $\mathbf{M_q}$ and $\mathbf{A_{q+1}^{-1} F_q M_q^{-1} P_q}$. It can be proved that $\mathbf{S_{q+1,q+1}} - \mathbf{A_{q+1}^{-1} F_q M_q^{-1} P_q}$ is invertible with probability at least $1 - \frac{n-f-1}{2^{L/\rho_k}}$ (see Appendix C.4 of [15]). According to the induction assumption, $\mathbf{M_q}$ is invertible with probability at least $\left(1 - \frac{n-f-1}{2^{L/\rho_k}}\right)^{q}$. So we have $\Pr\{\mathbf{M_{q+1}}$ is invertible$\} \geq \left(1 - \frac{n-f-1}{2^{L/\rho_k}}\right)^{q+1}$. This completes the induction. Now we can see that $\mathbf{M}_{\rho_k} = \tilde{\mathbf{M}}_H$ is invertible with probability $\geq \left(1 - \frac{n-f-1}{2^{L/\rho_k}}\right)^{\rho_k} \geq 1 - \frac{(n-f-1)\rho_k}{2^{L/\rho_k}} \to 1$, as $L \to \infty$. □

Now we have proved that there exists a set of coding matrices $\{\mathbf{C_e}|e \in \mathcal{E}_k\}$ such that the resulting $\mathbf{C_H}$ satisfies the condition that $\mathbf{D_H C_H} = 0$ if and only if $\mathbf{D_H} = 0$.

B.2 For all subgraphs in Ω_k

In this section, we are going to show that, for $\mathcal{G}_k$, if the coding matrices $\{\mathbf{C_e}|e \in \mathcal{E}_k\}$ are generated as described in Theorem 1, then with non-zero probability the set of square matrices $\{\mathbf{M_H}|H \in \Omega_k\}$ are all invertible *simultaneously*. When this is true, there exists a set of coding matrices that is correct. Note that the random coefficients are first chosen for all edges in $\mathcal{G}_k$, and then coefficients in graph H come from the corresponding edges in $\mathcal{G}_k$. This implies that the coefficients in the polynomials for different $\mathbf{M_H}$ for different H are overlapping sets.

According to Lemma 1, each $\mathbf{M_H}$ ($H \in \Omega_k$) is *not* invertible with probability at most $\frac{(n-f-1)\rho_k}{2^{L/\rho_k}}$. According to the union bound, it follows that the probability that all matrices $\{\mathbf{M_H}|H \in \Omega_k\}$ are simultaneously invertible with probability at least $1 - |\Omega_k|\frac{(n-f-1)\rho_k}{2^{L/\rho_k}}$. According to the way $\mathcal{G}_k$ is constructed and the definition of Ω_k, it should not be hard to see that $\mathcal{G}_k$ is a subgraph of $\mathcal{G}_1 = \mathcal{G}$, and $\Omega_k \subseteq \Omega_1$. Notice that $|\Omega_1| = \binom{n}{n-f}$. So $|\Omega_k| \le \binom{n}{n-f}$ and all $\mathbf{M_H}$ ($H \in \Omega_k$) are simultaneously invertible with probability at least $1 - \binom{n}{n-f}\frac{(n-f-1)\rho_k}{2^{L/\rho_k}}$.

This result shown here implies that for sufficiently large L, there exist a set of correct coding matrices $\{\mathbf{M_e}|e \in \mathcal{E}_k\}$. By considering *all* subgraphs in Ω_k, we essentially ensure that equality check is performed between all pairs of fault-free nodes in $\mathcal{G}_k$: for any pair of fault-free nodes (i, j), there exists an $H \in \Omega_k$ consisting of only fault-free nodes that includes i and j both; hence x_i and x_j will be checked for equality within this H. Then Theorem 1 follows.

C. THROUGHPUT OF NAB

First consider the time cost of each operation in instance k of NAB:

Phase 1: It takes $L/\gamma_k \le L/\gamma^*$ time units, since unreliable broadcast from the source node 1 at rate γ_k is achievable and $\gamma_k \ge \gamma^*$, as discussed in Section 2.

Phase 2 – Equality check: As discussed previously, it takes $L/\rho_k \le L/\rho^*$ time units.

Phase 2 – Broadcasting outcomes of equality check: To reliably broadcast the 1-bit flags from the equality check algorithm, a previously proposed Byzantine broadcast algorithm, such as [6], is used. The algorithm from [6], denoted as `Broadcast_Default` hereafter, reliably broadcasts 1 bit by communicating no more than $P(n)$ bits in a *complete* graph, where $P(n)$ is a polynomial of n. In our setting, $\mathcal{G}$ might not be complete. However, from each node i to each node j, $2f+1$ node-disjoint paths exists. In this case, since there are at most f faulty nodes, reliable *end-to-end* communication from node i to node j can be achieved by sending the same copy of data along a set of $2f+1$ node-disjoint paths and taking the majority at node j. By doing this, we can emulate a complete graph in an incomplete graph $\mathcal{G}$. Then it can be showed that, by running `Broadcast_Default` on top of the emulated complete graph, reliably broadcasting the 1-bit flags can be completed in $O(n^\alpha)$ time units, for some constant $\alpha > 0$.

Phase 3: If Phase 3 is performed in instance k, every node i in $\mathcal{V}_k$ uses `Broadcast_Default` to reliably broadcast all the messages that it claims to have received from other nodes,

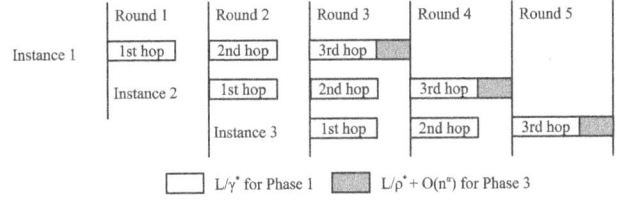

Figure 2: Example of pipelining

and sent to the other nodes, during Phase 1 and 2 of the k-th instance. Similar to the discussion above about broadcasting the outcomes of equality check, it can be showed that the time it takes to complete Phase 3 is $O(Ln^\beta)$ for some constant $\beta > 0$.

Now consider a sequence of $Q > 0$ instances of NAB. As discussed previously, Phase 3 will be performed at most $f(f+1)$ times throughout the execution of the algorithm. So we have the following upper bound of the execution time of Q instances of NAB: $t(\mathcal{G}, L, Q, NAB) \le Q\left(\frac{L}{\gamma^*} + \frac{L}{\rho^*} + O(n^\alpha)\right) + f(f+1)O(Ln^\beta)$. Given that $f < n$, throughput of NAB can be lower bounded by

$$
\begin{aligned}
T(\mathcal{G}, L, NAB) &= \lim_{Q \to \infty} \frac{LQ}{t(\mathcal{G}, L, Q, NAB)} \\
&\ge \lim_{Q \to \infty} \frac{LQ}{Q\left(\frac{L}{\gamma^*} + \frac{L}{\rho^*} + O(n^\alpha)\right) + f(f+1)O(Ln^\beta)} \\
&\ge \lim_{Q \to \infty} \left(\frac{\gamma^* + \rho^*}{\gamma^* \rho^*} + \frac{O(n^\alpha)}{L} + \frac{O(n^{\beta+2})}{Q}\right)^{-1}.
\end{aligned}
$$

Note that for a given graph $\mathcal{G}$, $n, \gamma^*, \rho^*, \alpha, \beta$ are all constants independent of L and Q. So for sufficiently large values of L and Q, the last two terms in the last inequality become negligible compared to the first term, and the throughput of NAB approaches to a value that is at least as large as $\frac{\gamma^* \rho^*}{\gamma^* + \rho^*}$.

In the above discussion, we implicitly assumed that transmissions during the unreliable broadcast in Phase 1 are performed all at the same time, by assuming no propagation delay. However, when propagation delay is considered, a node cannot forward a message/symbol until it finishes receiving it. So for the k-th instance of NAB, the information broadcast by the source propagates only one hop every L/γ_k time units. So for a large network, the "time span" of Phase 1 can be much larger than L/γ_k. This problem can be solved by pipelining: We divide the time horizon into rounds of $\left(\frac{L}{\gamma^*} + \frac{L}{\rho^*} + O(n^\alpha)\right)$ time units. For each instance of NAB, the L-bit input from the source node 1 propagates one hop per round, using the first L/γ^* time units, until Phase 1 completes. Then the remaining $\left(\frac{L}{\rho^*} + O(n^\alpha)\right)$ time units of the last round is used to perform Phase 2, using all the links. An example in which the broadcast in Phase 1 takes 3 hops is shown in Figure 2. By pipelining, we achieve the lower bound from Eq.1.

D. CONSTRUCTION OF Γ

A subgraph of $\mathcal{G}$ belonging to Γ is obtained as follows: We will say that edges in $W \subset \mathcal{E}$ are "explainable" if there exists a set $F \subset \mathcal{V}$ such that (i) F contains at most f nodes, and (ii) each edge in W is incident on at least one node in F. Set F is then said to "explain set W".

Consider each *explainable* set of edges $W \subset \mathcal{E}$. Suppose that

$F_1, \cdots, F_\Delta$ are all the subsets of $\mathcal{V}$ that *explain* edge set W. A subgraph Ψ_W of $\mathcal{G}$ is obtained by removing edges in W from $\mathcal{E}$, and nodes in $\bigcap_{\delta=1}^{\Delta} F_\delta$ from $\mathcal{V}$. [2] In general, Ψ_W above may or may not contain the source node 1. Only those Ψ_W's that do contain node 1 belongs to Γ.

E. PROOF OF THEOREM 2

In arbitrary point-to-point network $\mathcal{G}(\mathcal{V}, \mathcal{E})$, the capacity of the BB problem with node 1 being the source and up to $f < n/3$ faults satisfies the following upper bounds

E.1 $C_{BB}(\mathcal{G}) \leq \gamma^*$

PROOF. Consider any $\Psi_W \in \Gamma$ and let W is the set of edges in $\mathcal{G}$ but not in Ψ_W. By the construction of Γ, there must be at least one set $F \subset \mathcal{V}$ that explains W and does not contain the source node 1. We are going to show that $C_{BB}(\mathcal{G}) \leq MINCUT(\Psi_W, 1, i)$ for every node $i \neq 1$ that is in Ψ_W.

Notice that there must exist a set of nodes that explains W and does not contain node 1; otherwise node 1 is not in Ψ_W. Without loss of generality, assume that F_1 is one such set nodes.

First consider any node $i \neq 1$ in Ψ_W such that $i \notin F_1$. For $f > 0$, such a node i must exist since $|F_1| \leq f$ and Ψ_W contains $n - f$ nodes where $n > 3f$. Let all the nodes in F_1 be faulty such that they refuse to communicate over edges in W, but otherwise behave correctly. In this case, since the source is fault-free, node i must be able to receive the L-bit input that node 1 is trying to broadcast. So $C_{BB}(\mathcal{G}) \leq MINCUT(\Psi_W, 1, i)$.

Next we consider a node $i \neq 1$ in Ψ_W and $i \in F_1$. Since F_1 is non-empty, such a node i exists. Notice that node i cannot be contained in all sets of nodes that explain W, otherwise node i cannot be in Ψ_W. Then there are only two possibilities:
Case 1: There exist a set F explaining W that contains neither node 1 nor node i. In this case, $C_{BB}(\mathcal{G}) \leq MINCUT(\Psi_W, 1, i)$ according to the above argument by replacing F_1 with F.
Case 2: any set F that explains W and does not contain node i contains node 1. Let F_2 be one such set containing node 1 but not node i.

Define $V^- = \mathcal{V} - F_1 - F_2$. V^- is not empty since F_1 and F_2 both contain at most f nodes and there are $n \geq 3f + 1$ nodes in $\mathcal{V}$. Consider two scenarios with the same input value x: (1) Nodes in F_1 (which does not contain node 1) are faulty and they behave as if links in W are broken, but otherwise behave correctly; and (2) Nodes in F_2 (contains node 1) are faulty and they behave as if links in W are broken, but otherwise behave correctly. In both cases, nodes in V^- are fault-free.

Observe that among edges between nodes in V^- and $F_1 \cup F_2$, only edges between V^- and $F_1 \cap F_2$ could have been removed, because otherwise W cannot be explained by both F_1 and F_2. So nodes in V^- cannot distinguish between the two scenarios above. In scenario (1), the source node 1 is not faulty. Hence nodes in V^- must agree with the value x that node 1 is trying to broadcast, according to the validity condition. Since nodes in V^- cannot distinguish between the two scenarios, they must also set their outputs to x in scenario (2), even though in this case the source node 1 is faulty. Then according to the agreement condition, node i must agree with nodes in V^- in scenario (2), which means that node i also have to learn x. So $C_{BB}(\mathcal{G}) \leq MINCUT(\Psi_W, 1, i)$. Recall that γ^* equals to the

minimum of $MINCUT(\Psi_W, 1, i)$ over all $\Psi_W \in \Gamma$ and i. This completes the proof. □

E.2 $C_{BB}(\mathcal{G}) \leq 2\rho^*$

PROOF. For a subgraph $H \in \Omega_1$ and the corresponding $\overline{H} \in \overline{\Omega}_1$, denote $U_H = \min_{nodes\ i,j\ in\ \overline{H}} MINCUT(\overline{H}, i, j)$. We will prove the upper bound by showing that $C_{BB}(G) \leq U_H$ for every $H \in \Omega_1$.

Suppose on the contrary that Byzantine broadcast can be done at a rate $R > U_H + \epsilon$ for some constant $\epsilon > 0$. So there exists a BB algorithm, named $\mathcal{A}$, that can broadcast $t(U_H + \epsilon)$ bits in using t time units, for some $t > 0$.

Let E be a set of edges in H that corresponds to one of the minimum-cuts in $\overline{H}$. In other words, $\sum_{e \in E} z_e = U_H$, and the nodes in H can be partitioned into two non-empty sets $\mathcal{L}$ and $\mathcal{R}$ such that $\mathcal{L}$ and $\mathcal{R}$ are disconnected from each other if edges in E are removed. Also denote F as the set of nodes that are in $\mathcal{G}$ but not in H. Notice that since H contains $(n - f)$ nodes, F contains f nodes.

Notice that in t time units, at most $tU_H < t(U_H + \epsilon)$ bits of information can be sent over edges in E. According to the pigeonhole principle, there must exist two different input values of $t(U_H + \epsilon)$ bits, denoted as u and v, such that in the absence of misbehavior, broadcasting u and v with algorithm $\mathcal{A}$ results in the same communication pattern over edges in E.

First consider the case when F contains the source node 1. Consider the three scenarios using algorithm $\mathcal{A}$:

1. Node 1 broadcasts u, and none of the nodes misbehave. So all nodes should set their outputs to u.
2. Node 1 broadcasts v, and none of the nodes misbehave. So all nodes should set their outputs to v.
3. Nodes in F are faulty (includes the source node 1). The faulty nodes in F behave to nodes in $\mathcal{L}$ as in scenario 1, and behave to nodes in $\mathcal{R}$ as in scenario 2.

We show in [15] that nodes in $\mathcal{L}$ cannot distinguish scenario 1 from scenario 3, and nodes in $\mathcal{R}$ cannot distinguish scenario 2 from scenario 3. So in scenario 3, nodes in $\mathcal{L}$ set their outputs to u and nodes in $\mathcal{R}$ set their outputs to v. This violates the agreement condition and contradicts with the assumption that $\mathcal{A}$ solves BB at rate $U_H + \epsilon$. Hence $C_{BB}(\mathcal{G}) \leq U_H$.

Next consider the case when F does not contain the source node 1. Without loss of generality, suppose that node 1 is in $\mathcal{L}$. Consider the following three scenarios:

1. Node 1 broadcasts u, and none of the nodes misbehave. So all nodes should set their outputs to u.
2. Node 1 broadcasts v, and none of the nodes misbehave. So all nodes should set their outputs to v.
3. Node 1 broadcasts u, and nodes in F are faulty. The faulty nodes in F behave to nodes in $\mathcal{L}$ as in scenario 1, and behave to nodes in $\mathcal{R}$ as in scenario 2.

In this case, we show in [15] that nodes in $\mathcal{L}$ cannot distinguish scenario 1 from scenario 3, and nodes in $\mathcal{R}$ cannot distinguish scenario 2 from scenario 3. So in scenario 3, nodes in $\mathcal{L}$ set their outputs to u and nodes in $\mathcal{R}$ set their outputs to v. This violates the agreement condition and contradicts with the assumption that $\mathcal{A}$ solves BB at rate $U_H + \epsilon$. Hence $C_{BB}(\mathcal{G}) \leq U_H$. Recall that ρ^* equals to the minimum of $MINCUT(\overline{H}, i, j)$ over all $\overline{H} \in \Omega_1$ and (i, j). This completes the proof. □

---

[2]It is possible that Ψ_W for different W may be identical. This does not affect the correctness of our algorithm.

Brief Announcement: Network Formation Games Can Give Rise to Realistic Networks

András Gulyás, Attila Kőrösi, Gábor Rétvári, József Bíró, Dávid Szabó
Department of Telecommunications and Media Informatics
Budapest University of Technology and Economics
{gulyas,korosi,retvari,biro,szabod}@tmit.bme.hu

Categories and Subject Descriptors

C.2.1 [**Computer-communication networks**]: Network Architecture and Design—*Network topology*; G.2.2 [**Discrete Mathematics**]: Graph Theory; F.0 [**Theory of Computation**]: General

Keywords

network formation games, greedy routing, complex networks

1. INTRODUCTION

The purpose of network formation games [1] is to give a game-theoretical tool which can effectively explain the topological properties (clustering, degree distribution, small world property) and the emergence of Internet-like complex networks in an incentive centered economical fashion. In the influential book of the subject [2], the development of an incentive-oriented and *endogenous* model of network formation, that would generate more heterogeneous and realistic networks, is still attributed as an exciting open challenge. Although more recently several studies recovered realistic clustering and degree distribution by encoding these properties into the cost functions of the players, these still qualify as *exogeneous* models. In this paper, we define a network formation game in which realistic topologies naturally *emerge* as equilibrium networks, without enforcing topological concerns in the cost functions. Inspired by the wealth of studies concerning greedy search processes in networks, we define a modified game where players are placed in a metric space and, instead of the usual shortest path metric, we use the length of greedy paths as the measure of communication cost between players. We also present some preliminary results.

2. THE GREEDY NETWORK FORMATION GAME

Players, metric space and greedy routing. Let $\mathcal{P}$ be the set of players (identified with network nodes) with cardinality N. We place the players randomly (uniformly) into some metric space. Distance between two players u and v used in the greedy routing decision is calculated as their metric distance $d(u,v)$. A greedy routing step of player u operates above this metric space by choosing the neighbor whose distance is the smallest from the target t. If u has

PODC'12, July 16–18, 2012, Madeira, Portugal.
ACM 978-1-4503-1450-3/12/07.

no neighbor v such as $d(u,t) > d(v,t)$, then greedy routing gets stuck in a local minimum and fails.

Strategies. The strategy space for a player $u \in \mathcal{P}$ is to create some set of arcs to other players in the network: $S_u = 2^{\mathcal{P} \setminus \{u\}}$. Let s be a strategy vector: $s = (s_0, s_1 \dots s_{N-1}) \in (S_0, S_1 \dots S_{N-1})$ and $G(s)$ be the graph defined by the strategy vector s as $G(s) = \bigcup_{i=0}^{N-1} (i \times s_i)$.

Payoff. The objective of the players is to minimize their cost which is calculated as:

$$c_u = \sum_{\forall u \neq v} d_{G(s)}(u,v) + \alpha|s_u|, \quad u,v \in \mathcal{P} \qquad (1)$$

where $d_{G(s)}(u,v)$ is the number of players involved in the greedy routing process between u and v (including v itself) over $G(s)$ and α is a constant, characterizing the cost of building an edge. By definition, if greedy routing fails between u and v then $d_{G(s)}(u,v) = \infty$. Our cost function is a small modification of the one originally defined by Fabrikant [1] as:

$$c_u = \sum_{\forall u \neq v} d_{G(s)}^{\text{sh}}(u,v) + \alpha|s_u|, \quad u,v \in \mathcal{P} \qquad (2)$$

where $d_{G(s)}^{\text{sh}}(u,v)$ stands for the shortest path distance between u and v in $G(s)$. We show that this small modification in realistic equilibrium networks.

3. GREEDY NETWORK FORMATION GAME IN THE HYPERBOLIC PLANE

Now we present some preliminary results if, inspired by [3, 4], we choose the metric space to be hyperbolic. More specifically, the players are distributed uniformly (by assigning polar coordinates (r_u, ϕ_u) to player u) on an R-disk in the hyperboloid model of the hyperbolic plane. We are interested in the Nash-equilibria of this game. Easily, any Nash-equilibrium $G(s^*)$ is strongly connected (otherwise, for some pair of players u and v: $d_{G(s^*)}(u,v) = \infty$ and so $c_u = \infty$).

THEOREM 1. *Any Nash equilibrium of the hyperbolic GNFG contains a subgraph with scale-free (out-)degree distribution, regardless of α.*

Sketch of the proof: We show that there exists a well defined "frame" topology, which is contained in each Nash-equilibrium $G(s^*)$.

DEFINITION 1. *Let $G_{frame} = \bigcup_{u=0}^{N-1} (u \times g_u)$, where $g_u = \{v | \forall s_u, s_u \setminus v \Rightarrow c_u = \infty\}$.*

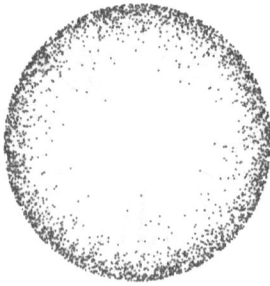

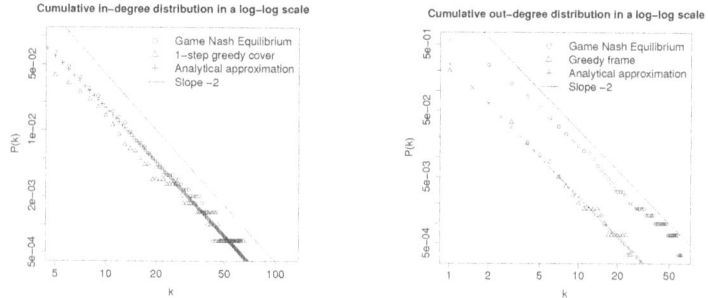

Figure 1: Equilibrium topology (left), in-degree distribution (middle) and out-degree (right) distribution.

Practically, the arc (u, v) is contained in G_{frame} if and only if the $d(u, v)$-disk centered at v does not contain any player other than u. This means that u cannot reach v by greedy routing through any other players then v, and so it must create an arc towards v. Note that the in-degree of each player in G_{frame} will be exactly one. The expected *out-degree* as the function of r_u is given by the integral:

$$k_{out}(r_u) = (N - 1) \int_{R-disk} \left(\frac{T_R - T_{uv}}{T_R} \right)^{N-2} dT \approx$$

$$\approx \delta \int_0^R \int_0^{2\pi} e^{-T_{uv}\delta} d\phi \sinh(r_v) dr_v,$$

where T_{uv} is the area of the intersection of the R-disk and the $d(u, v)$-disk at origin v and $\delta = N/T_R$ is the density of the players (T_R denotes the area of the R-disk). By calculating this integral it can be shown[1] that $k_{out}(r_u) \approx Ce^{-r_u/2}$, with $C = \frac{3e^{3R/2}(-1+\text{Cosh}(R))}{(-1+e^{R/2})^2(1+2e^{R/2}+3e^R)}$. Using this for the cumulative *out-degree* distribution we can obtain $P(k) = C_2 k^{-2}$. ☐
For some special cases of α the equilibria can be easily computed or characterized.

THEOREM 2. *For $\alpha < 1$ the only NE is the complete graph, and this is also the social optimum.*

THEOREM 3. *For $\alpha > N^2$ the only NE is a complex network with scale-free in- and out-degree distributions. This equilibrium is also a social optimum.*

Sketch of the proof: For $\alpha > N^2$ the only NE can be characterized for each player independently as follows: take a player u, and for all $v \in V \setminus u$ let $\mathbb{S}_v^u = \{w | d(v, w) < d(u, w)\}$. Trivially $\mathbb{S}_v^u \subset V$ and $\bigcup_{v \in V \setminus u} \mathbb{S}_v^u = V$. The optimal strategy s_u^{opt} of u is the minimal set cover of V with the sets $\mathbb{S}_v^u$, independently from the strategies of the other players. This means that $s = (s_1^{\text{opt}}, s_2^{\text{opt}} \ldots s_{N-1}^{\text{opt}})$ is both a NE and a social optimum.
The *out-degree* distribution of this network can be estimated by the degree distribution of G_{frame} described above. Regarding the *in-degree* distribution, it can be shown that for player u with $r_u \sim R$, there exists a player v such that $\forall t : d(v, t) < d(u, t)$ with high probability. Since most players fall under this characterization, we have a good estimate on the in-degree distribution with one-step greedy covers, meaning that each player is connected to the player that provides greedy path towards the largest fraction of the remaining players. The expected in-degree as the function

Table 1: Analytic approximations.

Network	GNFG	AS (97) [5]	AS (08) [6]
Nodes	3000	3112	17446
Edges	3112	5450	40805
Avg. degree	3.180	3.5	4.68
Avg. distance	5.981	3.8	3.69
Clust. coeff.	0.104	0.18	0.02
c/c_r	98.11	147.41	74.64

of r_u is given by $k_{in}(r_u) = \delta \int_0^R \int_0^{2\pi} P(u, v) d\phi \sinh(r_v) dr_v$, where $P(u, v)$ stands for the probability that v ensures the maximal cover for u. Using this integral, the cumulative *in-degree* distribution can be approximated by $P(k) \sim k^{-2}$. ☐

3.1 Simulations

The results of our simulations for a game with 3000 players distributed on a hyperbolic disk of radius 14 can be seen in Fig. 1 in the equilibrium state for large α. The simulations support our claim that the degree distribution of the emerging equilibrium topology is a power-law. Our estimation using one-step greedy covers works well for the hubs showing a very close in-degree distribution to the actual equilibrium. The G_{frame}, besides its omnipresence in every NE, explains only a smaller portion of the out-degree distribution, however, it guarantees that, regardless of α, a power-law subgraph is always present in the equilibrium state. Furthermore, the Table 1 suggests that the equilibrium is indeed a realistic graph, exhibiting the small-world property, realistic average degree, and 98 times higher clustering coefficient than the corresponding random graph.

Acknowledgements

This work was performed in the High Speed Networks Laboratory at BME-TMIT. The research was supported by OTKA-KTIA grant CNK77802.

4. REFERENCES

[1] A. Fabrikant et. al. On a network creation game. In *Proc. of PODC'03*, pages 347–351, 2003.
[2] N. Nisan. *Algorithmic game theory.* Cambridge Universiy Press, 2007.
[3] R. Kleinberg. Geographic routing using hyperbolic space. In *Proc. of INFOCOM*, 2007.
[4] D. Krioukov et. al. Hyperbolic geometry of complex networks. *Physical Review E*, 82(3):036106, 2010.
[5] Historical Internet AS level topology data recovered by NLANR. http://www.psc.edu/networking/nlanr/.
[6] Internet AS level topology data recovered from BGP tables by CAIDA Project. http://www.caida.org/.

---

[1] Note that this result is robust in δ.

Brief Announcement: Network-Destabilizing Attacks

Robert Lychev
Georgia Institute of
Technology, Atlanta, USA
robert.lychev@gatech.edu

Sharon Goldberg
Boston University,
Boston, USA
goldbe@cs.bu.edu

Michael Schapira
Hebrew University of
Jerusalem, Israel
schapiram@huji.ac.il

ABSTRACT

We provide an explanation for the observed stability of to-day's Internet in the face of common configuration errors and attacks.

Categories and Subject Descriptors

C.2.2 [**Network Protocols**]: Routing Protocols

Keywords

Interdomain routing, stability, security, BGP

1. MOTIVATION

The Internet is composed of smaller networks, called Autonomous Systems (ASes) (*e.g.*, AT&T, Bank of America, Google, *etc.*). ASes use the Border Gateway Protocol (BGP) to learn how to reach distant ASes on the Internet via announcements from their neighboring ASes. Each BGP announcement contains a list of every AS en route to a destination; an AS repeatedly applies its local routing policy to select a single available route to each destination, and announces that route to its neighbors. BGP routing suffers from a number of serious problems:

Bogus routing information. Because the Internet currently lacks infrastructure to validate the correctness of information in routing messages (*e.g.*, does the route actually exist? is one AS impersonating another?), an AS can announce bogus routes and, thus, influence the routes selected by other ASes. We see this quite frequently in practice [1]; a typical cause is a configuration error [7], but we also worry about attacks where a router deliberately manipulates routing information, thereby drawing traffic to its network [8].

Instability. BGP allows ASes great expressiveness in configuring local routing policies. Unfortunately, these routing policies can interact in ways that lead to persistent routing oscillations, *i.e.*, situations where some ASes endlessly change the route they select, even when the network structure is static (in terms of network topology, ASes' routing policies, *etc.*). BGP oscillations render the network unpredictable and can significantly harm network performance [5].

On the bright side, we have never seen events in which bogus routing information has inadvertently lead to a BGP instability. One might claim that the anomalies we have seen in the wild were never intended to create BGP instabilities. However, given the delicate conditions required to avoid BGP instabilities [3,4], the fact that a misbehaving AS has never caused the system to tip into an unstable state is quite surprising. How, then, can we explain the observed stability of today's Internet in the face of common errors and attacks?

This work sheds light on this phenomenon by first noticing that almost every observed misconfiguration/at- tack to date shares a common characteristic: even when a router announces egregiously bogus information, it will continue to announce the same bogus information for the duration of its misconfiguration/attack. We call this a "fixed-route attack", and show that although fixed-route attacks can destabilize a network in general, the routing policies used in today's Internet prevent such attacks from triggering instabilities.

2. OUR MODEL

We model (see [6]) BGP dynamics in the presence of fixed-route attackers, extending the standard model of BGP dynamics [4]. The network is modeled as an undirected graph $G = (V, E)$, where the node (vertex) set represents the ASes, and the edge set represents BGP communication links. The vertex set contains a unique destination node d to which all other nodes in V aim to establish routes.[1] The routing system evolves over an infinite sequence of discrete time steps, where at each time step a subset of the nodes is "activated".

Whenever a non-attacker node is activated it executes the following actions: (1) process the most recent BGP route announcements received from neighboring nodes; (2) select a single "best" available route according to a local ranking of routes; and (3) announce this route to a subset of the neighboring nodes via update messages according to a local "route-export policy". When an attacker node is activated, it announces a *fixed* route (list of nodes ending in d) to each neighbor. Other than requiring that the attacker announce the same route to a given neighbor for the duration of the attack, no other restrictions are imposed on the attacker. The attacker can pretend to be the destination (announce "d"), announce different (fixed!) routes to different neighbors, announce no route to some neighbors, *etc.*

We seek conditions which imply guaranteed network stability, *i.e.*, that from some moment forth, every non-attacker node's chosen route remain unchanged, for *every* choice of initial state of the system and of "fair" schedule of node activation and update message arrivals. (In "fair" schedules, no

---

[1]This is the standard model [4], as BGP establishes routes to every destination IP prefix independently.

node is indefinitely starved from acting, or from receiving update messages from a neighbor.) Update messages in our model can be arbitrarily delayed and even dropped, and our positive results do not require assumptions on the order of update message arrivals.

3. OUR RESULTS

Network-destabilizing fixed-route attacks. A stable network can be rendered unstable even by a single fixed-route attacker. Consider, for instance, the network in the figure, where each node's ranking of routes is as depicted beside it. Suppose each node is willing to export any route to any neighbor.

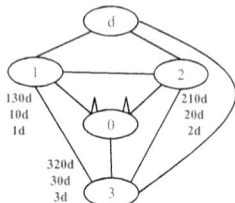

Before node 0 launches an attack, even though each of nodes $1, 2$, and 3 prefers the longer routes to d via node 0, these routes are not available as the link $(0, d)$ does not exist. Thus, each of these nodes will choose the direct route to d, and the network is stable. *After* 0 launches a fixed-route attack by announcing the bogus route "$0, d$" to all of its neighbors, this network becomes an instance of the classic BAD GADGET network [4], which is notoriously unstable! To understand why, suppose that nodes 1 and 2 think they are routing along $2, 1, 0, d$, while node 3 thinks it uses the route $3, 0, d$. This is unstable, since node 1 would rather be using the route $1, 3, 0, d$, and so it will change its route selection. By symmetry, this situation will repeat endlessly.

We identify two interesting environments where stability is maintained in the presence of fixed-route attackers. We also quantify convergence rate in terms of asynchronous rounds [2,9], *i.e.*, periods of time in which each node is activated (at least once) after receiving an update message from each neighbor. Our positive results hold for any network topology, and regardless of the number and locations of the fixed-route attackers, and of the specific fixed-route attacks launched.

Shortest-path routing is stable in the presence of fixed-route attacks. We first consider the scenario that all non-attackers have shortest-path rankings of routes, *i.e.*, always prefer shorter to longer routes. The following holds for all route-export policies:

Theorem 1: When all nodes have shortest-path rankings, convergence to a stable routing state is guaranteed within $|V|$ asynchronous rounds even in the presence of fixed-route attacks.

To gain intuition, suppose that there is a single fixed-route attacker that pretends to be the destination by announcing "d" to all of its neighbors and that every non-attacker node is willing to export all routes to every neighboring node. In a single asynchronous round, every (non-attacker) node that is directly connected to either the real destination node, or the attacker (or both), will inevitably learn of the existence of the (real or "fake") destination, select the direct route to the (real or "fake") destination, and not change its choice thereafter. We can use this argument to iteratively fix all nodes' routes within $|V|$ asynchronous rounds. In [6] we extend this argument to multiple attackers, and to arbitrary fixed-route attacks and route-export policies.

Commercial routing is stable in the presence of fixed-route attacks. While the exact routing policies ASes use in practice are proprietary and unknown, the following commercial routing framework of Gao and Rexford [3] is widely believed to capture most of the routing policies used in practice. Typically, neighboring ASes have one of two bilateral business relationships: *customer-provider*, in which the customer purchases connectivity from the provider, and *peering*, in which the two peers carry transit traffic between their customers for free. These business relationships naturally induce restrictions on ASes' routing policies: (1) an AS prefers revenue-generating routes through customers over routes through its peers and providers; and (2) an AS only carries traffic from one neighbor to another neighbor if at least one of them pays it, *i.e.*, is its customer. ([3] assumes that there can be no cycle of customer-provider edges in the AS-level digraph, as an AS cannot be an indirect customer of itself.) Our main result is in the Gao-Rexford framework:

Theorem 2: If all nodes have commercial routing policies, convergence to a stable routing state is guaranteed within $2X + 1$ asynchronous rounds even in the presence of fixed-route attacks, where X is the depth of the customer-provider hierarchy.

Like the proof of Theorem 1, the proof of Theorem 2 iteratively fixes nodes' routes. Here, however, this iterative stabilization argument is more delicate and involves two traversals of the customer-provider hierarchy (hence the $2X$ factor). In today's Internet, the depth of the customer-provider hierarchy is very shallow (roughly 5 levels on average). Hence, commercial routing guarantees not only network stability, but also fast convergence, even in the presence of fixed route attacks.

4. REFERENCES

[1] J. Cowie. Rensys blog: China's 18-minute mystery. http://www.renesys.com/blog/2010/11/chinas-18-minute-mystery.shtml.

[2] S. Dolev and N. Tzachar. Empire of colonies: Self-stabilizing and self-organizing distributed algorithms. In *OPODIS*, pages 230–243, 2006.

[3] L Gao and J Rexford. Stable Internet routing without global coordination. *Trans. on Networking*, 2001.

[4] T Griffin, F B Shepherd, and G Wilfong. The stable paths problem and interdomain routing. *Trans. on Networking*, 2002.

[5] N. Kushman, S. Kandula, and D. Katabi. Can you hear me now?!: it must be BGP. *SIGCOMM Comput. Commun. Rev.*, 37:75–84, March 2007.

[6] R. Lychev, S. Goldberg, and M. Schapira. Network destabilizing attacks. Arxiv Report 1203.1281, march 2012.

[7] S.A. Misel. "Wow, AS7007!". Merit NANOG Archive, apr 1997. http://www.merit.edu/mail.archives/nanog/1997-04/msg00340.html.

[8] Rensys Blog. Pakistan hijacks YouTube. http://www.renesys.com/blog/2008/02/pakistan_hijacks_youtube_1.shtml.

[9] R. Sami, M. Schapira, and A. Zohar. Searching for stability in interdomain routing. In *INFOCOM 2009, IEEE*, pages 549 –557, april 2009.

Brief Announcement:
Tolerating Permanent and Transient Value Faults

Zarko Milosevic
EPFL
Lausanne, Switzerland
zarko.milosevic@epfl.ch

Martin Hutle
Fraunhofer AISEC
Garching, Germany
martin.hutle@aisec.fraunhofer.de

André Schiper
EPFL
Lausanne, Switzerland
andre.schiper@epfl.ch

ABSTRACT

Transmission faults allow us to reason about permanent and transient value faults in a uniform way. However, all existing solutions to consensus in this model are either in the synchronous system, or require strong conditions for termination, that exclude the case where all messages of a process can be corrupted. We introduce eventual consistency in order to overcome this limitation. Eventual consistency denotes the existence of rounds in which processes receive the same set of messages. Eventually consistent rounds can be simulated from eventually synchronous rounds, and eventual consistent rounds can be used to solve consensus.

Depending on the nature and number of permanent and transient transmission faults, we obtain different conditions on n, the number of processes, in order to solve consensus in our weak model.

Categories and Subject Descriptors

C.2.4 [**Computer-Communication Networks**]: Distributed Systems; C.4 [**Computer Systems Organization**]: Performance of Systems — *Fault Tolerance*

Keywords

Consensus, Arbitrary Faults, Eventual Consistency

1. INTRODUCTION

We study the consensus problem, which is defined over a set of processes Π, where each process $p \in \Pi$ has an initial value v_i, and requires that all processes agree on a common value.

With respect to process faults, consensus can be considered with different fault assumptions. On the one end of the spectrum, processes fail only by crashing (so called *benign* faults); on the other end, faulty processes can exhibit an arbitrary (and even malicious) behavior. In distributed computing under arbitrary faults, when a process q receives a corrupted message from p, it makes no difference for q whether p is faulty and therefore sends a message that was not consistent with the protocol, or the message is corrupted by the link between p and q. Actually, for q these two cases are indistinguishable. This led to the definition of *transmission faults* that capture faults without blaming a specific component for the fault [10]. Transmission faults allow us

to deal, in a common framework, with — in the classical terminology — both permanent and transient faults, but also with static and dynamic faults. A *transient* fault is a non-permanent fault; a *dynamic* fault is a fault that can affect any process/link in the system — as opposed to *static* faults that affect at most f out of n processes per run [1].

Consensus under transmission faults in a synchronous system has been considered initially in [10] and later in [11]. In [3], this work combined with ideas from [6], is extended to non-synchronous systems with only benign transmission faults, leading to the *Heard-Of Model* (HO model). The paper gives several consensus algorithms under benign transmission faults. In [1], the HO model for benign faults is extended to value faults. There, consensus under transmission faults (both benign and value faults) is solved the first time in a non-synchronous setting. This was achieved by separating liveness conditions from safety conditions. For safety, only the number of corrupted messages is restricted, that is, in each round r of the round based model, every process p receives at most α corrupted messages. This assumption potentially allows corrupted messages on all links in a run; therefore it models dynamic faults. However, for liveness, some additional assumptions are necessary, namely *rounds in which some subset of processes does not receive any corrupted messages*. This means that, despite the possibility to handle dynamic and transient value faults in a non-synchronous system, [1] can not tolerate permanent faults located at a process p, where all messages from process p might be (always) corrupted. This raises the following question: is it possible to design a consensus algorithm in the general transmission fault model with non-synchronous assumptions but that does not require such strong conditions for liveness? If yes, such an algorithm can then be applied to a variety of system models: a partial synchronous system [4] with Byzantine processes, a partially synchronous system with Byzantine processes, eventually restricted to "symmetrical faults" [12] (also termed "identical Byzantine" in [9]), a partially synchronous system with Byzantine processes, where in addition, before stabilization time, in every round processes can receive some (bounded) number of corrupted messages from correct processes, etc. This spectrum of interpretations shows the benefit of considering the consensus problem in a model with (only) transmission faults.

2. RESULTS

We give a positive answer to the above question. We express algorithms in the round-based model of [3, 1]. Computations in this model are structured in rounds, which are communication-closed layers, i.e., any messages sent in a round can only be received in that round. Synchrony and fault assumptions are expressed uniformly by communication predicates.

As in [1], for safety, we assume that only the number of corrupted messages is restricted: in each round r of the round based model, every process p receives at most α corrupted messages. We denote this condition by $\mathcal{P}^\alpha_{dyn}$. However, for liveness, we want to consider conditions that do not exclude permanent faults located at a process (which is not the case in [1]). From [5] and [10] we know that in order to solve consensus, we need to restrict the asynchrony of communication and the dynamism of faults. Therefore, for liveness we assume that eventually there is a (sufficiently long) sequence of synchronous rounds where the messages of at most f processes are corrupted. We denote this condition by $\mathcal{P}^f_{\diamond sync}$.

At the center of our result is the notion of *eventual consistency*, a property that we already identified as a fundamental building block for ensuring termination of consensus algorithms with Byzantine process faults [7]. Eventual consistency ensures the existence of a round in which all processes receive the same set of messages (corrupted or not), and $n - f$ of these messages are received and correct. We denote this condition by $\mathcal{P}^f_{\diamond cons}$. Informally speaking, in a consensus algorithm this round is used to bring the system in the univalent configuration, and later rounds are used to "detect" univalence and decide.

We achieve consensus in our weak model in three steps: First, we simulate eventual consistency under $\mathcal{P}^f_{\diamond sync} \wedge \mathcal{P}^\alpha_{dyn}$, then we solve consensus under $\mathcal{P}^f_{\diamond cons} \wedge \mathcal{P}^\alpha_{dyn}$, and finally we combine both algorithms.

(a) Achieving eventual consistency ($\mathcal{P}^f_{\diamond cons}$) from $\mathcal{P}^f_{\diamond sync} \wedge \mathcal{P}^\alpha_{dyn}$. In [7], we showed how eventual consistency can be simulated in the stronger system model $\mathcal{P}^f_{\diamond sync} \wedge \mathcal{P}^f_{stat}$ (with $\mathcal{P}^f_{stat}$ denoting that the messages of a *static* set of at most f processes can be corrupted). Unfortunately, the simulation algorithm of [7] is no more correct under the weaker condition $\mathcal{P}^\alpha_{dyn}$.

Therefore, starting from the simulation algorithm from [7], we design a new algorithm, denoted as Algorithm A_{sim}. Similarly to the algorithm in [7], Algorithm A_{sim} simulates $\mathcal{P}^f_{\diamond cons}$ from $\mathcal{P}^f_{\diamond sync}$. In addition, it ensures a limit on the number of corrupted messages per round and process. More precisely, it simulates $\mathcal{P}^f_{\diamond cons} \wedge \mathcal{P}^\beta_{dyn}$ from $\mathcal{P}^f_{\diamond sync} \wedge \mathcal{P}^\alpha_{dyn}$, when $n > \frac{(\beta+1)(\alpha+f)}{\beta - \alpha + 1}$, $f \leq \alpha$ and $\beta \geq \alpha$. If we want to preserve $\mathcal{P}^\alpha_{dyn}$, i.e., $\alpha = \beta$, this leads to a quadratic dependency between n and α, since it requires $n > (\alpha+1)(\alpha+f)$. Surprisingly, allowing the number of corruptions increase during the simulation (i.e., $\beta > \alpha$) leads instead to a linear dependency between n and α: For any $\eta \in \mathbb{R}$, $\eta > 1$, if $n > \eta(\alpha + f)$, then A_{sim} simulates $\mathcal{P}^f_{\diamond cons} \wedge \mathcal{P}^{\lfloor \frac{\eta}{\eta-1}\alpha \rfloor}_{corr}$ from $\mathcal{P}^f_{\diamond sync} \wedge \mathcal{P}^\alpha_{dyn}$. It remains an open question whether there exists a simulation that preserves $\mathcal{P}^\alpha_{dyn}$ with n being linearly dependent on α.

(b) Solving consensus with eventual consistency ($\mathcal{P}^f_{\diamond cons}$) and $\mathcal{P}^\alpha_{dyn}$. In the second step, we design a consensus algorithm that is (i) safe under $\mathcal{P}^\alpha_{dyn}$, and (ii) live if eventual consistency holds. We obtain this algorithm by parameterizing the various thresholds that occur in our CL algorithm [7], itself inspired by PBFT, the Byzantine fault-tolerant state machine replication algorithm by Castro and Liskov [2]. Let us denote this algorithm with A_{cons}. Algorithm A_{cons} consists of a sequence of phases, where each phase has three rounds. It is safe if $n > 2(\alpha + f)$, and for termination it requires eventually a synchronous phase such that the first round of the phase is consistent, i.e., all processes receive the same set of messages.

(c) Combining (a) and (b). In the final step, we combine algorithms A_{sim} and A_{cons}; we use algorithm A_{sim} to simulate the first round of each phase of algorithm A_{cons}. Thereby we obtain a consensus algorithm for transmission faults that terminates under a condition that does not exclude permanent process faults and is safe under the weak conditions of [1]. When we use Algorithm A_{sim} to simulate the first round of A_{cons}, we have two options: (i) ensure $\mathcal{P}^\alpha_{dyn}$, or (ii) ensure $\mathcal{P}^{\lfloor \frac{\eta}{\eta-1}\alpha \rfloor}_{corr}$. In case (i), the consensus algorithm we obtain has a quadratic dependency between n and α, i.e. $n > (\alpha + 1)(\alpha + f)$. In case (ii), we deal with the additional corruptions at the level of the consensus algorithm. Interestingly, in this case, solving consensus requires $n > 3(\alpha + f)$, i.e., we have a linear dependency between n and α. Therefore, we solve consensus if either (i) $n > 3\alpha + 3f$, or (ii) $n > 4$ and $\alpha = f = 1$. The algorithms and our full results can be found in [8].

3. REFERENCES

[1] M. Biely, B. Charron-Bost, A. Gaillard, M. Hutle, A. Schiper, and J. Widder. Tolerating corrupted communication. In *PODC*, 2007.

[2] M. Castro and B. Liskov. Practical byzantine fault tolerance and proactive recovery. *ACM Transactions on Computer Systems*, 20(4):398–461, 2002.

[3] B. Charron-Bost and A. Schiper. The heard-of model: computing in distributed systems with benign faults. *Distributed Computing*, 22(1):49–71, 2009.

[4] C. Dwork, N. Lynch, and L. Stockmeyer. Consensus in the presence of partial synchrony. *Journal of the ACM*, 35(2):288–323, Apr. 1988.

[5] M. J. Fischer, N. A. Lynch, and M. S. Paterson. Impossibility of distributed consensus with one faulty process. *Journal of the ACM*, 32(2):374–382, 1985.

[6] E. Gafni. Round-by-round fault detectors: unifying synchrony and asynchrony. In *PODC*, 1998.

[7] Z. Milosevic, M. Hutle, and A. Schiper. Unifying Byzantine consensus algorithms with weak interactive consistency. In *OPODIS*, 2009.

[8] Z. Milosevic, M. Hutle, and A. Schiper. Tolerating permanent and transient value faults. Technical Report EPFL-REPORT-174935, EPFL, 2012.

[9] G. Neiger and S. Toueg. Automatically increasing the fault-tolerance of distributed algorithms. *J. Algorithms*, 11:374–419, September 1990.

[10] N. Santoro and P. Widmayer. Time is not a healer. In *STACS*, volume 349, pages 304–313, 1989.

[11] U. Schmid, B. Weiss, and I. Keidar. Impossibility results and lower bounds for consensus under link failures. *SIAM J. Comput.*, 38(5):1912–1951, 2009.

[12] U. Schmid, B. Weiss, and J. Rushby. Formally verified byzantine agreement in presence of link faults. In *ICDCS*, 2002.

Brief Announcement: Efficient Causality Tracking in Distributed Storage Systems With Dotted Version Vectors

Nuno Preguiça
CITI/DI-FCT-Univ. Nova de Lisboa
Portugal

Carlos Baquero, Paulo Sérgio Almeida,
Victor Fonte, Ricardo Gonçalves
HASLab, U. Minho & INESC TEC, Portugal

ABSTRACT

Version vectors (VV) are used pervasively to track dependencies between replica versions in multi-version distributed storage systems. In these systems, VV tend to have a dual functionality: identify a version and encode causal dependencies. In this paper, we show that by maintaining the identifier of the version separate from the causal past, it is possible to verify causality in constant time (instead of $O(n)$ for VV) and to precisely track causality with information with size bounded by the degree of replication, and not by the number of concurrent writers.

Categories and Subject Descriptors

C.2.4 [**Computer-communication networks**]: Distributed Systems

Keywords

Causality tracking, distributed storage systems.

1. INTRODUCTION

Tracking causality is one of the fundamental problems in distributed systems. Causality can be precisely characterized by *causal histories* [5]. Causal histories are sets of unique event identifiers. Each event, a, is assigned a new unique identifier, id_a, and its causal history, H_a, will include this identifier and the set, P_a, of identifiers for all events that causally precede a ($H_a = \{id_a\} \cup P_a$). The partial order of causality can be precisely tracked by comparing these sets by set inclusion. An history H_a causally precedes H_b iff $H_a \subset H_b$. Two histories are concurrent if neither include the other: $H_a \parallel H_b$ iff $H_a \nsubseteq H_b \wedge H_b \nsubseteq H_a$.

Version vectors (VV) [3] are an efficient mechanism to encode causal histories in distributed storage systems. When considering VV, unique identifiers are the composition of unique site ids and a monotonic integer counter. A version vector, V, maintains for each site, s_i, an integer $V[s_i] = n_i$ encoding that event identifiers $(s_i, 1), \ldots, (s_i, n_i)$ are included in the set represented by V (assuming that the first assigned identifier in s_i is $(s_i, 1)$). VV are used to verify the causality among replica versions: $V_a \leq V_b$, iff $\forall s, V_a[s] \leq V_b[s]$, which is no more that the application of set-inclusion defined for causal histories.

By the definition of causal history, it is clear that it is possible to verify if an event a causally precedes an event b by simply verifying if its identifier id_a is contained in the set P_b of events that precede event b : $a < b$, iff $id_a \in P_b$ (or $id_a \in H_b \wedge id_a \neq id_b$). Two events are concurrent if neither causally precedes the other: $a \parallel b$ iff $id_a \notin P_b \wedge id_b \notin P_a$. VV do not allow the use of the set-contains operation when verifying the causality dependencies of two events, as the version identifier is not known as it is diluted in the VV. In the next section, we present a causality tracking mechanism that decouples version identifiers and causality tracking information, correctly encoding the causal history.

2. DOTTED VERSION VECTORS

A dotted version vector (DVV) [4] is a logical clock which consists of a pair (d, v), where v is a traditional version vector and the dot d is a pair (i, n), with i a node identifier and n an integer. The dot is the version identifier and it represents the globally unique event being described, while the VV represents the causal past. Events represented by a DVV can be characterized by the following function from DVV to causal histories: $\mathcal{C}[\![((i,n),v)]\!] = \{i_n\} \cup \bigcup_j \{j_m \mid 1 \leq m \leq v[j]\}$ where i_n denotes the event with identifier (i, n).

From the definition of causal histories, it follows immediately that an event a with DVV $((i_a, n_a), v_a)$ causally precedes an event b with DVV $((i_b, n_b), v_b)$: $a < b$, iff $n_a \leq v_b[i_a]$ (i.e., the event identifier of a is in the causal past of b). Two events are concurrent if neither causally precedes the other: $a \parallel b$ iff $n_a > v_b[i_a] \wedge n_b > v_a[i_b]$.

As an example, we present the evolution of the versions of an object maintained in two storage servers using both causal histories (Figure 1a) and DVV (Figure 1c). DVV are the immediate representation of causal histories, with the version identifier decoupled from the causal past. Next, we discuss the advantages and disadvantages of DVV.

$O(1)$ **causality verification:** Verifying if one event a precedes some other event b can be done in constant time with adequate data structures, by simply verifying if the event identifier (dot) of a is reflected in the causal past of b. Although in many cases this is just a theoretical curiosity, with the growing number of sites involved in distributed systems, this is becoming increasingly important.

Efficient causality tracking in replicated storage systems: Distributed file systems (e.g. Locus, Coda, Ficus) usually use VV with one entry per server. This is sufficient for detecting concurrency between versions stored in servers. For detecting concurrency between the version in a server and the version a client wants to write, the client can record

(a) Causal histories (version identifier in underlined bold)

(b) Version vectors (problematic cases in underlined bold)

(c) Dotted version vectors

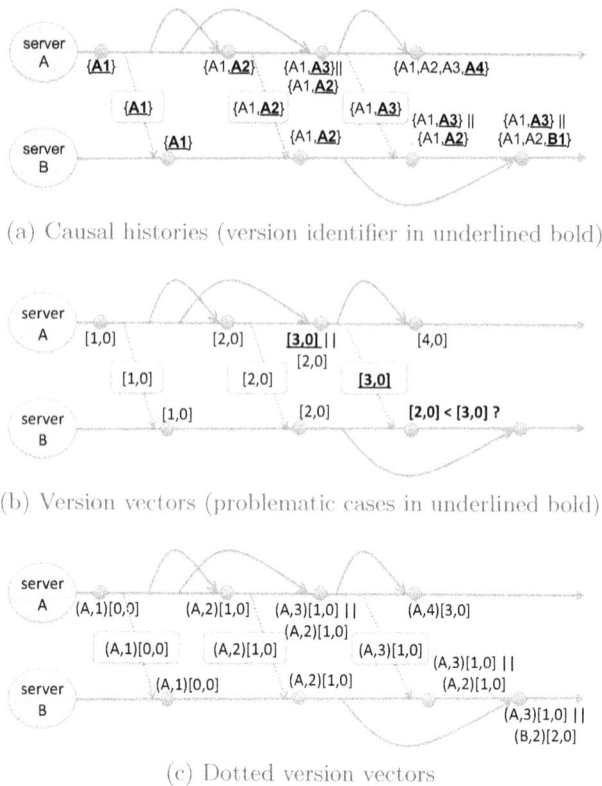

Figure 1: System with two servers and a single object. Client interactions are presented as curves. Server synchronizations depicted by dotted lines. The causality information maintained after each relevant event is shown close to each small circle, || meaning that concurrent versions are maintained.

the VV of the version it has read. When writing back its changes, if the VV in the server is different, a concurrent update is detected. In this case, systems as Coda require the conflict to be solved before the file can be accessed again. With DVV, conflicts can be detected by comparing only the dot, instead of the full VV – a different dot present in the server replica means a conflict.

When a storage system maintains multiple versions, the problems gets more complex. As exemplified in the replica A of Figure 1b, the same strategy can be used to detect concurrent writes from two clients. The problem that arises is what VV to use to identify the second version. When using an entry per server, any VV generated will dominate the VV of the previous version – in the example, $[2,0] < [3,0]$. This can cause problems if it is necessary to compare the two versions, as it would happen in server B, after receiving the version tagged with VV $[3,0]$. This shows that VV with one entry per server are insufficient to track causality among versions generated concurrently by multiple clients.

An alternative used in cloud storage systems, e.g. Riak version , is to keep one entry in the VV per client. This is inefficient as VV can grow very large. To address this problem these systems prune VV optimistically, which is unsafe, possibly leading to lost updates and/or to the introduction of false concurrency. Safe mechanisms for pruning VV, as the one proposed by Golding [1], require global knowledge.

DVV can precisely track causality among versions concurrently created by multiple clients using one entry per replica

server. When a client submits a version that is concurrent with the version in the server, a new DVV is generated that correctly tracks causality (as DVV decouple version identification and the causal past). In the example of figure 1c, we have $(A, 3)[1, 0] \parallel (A, 2)[1, 0]$.

DVV are a simple, practical and efficient solution to track causality - an evaluation with a modified version of Riak that includes DVV has shown a significant reduction in the size of metadata, and better latency when serving requests [4].

3. RELATED WORK AND CONCLUSIONS

Vector clocks (VC) are used to track causal dependencies among events in a distributed system. The same approach proposed in DVV could be used with VC, as VC use essentially the same mechanism as VV, with the difference that VV only record events that generate new data versions and VC record all events in a distributed system.

Wang et. al. [6] have proposed a variant of VV with $O(1)$ comparison time, but VV entries must be kept ordered, leading to non constant time for other operations. Furthermore, as a simple VV, it also incurs in the problems of VV for tracking causality among concurrent client updates.

WinFS [2] also maintains version identifiers for files separate from the causal past of the whole file system, recorded as a version vector with exceptions (VVE). VVE can express any causal history by recording non-continuous sequences of events.In most multi-version distributed storage systems, a client can only replace all versions in the repository by a new version, making DVV with a single dot sufficient for representing the causal histories that occur. Additionally, WinFS only tracks concurrency among clients running in different nodes, with their own replica and entry in the VVE.

By decoupling the version identifier and the causal past, DVV efficiently record causal dependencies that occurs among clients, allowing to verify causality in $O(1)$ time, instead of $O(n)$ for VV.

Acknowledgments.

We would like to thank Doug Terry for his comments on previous versions of this work. This work is funded by the ERDF, COMPETE Programme,and by National Funds through the FCT, projects FCOMP–01–0124–FEDER–010114, PTDC/EIA-EIA/108963/2008 and PEst-OE/EEI/UI0527/2011.

4. REFERENCES

[1] R. Golding. *Weak-consistency Group Communication and Membership*. PhD thesis, UCSC, 1992.

[2] Dahlia Malkhi and Douglas B. Terry. Concise version vectors in winfs. *Dist. Computing*, 20(3):209–219, 2007.

[3] D. Stott Parker and et. al. Detection of mutual inconsistency in distributed systems. *Trans. on Software Engineering*, 9(3):240–246, 1983.

[4] Nuno Preguiça, Carlos Baquero, Paulo Sérgio Almeida, Victor Fonte, and Ricardo Gonçalves. Dotted version vectors: Logical clocks for optimistic replication. *CoRR*, abs/1011.5808, 2010.

[5] R. Schwarz and F. Mattern. Detecting causal relationships in distributed computations: In search of the holy grail. *Dist. Computing*, 3(7):149–174, 1994.

[6] W. Wang and C. Amza. On optimal concurrency control for optimistic replication. In *Proc. ICDCS*, pages 317–326, 2009.

Brief Announcement: Increasing the Power of the Iterated Immediate Snapshot Model with Failure Detectors*

Michel Raynal
Institut Universitaire de France & IRISA
raynal@irisa.fr

Julien Stainer
IRISA, Université de Rennes
julien.stainer@irisa.fr

ABSTRACT

This short paper shows how to capture failure detectors so that the base asynchronous read/wite model and the distributed iterated model have the same computational power when both are enriched with the same failure detector. To that end it introduces the notion of a "strongly correct" process and presents simulations that prove the computational equivalence when both models are enriched with the same failure detector. Interestingly, these simulations, which work for a large family of failure detector classes, can be easily extended to the case where the wait-freedom requirement is replaced by the notion of t-resilience. A noteworthy and first class feature of the proposed approach lies in its simplicity.

Categories and Subject Descriptors

D.1.3 [**Programming Techniques**]: Concurrent Programming; F.1.1 [**Models of Computation**]: [Computability Theory]

Keywords

Asynchronous read/write model, Distributed computability, Failure detector, Immediate snapshot object, Iterated model, Model equivalence, Process crash, Wait-freedom.

Base read/write model and tasks.

The base asynchronous read/write (ARW) computation model consists of n asynchronous sequential processes that communicate only by reading and writing atomic registers. Moreover, any number of processes (but one) are allowed to crash in an unexpected way.

A decision task is the distributed analogous of the notion of a function encountered in sequential computing. Each process starts with its own input value (without knowing the input values of the other processes). The association of an input value with each process define an input vector of the task. Each process has to compute its own output value in such a way that the vector of output values satisfies a predefined input/output relation (this is the relation that defines the task). The most famous distributed task is the

consensus task: each process proposes a value and processes have to decide the very same value which has to be one of the proposed values. The progress condition that is usually considered is called *wait-freedom*. It requires that any process that does not crash eventually decides a value. It has been shown that the consensus task cannot be wait-free solved in the ARW model. The tasks that can be wait-free solved in this base model are sometimes called *trivial* tasks.

The iterated immediate snapshot (IIS) model and its power.

The fact that, in the ARW model, a process can issue a read or write on any atomic register at any time makes difficult to analyze the set of runs that can be generated by the execution of an algorithm that solves a task in this model.

To make such analyses simpler and obtain a deeper understanding of the nature of asynchronous runs, Borowsky and Gafni have introduced the *iterated immediate snapshot* (IIS) model [2]. In this model, each process (until it possibly crashes) executes asynchronously an infinite number of rounds and, in each round, processes communicate through a one-shot *immediate snapshot* object [1] associated with this round. Such an object provides the processes with a single operation denoted write_snapshot(). This operation allows the invoking process to deposit a value into the corresponding object and obtains a snapshot of the values deposited into it. It is important to notice that each immediate snapshot object is accessed at most once by each process but can be simultaneously accessed by any number of processes.

A *colorless* decision task is a task such that any value decided by a process can be decided by any number of processes. The main result associated with the IIS model is the following one: A colorless decision task can be wait-free solved in the ARW model if and only if it can be wait-free solved in the IIS model. This result, which is due to Borowsky and Gafni [2], states that the ARW model and the IIS model (which is more constrained as far as runs are concerned) have the same computational power for colorless decision tasks.

Enriching a model with a failure detector.

One way to enrich the base read/write model in order to obtain a stronger model consists in providing the processes with operations whose computational power in presence of asynchrony and process crashes is stronger than the one of the base read or write operations. An example of such an operation is the compare&swap operation. Another way to

*Full version in [6]. Supported by the French ANR project DISPLEXITY devoted to the study of computability and complexity in distributed computing.

enrich the base read/write model consists in adding to it a failure detector [3].

A failure detector is a device that provides each process with a read-only variable that gives it information on failures. According to the type and the quality of this information, several classes of failure detectors can be defined. As an example, a failure detector of the class Ω provides each process p_i with a read-only local variable denoted leader$_i$ that contains always a process identity. The property associated with these read-only local variables is the following: there is an unknown but finite time after which all the variables leader$_i$ contain forever the same identity and this identity is the one of a non-faulty process. A failure detector is nontrivial if it cannot be built in the base read/write model (i.e., if it enriches the system with additional power).

A natural question is then the following: Are the ARW model and the IIS model still equivalent for wait-free task solvability when they are enriched with the same non-trivial failure detector? It has been shown by Rajsbaum, Raynal and Travers that the answer to this question is "no" [5]. It follows that, from a computability point of view, the ARW model enriched with a non-trivial failure detector is more powerful than the IIS model enriched with the same failure detector.

An approach aiming at introducing the power of failure detectors into the IIS model has been investigated in [4]. This approach consists in requiring some property P to be satisfied by the successive invocations of write_snapshot() issued on the sequence of immediate snapshot objects. Hence the name *iterated restricted immediate snapshot* (IRIS) given to this model. For each failure detector class taken separately, this approach requires (a) to associate a specific property P with the considered failure detector class, (b) design an ad hoc simulation of the write_snapshot() operation suited to this failure detector class in order to simulate IIS in ARW and (c) design a specific simulation of the output of the failure detector to simulate ARW in IIS. Interestingly, this approach was the first to show that failure detectors are related to fairness and can be considered as schedulers.

The problem addressed and solved in this paper.

Let C be a failure detector class defined in the context of the base ARW model. Our work was motivated by the following question: Is it possible to associate with C (in a systematic way) a failure detector class C^* such that the ARW model enriched with C and the IIS model enriched with C^* are equivalent for wait-free task solvability? To answer that question, the paper [6] considers failure detector classes whose output eventually involves (a) at least one non-faulty process and possibly faulty processes (such as Ω_k) or (b) only non-faulty processes (such as P, Σ, $\Diamond P$ or $\Diamond S_x$). The contributions, presented in a detailed way in [6], are the following.

- The answer to the previous question is based on a simple modification of the definition of what is a *correct* process (i.e., a process that does not crash in a run of the base read/write model). The notion of a correct process is replaced in the IIS model by what we call a *strongly correct* process. Such a process is a process that does not crash and whose all invocations of write_snapshot() are seen (directly or indirectly) by all other non-crashed processes.

Given this definition, and a failure detector class C designed for the ARW model, its IIS counterpart C^* is obtained by a simple and systematic replacement of the words "correct process(es)" by "strongly correct process(es)" in the definition of C.

- An immediate benefit of the previous definition is the fact that, when we want to simulate the ARW model in the IIS model, we can directly benefit from the simulation of the read and write operations defined in [2] by Borowsky and Gafni. The only addition to that simulation that has to be done concerns the local outputs of the corresponding failure detector C.

- Given the ARW model enriched with a failure detector class C, [6] presents a generic simulation of the IIS model enriched with C^*. This simulation is generic in the sense that it works for any of the previously cited failure detectors. The simulation algorithm has only to be instantiated with a predicate associated with the corresponding failure detector C.

- An interesting consequence of the fact that, given a failure detector class C, we have "for free" a corresponding failure detector for the IIS model, not only makes simpler the understanding of IIS enriched with a failure detector but allows for relatively easy proofs.

- The paper also generalizes the previous wait-free simulations to t-resilient simulations (let us remind that, in a system of n processes, wait-freedom is $(n-1)$-resilience).

Among other benefits, an important corollary result of this research work is the fact that if C is the weakest failure detector to solve a given task T in the base read/write model, it follows from the previous simulations that (when considering all failure detector classes D^* obtained from a detector class D designed for the read/write model) C^* is the weakest failure detector to solve T in the IIS model and vice-versa. The reader will find all the technical developments in [6].

1. REFERENCES

[1] Borowsky E. and Gafni E., Immediate atomic snapshots and fast renaming. *Proc. 12th ACM Symposium on Principles of Distributed Computing (PODC'93)*, pp. 41-51, 1993.

[2] Borowsky E. and Gafni E., A simple algorithmically reasoned characterization of wait-free computations. *Proc. 16th ACM Symposium on Principles of Distributed Computing (PODC'97)*, pp. 189-198, 1997.

[3] Chandra T. and Toueg S., Unreliable failure detectors for reliable distributed systems. *Journal of the ACM*, 43(2):225-267, 1996.

[4] Rajsbaum S., Raynal M., Travers C., The iterated restricted immediate snapshot model. *Proc. 14th Annual Int'l Conference Computing and Combinatorics (COCOON 2008)*, Springer Verlag LNCS #5092, pp. 487-497, 2008.

[5] Rajsbaum S., Raynal M., Travers C., An impossibility about failure detectors in the iterated immediate snapshot model. *Inf. Processing Letters*, 108(3):160-164, 2008.

[6] Raynal M. and Stainer J., Increasing the power of the iterated Immediate snapshot model with failures detectors. *Proc. 19th Int'l Colloquium on Structural Information and Communication Complexity (SIROCCO'12)*, Springer Verlag, LNCS #7355, pp. 231-242, 2012.

Brief Announcement: Delay or Deliver Dilemma in Organization Networks

Shailesh Vaya
Xerox Research Center India
Bangalore, India - 560056
shailesh.vaya@xerox.com

ABSTRACT

Organization networks are hierarchical trees and were proposed by Papadimitrious and Schreiber to model interactions in an organization. Packets arrive from the outside world at (possibly intermediate) nodes of this directed rooted tree and are to be forwarded to the root. A fixed delivery cost is charged every time a link is used and a delay cost is charged in proportion to the total time packets wait in the network before they reach the root. This is a natural online optimization problem whose motivation also appears in multi-cast acknowledgment setting.

While the asynchronous distributed setting has been studied rigorously, it allows arbitrary large number of packets to arrive at nodes of the network. This is unrealistic. This work proposes a more sophisticated model, called the Bounded Bandwidth Model, which restricts the maximum number of packets that can be sent on a delivery to a constant M. For a complete binary tree of height k, we present a distributed online algorithm with a competitive ratio of $O(min(\sqrt{M}, k))$. We also give a constant competitive strategy for flat tree networks, a competitive strategy for arbitrary tree topologies and a lower bound for any oblivious distributed online algorithm for serial networks.

Categories and Subject Descriptors: F.0 [Theory of Computation]: General

General Terms: Online algorithms, competitive analysis.

Keywords: Organization networks, Multi-cast Acknowledgment Aggregation problem, Transportation networks, Delay Or Deliver Dilemma.

1. INTRODUCTION

Let T be a directed rooted weighted tree, with all edges in it directed towards the root. An arbitrary sequence of messages, containing one or more packets, arrive at the (leaf or possibly internal) nodes of the tree. All packets in the messages are to be sent up to the root of T. Two costs are incurred in this process. (1) *Delay cost:* This is a function of the the total time spent by the packet in the network before it reaches the root node. (2) *Communication cost:* This is a function of the weight of the edges on the path to the root and the number of packets that are delivered on them. The total cost incurred for handling an arrival sequence of packets is the sum of the delay cost incurred for

each packet and the communication cost for all deliveries. The goal is to minimize the total cost incurred cost for the entire arrival sequence. This is a classical distributed online optimization problem: Nodes of the network do not have any knowledge of the arrival sequence of packets ahead of time, but are required to make decisions under uncertainty of future: whether they should hold on to certain packets and make a combined delivery to save on delivery cost while paying additional delay cost or immediately deliver the packets waiting at them, [3], [2].

In the synchronous setting, packets can arrive only at the start of a clock edge and all nodes in the network are synchronized with respect to a centralized clock. This setting was considered elaborately by [3], who present initial results for r-ary trees and a lower bound for serial network. For synchronous setting, [4] present asymptotically tight bounds. For the more natural asynchronous distributed setting, [1] give tight lower and upper bounds up to a small additive constant. However, the vanilla asynchronous distributed model allows arbitrary large number of packets to simultaneously arrive at the nodes forcing them to make deliveries. This is not feasible practically as the links of the networks have a fixed bandwidth and only a bounded number of packets may be sent on the links at a time or may arrive at the nodes. This work considers the following more realistic version of asynchronous distributed setting:

The Bounded Bandwidth model assumes that the links inside the network have a bounded bandwidth M and only a maximum of M packets may be sent on a link per usage.

Also, it is the case that fixed cost c is charged per usage of a link of the network and p packets pay a total delay cost of $d \cdot t \cdot p$ for waiting for t time in the network.

2. A COMPETITIVE ALGORITHM FOR THE BOUNDED BANDWIDTH MODEL

We present an $O(min(\sqrt{M}, k))$-competitive distributed algorithm for the bounded bandwidth problem.

THEOREM 2.1. *There exists a distributed online algorithm which achieves a competitive ratio of $O(\sqrt{M})$ on a complete binary tree T.*

Proof: Let the complete binary tree have a height k and cost c be charged per delivery per link of the tree. Consider the online schema Σ_d captured by the following three rules (constant l_1 is to be specified later): *(1) When the packets arrive at the leaf nodes, they are forwarded by all intermediate nodes immediately till they reach the first node which is located at height l_1 from the leaf node called the rest node.*

(2) Messages wait at the rest node till they have accumulated a delay cost of $l_0 = (k - l_1) \cdot c$. (3) If t packets are waiting and s new packets arrive such that $s + t > M$, then all t packets, $M - s$ of the rest are forwarded to the parent node.

We show that for appropriate l_1, Σ_d achieves a competitive ratio of $\sqrt{M}$. Consider an arbitrary arrival sequence of packets and fix an optimal algorithm $\mathcal{O}$. Let $D = \{(\delta_1, \tau_1), (\delta_2, \tau_2), \ldots, (\delta_i, \tau_i)\}$ be the sequence of deliveries made by $\mathcal{O}$ under these arrivals, where δ_i denotes the time instance and τ_i denotes the delivery subtree.

Fix a delivery (δ_i, τ_i). For the simplification of notations, we refer to this delivery by (δ, τ). Let node $n_j \in \tau$ be a node that is at a height l_1 from the leaf node. Let P_j be the path from n_j to root. Let α_j packets be delivered by $\mathcal{O}$ that take the path to the root via node n_j. Recall that the total number of packets delivered in δ_i is $\leq M$.

Let w_j denote the delay cost accumulated by $\mathcal{O}$ for these α_j packets. Then, the total cost incurred by $\mathcal{O}$ with the packets in this delivery is given by $weight(\tau) + \sum_j w_j$.

We estimate the maximum cost incurred by Σ_d to handle the packets in this delivery. According to Σ_d, packets are delivered immediately by intermediate nodes on the path from leaf nodes till they encounter the *rest* node at height l_1. At n_j the packets that arrive from below pay a waiting cost of l_0 before they are delivered to the root. The maximum number of deliveries at node n_j amongst which the α_{i_j} packets can be distributed is at most $\lceil \frac{w_j}{l_0} \rceil$. This is upper bounded by $\lfloor \frac{w_j}{l_0} \rfloor + 1$. For each of these deliveries, Σ_d pays a maximum cost of $\alpha_j \cdot l_1 + l_0 + l_0$.

Σ_d may make a separate delivery for each of the α_j packets from a leaf node to the intermediate node n_j and l_0 represents the weight of the path from n_j to the root node, as well as the maximum waiting cost paid by any delivery from n_j to the root. Thus, the total cost incurred by Σ_d for the packets in the delivery from n_j is at most

$$\sum_j (\frac{w_j}{l_0} + 1) \cdot (\alpha_j \cdot l_1 + 2 \cdot l_0)$$

The ratio of the costs $C_\tau^{\Sigma_d}$ paid by Σ_d and $C_\tau^{\mathcal{O}}$ paid by $\mathcal{O}$ to handle the entire set of packets in delivery δ is

$$\leq \frac{\sum_{j \in \tau} (\frac{w_j}{l_0} + 1) \cdot (\alpha_j \cdot l_1 + 2 \cdot l_0)}{weight(\tau) + \sum_{j \in \tau} w_j}$$

The term in the numerator expands to

$$\sum_j \left(\alpha_j \cdot l_1 + 2 \cdot l_0 + w_j \cdot \frac{l_1}{l_0} \cdot \alpha_j + 2 \cdot w_j \right)$$

Using (1) and the fact that $\sum_j \alpha_{i_j} \leq M$ and (2) the inequality $\sum_j w_j \cdot \alpha_j \leq (\sum_j w_j) \cdot (\sum_j \alpha_j)$, we have that the numerator is

$$\leq \sum_j 2 \cdot l_0 + M \cdot l_1 + 2 \cdot \sum_j w_j + \frac{l_1}{l_0} \cdot (\sum_j w_j) \cdot M$$

The ratio of costs $C_\tau^{\Sigma_d}$ and $C_\tau^{\mathcal{O}}$ incurred by Online and Offline algorithms respectively is:

$$\leq \frac{\sum_j 2 \cdot l_0 + M \cdot l_1 + 2 \cdot \sum_j w_j + \frac{l_1}{l_0} \cdot (\sum_j w_j) \cdot M}{weight(\tau) + \sum_j w_j}$$

If the delivery of $\mathcal{O}$ includes t intermediate nodes n_j, then the $weight(\tau)$ is at least $t \cdot l_1 + l_0$. Thus, the ratio $C_\tau^{\Sigma_d}$ and $C_\tau^{\mathcal{O}}$ is

$$\leq \frac{2 \cdot t \cdot l_0 + M \cdot l_1 + 2 \cdot \sum_j w_j + \frac{l_1}{l_0} \cdot (\sum_j w_j) \cdot M}{t \cdot l_1 + l_0 + \sum_j w_j}$$

If we choose $l_0 = \sqrt{M} \cdot l_1$, then the above expression simplifies to

$$\leq \frac{2 \cdot t \cdot \sqrt{M} \cdot l_1 + M \cdot l_1 + 2 \cdot \sum_j w_j + \frac{1}{\sqrt{M}} \cdot (\sum_j w_j) \cdot M}{t \cdot l_1 + \sqrt{M} \cdot l_1 + \sum_j w_j}.$$

We can verify that each of the four terms in the numerator when divided by the denominator is less than $2 \cdot \sqrt{M}$. Summing up, we have that the ratio $C_\tau^{\Sigma_d}/C_\tau^{\mathcal{O}}$ to handle the packets in delivery (τ, δ) is upper bounded by $O(\sqrt{M})$, concluding the proof. ∎

Using a few observations about the combinatorial quantity $\chi^*(T)$ defined for arbitrary tree topology T in [1] and the result there in we have the following result:

COROLLARY 2.1. *There exists an distributed online algorithm which achieves a competitive ratio of $O(min(\sqrt{M}, \chi^*(T) + 1))$ on tree T.*

For arbitrary tree topologies we are able to show that:

THEOREM 2.2. *There exists an $O(min(M, \chi^*(T)))$-competitive distributed algorithm for arbitrary tree topology T.*

Oblivious distributed algorithms are those for which decisions at each node are based solely upon the statically local information available at the node:

THEOREM 2.3. *The competitive ratio of any oblivious distributed online algorithm for a serial network (considered in [1]) is at least $\Omega(min(k, \sqrt{M}))$.*

In future, we intend to design competitive strategies for arbitrary tree topologies and also capture transportation system in a city using complex hierarchical networks.

3. REFERENCES

[1] C. Brito and E. Koutsoupias and S. Vaya. *Multi-cast Acknowledgment: How much to wait? Or Competitive analysis of organization networks*, In Algorithmica 10.1007/s00453-011-9567-5.

[2] C. Papadimitrious and E. S. Schreiber. *Optimizing communication in organizations*, Presented at workshop on Complexity in Economic Games in Aix-en-Provence, 1999.

[3] S. Khanna and J. Naor and D. Raz. *Control message aggregation in group communication protocols*, In Proceedings of the 29th International Colloquium on Automata, Languages and Programming, ICALP 2002, pp. 135-146.

[4] Y. Oswald and S. Schmid and R. Wattenhofer. *Tight bounds for delay-sensitive aggregation*, In Proceedings of ACM Symposium on Principles of Distributed Computing, PODC 2008, pp. 195-202.

Brief Announcement: Live Streaming with Utilities, Quality and Cost

Ymir Vigfusson
Reykjavik University
101 Reykjavik, Iceland

Ken Birman
Cornell University
14850 Ithaca, New York

Daniel A. Freedman
Cornell University
14850 Ithaca, New York

Qi Huang
Cornell University
14850 Ithaca, New York

Kristján V. Jónsson
Reykjavik University
101 Reykjavik, Iceland

Gunnar Sigurbjörnsson
Reykjavik University
101 Reykjavik, Iceland

Categories and Subject Descriptors

C.2.4 [**Computer Communication**]: Distributed Systems

General Terms

Algorithms, Theory

Keywords

live streaming, utility, optimization, approximation algorithm

1. INTRODUCTION

The growth in Internet traffic associated with video streaming and sharing of live video content is so rapid that it may soon dwarf all other forms of Internet content. By late 2012, Internet video alone is projected to generate almost 10 exabytes of traffic per month, accounting for nearly 50 percent of all Internet traffic [3]. ISPs and content providers are faced with the challenge of devising and deploying technologies to accommodate the surging demand for bandwidth. Data generated in real-time such as by live video broadcasts (e.g. sports games or new episodes of popular TV shows), chat systems, immersive virtual reality applications and games typically can't be cached at all. In today's systems, each client may pull such information on its own point-to-point stream directly from the data center, even if large numbers of clients share interest in at least some aspects of the data.

Here, we lay the groundwork for a new overlay networking architecture called GRADIENT aimed at reducing the load on providers of live-streaming content. At the crux of GRADIENT is an algorithm to construct dissemination overlays for each data stream. Nodes express their utility for receiving each stream at a given rate, which allows us to explore the trade-off between offering a lower-quality stream to a greater number of nodes and high-quality transmissions for fewer nodes. Intermediate nodes can downgrade the quality of the streams they receive and transmit at a lower rate if needed.

We present a cost model of the network and users, and give an effective algorithm to route streams to balance user utility with bandwidth costs by transforming inflight data to match the live stream to the preferences and requirements of the consumer.

2. MODEL AND ALGORITHM

Consider a collection $\mathcal{S}$ of content streams that must be disseminated over an undirected graph $G = (V, E)$. Each edge $e \in E$

has a *cost* $c_e \geq 0$, reflecting e.g. actual unit bandwidth costs. For simplicity, we assume that the source streams originate at a single, abstract *source* node $s \in V$. This assumption is reasonable in our context since services must store media contents (such as a CDN) or maintain consistency (such as a virtual reality service) at some central location, but is not restrictive since one can model multiple content sources by connecting each to s at a zero cost.

Other nodes $v \in V$ subscribe to a subset of the streams in $\mathcal{S}$, and express preferences for the quality they receive for each stream in terms of a *utility* function. Note that some nodes in G need not be subscribed to any stream, but may instead act as proxies. In our scenarios, nodes tend to subscribe to multiple concurrent streams, such as different object update streams in the case of virtual reality, or media in the case where a node collectively represents the customers of an ISP. We express these subscriptions in terms of utility: each node $v \in V$ derives $u_i(v, r) \geq 0$ utility for receiving stream $i \in \mathcal{S}$ at rate r. For convenience, we assume that each rate r is chosen among finitely many rates $0 = r_0 < r_1 < \cdots < r_k$, and $u_i(v, 0) = 0$ always. For example, $(r_0, r_1, r_2) = (0, 200 \text{ Kbps}, 400 \text{ Kbps})$ means that stream i may be received by subscribers at either 200 or 400 Kbps, or not at all. Let $R = \{r_0, r_1, \ldots, r_k\}$.

Users receive zero utility, $u_i(i, \cdot) = 0$, if they are not interested in stream $i \in \mathcal{S}$. We further assume that utility grows monotonically in r, more specifically that receiving a stream i at rate $r_a > r_b$ provides more benefit for the user so $u_i(v, r_a) \geq u_i(v, r_b)$. Note that if a stream is not available at a high rate r_j then $u_i(v, r_j) = u_i(v, r_{j-1})$, i.e., the *marginal* utility is zero.

High-Level Goal. We define a *routing tree* here to be a directed tree $T \subseteq E$ rooted away from s, along with rates $\rho(T, e)$ for $e \in T$ such that rates along a directed path from s are non-increasing. With abuse of notation, for each $e \in T$ we let $\rho(T, v) = \rho(T, (u, v))$ be the incoming rate to vertex v in the tree. Set $\rho(T, v) = 0$ and $\rho(T, e) = 0$ for vertices v and edges e not in T.

At a high level, our goal is to find a collection of routing trees T_i in G for every stream $i \in \mathcal{S}$ to maximize the utilities of nodes who receive each stream, while simultaneously minimizing the pro-rated cost of the trees. More specifically, we wish to find a collection of trees $(T_i)_{i \in \mathcal{S}}$ to maximize

$$\sum_{i \in \mathcal{S}} \sum_{v \in V} u_i(v, \rho(T_i, v)) - \sum_{i \in \mathcal{S}} \sum_{e \in E} \rho(T_i, e) \cdot c_e. \quad (1)$$

The problem is clearly NP-complete since it generalizes the Steiner tree problem, which corresponds to unit rates and infinite utilities at terminal nodes.

Linear Program. We next formulate the optimization problem above as a linear program. Because the routing trees are independent from one another in our formulation, we will hereafter focus our

Algorithm 1 Primal-dual approximation algorithm Ls.

Input: A graph $G = (V, E)$, edge costs c_e for $e \in E$, streams $\mathcal{S}$ originating in $s \in V$, utility $u_i(v, r) \geq 0$ for node $v \in V$ receiving stream $i \in \mathcal{S}$ at rate $r \in R$ where R is a finite set of possible rates. We augment the graph G as described to produce $G' = (V', E')$ and $\pi_v^r \geq 0$ for $v \in V', r \in R$.

Output: A routing tree over G' for each stream $i \in \mathcal{S}$.

We run the remaining steps for each stream $i \in \mathcal{S}$.

  for each rate $r = r_1, r_2, \ldots, r_k$ in R **do**
    - Let $C(r) \leftarrow \{\{v\} : v \in V'\}$ be a spanning forest.
    - Grow y_S^r uniformly for each untagged component $S \in C(r)$ with $r_S = r$ until either dual inequality is tight.
    - If inequality (3) is tight due to an edge e connecting two distinct components in $C(r)$, we merge the components spanned by e in $C(r)$ and tag e.
    - If inequality (4) is tight, we tag the component $S \in C(r)$ which we intend to exclude from the graph.
    - Stop growing when there are no untagged components $S \in C(r)$ with $r_S = r$ left.
  end for
Traverse the list of tagged edges and components in reverse order, discarding items whose removal produce a feasible solution.

---

attention on computing the best routing tree for a single, fixed stream $i \in \mathcal{S}$. The routing trees for each stream can then be composed. We note that the resulting network could place burden on individual users. We defer link capacity concerns since we believe live streams will not represent a bandwidth bottleneck between ISPs, but note that methods from Steiner tree packing [6] may help to minimize the maximum congestion on network edges.

Augmented Graph. For the sake of analysis, it is convenient for each vertex $v \in V$ to demand the stream at a particular rate or not to demand it at all. To accomplish this, we transform the original graph G as follows. Replace each node $v \in V$ with interest in stream i with a chain of nodes $v_0, \ldots, v_k$ and zero cost edges between (v_j, v_{j+1}) for $0 \leq j < k$, such that the original neighbors of v connect to v_0. Node v_j demands stream i at rate r_j with a *prize* $\pi_{v_j, r_j} = u_i(v, r_j)$ for $1 \leq j < k$ and $\pi_{v_0, r_0} = 0$. We further modify the graph by replicating each edge $e \in E$ to create $k + 1$ parallel edges $(e, r_0), (e, r_1), \ldots, (e, r_k) \in E'$ of cost c_e. Let $G' = (V, E')$ denote the final modified graph.

We define r_S as the maximum rate demanded by the vertices $v \in S \subseteq V$ in G', specifically the highest rate which has a non-zero prize in S.

The problem we have been describing is equivalent to the following integer program [1].

$$\text{Min} \sum_{(e,r) \in E'} x_{e,r} \cdot r \cdot c_e + \sum_{\substack{T \subseteq V - \{s\} \\ r \in R}} z_{T,r} \sum_{v \in T} \pi_{v,r}$$
$$(2)$$

$$\sum_{\substack{(e,r) \in \delta(S) \\ r = r_S}} x_{e,r} + \frac{1}{2} \sum_{\substack{(e,r) \in \delta(S) \\ r > r_S}} x_{e,r} + \sum_{\substack{T \supseteq S \\ r = r_S}} z_{T,r} \geq 1 \; \forall S \subseteq V - \{s\}$$

$$x_{e,r}, z_{T,r} \in \{0, 1\}, \; \forall T \subseteq V - \{s\}, r \in R$$

Here, $\delta(S)$ denotes the set of edges crossing the $(S, V - S)$ cut, i.e. the edges with one endpoint in S and the other in $V - S$. The binary vector $\vec{x}$ corresponds to the edges and edge rates picked as part of the routing tree, and for which we pay a cost. Conversely, the $\vec{z}$ denotes the vertices outside of the routing tree, and for which we pay a penalty equal to the prizes we did not collect. Note that the new cost function (2) is equivalent to the original cost function (1), shifted by the total available prizes. The $\frac{1}{2}$-term allows traffic to

be tunneled via a component (requiring at least a pair of edges) at a faster rate than required by the nodes in the component.

We relax the integrality constraints: $x_{e,r}, z_{T,r} \geq 0$ for all $T \subseteq V - \{s\}$ and $r \in R$. The dual of the linear program is as follows.

$$\text{Max} \sum_{S \subseteq V - \{s\}} y_S$$

$$\sum_{\substack{S : e \in \delta(S) \\ r_S = r}} y_S + \frac{1}{2} \sum_{\substack{S : e \in \delta(S) \\ r_S < r}} y_S \leq r \cdot c_e \quad \forall (e, r) \in E'$$
$$(3)$$

$$\sum_{\substack{S \subseteq T \\ r = r_S}} y_S \leq \sum_{v \in T} \pi_{v,r} \quad r \in R, \quad \forall T \subseteq V - \{s\}$$
$$(4)$$

$$y_S \geq 0 \quad \forall S \subseteq V - \{s\}.$$

THEOREM 1. *The solution found by the algorithm in Fig. 1 for stream $i \in \mathcal{S}$ costs at most $5.986 \cdot OPT$.*

PROOF. *(Sketch)* The proof has four steps. We first use randomized doubling [2] to round each traffic rate r in an instance of the problem to $a^{\gamma + j} \geq r$ for a fixed α, value of $\gamma \in [0, 1]$ was uniformly at random, and the lowest integral value of j. The cost of the rounded instance is at most α factor greater than the original.

We next bound the cost of the solution found by the algorithm on the rounded instance as a multiple of the dual solution, since the value of any dual feasible solution is at most the value of the optimum solution for the primal. By looking at the edges (e, r) chosen by the algorithm when the constraint (3) is tight, we find that

$$\sum_{S : e \in \delta(S); r_S = r_j} y_S \geq c_e \left(r_j - \frac{r_j}{a} \cdot \frac{2\alpha}{2\alpha - 1} \right) = c_e r_j \frac{2\alpha - 3}{2\alpha - 1}$$

for $0 \leq j \leq k$. One can derive a similar bound on the cost of the graph components T included by the algorithm.

Next, we analyze Ls in the Prize-Collecting Steiner Tree (PCST) framework [4, 5]. If $C(r)$ is the set of active components in the output with $r_S = r$ for $S \in C(r)$, then the number of edges of rate r between the components in $C(r)$ is at most $2C(r)$. Using PCST arguments, the solution found by Ls costs at most

$$2 \cdot \frac{2\alpha - 1}{2\alpha - 3} \sum_{S \subseteq V - \{s\}} y_S \leq \frac{4\alpha - 2}{2\alpha - 3} \text{OPT} \quad (5)$$

where OPT is the cost of the optimal solution to the linear program of the rounded instance.

Finally, we determine the ideal value of α to minimize rounding error using calculus. Combined with (5), Ls produces a solution with cost within a $\frac{(4a-2)(a-1)}{(2a-3)\ln a}$ factor of the optimum. This expression is minimized numerically at $a = 3.447$, yielding a 5.986-approximation algorithm. □

ACKNOWLEDGMENT

We gratefully acknowledge Graduate Studies Grant #080520008 from the Icelandic Centre for Research (Rannís).

3. REFERENCES

[1] G. Calinescu, C. Fernandes, I. Mandoiu, A. Olshevsky, K. Yang, and A. Zelikovsky. Primal-dual algorithms for QoS multimedia multicast. In *Proceedings. of IEEE GLOBECOM*, pages 1–17, 2003.

[2] M. Charikar, J. S. Naor, and B. Schieber. Resource optimization in QoS multicast routing of real-time multimedia. *IEEE/ACM Trans. Netw.*, 12(2):340–348, 2004.

[3] Cisco. Approaching the zettabyte Era, *Cisco Visual Networking Index*, page 23, 2008.

[4] M. X. Goemans and D. P. Williamson. A general approximation technique for constrained forest problems. In *SODA '92: Proceedings of the third annual ACM-SIAM symposium on Discrete algorithms*, pages 307–316, Philadelphia, PA, USA, 1992. Society for Industrial and Applied Mathematics.

[5] M. X. Goemans and D. P. Williamson. The primal-dual method for approximation algorithms and its application to network design problems, pages 144–191, 1997.

[6] K. Jain, M. Mahdian, and M. R. Salavatipour. Packing Steiner trees. In *SODA '03: Proceedings of the fourteenth annual ACM-SIAM symposium on Discrete algorithms*, pages 266–274, Philadelphia, PA, USA, 2003. Society for Industrial and Applied Mathematics.

Brief Announcement: A Calculus of Policy-Based Routing Systems

Anduo Wang*   Carolyn Talcott†   Alexander J. T. Gurney*
Boon Thau Loo*   Andre Scedrov*
*University of Pennsylvania, Philadelphia, Pennsylvania, USA   †SRI, Menlo Park, California, USA
{anduo,agurney,boonloo}@cis.upenn.edu   clt@csl.sri.com
scedrov@math.upenn.edu

ABSTRACT

The BGP (Border Gateway Protocol) is the single inter-domain routing protocol that enables network operators within each autonomous system (AS) to influence routing decisions by independently setting local policies on route filtering and selection. This independence leads to fragile networking and makes analysis of policy configurations very complex. To aid the systematic and efficient study of the policy configuration space, this paper presents a reduction calculus on policy-based routing systems. In the calculus, we provide two types of reduction rules that transform policy configurations by merging duplicate and complementary router configurations to simplify analysis. We show that the reductions are sound, dual of each other and are locally complete. The reductions are also computationally attractive, requiring only local configuration information and modification. These properties establish our reduction calculus as a sound, efficient, and complete theory for scaling up existing analysis techniques.

Categories and Subject Descriptors

C.2.2 [**Computer-Communication Networks**]: Network Protocols

General Terms

Verification, Management

Keywords

Reduction, BGP, Calculus, Convergence Analysis

1. INTRODUCTION

The Internet today runs on a complex routing protocol called the *Border Gateway Protocol or BGP* [2] for short. BGP enables Internet Service Providers (ISPs) worldwide to exchange reachability information to destinations over the Internet. With policy-based routing, BGP enables network operators to influence routing decisions by independently setting local policies. Each ISP acts as an autonomous system and influences the Internet routing process for its own economic reasons through policy-based routing. This independence leads to fragile networking and makes analysis of policy configurations very complex. Given the set of local policy configurations at each router, a BGP system converges and is said to be safe, if it produces stable routing tables, given any sequence of routing message exchanges. To aid the systematic and efficient study

of the policy configuration space, this paper makes the following contributions.

- We propose an abstract model for modeling Internet topology and policies. This abstract model, which we call the *Extended Path Diagram* (EDP), extends prior models [1, 3], and provides a basis for our reduction calculus.

- We present a reduction calculus on policy-based routing systems. In the calculus we provide two types of reduction that transform policy configurations to simplify analysis. Using our EDP model, we show that the reductions are sound, dual of each other and are locally complete. The reductions are also computationally attractive, requiring only local configuration information and modification. As a result, they have the potential to significantly reduce analysis time, and also provide a basis for identifying network instances that have similar configuration patterns.

- Finally, to demonstrate the practical value of our reduction calculus, we have identified several use cases.

2. FORMAL MODEL

The development of our calculus requires support for both specification and analysis, rather than using existing model [1] or analysis structure [3] and switch between them, we develop our own abstract model – *EPD (Extended Path Digraph)*, which combines the strength of both. First, EPD specifies policy configuration by specifying the network topology (which node shares routing information with which) and the routing policy at each node (what are the available paths and routing preference among them). Second, EPD embeds the route preference dependency relation in the network topology, which enables reasoning directly on EPD. The fact that EPD includes the network topology and routing policy makes EPD convenient for reasoning in and about our calculus, especially the reasoning makes use of the network topology change.

We first provide the notations we will use throughout the paper. For a policy configuration, we write V for its network nodes, d for the fixed destination node in V^1, P for the union of all simple paths from nodes in V to d(i.e. P are the available routing paths produced by the routing system under the policy configuration), P_u for the subset of P consisting of paths from u to d, and (u, v) for the one-hop path from node u to v. We use the symbol '$\circ$' for concatenation of paths. Given a path p from v to d, we write $(u, v) \circ p$ or simply $u \circ p$ for the path from u to d. Similarly, given a p from u to v, and a path q from v to node w, we write $p \circ q$ to denote the concatenated path from u to w. Finally for two paths p, q in P_u from the same node u to d, we write $p \prec q$ to denote u's

---

¹Routing policies are configured separately for each destination, and assuming the Internet is symmetric, we can focus our discusses on a fixed destination.

preference of p over q^2. Using these notations, we define the EPD instance associated with a policy configuration as follows:

An EPD instance is a graph $G = \{(V, P, d), E\}$ where (V, P) are the vertexes in the graph, $d \in V$ the particular destination, and E is the set of arcs. V are node vertexes and P are path vertexes, available paths to d. The are two types of arc: (1) transmission arcs, (p, q) where p is proper suffix of q; and (2) preference arcs, (p, q) where p, q are path vertexes in P_u, the paths from u to d, and p is preferred over q according to the route preference relation of u ($p \prec q$).

Closely related with safety is the acyclicity of the configuration. We say a policy configuration is cyclic (acyclic) if its EPD is cyclic (acyclic). An EPD instance $G = \{(V, d, P), E\}$ is cyclic (acyclic) if the arcs E contains at least one (no) cycle. The following characterization was first proved by Sobrinho [3]:

If a policy configuration is acyclic, then it is safe. If a policy configuration is cyclic, then we can construct a trace of routing updates under which the routing system exhibits route oscillation.

3. THE CALCULUS

This section presents a calculus of policy based routing systems, in which one rewrites a configuration by reduction. There are two types of reduction - *duplicate* and *complementary* reductions that only require checking *local* policy configurations at the relevant nodes and their direct neighbors. The basic idea is to incrementally merge two node vertexes into one while preserving safety property. At the top level, the reduction proceeds by repeatedly: (1) locating two reducible nodes; (2) if reducible, merge the two node's local configuration according to the reduction; and (3) rewriting the remainder of the EPD instance to reflect that local change. In the following, assume we are working with a given EPD instance $G = \{(V, d, P), E\}$. We first introduce two auxiliary notions: "consistent node" and "node rewrite" that will simplify our presentation of the calculus.

Two EPD node vertexes u, v in V are consistent, if E does not contain a cycle consisting of only path vertexes in u, v.

Inconsistent vertexes implies the policy configuration is unsafe, and therefore is considered a mis-configuration. Our reductions will only be performed on configurations with no inconsistent pairs. Next, we define "node rewrite".

For two consistent node vertexes u, v in V, u rewrites to v by follows: Rewrite the path vertex $p \in P_u$ in u to $p' \in P_v$ in v by: If $p = u \circ w \circ r$, and $w \neq v$, then rewrite p to $w \circ r$; If $p = u \circ v \circ r$, then rewrite p to r; For all other cases, abort rewrite. Rewrite the preference among P_u to that among P_v by: Rewrite preference arc (p, q) to (p', q'), where $p(q)$ rewrites to $p'(q')$.

Duplicate and Complementary Nodes We define two notions of reducible nodes, which we call duplicate and complementary.

For two consistent node vertexes u, v in V, v is a duplicate of u, if after rewriting v to u, the following conditions hold: (1) v's path vertexes P_v' is equivalent to (or a subset of) the path vertexes P_u; (2) For every preference arc (p, q) in v, there exists (p', q') in u.

For two consistent node vertexes u, v in V, v is complementary to u, if for any two path vertexes p in P_u, q in P_v, the following condition holds: For any two node vertexes x, y from u, v's downstream neighbors, which route to the destination through u, v. A preference arc from $x \circ p$ to $x \circ q$ exists in x, iff a preference arc exists from $y \circ p$ to $y \circ q$ in y.

To merge u, v, if u, v are duplicate, we can simply remove u; if u is complementary to u, then we merge them by: (1) Let path

vertexes P_w to be the union of P_u and P_v; (2) Let transmission arcs in w be according to the consensus agreed by u, v's neighbors: transmission arc (p, q) is in w, if $(x \circ p, x \circ q)$ is in x for some downstream neighbor x.

4. PROPERTIES

The key properties of reduction are that the duplicate and complementary reductions preserve safety, that they are dual of each other by nature, and locally complete. Finally, we discuss confluence property of the reductions.

Soundness Our main soundness result is that the reductions rewrite cyclic (acyclic) EPDs into cyclic (acyclic) EPDs. This means that the reductions preserve safety, i.e. we never have false positives or false negatives, with respect to safety property, after applying the reduction.

Duality Duplicate and complementary reductions are *dual*. Assuming EPD G, two node vertexes u, v, the set of their upstream neighbors N_{from} (through which u, v route to the destination) and downstream neighbors N_{to} (which route to the destination through u, v). If all the nodes in N_{from} (N_{to}) can be merged into one node by (multiple steps of) complementary (duplicate) reduction, then u, v are duplicate (complementary) nodes. This duality implies a very interesting practical result: If two nodes' upstream (downstream) are complementary (duplicate), then these two nodes themselves are duplicate (complementary). Moreover, the reduction can be performed in either order: Merge either $N_{from}(N_{to})$ or u, v first.

Local Completeness Consider an EPD G, our reductions are "local reduction" for two nodes u, v in G, in the sense that we only need (and are allowed) to check the configuration at u, v and their direct neighbors (i.e. N_{from} or N_{to}). We assume no knowledge of the rest of configuration. We write N_{rest} to denote these nodes. That is, the local reduction we propose must preserve the safety property for any configuration N_{rest}. Duplicate and complementary reduction are locally complete. We do not exclude the existence of other safety preserving reduction that requires checking policy configuration beyond u, v and their neighbors.

Confluence Duplicate reduction is confluent while complementary is not. There is a counter-example. For a set of nodes V, if they are pair-wise duplicate, that is any pair of u, v in V can be merged by one-step duplicate reduction, then V can be merged into one single node by multiple steps of duplicate reduction, regardless the order in which the nodes merged. A counter-example for complementary nodes, consider an EPD with three node vertexes u, v, w who have the same set of downstream neighbors, we construct their path vertexes and preference such that, while u, v and v, w can be pairwise reduced into u' and w' respectively. While complementary reduction can be applied to either *u,v* or *v,w*, a further reduction step is not possible.

Acknowledgment

This research is funded in part by NSF grants (CCF-0820208, CNS-0830949, CNS-0845552, CNS-1040672, TC-0905607 and CPS-0932397), AFOSR grant FA9550-08-1-0352, and ONR grant N00014-11-1-0555.

5. REFERENCES

[1] T. G. Griffin and G. Wilfong. An analysis of BGP convergence properties. In *SIGCOMM*, 1999.

[2] Y. Rekhter., T. Li., and S. Hares. A border gateway protocol 4 (bgp-4). RFC 4271, 2006.

[3] J. Sobrinho. Network routing with path vector protocols: theory and applications. In *SIGCOMM*, 2003.

$^2 \prec$ specifies the route preference among paths. It is local to each node, i.e., it only relates paths from same node.

Distributed Algorithms for Scheduling on Line and Tree Networks

[Extended Abstract] [*]

Venkatesan T.
Chakaravarthy
IBM Research - India
New Delhi
vechakra@in.ibm.com

Sambuddha Roy
IBM Research - India
New Delhi
sambuddha@in.ibm.com

Yogish Sabharwal
IBM Research - India
New Delhi
ysabharwal@in.ibm.com

ABSTRACT

We have a set of processors (or agents) and a set of graph networks defined over some vertex set. Each processor can access a subset of the graph networks. Each processor has a demand specified as a pair of vertices $\langle u, v \rangle$, along with a profit; the processor wishes to send data between u and v. Towards that goal, the processor needs to select a graph network accessible to it and a path connecting u and v within the selected network. The processor requires exclusive access to the chosen path, in order to route the data. Thus, the processors are competing for routes/channels. A feasible solution selects a subset of demands and schedules each selected demand on a graph network accessible to the processor owning the demand; the solution also specifies the paths to use for this purpose. The requirement is that for any two demands scheduled on the same graph network, their chosen paths must be edge disjoint. The goal is to output a solution having the maximum aggregate profit. Prior work has addressed the above problem in a distibuted setting for the special case where all the graph networks are simply paths (i.e, line-networks). Distributed constant factor approximation algorithms are known for this case.

The main contributions of this paper are twofold. First we design a distributed constant factor approximation algorithm for the more general case of tree-networks. The core component of our algorithm is a tree-decomposition technique, which may be of independent interest. Secondly, for the case of line-networks, we improve the known approximation guarantees by a factor of 5. Our algorithms can also handle the capacitated scenario, wherein the demands and edges have bandwidth requirements and capacities, respectively.

[*]A full version of this paper is available as ArXiv report 1205.1924

Categories and Subject Descriptors

F.2.2 [**Theory of Computation**]: Analysis of Algorithms and Problem Complexity—*Nonnumerical Algorithms and Problems*

General Terms

Theory, Algorithms

Keywords

Scheduling, unsplittable flow problem, approximation algorithm

1. INTRODUCTION

Consider the following fundamental scheduling or routing problem. We have a set V consisting of n points or vertices. A set of r undirected graphs provide communication networks over these vertices. All the edges in the graphs provide a uniform bandwidth, say 1 unit. There are m processors (or agents) each having access to a subset of the communication networks. Each processor P has a demand/job a specified as a pair of vertices u and v, and a bandwidth requirement (or *height*) $h(a) \leq 1$. The processor P wishes to send data between u and v, and for this purpose, the processor can use any of the networks G accessible to it. To send data over a network G, the processor P requires a bandwidth of $h(a)$ along some path (or route) connecting the pair of vertices u and v in G. The input specifies a profit for each demand. A feasible solution is to select a subset of demands and schedule each selected demand on some graph-network. For each selected demand $\langle u, v \rangle$ scheduled on a graph-network G, the feasible solution must also specify which path connecting u and v must be used for transmission. The following conditions must be satisfied: (i) *Accessibility requirement:* If a demand $\langle u, v \rangle$ owned by a processor P is scheduled on a graph-network G, then P should be able to access G; (ii) *Bandwidth requirement:* For any network G and for any edge e in G, the sum of bandwidth requirements of selected demands that use the edge e must not exceed 1 unit (the bandwidth offered by the edge). We call this the *throughput maximization problem*[1]. We shall refer to the special case of

---

[1]The generalization in which the bandwidths offered by edges can vary has also been studied. For the case where there is only one graph, this is known as the *unsplittable flow problem* (UFP), which has been well-studied (see sur-

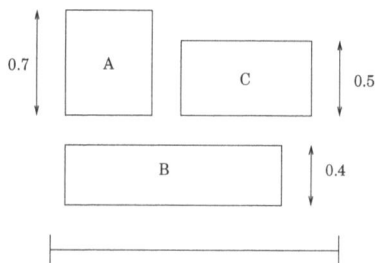

Figure 1: Line networks: Illustration

the problem wherein the heights of all demands is 1 unit as the *unit height case*. In this case, we see that the paths of any two demands scheduled on the same network should be edge disjoint. The general case wherein the heights can be arbitrary will be referred to as the *arbitrary height case*.

It is known that the throughput maximization problem is NP-hard to approximate within a factor of $\Omega(\log^{1/2-\epsilon} n)$, even for the unit height case of a single graph-network [1]. Constant factor approximations are known for special cases of the throughput maximization problem (c.f. [9]). Our goal in this paper is to study the problem in a distributed setting. Prior work has addressed the problem in a distributed setting for the special case of line networks. In our paper, we present distributed algorithms for the more general case of tree networks and also improve the known approximation ratios for the case of line networks. We first discuss the concept of line networks and summarize the known sequential and distributed algorithms for this case.

Line-Networks: A *line-network* refers to a graph which is simply a path. Consider the special case of the throughput maximization problem wherein all the graph-networks are identical paths; say the path is $1, 2, \ldots, n$. We can reformulate this special case by viewing the path as a timeline. We visualize each edge $(i, i+1)$ as a timeslot so that the number of timeslots is $n-1$, say numbered $1, 2, \ldots, n-1$; then the timeline consisting of these timeslots becomes a range $[1, n-1]$. Each demand pair $\langle u, v \rangle$ can be represented by the timeslots $u, u+1, \ldots, v-1$ and can be viewed as a interval $[u, v-1]$. Thus, each demand can be assumed to be specified as an interval $[s, e]$, where s and e are the starting and ending timeslots. Each graph network can be viewed as a resource offering a uniform bandwidth of 1 unit throughout the timeline. We see that a feasible solution selects a set of demands and schedules each demand on a resource accessible to the processor owning the demand such that for any resource and any timeslot, the sum of heights of the demands scheduled on the resource and active at the timeslot does not exceed 1 unit. The goal is to choose a subset of demands with the maximum throughput. See Figure 1 for an illustration. In the figure, the bandwidth/capacity offered by the resource is 1 unit throughout the timeline. The sets of demands $\{A, C\}$ and $\{B, C\}$ can be scheduled on the resource, but both A and B cannot be scheduled on the same resource.

In natural applications, a demand may specify a *window* [rt, dl] (release time and deadline) where it can be executed

vey [11]). In this paper, we shall only consider the case where the bandwidth offered by all the edges are uniform, say 1 unit

and a processing time ρ. The job can be executed on any time segment of length ρ contained within the window. The rest of the problem description remains the same as above. In the new setup, apart from selecting a set of demands and determining the resources where they must be executed, a feasible solution must also choose a execution segment for each selected demand. As before, the accessibility and the bandwidth constraints must be satisfied. The goal is to find a feasible solution having maximum profit.

The throughput maximization problem on line-networks has been well-studied in the realm of classical, sequential computation. For the arbitrary height case, Bar-Noy et al. [4] presented a 5-approximation algorithm. For the unit height case, Bar-Noy et al. [4], and independently Berman and Dasgupta [5] presented 2-approximation algorithms; both these algorithms can also handle the notion of windows. Generalizations and special cases of the problem have also been studied[2].

Panconesi and Sozio [14, 15] studied the throughput maximization problem on line-networks in a distributed setting. In this setup, two processors can communicate with each other, if they have access to some common resource. We shall assume the standard synchronous, message passing model of computation: in a given network of processors, each processor can communicate in one step with all other processors it is directly connected to. The running time of the algorithm is given by the number of communication rounds. This model is universally used in the context of distributed graph algorithms. We require that the local computation at any processor takes only polynomial time. To be efficient, we require the communication rounds to be polylogarithmic in the input size. We can construct a communication graph taking the processors to be the vertices and drawing an edge between two processors, if they can communicate (i.e., they share a common resource). Notice that the diameter of the communication graph can be as large as the number of processors m. So, there may be a pair of processors such that the path connecting them has a large number of hops (or edges). Hence, within the stipulated polylogarithmic number of rounds, it would be infeasible to send information between such a pair of processors. The above fact makes it challenging to design distributed algorithms with polylogarithmic number of rounds.

Under the above model, Panconesi and Sozio [15] designed distributed approximation algorithms for the throughput maximization problem on line networks. For the case of unit height demands, they presented an algorithm with an approximation ratio of $(20 + \epsilon)$ (throughout the paper, $\epsilon > 0$ is a constant fixed arbitrarily). For the general arbitrary height case, they devised an algorithm with an approximation ratio of $(55 + \epsilon)$. Both the above algorithms can also handle the notion of windows. The number of communication rounds of these algorithms is: $O\left(\frac{\text{Time(MIS)}}{\epsilon \cdot h_{\min}} \log \frac{L_{\max}}{L_{\min}} \log \frac{p_{\max}}{p_{\min}}\right)$. Here, $L_{\max}$ and $L_{\min}$ are the maximum and minimum length of any demand, and $p_{\max}$ and $p_{\min}$ are the maximum and minimum profit of any demand. The value $h_{\min}$ is the minimum height of any demand (recall that all demand heights

---

[2]For the case where there is only one line-network and there are no windows, improved approximations are known [4, 7]. The UFP problem on line-networks (where the bandwidth offered varies over the timeline) has also been well studied (see [3, 2, 8, 9, 10]) and a constant factor approximation algorithm is known [6].

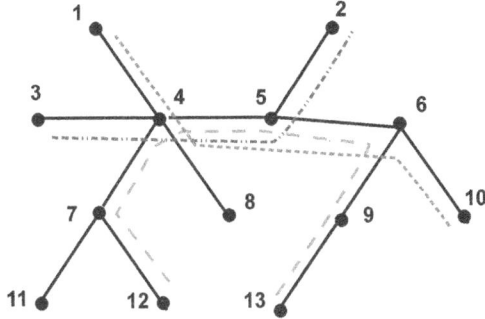

Figure 2: Tree-networks: Illustration

are at most 1 unit); in the case of unit height demands, $h_{\min} = 1$. The value Time(MIS) is the number of rounds needed for computing a maximal independent set (MIS) in general graphs. The randomized algorithm of Luby [13] can compute MIS in $O(\log N)$ rounds, where $N = nmr$ (n, m and r are the number of timeslots, demands and resources, respectively); if this algorithm is used, then the overall distributed algorithm would also be randomized. Alternatively, via network-decompositions, [16] present a deterministic algorithm with Time(MIS) $= O(2^{\sqrt{\log N}})$.

Our Contributions: In this paper, we make two important contributions. The first is that we provide improved approximation ratios for the throughput maximization problems on line-networks addressed by Panconesi and Sozio [15]. Secondly, we present distributed approximation algorithms for the more general case of tree-networks. A *tree-network* refers to a graph which is a tree. Notice that in a tree, the path between a pair of vertices u and v is unique and so, it suffices if the feasible solution schedules each selected demand on a tree-network and the paths will be determined uniquely. See Figure 2 for an illustration. In the figure, there are three demands $\langle 1, 10 \rangle$, $\langle 2, 3 \rangle$ and $\langle 12, 13 \rangle$. In the unit height case, only one of the three demands can be scheduled on the given tree-network (because they all share the edge $\langle 4, 5 \rangle$). To illustrate the arbitrary height case, suppose their heights are 0.4, 0.7 and 0.3, respectively. Then, the first and third demand can be scheduled together.

Prior work has addressed the throughput maximization problem for the scenario where the input consists of a single tree-network (and all processors have access to the sole tree-network). Under this setup, Tarjan showed that the unit height case can be solved in polynomial time [17]. Lewin-Eytan et al. [12] presented a 5-approximation algorithm for the arbitrary height case. In the setting of multiple tree-networks, the problem is NP-hard even for the unit height case. By extending the algorithm of Lewin-Eytan et al., we can show that the problem can be approximated within a factor of 3 and 8, for the unit height and arbitrary height cases, respectively.

One of the main goals of the current paper is to design distributed algorithms for the throughput maximization problems on tree-networks. Our main result is:

> **Main result**: We present a distributed $(7 + \epsilon)$-approximation algorithm for the unit height case of the throughput maximization problem on tree-networks.

The number of communication rounds is polylogarithmic in the input size: $O(\text{Time(MIS)} \cdot (1/\epsilon) \cdot \log n \cdot \log(p_{\max}/p_{\min}))$. Here, n is the number of vertices; $p_{\max}$ and $p_{\min}$ are the maximum and minimum profits. Time(MIS) is the number of rounds taken for computing MIS in arbitrary graphs with N vertices, where $N = mr$ (m is the number of processors/demands and r is the number of input tree-networks). As in the work of Panconesi and Sozio [15], the size of each message is $O(M)$ where M is the number of bits needed for encoding the information about a demand (such as its profit, end-points and height).

Recall that Panconesi and Sozio [15] presented a distributed $(20 + \epsilon)$-approximation algorithm for the unit height case of the line-networks problem. The main result provides improvements over the above work along two dimensions: the new algorithm can handle the more general concept of tree-networks and simultaneously, it offers an improved approximation ratio.

Extending the main result, we design a distributed $(20 + \epsilon)$-approximation algorithm for the arbitrary height case of the tree-networks problem. The number of communication rounds taken by this algorithm is $O(\text{Time(MIS)} \cdot (1/\epsilon) \cdot (1/h_{\min}) \cdot \log n \cdot \log(p_{\max}/p_{\min}))$. This algorithm assumes that the value $h_{\min}$ is known to all the processors. Alternatively, we assume that a value $h_{\min}$ is fixed a priori and all the demands are required to have height at least $h_{\min}$.

Next, we provide a 5-factor improvement in the approximation ratios for the case of line-networks with windows. We design distributed algorithms with approximation ratios $(4 + \epsilon)$ and $(11 + \epsilon)$, for the unit height case and arbitrary height case, respectively. The number of communication rounds taken by these algorithms is the same as that of Panconesi and Sozio [15].

For lack of space, we discuss only the main result (distributed $(7 + \epsilon)$-approximation algorithm for the unit height case of tree-networks) in the body of the paper. The other results are discussed in the full version of the paper.

Proof Techniques and Discussion: At a technical level, our paper makes two main contributions. The algorithms of Panconesi and Sozio [15], as well as our algorithms, go via the primal-dual method. The sequential algorithms of Bar-Noy et al. [4] and Lewin-Eytan et al. [12] use the local ratio technique, but they can also be reformulated as primal-dual algorithms. Given a demand/job, there are multiple tree-networks (or line-networks) where the demand can be scheduled and we call each such possibility as a demand instance. All of the above algorithms work in two phases: in the first phase, a subset of candidate demand instances are identified and an assignment to dual variables is computed. In the second phase, the candidate set is pruned and a feasible solution is constructed. The dual assignment is used as a lowerbound for the optimal solution, by appealing to the weak-duality theorem. In fact, approximation algorithms for many other packing problems utilize the above two-phase strategy.

We first formulate the above two-phase method as a framework. An important feature of the framework is that any algorithm following the framework must produce an ordering of the demand instances and also for each demand instance, it must determine the edges along the path whose dual variables will be increased (or *raised*). The ordering and the chosen edges should satisfy a certain property called the "interference property". The number of edges chosen, denoted Δ, is a factor in determining the approximation ratio. In the case of line-networks, Panconesi and Sozio [15] classify the demand instances into logarithmic many groups based on their lengths and obtain an ordering with $\Delta = 3$. In the case of tree-networks, it is more challenging to design an ordering satisfying the interference property. Towards that goal, we introduce the notion of "tree-decompositions". The efficacy of a tree-decomposition is measured by its depth and "pivot size" θ. As it turns out, the pivot size θ determines the parameter Δ and the depth determines the number of rounds taken by the algorithm. Our first main technical contribution is a tree-decomposition with depth $O(\log n)$ and pivot size $\theta = 2$. Using this tree-decomposition, we show how to get an ordering with $\Delta = 6$. Our tree-decompositions may be of independent interest.

Another feature of the framework is that an algorithm following the framework should produce an assignment for the dual variables in the first phase. This assignment need not form a dual feasible solution, but it should be approximately feasible: the dual assignment divided by a parameter λ ($0 < \lambda \leq 1$) should yield a feasible solution. The approximation ratio is inversely related to the parameter λ. The algorithm of Panconesi and Sozio [15] produces a dual assignment with parameter $\lambda = 1/(5 + \epsilon)$. Our second main technical contribution is a method for constructing a dual assignment with parameter $\lambda = (1 - \epsilon)$. Thus, we get a 5-factor improvement in the approximation ratio for the case of line-networks.

2. UNIT HEIGHT CASE OF TREE NETWORKS: PROBLEM DEFINITION

The input consists of a vertex set V containing n vertices, a set of m processors $\mathcal{P}$, a set of m *demands* $\mathcal{A}$ and a set of r *tree-networks* $\mathcal{T}$ (each defined over the vertex-set V). A demand $a \in \mathcal{A}$ is specified as a pair of vertices $a = (u, v)$ and it is associated with a profit $p(a)$; u and v are called the *end-points* of a. Each processor $P \in \mathcal{P}$ owns a unique demand $a \in \mathcal{A}$. For each processor $P \in \mathcal{P}$, the input also provides a set $\text{Acc}(P) \subseteq \mathcal{T}$ that specifies the set of tree-networks *accessible* to P. Let $p_{\max}$ and $p_{\min}$ be the maximum and minimum profits. We will assume that all the tree-networks are connected. Note that the tree-networks can have different sets of edges and so, they are allowed to define different trees.

A feasible solution S selects a set of demands $S \subseteq \mathcal{A}$ and schedules each $a \in S$ on some tree-network $T \in \mathcal{T}$. The feasible solution must satisfy the following properties: (i) for any $a \in S$, if a is owned by a processor P and a is scheduled on a tree-network T, then P must be able to access T (i.e., $T \in \text{Acc}(P)$); (ii) for any two selected demands $a_1 = (u_1, v_1)$ and $a_2 = (u_2, v_2)$, if both a_1 and a_2 are scheduled on the same tree-network T, then the path between u_1 and v_1, and the path between u_2 and v_2 in the tree-network T must be edge-disjoint (meaning, the two paths must not share any

edge). The profit of solution S is defined to be the sum of profits of the selected demands; this is denoted $p(S)$. The problem is to find the maximum profit feasible solution.

We next present a reformulation of the problem, which will be more convenient for our discussion. Consider each demand $a \in \mathcal{A}$ and let P be the processor which owns a. For each tree-network $T \in \text{Acc}(P)$, create a copy of a with the same end-points and profit; we call this the *demand instance* of a belonging to the tree-network T. Let $\mathcal{D}$ denote the set of all demand instances over all the demands; each demand instance $d \in \mathcal{D}$ can represented by its two end-points and the tree-network to which it belongs. For a demand a owned by a processor P, let $\text{Inst}(a)$ denote the set of all instances of a (we have $|\text{Inst}(a)| = |\text{Acc}(P)|$). The profit of a demand instance $d \in \mathcal{D}$ is defined to be the same as that of the demand to which it belongs; we denote this as $p(d)$. A feasible solution selects a subset of demand instances $S \subseteq \mathcal{D}$ such that: (i) for any two demand instances $d_1, d_2 \in S$, if d_1 and d_2 belong to the same tree-network T, then their paths (in the tree-network T) do not share any edge; (ii) for any demand $a \in \mathcal{A}$, at most one demand instance of a is selected. The profit of the solution is the sum of profits of the demand instance contained in it. The goal is to find a feasible solution of maximum profit.

The communication among the processors is governed by the following rule: two processors P_1 and P_2 are allowed to communicate, if they have access to some common resource ($\text{Acc}(P_1) \cap \text{Acc}(P_2) \neq \emptyset$).

Notation: The following notation will be useful in our discussion. Let $\mathcal{E}$ denote the set of all edges over all the tree-networks; any edge $e \in \mathcal{E}$ is represented by a triple $\langle u, v, T \rangle$, where u and v are vertices of e and T is the tree-network to which e belongs. For a tree-network T, let $\mathcal{D}(T)$ denote the set of all demand instances belonging to T. Any demand instance $d \in \mathcal{D}(T)$ can be viewed as a path in T and we denote this as $\text{path}(d)$. For a demand instance $d \in \mathcal{D}(T)$ and an edge e in T, we say that d is *active* on the edge e, if the $\text{path}(d)$ includes e; this is denoted $d \sim e$. We say that two demand instances d_1 and d_2 are *overlapping*, if d_1 and d_2 belong to the same tree-network, and $\text{path}(d_1)$ and $\text{path}(d_2)$ share some edge; the demands are said to non-overlapping, otherwise. Two demand instances d_1 and d_2 are said to be *conflicting*, if both d_1 and d_2 belong to the same demand or they overlap; otherwise, the demands are said to be non-conflicting. We shall alternatively use the term *independent* to mean a pair of non-conflicting demands. A set of demand instances D is said to be *independent set*, if every pair of demand instances in D is independent. Notice that a feasible solution is nothing but an independent set of demand instances.

3. LP AND TWO-PHASE FRAMEWORK

Our algorithm uses the well-known primal-dual scheme and goes via a two-phase framework. We first present the primal and the dual LPs and then discuss the framework.

3.1 LP Formulation

The LP is presented below. For each demand instance $d \in \mathcal{D}$, we introduce a primal variable $x(d)$. The first set of primal constraints capture the fact that a feasible solution cannot select two demand instances active on the same edge. Similarly, the second set of primal constraints capture the fact that a feasible solution can select at most one demand instance belonging to any demand.

$$\max \qquad \sum_{d \in \mathcal{D}} x(d) \cdot p(d)$$

$$\sum_{d \in \mathcal{D} \,:\, d \sim e} x(d) \leq 1 \quad (\forall e \in \mathcal{E})$$

$$\sum_{d \in \mathrm{Inst}(a)} x(d) \leq 1 \quad (\forall a \in \mathcal{A})$$

$$x(d) \geq 0 \quad (\forall d \in \mathcal{D})$$

The dual is presented next. For each demand $a \in \mathcal{A}$ and each edge $e \in \mathcal{E}$, the dual includes a variable $\alpha(a)$ and $\beta(e)$, respectively. Similarly, for each demand instance $d \in \mathcal{D}$, the dual includes a constraint; we call this the *dual constraint of d*. Let a_d denote the demand to which a demand instance d belongs.

$$\min \quad \sum_{a \in \mathcal{A}} \alpha(a) \;+\; \sum_{e \in \mathcal{E}} \beta(e)$$

$$\alpha(a_d) + \sum_{e \,:\, d \sim e} \beta(e) \geq p(d) \quad (\forall d \in \mathcal{D})$$

$$\alpha(a) \geq 0 \quad (\forall a \in \mathcal{A})$$

$$\beta(e) \geq 0 \quad (\forall e \in \mathcal{E})$$

3.2 Two-phase framework

We formulate the ideas implicit in [15, 4, 12] in the form of a two-phase framework, described next. Our algorithm would follow this framework.

First Phase: The procedure initializes all the dual variables $\alpha(\cdot)$ and $\beta(\cdot)$ to 0 and constructs an empty stack, and then it proceeds iteratively. Consider an iteration. Let U be the set of all demand instances whose dual constraints are still unsatisfied. We select a suitable independent set $I \subseteq U$ (how to select I is clarified below). For each $d \in I$, we wish to increase (or *raise*) the value of the dual variables suitably so that the dual constraint of d is satisfied tightly (i.e., the LHS becomes equal to the RHS). For this purpose, we adopt the following strategy. Consider each demand instance $d \in I$. We first determine the *slackness* s of the constraint, which is the difference between the LHS and RHS of the constraint: $s = p(d) - (\alpha(a_d) + \sum_{e \,:\, d \sim e} \beta(e))$. We next select a suitable subset $\pi(d)$ consisting of edges on which d is active (how to select $\pi(d)$ is clarified below). Next we compute the quantity $\delta(d) = s/(|\pi(d)| + 1)$. We then raise the value of $\alpha(a_d)$ by the amount $\delta(d)$; and for each $e \in \pi(d)$, we raise dual variable $\beta(e)$ by the amount $\delta(d)$. We see that the dual constraint is satisfied tightly in the process. The edges $\pi(d)$ are called the *critical edges* of d. We say that the demand instance d is *raised* by the amount $\delta(d)$. Finally, the independent set I is pushed on to the stack (as a single object). This completes an iteration. In the above framework, in each iteration, we need to select an independent set I and the critical set of edges $\pi(d)$ for each $d \in I$. These are left as choices that must be made by the specific algorithm constructed via this framework. Similarly, the algorithm must also decide the termination condition for the first phase.

Second Phase: We consider the independent sets in the reverse order and construct a solution S, as follows. We initialize a set $D = \emptyset$ and proceed iteratively. In each iteration, the independent set I on the top of the stack is popped. For each $d \in I$, we add d to D, if doing so does not violate feasibility (namely, $D \cup \{d\}$ is an independent set). The second

phase continues until the stack becomes empty. Let $S = D$ be the feasible solution produced by the second phase. This completes the description of the framework.

An important aspect of the above framework is that is parallelizable. The set I chosen in each iteration of the first phase is an independent set. Hence, for any two demand instances $d_1, d_2 \in I$, the LHS of the constraints of d_1 and d_2 do not share any dual variable. Consequently, all the demand instances $d \in I$ can be raised simultaneously.

As we shall see, we can derive an approximation ratio for any algorithm built on the above framework, provided it satisfies the following condition, which we call the *interference property*: for any pair of overlapping demand instances d_1 and d_2 raised in the first phase, if d_1 is raised before d_2, then path(d_2) must include at least one of the critical edges contained in $\pi(d_1)$.

The following notation is useful in determining the approximation ratio. Let $\xi \in [0, 1]$ be any real number. At any stage of the algorithm, we say that a demand instance $d \in \mathcal{D}$ is ξ-*satisfied*, if in the dual constraint of d, the LHS is at least ξ times the RHS: $\alpha(a_d) + \sum_{e \,:\, d \sim e} \beta(e) \geq \xi \cdot p(d)$. If the above condition is not true, then we say that d is ξ-*unsatisfied*.

We shall measure the efficacy of an algorithm following the above framework using three parameters. (1) *Critical set size* Δ: Let Δ be the maximum cardinality of $\pi(d)$, over all demand instances d raised by the algorithm. (2) *Slackness parameter* λ: Let $\lambda \in [0, 1]$ be the largest number such that at the end of the first phase, all the demand instances $d \in \mathcal{D}$ are λ-satisfied. (3) *Round complexity:* The number of iterations taken by the first phase. The parameters Δ and λ will determine the approximation ratio of the algorithm; we would like to have Δ to be small and λ to be close to 1. The round complexity determines the number of rounds taken by the algorithm when implemented in a distributed setting. We say that the algorithm is *governed* by the parameters Δ and λ.

The following lemma provides an approximation guarantee for any algorithm satisfying the interference property. The lemma is similar to Lemma 1 in the work of Panconesi and Sozio [14]. We provide a proof in the full version of the paper. Let Opt denote the optimal solution to the input problem instance.

Lemma 3.1. *Consider any algorithm satisfying the interference property and governed by parameters Δ and λ. Then the feasible solution S produced by the algorithm satisfies $p(S) \geq \left(\frac{\lambda}{\Delta+1}\right) \cdot p(\text{Opt})$.*

A local-ratio based sequential 3-approximation algorithm for the unit height case of tree-networks is implicit in the work of Lewin-Eytan [12]. This algorithm can be reformulated in the two-phase framework with parameters critical set size $\Delta = 2$ and slackness $\lambda = 1$ (however, the round complexity can be as high as n). We present the above algorithm in the full version of the paper. the purpose is to provide a concrete exposition of the two-phase framework.

Panconesi and Sozio [15] designed a distributed algorithm for the throughput maximization problem restricted to line-networks. In terms of the two-phase framework, their algorithm satisfies the interference property with critical set size $\Delta = 3$ and slackness $\lambda = 1/(5 + \epsilon)$. To this end, they partition the demand instances in to logarithmic number of

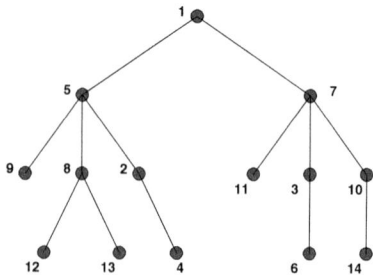

Figure 3: Tree-decomposition: Illustration

groups based on their lengths, wherein the lengths of any pair of demand instances found within the same group differ at most by a factor of 2. Then they exploit the property that if d_1 and d_2 are overlapping demand instances found within the same group, then d_2 is active either at the left end-point, the right end-point or the mid-point of d_1. This way, they satisfy the interference property with $\Delta = 3$. We do not know how to extend such a length-based ordering to our setting of tree-networks. Consequently, designing an ordering satisfying the interference property with a constant Δ turns out to be more challenging. Nevertheless, we show an ordering for which $\Delta = 6$. Furthermore, we shall present a method for improving the slackness parameter λ to $(1 - \epsilon)$. The notion of *tree-decompositions* and *layered decompositions* form the core components of our algorithms.

4. TREE-DECOMPOSITIONS, LAYERED DECOMPOSITIONS

We first define the notion of tree-decompositions and show how to construct tree decompositions with good parameters. Then, we show how to transform tree decompositions into layered decompositions.

Let H be a rooted tree defined over the vertex-set V with g as the root. For a node x, define its *depth* to be the number of nodes along the path from g to x; the root g itself is defined to have to depth 1. With respect to H, a node y is said to be an *ancestor* of x, if y appears along the path from g to x; in this case, x is said to be a *descendent* of y. By convention, we do not consider x to be an ancestor or descendent of itself. For a node z in H, let $C(z)$ be the set consisting of z and its descendents in H.

4.1 Tree-decomposition: Definition

Let $T \in \mathcal{T}$ be a tree-network defined over the input vertex-set V consisting of n vertices. A subset of nodes $C \subseteq V$ is called a *component*, if C induces a (connected) subtree in T. We say that a node $x \in V - C$ is a *neighbor* of C, if x is adjacent to some node in C. Let $\Gamma[C]$ denote the set of neighbors (or *neighborhood*) of C. Notice that for any two nodes $x \in C$ and $y \notin C$, the path between x and y must pass through some node in the neighborhood $\Gamma[C]$.

Let T be a tree-network and H be a rooted-tree defined over V with g as the root. We say that H is a *tree decomposition* for T, if the following conditions are satisfied: (i) for any demand instance $d \in \mathcal{D}(T)$, if d passes through nodes x and y then d also passes through $\text{LCA}(x,y)$, which is the least common ancestor of x and y in H; (ii) for any node z in H, $C(z)$ forms a component in T.

For a node $z \in H$, let $\chi(z)$ denote the set of neighbors of

the component $C(z)$, i.e., $\Gamma[C(z)]$. We call $\chi(z)$ the *pivot set* of z. Clearly, for any nodes $x \in C(z)$ and $y \notin C(z)$, the path between x and y in T must pass through one of the nodes in $\chi(z)$. We shall measure the efficacy of a tree decomposition H using two parameters: (i) *pivot size θ:* this is the maximum cardinality of $\chi(z)$ over all $z \in V$; (ii) the depth of the tree.

See Figure 3. This figure shows an example tree decomposition for the tree-network shown in Figure 6. The demand instance $\langle 4, 13 \rangle$ passes through nodes 2 and 8; it also passes through $\text{LCA}(2, 8) = 5$. For the node 2, the component $C(2) = \{2, 4\}$; its pivot set is $\chi(2) = \{1, 5\}$. On the other hand, $C(5) = \{5, 9, 8, 2, 12, 13, 4\}$ and its pivot set is $\chi(5) = \{1\}$. This tree-decomposition has depth 4 and pivot set size $\theta = 2$.

We note that it is not difficult to design tree-decompositions with parameters $\langle \text{depth} = n,\ \theta = 1 \rangle$ or $\langle \text{depth} = \log n,\ \theta = \log n \rangle$. As it turns out the depth of the tree-decomposition will determine the number of rounds, whereas the pivot size θ will determine the approximation ratio. Thus, neither of these two tree-decompositions would yield an algorithm that runs in polylogarithmic number of rounds, while achieving a constant factor approximation ratio. Our main contribution is a tree-decomposition with parameters $\langle \text{depth} = 2 \log n,\ \theta = 2 \rangle$ (we call this the *ideal tree-decomposition*). Interestingly, the ideal tree-decomposition builds on the two simpler tree-decompositions mentioned above. The two simpler tree-decompositions are discussed in the full version.

4.2 Ideal Tree-decomposition

The ideal tree-decomposition goes via the notion of *balancers*. Let $T \in \mathcal{T}$ be a tree-network. Consider a component $C \subseteq V$ and let $T(C)$ be the (connected) subtree induced by C. Let z be a node in C. If we delete the node z from $T(C)$, the tree $T(C)$ splits into subtrees $T_1, T_2, \ldots, T_s$ (for some s). Let $C_1, C_2, \ldots, C_s$ be the vertex-set of these subtrees. Every node in $C - \{z\}$ is found in some component C_i. We say that the node z *splits* C into components $C_1, C_2, \ldots C_s$. The node z is said to be a *balancer* for C, if for all $1 \leq i \leq s$, $|C_i| \leq \lfloor |C|/2 \rfloor$. Observe that any component $C \subseteq V$ contains a balancer z.

Fix a tree-network T and we shall construct an ideal tree decomposition H for T with pivot set size $\theta = 2$ and depth $O(\log n)$. Intuitively, the tree H will be constructed recursively. In each level of the recursion, we will add two nodes to the tree: a balancer and a node that we call a *junction*. The output tree-decomposition will have depth at most $2\lceil \log n \rceil$.

The construction works via a recursive procedure Build-dIdealTD (*build ideal tree decomposition*). The procedure BuildIdealTD takes as input a set $C \subseteq V$ forming a component in T. As a precondition, it requires the component C to satisfy the important property that C has at most two neighbors in T. It outputs a rooted-tree H with C as the vertex set having depth at most $2\lceil \log |C| \rceil$ such that for any node $x \in C$, the number of neighbors of $C(x)$ is at most 2, where $C(x)$ is the set consisting of x and its descendents in H.

The procedure BuildIdealTD works as follows. We first find a balancer z for the component C. The node z splits C into components $C_1, C_2, \ldots, C_s$. We shall consider two cases based on whether C has a single neighbor or two neighbors.

Case 1: This is the easier case where C has only one neighbor, say u_1. See Figure 4: for this case, ignore the nodes u_2

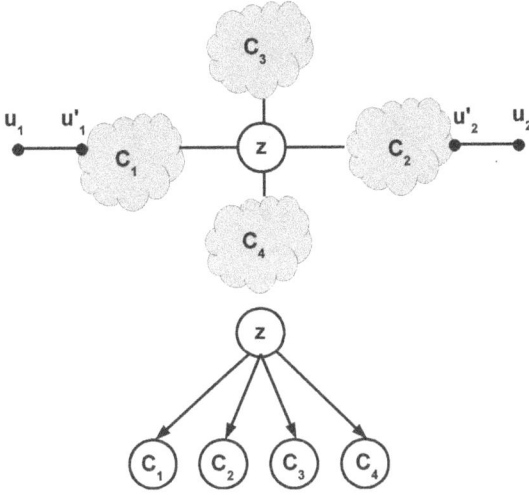

Figure 4: Illustration for ideal tree-decomposition

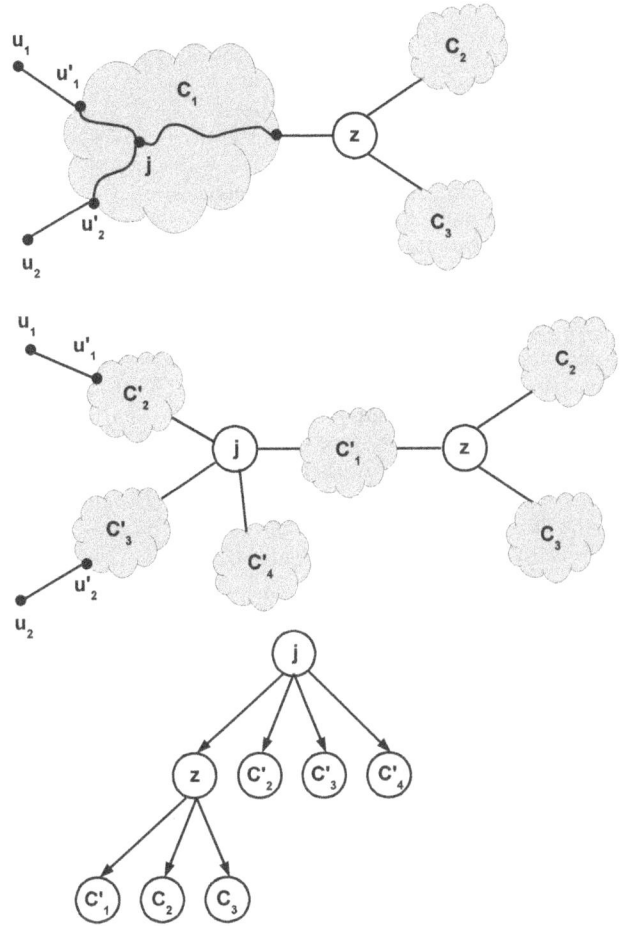

Figure 5: Illustration for Case 2(b)

and u_2'. Let u_1' be the node in C which is adjacent to u_1 and without loss of generality, assume that C_1 is the component to which u_1' belongs. Observe that $\Gamma(C_1) = \{u_1, z\}$ and for all $i \geq 2$, $\Gamma(C_i) = \{z\}$. In other words, all the components C_i have at most two neighbors. That is, they all satisfy the precondition set by the procedure. For each $1 \leq i \leq s$, we recursively call the procedure BuildIdealTD on the component C_i and obtain a tree H_i with g_i as the root. We construct a tree H by making z as the root and $g_1, g_2, \ldots, g_s$ as its children. Then, the rooted-tree H is returned.

Case 2: Now consider the case where C has two neighbors, say u_1 and u_2. Let u_1' and u_2' be the nodes in C which are neighbors of u_1 and u_2, respectively. We consider two subcases.

Case 2(a): The first subcase is when u_1' and u_2' lie in two different components, say C_1 and C_2, respectively. See Figure 4. Observe that $\Gamma(C_1) = \{u_1, z\}$, $\Gamma(C_2) = \{u_2, z\}$ and for all $i \geq 3$, $\Gamma(C_i) = \{z\}$. Hence all the components C_i satisfy the precondition set by the procedure. For each $1 \leq i \leq s$, we call the procedure BuildIdealTD with C_i as input and obtain a tree H_i. We construct a tree H by making the balancer z as the root and $g_1, g_2, \ldots, g_s$ as its children. Then, the rooted-tree H is returned.

Case 2(b): Now consider the second and comparatively more involved subcase wherein u_1' and u_2' belong to the same component, say C_1. See Figure 5. Observe that there exists a unique node $j \in C_1$ such that all the three paths $u_1 \rightsquigarrow u_2$, $u_1 \rightsquigarrow z$, and $u_2 \rightsquigarrow z$ pass through j. We call j as the *junction*. Spilt the component C_1 by the node j to obtain components $C_1', C_2', \ldots, C_{s'}'$ (for some s'). Observe that among $C_1', C_2', \ldots, C_{s'}'$, there exists three distinct components such that z is a neighbor of the first component, and u_1' and u_2' belong to the other two components; without loss of generality, let these components be C_1', C_2' and C_3', respectively. We see that for $2 \leq i \leq s$, $\Gamma(C_i) = \{z\}$; moreover, $\Gamma(C_1') = \{j, z\}$, $\Gamma(C_2') = \{u_1, j\}$, $\Gamma(C_3') = \{u_2, j\}$ and for $4 \leq i \leq s'$, $\Gamma(C_i') = \{j\}$. Thus, all the components $C_2, C_3, \ldots, C_s$ and $C_1', C_2', \ldots, C_{s'}'$ satisfy the precondition set by the procedure. For each $2 \leq i \leq s$, we call the procedure BuildIdealTD recursively with C_i as input and obtain

a tree H_i with g_i as the root. For each $1 \leq i \leq s'$, we call the procedure BuildIdealTD recursively with C_i' as input and obtain a tree H_i' with g_i' as the root. Construct a tree H as follows. Make the junction j as the root; make $g_2', g_3', \ldots, g_{s'}'$ as the children of j; make z as a child of j; make g_1' and $g_2, g_3, \ldots, g_s$ as the children of z. Return the rooted-tree H. This completes the description of the procedure BuildIdealTD.

By induction, we can argue that BuildIdealTD satisfies the intended property: for any node $x \in C$, the number of neighbors of $C(x)$ is at most 2. As an example, consider the subcase in which u_1' and u_2' belong to the same component (the case where a junction j is created). The procedure creates only two nodes j and z on its own and the rest of the nodes in H are created by the recursive calls. Consider the node j. It is guaranteed that the input component C has at most two neighbors (this is the precondition set by the procedure). Since $C(j) = C$, we see that j satisfies the property. Now, consider the node z. The component $C(z)$ is the union of $C_2, C_3, \ldots, C_s$ and C_1'. We have that $\Gamma[C(z)] = \{j\}$. Thus, z also satisfies the property. The rest of the nodes satisfy the property by induction.

Let us now analyze the depth of the tree H output by the procedure. Since z is a balancer for C, the components $C_1, C_2, \ldots, C_s$ have size at most $\lfloor C/2 \rfloor$. Moreover, since $C'_1, C'_2, \ldots, C'_{s'}$ are subsets of C_1, these components also have size at most $\lfloor C/2 \rfloor$. Thus, all the components input to the recursive calls have size at most $\lfloor C/2 \rfloor$. Thus, by induction, H has depth at most $2\lceil \log C \rceil$.

We next show how to construct a tree decomposition H for the tree-network T. First, find a balancer g for the entire vertex-set V and split V into components $C_1, C_2, \ldots, C_s$. For each component C_i, $\Gamma[C_i] = \{g\}$. For each $1 \leq i \leq s$, call the procedure `BuildIdealTD` with C_i as input and obtain a tree H_i with g_i as the root. Construct a tree H by making g as the root and each g_i as its children. Return H.

We can argue that for any node z in H, $C(z)$ forms a component in T. Furthermore, for any node z in H with children $z_1, z_2, \ldots, z_s$ (for some s), $C(z_1), C(z_2), \ldots, C(z_s)$ are nothing but the components obtained by splitting $C(z)$ by z. This implies that H satisfies the first property of tree decompositions. It follows that H is indeed a tree decomposition. The depth of H is at most $2\lceil \log n \rceil$. The properties of the `BuildIdealTD` procedure ensure that the pivot size of H is at most 2. We have the following result

Lemma 4.1. *For any tree-network $T \in \mathcal{T}$, there exists a tree decomposition H (called the ideal tree decomposition) with depth $O(\log n)$ and pivot size $\theta = 2$.*

4.3 Layered Decompositions

In this section, we define the notion of *layered decompositions* and show how to transform tree decompositions into layered decompositions.

Let $T \in \mathcal{T}$ be a tree-network. A layered decomposition of T is a pair σ and π, where σ is a partitioning of $\mathcal{D}(T)$ into a sequence of groups $G_1, G_2, \ldots, G_\ell$ and π maps each demand instance $d \in \mathcal{D}(T)$ to a subset of edges in $\text{path}(d)$. The following property should be satisfied: for any $1 \leq i \leq j \leq \ell$ and for any pair of demand instances $d_1 \in G_i$ and $d_2 \in G_j$, if d_1 and d_2 are overlapping, then $\text{path}(d_2)$ should include at least one of the edges in $\pi(d_1)$. The edges in $\pi(d)$ are called the *critical edges* of d. The value ℓ is called the *length* (or depth) of the decomposition.

Notice that similarity between the inference property and the notion of layered decompositions. We shall measure the efficacy of a layered decomposition by two parameters: (i) *Critical set size* Δ - this is the maximum cardinality of $\pi(d)$ over all demand instances $d \in \mathcal{D}(T)$; (ii) the length ℓ of the sequence. Our goal is to construct a layered decomposition with length $O(\log n)$ and critical set size $\Delta = 6$. Towards that goal we shall show how to transform tree-decompositions into layered decompositions. The following notations are useful for this purpose.

Let $T \in \mathcal{T}$ be tree-network and H be a tree-decomposition for T with pivot size θ and depth ℓ. For a demand instance d, let $\mu(d)$ be the node with the least depth in H among all the nodes that $\text{path}(d)$ passes through. The first property of tree decompositions ensure that $\mu(d)$ is unique. We say that d is *captured* at $\mu(d)$. See Figure 3; here, the demand $\langle 4, 13 \rangle$ will be captured at node 5. Let $d \in \mathcal{D}(T)$ be a demand instance and u be a node in T. Observe that there exists a unique node y belonging to $\text{path}(d)$ such that the path from u to y does not pass through any other node in $\text{path}(d)$. We call y as the *bending point* of d with respect to u. For a node y in $\text{path}(d)$, we call the edges on $\text{path}(d)$ adjacent to y as the *wings* of y on $\text{path}(d)$. If y is an end-point of d, there will be only one wing; otherwise, there will be two wings.

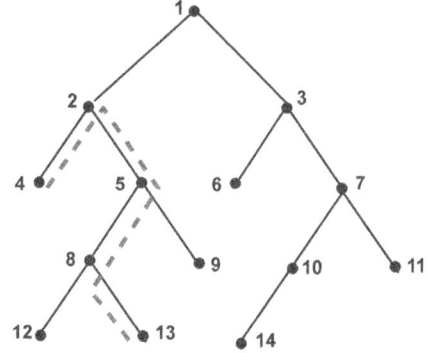

Figure 6: An example tree-network and a demand

See Figure 6: with respect to nodes 3 and 9, the bending points of the demand $d = \langle 4, 13 \rangle$ are 2 and 5, respectively; with respect to $\text{path}(d)$, node 4 has only one wing $\langle 4, 2 \rangle$, while node 8 has two wings $\langle 5, 8 \rangle$ and $\langle 8, 13 \rangle$.

Lemma 4.2. *Let $T \in \mathcal{T}$ be a tree-network and H be a tree decomposition for T with pivot size θ and depth ℓ. Then H can be transformed into a layered decomposition $\langle \sigma, \pi \rangle$ with critical set size $\Delta = 2(\theta + 1)$ and length ℓ.*

PROOF. For $1 \leq i \leq \ell$, let $\widetilde{G}_i$ to be the set consisting of all demand instances d such that depth of $\mu(d)$ is i. We define σ to be the reverse of $\widetilde{G}_1, \widetilde{G}_2, \ldots, \widetilde{G}_\ell$; namely, let $\sigma = G_1, G_2, \ldots, G_\ell$, where $G_i = \widetilde{G}_{\ell-i+1}$, for $1 \leq i \leq \ell$. Thus, in σ, the demand instances captured at the nodes having the highest depth are placed in G_1 and the demand instances captured at the root are placed in G_ℓ. We now show how to construct the critical set $\pi(d)$ for each demand instance $d \in \mathcal{D}(T)$. Let $z = \mu(d)$ be the node in H where d is captured. Add the wing(s) of z on $\text{path}(d)$ to $\pi(d)$. Then, consider the component $C(z)$ consisting of z and its descendents in H. Let $U = \{u_1, u_2, \ldots, u_s\}$ be the neighbors of $C(z)$, where $s \leq \theta$. For $1 \leq i \leq s$, let y_i be the bending point of d with respect to u_i; add the wing(s) of y_i on $\text{path}(d)$ to $\pi(d)$. Notice that $\pi(d)$ has at most $2(\theta+1)$ edges. This completes the construction of σ and $\pi(\cdot)$.

We now argue that the construction satisfies the properties of layered decompositions. Consider any two groups G_i and G_j such that $i \leq j$. Consider two overlapping demand instances $d_1 \in G_i$ and $d_2 \in G_j$. Let $z_1 = \mu(d_1)$ and $z_2 = \mu(d_2)$ be the nodes in H where d_1 and d_2 are captured, respectively. We consider two cases: (1) $z_2 \in C(z_1)$; (2) $z_2 \notin C(z_1)$.

Case 1: In this case, z_2 must be the same as z_1 (otherwise, we have $\text{depth}(z_2) > \text{depth}(z_1)$; this would contradict $i \leq j$). Therefore, $\text{path}(d_2)$ should include at least one of the wings of z_1 on $\text{path}(d_1)$. Recall that the wing(s) of z_1 on $\text{path}(d_1)$ are included in $\pi(d_1)$.

Case 2: We see that $\text{path}(d_2)$ goes through the node z_2 found outside $C(z_1)$; moreover, it also goes through some node found within $C(z_1)$ (since z_1 and z_2 overlap). By the second property of tree decompositions, such a path must also pass through one of the neighbors of $C(z_1)$; let u be such a neighbor. Let the bending point of $\text{path}(d_1)$ with respect to u be y. Since path(d_2) passes through u and overlaps with path(d_1), the path(d_2) must also pass through the bending point y. It follows that path(d_2) must include one of the wings of y on path(d_1). Recall that the wing(s) of y on path(d_1) are included in $\pi(d_1)$. □

By applying Lemma 4.2 for the ideal tree decomposition (given by Lemma 4.1), we establish the following result.

Lemma 4.3. *For any tree-network $T \in \mathcal{T}$, we can construct a layered decomposition with critical set size $\Delta = 6$ and length at most $O(\log n)$.*

5. DISTRIBUTED ALGORITHM

In this section, we prove the main result of the paper by exhibiting a two-phase procedure with critical set size $\Delta = 6$ and slackness parameter $\lambda = (1 - \epsilon)$, for any constant $\epsilon > 0$.

Let the input tree networks be $\mathcal{T} = \{T_1, T_2, \ldots, T_r\}$. For each tree-network T_q, invoke Lemma 4.3 and obtain a layered decomposition $\sigma_q = G_1^{(q)}, G_2^{(q)}, \ldots, G_{\ell_q}^{(q)}$ of length ℓ_q and a mapping π_q. Let $\ell_{\max} = \max_q \ell_q$. The lemma guarantees that $\ell_{\max}$ is $O(\log n)$ and all the critical set sizes are at most $\Delta = 6$. Let $\Delta' = \Delta + 1$ and $\xi = (2\Delta')/(2\Delta' + 1) = 14/15$. For the ease of exposition, we combine all the mapping functions into single mapping function π, as follows. For each tree-network T_q and demand instance $d \in \mathcal{D}(T_q)$, define $\pi(d) = \pi_q(d)$.

For each $1 \leq k \leq \ell_{\max}$, let G_k be union of the kth components of all the layered decompositions: $G_k = \cup_{q=1}^{r} G_k^{(q)}$. The algorithm would follow the two-phase framework. All the dual variables are initialized to zero and an empty stack is created. The first phase is split into $\ell_{\max}$ epochs. Epoch k will process the group G_k. Our goal is to ensure that at the end of the epoch, all the demand instances in G_k are $(1 - \epsilon)$-satisfied. Each epoch is divided into multiple stages, with each stage making a gradual progress towards the goal. We will ensure that at the end of stage j, all the demand instances in G_k are $(1 - \xi^j)$-satisfied. Each stage is split into multiple steps (each step corresponds to an iteration of the two-phase framework). A typical step is explained next. Let U be the set of all demand instances in G_k that are $(1 - \xi^j)$-unsatisfied. Find a maximal independent set I contained within U. For all demand instances $d \in I$, raise the demand instance d as prescribed by the framework, taking $\pi(d)$ to be the critical edges. Namely, for all demand instances $d \in I$, perform the raising as follows. Compute the slackness $s = p(d) - \alpha(a_d) - \sum_{e\,:\,d \sim e} \beta(e)$ and $\delta(d) = s/(|\pi(d)| + 1)$. Raise the dual variable $\alpha(a_d)$ by the amount $\delta(d)$ and for all $e \in \pi(d)$, raise the dual variable $\beta(e)$ by $\delta(d)$. The stage is completed when all the demand instances in G_k are $(1 - \xi^j)$-satisfied and we proceed to the next stage. The epoch is completed when all the demand instances in G_k are $(1 - \epsilon)$-satisfied. The second phase is the same as that of the two-phase framework. The pseudocode is provided in Figure 7. Certain aspects of implementing the algorithm in a distributed manner (including message size) are discussed in the full version.

Let us analyze the number of steps (or iterations) taken by the above algorithm. The number of epochs is $\ell_{\max}$, which is $O(\log n)$. Each epoch has at most $\log_\xi \epsilon = O(\log(1/\epsilon))$ stages. The lemma below provides a bound on the number of steps taken by each stage. It follows that the number of epochs is at most $O(\text{Time(MIS)} \log n \log(1/\epsilon) \log(p_{\max}/p_{\min}))$,

```
Begin
  For all a ∈ 𝒜, set α(a) = 0; for all e ∈ ℰ, set β(e) = 0.
  Initialize an empty stack.
  Let the input set of tree-networks be 𝒯 = {T₁, T₂, ..., Tᵣ}.
  For each tree-network T_q
    Invoke Lemma 4.3 on T_q and
    obtain layered decomposition:
      σ_q = G₁^(q), G₂^(q), ..., G_{ℓq}^(q) and a mapping π_q.
    Let ℓ_max = max_q ℓ_q.
    For each d ∈ 𝒟(T), define π(d) = π_q(d).
  For each k = 1 to ℓ_max,
    Define G_k = ∪_{q=1}^r G_k^(q).

  // First phase
  For k = 1 to ℓ_max      //Epochs
    Let b be the smallest integer such that (14/15)^b ≤ ε
    For j = 1 to b          //Stages
      While        // Steps or iterations.
        Let U = {d ∈ G_k  :  d is (1 − (14/15)^j)-unsatisfied}
        If U is empty, exit the loop.
        Find a maximal ind. set I contained within U
        For each d ∈ I
          Compute slackness:
            s = p(d) − α(a_d) − ∑_{e:d∼e} β(e).
          Compute δ(d) = s/(|π(d)| + 1).
          Raise the variables:
            α(a_d) ← α(a_d) + δ(d);
              for all e ∈ π(d), β(e) ← β(e) + δ(d).
        Push I into the stack (as a single object).

  // Second Phase
    S = ∅.
      While(stack not empty)
        Pop the top element I of the stack
        For each d ∈ I
          If S ∪ {d} is an independent set, then add d to S.
    Output S.
End
```

Figure 7: Pseudocode of the overall algorithm

where Time(MIS) is the number of (communication) rounds needed to find a maximal independent set (see Introduction).

Lemma 5.1. *Consider any epoch k and stage j within the epoch. The number of steps taken by the stage is at most $O(\log(p_{\max}/p_{\min}))$.*

PROOF. Let the number of steps taken by the stage be L. For $1 \leq i \leq L$, let U_i be the demand instances in G_k that are $(1 - \xi^j)$-unsatisfied at the beginning of step i. Let $I_1, I_2, \ldots, I_L$ be the sequence of maximal independent sets computed in these steps. For two demand instances $d_1, d_2 \in G_k$, we say that d_1 kills d_2 in step i, if $d_1 \in I_i$, $d_2 \in U_{i+1}$, and d_1 and d_2 are conflicting. Intuitively, both d_1 and d_2 are present in U_i, and both are contenders for the maximal independent I_i. Of the two, d_1 got selected in I_i and d_2 was omitted; even after the demand instances in I_i were raised, d_2 was still $(1 - \xi^j)$-unsatisfied. Since d_1 and d_2 are conflicting, only one of them can be included in the independent set. We imagine that d_1 "kills" d_2.

Claim 5.2. *Suppose d_1 kills d_2 in step i. Then, their profits satisfy $p(d_2) \geq 2p(d_1)$*

We now prove the claim. Since $d_1 \in I_i$, the demand instance is $(1 - \xi^j)$-unsatisfied at the beginning of step i.

Hence, the difference between the LHS and RHS of the constraint is at least $\xi^j \cdot p(d_1)$. The number dual variables raised for d_1 is at most $\Delta + 1$. Hence,

$$\delta(d_1) \geq \frac{\xi^j \cdot p(d_1)}{(\Delta + 1)}$$

Since d_1 and d_2 are conflicting, either it is the case that d_1 and d_2 belong to the same demand a or they belong to the same tree-network T_q (for some q) and overlap. In the former case, the dual constraints of d_1 and d_2 share the dual variable $\alpha(a_d)$. In the latter case, both d_1 and d_2 belong to the same group $G_k^{(q)}$. Hence, the properties of layered decompositions imply that one of the critical edges in $\pi(d_1)$ also appears in the path(d_2). Thus, in either case, when d_1 is raised, the LHS of d_2 is also raised by an amount $\delta(d_1)$. On the other hand, $d_2 \in U_{i+1}$ and so, even after the above raise in the LHS value, d_2 is still $(1 - \xi^j)$-unsatisfied. As we are considering stage j, all the demand instances in G_k are $(1 - (\xi)^{j-1})$-satisfied. The gap between $(1 - \xi^{j-1})p(d_2)$ and $(1 - \xi^j)p(d_2)$ is $(\xi^{j-1} - \xi^j)p(d_2)$. We see that even after the value of the LHS of the dual constraint of d_2 is raised by an amount $\delta(d_1)$, the above gap is not bridged. It follows that

$$(\xi^{j-1} - \xi^j)p(d_2) \geq \delta(d_1) \geq \frac{\xi^j \cdot p(d_1)}{(\Delta + 1)}$$

This implies that

$$\frac{p(d_2)}{p(d_1)} \geq \frac{\xi}{(1 - \xi)(\Delta + 1)}.$$

We derive the claim by substituting $\xi = 14/15$ and $\Delta = 6$.

Consider any demand instance $d_L \in U_L$. There must exist a demand instance d_{L-1} in U_{L-1} such that d_{L-1} kills d_L. In general, we can find a sequence of demand instances $d_L, d_{L-1}, \ldots, d_1$ such that for $1 \leq i \leq L-1$, d_i kills d_{i+1}. By the above claim, for $1 \leq i \leq L-1$, $p(d_{i+1}) \geq 2p(d_i)$. It follows that $p(d_L) \geq 2^{L-1}p(d_1)$. Hence, $L \leq 1 + \log(p(d_L)/p(d_1)) = O(\log(p_{\max}/p_{\min}))$. $\square$

The properties of layered decomposition imply that the above two-phase algorithm satisfies the interference property, governed by parameters $\Delta = 6$ and $\lambda = (1 - \epsilon)$. Therefore, by Lemma 3.1, it follows that the algorithm has an approximation ratio of $7/(1 - \epsilon)$. For $\epsilon' > 0$, we can choose ϵ suitably and obtain an approximation ratio of $(7 + \epsilon')$. We have proved the main result of the paper.

Theorem 5.3. *Fix any $\epsilon > 0$. There exists a distributed algorithm for the unit height case of the throughput maximization problem on tree-networks with approximation ratio $(7 + \epsilon)$ and number of (communication) rounds is at most $O(\text{Time}(\text{MIS}) \log n \log(1/\epsilon) \log(p_{\max}/p_{\min}))$.*

Recall that Panconesi and Sozio [14] presented an algorithm for the unit height case of line-networks. Their algorithm follows the two-phase framework with the slackness parameter $\lambda = 1/(5 + \epsilon)$. On the other hand, our algorithm has $\lambda = (1 - \epsilon)$. A comparison of the two algorithms is in order. We reformulate their algorithm to suit our framework. Their algorithm also classifies the demand instances into groups (based on length) and processes the groups in epochs. However, each epoch consists of only a single stage. They split the stage into multiple iterations/steps. In any iteration, a demand instance d which is $(1/(5 + \epsilon))$-satisfied is ignored for the rest of the first phase. In contrast, our

algorithm works in multiple stages, where in each stage, we make gradual progress towards making the demand instances within the group to be $(1 - \epsilon)$-satisfied. In particular, in stage j, a demand instance which is $(1 - \xi^j)$-satisfied is not ignored; it exits the current stage, but it is included in the MIS computations in the next stage.

6. REFERENCES

[1] M. Andrews, J. Chuzhoy, S. Khanna, and L. Zhang. Hardness of the undirected edge-disjoint paths problem with congestion. In *FOCS*, 2005.

[2] N. Bansal, A. Chakrabarti, A. Epstein, and B. Schieber. A quasi-PTAS for unsplittable flow on line graphs. In *STOC*, 2006.

[3] N. Bansal, Z. Friggstad, R. Khandekar, and M. Salavatipour. A logarithmic approximation for unsplittable flow on line graphs. In *SODA*, 2009.

[4] A. Bar-Noy, R. Bar-Yehuda, A. Freund, J. Naor, and B. Schieber. A unified approach to approximating resource allocation and scheduling. *Journal of the ACM*, 48(5):1069–1090, 2001.

[5] P. Berman and B. DasGupta. Improvements in throughout maximization for real-time scheduling. In *STOC*, 2000.

[6] P. Bonsma, J. Schulz, and A. Wiese. A constant factor approximation algorithm for unsplittable flow on paths. In *FOCS*, 2011.

[7] G. Calinescu, A. Chakrabarti, H. J. Karloff, and Y. Rabani. Improved approximation algorithms for resource allocation. In *IPCO*, 2002.

[8] V. Chakaravarthy, V. Pandit, Y. Sabharwal, and D. Seetharam. Varying bandwidth resource allocation problem with bag constraints. In *IPDPS*, 2010.

[9] A. Chakrabarti, C. Chekuri, A. Gupta, and A. Kumar. Approximation algorithms for the unsplittable flow problem. *Algorithmica*, 47(1):53–78, 2007.

[10] C. Chekuri, M. Mydlarz, and F. Shepherd. Multicommodity demand flow in a tree and packing integer programs. *ACM Transactions on Algorithms*, 3(3), 2007.

[11] S. Kolliopoulos. Edge-disjoint paths and unsplittable flow. In T. Gonzalez, editor, *Handbook of Approximation Algorithms and Metaheuristics*. Chapman and Hall/CRC, 2007.

[12] L. Lewin-Eytan, J. Naor, and A. Orda. Admission control in networks with advance reservations. *Algorithmica*, 40(4):293–304, 2004.

[13] M. Luby. A simple parallel algorithm for the maximal independent set problem. *SIAM Journal of Computing*, 15(4):1036–1053, 1986.

[14] A. Panconesi and M. Sozio. Fast distributed scheduling via primal-dual. In *SPAA*, 2008.

[15] A. Panconesi and M. Sozio. Fast primal-dual distributed algorithms for scheduling and matching problems. *Distributed Computing*, 22(4):269–283, 2010.

[16] A. Panconesi and A. Srinivasan. On the complexity of distributed network decomposition. *Journal of Algorithms*, 20(2):356–374, 1996.

[17] R. Tarjan. Decomposition by clique separators. *Discrete Mathematics*, 55(2):221–232, 1985.

Optimal Distributed All Pairs Shortest Paths and Applications [*]

[Extended Abstract]

Stephan Holzer
ETH Zurich, Switzerland
stholzer@ethz.ch

Roger Wattenhofer
ETH Zurich, Switzerland
wattenhofer@ethz.ch

ABSTRACT

We present an algorithm to compute All Pairs Shortest Paths (APSP) of a network in a distributed way. The model of distributed computation we consider is the message passing model: in each synchronous round, every node can transmit a different (but short) message to each of its neighbors. We provide an algorithm that computes APSP in $\mathcal{O}(n)$ communication rounds, where n denotes the number of nodes in the network. This implies a linear time algorithm for computing the diameter of a network. Due to a lower bound these two algorithms are optimal up to a logarithmic factor. Furthermore, we present a new lower bound for approximating the diameter D of a graph: Being allowed to answer $D+1$ or D can speed up the computation by at most a factor D. On the positive side, we provide an algorithm that achieves such a speedup of D and computes an $1 + \varepsilon$ multiplicative approximation of the diameter. We extend these algorithms to compute or approximate other problems, such as girth, radius, center and peripheral vertices. At the heart of these approximation algorithms is the S-Shortest Paths problem which we solve in $\mathcal{O}(|S| + D)$ time.

Categories and Subject Descriptors

F.1.2. [**Theory of Computation**]: Computation by abstract Devices—*Modes of Computation, Parallelism and concurrency*; F.2.3. [**Theory of Computation**]: Analysis of Algorithms and Problem Complexity—*Tradeoffs among Complexity Measures*

Keywords

Distributed Computing, Message Passing, CONGEST, All Pairs Shortest Paths, Diameter, Radius, Eccentricity, Girth, Center, Peripheral Vertices, Approximation, Lower Bound.

---

[*]A full version of this paper is available online [24].

1. INTRODUCTION

In networks, basically two types of routing algorithms are known: distance-vector and link-state. Link-state algorithms embody the school of centralized algorithms. First all the information about the network graph is collected, and then optimal routes between all nodes are computed, using an efficient centralized algorithm. Distance-vector routing protocols on the other hand represent the school of distributed algorithms. Nodes update their routing tables by constantly exchanging messages with their neighbors. Both approaches are used in the Internet, link-state for instance in OSPF or IS-IS, distance-vector in RIP or BGP[1]. Among network researchers there is a vivid debate on which approach is better. After all, both approaches essentially do the same thing – compute shortest paths between all nodes – a problem known as all pairs shortest paths (APSP). Despite its practical relevance, the distributed time-complexity of APSP was so far not known.

In this paper we present a new distributed algorithm that computes APSP in $\mathcal{O}(n)$ time. Because of a recent lower bound for computing the diameter [22], this APSP-algorithm is essentially optimal (up to a logarithmic factor). In addition this demonstrates that computing the diameter has about the same complexity as computing APSP in a distributed setting. These statements contrast the sequential setting: It is open to provide matching upper/lower bounds for APSP or to show whether determining the diameter of a graph can be done faster than computing APSP (or performing matrix multiplication.)

In addition, we present a new lower bound for approximating the diameter D of a graph: Being allowed to answer $D + 1$ (in addition to the correct answer D) can speed up the computation by at most a factor D. On the bright side, we provide an algorithm that achieves a speedup of D and computes an $1 + \varepsilon$ multiplicative approximation of the diameter. We extend these algorithms to compute/approximate other problems, such as girth, radius, center and peripheral vertices. At the heart of these approximation algorithms is the S-Shortest Paths problem. We essentially show that s breadth-first searches can be computed in time $\mathcal{O}(s + D)$ which is of interest on its own.

2. MODEL AND BASIC DEFINITIONS

Model: We study the message passing model with limited bandwidth (also known as CONGEST model, [32]): Our

---

[1]These are presented in many textbooks, e.g. [6].

network is represented by an undirected unweighted graph $G = (V, E)$. Nodes V correspond to processors (computers or routers), two nodes are connected by an edge from set E if they can communicate directly with each other. We denote the number of nodes of a graph by n, and the number of its edges by m. Furthermore we assume that each node has an unique identifier (ID) in the range of $\{1, \ldots, 2^{\mathcal{O}(\log n)}\}$, i.e. each node can be represented by $\mathcal{O}(\log n)$ bits. We assume that n is known to each node and there is a node with ID 1. These are valid assumptions since the time to compute n or to find the node with smallest ID and rename it to 1 would not affect the asymptotic runtime of the presented algorithms. For simplicity, we refer to $u \in V$ not only as a node, we use u to refer to u's ID as well when this is clear from the context. Nodes initially have no knowledge of the graph G – except that they know their immediate neighborhood. By $N_k(v)$ we denote the k-neighborhood of v, that is all nodes in G that can be reached from v using k hops/edges. We define that $v \in N_1(v)$. Given a set $S \subseteq V$, set $N_k(S)$ denotes the k-neighborhood of S, that is $\cup_{v \in S} N_k(S)$.

We consider a synchronous communication model, where every node can send B bits of information over all its edges in one synchronous round of communication. In principle it is allowed that in a round, a node can send different messages of size B to each of its neighbors (and likewise receive different messages from each of its neighbors). Typically we have $B = \mathcal{O}(\log n)$ bits, which allows us to send a constant number of node or edge IDs per message. Since communication cost usually dominates the cost of local computation, local computation is considered free. We are interested in the number of rounds that a distributed algorithm needs until a problem is solved – this is the time complexity of the algorithm. By solving a problem we refer to evaluating a function $h : \mathbb{C}_n \to SOL$ over the underlying network-structure. Here $\mathbb{C}_n$ is the set of all graphs over n vertices and SOL is e.g. $\{0, 1\}$ or $\mathbb{N}$. We define distributed round complexity as follows:

DEFINITION 1. *(distributed round complexity). Let $\mathcal{A}_\varepsilon$ be the set of distributed algorithms that use (public) randomness (indicated by "pub") and evaluate a function h on the underlying graph G over n nodes with an error probability smaller than ε. Denote by $R_\varepsilon^{dc-pub}(A(G))$ the distributed round complexity (indicated by "dc") representing the number of rounds that an algorithm $A \in \mathcal{A}_\varepsilon$ needs in order to compute $h(G)$ on G. We define*

$$R_\varepsilon^{dc-pub}(h) = \min_{A \in \mathcal{A}_\varepsilon} \max_{G \in \mathbb{C}_n} R_\varepsilon^{dc-pub}(A(G))$$

to be the smallest amount of rounds any algorithm needs in order to compute h.

Throughout the paper we often state results in a less formal way. Example: when h is *diam* (the function that maps a graph to its diameter) and $R_0^{dc-pub}(diam) = \mathcal{O}(n)$, we often just write "the deterministic round complexity of computing the diameter is $\mathcal{O}(n)$".

Let us denote by $d(u, v)$ the distance of nodes u and v in G, which is the length of a shortest $u - v$-path in G. The problems we consider are:

DEFINITION 2. *(APSP, S-SP) Let $G = (V, E)$ be a graph. The all pairs shortest paths (APSP) problem is to compute*
the shortest paths between any pair of vertices in $V \times V$. In the *S-Shortest Paths (S-SP)* problem, we are given a set $S \subseteq V$ and need to compute the shortest paths between any pair of vertices in $S \times V$.

Like in [18], at the end of an S-SP computation, each node in V knows its distances to every node in S. Accordingly we assume that the result of APSP/S-SP is stored in a distributed way as well. Note that there exist graphs where storing all distance information of all pairs at all nodes takes $\Omega(n^2)$ time, such that a distributed approach is crucial.

DEFINITION 3. *(eccentricity, diameter, radius, girth) The eccentricity $ecc(u)$ of a node $u \in V$ is defined to be $ecc(u) := \max_{v \in V} d(u, v)$ and is the maximum distance to any other node in the graph. The diameter $D := \max_{u \in V} ecc(u) = \max_{u, v \in V} d(u, v)$ of a graph G is the maximum distance between any two nodes of the graph. The radius of G denoted by $rad := \min_{u \in V} ecc(u)$ is the minimum eccentricity of any vertex. The girth g of a graph G is the length of the shortest cycle in G. If G is a forest its girth is infinity.*

DEFINITION 4. *(center vertices, peripheral vertices). The center of a graph G is the set of nodes whose eccentricity equals the radius of the graph. A node u is a peripheral vertex of a graph if its eccentricity equals the diameter of the graph.*

DEFINITION 5. *(approximation). Given an optimization problem P, denote by OPT the cost of the optimal solution for P and by sol_A the cost of the solution of an algorithm A for P. Let $\rho \geq 1$. We say A is a $(\times, \rho)$-approximation (multiplicative approximation) for P if $OPT \leq sol_A \leq \rho \cdot OPT$ for any input. Let $\gamma \geq 0$. We say A is a $(+, \gamma)$-approximation (additive approximation) for P if $OPT \leq sol_A \leq OPT + \gamma$ for any input.*

We extend the above definition to sets: assume we are given the problem of computing a set $S_c := \{v \mid cost(v) \leq c\}$ of nodes, where each node has a certain cost. A $(+, k)$-approximation to S_c is any subset of $\{v \mid cost(v) \leq c+k\}$ that includes S_c. As an example, consider the eccentricity of a node as its cost which allows us to think of the center of G as the set of nodes with cost $rad(G)$. A k-approximation to the center in unweighted graphs would be any subsets of the center's k-neighborhood such that $center \subseteq S \subseteq N_k(center)$.

DEFINITION 6. *In the problem of computing/approximating eccentricities, we require that each node in the graph knows (an approximation to) its own eccentricity in the end. In the problem of computing/approximating the diameter/radius /girth , we require that each node in the graph knows (the same estimate of) the networks diameter/radius /girth in the end. In the problem of computing (approximations to) the center/peripheral vertices, we require that each node in the graph knows whether it belongs to (the approximation of) the center/peripheral vertices.*

Sometimes we use the following facts and notion of (partial) BFS trees.

FACT 1. *It is well known that the eccentricity of any node is a good multiplicative approximation of the diameter: For any node $u \in V$ we know that $ecc(u) \leq D \leq 2 \cdot ecc(u)$.*

DEFINITION 7. *(k-BFS tree)*. *A (partial) k-BFS tree rooted in v is the subtree of a BFS tree rooted in v that contains only the nodes at distance at most k to v.*

3. RELATED WORK AND OUR CONTRIBUTIONS

3.1 All Pairs Shortest Paths

In the synchronous model, a link-state APSP algorithm will finish in D time, since nodes have to learn about all the edges. Likewise a distance-vector APSP algorithm will finish in D time: Nodes with distance d will learn about each other in round d. So both algorithms have the same time complexity. However, both algorithms severely violate our restriction for message size! A link-state algorithm must exchange information about all edges, hence potentially messages are of a size which is quadratic in the number of nodes. Likewise, nodes in a distance-vector algorithm may have to send routing table updates about almost all the nodes in each round. In real networks, one can often not exchange information about all nodes in one single message. If we restrict link-state and distance-vector algorithms to messages of size $\mathcal{O}(\log n)$ (by serializing the long messages), they will need strictly superlinear (and sometimes quadratic) time.

Due to its importance in network design, shortest path-problems in general and the APSP problem in particular were among the earliest studied problems in distributed computing. Developed algorithms were immediately used e.g. as early as in 1969 in the ARPANET (see [28], p.506). Routing messages via shortest paths were extensively discussed to be beneficial in [11, 29, 30, 38, 41] and in many other papers. It is not surprising that there is plenty of literature dealing with algorithms for distributed APSP, but most of them focused on secondary targets such as trading time for message complexity. E.g. papers [1, 12, 45] obtain a communication complexity of roughly $\mathcal{O}(n \cdot m)$ bits/messages and still require superlinear runtime. Also a lot of effort was spent to obtain fast sequential algorithms for various versions of computing APSP or related problems such as the diameter problem, e.g. [3, 4, 7, 13, 39, 40]. These algorithms are based on fast matrix multiplication such that currently the best runtime is $\mathcal{O}(n^{2.3727})$ due to [46]. Despite these advances the nature of distributed computing makes it unlikely to design fast algorithms based on matrix multiplication. It seems that combinatorial algorithms for APSP (not using fast matrix multiplication) are much better suited to be implemented in a distributed way. Combinatorial APSP algorithms were studied first in [21] and then [9, 10, 15, 19, 23, 42, 43, 49] but only yield polylogarithmic improvements over $\mathcal{O}(n^3)$.

In this paper we do not follow these approaches but present a simpler algorithm with simple analysis that computes APSP by extending a classical approach to compute APSP that is taught in many lectures: Perform a breadth-first search (BFS) from each node in the graph. The depth of a node in a BFS tree is its distance to the tree's root. Since one computes all BFS trees, all distances are known in the end. This takes time $\mathcal{O}(n^2 + n \cdot m)$ in most sequential models of computing. In the distributed model considered in this paper, this approach (if not modified) takes time $\mathcal{O}(n \cdot D)$ as mentioned e.g. in [18] since each BFS requires $\mathcal{O}(D)$

time. In Section 4.1 we modify this approach by starting the breadth-first searches in a special order at special times. We prove that the chosen start times and the order yield no congestion and thus a linear runtime. This is optimal up to a logarithmic factor due to a lower bound presented in [22] which extended the techniques used in [14].

3.2 s-Shortest Paths

Sometimes one might be satisfied by obtaining approximate distances in the sense that they differ by at most a small additive term. In the literature this problem is known as $APASP_k$ (All Pairs Almost Shortest Paths), where all computed estimates of the distances are at most an additive term k longer than the actual distances. In [2] a sequential algorithm for $APASP_2$ was presented that runs in time $\tilde{O}(\min\{n^{3/2} \cdot m^{1/2}, n^{7/3}\})$. Dor, Halperin and Zwick extended this to $APASP_k$ with a runtime of $\tilde{O}(\min\{n^{2-\frac{2}{k+2}} \cdot m^{\frac{2}{k+2}}, n^{2+\frac{2}{3 \cdot k-2}}\})$ in [17]. This line of research led to *approximate distance oracles* [44], where one is not interested in an additive but a multiplicative error (called stretch). These were recently extended to the distributed setting in [37]. Previously Elkin [18] suggested an approached to obtain distributed algorithms for $APASP_k$ (and APASP with small stretch) by considering almost shortest paths for the S-SP problem (denoted by S-ASP) and mainly focused on the number of bits exchanged. When comparing Elkin's results with our results we need to keep in mind that the aim of the two papers is different, which makes comparison difficult. For our model, the runtime provided in [18] is $\mathcal{O}(|S| \cdot D + n^{1+\xi/2})$ for computing almost shortest paths in the sense that the estimated distance is at most $(1 + \varepsilon) \cdot d(u, v) + \beta(\xi, \rho, \varepsilon)$, where $\beta(\xi, \rho, \varepsilon)$ is constant when ξ, ρ and ε are. The runtime of our algorithm for computing exact shortest paths runs in $\mathcal{O}(|S| + D)$ time, which is faster for all parameters. However, our approach requires the exchange of $\mathcal{O}((|S| + D) \cdot m \cdot \log n)$ bits while [18] needs only $\mathcal{O}(m \cdot n^\rho + |S| \cdot n^{1+\xi})$ bits. In the case $\max\{S, D\} \leq n^\rho/\log n$ and $m \leq n^{1+\xi}/\log n$ and $D \leq \frac{|S| \cdot n^{1+\xi}}{m \cdot \log n}$, our algorithm sends fewer bits. Besides the synchronous model that we study, [18] also investigated an asynchronous setting. While Elkin focused on very precise approximations, the authors of [26] were interested in rather loose approximation factors when considering the S-ASP problem and thus obtained better time complexities. It is stated in Theorem 4.11. of [26] that an (expected) $\mathcal{O}(\log n)$-multiplicative approximation to S-SP (called k-source shortest paths in [26]) can be computed in $\mathcal{O}(|S| \cdot D \cdot \log n)$ time using $\mathcal{O}(|E| \cdot (\min(D, \log n) + |S|) + |S| \cdot n \log n)$ messages in an unweighted graph. In contrast to this we can compute exact S-SP faster by using less messages, that is in time $\mathcal{O}(|S| + D)$ with $\mathcal{O}((|S| + D) \cdot |E|)$ messages.

Based on these results, lower and upper bounds for computing exact and approximate solutions of a variety of other problems can be derived, as listed in Table 1 . Note that our algorithm demonstrates how to compute s BFS trees from s nodes in just $\mathcal{O}(s + D)$ time, which is of independent interest.

3.3 Diameter

Based on the APSP algorithm we derive an algorithm that can compute the diameter in linear time. As for

Problem	exact	(+,1)	(×,1+ε)	(×,3/2−ε)	(×,3/2)	(×,2)
APSP	$\tilde{\Theta}(n)^{16)}$	$\tilde{\Theta}(n)^{1,13)}$	$\tilde{\Theta}(n)^{1,13)}$	$\tilde{\Theta}(n)^{1,13)}$	–	–
eccentricity	$\tilde{\Theta}(n)^{5,11)}$	$\Omega(\frac{n}{D\cdot\log n}+D)^{11)}$	$\mathcal{O}(\frac{n}{D}+D)^{3)}$	$\Omega\left(\frac{\sqrt{n}}{\log n}+D\right)^{11)}$		$\Theta(D)^{18)}$
diameter	$\tilde{\Theta}(n)^{6,20)}$	$\Omega(\frac{n}{D\cdot\log n}+D)^{2)}$	$\mathcal{O}(\frac{n}{D}+D)^{17)}$	$\Omega\left(\frac{\sqrt{n}}{\log n}+D\right)^{21)*}$	$\mathcal{O}(n^{3/4}+D)^{14)}$	$\Theta(D)^{18)}$
radius	$\mathcal{O}(n)^{8)}$	–	$\mathcal{O}(\frac{n}{D}+D)^{17)}$	–		$\Theta(D)^{18)}$
center	$\tilde{\Theta}(n)^{9,12)}$	$\Omega(\frac{n}{D\cdot\log n}+D)^{12)}$	$\mathcal{O}(\frac{n}{D}+D)^{17)}$	$\Omega\left(\frac{\sqrt{n}}{\log n}+D\right)^{12)}$		$0^{19)}$
p. vertices	$\tilde{\Theta}(n)^{10,11)}$	$\Omega(\frac{n}{D\cdot\log n}+D)^{11)}$	$\mathcal{O}(\frac{n}{D}+D)^{17)}$	$\Omega\left(\frac{\sqrt{n}}{\log n}+D\right)^{11)}$		$0^{19)}$
girth	$\mathcal{O}(n)^{7)}$	–	$\mathcal{O}\left(\min\left\{n/g+D\cdot\log\frac{D}{g},\,n\right\}\right)^{4)}$			–

10) Lem. 6
11) Lem. 8
12) Lem. 9
13) Lem.11
14) Cor. 1
15) Cor. 2
16) Cor. 3
17) Cor. 4
18) Rem. 1
19) Rem. 2

For the girth, two additional ratios are of interest:

Problem	(×,2−ε)	(×,2−1/g)
girth	$\Omega\left(\frac{\sqrt{n}}{\log n}+D\right)^{22)*}$	$\mathcal{O}\left(n^{2/3}+D\cdot\log\frac{D}{g}\right)^{15)}$

1) Thm. 1   4) Thm. 5   7) Lem. 7   20) [22]–Thm. 5.1
2) Thm. 2   5) Lem. 2   8) Lem. 4   21) [22]–Thm. 6.1
3) Thm. 4   6) Lem. 3   9) Lem. 5   22) [22]–Thm. 7.1

Table 1: **The two tables above summarize the results of this paper and show which parts remain open. All entries are annotated with a number that is associated to the according Theorem/Lemma/Corollary in the list next to the tables. Entries marked with an asterisk (*) were previously known. Some fields are marked by "–" or do not appear. This indicates open problems: where 1) no almost tight bounds are known 2) only trivial bounds such as $\Omega(D)$ are known, or 3) no better upper/lower bounds than those stated for stronger/weaker approximation ratios are known. All entries in the tables reflect a choice for bandwidth B of $B = \log n$. We denote by $\tilde{\Theta}$ that according upper and lower bounds differ by at most a factor of** polylog n.

APSP, this is optimal due to a lower bound stated in Theorem 5.1. of [22]. Since the authors of [22] also showed an $\Omega(\sqrt{n}/B + D)$-lower bound for any $(\times, 3/2 - \varepsilon)$-approximation it would be nice to obtain a matching upper bound. One approach towards this end is to consider a combinatorial $(\times, 3/2)$-approximation in a sequential setting by Aingworth, Chekuri, Indyk and Motwani [2]. According to the runtime of $\mathcal{O}(m \cdot \sqrt{n \cdot \log n} + n^2 \cdot \log n)$ it seems possible to implement it in our distributed model in time $\mathcal{O}(\sqrt{n} + D)$. As a first crucial step towards this approximation, [2] shows how to distinguish graphs of diameter 2 from graphs of diameter 4 in $\mathcal{O}(m \cdot \sqrt{n \cdot \log n} + n^2 \cdot \log n)$. This is a key insight that leads to their fast approximation-algorithm. They specifically mention that a step towards fast exact algorithms is being able to distinguish graphs of diameter 2 from graphs of diameter 3 in $o(n \cdot m)$ (instead of distinguishing 2 from 4 as needed for their approximation). Following this approach we show that a distributed algorithm can distinguish graphs of diameter 2 from graphs of diameter 4 in time $\mathcal{O}(\sqrt{n \cdot \log n})$, which is optimal. By extending the argument used in the proof of Theorem 5.1. in [22] we show that in contrast to this, distinguishing diameter 2 from 3 takes $\Omega(n/\log n)$ time by refining the construction of [22].

Although we were not able to transfer this $(\times, 3/2)$-approximation in such a way that it would result in distributed time $\mathcal{O}(\sqrt{n} + D)$, we are able to obtain an algorithm that yields a much better approximation factor. However, as expected, this is done by trading runtime for accuracy such that we use more than $\Omega(\sqrt{n}/\log n + D)$ time in most cases. Based on the S-SP-algorithm, we obtain a $(\times, 1 + \varepsilon)$-approximation to the diameter in time $\mathcal{O}(n/D + D)$. This result is complemented by an $\Omega(n/(D \cdot \log n) + D)$ lower bound for computing a $(+, 1)$-approximation in Theorem 2. Observe that if $D \geq \sqrt{n}$, we are unable to improve the runtime of the $(\times, 1 + \varepsilon)$-approximation, even when considering

a worse approximation factor. A reason for this is that the upper bound of the algorithm matches the lower bound for $(\times, 3/2 - \varepsilon)$-approximations for these parameters. For more recent results, see Section 3.6.

3.4 Girth

In the sequential setting various results to approximate the girth are known, e.g. [5, 25, 34, 35, 36, 48]. In a sequentially setting they run faster than e.g. a $(+, 1)$-approximation that takes $\mathcal{O}(n^2)$ time [25]. When trying to transfer these algorithms into a distributed setting one has to compute a partial BFS tree of a certain depth (i.e., depth $k - 1$ if the girth is $2 \cdot k - 1$) for each of the n nodes. We show that in general computing all partial BFS trees of a certain depth might be hard by constructing a family of graphs of girth 3 where computing all 2-BFS trees takes $\Omega(n/\log n)$ time.

In a model where all n processes are connected to all other processes which want to verifying whether a subgraph contains a cycle of length d, a deterministic distributed algorithm running in time $\mathcal{O}(n^{1 - 2/d}/\log n)$ is stated in [16]. In contrast to this model, our processes can only communicate by using edges in the graph on which we want to compute the girth. We show how to compute the girth in this model in time $O(n)$ and extend this to a $(\times, 1 + \varepsilon)$- and a $(\times, 2 - 1/g)$-approximation with better runtime.

For more recent results, see Section 3.6.

3.5 Further Problems

We extend the results from above to the problems of computing the eccentricity, radius, center and peripheral vertices of a graph. Computing the center of a graph turned out to be important in applications such as PageRank [20, 31] and the analysis of social networks (centers will be e.g. celebrities [8]) while in spam-detectors it is proven to be useful to investigate peripheral vertices [47]. These settings are predestined to be solved by large distributed systems: The data processed is huge and exact sequential algorithms (or good approximations) for these problems usually have superquadratic runtime. Computing the eccentricity and radius are strongly related to these two problems. Table 1 summarizes the results obtained in this paper

REMARK 1. *As in the case of approximating the diameter, a $(\times, 2)$-approximation to the radius/eccentricity of all nodes can be computed by taking the eccentricity of any node. This can be done in $\mathcal{O}(D)$ by performing a breadth-first search rooted in this node.*

REMARK 2. *Due to Fact 1, a $(\times, 2)$-approximation to the center/peripheral vertices is just the set of all nodes. Each node can decide to join the set internally thus the runtime would be 0.*

3.6 Combination with Independent Results by Peleg, Roditty and Tal

Independently, a similar algorithm to compute APSP and Diameter in time $\mathcal{O}(n)$ appears at ICALP 2012 [33]. In addition [33] demonstrates how to implement the sequential $(\times, 3/2)$-approximation algorithm mentioned in Section 3.3 in a distributed way in time $\mathcal{O}(D \cdot \sqrt{n})$. By combining this with our Corollary 4 (choosing $\varepsilon \leq 1/2$), we obtain:

COROLLARY 1. *Combining both algorithms yields a $(\times, 3/2)$-approximation to the diameter with runtime $\mathcal{O}(\min\{D \cdot \sqrt{n}, n/D + D\})$, which is $\mathcal{O}(n^{3/4} + D)$.*

Furthermore, [33] provides a $(\times, 2 - 1/g)$-approximation for the girth running in time $\tilde{\mathcal{O}}(D + \sqrt{gn})$. By combining this with Theorem 5 of our paper, (choosing $\varepsilon \leq 1/2$), we obtain:

COROLLARY 2. *By combining both algorithms, a $(\times, 2 - 1/g)$-approximation to the girth can be computed in time $\mathcal{O}\left(\min\left\{D + \sqrt{gn}, \min\left\{n/g + D \cdot \log \frac{D}{g}, n\right\}\right\}\right)$, which is $\mathcal{O}\left(n^{2/3} + D \cdot \log \frac{D}{g}\right)$.*

4. ALL PAIRS SHORTEST PATHS

4.1 An Almost Optimal Algorithm

In this section we present a simple algorithm with a simple analysis that allows us to compute APSP of the underlying network in the message passing model with limited bandwidth $B = O(\log n)$ in time $\mathcal{O}(n)$. We argue that this algorithm can be used to compute solutions to several other properties of the graph in linear time as well. Combined with the $\Omega(n/\log n)$ lower bound [22] for computing the diameter, the presented algorithm is asymptotically nearly optimal (see Corollary 3.) We start with some notation.

DEFINITION 8. *(Tree T_v) Given a node v, we denote the spanning tree of G that results from performing a breadth-first search BFS_v starting at v by T_v.*

REMARK 3. *A spanning tree of G can be traversed in time $\mathcal{O}(n)$ by sending a pebble over an edge in each time slot. This can be done using e.g. a depth-first search.*

Algorithm 1 below computes shortest paths between all pairs of nodes in a graph. Given a graph G, it computes

BFS tree T_1 (Line 1). Then it sends a pebble P to traverse tree T_1 (Lines 2–8). Each time pebble P enters a node v for the first time, P waits one time slot (Line 5), and then starts a breadth-first search (BFS) – using edges in G – from v with the aim of computing the distances from v to all other nodes (Line 6). Since we start a BFS from every node, each node learns its distance to all other nodes (that is APSP).

Algorithm 1 as executed by each node $v \in G$ simultaneously. Computes: APSP on G

1: **compute** T_1
2: **send** a pebble P to traverse T_1
3: **while** P traverses T_1 **do**
4:     **if** P visits a node v for the first time **then**
5:         **wait** one time slot //** avoid congestion
6:         **start** a BFS_v from node v
                //** compute all distances to v
7:     **end if**
8: **end while**

REMARK 4. *For simplicity of the write up of the algorithm and proofs we do not state actual computations of distances. Algorithm 1 could be easily modified to compute these: During each computation of a BFS_v, tell each node u its depth in T_v. The depth is equivalent to the distance $d(u, v)$. In the end all distances are known. Shortest paths are implicitly stored via BFS trees.*

LEMMA 1. *In Algorithm 1, at no time a node w is simultaneously active for both BFS_u and BFS_v.*

PROOF. Assume a BFS_u is started at time t_u at node u. Then node w will be involved in BFS_u at time $t_u + d(u, w)$. Now, consider a node v whose BFS_v is started at time $t_v > t_u$. According to Algorithm 1 this implies that the pebble visits v after u and took some time to travel from u to v. In particular, the time to get from u to v is at least $d(u, v)$, in addition at least node v is visited for the first time (which involves waiting at least one time slot), and we have $t_v \geq t_u + d(u, v) + 1$. Using this and the triangle inequality, we get that node w is involved in BFS_v strictly after being involved in BFS_u since $t_v + d(v, w) \geq (t_u + d(u, v) + 1) + d(v, w) \geq t_u + d(u, w) + 1 > t_u + d(u, w)$. $\square$

THEOREM 1. *Algorithm 1 computes APSP in time $O(n)$.*

PROOF. Since the previous lemma holds for any pair of vertices, no two BFS "interfere" with each other, i.e. all messages can be sent on time without congestion. Hence, all BFS stop at most D time slots after they were started. We conclude that the runtime of the algorithm is determined by the time $O(D)$ we need to build tree T_1, plus the time $O(n)$ that P needs to traverse tree T_1, plus the time $O(D)$ needed by the last BFS that P initiated. Since $D \leq n$, this is all in $O(n)$. $\square$

4.2 Applications

Given a solution for APSP, many other graph properties can be computed efficiently. The following lemmas and corollaries demonstrate several of these extensions.

LEMMA 2. *The eccentricity of all nodes can be computed in $\mathcal{O}(n)$.*

PROOF. Compute APSP in $\mathcal{O}(n)$. Based on this, each node v of the network computes its eccentricity internally by taking the maximum of all distances to v. The total complexity remains $\mathcal{O}(n)$. □

LEMMA 3. *The complexity of computing the diameter is* $\mathcal{O}(n)$.

PROOF. Compute APSP in $\mathcal{O}(n)$ and aggregate the maximum of all distances using T_1 in additional time $\mathcal{O}(D)$. The result is the diameter. □

COROLLARY 3. *Algorithm 1 is optimal up to a logarithmic factor due to Lemma 3 and Theorem 5.1 of [22].*

LEMMA 4. *The complexity of comp. the radius is* $\mathcal{O}(n)$.

PROOF. Compute all eccentricities in $\mathcal{O}(n)$ and aggregate the minimum of all eccentricities using T_1 in additional time $\mathcal{O}(D)$. The result is the radius. □

LEMMA 5. *The complexity of comp. the center is* $\mathcal{O}(n)$.

PROOF. Compute all eccentricities and the diameter in $\mathcal{O}(n)$. Each node checks internally if the radius equals its eccentricity. If yes, it is a center vertex of the graph. □

LEMMA 6. *The complexity of computing peripheral vertices is* $\mathcal{O}(n)$.

PROOF. Compute all eccentricities and the diameter in $\mathcal{O}(n)$. Each node checks internally if the diameter equals its eccentricity. If yes, it is a peripheral vertex of the graph. □

LEMMA 7. *The complexity of comp. the girth is* $\mathcal{O}(n)$.

CLAIM 1. *Executing BFS₁ can be used to check whether G is a tree or not.*

PROOF. Consider the following implementation of BFS: Node 1 starts by sending an arbitrary message to all its neighbors (each neighbor receives the same message). Consider a node v that receives this message for the first time in time slot t_v. Then v forwards this message in time slot $t_v + 1$ to all its neighbors from which v did not receive a message in time slot t_v. In all other time slots, node v remains silent. Then G is a tree if and only if no node received more than one message during the execution of BFS₁ and this can be verified in time $\mathcal{O}(D)$. □

PROOF. (of Lemma 7.) First, use Claim 1 to check in $\mathcal{O}(D)$ whether G is a tree or not. If yes, return ∞. If not, adopting a classical algorithm to compute the girth g: First, perform a BFS from each node (which is essentially done by Algorithm 1 in time $\mathcal{O}(n)$.) If during round t of a BFS$_v$, a vertex u that is already in T_v (or is included into T_v in round t) receives a second message in round t, we know that u and w belong to a cycle. If u is at depth d_u in T_v and receives a message from node w that is at depth d_w in T_v, then there is a cycle in G of length at most $d_u + d_w + 1$. In case v is the least common ancestor of nodes u and w in T_v, the cycle is exactly of size $d_u + d_w + 1$. If C is a minimal cycle in G – that is C defines the girth – the algorithm definitely detects C while performing a BFS from any node in C. At the same time the algorithm can never claim to have found a smaller cycle that does not exist. The overhead induced by this computation is only internal, min-aggregating at node 1 the size of the smallest cycle that any node is contained in takes time $\mathcal{O}(D)$. The total complexity of computing the girth is $\mathcal{O}(n)$. □

To be consistent with Definition 6, we could add in each corollary: Broadcasting the computed information to the whole network would take additional time at most $\mathcal{O}(n)$.

5. LOWER BOUNDS

In [22] we already gave lower bounds for computing/approximating the diameter as well as lower bounds for approximating the girth. In the full version [24] of this paper we use the general technique of transferring lower bounds from communication complexity into a distributed setting, but use different graph-constructions and arguments than in [22].

THEOREM 2. *For any $\delta > 0$, parameter $d \geq 4$, where d is even, and $n \geq d + 6$ and $B \geq 1$ and sufficiently small ε, any distributed ε-error algorithm A that computes a $(+, 1)$-approximation to the diameter requires at least $\Omega\left(\frac{n}{D \cdot B} + D\right)$ time for some n-node graph of diameter $D \in \{d, d+2\}$. This can be extended to odd d.*

PROOF. The proof of Theorem 2 can be found in the full version [24] of this paper. We essentially construct a family of graphs inspired by [22] and prove that for any approximation algorithm it is hard to distinguish whether they have diameter d or $d + 2$. □

In the remainder of this section we extend this lower bound to several other problems. In the according statements, we implicitly assume similar conditions as stated in those Theorems/Lemmas used in the reductions.

LEMMA 8. *The following problems: 1) computing APSP 2) computing the eccentricity of each node of a graph 3) finding a peripheral vertex, take $\Omega(n/B+D)$ time. Any $(\times, 3/2 - \varepsilon)$-approximation to the above problems takes $\Omega(\sqrt{n}/B + D)$ time. Any $(+, 1)$-approximation takes time $\Omega(n/(B \cdot D)+D)$.*

PROOF. Solutions for APSP, eccentricity and peripheral-vertex can directly be used to obtain (an estimate of) the diameter in additional time $\mathcal{O}(D)$: In case of APSP and eccentricity we can do so by computing the maximum of the known distances or eccentricities by max-aggregation. In case we are given the (approximate) peripheral vertices, we just compute the eccentricity of any of them. These reductions yield that, if any of these tasks could be done faster than $o\left(\frac{n}{B}\right)$, $o\left(\frac{\sqrt{n}}{B}\right)$ or $o\left(\frac{n}{D \cdot B}\right)$ respectively, this is in contradiction to the already established lower bounds of Theorem 2 of this paper as well as Theorems 5.1. and 6.1. of [22]. □

Note that in Lemma 11 we provide a better lower bound for $(\times, 3/2 - \varepsilon)$-approximating APSP.

LEMMA 9. *Computing the center of a graph takes $\Omega(n/B + D)$. Computing a $(\times, 3/2 - \varepsilon)$-approximation to the center takes $\Omega(\sqrt{n}/B + D)$ time. Computing a $(+, 1)$-approximation to the center takes $\Omega\left(\frac{n}{D \cdot B} + D\right)$ time.*

PROOF. The proof of Lemma 9 can be found in the full version [24] of this paper. □

6. APPROXIMATION ALGORITHMS

In the previous section we have seen lower bounds that demonstrated that obtaining $(+, 1)$-approximations takes

$\Omega(n/D + D)$ time for the diameter. In order to approach this by an upper bound, we present an algorithm running in time $\mathcal{O}(n/D + D)$ that computes a $(\times, 1 + \varepsilon)$-approximation of the diameter. Furthermore we present a $(\times, 1 + \varepsilon)$-approximation to the girth g running in time $\mathcal{O}\left(n/g + D \cdot \log \frac{D}{g}\right)$. At the heart of these two approximations is the S-shortest paths problem (S-SP). In this problem we are given a graph and a subset S of its vertices. We are interested in computing the distances between all pairs of nodes in $S \times V$.

6.1 S - Shortest Paths

The idea of the algorithm is that we compute BFS trees T_v from each node $v \in S$. Differently from Algorithm 1, the trees start growing at the same time from each node $v \in S$. This causes that while growing T_v, the development of T_v might be delayed once reaching a node that is already part of a BFS tree T_u started in u if ID u is strictly smaller then ID v. We will prove that the total delay of any BFS is $\mathcal{O}(|S|)$ and that the resulting trees are indeed BFS trees. Clearly this is directly an alternative (more complicated, less elegant) algorithm/proof for APSP running in time $\mathcal{O}(n)$.

Algorithm 2 is executed by each node $v \in V$, the pseudocode demonstrates what a node v does. Each node v locally stores $d(v)$ sets L_i, one for each of the $d(v)$ neighbors $v_1, \ldots, v_{d(v)}$, and a set L. These locally stored sets depend on v and therefore the content of these sets might be different in different nodes during the execution of Algorithm 2.

At the beginning all these lists of a node v contain ID v if and only if $v \in S$, else they are empty (lines 1–6). Furthermore v maintains an array δ that will eventually store at position u (indicated by $\delta[u]$ the distance of v to node u. Initially $\delta[u]$ is set to infinity for all u and will only get updated at the time the distance is known (Line 21).

At time t, set L contains all node-IDs corresponding to the BFS tree computations that reached v until time t. That is at the end of the algorithm L contains all nodes of S.

At any time L_i contains all IDs that are currently in L except those that were forwarded successfully to neighbor v_i in the past. We say an ID l_i is forwarded successfully to neighbor u_i, if u_i is not sending a smaller ID r_i to v at the same time.

To compute the trees in Algorithm 2, the unique node with ID 1 computes $D' := ecc(1)$ and thus a $(\times, 2)$-approximation to the distance-diameter D'. This value is subsequently broadcasted to the network (lines 7–9). Then the computation of the $|S|$ trees starts and runs for $|S| + D'$ time steps.

Lines 13–17 make sure that at any time the smallest ID, that was not already successfully forwarded to neighbor u_i is sent. If a node ID r_i was received successful for the first time (verified in lines 19 and 20), we update $\delta[r_i]$, add r_i to the according lists (Line 22) and remember in variable $parent[r_i]$ who v's parent in T_{r_i} is (Line 23). In case a node-ID u is received several times, the algorithm adds the edge to tree T_u through which ID u was received at the earliest point in time. In case ID u was received at this (first) time from several neighbors, the algorithm (as we stated it) chooses the edge with lowest index i due to iterating in this way in Line 18. On the other hand if we did not successfully receive a message from neighbor v_i but sent successfully a message

---

Algorithm 2 as executed by each node $v \in G$ simultaneously. Input: $S \subseteq V$ Computes: S-SP on G

//** INITIALIZATION
1: $L := \emptyset$; $\delta := \{\infty, \infty, \ldots, \infty\}$
2: **if** $v \in S$ **then**
3:    $L := \{v\}$
4:    $\delta[v] := 0$
5: **end if**
6: $L_1, \ldots, L_{d(v)} := L$
7: **if** $u = 1$ **then**
8:    **compute** $D' := 2 \cdot ecc(u)$ //** upper bound on D
9:    **broadcast** D'
10: **else**
11:    **wait until** D' was **received**
12: **end if**

//** COMPUTATION of S-SP
13: **for** $|S| + D'$ time steps **do**
14:    **for** $i = 1, \ldots, d(v)$ **do**
15:       $l_i := \begin{cases} \infty & : \text{if } L_i = \emptyset \\ \min(L_i) & : \text{else} \end{cases}$
16:    **end for**
17:    within one time slot:
      |**send** $(l_1, \delta[l_1] + 1)$ to neighbor v_1, receive (r_1, δ_{r_1}) from v_1
      |**send** $(l_2, \delta[l_2] + 1)$ to neighbor v_2, receive (r_2, δ_{r_2}) from v_2
      |...
      |**send** $(l_{d(v)}, \delta[l_{d(v)}] + 1)$ to neighbor $v_{d(v)}$, receive
      | $(r_{d(v)}, \delta_{r_{d(v)}})$ from $v_{d(v)}$
18:    **for** $i = 1, \ldots, d(v)$ **do**
19:       **if** $r_i < l_i$ **then**
            //** T_{l_i}'s message is delayed due to T_{r_i}
20:          **if** $r_i \notin L$ **then**
               //** first time received "r_i" successfully
21:             $\delta[r_i] = \delta_{r_i}$ //** updates distances
22:             $L := L \cup \{r_i\}$ //** updates lists
               $L_1 := L_1 \cup \{r_i\}$
               $\ldots$
               $L_{i-1} := L_{i-1} \cup \{r_i\}$
               $L_{i+1} := L_{i+1} \cup \{r_i\}$
               $\ldots$
               $L_{d(v)} := L_{d(v)} \cup \{r_i\}$
23:             $parent[r_i] := v_i$
24:          **end if**
25:       **else**
26:          $L_i := L_i \setminus \{l_i\}$ //** "l_i" was successfully
27:       **end if**   //** sent to neighbor i.
28:    **end for**
29: **end for**

---

to v_i, the transmitted ID is removed from L_i (Line 26).

THEOREM 3. *Algorithm 2 computes S-SP, in time* $\mathcal{O}(|S| + D)$.

PROOF. First we prove the correctness of Algorithm 2: Let us choose a node $u \in S$ and consider the computation T_u (for now ignoring that we actually want to compute S-SP.) In such a computation, at time t, nodes at distance t from u receive a message ID u from all neighbors that are at distance $t - 1$ to u. An edge incident to the neighbor with lowest index that sent such a message is added to tree T_u.

Now consider Algorithm 2 and node v at distance t from u, as well as two nodes $w_1, w_2 \subseteq N_1(v)$; we can ignore the case that v has only one neighbor. A message containing ID u is sent over the edge (w_1, v) earlier than over edge (w_2, v) if and only if $d(u, w_1) < d(v, w_2)$. To see this, note that the set of lower IDs which delay the messages of T_u is the same for both paths (u, w_1, v) and (u, w_2, v). To see this assume that T_i is delaying the message ID u sent over (u, w_1, v) at some point. Then ID i will reach (or will have reached in case ID i is coming from v's direction) v earlier then ID u. Thus it will also block the message ID u running through path (u, w_2, v), if it did not already block it earlier.

Now we prove that Algorithm 2 runs in time $\mathcal{O}(|S| + D)$: The BFS executed by node 1 to compute D' takes $\mathcal{O}(D)$. The for-loop in Lines 13–31 is executed for $|S| + D'$ times, each time taking 1 round of communication, which is $\mathcal{O}(|S| + D)$.

Note that during traveling on any $u - v$-path of T_u, the message ID u gets delayed at most once by the computation BFS$_i$ if ID i is strictly smaller then ID u. This happens either by waiting in the set L_i of some node or by trying to cross an edge of the path at the same time as ID i (which will not be successful during the according time slot). Thus the total delay of computing T_u is $|S|$ and the total runtime of Algorithm 2 is $\mathcal{O}(|S| + D)$.

Finally observe, that in Line 21, after $\delta[r_i]$ is changed from ∞ to the value received, $\delta[r_i]$ stores the correct distance between v and node r_i. This can be shown by induction over the levels in the computed BFS tree rooted in the node with id r_i. $\square$

6.2 A $(\times, 1+\varepsilon)$-Approximation to Diameter and Girth

The presented algorithms are based on computing a k-dominating set $\mathcal{DOM} \subseteq V$ and solving $\mathcal{DOM}$-SP. There is plenty of literature on k-dominating sets. We use the results provided in [27].

DEFINITION 9. (composed from [27]) A k-dominating set for a graph G is a subset $\mathcal{DOM}$ of vertices with the property that for every $v \in V$ there is some $u \in \mathcal{DOM}$ at distance of at most k from v. For every such k-dominating set we define a partition $\mathcal{P} = \{P_1, \ldots, P_{|\mathcal{DOM}|}\}$ such that each node of V is exactly in one P_i and of distance less than or equal k to the dominator in $\mathcal{DOM}$ of P_i.

LEMMA 10. (Version of Lemma 2.3 in [27]). Algorithm `Diam_DOM` of [27] computes a k-dominating set $\mathcal{DOM}$ of size $|\mathcal{DOM}| \leq \max\{1, \lfloor n/(k+1) \rfloor\}$ deterministically and its time complexity is $6 \cdot D + k$. A partition $\mathcal{P}$ can be computed in additional time $\mathcal{O}(k)$.

THEOREM 4. We can compute a $(\times, 1+\varepsilon)$-approximation of all eccentricities in $\mathcal{O}(\frac{n}{D} + D)$ time.

PROOF. To do so, we use Fact 1 and determine a $(\times, 2)$-estimate $D' := 2 \cdot ecc(1)$ of the diameter by computing the eccentricity $ecc(1)$ of the node with ID 1. Next we set $k := \lfloor \varepsilon \cdot D'/4 \rfloor$ and use Lemma 10 to compute a k-dominating set $\mathcal{DOM}$ of size $|\mathcal{DOM}| \leq \max\{1, \lfloor n/(k+1) \rfloor\}$ in time $\mathcal{O}(D+k)$. Then we solve $\mathcal{DOM}$-SP in time $\mathcal{O}(|\mathcal{DOM}| + D)$. At the end of this computation each node $v \in V$ knows its distance to all vertices in $\mathcal{DOM}$. Let $u \in \mathcal{DOM}$ be a node in $\mathcal{DOM}$ of maximal distance to v. Then $d(u, v)$ is at most k hops shorter than v's actual eccentricity due to the

use of k-dominating sets. Thus the computed estimate of the eccentricity of v is less than $k + \max_{u \in \mathcal{DOM}} d(u, v) \leq k + ecc(v) = \lfloor \varepsilon \cdot D'/4 \rfloor + ecc(v) = \lfloor \varepsilon \cdot ecc(1)/2 \rfloor + ecc(v) \leq (1 + \varepsilon) \cdot ecc(v)$ where the last bound follows due to Fact 1. The total time for this computation is $\mathcal{O}(|\mathcal{DOM}| + D + k) = \mathcal{O}(n/D + D)$. $\square$

COROLLARY 4. We can compute a $(\times, 1 + \varepsilon)$-approximation of the diameter, radius, center and peripheral vertices in time $\mathcal{O}(n/D + D)$.

THEOREM 5. We can compute a $(\times, 1+\varepsilon)$-approximation of the girth in time

$$\mathcal{O}\left(\min\left\{\left(n/g + D \cdot \log \frac{D}{g}\right), n\right\}\right).$$

PROOF. The proof of Theorem 5 can be found in the full version [24] of this paper. We essentially start with a loose upper bound on the girth which is improved over time. For each improvement, we run an instance of S-SP on a k-dominating set, where k depends on the current estimate of g (and ε in the last iteration). In each iteration we obtain a new estimate of g following an idea similar to the one used in 7. $\square$

7. DISTINGUISHING GRAPHS OF SMALL DIAMETER

7.1 Distinguishing Diameter 2 from 3 takes time $\Omega(n/B + D)$

THEOREM 6. Let $\mathcal{G}$ be the family of all graphs of diameter 2 or 3. For any $n \geq 6$ and $B \geq 1$ and sufficiently small ε any distributed randomized ε-error algorithm A that can decide whether a graph $G \in \mathcal{G}$ has diameter 2 or 3 needs $\Omega\left(\frac{n}{B} + D\right)$ time for some n-node graph.

REMARK 5. This is an improvement of Theorem 5.1. of [22]: computing the diameter of a graph takes time $\Omega(n/B + D)$ even if the diameter is 3 (compared to five as in [22]).

PROOF. The proof of Theorem 6 can be found in the full version [24] of this paper. We essentially construct a family of graphs inspired by [22] and prove that for any algorithm it is hard to distinguish whether they have diameter 2 or 3. $\square$

LEMMA 11. Computing a $(\times, 3/2 - \varepsilon)$-approximation for APSP takes $\Omega(\frac{n}{B} + D)$ time.

PROOF. From Theorem 6 we know that $\Omega(\frac{n}{B} + D)$ is needed to distinguish diameter 3 from 2. Any $(\times, 3/2 - \varepsilon)$-approximation algorithm for APSP can distinguishing graphs of diameter 2 from graphs of diameter 2 with only $O(D) = O(1)$ communication rounds overhead. This can be extended to the case of larger diameters: Construct a graph by adding a path of the desired length to one node in the graph. In this setting we are interested in deciding whether the diameter of a certain subgraph is 2 or 3. This subgraph is just the previously described graph to which we later added the path. $\square$

7.2 Distinguishing Diameter 2 from 4 in time $\mathcal{O}(\sqrt{n \cdot \log n})$

We now demonstrate how to distinguish graphs of diameter 2 from graphs of diameter 4 in time $\mathcal{O}(\sqrt{n})$. This algorithm is inspired by an algorithm called 2-vs-4 presented in [2]. The authors of [2] considered the idea leading to this algorithm to be an important step towards obtaining their $(\times, 3/2)$-approximation algorithm. In the light of Theorem 6 (and Theorem 2), where we showed that distinguishing diameter 2 graphs from diameter 3 graphs (and diameter k graphs from diameter $k+2$ graphs for $k \geq 4$, respectively) takes long time, it is intriguing that distinguishing diameter 2 graphs from 4 graphs can be done rather fast. Before we state Algorithm 3 (a.k.a. Algorithm 2-vs-4), we introduce some notation and review some results of [2] depending on a parameter s. Later in the paper they choose the parameter s to be $s := \sqrt{n \cdot \log n}$ and we do the same in our distributed setting.

DEFINITION 10. *We define* $L(V) := \{u \in V : |N_1(u)| < s\}$ *and* $H(V) := V \setminus L(V) = \{u \in V : |N_1(u)| \geq s\}$.

REMARK 6. *(Version of Remark 2.1. in [2]). Choosing a set of* $\Theta(s^{-1} \cdot n \cdot \log n)$ *vertices uniformly at random results in an 1-dominating set for* $H(V)$ *with high probability.*

THEOREM 7. *Algorithm 3 distinguishes diameter 2 from 4 and can be implemented in a distributed way (using randomness) terminating whp within* $\mathcal{O}(\sqrt{n \cdot \log n})$ *rounds of communication.*

Algorithm 3 – same as **Algorithm** 2-vs-4 from [2].
Input: G with diameter 2 or 4   Output: diameter of G

1: **if** $L(V) \neq \emptyset$ **then**
2:     choose $v \in L(V)$
3:     **compute** a BFS tree from each vertex in $N_1(v)$
4: **else**
5:     **compute** a dominating set $\mathcal{DOM}$ for $H(V)$
6:     **compute** a BFS tree from each vertex in $\mathcal{DOM}$
7: **end if**
8: **if** all BFS trees have depth 2 **then**
9:     **return** 2
10: **else**
11:     **return** 4
12: **end if**

PROOF. Correctness is shown in Theorem 3.1. in [2] and we only need to take care of analyzing the distributed runtime. Each node can decide internally without communication whether it belongs to set $L(V)$ or $H(V)$. Choosing the node v in Line 2 takes $\mathcal{O}(D)$. Computing the BFS trees from each vertex in $N_1(v)$ can be done in time $\mathcal{O}(|N_1(v)| \cdot D) = \mathcal{O}(s \cdot D) = \mathcal{O}(\sqrt{n \cdot \log n})$, due to the choice of v and s as well as the fact that $D \leq 4 = \mathcal{O}(1)$. (Note: This is already fast enough and we do not need to use $N_1(v)$-SP here.) Computing a dominating set $\mathcal{DOM}$ for $H(V)$ can be done locally without communication: each node in $H(V)$ independently joins $\mathcal{DOM}$ with probability $\sqrt{\frac{\log n}{n}}$. With high probability this results in a set $\mathcal{DOM}$ of size $\Theta(\sqrt{n \cdot \log n})$ which in turn is a dominating set with high probability according to Remark 6. Computing BFS trees from each of

the vertices in $\mathcal{DOM}$ takes $\mathcal{O}(|\mathcal{DOM}| \cdot D) = \mathcal{O}(\sqrt{n \cdot \log n})$. Deciding whether all computed BFS trees have depth at most 2 can be done by max-aggregation in an arbitrary node in time $\mathcal{O}(D) = \mathcal{O}(1)$. Thus the total time complexity is $\mathcal{O}(\sqrt{n \cdot \log n})$. $\square$

8. COUNTING THE NUMBER OF NODES IN THE GREATER NEIGHBORHOOD

In this section we argue that computing all depth k-BFS trees can be a hard task by giving a worst case example for $k = 2$. Towards this end we construct a family of graphs where computing all depth 2-BFS trees takes $\Omega(n/B + D)$ time. At the same time these graphs have girth 3.

THEOREM 8. *Let $\mathcal{G}$ be the family of all graphs of diameter 2 or 3. For any $n \geq 6$ and $B \geq 1$ and sufficiently small ε any distributed randomized ε-error algorithm A that can compute a 2-BFS trees for each nodes needs $\Omega(n/B + D)$ time for some n-node graph.*

PROOF. Consider the following problem: "Is there a node v, such that the number of nodes in the 2-neighborhood $N_2(v)$ (including v) is strictly less than n?" The problem of computing all 2-BFS trees can be reduced to this problem in time $\mathcal{O}(D) = \mathcal{O}(1)$: Simply check whether there is a node that is not included in some 2-BFS tree. This problem in turn can be reduced to distinguishing whether the graph used in the proof of Theorem 6 has diameter 2 or 3. If for all nodes the number of nodes in the k-neighborhood is $n - 1$, this means that the diameter is 2. Else the diameter is 3. Applying Theorem 6 immediately yields the lower bound. $\square$

Acknowledgments: We thank an anonymous reviewer for helpful comments on the presentation.

9. REFERENCES

[1] J. Abram and I. Rhodes. A decentralized shortest path algorithm. In *Proceedings of the 16th Allerton Conference on Communication, Control and Computing (Allerton)*, pages 271–277, 1978.

[2] D. Aingworth, C. Chekuri, P. Indyk, and R. Motwani. Fast estimation of diameter and shortest paths (without matrix multiplication). *SIAM Journal on Computing (SICOMP)*, 28(4):1167–1181, 1999.

[3] N. Alon, Z. Galil, and O. Margalit. On the exponent of the all pairs shortest path problem. In *Proceedings of the 32nd Annual IEEE Symposium on Foundations of Computer Science (FOCS)*, pages 569–575, 1991.

[4] N. Alon, O. Margalit, Z. Galilt, and M. Naor. Witnesses for boolean matrix multiplication and for shortest paths. In *Proceedings of the 33rd Annual Symposium on Foundations of Computer Science (FOCS)*, pages 417–426, 1992.

[5] N. Alon, R. Yuster, and U. Zwick. Finding and counting given length cycles. *Algorithmica*, 17(3):209–223, 1997.

[6] U. Black. *IP routing protocols: RIP, OSPF, BGP, PNNI and Cisco routing protocols*. Prentice Hall PTR, 2000.

[7] G. Blelloch, V. Vassilevska, and R. Williams. A new combinatorial approach for sparse graph problems. In *Proceedings of the 35th international colloquium on Automata, Languages and Programming, Part I (ICALP)*, pages 108–120, 2008.

[8] P. Carrington, J. Scott, and S. Wasserman. *Models and methods in social network analysis*. Cambridge University Press, 2005.

[9] T. Chan. All-pairs shortest paths for unweighted undirected graphs in o (mn) time. In *Proceedings of the 17th annual ACM-SIAM symposium on Discrete algorithm (SODA)*, pages 514–523. ACM, 2006.

[10] T. M. Chan. More algorithms for all-pairs shortest paths in weighted graphs. In *Proceedings of the 39th annual ACM symposium on Theory of computing*, (STOC), pages 590–598, New York, NY, USA, 2007. ACM.

[11] K. Chandy and J. Misra. Distributed computation on graphs: Shortest path algorithms. *Communications of the ACM (CACM)*, 25(11):833–837, 1982.

[12] C. Chen. A distributed algorithm for shortest paths. *IEEE Transactions on Computers (TC)*, 100(9):898–899, 1982.

[13] D. Coppersmith and S. Winograd. Matrix multiplication via arithmetic progressions. *Journal of symbolic computation (JSC)*, 9(3):251–280, 1990.

[14] A. Das Sarma, S. Holzer, L. Kor, A. Korman, D. Nanongkai, G. Pandurangan, D. Peleg, and R. Wattenhofer. Distributed verification and hardness of distributed approximation. *Proceedings of the 43rd annual ACM Symposium on Theory of Computing (STOC)*, 2011.

[15] W. Dobosiewicz. A more efficient algorithm for the min-plus multiplication. *International journal of computer mathematics*, 32(1-2):49–60, 1990.

[16] D. Dolev, C. Lenzen, and S. Peled. "tri, tri again": Finding triangles and small subgraphs in a distributed setting. *CoRR*, http://arxiv.org/abs/1201.6652, 2012.

[17] D. Dor, S. Halperin, and U. Zwick. All-pairs almost shortest paths. *SIAM Journal on Computing (SICOMP)*, 29:1740, 2000.

[18] M. Elkin. Computing almost shortest paths. In *Proceedings of the 20th annual ACM symposium on Principles of distributed computing (PODC)*, pages 53–62, 2001.

[19] T. Feder and R. Motwani. Clique partitions, graph compression and speeding-up algorithms. In *Proceedings of the 23rd annual ACM symposium on Theory of computing (STOC)*, pages 123–133, 1991.

[20] G. Flake, S. Lawrence, and C. Giles. Efficient identification of web communities. In *Proceedings of the 6th ACM SIGKDD international conference on Knowledge discovery and data mining (KDD)*, pages 150–160. ACM, 2000.

[21] M. Fredman. New bounds on the complexity of the shortest path problem. *SIAM Journal on Computing (SICOMP)*, 5:83, 1976.

[22] S. Frischknecht, S. Holzer, and R. Wattenhofer. Networks Cannot Compute Their Diameter in Sublinear Time. In *Proceedings of the 23rd annual ACM-SIAM Symposium on Discrete Algorithms (SODA)*, pages 1150–1162.

[23] Y. Han. Improved algorithm for all pairs shortest paths. *Information Processing Letters (IPL)*, 91(5):245–250, 2004.

[24] S. Holzer and R. Wattenhofer. Optimal distributed all pairs shortest paths and applications. *http://www.dcg.ethz.ch/ stholzer/PODC12-APSP-full.pdf (preliminary full version to be submitted to a journal)*.

[25] A. Itai and M. Rodeh. Finding a minimum circuit in a graph. *SIAM Journal on Computing (SICOMP)*, 7:413, 1978.

[26] M. Khan, F. Kuhn, D. Malkhi, G. Pandurangan, and K. Talwar. Efficient distributed approximation algorithms via probabilistic tree embeddings. In *Proceedings of the 27th Annual ACM SIGACT-SIGOPS Symposium on Principles of Distributed Computing (PODC)*, pages 263–272, 2008.

[27] S. Kutten and D. Peleg. Fast distributed construction of small k-dominating sets and applications. *Journal of Algorithms*, 28(1):40–66, 1998.

[28] N. Lynch. *Distributed algorithms*. Morgan Kaufmann, 1996.

[29] J. McQuillan, I. Richer, and E. Rosen. The new routing algorithm for the arpanet. *IEEE Transactions on Communications (TC)*, 28(5):711–719, 1980.

[30] P. Merlin and A. Segall. A failsafe distributed routing protocol. *IEEE Transactions on Communications (TC)*, 27(9):1280–1287, 1979.

[31] L. Page, S. Brin, R. Motwani, and T. Winograd. The pagerank citation ranking: Bringing order to the web. *Technical Report 1999-66, Stanford InfoLab*, 1999.

[32] D. Peleg. *Distributed computing: a locality-sensitive approach*. 2000.

[33] D. Peleg, L. Roditty, and E. Tal. Distributed algorithms for network diameter and girth. In *Proceedings of the 39th International Colloquium on Automata, Languages and Programming (ICALP), to appear*, 2012.

[34] L. Roditty and R. Tov. Approximating the girth. In *Proceedings of the 22nd annual ACM-SIAM symposium on Discrete algorithm (SODA)*, pages 1446–1454, 2011.

[35] L. Roditty and V. Williams. Minimum weight cycles and triangles: Equivalences and algorithms. In *Proceedings of the 52nd Annual IEEE Symposium on Foundations of Computer Science (FOCS)*, pages 180–189, 2011.

[36] L. Roditty and V. Williams. Subquadratic time approximation algorithms for the girth. In *Proceedings of the 23rd annual ACM-SIAM symposium on Discrete algorithm (SODA)*, pages 833–845, 2012.

[37] A. Sarma, M. Dinitz, and G. Pandurangan. Efficient computation of distance sketches in distributed networks. *24th ACM Symposium on Parallelism in Algorithms and Architectures (SPAA), to appear*, 2012.

[38] M. Schwartz and T. Stern. Routing techniques used in computer communication networks. *IEEE Transactions on Communications (TC)*, 28(4):539–552, 1980.

[39] R. Seidel. On the all-pairs-shortest-path problem in unweighted undirected graphs. *Journal of Computer and System Sciences (JCSS)*, 51(3):400–403, 1995.

[40] A. Shoshan and U. Zwick. All pairs shortest paths in undirected graphs with integer weights. In *Proceedings of the 40th Annual IEEE Symposium on Foundations of Computer Science (FOCS)*, pages 605–614, 1999.

[41] W. Tajibnapis. A correctness proof of a topology information maintenance protocol for a distributed computer network. *Communications of the ACM (CACM)*, 20(7):477–485, 1977.

[42] T. Takaoka. A new upper bound on the complexity of the all pairs shortest path problem. *Information Processing Letters (IPL)*, 43(4):195–199, 1992.

[43] T. Takaoka. A faster algorithm for the all-pairs shortest path problem and its application. *Proceedings of the 10th Annual International Computing and Combinatorics Conference (COCOON)*, pages 278–289, 2004.

[44] M. Thorup and U. Zwick. Approximate distance oracles. *Journal of the ACM (JACM)*, 52(1):1–24, 2005.

[45] S. Toueg. An all-pairs shortest-paths distributed algorithm. *Tech. Rep. RC 8327, IBM TJ Watson Research Center, Yorktown Heights, NY 10598, USA*, 1980.

[46] V. Williams. Multiplying matrices faster than coppersmith-winograd. *Proceedings of the 44th annual ACM Symposium on Theory of Computing (STOC)*, 2012.

[47] S. Yardi, D. Romero, G. Schoenebeck, and D. Boyd. Detecting spam in a twitter network. *First Monday*, 15(1), 2009.

[48] R. Yuster and U. Zwick. Finding even cycles even faster. *SIAM Journal on Discrete Mathematics (SIDMA)*, 10:209, 1997.

[49] U. Zwick. A slightly improved sub-cubic algorithm for the all pairs shortest paths problem with real edge lengths. *Algorithms and Computation*, pages 841–843, 2005.

Iterative Approximate Byzantine Consensus in Arbitrary Directed Graphs [*]

Nitin H. Vaidya
University of Illinois
Electrical and Computer
Engineering
Urbana, Illinois
nhv@illinois.edu

Lewis Tseng
University of Illinois
Computer Science
Department
Urbana, Illinois
ltseng3@illinois.edu

Guanfeng Liang
University of Illinois
Electrical and Computer
Engineering
Urbana, Illinois
guanfeng.liang@gmail.com

ABSTRACT

This paper proves a necessary and sufficient condition for the existence of *iterative* algorithms that achieve *approximate Byzantine consensus* in arbitrary directed graphs, where each directed edge represents a communication channel between a pair of nodes. The class of iterative algorithms considered in this paper ensures that, after each iteration of the algorithm, the state of each fault-free node remains in the *convex hull* of the states of the fault-free nodes at the end of the previous iteration. The following *convergence* requirement is imposed: for any $\epsilon > 0$, after a sufficiently large number of iterations, the states of the fault-free nodes are guaranteed to be within ϵ of each other.

To the best of our knowledge, *tight* necessary and sufficient conditions for the existence of such iterative consensus algorithms in synchronous *arbitrary* point-to-point networks in presence of *Byzantine faults* have not been developed previously.

The methodology and results presented in this paper can also be extended to asynchronous systems.

Categories and Subject Descriptors

C.2.4 [**Distributed Systems**]: Distributed applications

General Terms

Algorithms

Keywords

Consensus, Byzantine faults, iterative algorithms

[*]This research is supported in part by National Science Foundation award CNS 1059540 and Army Research Office grant W-911-NF-0710287. Any opinions, findings, and conclusions or recommendations expressed here are those of the authors and do not necessarily reflect the views of the funding agencies or the U.S. government.

1. INTRODUCTION

Dolev et al. [5] introduced the notion of *approximate Byzantine consensus* by relaxing the requirement of *exact* consensus [14]. The goal in approximate consensus is to allow the fault-free nodes to agree on values that are approximately equal to each other (and not necessarily exactly identical). In presence of Byzantine faults, while *exact* consensus is impossible in *asynchronous* systems [8], approximate consensus is achievable [5]. The notion of approximate consensus is of interest in *synchronous* systems as well, since approximate consensus can be achieved using distributed algorithms that do not require complete knowledge of the network topology [3]. The rest of the discussion in this paper – with the exception of Section 8 – applies to synchronous systems.

We consider "iterative" algorithms for achieving approximate Byzantine consensus in synchronous point-to-point networks that are modeled by arbitrary *directed* graphs. The *iterative approximate Byzantine consensus* (IABC) algorithms of interest have the following properties, which we will soon state more formally:

- *Initial state* of each node is equal to a real-valued *input* provided to that node.

- *Validity* condition: After each iteration of an IABC algorithm, the state of each fault-free node must remain in the *convex hull* of the states of the fault-free nodes at the end of the *previous* iteration.

- *Convergence* condition: For any $\epsilon > 0$, after a sufficiently large number of iterations, the states of the fault-free nodes are guaranteed to be within ϵ of each other.

In this paper, for the existence of a correct IABC algorithm, we derive a necessary condition that must be satisfied by the underlying communication graph. For graphs that satisfy this necessary condition, we show the correctness of a specific IABC algorithm, proving that the necessary conditions are tight. The rest of the paper is organized as follows. Section 2 present our system and network models. Related work is discussed in Section 3. Section 4 describes the iterative algorithms of interest. The necessary condition is derived in Section 5. A specific IABC algorithm is described in Section 6, and its correctness is proved in Section 7. Section 8 extends our results to an iterative algorithm in asynchronous environments. Some recent results that build on the results presented in this paper are summarized in Section 9. The paper concludes with Section 10.

2. SYSTEM MODEL

Communication model: The system is assumed to be *synchronous* (except in Section 8). The communication network is modeled as a simple *directed* graph $G(\mathcal{V}, \mathcal{E})$, where $\mathcal{V} = \{1, \ldots, n\}$ is the set of n nodes, and $\mathcal{E}$ is the set of directed edges between the nodes in $\mathcal{V}$. We assume that $n \geq 2$, since the consensus problem for $n = 1$ is trivial. Node i can reliably transmit messages to node j if and only if the directed edge (i, j) is in $\mathcal{E}$. Each node can send messages to itself as well, however, for convenience, we exclude self-loops from set $\mathcal{E}$. That is, $(i, i) \notin \mathcal{E}$ for $i \in \mathcal{V}$. With a slight abuse of terminology, we will use the terms *edge* and *link* interchangeably in our presentation.

For each node i, let N_i^- be the set of nodes from which i has incoming edges. That is, $N_i^- = \{ j \mid (j, i) \in \mathcal{E} \}$. Similarly, define N_i^+ as the set of nodes to which node i has outgoing edges. That is, $N_i^+ = \{ j \mid (i, j) \in \mathcal{E} \}$. Since we exclude self-loops from $\mathcal{E}$, $i \notin N_i^-$ and $i \notin N_i^+$. However, we note again that each node can indeed send messages to itself.

Failure Model: We consider the Byzantine failure model, with up to f nodes becoming faulty. A faulty node may *misbehave* arbitrarily. Possible misbehavior includes sending incorrect and mismatching (or inconsistent) messages to different neighbors. The faulty nodes may potentially collaborate with each other. Moreover, the faulty nodes are assumed to have a complete knowledge of the execution of the algorithm, including the states of all the nodes, contents of messages the other nodes send to each other, the algorithm specification, and the network topology.

3. RELATED WORK

As noted earlier, Dolev et al. presented the early results on Byzantine fault-tolerant iterative consensus [5]. The initial algorithms [5, 14] were proved correct in *fully connected* networks. Fekete [6] studied the convergence rate of approximate consensus algorithms.

There have been attempts at achieving approximate fault-tolerant consensus iteratively in *partially* connected graphs. Kieckhafer and Azadmanesh examined the necessary conditions in order to achieve "local convergence" in synchronous [10] and asynchronous [2] systems. [1] presents a specific class of networks in which convergence condition can be satisfied using iterative algorithms.

A restricted fault model – called "malicious" fault model – in which the faulty nodes are restricted to sending identical messages to their neighbors has also been explored recently [19, 11, 12, 13]. In contrast, our Byzantine model allows a faulty node to send different messages to different neighbors. Under the (restricted) malicious fault model, Zhang and Sundaram [19] develop sufficient conditions for iterative consensus algorithm assuming a "local" fault model (in their "local" model, a bounded number of each node's neighbors may be faulty).

LeBlanc and Koutsoukos [11] address a continuous time version of the consensus problem with malicious faults in complete graphs. Under both malicious and Byzantine fault models, LeBlanc and Koutsoukos [12] have identified some sufficient conditions under which the continuous time version of iterative consensus can be achieved with up to f faults

in the network; however, these sufficient conditions are *not* tight.

For the malicious fault model, LeBlanc et al. [13] have independently obtained *tight* necessary and sufficient conditions for tolerating up to f total number of faults in the network. Under the malicious model, since a faulty node must send identical messages to all the neighbors, the necessary and sufficient conditions are weaker than those developed here for the Byzantine fault model. For instance, under the malicious model, iterative consensus is possible in a complete graph consisting of $2f + 1$ nodes, whereas at least $3f + 1$ nodes are necessary for consensus under the Byzantine fault model.

Iterative approximate consensus algorithms that do not tolerate faulty behavior have been studied extensively (e.g., [9, 3]). The proof technique used for proving *sufficiency* in this paper is inspired by the prior work on non-fault-tolerant iterative algorithms [3].

4. IABC ALGORITHMS

In this section, we describe the structure of the *iterative approximate Byzantine consensus* (IABC) algorithms of interest, and state the validity and convergence conditions that they must satisfy.

Each node i maintains state v_i, with $v_i[t]$ denoting the state of node i at the *end* of the t-th iteration of the algorithm. Initial state of node i, $v_i[0]$, is equal to the initial *input* provided to node i. At the *start* of the t-th iteration ($t > 0$), the state of node i is $v_i[t-1]$. The IABC algorithms of interest will require each node i to perform the following three steps in iteration t, where $t > 0$. Note that the faulty nodes may deviate from this specification.

1. *Transmit step:* Transmit current state, namely $v_i[t-1]$, on all outgoing edges (to nodes in N_i^+).

2. *Receive step:* Receive values on all incoming edges (from nodes in N_i^-). Denote by $r_i[t]$ the vector of values received by node i from its neighbors. The size of vector $r_i[t]$ is $|N_i^-|$.

3. *Update step:* Node i updates its state using a transition function Z_i as follows. Z_i is a part of the specification of the algorithm, and takes as input the vector $r_i[t]$ and state $v_i[t-1]$.

$$v_i[t] = Z_i (r_i[t], v_i[t-1]) \tag{1}$$

We now define $U[t]$ and $\mu[t]$, assuming that $\mathcal{F}$ is the set of Byzantine faulty nodes, with the nodes in $\mathcal{V} - \mathcal{F}$ being fault-free.[1]

- $U[t] = \max_{i \in \mathcal{V} - \mathcal{F}} v_i[t]$. $U[t]$ is the largest state among the fault-free nodes at the end of the t-th iteration. Since the initial state of each node is equal to its input, $U[0]$ is equal to the maximum value of the initial input at the fault-free nodes.

- $\mu[t] = \min_{i \in \mathcal{V} - \mathcal{F}} v_i[t]$. $\mu[t]$ is the smallest state among the fault-free nodes at the end of the t-th iteration. $\mu[0]$ is equal to the minimum value of the initial input at the fault-free nodes.

---

[1]For sets X and Y, $X - Y$ contains elements that are in X but not in Y. That is, $X - Y = \{i \mid i \in X, i \notin Y\}$.

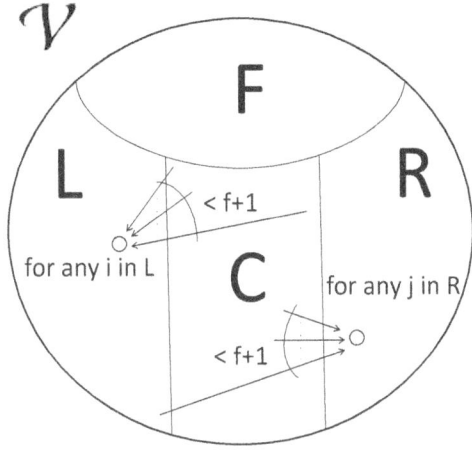

Figure 1: Illustration for the proof of Theorem 1. In this figure, $C \cup R \Rightarrow L$ and $L \cup C \not\Rightarrow R$.

The following conditions must be satisfied by an IABC algorithm in presence of up to f Byzantine faulty nodes:

- *Validity:* $\forall t > 0,\ \ \mu[t] \geq \mu[t-1]$ and $U[t] \leq U[t-1]$

- *Convergence:* $\lim_{t \to \infty} U[t] - \mu[t] = 0$

The objective in this paper is to identify the necessary and sufficient conditions for the existence of a *correct* IABC algorithm (i.e., an algorithm satisfying the above validity and convergence conditions) for a given $G(\mathcal{V}, \mathcal{E})$.

5. NECESSARY CONDITION

For a correct IABC algorithm to exist, the network graph $G(\mathcal{V}, \mathcal{E})$ must satisfy the necessary condition proved in this section. Theorems 1 and 2 below state equivalent necessary conditions. The form of the necessary condition in Theorem 2 is more intuitive, whereas the form in Theorem 1 is used later to prove sufficiency. We now define relations $\Rightarrow$ and $\not\Rightarrow$ that are used frequently in our discussion.

DEFINITION 1. *For non-empty disjoint sets of nodes A and B,*

- $A \Rightarrow B$ *iff there exists a node $v \in B$ that has at least $f+1$ incoming edges from nodes in A, i.e., $|N_v^- \cap A| > f$.*

- $A \not\Rightarrow B$ *iff $A \Rightarrow B$ is not true.*

THEOREM 1. *Suppose that a correct IABC algorithm exists for $G(\mathcal{V}, \mathcal{E})$. Let sets F, L, C, R form a partition[2] of $\mathcal{V}$, such that L and R are both non-empty, and $|F| \leq f$. Then, either $C \cup R \Rightarrow L$, or $L \cup C \Rightarrow R$.*

PROOF. The proof is by contradiction. Let us assume that a correct iterative consensus algorithm exists, and $C \cup R \not\Rightarrow L$ and $L \cup C \not\Rightarrow R$. Thus, for any $i \in L$, $|N_i^- \cap (C \cup R)| < f+1$, and for any $j \in R$, $|N_j^- \cap (L \cup C)| < f+1$. Figure 1 illustrates the sets used in this proof.

---

[2]Sets $X_1, X_2, X_3, ..., X_p$ are said to form a partition of set X provided that (i) $\cup_{1 \leq i \leq p} X_i = X$, and (ii) $X_i \cap X_j = \Phi$ if $i \neq j$.

Also assume that the nodes in F (if F is non-empty) are all faulty, and the other nodes in sets L, C, R are fault-free. Note that the fault-free nodes are not aware of the identity of the faulty nodes.

Consider the case when (i) each node in L has initial input m, (ii) each node in R has initial input M, such that $M > m$, and (iii) each node in C, if C is non-empty, has an input in the interval $[m, M]$.

In the *Transmit Step* of iteration 1, suppose that the faulty nodes in F (if non-empty) send $m^- < m$ on outgoing links to nodes in L, send $M^+ > M$ on outgoing links to nodes in R, and send some arbitrary value in interval $[m, M]$ on outgoing links to the nodes in C (if C is non-empty). This behavior is possible since nodes in F are faulty. Note that $m^- < m < M < M^+$. Each fault-free node $k \in \mathcal{V} - F$, sends to nodes in N_k^+ value $v_k[0]$ in iteration 1.

Consider any node $i \in L$. Denote $N_i' = N_i^- \cap (C \cup R)$. Since $|F| \leq f$, $|N_i^- \cap F| \leq f$. Since $C \cup R \not\Rightarrow L$, $|N_i'| \leq f$. Node i will then receive m^- from the nodes in $N_i^- \cap F$, and values in $[m, M]$ from the nodes in N_i', and m from the nodes in $\{i\} \cup (N_i^- \cap L)$.

Consider the following two cases:

- Both $N_i^- \cap F$ and N_i' are non-empty: Now $|N_i^- \cap F| \leq f$ and $|N_i'| \leq f$. From node i's perspective, consider two possible scenarios: (a) nodes in $N_i^- \cap F$ are faulty, and the other nodes are fault-free, and (b) nodes in N_i' are faulty, and the other nodes are fault-free.

  In scenario (a), from node i's perspective, the fault-free nodes have sent values in interval $[m, M]$, whereas the faulty nodes have sent value m^-. According to the validity condition, $v_i[1] \geq m$. On the other hand, in scenario (b), the fault-free nodes have sent values m^- and m, where $m^- < m$; so $v_i[1] \leq m$, according to the validity condition. Since node i does not know whether the correct scenario is (a) or (b), it must update its state to satisfy the validity condition in both cases. Thus, it follows that $v_i[1] = m$.

- At most one of $N_i^- \cap F$ and N_i' is non-empty: Thus, $|(N_i^- \cap F) \cup N_i'| \leq f$. From node i's perspective, it is possible that the nodes in $(N_i^- \cap F) \cup N_i'$ are all faulty, and the rest of the nodes are fault-free. In this situation, the values sent to node i by the fault-free nodes (which are all in $\{i\} \cup (N_i^- \cap L)$) are all m, and therefore, $v_i[1]$ must be set to m as per the validity condition.

Thus, $v_i[1] = m$ for each node $i \in L$. Similarly, we can show that $v_j[1] = M$ for each node $j \in R$.

Now consider the nodes in set C, if C is non-empty. All the values received by the nodes in C are in $[m, M]$, therefore, their new state must also remain in $[m, M]$, as per the validity condition.

The above discussion implies that, at the end of iteration 1, the following conditions hold true: (i) state of each node in L is m, (ii) state of each node in R is M, and (iii) state of each node in C is in the interval $[m, M]$. These conditions are identical to the initial conditions listed previously. Then, by a repeated application of the above argument (proof by induction), it follows that for any $t \geq 0$, $v_i[t] = m$ for all $\forall i \in L$, $v_j[t] = M$ for all $j \in R$ and $v_k[t] \in [m, M]$ for all $k \in C$.

Since L and R both contain fault-free nodes, the convergence requirement is not satisfied. This is a contradiction to the assumption that a correct iterative algorithm exists. $\quad\square$

COROLLARY 1. *Suppose that a correct IABC algorithm exists for $G(\mathcal{V},\mathcal{E})$. Let $\{F,L,R\}$ be a partition of $\mathcal{V}$, such that L and R are both non-empty and $|F| \le f$. Then, either $L \Rightarrow R$ or $R \Rightarrow L$.*

The proof follows by setting $C = \Phi$ in Theorem 1.

COROLLARY 2. *Suppose that a correct IABC algorithm exists for $G(\mathcal{V},\mathcal{E})$. Then n must be at least $3f + 1$, and if $f > 0$, then each node must have at least $2f + 1$ incoming edges.*

PROOF. The necessary condition of $n \ge 3f + 1$ has been shown previously [7]. We include a proof here for completeness. For $f = 0$, $n \ge 3f + 1$ is trivially true. For $f > 0$, the proof is by contradiction. Suppose that $2 \le n \le 3f$. In this case, we can partition $\mathcal{V}$ into sets L, R, F such that $0 < |L| \le f$, $0 < |R| \le f$ and $0 \le |F| \le f$. Since $0 < |L| \le f$ and $0 < |R| \le f$, we have $L \nRightarrow R$ and $R \nRightarrow L$, respectively. This violates the necessary condition in Corollary 1. Thus, $n \ge 3f + 1$.

The proof of the remaining corollary is also by contradiction. Suppose that $f > 0$, and for some node i, $|N_i^-| \le 2f$. Define set $L = \{i\}$. Partition N_i^- into two sets F and H such that $|H| = \lfloor |N_i^-|/2 \rfloor \le f$ and $|F| = \lceil |N_i^-|/2 \rceil \le f$. Define $R = \mathcal{V} - F - L = \mathcal{V} - F - \{i\}$. Since $|\mathcal{V}| = n \ge 3f + 1$, R is non-empty. Now, $N_i^- \cap R = H$, and $|N_i^- \cap R| \le f$. Therefore, since $L = \{i\}$ and $|N_i^- \cap R| \le f$, $R \nRightarrow L$. Also, since $|L| = 1 < f+1$, $L \nRightarrow R$. This violates Corollary 1 above. $\square$

In Section 7, we prove that the condition stated in Theorem 1 is also sufficient for the existence of a correct IABC algorithm. The condition in Theorem 1 is not very intuitive. In Theorem 2 below, we state another necessary condition that is equivalent to the necessary condition in Theorem 1, and is somewhat easier to interpret. To facilitate the statement of Theorem 2, we now introduce the notions of "source component" and "reduced graph" using the following three definitions.

DEFINITION 2. **Graph decomposition:** *Let H be a directed graph. Partition graph H into non-empty strongly connected components, $H_1, H_2, \cdots, H_h$, where h is a non-zero integer dependent on graph H, such that*

- *every pair of nodes within the same strongly connected component has directed paths in H to each other, and*

- *for each pair of nodes, say i and j, that belong to two different strongly connected components, either i does not have a directed path to j in H, or j does not have a directed path to i in H.*

Construct a graph H^d wherein each strongly connected component H_k above is represented by vertex c_k, and there is an edge from vertex c_k to vertex c_l if and only if the nodes in H_k have directed paths in H to the nodes in H_l.

It is known that the decomposition graph H^d is a directed *acyclic* graph [4].

DEFINITION 3. **Source component**: *Let H be a directed graph, and let H^d be its decomposition as per Definition 2. Strongly connected component H_k of H is said to be a source component if the corresponding vertex c_k in H^d is <u>not</u> reachable from any other vertex in H^d.*

DEFINITION 4. **Reduced Graph:** *For a given graph $G(\mathcal{V},\mathcal{E})$ and $F \subset \mathcal{V}$, a graph $G_F(\mathcal{V}_F, \mathcal{E}_F)$ is said to be a reduced graph, if: (i) $\mathcal{V}_F = \mathcal{V} - F$, and (ii) $\mathcal{E}_F$ is obtained by first removing from $\mathcal{E}$ all the links incident on the nodes in F, and then removing up to f other incoming links at each node in $\mathcal{V}_F$.*

Note that for a given $G(\mathcal{V},\mathcal{E})$ and a given F, multiple reduced graphs G_F may exist.

THEOREM 2. *Suppose that Theorem 1 holds for graph $G(\mathcal{V},\mathcal{E})$. Then, for any $F \subset \mathcal{V}$ such that $|F| < |\mathcal{V}|$ and $|F| \le f$, every reduced graph G_F obtained as per Definition 4 must contain exactly one source component.*

PROOF. Since $|F| < |\mathcal{V}|$, G_F contains at least one node; therefore, at least one source component must exist in G_F. We now prove that G_F cannot contain more than one source component. The proof is by contradiction. Suppose that there exists a set $F \subset \mathcal{V}$ with $|F| < |\mathcal{V}|$ and $|F| \le f$, and a reduced graph $G_F(\mathcal{V}_F, \mathcal{E}_F)$ corresponding to F, such that the decomposition of G_F includes at least two source components.

Let the sets of nodes in two such source components of G_F be denoted L and R, respectively. Let $C = \mathcal{V} - F - L - R$. Observe that F, L, C, R form a partition of the nodes in $\mathcal{V}$. Since L is a source component in G_F it follows that there are no directed links in $\mathcal{E}_F$ from any node in $C \cup R$ to the nodes in L. Similarly, since R is a source component in G_F it follows that there are no directed links in $\mathcal{E}_F$ from any node in $L \cup C$ to the nodes in R. These observations, together with the manner in which $\mathcal{E}_F$ is defined, imply that (i) there are at most f links in $\mathcal{E}$ from the nodes in $C \cup R$ to each node in L, and (ii) there are at most f links in $\mathcal{E}$ from the nodes in $L \cup C$ to each node in R. Therefore, in graph $G(\mathcal{V},\mathcal{E})$, $C \cup R \nRightarrow L$ and $L \cup C \nRightarrow R$, violating Theorem 1. Thus, we have proved that G_F must contain exactly one source component. $\square$

The above proof shows that Theorem 1 implies Theorem 2. Appendix A presents the proof that Theorem 2 implies Theorem 1. Thus, it follows that Theorems 1 and 2 specify equivalent conditions.[3]

COROLLARY 3. *Suppose that Theorem 1 holds true for graph $G(\mathcal{V},\mathcal{E})$. Then, for any $F \subset \mathcal{V}$ such that $|F| \le f$, the unique source component in every reduced graph G_F must contain at least $f + 1$ nodes.*

PROOF. Since the source component is non-empty, the claim is trivially true for $f = 0$.

Now consider $f > 0$. The proof in this case is by contradiction. Suppose that there exists a set F with $|F| \le f$, and a corresponding reduced graph $G_F(\mathcal{V}_F, \mathcal{E}_F)$, such that the decomposition of G_F contains a unique source component consisting of at most f nodes. Define L to be the set of nodes in this unique source component, and $R = \mathcal{V} - L - F$. Observe that F, L, R form a partition of $\mathcal{V}$. R must contain at least $f + 1$ nodes, since $|L| \le f$, $|F| \le f$, and by Corollary 2, $n \ge 3f + 1$.

Since $|L| \le f$, it follows that in graph $G(\mathcal{V},\mathcal{E})$, $L \nRightarrow R$, Then Corollary 1 implies that, in graph $G(\mathcal{V},\mathcal{E})$, $R \Rightarrow L$. Thus, there must be a node in L, say node i, that has at least $f + 1$ incoming links in $\mathcal{E}$ from the nodes in R. Since $i \in L$, it follows that $i \notin F$ (by definition of a reduced graph). Also, since i has at least $f + 1$ incoming links in $\mathcal{E}$ from nodes in R, it follows that in $\mathcal{E}_F$, node i must have at least one incoming link from the nodes in R. This contradicts that assumption that set L containing node i is a source component of G_F. $\square$

---

[3] An alternate interpretation of Theorem 2 is that in graph G_F non-fault-tolerant iterative consensus must be possible.

6. ALGORITHM 1

We will prove that there exists an IABC algorithm – particularly *Algorithm 1* below – that satisfies the *validity* and *convergence* conditions provided that the graph $G(\mathcal{V}, \mathcal{E})$ satisfies the necessary condition in Theorem 1. This implies that the necessary condition in Theorem 1 is also sufficient. *Algorithm 1* has the three-step structure described in Section 4, and it is similar to algorithms that were analyzed in prior work as well [5, 14, 10] (although correctness of the algorithm under the necessary condition in Theorem 1 has not been proved previously).

Algorithm 1

Steps to be performed by node $i \in \mathcal{V}$ in t-th iteration, $t > 0$:

1. *Transmit step:* Transmit current state $v_i[t-1]$ on all outgoing edges.

2. *Receive step:* Receive values on all incoming edges. These values form vector $r_i[t]$ of size $|N_i^-|$. When a fault-free node expects to receive a message from a neighbor but does not receive the message, the message value is assumed to be equal to some *default value*.

3. *Update step:* Sort the values in $r_i[t]$ in an increasing order, and eliminate the smallest f values, and the largest f values (breaking ties arbitrarily). Let $N_i^*[t]$ denote the set of nodes from whom the remaining $N_i^- - 2f$ values were received, and let w_j denote the value received from node $j \in N_i^*[t]$. For convenience, define $w_i = v_i[t-1]$ to be the value node i "receives" from itself. Observe that if $j \in \{i\} \cup N_i^*[t]$ is fault-free, then $w_j = v_j[t-1]$.

Define

$$v_i[t] = Z_i(r_i[t], v_i[t-1]) = \sum_{j \in \{i\} \cup N_i^*[t]} a_i w_j \qquad (2)$$

where

$$a_i = \frac{1}{|N_i^-| + 1 - 2f}$$

Note that $|N_i^*[t]| = |N_i^-| - 2f$, and $i \notin N_i^*[t]$ because $(i, i) \notin \mathcal{E}$. The "weight" of each term on the right-hand side of (2) is a_i, and these weights add to 1. Also, $0 < a_i \leq 1$. For future reference, let us define α as:

$$\alpha = \min_{i \in \mathcal{V}} a_i \qquad (3)$$

---

7. SUFFICIENCY (CORRECTNESS OF ALGORITHM 1)

In Theorems 3 and 4 in this section, we prove that Algorithm 1 satisfies *validity* and *convergence* conditions, respectively, provided that $G(\mathcal{V}, \mathcal{E})$ satisfies the condition below, which matches the necessary condition stated in Theorem 1.

Sufficient condition: For every partition F, L, C, R of $\mathcal{V}$, such that L and R are both non-empty, and $|F| \leq f$, either $C \cup R \Rightarrow L$, or $L \cup C \Rightarrow R$.

THEOREM 3. *Suppose that $\mathcal{F}$ is the set of Byzantine faulty nodes, and that $G(\mathcal{V}, \mathcal{E})$ satisfies the* sufficient *condition stated above. Then Algorithm 1 satisfies the* validity *condition.*

PROOF. Consider the t-th iteration, and any fault-free node $i \in \mathcal{V} - \mathcal{F}$. Consider two cases:

- $f = 0$: In this case, all nodes must be fault-free, and $\mathcal{F} = \Phi$. In (2) in Algorithm 1, note that $v_i[t]$ is computed using states from the previous iteration at node i and other nodes. By definition of $\mu[t-1]$ and $U[t-1]$, $v_j[t-1] \in [\mu[t-1], U[t-1]]$ for all fault-free nodes $j \in \mathcal{V} - \mathcal{F} = \mathcal{V}$. Thus, in this case, all the values used in computing $v_i[t]$ are in the interval $[\mu[t-1], U[t-1]]$. Since $v_i[t]$ is computed as a weighted average of these values, $v_i[t]$ is also within $[\mu[t-1], U[t-1]]$.

- $f > 0$: By Corollary 2, $|N_i^-| \geq 2f + 1$, and therefore, $|r_i[t]| \geq 2f + 1$. When computing set $N_i^*[t]$, the largest f and smallest f values from $r_i[t]$ are eliminated. Since at most f nodes are faulty, it follows that, either (i) the values received from the faulty nodes are all eliminated, or (ii) the values from the faulty nodes that still remain are between values received from two fault-free nodes. Thus, the remaining values in $r_i[t]$ are all in the interval $[\mu[t-1], U[t-1]]$. Also, $v_i[t-1]$ is in $[\mu[t-1], U[t-1]]$, as per the definition of $\mu[t-1]$ and $U[t-1]$. Thus $v_i[t]$ is computed as a weighted average of values in $[\mu[t-1], U[t-1]]$, and, therefore, it will also be in $[\mu[t-1], U[t-1]]$.

Since $\forall i \in \mathcal{V} - \mathcal{F}$, $v_i[t] \in [\mu[t-1], U[t-1]]$, the validity condition is satisfied. $\square$

DEFINITION 5. *For disjoint sets A, B, $in(A \Rightarrow B)$ denotes the set of all the nodes in B that each have at least $f + 1$ incoming edges from nodes in A. More formally,*

$$in(A \Rightarrow B) = \{ v \mid v \in B \text{ and } f + 1 \leq |N_v^- \cap A| \}$$

With an abuse of notation, when $A \nRightarrow B$, define $in(A \Rightarrow B) = \Phi$.

DEFINITION 6. *For non-empty disjoint sets A and B, set A is said to propagate to set B in l steps, where $l > 0$, if there exist sequences of sets $A_0, A_1, A_2, \cdots, A_l$ and $B_0, B_1, B_2, \cdots, B_l$ (propagating sequences) such that*

- $A_0 = A$, $\quad B_0 = B$, $\quad A_l = A \cup B$, $\quad B_l = \Phi$, $\quad B_\tau \neq \Phi$ *for $\tau < l$,* *and*

- *for $0 \leq \tau \leq l - 1$,*

  - $A_\tau \Rightarrow B_\tau$,
  - $A_{\tau+1} = A_\tau \cup in(A_\tau \Rightarrow B_\tau)$, *and*
  - $B_{\tau+1} = B_\tau - in(A_\tau \Rightarrow B_\tau)$

Observe that A_τ and B_τ form a partition of $A \cup B$, and for $\tau < l$, $in(A_\tau \Rightarrow B_\tau) \neq \Phi$. Also, when set A propagates to set B, the number of steps l in the above definition is upper bounded by $n - f - 1$, since set A must be of size at least $f + 1$ for it to propagate to B; otherwise, $A \nRightarrow B$.

LEMMA 1. *Assume that $G(\mathcal{V}, \mathcal{E})$ satisfies the* sufficient *condition stated above. For any partition A, B, F of $\mathcal{V}$, where A, B are both non-empty, and $|F| \leq f$, either A propagates to B, or B propagates to A.*

PROOF. Appendix B presents the proof. $\square$

The lemma below states that the interval to which the states at all the fault-free nodes are confined shrinks after a finite number of iterations of Algorithm 1. Recall that $U[t]$ and $\mu[t]$ (defined in Section 4) are the maximum and minimum over the states at the fault-free nodes at the end of the t-th iteration.

369

LEMMA 2. *Suppose that* $G(\mathcal{V}, \mathcal{E})$ *satisfies the* sufficient *condition stated above, and* $\mathcal{F}$ *is the set of Byzantine faulty nodes. Moreover, at the end of the s-th iteration of Algorithm 1, suppose that the fault-free nodes in* $\mathcal{V} - \mathcal{F}$ *can be partitioned into non-empty sets R and L such that (i) R propagates to L in l steps, and (ii) the states of nodes in R are confined to an interval of length* $\leq \frac{U[s] - \mu[s]}{2}$. *Then, with Algorithm 1,*

$$U[s+l] - \mu[s+l] \leq \left(1 - \frac{\alpha^l}{2}\right)(U[s] - \mu[s]) \qquad (4)$$

where α *is as defined in (3).*

PROOF. Appendix C presents the proof. □

THEOREM 4. *Suppose that* $\mathcal{F}$ *is the set of Byzantine faulty nodes, and that* $G(\mathcal{V}, \mathcal{E})$ *satisfies the* sufficient *condition stated above. Then Algorithm 1 satisfies the* convergence *condition.*

PROOF. Our goal is to prove that, given any $\epsilon > 0$, there exists τ such that

$$U[t] - \mu[t] \leq \epsilon \quad \forall t \geq \tau \qquad (5)$$

Consider s-th iteration, for some $s \geq 0$. If $U[s] - \mu[s] = 0$, then the algorithm has already converged, and the proof is complete, with $\tau = s$ (recall that we have already proved that the algorithm satisfies the validity condition).

Now consider the case when $U[s] - \mu[s] > 0$. Partition $\mathcal{V} - \mathcal{F}$ into two subsets, A and B, such that, for each node $i \in A$, $v_i[s] \in \left[\mu[s], \frac{U[s] + \mu[s]}{2}\right)$, and for each node $j \in B$, $v_j[s] \in \left[\frac{U[s] + \mu[s]}{2}, U[s]\right]$. By definition of $\mu[s]$ and $U[s]$, there exist fault-free nodes i and j such that $v_i[s] = \mu[s]$ and $v_j[s] = U[s]$. Thus, sets A and B are both non-empty. By Lemma 1, one of the following two conditions must be true:

- Set A propagates to set B. Then, define $L = B$ and $R = A$. The states of all the nodes in $R = A$ are confined within an interval of length $< \frac{U[s] + \mu[s]}{2} - \mu[s] \leq \frac{U[s] - \mu[s]}{2}$.

- Set B propagates to set A. Then, define $L = A$ and $R = B$. In this case, states of all the nodes in $R = B$ are confined within an interval of length $\leq U[s] - \frac{U[s] + \mu[s]}{2} \leq \frac{U[s] - \mu[s]}{2}$.

In both cases above, we have found non-empty sets L and R such that (i) L, R is a partition of $\mathcal{V} - \mathcal{F}$, (ii) R propagates to L, and (iii) the states in R are confined to an interval of length $\leq \frac{U[s] - \mu[s]}{2}$. Suppose that R propagates to L in $l(s)$ steps, where $l(s) \geq 1$. Then by Lemma 2,

$$U[s+l(s)] - \mu[s+l(s)] \leq \left(1 - \frac{\alpha^{l(s)}}{2}\right)(U[s] - \mu[s]) \qquad (6)$$

In Algorithm 1, observe that $a_i > 0$ for all i. Therefore, α defined in 3 in Algorithm 1 is > 0. Then, $n - f - 1 \geq l(s) \geq 1$ and $0 < \alpha \leq 1$; hence, $0 \leq \left(1 - \frac{\alpha^{l(s)}}{2}\right) < 1$.

Let us define the following sequence of iteration indices:

- $\tau_0 = 0$,

- for $i > 0$, $\tau_i = \tau_{i-1} + l(\tau_{i-1})$, where $l(s)$ for any given s was defined above.

If for some i, $U[\tau_i] - \mu[\tau_i] = 0$, then since the algorithm is already proved to satisfy the validity condition, we will have $U[t] - \mu[t] = 0$ for all $t \geq \tau_i$, and the proof of convergence is complete.

Now suppose that $U[\tau_i] - \mu[\tau_i] \neq 0$ for the values of i in the analysis below. By repeated application of the argument leading to (6), we can prove that, for $i \geq 0$,

$$U[\tau_i] - \mu[\tau_i] \leq \left(\Pi_{j=1}^{i}\left(1 - \frac{\alpha^{\tau_j - \tau_{j-1}}}{2}\right)\right)(U[0] - \mu[0]) \qquad (7)$$

For a given ϵ, by choosing a large enough i, we can obtain

$$\left(\Pi_{j=1}^{i}\left(1 - \frac{\alpha^{\tau_j - \tau_{j-1}}}{2}\right)\right)(U[0] - \mu[0]) \leq \epsilon$$

and, therefore,

$$U[\tau_i] - \mu[\tau_i] \leq \epsilon \qquad (8)$$

For $t \geq \tau_i$, by validity of Algorithm 1, it follows that

$$U[t] - \mu[t] \leq U[\tau_i] - \mu[\tau_i] \leq \epsilon$$

This concludes the proof. □

It should be easy to see that other correct IABC algorithms can be obtained by choosing "weights" differently than in Algorithm 1, and with other appropriate ways of eliminating values in the *Update step*. In recent work [18] we have developed an alternate proof of sufficiency, based on a transition matrix representation of the update step in Algorithm 1.

8. ASYNCHRONOUS NETWORKS

Dolev et al. [5] propose an iterative algorithm for asynchronous networks wherein message and processing delays may be arbitrary but finite. We extend their approach to arbitrary point-to-point networks. In particular, we consider the *Asynchronous IABC Algorithm* structure below, which is similar to the algorithm in [5]. This algorithm structure differs from the structure presented in Section 4 in two important ways: (i) the messages containing states are now tagged by the iteration index to which the states correspond, and (ii) each node i waits to receive only $|N_i^-| - f$ messages containing states from iteration $t - 1$ before computing the new state in its t-th iteration. Due to the asynchronous nature of the system, different nodes may potentially perform their t-th iteration at very different real times.

Asynchronous IABC Algorithm

Steps to be performed by each node $i \in \mathcal{V}$ in its t-th iteration, $t > 0$:

1. *Transmit step:* Transmit current state $v_i[t-1]$ on all outgoing edges. The message is tagged by index $t - 1$.

2. *Receive step:* Wait until $|N_i^-| - f$ messages tagged by index $t - 1$ are received on the incoming edges. Values received in these messages form vector $r_i[t]$ of size $|N_i^-| - f$.

3. *Update step:* Node i updates its state using a transition function Z_i.

$$v_i[t] = Z_i(r_i[t], v_i[t-1]) \qquad (9)$$

We now introduce relation $\stackrel{a}{\Rightarrow}$ that is analogous to relation $\Rightarrow$ defined previously.

DEFINITION 7. *For non-empty disjoint sets of nodes A and B,* $A \stackrel{a}{\Rightarrow} B$ *iff there exists a node* $v \in B$ *that has at least* $2f + 1$ *incoming edges from nodes in A, i.e.,* $|N_v^- \cap A| \geq 2f + 1$.

Theorem 5 states a necessary condition for asynchronous iterative algorithms with the above structure.

THEOREM 5. *If an* Asynchronous IABC Algorithm *satisfies* validity *and* convergence *conditions in graph* $G(\mathcal{V}, \mathcal{E})$, *then for any partition* F, L, C, R *of* $\mathcal{V}$, *such that* L *and* R *are both non-empty and* $|F| \leq f$, *then either* $C \cup R \stackrel{a}{\Rightarrow} L$, *or* $L \cup C \stackrel{a}{\Rightarrow} R$.

PROOF. The proof is similar to the proof of Theorem 1. More details can be found in [17]. □

The following corollary can be obtained from Theorem 5 [17].

COROLLARY 4. *If an* Asynchronous IABC Algorithm *satisfies* validity *and* convergence *conditions in graph* $G(\mathcal{V}, \mathcal{E})$, *then* $n > 5f$, *and when* $f > 0$, $|N_i^-| \geq 3f + 1$ *for all* $i \in \mathcal{V}$.

It can be shown that the necessary condition in Theorem 5 is tight. In particular, an *Asynchronous IABC Algorithm* with the structure above that performs the *Update step* shown below can be proved to satisfy the convergence and validity conditions [17]. Note that the *Update step* below, to be performed by each node $i \in \mathcal{V}$, is similar to that in *Algorithm 1* for the synchronous network.

- *Update step:* Sort the values in vector $r_i[t]$ in an increasing order, and eliminate the smallest f and the largest f values (breaking ties arbitrarily). Recall that $r_i[t]$ contains $|N_i^-| - f$ values. Let $N_i^*[t]$ denote the set of nodes from whom the remaining $|N_i^-| - 3f$ values were received, and let w_j denote the value received from node $j \in N_i^*[t]$. Define $w_i = v_i[t-1]$, and

$$v_i[t] = \sum_{j \in \{i\} \cup N_i^*[t]} a_i \, w_j \qquad (10)$$

where

$$a_i = \frac{1}{|N_i^-| + 1 - 3f}.$$

9. OTHER RESULTS

The results presented in this paper have led to other related results described elsewhere. Here we summarize the other results. An alternate proof of correctness of Algorithm 1, using a transition matrix representation of the algorithm, is presented in [18]. Our necessary conditions are useful to examine whether IABC algorithms exist for specific graph families [16]. For instance, IABC is feasible in an undirected "core" network consisting of a clique of $2f + 1$ nodes, with the remaining nodes being connected to all the nodes in this clique [16]. Our results can also be extended to other system models, particularly, the *partially* asynchronous algorithmic model of [3], as shown in [17], and networks with time-varying topologies, as briefly discussed in [18]. Finally, the results can also be extended to a *generalized* Byzantine fault model [15] wherein possible faults are specified using a set of feasible fault sets. The generalized fault model can be used to capture correlated failures as well as different levels of reliabilities for different nodes in the system.

10. CONCLUSIONS

This paper proves a *tight* necessary and sufficient condition for the existence of a class of synchronous iterative approximate Byzantine consensus algorithms (IABC) that can

tolerate up to f Byzantine fault in arbitrary directed graphs. These results can be extended to a class of iterative algorithms for asynchronous systems, as briefly discussed in Section 8. The work presented in this paper has led to further related results, as summarized in Section 9.

11. REFERENCES

[1] A. Azadmanesh and H. Bajwa. Global convergence in partially fully connected networks (PFCN) with limited relays. *Conf. of IEEE Industrial Electronics Soc. (IECON)*, 2001.

[2] M. H. Azadmanesh and R. Kieckhafer. Asynchronous approximate agreement in partially connected networks. *International Journal of Parallel and Distributed Systems and Networks*, 2002. http://ahvaz.unomaha .edu/azad/pubs/ijpdsn.asyncpart.pdf

[3] D. P. Bertsekas and J. N. Tsitsiklis. *Parallel and Distributed Computation: Numerical Methods*. Optimization and Neural Computation Series. Athena Scientific, 1997.

[4] S. Dasgupta, C. Papadimitriou, and U. Vazirani. *Algorithms*. McGraw-Hill Higher Education, 2006.

[5] D. Dolev, N. A. Lynch, S. S. Pinter, E. W. Stark, and W. E. Weihl. Reaching approximate agreement in the presence of faults. *J. ACM*, 33:499–516, May 1986.

[6] A. D. Fekete. Asymptotically optimal algorithms for approximate agreement. *ACM PODC*, 1986.

[7] M. J. Fischer, N. A. Lynch, and M. Merritt. Easy impossibility proofs for distributed consensus problems. *ACM PODC*, 1985.

[8] M. J. Fischer, N. A. Lynch, and M. S. Paterson. Impossibility of distributed consensus with one faulty process. *J. ACM*, 32:374–382, April 1985.

[9] A. Jadbabaie, J. Lin, and A. Morse. Coordination of groups of mobile autonomous agents using nearest neighbor rules. *Automatic Control, IEEE Transactions on*, 48(6):988 – 1001, June 2003.

[10] R. M. Kieckhafer and M. H. Azadmanesh. Low cost approximate agreement in partially connected networks. *J. of Computing and Information*, 1993. *http:// ahvaz.ist.unomaha.edu/azad/pubs/jci.syncpart.pdf*

[11] H. LeBlanc and X. Koutsoukos. Consensus in networked multi-agent systems with adversaries. *14th International conference on Hybrid Systems: Computation and Control (HSCC)*, 2011.

[12] H. LeBlanc and X. Koutsoukos. Low complexity resilient consensus in networked multi-agent systems with adversaries. *Int. Conf. on Hybrid Systems: Computation and Control (HSCC)*, 2012.

[13] H. LeBlanc, H. Zhang, S. Sundaram, and X. Koutsoukos. Consensus of multi-agent networks in the presence of adversaries using only local information. *Conference on High Confidence Networked Systems* (HiCoNS), 2012.

[14] N. A. Lynch. *Distributed Algorithms*. Morgan Kaufmann, 1996.

[15] L. Tseng and N. H. Vaidya, "Iterative Approximate Byzantine Consensus under a Generalized Fault Model," report under preparation, May 2012.

[16] N. H. Vaidya, L. Tseng, and G. Liang. Iterative approximate Byzantine consensus in arbitrary directed

graphs. Tech. Rep., University of Illinois, January 2012.
`http://arxiv.org/abs/1201.4183`

[17] N. H. Vaidya, L. Tseng, and G. Liang. Iterative approximate Byzantine consensus in arbitrary directed graphs – Part II: Synchronous and asynchronous systems. Tech. Rep., University of Illinois, February 2012. `http://arxiv.org/abs/1202.6094`

[18] N. H. Vaidya, "Matrix Representation of Iterative Approximate Byzantine Consensus in Directed Graphs," Tech. Rep., University of Illinois, March 2012. `http://arxiv.org/abs/1203.1888`

[19] H. Zhang and S. Sundaram. Robustness of information diffusion algorithms to locally bounded adversaries. `http://arxiv.org/abs/1110.3843`, October 2011. A version to appear at ACC 2012 as *Robustness of Distributed Algorithms to Locally Bounded Adversaries*.

APPENDIX

A. THEOREM 2 IMPLIES THEOREM 1

We now prove that Theorem 2 implies the correctness of Theorem 1. We achieve this by proving that, if the condition in Theorem 1 does not hold true for $G(\mathcal{V}, \mathcal{E})$, then the condition in Theorem 2 also does not hold true.

PROOF. Suppose that the condition stated in Theorem 1 does not hold for $G(\mathcal{V}, \mathcal{E})$. Thus, there exists a partition F, L, C, R of $\mathcal{V}$ such that $|F| \leq f$, L and R are non-empty, and $C \cup R \nRightarrow L$ and $L \cup C \nRightarrow R$.

We now construct a reduced graph $G_F(\mathcal{V}_F, \mathcal{E}_F)$ corresponding to set F. First, remove all nodes in F from $\mathcal{V}$ to obtain $\mathcal{V}_F$. Remove all the edges incident on F from $\mathcal{E}$. Then because $C \cup R \nRightarrow L$, the number of incoming edges at each node in L from the nodes in $C \cup R$ is at most f; remove all these edges. Similarly, for every node $j \in R$, remove all incoming edges from $L \cup C$ (there are at most f such edges at each node $j \in R$). The resulting graph G_F is a reduced graph that satisfies the conditions in Definition 4.

In $\mathcal{E}_F$, there are no incoming edges to nodes in R from the nodes in $L \cup C$; similarly, in $\mathcal{E}_F$, there are no incoming edges to nodes in L from the nodes in $C \cup R$. It follows that no single node in $\mathcal{V}_F$ has paths in G_F (i.e., paths consisting of links in $\mathcal{E}_F$) to all the other nodes in $\mathcal{V}_F$. Thus, G_F must contain more than one source component. Thus, Theorem 2 does not hold for $G(\mathcal{V}, \mathcal{E})$. □

B. PROOF OF LEMMA 1

To prove Lemma 1, we first prove the following Lemma.

LEMMA 3. *Assume that $G(\mathcal{V}, \mathcal{E})$ satisfies Theorem 1. Consider a partition A, B, F of $\mathcal{V}$ such that A and B are non-empty, and $|F| \leq f$. If $B \nRightarrow A$, then set A propagates to set B.*

PROOF. Since A, B are non-empty, and $B \nRightarrow A$, by Corollary 1, we have $A \Rightarrow B$.

Define $A_0 = A$ and $B_0 = B$. Now, for a suitable $l > 0$, we will build propagating sequences $A_0, A_1, \cdots A_l$ and $B_0, B_1, \cdots B_l$ inductively.

- Recall that $A = A_0$ and $B = B_0 \neq \Phi$. Since $A \Rightarrow B$, $in(A_0 \Rightarrow B_0) \neq \Phi$. Define $A_1 = A_0 \cup in(A_0 \Rightarrow B_0)$ and $B_1 = B_0 - in(A_0 \Rightarrow B_0)$.

  If $B_1 = \Phi$, then $l = 1$, and we have found the propagating sequence already.

If $B_1 \neq \Phi$, then define $L = A = A_0$, $R = B_1$ and $C = A_1 - A = B - B_1$. Since $B \nRightarrow A$, $R \cup C \nRightarrow L$. Therefore, by Theorem 1, $L \cup C \Rightarrow R$. That is, $A_1 \Rightarrow B_1$.

- For increasing values of $i \geq 0$, given A_i and B_i, where $B_i \neq \Phi$, by following steps similar to the previous item, we can obtain $A_{i+1} = A_i \cup in(A_i \Rightarrow B_i)$ and $B_{i+1} = B_i - in(A_i \Rightarrow B_i)$, such that either $B_{i+1} = \Phi$ or $A_{i+1} \Rightarrow B_{i+1}$.

In the above construction, l is the smallest index such that $B_l = \Phi$. □

A more detailed proof of the above lemma is presented in [16].

Proof of Lemma 1.

PROOF. Consider two cases:

- $A \nRightarrow B$: Then by Lemma 3 above, B propagates to A, completing the proof.

- $A \Rightarrow B$: In this case, consider two sub-cases:

  - *A propagates to B*: The proof in this case is complete.
  - *A does not propagate to B*: Recall that $A \Rightarrow B$. Since A does not propagate to B, propagating sequences defined in Definition 6 do not exist in this case. More precisely, there must exist $k > 0$, and sets $A_0, A_1, \cdots, A_k$ and $B_0, B_1, \cdots, B_k$, such that:
    * $A_0 = A$ and $B_0 = B$, and
    * for $0 \leq i \leq k - 1$,
      o $A_i \Rightarrow B_i$,
      o $A_{i+1} = A_i \cup in(A_i \Rightarrow B_i)$, and
      o $B_{i+1} = B_i - in(A_i \Rightarrow B_i)$.
    * $B_k \neq \Phi$ and $A_k \nRightarrow B_k$.

  The last condition above violates the requirements for A to propagate to B.

  Now, $A_k \neq \Phi$, $B_k \neq \Phi$, and A_k, B_k, F form a partition of $\mathcal{V}$. Since $A_k \nRightarrow B_k$, by Lemma 3 above, B_k propagates to A_k.

  Given that $B_k \subseteq B_0 = B$, $A = A_0 \subseteq A_k$, and B_k propagates to A_k, now we prove that B propagates to A.

  Recall that A_i and B_i form a partition of $\mathcal{V} - F$.

  Let us define $P = P_0 = B_k$ and $Q = Q_0 = A_k$. Thus, P propagates to Q. Suppose that $P_0, P_1, \ldots P_m$ and $Q_0, Q_1, \cdots, Q_m$ are the propagating sequences in this case, with P_i and Q_i forming a partition of $P \cup Q = A_k \cup B_k = \mathcal{V} - F$.

  Let us define $R = R_0 = B$ and $S = S_0 = A$. Note that R, S form a partition of $A \cup B = \mathcal{V} - F$. Now, $P_0 = B_k \subseteq B = R_0$ and $S_0 = A \subseteq A_k = Q_0$. Also, $R_0 - P_0$ and S_0 form a partition of Q_0. Figure 2 illustrates some of the sets used in this proof.

    * Define $P_1 = P_0 \cup (in(P_0 \Rightarrow Q_0))$, and $Q_1 = \mathcal{V} - F - P_1 = Q_0 - (in(P_0 \Rightarrow Q_0))$. Also, $R_1 = R_0 \cup (in(R_0 \Rightarrow S_0))$, and $S_1 = \mathcal{V} - F - R_1 = S_0 - (in(R_0 \Rightarrow S_0))$. Since $R_0 - P_0$ and S_0 are a partition of Q_0, the nodes in $in(P_0 \Rightarrow Q_0)$ belong to one of these two sets. Note that $R_0 - P_0 \subseteq R_0$. Also, $S_0 \cap in(P_0 \Rightarrow Q_0) \subseteq in(R_0 \Rightarrow S_0)$. Therefore, it follows that $P_1 = P_0 \cup (in(P_0 \Rightarrow Q_0)) \subseteq R_0 \cup (in(R_0 \Rightarrow S_0)) = R_1$.

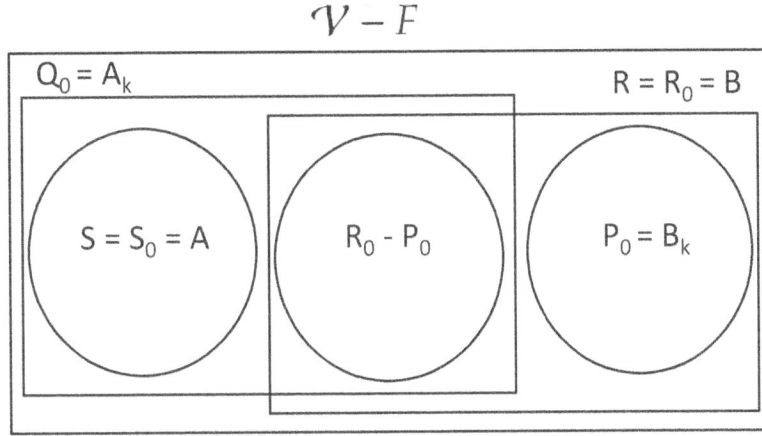

Figure 2: **Illustration for the last part of the proof of Lemma 1. In this figure,** $R_0 = P_0 \cup (R_0 - P_0)$ **and** $Q_0 = S_0 \cup (R_0 - P_0)$.

Thus, we have shown that, $P_1 \subseteq R_1$. Then it follows that $S_1 \subseteq Q_1$.

* For $0 \leq i < m$, let us define $R_{i+1} = R_i \cup in(R_i \Rightarrow S_i)$ and $S_{i+1} = S_i - in(R_i \Rightarrow S_i)$. Then following an argument similar to the above case, we can inductively show that, $P_i \subseteq R_i$ and $S_i \subseteq Q_i$. Due to the assumption on the length of the propagating sequence above, $P_m = P \cup Q = \mathcal{V} - F$ and $Q_m = \Phi$. Thus, there must exist $r \leq m$, such that for $i < r$, $R_i \neq \mathcal{V} - F$, and $R_r = \mathcal{V} - F$ and $S_r = \Phi$. The sequences $R_0, R_1, \cdots, R_r$ and $S_0, S_1, \cdots, S_r$ form propagating sequences, proving that $R = B$ propagates to $S = A$.

$\square$

C. PROOF OF LEMMA 2

We first present two additional lemmas (using the notation in Algorithm 1).

LEMMA 4. *Suppose that $\mathcal{F}$ is the set of faulty nodes, and that $G(\mathcal{V}, \mathcal{E})$ satisfies the "sufficient condition" stated in Section 7. Consider node $i \in \mathcal{V} - \mathcal{F}$. Let $\psi \leq \mu[t-1]$. Then, for $j \in \{i\} \cup N_i^*[t]$,*

$$v_i[t] - \psi \geq a_i (w_j - \psi)$$

Specifically, for fault-free $j \in \{i\} \cup N_i^*[t]$,

$$v_i[t] - \psi \geq a_i (v_j[t-1] - \psi)$$

PROOF. In (2) in Algorithm 1, for each $j \in \{i\} \cup N_i^*[t]$, consider two cases:

- j is fault-free: Then, either $j = i$ or $j \in N_i^*[t] \cap (\mathcal{V} - \mathcal{F})$. In this case, $w_j = v_j[t-1]$. Therefore, $\mu[t-1] \leq w_j \leq U[t-1]$.
- j is faulty: In this case, f must be non-zero (otherwise, all nodes are fault-free). By Corollary 2, $|N_i^-| \geq 2f+1$. Then it follows that, in step 2 of Algorithm 1, the smallest f values in $r_i[t]$ contain the state of at least one fault-free

node, say k. This implies that $v_k[t-1] \leq w_j$. This, in turn, implies that $\mu[t-1] \leq w_j$.

Thus, for all $j \in \{i\} \cup N_i^*[t]$, we have $\mu[t-1] \leq w_j$. Therefore,

$$w_j - \psi \geq 0 \text{ for all } j \in \{i\} \cup N_i^*[t] \tag{11}$$

Since weights in (2) in Algorithm 1 add to 1, we can re-write that equation as,

$$v_i[t] - \psi = \sum_{j \in \{i\} \cup N_i^*[t]} a_i (w_j - \psi) \tag{12}$$

$$\geq a_i (w_j - \psi), \ \forall j \in \{i\} \cup N_i^*[t] \quad \text{from (11)}$$

For fault-free $j \in \{i\} \cup N_i^*[t]$, $w_j = v_j[t-1]$, therefore,

$$v_i[t] - \psi \geq a_i (v_j[t-1] - \psi) \tag{13}$$

$\square$

LEMMA 5. *Suppose that $\mathcal{F}$ is the set of faulty nodes, and that $G(\mathcal{V}, \mathcal{E})$ satisfies the "sufficient condition" stated in Section 7. Consider fault-free node $i \in \mathcal{V} - \mathcal{F}$. Let $\Psi \geq U[t-1]$. Then, for $j \in \{i\} \cup N_i^*[t]$,*

$$\Psi - v_i[t] \geq a_i (\Psi - w_j)$$

Specifically, for fault-free $j \in \{i\} \cup N_i^*[t]$,

$$\Psi - v_i[t] \geq a_i (\Psi - v_j[t-1])$$

PROOF. The proof is similar to Lemma 4 proof. [16]. $\square$

Proof of Lemma 2.

PROOF. Since R propagates to L, as per Definition 6, there exist sequences of sets $R_0, R_1, \cdots, R_l$ and $L_0, L_1, \cdots, L_l$, where

- $R_0 = R$, $L_0 = L$, $R_l = R \cup L$, $L_l = \Phi$, for $0 \leq \tau < l$, $L_\tau \neq \Phi$, and
- for $0 \leq \tau \leq l-1$,

* $R_\tau \Rightarrow L_\tau$,
* $R_{\tau+1} = R_\tau \cup in(R_\tau \Rightarrow L_\tau)$, and
* $L_{\tau+1} = L_\tau - in(R_\tau \Rightarrow L_\tau)$

Let us define the following bounds on the states of the nodes in R at the end of the s-th iteration:

$$M = max_{j \in R}\ v_j[s] \tag{14}$$
$$m = min_{j \in R}\ v_j[s] \tag{15}$$

By the assumption in the statement of Lemma 2,

$$M - m \leq \frac{U[s] - \mu[s]}{2} \tag{16}$$

Also, $M \leq U[s]$ and $m \geq \mu[s]$. Therefore, $U[s] - M \geq 0$ and $m - \mu[s] \geq 0$.

The remaining proof of Lemma 2 relies on derivation of the three intermediate claims below.

CLAIM 1. *For $0 \leq \tau \leq l$, for each node $i \in R_\tau$,*

$$v_i[s+\tau] - \mu[s] \geq \alpha^\tau (m - \mu[s]) \tag{17}$$

Proof of Claim 1: The proof is by induction.
Induction basis: By definition of m, (17) holds true for $\tau = 0$.
Induction: Assume that (17) holds true for some τ, $0 \leq \tau < l$. Consider $R_{\tau+1}$. Observe that R_τ and $R_{\tau+1} - R_\tau$ form a partition of $R_{\tau+1}$; let us consider each of these sets separately.

* Set R_τ: By assumption, for each $i \in R_\tau$, (17) holds true. By validity of Algorithm 1 (proved in Theorem 3), $\mu[s] \leq \mu[s+\tau]$. Therefore, setting $\psi = \mu[s]$ and $t = s + \tau + 1$ in Lemma 4, we get,

$$
\begin{aligned}
v_i[s+\tau+1] - \mu[s] &\geq a_i\ (v_i[s+\tau] - \mu[s]) \\
&\geq a_i\ \alpha^\tau (m - \mu[s]) \quad \text{due to (17)} \\
&\geq \alpha^{\tau+1}(m - \mu[s]) \quad \text{due to (3)} \\
&\quad \text{and because} \quad m - \mu[s] \geq 0
\end{aligned}
$$

* Set $R_{\tau+1} - R_\tau$: Consider a node $i \in R_{\tau+1} - R_\tau$. By definition of $R_{\tau+1}$, we have that $i \in in(R_\tau \Rightarrow L_\tau)$. Thus,

$$|N_i^- \cap R_\tau| \geq f + 1$$

In Algorithm 1, $2f$ values (f smallest and f largest) received by node i are eliminated before $v_i[s + \tau + 1]$ is computed at the end of $(s + \tau + 1)$-th iteration. Consider two possibilities:

   – Value received from one of the nodes in $N_i^- \cap R_\tau$ is *not* eliminated. Suppose that this value is received from fault-free node $p \in N_i^- \cap R_\tau$. Then, by an argument similar to the previous case, we can set $\psi = \mu[s]$ in Lemma 4, to obtain,

$$
\begin{aligned}
v_i[s+\tau+1] - \mu[s] &\geq a_i\ (v_p[s+\tau] - \mu[s]) \\
&\geq a_i\ \alpha^\tau (m - \mu[s]) \quad \text{due to (17)} \\
&\geq \alpha^{\tau+1}(m - \mu[s]) \quad \text{due to (3)} \\
&\quad \text{and because} \quad m - \mu[s] \geq 0
\end{aligned}
$$

   – Values received from *all* (there are at least $f + 1$) nodes in $N_i^- \cap R_\tau$ are eliminated. Note that in this case f must be non-zero (for $f = 0$, no value is eliminated, as already considered in the previous case). By Corollary 2, we know that each node must have at least $2f + 1$ incoming edges. Since at least

$f + 1$ values from nodes in $N_i^- \cap R_\tau$ are eliminated, and there are at least $2f + 1$ values to choose from, it follows that the values that are *not* eliminated[4] are within the interval to which the values from $N_i^- \cap R_\tau$ belong. Thus, there exists a node k (possibly faulty) from whom node i receives some value w_k – which is not eliminated – and a fault-free node $p \in N_i^- \cap R_\tau$ such that

$$v_p[s+\tau] \leq w_k \tag{18}$$

Then by setting $\psi = \mu[s]$ and $t = s+\tau+1$ in Lemma 4, we have

$$
\begin{aligned}
v_i[s+\tau+1] - \mu[s] &\geq a_i\ (w_k - \mu[s]) \\
&\geq a_i\ (v_p[s+\tau] - \mu[s]) \quad \text{by (18)} \\
&\geq a_i\ \alpha^\tau (m - \mu[s]) \quad \text{due to (17)} \\
&\geq \alpha^{\tau+1}(m - \mu[s]) \quad \text{due to (3)} \\
&\quad \text{and because} \quad m - \mu[s] \geq 0
\end{aligned}
$$

Thus, we have shown that for all nodes in $R_{\tau+1}$,

$$v_i[s+\tau+1] - \mu[s] \geq \alpha^{\tau+1}(m - \mu[s])$$

This completes the proof of Claim 1.

CLAIM 2. *For each node $i \in \mathcal{V} - \mathcal{F}$,*

$$v_i[s+l] - \mu[s] \geq \alpha^l (m - \mu[s]) \tag{19}$$

Proof of Claim 2: Note that by definition, $R_l = \mathcal{V} - \mathcal{F}$. Then the proof follows by setting $\tau = l$ in the above Claim 1.

CLAIM 3. *For each node $i \in \mathcal{V} - \mathcal{F}$,*

$$U[s] - v_i[s+l] \geq \alpha^l (U[s] - M) \tag{20}$$

The proof of Claim 3 is similar to the proof of Claim 2 [16].

Now let us resume the proof of the Lemma 2. Note that $R_l = \mathcal{V} - \mathcal{F}$. Thus,

$$
\begin{aligned}
U[s+l] &= \max_{i \in \mathcal{V} - \mathcal{F}} v_i[s+l] \\
&\leq U[s] - \alpha^l(U[s] - M) \quad \text{by (20)} \tag{21}
\end{aligned}
$$

and

$$
\begin{aligned}
\mu[s+l] &= \min_{i \in \mathcal{V} - \mathcal{F}} v_i[s+l] \\
&\geq \mu[s] + \alpha^l(m - \mu[s]) \quad \text{by (19)} \tag{22}
\end{aligned}
$$

Subtracting (22) from (21),

$$
\begin{aligned}
&U[s+l] - \mu[s+l] \\
&\leq U[s] - \alpha^l(U[s] - M) - \mu[s] - \alpha^l(m - \mu[s]) \\
&= (1 - \alpha^l)(U[s] - \mu[s]) + \alpha^l(M - m) \\
&\leq (1 - \alpha^l)(U[s] - \mu[s]) + \alpha^l\ \frac{U[s] - \mu[s]}{2} \quad \text{by (16)} \\
&\leq (1 - \frac{\alpha^l}{2})(U[s] - \mu[s])
\end{aligned}
$$

This concludes the proof of Lemma 2. $\square$

---

[4]At least one value received from the nodes in N_i^- is not eliminated, since there are $2f + 1$ incoming edges, and only $2f$ values are eliminated.

Faster than Optimal Snapshots (for a While)

Preliminary Version

James Aspnes[*]
Department of Computer
Science, Yale University
aspnes@cs.yale.edu

Hagit Attiya[†]
Department of Computer
Science, Technion
hagit@cs.technion.ac.il

Keren Censor-Hillel[‡]
Computer Science and
Artificial Intelligence Lab, MIT
ckeren@csail.mit.edu

Faith Ellen[§]
Department of Computer
Science, University of Toronto
faith@cs.toronto.edu

ABSTRACT

This paper presents a novel implementation of a snapshot object for n processes, with $O(\log^2 b \log n)$ step complexity for update operations and $O(\log b)$ step complexity for scan operations, where b is the number of updates. The algorithm uses only reads and writes.

For polynomially many updates, this is an exponential improvement on previous snapshot algorithms, which have linear step complexity. It overcomes the existing $\Omega(n)$ lower bound on step complexity by having the step complexity depend on the number of updates. The key to this implementation is the construction of a new object consisting of a pair of max registers that supports a scan operation.

Applications of this construction include an implementation of a limited-use generalized counter with polylogarithmic step complexity. This can be used, for example, to monitor the number of active processes, which is crucial to adaptive algorithms.

Categories and Subject Descriptors

D.1.3 [**Programming Techniques**]: Concurrent Programming—*Distributed programming*; F.2.2 [**Analysis of Algorithms and Problem Complexity**]: Nonnumerical Algorithms and Problems

[*]Supported in part by NSF grant CCF-0916389.

[†]Supported in part by the *Israel Science Foundation* (grant number 1227/10).

[‡]Supported by the Simons Postdoctoral Fellows Program.

[§]Supported in part by the Natural Science and Engineering Research Council of Canada.

General Terms

Theory, Algorithms

Keywords

Concurrent objects, restricted-use objects, atomic snapshot, generalized counters

1. INTRODUCTION

Atomic snapshots [1] are fundamental data structures in shared memory computations. They allow processes to scan and update shared arrays so that the operations seem to take effect atomically.

Atomic snapshots provide a crucial tool for many shared-memory algorithms, as they simplify coordination between processes. A typical example is a *generalized counter*, which supports the addition of arbitrary positive or negative integers. This is a very useful concurrent data structure: It can be used for keeping track of the number of participants in an algorithm, as is done for mutual exclusion [9], where processes join and leave the competition for the critical section. With atomic snapshots, each process can store its "contribution" (the sum of the values by which it has incremented and decremented) in its component. Using a scan, a process gets an instantaneous view of the contributions, which it sums to obtain the value of the counter.

The best previously-known algorithms for atomic snapshots using only reads and writes [7, 12] have step complexity that is linear in the number of processes n. For a long time, this was taken to be the inherent cost of atomic snapshots, in light of the linear lower bound proved by Jayanti, Tan, and Toueg [15].

Recently, it was shown that a counter, which only allows updates that add one to the counter value, can be implemented with polylogarithmic (in n) step complexity using only reads and writes, assuming the number of increments is polynomial (in n) [4]. This is indeed the case for many applications of a counter. The construction is based on an implementation of a bounded *max register*. It extends to other concurrent data structures, provided that they can be represented by monotone circuits. However, it critically depends on the facts that the value of the counter is monotonically increasing and that all increment operations have the same effect. Therefore, the construction cannot be used to implement a generalized counter or an atomic snapshot.

In this paper, we present a linearizable implementation of atomic snapshots with $O(\log^3 n)$ step complexity, as long as the number of update operations that are performed is polynomial in n. Obtaining an implementation of a snapshot object with polylogarithmic step complexity using only reads and writes is particularly surprising, since all previous implementations had a process directly read a linear number of registers to perform an operation. Instead, our implementation allows processes performing scans and updates to cooperate to reduce the cost exponentially, provided the snapshot object is only updated polynomially many times, as is the case in many important applications. This implies implementations with polylogarithmic step complexity using only reads and writes for a wide variety of shared-memory objects, including generalized counters.

The key technical development behind our results is the definition and implementation of a linearizable 2-*component max array*, a new data structure consisting of two components, each of which is a max register that may be updated independently, and which supports a scan operation that returns the values of both components. The pairs (x_0, x_1) and (y_0, y_1) returned by different scans are always comparable in the sense that either $x_0 \le y_0$ and $x_1 \le y_1$ or $y_0 \le x_0$ and $y_1 \le x_1$. The implementation of the 2-component max array is based on inserting copies of the first component at all levels of a tree of registers implementing the second component using the construction of [4].

The 2-component max array is exactly the tool we need to coordinate the recursive construction of atomic snapshots. We use a binary tree of 2-component max arrays to manage the combination of increasingly wide snapshots of parts of an array of n values. The max registers store increasing indices into a table of partial snapshot values. The scan of a max array is used to guarantee that the two halves of a partial snapshot are consistent with each other. By requiring updaters to propagate their new values up the tree, we amortize the cost of constructing an updated snapshot of all n components across the updates that modify it. This allows a process to obtain a precomputed snapshot in sublinear time.

The reason our results do not contradict the linear lower bound [15] is because the proof uses executions that are exponentially long as a function of n. Specifically, it has been shown [5] that collect objects and, hence, snapshot objects have $\Omega(\min(\log b, n))$ step complexity, where b is the number of updates performed. This indicates that our implementation is close to optimal.

Due to their importance, there have been other implementations of atomic snapshots, e.g., [2, 10, 16]. An interesting implementation of atomic snapshots using f-arrays takes one step for a scan and $O(\log n)$ steps for an update, but it uses LL/SC [13]. There are also atomic snapshot implementations using CAS [14, 18], which take one step for an update and $O(n)$ steps for a scan.

2. MODEL AND PRELIMINARIES

Consider a deterministic asynchronous shared-memory system comprised of n processes, which communicate through shared registers that support read and write. We assume that any number of processes can fail by crashing.

An *implementation* of a shared object in this system pro-

vides a representation of the object using shared registers and an algorithm for each type of operation supported by the object. The implementation is *linearizable* [11] if, for every execution, there is a total order of all completed operations and a subset of the uncompleted operations in the execution that satisfies the sequential specifications of the object and is consistent with the real-time ordering of these operations (i.e. if an operation is completed before another operation begins, then the former operation occurs earlier in the total order).

There are a number of different shared objects we consider. A *counter*, r, supports two operations, $\texttt{Read}(r)$ and $\texttt{Increment}(r)$. If r is a *generalized counter*, then it also supports $\texttt{Add}(r, v)$, where $v \in \mathbb{Z}$, i.e. it allows the value of r to be atomically changed by an arbitrary integer, instead of simply being incremented by 1.

An *atomic snapshot* object consists of a finite array of m components. $\texttt{Update}(r, i, v)$ sets the value of component i of snapshot r to v. $\texttt{Scan}(r)$ atomically reads the values of all m components. In a *single-writer snapshot*, the number of components, m, is equal to the number processes, n, and only process i can update component i.

A *max register* r is an object that supports two operations, $\texttt{ReadMax}(r)$, which returns the value of r, and $\texttt{WriteMax}(r, v)$, which sets the value of r to $v \in \mathbb{N}$, if its value was less than v. Thus, a $\texttt{ReadMax}(r)$ operation returns the largest value of v in any $\texttt{WriteMax}(r, v)$ operation that is linearized before it. For any positive integer k, a *bounded max register* object of type $\texttt{MaxReg}_k$ is a max register whose values are restricted to $\{0, \ldots, k-1\}$; we say that it has *range* k.

A *2-component max array* consists of a pair of $\texttt{MaxReg}$ objects, with an atomic operation that returns the values of both of them. Specifically, an object r of type $\texttt{MaxArray}_{k \times h}$ supports three linearizable operations: $\texttt{MaxUpdate0}(r, v)$, where $v \in \{0, \ldots, k-1\}$, $\texttt{MaxUpdate1}(r, v)$, where $v \in \{0, \ldots, h-1\}$, and $\texttt{MaxScan}(r)$, with the following properties:

— $\texttt{MaxUpdate0}(r, v)$ sets the value of the first component of r to v.

— $\texttt{MaxUpdate1}(r, v)$ sets the value of the second component of r to v.

— $\texttt{MaxScan}(r)$ returns the value of r, i.e. it returns a pair (v, v') such that v and v' are the largest values in any $\texttt{MaxUpdate0}(r, v)$ and $\texttt{MaxUpdate1}(r, v')$ operations that are linearized before it.

The results of two $\texttt{MaxScan}(r)$ operations in a linearizable execution are never incomparable under the componentwise $\le$ partial order, i.e., it is never the case that $u < v$ and $u' > v'$, for any pair of $\texttt{MaxScan}$ operations returning (u, u') and (v, v').

A *b-limited-use* object limits the total number of update operations (e.g. $\texttt{Increment}$, $\texttt{Add}$, or $\texttt{Update}$) that can be applied to it during an execution to at most b. Operations that do not change the value of the object can be applied an unlimited number of times.

3. IMPLEMENTING A 2-COMPONENT MAX ARRAY

We begin with the description of the implementation of a $\texttt{MaxReg}_k$ object from registers [4], since our implementation of a $\texttt{MaxArray}_{k \times h}$ object is based on it. The smallest max register, the trivial $\texttt{MaxReg}_1$ object, requires no reads or writes and uses no space: $\texttt{WriteMax}(r,0)$ does nothing and $\texttt{ReadMax}(r)$ simply returns 0. To get larger max registers, smaller ones are combined recursively.

A max register r with range k consists of a single bit register, $r.\texttt{switch}$, and two smaller max registers, $r.\texttt{left}$ with range $m = \lceil k/2 \rceil$ and $r.\texttt{right}$ with range $k - m$. When $r.\texttt{switch} = 0$, the value of r is the value of $r.\texttt{left}$; when $r.\texttt{switch} = 1$, the value of r is m plus the value of $r.\texttt{right}$. This gives a simple recursive algorithm for $\texttt{ReadMax}$. If $v \geq m$, a process performs $\texttt{WriteMax}(r,v)$ by recursively calling $\texttt{WriteMax}(r.\texttt{right}, v-m)$ and then setting $r.\texttt{switch}$ to 1. Otherwise, it first checks that $r.\texttt{switch} = 0$ and, if so, recursively calls $\texttt{WriteMax}(r.\texttt{left}, v)$. If $r.\texttt{switch} = 1$, the value of r is already at least m, so no recursive call is needed. The construction results in a tree of depth $\lceil \log_2 k \rceil$.

Pseudocode for this implementation of a $\texttt{MaxReg}_k$ object is presented in Algorithm 1.

Next, we turn attention to the implementation of a $\texttt{MaxArray}_{2 \times 2}$ object, r. Suppose we use two $\texttt{MaxReg}_2$ objects, r_0 and r_1, one storing the value of each component. Then $\texttt{MaxUpdate0}(r,v)$ can be performed by performing $\texttt{WriteMax}(r_0, v)$ and $\texttt{MaxUpdate1}(r,v)$ can be performed by performing $\texttt{WriteMax}(r_1, v)$. However, it is incorrect to perform $\texttt{MaxScan}(r)$ by simply collecting the values of both components, i.e., by performing $\texttt{ReadMax}(r_0)$ followed by $\texttt{ReadMax}(r_1)$. For example, consider the execution in Figure 1.

In this execution, the steps of two scanners, p and p', are interleaved with those of an updater q, such that p returns $(0,1)$ and p' returns $(1,0)$, which are incomparable. Thus, it is impossible to linearize both these operations with this naive implementation.

However, since the only possible values are 0 and 1, there is a correct implementation of $\texttt{MaxScan}(r)$ that is only slightly more complicated: If a process obtains $(0,0)$ from a collect, it can return $(0,0)$ and its operation can be linearized at its first step. Similarly, a process that obtains $(1,1)$ can always return $(1,1)$ and be linearized at its last step. When a process obtains either $(0,1)$ or $(1,0)$, it can return the

pair of values resulting from performing $\texttt{ReadMax}(r_0)$ and $\texttt{ReadMax}(r_1)$ again. Since the value of each component is nondecreasing, its second collect will either return $(1,1)$ or the same pair as its first collect. In the latter case, we have an identical *double collect* [1], and the operation can be linearized between the two collects.

More generally, if r is a $\texttt{MaxArray}_{k \times h}$ object, then $\texttt{MaxScan}(r)$ can be performed by repeatedly performing $\texttt{ReadMax}(r_0)$ followed by $\texttt{ReadMax}(r_1)$ until the result is either $(0,0)$, (k,h), or the same pair twice in a row. Unfortunately, the worst case step complexity of this implementation is $\Theta((k+h)(\log k + \log h))$, since the values can change $k + h$ times.

The challenge in implementing a significantly faster $\texttt{MaxArray}_{k \times h}$ object is to ensure that, in each execution, all pairs returned by the $\texttt{MaxScan}$ operations are comparable. Our approach is to make the $\texttt{MaxScan}$ operations be responsible for this coordination. For the first component, we use the same binary tree as in the preceding implementation of a $\texttt{MaxReg}_k$ object. In addition, we insert a $\texttt{MaxReg}_h$ object for the second component at every node in the tree. To perform $\texttt{MaxUpdate0}(r,v)$, a process uses the algorithm for $\texttt{WriteMax}$, ignoring these additional objects. To perform $\texttt{MaxUpdate1}(r,v)$, a process simply performs $\texttt{WriteMax}$ on the $\texttt{MaxReg}_h$ object at the root of the tree, ignoring the rest of the $\texttt{MaxReg}_h$ objects at other nodes of the tree.

The $\texttt{MaxScan}$ operation uses a subtle helping mechanism that propagates values of the second component down the path in the tree, while it is being traversed to obtain the value of the first component. Specifically, a process performing $\texttt{MaxScan}(r)$ begins by performing $\texttt{ReadMax}$ on the $\texttt{MaxReg}_h$ object at the root of the tree. If the switch bit at the root of the tree is 0, it updates the $\texttt{MaxReg}_h$ object at the left child of the root with the value it obtained from the $\texttt{MaxReg}_h$ object at the root and recursively performs $\texttt{MaxScan}$ on the left subtree. If the bit at the root of the tree is 1, it repeats the $\texttt{ReadMax}$ on the $\texttt{MaxReg}_h$ object at the root of the tree before updating the $\texttt{MaxReg}_h$ object at the right child of the root with the value it receives and then recursively performs $\texttt{MaxScan}$ on the right subtree (and adds m to the first component of the result). Because the value of the $\texttt{MaxReg}_h$ object is nondecreasing, the value returned by the second $\texttt{ReadMax}$ is guaranteed to be at least as large as the value returned by the $\texttt{ReadMax}$ to any process that goes to the left subtree.

Formally, our implementation of a $\texttt{MaxArray}_{k \times h}$ object r is recursive. When $k = 1$, we use a single $\texttt{MaxReg}_h$ object, $r.\texttt{second}$. $\texttt{MaxScan}(r)$ returns $(0, x)$, where x is the result of performing $\texttt{ReadMax}(r.\texttt{second})$. $\texttt{MaxUpdate1}(r,v)$ performs $\texttt{WriteMax}$ on this object. $\texttt{MaxUpdate0}(r,v)$ does nothing.

When $k > 1$, r consists of a $\texttt{MaxArray}_{m \times h}$ object $r.\texttt{left}$, where $m = \lceil k/2 \rceil$, a $\texttt{MaxArray}_{(k-m) \times h}$ object $r.\texttt{right}$, a binary register $r.\texttt{switch}$, and a $\texttt{MaxReg}_h$ object $r.\texttt{second}$.

Pseudocode for these operations is presented in Algorithm 2.

3.1 Linearizability

We show that our implementation is linearizable. We do this by showing that, in any execution, the pairs returned by $\texttt{MaxScan}(r)$ operations are comparable under componentwise $\leq$ and use this total ordering to linearize these operations. Then we linearize the $\texttt{MaxUpdate0}(r,v)$ and $\texttt{MaxUpdate1}(r,v)$

Algorithm 1 An implementation of a $\texttt{MaxReg}_k$ object

Shared data:
    switch: a single bit multi-writer register, initially 0
    left: a $\texttt{MaxReg}_m$ object, where $m = \lceil k/2 \rceil$, initially 0,
    right: a $\texttt{MaxReg}_{k-m}$ object, initially 0

```
1:  WriteMax(r, v):
2:      if v < m
3:          if r.switch = 0
4:              WriteMax(r.left, v)
5:          else
6:              WriteMax(r.right, v - m)
7:              r.switch ← 1

8:  ReadMax(r):
9:      if r.switch = 0
10:         return ReadMax(r.left)
11:     else
12:         return ReadMax(r.right) + m
```

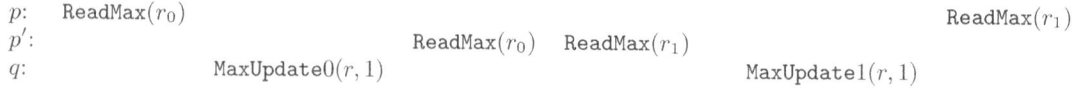

Figure 1: An execution of an incorrect implementation of a MaxArray$_{2\times 2}$ object

operations in a consistent manner before, after, and between them. We begin with some technical lemmas.

LEMMA 1. *For any execution, if v is the value of x the first time* WriteMax(r.right.second, x) *is performed on Line 18, then at all points in the execution, r.left.second $\leq v$.*

PROOF. Consider the MaxScan(r) operation op that first performs WriteMax(r.right.second, x) on Line 17. Prior to this step, op read r.switch = 1 on Line 12 and then received value v when it performed ReadMax(r.second) on Line 16.

The value of r.left.second is initially 0 and is changed only when a MaxScan(r) operation op' performs WriteMax(r.left.second, x) on Line 13, provided r.left.second $< x$. The value of x at this step is the value v' that op' obtained by performing ReadMax(r.second) on Line 11, prior to reading r.switch = 0 on Line 12.

Since r.switch only changes from 0 to 1, the ReadMax(r.second) by op' on Line 11 occurred before the ReadMax(r.second) by op on Line 16. Since r.second is a max register, $v' \leq v$. Thus, at all points in the execution, r.left.second $\leq v$. □

Algorithm 2 An implementation of a MaxArray$_{k\times h}$ object for $k > 1$

Shared data:
> switch: a 1-bit multi-writer register, initially 0
> left: a MaxArray$_{m\times h}$ object, where $m = \lceil k/2 \rceil$,
>   initially (0,0)
> right: a MaxArray$_{(k-m)\times h}$ object, initially (0,0)
> second: a MaxReg$_h$ object, initially 0

```
1:  MaxUpdate0(r, v):        // write to the first component
2:    if v < m
3:      if r.switch = 0
4:        MaxUpdate0(r.left, v)
5:    else
6:      MaxUpdate0(r.right, v − m)
7:      r.switch ← 1

8:  MaxUpdate1(r, v):    // write to the second component
9:    WriteMax(r.second, v)

10: MaxScan(r):
11:   x ← ReadMax(r.second)
12:   if r.switch = 0
13:     WriteMax(r.left.second, x)
14:     return MaxScan(r.left)
15:   else
16:     x ← ReadMax(r.second)
17:     WriteMax(r.right.second, x)
18:     return ((m, 0) + MaxScan(r.right))
```

LEMMA 2. *The second component of the pair returned by a MaxScan(r) operation is at most the value of r.second.*

PROOF. By induction on the range of the first component. If r is a MaxArray$_{1\times h}$ object, then the second component returned by a MaxScan(r) operation is the result of ReadMax(r.second), which is the value of r.second.

Now let r be a MaxArray$_{k\times h}$ object, where $k > 1$. Suppose the claim is true for r.left and r.right.

The second component of the pair returned by a MaxScan(r) operation on Line 14 is the second component of the pair returned by MaxScan(r.left), which, by the induction hypothesis, is at most the value of r.left.second. Similarly, the second component of the pair returned by a MaxScan(r) operation on Line 18 is the second component of the pair returned by MaxScan(r.right), which, by the induction hypothesis, is at most the value of r.right.second.

Whenever WriteMax(r.left.second, x) is performed on Line 13 or WriteMax(r.right.second, x) is performed on Line 17, the value of x is the result of a preceding ReadMax(r.second) operation. Thus r.left.second, r.right.second $\leq r$.second. □

LEMMA 3. *The second component of the pair returned by a MaxScan(r) operation is at least the value of r.second when the operation was invoked.*

PROOF. By induction on the range of the first component. If r is a MaxArray$_{1\times h}$ object, then the second component returned by a MaxScan(r) operation is the result of ReadMax(r.second). Then the claim follows from the fact that the value of the MaxReg$_h$ object r.second does not decrease.

Now let r be a MaxArray$_{k\times h}$ object, where $k > 1$. Suppose the claim is true for r.left and r.right. Let v' be the value of r.second when a MaxScan(r) operation op' is invoked. Then the value of x immediately after op' performs ReadMax(r.second) on Line 11 is at least v'.

If op' performs WriteMax(r.left.second, x) on Line 13, then the value of r.left.second will be at least v' when op' invokes MaxScan(r.left) on Line 14. Then, by the induction hypothesis, the second component of the pair returned by this operation (and, hence by MaxScan(r)) is at least v'.

Otherwise, on Line 16, op' sets x to the result of ReadMax(r.second), which is still at least v'. Then op' performs WriteMax(r.right.second, x) on Line 17. Hence, the value of r.right.second will be at least v' when op' invokes MaxScan(r.right) on Line 18. By the induction hypothesis, the second component of the pair returned by this operation (and, hence by MaxScan(r)) is at least v'. □

THEOREM 4. *The MaxArray$_{k\times h}$ implementation in Algorithm 2 is linearizable.*

PROOF. By induction on k. The linearizability of the MaxArray$_{1\times h}$ implementation follows immediately from the linearizability of the MaxReg$_h$ object that represents it.

Now let $k > 1$. Suppose that $1 \le m < k$, r.left is a linearizable $\mathtt{MaxArray}_{m \times h}$ object, and r.right is a linearizable $\mathtt{MaxArray}_{(k-m) \times h}$ object. We will show that r is a linearizable $\mathtt{MaxArray}_{k \times h}$ object.

Consider any execution and let (x_0, x_1) and (x'_0, x'_1) be the pairs returned by two $\mathtt{MaxScan}(r)$ operations op and op'. If both are the result of $\mathtt{MaxScan}(r$.left$)$ on Line 14, then, by the induction hypothesis, they can be ordered in a consistent manner. The same is true if both are $(m, 0)$ plus the result of $\mathtt{MaxScan}(r$.right$)$ on Line 18. Otherwise, one of the pairs, say (x_0, x_1), is the result of $\mathtt{MaxScan}(r$.left$)$ on Line 14 and (x'_0, x'_1) is equal to $(m, 0)$ plus the result of $\mathtt{MaxScan}(r$.right$)$ on Line 18.

The only instruction that updates the first component of r.left is $\mathtt{MaxUpdate0}(r$.left$, v)$ on Line 4. By Line 2, $v < m$. Hence $x_0 < m$. Initially, r.right $= 0$, so, by Line 18, $x'_0 \ge m$. Thus $x_0 < x'_0$.

By Lemma 2, $x_1 \le r$.left.second. Let v be the value of x the first time that $\mathtt{WriteMax}(r$.right.second$, x)$ is performed on Line 17 during the execution. Then, by Lemma 1, r.left.second $\le v$.

Since r.right.second is a $\mathtt{MaxReg}_h$ object, which never decreases in value, r.right.second $\ge v$ when op' invokes Line 18. By Lemma 3, $x'_1 \ge v$. Hence $x_1 \le x'_1$ and op is linearized before op'.

The only step performed by a $\mathtt{MaxUpdate1}(r, v)$ operation is $\mathtt{WriteMax}(r$.second$, v)$ on Line 9. It follows from Lemmas 2 and 3 that it can be linearized among the $\mathtt{MaxScan}(r)$ operations.

Provided r.switch $= 0$, the $\mathtt{MaxUpdate0}(r, v)$ operations with $v < m$ can be linearized where the $\mathtt{MaxUpdate0}(r$.left$, v)$ operations on Line 4 are linearized, which, by the induction hypothesis, can be linearized among the $\mathtt{MaxScan}(r$.left$)$ operations. When r.switch $= 1$, the $\mathtt{MaxUpdate0}(r, v)$ operations with $v < m$ have no effect and they can be linearized when they return.

Similarly, each $\mathtt{MaxUpdate0}(r, v)$ operation with $v \ge m$ performs a $\mathtt{MaxUpdate0}(r$.right$, v - m)$ operation on Line 6. By the induction hypothesis, these operations can be linearized among the $\mathtt{MaxScan}(r$.right$)$ operations, each of which corresponds to a $\mathtt{MaxScan}(r)$ operation that reads r.switch $= 1$ on Line 12. The $\mathtt{MaxScan}(r$.right$)$ operations all occur after r.switch becomes 1. Any $\mathtt{MaxUpdate0}(r, v)$ operation with $v \ge m$ that performs Line 6 when r.switch $= 0$ can be linearized when r.switch is changed to 1, which occurs at or before it performs Line 7. $\square$

3.2 Step complexity

Our $\mathtt{MaxArray}_{k \times h}$ implementation has step complexity that is polylogarithmic in h and k.

LEMMA 5. *For the $\mathtt{MaxArray}_{k \times h}$ implementation in Algorithm 2, the step complexity of $\mathtt{MaxUpdate0}$ is $O(\log k)$, the step complexity of $\mathtt{MaxUpdate1}$ is $O(\log h)$, and the step complexity of $\mathtt{MaxScan}$ is $O(\log k \log h)$.*

PROOF. A $\mathtt{MaxUpdate1}(r, v)$ operation performs one $\mathtt{WriteMax}$ operation on a $\mathtt{MaxReg}_h$ object, which has step complexity $O(\log h)$. A $\mathtt{MaxUpdate0}(r, v)$ operation accesses the binary register r.switch once and performs one $\mathtt{MaxUpdate0}(r', v')$ operation, where r' is a $\mathtt{MaxArray}_{m \times h}$ object or a $\mathtt{MaxArray}_{(k-m) \times h}$ object, and $m = \lceil k/2 \rceil$. If $T(k)$ is the step complexity of $\mathtt{MaxUpdate0}(r, v)$ for a $\mathtt{MaxArray}_{k \times h}$ object r, it follows that $T(1) = 1$ and $T(k) = T(\lceil k/2 \rceil) + 1$. Hence $T(k)$ is $O(\log k)$.

A $\mathtt{MaxScan}(r)$ operation reads r.switch once, performs at most two $\mathtt{ReadMax}(r$.second$)$ operations, performs one $\mathtt{MaxUpdate1}(r', v')$ operation, and performs one $\mathtt{MaxScan}(r')$ operation, where $m = \lceil k/2 \rceil$ and r' is a $\mathtt{MaxArray}_{m \times h}$ object or a $\mathtt{MaxArray}_{(k-m) \times h}$ object. If $T_h(k)$ is the step complexity of a $\mathtt{MaxScan}$ operation on a $\mathtt{MaxArray}_{k \times h}$ object, then $T_h(k) = T_h(\lceil k/2 \rceil) + 1 + 3 \cdot O(\log h)$. Since $T_h(1)$ is $O(\log h)$, it follows that $T_h(k)$ is $O(\log k \log h)$. $\square$

4. SINGLE-WRITER SNAPSHOTS FROM 2-COMPONENT MAX ARRAYS

We build a $(b - 1)$-limited-use snapshot object from $\mathtt{MaxArray}_{b \times b}$ objects, registers, and a $\mathtt{MaxReg}_b$ object. To do so, we construct a strict, balanced, binary tree in which each leaf holds a pointer to the value of one component and each internal node holds a pointer to a partial snapshot containing the values of all the components in the subtree of which it is the root. The pointers held by each pair of siblings in the tree are stored at their parent in a 2-component max array. The pointer held by the root is stored in a max register. Each pointer is a nondecreasing index into a different array of b registers. The initial value of component j is stored in $\mathtt{leaf}_j$.view$[0]$, for $j = 0, \ldots, n - 1$. The concatenation of these values, for each leaf in the substree rooted at an internal node u, is stored in u.view$[0]$. Figure 2 depicts this structure, with an $\mathtt{Update}(4, s)$ operation in progress.

To perform a $\mathtt{Scan}$, a process simply takes the result of a $\mathtt{ReadMax}$ of the $\mathtt{MaxReg}_b$ stored at the root and, if nonzero, uses it to index the array at the root. The step complexity of $\mathtt{Scan}$ is dominated by the step complexity of $\mathtt{ReadMax}$, which is $O(\log b)$.

When a process updates its component of the snapshot object, it writes the new value to the first empty location in the array at its leaf and increases the value of the pointer held in its leaf to point to the location of this new value. Then it propagates this new value up the tree, combining partial snapshots. Specifically, at an internal node, a process performs a $\mathtt{MaxScan}$ of ma, the 2-component max array containing the pointers held at its children, and reads the array elements to which they point to obtain a partial snapshot. Its new pointer is the sum of the two pointers held at its children. The process stores the partial snapshot at the location in the array to which it points. The 2-component max arrays ensure linearizability. Since each $\mathtt{MaxScan}$ operation takes $O(\log^2 b)$ steps and the tree has $O(\log n)$ height, the step complexity of $\mathtt{Update}$ is $O(\log^2 b \log n)$.

Pseudocode for our implementation is given in Algorithm 3.

The resulting algorithm is similar to the lattice agreement procedure of Inoue et al. [12], except that we use $\mathtt{MaxScan}$ in place of double collects and we allow processes to update their values more than once.

The length of the array at a node is one greater than the total number of updates that can be performed by processes whose components are in the subtree rooted at that node. The pointer to this array is initially 0 and its maximum value is one less than the length of the array. Thus, if the arrays at a pair of siblings have length k and h, respectively, a $\mathtt{MaxArray}_{k \times h}$ object can be used to store the pointers held by those nodes.

The size of each register in an array is the sum of the maximum sizes of the components in the partial snapshot

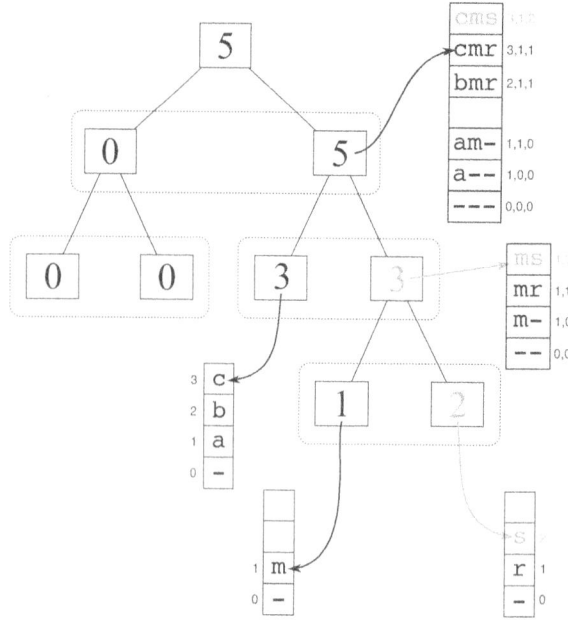

Figure 2: A limited-use single-writer snapshot object shared by 5 processes. Grayed values correspond to an update operation in progress. Sequences outside the view arrays represent entries of the seq arrays from the proof of correctness. Not all array locations are shown.

it stores. This may be impractical, unless it is possible to represent the important information in a partial snapshot in a condensed manner. For example, a generalized counter can be implemented using a single-writer snapshot in which component i contains the sum of the values process i has added to the counter. Then each partial snapshot stored in a register (in an array) can be replaced by the sum of its components. The upper bound on the number of `Add` operations that can be performed by each process in the generalized counter is the number of times that process can update its component in the single-writer snapshot. This construction is similar to Jayanti's f-arrays [13] for efficient computation of aggregate functions (such as max and sum) of the elements of an array. Because the pointers are non-decreasing, we can use 2-component max arrays instead of the more powerful primitives used in that paper.

4.1 Linearizability

Now we show that our implementation is linearizable. A `Scan` operation is linearized when it performs `ReadMax(root.mr)` on Line 20. If $ptr = d$ when an `Update` operation performs Line 16 with $u = $ root, then the `Update` operation is linearized the first time any process performs `WriteMax(root.mr, ptr)` on Line 18 with $ptr \geq d$. The `Update` operation performs Line 18 with $ptr = d$ before it returns, so its linearization point occurs before it returns. The following lemma shows that its linearization point occurs after it begins.

LEMMA 6. *If d is the index stored at root.mr when an* Update *operation begins, then $ptr > d$ when the operation performs* WriteMax(root.mr, ptr) *on Line 18.*

PROOF. We also prove that, when an `Update` operation tries to update a pointer stored in a component of a `MaxArray` to ptr on Line 8 or 10, ptr is greater than the index stored at the component when the `Update` began.

The proof is by induction. The claim is true for a pointer held at a leaf. This is because only one process updates the pointer, it is intially 0, and $count_i$ is incremented on Line 2 before it is assigned to ptr on Line 5.

Suppose the claim is true for a pointer held at a non-root node. The pointer held at its sibling never decreases. Since ptr is the sum of these two indices, the claim is true at the parent of this node, whether or not it is the root. □

Now, we prove that our linearization satisfies the specifications of a snapshot object. For the purpose of the proof, we introduce an auxiliary array, $seq[0..b-1]$, stored at each node. We imagine that, when Line 4 is performed, $leaf_i.seq[ptr] \leftarrow ptr$ is performed at the same time and, when Line 15 is performed, $u.seq[ptr] \leftarrow u.left.seq[lptr] \cdot u.right.seq[rptr]$ is performed at the same time. Thus, each element of $u.seq$ is a sequence of pointers, one into the array at each leaf of the subtree rooted at u. The following invariants are maintained:

— ptr is the sum of the elements in the sequence $u.seq[ptr]$,

— if $ptr \leq ptr'$, then each component of $u.seq[ptr]$ is less than or equal to the corresponding component of $u.seq[ptr']$, and

— the j'th component of $u.view[ptr]$ is equal to the element of view in the j'th leaf of the subtree rooted at node u pointed to by the j'th component of $u.seq[ptr]$, i.e. $(u.view[ptr])_j = \ell.view[(u.seq[ptr])_j]$, where ℓ is the j'th leaf of the subtree rooted at node u.

The second of these follows inductively from Line 12 and the fact that $u.ma$ is a linearizable max array.

Consider an `Update` operation by process i that is linearized when process j performs Line 18. Suppose that

$ptr = c$ when process j performs Line 18 and suppose that $ptr = d$ when the Update operation by process i performs Line 18. By the definition of the linearization points, $c \geq d$. Hence $(\mathsf{root.seq}[c])_i \geq (\mathsf{root.seq}[d])_i$. Only process i modifies the pointer at leaf_i (setting it to count_i) and its operation is linearized before it returns, so $(\mathsf{root.seq}[c])_i \leq \mathsf{count}_i \leq (\mathsf{root.seq}[d])_i$. Therefore $(\mathsf{root.seq}[c])_i = (\mathsf{root.seq}[d])_i = \mathsf{count}_i$. Similarly, any other Update operation that is linearized after this Update operation by process i is linearized, but before any other Update operation by process i is linearized, has $(\mathsf{root.seq}[ptr])_i = \mathsf{count}_i$ when it performs Line 18.

Consider any linearized Scan operation op. Suppose that

Algorithm 3 An implementation of a $(b-1)$-limited-use single-writer snapshot, code for process i.

Shared data:
   leaf_j, for $j \in \{0, \dots, n-1\}$:
      the leaf node corresponding to process j, with fields:
      parent: the parent of this leaf in the tree
      view$[0..b-1]$: an array, each of whose entries contains
         a partial snapshot,
         view$[0]$ contains the initial value of component j
   root: the root of the tree
   Each internal node has the fields:
      left: the left child of the node in the tree
      right: the right child of the node in the tree
      view$[0..b-1]$: an array, each of whose entries contains
         a partial snapshot, view$[0]$ contains the
         concatenation of leaf_j.view$[0]$ for all leaves
         leaf_j in the subtree rooted at this node
      ma: a $\mathsf{MaxArray}_{b \times b}$ object, initially $(0,0)$
   The root also has the field:
      mr: a MaxReg_b object, initially 0
   Each non-root internal node also has the field:
      parent: the parent of the node in the tree
Persistent local data: count_i, initially 0.

```
1:  Update(s, v)
2:      count_i ← count_i + 1
3:      u ← leaf_i
4:      ptr ← count_i
5:      u.view[ptr] ← v
6:      repeat
7:          if u = u.parent.left
8:              MaxUpdate0(u.parent.ma, ptr)
9:          if u = u.parent.right
10:             MaxUpdate1(u.parent.ma, ptr)
11:         u ← u.parent
12:         (lptr, rptr) ← MaxScan(u.ma)
13:         lview ← u.left.view[lptr]
14:         rview ← u.right.view[rptr]
15:         ptr ← lptr + rptr
16:         u.view[ptr] ← lview · rview
17:     until u = root
18:     WriteMax(root.mr, ptr)

19: Scan(s)
20:     ptr ← ReadMax(root.mr)
21:     return root.view[ptr]
```

$\mathsf{root.seq}[ptr] = (f_0, \dots, f_{n-1})$ when it performs Line 20. Then $\mathsf{root.view}[f] = (v_0, \dots, v_{n-1})$ is the view it returns, where $f = f_0 + \dots + f_{n-1}$ and $v_j = \mathsf{leaf}_j.\mathsf{view}[f_j]$ for $j = 0, \dots, n-1$. We need to show that v_j is the value written by process j in its last Update operation, op_j, linearized before op. Suppose that $ptr = c$ when op_j is linearized. From the preceding paragraph, it follows that $(\mathsf{root.seq}[f])_j = (\mathsf{root.seq}[c])_j = \mathsf{count}_j$. Since every Update by process j sets count_j to a new value on Line 2, op_j updated component j with value v_j in $\mathsf{leaf}_j.\mathsf{view}[\mathsf{count}_j]$. Similarly, if there is no Update operation by process j that is linearized before op, $\mathsf{count}_j = 0$ and $v_j = \mathsf{leaf}_j.\mathsf{view}[0]$ is the initial value of component j.

Thus, we have proved:

THEOREM 7. *The $(b-1)$-limited-use single-writer snapshot implementation in Algorithm 3 is linearizable.*

4.2 Step Complexity

LEMMA 8. *The step complexity of a Scan operation is $O(\log b)$ and the step complexity of an Update operation is $O(\log^2 b \log n)$, where $b-1$ is an upper bound on the number of Update operations it supports.*

PROOF. A Scan operation performs one ReadMax on a MaxReg_b object and reads one entry from the array $\mathsf{root.view}$. Hence it has step complexity $O(\log b)$.

An Update operation performs at most $\lceil \log_2 n \rceil$ iterations, one for each ancestor of leaf_i. In each iteration, there is one MaxUpdate operation and one MaxScan operation applied to $\mathsf{MaxArray}_{b \times b}$ objects and a constant number of accesses to entries of view arrays. Finally, one WriteMax operation is performed on the MaxReg_b at root. This implies the claimed step complexity of $O(\log^2 b \log n)$. □

This immediately gives us an $O(\log^3 n)$ implementation of any object that can be built from a snapshot object, including counters, generalized counters, and (by [3, 6]) any object with the property that for each pair of operations, either the operations always commute or one always overwrites the other—provided we only want to use the implementation polynomially many times.

5. MULTI-WRITER SNAPSHOTS

The previous section considered a single-writer snapshot object, that is, each component can be updated by a single process. Here, we extend this to implement a multi-writer snapshot object, where each component can be updated by every process. This is done by using a single-writer snapshot object and having each process record its own updates to each multi-writer component along with a *timestamp*. When these records are scanned, the value for each multi-writer component is the value written with the largest timestamp. Ties are broken using process ids. To produce a timestamp, Lamport's linearizable timestamp algorithm [17] is used: a process scans the single-writer snapshot object and adds one to the largest timestamp for the corresponding multi-writer component. The creation of timestamps can be linearized in increasing order, with ties broken using process ids.

It is easy to see that the step complexity of MW-Scan(s) is the same as that of Scan(snp), and that the step complexity of MW-Update(s, j, v) is the sum of the step complexities of Scan(snp) and Update(snp, v).

We linearize a MW-Scan(s) operation at Line 7, which is the linearization point of the Scan(snp) operation. We linearize a MW-Update(s, j, v) operation which uses timestamp t the first time after it performs Line 2 at which the timestamp of the j'th pair of the component of some process is updated on Line 5 with a timestamp $t' \geq t$, with ties broken by process id. This is at or before the linearization point of the Update(snp, record) operation. Since every operation is linearized after it begins and before it returns, the order of non-overlapping operations is preserved.

If a MW-Scan(s) operation op returns a view $(v_0, \ldots, v_{c-1})$, then, for $0 \leq j < c$, the last MW-Update(s, j, v) operation op_j linearized before op has $v = v_j$. This follows because we are using a linearizable single-writer snapshot object, because the timestamps are linearized in increasing order, and because of the linearization points we chose for MW-Update operations. Thus, the linearization satisfies the specifications of a multi-writer snapshot object.

THEOREM 9. *The $(b-1)$-limited-use multi-writer snapshot implementation in Algorithm 4 is linearizable. The step complexity of a MW-Scan(s) operation is $O(\log b)$ and the step complexity of a MW-Update(s, j, v) operation is $O(\log^2 b \log n)$.*

6. DISCUSSION

This paper gives a linearizable implementation of a snapshot object with $O(\log^3 n)$ step complexity, as long as the number of update operations is at most polynomial in the number of processes, n. This is an exponential improvement over the best previously known algorithms, which have step complexity linear in n.

In [4], an implementation is given for an *unbounded* max register that can support an unbounded number of values and has a step complexity of $O(\min(\log v, n))$, where v is the

---

Algorithm 4 An implementation of a $(b-1)$-limited-use c-component multi-writer snapshot, code for process i.

Shared data:
    snp: a single-writer snapshot object,
        each component is an array of c pairs (val,ts),
        each pair is initialized to $(-, 0)$
Persistent local data:
    record$[0..c-1]$: an array of pairs (val,ts),
        each is initialized to $(-, 0)$

1: MW-Update(s, j, v)
2:    $view \leftarrow$ Scan(snp)
3:    $t \leftarrow 1 + \max\{view_k[j].\text{ts} \mid 0 \leq k < n\}$
4:    record$[j] \leftarrow (v, t)$
5:    Update(snp, record)

6: MW-Scan(s)
7:    $view \leftarrow$ Scan(snp)
8:    for $0 \leq j < c$ do
9:      $k \leftarrow \text{argmax}\{(view_k[j].\text{ts}) \times n + k \mid 0 \leq k < n\}$
           // find process with largest timestamp for
           // component j, use process id to break ties
10:     $result_j \leftarrow view_k[j].\text{val}$
           // use its value for component j
11:    return $result$

---

value written or read. It may be possible to implement 2-component max arrays that support unbounded values and use them to construct unbounded snapshot objects whose step complexity is both $O(n)$ and polylogarithmic in the number of update operations. However, direct use of the unbounded tree construction from [4] seems to give worse complexity bounds. We leave this for future research.

Our 2-component max array implementation easily extends to c-component max arrays in a recursive manner, by having r.second be a $(c-1)$-component max array. The complexity of a MaxUpdate operation is then $O(\log k)$, where k is the range of each component, and the complexity of a MaxScan operation is $O(\log^c k)$. As with 2-component max arrays, this can also support components with different ranges, as well as unbounded ranges, with corresponding step complexities.

Our constructions use multi-writer registers. A very intriguing question is to extend them to obtain a snapshot object with $O(n)$ step complexity using only *single-writer* registers, improving on the $O(n \log n)$ best previously-known upper bound [8].

7. REFERENCES

[1] Y. Afek, H. Attiya, D. Dolev, E. Gafni, M. Merritt, and N. Shavit. Atomic snapshots of shared memory. *J. ACM*, 40(4):873–890, 1993.

[2] J. H. Anderson. Composite registers. *Distributed Computing*, 6(3):141–154, 1993.

[3] J. H. Anderson and M. Moir. Towards a necessary and sufficient condition for wait-free synchronization (extended abstract). In A. Schiper, editor, *Distributed Algorithms, 7th International Workshop, WDAG '93, Lausanne, Switzerland, September 27-29, 1993, Proceedings*, volume 725 of *Lecture Notes in Computer Science*, pages 39–53. Springer, 1993.

[4] J. Aspnes, H. Attiya, and K. Censor-Hillel. Polylogarithmic concurrent data structures from monotone circuits. *J. ACM*, 59(1):2:1–2:24, Mar. 2012.

[5] J. Aspnes, H. Attiya, K. Censor-Hillel, and D. Hendler. Lower bounds for resricted-use objects. In *The 24th ACM Symposium on Parallelism in Algorithms and Architectures (SPAA)*, 2012. to appear.

[6] J. Aspnes and M. Herlihy. Wait-free data structures in the asynchronous PRAM model. In *Second Annual ACM Symposium on Parallel Algorithms and Architectures*, pages 340–349, July 1990.

[7] H. Attiya and A. Fouren. Adaptive and efficient algorithms for lattice agreement and renaming. *SIAM J. Comput.*, 31(2):642–664, 2001.

[8] H. Attiya and O. Rachman. Atomic snapshots in $O(n \log n)$ operations. *SIAM J. Comput.*, 27(2):319–340, 1998.

[9] M. A. Bender and S. Gilbert. Mutual exclusion with $O(\log^2 \log n)$ amortized work. In *IEEE 52nd Annual Symposium on Foundations of Computer Science, (FOCS)*, pages 728–737, 2011.

[10] F. E. Fich. How hard is it to take a snapshot? In *Proceedings of 31st Annual Conference on Current Trends in Theory and Practice of Informatics*, volume 3381, pages 27–35. LNCS, 2005.

[11] M. P. Herlihy and J. M. Wing. Linearizability: a

correctness condition for concurrent objects. *ACM Transactions on Programming Languages and Systems*, 12(3):463–492, July 1990.

[12] M. Inoue and W. Chen. Linear-time snapshot using multi-writer multi-reader registers. In *WDAG '94: Proceedings of the 8th International Workshop on Distributed Algorithms*, pages 130–140, London, UK, 1994. Springer-Verlag.

[13] P. Jayanti. *f*-arrays: implementation and applications. In *Proceedings of the twenty-first annual symposium on Principles of distributed computing*, PODC '02, pages 270–279, New York, NY, USA, 2002. ACM.

[14] P. Jayanti. An optimal multi-writer snapshot algorithm. In *Proceedings of the 37th Annual ACM Symposium on Theory of Computing (STOC)*, pages 723–732, 2005.

[15] P. Jayanti, K. Tan, and S. Toueg. Time and space lower bounds for nonblocking implementations. *SIAM J. Comput.*, 30(2):438–456, 2000.

[16] L. Kirousis, P. Spirakis, and P. Tsigas. Reading many variables in one atomic operation: Solutions with linear or sublinear complexity. *IEEE Trans. on Parallel and Distributed Systems*, 5(7):688–696, July 1994.

[17] L. Lamport. A new solution of Dijkstra's concurrent programming problem. *Commun. ACM*, 17(8):453–455, Aug. 1974.

[18] Y. Riany, N. Shavit, and D. Touitou. Towards a practical snapshot algorithm. *Theor. Comput. Sci.*, 269(1-2):163–201, 2001.

Strongly Linearizable Implementations: Possibilities and Impossibilities

Maryam Helmi[*]
Dept. of Computer Science
University of Calgary
Calgary, AB T2N 1N4, Canada
mhelmikh@ucalgary.ca

Lisa Higham[*]
Dept. of Computer Science
University of Calgary
Calgary, AB T2N 1N4, Canada
higham@ucalgary.ca

Philipp Woelfel[*]
Dept. of Computer Science
University of Calgary
Calgary, AB T2N 1N4, Canada
woelfel@ucalgary.ca

ABSTRACT

Herlihy and Wing [11] established that the set of possible outcomes of a shared memory distributed algorithm remains unchanged when atomic objects are replaced by their linearizable implementations. Since then, linearizability has been the correctness condition of choice for distributed algorithm designers. In 2011, however, Golab, Higham and Woelfel [9] showed that, if an algorithm employs randomization, then the probability distribution over the set of possible outcomes can differ between the atomic and implemented versions. They also proved that a stronger condition, called strong linearizability, is necessary and sufficient to guarantee the same probability distributions for these two cases when the randomized algorithm is under the control of an adaptive adversary. Therefore, we are motivated to construct strongly linearizable implementations of common distributed objects whenever possible. In this paper we prove

- for several objects including multi-writer registers, max-registers, snapshots, and counters there is no strongly linearizable, non-blocking implementation from multi-reader/single-writer atomic registers, even though each of these objects has a linearizable implementation meeting the stronger wait-free progress requirement.

- There is a universal strongly linearizable obstruction-free implementation of any object from multi-reader/single-writer atomic registers.

- There is a strongly linearizable wait-free implementation of bounded max-registers from multi-reader/multi-writer atomic registers.

[*]Supported by Discovery Grants from the Natural Sciences and Research Council of Canada (NSERC)

Categories and Subject Descriptors

F.2.2 [**Analysis of Algorithms and Problem Complexity**]: Nonnumerical Algorithms and Problems; D.1.3 [**Programming Techniques**]: Concurrent Programming—*Distributed programming*

Keywords

strong linearizability, linearizability, randomization, wait-free, obstruction-free, non-blocking

1. INTRODUCTION

Abstraction is an essential technique for both designing algorithms and proving they are correct. In the domain of distributed algorithms, it is standard to first design a system using some appropriately powerful shared objects, while assuming that each operation on these objects happens in one atomic step. That is, no other changes happen to the system between the beginning and the end of the operation. Once this abstract version of the algorithm is proved correct, we need to ensure, as a second step, that the algorithm remains correct when the operations on the abstract shared objects are replaced by method calls that implement the operations. These two steps are typically iterated so that eventually a high level specification is implemented on existing hardware.

Ever since Herlihy and Wing [11] defined *linearizability* and established its properties, it has been the correctness condition of choice for the implementation of shared objects. Linearizability is an extremely useful correctness condition because it guarantees that for any distributed algorithm, the set of outcomes of the algorithm when executed using atomic objects does not change when any of the atomic objects are replaced by their linearizable implementations. This means that the correctness of any deterministic distributed algorithm using linearizable implementations of objects can be inferred from its correctness using the corresponding atomic objects. That is, we get the second step in the design process for free, if we write deterministic algorithms and use linearizable implementations.

More and more however, algorithms researchers are discovering that randomization can be used effectively in distributed algorithms to circumvent deterministic impossibilities, to increase efficiency, and to simplify complicated code [2, 3, 5, 10]. Unfortunately, however, we lose the free second step in algorithm design when algorithms are randomized. Golab, Higham and Woelfel [9] showed that the probability distribution over the set of outcomes can change (dramatically) when atomic objects in randomized algorithms are replaced by (deterministic) linearizable implementations. Their paper contains several examples that illustrate how the adversary gains additional power to control the distribution of outcomes. One reason for the gain in power arises because an operation can be "stretched-out" to the interval of the method call. Thus, the adversary can begin a method call and then schedule other processes including their random choices. It can then choose how to schedule the remainder of the method call, and consequently influence where it will be linearized, depending on the outcome of these random choices. The paper includes examples for several adversary models. The weakest considered is an *oblivious adversary*, which must determine the entire sequence of process steps before the algorithm begins. The strongest is an *adaptive adversary*, which can choose the next process based on the entire history of the execution so far. There are examples that show that even the oblivious adversary, when controlling an algorithm with linearizable implemented objects, has more power to influence the outcome than the adaptive adversary has when controlling the same algorithm with atomic objects.

In the same paper, Golab, Higham and Woelfel derive a new correctness condition called *strong linearizability* that is stronger than linearizability. They prove that strong linearizability is sufficient to ensure that the probability distribution over the outcomes of a randomized algorithm under the control of an adaptive adversary does not change when atomic objects are replaced by implemented ones. They also show that strong linearizability is necessary. That is, to ensure that an atomic object can be replaced by its implementation in any algorithm that uses the object, without changing the probability distribution over the algorithm's outcomes, it is necessary that the implementation be strongly linearizable. We need to be certain of the correctness of our randomized implementations when they are designed hierarchically — by (possibly repeatedly) replacing atomic objects with implemented ones. We are, therefore, motivated to find strongly linearizable implementations of useful objects, and to determine under what conditions they do not exit. This paper begins to address this question.

Our Contributions

1. We define a class of objects, called *nontrivial* objects, that includes snapshots, max-registers, counters, and multi-reader/multi-writer registers. Each of these objects supports an operation that we call the *inspect* operation, which returns some information about the state of the object. We prove that no object in this class has a strongly linearizable non-blocking implementation from multi-reader/single-writer atomic registers. This impossibility holds even if restricted to just 3 processes executing only one operation each. This is in sharp contrast to linearizability. There are linearizable wait-free implementations of snapshots, max-registers, counters and multi-reader/multi-writer registers from multi-reader/single-writer registers and these implementations work for any number of processes each executing any sequence of operations on the object.

2. There is a strongly linearizable obstruction-free universal construction of any object from multi-reader/single-writer registers.

3. There is a strongly linearizable wait-free implementation of bounded max-registers from multi-reader/multi-

writer registers. This means that to resolve the current impasse of whether or not objects such as max-registers, counters and snapshots have strongly linearizable implementations for multi-reader/multi-writer registers will likely require investigating unbounded executions.

Section 2 contains our model and the required definitions including that of strong linearizability. The remaining sections address the three items above.

2. PRELIMINARIES

Our model of computation is a system of asynchronous processes communicating through shared objects. We are concerned with the problem of implementing the abstraction of objects that are more complex than shared than registers, on a system whose only real shared objects are registers.

A *(shared) object* can be defined operationally by specifying the states of the object and the next states and return values that can arise when a process applies an operation invocation to the current state of the object. More formally, an operational definition of an object O is a 5-tuple (Q, s, I, R, Δ) where Q is the set of *states* of the object; $s \in Q$ is the designated *initial state*; I is the set of the *operation invocations* that can be applied to the object; R is the set of the *operation responses* that can be produced by the object; $\Delta \subseteq (Q \times I) \times (Q \times R)$ is the *transition relation*. An operation invocation $o \in I$ is a 3-tuple containing the name of an operation, the name of the invoking process, and a value for each input parameter; an operation response is a sequence of values, one for each output parameter, which is returned to a process. The transition relation Δ specifies the set of pairs, each consisting of a state and an operation response, that can arise when a given operation invocation is applied to a given state. This definition is similar to that given by Attiya, Guerraoui, Hendler and Kuznetsov [7].

An *operation* consists of an operation invocation together with an operation response. For operation op, denote its invocation by $\text{inv}(op)$ and its response by $\text{rsp}(op)$. Given an operational definition (Q, s, I, R, Δ) of object O, there is a corresponding set of sequences of operations $\mathcal{S}$ defined by: $(op_1, op_2, \ldots) \in \mathcal{S}$ if and only if there is a sequence of states $(s_1, s_2, \ldots)$ satisfying $(s_i, \text{inv}(o_i)), (s_{i+1}, \text{rsp}(op_i)) \in \Delta$ for each $i \in \{1, 2, \ldots\}$ and $s_1 = s$. Thus we see that, equivalently, a shared object can be defined by a set of sequences of operations, which we call the *sequential specification* of the object. Whether it is most natural to define an object operationally or by giving its sequential specification typically depends on the object and the properties that are being explored. We now define the most prominent objects used in this paper. We use $O.\text{opName}_p(\Upsilon)$ to denote the operation invocation $(\text{opName}, p, \Upsilon)$ on an object O, and we omit the process name p if it is arbitrary.

A *register* R, initialized to a value χ, supports the operations $R.\text{read}()$, which returns a value, and $R.\text{write}(\cdot)$, where $R.\text{write}(x)$ changes the value of R to x. We are concerned with two variants of registers. If any process can apply $R.\text{read}()$ and $R.\text{write}(\cdot)$ to register R, then R is a *multi-reader/multi-writer register*, which has the sequential specification: the set of all sequences of the operations $R.\text{read}()$ and $R.\text{write}(\cdot)$ such that each $R.\text{read}()$ returns the value written by the most recent preceding $R.\text{write}(\cdot)$, or χ if no such $R.\text{write}(\cdot)$ exists. If any process can apply $R.\text{read}()$ but only one process, say p, can apply $R.\text{write}(\cdot)$ to register R, then R is a *multi-*

reader/single-writer register, with the sequential specification: the set of all sequences of the operations $R.\texttt{read}()$ and $R.\texttt{write}_p(\cdot)$ such that each $R.\texttt{read}()$ returns the value written by the most recent preceding $R.\texttt{write}_p(\cdot)$, or χ if no such $R.\texttt{write}_p(\cdot)$ exists. Since all the shared registers considered in this paper allow multiple readers, henceforth we refer to a multi-reader/multi-writer register (respectively, a multi-reader/single-writer register) as a *multi-writer* register (respectively, a *single-writer* register).

A *max-register* R is initialized to 0 and supports the operations $R.\texttt{maxRead}()$ which returns a value, and $R.\texttt{maxWrite}(x)$, where x can be any natural number. The sequential specification of max-register R is the set of all sequences of the operations $R.\texttt{maxRead}()$ and $R.\texttt{maxWrite}(\cdot)$, such that each $R.\texttt{maxRead}()$ operation returns the largest value written by any preceding $R.\texttt{maxWrite}(\cdot)$ operation, or 0 if no such $R.\texttt{maxWrite}(\cdot)$ exists. A max-register is *bounded* with bound B if it can only hold integers in $\{0, 1, \ldots, B\}$ [4].

A *counter object* C, is initialized to 0, and supports the operations $C.\texttt{read}()$, which returns the current value of C and does not change the state of C, and $C.\texttt{increment}()$ which adds 1 to the current value of C. Thus, the sequential specification of C is the set of all sequences of $C.\texttt{read}()$ and $C.\texttt{increment}()$ operations such that each $C.\texttt{read}()$ operation returns the number of preceding $C.\texttt{increment}()$ operations.

A *snapshot object with m segments* [1] supports the two operations $\texttt{scan}()$ and $\texttt{update}(\cdot, \cdot)$ for each process. Operation $\texttt{scan}()$ by process i returns an m element vector, and $\texttt{update}(i, \nu)$ changes the value of the ith segment to ν. In any sequence of $\texttt{scan}()$ and $\texttt{update}(\cdot, \cdot)$ operations, each $\texttt{scan}()$ operation returns the vector $(\nu_1, \ldots, \nu_m)$ where, for each $j \in \{1, \ldots, m\}$, the most recent preceding $\texttt{update}(j, \cdot)$ operation is $\texttt{update}(j, \nu_j)$ (or ν_j is the initial value of segment j, if there is no preceding $\texttt{update}(j, \cdot)$).

An object can be *atomic* or *implemented*. If it is atomic, then each operation on the object completes in one step and the outcome of any sequence of operations on the object agrees with its sequential specification. An object is implemented by implementing each operation type. This is done by supplying a method for each operation type. A process p executes an operation o by executing the steps of the method beginning with an invocation step and ending with a response step. In this case, other processes can be taking their own steps during the interval that p is executing the method for o and these steps by the processes interleave.

This interleaving of steps that results as processes execute is called a *history*. Consider an object O and the histories that can arise as processes execute operations on O. If O is atomic, each of these histories is in the sequential specification of O. Such histories are called *sequential* histories. An *implemented history* on O arises when the operations on O are implemented. The *interpretation* of an implemented history H, denoted $\Gamma(H)$, is formed by removing from H all the steps of every method call except the invocation and response steps.

Let H be an implemented history arising from method calls for operations on O. Operation o *completes* in H if H contains both the invocation and response of o. $\text{Cmp}(H)$ denotes the set of operations that complete in H. Operation o is *pending* in H if H contains the invocation but not the response of o. For implemented operations o_1 and o_2, o_1 *happens-before* o_2 in H, denoted $o_1 \prec o_2$, if the response

of o_1 precedes the invocation of o_2 in H. H is *linearizable* if, for some subset S of the pending operations in H, there is a permutation of $\text{Cmp}(H) \cup S$ that is in the sequential specification of O and preserves $\prec$. An implementation of O is linearizable if every history that can arise from the implementation is linearizable.

Let $\text{close}(\mathcal{H})$ denote the prefix-closure of a set of histories $\mathcal{H}$. That is, $G \in \text{close}(\mathcal{H})$ if and only if there is a sequence, S, of invocation and response steps such that $G \circ S \in \mathcal{H}$. (The operator $\circ$ denotes concatenation.) A function f that maps a set $\mathcal{H}$ of histories to a set $\mathcal{H}'$ of histories, is *prefix preserving*, if for any two histories $G, H \in \mathcal{H}$, where G is a prefix of H, $f(G)$ is a prefix of $f(H)$.

DEFINITION 2.1. *[9] A set of histories $\mathcal{H}$ is strongly linearizable if there exists a function f mapping histories in $\text{close}(\mathcal{H})$ to sequential histories, such that*

(L) for any $H \in \text{close}(\mathcal{H})$, $f(H)$ is a linearization of the interpreted history $\Gamma(H)$, and

(P) f is prefix-preserving.

A function satisfying properties (L) and (P) is called a strong linearization function *for $\mathcal{H}$.*

Let $\mathcal{H}$ be the set of all histories that can arise as processes execute the method calls of an implementation of an object O. This implementation of O is *strongly linearizable* if $\mathcal{H}$ is strongly linearizable. As the name suggests, strong linearizability, is strictly stronger than linearizability. To determine that our implementation is linearizable, it suffices to show a linearization of $\Gamma(H)$ for each $H \in \mathcal{H}$. In contrast, strong linearizability is defined for the whole set $\mathcal{H}$: the linearizations of all the possible histories must together satisfy the prefix property P. Furthermore, the prefix property is defined on the implemented histories, not just their interpretations. It must be satisfied at all points within the method calls, and not just at invocation and response steps.

Intuitively, strong linearizability requires that the linearization points of method calls are determined as the history is created. As soon as a step is taken, whether or not a particular method is linearized at the step is uniquely determined by the history up to this step; it cannot be influenced by future steps.

A *configuration* C of a system with n processes an m registers is a tuple $(s_1, \ldots, s_n, v_1, \ldots, v_m)$, which denotes that process p_i, $1 \leq i \leq n$, is in state s_i, and register r_j, $1 \leq j \leq m$, has value v_j. The initial configuration is denoted C_0.

A *schedule* σ is a (possibly infinite) sequence of process indices. An *execution* $(C; \sigma)$ is a sequence of steps beginning in configuration C and moving through successive configurations one at a time. At each step, the next process p indicated in the schedule σ, takes the next step in its deterministic program. If σ is a finite schedule, the final configuration of the execution $(C; \sigma)$ is denoted $\sigma(C)$. If σ is a sequence of length one, say $\sigma = (p)$, we simplify notation by writing $(C; p)$ and $p(C)$ instead of $(C; (p))$ and $(p)(C)$ respectively.

A configuration, C, is *reachable* if there exists a finite schedule, σ, such that $\sigma(C_0) = C$. If σ and π are finite schedules then $\sigma\pi$ denotes the concatenation of σ and π. Let P be a set of processes, and σ a schedule. We say σ is *P-only* if only indices of processes in P appear in σ.

Two configurations $C_1 = (s_1, \ldots, s_n, r_1, \ldots, r_m)$ and $C_2 = (s'_1, \ldots, s'_n, r'_1, \ldots, r'_m)$ are *indistinguishable* to a process p_i, denoted $C_1 \overset{p_i}{\sim} C_2$, if $s_i = s_i'$ and $r_j = r_j'$ for $1 \leq j \leq m$. If S is a set of processes, and for every process $p \in S$, $C_1 \overset{p}{\sim} C_2$ then we write $C_1 \overset{S}{\sim} C_2$. If $C_1 \overset{S}{\sim} C_2$, then for any S-only schedule σ, $\sigma(C_1)$ and $\sigma(C_2)$ are indistinguishable to every process in S.

We consider three different progress conditions. An operation o by a process p is *pending* in a configuration C if the one step execution $(C; p)$ is between the invocation and the response of the method call of o. An implementation is *obstruction-free* [12] if, for every reachable configuration C, and for every pending operation o by a process p in C, there is a finite p-only schedule σ such that o is not pending in $\sigma(C)$. An implementation is *wait-free* [8] if, starting from any reachable configuration, any process with a pending operation will complete the method of that operation in a finite number of its own steps (regardless of the steps taken by other processes). An implementation is *non-blocking* if, for any reachable configuration, C, and every infinite schedule σ, if there is a pending operation in C, then some operation completes during the execution $(C; \sigma)$.

3. IMPOSSIBILITIES

In this section, we first define a very general and natural class of objects. We then prove that no object in this class has a strongly linearizable non-blocking implementation from single-writer registers. In fact we show that no such implementation exists even when the use of the object is restricted to at most one operation by each of only 3 processes.

3.1 Nontrivial objects

Let O be an object that supports three (not necessarily distinct) operations, say $O.\text{inspect}()$, $O.\text{change1}()$, and $O.\text{change2}()$. Operation $O.\text{inspect}()$ returns a value from some domain D_O, and operations $O.\text{change1}()$, and $O.\text{change2}()$ may or may not return values.

Let $\mathcal{S}_O$ be the subset of all histories in the sequential specification of O that contains exactly the three operations $O.\text{inspect}_v()$, $O.\text{change1}_{u_1}()$, and $O.\text{change2}_{u_2}()$. (Notice that there are three different processes; each one is designated to execute one of these three operations.) Then $\mathcal{S}_O$ is the set of histories that are generated by Program Basic depicted in Figure 1, when each process completes its execution. For each history $H \in \mathcal{S}_O$, let $\text{insp}(H) \in D_O$ be the value returned by $O.\text{inspect}_v()$. We say object O is *nontrivial* if D contains three distinct values, χ, c, and d, such that

$$
\begin{aligned}
v : &\quad O.\text{inspect}() \\
u_1 : &\quad O.\text{change1}() \\
u_2 : &\quad O.\text{change2}()
\end{aligned}
$$

Figure 1: Program Basic

(a) for every history $H \in \mathcal{S}_O$, $\text{insp}(H) = \chi$ if and only if $O.\text{inspect}_v()$ is the first operation in H, and

(b) $\{\chi, c, d\} \subseteq \{\text{insp}(H) | H \in \mathcal{S}_O\}$.

Informally speaking, an object O is nontrivial if it has the property that at least two process can change O in such a way that later inspections of O can reveal those changes. For example, multi-writer registers, max-registers, counters, and snapshot objects are nontrivial, as discussed below.

3.1.1 Multi-writer registers

Let M be a multi-writer register. Set $O.\text{inspect}()$ to $M.\text{read}()$, $O.\text{change1}()$ to $M.\text{write}(1)$ and $O.\text{change2}()$ to $M.\text{write}(2)$ in the definition of a nontrivial object. Then $M.\text{read}()$ returns the initial value $\chi = 0$ in exactly those histories in $\mathcal{S}_M$ that begin with $M.\text{read}()$. Also, $M.\text{read}()$ returns $c = 1$ in the history

$$(M.\text{write}_{u_1}(1), \ M.\text{read}_v(), \ M.\text{write}_{u_2}(2)),$$

and $M.\text{read}()$ returns $d = 2$ in the history

$$(M.\text{write}_{u_2}(2), \ M.\text{read}_v(), \ M.\text{write}_{u_1}(1)).$$

3.1.2 Max-Registers

Let R be a max-register. Set $O.\text{inspect}()$ to $R.\text{maxRead}()$, $O.\text{change1}()$ to $R.\text{maxWrite}(1)$ and $O.\text{change2}()$ to $R.\text{maxWrite}(2)$ in the definition of a nontrivial object. Then $R.\text{maxRead}()$ returns the initial value $\chi = 0$ exactly in those histories in $\mathcal{S}_R$ that begin with $R.\text{maxRead}()$. Just as in the case of the multi-writer register, $R.\text{maxRead}()$ returns $c = 1$ in

$$(R.\text{maxWrite}_{u_1}(1), \ R.\text{maxRead}_v(), \ R.\text{maxWrite}_{u_2}(2)),$$

and $R.\text{maxRead}()$ returns $d = 2$ in

$$(R.\text{maxWrite}_{u_2}(2), \ R.\text{read}_v(), \ R.\text{write}_{u_1}(1)).$$

3.1.3 Counters

Let C be a counter object. Set $O.\text{inspect}()$ to $C.\text{read}()$ and both $O.\text{change1}()$ and $O.\text{change2}()$ to $C.\text{increment}()$ in the definition of a nontrivial object. Then $C.\text{read}()$ returns the initial value $\chi = 0$ exactly in those histories in $\mathcal{S}_C$ that begin with $C.\text{read}()$. Also, $C.\text{read}()$ returns $c = 1$ in

$$(C.\text{increment}_{u_1}(), \ C.\text{read}_v(), \ C.\text{increment}_{u_2}()),$$

and $C.\text{read}()$ returns $d = 2$ in

$$(C.\text{increment}_{u_1}(), \ C.\text{increment}_{u_2}(), \ C.\text{read}_v()).$$

3.1.4 Snapshots

Let S be a snapshot object with two segments (one for u_1 and one for u_2) that store integers and is initialized to $\chi = (0,0)$. Set $O.\text{inspect}()$ to $S.\text{scan}()$, $O.\text{change1}$ to $S.\text{update}(1,1)$ and $O.\text{change2}$ to $S.\text{update}(2,2)$ in the definition of a nontrivial object. Then $S.\text{scan}()$ returns $\chi = (0,0)$ exactly in those histories in $\mathcal{S}_S$ that begin with $S.\text{scan}()$. Also, $S.\text{scan}()$ returns $c = (1,0)$ in

$$(S.\text{update}_{u_1}(1,1), \ S.\text{scan}_v(), \ S.\text{update}_{u_2}(2,2)),$$

and $S.\text{scan}()$ returns $d = (0,2)$ in

$$(S.\text{update}_{u_2}(2,2), \ S.\text{scan}_v(), \ S.\text{update}_{u_1}(1,1)),$$

3.1.5 Single-updater objects are not nontrivial

Suppose only one process can change the value of O, meaning that an $O.\text{inspect}()$ operation by v is not affected by a previous operation of one of the other two processes. W.l.o.g. suppose operation $O.\text{change1}_{u_1}()$ does not change the object's value. In this case, method $O.\text{inspect}()$ returns the same value in the two sequences

$$(O.\text{inspect}_v(), \ O.\text{change1}_{u_1}(), \ O.\text{change2}_{u_2}())$$

and

$$(O.\texttt{change1}_{u_1}(), \; O.\texttt{inspect}_v(), \; O.\texttt{change2}_{u_2}()).$$

Therefore condition (a) of the definition of nontrivial objects can only be satisfied if one of these histories is not in $\mathcal{S}_O$. But if the sequential specification of O excludes one of the permutations over $\{O.\texttt{inspect}_v(), O.\texttt{change1}_{u_1}(), O.\texttt{change2}_{u_2}()\}$, then either O cannot be implemented at all from registers or $\mathcal{S}_O = \emptyset$. In the latter case condition (b) cannot be satisfied. So, only objects that can be updated by more than one process can satisfy the definition of a nontrivial object. An example of an object that is not nontrivial is a single-writer register. In contrast, even when constrained so that each component can be updated by only one process, a snapshot object remains nontrivial because the entire object can be changed by more than one process.

3.2 Impossibilities for nontrivial objects

The goal of this subsection is to establish that even for very restricted use, and even for progress requirements weaker than wait-freedom, there is no strongly linearizable implementation of any nontrivial object. Specifically, after a short sequence of lemmas, we will have proved the following theorem.

THEOREM 3.1. *No nontrivial object has an implementation from single-writer registers that satisfies:*

- *the implementation of Program Basic is non-blocking;*

- *the set of all histories that arise from the implemented Program Basic is strongly linearizable.*

For the following definitions and lemmas, configurations and executions refer to those that can arise when the atomic operations inspect(), change1(), and change2() in Program Basic are implemented by replacing them with linearizable method calls that access only single-writer registers. We also assume that Program Basic remains non-blocking, if the implemented method calls are used. (No assumptions are made about the correctness or progress of these method calls if they are used in some other program.) We eventually conclude that any such implementation is not strongly linearizable.

DEFINITION 3.2.

(a) *The* valence *of a configuration C, denoted $\text{val}(C)$, is the set of all values ν such that one of the following is true:*

- *in some (and thus all) of the executions leading to configuration C, process v's operation inspect() returns ν, or*

- *there exists a schedule σ such that v's operation inspect() returns ν during execution $(C; \sigma)$.*

(b) *A process is* active *if it has not yet terminated.*

(c) *Valence $\text{val}(C)$ is* super-initial *if $\chi \in \text{val}(C)$ and $\{c, d\} \cap \text{val}(C) \neq \emptyset$.*

If a process p has terminated in configuration C, then we assume the execution $(C; p)$ is a no-op. The following observation is straight-forward.

OBSERVATION 3.3. *For any configuration C and for any process $p \in \{v, u_1, u_2\}$:*

- $\text{val}(p(C)) \subseteq \text{val}(C)$, *and*

- $\text{val}(v(C)) \cup \text{val}(u_1(C)) \cup \text{val}(u_2(C)) = \text{val}(C)$.

LEMMA 3.4. *Let $p, q \in \{v, u_1, u_2\}$ and let C be a configuration. If $p\alpha$ and $q\beta$ are two schedules over $\{v, u_1, u_2\}$ such that $p\alpha(C) \overset{v}{\sim} q\beta(C)$ then $\text{val}(p(C)) \cap \text{val}(q(C)) \neq \emptyset$.*

PROOF. Let σ be the shortest v-only schedule such that v's method call for inspect() returns in execution $(p\alpha(C); \sigma)$. Since Program Basic is non-blocking, there must be such a v-only schedule. Then $|\text{val}(p\alpha\sigma(C))| = 1$; so let $\{b\} = \text{val}(p\alpha\sigma(C))$. Since $p\alpha(C) \overset{v}{\sim} q\beta(C)$, $\text{val}(q\beta\sigma(C)) = \{b\}$. Thus, by Observation 3.3, b is an element of both $\text{val}(p(C))$ and $\text{val}(q(C))$. $\square$

LEMMA 3.5. *Let C be a configuration where each of v, u_1 and u_2 are active and where $\text{val}(C)$ is super-initial. Suppose the valences in $\{\text{val}(v(C)), \text{val}(u_1(C)), \text{val}(u_2(C))\}$ can be renamed so that $\{\text{val}(v(C)), \text{val}(u_1(C)), \text{val}(u_2(C))\} = \{V_1, V_2, V_3\}$ and the renaming satisfies $V_1 \cap V_2 \neq \emptyset$ and $V_3 \cap V_2 \neq \emptyset$. Then, for some $i \in \{1, 2, 3\}$, V_i is super-initial.*

PROOF. Since $\text{val}(C)$ is super-initial, by Observation 3.3, there are i and j in $\{1, 2, 3\}$ such that V_i contains χ, and V_j contains $b \in \{c, d\}$. If V_2 is super-initial, the lemma holds. So suppose, V_2 is not super-initial. Then either $V_2 = \{\chi\}$ or $\chi \notin V_2$. If $V_2 = \{\chi\}$ then, because $V_2 \cap V_1 \neq \emptyset$ and $V_2 \cap V_3 \neq \emptyset$ both V_1 and V_3 contain χ and one of them must also contain b. Similarly, if $\chi \notin V_2$, then, because $V_2 \cap V_1 \neq \emptyset$ and $V_2 \cap V_3 \neq \emptyset$ each of V_1 and V_3 contain a value not equal to χ and one of them must also contain χ. So in either case at least one of V_1 and V_3 is a set that contains χ and b; hence, that set is super-initial. $\square$

LEMMA 3.6. *Let C be a configuration where each of v, u_1 and u_2 are active and where $\text{val}(C)$ is super-initial. Then there is a process $p \in \{v, u_1, u_2\}$ such that $\text{val}(p(C))$ is super-initial.*

PROOF. For each $p \in \{v, u_1, u_2\}$, denote by R_p, the single-writer register accessed in the one-step execution $(C; p)$. We consider two cases.

Case 1: $|\{R_v, R_{u_1}, R_{u_2}\}| \geq 2$.

In this case there is a process $p \in \{v, u_1, u_2\}$ that accesses a register that is distinct from the register accessed by each of the other two processes, say q and s, in $\{v, u_1, u_2\}$. Thus the two-step executions $(C; pq)$ and $(C; qp)$ commute, and hence configurations $pq(C)$ and $qp(C)$ are indistinguishable to all three processes. Thus, $pq(C) \overset{v}{\sim} qp(C)$, so by Lemma 3.4, $\text{val}(p(C)) \cap \text{val}(q(C)) \neq \emptyset$. Similarly, configurations $ps(C)$ and $sp(C)$ are indistinguishable to all three processes. So $\text{val}(p(C)) \cap \text{val}(s(C)) \neq \emptyset$. Hence by Lemma 3.5, at least one of $\text{val}(v(C), \text{val}(u_1(C)))$, $\text{val}(u_2(C))$ is super-initial.

Case 2: $|\{R_v, R_{u_1}, R_{u_2}\}| = 1$.

In this case, let R denote the register that is accessed in each one-step execution $(C; v)$, $(C; u_1)$, and $(C; u_2)$. Because register R is single-writer, either all these accesses are reads or there is exactly one write and two reads.

Case 2a: Each of these one-step executions is a read. Then $v(C) \overset{v}{\sim} u_1v(C)$, and also $v(C) \overset{v}{\sim} u_2v(C)$. So by Lemma 3.4, $\text{val}(v(C)) \cap \text{val}(u_1(C)) \neq \emptyset$ and $\text{val}(v(C)) \cap \text{val}(u_2(C)) \neq \emptyset$. Thus, by Lemma 3.5, at least one valence in $\{\text{val}(v(C)), \text{val}(u_1(C)), \text{val}(u_2(C))\}$ is super-initial.

Case 2b: There is exactly one write and two reads in the three executions $(C; v)$, $(C; u_1)$, and $(C; u_2)$. If the write to R is by v, then $v(C) \overset{v}{\sim} u_1v(C)$, and also $v(C) \overset{v}{\sim} u_2v(C)$. So by Lemma 3.4, $\text{val}(v(C)) \cap \text{val}(u_1(C)) \neq \emptyset$ and $\text{val}(v(C)) \cap \text{val}(u_2(C)) \neq \emptyset$. Hence, by Lemma 3.5 at least one of $\text{val}(v(C))$, $\text{val}(u_1(C))$, $\text{val}(u_2(C))$ is super-initial. Now suppose the write to R is by one of u_1 or u_2, and thus the other two processes read register R. Without loss of generality, suppose $(C; u_1)$ is a read step, and $(C; u_2)$ is a write step, and $(C; v)$ is a read step, each to register R. Then $vu_1(C) \overset{v}{\sim} u_1v(C)$ implying, by Lemma 3.4, that $\text{val}(v(C)) \cap \text{val}(u_1(C)) \neq \emptyset$. Furthermore, $u_1u_2(C) \overset{v}{\sim} u_2(C)$ implying $\text{val}(u_1(C)) \cap \text{val}(u_2(C)) \neq \emptyset$. Thus, by Lemma 3.5, at least one of $\text{val}(v(C))$, $\text{val}(u_1(C))$, $\text{val}(u_2(C))$ is super-initial. $\square$

We are now ready to prove the main result claimed at the beginning of this section.

PROOF OF THEOREM 3.1. Consider any execution of Program Basic where the atomic operations `inspect()`, `change1()`, and `change2()` are replaced with linearizable method calls that access only multi-reader/single-writer registers.

Clearly, in the initial configuration, C_0, all processes are active and $\text{val}(C_0)$ is super-initial. Starting with C_0, by Lemma 3.6, as long as all processes v, u_1 and u_2 are active, we can inductively construct C_i from C_{i-1}, such that $\text{val}(C_i)$ is super-initial. Since our implementation is non-blocking, eventually one process must terminate. Let C_k be the first configuration in this construction such that some process has terminated. Observe that $\text{val}(C_k)$ is super-initial so $|\text{val}(C_k)| \geq 2$.

It cannot be v that has already terminated in configuration C_k because, otherwise, $|\text{val}(C_k)| = 1$. Hence, there exists $i^* \in \{1, 2\}$ such that u_{i^*} has terminated. Since $\text{val}(C_k)$ is super-initial, there is some schedule α such that in execution $(C_k; \alpha)$, v returns χ, and there is some schedule β such that in execution $(C_k; \beta)$ v returns $b \in \{c, d\}$.

Let G denote the history of the constructed execution from C_0 up to C_k; Let H_1 denote the history of the constructed execution starting at C_0 continuing to C_k and then to $\alpha(C_k)$. Let H_2 denote the history of the constructed execution starting at C_0 continuing to C_k and then to $\beta(C_k)$. Clearly, G is a prefix of both H_1 and H_2.

For any strong linearization function f:

- In $f(H_1)$, $\text{inspect}_v()$ occurs before both $\text{change1}_{u_1}()$ and $\text{change2}_{u_2}()$ because otherwise the $\text{inspect}()$ operation could not return the initial value χ.

- In $f(H_2)$ $\text{inspect}_v()$ occurs after at least one of $\text{change1}_{u_1}()$ or $\text{change2}_{u_2}()$ because otherwise the $\text{inspect}()$ operation would be first and must return the initial value χ.

- $f(G)$ must include one of the operations $\text{change1}_{u_1}()$ or $\text{change2}_{u_2}()$ since one of these operations completes in G.

We conclude that $f(G)$ cannot be a prefix of both $f(H_1)$ and of $f(H_2)$. Hence, the set of all histories that arise from Program Basic cannot be strongly linearizable. $\square$

COROLLARY 3.7. *There is no strongly linearizable non-blocking implementation from single-writer registers of multi-writer registers, max-registers, counters, or snapshot objects. These impossibilities hold even for 3 process each of which accesses the object at most once.*

An alternative proof of the impossibility in Corollary 3.7 in the case of snapshots can be derived by a reduction. There is a strongly linearizable implementation of a max-register shared by n processes from a snapshot object with n segments as follows. Process p_j executes $\text{maxWrite}(x)$ by applying $\text{update}(j, x)$. Process p_j executes $\text{maxRead}()$ by applying $\text{scan}()$ and returning the maximum value of the scan. Since the composition of strong linearizability objects is strongly linearizable, the impossibility of constructing a strongly linearizable snapshot object from single-writers registers follows from the impossibility of constructing a max-register from single-writer registers.

Theorem 3.1 and Corollary 3.7 are in sharp contrast to the possibility of Section 4, which shows that removing the non-blocking requirement circumvents the impossibilities for any collection of processes executing any number of method calls.

4. POSSIBILITIES

4.1 Obstruction-Free Universal Construction

We now present an obstruction-free strongly linearizable implementation of any object that has a sequential specification. The algorithm uses only multi-reader/single-writer registers. The algorithm itself is not new; we simply combine a derandomized version of Aspnes and Herlihy's randomized consensus protocol [6] with a basic obstruction-free universal construction from consensus objects. We then observe that the result is in fact strongly linearizable. Since universal constructions are standard and the focus of this paper is on the (non-)existence of strongly linearizable implementations, we do not attempt to optimize time- or space-efficiency.

A *consensus* object over domain D is an object that provides a single operation, $\text{decide}(x)$, that returns some value y, where x and y are values from the set D. If a process calls $\text{decide}(x)$ and that call returns y, then we say the process *proposes* x and *decides* y. The safety condition of consensus is that processes have to agree on one of the proposed values. More formally, the sequential specification of a consensus object C contains every sequence S of atomic $C.\text{decide}(\cdot)$ operations that satisfies

agreement, i.e., all operations return the same value $y^* \in D$; and

validity, i.e., y^* is the argument of at least one of the $\text{decide}(\cdot)$ operations.

Sometimes it is assumed that a process can call $C.\text{decide}(\cdot)$ only once. But if a process memorizes the return value of its first $C.\text{decide}(\cdot)$ call and uses that same return value for subsequent $C.\text{decide}(\cdot)$ operations, then agreement and validity is trivially preserved. Therefore, we don't restrict the number of $C.\text{decide}(\cdot)$ operations each process can execute.

Any implementation of a consensus object is trivially linearizable if any history H that can be generated from the implemented object satisfies agreement and validity. If $\Gamma(H)$ contains no complete operations, then its linearization is the empty sequence. Otherwise, if $\Gamma(H)$ contains at least one response with return-value y^*, a linearization $L(H)$ of $\Gamma(H)$ if formed by ordering all pending and completed operations of $\Gamma(H)$ in an arbitrary way that preserves the happens-before relation and by adding the responses with return-value y^* to all operations that have no response in $\Gamma(H)$. Since $L(H)$ is a sequential history that satisfies agreement and validity, it is in the sequential specification of a consensus object. Since $L(H)$ extends the happens-before relation of operations in $\Gamma(H)$, it is is a linearization of $\Gamma(H)$.

It turns out that any linearizable implementation of a consensus object is even strongly linearizable.

CLAIM 4.1. *Let $\mathcal{H}$ be a set of histories over an implemented consensus object such that any history $H \in \mathcal{H}$ satisfies agreement and validity. Then $\mathcal{H}$ is strongly linearizable.*

PROOF. We specify the strong linearization function f for each history $H \in \mathcal{H}$. If H contains no complete `decide(·)` operations, then $f(H)$ is the empty history. Now suppose H contains at least one `decide(·)` operation that responds with return value $y^* \in D$. Then $f(H)$ is the sequence of all operations from $\Gamma(H)$ ordered by the position of their invocations in $\Gamma(H)$. Every operation that has no response in $\Gamma(H)$ is equipped with the response with return-value y^* in $f(H)$.

Obviously, $f(H)$ extends the happens-before ordering of $\Gamma(H)$. Hence, as argued above, $f(H)$ is a linearization of $\Gamma(H)$.

It remains to show that $f(H)$ is prefix-preserving. Let $G, H \in \mathcal{H}$ such that G is a prefix of H. If $\Gamma(G)$ contains no complete operation, then $f(G)$ is the empty history and thus a prefix of $f(H)$. Otherwise, if $\Gamma(G)$ contains some response with return value y, then that same response is also in $\Gamma(H)$. Then all responses in $\Gamma(G)$ and $\Gamma(H)$ have return value y, and also all responses in $f(G)$ and $f(H)$. Moreover, since $f(G)$ and $f(H)$ contain all complete and pending operations of $\Gamma(G)$ and $\Gamma(H)$, respectively, every operation in $f(G)$ also appears in $f(H)$. Now suppose some operation op_1 precedes another operation op_2 in $f(H)$ and op_2 is in $f(G)$. Then the invocation of op_1 precedes the invocation of op_2 in $\Gamma(H)$ and thus both invocations occur in $\Gamma(G)$ and in the same order. Thus, op_1 appears in $f(G)$ and precedes op_2. $\square$

Aspnes and Herlihy [6] presented a randomized implementation of a *binary* consensus object, that is, one over the domain $D = \{0, 1\}$. In their algorithm, each process p writes only to a unique single-writer register R_p. Process p writes pairs (*prefer*, *round*), where *prefer* denotes the value p would choose if it were to complete the protocol executing in isolation (p's preferred value), and *round* is a counter that keeps track of how many times p has updated its register R_p so far. A process p is a *leader* if the *round* value stored in R_p is greater than or equal to any other process' *round* value. In each round, a process p reads all registers of other processes. If p finds that it is a leader and every process whose counter trails p's by less than two agrees with p (i.e., its *prefer* value matches that of p), then p can safely decide its preferred value. Otherwise, if all leaders agree, p adopts the leaders' opinion by setting its value *prefer* to the leaders' preferred value. If the leaders don't agree, p changes its *prefer* value

to $\perp$, which is a unique value not in D. If p's *prefer* value is already $\perp$, then p chooses a new *prefer* value uniformly at random from $\{0, 1\}$.

It is known that the algorithm can easily be adjusted to solve consensus for arbitrary finite domains D: instead of choosing a new *prefer* value uniformly at random from $\{0, 1\}$, process p chooses a value at random that is preferred by one of the leaders. Moreover, Herlihy, Luchangco and Moir [12] observed that this algorithm can easily be derandomized to obtain an obstruction-free consensus algorithm: Instead of choosing a new preference at random, a process adopts the preference with the smallest value among all *prefer* values of the leaders. (We can use an arbitrary total order over D.) Thus, from Claim 4.1 we obtain the following corollary.

COROLLARY 4.2. *There is a strongly-linearizable obstruction-free implementation of consensus objects from multi-reader/single-writer registers.*

A very basic strongly linearizable and obstruction-free implementation of an arbitrary object O from an infinite number of consensus objects, $C_1, C_2, \ldots$, is as follows. The domain D of these consensus objects is the set of all possible invocations of operations on O (recall that an invocation description also determines the process who executes the invocation). To invoke an operation on the object O, process p determines the corresponding invocation description inv and executes $C_i.\texttt{decide}(inv)$ for $i = 1, 2, \ldots$, until the one of these `decide(inv)` calls returns the value inv. Suppose the k-th `decide(inv)` call if the first that returns inv, and let inv_j, $j = 1, \ldots, k$, be the return value of p's j-th `decide(inv)` call. Then p computes the value val that would be returned by the last operation on O in a sequential execution with k operations with invocations $inv_1, \ldots, inv_k$. Process p returns this value val as its return value of the operation it invoked.

Note that if the `decide(·)` operations are atomic, then this universal construction is strongly linearizable. Consider a history H in which `decide(·)` operations on k distinct consensus objects complete. Then these k objects must be $C_1, \ldots, C_k$, and for $i \in \{1, \ldots, k\}$ all $C_i.\texttt{decide}(·)$ operations on object C_i return the same value inv_i. We define $f(H)$ to be the unique sequential history with k operations, where the i-th operation has invocation inv_i. It is immediate from the agreement and validity properties of consensus objects that f is a strong linearization function. Hence, the implementation of object O is strongly linearizable. Since strong linearizability is a composable property, we can replace the atomic consensus objects with the obstruction-free implementation guaranteed in Corollary 4.2, and the resulting universal construction is still strongly linearizable.

COROLLARY 4.3. *There is a strongly linearizable obstruction-free universal construction from multi-reader/single-writer registers.*

4.2 Bounded Max-Registers

There is a linearizable wait-free implementation of a multi-writer register from single-writer registers [13]. Therefore, if an object has no linearizable wait-free implementation from single-writer registers, we can conclude that it does not have a linearizable wait-free implementation from multi-writer registers. The comparable situation does not hold for strongly linearizable implementations because, as shown in

Section 3, there is no strongly linearizable implementation of a multi-writer register from single-writer registers, even if the progress requirement is weakened to non-blocking instead of wait-free.

Indeed, as we establish in Theorem 4.4 below, Algorithms 1 and 2 in Figure 2 constitute a (not very efficient!) strongly linearizable wait-free implementation of a bounded max-register from multi-writer registers even though this is impossible from single-writer registers. Let M_B denote a bounded max-register with bound B. The idea of the implementation is to represent M_B by an array of $B+2$ multi-writer registers $R[0], \ldots, R[B+1]$, where the current value of M_B is interpreted to be b if and only if $R[b] = b$ and $R[b+1] = 0$. The operation maxWrite(x) is implemented by writing x successively to $R[1]$ through $R[x]$. Thus, if the current value is c, and a subsequent maxWrite(d) where $d < c$ is executing, d can never be interpreted as the value of M_B. A maxRead() operation helps execute potentially incomplete maxWrite() operations that could possibly become the current value, until it finally completes a maxWrite(t) and then reads that $R[t+1]$ is still 0. At that point the maxRead() can safely return t.

```
/* R[0...B + 1] is an array of shared multi-writer
   registers, each initially 0                      */
```

Algorithm 1: maxWrite(x)

---

for $i = 1 \ldots x$ **do**
   $R[i] := x$

Algorithm 2: maxRead()

```
/* t is local and initially 0                      */
```
repeat
   maxWrite(t)
   $r := R[t+1]$
   if $r == 0$ **then**
     $return(t)$
   else
     $t := r$
until *True*

Figure 2: A strongly linearizable implementation of a bounded max-register

THEOREM 4.4. *Algorithms 1 and 2 together provide a strongly linearizable and wait-free implementation of a bounded max-register with bound B.*

PROOF. Let H be any history that arises from a partial or complete execution of maxRead() and maxWrite() method calls. For each maxWrite(x) method call in $\Gamma(H)$, say $mw(x)$, we let $pt(mw(x))$ be

- undefined if register $R[x]$ has not been written in H;

- the operation in H where $R[x]$ is first written by some process if that write is after the invocation of $mw(x)$;

- the first step of $mw(x)$ if register $R[x]$ is first written before the invocation of $mw(x)$.

For each maxRead() method call in $\Gamma(H)$, say mr, if the last step of mr is in H, define $pt(mr)$ to be the last read

of shared memory by mr and undefined otherwise. Notice that each completed method call in $\Gamma(H)$ and some pending method calls in $\Gamma(H)$ are mapped to steps in H. We define the function f to map each history H to the sequential history that is determined by the points $pt(op)$ of all of $\Gamma(H)$'s operations op. More precisely, let $S(H)$ be the set of all operations op in $\Gamma(H)$ such that $pt(op)$ is defined and thus a step in H. Define $f(H)$ to be the sequential history H^* consisting of the operations in $S(H)$ ordered so that op_1 precedes op_2 in H^* if and only if $pt(op_1)$ precedes $pt(op_2)$ in H.

First we prove that $f(H)$ is a linearization of $\Gamma(H)$. Any maxRead() method call is clearly mapped by pt to a point between its invocation and response because it is mapped to its last read of a shared register. For any maxWrite(x) method call, say $mw(x)$, by the definition of pt, $pt(mw(x))$ must follow the invocation of $mw(x)$. Also, $pt(mw(x))$ must preceded the response of $mw(x)$ because the method call $mw(x)$ itself writes x to $R[x]$. So we need to show that if a maxRead$_p$() method call, mr, returning value x is mapped to some point in H, at least one maxWrite(x) method call is mapped to a point that precedes $pt(mr)$, and no maxWrite(y) method call where $y > x$ is mapped to any point that precedes $pt(mr)$. Observe from the algorithm that once a register $R[j]$ becomes non-zero, it cannot subsequently become 0, and if $R[j]$ is non-zero, all registers $R[1], \ldots, R[j-1]$ are also non-zero. Since $pt(mr)$ is defined in H, in the method call mr, p must have written x to $R[x]$ and then read $R[x+1] == 0$. Any execution of a maxRead() method call, however, can only write values that were previously written. Therefore, there must be a maxWrite(x) method call $mw(x)$ that began before p read $R[x+1] == 0$. By definition of pt, $pt(mw(x))$ is the first write of x to $R[x]$, so it is at or before the write by p of x to $R[x]$, which precedes the last read by p, which is the point $pt(mr)$. Furthermore, in this last read by method call mr, p read $R[x+1] == 0$. So there can be no $y > x$ for which y had been written to $R[y]$ when p read $R[x+1]$. Thus there is no maxWrite(y) method call, where $y > x$, that is mapped to a point that precedes $pt(mr)$.

Now we observe that f satisfies the prefix property P of strong linearizability. For each step h of a history H, we see from the definition of f, that a method call op in $\Gamma(H)$ satisfies $pt(op) = h$ if:

- op is a maxRead() method call and h is the last read of op; or

- op is a maxWrite(j) that is pending at h, and h is the first write in H of j to $R[j]$; or

- op is a maxWrite(j) and h is the first write of op and there is an h' preceding h in H that is the first write of j to $R[j]$.

Thus, for each successive step $h \in H$, exactly which method calls op satisfy $pt(op) = h$ is entirely determined at step h. Therefore, if history G is a prefix of history H, then $f(G)$ is a prefix of $f(H)$.

Finally, observe that Algorithms 1 and 2 are both wait-free. Clearly, maxWrite(x) is wait-free for any $1 \leq x \leq B$ since its single instruction for-loop executes exactly $x \leq B$ times. Each iteration of the repeat-loop of maxRead() includes one read of shared memory and an execution of maxWrite(y), where y increases with each iteration. So the repeat-loop can iterate at most B times implying that `maxRead()` is also wait-free.

Since f is a strong linearization function, and Algorithms 1 and 2 are wait-free, they constitute a strongly linearizable and wait-free implementation of a bounded max-register. $\square$

5. OPEN PROBLEMS

There are more questions than answers concerning strong linearizability. It appears that new techniques are required to determine what objects have strongly linearizable wait-free implementations from multi-writer registers. Given the bounded max-register construction from multi-writer registers, impossibilities will likely need to consider unbounded executions. It is curious that the impossibility from single-writer registers applies even to non-blocking implementations that require the `inspect()` operation to be obstruction-free; yet removing the non-blocking requirement and adding an obstruction-free requirement for all operations is possible for any object. A better understanding of the impact of various progress requirements is needed. Finding efficient strongly linearizable implementations of useful objects is an obvious topic for future work.

Acknowledgments

We are grateful to Hagit Attiya, Keren Censor-Hillel, Rotem Oshman, Eric Ruppert, and three anonymous referees whose comments and questions have helped us improve and extend this work.

6. REFERENCES

[1] Yehuda Afek, Danny Dolev, Hagit Attiya, Eli Gafni, Michael Merritt, and Nir Shavit. Atomic snapshots of shared memory. In *Proceedings of the 9th SIGACT-SIGOPS Symposium on Principles of Distributed Computing (PODC)*, pages 1–13, 1990.

[2] Dan Alistarh and James Aspnes. Sub-logarithmic test-and-set against a weak adversary. In *Proceedings of the 25th International Symposium on Distributed Computing (DISC)*, pages 97–109, 2011.

[3] James Aspnes, Hagit Attiya, and Keren Censor. Randomized consensus in expected o(n log n) individual work. In *PODC27th*, pages 325–334, 2008.

[4] James Aspnes, Hagit Attiya, and Keren Censor. Max registers, counters, and monotone circuits. In *Proceedings of the 28th SIGACT-SIGOPS Symposium on Principles of Distributed Computing (PODC)*, pages 36–45, 2009.

[5] James Aspnes and Keren Censor. Approximate shared-memory counting despite a strong adversary. *ACM Transactions on Algorithms*, 6(2), 2010.

[6] James Aspnes and Maurice Herlihy. Fast randomized consensus using shared memory. *Journal of Algorithms*, 11(3):441–461, 1990.

[7] Hagit Attiya, Rachid Guerraoui, Danny Hendler, and Petr Kuznetsov. The complexity of obstruction-free implementations. *Journal of the ACM*, 56(4), 2009.

[8] Michael J. Fischer, Nancy A. Lynch, and Mike Paterson. Impossibility of distributed consensus with one faulty process. *Journal of the ACM*, 32(2):374–382, 1985.

[9] Wojciech M. Golab, Lisa Higham, and Philipp Woelfel. Linearizable implementations do not suffice for randomized distributed computation. In *Proceedings of the 43rd Annual ACM Symposium on Theory of Computing (STOC)*, pages 373–382, 2011.

[10] Danny Hendler and Philipp Woelfel. Randomized mutual exclusion with sub-logarithmic RMR-complexity. *Distributed Computing*, 24(1):3–19, 2011.

[11] M. Herlihy and J. M. Wing. Linearizability: A correctness condition for concurrent objects. *ACM Transactions on Programming Languages and Systems*, 12(3):463–492, July 1990.

[12] Maurice Herlihy, Victor Luchangco, and Mark Moir. Obstruction-free synchronization: Double-ended queues as an example. In *Proceedings of the 23rd International Conference on Distributed Computing Systems (ICDCS)*, pages 522–529, 2003.

[13] Paul M. B. Vitányi and Baruch Awerbuch. Errata to "atomic shared register access by asynchronous hardware". In *Proceedings of the 28th Annual IEEE Symposium on Foundations of Computer Science (FOCS)*, page 487, 1987.

Author Index

www.ingramcontent.com/pod-product-compliance
Lightning Source LLC
Chambersburg PA
CBHW080656220326

41598CB00033B/5227